WORLD POPULATION DYNAMICS
An Introduction to Demography

BARBARA A. ANDERSON
UNIVERSITY OF MICHIGAN

PEARSON

Boston   Columbus   Indianapolis   New York   San Francisco   Upper Saddle River
Amsterdam   Cape Town   Dubai   London   Madrid   Milan   Munich   Paris   Montréal   Toronto
Delhi   Mexico City   São Paulo   Sydney   Hong Kong   Seoul   Singapore   Taipei   Tokyo

Editor in Chief: Ashley Dodge
Publisher: Nancy Roberts
Editorial Assistant: Molly White
Marketing Coordinator: Jessica Warren
Managing Editor: Denise Forlow
Program Manager: Mayda Bosco
Senior Operations Supervisor: Mary Fischer
Operations Specialist: Diane Peirano
Art Director: Jayne Conte
Cover Designer: John Christiana

Director of Digital Media: Brian Hyland
Digital Media Project Manager:
Tina Gagliostro
Digital Media Project Management:
Learning Mate Solutions, Ltd./Lynn Cohen
Full-Service Project Management and
Composition: Aravinda Doss/PreMediaGlobal
Printer/Binder: LSC Communications
Cover Printer: LSC Communications
Text Font: 10/11 ITC New Baskerville Std

Credits and acknowledgments borrowed from other sources and reproduced, with permission, in this textbook appear in the Notes at the end of each chapter.

Cover Image:
From *The Atlas of the Real World: Mapping the Way We Live* by Daniel Dorling, Mark Newman and Anna Barford. © 2008 Daniel Dorling, Mark Newman and Anna Barford. Published by Thames & Hudson, Ltd., London, 2008 and 2010.

Many of the designations by manufacturers and seller to distinguish their products are claimed as trademarks. Where those designations appear in this book, and the publisher was aware of a trademark claim, the designations have been printed in initial caps or all caps.

Library of Congress Cataloging-in-Publication Data

Anderson, Barbara A.
World population dynamics : an introduction to demography / Barbara
Anderson, University of Michigan.
pages cm
ISBN-13: 978-0-205-74203-5
ISBN-10: 0-205-74203-3
1. Demography.   2. Population.   I. Title.
HB871.A517 2014
304.6—dc23

2014000583

6   17

PEARSON

ISBN 10: 0-205-74203-3
ISBN 13: 978-0-205-74203-5

To my husband, John H. Romani

CONTENTS

Chapter 6	Mortality Decline in the Less Developed Region	177

Chapter 7	Mortality Issues in the More Developed Region	206

Chapter 8	Fertility Patterns in the Modern Era	245

Chapter 10   Fertility in the More Developed Region   321

| Chapter 12 | Migration and Urbanization | 402 |

LIST OF FIGURES

CHAPTER 5

CHAPTER 6

CHAPTER 7

CHAPTER 8

CHAPTER 9

CHAPTER 10

CHAPTER 11

CHAPTER 12

LIST OF TABLES

CHAPTER 6

CHAPTER 7

CHAPTER 8

CHAPTER 9

LIST OF BOXES

PREFACE

This book is an introduction to social demography for undergraduate and graduate students. Although some methodological and technical material is included, its main purpose is to make the substantive material understandable.

I first was introduced to demography as an undergraduate math major at the University of Chicago in the 1960s. I was always interested in what made things work, and in that setting, I was trying to understand the massive social and political changes in the United States, at a time of the struggle for civil rights, the emergence of feminism, and the turmoil related to the Vietnam War.

I was concerned with social change, and I had never been impressed by "great men theories" of history. I did not believe that the king sneezed and the world changed. I also did not care very much about the fate of a small, privileged elite. What first attracted me to demography was its populist nature. If there was a change in some demographic indicator, you did not immediately know the causes or consequences of that change, but you could be sure that something had happened that affected the lives of a large part of the population.

Although I remained concerned about the challenges and the problems facing the U.S. population, as I learned about developing countries, their problems seemed even more daunting than those in the United States. In addition, I became increasingly convinced that understanding the historical and cultural setting was key to understanding the meaning of all social change, including demographic change.

These perspectives have informed how I have taught undergraduate and graduate students about demographic and social change for almost 40 years at Yale University, Brown University, and the University of Michigan. I take an historical and comparative approach that places demographic conditions and changes in context and illuminates their importance in the past, in the present, and in years to come.

Many people have provided helpful input to this book. Mary Beth Ofstedal, Arland Thornton, Silvia Pedraza, and Elizabeth Mosley of the University of Michigan; Hania Zlotnik, Gerhard Heilig, and Patrick Gerland of the United Nations Population Division; Victoria Velkoff of the U.S. Census Bureau; Wayne Parent of Louisiana State University; Bryan Vincent of House Legislative Services of the Louisiana Legislature; and Yunah Sung, Korean Studies Librarian of the Asia Library at the University of Michigan, answered specific questions. Howard Kimeldorf and Kiyo Tsutsui of the University of Michigan gave helpful comments and reactions. Renee Anspach of the University of Michigan and Arun Rajmohan of Argon ST, a subsidiary of Boeing Company, read extensive sections and provided comments. Michael McCarthy of the University of Michigan, Theresa Anderson of the Urban Institute, Claudette Smith of Wayne State University, Pamela McMullin-Messier of Central Washington University, Josh Packard of the University of Northern Colorado, and Veena Kulkarni of Arkansas State University read the entire manuscript and provided numerous helpful comments. John Romani of the University of Michigan was supportive, helpful, and constructive throughout the entire book production process.

Barbara A. Anderson
Ronald Freedman Collegiate Professor
of Sociology and Population Studies
University of Michigan
Ann Arbor, Michigan

CHAPTER 1

THE FIELD OF DEMOGRAPHY

LEARNING OBJECTIVES

- List four questions that demography can address.
- List four social problems or policies in which the application of demography is useful.
- Describe the two main ways to think about population change.
- Outline the major historical patterns that have shaped population thinking and the theories that have been developed to explain these patterns.
- Describe the influence of anthropological, psychological, political, and statistical perspectives on population thinking.
- Discuss the difference between neo-Malthusian thinking and neo-Marxist thinking about the relation between population growth and the availability of food and other resources.

((• Listen to the Chapter Audio

OVERVIEW

This book examines the three major population processes: mortality, fertility, and migration. It is an introduction to the technical and substantive aspects of demography—the study of the growth and structure of human populations, with an emphasis on substantive issues.

If you look at the size of the population of a geographic area at two points in time, people are added to the original population through births and migrants into the area, and people are removed from the original population through deaths and migrants out of the area. The sum of these changes is the difference between the size of the population at the first time and the size of the population at the second time. The study of the determinants of the basic population processes of mortality, fertility, and migration is, thus, the study of the determinants of population growth and decline.

There are large differences in fertility and mortality throughout the world, and there have been large changes over time in the rate of population growth. The way that fertility, mortality, and migration interrelate to result in population change is important as a background for understanding many social, economic, and political issues. This book concentrates on the *causes* of population processes rather than the *effects* of population processes.

The student will be introduced to several measures of each of these processes and how to interpret these measures. Technical and methodological material is examined to enable the student to understand the meaning and interpretation of the measures but without detailed consideration of the underlying mathematics and statistics. Other books focus on more technical aspects of demographic measures and methods.[1]

After using this book, a student will be familiar with the major theoretical perspectives and policy controversies about demographic processes. A student will be able to read an article in a newspaper or magazine that deals with population issues and be able to understand what the issue is about, to assess the likely validity of the article, and to identify possible problems or additional considerations. A student will also be prepared to take more advanced or specialized courses related to population and to understand the importance of population considerations in fields such as sociology, economics, psychology, history, political science, and public health as well as in a wide variety of policy debates.

This first chapter discusses the nature of and the subjects in the field of demography. The "demographic perspective" is introduced. Demographic trends and problems that have focused the interest of researchers and policy makers on demography are described. The major theories and perspectives about population growth and the components of population growth—mortality, fertility, and migration—are discussed briefly.

THE STUDY OF DEMOGRAPHY

There have been many definitions of **demography**. Demography has been defined as the scientific study of human populations. Demography has also been defined as the study of the growth, structure, and composition of human populations. Often, study of the causes and consequences of the growth, structure, and composition of populations is also considered part of demography. Much of demography focuses on estimates and projections of the size and characteristics of the population and of the components of population change.[2]

Sometimes, people distinguish demography from population studies. Population studies is often concerned with the consequences of demographic processes, while demography is more concerned with the causes of those processes. Other people do not distinguish between demography and population studies.

The term "demographics" has been used increasingly in popular discussion: it means the most recent statistical information about a population, often with little interpretation or analysis. Most researchers and teachers of demography do not like the term "demographics." They think it emphasizes raw data over understanding of causes, consequences, or processes.

Hauser and Bogue defined demography as "the study of the size, territorial distribution, and composition of population, changes therein, and the components of such changes."[3] Xie argued that the inclusion of "composition" and "changes therein" in this definition situates demography as the basis upon which all social science is based.[4] Other people would not define demography quite so broadly.

Demography studies the following:

1. **Population size:** the number of people in a country, a state, a city, a region, or the world at a given time
2. **Population growth or decline:** changes in the number of people in a given geographic area over time
3. **Population processes:** fertility, mortality, and migration
4. **Factors related to population processes:** diseases and socioeconomic characteristics related to mortality, family formation, labor force participation, government policies related to fertility, differences in income and opportunities in various areas, war and immigration policies, and economic conditions motivating migration
5. **Population distribution:** geographic distribution, such as among states or between rural and urban areas
6. **Population structure:** age and sex composition, the growing proportion of the population at advanced ages, the sex ratio at birth, and the increasing proportion of the population that is female with increasing age
7. **Population characteristics:** education, income, labor force participation, marital status, and race or ethnic group membership—anything that has a value for each member of the population and does not have the same value for everyone

USES OF DEMOGRAPHY

Demographic analysis is used to address a wide variety of scientific and policy questions.[5] Any field in which the number of people and their characteristics relate to utilization of a service, such as health care or public transport, uses the results of demographic analysis. Demography is important for estimating future school enrollment and for projecting demand for utilities and services, such as electricity and ridership on public transportation. In addition, in trying to understand the dynamics or causes of phenomena such as crime rates or educational attainment, where there is variation in the outcomes of interest by characteristics such as age, sex, education, and race or ethnicity, demographic considerations and demographic analysis are important. Often, as a first step to understanding the causes and consequences of a demographic phenomenon, it is important to actually know the magnitude of the phenomenon or the magnitude of change over time and how controlling for characteristics such as age changes the view of the situation.

Young males are more likely to commit violent crimes than women or older men. In order to understand whether the tendency to commit violent crimes has changed, it is necessary to adjust for changes in the age composition of the population.[6] If the population has grown older, the violent crime rate will usually fall, even if the rates of criminal activity by age have not changed.

Similarly, in a country where schooling opportunities are increasing, people born later are likely to have higher educational attainment than people who were born earlier. The average educational attainment can be higher in Country A than in Country B, but the educational attainment at each age can be higher in Country B than in Country A. This can happen if Country B has a much older population than Country A. This situation is illustrated in Box 1.1, which looks at the literacy rates of people at least age 10.

BOX 1.1

A Hypothetical Example of the Effect of Age Composition on the Percentage of Literate People among Those Age 10 or Older

In this table, Country B has a higher percentage of literate people at every age than does Country A. In both countries, younger people are more likely to be literate than older people. Also, Country A has a younger population than Country B. In Country B, 31% of all persons age 10 or older are age 10–19, but in Country A, 83% of all persons age 10 or older are age 10–19. Due to the younger population of Country A than Country B, a higher percentage of people at least age 10 are literate in Country A (23%) than in Country B (20%), even though within every age group, persons in Country B are more likely to be literate than persons in Country A.

Age	Country A		Country B	
	% Literate	% of Population Age 10+	% Literate	% of Population Age 10+
10–19	25%	83%	30%	31%
20–39	15%	15%	20%	34%
40+	5%	2%	10%	35%
Age 10+	23%	100%	20%	100%

DEMOGRAPHIC PERSPECTIVES

In this section, first we discuss two different ways to think about population change. Then we give examples of the influence of the demographic perspective in various areas of social science.

Two Ways to Think about Population Change

There are two ways to think about population change: an aggregate approach and a microbehavioral approach. They are used to answer different kinds of questions.

1. **An aggregate approach:** What are the components of population change (e.g. what are the roles of births, deaths, and migration in changes in population size)?

   This perspective deals with macrosocial demographic processes. It looks at how the levels of childbearing, mortality, and population movement result in the growth or decline of a population. This perspective is important for understanding when and where the population is increasing or declining.

   This perspective alerted the world to the future implications of high rates of population growth in the less developed region of the world in the 1960s and 1970s. Awareness that high fertility (many more births than deaths) was the main reason for high population growth motivated the development of family-planning programs in the less developed region of the world.

   However, devising effective policies and programs to influence behavior that would lead to lower fertility depended on a microbehavioral approach (discussed next) that understood the reasons why women and couples wanted to limit the number of children they had in different circumstances.

2. **A causal or microbehavioral approach:** What are the causal factors or behavioral mechanisms that lead to the decisions that people make? What behaviors do individuals adopt to implement their decisions?

People make decisions related to fertility and migration. Individual choices and behaviors also affect the chance that a person will die. Researchers and policy makers need to understand why people have children in order to motivate people in countries with a high rate of population growth to have fewer children. In some areas, the provision of effective, easy-to-use contraceptives resulted in a rapid decline in the number of births. In other regions, the process of convincing women and couples to reduce their fertility was more complicated and required an in-depth understanding of their views of children and concerns about whether reductions in mortality in the past might be reversed in the future.

Recently, several more developed countries have become very worried as their fertility rate has become so low that it can lead to population decline. Concern with population decline has led to a theoretical and policy debate about why people have children that is somewhat different from the debate when the concern was a high rate of population growth. Is having a child a necessary part of being an adult woman or an adult man? Are increased employment opportunities for women providing an alternative path to self-fulfillment that raising children provided in the past? Sociological and economic explanations often disagree about what policies would be most effective in maintaining or raising fertility in very-low-fertility settings.

Behaviors also influence mortality. Although people would prefer to live a longer rather than a shorter life, increasingly behaviors, such as smoking, alcohol consumption, and poor diet, affect the chances that people will die early. What motivates people to change from these unhealthy behaviors to more healthy behaviors?

Individual decisions also affect migration. Migrating to an unfamiliar setting can be a scary proposition. Why are some people willing to take this risk while others are not? What is the role of other family members in whether a person migrates? When the economy worsens or violence erupts in an area, what kind of people decide to leave while others stay?

Ecological or structural factors also influence demographic outcomes. A woman might want to limit her childbearing, but this will be difficult if no effective contraceptives are available or if there are strong family or cultural pressures against contraceptive use. A person might engage in healthy personal behaviors but will still face high mortality risks if he or she lives in a polluted environment or if clean drinking water is not available, situations over which the person or household has little control. A person might want to live a healthy life, but if racial residential segregation contributes to unclean air and a lack of social services, that person will have a difficult time remaining healthy. People might want to migrate for work and other opportunities from a poorer to a better-off country, but this might not be possible if the better-off country has restrictive immigration laws.

The Influence of the Demographic Perspective in Other Areas of Social Science

The demographic perspective has influenced the conceptualization of problems and analytic approaches in many areas of social science. Next we discuss the influence of the demographic perspective in several areas, with examples of studies that have applied the demographic perspective.

The Demographic Perspective and Social Statistics

Much of the microbehavioral perspective in demography concerns decisions that people make given the choices or risks that they face. Not all women are able to have a second child. Naturally, only those women who have already had one child are able to have a second child. Similarly, only those who are currently married are able to be divorced.

A major part of the demographic perspective involves looking at mortality through what is called a life table. In a life table, the chance of dying at each age is considered among those who have survived to that age. For example, the chance of dying between the twentieth birthday and the twenty-fifth birthday is considered for those who are alive on their twentieth birthday. A life table looks at the chances of dying at various ages at a given point of time and calculates how many years on average a person would live if he or she were exposed to these chances in a given time and place. This approach looks at whether a particular phenomenon occurs to members of the "population at risk" of that phenomenon occurring.

The life table is discussed in detail in Chapter 4. Although often applied to mortality, the life table approach can be applied in many other areas. For example, a life table approach can be used to calculate the average number of years that a person in a population works for pay or the expected number of years that a person will remain married after marrying for the first time. The life table approach is behind the statistical methods of survival analysis and hazard analysis.[7]

The Demographic Perspective and the Study of Voting Behavior

An example from the study of voting behavior can make the "population at risk" perspective clearer.[8] The American National Election Studies conducts a survey before each congressional and presidential election in which people are asked if they intend to vote. After the election, the survey participants are re-interviewed and asked if they actually did vote.

For many National Election Surveys, a vote validation is conducted in which survey staff check who actually voted. Almost everywhere in the United States, whether or not a person voted is a matter of public record, although, of course, who the person voted for is secret. When the vote is validated, it is possible to determine whether or not the person told the truth about their voting behavior.

Validating the vote is very expensive, since survey staff need to check local records. Thus, National Election Survey researchers wanted to know how good an indicator *reported* voting behavior was of *actual* voting behavior. If they could accept reported voting behavior as a reasonably accurate indicator of actual voting behavior, a lot of money could be saved by not validating the vote. In this budgetary investigation of whether there needed to be vote validation, analysts looked at the proportion of those who claimed to have voted but did not actually vote or the proportion of all respondents who accurately reported their voting behavior.

Voting is normatively approved behavior. Almost no one who actually votes lies about it and says they didn't vote. In the National Election Studies, only 1% of actual voters say they didn't vote—over 90% of vote misreporters are actual nonvoters. Thus, the population at risk of misreporting their voting is not all people; the population at risk of misreporting their voting is *actual nonvoters.*

Earlier work concluded that respondent characteristics, such as education or political attitudes, were unrelated to vote misreporting. It also claimed that the only respondent characteristic related to vote misreporting was race, with *African Americans* **twice** *as likely as Whites to misstate their voting behavior.* A problem with this earlier work was that researchers were looking at all persons, both actual voters and actual nonvoters, when only actual nonvoters were at risk of misstating their voting behavior, and a higher proportion of African Americans than of Whites were actual nonvoters.

Anderson and her colleagues looked at actual nonvoters and obtained results that changed these interpretations. They found that even though more educated people are more likely to actually vote, those more educated people who *don't* vote are very likely to lie about it and say they voted. When you look at actual nonvoters, *African Americans are* **20%** *more likely to (falsely) claim they voted than Whites—not* **100%** *more likely.* In this case, applying a demographic perspective completely changes the understanding of what was going on.

The Demographic Perspective and the Study of the Labor Force and Employment

In the study of the labor force, employment, and unemployment, one approach would be to look at the percentage of all people aged 15–64 who are working for pay. However, we know that young people often are not working for pay because they are in school, and that as people age, many withdraw from the labor force even before typical retirement age. Thus, if a population has a high proportion of members aged 15–24 or over age 50, the percentage which is working for pay will be lower than otherwise due to the age composition of the population. A demographic approach would look at how many years a person would work for pay in their entire life if the person were working for pay at each age at the rate existing in the population at that time. This could be known by applying a life table approach to

estimating the average number of years of working for pay.

Applying a demographic perspective, Smith looked at the number of years that men and women would have worked for pay over their lifetimes given the employment rates by age and sex in 1970 and 1977.[9] She found that in both 1970 and 1977, men on average would have worked 38 years, while the number of years that women would have worked increased from 22 years in 1970 to 28 years in 1977. Her work provided a good picture of increasing female labor force participation in the United States.

The Demographic Perspective and the Study of Marriage and the Family

A population at risk demographic approach has revolutionized the study of marriage and the family.[10] The only people at risk of divorce are those who are currently married. A life table approach to the study of divorce could look at the chance of being divorced before 5 years of marriage among those who were still married one year after marriage. This perspective involves a dynamic, life cycle approach that illuminates how people make decisions as they pass through their lives.[11]

For example, Schoen and Standish used a life table approach to look at changes in marriage and divorce between 1970 and 1995. They found that women experiencing the risks of marriage, divorce, and widowhood that were present in 1970 would have married at age 22. If they divorced, it would have occurred on average at age 36, and 80% of the divorced women would have eventually remarried. Under the conditions in 1995, women would have married at age 27. If they divorced, it would have occurred at age 37, and only 69% of divorced women would have ever remarried.[12]

Bumpass and Lu used a life table approach to look at the average number of years that a child would spend in a single-parent household before age 16 in the early 1980s and in the early 1990s. They found that a non-Hispanic White child would have lived with a single parent on average for 2 years in both periods, whereas an African-American child would have lived with a single parent for 8 years before age 16 in the early 1980s but would have lived on average 10 years with a single parent before age 16 in the early 1990s.[13]

The Demographic Perspective and the Study of Organizations

The demographic perspective has also become important in the study of organizations. Just as demographers apply demographic reasoning to understand patterns of the birth and death of people, researchers in the area of organizations applied demographic reasoning to thinking about the birth and death of organizations.

Brüderl and his colleagues did a life table analysis of factors related to failure of German businesses that were founded in 1985–1986. They found that 37% of all businesses had gone out of business within 5 years. However, the more educated the founder, the less likely it was that a business would fail within 5 years. Forty-five percent of businesses where the founder had fewer than 12 years of education failed within 5 years, while only 28% of businesses where the founder had 15 or more years of education failed in the first 5 years. Also, the larger the initial capital investment, the lower the chance that the business failed, with 55% of businesses with 20,000 Deutschmarks or less (about $11,111) in initial capital failing within 5 years, but 16% of businesses with 50,000 Deutschmarks or more (about $28,000) in initial capital failing within 5 years.[14]

The Demographic Perspective and the Study of Criminology

The demographic perspective also has influenced research in the area of criminology. Pettit and Western used a life table approach to estimate the percentage of men born 1965–1969 and still alive in 1999 who had ever been incarcerated. They had survey data on rates of imprisonment by age, and they also had data on whether it was the first time the person had been imprisoned. They calculated what percentage of men would have been imprisoned at least once by 1999 if they had been exposed to the rates of first-time incarceration found in the surveys. They found that 3% of White men and 22% of African-American men born 1965–1969 would have been imprisoned by 1999. These results make clear that there are large differentials in incarceration both by race, and also by education: For men who had not attended college, 6% of White men and 32% of African-American men would have been imprisoned by 1999.[15]

MAJOR POPULATION PHENOMENA AND RELATED THEORIES AND FRAMEWORKS

Population theories and population policies are not created in isolation. They stem from actual population phenomena that are seen as important, in need of explanation, or problematic. Next, we look at historical patterns of population growth, mortality, fertility, and migration. In each area, after we have summarized historical changes, we look at theories and frameworks that have been developed in the given area. Often, the theories and frameworks were motivated by empirical patterns. Most of the population phenomena, theories, and frameworks are explored in more detail in later chapters.

Changes in Population Size and the Population Growth Rate

Through much of human history, the population grew slowly. Famines and wars sometimes decimated the population in a local area or, in the case of the Black Death in the fourteenth century, over a very large area.

In Europe, the population grew rapidly after 1750. This was both an opportunity and a problem. On the one hand, a growing labor force facilitated industrialization. On the other hand, the growth in the number of the poor, especially the urban poor, led to the development of competing theories about the causes of population growth and whether population growth or economic organization was the cause of poverty. The rate of world population growth increased very rapidly in the twentieth century, which led to great alarm. However, in the late twentieth century, the growth rate fell to a very low level in some highly developed countries, leading to worry about the possibilities and likely negative consequences of population decline.

Theories and Perspectives about Population Growth

Throughout the ages, many thinkers have had definite views about population growth. This thinking about population growth and population processes has been influenced by many of the phenomena discussed in this chapter. Table 1.1 summarizes various theoretical views and frameworks about population growth. The theorists and frameworks are listed chronologically in the table, although some of the discussion deals with thinkers thematically rather than completely chronologically. Some have thought that a growing population was always good for society, and the more rapid the growth, the better. Others thought that there were problems with both a rapidly growing and a rapidly declining population, but they differed regarding which they saw as the greater threat.

When thinkers and policy makers have been concerned with keeping the population from declining or from growing too slowly, this has often been expressed in **pronatalist** policies that promote fertility, whether through incentives for having children or through penalties for intentional fertility limitation. At other times, the concern has been about too-rapid population growth, and policies to limit fertility have been advocated. This section discusses positions about population growth per se. The "Changes in Fertility" section discusses theories of fertility change.[16]

Population Theorists and Perspectives before Thomas Malthus

The Babylonian Code of Hammurabi (2130–2088 BCE[17]), which is the oldest known legal code, addressed the concern to maintain a growing

TABLE 1.1   Theories and Frameworks about Population Growth

Theorist, Theory, or Framework	Date	Brief Description
Code of Hammurabi	~2100 BCE	Population growth is important for military and state power.
Confucius	~500 BCE	A large population is helpful for a productive society and would work well if the population was educated and trusted the rulers.
Plato	~400 BCE	Population should not grow or shrink rapidly. Only fit men should have children. Rapid population growth could lead to social disruption. Fertility limitation is acceptable to slow population growth.
Aristotle	~350 BCE	Population growth should be moderate. Too large a population could impair democratic government. Abortion and infanticide are acceptable means of limiting population growth.
Kautilya	~300 BCE	A large population is important for military and political reasons. Both a growing and a shrinking population create problems, but a declining population is a greater threat.
Roman rulers	~15 BCE	Population growth is necessary to produce a large army and colonists for the Roman Empire.
Ibn Khaldun	~1350	Population growth, and especially a high population density, is necessary for specialization in society.
Mercantilism	1600–1750	Population growth is essential for staffing the military and supplying colonists.
Physiocrats	~1750	A decent standard of living is important. Agriculture is an important sector, and there is a relation between agricultural production and the size of a supportable population. The solution is increasing agricultural production.
Thomas Malthus	~1800	Population grows exponentially and agricultural output linearly, so population growth must be curbed. If this is not done through reduction in fertility, mortality will increase. The only acceptable way to limit fertility is by premarital celibacy and postponement of marriage until a family can be supported.
John Stuart Mill: utilitarianism	1848	A societal goal should be the maximization of happiness, and overpopulation is a serious threat to this. Fertility limitation is acceptable.
Karl Marx	~1870	Poverty and inequality in distribution of resources are the problems, rather than population growth. There is no reason why agricultural output cannot increase more rapidly than linearly.
Émile Durkheim	1893	Specialization in society is desirable, and it is facilitated by population growth and, more specifically, a high population density.
Joseph Spengler: fear of population decline	1938	Further population decline in Europe was inevitable with bad consequences. Selfishness of low-fertility women was one cause.
Development economists and many international organizations	1960s and later	Continued high population growth rates in less developed countries would make economic development and goals such as universal primary education impossible to achieve.
Kingsley Davis: Theory of Demographic Change and Response	1963	Under pressures resulting from population increase, people have a variety of possible responses, including migration, abortion, and infanticide in addition to postponement of marriage, sterilization, and contraception.
Paul Ehrlich: *The Population Bomb*	1968	World disaster would result if population growth rates did not decline.
Club of Rome: *The Limits of Growth*	1972	This is a Malthusian analysis of the relation between population and agricultural output.
Fear of depopulation in developed countries	~2000	Very low fertility in highly developed countries, such as in Western Europe and Japan, could continue and lead to population decline with bad results.
Global warming concerns	~2005	Since global warming is mainly the result of human activity, overpopulation is a major cause of global warming.
Sustainability concerns	~2010	Population growth is a major threat to sustainability, and a lower rate of population growth or population decline would be desirable.
Craig Gurian	2012	Developed countries should be concerned about population growth. The labor problem in developed countries is the result of too-low wage rates for many jobs rather than a shortage of American labor.

population. Many of its provisions were explicitly pronatalist, including allowing a man to take a concubine if his wife was childless. Babylonian rulers saw a large population and a positive rate of population growth as resulting in increased state power, especially as reflected in the size of the army that could be raised. Pronatalist government policies have been motivated by military concerns up to recent times.

Plato (427–347 BCE) thought that both a rapidly growing and a rapidly shrinking population presented problems, and he supported fertility control. He had eugenic views, believing that only fit men, especially warriors and philosophers, should be allowed to have children. He thought that since the amount of resources available in society was limited, population size needed to be limited. He was somewhat worried that population growth could lead to social disruption, and he saw emigration (out-migration) and colonization as possible ways to remove excess population. Plato also thought that population decline could be injurious to society. In the case of population decline, he supported pronatalist policies that rewarded those with many children and thought that immigration (in-migration) might be a good idea.

The willingness of Plato to adopt strong policies to encourage a slowing or increasing of the rate of population growth as needed is consistent with the positions of countries later in history. In Chapter 9, policies in Singapore are discussed. In Singapore, when population was seen as growing too rapidly, strong fertility limitation policies were implemented; later, when population decline was a concern, pronatalist and semi-eugenic policies were implemented that encouraged increased fertility, especially among college-educated women.

Aristotle (384–322 BCE) also thought that population size should be limited, although he was not as concerned with this as Plato was. He worried that if the population grew rapidly and adequate resources were not bequeathed to children, then social disorder and revolution might result. He also worried that if the population grew too large, Greek democratic government could not function adequately. The main methods of population limitation that he advocated were abortion and exposure (infanticide) of children with disabilities or deformities.

Roman rulers also saw a growing population as a social benefit. The need for a large Roman army and the Roman colonial policies called for an ever-increasing number of people. Pronatalist laws that encouraged marriage among the upper classes were implemented in 18 BCE and again in 9 BCE.[18]

The value of a growing population was also recognized by Asian thinkers. Confucius in China saw a large population as helpful for a productive society, but he was also concerned that the population

needed to be well educated and have confidence in their rulers. Kautilya, who lived in India in about 300 BCE, saw population growth as important to the state for political, economic, and military reasons. Although he recognized that too many people and too high a rate of population growth could be problems, he also thought that too small a population and a negative growth rate were more serious threats than high population growth.[19]

Ibn Khaldun was a Tunisian historian who lived 1332–1406. He had complicated views of population growth that echo those of more modern thinkers. He thought that specialization in society was essential for prosperity. He pointed out that the key to specialization was high population density rather than a high population growth rate, but he saw high density as resulting from population growth. His views were precursors of Émile Durkheim's ideas about the importance of specialization in society.[20]

Mercantilism was an economic doctrine and philosophy that was very important in Western Europe from the sixteenth through the eighteenth centuries. It saw international conflict and war as a normal state of affairs. Foreign trade and military power were seen as the key aspects of national power. Economic growth was seen as the result of the exploitation of natural resources from colonies, preferably helped by monopolies over every market possible. To provide soldiers and colonists, a high rate of population growth was seen as essential.

One manifestation of mercantilism was the triangle trade (also called the "triangular trade"), in which textiles, rum, and other manufactured goods went from Europe to Africa; slaves went from Africa to the Americas; and sugar, cotton, and tobacco went from the Americas to Europe. A schematic representation of the triangle trade is depicted in Figure 1.1.[21]

After the mid-eighteenth century, the physiocrats arose, mainly in France. They criticized the mercantilist neglect of agriculture, and they rejected the idea that state power should be pursued for its own sake. They argued that the population's welfare

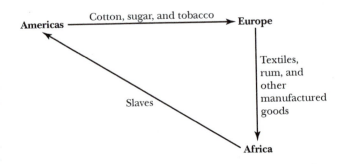

FIGURE 1.1   A Schematic Representation of the Triangle Trade

and the achievement of a decent standard of living for all people should be among society's goals. The physiocrats recognized a relation between agricultural productivity and the size of the population that could be supported, but they thought this problem should be solved by increasing agricultural productivity rather than by limiting population growth. However, the connection in people's minds between agriculture and population paved the way for Malthus, which is discussed next.

Malthusian and Marxist Perspectives on Population Growth: Arguments and Criticisms

The two main perspectives on the causes and consequences of population growth are the Malthusian perspective and the Marxist perspective. These two perspectives still influence thinking on the relation between population growth and social and economic well-being.

Malthusian Approaches to Population Growth   Thomas Malthus was a late eighteenth-century minister who maintained that although population grows exponentially, food supply grows arithmetically (or linearly). He believed that poverty is the result of population growth outstripping the availability of resources, especially food. He saw the source of too-high population growth to be the absence of moral restraint. He thought that people have a natural urge to reproduce. In Malthus's view, the only acceptable way to restrict fertility was for people to remain celibate before marriage and for marriage to be postponed until the couple could afford to support whatever children resulted. Celibacy before marriage and postponement of marriage were called **preventive check** on population growth. If a preventive check was not employed, Malthus thought that population growth eventually would be curbed by a **positive check**, which was increased mortality.[22] Preventive checks were also called **moral restraint**.

Various social customs have evolved consistent with the view that marriage and childbearing should be postponed until a family can be supported. Primogeniture, in which the oldest son inherits everything, promotes marriage (and childbearing) for the oldest son and a single life or postponement of marriage for other sons. The belief that a man should not marry until he had the financial security to support a family led to an advanced age of marriage in countries such as Ireland, where in 1941 34% of men and 26% of women in their late 40s had never married.[23]

Polyandry, in which one woman has two or more husbands, has long been reported in some areas of northern India and Tibet. One explanation for this practice is a Malthusian argument. The areas in which polyandry is practiced have low levels of agricultural productivity, and a high rate of population growth would soon exhaust resources. With more than one man for each woman, marriage can occur early, but fewer children are born than would have occurred with one husband for each wife and a similar early age at marriage. Recently in these areas, it is reported that polyandry has started to disappear.[24] The explanation seems to be that the economy has become more diverse and incomes have risen, which has allowed each man to have one wife.[25]

By about 1800, some neo-Malthusians came to the view that birth control measures are appropriate checks on population growth. By the twentieth century, almost all Malthusians came to see contraception as acceptable. John Stuart Mill, who lived in the nineteenth century, was among the neo-Malthusians who supported the use of birth control. Mill was in the utilitarian philosophical tradition, which maintains that the right thing to do is that which maximizes happiness in society, and the worth of an action cannot be assessed until the consequences of that action are known. He thought that overpopulation was a serious threat to prosperity and human happiness and saw nothing wrong with the use of methods to inhibit fertility. He also thought that fear of hunger and want rather than actual hunger could motivate fertility limitation.[26]

Malthus's views were a substantial influence on the thinking of Charles Darwin. Although Darwin is best known for his theory of natural selection, which describes how species compete and change in nature, an outgrowth of Darwin's thought was **social Darwinism**. Social Darwinism is the following position:

> There are underlying, and largely irresistible, forces acting in societies which are like the natural forces that operate in animal and plant communities. One can therefore formulate social laws similar to natural ones. These social forces are of such a kind as to produce evolutionary progress through the natural conflicts between social groups. The best-adapted and most successful social groups survive these conflicts, raising the evolutionary level of society generally (the "survival of the fittest").[27]

Although Malthus's writings directly addressed overpopulation, Malthus's work has often been interpreted as a concern with rapid population growth among the poor. The English Poor Laws were designed to some extent to improve the situation of the poor. Malthus was a strong critic of the modest Poor Law provisions because he thought that they simply encouraged poverty and lack of productivity, thus increasing population growth among the poor and exacerbating general overpopulation and other social problems.

One outgrowth of Malthus's ideas has been support of eugenic positions. **Eugenics** is "a science that deals with the improvement (as by control of human mating) of hereditary qualities of a race or breed."[28] Malthus supported the idea of eugenics, but he was not sure that its implementation would be feasible. Commenting on eugenics, he wrote,

It does not . . . by any means seem impossible that by an attention to breed, a certain degree of improvement, similar to that among animals, might take place among men. Whether intellect could be communicated may be a matter of doubt; but size, strength, beauty, complexion, and perhaps longevity are in a degree transmissible. . . . As the human race, however, could not be improved in this way without condemning all the bad specimens to celibacy, it is not probable that an attention to breed should ever become general.[29]

Eugenic views have been the motivation for many laws limiting intermarriage between racial and ethnic groups. They have also been the motivation for programs such as those by the Nazis to encourage childbearing among Aryans and discourage fertility among other groups. Eugenic positions contributed to Plato's views that only fit men should be allowed to have children and to recent fertility policies in Singapore.

In the nineteenth and early twentieth centuries, eugenic views were quite popular in the United States. Much of this was melded with views about health care and public health. In the early twentieth century, eugenic-inspired laws were passed in several states, including compulsory sterilization of patients in state mental institutions in Virginia in 1927.[30]

Not all eugenic-based views are generally viewed with disapproval. Laws against marriage between first cousins in the United States are least partly eugenic based, because one of their purposes is to minimize the passing on of damaging recessive traits to children from both parents. Most people in the United States do not think these laws are unreasonable.[31]

General Malthusian arguments about population also continued to be strong. In 1972, the Club of Rome published *The Limits of Growth*, which is a Malthusian critique of population policies. Updated analyses were published in 1992 and in 2004.[32] All of these works are based on the Malthusian assumption that population grows at a positive exponential rate, while resources, especially food, increase at a positive linear rate. With such a model, the amount growing at an exponential rate will always eventually overtake the amount growing at a linear rate.

Figure 1.2 shows the basic mechanism that concerns Malthusians. Food production and population size are shown on the left-hand axis. Food output grows linearly (in a straight line), while population grows exponentially (in an upward curving line). In

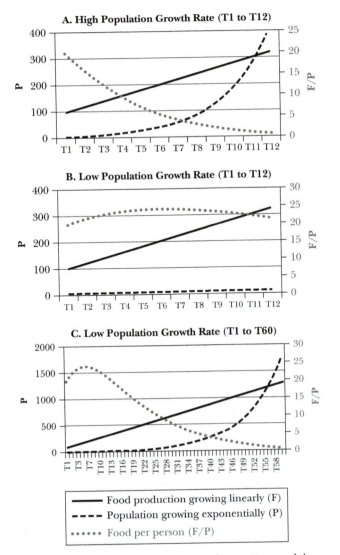

FIGURE 1.2 Food Production, Population Size, and the Food–Population Ratio

the figure, the ratio of food production to population (F/P) is also shown on the right-hand axis.

In all three panels of Figure 1.2, the line for food production is the same. Also, in all three panels, the population size at T1 is the same. Under the scenario of a high population growth rate, population grows at a higher rate than in the scenario of a low population growth rate. The first two panels show the high- and low-population-growth scenarios over a short time period, from T1 to T12. Between T1 and T12, the population size grows much less under the low-growth-rate scenario than under the high-growth-rate one. The third panel shows the low-growth-rate scenario, but over a longer time period, from T1 to T60. No matter the growth rate, as long as population is growing at a positive exponential rate and food production is growing linearly at a positive rate, the population size curve eventually will cross the food production curve. For the high-growth-rate scenario, this occurs between T11 and T12. In the low-growth-rate scenario, the curves cross between T55 and T56.

In Figure 1.2, the values of food per person are shown on the right-hand axis. In the high-population-growth situation in Panel A of Figure 1.2, the F/P ratio declines steadily. In the low-population-growth situation, the F/P ratio increases before then declining. Panel C shows the ratio over a longer time period, from T1 to T60. It is clear from Panel B that as long as population increases at a positive *exponential* rate and food production increases at a positive *linear* rate, the F/P ratio eventually will fall below any value that one wants to specify. However, the rates at which population and food production are increasing matters a lot for how long in the future the F/P ratio will fall below any given value.

Other neo-Malthusian ideas also became prominent in the twentieth and twenty-first centuries. The neo-Malthusians generally did not oppose the use of contraception, but they saw a high rate of population growth as the most or one of the most important causes of world problems. Some of this concern was motivated by the high population growth rates in the less developed region in the 1960s and 1970s. Paul Ehrlich published *The Population Bomb* in 1968, in which he warned about worldwide starvation and social upheaval if the population growth rate did not quickly decline.[33] The family-planning efforts launched by governments and nongovernmental organizations in the 1960s and 1970s were also motivated by Malthusian concerns stimulated by very high population growth rates in some less developed countries.

Concerns about global warming have often focused on the role of population growth in the production of greenhouse gases and have seen a lower population growth rate and a smaller world population as one solution to these problems.[34] Related to global warming concerns are concerns about population sustainability, in which it is often argued that a nonincreasing or decreasing world population would facilitate sustainable practices.[35]

Marxist Approaches to Population Growth   Karl Marx had a very different explanation of population growth than Malthus. Marx saw the basis of capitalism as the profit that the owner makes from the surplus value of the worker's productivity, which is the difference between the true value of the worker's activities and the wage paid to the worker. Thus, his view was that the source of poverty was not a high rate of population growth but, rather, was inequality in the distribution of resources, with a small portion of the population consuming most resources, leaving little for the rest of the population.[36]

Marx also questioned the assumption that food production could only increase linearly. He had a great deal of confidence in the potential of technological developments to increase food production, perhaps at a positive exponential rate. The Green Revolution increases in rice and wheat production, especially in Asia and Latin America, are examples of the potential for increased production of food through technological advances.[37] Lam has pointed to Ehrlich's dire predictions about food production in India, which was thought to have peaked in the late 1960s. Actually food production in India grew much more rapidly than had been anticipated, and in 1990 it was almost twice the level it was in 1961.[38] Malakoff discusses the Machakos region of Kenya, which in 1937 with a population of 250,000 was seen as disastrously overpopulated.[39] In 2011, the region had a population of 1.5 million and was thriving as a result of agricultural changes. Boserup argued that increased population density could lead to changes in agricultural technique that resulted in higher productivity.[40] She thought that the productivity of the land should not be viewed as a constant, while population size was viewed as variable.

In the early twenty-first century, many expressed concern about possible population decline in developed countries and saw immigration as the solution to a shrinking working-age population. At that time, a new Marxist argument emerged that developed countries such as the United States do not need population growth. Gurian argued that the United States and other developed countries should be concerned about too-high population growth. He maintained that the problem in highly developed countries such as the United States was not a labor shortage but rather was the setting of too-low wage rates for many jobs, which meant that citizens of the developed countries would not take the jobs, and only immigrants from very low-wage-rate, less developed countries would be willing to do these jobs for the pay that was offered.[41]

Other Important Thinkers about Population Growth
Durkheim wrote in the late nineteenth century. He saw societies as going through various stages. He saw progress as occurring through increased specialization in society, which was facilitated by an increasing population and a high population density.[42] His ideas harked back to those of Ibn Khaldun.

Spengler was worried about incipient population decline in Europe, especially France. In 1938, he wrote,

Within the next quarter century true depopulation—a persistent long-run excess of deaths over births—will manifest itself in nearly all the countries of Europe and in those non-European countries to which Western civilization has spread.[43]

These fears were triggered by very low fertility in France during the Great Depression. Spengler despaired that long-term population decline could be avoided. The population of France had declined during World War I, which people thought was understandable. The French population increased slowly from 1920 through 1934 and then again began to decline due to reduced fertility. Spengler attributed low French fertility in the 1930s to a combination of Malthusian fears about the economy and selfishness or egoism on the parts of women who did not want to occupy themselves with the tasks of motherhood. Thus, Spengler thought that a higher rate of population growth was desirable due to fear of massive population loss rather than a desire to produce an excess of persons for an army or colonization.

Davis proposed the **Theory of Demographic Change and Response**. He thought that people's behavior is affected by population growth, especially problems that accompany a high rate of population growth, but he thought that people have a variety of ways in which they can respond in addition to postponing marriage or adopting contraception. Possible alternative responses include using abortion, becoming sterilized, committing infanticide, and migrating. Which response is chosen depends on the socioeconomic conditions at the time and the individual or household's characteristics.[44]

With falling fertility in many developed countries, fears of depopulation and its possible dire consequences have reemerged, similar to the concerns of Spengler in the 1930s. Concerns about depopulation have been linked to the fact that in low-mortality populations, a lower growth rate or a negative growth rate leads to a much older age distribution.[45] Japan has the oldest population in the world, and by 2015 the Japanese population is expected to decrease in size. That country is already facing severe social strains stemming from the high proportion of the population comprised by the elderly.

Changes in Mortality and Disease

Through much of history, periods of fairly constant mortality risks were punctuated by spurts of greatly increased mortality, called mortality crises. These crises could be caused by famine, an epidemic, or war. Gradually, these crises became less frequent, and the mortality risks that people faced became somewhat more predictable.

The growth of the European population after 1750 was mainly due to a decline in the death rate that accompanied the Industrial Revolution. Various views of the causes of this mortality decline are still debated. There is still disagreement about the role of an improved standard of living, manifested in better nutrition, public health advances such as improved sanitation and clean drinking water, the development of vaccines, and changes in curative medical care, in mortality decline in historical Europe.

Since World War II, mortality has declined in most of the less developed region of the world, leading to increased growth rates. Mortality has declined mainly from infectious diseases, such as malaria and measles, aided by vaccines from the more developed countries.

In the more developed countries, deaths are increasingly concentrated at advanced ages. The causes of death have shifted from infectious diseases to noncommunicable causes of death such as heart disease and stroke. Unhealthy behaviors, such as smoking, obesity, and excessive alcohol consumption, are major factors in death from these noncommunicable diseases. In developing countries, these unhealthy behaviors have increased, leading to increased concern about the development of obesity, hypertension (high blood pressure), and high cholesterol.

As mortality has declined, the average age of death has increased to the point where in many more developed countries, almost all deaths occur at advanced ages. With low mortality in developed countries, although people can die from chronic conditions, such as emphysema or Alzheimer's disease, they also can live for many years without functioning fully and thus pose a substantial burden on relatives and society. This has led to interest in healthy aging in an effort to decrease the number of years that people live in a dependent state. This is discussed more in Chapter 7.

Mortality Theories and Perspectives

Discussions about mortality have not debated whether death is a good or a bad thing. Rather, they have focused on whether the causes of disease and death were supernatural, biological, or social. Table 1.2 indicates some of the major theories and perspectives about disease and mortality over time.

The Struggle for a Scientific Understanding of the Causes of Disease

In ancient times, it was commonly believed that disease and death were supernaturally caused, whether through the arbitrary act of a spirit or god or as punishment for some misdeed. Hippocrates, in about 400 BCE, stated that disease was naturally caused, a point of view that has strongly influenced medical practice to the present day. He saw disease as the result of an imbalance in the body of four humors. The idea of imbalance of humors as a cause of

TABLE 1.2   Theories and Perspectives about Disease and Mortality

Theorist, Theory, or Framework	Date	Brief Description
Supernatural causes of disease	From ancient times	Disease and death are caused supernaturally or by evil spirits.
Hippocrates: natural disease causation	~400 BCE	Disease is naturally caused, often as a result of the mixture of different humors in the body.
Girolamo Fracastoro: contagion theory of disease	1546	Many diseases are caused by transmission from one ill person to another.
Miasma theory of disease	Ancient times to mid-19th century	Many diseases are caused by a miasma or mist, often from decomposing materials.
Louis Pasteur, Joseph Lister, and the germ theory of disease	~1870	Many diseases are caused by microorganisms, and the disease can be countered by attacking the disease-causing organism. This view also led to the promotion of greater hygiene during surgery.
Allopathic view of medical care	Mid-19th–20th centuries	The way to treat a disease or injury is through focus on the specific problem with little attention to other aspects of the person's health or life.
Homeopathic view of medical care	Mid-19th–20th centuries	A person's health, including recovery from a specific disease or injury, is linked to all other aspects of the person's health and life.
World Health Organization's definition of health	1946	Health is defined as a state of complete physical, mental, and social well-being and not merely the absence of disease or infirmity.
Thomas McKeown	1976	Improvements in nutrition and the standard of living are seen as the main causes of mortality decline in Western Europe from the 18th through the early 20th centuries.
Davidson Gwatkin	1980	People in less developed countries are vulnerable to any new disease if they do not have a good nutritional state and thus are not very hardy.
Fries: compression of morbidity	1983	As the age at death increases, the age of onset of disability or dependency also increases.
Global Burden of Disease Project	1990	This project estimates the roles of diseases and injuries and of risk factors in death and disability for countries by income level and region.
Resurgence of homeopathic medical care	1993	This is recognition of some increase in a holistic or integrative care approach in medical care and in integration of social scientific and biomedical perspectives in explanations of disease and death.
Bruce Link and Jo Phelan: fundamental causes of disease approach	1995	Social factors are often the root causes of diseases and chronic conditions that lead to disability or death.

disease was important in Western medicine until the mid-nineteenth century and was the rationale for bleeding a sick person (also known as "bloodletting"). Girolamo Fracastoro, an Italian physician and scholar, wrote in 1546 that "such things as clothes, linen, etc., which although not themselves corrupt, can nevertheless foster the essential seeds of the contagion and thus cause corruption."[46] He was the first person to describe how infectious diseases are transmitted in a manner that is consistent with modern understandings.

The miasma theory of disease claimed that bad air or bad humors caused disease. As mentioned, it was popular from ancient times through the mid-nineteenth century. The contagion theorists and the miasma theorists were often in conflict, with contagion advocates saying that disease transmission had to be through contact, while miasma adherents saw transmission as occurring through the air. When John Snow demonstrated in 1855 that cholera was transmitted through contaminated water, he was on one side of an argument in which the other side maintained that cholera was transmitted through "bad air," or a miasma. Snow's work is discussed more in Chapter 5.

Since some diseases are airborne, miasma theory was not totally wrong. One of the major contributions of miasma theory was that it was a motivation for public health efforts that led to improvements in sanitation. Many of these efforts were aimed at reducing or eliminating bad smells.[47]

The germ theory of disease brought together contagion theory and miasma theory. The germ theory of disease contended that many diseases are caused by microscopic organisms. Two of the main proponents of the germ theory were Louis Pasteur and Joseph Lister. Even though the germ theory was proposed in the last half of the nineteenth century, it took some time for its recommendations regarding disease transmission and sanitary conditions for surgery to have a major effect on medical practice.

Biomedical and Social Scientific Perspectives: The Disease, the Whole Person, and Population Implications

In the early twentieth century, there were major conflicts between two approaches to medical treatment. One was the allopathic approach, which was based on the germ theory of disease view that each disease or ailment had a specific cause. This approach contended that the way to treat an afflicted person was to address the specific cause of the person's ailment. The other was the homeopathic approach. Adherents of the homeopathic approach accepted the germ theory of disease, but they thought that other aspects of a person's situation and health also affected a person's recovery. The allopathic approach saw treating a broken arm as treating the arm in isolation, while the homeopathic approach saw the recovery of a person with a broken arm as affected also by the patient's state of mind and the other health problems that the person might face.[48]

In the late nineteenth century in the United States, both approaches to medicine were popular. The Rockefeller Foundation commissioned Abraham Flexner to make a study of American medical schools, both those that applied the allopathic approach and those that applied the homeopathic approach. The Flexner Report was published in 1910 and was very critical of homeopathic medicine. As a result of this report, many homeopathic medical schools were shut down. By the 1920s, the allopathic approach almost completely won out over the homeopathic approach in American medicine. Some have contended that the findings of the Flexner Report were predetermined in collaboration with the allopathic medical community.[49]

Recently, there has been increased interest in and recognition of the value of homeopathic medical care, also called integrative, holistic, or complementary and alternative medicine. In 1993, a *New England Journal of Medicine* article pointed out that, based on a telephone survey in 1991, 34% of American adults used one of these homeopathic-based therapies.[50] A study in 2007 found that 38% of American adults used one of these therapies, and people who had more education were more likely to use one of these therapies.[51] Allopathic medicine has increasingly integrated these alternative approaches, especially in areas such as pain management.[52]

Many medical practitioners have thought that the World Health Organization (WHO) definition of health is too broad and gives too much consideration to nonbiological factors. WHO defines health as "a state of complete physical, mental, and social well-being and not merely the absence of disease or infirmity."[53] This definition of health includes the role of the social and physical environments in which a person is situated. Demography and social science have viewed consideration of the social environment and behaviors that people engage in as an important part of the explanation of disease and mortality. Social scientists have been supportive of the WHO definition. As discussed in Chapters 5–7, health behaviors and other social factors, including the social environment in which people function, are increasingly thought to explain mortality differentials, especially in more developed countries.

Even as vaccines for diseases reduced mortality from specific causes, Gwatkin was concerned that the mortality gains in less developed countries could be reversed if the people being vaccinated still did not have good nutritional status, and if they were not hardier than people in their countries had been in earlier times. He thought that if they had poor nutrition, they were vulnerable to any new disease that might come along. He was criticizing the allopathic medical approach that addressed the threat of each individual disease, without sufficient concern with the overall healthiness of the person.[54] Gwatkin wrote before the HIV epidemic, but the more rapid death of HIV-positive people who are poorly nourished is consistent with his concerns.

Link and Phelan developed the **fundamental causes of disease approach**, which views social conditions, poverty, and socioeconomic characteristics as the underlying causes of disease and death.[55] Hypertension and high cholesterol contribute to disease or death in the fundamental causes of disease approach, due to the social conditions that lead to hypertension and high cholesterol. For example, being obese contributes to hypertension and in turn to a wide variety of diseases and causes of death. However, eating healthy food, which could reduce the risk of obesity, is related to the cost of those foods and their availability. People who live in poor areas often have less access to fresh and nutritious food, and, when available, these foods are often more expensive than in better-off neighborhoods. Thus, poverty and living in a poor area contribute to obesity, which in turn has negative consequences. In the view of the fundamental causes approach, focusing only on directly treating hypertension or high cholesterol is shortsighted and does not address the roots of the problem. Link and Phelan were mainly thinking about more developed countries, but their argument is similar to that of Gwatkin for less developed countries.

Integration of Biomedical and Social Scientific Perspectives

Many researchers have become interested in combining biological and social scientific knowledge in their explanations of mortality. For example, Kujaha and his colleagues found in a study of twins in Finland that although physical activity and alcohol consumption affected the risk of dying, genetic differences caused lack of activity and drinking to be greater risks for some individuals than others.[56] Social surveys have incorporated physical measures, such as height and weight, and have taken biological samples, such as saliva and blood, to allow investigation of the joint behavioral and biological determinants of health outcomes. Many conditions, such as high blood pressure and type II diabetes, often have no symptoms for afflicted individuals. A biological measure of whether a person has a condition is a better indicator of the prevalence of the condition than is whether a person thinks he or she has high blood pressure (hypertension) or diabetes or whether a health practitioner has told the person that he or she has a particular condition. Those with regular health care are more likely to know whether they have a particular condition, but those without regular health care are often more likely to actually have the condition. Knowing both the actual prevalence of hypertension and how it is related to other characteristics are important. As discussed in Chapter 5, high blood pressure (hypertension) was the leading risk factor for death in the world in 2004. Although there are genetic predispositions to hypertension, behaviors such as diet, smoking, and exercise also contribute to whether a person is hypertensive.

The World Health Organization Global Burden of Disease (GBD) Project has promoted integration of thinking and research about biological and social factors in disease and mortality. This project has estimated the portion of deaths and of disability due to various causes for countries grouped by income level and by region. It has also estimated the contribution of various risk factors, such as high cholesterol, smoking, lack of exercise, poor sanitation, and unclean water, to death and disability. Since these risk factors span biomedical, behavioral, and social structural aspects, the GBD project promotes integration of biomedical and social scientific perspectives. This project is discussed in Chapter 5.

Public Health Perspectives on Mortality and Disease
Public health perspectives are situated between biomedical and social scientific perspectives. Public health is oriented toward promoting the health of the entire population and thus, like demography, typically has a population rather than a clinical perspective. Schools of public health often include a department of health education and health behavior, which focuses on understanding and developing policies to encourage healthy lifestyles, an area that is increasingly important in reducing mortality in developed countries. A major example of the role of health behaviors in mortality is smoking. Other areas include alcohol consumption and seat belt use. Health education and health behavior studies also include understanding why women use contraception or choose or reject particular contraceptive methods.

Schools of public health virtually always include a department of epidemiology, whose methodological concerns are very similar to concerns in demography. Epidemiology has been defined as the "study of the distribution and determinants of health-related states or events in specified populations, and the application of this study to control of health problems."[57] Within epidemiology is the area of **social epidemiology**, which "is a branch of epidemiology that focuses particularly on the effects of social-structural factors on states of health."[58] Research in this area has included an examination of the relation of health and mortality to factors such as social class and income distribution. Epidemiological research in public health explicitly includes a programmatic component, while research in demography, although it often is applied to policy questions, can be undertaken for purely scientific purposes. Also, although demography is concerned with patterns and causes of mortality due to their role in population growth, epidemiology is concerned both with mortality and with patterns and causes of ill health or sickness, called morbidity. Mortality and morbidity are discussed more in Chapters 4–7.

As the causes of death have changed from conditions that kill rapidly, such as measles or smallpox, to long-lasting chronic conditions that can eventually kill people but more often lead to disabling health problems, such as diabetes, interest in population health has emerged, which bridges demography and epidemiology. Kindig and Stoddart defined **population health** as "the health outcomes of a group of individuals, including the distribution of such outcomes within the group."[59] With declines in mortality, an increasing proportion of people live to advanced ages. A concern is whether the additional years of life are spent in an active independent state or in a disabled state that requires substantial expenditures of time and money by others to support what is often seen as a poor quality of life.

A concern with population health and with active life has also been stimulated by Fries's idea of the compression of morbidity. Fries thought that as the age of death increased, the age of the onset of disability would also increase. If this occurred, then the time a person spent in a disabled or dependent state would be much less than if people became disabled at the same age as they had earlier and spent their additional years of life disabled and dependent on others. There has been mixed evidence as to the extent to which compression of morbidity has occurred.[60]

The Clinical Perspective and the Population Perspective

In the study of human health and its treatment, people discuss a clinical perspective versus a population perspective. In the clinical perspective, the health care provider uses what is known to diagnose and treat an individual patient. The individually based clinical perspective asks, "Why did this person die?" Or, "What could have been done to prevent this person from dying so soon?" The population perspective is concerned with causes of disease, but it is also concerned with structural factors related to mortality risks and overall patterns of disease and mortality. The population perspective asks, "What could be done to reduce death rates from a particular cause?" Understanding the population perspective can aid physicians in contextualizing and understanding the situation in treating individual patients. Demography employs the population perspective.[61]

Changes in Fertility

Through most of human history, mortality has been high enough that women and couples have struggled to bear enough children to assure that some would survive to adulthood and subsequently have children of their own. As mortality declined and fertility did not, more children survived to adulthood, and population growth rates increased.

In Europe, starting with France in the eighteenth century, fertility declined, which reduced population growth. By the early twentieth century, fertility declined considerably in all of the currently developed countries to the point where population growth rates were moderate.

As mortality declined in the less developed countries and fertility did not decline as rapidly, growth rates in some countries became very high, making efforts to extend education and health care to a larger proportion of the population more difficult. Since the 1970s, fertility has declined in much of the less developed region, although it is still very high in much of Africa and in some other countries.

In the late twentieth century, fertility had become so low in most of the more developed region that population decline seemed very likely. Countries do not want a declining population because of anticipated negative effects on economic growth: For example, population aging accompanies a declining population and reduces the proportion of the population working for pay to support those too old or too young to work for pay. The United States has continued to have high fertility for a developed country and is unlikely to face population decline in the foreseeable future, a situation that many other developed countries would like to have.

In almost all developed countries, childbearing has shifted to an older age. In some cases, this seems to have led to continued fertility decline. In other cases, fertility rates have increased enough at older ages to compensate for the declines at younger ages, sometimes reaching a level of fertility that would avoid population decline.

Fertility Theories and Perspectives

We talked earlier in this chapter about views of the desirability or undesirability of increased population growth. In this section, we discuss views and theories about fertility. There have been various philosophical or moral views about fertility limitation or encouragement, and there have been a variety of theories about why women and couples have children. Fertility is discussed more in Chapters 8–10. Table 1.3 summarizes the main theories and perspectives about fertility.

Much of the discussion about fertility is about how fertility affects the rate of population growth. If population growth is viewed as too high, people discuss what might be done to reduce fertility; if population growth is viewed as too low, there is discussion about what might be done to increase fertility. The Roman rulers supported high fertility because they wanted a high rate of population growth. Much of the controversy between Malthusians and Marxists, discussed in this chapter in the context of population growth, was an argument about whether a high rate of population growth necessitated specific attention to trying to lower fertility. Malthusians thought there needed to be fertility-limiting policies, while the Marxists thought the problem was not high fertility but rather a need for technological advances and a fairer distribution of resources.

Religions have taken various positions on the acceptability of intentional fertility limitation. Saint Augustine (354–430) wrote that any form of fertility limitation among married persons was wrong and saw procreation as the only legitimate purpose of sexual intercourse. These views helped form much of later Roman Catholic thought about fertility limitation and its relation to population growth.[62] In 1930, the Anglican Church was the first Christian denomination to decree that use of contraception was acceptable.[63] Some religions, such as Buddhism, have no general position on the use of contraception. Hinduism has no proscription on the use of contraception and provides believers advice on how to either increase or decrease the chance that a woman becomes pregnant. In Judaism, views of contraceptive use differ by the branch of Judaism. The Qur'an does not discuss contraception, but Muhammad knew of the use of coitus interruptus (withdrawal) and did not forbid it. Historically, the use of fertility-limiting practices was acknowledged and widespread in Islam, but there has been controversy within Islam about the legitimacy of contraceptive use.[64]

TABLE 1.3   Theories and Perspectives about Fertility

Theorist, Theory, or Framework	Date	Brief Description
Roman rulers	~15 BCE	High fertility is desirable because of the need for a large army and colonists for the Roman Empire.
Positions of religions		Religions differ in their positions about contraception: Christianity is often opposed, in Judaism the position varies by branch, in Islam the position varied over time and by school of thought, Buddhism takes no position, and Hinduism has no proscription.
Thomas Malthus	~1800	High fertility is the main cause of high population growth rates and must be controlled by postponement of marriage.
Karl Marx	~1870	High fertility is not a problem. Sufficient resources per person can be provided by economic growth fueled by technology and a fair distribution of resources.
Arsene Dumont: social capillarity	1890	When social mobility is possible, having fewer children facilitates mobility.
W. S. Thompson Demographic Transition Theory	1929	This is a description of population change in Europe historically in which first mortality declined and later fertility declined to the level of mortality.
Role incompatibility between motherhood and paid work	1976	Childbearing and female labor force participation are inherently incompatible.
Gary Becker: shift from child quantity to child quality	1960, 1973	The implications of viewing children as desirable consumer durables, in the context of a shift from concern with child quantity to child quality, are examined.
Richard Easterlin: relative cohort size hypothesis	1966, 1974	People decide what resources are needed to raise a child based on the resources that their family had available when they were young.
Bernard Berelson: beyond family planning	1969	This discusses a variety of policies that less developed countries could implement to try to reduce fertility.
James Fawcett: value of children studies	1972	These studies examined the social-psychological reasons for having children, such as old age security or to carry on the family name.
Ansley Coale: preconditions for fertility limitation	1972	The preconditions for fertile sexually active women and couples to intentionally limit their fertility are that (1) fertility limitation was morally acceptable and possible, (2) fertility limitation was in their interest, and (3) they had available an effective and acceptable means of limiting fertility.
John Caldwell: intergenerational wealth flows	1976	Voluntary fertility limitation is motivated by a shift in the flow of resources from upward with the older generation to downward to the younger generation.
Karen Oppenheim Mason: reconsideration of role incompatibility	1981	Whether women's labor force activity is incompatible with childbearing and childrearing depends on the nature of the work.
Coale: European Fertility Project	1986	This challenges the Demographic Transition Theory, emphasizing the role of culture and the diffusion of ideas.
Ron Lesthaeghe and Chris Wilson: FLIMP	1986	In the family labor-intensive mode of production (FLIMP), the household is the productive unit, and having many children is economically rational.
Caldwell: persistence of high fertility	1987	A fear of unpredictable future, high mortality, and destitution of many elderly persons without adult sons supports continued high fertility.
Cairo Population Conference	1994	At this conference, the attention of the population community was redirected from family planning to facilitating reproductive choice.
Dirk van de Kaa: the Second Demographic Transition	2001	Postponement of marriage and childbearing and increased childlessness led to very low fertility in some Western European countries.
Massimo Livi-Bacci: too much family	2001	Based on Italy, this theory posits that very low fertility can result from norms that allow long co-residence of adult children and high economic requirements for starting a family.
Brienna Perelli-Harris: another path to very low fertility	2005	Very low fertility was achieved in some Eastern European countries without all of the changes that are described in the Second Demographic Transition.
Arland Thornton: developmental idealism	2005	A set of views about what is good about modern society and the modern family that people internalize when they decide to control their fertility.
James Feyrer and Bruce Sacerdote: gender equity and fertility	2008	Societal gender equity is essential for highly developed countries to have a fertility level high enough to avoid population decline.
Jason Linde: children as inferior goods	2010	With changing attitudes, there can be other goods that can substitute for the material and psychological benefits that people obtain from their children.

The First and Second Demographic Transitions: Generalizations from Experience in Western Europe

Some scholars have theorized that certain conditions or changes are essential for fertility change based on observation of the empirical situation where fertility has declined. This occurred in the Theory of the Demographic Transition and the Second Demographic Transition. In each case, other thinkers have challenged these conclusions.

The Theory of the Demographic Transition is a description of the pattern of mortality and fertility decline in Europe historically. Some have looked at the social and economic changes that accompanied that transition and posited that changes such as urbanization and industrialization were essential to these demographic changes, especially to fertility decline.[65] The European Fertility Project pursued more detailed research that challenged the causal role of socioeconomic factors in the decline of European fertility and pointed to the importance of cultural factors and the diffusion of information.[66]

When fertility became very low in some Western European countries in the 1990s, scholars summarized the changes that had accompanied those fertility changes, including an older age at first birth, more permanent childlessness, an increase in cohabitation, and an increase in nonmarital births. Van de Kaa described this set of changes as a Second Demographic Transition. Some researchers thought that these changes were necessary in order for very low fertility to occur.[67] Livi-Bacci looking at Italy, and Perelli-Harris looking at Eastern Europe, described situations in which very low fertility occurred without all of the changes described in the Second Demographic Transition, suggesting that there is a variety of paths to very low fertility.[68]

Supports for Continued High Fertility

Much theorizing has been about what leads people to limit their fertility. In some historical and contemporary settings, fertility has remained high even after mortality had declined substantially and other social changes had occurred that people would have expected to lead to fertility decline.

Lesthaeghe and Wilson pointed out that in situations that employ what they called the family labor-intensive mode of production (FLIMP), the productive unit is the family. In these situations, in which the productive unit is often a household engaged in agriculture, as much labor as is available can be utilized, making continued high fertility rational.[69]

Caldwell points out that in some less developed countries, cultural pressure to have many children has made it very difficult for people to voluntarily limit the total number of children they have. Often, many women in these populations have faced serious problems in getting pregnant and having live births

and are happy to successfully have many children. Also, in some less developed settings, older widows with no adult sons are one of the most impoverished groups in the community. In these situations, it is rational for a woman to want to have as many sons as possible to try to ensure that at least one son is alive when she reaches old age. Also, with mortality fluctuations from epidemics, famine, and war, women and couples sometimes want to have "extra children" to try to insure against unforeseen high mortality in the future.[70]

Motivations for Fertility Limitation

Several theorists have proposed ideas about what motivates people to limit their fertility. One of the first was Dumont, who in 1890 put forward the idea of "social capillarity." He thought that in a society in which social mobility was possible, those who wanted to be mobile needed to direct their resources to that end and make sacrifices. One of the sacrifices that could facilitate social mobility was remaining childless or having a small number of children.[71]

Caldwell, thinking about high fertility in less developed countries, saw the shift from a set of social norms and practices where resources flowed from the younger generation to the older generation to a situation in which resources flowed from the older generation to the younger generation as crucial for people to decide to try to limit the number of children they have.[72]

Models and typologies based on sociology and social psychology have also been useful in understanding motivations for fertility control. The Value of Children studies were explicitly based on social psychology.[73] These studies were conducted in numerous countries. They looked at the reasons why people thought having children was valuable and how these values varied across societies. One aim was to determine whether different values of children were associated with situations in which there was little voluntary fertility limitation and situations in which there was substantial voluntary fertility limitation. Parents were asked whether they valued children for economic reasons such as help around the house or old age security and whether they thought that children tied parents down. For example, in higher fertility settings, parents were more likely to mention economic reasons and were less likely to think that children tied them down. In the same tradition, Thornton developed the model of developmental idealism.[74] He saw that throughout the world, a set of ideas has spread about what constitutes modern society and the modern family, including low fertility and the use of family planning. Other parts of developmental idealism include a society that is industrialized and highly educated. As people come to see modern society and the modern family as desirable, they become receptive to the use of family planning, and thus fertility declines.

An economist, Gary Becker, thought fertility limitation was motivated by a shift from a concern with "child quantity" to "child quality." Higher child quality is usually interpreted as more expensive children due to costs such as paying for schooling, so the shift to a smaller family size is explained by the observation that the fewer children a couple has, the more they can afford to invest in each child. This approach grew out of the application of ideas from economic theories of consumption to the bearing of children. Children were seen as consumer durables, and like other consumer durables, children were satisfying to parents to the extent that they satisfied their parents' tastes. As tastes changed from a desire for child quantity to one for child quality, a different kind of child was produced for the parents' satisfaction—a higher quality child.[75] In Becker's view, children were superior goods, that is, they were inherently desirable. Also, there were few if any acceptable substitutes for what children could provide to parents in areas such as affection, respect, and carrying on the family name.

Coale proposed a set of three preconditions for voluntary fertility limitation that need to be simultaneously fulfilled. He thought that a woman or couple needed to think that (1) fertility limitation was morally acceptable and possible, (2) fertility limitation was in their interest, and (3) they had available an effective and acceptable means of limiting fertility.[76] With changes in the tastes of potential parents and some Second Demographic Transition arguments that people no longer needed to have children to feel they are adults, some have speculated that one reason fertility has become very low and childlessness has increased in many more developed countries is that children have changed from being superior goods to being inferior goods. An "inferior good" is something that people consume when they have a low income and cannot afford more desirable goods.[77]

Female Labor Force Participation and Fertility
There has been a variety of views about the relation between female labor force participation and fertility. Many have assumed that in less developed countries, female labor force participation and childbearing (or the presence of a young child) are incompatible. This has sometimes led to expectations that increasing female income-producing activity in less developed countries would lead to lower fertility.[78] Mason, however, points out that whether the presence of young children conflicts with female labor force participation in less developed countries depends on the nature of the woman's work. For example, a woman can resell goods on the street in a city in a less developed country and have young children present with little conflict.[79]

Until recently, economic theories of fertility in developed countries have also assumed that a woman with a child, especially a young child, would not be able to work for pay or that she would avoid working for pay if at all possible. In addition, legal barriers to women's employment in developed countries strengthened the negative relationship between fertility and female labor force participation.[80] Especially before the large increase in labor force participation of American women with young children that began in about 1970, a main economic explanation of childbearing decisions focused on the education of the wife. The economic interpretation of why more educated women had fewer children than less educated women was that a woman would have less income for some time if she had a child and that the amount of income lost due to childbearing would be directly related to her education, because the more highly educated the woman was, the higher her wage rate if she worked for pay. The assumption was that having a child led to the woman withdrawing from paid work for some time and, in doing so, losing the income she would have received if she had continued to work for pay. This was viewed as the opportunity cost of childbearing, with foregone income being the missed opportunity.[81]

This assumed connection between fertility and women not working for pay in more developed countries weakened as labor force participation rates of women increased, regardless of how young their children were. By the mid-1990s, there had emerged a positive relation among more developed countries between female labor force participation and fertility. This led to research on the relation between government policies and fertility. Also, as fertility at older ages increased in some developed countries, sometimes enough to raise the overall fertility level, scholars thought about what conditions were necessary for this fertility increase to occur. Feyrer put forth the view that a high level of societal gender equity was necessary for fertility to increase enough at older ages to compensate for the fertility decline at younger ages.[82]

Changes in Fertility Policy Positions
In the 1960s and 1970s, some policy planners became very agitated about how to reduce fertility in the face of very high growth rates in many less developed countries. In 1969, Berelson discussed a wide variety of policies that had been proposed to reduce fertility, including requiring licenses to have children and compulsory sterilization of men with more than three children.[83]

By the mid-1990s, fertility in the less developed countries as a whole had fallen considerably, and there were emerging concerns in some developed countries about very low fertility. At the World

Population Conference in Cairo in 1994, the emphasis shifted from a concern with fertility limitation and reducing population growth rates to an emphasis on reproductive health.[84] The four goals agreed on at the meeting were as follows:

1. Universal primary education and improved access of women to postprimary education
2. Reduction of infant and child mortality
3. Reduction of maternal mortality
4. Access to reproductive and sexual health services, including family planning, prevention and treatment of infertility, treatment of sexually transmitted diseases, and discouragement of female genital mutilation

It is interesting that only the fourth goal directly addressed fertility, and that goal concerned both the limitation of fertility and the prevention and treatment of infertility. The other goals addressed factors thought to be related to the decision to limit fertility but were not immediately related to reduction of population growth rates.

Changes in Migration

Human populations have always migrated. Humans originated in Africa and, through migration, spread through Europe, Asia, and the Americas. As people settled in different climates and physical settings, ways of life and social organization changed.

Migration as a part of daily life has been common throughout history. Hunters and gatherers moved frequently to new areas to find game and gatherable food. Pastoral nomads moved at least seasonally to take their animals to fresh grazing areas.

The establishment of towns and cities entailed a shift in the location of part of the population. Also, there was a major change in occupational structure, from almost everyone being engaged in agriculture to the growth in the number of full-time artisans, traders, and others providing services. Members of these new occupations did not produce their own food but received money or other goods in exchange for their services. This was a key part of the development of the market economy.

Since at least 1500, international migration has led to denser settlement of much of the world, especially in North America, Australia, and parts of Africa. This was part of the process of colonization, with accompanying implications for the spread of disease and changes in social and economic practices.

Since the late twentieth century, international migration from less developed countries has helped many developed countries avert population decline. Many developed countries have had programs that allow workers from less developed countries to come and work for some period of time, but without the chance for permanent residence or citizenship. Often, immigration to more developed countries becomes an issue of policy formation and legislation in the more developed country rather than an issue of the desires and motivations of potential international migrants.

Natural disasters and political disturbances have led to large movements of refugees. Most refugees from less developed countries move temporarily to other less developed countries. This can cause a major strain on the resources of the receiving countries. In addition, while international laws promote the consideration of refugees for permanent residence, many more developed countries struggle with the question "Who is a true refugee?" as they perceive a much larger number of people who would like to immigrate than they would be willing to admit. Migration is discussed further in Chapter 12.

Theories of and Perspectives on Migration

Table 1.4 summarizes the main theories of and perspectives on migration. Some of the theories and perspectives were developed with internal migration (migration within one country) in mind, and some were developed to apply to international migration, but most are applicable to both internal and international migration. A major difference between explanations of internal and international migration is that legal restrictions play a much greater role in international migration. Also, the difference in wage rates is typically greater between less developed and more developed countries, even for labor-intensive jobs, than is the case within one country. However, there often is a substantially higher wage rate (even for labor-intensive jobs) in urban areas than in rural areas of less developed countries. Also, some theories involve aspects of international economic activity that influence international migration.

Geographical Perspectives on Migration

The discipline of geography has had a large impact on thinking in the area of migration. Some of this has been manifested in attraction models, such as that of Young and Zipf. These models are based on the attraction between particles in physics and the decrease in attraction with distance, and they have been used to try to model the number of migrants between places.[85] Stouffer added to earlier work by including consideration of the presence of intervening opportunities or alternative destinations as affecting the volume of migration between the two places. These intervening opportunities did not need to be physically between the two places under consideration, but would include the presence of a large city located west of both places.[86]

TABLE 1.4   Theories and Perspectives about Migration

Theorist, Theory, or Framework	Date	Brief Description
E. G. Ravenstein: laws of migration	1885, 1889	There are ten laws, which include considerations of gender, age, motivation, and distance.
E. C. Young	1928	The number of migrants between two places is positively related to the "force of attraction" between the places and inversely related to distance.
Samuel Stouffer: intervening opportunities	1940, 1960	The number of intervening opportunities or alternative destinations will influence migration between two places in addition to the characteristics of the two places.
George Kingsley Zipf: inverse distance law	1946	The number of migrants between two places is positively related to the population of the two places and inversely related to distance.
Gunnar Myrdal: cumulative causation model	1957	When migration occurs, it alters the context of migration decisions and makes subsequent migration more likely.
John MacDonald and Leatrice MacDonald: chain migration	1964	The earlier international migration of friends and relatives facilitates later migration through informational, economic, and legal help.
Everett Lee: theory of migration	1966	Four factors influence migration: (1) origin characteristics, (2) destination characteristics, (3) intervening obstacles, and (4) personal factors.
John Caldwell: rural-urban migration in Ghana	1969	Networks are important, and institutions develop in urban areas to facilitate migrants and migrant adaptation.
John Harris and Michael Todaro: rural-urban migration in developing countries	1970	Based on the existence of a dual labor market, rural-urban migration is related to the difference between the expected wage rate at the destination and at the origin, especially among workers in the labor-intensive sector.
Wilbur Zelinsky: mobility transition model	1971	There are five stages of the mobility transition, which are generally related to the demographic transition.
Michael Piore: dual labor markets and international migration	1979	International migration is caused by the demand for low-cost labor in developed countries in the labor-intensive sector.
Graeme Hugo: network theory	1981	Interpersonal ties between people at the origin and destination facilitate international migration by improving information and decreasing economic and other costs to potential migrants.
Alejandro Portes and Michael Piore: world systems theory	1981	International migration is motivated by the global capitalist market. Labor flows in the opposite direction of goods and capital, often to former colonial powers.
Oded Stark and David Bloom: new economics of labor migration	1985	Migration decisions involve the entire household, not just the individual potential migrant.
Oded Stark and J. Taylor: relative deprivation and international migration	1989	The decisions of whether a household member will migrate and the choice of who will migrate are influenced by comparison, with wanting the household to have a good standard of living and good opportunities held in comparison with the household's reference group.
Douglas Massey: institutional theory	1993	After international migration to developed countries begins, legal and illegal institutions emerge to facilitate this migration and overcome practical and legal obstacles.

Lee developed a model of migration that combined earlier geographically based work with more social scientific thinking. Migration between places resulted from four sets of factors: (1) factors associated with the origin, (2) factors associated with the destination, (3) intervening obstacles, and (4) personal factors. The origin and destination factors could include economic conditions at the origin and destination. Personal factors could include education, gender, and age. Intervening obstacles included the distance between the origin and the destination, the difficulty of travel, and alternative destinations.[87]

Zelinsky's Model of the Mobility Transition
Zelinsky developed a model of what he called the mobility transition that had five phases. The five phases were related to phases of the demographic transition. Phase 1 is a premodern traditional society with little migration and little population growth. Phase 5 is a future superadvanced society in which almost all migration is between or within urban places.[88]

Economic Perspectives on Migration
Economic models have long dominated explanations of migration. In the 1880s, Ravenstein proposed ten laws of migration, one of which was that people usually migrate for economic reasons.[89] The most prominent model of rural-urban migration in less developed countries is that of the economists Harris and Todaro, which sees the potential migrant in the rural area assessing his (or her) likely wage rate if he remained in the rural area and his likely wage rate

if he migrated to an urban destination. If the likely increment to the wage rate is sufficient, the person will migrate.[90]

Stark and Bloom are economists who expanded the range of actors making migration decisions. While the Harris–Todaro model assumed the potential migrant was the sole decision maker, Stark and Bloom thought that the migration decision was made by the entire household, with the decision of whether anyone would migrate and who would migrate made with the interests of *all* household members in mind.[91]

Stark and Taylor further developed the role of all household members in migration decisions in the relative deprivation perspective. In this perspective, migration decisions by households are made with the standard of living and opportunities of the household's reference group in mind. If other households in the community have obtained goods due to earnings from migrants, this can motivate a household to send a member to become a labor migrant when otherwise household members would not have aspired to those goods.[92]

Sociological Perspectives on Migration

In the area of rural-urban migration in developing countries, sociologists have also emphasized perceptions, norms, values, and other non-economic factors. Migration to an alien destination can be off-putting to a potential migrant, and for both internal and international migration there are often numerous practical difficulties that must be overcome. Thus, people are more likely to migrate if they are less risk-averse. This is one reason why migrants disproportionately tend to be people with relatively high education among those at their place of origin.

In 1957, Myrdal proposed the idea of cumulative causation, in which once a migration stream between two places begins, this in itself alters the context in which subsequent migration decisions are made and typically increases the volume of migration.[93] MacDonald and MacDonald showed that chain migration, in which subsequent migrants receive information and practical help from friends and relatives who migrated earlier, is important. Caldwell for Ghana and Hugo for Indonesia showed that networks in urban destinations, sometimes based on ethnic group membership, can ease the adjustment process for new migrants from rural areas. Thinking about international migration, Massey made a similar argument about the development of networks and institutions to facilitate migration.[94]

Some Considerations about International Migration

Piore and Portes have addressed how the world economy influences the international migration of workers with a low skill level. They took a somewhat Marxist approach and saw international migration as driven by the demand for low-cost workers in the labor-intensive sector of developed countries.[95]

THE INFLUENCE OF HISTORY, ANTHROPOLOGY, PSYCHOLOGY, POLITICAL SCIENCE, AND STATISTICS ON POPULATION THINKING

Disciplines other than economics and sociology have not had as pervasive an influence on population thinking, although their influence has been substantial. Next, we discuss the perspectives and influence of history, anthropology, political science, psychology, and statistics.

Historical Perspectives

Historical and anthropological perspectives address the need to have sufficient cultural and historical understanding to know what things mean in a specific context. In terms of data analysis, cultural and historical understanding relates to the question of **validity**. When you have a particular indicator or measure, it is intended that it represents some underlying concept. The measure is valid if in fact it does represent the underlying concept.

A lack of cultural and historical understanding can lead to the choice of an invalid indicator, which means that the interpretation of the results can be wrong. For example, Buckley in a discussion of surveys conducted in Russia involving foreign scholars refers to difficulties of translating concepts from one language (English) in which they are well understood to another language (Russian) in which the concept is not present or is uncommon. She noted that one survey studying depression translated "Do you sometimes feel blue?" literally into Russian, even though in Russian the word "blue" does not necessarily mean depressed and can refer to gay sexual orientation. Jones notes that it has often been observed that people in Southeast Asia tend to be extremely eager to please interviewers and to give the desired answer. She argues that this tendency is real, but that it can be overcome by the interviewer establishing a good rapport with the respondent and by careful construction of survey questions so that there does not seem to be any preferred or "right" answer.[96]

There is a long tradition in historical demography of attempting to understand the life of ordinary people. History had been limited because often common people were not literate and did not leave letters or diaries. In the 1960s, there emerged an interest of what was sometimes called studying history "from the bottom up," which focused on the lives of common people. The application of demographic methods to religious and administrative records collected for other purposes, often using church parish registers or village listings, has allowed a great deal to be discovered about mortality and fertility conditions, as well as the household and family structure of people in the past.[97]

Anthropological Perspectives

Populations typically studied by anthropologists have sometimes been studied by demographers intending to make inferences about the demographic conditions experienced by populations that lived long in the past, such as hunters and gatherers. Howell's book in this vein was published in a series in historical demography.[98] However, increasingly anthropologists have applied demographic approaches to studying mainstream anthropological questions.[99]

Since the 1970s, there has been increasing awareness of the importance of anthropological and cultural perspectives among demographers. Some of this was motivated by research in the Princeton European Fertility Project, which aimed to test the Theory of the Demographic Transition. In its assessment of historical fertility decline across Europe, there was substantial evidence that the geographic spread of the intentional limitation of childbearing was more strongly related to the diffusion of various cultural views and practices than it was to the extent to which a locale had become industrialized.[100] These observations led demographers who were usually economists or sociologists to take consideration of the role of culture more seriously than had generally been true previously. This new awareness also led to an increase in research that combined quantitative and qualitative methods, as demographers become aware that qualitative research (observing and talking to people about their views and feelings) is often necessary in order to understand demographic decision-making behavior.[101]

Political Perspectives

Much of demography is concerned with the likely implications of alternative policies, something that immediately involves political considerations and political positions. Some political issues directly involve demographic considerations, including the U.S. constitutional requirement that seats in the U.S. House of Representatives be reallocated across states after each decennial census proportionate to the distribution of the U.S. population across states.

Political considerations can also lead to demographic data not being collected. For example, Lebanon has not had a census since 1932, mainly because the Lebanese Parliament is allocated 50/50 between Christians and Muslims. It is clear that a census would show that a substantial majority of the Lebanese population is Muslim. This result would almost certainly lead to calls for change in the composition of the Lebanese legislature, which could lead to political unrest.

Sometimes, there are intense disagreements about the wisdom or efficacy of particular programs or policies. These disagreements often reduce to different views of which groups are most deserving of government social program support, which is a political or policy judgment. For example, Ben-Shalom and his colleagues concluded that social welfare programs in the United States have had only a modest effect on reduction of poverty because they favor the employed, disabled, and elderly, groups that are viewed as deserving. These programs are less focused on the poorest segment of the population, even though the poorest segment has the worst health and the highest mortality.[102]

Politics also influences fertility-related policies and programs. For example, there has been a heated policy debate in the United States about sex education programs for adolescents, which has focused on whether abstinence should be the only pregnancy prevention method discussed in schools or contraception should also be included. These debates concern whether sex education that includes more than abstinence education promotes sexual activity and also include disagreements about the effectiveness of abstinence-only programs.[103]

An area of demography that directly involves political considerations is international migration. Although most countries do little to limit emigration, many countries, especially more developed countries, have strict rules about legal immigration. Illegal immigration has become an increasingly important issue of policy concern in many countries. There are also policy choices about what the penalties and enforcement procedures should be for undocumented immigrants.[104] Thus, the causes of immigration are sometimes more strongly related to laws and policies rather than to incentives to emigrate from the origin country or preferences of potential international migrants. Thus, much of immigration is determined by the process by which immigration laws are passed, an issue of agenda-setting and legislative dynamics that is studied by political scientists.[105]

Psychological Perspectives

Sometimes, psychologists have studied the personality or psychological consequences that result from demographic phenomena. For example, Falbo studied the personality and other characteristics of only children in China. The large proportion of only children resulted from China's fertility limitation (one-child) policy.[106] Also, research on the psychological adjustment of older persons has become increasingly relevant in aging populations.[107] An increasing part of research on health and mortality has focused on the role of psychological conditions such as stress or depression.[108]

The Influence of Statistics and Advances in Computing

Advances in statistics and in computing have long been important in demographic analysis. Through the 1880 U.S. Census, results were tabulated by hand. For the 1890 Census, a punch card tabulating machine, developed by Hollerith, was used, which speeded up and reduced the cost of census tabulation. The resulting company eventually became IBM.[109]

Advances in statistical methods, in combination with improvements in computing power, have continued to be important. Better sampling methods have improved the value of surveys. Also, more powerful computing allowed multidimensional analysis of very large files, such as individual data from census files. These developments have allowed researchers and policy analysts to answer increasingly complex questions using empirical data.

Space and geographic location have played increasing roles in demographic analysis. This has been facilitated by advances in spatial statistical methods and in the availability of low-cost Global Positioning System (GPS) units so that the locations of residences, schools, and health clinics can be used as variables to analyze the impact of proximity to health care, schools, stores, and water sources on outcomes such as infant and child mortality and use of contraception. For example, Szwarcwald and her colleagues used spatial analysis methods in a study of infant mortality in Rio de Janeiro to show that infant death from 1 to 11 months of age was related to the concentration of poverty in an area, even after the local poverty level had been taken into account.[110] Much research about the role of geographic location addresses the role of neighborhood effects in health and other outcomes.[111]

DEMOGRAPHY AS A FIELD

In the United States, demography is usually not considered a separate discipline. At American universities and colleges, students cannot get a bachelor's degree in demography, and there are only a few American universities where a doctoral degree in demography is available.[112] Most American demographers are either sociologists or economists, although some are historians, political scientists, psychologists, statisticians, or public health specialists. The dominant American perspective is that work in demography is enriched by a disciplinary theoretical and conceptual perspective, such as that from sociology or economics. Thus, most American demographers with doctorates receive their degree in a field such as sociology or economics, with demography as a specialization.

In most of the rest of the world, demography is considered a separate discipline. In many countries, students can receive bachelor's degrees and advanced degrees, such as doctoral degrees, in demography. There are many excellent demographers throughout the world. However, the lack of a disciplinary base can lead demographic work to be excessively descriptive and atheoretical.

DEMOGRAPHIC PATTERNS, DEVELOPMENT, AND SOCIAL CHANGE

Many demographic phenomena are related to the population's standard of living, its education, the infrastructure in the country, or some other aspect of the development level of the country. Poorer and less educated populations typically have higher mortality and higher fertility than more prosperous and better educated populations.

There is often value in comparing the demographic situation and demographic changes in (1) the currently more developed countries in the past, (2) current less developed countries, and (3) the more developed countries. Both Marxist models of development and modernization theory have been dismissed by many as simplistic and not fitting empirical reality. However, examining the differences and similarities in the relation of social, economic, and demographic change in various circumstances can be informative.[113]

One major difference between the historical situation of currently more developed countries and that of the less developed countries is the pace of change and the role of technology. In the currently developed countries in the past, demographic change was fairly gradual, and technological innovation was developed at the same time that it was applied. In currently less developed countries, social and technological change has occurred much more rapidly, and there have been substantial social, economic, and cultural shocks from these changes. The introduction of vaccines sped mortality decline, and the availability of modern contraceptives often facilitated fertility decline in less developed countries.

The trajectory of the more developed countries from the past to the present gives an extended timeline of social and demographic change that is useful in thinking about likely future changes in the less developed part of the world. However, discerning which aspects of historical change in the currently more developed countries are relevant to less developed countries and which aspects are irrelevant is a major challenge to social research and policy formulation.

CONCLUDING COMMENTS

A survey was conducted in 2009 of 970 members of the International Union for the Study of Population, the major world professional organization for demographers. The survey asked questions about views of the field of demography and about the importance of various policy issues.[114]

Demographers thought that the most important characteristic for a demographer was to be "highly empirical." That means that conclusions should be based on analysis of data and familiarity with actual population situations, rather than based on unfounded speculation or untested theories. Demographers also recognized and valued the multidisciplinary nature of demography and tended to read and publish widely across disciplines.

Table 1.5 shows the ranking of what are expected to be the most important population issues in the next 20 years. The percentage of demographers who thought that the given issue was the most important is shown. The issues span the areas of demographic concern: population growth, fertility, mortality, and migration. Population aging is by far the leading issue of concern. The second and third issues, large-scale migration flows and HIV, were cited by less than half as many demographers as population aging. It is interesting that above-replacement fertility, which is fertility high enough for the population to grow,

TABLE 1.5   Demographers' Views of the Importance of World Population Issues in the Next 20 Years

Rank	Issue	Percentage with that view
1	Population aging	30%
2	Large-scale migration flows	14%
3	HIV	13%
4	Above-replacement fertility	12%
4	Urbanization	12%
6	Infant mortality	10%
7	Women's reproductive rights	7%
8	Population decline	2%
Total		100%

is tied for fourth place. In the 1960s and 1970s, it almost certainly would have held first place. Population decline, although an increasing concern in highly developed countries, was cited as the most important population issue by only 2% of demographers.

Later chapters examine population growth, mortality, fertility, and migration in detail. A great deal of empirical information is presented. Hopefully, the student will come to understand the data behind population trends and concerns as well as the complexity of the issues. Also, the multidisciplinary nature of research and thinking in demography should be even clearer than what has been shown in this introductory chapter.

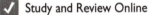 Study and Review Online

SUMMARY

1. Demography is often defined as the scientific study of human populations or as the study of the growth and structure of human populations.
2. Demography studies the size and characteristics of populations as well as the processes that lead to population change: fertility, mortality, and migration.
3. Demography is used to help answer scientific and policy questions in a wide variety of areas.
4. Demography can either focus on change in demographic mechanisms at an aggregate level, such as changes in the number of births or in the size of the population, or take a microbehavioral approach, looking at factors related to the behavioral mechanisms and external influences that lead individuals or households to have a child, to die from a particular cause, or to move to another place.
5. The demographic perspective has become very influential in many fields, including social statistics,

the study of the labor force, research on organizations, and the study of marriage and the family.
6. Population theories and policies have been developed over time in response to population phenomena that were seen as important, in need of explanation, or problematic.
7. Malthus and Marx had very different explanations of the causes and consequences of population growth. These different perspectives have persisted over time.
8. Economics and sociology have had different kinds of explanations of population growth and population dynamics.
9. There have been controversies over time about the causes of disease and biomedical researchers, and social scientists have differed in their views of the causes of disease and death. In recent years, there has been some merging of perspectives.

10. Explanations of motivations for fertility decline have focused sometimes on economic or practical considerations and sometimes on changes in norms, values, and views of children.
11. Explanations of migration have broadened over time from consideration of the potential migrant as an individual decision maker to inclusion of the entire household in the decision-making process.
12. In the United States, demography is not considered a separate discipline, and there are few departments of demography or degrees in demography granted. Most American demographers are sociologists or economists, although some demographers come from anthropology, history, political science, or other disciplines. In most other countries, demography is viewed as a separate discipline, and degrees in demography are granted.
13. Demographers see population aging as the most important population issue in the next 20 years.

KEY TERMS

demography 2
pronatalist 6
mercantilism 8
preventive check 9
positive check 9

moral restraint 9
social Darwinism 9
eugenics 9
Theory of Demographic Change
    and Response 12

fundamental causes of disease
    approach 14
social epidemiology 15
population health 15
validity 22

QUESTIONS FOR DISCUSSION AND REVIEW

1. What is the difference between a demographic (or a population) approach and a clinical approach to addressing a question such as infant death? Describe a situation in which the demographic approach is more relevant, and describe another situation in which the clinical approach is more relevant.
2. Discuss how changes in mortality, fertility, and migration levels have influenced theory and policy concerns.
3. Briefly describe the difference between the Malthusian and the Marxist views of the relation between population growth and the growth of food production and other resources.
4. Briefly describe the difference in views of the causes of disease and death between biomedical researchers and social scientists.
5. Briefly describe the role of economic factors and of norms and values in explanations of decisions by women and couples to have more or less children.
6. Briefly describe the economic approach to explanations of migration and how sociological explanations modify that approach.

NOTES

1. cf. Colin Newell. 1988. *Methods and Models in Demography*, New York: Guilford Press; and Samuel H. Preston, Patrick Heuveline, and Michel Guillot. 2001. *Demography: Measuring and Modeling Population Processes*, Malden, MA: Blackwell.
2. Samuel H. Preston. 1993. "The Contours of Demography: Estimates and Projections," *Demography*, 30: 593–606.
3. Philip H. Hauser and Otis Dudley Duncan. 1959. *The Study of Population: An Inventory and Appraisal*, Chicago: University of Chicago Press, 2.
4. Yu Xie. 2000. "Demography: Past, Present, and Future," *Journal of the American Statistical Association*, 95: 670–673.
5. R. J. Graham. 1984. "Population Issues in Economic Planning: Uses of Demography in Business," *Population Research*, 1: 82–88; and Charles Hirschman. 1981. "The Uses of Demography in Development Planning," *Economic Development and Cultural Change*, 29: 561–575.
6. Darrell Steffensmeier and Miles D. Harer. 1993. "Bulging Prisons, an Aging U. S. Population, and the Nation's Violent Crime Rate," *Federal Probation*, 57: 3–10.
7. Eugene K. Harris. 1991. *Survivorship Analysis for Clinical Studies*, New York: Marcel Dekker; and N. Balakrishnan and C. R. Rao, eds. 2004. *Advances in Survival Analysis*, Amsterdam: Elsevier.
8. Barbara A. Anderson and Brian D. Silver. 1986. "Measurement and Mismeasurement of the Validity of the Self-Reported Vote," *American Journal of Political Science*, 30: 771–785; and Brian D. Silver, Barbara A. Anderson, and Paul R. Abramson, 1986. "Who Overreports Voting?" *American Political Science Review*, 80: 613–624.

9. Shirley J. Smith. 1982. "New Worklife Estimates Reflect Changing Profile of Labor Force," *Monthly Labor Review*, 105: 15–20.

10. Heather Juby and Celine Le Bourdais. 1998. "The Changing Context of Fatherhood in Canada: A Life Course Analysis," *Population Studies*, 52: 163–175.

11. Jay D. Teachman. 1983. "Analyzing Social Processes: Life Tables and Proportional Hazards Models," *Social Science Research*, 12: 263–301; and Zeng Yi. 1991. *Family Dynamics in China: A Life Table Analysis*, Madison: University of Wisconsin Press.

12. Robert Schoen and Nicola Standish. 2001. "The Retrenchment of Marriage: Results from Marital Status Life Tables for the United States, 1995," *Population and Development Review*, 27: 553–563.

13. Larry Bumpass and Hsien-Hen Lu. 2000. "Trends in Cohabitation and Implications for Children's Family Contexts in the United States," *Population Studies*, 54: 29–41.

14. Josef Brüderl, Peter Preisendörfer, and Rolf Ziegler. 1992. "Survival Chances of Newly Founded Business Organizations," *American Sociological Review*, 57: 227–242.

15. Becky Pettit and Bruce Western. 2004. "Mass Imprisonment and the Life Course: Race and Class Inequality in U.S. Incarceration," *American Sociological Review*, 69: 151–169.

16. Much of this section is based on J. Overbeek. 1974. *History of Population Theories*, Rotterdam: Rotterdam University Press.

17. BCE stands for "before the Christian era." It often has been referred to as BC, which stands for "before Christ."

18. C. E. Strangeland. 1904. *Pre-Malthusian Doctrines of Population*, New York: Columbia University Press, 29.

19. Paul Neurath. 1994. *From Malthus to the Club of Rome and Back*, Armonk, NY: M. E. Sharpe.

20. Charles Issawi. 1987. *An Arab Philosophy of History: Selections from the Prolegomena of Ibn Khaldun of Tunis (1322–1406)*, Princeton, NJ: Princeton University Press.

21. J. Overbeek. 1973. "Mercantilism, Physiocracy and Population Theory," *South African Journal of Economics*, 41: 108–113. A schematic representation is a symbolic picture that shows the idea or the structure of something without showing specific numeric values or realistic distances between places.

22. William Petersen. 1999. *Malthus: Founder of Modern Demography*, New Brunswick, NJ: Transaction Publishers.

23. John Hajnal. 1953. "Age at Marriage and Proportions Marrying," *Population Studies*, 7: 112.

24. Lydia Polgreen. 2010. "One Bride for 2 Brothers: A Custom Fades in India," *New York Times*, July 16, http://www.nytimes.com/2010/07/17/world/asia/17polyandry.html?scp=1&sq=polyandry&st=cse (accessed October 20, 2013).

25. Mervyn C. Goldstein. 1978. "Pahari and Tibetan Polyandry Revisited," *Ethnology*, 17: 325–337; and Eric Alden Smith. 1998. "Is Tibetan Polyandry Adaptive?" *Human Nature*, 9: 225–261.

26. J. S. Mill. 1929. "Two Speeches on Population," *The Journal of Adult Education*, 4: 38–61.

27. Nicholas Abercrombie, Stephen Hill, and Bryan Turner. 2000. "Social Darwinism," *Penguin Dictionary of Sociology*, 4th ed., London: Penguin.

28. Merriam-Webster Dictionary, "Eugenics," http://www.merriam-webster.com/medical/eugenics?show=0&t=1335365502 (accessed April 25, 2012).

29. Thomas Robert Malthus. 1798. *An Essay on the Principle of Population as It Affects the Future Improvement of Society*, London: J. Johnson, 72.

30. Daniel J. Kevles. 1985. *In the Name of Eugenics: Genetics and the Uses of Human Heredity*, New York: Knopf.

31. I. Rudan, D. Rudan, H. Campbell, A. Carothers, A. Wright, N. Smolej-Narancic, B. Janicijevic, L. Jin, R. Chakraborty, R. Deka, and P. Rudan. 2003. "Inbreeding and Risk of Late Onset Complex Disease," *Journal of Medical Genetics*, 40: 925–932.

32. Donella H. Meadows, Dennis L. Meadows, Jorgen Randers, and William W. Behrens III. 1972. *The Limits to Growth*, New York: Universe Books; Donella H. Meadows, Dennis L. Meadows, and Jorgen Randers. 1992 *Beyond the Limits*, Post Mills, VT: Chelsea Green; and Donella H. Meadows, Jorgen Randers, and Dennis L. Meadows. 2004. *Limits to Growth: The 30-Year Update*, White River Junction, VT: Chelsea Green.

33. P. R. Ehrlich. 1968. *The Population Bomb*, New York: Ballantine.

34. David Houle. 2007. "Over Population of the Planet and Global Warming," *Science20*, November 19, http://www.science20.com/a_future_look_at_today/over_population_of_the_planet_and_global_warming (accessed April 25, 2012).

35. Views of population and sustainability are discussed in Blake D. Ratner. 2004. "Equity, Efficiency, and Identity: Grounding the Debate over Population and Sustainability," *Population Research and Policy Review*, 23: 55–71. They are also discussed on websites such as Overpopulation.org. 2012. "Sustainability, Carrying Capacity, and Overconsumption," http://www.overpopulation.org/solutions.html (accessed April 26, 2012).

36. Ronald L. Meek, ed. 1971. *Marx and Engels on the Population Bomb*, 2nd ed., Berkeley, CA: Ramparts Press.

37. R. E. Evenson and D. Gollin. 2003. "Assessing the Impact of the Green Revolution, 1960 to 2000," *Science,* 300(5620): 758–762.

38. David Lam. 2011. "How the World Survived the Population Bomb: Lessons from 50 Years of Exceptional Demographic History," *Demography,* 48: 1231–1262.

39. David Malakoff. 2011. "Are More People Necessarily a Problem?" *Science,* 333: 544–546.

40. Ester Boserup. 1965. *The Conditions of Agricultural Growth.* Chicago: Aldine.

41. Craig Gurian. 2012. *On Population, U.S. Remains in Full Denial Mode.* Remapping Debate, May 2 http://www.remappingdebate.org/article /population-us-remains-full-denial-mode (accessed May 4, 2012).

42. Emile Durkheim. 1893. *De la division du travail social; étude sur l'organisation des sociétés supérieures* [The Division of Labor in Society: A Study of the Higher Organization of Societies], Paris: F. Alcan.

43. Joseph J. Spengler. 1938. *France Faces Depopulation,* Durham, NC: Duke University Press, 3.

44. Kingsley Davis. 1963. "The Theory of Change and Response in Modern Demographic History," *Population Index,* 29: 345–366.

45. Phillip Longman. 2004. "The Global Baby Bust," *Foreign Affairs,* 83: 64–79.

46. Wilmer Cave Wright. 1930. *Hieronymus Fracastorius. Contagion, Contagious Diseases and Their Treatment,* New York: Putnam.

47. John P. Mackenbach. 2007. "Sanitation: Pragmatism Works," *British Medical Journal,* 334 (online supplement): s17, http://www.bmj.com.proxy .lib.umich.edu/content/334/suppl_1/s17.short (accessed April 27, 2012).

48. Janet McKee. 1988. "Holistic Health and the Critique of Western Medicine," *Social Science & Medicine,* 26: 775–784; and Wayne B. Jonas, Ted J. Kaptchuk, and Klaus Linde. 2003. "A Critical Overview of Homeopathy," *Annals of Internal Medicine,* 138: 393–399.

49. E. Richard Brown.1979. *Rockefeller Medicine Men: Medicine and Capitalism in America,* Berkeley: University of California Press; and Howard S. Berliner. 1975. "A Larger Perspective on the Flexner Report," *International Journal of Health Services,* 5: 573–592.

50. David M. Eisenberg, Ronald C. Kessler, Cindy Foster, Frances E. Norlock, David R. Calkins, and Thomas L. Delbanco. 1993, "Unconventional Medicine in the United States," *New England Journal of Medicine,* 328: 246–252.

51. Patricia M. Barnes, Barbara Bloom, and Ruchard L. Nahin. 2008. *Complementary and Alternative Medicine Use among Adults and Children: United States, 2007,* National Health Statistics Reports, no. 12, Hyattsville, MD: National Center for Health Statistics.

52. James N. Dillard and Sharon Knapp. 2005. "Complementary and Alternative Pain Therapy in the Emergency Department," *Emergency Medicine Clinics of North America,* 23: 529–549.

53. Preamble to the Constitution of the World Health Organization as adopted by the International Health Conference, New York, June 19–22, 1946; signed on July 22, 1946, by the representatives of 61 states (Official Records of the World Health Organization, no. 2, p. 100) and entered into force on April 7, 1948.

54. Davidson R. Gwatkin. 1980. "Indications of Change in Developing Country Mortality Trends: The End of an Era?" *Population and Development Review,* 6: 615–644.

55. Bruce G. Link and Jo Phelan, 1995. "Social Conditions as Fundamental Causes of Disease," *Journal of Health and Social Behavior,* 35 (extra issue): 80–94.

56. U. M. Kujala, J. Kaprio, and M. Koskenvuo. 2002. "Modifiable Risk Factors as Predictors of All-Cause Mortality: The Roles of Genetics and Childhood Environment," *American Journal of Epidemiology,* 156: 985–993.

57. John M. Last, ed. 1995. *A Dictionary of Epidemiology,* New York: Oxford University Press, 55.

58. Kaori Honjo. 2004. "Social Epidemiology: Definition, History, and Research Examples," *Environmental Health and Preventive Medicine,* 9: 193–199.

59. David Kindig and Greg Stoddart. 2003. "What is Population Health?" *American Journal of Public Health,* 93: 380–383; Alberto Palloni and Jeffrey D. Morenoff. 2001. "Interpreting the Paradoxical in the Hispanic Paradox," in *Population Health and Aging: Strengthening the Dialogue between Epidemiology and Demography,* ed. M. Weinstein, A. I. Hermalin, and M. A. Stoto, Annals of the New York Academy of Sciences, vol. 954, New York: New York Academy of Sciences, 140–174; and Ichiro Kawachi and S. V. Subramanian. 2005. "Health Demography," in *Handbook of Population,* ed. Dudley L. Poston and Michael Micklin, New York: Kluwer Academic, 787–808.

60. James F. Fries. 1983. "The Compression of Morbidity," *The Milbank Memorial Fund Quarterly. Health and Society,* 61 (Special Issue: Aging: Demographic, Health, and Social Prospects): 397–419.

61. cf. Scott D. Grosse and Muin J. Khoury. 2006. "What is the Clinical Utility of Genetic Testing?" *Genetics in Medicine,* 8: 448–450; and Ralph P. Insinga, Andrew G. Glass, and Brenda B. Rush. 2004. "Diagnoses and Outcomes in Cervical Cancer Screening: A Population-Based Study,"

American Journal of Obstetrics and Gynecology, 191: 105–113.

62. Angus McLaren. 1990. *A History of Contraception: From Antiquity to the Present Day*, Cambridge, MA: Blackwell.

63. Church of England. 2012. "Contraception," http://www.churchofengland.org/our-views /medical-ethics-health-social-care-policy /contraception.aspx (accessed May 1, 2012).

64. Basim Musallam. 1983. *Sex and Society in Islam: Birth Control before the Nineteenth Century*, New York: Cambridge University Press; and Heather Boonstra. 2001. "Islam, Women and Family Planning: A Primer," *The Guttmacher Report on Public Policy*, 4: 4–7, http://www.guttmacher.org/pubs/tgr/04/6 /gr040604.html (accessed June 12, 2012).

65. W. S. Thompson. 1929. "Population," *American Journal of Sociology*, 34: 959–975.

66. Ansley J. Coale and Susan Cotts Watkins, Susan Cotts, eds. 1986. *The Decline of Fertility in Europe: The Revised Proceedings of a Conference on the Princeton European Fertility Project*. Princeton, NJ: Princeton University Press.

67. Dirk J. van de Kaa. 2001. "Postmodern Fertility Preferences: From Changing Value Orientation to New Behavior," *Population and Development Review*, 27 (Supplement: Global Fertility Transition): 290–331.

68. Massimo Livi-Bacci. 2001. "Too Few Children and Too Much Family," *Daedalus*, 130: 139–155; and Brienna Perelli-Harris. 2005. "The Path to Lowest-Low Fertility in Ukraine," *Population Studies*, 59: 55–70.

69. Ron Lesthaeghe and Chris Wilson. 1986. "Modes of Production, Secularization, and the Pace of the Fertility Decline in Western Europe, 1870–1930," in *The Decline of Fertility in Europe*, ed. Ansley J. Coale and Susan Cotts Watkins, Princeton, NJ: Princeton University Press, 261–292.

70. John C. Caldwell and Pat Caldwell. 1987. "The Cultural Context of High Fertility in Sub-Saharan Africa," *Population and Development Review*, 13: 409–437; and John C. Caldwell, P. H. Reddy, and Pat Caldwell. 1984. "The Determinants of Family Structure in Rural South India," *Journal of Marriage and Family*, 46: 215–229.

71. Arsene Dumont. 1890. *Depopulation et Civilisation: Etude Demographique*, Paris: Lecrosnier & Babe.

72. John C. Caldwell. 1978. "A Theory of Fertility: From High Plateau to Destabilization," *Population and Development Review*, 4: 553.

73. James T. Fawcett, ed. 1972. *The Satisfactions and Cost of Children: Theories, Concepts and Methods*, Honolulu: East-West Population Institute.

74. Arland Thornton. 2005. *Reading History Sideways: The Fallacy and Enduring Impact of the Developmental Paradigm on Family Life*, Chicago: University of Chicago Press.

75. Gary S. Becker. 1960. "An Economic Analysis of Fertility," in *Demographic and Economic Change in Developed Countries*, Universities–National Bureau of Economic Research series, Princeton, NJ: Princeton University Press, 225–256; G. S. Becker and H. G. Lewis. 1973. "On the Interaction between the Quantity and Quality of Children," *Journal of Political Economy*, 81: S279–S288; and Boone Turchi. 1975. "Microeconomic Theories of Fertility: A Critique," *Social Forces*, 51: 107–125.

76. Ansley J. Coale. 1973. "The Demographic Transition Reconsidered," in *International Population Conference, Liege, 1973*, vol. 1, Liege: International Union for the Scientific Study of Population, 53–72.

77. Jason M. Linde. 2010. "Are Children Really Inferior Goods? Evidence from Displacement-Driven Income Shocks," *Journal of Human Resources*, 45: 301–327.

78. James L. McCabe and Mark R. Rosenzweig. 1976. "Female Labor-Force Participation, Occupational Choice, and Fertility in Developing Countries," *Journal of Development Economics*, 3: 141–160.

79. Karen Oppenheim Mason and V. T. Palan. 1981. "Female Employment and Fertility in Peninsular Malaysia: The Maternal Role Incompatibility Hypothesis Reconsidered," *Demography*, 18: 549–575.

80. Valerie Kincade Oppenheimer. 1970. *The Female Labor Force in the United States: Demographic and Economic Factors Governing Its Growth and Changing Composition*, Berkeley: Institute of International Studies, University of California; and Claudia Goldin. 1994. "Understanding the Gender Gap: An Economic History of American Women," in *Equal Employment Opportunity: Labor Market Discrimination and Public Policy*, ed. Paul Burstein, Hawthorne, NY: Aldine de Gruyter, 17–26.

81. Charles A. Calhoun and Thomas J. Espenshade. 1988. "Childbearing and Wives' Foregone Earnings," *Population Studies*, 42: 5–37.

82. James Feyrer, Bruce Sacerdote, and Ariel Dora Stern. 2008. "Will the Stork Return to Europe and Japan? Understanding Fertility within Developed Nations," *The Journal of Economic Perspectives*, 22: 3–22.

83. Bernard Berelson. 1969. "Beyond Family Planning," *Studies in Family Planning*, 1: 1–16.

84. C. Alison McIntosh and Jason L. Finkle. 1995. "The Cairo Conference on Population and Development: A New Paradigm?" *Population and Development Review*, 21: 223–260; and UNFPA. 1995. *International Conference on Population and Development—ICPD—Programme of Action*,

New York: United Nations, http://www.unfpa.org/public/site/global/publications/pid/1973 (accessed May 4, 2012).

85. E. C. Young. 1928. *The Movement of Farm Population*, Cornell Agricultural Experiment Station Bulletin 426, Ithaca, NY: Cornell University; and George Kingsley Zipf. 1946. "The $P_1 P_2/D$ Hypothesis: On the Intercity Movement of Persons," *American Sociological Review*, 11: 677–686.

86. Samuel A. Stouffer. 1940. "Intervening Opportunities: A Theory Relating Mobility and Distance," *American Sociological Review*, 5: 845–867; and Stouffer, Samuel A. Stouffer. 1960. "Intervening Opportunities and Competing Migrants," *Journal of Regional Science*, 2: 1–26.

87. Everett S. Lee. 1966. "A Theory of Migration," *Demography*, 3: 47–57.

88. Wilbur Zelinsky. 1971. "The Hypothesis of the Mobility Transition," *Geographical Review*, 61: 219–249.

89. E. G. Ravenstein. 1885. "The Laws of Migration," *Journal of the Statistical Society of London*, 48: 167–235; and E. G. Ravenstein. 1889. "The Laws of Migration, Part II," *Journal of the Statistical Society of London*, 52: 241–301.

90. John R. Harris and Michael P. Todaro. 1970. "Migration, Unemployment and Development: A Two-Sector Analysis," *The American Economic Review*, 60: 126–142; and S. V. Lall, H. Selod and Z. Shalizi. 2006. *Rural-Urban Migration in Developing Countries: A Survey of Theoretical Predictions and Empirical Findings*, Washington, DC: World Bank, Policy Research Working Paper No. 3915, http://www-wds.worldbank.org/external/default/WDSContentServer/IW3P/IB/2006/05/05/000016406_20060505110833/Rendered/PDF/wps (accessed October 19, 2013).

91. Oded Stark and David E. Bloom. 1985. "The New Economics of Labor Migration," *The American Economic Review*, 75: 173–178.

92. Oded Stark and J. Taylor. 1989. "Relative Deprivation and International Migration," *Demography*, 26: 1–14.

93. Gunnar Myrdal. 1957. *Rich Lands and Poor*, New York: Harper and Row.

94. John S. MacDonald and Leatrice D. MacDonald. 1964. "Chain Migration Ethnic Neighborhood Formation and Social Networks," *The Milbank Memorial Fund Quarterly*, 42: 82–97; J. C. Caldwell. 1969. *African Rural-Urban Migration. The Movement to Ghana's Towns*, Canberra: Australian National University Press; Graeme J. Hugo. 1981. "Village-Community Ties, Village Norms, and Ethnic and Social Networks: A Review of Evidence from the Third World," in *Migration Decision Making: Multidisciplinary Approaches to Microlevel Studies in Developed and Developing Countries*, ed. Gordon F. De Jong and Robert W. Gardner, New York: Pergamon, 186–225; and Douglas S. Massey, Joaquin Arango, Graeme Hugo, Ali Kouaouci, Adela Pellegrino, and J. Edward Taylor. 1993. "Theories of International Migration: A Review and Appraisal," *Population and Development Review*, 19: 431–466.

95. Michael J. Piore. 1979. *Birds of Passage: Migrant Labor in Industrial Societies*, Cambridge: Cambridge University Press; and Alejandro Portes and John Walton. 1981. *Labor, Class, and the International System*, New York: Academic Press.

96. Cynthia J. Buckley. 1998. "Ideology, Methodology, and Context: Social Science Surveys in the Russian Federation," *American Behavioral Scientist*, 42: 223–236; and Emily L. Jones. 1993. "The Courtesy Bias in South-East Asian Surveys," in *Social Research in Developing Countries: Surveys and Censuses in the Third World*, ed. Martin Bulmer and Donald P. Warwick, London: UCL Press, 253–260.

97. Jesse Lemisch. 1968. "Jack Tar in the Streets: Merchant Seamen in the Politics of Revolutionary America," *William and Mary Quarterly*, 25: 371–407. This article is an example of "history from the bottom up." Jesse Lemisch coined the term "history from the bottom up." Peter Laslett and Richard Wall, eds. 1972. *Household and Family in Past Time: Comparative Studies in the Size and Structure of the Domestic Group over the Last Three Centuries in England, France, Serbia, Japan and Colonial North America, with Further Materials from Western Europe*, Cambridge: Cambridge University Press; Bennett Dyke and Warren T. Morrill, eds. 1980. *Genealogical Demography*, New York: Academic Press; Tommy Bengtsson, Cameron Campbell, and James Z. Lee. 2004. *Life under Pressure: Mortality and Living Standards in Europe and Asia, 1700–1900*, Cambridge, MA: MIT Press; Ansley J. Coale and Susan Cotts Watkins, eds. 1986. *The Decline of Fertility in Europe*, Princeton, NJ: Princeton University Press; Daniel Scott Smith. 1973. "Parental Power and Marriage Patterns: An Analysis of Historical Trends in Hingham, Massachusetts," *Journal of Marriage and the Family*, 35: 419–428; and Thomas C. Smith. 1977. *Nakahara: Family Farming and Population in a Japanese Village, 1717–1830*. Stanford, CA: Stanford University Press.

98. Nancy Howell. 1979. *Demography of the Dobe !Kung*. New York: Academic Press.

99. David I. Kertzer and Tom Fricke, eds. 1997. *Anthropological Demography: Toward a New Synthesis*, Chicago: University of Chicago Press; and Laura Bernardi and Inge Hutter,

"The Anthropological Demography of Europe," *Demographic Research*, 17: 541–566.

100. Barbara A. Anderson. 1986. "Cultural and Regional Factors in the Decline of Marital Fertility in Europe," in *The Decline of Fertility in Europe*, ed. Susan Cott Watkins and Ansley J. Coale, Princeton, NJ: Princeton University Press, 293–313.

101. Brent Wolff, John Knodel, and Werasit Sittrai. 1993. "Focus Groups and Surveys as Complementary Research Methods: A Case Example," in *Successful Focus Groups: Advancing the State of the Art*, ed. D. L. Morgan, Newbury Park, CA: Sage, 118–136: William G. Axinn and Lisa D. Pearce, eds. 2006. *Mixed Method Data Collection Strategies.* New York: Cambridge University Press; John C. Caldwell, Allen G. Hill, and Valerie J. Hull, eds. 1988. *Micro-Approaches to Demographic Research*, London: Kegan Paul International; and A. M. Basu and P. Aaby. 1998. *Methods and Uses of Anthropological Demography*, New York: Clarendon Press.

102. Yanatan ben-Shalom, Robert A. Moffitt, and John Karl Scholz. 2011. *An Assessment of the Effectiveness of Anti-poverty Programs in the United States*, NBER Working Paper 17-042, Cambridge, MA: National Bureau of Economic Research, http://www.nber.org/papers/w17042.pdf (accessed May 4, 2012).

103. Karen (Kay) Perrin and Sharon Bernecki DeJoy. 2003. "Abstinence-Only Education: How We Got Here and Where We're Going," *Journal of Public Health Policy*, 24: 445–459.

104. Anne E. Kornblut and Spencer S. Hsu. 2010. "Arizona Governor Signs Immigration Bill, Reopening National Debate," *Washington Post*, April 24, http://www.washingtonpost.com/wp-dyn/content/article/2010/04/23/AR2010042301441.html (accessed May 4, 2012).

105. John W. Kingdon. 1984. *Agendas, Alternatives and Public Policies*, Boston: Little, Brown.

106. Toni Falbo and Dudley L. Poston. 1993. "The Academic, Personality, and Physical Outcomes of Only Children in China," *Child Development*, 64: 18–35.

107. Arthur D. Fisk and Wendy A. Rogers. 2002. "Psychology and Aging: Enhancing the Lives of an Aging Population," *Current Directions in Psychological Science*, 11: 107–110.

108. James S. House. 2002. "Understanding Social Factors and Inequalities in Health: 20th Century Progress and 21st Century Prospects," *Journal of Health and Social Behavior*, 43: 125–142; and Edna Maria Vissoci Reiche, Sandra Odebrecht Vargas Nunes, and Helena Kaminami Morimoto. 2004. "Stress, Depression, the Immune System, and Cancer," *The Lancet Oncology*, 5: 617–625.

109. U.S. Census Bureau. 2012. *Herman Hollerith*, http://www.census.gov/history/www/census_then_now/notable_alumni/herman_hollerith.html (accessed April 26, 2012).

110. Celia Landmann Szwarcwald, Carla Lourenco Tavares de Andrade, and Francisco Inacio Bastos. 2002. "Income Inequality, Residential Poverty Clustering and Infant Mortality: A Study in Rio de Janeiro, Brazil," *Social Science & Medicine*, 55: 2083–2092.

111. Robert J. Sampson, Jeffrey D. Morenoff, and Thomas Gannon-Rowley. 2002. "Assessing 'Neighborhood Effects': Social Processes and New Directions in Research," *Annual Review of Sociology*, 28: 443–478.

112. As of 2013, a doctorate in demography is available in the United States at Princeton University, University of Pennsylvania, and University of California, Berkeley.

113. Dean C. Tipps. 1973. "Modernization Theory and the Comparative Study of Societies: A Critical Perspective," *Comparative Studies in Society and History*, 15: 199–226; David Harrison. 1988. *The Sociology of Modernization and Development*, New York: Routledge; and Peter Evans and John D. Stephens. 1988. "Studying Development since the Sixties," *Theory and Society*, 17: 713–745.

114. Henrik P. van Dalen and Kene Henkens. 2012. "What Is on a Demographer's Mind? A Worldwide Survey," *Demographic Research*, 26: 363–408.

CHAPTER 2

WORLD DEMOGRAPHIC PATTERNS

LEARNING OBJECTIVES

- Describe the trajectory of world population growth since 1400.
- Contrast the trajectory of population growth in the less developed region and in the more developed region since 1950.
- Discuss how population size can aid or hinder countries in achieving their goals.
- Contrast demographic patterns in the less developed region and in the more developed region, and discuss the consequences of these patterns.
- Describe the aging of the world's population since 1950 and the extreme pattern of aging in Japan.
- Discuss the major population policy concerns of the governments in the less developed regions compared to those in the more developed region. Why do these concerns differ, and why have they changed over time?

((Listen to the Chapter Audio

OVERVIEW

This chapter presents patterns of world population growth since the fifteenth century, with a focus on the situation since 1950. Population growth has been a subject of great scholarly and policy concern. In the 1960s, many were worried about the consequences of a population explosion and feared that in the future, people would be packed together with only a few square feet available per person.[1] Concerns about the environment and about challenges to sustainable use of resources have also stimulated interest in population growth, its sources, and its consequences.[2]

More recently, many developed countries have become concerned about the possible negative consequences of slow or negative population growth.[3] However, in the late 1930s, population decline by the early 1960s was predicted for most of Europe,[4] and in the late 1940s the U.S. population was predicted to decline after 1985,[5] neither of which happened.

This chapter looks at the growth of the population of the entire world and of major world divisions. It explains measures of population growth and discusses their interpretation. The components of population change—fertility, mortality, and migration—and how changes in these components have resulted in different patterns of population growth in different regions and at different times are examined.

Chapter 3 discusses sources of demographic data that are behind the graphs and tables in this and later chapters, and Chapters 4–12 discuss mortality, fertility, and migration in detail. Hopefully, the discussion of empirical patterns in this chapter will stimulate interest in understanding the sources of the underlying data, and motivate interest in understanding fertility, mortality, and migration processes more completely.[6]

WORLD POPULATION GROWTH

Figure 2.1 shows estimates of the population of the world from 1400 to 2100.[7] The size of the world's population fluctuated until about 1650, after which it increased steadily until about 1900. Note that the history of world population size has not been one of constant increase. Figure 2.1 shows that the world's population decreased slightly between 1600 and 1650 (from 0.56 billion to 0.51 billion) due to famine, epidemics, and social disruptions.[8] Population increase after the mid-seventeenth century was mainly due to declines in mortality. Causes of mortality decline and

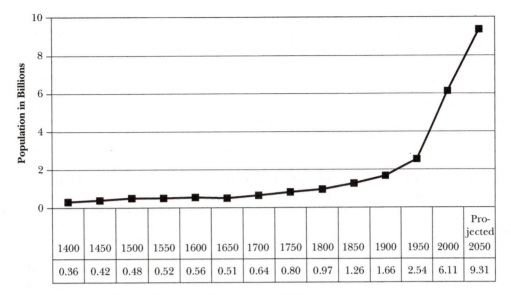

FIGURE 2.1 World Population in Billions, 1400–2050

	1400	1450	1500	1550	1600	1650	1700	1750	1800	1850	1900	1950	2000	Projected 2050
	0.36	0.42	0.48	0.52	0.56	0.51	0.64	0.80	0.97	1.26	1.66	2.54	6.11	9.31

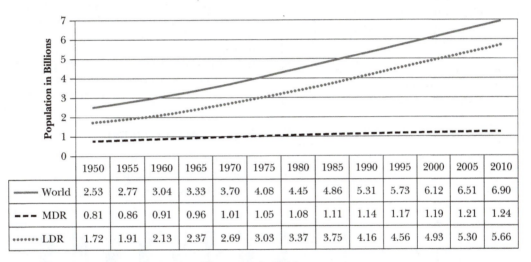

FIGURE 2.2 World Population in Billions, 1950–2010

	1950	1955	1960	1965	1970	1975	1980	1985	1990	1995	2000	2005	2010
—— World	2.53	2.77	3.04	3.33	3.70	4.08	4.45	4.86	5.31	5.73	6.12	6.51	6.90
- - - MDR	0.81	0.86	0.91	0.96	1.01	1.05	1.08	1.11	1.14	1.17	1.19	1.21	1.24
•••••• LDR	1.72	1.91	2.13	2.37	2.69	3.03	3.37	3.75	4.16	4.56	4.93	5.30	5.66

MDR: more developed region; LDR: less developed region.

sources of fluctuations in premodern population size are discussed in Chapter 5.

As shown in Figure 2.1, world population increased rapidly after 1900. World population was not quite 1 billion in 1800, increased more than six-fold by 200 years later in 2000, and is expected to increase by 52% between 2000 and 2050. The rapid rise in world population in the twentieth century led to great concern among governments and international agencies about the possible consequences of (1) a rapid increase in population and (2) a very large world population. It is clear that the increase in world population is expected to be less between 2000 and 2050 (3.20 billion) than it was between 1950 and 2000 (3.68 billion).[9]

Population Growth in the World, the More Developed Region, and the Less Developed Region since 1950

Figure 2.2 presents the population of the world as a whole from 1950 to 2010, and also the population divided into the more developed region of the world (MDR) and the less developed region of the world (LDR) in billions of people. It is clear that world population growth since 1950 has been almost totally due to growth in the LDR.[10]

The distinction between the MDR and the LDR is a UN designation. The **more developed region (MDR)** includes all of the countries of Europe, Northern America (the United States,

Canada, Bermuda, Greenland, and Saint Pierre and Miquelon), Australia, New Zealand, and Japan. The **less developed region (LDR)** includes all other countries in the world.

Some countries in the LDR, such as Brazil and South Korea, are very developed by many measures, while some countries in the MDR, such as Albania, are not very developed. For example, in 2010 Brazil (in the LDR) had a gross national income per capita of $10,920, while Albania (in the MDR) had a gross national income per capita of $8,840.[11]

Whether the more developed–less developed distinction is useful is an issue of controversy. It has been argued that the developed–developing or more developed–less developed distinction is not helpful and that the implication is that "developing countries" are backward.[12] The World Bank has used a division into high-income, moderate-income, and low-income countries, but the cutoffs between categories and the countries included in each category change every 2 years, which makes it difficult to trace trends.

An advantage of the MDR–LDR distinction is that it yields a consistent classification that generally distinguishes between wealthier, better educated, and healthier countries and poorer, less educated, and less healthy countries. In this book, an MDR–LDR division is often used, although a division by the income level of countries is used in the presentation of some results in Chapter 5.

Figure 2.2 and many other figures in this book begin with data for 1950. This is because a major source of data for figures and tables is the UN Population Division. The United Nations was founded in 1945, and the Population Division has published estimates of the population and other characteristics of countries and world regions from 1950 onward.

Between 1950 and 2010, the population of the world increased more than 2.7 times; the population of the MDR increased by more than 50%, but the population of the LDR more than tripled. Thus, concern with world population growth since World War II has been mainly a concern with population growth in the LDR.

Although there has been concern with conservation of resources in countries in the MDR, population concerns in the MDR have increasingly focused on very low fertility, the negative consequences of likely future population decline, and the consequences of an aging population. These issues are discussed in more detail in Chapters 10 and 11.

The Increasing Proportion of World Population in the Less Developed Region

Figure 2.3 shows the changing distribution of the world's population between the MDR and the LDR in 1950–2010. The more rapid increase in the population of the LDR (seen in Figure 2.2) resulted in an increasing percentage of the world population being located in the LDR—from 68% in 1950 to 82% in 2010. The fraction of the world's population in the MDR similarly declined from one-third to less than one-fifth.

Population Growth Rates

When one looks at the change in population size over time, as shown in Figures 2.1 and 2.2, the steeper the ascent or the slope of the graph of population size,

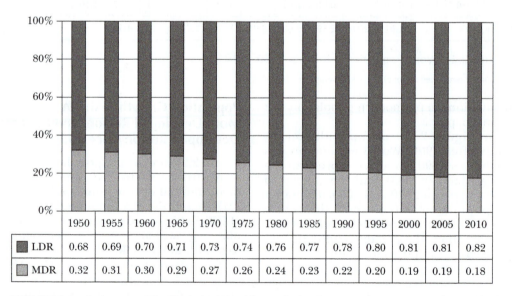

	1950	1955	1960	1965	1970	1975	1980	1985	1990	1995	2000	2005	2010
■ LDR	0.68	0.69	0.70	0.71	0.73	0.74	0.76	0.77	0.78	0.80	0.81	0.81	0.82
▨ MDR	0.32	0.31	0.30	0.29	0.27	0.26	0.24	0.23	0.22	0.20	0.19	0.19	0.18

FIGURE 2.3 Percentage Distribution of World Population between the More Developed Region (MDR) and the Less Developed Region (LDR), 1950–2010

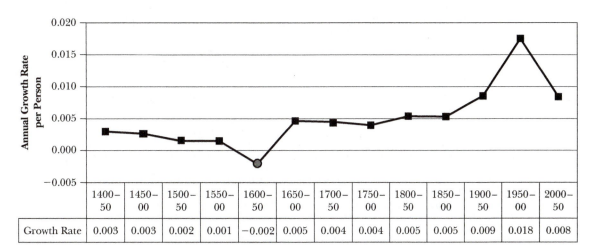

BOX 2.1

Calculation of the Annual Population Growth Rate

Exponential growth occurs when the population (or money) is compounded continuously between two points in time, Time 1 (T1) and Time 2 (T2).
  Then:

  Amount T2 = Amount T1 $\times$ e^{rt}

where:

  t = the number of years between T1 and T2;
  r = the annual interest rate or growth rate; and
  e = the base of the natural logarithm, e = 2.72.

  $P_{T2} = P_{T1}e^{rt}$

where:

  P_{T1} = population at T1;
  P_{T2} = population at T2;
    t = number of years between T1 and T2; and
    r = annual growth rate between T1 and T2.

Then:

  $r = (\ln(P_{T2}/P_{T1}))/t$

Annual population growth rates are often calculated based on data for 5- or 10-year time periods, but they can be calculated based on any time period, such as 50 years or 100 years.

the more rapidly the population is increasing. A way to measure how rapidly a population is increasing is to calculate the annual **population growth rate**.

A population grows (or declines) exponentially in the same manner as money earning compound interest increases in a bank. A growth rate above zero means the population size is increasing; a growth rate less than zero (a negative growth rate) means the population size is declining. Box 2.1 shows how the population growth rate between two points in time is calculated.

Figure 2.4 shows the growth rate of the world's population in 1400–2050 based on data for 50-year intervals, applying the method described in Box 2.1

to the data shown in Figure 2.1. Recall that in Figure 2.1, world population increased in 1400–1600 and then decreased between 1600 and 1650. We see in Figure 2.4 that the population growth rate declined in 1400–1650 and was *negative* for 1600–1650.

Thus, from 1400 through 1600, the world population had a positive growth rate (which means that the population was increasing), although the *rate* of growth was declining. For 1600–1650, the growth rate was negative, and world population declined.

As shown in Figure 2.1, it is estimated that the world population in 1600 was 0.56 billion but

	1400–50	1450–00	1500–50	1550–00	1600–50	1650–00	1700–50	1750–00	1800–50	1850–00	1900–50	1950–00	2000–50
Growth Rate	0.003	0.003	0.002	0.001	−0.002	0.005	0.004	0.004	0.005	0.005	0.009	0.018	0.008

FIGURE 2.4   Annual Growth Rate of the World Population per Person in 50-Year Periods, 1400–2050

declined to 0.51 billion by 1650. Population decline in the early seventeenth century was probably the result of very poor crop yields and other disruptions in the European economy.[13]

As indicated by the positive growth rates in Figure 2.4, world population grew in 1650–1900 and grew **much** more rapidly after 1900. If, as projected in Figure 2.1, world population increases from over 6 billion in 2000 to over 9 billion in 2050, the rate of population growth for 2000–2050 will be much **lower** than the rate was in 1950–2000, even though there will be a large increase in population size. If world population grows as projected in 2000–2050, the growth rate for 2000–2050 would be almost the same as the growth rate for 1900–1950. The reason for this likely decline in the population growth rate from 1950–2000 to 2000–2050 is that fertility is expected to decline worldwide through 2050, leading to a reduction in the population growth rate. This is discussed later in this chapter and also in Chapters 8–10.

Figure 2.5 shows annual population growth rates for the world, the MDR, and the LDR since 1950. The growth rates for the United States are also shown. The growth rates in Figure 2.5 are calculated for 5-year time periods. From looking at growth rates for 50-year periods in Figure 2.4, it is clear that the world population growth rate increased in the 50-year periods of 1900–1950 and 1950–2000. It is clear from Figure 2.5 that when one looks at 5-year periods between 1950 and 2010, the rate of growth of the world population increased in 1950–1970 and then declined in 1970–2010. The growth rates in Figures 2.4 and 2.5 are shown per person, while the growth rates in Figure 2.7 and most of the rest of the figures in this chapter are shown per thousand population. Either way is fine as long as the basis used is clear. This is explained further in Box 2.2.

The picture of population growth rates in the MDR is very different than for the world as a whole.

We see in Figure 2.5 that in the early 1960s, the annual growth rate in the LDR was 2.5%, and it declined to 1.3% by 2005–2010. The increase in the growth rate in the LDR through the early 1970s was due to a more rapid decline in mortality than in fertility. The increase in the rate of population growth in the world as a whole, and especially in the LDR, in the late 1960s alarmed many world leaders and policy makers. The high rate of population growth in the late 1960s led to fears about what the size of the world population would be if these high growth rates continued unchecked into the future. These concerns led to the development of family-planning programs, especially ones targeted at the LDR. The world and LDR growth rates began to decline when fertility began to decline more rapidly than mortality. After 1970, the growth rates in the world and in the LDR declined somewhat, and these rates declined more rapidly after 1990. The increase and then the

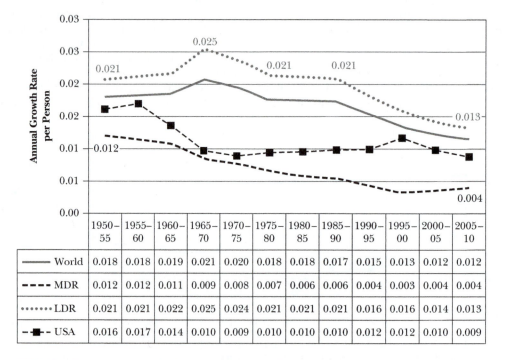

	1950–55	1955–60	1960–65	1965–70	1970–75	1975–80	1980–85	1985–90	1990–95	1995–00	2000–05	2005–10
—— World	0.018	0.018	0.019	0.021	0.020	0.018	0.018	0.017	0.015	0.013	0.012	0.012
---- MDR	0.012	0.012	0.011	0.009	0.008	0.007	0.006	0.006	0.004	0.003	0.004	0.004
······ LDR	0.021	0.021	0.022	0.025	0.024	0.021	0.021	0.021	0.016	0.016	0.014	0.013
--■-- USA	0.016	0.017	0.014	0.010	0.009	0.010	0.010	0.010	0.012	0.012	0.010	0.009

FIGURE 2.5 Annual Growth Rates per Person, 1950–2010

MDR: more developed region; LDR: less developed region; USA: the United States of America.

BOX 2.2
Alternative Expressions of an Annual Population Growth Rate

You can express a rate, such as a growth rate, per person, per hundred, per thousand, per ten thousand, or per hundred thousand:

per person	0.015
per hundred population (%)	1.500
per thousand population	15.000
per ten thousand population	150.000
per hundred thousand population	1500.000

Which way it is expressed is a matter of preference, as long as what is meant is clear. Usually, researchers and policy analysts present a rate in a form that is understandable by using the information to the left of the decimal point or using, at most, two decimal places. It can be confusing when all of the relevant information appears after five or six zeroes to the right of the decimal point.

---

decline in the growth rate are referred to as the Demographic Transition, which is discussed later in this chapter.

The growth rate in the LDR reached a maximum of 25 per thousand, or 2.5%, in 1965–1970, which many governments and international agencies and organizations found alarmingly high. One way to think about the meaning of a growth rate of 2.5% is in terms of the challenges facing a country. Imagine that a developing country has 35% of 6-year-olds in school and is trying to raise this percentage. If the population is increasing by 2.5% per year, this means that the number of seats for 6-year-olds in school needs to increase by 2.5% per year just to not fall further behind. If the number of seats increases by only 1% a year, then the percentage of 6-year-olds who are in school will decline.

In the MDR, the growth rate declined fairly steadily in 1950–1990, and then it was almost constant in 1990–2010 at 3–4 per thousand. The growth rate in the United States was higher than the growth rate in the MDR as a whole at every date, and the gap in the growth rates between the United States and the MDR increased after the early 1970s. The United States had a higher growth rate than the MDR in 1950–1965 mainly because of the Baby Boom that occurred there from the mid-1940s through the mid-1960s. Since the mid-1970s, the gap in the growth rate between the United States and the MDR as a whole increased due to fertility decline in the rest of the MDR to a very low level, while fertility in the United States remained relatively constant. Immigration has also been higher to the United States than to the MDR as a whole. The roles of fertility and immigration in the higher growth rate in the United States than in the MDR are discussed further later in this chapter and more in Chapters 10 and 12.

Population Doubling (Halving) Time in Years

When looking at population growth rates, it can be difficult to appreciate what a difference in growth rates means. Both a 1% growth rate and a 3% growth rate sound low. However, a small difference in rates can make a big difference in the pace of growth of a population. For example, if a population increased steadily at 1% per year, that population would double in size in 69 years; if it increased at 3% a year, it would double in size in 23 years.

The **population doubling time** is the number of years required for a population to double if a given rate of population growth continued indefinitely. The population doubling time will be the number of years for the population to double if the annual population growth rate is positive (above zero), and the **population halving time** will be the number of years for the population to be reduced to one-half its size if the annual population growth rate is negative (below zero).

The doubling time is approximately equal to 69 divided by the growth rate per hundred population. The world's rate of growth in 2005–2010 was 1.16% per year, which implies a doubling time of 60 years. The population doubling time is not a prediction of what will happen—it is a way to see the impact of different growth rates. Box 2.3 shows how the population doubling time is calculated.

As shown in Figure 2.6, the world population doubling time decreased from 38 years in 1950–1955 to 34 years in 1965–1970, reflecting the increasing population growth rate from 1950–1955 through 1965–1970. Then it increased to 60 years in 2005–2010. Since the LDR comprised 80% of the population by 2005–2010, these fluctuations in the doubling time of the world population are mirrored

BOX 2.3

Calculating the Population Doubling Time: The Number of Years for the Population to Double

With a population growing exponentially, the relation of the size of the population at Time 1 (T1) and Time 2 (T2) is as follows:

$$P_{T2} = P_{T1}e^{rt}$$

Dividing both sides by P_{T1}: $P_{T2}/P_{T1} = e^{rt}$

We know that the natural logarithm of e^x is

$$\ln(e^x) = x.$$

Then, taking the natural logarithm of both sides of the equation:

$$\ln(P_{T2}/P_{T1}) = rt$$

For a population to double in size:

$$2 = P_{T2}/P_{T1} = e^{rt}$$

Natural logarithm of $2 = \ln(2) = 0.693 = rt$

Years to double $= t = (\ln(2))/r$

$t = (0.693/r) =$ years needed for the population to double (or be reduced to one-half its size), with the given annual growth rate, r:

r	−0.010	−0.005	0.005	0.010	0.020	0.030	0.040
t	69	139	139	69	35	23	17

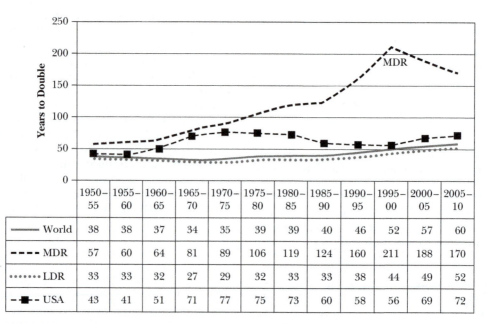

	1950– 55	1955– 60	1960– 65	1965– 70	1970– 75	1975– 80	1980– 85	1985– 90	1990– 95	1995– 00	2000– 05	2005– 10
——— World	38	38	37	34	35	39	39	40	46	52	57	60
- - - - MDR	57	60	64	81	89	106	119	124	160	211	188	170
•••••••• LDR	33	33	32	27	29	32	33	33	38	44	49	52
- -■- - USA	43	41	51	71	77	75	73	60	58	56	69	72

FIGURE 2.6   Population Doubling Time in Years, 1950–2010

MDR: more developed region; LDR: less developed region; USA: the United States of America.

by fluctuations in the population doubling time in the LDR, which went from 33 years in 1950–1955 to a low of 27 years in 1965–1970 before increasing to 52 years in 2005–2010.

In the same hypothetical developing country that was discussed in the "Population Growth Rates" section with a growth rate of 2.5%, the number of 6-year-olds would double every 28 years. If

the growth rate were 1.5%, then the doubling time would be 46 years, which would make it much easier to increase the proportion of 6-year-olds in school.

The population doubling time in the MDR almost quadrupled between 1950–1955 and 2005–2010. In 2005–2010, the population doubling time in the United States was less than half that of the MDR as a whole, due to higher fertility in the United States than in the MDR as a whole.

Alarm over the possible negative effects of a population doubling time in the LDR of less than 30 years in the late 1960s and early 1970s was an impetus to the development of family-planning programs in the world. Changes in governments' views of population problems are discussed at the end of this chapter, and policies and programs that were developed to reduce fertility and thus reduce population growth are discussed in Chapter 9.

CHARACTERISTICS OF WORLD REGIONS AND OF THE TEN MOST POPULOUS COUNTRIES

Table 2.1 shows some characteristics of the world as a whole and of major world regions in 2010. Besides a division into the MDR and the LDR, information is shown for each continent. Europe and Northern America are classified as completely within the MDR, while Latin America and the Caribbean are classified as completely in the LDR. Asia is composed mostly of LDR countries, although Japan is in the MDR. Oceania includes both MDR countries, Australia and New Zealand, and LDR countries, such as Papua New Guinea. However, many of the countries in Oceania have very small populations, and 73% of the population of Oceania resides in Australia or New Zealand.[14]

The LDR has a much higher population density than the MDR. Asia has the highest population density of any region, while Oceania has the lowest population density. Europe is often thought of as very densely populated, but actually it has a somewhat lower population density than Africa. The population density of Europe is affected by the very low density in Russia at 3 persons per square mile, while Germany had a population density of 89 persons per square mile.

Growth rates among world regions vary much more than the difference in growth rates between the LDR and the MDR. The growth rate in Africa was 23 per thousand, 77% higher than in the LDR as a whole. On the other hand, the growth rate in Europe in 2005–2010 was only 2 per thousand, one-half of the value for the MDR as a whole. At 2005–2010 growth rates, the population of Africa will double in 23 years, while it would take 341 years for the population of Europe to double. While Northern America had a growth rate of almost 1% (9 per thousand), Europe had a 2 per thousand growth rate in 2005–2010.

The large portion of the world's population that is located in Asia is clear in Table 2.1. Sixty percentage of the population of the world was in Asia in 2010.

Table 2.2 shows similar information to that in Table 2.1 for the ten largest countries in population in 2010. As seen in Column (3), China and India have by far the largest populations. The United States, ranked third in population size, had about one-fourth of the population of either of the two largest countries. The size of countries drops off quickly, with Japan, the tenth-largest country, having less than one-tenth of the population of China.

Three of the largest 10 countries, United States, Russia, and Japan, are in the MDR, and the rest are in the LDR. The ten largest countries span five continents, with six from Asia, one from Latin America and the Caribbean, one from Northern America, one from Europe, and one from Africa.

TABLE 2.1   Characteristics of World Regions, 2010

(1)	Population in Millions, 2010 (2)	Growth Rate per Thousand, 2005–2010 (3)	Doubling (Halving) Time Based on Growth Rate, 2005–2010 (4)	Population Density (Persons per Square Mile), 2010 (5)
World	6,896	12	60	132
MDR	1,236	4	170	60
LDR	5,660	13	52	176
Europe	738	2	341	83
Northern America	345	9	76	41
Latin America and Caribbean	590	12	60	75
Asia	4,164	11	64	337
Africa	1,022	23	30	88
Oceania	37	18	40	4

MDR: more developed region; LDR: less developed region.

TABLE 2.2 Characteristics of the World's Ten Most Populous Countries, 2010

(1)	(2)	Population in Millions, 2010	Growth Rate per Thousand, 2005–2010	Doubling (Halving) Time Based on Growth Rate, 2005–2010	Population Density (Persons per Square Mile), 2010[16]	GNI per Capita (PPP), 2010[17]	% Population Living on Less Than US$1.25 per Day (PPP), Latest Available Year[18]	Income of Richest 10% of Households Divided by Income of Poorest 10% of Households, Latest Available Year[19]
		(3)	(4)	(5)	(6)	(7)	(8)	(9)
1	China (PRC)	1,341	5	136	363	$7,570	13	13.2
2	India	1,225	14	48	966	$3,560	33	8.6
3	United States	310	9	78	83	$47,020	NA	15.9
4	Indonesia	240	11	64	323	$4,300	18	10.8
5	Brazil	195	9	74	60	$10,920	6	40.6
6	Pakistan	174	18	38	565	$2,780	21	6.7
7	Nigeria	158	25	28	443	$2,160	68	16.3
8	Bangladesh	149	11	62	2675	$1,620	43	6.2
9	Russia	142	−1	(562)	21	$19,190	0	11.0
10	Japan	127	0	3065	868	$34,790	NA	4.5

GNI: gross national income; PPP: purchasing power parity; NA: Not available.

As shown in Column (4), these ten countries differ enormously in how rapidly they are growing. If the growth rate of 2005–2010 continued indefinitely, the population of Nigeria would double in 28 years—by 2038 (Column (5)). However, at 2005–2010 rates, China's population would double its 2010 size in 2146, and the United States would be double its 2010 size in 2088.

Japan had a growth rate of 0 (actually, a very slightly positive rate at 0.2 per thousand) in 2005–2010, and Russia had a negative growth rate. If the 2005–2010 rates continued in those countries, the population of Japan would double by the year 5075, and the population of Russia would be one-half its 2010 size in the year 2572.

The ten largest countries also differ greatly in their density of population (persons per square mile). Of course, countries differ in how densely it is feasible for them to be settled. Even with extensive irrigation, it is unlikely that a country with a large desert will have as high a density as a country with adequate rainfall in all regions.[15] In addition, supportable population density differs according to the type of agriculture practiced and the kind of economic organization. Nonetheless, comparisons of population density among countries can reveal meaningful differences in how crowded countries are. As shown in Column (6), the ten largest countries range from a density of 21 persons per square mile in Russia to 2,675 persons per square mile in Bangladesh. In 2010, only a few city-states and small island countries (Macao, Singapore, Bahrain, Malta, and the Maldives) had a higher population density than Bangladesh. People often think of China as a very crowded country due to its large population, but among the ten largest countries, China ranks sixth in population density.

Table 2.2 also shows some information about income and poverty. GNI stands for **gross national income**.[20] This is shown per capita (per person), on a **purchasing power parity** (PPP) basis. PPP adjusts income for each country for international currency exchange rates and for the cost of living in the given country, based on the cost of a particular market basket of goods.[21] The question of a market basket for PPP calculation is similar to the issue of a market basket for calculation of the Consumer Price Index (CPI). As consumption patterns change, the goods in the market basket can also change. A PPP approach is also helpful when countries experience different inflation rates. Thus, the PPP approach adjusts for differences in the cost of living across locales.

When GNI per capita is determined using the PPP approach, it is usually higher than when the PPP approach is not used, since in poorer countries the cost in terms of a currency such as the U.S. dollar is usually less than in higher income countries. For example, the PPP GNI per capita of Laos in 2010 was $2,300, but the non-PPP value for Laos in 2010 was $1,010. The rank order of countries for GNI per capita is similar whichever approach is used.[22]

There are enormous differences in the material standard of living among the ten largest countries. In 2010, the GNI per capita of the United States was 22 times that of Nigeria and 29 times that of Bangladesh. Japan is a very prosperous country, but the GNI per capita of the United States was 35% higher than that of Japan.

The GNI per capita indicates an average level of welfare, but this income can be more evenly or less evenly distributed. The percentage of the population living on less than $1.25 a day is an indicator of the proportion of the population in an impoverished state.[23] Table 2.2 also shows the percentage of households living on less than $1.25 a day in Column (8), based on the most recently available data. In India, Pakistan, and Nigeria, it is estimated that more than one-third of the population lives on less than $1.25 a day.

International media have written extensively about economic growth and vitality in China and India and about economic problems in Russia.[24] It is interesting to note that these three countries have enormously different economic and social circumstances. The GNI per capita of China in 2010 was more than twice that of India, and the GNI per capita of Russia in 2010 was more than twice as high as that of China. Also, around 2010, more than twice as high a proportion of people in India live on less than $1.25 a day than in China. While 13% of China's population lives on less than $1.25 a day, this is estimated to be true for 0% of the population of Russia. Thus, Russia is much more prosperous than China, and China is much more prosperous than India. Therefore, although in recent years China and India have experienced higher rates of economic growth than Russia, it is important to keep in mind the much better level of material welfare of the population of Russia than of India or China.

Nigeria has a higher GNI per capita than Bangladesh, but also a higher percentage of the population living on less than $1.25 a day than Bangladesh. These differences reflect the higher level of income inequality in Nigeria than in Bangladesh.

Column (9) shows a measure of the inequality in the distribution of income in the ten largest countries—the income of the richest 10% of households in the given country divided by the income of the poorest 10% of households. The larger this value, the more unequal the distribution of income in the country. Japan has the most equal income distribution, with the richest 10% of households having 4.5 times as much income as the poorest 10% of households. Brazil has the most unequal income distribution, with the richest 10% of households having more than 40 times the income of the poorest 10% of households. In China, the United States, Indonesia, Nigeria, and Russia, the richest 10% of households has 10–16 times the income of the poorest 10%. In India, Pakistan, and Bangladesh, the richest 10% has 6–9 times the income of the poorest 10%.

When Will the Population of India Surpass That of China?

As shown in Table 2.2, although China had a larger population than India in 2010, India had over twice the growth rate of China. Clearly, if these rates continue unchanged into the future, then eventually the population of India will surpass that of China. Applying the method shown in Box 2.1, the population of China and India would be equal in the year 2020, after which the population of India would be larger than that of China. Box 2.4 shows the calculation that leads to this conclusion.

BOX 2.4

Calculation of When the Size of the Population of India Will Surpass That of China

Here we calculate when the population of India will surpass that of China. This is done with the assumption that the 2005–2010 growth rates in each country continue indefinitely into the future. The method shown in Box 2.1 is used. The Year 2010 is T1. The annual growth rates 2005–2010 are as shown in Table 2.2. This calculation assumes that India and China each maintain the population growth rate of 2005–2010 indefinitely into the future. It is unlikely this will be true.

	Population in Millions (2010)	GR (2005–2010)
China (PRC)	1,341	0.005
India	1,225	0.014

$$PopChina \times e^{0.005t} = PopIndia \times e^{0.014t}$$
$$1341 \times e^{0.005t} = 1225 \times e^{0.014t}$$
$$(1341/1225) = (e^{0.014t}/e^{0.005t})$$
$$= e^{(0.014t - 0.005t)} = e^{0.009t}$$
$$1.1095 = e^{0.009t}$$
$$\ln(1.1095) = 0.0905 = 0.009t$$
$$t = (0.0905/0.009) = 10.06$$

At 2005–2010 growth rates, India and China will have the same population size 10 years after 2010, in 2020. In 2020, the population of each country would be 1,409 million.

Population Growth Rate and Doubling Time in China, in the Less Developed Region (LDR), and in the LDR without China

As shown in Tables 2.1 and 2.2, in 2005–2010 the population growth rate in China was less than half of that of the LDC as a whole (5 per thousand versus 13 per thousand). Also, in 2010 China had a larger population than the entire MDR. In 2010, China comprised 24% of the population of the LDR and 19% of the population of the world.

Figure 2.7 shows the population growth rate in China and in the LDR as a whole for 1950–2010. By 1965–1970, the population growth rate in China was higher than in the LDR as a whole. In the late 1950s and early 1960s, at the time of the Great Leap Forward in China, there was widespread famine.[25] After the end of the Great Leap Forward, the Chinese population grew rapidly.

The very rapid population growth rate in China in the late 1960s caused great concern on the part of Chinese authorities. In the late 1960s, the population growth rate of China exceeded that of the LDR excluding China (2.7% versus 2.5%). This high growth rate in China motivated Chinese leaders to implement a strong fertility limitation program. This policy included postponement of marriage, limitation of the number of children, and longer intervals between births.[26] This policy is discussed further in Chapter 9. The fertility limitation program resulted in a rapid decline in the growth rate of China's population. In 2005–2010, the growth rate in China was less than half that of the LDR as a whole. The

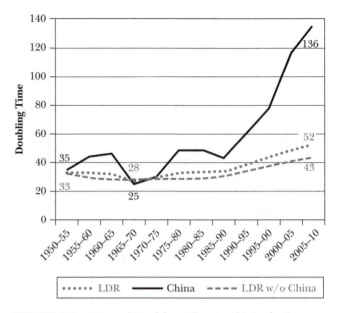

FIGURE 2.8   Years of Doubling Time in China, the Less Developed Region (LDR), and the LDR without China, 1950–2010

concern of Chinese leaders with rapid population growth in China mirrored the concern of MDR governments and NGOs about population growth in the LDR generally.

The very different paths of the growth rate in China and that of the rest of the LDR population has led people to also look at the characteristics of all of the LDR but exclude China. The growth rate of the LDR excluding China also is shown in Figure 2.7. In 2005–2010, the growth rate in China was less than one-third of the growth rate of the LDR excluding China. Note in Table 2.2 that in 2005–2010, the growth rate of China was less than that of the United States. Thus, the goal on the part of China's leaders to lower the population growth rate was fulfilled. Programs intended to reduce fertility in China and elsewhere are discussed in Chapter 9.

Figure 2.8 shows the population doubling time for China, the LDR, and the LDR without China. Population doubling time in China increased from 25 years in the late 1960s to 136 years in 2005–2010, while in the LDR excluding China the population doubling time was 28 years in 1965–1970 and 43 years in 2005–2010.

CONSEQUENCES OF POPULATION SIZE

Much of demography is concerned with the dynamics of population change, such as growth rates, where the rate is adjusted for total population size. For example, the population growth rate is calculated

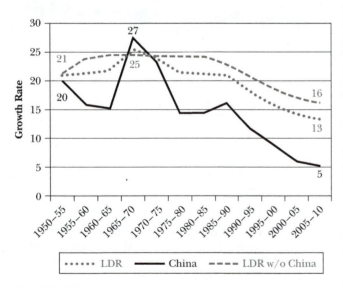

FIGURE 2.7   Growth Rate per Thousand Population in China, in the Less Developed Region (LDR), and in the LDR without China, 1950–2010

TABLE 2.3 The Ten Most Populous Countries in 1950, 2000, and 2010 and as Projected to 2050

Rank	1950 Country	Pop. in Millions	2000 Country	Pop. in Millions	2010 Country	Pop. in Millions	2050 (projected) Country	Pop. in Millions
1	China (PRC)	551	China (PRC)	1,274	China (PRC)	1,341	India	1,692
2	India	372	India	1,021	India	1,225	China (PRC)	1,296
3	USSR	181	United States	284	United States	310	United States	403
4	United States	158	Indonesia	209	Indonesia	240	Nigeria	390
5	Pakistan	85	Brazil	174	Brazil	195	Indonesia	293
6	Japan	82	Russia	147	Pakistan	174	Pakistan	275
7	Indonesia	75	Pakistan	143	Nigeria	158	Brazil	223
8	Brazil	54	Bangladesh	129	Bangladesh	149	Bangladesh	194
9	West Germany	51	Japan	127	Russia	142	Democratic Republic of the Congo	149
10	United Kingdom	50	Nigeria	2–3	Japan	127	Ethiopia	145

per person or per thousand population. Knowing that a country has a large or a small population by itself does not tell you anything about whether that country has a high or low rate of population growth.

However, total population size and the changes in the size of the population of countries and subdivisions of countries are important for social, cultural, economic, and political (including military) reasons. Table 2.3 shows the ten largest countries in population in 1950, in 2000, in 2010, and as projected for 2050.

There are substantial changes over time regarding which ten countries have the largest populations. In 1950, five of the ten largest countries were from the MDR, three were in 2000, and only one (the United States) is expected to be from the MDR in 2050. These changes occurred mainly because of the much higher population growth rate in the LDR than in the MDR, as shown in Figure 2.5, and the increasing proportion of the world population in the LDR, as shown in Figure 2.3, rather than due to population decline in the countries in the MDR. For example, between 1950 and 2010, the population of Japan increased from 82 million to 127 million, but Japan fell from sixth place in population in 1950 to tenth place in 2010.

Political changes also affect the size of countries. Table 2.3 shows the rank order of the largest countries according to how countries were defined at the given date. In 1950, the USSR was the third-largest country in the world, with a population of 181 million. In 1950, Russia was a part of the USSR and was not a separate country. In 1950, the population of Russia was 103 million and would have ranked between the United States and Pakistan in population. In 1991, the USSR dissolved. In 2000, the largest country that had been part of the USSR in 1950 was

Russia. When the USSR dissolved in 1991, the population of the USSR was 293 million and the population of Russia was 149 million. This decline in the population of the country to 51% of its earlier value was one source of a sense of status loss on the part of the Russian people. The total population of the 15 countries that had been part of the USSR in 1950 was 289 million in 2000. If the USSR had still existed in 2000, it would have been the world's third-largest country in population.

In 1950, West Germany was the eighth-largest country in the world. By 2000, former West Germany and former East Germany had merged into one country—Germany. West and East Germany together had a population of 68 million in 1950, which would have made them together the seventh-largest country in the world in 1950.

In 1950, Pakistan included what later became the separate countries of Pakistan and Bangladesh. Bangladesh became an independent country in 1971. In 1950, the area that became Bangladesh had a population of 46 million, and the area that remained Pakistan after Bangladesh gained independence had a population of 39 million. Thus although both Pakistan and Bangladesh were included in the ten largest countries in 2000, neither of them would have been included in the ten largest countries in 1950 on their own.

China and India remain the two largest countries at all three dates, but in 2050 India is projected to have a substantially larger population than China in 2050—396 million larger. The population of China is projected to begin to decline in size between 2025 and 2030, while the population of India is projected to continue to increase through 2050.

Usually demographers are concerned with rates or proportions rather than the total number of persons or events. But total population size matters for several reasons:

1. **Larger Market:** A country with a larger population can generate a larger market than a smaller country. For example, China and India have large markets even though they are relatively poor countries. With a large total population or a large urban population, only a small proportion of the population needs to be potential buyers of a particular product for there to be a very large absolute number of potential consumers of the product.
2. **Larger Military:** A country with a larger population can raise a larger military. In the 1970s in Zaire (later renamed the Democratic Republic of the Congo), all dissemination of birth control materials was illegal because the Zairois government saw population as power and was concerned with the ability to raise a large army.[27]
3. **More Highly Accomplished Persons with Rare Qualifications:** A country with a larger population has a greater chance of producing persons with rare qualifications, such as medal-winning Olympic athletes. Small countries rarely have many Olympic medal winners, partly because with a small population the likelihood of generating a top athlete is low.
4. **More Funds for Public Projects:** A large population can more easily generate funds for public projects. The larger the taxed population, the lower the tax rate necessary to generate any specific amount of money. Many countries have used profits from an agricultural surplus to finance national projects, such as construction of palaces or factories. With a large rural population, a small tax per person or per household can generate a large amount of money for projects that are usually located in urban areas. Both Japan and Russia financed a substantial part of their industrial development in the nineteenth century through a tax on rural landowners.[28]
5. **Problems of Very Small Populations:** A small population can also be seen as a problem. Focusing on Greenland, which has a population of 60,000, Sibert argued that a country with a small population tends to have erratic economic production and consumption and less competent civil servants.[29]

THE POPULATION BALANCING EQUATION AND COMPONENTS OF POPULATION GROWTH

The population of the world increases due to births and decreases due to deaths. Except for astronauts leaving the Earth to colonize other planets, the world population is unaffected by migration. A population,

such as that of the entire world, which does not experience migration across its geographic borders is called a **closed population**.

Populations of actual countries or regions are not closed to migration. The population of a particular geographic area grows due to births and migrants into the geographic area. The population of the geographic area declines due to deaths and migrants out of the geographic area. Births, deaths, in-migrants, and out-migrants are the only sources of change in the population of a geographic area.

When there are too many people for a given land area to support, this is often considered a situation of **population pressure**. Population pressure is defined as the force exerted by a growing population upon its environment, resulting in dispersal or reduction of the population. An idea closely related to population pressure is **carrying capacity**, which is the maximum population size that the environment can sustain, given the food, habitat, water, and other necessities available in the environment.[30] The carrying capacity of an area differs depending on the basis of the economy. An area in which the inhabitants are supported by hunting and gathering has a lower carrying capacity than if the inhabitants of the area were supported by settled agriculture.

The limited ways that population size can change has motivated many thoughts about population growth. Ignoring migration, Malthus saw that an unacceptably high population growth rate could be remedied only by decreasing the number of births or increasing the number of deaths. He thought that a high rate of population growth was self-limiting at some point. Thus, he concluded that if births were not limited, then the population would face the undesirable alternative of an increase in the number of deaths.

Davis and Blake thought that thinking about how people respond to a high population growth rate had been too limited. In the Theory of Demographic Change and Response, they argued that people have more options than to limit their fertility through averting pregnancy, including migration and use of abortion.[31]

The observation of how the size of a population changes is summarized in the **population balancing equation**:

$$P_{T2} = P_{T1} + B - D + I - O$$

where:

P_{T2} = population at Time 2

P_{T1} = population at Time 1

B = births between Time 1 and Time 2

D = deaths between Time 1 and Time 2

I = migrants into the area (country, state, or world) between Time 1 and Time 2

O = migrants out of the area between Time 1 and Time 2

The population will grow between Time 1 and Time 2 if the number of people added by births and in-migration is **greater** than the number lost through deaths and out-migration. The population will decline between Time 1 and Time 2 if the number of people added by births and in-migration is *less* than the number lost through deaths and out-migration.

Rearranging terms in the population balancing equation results in the following equation for change in the size of the population between two dates:

Population change between
T1 and T2 = $P_{T2} - P_{T1}$ = B − D + I − O

Rather than looking only at the total magnitude of the change in population size between two dates, it is useful to take into account population size.

Population size is taken into account by calculating crude rates. A crude rate is usually expressed as the rate per thousand population. Thus, in a year, the **crude death rate** is the number of deaths in that year divided by the midyear population in thousands, and the **crude birth rate** is the number of births in the year per thousand midyear population. The **midyear population** is the population in the middle of the year, usually considered as July 1.

Dividing both sides by the midperiod population:

(Pop change/Pop in thousands)
= (B/Pop in 1000s) − (D/Pop in 1000s)
+ (I/Pop in 1000s) − (O/Pop in 1000s)

(Pop change/(Pop in 1000s))
= (B/(Pop in 1000s)) − (D/(Pop in 1000s))
+ (I/(Pop in 1000s)) − (O/(Pop in 1000s))

Growth Rate per 1000 Population
= (Births per 1000 Pop)
− (Deaths per 1000 Pop)
+ (In-migrants per 1000 Pop)
− (Out-migrants per 1000 Pop)

Growth Rate (GR) = Crude Birth Rate (CBR)
− Crude Death Rate (CDR)
+ In-Migration Rate (IMigR)
− Out-Migration Rate (OMigR)

Rate of Natural Increase per Thousand
Population (Nat r) = Growth (or decline) per thousand population due to births and deaths (natural processes) = CBR − CDR

Net Migration Rate per Thousand (NetMigR)
= Growth (or decline) per thousand population due to in-migration and out-migration

Growth Rate (GR)
= Crude Birth Rate (CBR)
− Crude Death Rate (CDR)
+ In-Migration Rate (IMigR)
− Out-Migration Rate (OMigR)
= CBR − CDR − NetMigR

so

GR = Nat r + NetMigR

If net migration = 0

GR = Nat r

Estimation of the Net Migration Rate

Often, there are no direct data on migration. In such cases, the net migration rate is estimated as

NetMigR = GR − Nat r

Now we will look at trends in each of the following: CDR, CBR, Nat r, and NetMigR.

Trends in Crude Rates

Crude rates do not take the age distribution of a population into account; they just look at the number of events (such as deaths or births) divided by the size of the total population. We now look at trends in the crude death rate. Babies younger than a year old and people older than age 65 have a higher chance of dying than people between ages 1 and 65. Also, some populations (such as that of Japan) are older than most other populations, and some (such as Nigeria's) are younger than most others. In Chapter 4, we look in detail at death rates by age.

Figure 2.9 shows the crude death rate in the world, the MDR, the LDR, and the United States. There was almost no change in the crude death rate in the MDR or the United States between 1950 and 2010. The crude death rate did not decline in the United States or the MDR, even though the chances of dying by age were declining. The lack of decline in the crude death rate in the MDR is a result of changes in the age distribution of these populations, particularly in the aging of these populations. This will be discussed further in this chapter and in Chapters 4, 5, and 11. Worldwide, the crude death rate declined by more than 50% from the early 1950s through 2005–2010. The downward path of the CDR in the LDR indicates the huge decline in mortality in the LDR since the end of World War II. In the LDR, the 2005–2010 value was only 35% of the 1950–1955 value. The decline in mortality in the LDR was mainly the result of declines in mortality of infants and children.

Figure 2.10 shows the crude birth rate in the same world divisions as were shown for the CDR in Figure 2.9. However, in light of the earlier discussion of rapid fertility decline in China compared to the LDR as a whole, Figure 2.9 also shows the crude birth rate for China. The CBR declined among all groups shown in Figure 2.9. In both the MDR and the LDR, the CBR in 2005–2010 was one-half its value in 1950–1955. In the United States, the CBR

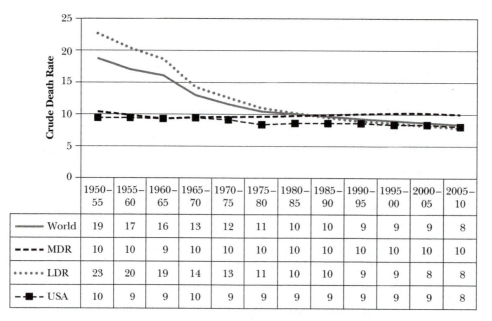

FIGURE 2.9 Crude Death Rate per Thousand Population, 1950–2010

	1950–55	1955–60	1960–65	1965–70	1970–75	1975–80	1980–85	1985–90	1990–95	1995–00	2000–05	2005–10
—— World	19	17	16	13	12	11	10	10	9	9	9	8
- - - MDR	10	10	9	10	10	10	10	10	10	10	10	10
····· LDR	23	20	19	14	13	11	10	10	9	9	8	8
-■- USA	10	9	9	10	9	9	9	9	9	9	9	8

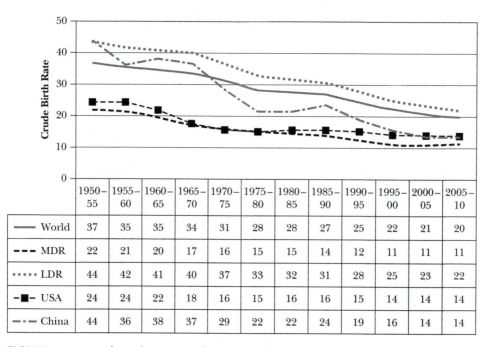

FIGURE 2.10 Crude Birth Rate per Thousand Population, 1950–2010

	1950–55	1955–60	1960–65	1965–70	1970–75	1975–80	1980–85	1985–90	1990–95	1995–00	2000–05	2005–10
—— World	37	35	35	34	31	28	28	27	25	22	21	20
- - - MDR	22	21	20	17	16	15	15	14	12	11	11	11
····· LDR	44	42	41	40	37	33	32	31	28	25	23	22
-■- USA	24	24	22	18	16	15	16	16	15	14	14	14
-·-·- China	44	36	38	37	29	22	22	24	19	16	14	14

in 2005–2010 was 58% of the 1950–1955 value. In China, the CBR declined from having the same value as the LDR as a whole in 1950–1955 to having the same value as the United States in 2005–2010.

The difference between the crude birth rate and the crude death rate is the **rate of natural increase**, also called natural r. When these rates are expressed per thousand population, the rate of natural increase is the number per thousand by which the population increases (or declines) due to the excess of births over deaths. If the number of births equals the number of deaths, the size of the population will not change, apart from the influence of migration. If there are more births than deaths, the population will increase (apart from the effects of migration), and if there are more deaths than births, the size of

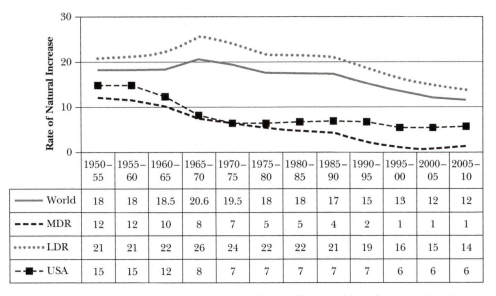

	1950–55	1955–60	1960–65	1965–70	1970–75	1975–80	1980–85	1985–90	1990–95	1995–00	2000–05	2005–10
World	18	18	18.5	20.6	19.5	18	18	17	15	13	12	12
MDR	12	12	10	8	7	5	5	4	2	1	1	1
LDR	21	21	22	26	24	22	22	21	19	16	15	14
USA	15	15	12	8	7	7	7	7	7	6	6	6

FIGURE 2.11   Rate of Natural Increase (Natural r) per Thousand Population, 1950–2010

the population will decline (apart from the effects of migration).

The rate of natural increase in the same geographic divisions considered in Figure 2.9 is shown in Figure 2.11. In the MDR and the United States, the rate of natural increase declined over time. Worldwide, natural r increased from 1950–1955 through 1965–1970, after which it declined. In the LDR, natural r also increased through 1965–1970, after which it declined. If you look at Figures 2.9 and 2.10, you can see that in the world and in the LDR, natural r rose and then declined because through 1965–1970, the CDR declined more rapidly than the CBR; after 1965–1970, the CBR declined more rapidly than the CDR.

If there is no migration in or out of an area or if the number of people migrating into an area equals the number of people migrating out of the area, the population growth rate and the rate of natural increase will be equal. The difference between the population growth rate and the rate of natural increase is the net migration rate.

Figure 2.12 shows the net migration rate in the same geographic divisions used earlier in this chapter. Recall that the **net migration rate** is the number of people by which the population increases (or decreases) annually due to the net number of migrants into the area. The net migration rate is estimated as the growth rate minus the natural rate of increase.

For the world as a whole, the net migration rate is zero, as it should be.[32] Over time, the net migration rate increased in the MDR and declined in the LDR. A positive net migration rate means that, on balance, people are migrating into the region or country; a negative net migration rate means that, on balance, people are migrating out of the region or country. Thus, the results in Figure 2.12 mean that increasingly since 1950, people have been migrating from the LDR to the MDR.

Since all of the world's population is either in the MDR or the LDR, the net number of people migrating out of the LDR equals the net number of people migrating into the MDR. The two net migration rates have opposite signs (+ for net in-migration and − for net out-migration), but the denominators of the two net migration rates are also different. Recall from Figure 2.3 that in 2005–2010, four times as many people lived in the LDR as in the MDR. Thus, a given number of people migrating from the LDR to the MDR results in a positive net migration rate for the MDR that is four times the magnitude of the negative net migration rate that is generated for the LDR. This is what we find. In Figure 2.12, in 2005–2010, the net migration rate into the MDR is a little more than four times the net migration rate out of the LDR.

Table 2.4 shows the crude death rate, crude birth rate, rate of natural increase, net migration rate, and growth rate for 2005–2010 for the world as a whole, as well as for the regions of the world, the MDR, and the LDR. The rates are shown per thousand population.

Europe is the only region that has a negative rate of natural increase, although the growth rate is positive due to net in-migration. The growth rate of Northern America is more than four times that of Europe. Northern America has a higher rate of natural increase than Europe as well as a higher net migration rate. The growth rates in Latin American and the

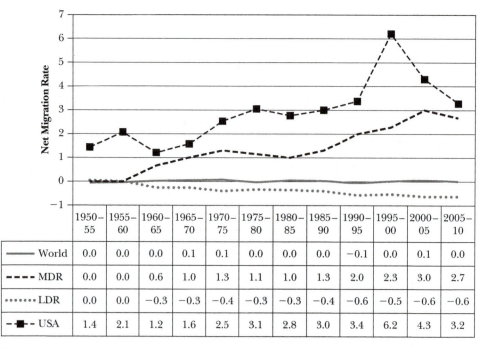

FIGURE 2.12   Net Migration Rate (NetMigR) per Thousand Population, 1950–2010

TABLE 2.4   Population Dynamics per Thousand Population in World Regions, 2005–2010

	Crude Death Rate, 2005–2010	Crude Birth Rate, 2005–2010	Natural r, 2005–2010	Net Migration Rate, 2005–2010	Growth Rate, 2005–2010
World	8.4	20.0	11.6	0.0	11.6
MDR	10.0	11.4	1.4	2.7	4.1
LDR	8.0	21.9	13.9	−0.6	13.3
Europe	11.2	10.8	−0.4	2.4	2.0
Northern America	8.2	13.7	5.5	3.6	9.1
Latin America and the Caribbean	5.9	19.3	13.4	−1.9	11.5
Asia	7.4	18.6	11.2	−0.4	10.8
Africa	11.9	35.6	23.7	−0.7	23.0
Oceania	6.9	18.0	11.1	0.6	11.8

Caribbean, Asia, and Oceania are approximately equal (11.5, 10.8, and 11.8 per thousand). There is a higher net migration rate out of Latin America and the Caribbean than out of Asia, perhaps due to the proximity of Northern America to Latin America. The net migration rate for Oceania is positive, because in 2010 73% of the population of Oceania was from the MDR countries of Australia and New Zealand, although it includes LDR countries such as Papua New Guinea.

We saw in Figure 2.12 that international migrants tend to move from the LDR to the MDR. We see in Table 2.4 that economically poorer areas (such as Africa) on balance send migrants to economically better off areas (such as Europe).

Some of the main international migration flows are as follows:

From Latin America and Asia to the United States

From Asia to Canada

From Africa and Asia to Europe

We see in Table 2.4 that although Asia on net loses population through migration, less than 0.5 a person per thousand population (0.4 persons per

BOX 2.5
Magnitude of Net Migration Out of Asia, 2005–2010

Population of Asia in Thousands, 2005: 3,944,992; 2010: 4,164,252

Average Population, 2005–2010: 4,054,622

Net Migration Rate per Thousand Population, 2005–2010: −0.4

Net Migration Rate per Person, 2005–2010: −0.0004

0.0004 × 4,054,622,000 = 1,621,848
net out-migrants from Asia per year

Over five years (mid 2005–mid 2010), there would be

5 × 1,621,848 = 8,109,244
net out-migrants from Asia

---

thousand) left Asia per year in the 2005–2010 period. This might seem like a trivially low rate of net out-migration. However, the huge size of Asia's population translates this low out-migration rate into a large number of migrants leaving Asia. This low rate of net out-migration, combined with Asia's large population size, results in more than 8 million people on balance leaving Asia in the 5-year period of 2005–2010. The calculations behind this are shown in Box 2.5.

Population Dynamics in the Less Developed Region of the World: Falling Mortality Followed by (Usually) Falling Fertility

In this section, we look at how the components of population growth worked together in the LDR in 1950–2010. The components of population growth for the LDR are shown in Figure 2.13. The crude death rate declined by 1965–1970 to 61% of the 1950–1955 value. Between 1965–1970 and 2005–2010, the crude death rate further declined from 14 to 8 per thousand, a decline to 57% of the 1965–1970 value. The crude birth rate also declined throughout the period, but through 1965–1970, the CBR declined more slowly than the CDR. Thus, the rate of natural increase (CBR–CDR) increased from 1950–1955 to 1965–1970 by 24% (from 21 to 26 per thousand), after which the rate of natural increase declined to three-quarters of its 1950–1955 value by 2005–2010.

The net migration rate was close to zero in the LDR throughout the period, with a negative value of −1 per thousand in 2005–2010. Thus, in 2005–2010, net out-migration from the LDR slightly depressed overall population growth. Due to the zero or near-zero value of the net migration rate, the growth rate in the LDR was virtually identical to the rate of natural increase. The growth rate is not shown in Figure 2.13, since the lines for the growth rate and for the rate of natural increase would have been on top of each other.

The Demographic Transition

Figure 2.13 illustrates the pattern of changes that encompass a large part of what is called the Demographic Transition or the First Demographic Transition. The **Theory of the Demographic Transition** was first proposed by Thompson in 1929.[33] Demographic transition theory describes the changes in the crude birth rate and the crude death rate that have resulted in a particular pattern of change in population size in the developed countries historically and in many less developed countries since World War II.[34]

Figure 2.14 schematically shows the changes in the CBR and CDR in the course of the Demographic Transition. The rate of natural increase (CBR–CDR) is also shown. The rates are illustrative and are not exactly what the rates have been in real populations.

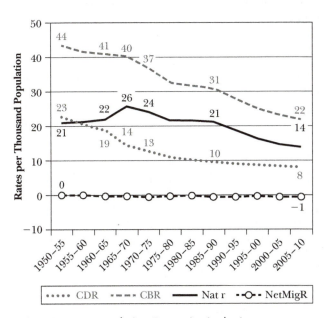

FIGURE 2.13 Population Dynamics in the Less Developed Region

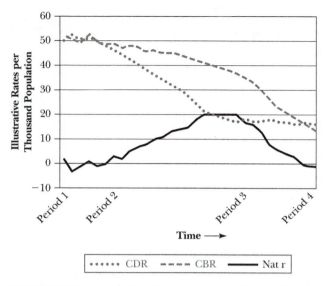

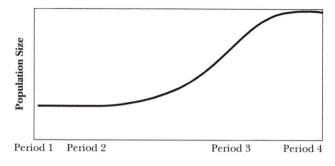

FIGURE 2.15   Population Size in the Course of the Demographic Transition

FIGURE 2.14   Population Dynamics in the Course of the Demographic Transition

Before the Demographic Transition begins (Period 1), the CBR and CDR both fluctuate. They are high and have values that are close to each other. Since the CDR and the CBR are approximately the same during Period 1, the rate of natural increase is close to zero. During Period 2, mortality conditions improve, and the CDR begins to decline, but the CBR either is virtually unchanged or declines much more slowly than the CDR. As the gap between the CBR and the CDR widens, the rate of natural increase (natural r) rises. Eventually, the CBR declines more rapidly, and decline in the CDR stops or slows considerably (Period 3). This leads to a halt in the rise in natural r and then a decline in natural r. By Period 4, the CDR and CBR again have values close to each other, resulting again in a rate of natural increase close to zero, but with both the CBR and the CDR having much lower values than they did in Period 1. In Chapter 5, we discuss the causes of the decline in mortality, and in Chapter 9, we discuss the causes of the decline in fertility.

Figure 2.15 shows the population size that would result from the dynamics shown in Figure 2.14, under the assumption of zero net migration. In Period 1, population size is essentially unchanged, because natural r is close to zero. In Period 2 and Period 3, population size increases as natural r rises. By Period 4, natural r is again close to zero, so the population no longer grows, but the size of the population in Period 4 is much larger than it was in Period 1.

Kenya and Botswana as Examples of Extreme Population Dynamics

In this section, we look at population dynamics in two distinctive, less developed countries—Kenya and

Botswana. Both countries are in sub-Saharan Africa, and their locations are shown in Figure 2.16.[35]

Kenya has the distinction of having had the highest reliably recorded population growth rate of any country in the world—3.8% in 1980–1985. That growth rate translates into a population doubling time of only 18 years.

Botswana has the distinction of being the first country for which the impact of deaths from HIV could be seen in national mortality data. For 2008, Botswana was estimated to have the third highest adult prevalence of people who were HIV positive—23% of those age 15 or older. Only Lesotho and Swaziland were estimated to have had a higher adult HIV prevalence.

Figure 2.17 shows population dynamics in Kenya. Although in 1950–1955 the rate of natural increase in Kenya was 28 per thousand, indicating earlier substantial mortality decline, the increase in natural r between the 1950s and the 1980s and its subsequent decline look similar to part of the schematic picture of the Demographic Transition in Figure 2.14. It is also a more extreme example of what we saw for the LDR in Figure 2.13. The very high growth rate in Kenya and the short implied population doubling time in 1980–1985 served as a warning to many policy makers of what could happen throughout the LDR if crude birth rates did not decline. Factors related to fertility decline in Kenya are discussed more in Chapter 9.[36]

Figure 2.18 shows population dynamics in Botswana. The large increase in the CDR after 1990–1995 is likely due to increasing mortality from HIV. The decline in the crude death rate in 2005–2010 is likely due to effective HIV prevention and treatment programs. Mortality in Botswana is discussed more in Chapter 4.

There was also an increase in the CDR in Kenya between 1990 and 2005, although not as large as what occurred in Botswana. This increase was probably due to increased HIV mortality in Kenya,[37] as well as some increases in malaria mortality.[38]

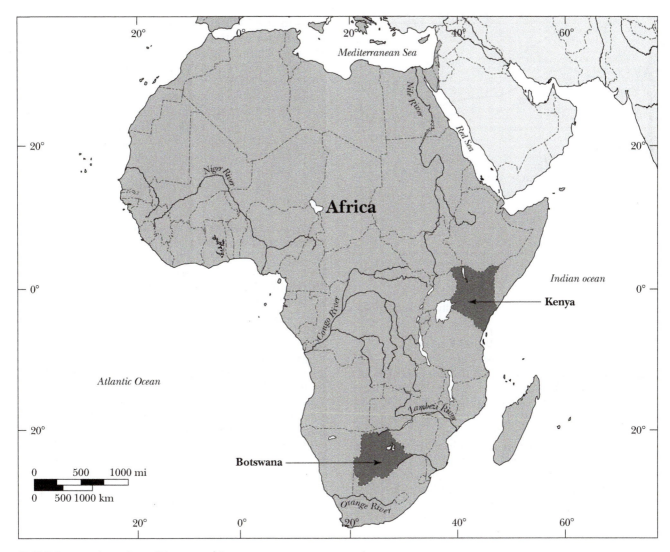

FIGURE 2.16   Location of Kenya and Botswana

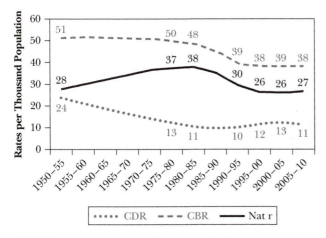

FIGURE 2.17   Population Dynamics in Kenya

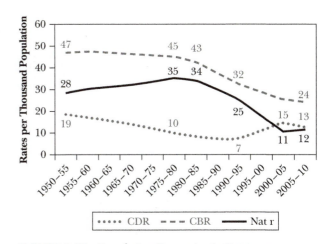

FIGURE 2.18   Population Dynamics in Botswana

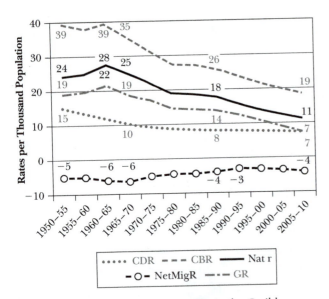

FIGURE 2.19   Population Dynamics in the Caribbean

The Caribbean: A Less Developed Region with a High Net Out-migration Rate

We saw in Figures 2.12 and 2.13 that for the LDR as a whole, the net migration rate has been close to zero, and after 1980 it has been slightly negative. A negative net migration rate means that more people are migrating out of the country or region than are migrating into the country or region in a given time period. Although for the LDR overall, the net migration rate has a trivial effect on population growth, in some regions the level of net out-migration is much higher

than in the LDR as a whole. One region where the net migration rate plays a substantial role in dampening population growth is the Caribbean.[39]

Figure 2.19 shows population dynamics in the Caribbean. Throughout the period of 1950–2010, the population growth rate was substantially lower than the rate of natural increase. The difference between the two lines is the value of the net migration rate, which varied between −3 and −6 per thousand. For the Caribbean, in 2005–2010 the growth rate is less than two-thirds of the value of natural r, due to the dampening effect of net out-migration on population growth.

Population Dynamics in the Least Developed Countries of the World

Within the LDR, there is a group of countries with an especially low development level, called the **Least Developed Countries (LeastDC)**. They are defined by a combination of low income, human resource weakness, and economic vulnerability.[40] Most of the least developed countries are in Africa. Haiti is the only least developed country in the Western Hemisphere. Countries can move off the list of LeastDC. Botswana moved off in 1994, Cape Verde in 2007, and Maldives in 2011. In 2012, there were 47 countries in the LeastDC group. Figure 2.20 shows the location of the LeastDC as of 2012. The list of the LeastDC in 2012 also appears in Appendix A.[41]

The population dynamics in the LeastDC are shown in Figure 2.21. The picture is similar to that for the LDR in Figure 2.13, but is more extreme. In the LeastDC, the crude birth rate began to decline more

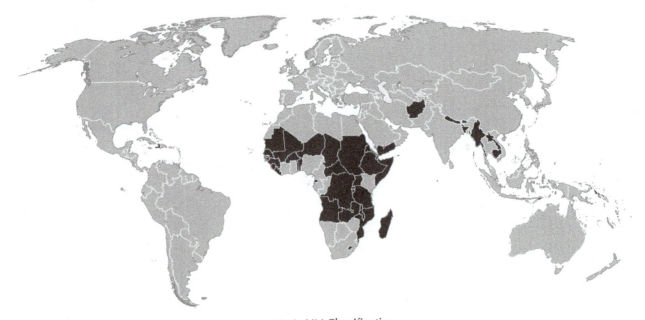

FIGURE 2.20   The Least Developed Countries, 2012: UN Classification

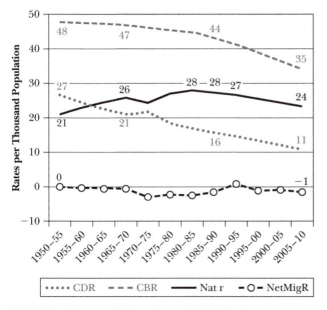

FIGURE 2.21 Population Dynamics in the Least Developed Countries (LeastDC) of the World

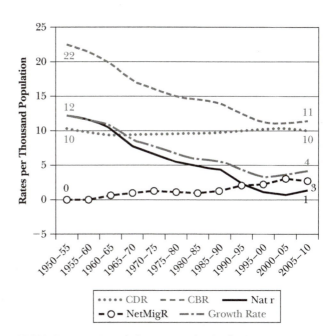

FIGURE 2.22 Population Dynamics in the More Developed Region

rapidly than the crude death rate only in the 1990s, as can be seen by the fact that the rate of natural increase only began to decline in the 1990s. Even in 2005–2010, the growth rate in the LeastDC was 2.4%, which results in a doubling time of 29 years. In the LDR, the rate of natural increase began to decline by the early 1970s. Thus, the Demographic Transition occurred about 20 years later in the LeastDC than in the LDR as a whole.

Population Dynamics in the More Developed Region of the World: The Increasing Importance of Immigration in Population Growth

While in the LDR, the main dynamic behind population growth has been the magnitude of the difference between the crude birth rate and the crude death rate, recently in the MDR of the world the rate of natural increase has been low, often close to or below zero. In this situation, a positive net migration rate—immigration into countries—has become the most important determinant of the rate of population growth.

Figure 2.22 shows changes in the components of population growth in the MDR. Natural r declined from 12 per thousand in 1950–1955 to 1 per thousand in 2005–2010. Also, in 1950–1955, the rate of natural increase and the growth rate were identical—at that time, the net migration rate was zero. Over time, the growth rate and natural r increasingly diverged, as net migration into the MDR increased. By 1990–1995, the rate of natural increase and the net migration rate were equal in magnitude—each at

2 per thousand. By 2005–2010, in the MDR 75% of growth was due to net migration and 25% was due to natural increase (the excess of births over deaths).

The contribution of the rate of natural increase and of the net migration rate to the population growth rate differs in different parts of the MDR. Figure 2.23 shows the roles of natural r and of the net migration rate in the population growth rate in Europe, on the one hand, and in the United States, on the other hand.

Europe is a more extreme example of what is seen in Figure 2.22 for the MDR. In Europe, the rate of natural increase has not been positive since the late 1980s. Thus, without net in-migration, Europe as a whole would have had a declining population since 1990–1995. Net migration to Europe increased since the early 1950s. By 1990–1995 in Europe, the net migration rate exceeded the rate of natural increase. The positive growth rate in Europe in 2005–2010 of 2 per thousand was entirely due to immigration, a net migration rate of +2 per thousand. The low level of natural r in Europe was due to very low fertility. Theories about causes of this low fertility are discussed in Chapter 10.

The United States shows a different pattern. For the United States, the rate of natural increase was positive throughout 1950–2010, which is unusual for a more developed country. The net migration rate was higher at every date in the United States than in Europe, but due to the higher rate of natural increase in the United States than in Europe, even in 2005–2010 in the United States the excess of births over death (natural growth) accounted for two-thirds of population

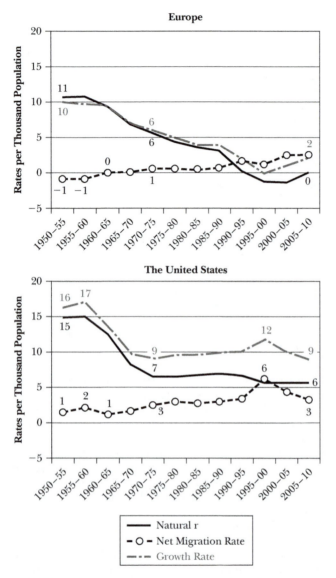

FIGURE 2.23 The Role of Natural Growth and Net Migration in Population Growth in Europe and the United States

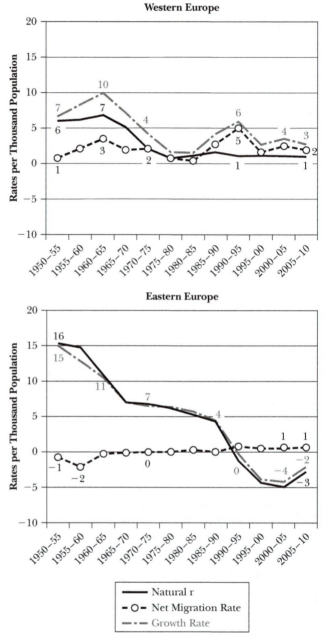

FIGURE 2.24 Role of Natural Growth and Net Migration in Population Growth in Western and Eastern Europe

growth. The rate of natural increase exceeded the net migration rate except in 1995–2000, when they were equal at 6 per thousand. Policies related to immigration in the United States and other more developed countries are discussed in Chapter 12.

Figure 2.24 shows the role of the rate of natural increase and of the net migration rate in population growth (or decline) in Western Europe in comparison to Eastern Europe. Both panels have the same vertical scale to make comparisons easier. The growth rate declined since the 1950s in Eastern Europe, with some recovery in 2005–2010. In Western Europe, the growth rate declined from 1960 through 1985 and then increased before declining again in the years since 1995. In 2005–2010, the net migration rate was

2 per thousand in Western Europe and 1 per thousand in Eastern Europe. Since the late 1970s, the rate of natural increase in Western Europe has been about 1 per thousand. The growth rate in Western Europe has fluctuated due to the fluctuating net migration rate. In Eastern Europe, the growth rate and natural r have been virtually identical since 1950, because the net migration rate has been close to zero throughout the period. Thus, in Western Europe, the growth rate has been mainly determined by the net migration rate,

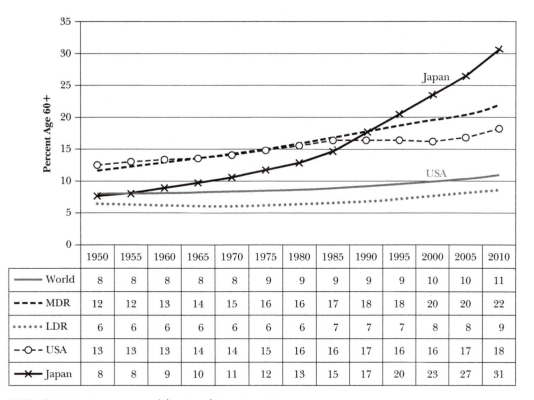

	1950	1955	1960	1965	1970	1975	1980	1985	1990	1995	2000	2005	2010
——— World	8	8	8	8	8	9	9	9	9	9	10	10	11
- - - - MDR	12	12	13	14	15	16	16	17	18	18	20	20	22
•••••• LDR	6	6	6	6	6	6	6	7	7	7	8	8	9
- -○- - USA	13	13	13	14	14	15	16	16	17	16	16	17	18
—✕— Japan	8	8	9	10	11	12	13	15	17	20	23	27	31

FIGURE 2.25 Percentage of the Population Age 60+

while in Eastern Europe, the growth rate has been mainly determined by the rate of natural increase.

WORLD POPULATION AGING

The population of the world has become older over time. Figure 2.25 shows the percentage of the population of the world, the LDR, and the MDR that was aged 60 or older. It also shows the results for the United States and for Japan. In 2010, Japan had the oldest population in the world. As the proportion of the population above an age such as 60 or

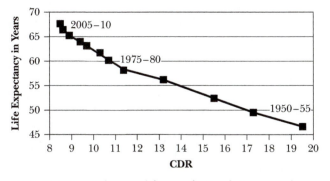

FIGURE 2.26 Relation of the Crude Death Rate (CDR) and Life Expectancy in Years for the World, 1950–1955 through 2005–2010

65 increases, the burdens on working-age family members and on social services increase.

Two common indicators of the mortality situation of a population are the crude death rate (CDR), which is the number of deaths at all ages per thousand population, and the expectation of life at birth or life expectancy at birth, which is the number of years that a person on average would live if subject to the chances by age that a person will die in a given population. The lower the crude death rate and the higher the life expectancy at birth, the better the mortality situation.

Figure 2.26 shows the relation between the CDR and life expectancy at birth for the world as a whole from 1950–1955 through 2005–2010. Over time, as the CDR declined, life expectancy increased—the higher the crude death rate, the lower life expectancy. This seems obvious. However, next we look at the situation in Japan, which contradicts this obvious expectation.

A Cautionary Note about the Influence of Age Structure on the Crude Death Rate

Consideration of mortality changes in Japan shows why people should be cautious in interpreting the meaning of trends in the crude death rate. Recall that in 2010, Japan had the oldest population in the world.

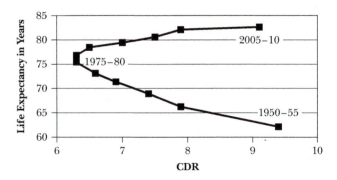

FIGURE 2.27 Relation of the Crude Death Rate (CDR) and Life Expectancy in Years for Japan from 1950–1955 through 2005–2010

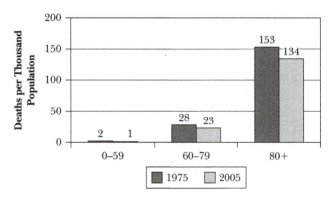

FIGURE 2.28 Female Death Rates by Age in Japan, 1975 and 2005

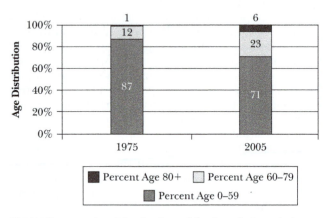

FIGURE 2.29 Age Distribution of the Female Population of Japan, 1975 and 2005

Figure 2.27 shows the same information for Japan as was shown in Figure 2.26 for the world as a whole. In the period from 1950–1955 through 1975–1980, the relation of the crude death rate and life expectancy in Japan is the same as in the world as a whole. However, in the period 1975–1980 through 2005–2010, as life expectancy has increased, the CDR

has also increased. Why has this happened in Japan? Have mortality conditions in Japan improved or worsened between 1975–1980 and 2005–2010?

Note in Figure 2.25 that the proportion of the Japanese population over age 60 increased rapidly, more than doubling from less than 13% in 1980 to 31% in 2010. In every population, the elderly—those over age 60—have a higher chance of dying than younger people in the same population.

Figures 2.28 and 2.29 make the situation even clearer. Figure 2.28 shows female death rates per 1,000 population in Japan in 1975 and 2005 for the population age 0–59, age 60–79 and age 80 or older. Death rates are higher at older than at younger ages. Also, in every age group, the death rate is lower in 2005 than in 1975. Figure 2.29 shows the distribution of the female population of Japan in 1975 and 2005. It is clear that the Japanese population has become older, with increasing proportions in the older age groups that have high death rates.

As an increasing proportion of the population is at the older ages, the mortality of these older people has an increasing influence on the CDR. Thus, although in Japan over time individuals have tended to live longer, the shift in the composition of the population to older ages has resulted in a higher CDR even while life expectancy has increased, as shown in Figure 2.27.

The example of Japan shows that changes in the crude death rate cannot be directly interpreted as similar changes in the survival chances in the population as a whole when the proportion of the population at older ages is increasing rapidly. This issue is examined in more detail in Chapter 4.

WORLD POPULATION POLICY CONCERNS

As the dynamics of world population have changed, similarly the kinds of population problems that have concerned governments and motivated the formulation of policies have changed. The United Nations conducted surveys of member governments since 1976 to determine the extent to which governments were concerned about different population areas.[42]

In this section, we look at changing governmental views of the seriousness of various population problems. In some cases, these changing views seem logically related to changes in the components of population growth, while in other cases, the connection between empirical changes and changing views is less obvious.

Figure 2.30 shows changes over time in the views of governments about their country's population growth rate. Governments could respond that the

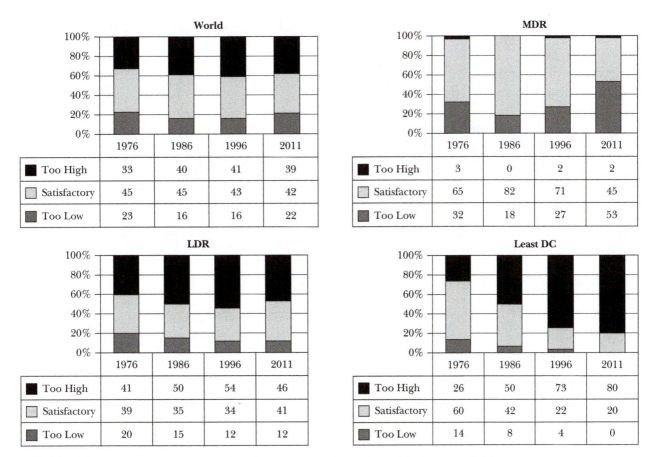

FIGURE 2.30 Government Views on Their Country's Population Growth Rate, 1976–2011

country's population growth rate was too high, satisfactory, or too low. The results are shown for the countries in the world as a whole, in the MDR, in the LDR, and in the LeastDC. For each date, the percentage distribution of views of countries in the given category is shown.

In the world as a whole, there was an increase in the percentage of countries that perceived their country's population growth rate as too high from 1976 through 1996 and then a decline by 2011. This variable pattern for the world is the result of very different patterns in different divisions of the world. Almost no MDR governments viewed their population growth rates as too high at any date from 1976 to 2011. However, at every date a substantial portion of MDR governments viewed their growth rates as too low (over 50% in 2011). There was some fluctuation in the views of LDR governments as to whether their growth rates were too high, but Figure 2.5 shows that in the LDR as a whole, the growth rate has declined since the late 1960s.

Governmental concern about the country's growth rate results from both (1) observation of the actual level of the growth rate, and (2) whether leaders see

a high growth rate as presenting a problem. In the LeastDC, there was a steady increase in the percentage of governments that viewed their growth rates as too high, with 80% of the LeastDC governments holding this view in 2011. Figure 2.21 showed that the growth rate in the LeastDC was high since 1950 and has declined only slightly since the 1980s. Even in 2005–2010, the LeastDC had a population doubling time of 30 years, an increase from a doubling time of 25 years in the late 1980s. Thus, it seems that LeastDC governments have become increasing convinced of the likely negative consequences of a continued high growth rate, even as the actual growth rate in the LeastDC has declined somewhat.

Figure 2.31 shows changes between 1976 and 2011 in the percentage of governments that viewed their country's life expectancy as unacceptably low. Recall that by 1976, as shown in Figures 2.13 and 2.21, the CDR had declined considerably both in the LDR and in the LeastDC from its level in the early 1950s. A declining percentage of LDC countries viewed their life expectancy as unacceptably low over time, but the percentage of LeastDC countries that viewed their life expectancy as too low increased between 1976 to

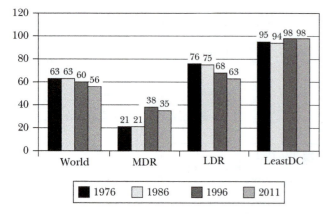

FIGURE 2.31 Percentage of Governments Viewing Their Life Expectancy as Unacceptably Low, 1976–2011

2011, with almost all LeastDC governments holding this view at every date.

Although only slightly more than half of the world's countries viewed their life expectancy as unacceptably low in 2011, there still were major mortality concerns. Since 1996, the United Nations has been asking about the level of governmental concern about HIV. The responses to this inquiry are shown in Figure 2.32. In the world as a whole, concern increased between 1996 and 2009 and then decreased somewhat by 2011. In the MDR, concern with HIV declined after 2005, as antiretroviral therapy (ART) became increasingly available. There was a decline in concern with HIV in the LDR after 2009, likely due to the increased availability of ART. In the LeastDC, there was no decline in concern with HIV through 2011.

Figure 2.33 shows changes over time in governmental views of their country's fertility level. Recall that high rates of population growth in many less developed countries in the 1960s and 1970s were

fueled by higher fertility than mortality, and this motivated much of the modern impetus to control population growth. Between 1976 and 1996, the percentage of LDR governments who thought their fertility level was too high increased from 47% to 59% before declining to 52% in 2011. However, in the LeastDC, the percentage of governments that thought their fertility level was too high increased from 31% in 1976 to 92% in 2011. At the same time, the percentage of MDR governments that thought their fertility level was too low increased from 21% to 65%, which is consistent with the fertility declines in the MDR, reaching a very low level of fertility by 2010.

We saw in Figure 2.25 that the percentage of the population over age 60 has increased throughout the world. Since 2005, the United Nations has been asking governments about their level of concern about population aging in their country. Figure 2.34 indicates the responses to that question in 2005 and 2011. At both dates, population aging was a greater concern in the MDR than in the LDR and greater in the LDR than in the LeastDC, which is consistent with the extent of population aging in these different groups of countries. There was a small decline in the extent of concern with population aging between 2005 and 2011 in the LDR and the LeastDC, while in the MDR, major concern with population aging increased from 76% of governments to 88% of governments. Population aging is discussed in detail in Chapter 11.

U.S. Government Population Policy Concerns

The responses of the United States to the questions from the United Nations Population Division are generally similar to those from the other MDR countries, but with some differences. At all four dates, the United States replied that the country's population growth rate was satisfactory, even as an increasing proportion of MDR countries found their growth rate too low. In light of the much higher growth rate in the United States than in the MDR, as shown in Figure 2.5, this divergence of views seems reasonable.

In 1976 and 1986, the United States viewed its life expectancy as acceptable, but in 1996 and 2011, the United States reported that its life expectancy was unacceptably low. The U.S. life expectancy did not decline over time, but some more developed countries increased their life expectancy to many more years than seen for the United States. Perhaps this growing gap in life expectancy between the United States and some other countries led to this change in the U.S. government's view. Mortality determinants

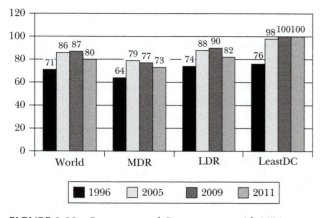

FIGURE 2.32 Percentage of Governments with HIV as a Major Concern, 1996–2011

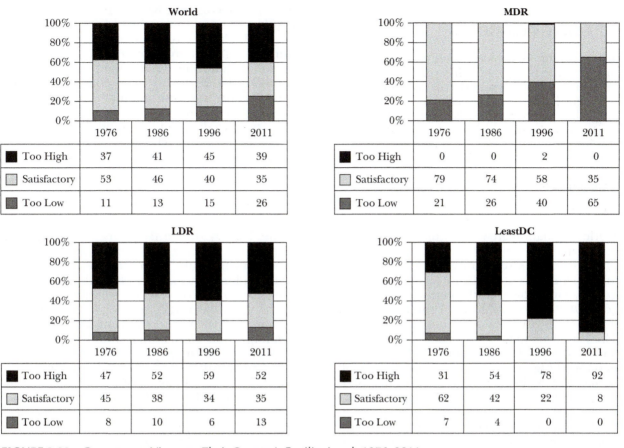

FIGURE 2.33   Government Views on Their Country's Fertility Level, 1976–2011

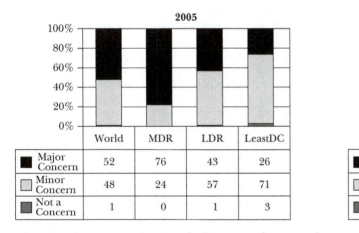

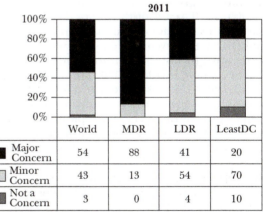

FIGURE 2.34   Government Level of Concern about Population Aging, 2005 and 2011

in more developed countries are discussed in Chapter 7. Like the vast majority of the world's countries, the United States viewed HIV as an area of major concern both in 1996 and in 2011.

While by 2011, 65% of MDR countries thought their fertility level was too low, the United States viewed its fertility level as satisfactory, which is reasonable, given the higher CBR in the United States than in the MDR as a whole, as shown in Figure 2.10. Along with 88% of the MDR countries, the United States in 2011 viewed population aging as an area of major concern.

CONCLUDING COMMENTS

We have seen that there have been massive changes in demographic patterns in the world since 1950. Mortality has declined everywhere, and, after some delay, fertility levels also have declined. International migration has played an increasingly important role in population growth, especially in the MDR.

Population concerns have shifted between 1976 and 2011 from a concern in the LDR with high mortality and high fertility to a concern with HIV and continued high fertility in some regions, while concern with high fertility has declined greatly in other regions. In the MDR, the main concerns are with too-low fertility and with population aging. These changing policy concerns set a context for the discussion of mortality, fertility, migration, and aging dynamics in subsequent chapters.

✅ Study and Review Online

SUMMARY

1. World population grew slowly up to about 1800, more rapidly in 1800–1900, and much more rapidly after 1900. Growth rates declined after the mid-twentieth century. If the world population growth rate in 2005–2010 continued indefinitely after 2010, the population of the world would double in 59 years—by 2069.

2. The less developed region (LDR) of the world has grown much more rapidly than the more developed region (MDR) of the world. In 1950, 32% of the world's population was in the MDR; by 2010, only 13% of the world's population was in the MDR.

3. In 2010, three of the ten largest countries in the world (United States, Russia, and Japan) were in the MDR. China and India were the largest countries in the world.

4. Population growth rates in the LDR peaked in 1965–1970 at a growth rate of 2.5%. If these growth rates had not declined, the population of the LDR would have doubled in 29 years.

5. China was growing even more rapidly than the LDR as a whole in 1965–1970. This rapid growth rate alarmed China's leaders and led to the implementation of fertility limitation programs. China's growth rate declined rapidly after 1970. In 2005–2010, China's population growth rate was less than half that of the LDR excluding China.

6. The population balancing equation is useful in decomposing population growth. Between two points in time, a population grows through the addition of births and in-migrants and declines through deaths and out-migrants.

7. High growth rates in the LDR were the result of a decline in the crude death rate while the crude birth rate remained high.

8. Population growth rates declined when the crude birth rate declined and approached the value of the crude death rate.

9. The Theory of the Demographic Transition describes the process by which the decline in death rates results in an increase in the rate of population growth, after which the growth rate declines once birth rates have declined.

10. International migration has mainly flowed from the LDR to the MDR. In 2005–2010, net in-migration contributed about two-thirds of the growth of the population in the MDR, and natural growth (the excess of births over deaths) contributed about one-third. Net migration out of the LDR had only a slight effect on the growth rate in the LDR. Net migration out of the LDR resulted in the growth rate in the LDR being about 96% of what it would have been with no emigration.

11. Throughout the world, the proportion of the population over age 60 has increased. In the LDR, the percentage aged 60+ years went from 6% in 1950 to 9% in 2010; in the MDR, the percentage aged 60+ went from 12% in 1950 to 22% in 2010. Japan, the oldest country in the world, had 31% of its population aged 60+ in 2010.

12. The crude death rate, which is the number of deaths per thousand population, does not take the age distribution of the population into account. In every population, death rates are higher at older ages (over age 60) than at younger ages. Japan is an example where the expectation of life at birth (average length of life) has increased, but the crude death rate has also increased. This is because as mortality at all ages declined, the population also became older. The increasing proportion of the population above age 60 led to an increase in the crude death rate, even as the chance of dying at each age declined.

13. Population concerns of governments have shifted over time. Since 1976, in the world as a whole, concern about population growth rates has fluctuated, concern about the overall mortality

level has declined, while HIV has emerged as a major area of concern. There is also substantial concern about population aging. In the MDR, there is a high level of concern about too-low fertility, and almost 90% of MDR governments view population aging as a major concern. In the LDR and especially in the LeastDC, there have been high and increasing concerns about a too-high population growth rate, fueled by high fertility. In the LDR, concern about overall mortality has declined, while all LeastDC governments view their mortality level as unacceptably high. Over 40% of LDR governments and 20% of LeastDC governments view population aging as an area of major concern.

KEY TERMS

more developed region (MDR)   33
less developed region (LDR)   34
population growth rate   35
population doubling time   37
population halving time   37
gross national income   40
purchasing power parity   40

closed population   44
population pressure   44
carrying capacity   44
population balancing equation   44
crude death rate   45
crude birth rate   45
midyear population   45

rate of natural increase   46
net migration rate   47
Theory of the Demographic Transition   49
least developed countries (LeastDC)   52

QUESTIONS FOR DISCUSSION AND REVIEW

1. Imagine the following countries. The rates are all per thousand population:

	Country A	Country B	Country C	Country D	Country E	Country F
Crude birth rate	50.0	10.0	13.0	14.0	13.0	40.0
Crude death rate	20.0	12.0	5.0	10.0	5.0	30.0
Rate of natural increase	30.0	−2.0	8.0	4.0	8.0	10.0
Net migration rate	−3.0	2.0	−0.2	4.0	3.0	−0.3

Rank the countries from the highest population growth rate to the lowest population growth rate. Why do you think this is the order?

Discuss the role of fertility, mortality and migration in the growth rate of each country.

Which country, if any, is likely a popular destination for international migrants? Which country, if any, is likely a popular origin for international migrants?

Which of these countries are probably in the more developed region of the world? Which of these countries are probably in the less developed region of the world? Why do you think this?

2. Why have some countries been concerned about the total size of their population?

3. Look at the following data for Algeria and France. If the growth rate in each country continues unchanged into the future, when will the population of Algeria surpass that of France in size?

	Population in thousands 2000	Population in thousands in 2010
Algeria	30,506	35,423
France	59,128	62,637

4. Look at the graphs of demographic rates for Country G and for Country H. Describe the changing population situation in each country over time. Is each of these countries probably in the LDR or the MDR? What problems or challenges is each country probably facing and how have these problems changed over time?

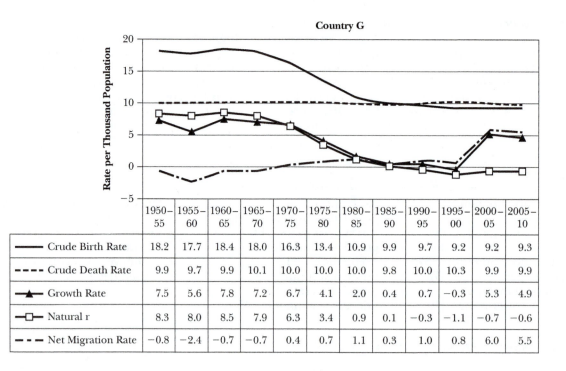

	1950–55	1955–60	1960–65	1965–70	1970–75	1975–80	1980–85	1985–90	1990–95	1995–00	2000–05	2005–10
——— Crude Birth Rate	18.2	17.7	18.4	18.0	16.3	13.4	10.9	9.9	9.7	9.2	9.2	9.3
- - - - Crude Death Rate	9.9	9.7	9.9	10.1	10.0	10.0	10.0	9.8	10.0	10.3	9.9	9.9
—▲— Growth Rate	7.5	5.6	7.8	7.2	6.7	4.1	2.0	0.4	0.7	−0.3	5.3	4.9
—□— Natural r	8.3	8.0	8.5	7.9	6.3	3.4	0.9	0.1	−0.3	−1.1	−0.7	−0.6
- - - Net Migration Rate	−0.8	−2.4	−0.7	−0.7	0.4	0.7	1.1	0.3	1.0	0.8	6.0	5.5

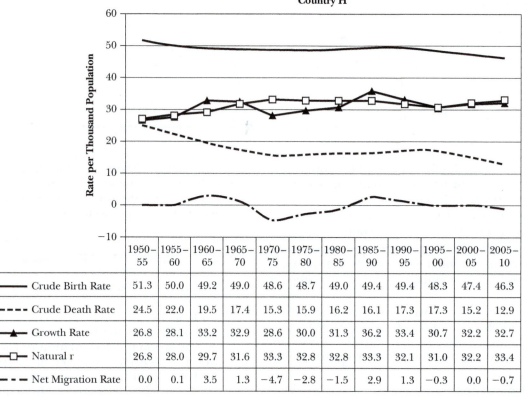

	1950–55	1955–60	1960–65	1965–70	1970–75	1975–80	1980–85	1985–90	1990–95	1995–00	2000–05	2005–10
——— Crude Birth Rate	51.3	50.0	49.2	49.0	48.6	48.7	49.0	49.4	49.4	48.3	47.4	46.3
- - - - Crude Death Rate	24.5	22.0	19.5	17.4	15.3	15.9	16.2	16.1	17.3	17.3	15.2	12.9
—▲— Growth Rate	26.8	28.1	33.2	32.9	28.6	30.0	31.3	36.2	33.4	30.7	32.2	32.7
—□— Natural r	26.8	28.0	29.7	31.6	33.3	32.8	32.8	33.3	32.1	31.0	32.2	33.4
- - - Net Migration Rate	0.0	0.1	3.5	1.3	−4.7	−2.8	−1.5	2.9	1.3	−0.3	0.0	−0.7

NOTES

1. Paul R. Ehrlich. 1968. *The Population Bomb*, New York: Ballantine.

2. cf. United Nations Fund for Population Activities (UNFPA). 2001. *Footprints and Milestones: Population and Environmental Change*, New York: UNFPA.

3. M. S. Teitelbaum and J. M. Winter. 1985. *The Fear of Population Decline*, Orlando, FL: Academic Press; and Wolfgang Lutz, Brian C. O'Neill, and Sergei Scherbov. 2003. "Europe's Population at a Turning Point," *Science*, 299: 1991–1992.

4. J. J. Spengler. 1938. *France Faces Depopulation*, Durham, NC: Duke University Press.

5. K. Davis. 1948. *Human Society*, New York: Macmillan, 608.

6. For a discussion of the world population situation in 2010, see Population Reference Bureau. 2010. "World Population Highlights: Key Findings from PRB's 2010 World Population Data Sheet," *Population Bulletin*, 64 (3), http://www.prb.org/Publications/PopulationBulletins/2009/worldpopulationhighlights2009.aspx (accessed April 11, 2010).

7. The population size for 2050 and 2100 is a UN Population Division estimate of what the world population will be at that date.

8. David Hackett Fischer. 2000. *The Great Wave: Price Revolutions and the Rhythm of History*, Oxford: Oxford University Press, 95–97.

9. Estimates from the U.S. Census Bureau. Results shown for 1400–1950 are the average of the upper and lower estimates in the "Summary Table for 1400–1950," http://www.census.gov/ipc/www/worldhis.html (accessed March 4, 2010). Estimates for 2000–2100 are from United Nations. 2011. *World Population Prospects 2010*, http://esa.un.org/unpd/wpp/unpp/p2k0data.asp (accessed June 10, 2011).

10. Numbers upon which figures and tables are based are obtained from United Nations Population Division. 2011. *World Population Prospects: The 2010 Revision*, http://www.un.org/esa/population/unpop.htm (accessed October 21, 2013), or on calculations based on numbers from that source, unless otherwise indicated.

11. World Bank estimates are available at http://siteresources.worldbank.org/DATASTATISTICS/Resources/GNIPC.pdf (accessed March 18, 2013). These are purchasing power party (PPP) estimates, which adjust for differences in currency exchange rates and in the cost of living among countries.

12. Arland Thornton. 2012. "Developed and Developing Societies," in *The Wiley-Blackwell Encyclopedia of Globalization*, ed. G. Ritser, vol. 1, Oxford: Wiley-Blackwell, 411–417.

13. E. J. Hobsbawn. 1954. "The General Crisis of the European Economy in the 17th Century," *Past & Present*, 5: 33–53.

14. Data on population per square kilometer from United Nations. 2011. *World Population Prospects 2010*. Density converted as 1 square kilometer = .3861 square miles.

15. The number of people that a given amount of land can support with a given economic organization and type of land use is called that area's "carrying capacity." For further discussion of economic development and carrying capacity, see Kenneth Arrow et al. 1996. "Economic Growth, Carrying Capacity, and the Environment," *Environment and Development Economics*, 1: 104–110.

16. Data on population per square kilometer from United Nations. 2011. *World Population Prospects 2010*, New York: United Nations. Converted as 1 square kilometer = .3861 square miles.

17. World Bank. 2011. World Development Indicators database, July 1, http://siteresources.worldbank.org/DATASTATISTICS/Resources/GNIPC.pdf (accessed March 18, 2013).

18. United Nations Development Programme. 2013. *Human Development Report 2013*, New York: United Nations, http://hdr.undp.org/en/reports/global/hdr2013/download/ (accessed March 18, 2013). The percentage of the population living on less than $1.25 a day was not reported for the United States, Japan, and many other more developed countries, under the assumption that it was zero.

19. United Nations Development Programme. 2009. *Human Development Report 2009*, New York: United Nations, http://hdr.undp.org/en/reports/global/hdr2009/ (accessed April 20, 2011). The estimates are from surveys conducted in various years.

20. GNI should not be confused with the Gini coefficient. The Gini coefficient is a measure of inequality in the distribution of something, such as income or wealth.

21. About.com. "U.S. Economy," http://useconomy.about.com/od/glossary/g/ppp.htm (accessed May 4, 2010).

22. Michael J. Boskin, Ellen R. Dulberger, Robert J. Gordon, Zvi Griliches, and Dale W. Jorgenson. 1997. "The CPI Commission: Findings and Recommendations," *The American Economic Review*, 87: 78–83; and Saeid Mahdavi and Su Zhou. 1994. "Purchasing Power Parity in High-Inflation

Countries: Further Evidence," *Journal of Macro-economics*, 16: 403–422.

23. Living on less than $1.25 a day is usually interpreted as having expenditures of less than $1.25 a day. Thus, this does not include the value of food raised for home consumption and other materials produced or gathered for home use, such as the value of wood or dung that is gathered for fuel.

24. cf. Prashanth N. Bhadadwaj. 2005. "On the Re-emergence of China and India as Global Economic and Political Powers," *Global Competitiveness*, January 1, http://www.allbusiness.com/specialty-businesses/601843-1.html (accessed May 30, 2010); and Luke Harding. 2009. "Russia Has Huge Political and Economic Problems, Says Dmitry Medvedev," *The Guardian*, September 11, http://www.guardian.co.uk/world/2009/sep/11/russia-trouble-dmitry-medvedev-putin (accessed May 30, 2010).

25. B. Ashton, K. Hill, A. Piazza, and R. Zeitz. 1984. "Famine in China 1958–61," *Population and Development Review*, 10: 613–645; Xizhe Peng. 1987. "Demographic Consequences of the Great Leap Forward in China's Provinces," *Population and Development Review*, 13: 639–670; and Wei Li. 2005. "The Great Leap Forward: Anatomy of a Central Planning Disaster," *Journal of Political Economy*, 113: 840–877.

26. Susan Greenhalgh. 1987. "Fertility Policy in China: Future Options," *Science*, 235: 1167–1172.

27. Barbara A. Anderson and James L. McCabe. 1977. "Nutrition and the Fertility of Younger Women in Kinshasa, Zaire," *Journal of Development Economics* 4: 343–363.

28. Alexander Gerschenkron. 1962. *Economic Backwardness in Historical Perspective: A Book of Essays*, Cambridge, MA: Belknap Press of Harvard University; and Henry Rosovsky. 1961. *Capital Formation in Japan, 1868–1940*, Glencoe, IL: The Free Press.

29. Anne Sibert. 2009. "Undersized: Could Greenland Be the New Iceland? Should It Be?" VOX, http://www.voxeu.org/index.php?q=node/3857 (accessed June 14, 2010).

30. C. Hui. 2006. "Carrying Capacity, Population Equilibrium, and Environment's Maximal Load," *Ecological Modelling*, 192: 317–320.

31. Kingsley Davis and Judith Blake. 1956. "Social Structure and Fertility: An Analytic Framework," *Economic Development and Cultural Change*, 4: 211–235; and Kingsley Davis. 1963. "The Theory of Change and Response in Modern Demographic History," *Population Index*, 29: 345–366.

32. The net migration rate is calculated as the growth rate minus the rate of natural increase. Any error in the growth rate or in the rate of natural increase can result in error in the estimate of the net migration rate. This can lead to an estimated nonzero world net migration rate. That the estimated net migration rate for the world in Figure 2.12 is zero or close to zero indicates good overall data quality in the estimates of the growth rate and the rate of natural increase for the world as a whole.

33. W. S. Thompson. 1929. "Population," *American Journal of Sociology*, 34: 959–975.

34. Dudley Kirk. 1996. "Demographic Transition Theory," *Population Studies*, 50: 361–387.

35. Map from http://www.maps.com/map.aspx?pid=3579 (accessed April 20, 2011).

36. Odile Frank and Geoffrey McNicoll. 1987. "An Interpretation of Fertility and Population Policy in Kenya," *Population and Development Review*, 13: 209–243; Warren C. Robinson. 1992. "Kenya Enters the Fertility Transition," *Population Studies*, 46: 445–457; and Thomas E. Dow Jr., Linda Archer, Shansiya Khasiani, and John Kekovole. 1994. "Wealth Flow and Fertility Decline in Rural Kenya, 1981–92," *Population and Development Review*, 20: 343–364.

37. Thomas C. Quinn. 2008. "HIV Epidemiology and the Effects of Antiviral Therapy on Long-term Consequences," *AIDS*, 22 (Suppl. 3): S7–12; UNAIDS. 2010. *Progress Report of the National Response to the 2001 Declaration of Commitment on HIV and AIDS, Botswana Country Report 2010*, http://data.unaids.org/pub/Report/2010/botswana_2010_country_progress_report_en.pdf (accessed May 30, 2010); and Kenneth Hill, Boaz Cheluget, Sian Curtis, George Bicego, and Mary Mahy. 2004. *HIV and Increases in Childhood Mortality in Kenya in the Late 1980s to the Mid-1990s*, June, report SR-04-26, Washington. DC: USAID.

38. G. Dennis Shanks, Simon I. Hay, Judy A. Omunmbo, and Robert W. Snow. 2005. "Malaria in Kenya's Western Highlands," *Emerging Infectious Diseases*, 11, http://www.cdc.gov/ncidod/eid/vol11no09/04-1131.htm (accessed April 25, 2011).

39. Prachi Mishra. 2006. *Emigration and Brain Drain: Evidence from the Caribbean*, IMF Working Paper WP/06/25, www.imf.org/external/pubs/ft/wp/2006/wp0625.pdf (accessed April 25, 2011).

40. See the UN website for criteria for being included in the least developed countries, http://www.un.org/special-rep/ohrlls/ldc/ldc%20criteria.htm

(accessed March 4, 2010). A list of the least developed countries as of April 2012 also appears in Appendix A.

41. Figure 2.20 is from Wikipedia, http://commons .wikimedia.org/wiki/File:Least_Developed _Countries_map.svg (accessed September 2, 2012).

42. Figures 2.30 through 2.34 from United Nations Population Division. 2010. *World Population Policies 2009*, New York: United Nations, http:// www.un.org/esa/population/publications /wpp2009/wpp2009.htm (accessed June 12, 2011); and United Nations Population Division. 2012. *World Population Policies 2011*, New York: United Nations, http://www.un.org/en /development/desa/population/publications /policy/world-population-policies-2011.shtml (accessed April 15, 2013).

CHAPTER 3

SOURCES OF DEMOGRAPHIC DATA

LEARNING OBJECTIVES

- List the four main sources of demographic data.
- Discuss the strengths and weaknesses of censuses in less developed countries and in more developed countries.
- Compare the reasons why demographic surveys are done in less developed countries and in more developed countries.
- Discuss the reasons why collection and interpretation of vital registration data are complicated by political considerations.

- Describe why collection and interpretation of data on race and ethnicity are complicated in the United States and in other countries.
- Explain why the protection of human subjects is important in the collection and use of demographic data, and describe some of the measures taken to protect human subjects.

((• Listen to the Chapter Audio

OVERVIEW

Demographic data do not fall from the sky. Information about births, deaths, and migration is gathered through a process in which either people respond to verbal questions or they fill out information on a form. Sometimes the data are gathered for the purpose of estimation of demographic measures, and sometimes for other purposes. In this chapter, the major methods of collection of demographic data are discussed, as well as the strengths and weaknesses of each method. Political considerations also enter into data collection decisions in both more developed and less developed countries. Some of these considerations are discussed. In collecting data for administrative, policy, and scientific purposes, protection of the privacy of individuals is important. Some of the considerations and problems with protecting the rights of respondents are discussed.

DEMOGRAPHIC DATA SOURCES: BRIEFLY CONSIDERED

The main sources of demographic data are censuses, vital statistics, population registers, and surveys.

Census of population: A census is a onetime enumeration of the total population of a country. It mainly collects data about current status such as age, sex, educational attainment, labor force status, and current occupation. Sometimes, data about the situation at an earlier point in time are also collected, such as place of birth or where the person lived 5 years ago. For example, a census often asks labor force status but rarely asks what age the person was when he or she first worked for pay. A census usually does not collect data about the flow of events, such as whether a birth or death occurred recently in the household.

Registration of vital statistics: This is the recording of events (births, deaths, and sometimes marriages and divorces) close in time to when the event occurs. It gives information about the flow of events.

Population register: A population register is the continual update of the population in the area and their characteristics (survival, educational enrollment, marital status, number of children, deaths of household members, employment status, and migration of household members).

Survey: In a survey, many questions are asked of a sample of the population. A survey can be cross-sectional (interviews of the same individuals or households once) or longitudinal (interviews of the same individuals or households two or more times). Surveys, especially longitudinal surveys, often collect data on the flow of events.

COMBINING OF CENSUS AND VITAL REGISTRATION DATA TO CALCULATE RATES

The main way that basic demographic rates are calculated is through a combination of vital registration data and census counts. The numerator for the rate is the number of events (number of births or number of deaths) from vital statistics, and the denominator for the rate (population size) comes from a census. The most basic rate is calculated as follows:

Crude Rate = Events/(Midperiod population)

The calculation of a rate combines a stock and flow. There is a stock of population in which events occur, and there is a flow of events (births, deaths, etc.) occurring in that population.

With a population register system, there is (supposedly) information about all of the people in the register on a continuous basis and also about all events that occur to them (births and deaths). Then for any time period, the number of events in that period (such as deaths) can be tabulated to give the numerator for a rate, and the population in the area can be tabulated to give the denominator.

If you have the population size at two points in time from two censuses

and

if you have births and deaths from vital registration
then you can calculate the population growth rate (GR), the crude birth rate (CBR), and the crude death rate (CDR).

You rarely have direct data about migration, so by using the population balancing equation discussed in Chapter 2, people often calculate the net migration rate as the difference between the growth rate (GR) and the rate of natural increase (natural r).

POPULATION CENSUSES: CONSIDERATIONS AND PROBLEMS

A census is the total process of collecting, compiling, and publishing demographic, economic, and social data pertaining, at a specified time or times, to all persons in a country or geographic area.

A census can be thought of as a survey with a large number of respondents and a small number of questions that are asked of everyone, although often one person answers for the entire household.

A census always asks each person's age or date of birth and sex. Usually, the census also asks about each person's marital status, education, relation to head of household, and labor force participation.

De Facto (Present) and De Jure (Permanent) Populations

The **population** of a geographic area is all persons in that area at a particular time. There are two different bases on which data are collected about the population, the de facto basis and the de jure basis.

De facto population: The de facto population is also called the present population. This is a count of people who are physically in a given territory on Census Day, regardless of where their place of permanent residence or legal residence is located.

De jure population: The de jure population is also called the permanent population. This is a count of people who legally "belong" to a given area, or have their legal or permanent residence there, regardless of whether they are there on the day of the census.

Almost all countries collect some data each way. However, countries differ on whether the data from the census are mainly organized on a de facto basis or on a de jure basis.

A de jure basis gives a larger rural population: In this case, rural-urban temporary migrants are counted at their rural place of permanent residence.

A de facto basis gives a larger urban population: In this case, rural-urban temporary migrants are counted at their urban destination.

The main difference between the de facto and the de jure bases is how migrants are dealt with. With a de facto basis, the urban population is more ethnically diverse, since rural-urban migrants are typically drawn from many rural sources.

Whether the de facto or de jure system is better depends on the purpose. Data on the de facto population data are useful for purposes such as planning the demand for public transportation. Data on the de jure population are useful for purposes such as calculating the tax base for many kinds of taxes.

Many countries have a legal place of residence for all citizens. Sometimes, this place is entered on an identity card. That place of legal residence is the de jure location of people, regardless of where they are physically located at a given time. The United States does not have a single legal place of residence, although a permanent or usual place of residence is important for some purposes, such as granting the right to a local library card or a student receiving in-state tuition at a public college or university.

Change from a De Facto to De Jure Population Basis in the Soviet Union

Sometimes, countries change the basis on which they collect and report data. There was a change in the major basis of population data in the Soviet Union between 1970 and 1979 censuses from de facto to de jure.[1]

For 1970, Soviet Census data on the ethnic composition of the population were published on only a de facto basis—but for 1979, they were published on only a de jure basis. In Table 3.1, we see that in both 1970 and 1979, there is a higher de facto than de jure population for Alma-Ata, the largest city and at that time the capital of Kazakhstan.[2] This is not surprising since Alma-Ata is a major city. Thus, the city's de facto population was larger than its de jure population. Ethnic Kazakhs are the main group indigenous to Kazakhstan. Many Russians in the capital city of Kazakhstan would have been recent migrants, perhaps temporary migrants. We also see that there is a higher proportion of the non-indigenous group (Russians) in Alma-Ata on a de facto basis than on a de jure basis.

Turkish Censuses Conducted in One Day: A De Facto Population Approach

Turkish Censuses are conducted on a single day on a de facto basis.[3] Everyone in Turkey is required to stay home all day. In 2000, there was a national curfew on Census Day from 8:00 AM to 5:00 PM to facilitate the census enumerators finding people. An interviewer conducted each interview and filled out the census form. It was a true de facto enumeration because no person not physically in Turkey on Census Day was enumerated in the census, but foreigners who were in Turkey on Census Day were enumerated. This strict de facto basis has led to some problems. In 1985, 14% of the households could not be classified by type since the actual head of household was absent because he was working as a labor migrant in a foreign country.

The United States Census 2010: A Mixed De Facto and De Jure Approach

The 2010 U.S. Census employed a mixed de facto and de jure approach. Table 3.2 shows where people in different situations were counted and whether they were treated on a de facto or a de jure basis.[4]

For people at home on Census Day, the de facto and the de jure approach yield the same result. For those temporarily away from home on a vacation or on a business trip, a de jure approach is used, attributing the person to his or her usual place of residence. For people in group quarters, such as a prison or a group home, the person is counted at the group quarters location. This means that a person from a city who is an inmate at a rural prison is counted in the census at the location of the prison. Thus, the prisoner contributes to the population of the district in which the prison is located for the purpose of allocating members of the state legislature and in distributing population-based funds. This practice led to a major controversy in New York State, where many prisoners from New York City were inmates in prisons in northern New York State, thus giving more weight in redistricting to rural counties that include prisons.[5] However, facing a similar situation in 2010, the Maryland legislature passed a law requiring that for the purpose of redistricting, prisoners would be counted at their home address rather than at the address of the prison.[6]

College students who live apart from their parents are counted at the place they live at college if that is where they actually spend most of their time. This means that the students are eligible to vote in local elections. The right of college students to vote in local elections in the city or town where the college is located has been challenged by some college towns, but the courts have ruled that the students are eligible to vote in local elections.[7]

On the other hand, high school students who are at boarding schools are counted in the census at the place of residence of their parents, even though their living situation is very similar to that of college students away at college. Seemingly, the rationale is that the high school students are only temporarily away from home at the boarding school. College students, however, are assumed to have somewhat looser ties to their parents and could be on their way to an independent life.

TABLE 3.1 Population of Alma-Ata, Capital of Soviet Kazakhstan, 1970 and 1979

	Total Population	% Kazakh	% Russian
1970 de facto	729,633	12.1%	70.3%
1970 de jure	725,522	NA	NA
1979 de facto	910,000	NA	NA
1979 de jure	899,644	16.4%	66.0%

NA: Not available.

TABLE 3.2   Location Where People Were Counted in the 2010 U.S. Census

Living Situation	Where Counted	De Facto or De Jure
Typical Living Situations		
At home	At home	De facto and de jure agree
On vacation or on a business trip	At home	De jure
No regular living place or homeless	Residence on Census Day	De facto and de jure agree
People in group-living situations such as in prisons, group homes, or emergency shelters	Group location	De facto
U.S. Military		
In barracks in the United States	Barracks location	De facto
On base or off base in the United States but not in barracks	Where they usually live and sleep	De jure
In military overseas	At place of home address in military records	De jure
High School and College Students		
Live with parents while attending college or high school	Parental home	De facto and de jure agree
Live apart from parents while attending high school	Parental home	De jure
Live apart from parents while attending college in the United States	Housing location at college	De facto or de jure, depending on view of independence of college student
Attend college outside of the United States	Not counted in census	De facto
Foreign Citizens in the United States		
Foreign citizens living in the United States	Where they usually live and sleep	De facto and de jure agree
Foreign citizens in the United States on a vacation or on a business trip	Not counted in census	De jure
People Who Move throughout the Year		
Those staying at more than one place, such as those with two homes, who live in a vehicle, or who travel with carnivals	Where they live or sleep most of the time—if time is equally divided between locations, the place they are on Census Day	Mixed de facto and de jure

Households, Group Quarters, and Residence in Institutions

A census collects information about every person, but not every person individually supplies information about himself or herself. Children do not answer for themselves, and usually one person answers for an entire household. Often information is collected on the level of the household. Sometimes, this refers to characteristics that truly refer to the household as a whole, such as whether the household has running water, and sometimes they are essentially an average or sum over all household members, such as income per household member or household size.

Countries differ in their definition of who is a member of a **household**. Household membership usually requires some aspects of co-residence, such as sharing a budget or eating meals together.

The United Nations definition of a household is as follows:

The concept of "household" is based on the arrangements made by persons, individually or in groups, for providing themselves with food or other essentials for living. A household may be either: (a) a one-person household, that is, a person who makes provision for his own food or other essentials for living without combining with any other person to form part of a multi-person household; or (b) a multi-person household, that is, a group of two or more persons who make common provision for food or other essentials for living. The persons in the group may pool their incomes and have a common budget to a greater or lesser extent; they may be related or unrelated persons, or a combination of both.

Households usually occupy the whole, part of, or more than one housing unit, but they may also be found in camps, in boarding houses or hotels, or as administrative personnel in institutions, or they may be homeless. Households consisting of extended families which make common provision for food, or of potentially separate households with a common head, resulting from polygamous unions, may occupy more than one housing unit.[8]

In censuses and in surveys, there is sometimes a lack of clarity as to who is a household member. This is especially a problem in a census, since the aim is to enumerate every person once and only once. People are sometimes not listed as household members if they are viewed as living in the household temporarily, such as adult children who always are "about to move out and find their own place." Also, older relatives can be missed when they spend part of the year living on their own and part of the year living with younger adult relatives. Mobile young adults, especially males, who have been in the household a short time can also be omitted from the list of household members.[9]

People reside in households or in group quarters. Group quarters can either be in an institution or in a non-institutional setting. In an **institution**, there is formally supervised care of inmates or patients. Examples of group quarters in an institution are those in a prison or in a nursing home. Examples of group quarters not in an institution are college dormitories and adult group homes.

The U.S. Census Bureau defines households as follows:

> all the persons who occupy a housing unit as their usual place of residence. A housing unit is a house, an apartment, a mobile home, a group of rooms, or a single room that is occupied (or if vacant, is intended for occupancy) as separate living quarters. Separate living quarters are those in which the occupants live and eat separately from any other persons in the building and which have direct access from outside the building or through a common hall. The occupants may be a single family, one person living alone, two or more families living together, or any other group of related or unrelated persons who share living arrangements.[10]

The U.S. Census Bureau defines **group quarters** as follows:

> A group quarters is a place where people live or stay, in a group living arrangement that is owned or managed by an entity or organization providing housing and/or services for the residents. This is not a typical household-type living arrangement. These services may include custodial or medical care as well as other types of assistance, and residency is commonly restricted to those receiving these services. People living in group quarters are usually not related to each other. Group quarters include such places as college residence halls, residential treatment centers, skilled nursing facilities, group homes, military barracks, correctional facilities, and workers' dormitories.[11]

Most surveys only include persons in households. However, since a census aims to enumerate the entire population, both those in households and those in group quarters are included. In the United States, about half of those in group quarters are in institutions and about half of those in group quarters are not in institutions.

The percentage of the population in group quarters differs greatly according to population characteristics. Table 3.3 shows the percentage of the population living in group quarters in 2000 in the United States by age, race, and sex.[12] A very small percentage of children under the age of 18 are in group quarters. The percentage in group quarters is the highest for the 18–29 age group. This age group encompasses students in dormitories and also much of the population in military barracks. This is also an age group with high incarceration rates. Seventeen percent of African-American males aged 18–29 were in group quarters in 2000.

Census Administration and Completeness

Most countries conduct censuses every 10 years or every 5 years. In the United States, censuses have been taken every 10 years since 1790. Canada

TABLE 3.3 Percentage of Population in Group Quarters, 2000 U.S. Census

	Total	African American
Both sexes	2.8%	5.0%
<18 years	0.4%	1.0%
18–29 years	7.2%	11.2%
30–49 years	1.9%	5.9%
50+ years	3.2%	4.0%
Male	3.3%	7.7%
<18 years	0.6%	1.3%
18–29 years	8.8%	16.7%
30–49 years	3.2%	10.8%
50+ years	2.5%	4.9%
Female	2.3%	2.5%
<18 years	0.3%	0.6%
18–29 years	5.5%	6.0%
30–49 years	0.7%	1.7%
50+ years	3.8%	3.4%

conducted censuses every 10 years starting in 1851 and has been conducting them every 5 years since 1951. Also, Mexico conducted censuses every 10 years starting in 1900, and then every 5 years since 1990. On the other hand, South Africa changed from taking a census every 5 years (1996 and 2001) to every 10 years (2011), because with 5 years between censuses, there was not sufficient time to plan the next census. A large national survey was done in South Africa in 2007, about midway between census dates.

Many countries conduct censuses in years that end in 0 (or 0 and 5), such as 1990, 2000, and 2010, including the United States, China, Switzerland, Indonesia, Japan, and Costa Rica. Other countries conduct censuses in years that end in 1 (or 1 and 6), such as 1991, 2001, and 2011, especially those that were part of the British Empire, including the United Kingdom, Canada, South Africa, Australia, New Zealand, and India. Austria, Italy, and Spain also conduct censuses in years ending in 1. But some countries have other census dates such as 1999 (France, Cayman Islands), 2002 (Cuba and Paraguay), 1997 (Iraq), and 1998 (Cambodia).

For a census to be self-administered, people need to be literate, and there needs to be a reliable mail and address system for the census forms to be mailed. In a self-administered census, if the form is not returned, then an interviewer shows up. The census bureau needs a reliable list of places of residence to send the forms to. If a census is interviewer administered, unreasonable answers can be rejected, and the question can be explained to the respondent.

Every census misses people. It misses people who live in nonstandard locations—homeless persons, or people who live in alleys or above stores. It misses people who are very mobile—young adults, especially males. It misses young children and the entire (mobile) young family. It misses poor people and members of ethnic minorities. It misses people who want to avoid authorities, such as undocumented aliens.

A census also can overcount people—they can be counted twice or perhaps more. This can include people who have two homes and spend part of the year in one place and part of the year in another place. On balance, censuses almost always undercount the population.

By law, undocumented immigrants are supposed to be included in the U.S. Census. In 2000, the U.S. government suspended raids to locate undocumented immigrants for several months around the census date in order to improve census coverage of the undocumented population. The U.S. government did not suspend immigration raids at the time of the 2010 Census. However, the time period for collection of census data was longer in 2010 than in 2000. Also in 2010, the Census Bureau had an outreach program to more than 250,000 local organizations, which involved a publicity campaign that emphasized that being counted in the census helps the local community. The program also sought to reassure people that information gathered in the census would not be used to harm individuals. These efforts were intended to minimize the overall undercount and the undercount of undocumented persons.[13]

Figure 3.1 shows the estimated percentage census undercount by age and sex for the 1996 Australian Census.[14] The **net percent undercount** is the percentage of the actual population that is estimated to have been missed by the census. It shows a typical pattern of census undercount by age and sex. The higher percentage undercount for males than females and

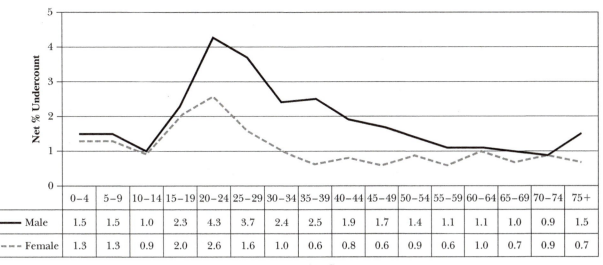

Age Group	0–4	5–9	10–14	15–19	20–24	25–29	30–34	35–39	40–44	45–49	50–54	55–59	60–64	65–69	70–74	75+
——— Male	1.5	1.5	1.0	2.3	4.3	3.7	2.4	2.5	1.9	1.7	1.4	1.1	1.1	1.0	0.9	1.5
- - - - Female	1.3	1.3	0.9	2.0	2.6	1.6	1.0	0.6	0.8	0.6	0.9	0.6	1.0	0.7	0.9	0.7

Age Group

FIGURE 3.1   Estimated Net Percentage Census Undercount, Australia, 1996

for young adults at highly mobile ages is clear. It is thought that young adults are missed because they often are highly mobile and have no fixed place of residence. The male undercount is higher than the female undercount because young men tend to be more mobile than young women.

Figure 3.2 shows the estimated percentage undercount in the 1940 through 2010 U.S. Censuses for the entire population, the African-American population, and the non-African-American population.[15] For the total population, the estimated undercount falls from over 5% in 1940 to 0% (actually −0.01%) in 2010. However, this overall population

undercount is the result of a much larger undercount of the African-American population than of the non-African-American population. In fact, for the non-African-American population for 2000 and 2010, there is an estimated slight overcount, resulting mainly from double counting of people with two homes who spend part of the year in one location and part of the year in another location. Even in 2010, the African-American population is estimated to have been undercounted by over 2%.

Figure 3.3 shows the estimated undercount for the 1940 through 2000 Censuses by race and sex.[16] For both African Americans and non–African Americans,

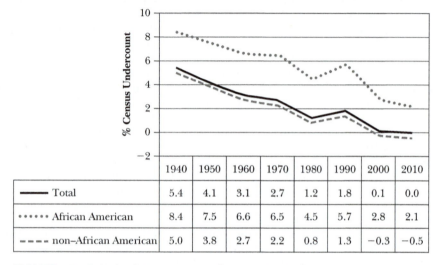

	1940	1950	1960	1970	1980	1990	2000	2010
—— Total	5.4	4.1	3.1	2.7	1.2	1.8	0.1	0.0
•••••• African American	8.4	7.5	6.6	6.5	4.5	5.7	2.8	2.1
– – – – non–African American	5.0	3.8	2.7	2.2	0.8	1.3	−0.3	−0.5

FIGURE 3.2   Estimated Percentage Undercount in U.S. Censuses, 1940–2010, Total Population, African Americans, and non–African Americans

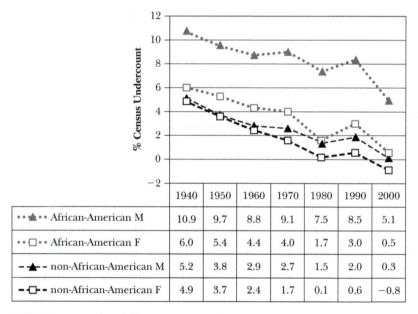

	1940	1950	1960	1970	1980	1990	2000
••▲•• African-American M	10.9	9.7	8.8	9.1	7.5	8.5	5.1
••□•• African-American F	6.0	5.4	4.4	4.0	1.7	3.0	0.5
–▲– non-African-American M	5.2	3.8	2.9	2.7	1.5	2.0	0.3
–□– non-African-American F	4.9	3.7	2.4	1.7	0.1	0.6	−0.8

FIGURE 3.3   Estimated Percentage Undercount in U.S. Censuses, 1940–2000, by Race and Sex

in each census males of a given race are more likely to be missed than females, consistent with the results for Australia shown in Figure 3.1. What is most striking about the results in Figure 3.3 in that African-American males are much more likely to be undercounted than the other three groups. Males, especially young adult males, are more likely to be mobile and to have no fixed address than females, and this is likely more true of African-American than non-African-American males. Also, African Americans tend to be poorer than non–African Americans and thus are more likely to be missed in the census. It is estimated that in 2000, non-African-American females were overcounted by almost 1%.

Politics and Censuses: United States

The original purpose of the U.S. Census was to allocate members of the House of Representatives. Over time, as the location of the U.S. population shifted, the South and the West gained in population, and the East and North lost. As shown in Table 3.2, the U.S. Census is conducted mainly on a de facto population basis that includes federal employees (civilian and military) and their families who are overseas. Recall that college students are counted at the location of the college, whereas high school students at boarding school are counted at the place of residence of their parents.

No census count is perfect. As discussed in this chapter, every census misses some people. One way to estimate the percentage of the population missed in a census is the demographic analysis approach. In this approach, the population at a census date is estimated independently from the census count by looking at births, deaths, and international migration in the past. For example, for 2010, the number of people aged 40 is estimated by taking the number of births in 1970 (40 years earlier), the number of deaths between 1970 and 2010 to those born in 1970, and the estimated number of net international migrants who were also born in 1970. When this is done for every age group, one obtains an independent estimate of the 2010 population. This independent estimate takes into account the estimated incompleteness of birth and death registration.

A demographic analysis approach was the basis of the census undercount estimates by race for the United States shown in Figures 3.2 and 3.3. The demographic analysis approach only yields estimates of census undercount for the country as a whole and cannot be used to estimate the undercount in subnational geographic areas, due to the difficulty of accurately assessing internal migration. In 2000 and 2010 in the United States, the most difficult part of applying the demographic analysis approach has been estimation of international migration, especially due to the large amount of undocumented migration.

The other approach to estimating the completeness of coverage of a census is to conduct a large independent survey (usually called a **post-enumeration survey**) shortly after the census. Estimates from a post-enumeration survey are the basis of the census undercount estimates for Australia shown in Figure 3.1. The major assumption in the estimation of census undercount from a post-enumeration survey is that inclusion in the census count and inclusion in the post-enumeration survey count are independent of each other.

Imagine that you capture a number of rabbits in the woods, spray a red mark on the back of each rabbit, and then release the rabbits back into the woods. You assume that the earlier captured rabbits randomly mix with the other rabbits in the woods. Then you capture some more rabbits. By seeing how many rabbits in the second batch have a red mark on their backs, you can estimate the total number of rabbits in the woods. How this is done is shown in more detail in Box 3.1.

One problem with the post-enumeration survey approach is that whatever characteristics of a person contributed to the probability that they were missed in the original census enumeration are likely to contribute to the probability that they will be missed in the post-enumeration survey as well. For example, people who tend to be missed in a census because they are highly mobile, have no regular place of residence, or live in an unusual place of residence also are more likely than other people to be missed in the post-enumeration survey. This problem is called correlation bias.[17] Thus, this kind of undercount estimate is usually an underestimate of the undercount.

One advantage of the post-enumeration survey approach is that it allows estimates of undercount for geographic areas smaller than the country as a whole. The estimates of the census undercount for subnational geographic units, such as states, counties, or cities, are developed by a method called statistical estimation. Statistical estimates are discussed a little later in this chapter.

Gain and Loss of Congressional Seats

The census count is the basis for the reallocation of the 435 seats in the House of Representatives. Table 3.4 shows the states that lost and the states that gained congressional seats as a result of the enumerations in the 2000 and 2010 Censuses.

In both censuses, states in the West and the South tended to gain seats, and states in the Midwest and the Northeast tended to lose seats. One exception is the loss of a seat by Oklahoma after the 2000 Census and the loss of a seat in Louisiana after the 2010 Census. The loss of a seat by Louisiana after the 2010 Census

BOX 3.1

Example of Post-Enumeration Survey Estimation of Census Undercount

Number Counted in the Census and in the Survey

		Survey		
		No	Yes	Total
Census	No	**X**	20	
	Yes	920	80	1,000
	Total		100	

In this example, **X** is the number missed both in the census and in the survey.

Assuming independence of the census and the survey,

$$(20/80) = (X/920),$$

so

$$X = 920 \times (20/80) = 920 \times 0.25 = 230.$$

Then you can solve for the rest of the table.

The proportion missed is

$$(1{,}250 - 1{,}000)/1{,}250 = 250/1{,}250 = 0.2,$$

so 20% were missed in the census.

Number Counted in the Census and the Survey and Number Estimated as Missed in Both the Census and the Survey

		Survey		
		No	Yes	Total
Census	No	230	20	250
	Yes	920	80	1,000
	Total	1,150	100	1,250

is related to population loss after Hurricane Katrina, which was only partially offset by other sources of Louisiana population increase. Between 2000 and 2010, the population of the United States increased by 9.7%, but the population of Louisiana increased by only 1.4% (64,396 persons).

Since the number of seats in the U.S. House of Representatives is fixed at 435, when the population of the United States as a whole grows, a state can increase in population but lose one or more seats if the rate of population growth in the state is less than in the United States as a whole. For example, Oklahoma

lost a seat from 1990 to 2000, during which time its population grew by 9.7%, but the population of the United States as a whole grew by 13.2%. The only state that lost population between 1990 and 2000 or 2000 and 2010 was Michigan, which lost 0.6% of its population (54,804 persons) between 2000 and 2010.

According to the law, all those present within the geographic limits of the United States are to be included in the census enumeration, whether they are present legally or not. U.S. usual residents or citizens who are not present in the United States on Census Day are to be included in the census enumeration

TABLE 3.4   Gain and Loss of Congressional Seats by State in 2000 and 2010

2000				2010			
Total gain	12	Total loss	12	Total gain	12	Total loss	12
Arizona	2	New York	2	Texas	4	New York	2
Florida	2	Pennsylvania	2	Florida	2	Ohio	2
Georgia	2	Connecticut	1	Arizona	1	Illinois	1
Texas	2	Illinois	1	Georgia	1	Indiana	1
California	1	Indiana	1	Nevada	1	Iowa	1
Colorado	1	Michigan	1	South Carolina	1	Louisiana	1
Nevada	1	Mississippi	1	Utah	1	Massachusetts	1
North Carolina	1	Ohio	1	Washington	1	Michigan	1
		Oklahoma	1			New Jersey	1
		Wisconsin	1			Pennsylvania	1

only if they are federal government employees or dependents of federal government employees. This would include members of the State Department posted abroad but also, more significantly, members of the U.S. Armed Forces.

After the 2000 U.S. Census, there was a question of whether an additional seat would go to North Carolina or Utah. A large number of North Carolina military personnel overseas were counted as in North Carolina. Military personnel were U.S. government employees. Mormon missionaries from Utah who were overseas at the time of the 2000 Census were not counted as in Utah. These missionaries were not U.S. government employees. From the census count, North Carolina had 657 more people than Utah. But Utah had 11,176 Mormon missionaries abroad at the time of the 2000 Census, while North Carolina had 106 Mormon missionaries abroad. If the Mormon missionaries from Utah had been enumerated in the 2000 U.S. Census and attributed to Utah, Utah would have gained a representative rather than North Carolina.[18]

Detroit Population Loss and Loss of Funding
Many large U.S. cities have lost population in recent decades. The characteristics that lead to omission in the census (young mobile people, a large poor and minority population, and people residing in nonstandard dwelling units) are likely to contribute to the undercount of the population of large cities. The City of Detroit sued after the 1980 Census and again after the 1990 Census. It maintained that additional people should be added to the count of Detroit's population due to the omission of poor persons and minority group members. The City of Detroit lost both cases.

In 1961–1962, there was a constitutional convention in Michigan. In the new constitution, special taxing authority was given to cities with a population of 1 million or more. Detroit was the only city with a population greater than 1 million. These provisions were added to the constitution due to a desire to help Detroit.

The population of Detroit was counted as greater than 1 million in the 1930–1990 Censuses. The population peaked in 1950 at 1,849,568. The 1990 final census count of the population of Detroit was 1,027,974. There was great concern in Detroit about what the 2000 Census would show.[19] The 2000 Census recorded the population of Detroit as 951,270. When less than 1,000,000 Detroit residents were counted in the 2000 Census, the direct consequences to the city included a loss of over $55 million from no longer being able to levy a utility tax that had been dedicated to public protection and enabled Detroit to hire additional police officers, and a loss of over $103 million due to a reduction by one-third in the allowable income tax rates that Detroit could levy on residents and on nonresidents who worked in Detroit.[20]

By 2000, the main growth in the Detroit area was in the near suburbs. By that time, there was much less concern in the Michigan legislature with helping Detroit with its problems than there had been in the 1960s. In 1998, when Dennis Archer was mayor of Detroit, the Michigan House voted to change the population cutoff for special taxing authority to 750,000, but the bill was not passed in the Michigan Senate.[21] Bills lowering the cutoff to 750,000 were passed in 2001 and went into effect in January 2002.[22] In 2011, the population cutoff for special taxation authority was lowered to 600,000, as the 2010 Census population of Detroit was 713,777.[23]

New Orleans, Population Loss, and Hurricane Katrina
In Louisiana, there were benefits to a city that had over 400,000 people.[24] New Orleans is the only Louisiana city that has ever had a population of over 400,000, and the laws were written with New Orleans in mind. However, as in the case in Michigan, where the law referred to cities with a population over 1 million, rather than naming Detroit as the beneficiary, in Louisiana, laws intended to benefit New Orleans referred to cities with a population size of above 400,000 and did not mention New Orleans by name. After Hurricane Katrina, many people did not return to New Orleans, and the 2010 population of New Orleans was only 343,829. The Louisiana legislature passed a stopgap law that specified that the impact of the decreased population from the 2010 Census results would not have an effect on state laws until September 2011. New laws lowering the population threshold to 300,000 were passed in August 2011. Thus there were no financial impacts on New Orleans due to the lapse of the old laws that had the 400,000 population threshold.[25]

Controversies about Census Statistical Adjustment
There have been arguments for years about whether to use an approach called statistical adjustment to improve the count obtained through the census enumeration. Statistical adjustment is usually based on estimation of the correct population based on a large post-enumeration study. Then, the enumeration of the population in each small area is adjusted based on the estimated undercount of the small area. The larger the size of the post-enumeration survey, the more accurate the statistical adjustment estimates are, but the estimates have some uncertainty.[26]

The United States does not use statistical adjustment to improve on the census count for the purpose of allocation of seats in the House of Representatives. In 1996, the Supreme Court ruled that the results of the 1990 Census were valid, despite clear evidence that the 1990 Census was affected by an undercount.[27] The U.S. Courts have not supported statistical estimation. They have decreed that the official census count must be the result of an actual enumeration, not a statistical estimate based on a survey of part of the population.

However, the census *can* estimate the number of people in residential units for which no information was gathered from the occupants of the unit, using methods such as talking with neighbors or estimating the number of occupants based on similar residential units in the area. The results of these estimates are added to the census count.

Statistical adjustments can be made to census results for purposes other than reapportionment of seats in Congress.[28] As discussed further in this chapter, the American Community Survey replaced the long form of the U.S. Census beginning in 2010. The results of the American Community Survey are adjusted using statistical methods, and the adjusted counts are the basis of allocation of many government funds, but by law the American Community Survey cannot be used for the purpose of allocation of seats in the House of Representatives among states.

Politics and Censuses: Other More Developed Countries

In 1983 and more strongly in 1987, there were campaigns in Germany to boycott the census. Related to these concerns, a planned 1983 census was cancelled. There were many objections to a German law that would have allowed fairly free sharing of personal information among agencies. The last German Census was in 1987, and since then census-type information has been compiled from population registers.[29] The British government is considering alternatives to a full census, and 2011 might have been the last full British Census.[30] Developed countries that have ceased conducting full censuses usually rely on a population register, which is discussed later in this chapter.

Politics and Censuses: Less Developed Countries

Over time, more and more less developed countries have conducted censuses. Only five countries (Iraq, Lebanon, Myanmar, Somalia, and Uzbekistan) did not plan to conduct a census between 2005 and 2015, while 27 countries did not conduct a census between 1995 and 2005. A census is a massive national effort, and in less developed countries the coverage of censuses can be quite incomplete. It was estimated that the 1981 census of Venezuela missed 7% of the population.[31] There are methods that can estimate the extent of census undercount, such as those discussed in this chapter, and

the census results can be adjusted to obtain a more accurate estimate, but as accurate a census as possible is desirable.

In many less developed countries, political considerations have influenced the timing of censuses and the information collected through them. For example, censuses were postponed in many countries for a mixture of political and financial reasons, including Sudan in 2008; Uganda in 1990, 2001, and 2012; Pakistan and Nepal in 1991; Burundi in 2000; and Bosnia in 2013.[32] Next, we discuss some examples of political influences on censuses from Nigeria, Lebanon, and Botswana.

Ethnic Representation and the Nigerian Census of 1962

The Nigeria Census of 1962 has been severely criticized. Although there has been disagreement about the extent to which results were deliberately falsified, most agree that there was substantial falsification of the regional results. The three major ethnic groups in Nigeria are the Yoruba, Hausa, and Ibo. These groups tend to live in separate regions. As in the United States, in Nigeria census results determine legislative representation, and the regional aspect of ethnic group location means that the regional results are an object of strong political concern. Thus, there was thought to be inflation of the census results in the various regions in an attempt to increase the representation of the major ethnic group in the given region.[33]

Religious Representation and No Census in Lebanon Since 1932

In Lebanon, there has long been political conflict between Christians and Muslims. The last official census in Lebanon was conducted in 1932, and based on the results of that census, the Lebanese Parliament has been divided 6:5 between Christians and Muslims.[34] A survey and other estimates of the religious composition of Lebanon in the 1980s indicated that at least 60% of the Lebanese population was Muslim.[35] A major reason for the continued lack of a more recent census is that any reasonable census would show many more Muslims than Christians in Lebanon, but a reallocation of parliamentary representation reflecting the greater size of the Muslim population would lead to increased political conflict.

Census Resistance in Botswana

About 500–700 Bushmen live in a game reserve in Botswana. The Bushmen are an indigenous population in Botswana and other areas of southwest Africa. Bushmen have struggled with the Botswana government over many issues. In 2002, the Botswana government closed a borehole, which had been a main water source for the Bushmen in the reserve. In the 2009 elections, the government did not put any polling stations in the game reserve. The Bushmen won a long legal battle in January 2011, and the Botswana government was ordered to redrill the borehole and thus restore the Bushmen's water supply. Motivated by anger over the borehole controversy and what was viewed as the disenfranchisement of Bushmen in the 2009 Botswana elections, the Bushmen boycotted the 2011 Botswana Census. A Botswana Census official said, "The community is not even willing to speak to our enumerators."[36]

Items Typically Asked in Censuses

Almost always, a census asks about each person's sex and age (or date of birth). Typically, censuses also ask about each person's marital status, educational attainment, and relation to the head of the household. Most countries ask some questions about race or ethnic group membership. Race and ethnicity often are sensitive issues, and these are discussed later in this chapter.

Through 2000, the U.S. Census had two forms, a short form that asked a limited number of questions and a long form that was sent to about one-sixth of all households and asked about 60 questions. Starting in 2010, the U.S. Census used only a single form. This was the shortest form ever used in a U.S. Census. One reason for the elimination of the long form and for the very small number of questions in the remaining census form was to try to increase census response rates. The only items asked in the 2010 U.S. Census were as follows:

- Age and date of birth
- Relation to person 1 (usually the head of household, but the person who owns or rents the residence or any adult)
- Race
- Ethnicity (Hispanic or not)
- Whether the person sometimes lives somewhere else
- Whether the residence is a house, apartment, or mobile home
- Whether the residence is owned or rented
- Name of each person and household telephone number for verification

No questions were asked on the 2010 U.S. Census about marital status, education, or income. Detailed questions about issues such as marital status, education, and income were asked in the American Community Survey, which was the replacement for the long form of the census. The American Community Survey is discussed further in this chapter.

REGISTRATION OF VITAL EVENTS: CONSIDERATIONS AND PROBLEMS

A vital statistics system aims for the timely registration of all births and deaths. Vital statistics systems sometimes register other events, such as marriages and divorces.

Definitions of a Live Birth and a Death

The events that demographers study are births, deaths, and migrations. We discuss definitional issues about migration in Chapter 12. What constitutes each of these events could seem to be straightforward, but it can be complicated.

The World Health Organization (WHO) defines a **live birth** as

> the complete expulsion or extraction from its mother of a product of conception, irrespective of the duration of the pregnancy, which, after such separation, breathes or shows any other evidence of life—e.g. beating of the heart, pulsation of the umbilical cord or definite movement of voluntary muscles—whether or not the umbilical cord has been cut or the placenta is attached. Each product of such a birth is considered live born.[37]

The United States uses the WHO definition, but some other developed countries use a narrower definition of a live birth. The differences relate to whether an event is classified as a live birth or as a fetal death, whether the fetal death is a stillbirth or a miscarriage. Fetal deaths that occur before 20 weeks of gestation are usually called miscarriages, and fetal deaths that occur at 20 weeks or more of gestational age are usually called stillbirths.

Infant deaths in developed countries tend to occur shortly after birth. These babies tend to have a very low birth weight or tend to be of short gestational age and are not in very good health. Among babies born in the United States in 1960, although only 0.6% of all infants at birth weighed less than 1,000 grams, deaths to babies who weighed less than 1,000 grams at birth constituted 21% of all infant deaths. Similarly, although only 0.6% of all births are less than 28 weeks in gestational age, deaths to these very premature babies constituted 19% of all infant deaths.[38] As of 2004, in France and the Netherlands, an infant needs to be 22 weeks or more in gestational age and have a birth weight of 500 grams or more to be counted as a live birth. If the infant does not meet these criteria and dies, he or she is classified as a stillbirth, even if the infant lived for some time.[39] Kramer and colleagues concluded that despite the fact that Sweden used the same definition of a live birth as the United States, many infants who weighed less than 500 grams and then died were not recorded as either live births or infant deaths in Sweden, thus lowering Swedish infant mortality rate (IMR) estimates.[40]

In the Soviet Union, the only sign of life accepted as defining a live birth was whether the infant breathed. Other signs of life, such as a heartbeat, did not qualify a birth as a live birth if the infant did not breathe. In addition, babies at less than 28 weeks of gestational age, who weighed less than 1,000 grams, or who were less than 35 centimeters in length and who died in the first 7 days were to be counted as miscarriages and not recorded as either live births or infant deaths. Anderson and Silver calculated that if the WHO definition of a live birth and an infant death had been applied in the Soviet Union in the 1980s, the estimated IMR would have been about 25% higher.[41]

If a birth occurs in a hospital, the formal definition of a live birth and an infant death can be quite important. In countries where many births do not occur in hospitals, vital registration of births depends on the parent voluntarily reporting the birth and any death. In many countries, there are benefits related to having children. However, there rarely are benefits for having had a baby who died very soon after birth. Thus, there is little incentive to report either the birth or the death of a child who died soon after birth.

There is large variation in the extent to which births of children are registered even when the children survive. The World Bank looked at the percentage of children under age 5 in World Bank Surveys conducted in 2006–2009 whose births had been registered. They estimated that while 99% of the births had been registered in El Salvador, only 41% had been registered in India, 53% in Indonesia, and 88% in Vietnam.[42]

Sometimes, registration of the birth of a surviving child is delayed. The necessity of a birth certificate for enrolling in school in some countries can motivate birth registration when the child is 6 or 7 years old. Sometimes, the birth is only registered when the child needs to apply for a national identity card.[43]

The definition of a death when the person is not an infant is much more straightforward than when the deceased is an infant. A **death** is often defined as the cessation of life. Brain death is "irreversible unconsciousness with complete loss of brain function."[44] Brain death is the official definition of death in the United States. There are important legal and ethical controversies about when an individual in a coma or who has suffered a severe accident has died, but the resolution of these issues has little impact on demographic measures.[45]

Countries differ in the percentage of deaths that are registered in the vital statistics system. For example, the WHO estimated the percentage of deaths that were registered in the vital statistics systems in many countries. For the most recent data available as of 2006, they concluded that while 100% of deaths were registered in the United States and most other developed countries, only 86% of deaths in Thailand, 68% in Armenia, 67% in Peru, 64% in the Dominican Republic, and 58% in Albania were registered.[46] Besides the omission of deaths to infants who die soon after birth, vital statistics systems sometimes miss deaths of the elderly and others who are not actively engaged in the productive economy.

Vital Statistics Often Are Not Collected Mainly for the Purpose of Population Statistics

In some countries, recording of vital statistics (births, deaths, and sometimes other events) is not under the control of a statistical or health agency, but rather under the control of another ministry, such as the Ministry of Justice. In 1995, in 34% of countries with a central registration system, vital statistics registration was under the control of the Ministry of Justice.[47] In such situations, the main concern in recording vital events is not obtaining a complete count but rather making certain that no one obtains a legal document who does not have a right to that document.

In the United States, birth registration is usually completed before the mother leaves the hospital. However, in the Soviet Union, although a hospital could encourage parents to register the baby's birth and could give the mother a form that would allow her to obtain health care for the baby, the actual registration of the birth required the mother or another relative to register the birth at the registration office, which was under the control of the Ministry of Justice. Most parents would register the birth, but there were few sanctions if the birth was not registered.[48]

Vital Statistics Problems and Unusual Census Questions in China

China is a country in which vital registration is under control of the Ministry of Justice. Ministries in China tend to be vertically organized, with few responsibilities extending horizontally across ministries. Thus, there is no requirement that the collectors of vital statistics cooperate with those concerned with population statistics or calculation of demographic measures. In each locale, all that is required is that annually the population statistics office be told the total number of births (not classified by age of the mother) and the total number of deaths (not classified by age or sex). Since 1982, the population statistics authorities have conducted a large annual survey, called the Population Change Survey, that asks about births and deaths that occurred in the household in the previous year, including the age of the mother and the age and sex of any persons who died. Chinese censuses also ask vital statistics–type questions that are unusual for censuses to include, such as those about the age of the mother of any recent births and the age and sex of any household members who have recently died. This information in combination with answers in the census about the number of persons by age and sex is used to construct age-specific birth and death rates.[49] The data from the Population Change Survey are used for numerators to construct age-specific fertility and mortality rates for noncensus years.

POPULATION REGISTERS: CONSIDERATIONS AND PROBLEMS

A population register seeks to record, on a continuous basis, information about all members of households living permanently in a given geographic area. Information about events, such as births, deaths, marriages, divorces, and sometimes migration, is to be recorded in the register in a timely manner. A population register works best in an ethnically homogeneous population that is not highly geographically mobile. Data from population registers refer almost exclusively to the de jure population. Sometimes, registers do not work exactly the way they should, as illustrated by the example in this section from South Korea.

Temporary Migration in South Korea

Choi investigated return migration to rural South Korea among persons who had migrated to the cities of Seoul or Daegu and then returned to their native village. He was interested in whether these return migrants were failures who upon their return demoralized the rural residents or whether they were agents of change in the rural areas who brought new ideas back from the city.[50]

Choi needed to locate return migrants in order to administer a survey to them. In principle, this temporary migration should have been recorded in the village household register. However, upon inspection of the village registers in rural Korea, he found that few such temporary moves were recorded. He then thought that the village headman would be able to identify return migrants. But the village headmen did not know who was a return migrant either. To locate return migrants, Choi conducted a semicensus in the target villages, in which a short questionnaire was administered to every household to determine whether the household included any eligible return migrants. If the household included any eligible return migrants, those return migrants were administered a longer survey.

Replacement of the Census by Data from Population Registers in Some Countries

Some countries have completely replaced their censuses by collation of data from population registers. When census data are based on a population register, it almost always means that the census refers only to the de jure population. Depending on the registration system, temporary and sometimes longer-term migrants will not be counted.

Changing to a register-based census has been especially common in Europe. Austria has had a register-based census since 2011.[51] Norway has progressively moved toward assembling more and more census data from population registers, and starting in 2010, the census has been completely register based.[52] Denmark moved toward a register-based census in 1976 and fully implemented a register-based census in 1981.[53] In 1976, there was found to be a problem because information from the workplace was not fully integrated into the census effort. In 1981, information about workplaces was more adequately collected. The 1981 Census drew information from several different administrative registers, including the population register, the register of buildings and dwellings, tax registers, and registers of employment insurance and benefits. A key issue in Denmark was making sure that registers recorded when events had occurred rather than only when the event was entered into the register.

SAMPLE SURVEYS

Sample surveys ask many questions of a subset of the population of persons or households. The purposes of these surveys are somewhat different in less developed countries than they are in more developed countries.

Cross-Sectional and Longitudinal Surveys

Surveys can be either cross-sectional or longitudinal. In a **cross-sectional survey**, a different set of individuals or households is interviewed each time the survey is conducted. In a **longitudinal survey**, the same individuals or households are interviewed repeatedly.

Cross-sectional surveys can supply a time series that collects indicators of social and demographic changes in a population. The survey results will be comparable if each survey is representative of the population at the time the survey is conducted and if the same questions are asked each time. Since the surveys do not interview the same individuals or households, it is not possible to directly measure change for individuals or households from cross-sectional surveys.

Longitudinal surveys are designed to track changes in individuals or households. Not all people or households are tracked from one round of a longitudinal survey to the next. For a survey of individuals, some people will have died between survey rounds. Households or individuals could move, and often it is not possible to track them. Also, individuals or households could refuse to continue to participate in a longitudinal survey after they have been interviewed one or more times. The characteristics of those who withdraw from a longitudinal survey can be different from those who remain in the survey. Due to loss of respondents over time from longitudinal surveys (called sample attrition), it is necessary to start a longitudinal survey with enough respondents that reliable results can be obtained even after several rounds have been conducted and even if there is a high level of sample attrition.

Another consideration is that a longitudinal survey can start by being representative of the total population, but it becomes unrepresentative in later rounds. One reason is sample attrition. Another reason is that in a survey of individuals, if the second round of the survey occurs 2 years after the first round, the respondents are 2 years older. Thus, if the respondents were representative of the population in the first round, they will be older than the population in the second round and thus no longer representative of the total population. In the second and later rounds, additional persons can be interviewed to make the survey again representative, but of course comparisons cannot be made between responses in the first round and later rounds for those who were only added in later rounds.

Reasons to Do a Survey: Less Developed Countries

A major reason to do a survey in a less developed county is a lack of other sources of information. Without a reliable and fairly complete system of vital statistics and censuses, surveys are one way to gather data that can be used to estimate demographic measures. Sometimes, the measures are calculated directly from the information collected in the survey, and sometimes the data collected are used to fit models to estimate demographic measures. In countries that do not have a reliable census or a reliable vital statistics system, an advantage of a survey is that information can be collected about recent births and deaths that together with the population information can be used to calculate demographic indicators.[54]

When information about births and deaths is collected in a survey, one is relying on recollection of events in the past. Children who died very soon after birth might not be reported in the survey as live births and infant deaths but instead might be omitted from survey responses entirely. This problem is similar to the problem of nonreporting the vital statistics of a live birth that is followed quickly by a death at the time that the birth and death occurred.

Sometimes intensive local surveys combined with anthropological qualitative research can lead to a better understanding of demographic behavior. For example, Axinn and his colleagues describe how they have combined a structured survey with ongoing ethnographic data collection to improve the validity and interpretation of their survey data in Nepal. In the course of their fieldwork, the researchers discovered a development program, the Small Farmers Development Program (SFDP), that gave small loans to farmers. The presence of the SFDP varied across localities. In the statistical analysis of factors related to contraceptive use, it was thought that whether the husband worked outside of his family before marriage might be important. When that factor was included along with other family characteristics, it seemed that nonfamily work experience was important. However, when participation in the SFPD was also included in the analysis, both the husband's nonfamily work experience and participation in SFDP were positively related to the married couple's contraceptive use. Without the ethnographic fieldwork, the potential importance of the SFDP would not have been understood.[55]

Many experiences with survey research point to the importance of understanding the local cultural and political situation in order to collect good-quality data and to assure researcher safety. The following example from Sri Lanka illustrates some of the risks in data collection.

Suspicion of Strangers in Sri Lanka

There are sometimes unexpected dangers in conducting a survey. Abeysekara conducted a survey to determine reasons why residents in one part of Sri Lanka might migrate to another part of Sri Lanka. Sri Lankan college students administered the survey in teams of two. A team of interviewers arrived in a village one evening. Early the next morning, a dead body was found in the village well. The college students feared that since they were strangers, they might be blamed; the students quickly left the village and decided not to try to conduct interviews there, which was certainly a wise decision.[56]

Demographic Surveillance Systems

In a demographic surveillance system (DSS), intensive efforts are made to collect information on demographic events at frequent intervals, usually in a setting in which other sources of demographic information do not exist or are of questionable quality.

Such systems operate in a very limited geographic area. The idea is that it is better to have good-quality data about the demographic situation in one locale of a country than to not know anything with certainty about the country's demography, even though the site studied might not be representative of the

BOX 3.2
Ethical Considerations in Demographic Surveillance Systems

One concern in DSS projects is under what conditions those directing the project, who typically have high educational attainment and often include researchers from more developed countries, should intervene. The purpose of the project is to collect data reflecting typical or normal conditions in the country of interest. On one hand, providing medicines or health care that would not be available otherwise can affect demographic indicators for the site. On the other hand, providing care or medicine that can that save human life is a basic humanitarian imperative.

---

country as a whole. Ethical issues in DSS systems are discussed further in Box 3.2.

Another concern regarding demographic surveillance sites regards data access. The persons directing and conducting data collection invest a huge amount of effort. They are often reluctant to turn over the data to external researchers who have not devoted the same amount of energy to the data collection. On the other hand, scientific standards require that data be available for independent examination and validation. If other researchers do not have access to the data, it is not possible for alternative explanations to be investigated, and it can lead to questioning the value of research results based on the data. In addition, since data collection is so time intensive, researchers often need to turn their attention to the next round of data collection as soon as one round is completed. Thus, much data from such sites are analyzed locally to only a limited extent. These issues have led to a lively debate about the conditions under which data from a demographic surveillance site should be available to the larger scholarly community.[57]

One of the first demographic surveillance sites was the Matlab project in Bangladesh, founded in 1966.[58] Data collected at Matlab have generated numerous publications on topics, including sex differences in childhood mortality, maternal mortality, fertility decline, and breastfeeding.[59]

In 2006, there were about 30 demographic surveillance sites throughout the less developed region of the world. Many of these sites, including Matlab, have been organized into a network that coordinates work and cooperates on some projects. It is called the INDEPTH network.[60]

National Surveys
There are many reasons to do national surveys in less developed countries. The World Fertility Surveys were undertaken in 41 countries in the 1970s and the early 1980s, and their successor, the Demographic and Health Surveys, began in 1984. The Demographic and Health Surveys have provided technical assistance in more than 84 countries.[61]

The World Fertility Surveys and the Demographic and Health Surveys have collected information mainly intended for the analysis of fertility. The surveys had a core of questions that were included for all countries and some questions that were specific to particular countries. The common core of questions allowed comparative analysis across a large number of countries. Although these were national surveys, usually they interviewed only women of childbearing age. Even though the main purpose of these surveys was to allow analysis of fertility, they yielded data that are useful for investigating many topics, including mortality, school enrollment, treatment of fever, and school dropout.[62] The development of a reasonably complete census in a country also helps in planning national surveys, since the census enumeration provides a good basis for choosing respondents for a survey that are representative of the population of the country as a whole.

Reasons to Do a Survey: More Developed Countries

Typically, more developed countries have reliable censuses and vital statistics systems, so surveys are not needed to estimate basic demographic measures. The main reasons to conduct population surveys in more developed countries are (1) to provide more timely information about the population than is available from a census that is conducted every 5 or 10 years, and (2) to obtain more detailed information about a wider range of topics than is collected in a census. Surveys collect more detailed information about topics that are usually addressed in censuses, such as education and employment. Often, they also ask questions about topics that are relevant to demographic analysis but are rarely included in censuses, such as about health behaviors, including smoking and alcohol consumption.

U.S. Current Population Survey
The U.S. Current Population Survey (CPS) has been administered monthly since 1946. It interviews about

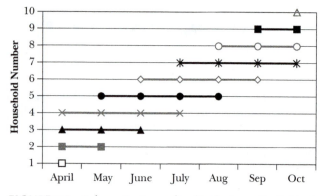

FIGURE 3.4   Schematic Example of Inclusion of Individual Households in the Current Population Survey

50,000 non-institutional households every month.[63] The CPS has a combined cross-sectional and longitudinal design. Each household is interviewed once a month for 4 months. Thus, one-fourth of the households in the survey are new each month. Figure 3.4 shows schematically how households enter and exit the survey.

The longitudinal aspect allows examination of short-term changes, such as entries and exits from the labor force. The short time that a household is in the survey (4 months) allows the CPS to remain representative of all non-institutional American households at every point in time.

In several months, the CPS has a special topic. For example, supplemental questions about school enrollment are asked in October, and an annual Social and Economic Supplement (originally administered in April and then in March) asks detailed questions about poverty, income, and health insurance. Often researchers who are interested in a particular topic combine CPS surveys for several years for the month in which their topic of interest was investigated.

American Community Survey
The American Community Survey (ACS) was tested beginning in 1996, and the actual survey began in 2005. It includes both non-institutional and institutional households. Data are collected every month of the year, covering about 3 million households in the course of a year. It includes about 60 questions.[64]

There was no long-form version of the 2010 U.S. Census. Instead, results from the ACS replaced the long form by supplying detailed information to researchers and business concerns. By law, results from the ACS are not to be used for redistricting of seats in the House of Representatives. However, ACS results can be used as the basis to distribute a variety of government funds, such as through grants, in which the amount available to each state is based on the number of low- or moderate-income families in the state, or the percentage of children living in poverty.[65]

Other Large National Population-Related Surveys in the United States
The U.S. government has supported several population-related national surveys that collect data on a wider range of topics or in more specialized areas than the CPS or the ACS. Next, we discuss a few of these surveys.

Some of the surveys, such as the National Health Interview Survey, are conducted directly by U.S. government agencies. Others, such as the Panel Study of Income Dynamics and the National Longitudinal Surveys, are conducted by universities with government funding. Some surveys, such as the Panel Study of Income Dynamics, cover the entire population, while others, such as Monitoring the Future and the National Longitudinal Adolescent Health Survey, focus on young adults, while the Health and Retirement Study focuses on the older population. The National Survey of Family Growth and the National Survey of Families and Households collect data to investigate family formation and childbearing.

Surveys have increasingly added physical measurements, such as height, weight, and blood pressure, as well as the collection of biological samples, such as saliva and blood. These measurements and samples have been added due to increased interest and understanding of the relation between social life, physical health, and physical manifestations of personal conditions, such as stress. Table 3.5 summarizes some information about the surveys that are discussed next.

Panel Study of Income Dynamics   The Panel Study of Income Dynamics (PSID) is a longitudinal study of households. It began in 1968 with 5,000 families, including more than 18,000 persons. Data from the individuals in these households and their descendants have been collected on topics including employment, income, wealth, expenditures, health, marriage, childbearing, child development, philanthropy, and education. Low-income households are oversampled to facilitate analysis of poverty. Similar national panel studies have been implemented in several countries, including Germany, Britain, and Canada. Between 1972 and 2004, 1,437 journal articles were published using PSID data.[66]

The PSID is directed by faculty at the University of Michigan and is supported by the National Science Foundation (NSF). In 2010, the NSF recognized the PSID as one of the 60 most significant advances funded by the NSF since the founding of NSF in 1950.

National Health Interview Survey   The National Health Interview Survey (NHIS) has been collecting survey data since 1957 through personal interviews on a broad range of topics, including health status and health care access, as well as questions about the

TABLE 3.5   Some Major American Population Surveys

Survey	Year Began	Description
Panel Study of Income Dynamics	1968	A longitudinal study of household focusing on economic issues and poverty
National Health Interview Survey	1957	A cross-sectional survey focusing on health status and health care
National Survey of Family Growth	1973	A cross-sectional survey focusing on family life, fertility, and health
National Survey of Families and Households	1987–1988	A longitudinal survey of households, including cohabiting households, that examines family, fertility, education, and employment
National Health and Nutrition Examination Survey	Early 1960s	A longitudinal survey that combines an interview and a physical exam
Survey of Income and Program Participation	1992	A series of longitudinal studies that measures the effectiveness of federal, local, and state programs and estimates future program costs and coverage
National Longitudinal Surveys of Labor Market Experience	1966	A series of longitudinal surveys that focuses on labor force participation and a variety of factors that influence labor market behavior
Monitoring the Future	1975	A series of cross-sectional and longitudinal surveys of high school students and young adults focusing on alcohol and substance abuse, health, and the transition to adulthood
National Longitudinal Survey of Adolescent Health	1994–1995	A longitudinal study of adolescents' well-being and family, community, and peer relationships, with biological samples collected in later rounds
Health and Retirement Study	1992	A longitudinal study of persons over age 50 that is concerned with the changes that occur in the later working years and retirement. It includes an interview as well as physical measurements and biological samples.
The National Survey of Black Americans and National Survey of American Life	1979–1980	Surveys that focused on the mental health of the Black population and on neighborhoods with a substantial Black population
New Immigrant Survey	2003–2004	A longitudinal survey of new legal immigrants focusing on health, education, and economic status
National Health and Aging Trends Study	2011	A longitudinal study of Medicare beneficiaries aged at least 65 that focuses on health and functional status

socioeconomic status of persons. The NHIS only covers the non–group quarters population, so people in long-term care facilities, the Armed Forces, and prisons are not included. The exclusion of people in group quarters somewhat limits its representativeness, especially at advanced ages. Data are collected by the U.S. Census Bureau for the National Center for Health Statistics, which is part of the Centers for Disease Control and Prevention.[67]

National Survey of Family Growth   The National Survey of Family Growth (NSFG) began in 1973, and the tenth cycle of NSFG was conducted in 2010. In the first five cycles through 1995, the NSFG surveyed women aged 15–44, but since the sixth cycle in 2002, it has been interviewing both men and women aged 15–44. NSFG collects data about family life, marriage and divorce, pregnancy, infertility, use of contraception, and men's and women's health. The NSFG is a project of the National Center for Health Statistics, which is part of the Centers for Disease Control and Prevention. Since 1999, it has been conducted under contract to faculty at the University of Michigan.[68]

National Survey of Families and Households   The National Survey of Families and Households (NSFH) is a longitudinal survey designed to collect a broad range of information about family life, including information about marriage, cohabitation, education, fertility, and employment. The first round of the survey took place in 1987–1988, and subsequent interviews took place in 1992–1994 and 2001–2003. The initial 1987–1988 survey interviewed 13,007 persons, with an oversampling of African Americans, Puerto Ricans, Mexican Americans, single-parent families, families with stepchildren, cohabiting couples, and recently married persons. The aim was to include a wide variety of family situations.

The NSFH is supported by the National Institute for Child Health and Human Development and the National Institute for Aging. There have been over a thousand publications using NSFH data on a wide variety of topics, including childbearing, marriage, cohabitation, household task allocation, co-residence, and the consequences of divorce. The NSFH is conducted by researchers at the Center for Demography at the University of Wisconsin.[69]

National Health and Nutrition Examination Survey   The National Health and Nutrition Examination Survey (NHANES) is designed to assess the health and nutritional status of adults and children in the United States. It combines interviews and physical examinations. The NHANES program began in the early 1960s. It was placed on a more consistent basis in 1999. Since 1999, the survey has interviewed a nationally representative sample of about 5,000 persons each year. It asks demographic, socioeconomic, dietary, and health-related questions. It includes medical, dental, and physiological measurements as well as laboratory tests. Survey results are used to determine the prevalence of major diseases and risk factors for diseases. NHANES findings are also the basis for national standards for measurements such as height, weight, and blood pressure. The NHANES is a program of the National Center for Health Statistics, which is part of the Centers for Disease Control and Prevention.

In 1982–1984, NHANES conducted special surveys of the Hispanic population of the United States. Although Hispanics are included in NHANES, the new surveys were conducted in order to increase the number of Hispanic respondents so that a greater variety of data analyses would be possible. These special surveys are called Hispanic HANES (HHANES). About 16,000 Hispanic respondents were interviewed.[70]

Survey of Income and Program Participation   The Survey of Income and Program Participation (SIPP) is a series of longitudinal studies, with each panel interviewed for 2.5 to 4 years. It began in 1992, and new panels were begun in most years through 2004. SIPP includes a nationally representative sample of about 14,000 to 36,700 households, and low-income households are oversampled. SIPP collects data about labor force participation, government program participation and eligibility, and general demographic characteristics. The purpose is to measure the effectiveness of existing federal, state, and local programs, and to estimate future costs and coverage for government programs, such as food stamps, which was renamed the Supplementary Nutrition Assistance Program (SNAP) in 2008. SIPP also provides improved statistics on the distribution of income and measures of economic well-being in the country. SIPP is conducted by the U.S. Census Bureau.[71]

National Longitudinal Surveys of Labor Market Experience   The National Longitudinal Surveys of Labor Market Experience (NLS) is a series of longitudinal studies that began in the 1960s and 1970s. The NLS has interviewed cohorts of men and women repeatedly in order to trace interrelated changes over the life course. A cohort is a group of people who can be traced as they age, such as people who are a

given age in a given year. The first surveys were of cohorts of men who were aged 14–24 and men who were aged 45–59 in 1966. The younger cohort were re-interviewed periodically until 1981, and the older cohort until 1990. In 1968, a cohort of women aged 14–24 and another aged 30–44 were first interviewed. These cohorts were re-interviewed periodically until 2003. In 1979 the National Longitudinal Survey of Youth first interviewed young men and women who were aged 14–24 in that year. A new cohort of young men and women who were aged 12–17 in 1997 also were interviewed. The cohorts who were first interviewed in 1979 and 1997 are still being periodically re-interviewed. The children of the young people first interviewed in 1979 also have been periodically re-interviewed. NLS has collected data on a wide variety of topics, including labor force participation, income, job search, job loss, and participation in government programs, as well as on social, demographic, and social-psychological factors that might influence labor force behavior. NLS is directed by faculty at the Ohio State University with major support from the Bureau of Labor Statistics and additional support from other government agencies and private foundations.[72]

Monitoring the Future   Monitoring the Future is an ongoing study of the behaviors, attitudes, and values of American secondary school students, college students, and young adults. The Monitoring the Future study has surveyed 12th-grade students since 1975 and 8th- and 10th-grade students since 1991. About 50,000 high school students are interviewed every year. Also, a sample of each graduating class is re-interviewed several times. Monitoring the Future collects data designed to study how alcohol use, drug use, and various aspects of health change across adolescence and the transition to adulthood in relation to age, education, labor force experience, and changes in roles, such as becoming married. Monitoring the Future is directed by faculty at the University of Michigan and is supported by the National Institute on Drug Abuse.[73]

National Longitudinal Survey of Adolescent Health   The National Longitudinal Study of Adolescent Health (Add Health) is a longitudinal study of a nationally representative sample of adolescents in grades 7–12 during the 1994–1995 school year. The Add Health respondents were re-interviewed several times, most recently in 2007–2008. Add Health collected data on respondents' social, economic, psychological, and physical well-being, as well as data on the respondents' family, neighborhood, community, school, friendships, peer groups, and romantic relationships. The 2001–2002 and 2007–2008 interviews also collected biological samples. Add Health has been supported by a variety of government agencies and is directed by faculty at the University of North Carolina.[74]

Health and Retirement Study   The Health and Retirement Study (HRS) began in 1992. It is a nationally representative survey of Americans over the age of 50. Respondents are re-interviewed every 2 years. If a respondent is married, both members of the couple are interviewed. The study is concerned with labor force participation, health transitions, and family structure changes and transfers that individuals undergo toward the end of their work lives and in the retirement years. Data are collected on many topics, including income, work, assets, pension plans, health insurance, disability, physical health and functioning, cognitive functioning, and health care expenditures. The HRS has increasingly collected physical measurements, such as height, weight, blood pressure, lung strength, and walking speed, and biological specimens, such as saliva and dried blood spots. The HRS is directed by faculty at the University of Michigan and is supported by the National Institute on Aging and the Social Security Administration.

Studies developed in consultation with the HRS and those that are based on the HRS approach have been implemented in several other countries, including Mexico since 2001, England since 2004, nine European countries since 2004, and Korea since 2006.[75]

The National Survey of Black Americans and the National Survey of American Life: Coping with Stress in the 21st Century   The National Survey of Black Americans (NSBA) is a survey of 2,107 self-identified Black Americans that was conducted in 1979–1980. Respondents were re-interviewed 8, 9, and 12 years later. Questions were asked on a wide variety of topics, including social and economic characteristics, and focused on issues of mental health. The National Survey of American Life: Coping with Stress in the 21st Century (NSAL) built on the NSBA and interviewed over 7,000 persons who lived in locations in which there was a substantial Black population. The fieldwork took place in 2001–2003. The survey covered a variety of topics, including economic, social, and structural conditions, as well as physical health, but the main focus was on mental health. The NSBA and NSAL were conducted by faculty at the University of Michigan and were supported by the National Institute of Mental Health.[76]

New Immigrant Survey   The New Immigrant Survey (NIS) is a longitudinal study of new legal immigrants to the United States. A pilot survey was conducted in 1996, and a baseline survey of over 9,000 respondents was conducted in 2003–2004, with a follow-up survey in 2007–2010. The NIS asks a wide variety of questions about health and health behaviors; background characteristics such as education, marital history, fertility history, and migration history; and questions about income, assets, and possession of consumer durables. The NIS is directed by faculty and researchers from the RAND Corporation, Princeton University, New York University, and Yale University, with support from the National Institutes of Health and other government agencies and private foundations.[77]

National Health and Aging Trends Study   The National Health and Aging Trends Study (NHATS) is a longitudinal study of Medicare beneficiaries aged 65 or older. The first wave of interviews was conducted in summer 2011 and included 9,000 respondents. The respondents are to be re-interviewed every year, with a new group of respondents added every 5 years. The purpose of NHATS is to collect data about trends in life functioning, disability, use of medical care, and living arrangements among older Americans. The NHATS is directed by researchers from Johns Hopkins University and is funded by the National Institute on Aging.[78]

HISTORICAL SOURCES

Historical sources that are useful for population analysis include parish registers and village registers. Parish registers are records of events that occurred to church members, especially baptisms, marriages, and burials. In the absence of a reliable vital statistics system, baptisms are a proxy for births, and burials are a proxy for deaths. Historical demographers have done extensive research that links information about the same people from baptism to marriage to burial, using a method called family reconstitution.[79] Using this approach, fertility and mortality rates and family size can be calculated to give a rich picture of the demographic situation of people in the past. This method works best when almost everyone in an area is the same religion and when there is little migration in or out of the area. Using non–religiously based village registers, Lee and Campbell produced a wide variety of information about the demography and social structure of Liaoning Province in northeast China from the mid-eighteenth through mid-nineteenth centuries.[80] Smith used village registers to investigate demographic and social structure in a village in Japan from the early eighteenth through mid-nineteenth centuries.[81]

ADMINISTRATIVE DATA

Administrative data that are useful sources of demographic information include immigration records, school enrollment data, and utilities data. Countries that are top destinations for international migrants have good records on the number and origin of legal migrants. To calculate the balance of international migrants, these countries need to know where their emigrants went. Immigration records from countries that are the main destinations of international migrants have been used to estimate the number of emigrants from countries such as the United States and South Africa.[82] The top destinations for emigrants from the United States are Mexico, the United Kingdom, Canada, and Germany. The top destinations for emigrants from South Africa are the United Kingdom, Ireland, Canada, Australia, New Zealand, and the United States.

School enrollment data and housing data are often used in the estimation of local area population. Plyer and colleagues discuss the use of administrative data, including utilities connections, to estimate population movements after a natural disaster.[83]

Population registers and other data sources used in register-based censuses are administrative records that were not constructed mainly for the purpose of collecting demographic data. With decreasing response rates in many surveys and with resistance to long census forms, countries that do not have a population register system have increasingly looked to administrative data for demographic estimates.

The U.S. Census Bureau is part of the Department of Commerce. It has been instructed to use administrative data wherever possible to minimize the burden on respondents:

(a) The Secretary [of Commerce], whenever he considers it advisable, may call upon any other department, agency, or establishment of the Federal Government, or of the government of the District of Columbia, for information pertinent to the work provided for in this title. (b) The Secretary may acquire, by purchase or otherwise, from states, counties, cities, or other units of government, or their instrumentalities, or from private persons and agencies, such copies of records, reports, and other material as may be required for the efficient and economical conduct of the censuses and surveys provided for in this title. (c) To the maximum extent possible and consistent with the kind, timeliness, quality and scope of the statistics required, the Secretary shall acquire and use information available from any source referred to in subsection (a) or (b) of this section instead of conducting direct inquiries.[84]

Use of administrative records requires linking together information about the same individual across various administrative sources. With the census refusal problems in Germany in mind, this record-linking effort is undertaken with a large number of safeguards to assure that the linked records are used only for aggregate and statistical purposes.

ASSUMPTIONS AND ACCURACY OF ESTIMATES: UNAIDS REVISION OF HIV PREVALENCE ESTIMATE FOR INDIA IN 2007

Estimates of the number of deaths by age or from some particular cause are sometimes based on results of a survey. In order for the estimates to be accurate, the survey respondents must be representative of the population as a whole, or the way in which the respondents differ from the population as a whole must be well understood so that estimates for the entire population can be made.

UNAIDS revised downward its estimate of the number of HIV-positive people in India from 5.7 million for 2006 to 2.5 million for 2007. This downward revision was not due to an actual enormous decline in HIV, but rather due to a change in the basis for the estimates. UNAIDS changed from basing their estimates on clinic data for high-risk groups (pregnant women, injection drug users, and commercial sex workers) to basing their estimates on a more representative population-based survey. It was clear that the earlier estimates had greatly overestimated the prevalence of HIV in the general Indian population.[85]

The new estimates are clearly more accurate than the old estimates. However, some are not happy about this change because they think it could lead to less attention and less money being allocated to fight HIV. Also, some interpret this reported change as real and thus exaggerate the extent of real declines in HIV. This example shows that how data are collected and how survey respondents are chosen for collection of data can have a large impact on what conclusions are drawn.

COLLECTION OF DATA ABOUT RACE AND ETHNICITY

In the United States, which ethnic groups are separately listed on the census is a political issue. The census questions are approved by Congress, and which groups are listed is argued about. Being separately listed, rather than needing to write in the name of a group, increases the number of people who indicate on the census that they are members of a given group.[86]

In many countries, there have been serious questions raised about whether data about race or ethnicity should be collected. On one hand, race and ethnicity are often important aspects of identity; racial and ethnic groups differ in their needs for social services, and information about race and ethnicity can be helpful in planning service provision. Also, if particular racial and ethnic groups are being discriminated against currently or have been in the past, resulting in disadvantages in education, employment, or other areas, it can be difficult or impossible to know this on more than an idiosyncratic or anecdotal basis without systematic data, such as from a census. As was written in a 2011 U.S. Census Bureau publication:[87]

> The Census Bureau collects data on Hispanic origin and race to fulfill a variety of legislative and program requirements. Data on Hispanic origin and race are used in the legislative redistricting process carried out by the states and in monitoring local jurisdictions' compliance with the Voting Rights Act. More broadly, data on Hispanic origin and race are critical for research that underlies many policy decisions at all levels of government. . . .
>
> All levels of government need information on Hispanic origin and race to implement and evaluate programs, or enforce laws, such as the Civil Rights Act, Voting Rights Act, Fair Housing Act, Equal Employment Opportunity Act, and the 2010 Census Redistricting Data Program.
>
> Both public and private organizations use Hispanic origin and race information to find areas where groups may need special services and to plan and implement education, housing, health, and other programs that address these needs. For example, a school system might use this information to design cultural activities that reflect the diversity in their community, or a business could use it to select the mix of merchandise it will sell in a new store. Census information also helps identify areas where residents might need services of particular importance to certain racial or ethnic groups, such as screening for hypertension or diabetes.

For the first time since 1931, the 2011 Census of India asked about caste.[88] While members of low castes have done quite well in southern India, this is reported to be less true in northern India, where caste-based political parties remain influential. Some in India think that the collection of data about caste will be helpful in detecting persistent discrimination, while others think that the collection of these data contributes to intercaste conflict.[89]

South Africa is a country where collection of data about race has been quite a sensitive issue. Under apartheid, there were four official population groups in South Africa (African, Coloured, Asian, and White). Population group membership was a matter of law, and official commissions would sometimes change a person's population group membership in an arbitrary way. Since there were laws under apartheid governing where members of different population groups were allowed to live, this could lead to the tearing apart of families when one member was classified as "African" and a sibling classified as "Coloured." Also, under apartheid some jobs were reserved for Whites, and in jobs that were not racially restricted the pay scale for non-Whites was much lower than for Whites. Thus, population group membership related to a mass of legal restrictions on what people could do and where they could go.

In post-apartheid South Africa, population group membership is a matter of self-identification. However, population groups in South Africa continue to differ greatly in almost every aspect of their lives. Many argue that to track progress from the poor situation of the Coloured and African population under apartheid, it is necessary to track conditions of life by population group.

In 1994, the new post-Apartheid South African government came to power. In 2010, the Federal Congress of the Democratic Alliance, the main opposition party to the African National Congress that was the party in power in South Africa, passed a resolution encouraging people to write "South African" on any official document that requested a racial identification.[90]

Figure 3.5 shows the percentage of households with clean drinking water, with a flush toilet in the dwelling, and in which there was a telephone landline or a household member had a cellphone, by population group in 1996 and 2006. There has been some closing of the gap, but much remains to be done, and Africans remain far worse off in terms of material standard of living than members of other groups. Some argue that without data on living conditions, education, and employment by population group, it will be impossible to know whether past differentials have narrowed or disappeared.

The collection of data about race has also been controversial in the United States. Many agree that race is a socially constructed category. Because of this, some think it is meaningless and unnecessary to collect data about race. Hasnain-Wynia and Baker report that many hospitals do not collect data on the race of patients, because the hospitals think the data are unnecessary and that collecting racial data can be disturbing to patients. Many demographers and other social scientists argue that collection of data by race in the United States is important in order to track disparities, as mentioned in this chapter.[91]

Racial and Ethnic Identification and U.S. Official Statistics

There have been important changes in how racial and ethnic group membership has been recorded in official U.S. statistics. The issues with Hispanic, African-American, and Native American identities are somewhat different from each other.

Changes in Recording of Hispanic Identity

The official recognition of Hispanic identity in the United States has evolved gradually over time. At

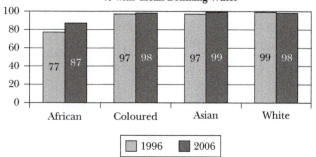

% with Clean Drinking Water

	African	Coloured	Asian	White
1996	77	97	97	99
2006	87	98	99	98

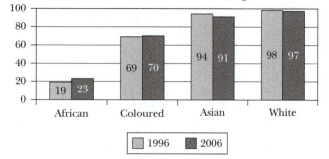

% with a Flush Toilet in the Dwelling

	African	Coloured	Asian	White
1996	19	69	94	98
2006	23	70	91	97

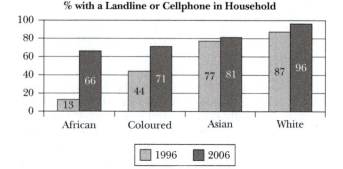

% with a Landline or Cellphone in Household

	African	Coloured	Asian	White
1996	13	44	77	87
2006	66	71	81	96

FIGURE 3.5 Characteristics of Population Groups in South Africa, 1996 and 2006

one time, having come from (or having one's forebears come from) Mexico, Cuba, or elsewhere in Spanish-speaking Latin America was officially viewed no differently than having come from Ireland or Poland. Hispanics in the United States, however, developed their identity in ways that were somewhat different from those with European backgrounds. For example, those with roots in Spanish-speaking Latin America retained Spanish as a home language more than did immigrants with European backgrounds retain a non-English language. Also, there seemed to be greater recognition by the public that having a background in Spanish-speaking Latin America was distinctive compared to those from a European background.

Those concerned with government statistics used several approaches to identify Hispanics. One approach was to try to identify those with Spanish surnames from official records in order to try to understand the size and characteristics of this population. The surname Martin, either could be of English origin, with the "i" pronounced as a short "i," or could be of Spanish origin, with the "i" pronounced like a long "e." This presented a problem, since Martin was the third most common surname for those with a Spanish-speaking Latin American background.[92]

Gradually, states started including a question designed to tap Hispanic identity on birth and death certificates. By 1990, all states recorded some version of Hispanic identity on birth and death certificates.

Multiple-Race Identification

A major change in collection of data by race was implemented in the U.S. 2000 Census and continued in the 2010 Census. This change allowed individuals to indicate that they considered themselves a member of two or more racial groups. There was not a separate "multiracial" category. In addition, people responded whether they considered themselves Hispanic or not. Whether a person was Hispanic was considered an issue of ethnicity, and Hispanics could be of any race.[93]

People could also indicate if they considered themselves a member of "some other race" than the listed races and could write in what race they felt they belonged to. Many people indicated that they were a member of "some other race" and filled in Hispanic as a race, which according to the instructions they were not supposed to do.[94] The write-in of "Hispanic" as a race was likely in some cases to be the expression of a point of view rather than a failure to follow instructions. Starting in the 1960s, some Mexican Americans argued that Mexican Americans were not White, but that Chicanos were a new race.[95] In 2010, 95% of Hispanics that indicated a race identified as White, but 40% of those who identified as Hispanic checked the "some other race" box.

Based on the 2000 Census, it was reported that there were more Hispanics than Blacks and African Americans in the United States.[96] Whether this conclusion was accurate depends on how you look at the data. Table 3.6 shows the number of people who were Black or Hispanic according to different definitions in 2000 and 2010. In 2000, if you count as Black only those who stated Black as a race and claimed no other racial identification, there were more Hispanics than Blacks (12.5% versus 12.3%). If you count as Black all those who stated Black racial identification regardless of whether they claimed any additional racial identification, there were more Blacks than Hispanics (12.9% versus 12.5%).

TABLE 3.6 Single and Multiple Racial Identifications in the 2000 and 2010 U.S. Censuses

Racial Group	% of Population 2000	% of Population 2010
Black only	12.3	12.6
Black and any other race	0.6	1.0
Total Black (by any definition)	12.9	13.6
White race (only) and Hispanic ethnicity	6.0	8.7
Black race (only) and Hispanic ethnicity	0.3	0.4
"Some other" race and Hispanic ethnicity	5.1	6.0
American Indian, Alaskan Native, Asian, Native Hawaiian, or other Pacific Islander race and Hispanic ethnicity	0.2	0.3
Two or more races and Hispanic ethnicity	0.8	1.0
Total Hispanic (by any definition)	12.5	16.3

In the 2010 Census, more people in the United States identified as Hispanic than as Black by any definition. In the 2010 U.S. Census, 16.3% of the population identified as Hispanic, while 12.6% identified as Black or African American and indicated no other racial group, while 1.0% identified as Black and at least one other racial group, for a total of 13.6% of the population identifying as Black either alone or in combination with another racial group.[97]

Methods have been proposed to translate multi-race responses into single-race categories. People apply such translations because they want to look at trends over time. In 1997–2002, the National Health Interview Survey allowed respondents to identify with more than one race but then asked each respondent what single race response they preferred. Liebler and Halpern-Manners used these data along with the respondent's age, sex, and Hispanic ethnicity and regional location to develop a statistical model to bridge between multirace and single-race responses. On average, about 39% of those who identified as both Black and White would have identified as White in a single-race forced choice, and about 78% of those who identified both as White and as American Indian or Alaskan Native would have identified as White in a single-race forced choice.[98] As of June 2012, the Census Bureau had published information about single-race and multiple-race reporting, as indicated in Table 3.6, but no translations of racial reports into single-race equivalents from earlier censuses or surveys had been published.

Official U.S. government data collection is not always consistent about what is a racial category and what is not a racial category. For example, although the U.S. Census Bureau considers Hispanic to be an ethnic group and not a race, Hispanic has been a racial classification, along with White, African American, and Asian, in Medicare data since 1980.[99]

Some parts of the U.S. government have used translation schemes to code multiracial individuals onto single-race categories. The U.S. National Vital Statistics System presents vital statistics data on births and deaths by state using bridged race categories based on results in surveys in which people could identify with several racial groups but also were forced to choose one racial group for identification. Other approaches have used reclassification schemes based on a statistical analysis that takes into account available information about the individual and the geographic location to reclassify multiracial respondents into a single racial group.[100]

Native American Classification

The classification of persons as Native American is very complicated. People can claim whatever racial group membership they wish on census returns, in vital statistics registration, or in response to surveys. However, for many purposes, there are barriers to recognition as a member of a Native American tribe, even for people who consider themselves to be Native Americans. Different definitions of who is Native American present a problem for demographers when a different definition leads to inclusion in the numerator of a rate than leads to inclusion in the denominator of a rate. For example, Sugarman and his colleagues found that in Oregon, injured people were less likely to be recorded as Native American in the injury surveillance system than in the census, which led to an underestimate of Native American injury rates.[101] Also, due to the rights and benefits that members of some Native American tribes receive, the issue of who is a member of an Indian tribe has social, political, and economic significance. Some tribes use indicators of participation in the community, and others use the concept of "blood quantum" that requires that a member of a tribe have at least one grandparent who was a tribal member.[102]

In 2011, there was a major dispute about whether African Americans whose families had lived in the Cherokee community for many generations were Cherokee tribal members. One issue was that after the Civil War, government lists of Cherokee tribal members sometimes designated those who were part White and part Cherokee as both White and Cherokee, but African Americans were only designated as Black on the lists, whether or not they had Cherokee ancestry.[103]

In 2011, there also were several members of the Chukchansi tribe in California who were removed from tribal rolls. The tribal membership of an ancestor who died in 1942 was questioned, and all of

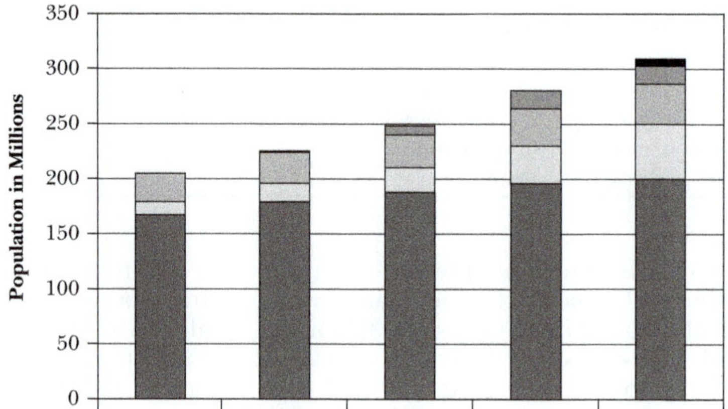

	1970	1980	1990	2000	2010
■ Two or More Races	0.0	0.0	0.0	3.9	5.5
■ Asian	1.4	3.5	7.3	10.6	14.4
■ Native American	0.8	1.4	2.0	2.7	3.2
□ non-Hispanic African American	22.4	26.5	29.0	32.9	36.0
□ Hispanic	9.6	14.6	22.4	35.3	49.7
■ non-Hispanic White	169.0	180.3	188.1	195.6	200.9

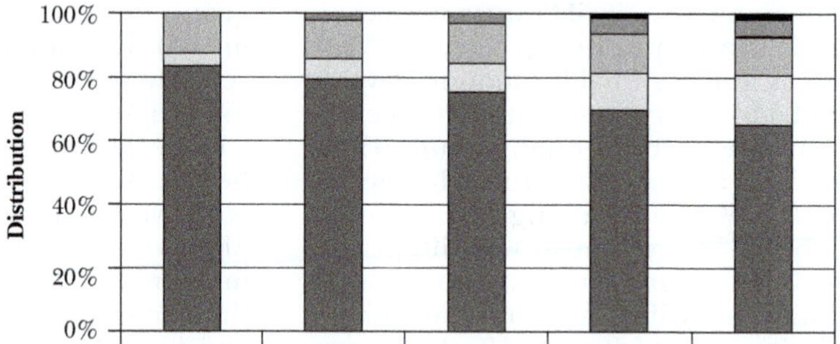

	1970	1980	1990	2000	2010
■ Two or More Races	0	0	0	1	2
■ Asian	1	2	3	4	5
■ Native American	0	1	1	1	1
■ non-Hispanic African American	11	12	12	12	11
□ Hispanic	5	6	9	12	16
■ non-Hispanic White	83	80	75	69	64

FIGURE 3.6 Estimated Racial and Ethnic Composition of the United States, 1970–2010

his descendants were removed from the tribal rolls, including one 87-year-old woman who was an expert basket weaver and one of the few remaining people who was a native speaker of the Chukchansi language. These issues had become hotly contested partly due to tribal income from a gambling casino that was distributed to all members of the tribe.[104]

Changes over Time in the Racial and Ethnic Composition of the United States

The racial and ethnic composition of the United States has changed considerably over time. Figure 3.6 shows the estimated distribution of U.S. population among non-Hispanic Whites, Hispanics, non-Hispanic African Americans, Native Americans, and Asians. In 2000 and 2010, the number of people who identified with two or more racial groups is also shown. Estimates are shown for census dates 1970–2010. The top panel shows the number of members of each group in 100,000s, and the bottom panel shows the percentage distribution among groups.[105]

The percentage of U.S. population comprising non-Hispanic Whites has decreased over time, falling to 64% of the total population in 2010. In 2010, 54% of children under age 18 were non-Hispanic Whites. In 2010, in ten states and in 35 large metropolitan areas, less than half of all children were non-Hispanic Whites.[106]

The percentage composed of Asians and of Hispanics has increased greatly. The increase in Asians from 1% to 5% of the population is related to increased immigration from Asia after 1965. This is discussed in Chapter 12 and is shown in Figures 12.15 and 12.16. The number of Hispanics also increased over time, which is partially related to increased legal immigration from Latin America, as shown in Figures 12.15 and 12.16. As discussed earlier, data on Hispanic identity have been collected in the U.S. Census only since 1980. In 1970, the Hispanic population was estimated based on information about Spanish language use and having a Spanish surname.

There has been little change in the percentage of the population composed of non-Hispanic African Americans or of Native Americans. The constancy of both the non-Hispanic African-American share and of the Native American share of the population has been affected by the opportunity for people to designate more than one racial group since the 2000 Census.

Shifting Racial and Ethnic Identification in Various Settings

Barth wrote about the shifting boundaries between ethnic groups. There is substantial evidence of shifts in the identification of individuals by race or

TABLE 3.7   Percentage of Children of Mixed-Race Unions Reported as White in the 1910 and 1920 Censuses in Puerto Rico

Parental Race	1910	1920
Black and White	6%	9%
Black and Mulatto	0%	1%
White and Mulatto	17%	22%

ethnicity. We discuss some examples from the Soviet Union, Puerto Rico, and Brazil.[107]

Shifting Ethnic Identification in the Soviet Union

In the Soviet Union, there were some advantages to being an ethnic Russian. A person's ethnic group membership was a matter of official record on the Soviet internal passport, but in the 1959 and 1970 Censuses, enumerators were supposed to record whatever ethnic group the person claimed and not to ask for other documentation. Anderson and Silver estimated that about 1% of all non-Russians who were aged 0–38 in 1959 claimed to be Russians in 1970, and among small ethnic groups, such as the Karelians and Mordvinians, more than 15% of those aged 0–38 who claimed to be members of these minority groups in 1959 claimed to be Russians in 1970.[108]

Changing Whiteness in Puerto Rico in the Early Twentieth Century

The percentage of residents of Puerto Rico who stated they were White increased from 65% in 1910 to 74% in 1920. Loveman and Muniz conclude that the major source of the increase in the percentage of Whites was changes in racial identification over time. The main racial groups in Puerto Rico were White, Black, and Mulatto.[109]

Table 3.7 shows the percentage of children who were reported as White in the 1910 and 1920 Censuses according to the racial identification of parents for mixed-race children. For every combination of mixed-race parents, the percentage of their children who were reported as White increased between the 1910 and 1920 U.S. Censuses.

Shifting Racial Categories in Brazil

Brazil provides a striking example of change in racial self-identification from White and Black into Brown between the 1950 and 1980 Brazilian Censuses, as shown in Table 3.8. In Brazilian parlance, race was referred to as "colour." Since there was little immigration before 1980, it is unlikely the change is due to an influx of people who always would have identified their race as "Brown."

Table 3.9 shows the estimated net percentage changing their racial identification between the 1950

TABLE 3.8 Reported Racial Distribution in the 1950 and 1980 Brazil Censuses

Colour	1950 (%)	1980 (%)
White	61.7	51.6
Brown	26.5	42.6
Black	11.0	5.0
Yellow	0.6	0.4
Missing	0.2	0.4
Total	100.0	100.0

TABLE 3.9 Estimated Percentage Reclassified by Racial Group between the 1950 and 1980 Brazilian Censuses

Sex	Colour	% Changing Racial Identification, 1950–1980
Male	Black	−38
	Brown	+36
	White	−9
Female	Black	−39
	Brown	+31
	White	−6

and 1980 Brazilian Censuses. There was a substantial shift out of the Black and the White racial categories and into the Brown racial category. De Calvalho and his associates argue that in Brazil, a dark-skinned poor person was likely to self-identify as Black, while a person with a similar shade of skin but a higher status was likely to identify as Brown. Between 1950 and 1980, income and educational attainment increased in Brazil. The shift from identification as Black to identification as Brown is viewed as reflecting upward mobility as well as perhaps changing mobility aspirations in Brazil. The authors were less certain about the explanation of the shift out of White identification. They thought either it could be due to a decline in the social stigma associated with Brown racial identification after 1950, or some Whites could have experienced downward mobility that was manifested as change in racial identification from White to Brown.[110]

DATA COLLECTION, DEVELOPMENT LEVEL, AND PRECISION OF KNOWLEDGE

This chapter has discussed the main types of demographic data collection, the challenges they face, and the information they are designed to provide. Table 3.10 summarizes the availability and usefulness of data sources according to the development level of the country.

At a very low development level, almost none of the usual data sources are available, and all population indicators are estimated. Sometimes, the estimates are based on local surveys in the absence of other information. Sometimes, the estimates are based on the situation in another country which is thought to be similar but for any of various reasons has better data.

TABLE 3.10 Demographic Data Sources at Different Development Levels

Data Source and Development Level	Very Low Development	Low Development	Moderate Development	High Development	Very High Development
Census	Not available	Sometimes available; questionable completeness and accuracy	Available; fairly complete coverage and fairly good data quality	Available; almost complete coverage and high data quality	Complete or almost complete coverage when done; sometimes replaced by register and survey data
Vital Statistics	Not available	Sometimes available; questionable completeness	Available; fairly complete coverage	Available; complete or almost complete coverage	Available complete coverage
Surveys	Local surveys sometimes the only basis for estimates	Local surveys; sometimes national surveys available	National surveys available	National surveys available; increasing range of data collected	National surveys available; large range of data available, sometimes replaces some data from census
Population Register	Not available	Rarely available	Sometimes available	Often available	Often available; sometimes replaces census

Sometimes, indicators of mortality and fertility are estimated based on answers to survey questions. It can be quite challenging to collect even these data if people do not know their age and if they are not literate.

As countries develop somewhat more infrastructure and capacity to collect data, censuses are often implemented. At this development level, more people are literate, and numbers are more meaningful to them. This means that the data from surveys, whether local or national, are better quality than are similar data from countries at a very low development level. The censuses conducted in countries with a low development level often have substantial shortcomings regarding completeness and accuracy but can provide a better basis for demographic estimates than a local survey. Similarly, vital statistics data begin to be collected, although there are often severe shortcomings in the completeness of coverage.

At a moderate level of development, the availability and quality of census and vital statistics data improve. Often national surveys are implemented that provide more detailed information than that available from censuses or local surveys. At a moderate development level, it is common for surveys to collect information about fertility and related experiences from women of childbearing age. Sometimes, there are population registers from which useful information can be obtained.

In countries at a high level of development, census and vital statistics data are of high quality, and many countries have useful population registers. Increasingly, there are national surveys that collect a variety of information about fertility, health, and labor market experiences.

In countries at a very high development level, censuses are sometimes eliminated or are greatly shortened in length. Information from a population register and other administrative records replaces the data previously collected in the census. Sometimes, large national surveys replace the detailed information about topics such as education and labor market activity that was earlier collected in the census.

TIMELINESS OF AVAILABLE DEMOGRAPHIC DATA

Detailed demographic data take time to assemble. Although a Gallup poll can report the results of a poll of presidential approval within 24 hours, more complex data are not available for some time. For example, in 2012, the most recent national data on death rates by age for the United States as a whole referred to 2010.[111] For the United States, vital statistics data are collected at the level of states, and those data must be assembled and sent on to be combined with data from all other states. The data must be examined for obvious errors before they are published. All this requires time and staff effort. The data on urban and rural populations published by the United Nations in 2012 relied on the most recent data available for each country. For Australia, the most recent data were from the 2001 Census, and for the Democratic Republic of the Congo from the 1984 Census.

Assessment of the demographic situation always entails looking at data from the past, and the more detailed the data required and the less developed the demographic data collection system in a country, the farther in the past are the data on which analysis and planning are based. There are models and ways to estimate values of demographic variables for more recent times, but all of these methods have strengths and weaknesses. The demographic situation in a country usually does not change very rapidly. However, it is always possible for a country's leaders to criticize an analysis of the country's demographic situation by saying, "Maybe you are correct about what things were like before, but now things are different, and your analysis is completely irrelevant to the current situation."

ETHICAL ISSUES IN DEMOGRAPHIC DATA COLLECTION

There are two kinds of concerns regarding the protection of persons in demographic data collection. The first involves the protection of respondents from physical or psychological harm in surveys and other studies where there are individual participants. An example is the concern about adequate protection of participants in drug tests from dangerous side effects. The second kind of concern involves the misuse of data from a census, population registration system, or survey that leads to persecution or mistreatment of persons or households. Usually this relates to the individual identification of persons when their personal data should have been used for statistical or aggregate analyses only.[112]

Protection of Human Subjects in Research Projects or Surveys

Research using **human subjects** includes surveys, interviews and focus group participation, as well as analysis of biological samples or other medical studies. There has been increasing concern with the protection of human subjects in research.

The Nazi medical experiments have often been discussed as horrific examples of disregard for the welfare of human subjects. These experiments involved a wide variety of torture, poisoning, and exposure to freezing conditions, without any scientific purpose that the experiments could have served. Many died in the course of these experiments. The subjects of these experiments were Jews and others who otherwise would have been put to death in the Nazi camps.[113]

However, there have been many more recent incidents of egregious mistreatment of human subjects. These mistakes and bad acts have led to the development of guidelines for research involving human beings. The motivation for much of the concern with the protection of human subjects was biomedical research, but human subjects protections extend to subjects in social science research, where there are limits on deception of survey participants and concerns about whether subjects would be extremely disturbed by participation or whether their participation could lead to harm.

Next we discuss some of these studies. The Tuskegee Study motivated much of the development of human subjects rules. The Guatemala STD study shows that unethical practices are still being revealed. The San Antonio birth control pill study is an example of recent unethical practices. A study of obedience and willingness to inflict pain also illustrates some psychological dangers in social science research. A study of persons with post-traumatic stress disorder illustrates that concerns about human subjects are also justified when thinking about surveys with vulnerable participants.

Tuskegee Study

In the 1930s, there was increasing concern about syphilis and a desire to understand more about how to treat it. From 1932 through 1972, there was a study of 600 poor African-American men in Tuskegee, Alabama, 399 of whom already had syphilis.[114]

Participants were not told they had syphilis and were not treated for syphilis, even after penicillin was accepted as an effective syphilis treatment in 1947. Many participants and their wives and children died of syphilis. In 1972, information about the study was leaked, which led to the study's termination. Outrage over the Tuskegee Study led to the *Belmont Report*, discussed in this chapter.

Guatemala STI Study

In 2010, the U.S. government apologized to people in Guatemala for a study conducted in 1946–1948 in which people in Guatemala were deliberately infected with syphilis and other sexually transmitted infections (STIs) without their consent or knowledge. Unlike in the Tuskegee Study, they treated the persons in Guatemala with penicillin and cured many of the infected persons. The purpose of the study was to better understand how penicillin could be effectively used to treat syphilis and other sexually transmitted infections. The research was carried out by a U.S. Public Health Service physician. The details of the study were disclosed after a historian,

Susan Reverby, examined Dr. John Cutler's unpublished notes on the study in the University of Pittsburgh archive. Dr. Cutler was also involved in the Tuskegee Study in the 1960s.[115]

Birth Control Pill Tests in San Antonio

In 1971 in San Antonio, Texas, 398 Mexican-American women came to a clinic to obtain contraceptives. As part of an experiment about the effectiveness of various oral contraceptives and to determine whether psychological factors affected whether a woman became pregnant, 76 of the women were given a placebo. Ten of the women given placebos became pregnant. The women had offered no consent, and all thought they had received contraception.[116]

The Milgram Obedience Experiment

Stanley Milgram was a psychologist at Yale who wanted to study the psychological processes at work that allowed people in Nazi Germany to torture and inflict other cruelties on persons toward whom they had no personal animosity. In 1961, volunteer participants were told that another person whom they could see was connected to an apparatus by which the subject could administer an electric shock. There was an indicator of the strength of the shock. The person was asked a series of questions. If an incorrect answer was given, the subject was to increase the level of the shock. The purpose of the experiment was to see how willing people would be to administer strong and potentially lethal shocks to others. It was found that most people were willing to deliver dangerously strong electric shocks.[117]

The person receiving the shocks was a collaborator in the experiment, and no actual shocks were administered. The researchers were astounded at how willing people were to harm others when instructed to do so. The participants were informed about the actual purposes of the study after they participated. This study has been strongly criticized for its deception and its possible psychological harm to the participants.

Psychological Distress and Post-traumatic Stress Disorder

There has also been concern that participation in a survey could cause psychological distress to especially vulnerable persons. In 1990–1993, Parslow and her colleagues interviewed Australian Vietnam War veterans to determine whether they had symptoms of post-traumatic stress disorder (PTSD).[118] Nineteen percent of the participants had PTSD. The concern was whether participation in the interview significantly increased participants' stress. The interview was found to significantly increase participants' stress, especially among those with PTSD. The additional stress did disappear over time and was not related to increased seeking of medical treatment. Participation was voluntary, and participants were informed of the risks. However, the study makes clear the potential for distress or harm to subjects from an interview.

Belmont Report

In response to the Tuskegee Study, in 1974 a law was passed creating the National Commission for the Protection of Human Subjects of Biomedical and Behavioral Research. This commission developed guidelines for the ethical conduct of research on humans. The conclusions were put forth in the *Belmont Report*. The three ethical principles for using human subjects in research elaborated in the *Belmont Report* are as follows:[119]

1. **Respect for Persons:** Research participants should be treated as autonomous agents. This motivates the principle of obtaining "informed consent." Informed consent means that the risks of the research are clearly explained to the potential participant and the potential participant is free to refuse to participate in all or part of the project. Respect for persons also means that those who are not fully capable or free to give informed consent (such as minor children and prisoners) are protected and additional safeguards are implemented to protect such persons from harm. Some research requires deception or lack of disclosure of the true research goals until after the research is concluded. In these cases, the deception needs to (1) be assessed as necessary to the research goals, (2) provide at most minimal undisclosed risks to participants, and (3) be followed by a debriefing that informs participants about the true research goals after the research has concluded.

2. **Beneficence:** Research is not supposed to harm subjects. The benefits to the research project should be maximized, and the risks to participants should be minimized.

3. **Justice:** The principle of justice involves the personal costs and benefits of research. Research participants should be treated equally within the parameters of the project, and there should be some benefit to participants, whenever possible. Research should include subjects whenever feasible from throughout the population, rather than only including the groups that are easiest to study. This principle has led to increased attention to the inclusion of women and members of racial and ethnic minorities in research studies.

The *Belmont Report* is the basis of the guidelines for the involvement of human subjects in research that covers all social and biomedical research. Protection of human subjects in academic research is monitored by Institutional Review Boards (IRBs) at colleges and universities to assure that the *Belmont Report* principles are followed.

Human Rights Abuses and Official Statistics

Officially collected demographic data have sometimes been used in human rights abuses.[120] Besides cruel medical experiments on individuals, the Nazis also used data from censuses and population registration systems in several countries, including Poland, France, the Netherlands, and Norway, to identify Jews and gypsies in order to ship them to camps and later kill them. The United States used the results of the 1940 Census to identify Japanese Americans to place them in internment camps and confiscate their property. In 1994 in Rwanda, population registration data were used to locate members of the Tutsi ethnic group for persecution and often death.

Fundamental Principles of Official Statistics

Interest in the transformation of national statistical systems in formerly state socialist countries in the late 1980s and 1990s led the United Nations to develop a set of Fundamental Principles of Official Statistics that should be adhered to by all national statistical agencies. There were ten principles, including providing official statistics to aid in government planning, facilitating correct interpretation of data, and commenting on erroneous interpretation or misuse of statistics.

The principles that are most relevant to protecting human subjects and preventing human rights abuses are Principle 2 and Principle 6. Principle 2 states that "the statistical agencies need to decide according to strictly professional considerations, including scientific principles and professional ethics, on the methods and procedures for the collection, processing, storage and presentation of statistical data." Principle 6 specifies that "individual data collected by statistical agencies are to be strictly confidential and used exclusively for statistical purposes."[121]

In 2003, the United Nations conducted a survey regarding how well countries had complied with the fundamental principles. One hundred and twelve out of 194 countries responded to the survey. Regarding Principle 2, many countries saw the need for more training for their staff. Many countries had formal ethical guidelines, others were developing such guidelines, while some countries saw no need for such guidelines. Regarding Principle 6, most countries had procedures to assure that individual identities could not be determined from the data, mainly through safeguards during data processing and transfer of personally identifiable information within the statistical office, although there were some reported cases of data being stolen or illegally sold for cash by government employees.[122] The United Nations also has a website where information about the practices of each country's national statistical agency is available.[123]

Other Issues in the Protection of Human Subjects

Next we discuss some other issues regarding research conduct and the protection of human subjects. We discuss dilemmas involved in research in authoritarian societies. Also there is research where the aim is worthwhile but there are inherent risks to subjects. Next, we describe an approach to collecting data on very sensitive topics. Finally, we consider some issues involved in protecting respondent identity.

Research about Authoritarian Societies and Informed Consent

Issues involving the conduct of research and research ethics about authoritarian societies can be complicated. Often, access by researchers to persons in authoritarian societies is quite limited. Thus, scholars have sometimes interviewed people who have left the country in order to find out about daily life in a country to which researchers have very limited or no access.

Hong Kong was under British control until 1997. At one time, the only way for Western researchers to obtain information about daily life in China was to interview Chinese who had immigrated to Hong Kong.[124] After World War II, there was a study of Soviet citizens who were forced west by the retreating Nazi army.[125] Starting in the 1970s, many Jews were allowed to leave the Soviet Union for the purpose of family reunification. There was a survey conducted in the 1980s of Soviet Jews who had come to the United States between 1979 and 1982. The intention of the survey was to obtain information about daily life in the Soviet Union.[126]

In surveys of emigrants from authoritarian societies, there are special considerations to protect human subjects. If it is known that a person participated in such a survey, there is the risk that there might be retaliation against family members who are still in the home country. Also, such countries have often been political enemies of the United States. If a legal immigrant to the United States had ever been a member of a Communist Party and does not admit it on his or her immigration interview, this is grounds for later deportation. Partly for this reason, the survey of immigrants from the Soviet Union conducted in the 1980s did not ask about Communist Party membership.

Sometimes, human subjects issues are problematic even after countries have become more open

to research. In the late Gorbachev period, sometimes Western researchers collaborated with Soviet researchers to conduct fairly normal social surveys, although the questionnaires had to be approved by state organs.[127] At other times, survey research in China has confronted substantial problems in dealing with Chinese cultural and governmental sensitivities.[128]

Goduka, a Black South African, wrote about her fieldwork experience in South Africa during the apartheid period. She interviewed 300 African children and their parents. Although she used standard informed consent forms and only interviewed those subjects where the parents consented, a substantial proportion of the parents were illiterate, and she wasn't sure whether they actually understood the concept of informed consent. This is a problem in many less developed country settings. In addition, she wanted to gather some information about White farms, but the apartheid laws limited her access to these farms. She wondered whether she should engage in deception to obtain the information she wanted. Deception of White South Africans or the South African authorities did not bother some other researchers.[129]

When research is conducted in countries whose human rights provisions do not meet U.S. standards, the researcher needs to think how to deal with the situation. Of course, if the researcher is American, all relevant human subjects protections need to be observed. However, the researcher needs to decide to what extent the topics and questions asked will be influenced by local and governmental concerns. If social scientists studied only "nice" societies, there would develop a social science of "nice" societies, the value of which would be limited if one wants to understand all of human experience. Often, the researcher faces a choice of operating under restrictions with which he or she does not agree or not doing the research at all.

Even when it is very difficult for researchers to do research within some countries, the country governments still publish some demographic information and often cooperate in many UN data dissemination efforts.

Studies with Inherent Risks: The Minnesota Starvation Experiment

The Minnesota Starvation Experiment is an example of a study with risks to the participants, but where the participants were informed of the risks, and the results served an important goal. After World War II, there was concern about starvation and near starvation caused by famine during World War II. There was a desire to assess the effectiveness of various strategies to help near-starved people return to a healthy state.

Two hundred men from the Civilian Public Service volunteered to participate in what was called the Minnesota Starvation Experiment, and 36 men were chosen as participants. Participants were reduced to near-starvation status and on average lost one-fourth of their pre-study weight. Then, various feeding programs were introduced to try to assess their effectiveness. The results of this study were helpful in treating victims of World War II famines. Participation was voluntary, and the participants were informed of the risks involved in participation. There clearly were risks to the long-term health of the participants, but many participated because they believed that doing so would help improve the situation of famine victims.[130]

An Approach to Sensitive Topics: The Randomized Response Technique and Abortion

Sometimes a subject is considered extremely sensitive, but there are strong reasons to want to know something about the behavior. The randomized response technique was developed in the 1960s.[131] It has been used to study several sensitive topics, including cheating on exams[132] and illegal drug use.[133] It also has been used since the late 1960s to study abortion, which was not legal in the United States until 1973 and remained a topic of shame for many women long after 1973.[134]

In the randomized response technique, there are two alternative questions: one that is sensitive, such as "Have you had an abortion in the last 12 months?" and one that is not sensitive, such as "Were you born in April?" One question had a red ball by it, and the other question had a blue ball by it. There is a clear box containing both red and blue balls. The respondent shakes the box, and one ball comes out. If it is a red ball, the respondent answers one question, and if it is a blue ball, the respondent answers the other question. The interviewer cannot see which color ball the respondent drew.

If the frequency of answers to the nonsensitive question ("Were you born in April?") is known, and since the proportion of balls in the box that are red is known, the answers from a large group of respondents can be used to calculate the percentage who replied they had an abortion in the last year. The respondent needs to believe that the interviewer does not know which ball was chosen and that the interviewer does not know the answer to the nonsensitive question for individual respondents. A fairly large sample size is necessary to make reliable estimates.

In a randomized response study in 1968 of abortion in the previous year among women age 18–44 in urban North Carolina, it was estimated that 1.4% of White women and 6.8% of non-White women had an abortion in the previous year. Questions were also asked about whether the respondent thought her friends would reply truthfully to a direct question about their abortion experience, and 67% responded, "No." When a question was also asked about whether the respondent thought other people would think there was a trick employed in the technique,

60% replied, "No," and an additional 20% were undecided. The abortion estimates from this study probably were low, but they likely were closer to the actual situation than would have been obtained from direct questions about abortion.

Protecting Respondent Identity

A principle of protection of human subjects is to keep the identity of respondents in censuses and surveys confidential. A number of approaches are used to achieve this result, including reporting ages in intervals, such as 5-year age groups, or slightly adjusting the ages of individuals. The slight adjustment of ages can sometimes lead to anomalous results, such as implausible sex ratios (the ratio of the number of males to the number of females).[135] Adjustment of the reported data to mask the identity of those over age 65 can also lead to inaccurate estimates of characteristics of the elderly, such as their income.[136]

To preserve the confidentiality of survey respondents, often there is masking of the detailed geographic location of the respondent.[137] Thus, information might be available only at the level of the county or the state of residence of the respondent. This does not cause a problem if a researcher does not require any more detailed information about geographic location for the planned analysis. However, researchers have increasingly incorporated detailed information about the characteristics of small geographic areas in analysis of a variety of research questions. For example, researchers who wish to identify clusters of people with particular diseases need very detailed geographic information to do so.[138] A researcher can apply to the body that controls the data and ask for more detailed information. If the controlling body sees the proposed research as sufficiently valuable, the researcher could obtain the more detailed data, but the approval process can take a long time and is often not successful.

Respondent Confidentiality and Biological Samples

As population surveys have begun to collect biological samples, such as urine, saliva, and blood, and with advances in DNA analysis, new concerns about respondent confidentiality have been raised. Additional safeguards have been implemented for release of data, and strong controls on the security of the biological samples have been implemented.[139]

CONCLUDING COMMENTS

In this chapter, the sources of demographic data and some problems and concerns with data quality and with ethical issues in data collection have been discussed. Data are needed for planning and policy development. Improvements in surveys and the integration of social and biomedical information lay the groundwork for a much fuller understanding of the causes of disease and death, as well as of fertility and migration behavior. As data sources become more numerous and data quality improves in less developed countries, the basis for planning and policy development will also improve for those countries. At the same time, attention to the protection of individuals supplying information will continue to be important.

☑ Study and Review Online

SUMMARY

1. The main sources of demographic data are censuses, vital registration, population registers, and surveys.

2. Data from vital registration and a census are combined to calculate birth and death rates.

3. Censuses are conducted every 5 or 10 years and aim to enumerate all persons in a country.

4. A census focuses either on the de facto (present) population or the de jure (permanent) population. Which population base is used makes a difference. Which population base is appropriate depends on the question being investigated.

5. Censuses are either self-administered or enumerator administered. If a self-administered census form is not returned, often an enumerator visits the household. Whether a census is self-administered depends partially on population characteristics, such as the educational level of the population.

6. All censuses miss some people. People who are mobile, such as young adults and those who dwell in nonstandard locations, such as behind a store, are often missed. Often, the poor and members of minority groups also are missed. People who wish to avoid the authorities or not to cooperate with authorities are often missed, which includes undocumented migrants.

7. Census counts influence allocation of funds to localities and allocation of seats in legislative bodies in the United States and other countries. Thus, the count and the estimated undercount are matters of great political concern in both more developed and less developed countries.

8. Population registers keep a continuously updated record of the population of a country. Some countries have abandoned conducting censuses and rely on tabulations from the population register as a substitute for a census. Often, data from other administrative sources are combined with population register data.

9. Population registers record only the de jure population and work best where the population is relatively homogeneous and is not very geographically mobile.

10. In some parts of the world, registration of births and deaths is mainly for the purpose of assuring that only people who are qualified for various official documents actually receive these documents. This is a different consideration than assuring that all births and deaths are registered to contribute to high-quality population statistics.

11. Surveys can be either cross-sectional or longitudinal. Cross-sectional surveys interview a new set of persons or households each time. Longitudinal households interview the same persons or households repeatedly.

12. In less developed countries, population surveys are often done when there is not a sufficient system of censuses and vital statistics to generate demographic estimates. Often, it is a question of preferring to know something rather than to know nothing. In less developed countries, population surveys are also done to obtain data not available in censuses.

13. In more developed countries, population surveys are done to generate more detailed and more frequent data than are available from the census.

14. In the United States, the American Community Survey (ACS) replaced the long form of the U.S. Census in 2010. The results of the ACS cannot be used to allocate members of the House of Representatives among states, but the ACS results can be used as the basis of distributing a wide variety of government funds.

15. Useful population data can come from administrative sources, such as school enrollment or tax, utilities, or immigration records, and from historical sources, such as church parish registers.

16. There has been increasingly systematic collection of data about the Hispanic population of the United States over time. By 2010, the Hispanic population was larger than the African-American population.

17. The percentage of the population of the United States composed of non-Hispanic Whites has fallen over time. In several states and metropolitan areas, non-Hispanic Whites comprise less than half of all children.

18. The collection of data about race and ethnicity in censuses and surveys has been a subject of controversy.

19. Ethical issues in data collection have become an increasing concern. The United States and many

other countries have strict rules about the release of government-collected data that could identify respondents. Surveys in the United States and other countries must pass a review to assure that respondents are subject to no risk or minimal risk related to possible trauma from data collection or to the possibility of others finding out embarrassing or harmful information about respondents.

KEY TERMS

census 66
vital statistics 67
population register 67
survey 67
population 67
de facto population 67

de jure population 67
household 69
institution 70
group quarters 70
net percent undercount 71
post-enumeration survey 73

live birth 77
death 78
cross-sectional survey 79
longitudinal survey 79
human subjects 93

QUESTIONS FOR DISCUSSION AND REVIEW

1. What are the reasons why surveys are used to collect demographic data? How do these reasons differ between more developed countries and less developed countries?

2. What difference can it make whether a census operates primarily on a de facto or primarily on a de jure basis? Does it matter for the size of the total population? Does it matter for estimates of the size of the urban population? Does it matter for the distribution of members of ethnic groups?

3. Why do political considerations arise in the collection of demographic data?

4. Why are concerns about the protection of human subjects in demographic research important? Is there too much concern or not enough concern about this area?

5. Is it a good idea to collect data on the racial and ethnic composition of a population, or does this just create problems and generate animosity?

NOTES

1. This section is from Barbara A. Anderson and Brian D. Silver. 1985. "'Permanent' and 'Present' Populations in Soviet Statistics," *Soviet Studies,* 37: 386–402.

2. The capital of Kazakhstan was changed from Alma-Ata to Astana in 1997.

3. Turkey, Census of Population. 2000. *Social and Economic Characteristics of Population, Turkey,* http://www.turkstat.gov.tr/Kitap .do?metod=KitapDetay&KT_ID=11&KITAP_ ID=12 (accessed October 22, 2013); and Integrated European Census Microdata, http:// www.iecm-project.org/index.php?module= metadata&c=tur (accessed June 20, 2011).

4. U.S. Census Bureau. 2010. *The 2010 Census: How People Are Counted,* http://2010.census .gov/partners/pdf/brochure_NHPI_How PeopleAreCounted.pdf (accessed July 17, 2010).

5. Sam Roberts. 2008. "Census Bureau's Counting of Prisoners Benefits Some Rural Voting Districts," *New York Times,* October 23, http://www.nytimes.com/2008/10/24/us /politics/24census.html (accessed February 12, 2011).

6. Kamika Dunlap. 2010. "New Maryland Law Changes Prisoner Census Head Count," http:// blogs.findlaw.com/blotter/2010/04/new-mary land-law-changes-prisoner-census-head-count .html (accessed February 12, 2011).

7. D'Vera Cohn. 2010. *The Census: College Students Count—but Where?* Pew Research Center Publications, http://pewresearch.org/pubs/1525 /census-college-students-where-to-count-them (accessed February 12, 2011); Kristen Mack. 2010. "Clear Census Lines for College Students: Students Should Be Counted Where They Spend Majority of Time," *Chicago Tribune,* March 18, http://articles.chicagotribune .com/2010-03-18/news/ct-met-census-q-and- a-20100318_1_census-bureau-census-counts- census-taker (accessed February 12, 2011); and Tamar Lewin. 2008. "Voter Registration by Students Raises Cloud of Consequences," *New York Times,* September 7, http://www.nytimes .com/2008/09/08/education/08students .html?_r=1&scp=1&sq=college%20students%20 voting%20local%20elections&st=cse (accessed February 12, 2011).

8. United Nations. 1969. *Principles and Recommendations for the 1970 Population Censuses*, 2nd printing, New York: United Nations, 14, http://unstats.un.org/unsd/demographic/standmeth/principles/Series_M44v2en.pdf (accessed December 7, 2011).

9. Elizabeth Martin. 1999. "Who Knows Who Lives Here? Within-Household Disagreements as a Source of Survey Coverage Error," *The Public Opinion Quarterly*, 63: 220–236; and Barbara A. Anderson and Brian D. Silver, 1987. "The Validity of Survey Responses: Insights from Interviews of Married Couples in a Survey of Soviet Emigrants," *Social Forces*, 66: 537–554.

10. U.S. Census Bureau, *Households, Persons per Household, and Households with Individuals under 18 Years*, http://quickfacts.census.gov/qfd/meta/long_HSD410209.htm (accessed September 7, 2011).

11. U.S. Census Bureau. 2007 *American Community Survey Group Quarters Definitions*, http://www.census.gov/acs/www/Downloads/data_documentation/GroupDefinitions/2007GQ_Definitions.pdf (accessed September 7, 2011).

12. U.S. Census Bureau. *Group Quarters Population by Race and Hispanic Origin: 2000*, http://www.census.gov/population/www/cen2000/briefs/phc-t7/index.html (accessed September 7, 2011).

13. U.S. Census Bureau. *Fact Sheets for Partners*, http://2010.census.gov/partners/materials/outreach-materials.php (accessed February 18, 2011); and U.S. Census Bureau, "Partners Home," http://2010.census.gov/partners/ (accessed February 18, 2011).

14. Australia, Australian Bureau of Statistics. 1997. *Information Paper: Census of Population and Housing: Data Quality—Undercount 1996*, Canberra: Australian Bureau of Statistics.

15. Sources for Figures 3.2 and 3.3: J. Gregory Robinson, Bashir Ahmed, Prithwis Das Gupta, and Karen A. Woodrow. 1993. "Estimation of Population Coverage in the 1990 United States Census Based on Demographic Analysis," *Journal of the American Statistical Association*, 88: 1061–1071; J. Gregory Robinson, Kirsten K. West, and Arjun Adlakha. 2002. "Coverage of the Population in Census 2000: Results from Demographic Analysis," *Population Research and Policy Review*, 21: 19–38; U.S. Census Bureau 2010. *2010 Demographic Analysis Estimates*, http://www.census.gov/newsroom/releases/archives/news_conferences/120610_demoanalysis.html (accessed July 23, 2011); and Thomas Mule. 2012. *Census Coverage Measurement Estimation Report*, U.S. Census Bureau, http://2010.census.gov/news/pdf/g-01.pdf (accessed June 12, 2012).

16. As of June 2012, undercount estimates by race and sex for the 2010 U.S. Census had not been published.

17. William R. Bell. 1993. "Using Information from Demographic Analysis in Post-Enumeration Survey Estimation," *Journal of the American Statistical Association*, 89: 1106–1118.

18. Linda Greenhouse. 2001. "Justices Deal Utah a Setback in Its Bid to Gain a House Seat," New York Times, November 27, http://www.nytimes.com/2001/11/27/us/justices-deal-utah-a-setback-in-its-bid-to-gain-a-house-seat.html?scp=1&sq=utah%20mormon%20abroad%20census&st=cse (accessed June 14, 2010).

19. Nichole M. Christian. 2000. "All-Out Fight in Detroit to Keep Census above a Million," New York Times, May 2, http://www.nytimes.com/2000/05/02/us/all-out-fight-in-detroit-to-keep-census-above-amillion.html?pagewanted=all (accessed June 9, 2010).

20. The United States Conference of Mayors. 1999. *The Fiscal Impact of the Census Undercount on Cities: A 34-City Survey January 1999. Findings*, http://www.usmayors.org/ced/census/census_findings.htm (accessed June 11, 2010).

21. Harold Wolman, Todd Swanstrom, and Margaret Weir. 2003. *Cities and State Legislatures: Changing Coalitions and the Metropolitan Agenda*, George Washington Institute of Public Policy Working Paper no. 3, http://www.gwu.edu/~gwipp/papers/wp003.pdf (accessed July 23, 2011).

22. Michigan Legislature. 2002. *2001 Public Acts*, http://www.legislature.mi.gov/documents/2001-2002/publicacttable/PDF/2001-PAT.PDF (accessed August 31, 2011).

23. Michigan Office of the Governor. 2011. *Detroit Tax Bills Signed into Law; Governor Says Bipartisan Legislation Shows Support for City*, June 9, http://www.michigan.gov/snyder/0,1607,7-277-257641-,00.html (accessed July 23, 2011).

24. "Exodus from a Neglected American City," *The Independent*, http://www.independent.co.uk/opinion/leading-articles/leading-article-exodus-from-a-neglected-american-city-2204988.html# (accessed February 12, 2011); and John Grand. 2006. "Tax Increment Financing: Louisiana Goes Fishing for New Business," *Louisiana Law Review*, 66: 851–884, http://digitalcommons.law.lsu.edu/cgi/viewcontent.cgi?article=6141&context=lalrev (accessed March 23, 2013).

25. Personal communication, Bryan Vincent, division director, Government Affairs Division, House Legislative Services, State of Louisiana, July 28, 2011.

26. Lawrence D. Brown, Morris L. Eaton, David A. Freedman, Stephen P. Klein, Richard A. Olshen,

Kenneth W. Wachter, Martin T. Wells, and Donald Ylvisaker. 1999. "Statistical Controversies in Census 2000," *Jurimetrics*, 39: 347–375.

27. Document. 1996. "The Supreme Court on the Adjustment of the US Census," *Population and Development Review*, 22: 399–405.

28. Nathaniel Persily. 2011. "The Law of the Census: How to Count, What to Count, Whom to Count, and Where to Count Them," *Cardozo Legal Review*, 32: 755–789.

29. Matthew Hannah. 2008. "Mapping the Under-Scrutinized: The West German Census Boycott Movement of 1987 and the Dangers of Information-Based Security," in *Geospatial Technologies and Homeland Security*, ed. Daniel Z. Sui, 301–314, http://www.springerlink.com /content/T71050PV30044788 (accessed June 14, 2010); and Gerrit Hornung and Christoph Schnabel. 2009. "Data Protection in Germany I: The Population Census Decision and the Right to Informational Self-Determination," *Computer Law & Security Report*, 25: 84–88, http://www.sciencedirect.com/science?_ ob=ArticleURL&_udi=B6VB3-4TY9MVH-2&_ user=99318&_coverDate=12%2F31%2F2009& _rdoc=1&_fmt=high&_orig=search&_ sort=d&_docanchor=&view=c&_search StrId=1369524129&_rerunOrigin=google&_ acct=C000007678&_version=1&_urlVersion=0&_ userid=99318&md5=9c42801e945751958b2bf48 c1c7cf01b (accessed June 14, 2010).

30. BBC News. 2010. "National Census in 2011 Could Be Last of Its Kind," July 10, http://www .bbc.co.uk/news/10584385 (accessed June 20, 2011); and Danny Dorling. 2013. "Local Government without the Census—It's a Frightening Vision," *The Guardian*, http://www.guardian .co.uk/local-government-network/2013 /jan/24/local-government-without-census-frightening (accessed March 23, 2013).

31. K. S. Gnanasekaran and Alice Clague. 1986. "Population Census Evaluation in the 1980 Round: National Practices and Issues," *Proceedings of the Social Research and Methodology Section of the American Statistical Association*, 128–137.

32. IRIN Africa. 2008. "Sudan: Census Setback as Count Postponed Again," April 14, http://www .irinnews.org/Report/77751/SUDAN-Census-setback-as-count-postponed-again (accessed March 23, 2013); XINHUA. 2012. "Uganda Postpones National Census Due to Lack of Funds," Africa Review, May 19, http://www.africareview .com/News/Uganda-postpones-census-over-cash-crunch/-/979180/1409240/-/o87bouz /-/index.html (accessed March 23, 2013); Reuters. 2013. "Bosnia Delays First Postwar Census as Regions Fail to Cooperate," January 23, http://www.reuters.com/article/2013/01/23 /us-bosnia-census-idUSBRE90M1AH20130123 (accessed March 23, 2013); and Richard Leete. 2001. *Funding Crisis in the 2000 Round of Population Censuses.* Pretoria: UNFPA, www.paris21.org/sites /default/files/985.ppt (accessed March 23, 2013).

33. Babatunde A. Ahonsi. 1988. "Deliberate Falsification and Census Data in Nigeria," *African Affairs*, 87: 553–562. S. A. Aluko. 1965. "How Many Nigerians? An Analysis of Nigeria's Census Problems, 1901–63," *The Journal of Modern African Studies*, 3: 371–392.

34. Andrew Rigby. 2000. "Lebanon: Patterns of Confessional Politics," *Parliamentary Affairs*, 53: 169–180; and Arnon Soffer. 1986. "Lebanon: Where Demography Is the Core of Politics and Life," *Middle Eastern Studies*, 22: 197–205.

35. Muhammad Faour. 1991. "The Demography of Lebanon: A Reappraisal," *Middle Eastern Studies*, 27: 631–641.

36. *Mail & Guardian Online* (South Africa). 2011. "Bushmen Boycott Botswana Census," June 27, http://mg.co.za/article/2011-06-27-bushmen-boycott-botswana-census (accessed September 7, 2011); *Mail & Guardian Online* (South Africa). 2010. "Kalahari Bushmen Win Appeal," January 28, http://mg.co.za/article/2011-01-28-kalahari-bushmen-win-appeal (accessed September 7, 2011); and Portal to Africa. 2011. "Botswana: Botswana's Bushmen Boycott Census," August 20, http:// portaltoafrica.com/news/africa/general /botswanas-bushmen-boycott-census/ (accessed September 7, 2011).

37. World Health Organization. *Health Status Statistics: Mortality*, http://www.who.int/healthinfo /statistics/indneonatalmortality/en/ (accessed September 2, 2011).

38. Robert J. Armstrong. 1972. *A Study of Infant Mortality from Linked Records by Birth weight, Period of Gestation and Other Variables: United States, 1960 Live Birth Cohort*, Vital and Health Statistics Series 20, no. 12. http://stacks.cdc.gov/view /cdc/12875 (accessed November 14, 2013).

39. Marian F. MacDorman and T. J. Mathews. 2009. *Behind International Rankings of Infant Mortality: How the United States Compares with Europe*, NCHS Data Brief, no. 23, http://www.cdc.gov/nchs/data/data-briefs/db23.pdf (accessed September 4, 2011).

40. Michael S. Kramer, Robert W. Platt, Hong Yang, Bengt Haglund, Sven Cnattingius, and Per Bergsjo. 2002. "Registration Artifacts in International Comparisons of Infant Mortality," *Obstetrical & Gynecological Survey*, 57: 429–430.

41. Barbara A. Anderson and Brian D. Silver. 1986. "Infant Mortality in the Soviet Union: Regional Differences and Measurement Issues," *Population and Development Review*, 12: 705–738.

42. World Bank. 2011. *Indicators, Completeness of Birth Registration*, http://data.worldbank.org/indicator/SP.REG.BRTH.ZS (accessed September 4, 2011).

43. UNICEF. 2002. "Birth Registration: Right from the Start," *Innocenti Digest*, no. 9, March, http://www.childinfo.org/files/birthregistration_Digestenglish.pdf (accessed March 23, 2013).

44. U.S. Legal. *Brain Death Law & Legal Definition*, http://definitions.uslegal.com/b/brain-death (accessed September 7, 2011).

45. The President's Council on Bioethics. 2009. "Terminology," *Controversies in the Determination of Death*, http://bioethics.georgetown.edu/pcbe/reports/death/chapter2.html (accessed September 7, 2011).

46. WHO. 2006. "Table 3: Estimated Completeness of Mortality Data for Latest Year," http://apps.who.int/whosis/database/mort/table3.cfm (accessed September 4, 2011).

47. International Institute for Vital Registration and Statistics. 1995. *Organization of National Civil Registration and Vital Statistics Systems: An Update*, IIVRS Technical Paper no. 63, http://unstats.un.org/unsd/demographic/CRVS/IIVRS%20papers/IIVRS_paper63.pdf (accessed June 20, 2011).

48. Barbara A. Anderson and Brian D. Silver. 1988. "The Effects of the Registration System on the Seasonality of Births: The Case of the Soviet Union," *Population Studies*, 42: 303–320.

49. Guangyu Zhang and Zhongwei Zhao. 2005. "Searching for the Answer to China's Fertility Puzzle: Data Collection and Data Use in the Last Two Decades," paper presented at the annual meeting of the Population Association of America, http://paa2005.princeton.edu/download.aspx?submissionId=50430 (accessed June 20, 2011); Barbara A. Anderson and Brian D. Silver. 1995. "Ethnic Differences in Fertility and Sex Ratios at Birth in China: Evidence from Xinjiang," *Population Studies*, 49: 211–226; and Barbara A. Anderson and Jinyun Liu. 1997. "Son Preference and Excess Female Infant Mortality among Koreans and non-Koreans in Yanbian Prefecture, Jilin Province, China, with Implications for the Republic of Korea," in *Population Process and Dynamics for Koreans in Korea and China*, ed. Doo-Sub Kim and Barbara A. Anderson, Seoul: Hanyang University Press, 189–243.

50. Jin Ho Choi. 1981. *Determinants and Consequences of Urban to Rural Return Migration in Korea*, doctoral dissertation, Department of Sociology, Brown University, Providence, RI.

51. Manuela Lenk. 2009. *Methods of Register-based Census in Austria*, Statistik Austria, http://unstats.un.org/unsd/statcom/statcom_09/seminars/innovation/Innovation%20Seminar/StatisticsAustria_register%20based%20census.pdf (accessed November 24, 2010).

52. The Norwegian Historical Data Centre. *Documenting the Norwegian Censuses*, http://www.rhd.uit.no/nhdc/census.html (accessed July 23, 2011); and Statistics Norway. 2005. *Plans for 2010 Population and Housing Census in Norway*, http://unstats.un.org/unsd/demographic/sources/census/2010_PHC/Norway/PHC.pdf (accessed July 23, 2011).

53. Lars Borchsenius. 2000. "From a Conventional to a Register-Based Census of Population," Eurostat Seminar on the Censuses after 2001, Paris, November 20–21, http://www.insee.fr/en/insee-statistique-publique/colloques/insee-eurostat/pdf/borchsenius.pdf (accessed November 2, 2011).

54. United Nations. 1983. *Manual X: Indirect Techniques for Demographic Estimation*, New York: United Nations; United Nations. 2002. *Methods for Estimating Adult Mortality*, New York: United Nations; William Brass, Ansley J. Coale, Paul Demeny, Don F. Heisel, Frank Lorimer, Anbatole Romaniuk and Etienne van de Walle. 1968. *The Demography of Tropical Africa*, Princeton, NJ: Princeton University Press.

55. William G. Axinn, Thomas E. Fricke, and Arland Thornton. 1991. "The Microdemographic Community-Study Approach: Improving Survey Data by Integrating the Ethnographic Method," *Sociological Methods & Research*, 20: 187–217.

56. Dayalal Abeysekera. 1980. *Determinants and Consequences of Internal Migration: The Rural Wet Zone to Rural Dry Zone in Sri Lanka*, doctoral dissertation, Department of Sociology, Brown University, Providence, RI.

57. Frank Baiden, Abraham Hodgson, and Fred N. Binka. 2006. "Demographic Surveillance Sites and Emerging Challenges in International Health," Editorial, *Bulletin of the World Health Organization*, 86: 163–164; and Daniel Chandramohan, Kenji Shibuya, Philip Setel, Sandy Cairncross, Alan D. Lopez, Christopher J. L. Murray, Basia Żaba, Robert W. Snow, and Fred Bink. 2008. "Should Data from Demographic Surveillance Systems Be Made More Widely Available to Researchers?" *PLoS Medicine*, 5: 0169–0170.

58. Abdur Razzaque and Peter Kim Streatfield. "Matlab DSS Bangladesh," *Indepth Monograph*, vol. 1, pt. C, http://www.indepth-network.org/dss_site_profiles/matlab.pdf (accessed July 2, 2011).

59. Pradip K. Muhuri and Samuel H. Preston. 1991. "Effects of Family Composition on Mortality Differentials by Sex among Children in Matlab, Bangladesh," *Population and Development Review*, 17: 415–434; Mahbub Elahi Chowdhury, Roslin

Botlero, Marge Koblinsky, Sajal Jumar Saha, Greet Dieltiens, and Carine Ronsmans. 2007. "Determinants of Reduction in Maternal Mortality in Matlab, Bangladesh: A 30-year Cohort Study," *The Lancet*, 370: 1320–1328; and Jeroen van Ginneken and Abdur Razzaque. 2004. "Supply and Demand Factors in the Fertility Decline in Matlab, Bangladesh in 1977–1999," *European Journal of Population*, 19: 29–45.

60. INDEPTH Network. http://www.indepth-network.org (accessed July 2, 2011).
61. J. Timothy Sprehe. 1974. "The World Fertility Survey: An International Program of Fertility Research," *Studies in Family Planning*, 5: 35–41; and Measure DHS, "Demographic and Health Surveys," http://www.measuredhs.com /aboutdhs/history.cfm (accessed July 9, 2011).
62. Limin Wang. 2003. "Determinants of Child Mortality in LDCs: Empirical Findings from Demographic and Health Surveys," *Health Policy*, 65: 277–299; Frederick Mugisha. 2006. "School Enrollment among Urban Non-slum, Slum and Rural Children in Kenya: Is the Urban Advantage Eroding?" *International Journal of Educational Development*, 26: 471–482; Deon Filmer. 2005. "Fever and Its Treatment among the More and Less Poor in Sub-Saharan Africa," *Health Policy Plan*, 20: 337–346; and C. B. Lloyd and B. S. Mensch. 2008. "Marriage and Childbirth as Factors in Dropping Out from School: An Analysis of DHS Data from Sub-Saharan Africa," *Population Studies*, 62: 1–13.
63. The Current Population Survey website, which has a wide range of information about the survey, is available at http://www.census.gov/cps (accessed October 1, 2011).
64. The U.S. Census Bureau American Community Survey website, with a wide range of information about the survey, is available at http://www .census.gov/acs/www/ (accessed July 9, 2011).
65. Andrew D. Reamer. 2010. *Surveying for Dollars: The Role of the American Community Survey in the Geographic Distribution of Federal Funds*, Brookings Institution, Metropolitan Policy Program, http:// www.brookings.edu/reports/2010/0726_acs_reamer.aspx (accessed August 28, 2011).
66. The Panel Study of Income Dynamics website, with a wide range of information about the survey, is available at http://psidonline.isr.umich .edu (accessed October 1, 2011); and Katherine A. McGonagle and Robert F. Schoeni. 2006. "The Panel Study of Income Dynamics: Overview & Summary of Scientific Contributions after Nearly 40 Years," paper presented at *Conference on Longitudinal Social and Health Surveys in an International Perspective*, Montreal, January 25–27, http://www.ciqss.umontreal.ca/Longit/Doc /Robert_Schoeni.pdf (accessed December 8, 2011).
67. The National Health Interview Survey website, with a wide range of information about the survey, is available at http://www.cdc.gov/nchs /nhis.htm (accessed October 1, 2011).
68. National Survey of Family Growth website, with a wide range of information about the survey, is available at http://www.cdc.gov/nchs/nsfg.htm (accessed October 1, 2011).
69. The NSFG website, with a wide range of information about the survey, is available at http://www .ssc.wisc.edu/nsfh/ (accessed December 14, 2011).
70. The National Health and Nutritional Examination Survey, with a wide range of information about the survey, is available at http://www.cdc.gov/nchs /nhanes.htm (accessed October 1, 2011).
71. The SIPP website, with a wide range of information about the survey, is available at http://www .census.gov/sipp/index.html (accessed October 2, 2011).
72. The National Longitudinal Surveys website, with a wide range of information about the surveys, is available at http://www.bls.gov/nls/home.htm (accessed October 1, 2011). There is also useful information about the NLS at the Center for Human Resource Research, http://www.chrr.ohio-state.edu/about-us (accessed October 1, 2011).
73. The Monitoring the Future website, with a wide range of information about the survey, is available at http://monitoringthefuture.org (accessed October 1, 2011).
74. The National Longitudinal Survey of Adolescent Health website, with a wide range of information about the survey, is available at http:// www.cpc.unc.edu/projects/addhealth (accessed October 1, 2011).
75. The HRS website, with a wide range of information about the survey, is available at http://hrsonline.isr.umich.edu (accessed October 1, 2011).
76. The Program of Research on Black Americans has substantial information about NSBA and NSAL and is available at http://www.rcgd.isr .umich.edu/prba/ (accessed October 2, 2011).
77. The New Immigrant Survey website, with a wide range of information about the survey, is available at http://nis.princeton.edu/index.html (accessed October 11, 2011).
78. Information about NHATS is available at http:// www.nhats.org (accessed April 11, 2012).
79. Edward Anthony Wrigley. 1997. *English Population History from Family Reconstitution, 1580–1837*, Cambridge: Cambridge University Press.
80. James Z. Lee and Cameron D. Campbell. 1997. *Fate and Fortune in Rural China: Social Organization and Population Behavior in Liaoning 1774–1873*, Cambridge: Cambridge University Press.

81. Thomas C. Smith. 1977. *Nakahara: Family Farming and Population in a Japanese Village, 1717–1830*, Palo Alto, CA: Stanford University Press.

82. J. Gibbs, G. Harper, M. Rubin, and H. Shin. 2003. *Evaluating Components of International Migration: Native-Born Emigrants*, Population Division Working Paper no. 63, U.S. Census Bureau; and Haroon Bhorat, Jean-Baptiste Meyer, and Cecil Mlatsheni. 2002. *Skilled Labour Migration from Developing Countries: Study on South and Southern Africa*, International Migration Papers no. 52, Geneva: International Labour Office, http://www.ilo.int/public/english/protection/migrant/download/imp/imp52e.pdf (accessed September 4, 2011).

83. Allison Plyer, Joy Bonaguro, and Ken Hodges. 2010. "Using Administrative Data to Estimate Population Displacement and Resettlement Following a Catastrophic U.S. Disaster," *Population & Environment*, 31: 150–175.

84. 13 U.S.C. §6. "US Code—Section 6: Information from Other Federal Departments and Agencies; Acquisition of Reports from Other Governmental and Private Sources."

85. UNAIDS. "Q + A on India's Revised AIDS Estimates," http://data.unaids.org/pub/Information-Note/2007/070701_india%20external_qa_en.pdf (accessed June 8, 2010); UNAIDS. "2.5 Million People Living with HIV in India," http://www.unaids.org/en/KnowledgeCentre/Resources/FeatureStories/archive/2007/20070704_India_new_data.asp (accessed October 29, 2013); and Robert Steinbrook. 2008. "HIV in India: A Downsized Epidemic," *New England Journal of Medicine*, 358: 107–109.

86. David L. Kertzer and Dominique Arel, eds. 2002. *Census and Identity: The Politics of Race, Ethnicity and Language in National Censuses*, Cambridge: Cambridge University Press.

87. Karen R. Humes, Nicholas A. Jones, and Roberto R. Ramirez. 2011. "Overview of Race and Hispanic Origin: 2010," *2010 Census Briefs*, http://www.census.gov/prod/cen2010/briefs/c2010br-02.pdf (accessed July 23, 2011).

88. Sara Sidner. "Caste Question on Census Angers Indians," CNN, http://www.cnn.com/2010/WORLD/asiapcf/06/27/india.census.caste/index.html?iref=allsearch (accessed September 11, 2010); and Harmeet Shah Singh, "India Revives Colonial-Era Caste Count," CNN, http://www.cnn.com/2010/WORLD/asiapcf/09/10/india.caste.count/index.html?iref=allsearch (accessed September 11, 2010).

89. Lydia Polgreen. 2010. "Business Class Rises in Ashes of Caste System," *New York Times*, September 10, http://www.nytimes.com/2010/09/11/world/asia/11caste.html?_r=1&hp (accessed September 11, 2010).

90. Jack Bloom. 2010. "Away with Race Classification," Politicsweb, http://www.politicsweb.co.za/politicsweb/view/politicsweb/en/page71619?oid=190845&sn=Marketingweb+detail (accessed August 21, 2010).

91. Peter L. Berger and Thomas Luckman. 1966. *The Social Construction of Reality: A Treatise on the Sociology of Knowledge*, New York: Irvington; Ian F. Haney Lopez. 1994. "The Social Construction of Race: Some Observations on Illusion, Fabrication, and Choice," *Harvard Civil Rights-Civil Liberties Law Review*, 29: 1–62; Romana Hasnain-Wynia and David W. Baker. 2006. "Obtaining Data on Patient Race, Ethnicity, and Primary Language in Health Care Organizations: Current Challenges and Proposed Solutions," *Health Services Research*, 41: 1501–1518; Sari Siegel, Ernest Moy, and Helen Burstin. 2004. "Assessing the Nation's Progress toward Elimination of Disparities in Health Care," *Journal of General Internal Medicine*, 19: 195–200; and C. D. Lee. 2007. *Culture, Literacy and Learning: Taking Bloom in the Midst of the Whirlwind*, New York: Teachers College Press.

92. David L. Word and R. Colby Perkins Jr. 1996. *Building a Spanish Surname List for the 1990's: A New Approach to an Old Problem*, Technical Working Paper no. 13, Washington, DC: U.S. Census Bureau, https://www.census.gov/population/documentation/twpno13.pdf (accessed October 4, 2012).

93. C. Matthew Snipp. 2003. "Racial Measurement in the American Census: Past Practices and Implications for the Future," *Annual Review of Sociology*, 29: 563–588; and Karen R. Humes, Nicholas A. Jones, and Roberto R. Ramirez. 2011. "Overview of Race and Hispanic Origin: 2010," *2010 Census Briefs*, http://www.census.gov/prod/cen2010/briefs/c2010br-02.pdf (accessed July 23, 2011).

94. Joel Perlmann and Mary C. Waters, eds. 2002. *The New Race Question: How the Census Counts Multiracial Individuals*, New York: Russell Sage Foundation.

95. Guillermo Fuenfrios. 1972. "The Emergence of the New Chicano," in *Axtlan: An Anthology of Mexican American Literature*, ed. Luis Valdez and Stan Steiner, New York: Vintage Books.

96. cf. Justin O'Brien. 2011. "Census Shows Hispanics Now Largest Ethnic Minority Other Surveys: Latino Population Increases Will Continue," U.S. Conference of Mayors, http://www.usmayors.org/usmayornewspaper/documents/04_16_01/census.asp (accessed July 11, 2011).

97. Karen R. Humes, Nicholas A. Jones, and Roberto R. Ramirez. 2011. "Overview of Race and Hispanic Origin: 2010," *2010 Census Briefs*, http://www.census.gov/prod/cen2010/briefs/c2010br-02.pdf (accessed July 23, 2011).

98. Carolyn A. Liebler and Andrew Halpern-Manners. 2008. "A Practical Approach to Using Multiple-Race Response Data: A Bridging Methods for Public-Use Microdata," *Demography*, 45: 143–155.

99. C. G. Scott. 1999. "Identifying the Race or Ethnicity of SSI Recipients," *Social Security Bulletin*, 62: 9–20.

100. D. D. Ingram, J. D. Parker, N. Schenker, J. A. Weed, B. Hamilton, E. Arias, and J. H. Madans. 2003. *United States Census 2000 Population with Bridged Race Categories*, National Center for Health Statistics. Vital and Health Statistics, http://www.cdc.gov/nchs/data/series/sr_02/sr02_135.pdf (accessed November 5, 2011); and Carolyn A. Liebler and Andrew Halpern-Manners. 2008. "A Practical Approach to Using Multiple-Race Response Data: A Bridging Methods for Public-Use Microdata," *Demography*, 45: 143–155.

101. Jonathan R. Sugarman, Robert Soderberg, Jane E. Gordon, and Frederick P. Rivara. 1983. "Racial Misclassification of American Indians: Its Effect on Injury Rates in Oregon, 1989–1990," *American Journal of Public Health*, 83: 681–684.

102. Russell Thornton. 1977. "Tribal Membership Requirements and the Demography of 'Old' and 'New' Native Americans," *Population Research and Policy Review*, 16: 33–42.

103. Alex Kellogg. 2011. "Cherokee Nation Faces Scrutiny for Expelling Blacks," September 19, NPR, http://www.npr.org/2011/09/19/140594124/u-s-government-opposes-cherokee-nations-decision (accessed September 20, 2011).

104. James Dao. 2011. "In California, Indian Tribes with Casino Money Cast Off Members," *New York Times*, December 12, http://www.nytimes.com/2011/12/13/us/california-indian-tribes-eject-thousands-of-members.html?_r=1&hp (accessed December 13, 2011).

105. Campbell Gibson and Kay Jung. 2005. *Historical Census Statistics on Population Totals by Race, 1790 to 1990, and by Hispanic Origin, 1970 to 1990, for Large Cities and Other Urban Places in the United States*, Population Division Working Paper, Washington, DC: U.S. Census Bureau, http://www.census.gov/population/www/documentation/twps0076/twps0076.html (accessed October 8, 2012); and U.S. Census Bureau. 2012. *The 2012 Statistical Abstract: The National Data Book*, Washington, DC: U.S. Census Bureau, Tables 10 and 12, http://www.census.gov/prod/2011pubs/12statab/pop.pdf (accessed October 8, 2012).

106. William H. Frey. 2011. *America's Diverse Future: Initial Glimpses at the U.S. Child Population from the 2010 Census*, April, Washington, DC: Brookings Institution, http://www.brookings.edu/~/media/research/files/papers/2011/4/06%20census%20diversity%20frey/0406_census_diversity_frey.pdf (accessed October 7, 2012).

107. Fredrik Barth, ed. 1969. *Ethnic Groups and Boundaries: The Social Organization of Cultural Differences*, Bergen-Oslo: Universitete Forgalet.

108. Barbara A. Anderson and Brian D. Silver. 1983. "Estimating Russification of Ethnic Identity among Non-Russians in the USSR," *Demography*, 20: 461–489.

109. Mara Loveman and Jeronimo O. Muniz. 2007. "How Puerto Rico Became White: Boundary Dynamics and Intercensus Racial Reclassification," *American Sociological Review*, 72: 915–939.

110. Jose Alberto Magno de Carvalho, Charles H. Wood, and Flavia Cristina Drumond Andrade. 2004. "Estimating the Stability of Census-Based Racial/Ethnic Classifications: The Case of Brazil," *Population Studies*, 58: 331–343.

111. Arialdi M. Minimo and Sherry L. Murphy. 2012. "Death in the United States, 2010," *NCHS Data Brief*, no. 99, July, http://www.cdc.gov/nchs/data/databriefs/db99.pdf (accessed August 22, 2012).

112. William Seltzer. 2005. "Official Statistics and Statistical Ethics: Selected Issues," *Proceedings of the 55th Session of the International Statistical Institute*, https://classshares.student.usp.ac.fj/OS201/ethics%20and%20official%20stats%2020paper.pdf (accessed June 16, 2010).

113. Kenneth Mellanby. 1947. "Medical Experiments on Human Beings in Concentration Camps in Nazi Germany," *British Medical Journal*, 1: 140–150.

114. Amy L. Fairchild and Ronald Bayer. 1999. "Uses and Abuses of Tuskegee," *Science*, 284: 919–921; J. H. Jones. 1981. *Bad Blood: The Tuskegee Syphilis Experiment*, New York: The Free Press.

115. CNN. 2010. "US Apologizes for Infecting Guatemalans with STDs in the 1940s," October 1, http://www.cnn.com/2010/WORLD/americas/10/01/us.guatemala.apology/index.html?iref=allsearch (accessed November 15, 2011); Reuters. 2011. "US Researchers Broke Rules in Guatemala Syphilis Study," August 29, http://www.reuters.com/article/2011/08/29/usa-guatemala-syphilis-idUSN1E77S0XW20110829 (accessed August 30, 2011); Donald G. McNeil, Jr. 2011. "Panel Hears Grim Details of Venereal Disease Tests," *New York Times*, August 31, http://www.nytimes.com/2011/08/31/world/americas/31syphilis.html?_r=1&scp=2&sq=Guatemala&st=cse (accessed August 31, 2011); and Susan M. Reverby. 2011. "'Normal Exposure' and Inoculation Syphilis: A PHS 'Tuskegee' Doctor in Guatemala, 1946–1948," *Journal of Policy History*, 23: 6–28.

116. Robert M. Veatch. 1971. "'Experimental'' Pregnancy," *The Hastings Center Report*, 1: 2–3.

117. Stanley Milgram. 1963. "Behavioral Study of Obedience," *The Journal of Abnormal and Social Psychology*, 67: 371–378.

118. Ruth A. Parslow, Anthony F. Jorm, Brian I. O'Toole, Richard P. Marshall, and David A. Grayson. 2000. "Distress Experienced by Participants during an Epidemiological Survey of Post-traumatic Stress Disorder," *Journal of Traumatic Stress*, 13: 465–471.

119. *The Belmont Report: Ethnical Principles and Guidelines for the Protection of Human Subjects of Research*, http://www.fda.gov/ohrms/dockets/ac/05/briefing/2005-4178b_09_02_Belmont%20Report.pdf (accessed July 11, 2011).

120. William Seltzer and Margo Anderson. 2001. "The Dark Side of Numbers: The Role of Population Data Systems in Human Rights Abuses," *Social Research*, 68: 481–513.

121. United Nations. 2006. *Fundamental Principles of Official Statistics*, http://unstats.un.org/unsd/methods/statorg/FP-English.htm (accessed December 11, 2011).

122. United Nations. 2004. *Implementation of the Fundamental Principles of Official Statistics*, New York: United Nations, http://unstats.un.org/unsd/statcom/doc04/2004-21e.pdf (accessed December 12, 2011).

123. United Nations. 2007. *Country Practices on National Official Statistics*, http://unstats.un.org/unsd/dnss/gp/searchgp.aspx (accessed December 12, 2011).

124. Andrew G. Walder. 1988. *Communist Neo-traditionalism: Work and Authority in Chinese Industry*, Berkeley: University of California Press.

125. Alex Inkeles and Raymond Bauer. 1960. *The Soviet Citizen: Daily Life in a Totalitarian Society*, Cambridge, MA: Harvard University Press.

126. James R. Millar. 1987. *Politics, Work, and Daily Life in the USSR: A Survey of Former Soviet Citizens*, Cambridge, MA: Cambridge University Press.

127. Mikk Titma, Brian D. Silver, Rein Voorman, and Douglas Johnson. 1996. "The Estonian Longitudinal Survey," *International Journal of Sociology*, 26: 76–93.

128. A. F. Thurston and B. Pasternak, eds. 1983. *The Social Sciences and Fieldwork in China: Views from the Field*, Boulder, CO: Westview Press; and Bin Liang and Hong Lu. 2006. "Conducting Fieldwork in China: Observations on Collecting Primary Data Regarding Crime, Law, and the Criminal Justice System," *Journal of Contemporary Criminal Justice*, 22: 157–172.

129. Ivy N. Goduka. 1990. "Ethics and Politics of Field Research in South Africa," *Social Problems*, 37: 329–340; and P. R. van den Berghe. 1968. "Research in South Africa: The Story of My Experiences with Tyranny," in *Ethics, Politics, and Social Research*, ed. G. Sjoberg, Cambridge: Schenkman, 185–186.

130. A. Keys, J. Brozek, A. Henschel, O. Mickelsen, and H. L. Taylor. 1950. *The Biology of Human Starvation*, 2 vols., St. Paul, MN: University of Minnesota Press; and Todd Tucker. 2006. *The Great Starvation Experiment: Ancel Keys and the Men Who Starved for Science*, New York: The Free Press.

131. Stanley L. Warner. 1965. "Randomized Response: A Survey Technique for Eliminating Evasive Answer Bias," *Journal of the American Statistical Association*, 60: 63–69.

132. N. J. Scheers and C. Mitchell Dayton. 1987. "Improved Estimation of Academic Cheating Behavior Using the Randomized Response Technique," *Research in Higher Education*, 26: 61–69.

133. Michael S. Goodstadt and Valerie Gruson. 1975. "The Randomized Response Technique: A Test on Drug Use," *Journal of the American Statistical Association*, 70: 814–818.

134. James Abernathy, Bernard Greenberg, and Daniel Horvitz. 1970. "Estimates of Induced Abortion in Urban North Carolina," *Demography*, 7: 19–29; Diana Lara, Sandra G. Garcia, Charlotte Ellertson, Carol Camlin, and Javier Suarez. 2006. "The Measure of Induced Abortion Levels in Mexico Using Random Response Technique," *Sociological Methods & Research*, 35: 279–301; and Bernard G. Greenberg, Roy R. Kuebler Jr., James R. Abernathy, and Daniel G. Horvitz. 1971. "Application of the Randomized Response Technique in Obtaining Quantitative Data," *Journal of the American Statistical Association*, 66: 243–250.

135. U.S. Census Bureau. 2010. "Analysis of Perturbed and Unperturbed Age Estimates: 2008," http://www.census.gov/cps/user_note_age_estimates.html (accessed July 2, 2010); and J. Trent Alexander, Michael Davern, and Betsey Stevenson. 2010. *Inaccurate Age and Sex Data in the Census PUMS Files: Evidence and Implications*, National Bureau of Economic Research Working Paper no. 15703, http://www.nber.org/papers/w15703.pdf (accessed September 4, 2011).

136. T. Lynn Fisher. 2010. "The Income of the Elderly: The Effect of Changes to Reported Age in the Current Population Survey," paper presented at the annual conference of the Association for Public Policy Analysis and Management, Boston, October 13, https://www.appam.org/conferences/fall/boston2010/sessions/downloads/4555.1.pdf (accessed July 9, 2011).

137. Jill E. Sherman and Tamara L. Fetters. 2007. "Confidentiality Concerns with Mapping Survey Data in Reproductive Health Research," *Studies in Family Planning*, 38: 309–321.

138. L. H. Cox. 1996. "Protecting Confidentiality in Small Population Health and Environmental Statistics," *Statistics in Medicine*, 15: 1895–1905; and Marc P. Armstrong, Gerard Rushton and Dale L. Zimmerman. 1999. "Geographically Masking Health Data to Preserve Confidentiality," *Statistics in Medicine*, 18: 497–525.

139. P. A. Schulte and M. Haring Sweeney. 1995. "Ethical Considerations, Confidentiality Issues, Rights of Human Subjects, and Uses of Monitoring Data in Research and Regulation," *Environmental Health Perspectives*, 103 (Suppl. 3): 69–74.

CHAPTER 4

MORTALITY PATTERNS IN THE MODERN ERA

LEARNING OBJECTIVES
- Explain what the infant mortality rate and expectation of life at birth are and why they are good indicators of the level of mortality in a population.
- Describe the age-specific patterns of risk of dying in high-mortality, moderate-mortality, and low-mortality populations.

- Explain why patterns of HIV mortality by age and sex differ from non-HIV causes of death.
- Explain what a cohort is and how examination of cohort mortality rates and period mortality rates can lead to different conclusions.

(((Listen to the Chapter Audio

OVERVIEW

There is a demographic joke that goes, "Death is not a question of whether it will happen—it's all a matter of timing." All people die, but the timing of these deaths matters a great deal to individuals, families, and society. Deaths of infants and young children, of people of working age, and of the elderly all are mourned and have individual and societal impacts, but these impacts differ based on the age of the person who died. Deaths of infants are sad, but in many societies infant deaths have been so common that social customs have developed to minimize their effect on the community. The death of a person in the working ages often removes a parent or an income-producing member from the family, which has large social and economic implications. Deaths of the elderly are expected at some point, but as life expectancy has increased and many elderly are healthy, what is seen as old has changed. Whereas the death of a person in their sixties once would have seemed normal, in many countries the sixties is now seen as an unreasonably early age at death.

Mortality has declined greatly since 1950. In the Less Developed Region (LDR) in 1950–1955, more than 15% of babies died before their first birthday; in 2005–2010, 5% of babies died before their first birthday, signifying a huge improvement in infant

survival. On the other hand, in the More Developed Region (MDR) in 2005–2010, only 0.6% of babies died before their first birthday. Thus, the LDR still has a long way to go in improvement of infant survival. In the LDR, life expectancy increased from 43 years in 1950–1955 to 68 years in 2005–2010, again a large improvement in survival. However, there remain countries with very high mortality. In Nigeria in 2009, life expectancy was 54 years, 14% died before their fifth birthday, and over 50% died before their sixty-fifth birthday. In the MDR, people on average lived 11 years longer in 2005–2010 than in 1950–1955, with a 2005–2010 average life expectancy of 78 years. In 2005–2010, Japanese women had the highest expectation of life at birth in the world at 86 years. In Japan in 2008, 91% of women were alive on their seventieth birthday, truly making the death of women aged 60–69 an unusual event.

This is the first of four chapters about mortality. Each chapter has a different focus, but they are interrelated and build on each other.

In this chapter, we look at variation in mortality levels and trends. We also discuss how demographers typically represent mortality indicators. The main tool used to represent mortality experience is the life table, which shows the risks of dying by age that a group of people would encounter if exposed to the mortality conditions in a given place (usually a country) at a given time. We also look at typical patterns and variations in the sex differential in mortality, in which male mortality is compared to female mortality.

Chapter 5 discusses the Epidemiological Transition, a characterization of changes in the level and causes of mortality over time. Chapter 5 also examines the course of mortality decline in historical Europe and ideas and findings about the causes of the decline. Studying historical mortality decline in other parts of the world, such as Africa and Asia, would be interesting. However, mortality declined first in Europe, and much thinking about mortality decline was based on the European experience. Also, reliable data on mortality in the past are very sparse in much of the world. After that, typical changes in mortality risks by age and the relation between mortality and morbidity (illness) are discussed. Finally, the results of the Global Burden of Disease (GBD) Project for 2004 are shown, which present a context for understanding the leading causes of death and of disability in countries across the world by national income levels. The GBD Project results provide a background for a more detailed discussion of mortality in the LDR in Chapter 6 and in the MDR in Chapter 7.

OVERALL MORTALITY TRENDS— THE INFANT MORTALITY RATE AND EXPECTATION OF LIFE AT BIRTH

The crude death rate (CDR), introduced in Chapter 2, shows the number of deaths that will occur in a year per 1,000 population. The CDR would be a good indicator of overall mortality conditions if every person in a population had the same risk of dying. But this is far from true. Older people in every population have a higher chance of dying than do younger people. In addition, infants and young children have a higher chance of dying than somewhat older children and young adults. Also, almost everywhere at every age men have a higher risk of dying than women. We saw in Figures 2.26 and 2.27 that although for the world as a whole the CDR and life expectancy tell the same story, for a population with a high proportion of older people, such as Japan, they tell very different stories.

Two important aspects of mortality experience are the probability of babies dying before they reach their first birthday and the average number of years that a person lives under a set of mortality conditions. The probability of a baby dying is examined through the infant mortality rate, and the average number of years that a person lives is measured as the expectation of life at birth, which is also called life expectancy at birth. Both of these indicators are important not only in themselves but also as signals of the well-being of countries. The infant mortality rate is often used as an indicator of a country's overall health situation. This is partially because in high- and moderate-mortality situations, a large portion of deaths occur to babies before their first birthday.[1]

The United Nations developed a single indicator of the development level of a country that focuses on the population's well-being: the Human Development Index (HDI). The HDI is constructed for each country based on three components: (1) the life expectancy at birth, (2) an indicator of educational attainment, and (3) an indicator based on gross national income per capita.[2] The HDI ranges from 0 to 1, with a higher value indicating a higher level of development. Governments care about their country's expectation of life at birth not only because of concern for the welfare of their citizens but also because of how it will make their country look in international comparisons. For example, the HDI for South Africa fell from 0.741 in 1995 to 0.604 in 2001. This was due to a decline in life expectancy in South Africa mainly due to high HIV mortality. The drop was also partly caused by the drop in the value of the South African rand, which lowered the estimate of gross national income per capita. Although South Africa has been criticized for its efforts to combat HIV, some in South Africa felt that since HIV was introduced to South Africa from other countries, the decline in life expectancy due to a new cause of death should not so severely influence their international rating in development as reflected in the HDI.[3] By 2011, the South African HDI had increased to 0.619, but this was still below its 1995 level.

Infant Mortality Rates by Region

The **infant mortality rate** (IMR), calculated for every 1,000 newborns, is the number of babies who will die before they reach their first birthday. The IMR is a major indicator of the overall health and mortality level of a population. It also is very important to the community since the death of a baby is wrenching to families. On the other hand, in settings in which a very high proportion of babies die soon after birth, social mechanisms develop to deal with this early loss. In some cultures with high infant mortality, a child is not named until he or she reaches a certain age.[4] This is a practice that helps the family maintain some emotional distance from the child until it seems likely that the child will survive.

The **child mortality rate**, calculated for every 1,000 births, is the number of children who die before their fifth birthday. The child mortality rate is examined less often than the infant mortality rate, but it is still a useful indicator of the mortality situation in a country.

Figure 4.1 shows the IMR during 1950–2010 for the world, the MDR, the LDR, the United States, and the least developed countries (LeastDC). Between

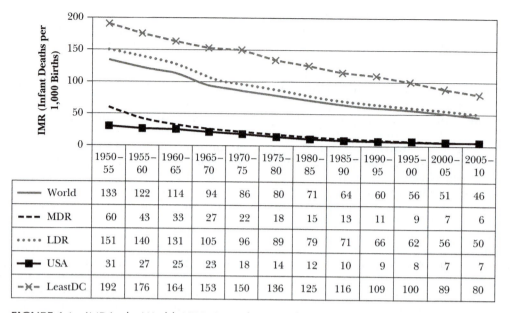

FIGURE 4.1 IMR in the World, MDR, LDR, the United States, and LeastDC

	1950–55	1955–60	1960–65	1965–70	1970–75	1975–80	1980–85	1985–90	1990–95	1995–00	2000–05	2005–10
World	133	122	114	94	86	80	71	64	60	56	51	46
MDR	60	43	33	27	22	18	15	13	11	9	7	6
LDR	151	140	131	105	96	89	79	71	66	62	56	50
USA	31	27	25	23	18	14	12	10	9	8	7	7
LeastDC	192	176	164	153	150	136	125	116	109	100	89	80

1950–1955 and 2005–2010, the IMR declined in all of these groups. In 1950–1955, in the world as a whole, over 13% of all newborns died before their first birthday, and in the LDR over 15% died before their first birthday. Between 1950–1955 and 2005–2010, the IMR in the MDR fell from 60 to 6 per 1,000—a decline to 10% of its earlier value; in the LDR it fell from 151 to 50, or 33% of its earlier value. In the LeastDC, it fell from 192 to 80—to 42% of its earlier value. By 2005–2010, the IMR in the LDR was less than it had been in the MDR in 1950–1955. Even in 2005–2010, 8% (80 per 1,000) of all babies born in the LeastDC died before their first birthday. Infant mortality decline in the LeastDC is about 25 years behind that in the LDR as a whole.

The infant mortality situation in the United States relative to other MDR countries changed over time. In 1950–1955 the IMR in the United States was half that of the MDR as a whole, but by 2005–2010 the IMR in the United States was slightly higher (7 per 1,000 births) than in the MDR as a whole (6 per 1,000 births).

The relatively high IMR in the United States has been a source of policy concern.[5] A difference of 1 death per 1,000 births in the IMR between the United States and Europe is not big enough to cause concern. In 2005–2010, the lowest IMR in the world was 2 deaths per 1,000 births, which was attained by Iceland, Luxembourg, and Singapore. Of more concern for the United States is the racial gap in the IMR. In 2005, the white IMR in the United States was 6, and the African-American IMR was 14.[6] In 2005–2010, Romania, Barbados, and French Guiana

had an IMR of 14. Racial differences in mortality in the United States are discussed in Chapter 7.

Figure 4.2 shows the IMR in 1950–2010 for world regions. Although the IMR declined in all regions, the declines in Asia and in Latin America and the Caribbean were much more rapid than in Africa. Also, at every date, the IMR in Africa is much higher than in the other regions. In 1950–1955 the IMR in Africa was 23% higher than in Asia, but in 2005–2010 the IMR in Africa was almost twice that of Asia. The rapid decline in the IMR in Asia in the 1960s was almost entirely due to the decline in infant mortality in China. The IMR in China declined from 121 in 1960–1965 to 63 in 1965–1970.

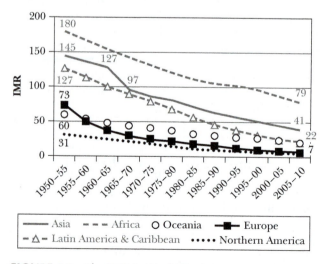

FIGURE 4.2 The IMR in World Regions

BOX 4.1

Expectation of Life at Birth: The Average Number of Years Lived from Birth

The expectation of life at birth is the average number of years lived by people under the mortality conditions by age in a given place and time. Since this is an average, it does not mean that most or even any people actually live for the number of years of the expectation of life at birth.

Imagine a hypothetical example where one-half of the people die 1 second after they are born. Imagine further that those 50% of the babies who live to 2 seconds of age die on their eightieth birthday.

In this case half of the people live for 1 second, and half live for 80 years. Thus, the average length of life (the expectation of life at birth) in this example is 40 years, even though NO ONE in this population dies at age 40.

It is also important to remember that the expectation of life at birth is a measure based on the mortality experience of people alive at a given point in time. Thus, the expectation of life at birth in the United States in 1990 does not reflect the chance of dying of any group of actual people. In 1990, those aged 0–4 were born in 1985–1990, and those aged 80–84 were born in 1905–1910. In 1905–1910 the death rate at age 0–4 was higher than in 1985–1990, and when those aged 0–4 in 1990 are aged 80–84, which will occur in 2065–2075, the death rate for those aged 80–84 will be lower than it was for those aged 80–84 in 1990. However, the expectation of life at birth remains a useful way to look at changing risks of dying across time. This is discussed further in this chapter.

In 1950–1955 the IMR in Europe was more than twice that in Northern America, but by 2005–2010 the IMRs in Europe and in Northern America were identical. The narrowing of the gap between Northern America and Europe seen in Figure 4.2 mirrors that shown between the United States and the MDR in Figure 4.1.

At every date, the IMR in Latin America and the Caribbean is intermediate between that in Europe and Northern America, on one hand, and that in Asia, on the other hand.[7] For most demographic indicators, Latin America and the Caribbean considered as one region has values that are intermediate between the values for the LDR and the MDR. Oceania changed over time from having an IMR similar to that of Europe in 1950–1955 to having an IMR similar to that of Latin America and the Caribbean in 2005–2010.

Expectation of Life at Birth by Region

The **expectation of life at birth**, which is also called life expectancy at birth, was discussed briefly in Chapter 2. It is the number of years on average that a person would live if exposed to the risk of dying by age present in a given population at a given time. It is abbreviated as e_0^0. Box 4.1 further explains the expectation of life at birth.

Expectation of life at birth is almost always calculated separately by sex because the value of e_0^0 is almost always different for the two sexes, as are the causes of death. Figure 4.3 shows female e_0^0 for the same group of regions and countries shown in Figure 4.1.

In all periods, female e_0^0 in the United States was virtually identical to that in the MDR as a whole, increasing from about 70 years to about 80 years. Although female e_0^0 increased in the LDR and the LeastDC, the gap between female e_0^0 in the LDR and in the LeastDC widened from 5 years in 1950–1955 to 10 years in 2005–2010. Thus, the poorest countries were not improving their female mortality as rapidly as less developed countries as a whole. Female e_0^0 in the LeastDC in 2005–2010 was about the same as in the LDR in 1975, indicating that the LeastDC were about 30 years behind the LDR in mortality decline.

Figure 4.4 shows female e_0^0 by world region. Female e_0^0 was approximately equal in Europe and Northern America at every date, with usually a slightly lower value for Europe. Female e_0^0 in Oceania (73% of the population of which was composed of Australia and New Zealand) improved from being 9 years less than Europe in 1950–1955 to being identical to Europe (at 79 years) in 2005–2010. In 1950–1955 Latin America and the Caribbean had a female e_0^0 19 years less than that of Northern America, but by 2005–2010, it was only 4 years less, a huge improvement in female survival in Latin America and the Caribbean. The improvement in female e_0^0 in Asia is even more striking. In 1950–1955, it was 32 years less than in Northern America, but by 2005–2010 it was only 10 years less. Female e_0^0 in Africa increased over time, but much more slowly than in the other LDR regions. The improvement in Africa was 16 years, compared to 28 years in Asia and 24 years in Latin America and the Caribbean. Also, female e_0^0 in

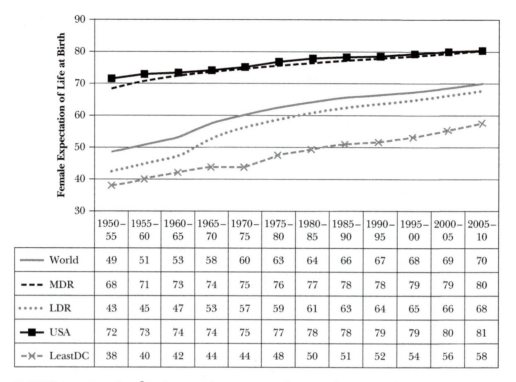

	1950–55	1955–60	1960–65	1965–70	1970–75	1975–80	1980–85	1985–90	1990–95	1995–00	2000–05	2005–10
—— World	49	51	53	58	60	63	64	66	67	68	69	70
- - - MDR	68	71	73	74	75	76	77	78	78	79	79	80
····· LDR	43	45	47	53	57	59	61	63	64	65	66	68
—■— USA	72	73	74	74	75	77	78	78	79	79	80	81
-✕- LeastDC	38	40	42	44	44	48	50	51	52	54	56	58

FIGURE 4.3   Female e_0^0 in the World, MDR, LDR, the United States, and LeastDC

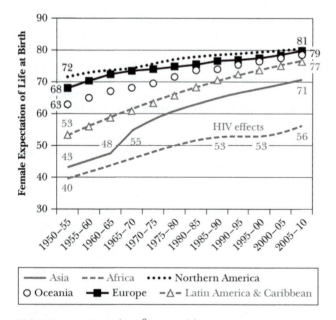

FIGURE 4.4   Female e_0^0 in World Regions

Africa only increased by 3 years between 1985–1990 and 2005–2010. A major reason for the slowdown in improvement in female e_0^0 in Africa since the late 1980s is HIV. The effect of HIV on mortality in Africa is discussed later in this chapter and in Chapter 6.

Figure 4.5 shows male e_0^0 in the world, the MDR, the LDR, the LeastDC, and the United States. The vertical scale in Figure 4.5 is the same as in Figure 4.3 for females to facilitate comparisons. As for females, male e_0^0 figures in the United States and in the MDR region as a whole are similar, but in 1950–1955 and in 1995–2010, male e_0^0 is noticeably higher in the United States than in the MDR.

The decline in male e_0^0 in the LeastDC in 1970–1975 is mainly due to an increase in male deaths in Bangladesh during their Liberation War in 1971.[8] In 1970–1975 Bangladesh constituted 21% of the population of the LeastDC. We do not see a decline in female e_0^0 for 1970–1975 in the LeastDC in Figure 4.4 because the war in Bangladesh had a much greater impact on male than on female mortality.

Figure 4.6 shows male e_0^0 in world regions. There is a growing gap after 1970–1975 between male e_0^0 in Europe and in Northern America, with greater male e_0^0 in Northern America. Male e_0^0 in Europe is pulled down by low male e_0^0 in Eastern Europe, especially in Russia, where it was 62 years in 2005–2010. High male mortality in Russia is discussed later in this chapter and in Chapter 7. Male e_0^0 in Latin America and the Caribbean almost caught up to Europe by 2005–2010. This was mainly because the chances of survival kept improving in Latin America and the Caribbean (11 years of increase from 1970–1975

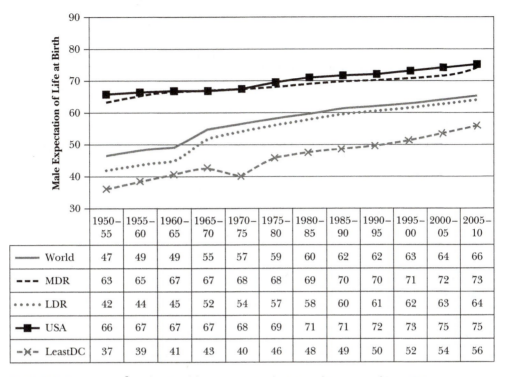

FIGURE 4.5 Male e_0^0 in the World, MDR, LDR, the United States, and LeastDC

	1950–55	1955–60	1960–65	1965–70	1970–75	1975–80	1980–85	1985–90	1990–95	1995–00	2000–05	2005–10
World	47	49	49	55	57	59	60	62	62	63	64	66
MDR	63	65	67	67	68	68	69	70	70	71	72	73
LDR	42	44	45	52	54	57	58	60	61	62	63	64
USA	66	67	67	67	68	69	71	71	72	73	75	75
LeastDC	37	39	41	43	40	46	48	49	50	52	54	56

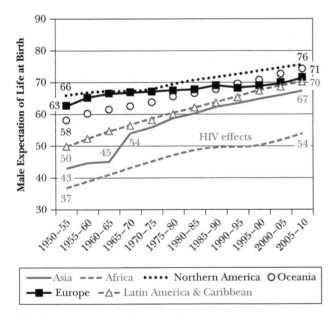

FIGURE 4.6 Male e_0^0 in World Regions

through 2005–2010), while in Europe as a whole there was an increase of only 4 years in the same period. Male e_0^0 in Africa also shows the impact of HIV, with no improvement between 1985–1990 and 1995–2000. Male e_0^0 in Asia increased by 9 years between 1960–1965 and 1965–1970. This is mainly due

to improvements in survival in China after the 1958–1961 famine. The improvement in male e_0^0 of 9 years is greater than the improvement in female e_0^0 of 7 years in the same period.

Figure 4.7 shows the number of years by which female e_0^0 exceeds male e_0^0. For the world as a whole, females have consistently lived on average 2–4 years longer than males. The female advantage is greater in the MDR than in the LDR. The large sex differential in the MDR is partially due to more negative health behaviors among men than women. The effects of health behaviors on mortality are discussed in Chapters 6 and 7. After increasing to a gap of 8 years in the United States in 1975–1980, the female advantage in survival has declined. The decline in the sex differential in the United States after 1975–1980 is partially due to a greater reduction in smoking among American men than among American women. The female advantage in survival in the LDR increases over time. This is partially due to decreasing female deprivation in the LDR. It is also probably due to greater adoption of unhealthy behaviors such as smoking and heavy alcohol consumption by men than by women in the LDR. The gender gap in e_0^0 increased from 2 years to 4 years in the LeastDC between 1965–1970 and 1970–1975 before falling to 2 years in 1975–1980. This spike in the sex differential in e_0^0 in the LeastDC is mainly due to greater male than female mortality in

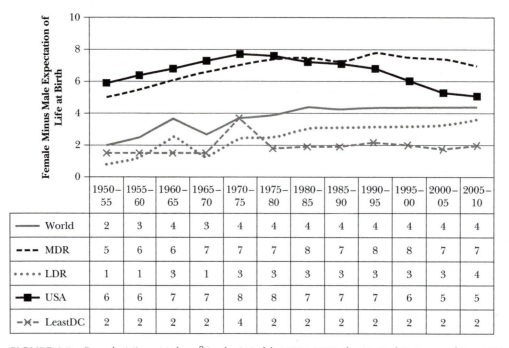

	1950–55	1955–60	1960–65	1965–70	1970–75	1975–80	1980–85	1985–90	1990–95	1995–00	2000–05	2005–10
—— World	2	3	4	3	4	4	4	4	4	4	4	4
--- MDR	5	6	6	7	7	7	8	7	8	8	7	7
····· LDR	1	1	3	1	3	3	3	3	3	3	3	4
—■— USA	6	6	7	7	8	8	7	7	7	6	5	5
–✕– LeastDC	2	2	2	2	4	2	2	2	2	2	2	2

FIGURE 4.7   Female Minus Male e_0^0 in the World, MDR, LDR, the United States, and LeastDC

Bangladesh in their 1971 Liberation War, discussed earlier in this section. The causes of these different levels and trends in the gender gap in mortality are discussed further in this chapter and in Chapters 6 and 7.

MORTALITY TRENDS BY REGION OF AFRICA

In this section, we look at mortality trends within Africa, which is the region with the highest mortality. We saw in Figure 4.2 that Africa had a much higher IMR than other regions since 1950. We also saw in Figures 4.4 and 4.6 that while e_0^0 in Africa was only a few years lower than in Asia in the early 1950s, by 2005–2010, e_0^0 in Africa lagged far behind Asia.

In this section, we look at trends in the IMR and e_0^0 among regions of Africa. The regions of Africa are as defined by the UN Population Division. The countries in each region are listed in Appendix A.

Figure 4.8 shows e_0^0 for females and for males and the IMR by region of Africa. Northern Africa is shown as a solid line. Eastern Africa, Middle Africa, Western Africa, and Southern Africa are the regions that together comprise sub-Saharan Africa; Northern Africa is not part of sub-Saharan Africa. This is important to remember because when people refer to "Africa," they often mean sub-Saharan Africa. In some ways, the social characteristics and demographic patterns in Northern Africa are more similar to those in the Middle East than to those of sub-Saharan Africa.

Thus, people sometimes refer to "the Middle East and North Africa" as a region, although that is not a regional designation used by the UN Population Division.

The trend in e_0^0 and in the IMR in Northern Africa shows a different pattern from the rest of Africa. Northern Africa had higher male and female e_0^0 than every other African region except Southern Africa at every date. After 1975–1980, the IMR in Northern Africa was lower than in every other African region except Southern Africa. The IMR trajectory for Northern Africa looks very similar to that in Asia as a whole, as shown in Figure 4.2.

Southern Africa also has a different IMR trajectory than the other regions of sub-Saharan Africa. In 1950–1955, the IMR in Southern Africa was low by international standards—even lower than in Latin America and the Caribbean, for which the IMR was 127. In Southern Africa, the IMR continued to decline until 1990–1995, when it was 52. Between 1990–1995 and 2000–2005, the IMR in Southern Africa increased to a value of 60. Between 2000–2005 and 2005–2010, the IMR in Southern Africa resumed its decline, reaching a value of 49 in 2005–2010. By 2005–2010, the IMR in Northern Africa was lower than in Southern Africa, but the IMR in Southern Africa was lower than in Middle Africa, Eastern Africa, or Western Africa.

The increase in IMR in Southern Africa was due to HIV. In the countries of Southern Africa in 2010,

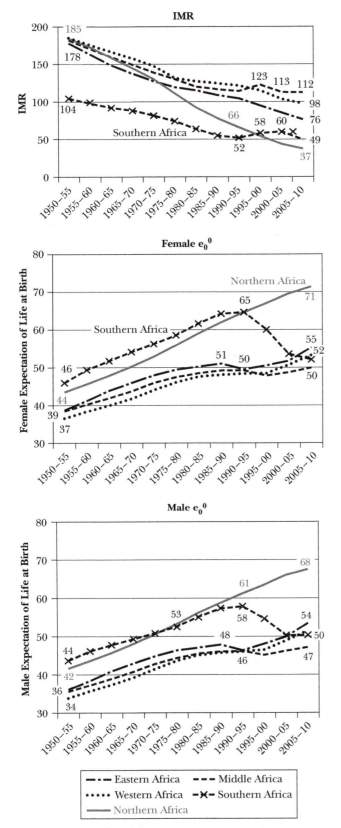

FIGURE 4.8 e_0^0 and the IMR in Regions of Africa

the estimated percentage of adults aged 15–49 who were HIV-positive ranged from 14% in Namibia to 26% in Swaziland. In South Africa, which comprised 87% of the population of Southern Africa in 2010, 18% of those aged 15–49 were HIV-positive.[9] The HIV epidemic was estimated to have reached a peak in 2004. Drugs administered during labor have substantially reduced the percentage of infants of HIV-positive mothers who are HIV-positive, which has led to a decline in HIV-caused infant mortality.

The economic situation in Southern Africa also differs from elsewhere in sub-Saharan Africa. South Africa has the best economy and infrastructure in sub-Saharan Africa. South Africa had a gross national income per capita in 2009 of $5,760, and the GNI per capita of Botswana was $6,260. In comparison, the average GNI per capita for sub-Saharan Africa in 2009 was $1,130.[10] Although HIV has increased mortality in Southern Africa, the region's relatively high development level and extensive infrastructure make it better able to address mortality concerns than countries at a lower development level.

Middle Africa, Western Africa, and Eastern Africa show similar levels of IMR through 1990–1995. Between 1990–1995 and 1995–2000, the IMR in Middle Africa increased from 114 to 123 before declining to 112 in 2005–2010. The deterioration in the IMR in Middle Africa was partially due to violent conflict in the Democratic Republic of the Congo, which comprised 52% of the population of Middle Africa in 2010.

Next, we compare trends in e_0^0 among regions of Africa. Note that the vertical axes in the second and third panels of Figure 4.8 are different than in Figures 4.4 and 4.6. This is because e_0^0 across African regions tends to be low by world standards and a scale that stopped at $e_0^0 = 80$ rather than $e_0^0 = 90$ made it easier to see the differences among African regions. The second and third panels of Figure 4.8 have the same vertical axes to facilitate comparisons between males and females. Middle Africa, Western Africa, and Eastern Africa had similar levels of female e_0^0 in 1950–1955, ranging from 37 to 39 years. This is lower than the value for Asia in 1950–1955, which was 43 years. In Eastern Africa, female e_0^0 increased to 51 years in 1985–1990, declined to 50 in 1990–1995, and then increased to 55 years by 2005–2010. In Eastern Africa, HIV mortality affected e_0^0, although not as severely as in Southern Africa. In Middle Africa and Western Africa, female e_0^0 increased to about 50 by 1990–1995 and then remained almost unchanged.

In Northern Africa, female e_0^0 rose steadily between 1950–1955 and 2005–2010, with values at the beginning and at the end of the 60-year period almost identical to those for Asia. HIV levels in Northern Africa are extremely low.

As for the IMR, e_0^0 in Southern Africa shows a distinctly different trend than in other regions. Female e_0^0 in Southern Africa started at a higher level than in Asia and was higher than in any other African region, rising to 65 years in 1990–1995. After 1995, female e_0^0 in Southern Africa declined sharply to 52 years in 2005–2010, lower than in Eastern Africa and in Northern Africa. The decline in e_0^0 for both sexes in Southern Africa was due to rapidly increasing mortality, but there was an especially large decline in female e_0^0. The effect of HIV on female e_0^0 was much greater than on the IMR.

Slowed or stagnating mortality decline in sub-Saharan Africa since the 1980s has motivated consideration of whether the mortality improvements in Africa in the past are sustainable into the future. This is discussed in Chapter 6, as new negative health behaviors in sub-Saharan Africa and other less developed countries have somewhat countered mortality improvements.

MORTALITY TRENDS BY REGION OF EUROPE

In this section, we look at trends in the IMR and e_0^0 in regions of Europe and in the United States. The regions of Europe are as defined by the UN Population Division. The countries in each region are listed in Appendix A.

Figure 4.9 shows the IMR and e_0^0 for females and for males by region of Europe and for the United States. The United States is indicated by a solid line.

In 1950–1955, the IMR in the United States was lower than in any European region. By 1955–1960, the IMR in Northern Europe was lower than in the United States, and in 2005–2010, the IMR was higher in the United States than in every European region except Eastern Europe. The decline in IMR in Southern Europe is especially impressive. In 1950–1955, the IMR in Southern Europe was almost three times as high as in the United States, while in 2005–2010 it was 5—lower than the United States, where the IMR was 7. Only Western Europe had a lower value at 4. In Eastern Europe, the IMR declined rapidly from 1950 through the mid-1970s and then declined more slowly.

In 1950–1955, female e_0^0 was higher in the United States than in any European region, but it was only one year higher than in Northern Europe. By 2005–2010, as with the IMR, female e_0^0 in the United States was lower (i.e., worse) than in every European region except Eastern Europe. Female e_0^0 in Southern Europe rose from the lowest of all European regions in 1950–1955 at 65 years to tying with Western Europe for the highest value at

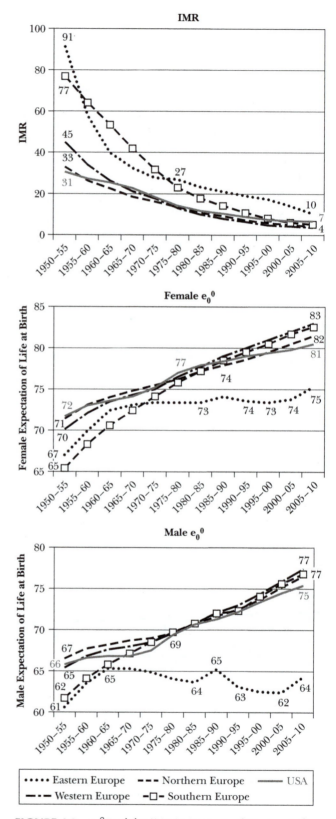

FIGURE 4.9 e_0^0 and the IMR in Regions of Europe and in the United States

83 years in 2005–2010. As with the IMR, female e_0^0 in Eastern Europe rose rapidly from 1950 through the mid-1970s and then remained almost constant until a slight improvement in 2005–2010.

Male e_0^0 in the United States was higher in 1950–1955 than in any European region except Northern Europe, but, like the IMR and like female e_0^0, in 2005–2010 male e_0^0 in the United States was lower than in any European region except Eastern Europe. Male e_0^0 in Eastern Europe increased rapidly from 1950 through the mid-1960s and then declined through the early 1980s. There was a brief increase in male e_0^0 in 1985–1990, which was due to the effects of then Soviet president Mikhail Gorbachev's anti-alcohol campaign in the Soviet Union. This campaign, which had a temporary substantial effect on adult male survival, is discussed more in this chapter and in Chapter 7.

Thus, we see that since 1950, the United States has gone from having the best or close to the best mortality situation compared to European regions to having a worse mortality situation than every region except Eastern Europe. Some of the reasons for the loss of the mortality advantage in the United States are discussed in Chapter 7.

MORTALITY INDICATORS IN THE WORLD'S TEN MOST POPULOUS COUNTRIES IN 2010

Table 4.1 shows some mortality indicators for the ten most populous countries in 2010. The IMR is shown in both 1950–1955 and 2005–2010. The decline in the IMR in all of the countries is impressive. Also, in every country, women had a higher e_0^0 than men in 2005–2010.

In the more developed countries, the gender gap in e_0^0 is mainly due to worse health behaviors among men than women. The difference in e_0^0 between men and women is especially striking in Russia, which had the largest sex differential in e_0^0 of any country in the world in 2005–2010. The large gender gap in Russia was mainly due to sex differences in alcohol consumption. Gender differences in health behaviors in the MDR are discussed more in Chapter 7.

The range in the IMR across the countries is also striking. In 2005–2010, a baby was more than 30 times likelier to die before his or her first birthday in Nigeria than in Japan. Also, women on average lived 35 years longer in Japan than in Nigeria, and men on average lived 29 years longer in Japan than in Nigeria.

TRENDS IN THE INFANT MORTALITY RATE AND EXPECTATION OF LIFE AT BIRTH IN SELECTED COUNTRIES

Next, we look at the trends in the IMR and in e_0^0 in a set of countries that illustrate the diversity in world mortality. Japan and Sweden are MDR countries that have extremely low mortality. Russia is in the MDR, but its mortality trajectory has been impacted by economic problems along with increases in homicide, suicide, and accidents after the dissolution of the Soviet Union in 1991. Also, there has been extremely high alcohol consumption among Russian males. China had high mortality in the early 1950s. After a the 1959–1961 famine in China, mortality conditions in that country improved rapidly. Nigeria is an example of a very-high-mortality country. Botswana was the first country in which the impact of HIV could be seen in a decline in e_0^0.

Figure 4.10 shows infant mortality rates in all of these countries in 1950–2010. The countries in the

TABLE 4.1 Mortality Indicators for the World's Ten Most Populous Countries in 2010

		Infant Mortality Rate (IMR), 1950–1955	IMR, 2005–2010	Female e_0^0, 2005–2010	Male e_0^0, 2005–2010	Female Minus Male e_0^0, 2005–2010*
1	China (PRC)	122	22	75	71	3
2	India	165	53	66	63	3
3	United States	31	7	81	76	5
4	Indonesia	192	29	68	66	2
5	Brazil	135	24	76	69	7
6	Pakistan	177	71	65	64	2
7	Nigeria	189	96	51	50	1
8	Bangladesh	165	49	68	67	1
9	Russia	98	11	74	62	13
10	Japan	50	3	86	79	7

*Values are calculated from estimates with more significant figures than those shown in the table.

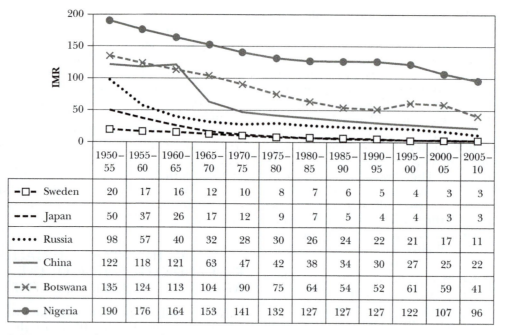

FIGURE 4.10 The IMR in Selected Countries

	1950–55	1955–60	1960–65	1965–70	1970–75	1975–80	1980–85	1985–90	1990–95	1995–00	2000–05	2005–10
–□– Sweden	20	17	16	12	10	8	7	6	5	4	3	3
– – – Japan	50	37	26	17	12	9	7	5	4	4	3	3
····· Russia	98	57	40	32	28	30	26	24	22	21	17	11
—— China	122	118	121	63	47	42	38	34	30	27	25	22
–✕– Botswana	135	124	113	104	90	75	64	54	52	61	59	41
–●– Nigeria	190	176	164	153	141	132	127	127	127	122	107	96

LDR are distinguished from the countries in the MDR by the color of the lines. Sweden and Japan had the lowest recorded IMR in the world in 2005–2010, with 3 out of every 1,000 babies dying before their first birthday. In Russia the IMR first declined rapidly and then after the 1970s declined slowly. The IMR in Russia declined in every 5-year period since 1950–1955, except for a slight increase in the late 1970s, which was almost certainly an artifact of an administrative change in the recording of live births and infant deaths in Russia.[11] Although economic conditions worsened in Russia after the dissolution of the Soviet Union in 1991, and although we shall see that e_0^0 declined after 1991, the IMR in Russia continued to decline in every 5-year period after 1975–1980.

China, Botswana, and Nigeria are in the Less Developed Region of the world. The IMRs in China and Botswana were approximately equal in 1950–1965, and in fact the IMR was higher in China than in Botswana in 1960–1965, due to the famine in China in 1959–1961. However, the IMR in China declined rapidly after the early 1960s, and in 2005–2010 the IMR in China was 54% of that in Botswana.

One possible reason for the decline in the IMR in China in the 1960s was the barefoot doctor program, which began in 1968.[12] This was a program of preventive health care that was administered by health personnel, many of whom had very little training. In 2005–2010, only 2% of babies in China died before

their first birthday, a decrease from 12% in 1950–1955. Although the IMR in China declined greatly, even in 2005–2010 it was twice as high in China as in Russia.

The IMR in Botswana declined almost as rapidly as in China from the early 1950s until the early 1990s. But between 1990–1995 and 1995–2000, the IMR in Botswana increased from 52 to 61. This increase was almost totally due to HIV. By 2005–2010, the IMR in Botswana had declined from the 2000–2005 level and was lower in 2005–2010 than it had been in 1990–1995.

The IMR in Nigeria declined from 1950–1955 through 1975–1980. It was almost unchanged from 1975–1980 through 1990–1995, and then declined from 1995–2000 through 2005–2010. Nigeria has not been affected by HIV as much as Botswana and thus did not experience the HIV-related increase in the IMR that occurred in Botswana. However, even in 1995–2000 when the IMR in Botswana was elevated as a result of HIV, the IMR in Nigeria was twice as high as in Botswana.

Figure 4.11 shows female expectation of life at birth in the same set of countries shown in Figure 4.10. The very low mortality in Sweden and Japan is striking—female expectation of life at birth was more than 80 years in both countries in 2005–2010. Sweden had relatively high female e_0^0 even in 1950–1955, so the increases in female e_0^0 in Japan (19 years) and in China (30 years) are notable. In China, we can see the effect of the

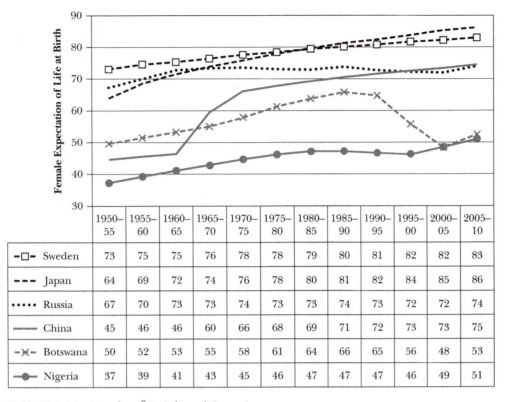

	1950–55	1955–60	1960–65	1965–70	1970–75	1975–80	1980–85	1985–90	1990–95	1995–00	2000–05	2005–10
-□- Sweden	73	75	75	76	78	78	79	80	81	82	82	83
--- Japan	64	69	72	74	76	78	80	81	82	84	85	86
••••• Russia	67	70	73	73	74	73	73	74	73	72	72	74
— China	45	46	46	60	66	68	69	71	72	73	73	75
-✕- Botswana	50	52	53	55	58	61	64	66	65	56	48	53
-●- Nigeria	37	39	41	43	45	46	47	47	47	46	49	51

FIGURE 4.11   Female e_0^0 in Selected Countries

1959–1961 famine in the lack of improvement in female expectation of life at birth between 1955–1960 and 1960–1965. After 1965, however, female e_0^0 in China increased rapidly. The relative positions of China and Russia in female survival reversed between 1950 and 2010. In 1950–1955 female e_0^0 was 22 years greater in Russia than in China, but it was one year greater in China than in Russia in 2005–2010. Female e_0^0 in Russia increased from 1950 through the early 1960s and then was almost unchanged through 2005–2010, not varying by more than one year from the 1960–1965 value.

Between 1950–1955 and 1985–1990, female e_0^0 in Botswana increased by 16 years. Then the value declined by 12 years between 1985–1990 and 2000–2005. The value for Botswana recovered somewhat in 2005–2010, reaching its 1960–1965 value. The decline in female e_0^0 in Botswana was almost totally due to the impact of HIV. The impact of HIV was much greater on female e_0^0 than on the IMR in Botswana. Female e_0^0 in Nigeria was always low by international standards, but it increased by 14 years between 1950–1955 and 1905–1910. At its low point in 2000–2005, female e_0^0 in Botswana was 1 year lower than in Nigeria.

By 2005–2010, female e_0^0 in Botswana was 2 years greater than in Nigeria.

Figure 4.12 shows male e_0^0 in the same set of countries shown in Figures 4.10 and 4.11. Figures 4.11 and 4.12 use the same vertical scale to facilitate comparisons between males and females. Higher female than male e_0^0 is clear. As for females, males in Sweden and Japan had very high e_0^0 in 2005–2010, 79 in each country. Only Iceland had a higher male e_0^0 in 2005–2010, at 80 years. Singapore, Italy, Australia, and Switzerland also had a male e_0^0 of 79 years in 2005–2010. Similar to females, the increases in male e_0^0 in Japan of 19 years and China of 26 years are notable.

In China, we can see the effects of the 1959–1961 famine in the decline in male e_0^0 between 1955–1960 and 1960–1965, similar to the increase in the IMR that we saw in Figure 4.10. For females, the famine slowed progress in e_0^0, while we see a decline of 3 years for males.

After 1965, male e_0^0 in China increased rapidly, going from 5 years less than Russia in 1965–1970 to 9 years more than Russia in 2005–2010. Male e_0^0 in Russia increased from 1950 through the mid-1960s and then declined through the early 1980s. Male e_0^0 in Russia rose briefly in the late 1980s,

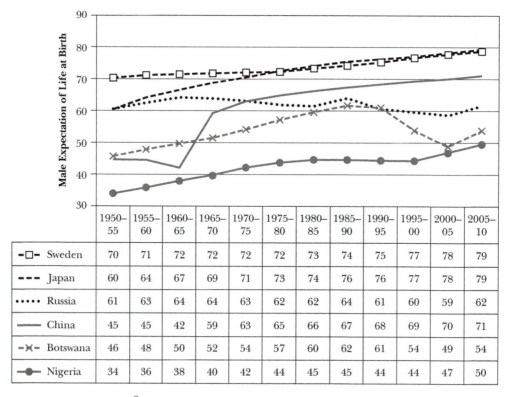

FIGURE 4.12   Male e_0^0 in Selected Countries

	1950–55	1955–60	1960–65	1965–70	1970–75	1975–80	1980–85	1985–90	1990–95	1995–00	2000–05	2005–10
-□- Sweden	70	71	72	72	72	72	73	74	75	77	78	79
--- Japan	60	64	67	69	71	73	74	76	76	77	78	79
••••• Russia	61	63	64	64	63	62	62	64	61	60	59	62
—— China	45	45	42	59	63	65	66	67	68	69	70	71
-×- Botswana	46	48	50	52	54	57	60	62	61	54	49	54
-●- Nigeria	34	36	38	40	42	44	45	45	44	44	47	50

mainly as a result of Gorbachev's anti-alcohol campaign. After the dissolution of the Soviet Union, male e_0^0 declined and then recovered somewhat in 2005–2010, although it did not reach its 1985–1990 value. Adult mortality in Russia is discussed further in Chapter 7.

Between 1950–1955 and 1985–1990, male e_0^0 in Botswana increased by 15 years. Then the value declined by 13 years between 1985–1990 and 2000–2005. The value for Botswana recovered somewhat in 2005–2010, reaching its 1970–1975 value. As for females, the decline in male e_0^0 in Botswana was due to the impact of HIV. The impact of HIV was less on male than on female e_0^0—between 1990–1995 and 1995–2000, male e_0^0 in Botswana declined by 7 years, while female e_0^0 declined by 9 years. In countries where HIV is mainly transmitted through heterosexual intercourse, such as in sub-Saharan Africa, the impact on adult female mortality is greater than on adult male mortality. Male e_0^0 in Nigeria was always low by international standards, but it increased by 11 years between 1950–1955 and 1980–1985. Even at its low point in 2000–2005, male e_0^0 in Botswana was 2 years greater than in Nigeria. By 2005–2010, male e_0^0 in Botswana was 4 years greater than in Nigeria.

Figure 4.13 shows female e_0^0 minus male e_0^0, similar to what was shown in Figure 4.7. The increase in the gender gap in mortality in Russia over time is clear. The gap declines in 1985–1990 because Gorbachev's anti-alcohol program had a greater impact on male than on female survival. The differential effect of the Chinese famine on the two sexes is clear in the changes in the gender gap in China in the 1950s. The effects of the Chinese famine were especially severe for males and for those over age 40 due to a food allocation system during the famine that favored the young.[13] In Sweden, the gap is fairly constant, while in Japan there is some increase over time. Botswana goes from females having a 4-year advantage in 1950–1955 to a 1-year disadvantage by 2005–2010. This change in the sex differential is because HIV in sub-Saharan Africa results in higher death rates for females than males.

TYPICAL MORTALITY PATTERNS

In this section, we look at typical mortality patterns by age for females in three populations that were chosen due to their different mortality levels, in order to look at how chances of dying by age

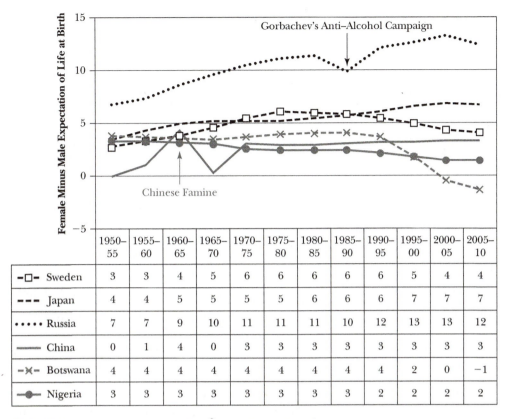

	1950– 55	1955– 60	1960– 65	1965– 70	1970– 75	1975– 80	1980– 85	1985– 90	1990– 95	1995– 00	2000– 05	2005– 10
–□– Sweden	3	3	4	5	6	6	6	6	6	5	4	4
– – – Japan	4	4	5	5	5	5	6	6	6	7	7	7
• • • • Russia	7	7	9	10	11	11	11	10	12	13	13	12
——— China	0	1	4	0	3	3	3	3	3	3	3	3
–✕– Botswana	4	4	4	4	4	4	4	4	4	2	0	−1
–●– Nigeria	3	3	3	3	3	3	3	3	2	2	2	2

FIGURE 4.13 Female Minus Male e_0^0 at Birth in Selected Countries

differ at various mortality levels. None of the three populations are substantially affected by HIV. The populations are (1) India in 1990 (a high-mortality population: female e_0^0 of 58 years, IMR 84), (2) the United States in 1990 (a low-mortality population: female e_0^0 of 79 years, IMR 8), and (3) Japan in 2008 (a very-low-mortality population: female e_0^0 of 86 years, IMR 2).[14]

Figure 4.14 shows, among women alive at a given age, the chance that a woman will die before she reaches an older age. The life table value that looks at this is called $_nq_x$, which is the chance that a person who has just turned age x will die before he or she reaches age x + n. In Figure 4.14, $_nq_x$ is multiplied by 1,000 in order to make the results easier to understand.

In every population, the chance of dying is relatively high at very young ages. The risk of dying then falls to a low level and increases after about age 50. Mortality data by age are often shown for people by 5-year age groups, except for those under age 5. The chance of dying between birth and age 1 is higher than the chance of dying between age 1 and age 5. Thus, for those younger than age 5, mortality data are typically shown separately for those aged 0 (not

yet age 1), and those aged 1–4 (at least aged 1 but not yet aged 5).

The elevated risk of dying at very young ages is clear in Figure 4.14 in the results from India. This U-shaped pattern of mortality risks by age is typical of virtually all populations. For the United States and Japan, the higher chance of dying when younger than age 5 is not as apparent in Figure 4.14 due to the scale used. However, the values in the data table make clear that even in the United States and Japan, the risks of dying are higher before the first birthday than they are between the first and fifth birthdays. In the United States in 1990, 8 out of every 1,000 babies died before their first birthday, but among those alive on their first birthday only 2 out of every 1,000 died before their fifth birthday. Among those alive on their fifth birthday, only 1 out of every 1,000 died before their tenth birthday.

Another way to look at mortality risks by age is to ask: Out of 100,000 newborn babies, how many will still be alive at later ages? The indicator for this in the life table is called l_x, which answers the question: Out of 100,000 births, how many persons will still be alive on their xth birthday? Thus, the value for age 10, l_{10},

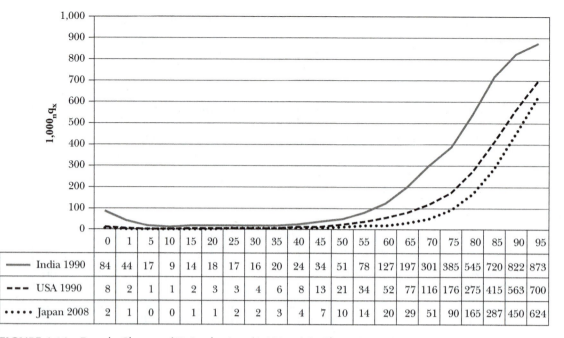

	0	1	5	10	15	20	25	30	35	40	45	50	55	60	65	70	75	80	85	90	95
—— India 1990	84	44	17	9	14	18	17	16	20	24	34	51	78	127	197	301	385	545	720	822	873
--- USA 1990	8	2	1	1	2	3	3	4	6	8	13	21	34	52	77	116	176	275	415	563	700
••••• Japan 2008	2	1	0	0	1	1	2	2	3	4	7	10	14	20	29	51	90	165	287	450	624

FIGURE 4.14   Female Chance of Dying by Age ($1,000_nq_x$) in Three Countries

answers the question, out of 100,000 births, how many will still be alive on their 10th birthday? This is shown in Figure 4.15 for females for the same three populations examined in Figure 4.14.

In India in 1990, the number of survivors declined rapidly from birth (age 0) to age 5. Only 88% of Indian baby girls survived to their fifth birthday. On the other hand, 98% of American girls in 1990 survived to age 5, and 99% of girls in Japan in 2008 survived to age 5. The rapid decline in the number

of survivors between birth and age 5 in India is consistent with the relatively high chance of dying below age 5 shown in Figure 4.14. The number of survivors in India declined more slowly from age 5 to about age 50, after which the number of survivors declined rapidly, with only about 9% of women surviving from birth to age 80. The rapid decline in the number of survivors after age 50 shown in Figure 4.15 is consistent with the increase in the proportions dying after age 50 shown in Figure 4.14.

For the United States in 1990, 57% survived to age 80, and for Japan in 2008, 78% survived to age 80. The cumulative effect of the lower chances of dying in Japan than in the United States above age 50 is shown in Figure 4.15 in the substantially higher proportion of females surviving to advanced ages in Japan than in the United States. This is apparent in Figure 4.15 since the line for Japan is above that for the United States, and the gap between Japan and the United States increases after age 50.

RECTANGULARIZATION OF MORTALITY: THE EXAMPLE OF SWEDEN

The pattern of change in survival to various ages as overall life expectancy increases is often referred to as the **rectangularization of mortality**.[15] As shown in Figure 4.15, in India, with a life

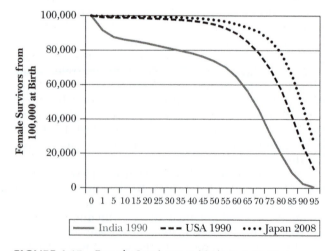

FIGURE 4.15   Female Survivors to Various Ages Out of 100,000 at Birth (l_x) in Three Countries

expectancy of 60 years in 1990, the number of survivors decreases rapidly after birth and then more
slowly until about age 55. In the United States in
1990 and even more so in Japan in 2008, there
is almost no decrease in the number of survivors
until about age 50 and only a slow decline until
about age 65, after which the number of survivors
declines more rapidly. In lower mortality populations, the graph of survivors by age increasingly
resembles half of a rectangle, with little change in
the number of survivors until an advanced age and
then a rapid decline.

This rectangularization of mortality is even clearer
when looking at the graphs of survival to various ages
across time periods in a given country. This is shown
for females in Sweden in Figure 4.16.[16] Sweden is a
good example to look at because it is known for having had high-quality mortality data even in the nineteenth century. Also, Sweden and Japan in 2008 had
the highest e_0^0 for females among all countries—
83 years.

In Sweden in 1816–1840, female e_0^0 was 44
years. There was high infant and child mortality,
as indicated in the rapid decline in the number
of survivors from birth. After age 5, the number
of survivors continues to decline, but more gradually, with the number of survivors from age 10 to
95 plotting an almost diagonal line. In 1891–1900,
female e_0^0 was 54 years, and the graph of survivors
looks similar to that for India in Figure 4.15, when
female e_0^0 was 60 years. In 1936–1940, female e_0^0 in
Sweden was 67 years. In the 1936–1940 graph, the
decline in survivors between age 0 and 5 is much
more gradual, reflecting a substantial reduction in

infant and child mortality. In 1936–1940, the graph
of survivors declines slowly until about age 50 or 55,
after which the number of survivors declines more
rapidly. By 1966–1970 and even more so in 2008,
the graph of the number of survivors resembles
half of a rectangle. Under female mortality conditions in Sweden in 2008, 92% of newborn babies
would survive to age 65, and 81% would survive to
age 75. The graph ends at age 95, but under Swedish mortality conditions in 2008, 11% of women
would survive to age 95, and 2% of women would
survive to age 100.

AGE-ADJUSTED DEATH RATES

As shown in Figure 4.14, the chances of dying vary
by age. They have a U-shaped pattern, being high
at young ages and at advanced ages. In fairly low-
mortality populations, such as in the United States
in 1990 or Japan in 2008, the main characteristic of
death rates by age is that after age 5 they increase
by age and increase more rapidly after about age
60. The chance of dying for a 65-year-old in Japan
in 2008 is higher than that for a 40-year-old in India in 1990, even though at every age, death rates
in Japan in 2008 are lower than in India in 1990.
A drawback of the crude death rate is that after
age 5 it does not adjust for the age structure of the
population.

One overall mortality measure that is not affected
by the age structure of the population is e_0^0. Another
measure is an **age-adjusted death rate**, which adjusts
for the changing age distribution over time in a
population.

An age-adjusted death rate, also called an age-
standardized death rate, adjusts for changes in the
age structure over time in one population or for differences in age structure between populations. An
age-adjusted rate can be calculated for the entire
population or for those in a particular age range.
An age-adjusted death rate shows what the crude
death rate would have been if the population had
a particular unchanging age distribution over time.
That unchanging age distribution is called the standard population. The standard population used can
be the age distribution of the actual population at
a given point in time, or it can be some other age
distribution.

An age adjustment can make a substantial difference in the picture that is obtained from mortality
trends. Figure 4.17 shows the crude death rate and
the age-adjusted death rate for the United States in
1980–2008.[17] The standard population is that for the
United States in 2000.

We see that the age-adjusted rate declines over
time because death rates at most ages were steadily
declining between 1940 and 2008. However, the

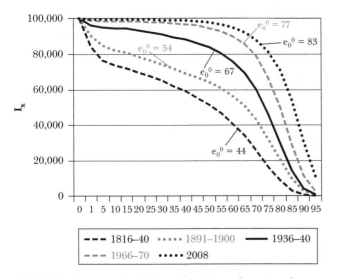

FIGURE 4.16 Rectangularization of Mortality: Female
Survivors from Birth in Sweden at Various Dates

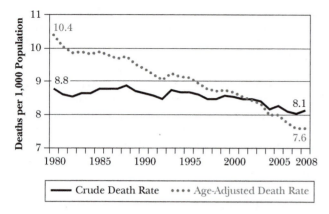

FIGURE 4.17 Crude Death Rates and Age-Adjusted Death Rates, the United States, 1980–2008

crude rate is almost constant, declining only from 8.8 to 8.1. This is because the lower mortality risks by age over time in the United States were offset by the aging of the population and the increasing proportion of the population at advanced ages, where death rates are higher than at younger ages in all populations. Since the crude death rate was affected both by the declining death rates by age and by the increasing proportion of the population at older ages, these two factors counterbalanced each other to result in very little change in the crude death rate.

Age-adjusted death rates also are useful for showing the death rate from a particular cause for a segment of the population, such as for the adult population. For example, in Chapter 6, Figure 6.13 shows the age-adjusted death rate from diabetes and obesity for those aged 15–64 in South Africa.

THE LIFE TABLE

The **life table** is a way of summarizing the mortality situation of a given place at a given time. A life table is usually calculated and presented separately for males and females, because the mortality patterns of men and women are different. A life table looks at what would happen to a group of people from birth if they were exposed to the risks of dying that occurred in a given time and place. The number of births that the life table begins with is called the **radix** of the life table. Usually a life table has a radix of 100,000 births.

Age Last Birthday and Exact Age

Demographers use the term **age** in two different ways. When used just as "age," it typically means **age last birthday**. Thus, a person age 18 has already had his or her 18th birthday and has not yet had his or her 19th birthday.

Exact age means age on a birthday. On your fifth birthday, you are exact age 5. Between exact age 5 and exact age 6, you are age 5. If you are born January 1, 1985, then on January 1, 2005, you are exact age 20. On July 1, 2005, you are exact age 20.5.

Columns of the Life Table: U.S. Female Life Table 2000 as an Example

Table 4.2 describes the columns of a life table. The meaning of these columns will become clearer as we look at subsequent graphs. The life table for U.S. females in 2000 is shown in Table 4.3.

The l_x column shows the number of survivors out of 100,000 babies to various later exact ages. The l_x column declines with each successive age, since people are only born at age 0. Figures 4.15 and 4.16 showed l_x values.

Figure 4.18 graphs the values of l_x from Table 4.3. Figure 4.18 also shows the l_x values for males in the United States in 2000.[18] In Figure 4.18, the line for females is higher than the line for males. This is because at every age, females in the United States had lower death rates than males. Thus, from birth, a higher proportion of females than males survived to every successive age. This is similar to the higher line for Japanese females than for American females in Figure 4.15 because Japanese women in 2008 had lower death rates at every age than American women in 1990.

The $_nd_x$ column shows the distribution of the deaths of the 100,000 babies across all ages, given the mortality conditions shown in the life table. This is shown as the number of deaths between exact age x and exact age x + n. The $_nd_x$ values are just the difference between successive values of l_x, expressed in an equation $_nd_x = l_x - l_{x+n}$. The values from the $_nd_x$ column in Table 4.3 are graphed in Figure 4.19. In Figure 4.19, the $_nd_x$ values for males in the United

TABLE 4.2 Columns of the Life Table

x	l_x	$_nd_x$	$_nq_x$	$_np_x$	$_nm_x$	$_nL_x$	T_x	e_x^0

x: age, or age at beginning of the interval

l_x: number of survivors to the beginning of the interval, to exact age x (age on your birthday), usually assume $l_0 = 100,000$

$_nd_x$: number dying between exact age x and exact age x + n

$_nq_x$: proportion dying between exact age x and exact age x + n

$_np_x$: proportion surviving between exact age x and exact age x + n

$_nm_x$: age-specific death rate between age x and x + n

$_nL_x$: number of person-years lived between age x and age x + n

T_x: years lived in the life table above exact age x

e_x^0: average number of years lived after exact age x

TABLE 4.3   Life Table for U.S. Females, 2000

x	l_x	$_nd_x$	$_nq_x$	$_nP_x$	$_nm_x$	$_nL_x$	T_x	e_x^0
0	100,000	660	0.00660	0.99340	0.00663	99,406	7,957,469	79.6
1	99,340	114	0.00115	0.99885	0.00029	397,088	7,858,062	79.1
5	99,227	69	0.00070	0.99930	0.00014	495,959	7,460,974	75.2
10	99,157	80	0.00080	0.99920	0.00016	495,586	6,965,015	70.2
15	99,077	195	0.00196	0.99804	0.00039	494,900	6,469,428	65.3
20	98,883	233	0.00235	0.99765	0.00047	493,832	5,974,528	60.4
25	98,650	260	0.00264	0.99736	0.00053	492,600	5,480,696	55.6
30	98,390	361	0.00367	0.99633	0.00074	491,046	4,988,096	50.7
35	98,028	553	0.00564	0.99436	0.00113	488,759	4,497,050	45.9
40	97,475	841	0.00863	0.99137	0.00173	485,273	4,008,290	41.1
45	96,634	1,210	0.01252	0.98748	0.00252	480,144	3,523,018	36.5
50	95,424	1,802	0.01889	0.98111	0.00381	472,614	3,042,873	31.9
55	93,622	2,804	0.02995	0.97005	0.00608	461,099	2,570,259	27.5
60	90,818	4,317	0.04753	0.95247	0.00974	443,297	2,109,160	23.2
65	86,501	6,316	0.07302	0.92698	0.01516	416,713	1,665,864	19.3
70	80,184	8,868	0.11059	0.88941	0.02341	378,752	1,249,150	15.6
75	71,316	12,257	0.17186	0.82814	0.03760	325,941	870,398	12.2
80	59,060	16,066	0.27202	0.72798	0.06297	255,135	544,457	9.2
85	42,994	17,776	0.41344	0.58656	0.10424	170,531	289,323	6.7
90	25,218	14,228	0.56417	0.43583	0.17057	83,410	118,791	4.7
95	10,991	7,714	0.70185	0.29815	0.27594	27,956	35,382	3.2
100	3,277	3,277			0.44127	7,426	7,426	2.3

States in 2000 are also shown. The values of $_nd_x$ increase with age and then decrease. The values become zero when all 100,000 persons die under the life table conditions. The $_nd_x$ values for females peak at a later age than the $_nd_x$ values for males because the female death rates are lower than the male rates at every age. This means that women tend to live longer than men, and thus their deaths are bunched at an older age than the deaths of men.

Table 4.3 also shows $_nm_x$ values, which are **age-specific death rates**. Just as the crude death rate is the number of deaths divided by the total population, an age-specific death rate is the deaths to persons in

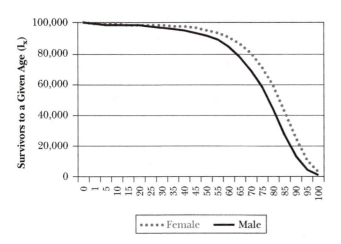

FIGURE 4.18   Survivors to a Given Age from 100,000 at Birth (l_x): the United States, 2000

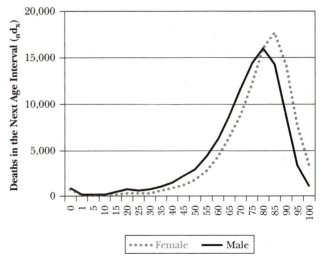

FIGURE 4.19   Deaths in the Next Interval from 100,000 at Birth ($_nd_x$): the United States, 2000

BOX 4.2
Proportions and Rates: $_nq_x$ and $_nm_x$

Two different, but similar, measures of the chances of dying in an age interval are $_nq_x$ and $_nm_x$. $_nq_x$ is among people alive at exact age x, the proportion who will die before reaching exact age x + n. $_nm_x$ is among those who are at least exact age x and not yet exact age x + n, the number who will die between exact ages x and x + n divided by the number of people alive between ages x and x + n in the life table.

Imagine that there are 2,000 people alive at exact age 20 and there are 1,800 people alive at exact age 21.
Then,

$$_1q_{20} = (2,000 - 1,800)/2,000 = 200/2,000 = 0.100$$

The denominator of $_1m_{20}$ is estimated as the average of the number of people alive at exact age 20 and the number of people alive at exact age 21. Then,

$$_1m_{20} = (2,000 - 1,800)/(0.5 \times (2,000 + 1,800))$$
$$= 200/1,900 = 0.105$$

$_nq_x$ is always somewhat less than $_nm_x$ because they both have the same numerator, but the denominator for $_nq_x$ is somewhat larger than the denominator for $_nm_x$.

The patterns shown by $_nq_x$ and by $_nm_x$ always tell the same story.

---

an age group divided by the number of people in that age group.

The $_nq_x$ column shows the proportion of persons dying between exact age x and exact age x + n, among those alive at exact age x. Figure 4.14 shows $_nq_x$ values. It is clear in Table 4.3 that even for the United States in 2000, the chance of dying is greater between birth and a baby girl's first birthday than between the girl's first and fifth birthdays, and the chance of dying between the first and fifth birthdays is higher than it is between the fifth and

tenth birthdays or between the tenth and fifteenth birthdays.

$_nq_x$ is similar to the age-specific death rate, $_nm_x$. The numerator of both measures is identical, but the denominators are slightly different. The values of $_nm_x$ are shown in Table 4.3. The difference between $_nq_x$ and $_nm_x$ is explained in Box 4.2.

The values of $_nq_x$ for females in the United States 2000 in Table 4.3 are graphed in Figure 4.20, along with the $_nq_x$ values for males for the United States in 2000. The line for females in Figure 4.20 lies below the line for males, again indicating that the risks of dying for females are lower than the risks of dying for males.

The probability of surviving from age x to age x + n among those alive at age x is $_np_x$. Since people either die or do not die between age x and age x + n, $_np_x = 1 - _nq_x$. The values of $_np_x$ are also shown in Table 4.3.

Presentation of $_nq_x$ Values

Sometimes, rather than showing the actual $_nq_x$ values (or 1,000 × $_nq_x$), the base 10 logarithm of the $_nq_x$ (or 1,000 × $_nq_x$ values) is shown. The logarithm spreads out differences in values at low values and compresses differences in higher values. Thus, the difference between 1,000 × $_nq_x$ values of 5 and of 10 is shown as larger than the difference between 1,000 × $_nq_x$ values of 200 and of 205.

Figure 4.21 shows the base 10 logarithm of the $_nq_x$ values for females from Table 4.3 and also shows the base 10 logarithm of the $_nq_x$ values for males in the

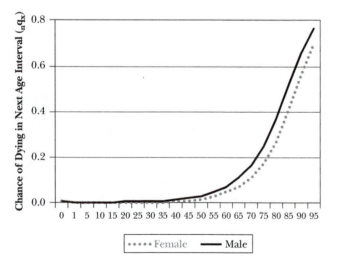

FIGURE 4.20   Chance of Dying in the Next Interval ($_nq_x$): the United States, 2000

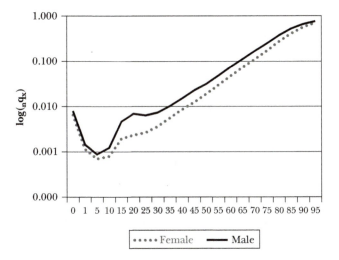

$\log(_nq_x)$

1.000

0.100

0.010

0.001

0.000

0 1 5 10 15 20 25 30 35 40 45 50 55 60 65 70 75 80 85 90 95

$\cdots$ Female   —— Male

FIGURE 4.21   Base 10 Logarithm of Chance of Dying in the Next Interval $\log(_nq_x)$: the United States, 2000

United States in 2000. In Figure 4.20, the $_nq_x$ values for males and females below age 40 looked identical, and for both sexes the values seemed to be close to zero. In Figure 4.21, the decline in the chance of dying shortly after birth is clear before the chance of dying begins to increase in the 10–14 age group. Also, in Figure 4.21, the much higher risk of dying for males than for females between ages 10 and 30 is clear, due to the greater tendency of young men than of young women to engage in risky behaviors. This is discussed further in Chapter 7.

Person-Years of Life and $_nL_x$ Values

The life table uses the concept of **person-years of life**. If one person lives one year, he or she contributes one person-year of life to the population. If 12 people each live one month, they also in total contribute one person-year of life. In a life table, l_x indicates the number of people living to exact age x (i.e., to their xth birthday). As shown in Table 4.3, $_nL_x$ shows the number of person-years lived between exact age x and exact age x + n. In a life table, above age 5, we usually look at the mortality situation in 5-year age intervals. In Table 4.3, out of 100,000 births, 99,157 females would be alive at exact age 10, and 99,077 would be alive at exact age 15—these are the l_{10} and the l_{15} values shown. Thus, the number of deaths between exact age 10 and exact age 15 is 80, which is the $_5d_{10}$ value shown in the table.

Imagine that females who died between exact age 10 and exact age 15 on average died halfway through the age interval, at exact age 12.5. Then each person who died in the age interval would have contributed 2.5 person-years of life to the population. In this case,

the number of person-years lived between exact age 10 and exact age 15 would be:

$$(5 \times 99{,}077) + (2.5 \times 80) = 495{,}586$$

Each person who survived to age 15 contributed 5 person-years, and each person who died in the age interval contributed 2.5 years. In this situation, 100,000 newborn girls would have 495,586 person-years of life between exact age 10 and exact age 15. $_nL_x$ is the number of person-years lived between exact age x and exact age x + n. In Table 4.3, $_5L_{10}$ is 495,959 because for American females in 2000, deaths between exact age 10 and exact age 15 on average occurred halfway through the interval.

At very young ages, those who die usually die much earlier than halfway through an age interval. In more developed countries, those who die before their first birthday usually die very soon after birth. This is because in more developed countries, most infant deaths are due to congenital problems that began before birth or are related to being very premature. These babies are not very healthy at birth.[19]

In Table 4.3, l_0 is 100,000 and l_1 is 99340. If those who died in their first year of life on average died at 0.5 years of age, $_1L_0$ would be

$$l_1 + 0.5_1d_0 = 99{,}340 + 0.5 \times 660 = 99{,}670$$

But $_1L_0$ is not 99,670. Rather, it is 99,406, which is less than it would have been if those who died before their first birthday lived halfway through the interval. In fact, those who died in the first year on average lived 0.10 of a year. Those who die between their first and their fifth birthdays also tend to die less than halfway through the age interval, which would be at exact age 3. In 2000, American females who died between exact age 1 and exact age 5 on average died at exact age 2.6. One can check the $_5L_x$ values in Table 4.3 and see that above age 5, $_5L_x$ is very close to $5 \times (l_{x+5}) + 0.5 \times 5 \times _5d_x$.

In a life table, $_nm_x = _nd_x/_nL_x$, which means that the age-specific death rate for age x to x + n is the number of deaths between age x and x + n (which is $_nd_x$) divided by the number of person-years lived between age x and x + n (which is $_nL_x$).

Years of Life Remaining T_x and Expectation of Remaining Life e_x^0

T_x is the number of years lived above exact age x by people in a life table who survive to exact age x. In a situation such as that in Table 4.3, T_x is the number of years lived above exact age x among 100,000 persons from birth. T_x is calculated by cumulating the $_nL_x$ values from age x to the oldest age. Expectation of life at birth, which is discussed in this chapter, is

FIGURE 4.22 Expectation of Remaining Life (e_x^0): the United States, 2000

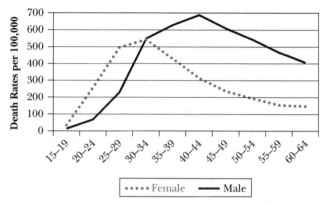

FIGURE 4.23 Adult Death Rates per 100,000 Population by Age and Sex Reported as Due to HIV: South Africa, 2004

the average number of years lived by a person from birth in terms of a given life table. Thus,

$$e_0^0 = T_0/l_0 = 7,957,469/100,000 = 79.6$$

which means that the average number of years lived from birth is the total number of person-years lived above age 0 divided by the number of people alive at age 0.

One can also look at the average number of years lived above exact age x among those who are alive at exact age x. **Expectation of remaining life at age x** is the number of years that a person can expect to live given the person is alive on his or her xth birthday. Thus, using the values from Table 4.3, expectation of remaining life at age 65 is as follows:

$$e_{65}^0 = T_{65}/l_{65} = 1,665,864/86,501 = 19.3$$

In the female life table for the United States for 2000, $e_{65}^0 = 19.3$. Thus, a woman who survived to her 65th birthday on average would survive 19.3 more years to age 84.3, which is considerably older than the e_0^0, which was 79.6 years.

Figure 4.22 shows expectation of remaining life by sex for the United States in 2000. At every age, females have more years of expected remaining life than males, reflecting the lower chances of dying for females than males at each age.

THE EFFECTS OF HIV ON MORTALITY BY AGE AND SEX

The increase in HIV has affected the level of mortality in several countries, especially those in sub-Saharan Africa. The effects of HIV on the IMR and e_0^0 are clear in Figures 4.10, 4.11, and 4.12 for Nigeria and even more so for Botswana. HIV increases death rates differentially at different ages, and in populations in which HIV is mainly transmitted through heterosexual

intercourse, the age patterns of the effects on mortality are different for men than for women.

Good-quality data on death rates from HIV by age and sex in less developed countries are difficult to find. South Africa is one less developed country with high HIV death rates for which good-quality data are available. Figure 4.23 shows death rates per 1,000 population reported as due to HIV for South Africa in 2004 by age and sex.[20]

It is thought that deaths from HIV for South Africa are underreported, but there is agreement that the mortality pattern by age and sex shown in Figure 4.23 reflects the pattern of mortality found in high-HIV-mortality populations in which HIV is mainly spread through heterosexual contact, which is the situation throughout sub-Saharan Africa. It is almost certain that the pattern of death rates from HIV by age and sex in Botswana would look similar to what is seen in Figure 4.23.

We see in Figure 4.23 that HIV death rates increase after the teenage years for each sex, peak, and then decline. The peak occurs at an earlier age for women than for men. Also, the death rates below the peak age are higher for women than for men. HIV death rates peak at a younger age for women partially because women tend to be younger than their sexual partners. Also, due to reproductive physiology, women are more easily infected by HIV than men. A woman who has intercourse once with an HIV-positive male is more likely to become HIV-positive from that encounter than is a man who has intercourse once with an HIV-positive woman.[21]

Figure 4.24 shows age-specific death rates from all causes in populations heavily affected by HIV. It is based on mortality data from eight demographic surveillance sites in the INDEPTH network where mortality (especially after infancy) was thought to be substantially due to HIV.[22] The INDEPTH Network is discussed

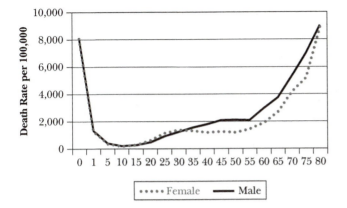

FIGURE 4.24 Death Rates per 100,000 Population ($_nm_x$) Based on African Populations with Substantial HIV Mortality in the INDEPTH Network

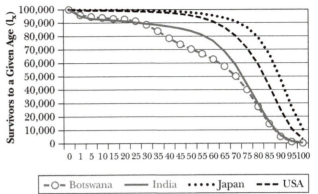

FIGURE 4.25 Female Survivors to a Given Age from 100,000 at Birth (l_x), 2009: Botswana, India, Japan, and the United States

in Chapter 3. The death rates peak for females in their twenties and early thirties and peak for males in their forties. For each sex, the rates then decline before increasing with advancing age. The patterns by age in Figure 4.24 are consistent with the age and sex patterns for HIV mortality apparent in Figure 4.23.

HIV is not the only disease for which death rates peak at a young adult age. Tuberculosis (TB) death rates also have typically peaked in the young adult ages.[23] However, even in populations with high TB rates, TB has not contributed such a large portion of mortality that it results in a peak in age-specific death rates in the working ages, unlike what is seen for HIV in Figure 4.24.

LIFE TABLE PATTERNS IN INDIA, THE UNITED STATES, JAPAN, AND BOTSWANA IN 2009

In this section, we look at life table values for females in India, the United States, and Japan for 2009. These are good examples of a high-mortality, a low-mortality, and a very-low-mortality population. Botswana was the first country for which HIV can be seen to lead to a decline in e_0^0. We saw in Figures 4.11 and 4.12 that e_0^0 in Botswana fell between the 1985–1990 period and the 1990–1995 period for each sex. The life table for Botswana in 2009 is very much affected by HIV mortality and shows a different age pattern of mortality than life tables for populations that are not seriously affected by HIV mortality.

Figure 4.25 shows the l_x values for 2009 for the four countries. The effects of HIV mortality on the values for Botswana are indicated in the rapid decline in the l_x values between ages 25 and about 60. The l_x values for Botswana are higher than for India below age 30, but the l_x values for Botswana fall below those for India for ages 35 through 75.

Figure 4.26 shows the $_nd_x$ values for the four populations. The jump in the values for Botswana visible for

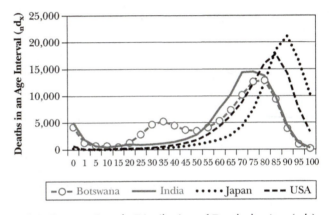

FIGURE 4.26 Female Distribution of Deaths by Age ($_nd_x$), 2009: Botswana, India, Japan, and the United States

those aged 25–50 is due to HIV deaths. The $_nd_x$ values for the United States peak at a later age than for India, and those for Japan peak at an even later age than for the United States, reflecting the lower age-specific death rates in the United States than in India and the even lower age-specific death rates in Japan.

Figure 4.27 shows $1,000 \times {}_nq_x$ values for the four populations. The $_nq_x$ are multiplied by 1,000 to make the results clearer. The jump at ages 25–50 for Botswana is also clear in the $_nq_x$ values, although it is not as obvious as in Figure 4.26, which showed the $_nd_x$ values. The higher death rates in Botswana than India at ages 25–50 are why the l_x values for India shown in Figure 4.25 are higher than for Botswana at ages 35–75.

The logged $1,000 \times {}_nq_x$ values in Figure 4.28 make the effects of HIV on the age pattern of mortality risk for Botswana quite clear. Also, the falling risk of death after birth is apparent even for Japan with its very low overall mortality.

Figure 4.29 shows e_x^0 values for the four countries. This is the average number of years that a person

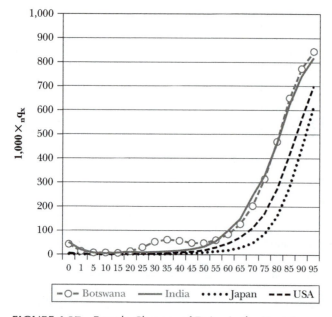

FIGURE 4.27   Female Chances of Dying in the Next Age Interval ($1,000 \times {}_nq_x$) 2009: Botswana, India, Japan, and the United States

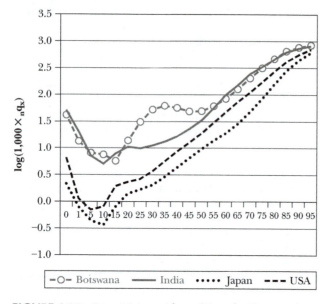

FIGURE 4.28   Base 10 Logarithm of Female Chance of Dying in the Next Age Interval ($\log(1,000 \times {}_nq_x)$), 2009: Botswana, India, Japan, and the United States

would live after their xth birthday, given the person is alive on his or her xth birthday. For example, e_{40}^0 is the average number of years that a person would live after his or her 40th birthday if he or she survived to age 40. The high death rates for Botswana after age 25 influence the e_x^0 values at all younger ages down to e_0^0. By age 50, the e_x^0 values for Botswana

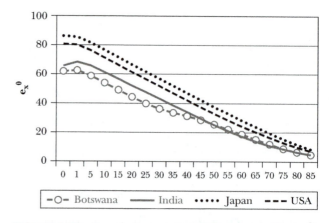

FIGURE 4.29   Female Expectation of Remaining Life (e_x^0), 2009: Botswana, India, Japan, and the United States

are equal to or higher than those for India. This is because, as seen in Figures 4.27 and 4.38, by age 50 the chances of dying in Botswana are almost as low as in India, and by age 60 the chances of dying in Botswana are as low as or lower than in India. In all populations, the e_x^0 values increase after birth because those who survive the high death rates just after birth can look forward to more years of survival than they could have expected at birth. This situation is explained in Box 4.2.

LIFE TABLE VALUES RELATED TO FERTILITY AND OLD-AGE SUPPORT FOR THE TEN LARGEST COUNTRIES IN 2010

Table 4.4 shows calculations based on life table values for each of the ten largest countries in 2010. The values refer to 2009, which was the most recent year for which these data were available.

Column (1) shows the ranking in population size in 2010, and Column (2) indicates the country.

Column (3) shows female e_0^0 in 2009. In the United States and in Japan female e_0^0 was greater than 80 years, while in Nigeria female e_0^0 was less than 55 years.

Column (4) shows $1,000 \times (1 - (l_5/l_0))$, which asks the following question: Out of 1,000 babies born, how many die before they reach their fifth birthday? In Nigeria, 13% of all female babies died before their fifth birthday, while in the United States and Japan, less than 1% of female babies died before their fifth birthday.

In most populations, the mean age of female childbearing is close to 30 years. Column (5) shows $l_{30}/100$, which asks the question, out of 1,000 baby girls, how many survive to their 30th birthday? One way to interpret Column (5) is as the chance that a woman survives long enough to have children. In China, the United States, Brazil, Russia, and Japan, over 95% of

TABLE 4.4   Female Life Table Values for the Ten Most Populous Countries in 2010

(1)	(2)	(3)	(4)	(5)	(6)	(7)
		$F\, e_0^0$ 2009	$F\, 1{,}000 \times (1 - (l_5/l_0))$ 2009	$F\, l_{30}/1{,}000$ 2009	$F\, e_{65}^0$ 2009	$F\, 1{,}000 \times (l_{65}/l_{30})$ 2009
Rank	Country					
1	China(PRC)	76	22	968	16	873
2	India	66	70	893	14	770
3	United States	81	7	985	20	891
4	Indonesia	71	35	945	15	807
5	Brazil	77	19	970	18	856
6	Pakistan	64	87	879	14	757
7	Nigeria	54	132	785	13	600
8	Bangladesh	66	51	912	14	721
9	Russia	74	11	973	16	811
10	Japan	87	3	992	24	943

women survive to their 30th birthday, while in Nigeria less than 79% of women survive to their 30th birthday.

Column (6) shows e_{65}^0, which is the average number of years a woman will survive after her 65th birthday, if she is alive on her 65th birthday. It is striking how little variation there is in the values in Column 6. For example, female e_0^0 in China is ten years greater than in India, but expectation of remaining life at age 65 is only 2 years greater in China than in India. Also, although female e_0^0 in the United States is 17 years greater than in Pakistan, female e_{65}^0 is only 6 years greater in the United States than in Pakistan. This is because high mortality (when e_0^0 is low) is mainly because of high infant and child mortality. In all populations, those who survive to an advanced age, such as age 65, are likely to survive for many more years.

Column (7) shows $1{,}000 \times (l_{65}/l_{30})$, which asks the question: For every 1,000 women who survive to their 30th birthday, how many will still be alive on their 65th birthday? One way to interpret this is: If a woman lives long enough to have children, what is the chance that she will live long enough to need someone to take care of her? Even in Nigeria with female e_0^0 of 54 years, 60% of women alive at age 30 will survive to age 65, and we see from Column (6) that in Nigeria those women alive at age 65 can expect to live for 13 more years, to age 78. In India, Indonesia, and Bangladesh, over 70% of women alive on their 30th birthday can expect to be alive on their 65th birthday, and if they live to age 65, they can expect to live 14 more years.

One theory about the reasons for high fertility is that people have many children as a form of old age insurance. That is, they want to be sure to have surviving children when they are elderly and unable to provide for all of their own needs. Some people think that if e_0^0 is less than 65 years, then this is a silly concern, because they (incorrectly) think that no one is going to survive to old age in a population with e_0^0 less than 65 years. We see from Table 4.4 that even in high-mortality populations, people who live to be parents have a rational basis to be concerned about their support when they become elderly.

SEX DIFFERENCES IN MORTALITY BY AGE: THE UNITED STATES, RUSSIA, AND INDIA

In most populations, females have lower death rates than males at every age. There is some evidence that there is a biological basis for this female advantage. It has been found that among chimpanzees, the closest primate relative to humans, females have lower age-specific mortality rates than males.[24] Also, women typically have better health behaviors (less smoking, lower alcohol consumption, and fewer risky behaviors) than men. Also, women tend to acknowledge they are ill and seek medical treatment more readily than men. Thus, ailments of women are likely to be diagnosed relatively early, which increases the chance of survival.[25]

The difference between male and female death rates by age is shown for the United States and Russia for 2000 in Figure 4.30. This difference is indicated by the chance of dying in an age interval for males divided by the chance of dying in that age interval for females.

The values are above 1.0 at every age for the United States, indicating higher male than female mortality at every age. The values peak in the early twenties; males are almost three times as likely as females to die between their twentieth and twenty-fifth birthdays. This is mainly due to more risk-taking behavior among young adult males than among young adult females. In Russia, a similar, but more

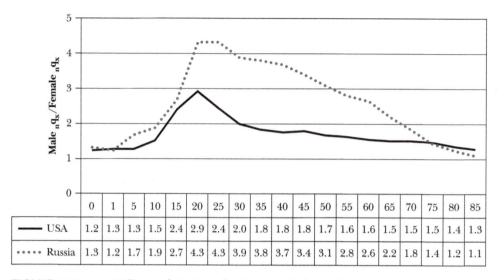

	0	1	5	10	15	20	25	30	35	40	45	50	55	60	65	70	75	80	85
—— USA	1.2	1.3	1.3	1.5	2.4	2.9	2.4	2.0	1.8	1.8	1.8	1.7	1.6	1.6	1.5	1.5	1.5	1.4	1.3
····· Russia	1.3	1.2	1.7	1.9	2.7	4.3	4.3	3.9	3.8	3.7	3.4	3.1	2.8	2.6	2.2	1.8	1.4	1.2	1.1

FIGURE 4.30 Sex Differentials in Mortality by Age (Male $_nq_x$/Female $_nq_x$), the United States and Russia, 2000

extreme, pattern is seen. In Russia, in every 5-year age group from age 15 through 55, males were more than 2.5 times as likely as females to die, and between ages 20 and 55 males were more than three times as likely as females to die.

Figure 4.31 shows similar information for India in 2000. The picture for India is very different from that of either the United States or Russia. In India below age 25, the ratio of the male to the female chance of dying is less than 1.00, which means that below age 25 at every age females in India are more likely to die than males. Under normal conditions, females are less likely than males to die at every age. It is likely that the pattern shown below age 25 for India results from extreme female disadvantage.[26]

We saw in Table 4.1 that in India in 2005–2010, female life expectancy at birth was three years longer than male life expectancy at birth. We also see in

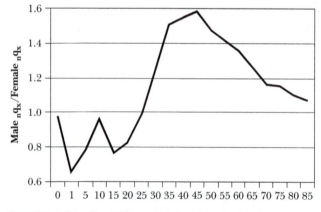

FIGURE 4.31 Sex Differentials in Mortality by Age (Male $_nq_x$/Female $_nq_x$), India, 2000

Figure 4.31 that in India in 2000, young females had higher mortality than young males. Figure 4.32 shows e_0^0 for each sex for India through the period 1950–2010. The values for male and female e_0^0 are indicated on the left-hand axis. Figure 4.32 also shows the number of years by which female e_0^0 exceeded or fell short of male e_0^0, with the values for the sex difference indicated on the right-hand axis. In 1950–1955, males in India had two years longer e_0^0 than females. Expectation of life at birth became equal for the two sexes in the early 1980s. The declining male advantage shown in Figure 4.32 probably reflects decreasing discrimination against females in India over time in access to food and health care.

SEX RATIOS BY AGE

Differences in death rates for the two sexes by age influence the sex ratio by age. A **sex ratio** is calculated as the number of males per hundred females. It can be calculated for the population as a whole, for a specific age group, or for births.

The **sex ratio at birth** in populations without sex-selective abortion or unreported female infanticide typically is in the range of 103–107 male births per 100 female births. There is evidence that in African-background populations, sex ratios at birth are at the low end of the range. A survey of sex ratios at birth in African populations found an average of 103 male births per 100 female births.[27] Sex ratios at birth in the context of sex-selective abortion are discussed in Chapter 9.

Since in almost all populations males at every age have higher death rates than females, there is usually a decline in the sex ratio with age. Figure 4.33 shows sex ratios by age in 2010 for the United States, Russia,

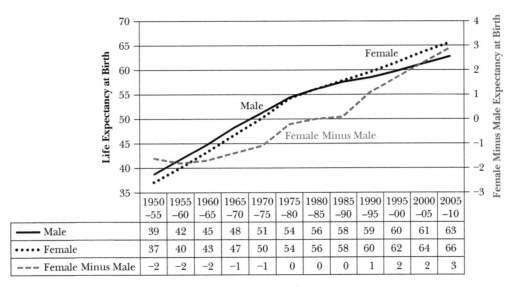

	1950 –55	1955 –60	1960 –65	1965 –70	1970 –75	1975 –80	1980 –85	1985 –90	1990 –95	1995 –00	2000 –05	2005 –10
—— Male	39	42	45	48	51	54	56	58	59	60	61	63
•••• Female	37	40	43	47	50	54	56	58	60	62	64	66
– – – Female Minus Male	–2	–2	–2	–1	–1	0	0	0	1	2	2	3

FIGURE 4.32 e_0^0 by Sex and the Sex Difference in e_0^0: India, 1950–2010

and Botswana. The sex ratios for the United States show a typical pattern of decline with age; the number of females equals the number of males for those in their early forties. The sex ratios by age for Russia show a similar pattern, but after age 10 they are lower at every age than in the United States. This reflects the substantially higher male than female mortality in Russia (indicated in Figure 4.30 for 2000) and by the 13-year-greater female than male e_0^0 in 2010, as shown in Table 4.1. The number of females equals the number of males in Russia by about age 30, about 10 years younger than the age at which the number of males equals the number of females in the United States. Figure 4.33 also shows the sex ratios by age for Botswana. Below age 25, the sex ratio in Botswana is lower than in the United States or Russia, reflecting the typically low African sex ratio at birth in Botswana. The sex ratio in Botswana increases for the 20–24 age group and increases more rapidly through the 35–39 age group before falling. The increase in the sex ratio from ages 20 through 44 is the result of the fact that HIV is a major cause of death in Botswana, and HIV death rates

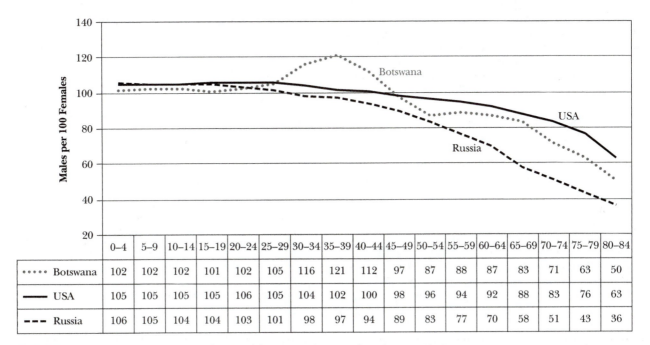

	0–4	5–9	10–14	15–19	20–24	25–29	30–34	35–39	40–44	45–49	50–54	55–59	60–64	65–69	70–74	75–79	80–84
•••• Botswana	102	102	102	101	102	105	116	121	112	97	87	88	87	83	71	63	50
—— USA	105	105	105	105	106	105	104	102	100	98	96	94	92	88	83	76	63
– – – Russia	106	105	104	104	103	101	98	97	94	89	83	77	70	58	51	43	36

FIGURE 4.33 Sex Ratios by Age in the United States, Russia, and Botswana, 2010

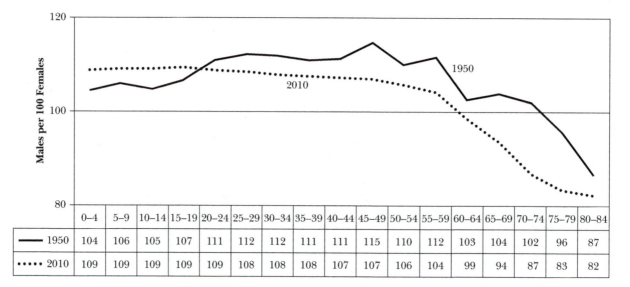

	0–4	5–9	10–14	15–19	20–24	25–29	30–34	35–39	40–44	45–49	50–54	55–59	60–64	65–69	70–74	75–79	80–84
—— 1950	104	106	105	107	111	112	112	111	111	115	110	112	103	104	102	96	87
••••• 2010	109	109	109	109	109	108	108	108	107	107	106	104	99	94	87	83	82

FIGURE 4.34   Sex Ratios by Age in India, 1950 and 2010

in populations where HIV is spread by heterosexual contact are higher for females than for males.

Figure 4.34 shows the sex ratios by age for India in 1950 and in 2010. After age 15, the sex ratios are higher in 1950 than in 2010, reflecting greater female disadvantage in mortality in 1950 than in 2010. The extent of female disadvantage declined over time, as indicated by the change in the sex difference in e_0^0 over time from a male advantage to a female advantage that is shown in Figure 4.32. However, with the development of ultrasound technology, female sex-selective abortion, which was unknown in 1950, had become common in India by 2010.[28] Thus, although the female disadvantage in mortality declined in the 60 years between 1950 and 2010, the female disadvantage in being born had increased. Sex-selective abortion is discussed more in Chapter 9.

SEX DIFFERENTIALS IN INFANT AND CHILD MORTALITY

A major concern in less developed countries has been excess female infant and child mortality. As noted in this chapter, under normal circumstances females at every age have lower death rates than males. There has been some controversy about the conditions under which female children are deprived relative to male children. In a study in rural Bangladesh using data from the 1970s, D'Souza and Chen found that excess mortality of girls occurred mainly in conditions of severe food shortage. When there was a severe shortage of resources such as food, families favored sons, but when economic circumstances were even slightly better, excess female mortality was substantially reduced.[29] In Egypt, Yount also found that

daughters with diarrhea were less likely to be taken to a physician than sons, and less money was spent on the care of daughters than sons.[30]

A UN study examined sex differentials in infant and child mortality throughout the world from the 1970s through the 2000s, doing the best they could with the available data.[31] The UN study found that in most of the world, there has been a decline in excess female infant and child mortality. Two major exceptions are the largest countries in the world: China and India.

Figure 4.35 shows the ratio of male mortality under age 5 to female mortality under age 5

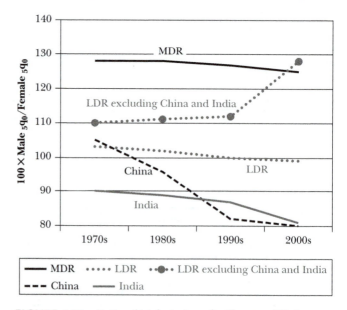

FIGURE 4.35   Ratio of Male to Female Chance of Dying before Age 5

$(100 \times$ Male $_5q_0$/Female $_5q_0)$ for the LDR as a whole, for the LDR excluding China and India, for China, and for India. Under normal circumstances, this ratio will always be greater than 100.

When the ratio is greater than 100, boys have a greater chance than girls of dying before their fifth birthday. This is true at every date in the MDR. However, for the LDR as a whole, this ratio declines from slightly greater than 100 in the 1970s to less than 100 in the 2000s. This suggests that in the LDR as a whole, there has been an increase over time in deprivation of female children in comparison to male children. We see that this downward trend can be completely explained by what happened in China and in India. When the ratio is calculated for the LDR excluding India and China, the ratio rises to the level of the MDR by the 2000s. We see that the substantial decline in the ratios in China and in India affect the trend for the entire LDR due to the large proportion of the population of the LDR composed of India and China. In both China and India, the ratio declines over time, suggesting increasing female deprivation relative to males. This is true even though we saw in Table 4.1 that the IMR declined considerably in both India and China between 1950–1955 and 2005–2010.

Figure 4.36 shows in more detail what happened in China and India. The male and female chances of dying by age five are shown, with male values indicated by triangular markers and female values indicated by X markers. In both countries, the chance of dying before the fifth birthday declined for each sex. However, the rate of decline was greater for boys than for girls.

In India, although the chances of dying declined, the chance that a girl would die before her fifth birthday was always higher than the chance that a boy would die before his fifth birthday. This female disadvantage in under age 5 mortality persisted even though, as seen in Figure 4.32, by the 1990s, female e_0^0 was higher than male e_0^0. The gap between male and female survival to age 5 in India was unchanged across time—at 18 per thousand births in the 1970s and still at 18 per thousand births in the 2000s. Even though the gap between male and female $_5q_0$ was unchanged over time, as the $_5q_0$ values fell for each sex, the gap relative to the $_5q_0$ values increased.

In China in the 1970s, male under 5 mortality was slightly higher than female under 5 mortality. In the 1980s, the values for males and females were virtually identical. However, in the 1990s and 2000s, the chances of dying before age 5 were higher for girls than for boys. There was an increasing female child survival disadvantage over time, even though we saw in Figure 4.13 that in China female e_0^0 was always equal to or greater than male e_0^0.

This emergence of a female disadvantage in survival to age 5 in China differs from the experience of other countries. Generally female disadvantage has been seen as a result of difficult choices in a situation of resource scarcity. In Egypt and in Bangladesh, by the 2000s the ratio of male-to-female child mortality was at least equal, although earlier there was evidence of a female disadvantage. However, in China, male preference has manifested itself more strongly in survival over time, even as mortality risks declined for both sexes and China became more prosperous. Thus, the emergence of a female disadvantage in China does not seem to be the result of poverty or desperation.

Anderson and Romani studied the IMR by sex and by education of mothers in northwest China in 1990.[32] Figure 4.37 shows male and female infant mortality rates by the education of the mother.

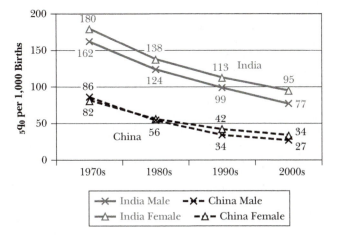

FIGURE 4.36 The Chance of Dying by Age 5 ($_5q_0$) in China and India by Sex

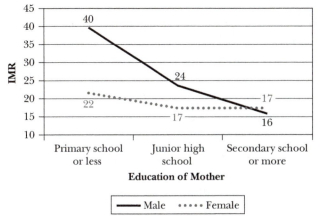

FIGURE 4.37 IMR by Sex and Education of Mother, Northeast China, 1990

A male preference does not instantly disappear as people acquire more education. People with more education typically have more resources and are more effective at using these resources to achieve their goals than are people with less education. We see in Figure 4.37 that having a more educated mother helped the survival of both boy and girl babies, but it helped baby boys more than it helped baby girls. Apparently, with persistent male preference, households with more knowledge and material resources were more motivated and more effective in using those resources to improve the survival chances of baby boys than of baby girls.

WHAT IS THE LIMIT OF THE HUMAN LIFE SPAN?

The human **life span** is the maximal age to which a person can live. It is clear that generally death rates have declined over time, and it seems possible that the maximal age to which persons can survive has also increased. There are two challenges to determining whether human life span has increased. One is the problem of inaccuracy in the reporting of the ages of very old people. The other challenge involves the small proportion of people who survive to an advanced age in light of mortality below that advanced age.

In many populations, there is substantial age exaggeration at older ages. Often, once a person becomes somewhat old, there is more status associated with being *very* old. Thus, in many populations the reported death rates at older ages are not reliable because a substantial proportion of people is actually younger than their reported age and thus subject to lower actual death rates than for the age they report.[33]

When one is constructing a life table, the decision must be made about the maximal age (a) for which values are tabulated. Above that maximal age, a, the values are shown for all those age a or older.

As e_0^0 has increased and death rates at older ages have declined, increasingly there are data available about mortality at older ages from countries such as Japan and Sweden, where there is a high degree of confidence in the accuracy of the age data. In Sweden, the maximal recorded age at death increased from 101 in the 1860s to 108 in the 1990s. Accurate data in very-low-mortality populations have provided the basis for knowing more about actual death rates at advanced ages.[34]

There are also data from human and animal populations that suggest that at advanced ages, the rate of increase in the death rate decelerates. It has been difficult to know whether this is true when the l_x values at advanced ages are very low. Through the 1980s some people thought the maximal age to which people could survive has been between 110 and 120 years for all of human history. However, a French woman,

Jeanne Calment, died at age 122 in 1997. It is not known what the maximal human life span is, but it could be 130 or older.[35]

There is a lively debate among scholars concerning whether there is an absolute maximal age to which humans could ever survive or whether it will continue to gradually increase over time.[36] As the completeness of birth registration has improved, it has become easier to verify the actual ages of very old people. In January 2012, the oldest person living person with a well-recorded year of birth was an American, Besse Cooper, who was age 115.[37]

Fries published an influential article in 1983 that assumed that there was a maximal age for human survival and that as death rates at younger ages declined, the l_x values would necessarily appear as those shown for recent years for Sweden.[38] This rectangularization of mortality means the age at death of almost all people narrows to a small range, so that many people live to an advanced age and then essentially fall off the end of a cliff as they approach the maximal age. This is consistent with the steeper rise and fall of $_nd_x$ values with higher values of e_0^0 shown in Figure 4.26.

Fries was also concerned with whether as e_0^0 increased and almost all people lived to an advanced age, there would be a **compression of morbidity** (illness). If compression of morbidity occurred, people would spend less and less of their lives in an unhealthy or disabled state. In this situation, they would become disabled only shortly before death. The alternative view, which other researchers held, was that people would become disabled at the same age as had earlier been the case, and they would spend many years in a disabled state before they died.[39] Morbidity and years spent in a disabled or functionally limited state are discussed more in Chapter 11.

FEMALE LIFE TABLE PATTERNS WITH e_0^0 FROM 25 TO 100 YEARS

For countries with low or moderate e_0^0, there are few survivors to older ages. Often, there are questions of the quality of reporting of ages of older persons and of the age at death of those who have died. In such situations, it is sensible to restrict attention to ages below 80 and to consider all those above age 80 as one group. However, as indicated in Table 4.1, e_0^0 for Japanese females reached 86 years for 2005–2010. Thus, there is reason to look in detail at the chance of dying at advanced ages, especially in very-low-mortality populations.

In the following graphs, life table measures are shown for females with e_0^0 25, 50, 75, and 100 years. The values are shown up to age 130. These life tables are based on typical patterns of variation in the risk of death by age based on well-recorded life tables. In these figures, results are shown at intervals of

25 years in expectation of life at birth. These figures make clear that although the overall increments to life expectancy are the same between successive levels, the changes in mortality by age at different levels of mortality vary enormously. If life tables had been shown for males at the same levels of e_0^0, the figures would appear similar to those for females.[40] The results are shown for life tables not impacted by HIV.

Figure 4.38 shows the number of females surviving from birth to various ages. This figure looks similar to the rectangularization of mortality in Sweden shown in Figure 4.16. As e_0^0 increases from 25 years to 50 years, survival at the younger ages, especially below age 10, increases greatly. At e_0^0 25 years, 51% of girls survive to age 10, while at e_0^0 50 years, 80% of girls survive to age 10. At e_0^0 75 years, 98% of girls survive to their tenth birthday, and at life expectancy of 100 years, 99.9% of girls survive to their tenth birthday.

At e_0^0 25 years, survival declines almost linearly from age 10 to about age 80. At e_0^0 75 years, 88% of females are alive at age 60, and 75% are alive at age 70. After age 70, the chance of further survival declines fairly rapidly. At e_0^0 100 years, 97% are still alive at age 80; after age 80, the number of survivors declines fairly rapidly, although 56% are still alive at age 100.

Figure 4.39 shows the number of deaths by age from 100,000 births from the same life tables used in Figure 4.38. At e_0^0 25 years, the vast majority of deaths occur below age 10. This is consistent with the l_x values in Figure 4.38. By age 10, at e_0^0 25 years, almost half of all females would be dead. With e_0^0 25 years, few deaths occur around age 25. Most deaths occur below age 5, and among those who survive to their fifth birthday, the greatest number of deaths occurs in the 65–69 age group. This is similar to the situation that was explained in Box 4.1. In Figure 4.39, at e_0^0 50 years, the largest number of deaths after infancy and early childhood occurs when people are in their seventies. With e_0^0 75 years, the largest number of deaths occurs to those in the 80–84 age group. This is consistent with the fall in the l_x values for those in their 70s and 80s at e_0^0 age 75 in Figure 4.38. With e_0^0 100 years, the largest number of deaths occurs in the 105–109 age group.

When mortality is very low, e_0^0 is very close to the modal age at death, as shown in Figure 4.39 for e_0^0 of 75 years and 100 years. This is very different from the situation at high or moderate mortality and is different from the situation discussed in Box 4.1.

Figure 4.40 shows, for each value of e_0^0 out of 1,000 women alive at the beginning of an age interval, the number who would die in the following age interval. At e_0^0 25 years, the chances of dying are high just after birth and decline to age 10, after which they rise

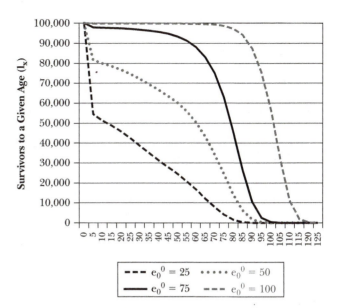

FIGURE 4.38 Female Survivors to a Given Age (l_x) at Varying Life Expectancies

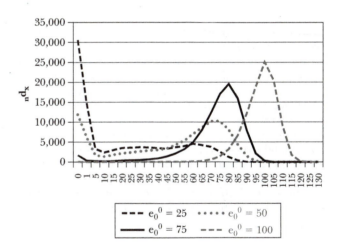

FIGURE 4.39 Female $_nd_x$ at Varying Life Expectancies

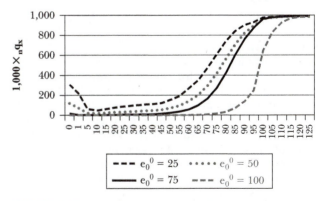

FIGURE 4.40 Female $1,000 \times {}_nq_x$ at Varying Life Expectancies

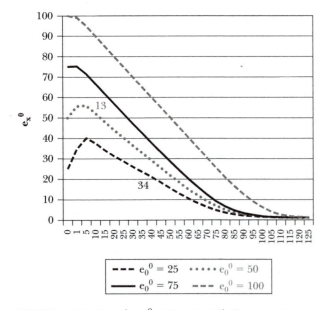

FIGURE 4.41   Female e_x^0 at Varying Life Expectancies

increase in e_x^0 between birth (age 0) and age 5 is clear. At e_0^0 25 years, e_5^0 is 40 years. Thus, in a situation with female e_0^0 of 25 years, a newborn baby girl can expect to live 25 years, but if that girl survives to her fifth birthday, on average she will survive 40 more years—to her forty-fifth birthday. In such a situation, high death rates below age 5 are a hurdle. If people can survive past that hurdle, their survival chances are better than they were at birth. This is the situation that was explained in Box 4.1.

In Figure 4.41, for $e_0^0 = 25$ and $e_0^0 = 50$, the age x is indicated at which $e_x^0 = e_0^0$. At e_0^0 25 years, expectation of (remaining) life is 25 years at age 0 (at birth) and also is 25 years at age 34; in this situation, a woman alive at age 34 can expect to live to age 59. With e_0^0 of 50 years, those who survive to their first birthday can expect to live 56 more years. For e_0^0 50 years, expectation of remaining life is also 50 years at exact age 13; in this situation, a young woman alive at age 13 can expect to live until age 63.

Sometimes journalists and others are very confused about the meaning of expectation of life at birth and expectation of remaining life. An example of this confusion is described in Box 4.3.

gradually until about age 50. After age 50, the chance of dying increases rapidly. At e_0^0 25 years, Figure 4.39 showed no increase in the number of deaths at older ages because at e_0^0 25 years, there are very few survivors to older ages. As shown in Figure 4.38, with e_0^0 at 25 years, only 17% of women live to age 60. In Figure 4.40, at every higher value of e_0^0, the chances of dying are lower at each age. At every value of e_0^0, the $_nq_x$ values eventually stop increasing when they approach 1.00, since there cannot be greater than a 1.00 (or 100%) chance that a person will die in an interval.

Figure 4.41 shows the expectation of remaining life (e_x^0) at each value of e_0^0. At e_0^0 25 years, the

THE CONCEPT OF A COHORT

A **cohort** is a group of people who start something at the same time. A birth cohort is people who were born at the same time (or in the same range of years). **Cohort mortality** traces the mortality experience of a birth cohort as they go through life. You can calculate a cohort e_0^0 just as you calculate a period e_0^0.

A college graduation cohort is people who graduated from college in the same year (or group of years). You might want to track a college graduation cohort to look at income and job position a certain

---

BOX 4.3

A Misleading *New York Times* Article about Expectation of Remaining Life

In her July 11, 2010, *New York Times* "Week in Review" article "Turn 70. Act Your Grandchild's Age," Kate Zernike noted that life expectancy (at birth) in the United States was 78 years. She implied that people age 70 can expect to live only 8 years longer. In fact, those alive at age 70 could expect to live for 15 more years. Seventy-seven percent of people in the United States currently live to their seventieth birthday, according to the U.S. life table. People alive at age 70 have survived the risks of death at younger ages, so their average age at death

will be substantially older than their life expectancy at birth.

Nonetheless, perhaps frightening those reaching age 70, Zernike wrote:

> In fact, for most people, the 70s represents the end, not a beginning. Life expectancy in this country is still 78—higher for white women, lower for men and blacks. It is rising, but not as fast, perhaps, as our expectations. As Gloria Steinem said of her 70th birthday in 2004, "This one has the ring of mortality."

number of years after college graduation. For example, Wolniak and his colleagues looked at cohorts of college graduates from 1974–1976, 1984–1986, and 1994–1996 to study the effects of various college majors on earnings in 2000 among people who attended college in different decades.[41]

Rogers and Amato studied various first-marriage cohorts to look at the contribution of wives to household income, the extent to which husbands did housework, and how these factors related to marital discord. They were especially interested in whether the relations between these factors were different in more recent marriage cohorts than in earlier marriage cohorts.[42]

Davis studied the relation of cohort membership to political attitudes. He found that those who reached age 16 in the 1960s had more liberal political attitudes than those who were born somewhat earlier or later, even after trends in political attitudes had been taken into account. The interpretation is that the events in the 1960s surrounding the Vietnam War and the Sexual Revolution made a particular impression on those who reached adulthood at that time, which influenced their political views throughout the rest of their lives.[43]

Putnam looked at the decline in voting and in interest in public affairs from the 1960s through the 1990s and concluded that the decline was almost entirely due to less political activity among members of more recent cohorts (those who were born more recently) rather than changes in political behavior among members of a birth cohort.[44]

Alwin examined changes over time in parental socialization values that moved toward increased preference for autonomy in children and less preference for obedience. He used data collected in 1958, 1971, and 1983 in the Detroit area. He found that cohorts of parents born since 1930 expressed greater support for these new parental socialization values at every point in time than did parents who were born earlier than 1930, and that because those born since 1930 comprised an increasing portion of all parents, the overall distribution of parental attitudes shifted.[45]

Period and Cohort Approaches and Tuberculosis in Massachusetts[46]

In this section, we present an example of how using a period perspective and using a cohort perspective result in completely different interpretations of what has happened. The controversy is about whether or not the age pattern of mortality from TB changed over time.

Period Death Rates

In the late nineteenth century, TB was known as having high death rates among young adults that then

TABLE 4.5   Death Rates per 100,000 from Tuberculosis, Massachusetts Males, 1880–1940

	1880	1890	1900	1910	1920	1930	1940
10–19	126	115	90	63	49	21	4
20–29	*444*	361	288	207	149	81	35
30–39	378	*368*	*296*	*253*	164	115	51
40–49	364	336	253	*253*	*175*	118	86
50–59	366	325	267	252	171	*127*	92
60–69	475	346	304	246	172	95	*109*
70+	672	396	343	163	127	95	79

fell before rising again at older ages. TB death rates for males in Massachusetts are shown for ten-year intervals from 1880 to 1940 in Table 4.5 and are graphed in Figure 4.42. The rates in Table 4.5 and Figure 4.42 are **period mortality**—the death rates across ages in a given year.

Looking across rows of Table 4.5, it is clear that for every age group, death rates from TB declined over time. From 1880 to 1940, death rates per 100,000 from TB for men aged 40–49 declined from 364 to 86.

Looking down the columns of Table 4.5 shows the death rates by age of men in Massachusetts in a given year. In 1880, the death rates increase from those aged 10–19 to those aged 20–29, after which they decline through ages 50–59, after which they increase. In 1940, the rates increase from the 10–19 age group through the 60-69 age group after which the rates decline for those age 70+. The highest rate for an age group in a given year is indicated by italics. The age group with the highest rate tended to increase over time.

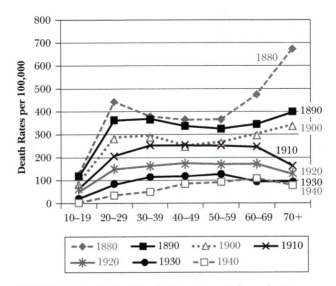

FIGURE 4.42   Period Death Rates from Tuberculosis, Massachusetts Males, 1880–1940

In Figure 4.42, the graph for 1880 shows the age pattern for TB mortality that was familiar to people, with a peak for those aged 20–29. Over time, this age pattern changed. By 1940, TB death rates increased with age and no longer showed a peak for those in their 20s. The change in the age pattern of TB mortality from peaking at a young adult age to generally increasing with age made people wonder whether the TB virus had mutated in a way that made young adults less susceptible to TB mortality than older people.

Cohort Death Rates

Table 4.6 and Figure 4.43 show death rates by age in a different way. In Table 4.6, the columns show the death rates by age for a cohort of men. The year at the top of each column indicates when the cohort was aged 10–19. Similarly, Figure 4.43 shows the death rates for the same cohort over time. The year designated in Figure 4.43 is the year when the given cohort was aged 10–19. The same vertical scale is shown in Figure 4.43 as in Figure 4.42. When looking at data for cohorts, it is only possible to look at their behavior up to the age the cohort was when the data were assembled. Thus, in 1940, the experience of who were ages 10–19 in 1940 cannot be observed for when they were ages 20–29. Similarly, those who were ages 10–19 in 1910 were ages 40–49 in 1940, so the experience of that cohort when they were age 50 or older was not known in 1940.

Looking across rows of Table 4.6 shows the death rates from TB for a given age across different cohorts. It is clear that rates were lower for members of cohorts who were born later. Looking down columns of Table 4.5 shows the TB death rates by age for a given cohort as it aged. The age group for which the rates peak is shown in italics. For every cohort, there is a peak for those age 20–29, which does not change across cohorts. Thus, the cohort data show no indication of a change in the age pattern of TB mortality. It is also clear in Figure 4.43 that TB mortality peaked at ages 20–29 for all cohorts.

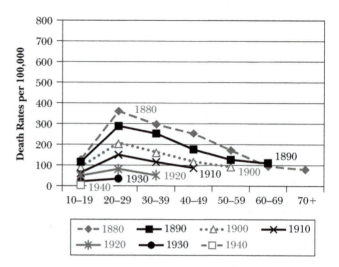

FIGURE 4.43   Cohort Death Rates from Tuberculosis, Massachusetts Males, Year When Cohort Was Aged 10–19, 1880–1940

When period death rates in 1920 are shown in Figure 4.42, we see the rates increase with age through the 60–69 age group. But those at younger ages in 1920 were born at a later date than those at older ages in 1920. The cross-sectional rates for 1920 in Figure 4.42 combine the rates for more recently born people, by which time rates at all ages were relatively low, with rates at older ages for people who were born at a time when rates at every age were higher. For every cohort, rates were lower after the cohort was age 30 than when the men in that cohort were ages 20–29. This analysis convinced people that the age pattern of risk of dying from TB had not changed.

One can think of the risk of dying from TB as having a trajectory by age that each cohort is assigned at birth. Later birth cohorts have a lower trajectory. When one is looking cross-sectionally at age-specific death rates from TB—looking at period rates—one is combining a higher trajectory at older ages from an earlier birth cohort with a lower trajectory at younger ages from a more recent birth cohort. In this situation, the (relatively) low TB death rates at older ages for the earlier birth cohort are actually higher than the (relatively) high death rates at younger ages for more recent birth cohorts. This is the situation when the period mortality from TB for 1920 appears in Figure 4.42 and Table 4.5. Those aged 20–29 in 1920 had a TB death rate per 100,000 of 149, while those aged 40–49 in 1920 had a TB death rate per 100,000 of 175. Those aged 20–29 in 1920 were aged 10–19 in 1910, and we see in Figure 4.43 and Table 4.6 that ages 20–29 experienced a high level of TB mortality for that birth cohort. Those aged 40–49 in 1920 were ages 10–19 in 1890, and the TB death rates for that cohort declined steadily from the time they were aged 20–29.

TABLE 4.6   Cohort Death Rates from Tuberculosis, Massachusetts Males, Year When Cohort Was Aged 10–19

	1880	1890	1900	1910	1920	1930	1940
10–19	126	115	90	63	49	21	4
20–29	*361*	*288*	*207*	*149*	*81*	*35*	
30–39	296	253	164	115	51		
40–49	253	175	118	86			
50–59	171	127	92				
60–69	95	109					
70+	79						

REAL COHORTS AND SYNTHETIC COHORTS

One could construct a life table for a real cohort by tracking the cohort from birth until all the members of that cohort die. However, that would take 100 years or more. Thus, life tables for true cohorts are rarely constructed, although as in the TB in Massachusetts example, looking at cohort age-specific death rates even for a limited age range can be quite revealing.

Typically, life tables are constructed based on the mortality experience of people at all ages at a particular point of time—in a particular time period. Thus, a period life table shows what the mortality experience would be if a group of people from birth were exposed to a set of risks of dying by age. This is often referred to as the mortality experience of a **synthetic cohort**.

Usually chances of dying at every age decline over time. Thus, the life table of any period of time does not reflect the mortality risks that any real cohort experiences. A period life table strings together the somewhat elevated mortality risks of earlier birth cohorts with the scaled-down mortality risks of more recent birth cohorts.

As Figure 4.3 showed, the female life expectancy at birth in the United States has increased steadily. In 2005–2010, its value was 81 years. However, for baby girls born in 2005–2010, their average life expectancy (their cohort e_0^0) is almost certainly longer than 81 years. Similarly, the cohort life expectancy at birth of the cohort that was at an advanced age in 2005–2010 was certainly lower than 81 years.

CONCLUDING COMMENTS

The decline in mortality at all ages and in all world regions since 1950 is very impressive, although Africa still has very high mortality. As e_0^0 increases, age-specific death rates change in different ways at different ages. Understanding these age patterns of change is central to understanding how mortality challenges shift over time.

A key to understanding mortality patterns and trends is the life table and being able to interpret results based on life table measures. This chapter aimed to equip the student with the understanding of the life table necessary to understand the material in the rest of this book as well as discussions of mortality in the popular press.

✔ Study and Review Online

SUMMARY

1. The infant mortality rate (IMR) is a good indicator of the overall health and mortality status of a population. Since the 1950s, the IMR has declined virtually everywhere in the world, although it remains very high in Africa.

2. The expectation of life at birth (e_0^0) is the number of years that a person would live on average if subject to the mortality risks by age in a given place and time. In almost every area in every time period, e_0^0 for each sex has increased. Some notable exceptions are (1) countries where HIV became a major cause of death, especially for females; and (2) countries where a war or famine caused temporary very high death rates, such as (a) the war in Bangladesh in 1971, which resulted in a decline in male e_0^0, and (b) famine in China in 1959–1961, which resulted in a decline in male e_0^0.

3. Typically, women live longer than men. The largest sex differential in 2005–2010 was in Russia, in which female e_0^0 was 13 years longer than male e_0^0. In some countries, female disadvantage can result in higher male than female e_0^0. India moved from having a 2-year female disadvantage in e_0^0 in 1950–1955 to a 3-year female advantage in 2005–2010, probably resulting from decreases in female disadvantage in access to food and health care. The extent of excess female mortality below age 5 decreased in most of the world, although it increased in China and India. Even though the chance of dying before age 5 declined in both countries, the decline was greater for boys than girls, probably reflecting greater allocation of resources to assure the survival of male than female children.

4. Chances of dying typically are very high immediately after birth, after which they decline to a low point at about age 10. Chances of dying then increase with age, with acceleration in death rates after about age 50.

5. The life table is a powerful analysis tool that allows the complexities of mortality patterns by age and sex to be seen. The life table summarizes the mortality situation of a given place at a given time. It shows the chances of dying by age, the chances of surviving from one age to the next (including survival from birth), and the average number of years that a person can expect to live after they have reached a given age.

6. High mortality from HIV can lead to a peak in death rates at ages 20–45, especially for females, a pattern not found in populations that are not strongly affected by HIV.

7. In high- and moderate-mortality populations, e_0^0 is quite different from the modal age at death. This is due to high infant and child mortality, in which a high proportion of all deaths occurs before age 5 or 10. Those persons who survive past early childhood have a higher expectation of remaining life than the population's e_0^0. In very-low-mortality populations, e_0^0 is close to the modal age at death.

8. A cohort is a group of people who start something at the same time. A birth cohort is a group of people who were all born in the same time period (a year or group of years).

9. Looking at the age-specific mortality experience of a cohort can lead to a different interpretation of the mortality levels and trends than looking at death rates for people of different ages in a particular time period.

KEY TERMS

infant mortality rate 109	age 124	sex ratio at birth 132
child mortality rate 109	age last birthday 124	life span 136
expectation of life at birth 111	exact age 124	compression of morbidity 136
rectangularization of	age-specific death rate 125	cohort 138
mortality 122	person-years of life 127	cohort mortality 138
age-adjusted death rate 123	expectation of remaining life at	period mortality 139
life table 124	age x 128	synthetic cohort 141
radix 124	sex ratio 132	

QUESTIONS FOR DISCUSSION AND REVIEW

1. Imagine a country with the following characteristics:

Male Infant Mortality Rate	250
Female Infant Mortality Rate	220
Male e_0^0	32 years
Female e_0^0	35 years
Male Proportion Surviving to Age 30	0.512
Female Proportion Surviving to Age 30	0.531
Proportion Surviving to Age 70	0.172

A newspaper reporter writes:

> In this country children never get to know their parents, since their parents die before the children reach their teens. Also, admiration for the elderly doesn't matter at all because no one lives to old age and any old people who are still alive die very soon anyway.

Comment on what this newspaper reporter wrote. What do you agree with? What do you not agree with? For what things can the truth not be verified, based on what you have been told about the characteristics of the country? What else would you like to know about the country?

2. The expectation of life at birth in the United States in 2000 was 80 years. Does this mean that baby girls born in the United States in 2000 on average would die in the year 2080? Why or why not?

3. What is the typical pattern of sex differentials in mortality? What are some sources of exceptions to this typical pattern?

4. How does a high level of HIV mortality affect death rates by age?

5. As overall mortality declines, what is the time sequence of typical changes in the risk of dying younger than age 10, at ages 10–59, and older than age 60?

6. How does the relation between e_0^0 and the modal age of death change as mortality declines?

7. Imagine the following countries:

	Country A	Country B	Country C	Country D
e_0^0	35	35	55	75
% of population HIV-positive	0.2%	10.0%	0.2%	0.1%

a. Draw a graph showing what age-specific mortality rates from age 0 through age 90 might look like in each country.

b. Draw a graph showing what the number of survivors from age 0 through age 90 might look like in each country.

c. Draw a graph showing what expectation of (remaining) life might look like from age 0 through age 90 in each country.

NOTES

1. D. D. Redpath and P. Allotey. 2003. "Infant Mortality Rate as an Indicator of Population Health," *Journal of Epidemiology and Community Health*, 57: 344–346.

2. United Nations Development Program (UNDP), "Human Development Index (HDI)," http://hdr .undp.org/en/statistics/hdi/ (accessed April 10, 2012).

3. Dirk A. Prinsloo. 2004. "The Human Development Index: Where South Africa Stands," *Urban Studies*, http://www.urbanstudies.co.za/Publications _The%20human%20development%20index .html (accessed April 10, 2012).

4. M. W. de Vries. 1987. "Cry Babies, Culture, and Catastrophe: Infant Temperament among the Masai," in *Child Survival*, ed. Nancy Scheper-Hughes, Dordrecht, the Netherlands: Reidel: 165–186; and Peter Garnsey. 1991. "Child Rearing in Ancient Italy," in *The Family in Italy from Antiquity to the Present*, ed. David I. Kertzer and, Richard P. Saller, New Haven, CT: Yale University Press, 48–65.

5. Save the Children. 2006. *State of the World's Mothers 2006: Saving the Lives of Women and Newborns*, http://www.savethechildren .org/atf/cf/%7B9def2ebe-10ae-432c-9bd0 -df91d2eba74a%7D/SOWM_2006_FINAL.PDF (accessed September 1, 2011); and Daniel L. DeNoon. 2008. "Infant Mortality: U.S. Ranks 29th," October 15, WebMSNews, http://www .webmd.com/parenting/baby/news /20081015/infant-mortality-us-ranks-29th (accessed September 1, 2011).

6. Marian F. MacDorman and T. J. Mathews. 2008. *Recent Trends in Infant Mortality in the United States*, NCHS Data Brief, Hyattsville, MD: National Center for Health Statistics, http://www.cdc.gov/nchs /data/databriefs/db09.pdf (accessed April 10, 2012).

7. The mortality values for Northern America are dominated by the United States, which in 2010 comprised 90% of the population of Northern America. A listing of countries by UN region is shown in Appendix A.

8. United Nations Population Division, personal communication, June 6, 2011.

9. Keep in mind that Southern Africa is a region composed of five countries, and South Africa is the largest country within Southern Africa.

10. World Bank. 2011. *Africa Development Indicators 2011*, Washington, DC: World Bank, http://data .worldbank.org/sites/default/files/adi_2011 -web.pdf (accessed April 10, 2012).

11. Barbara A. Anderson and Brian D. Silver, 1986. "Infant Mortality in the Soviet Union: Regional Differences and Measurement Issues," *Population and Development Review*, 12: 705–738.

12. Daqing Zhang and Paul U. Unschuld. 2008. "China's Barefoot Doctor: Past, Present, and Future," *Lancet*, 372: 1865–1866; Dean T. Jamison. 1985. "China's Health Care System: Policies, Organization, Inputs and Finance," in *Good Health at Low Cost: Proceedings of a Conference Held at the Bellagio Conference Center, Bellagio, Italy, April 29–May 2, 1985*, ed. Scott B. Halstead, Julia A. Walsh, and Kenneth S. Warren, New York: Rockefeller Foundation, 21–32.

13. Basil Ashton, Kenneth Hill, Alan Piazza, and Robin Zeitz. 1984. "Famine in China, 1958–61," *Population and Development Review*, 10: 613–645.

14. The data for these three populations in Figures 4.14 and 4.15 are from World Health Organization, *Life Tables for WHO Member States*, http:// www.who.int/healthinfo/statistics/mortality _life_tables/en/ (accessed June 6, 2011).

15. John Wilmoth and Shiro Horiuchi. 1999. "Rectangularization Revisited: Variability of Age at Death within Human Populations," *Demography*, 36: 475–495.

16. Data on survival for Sweden are from the Human Life-Table database, http://www.lifetable .de (accessed May 8, 2010).

17. Arialdi M. Minino, Sherry L. Murphy, Jiaquan Xu, and Kenneth D. Kochanel. 2011. *Deaths: Final Data for 2008*, National Vital Statistics Reports, Vol. 59, No. 10, Hyattsville, MD: National Center for Health Statistics, http://www.cdc .gov/nchs/data/nvsr/nvsr59/nvsr59_10.pdf (accessed April 11, 2012).

18. The World Health Organization (WHO) published life tables by sex for 1990, 2000, and 2009 for every WHO member country at http://www .who.int/whosis/mort/en/ (accessed March 21, 2013). The life tables for countries in this chapter are from that source unless otherwise indicated.

19. Dean T. Jamison, Sonbol A. Shahid-Salles, Julian Jamison, Joy E. Lawn, and Jelka Zupan. 2006. "Incorporating Deaths Near the Time of Birth into Estimates of the Global Burden of Disease," in *Global Burden of Disease and Risk Factors*, ed. Alan D. Lopez, Colin D. Matthews, Majid Ezzati, Dean T. Jamison, and Christopher J. L. Murray, Washington, DC: World Bank, http://files.dcp2.org/pdf /GBD/GBD06.pdf (accessed October 15, 2011).

20. Barbara A. Anderson and Heston E. Phillips. 2006. *Adult Mortality (Age 15–64) Based on Death Notification Data in South Africa: 1997–2004*, Pretoria: Statistics South Africa, 73.

21. Alfredo Nicolosi, Maria Léa Corrêa Leite, Massimo Musicco, Claudio Arici, Giovanna

Gavazzeni, and Adriano Lazzarin. 1994. "The Efficiency of Male-to-Female and Female-to-Male Sexual Transmission of the Human Immunodeficiency Virus: A Study of 730 Stable Couples," *Epidemiology*, 5: 570–575; and Stéphane Hugonnet, Frank Mosha, James Todd, Kokugonza Mugeye, Arnoud Klokke, Leonard Ndeki, David Ross, Heiner Grosskurth, and Richard Hayes. 2002. "Incidence of HIV Infection in Stable Sexual Partnerships: A Retrospective Cohort Study of 1802 Couples in Mwanza Region, Tanzania," *Journal of Acquired Immune Deficiency Syndromes*, 30: 73–80.

22. INDEPTH Network. 2004. *INDEPTH Model Life Tables for Sub-Saharan Africa*, Aldershot, UK: Ashgate; age-specific death rates are calculated from data on p. 21.

23. Jean Downes. 1931. "The Accuracy of Official Tuberculosis Death Rates," *Journal of the American Statistical Association*, 26: 393–403; and Kevin M. White. 1999. "Cardiovascular and Tuberculosis Mortality: The Contrasting Effects of Changes in Two Causes of Death," *Population and Development Review*, 25: 289–302.

24. Kim Hill, Christophe Boesch, Jane Goodall, Anne Pusey, Jennifer Williams, and Richard Wrangham. 2001. "Mortality Rates among Wild Chimpanzees," *Journal of Human Evolution*, 40: 437–450.

25. Deborah L. Wingard. 1984. "The Sex Differential in Morbidity, Mortality, and Lifestyle," *Annual Review of Public Health*, 5: 433–458; and Francis C. Madigan. 1957. "Are Sex Mortality Differences Biologically Caused?" *Milbank Memorial Fund Quarterly*, 35: 202–223.

26. In high-HIV situations, female death rates at some ages can be higher than male death rates, but India did not have high enough HIV prevalence below age 25 in 2000 for that to be a plausible explanation of the pattern in Figure 4.31.

27. Michel Garenne. 2002. "Sex Ratios at Birth in African Populations: A Review of Survey Data," *Human Biology*, 74: 889–900.

28. Amartya Sen. 2003. "Missing Girls—Revisited," *British Medical Journal*, 327: 1297–1298.

29. Stan D'Souza and Lincoln C. Chen. 1980. "Sex Differentials in Mortality in Rural Bangladesh," *Population and Development Review*, 6: 257–270; and Lincoln C. Chen, Emdadul Huq, and Stan D'Souza. 1981. "Sex Bias in the Family Allocation of Food and Health Care in Rural Bangladesh," *Population and Development Review*, 7: 55–70.

30. Kathryn M. Yount. 2003. "Gender Bias in the Allocation of Curative Health Care in Minia, Egypt," *Population Research and Policy Review*, 3: 267–295.

31. United Nations. 2011. *Sex Differentials in Childhood Mortality*, New York: United Nations, http://www.un.org/esa/population/publications/SexDifChildMort/SexDifferentialsChildhoodMortality.pdf (accessed January 7, 2012).

32. Barbara A. Anderson and John H. Romani. 2009. "Socio-economic Characteristics and Excess Female Infant Mortality in Jilin Province, China," *Population and Society*, 5: 1–25.

33. Ira Rosenwaike and Samuel H. Preston. 1984. "Age Overstatement and Puerto Rican Longevity," *Human Biology*, 56: 503–525; Lea Keil Garson. 1991. "The Centenarian Question: Old-Age Mortality in the Soviet Union, 1897 to 1970," *Population Studies*, 45: 265–278; and Barbara A. Anderson and Brian D. Silver. 1989. "The Changing Shape of Soviet Mortality, 1958–1985: An Evaluation of Old and New Evidence," *Population Studies*, 43: 243–265.

34. J. R. Wilmoth, L. J. Deegan, H. Lungstrom, and S. Horiucji. 2000. "Increase of Maximum Life-Span in Sweden, 1861–1999," *Science*, 289: 2366–2368.

35. Shiro Horiuchi and John R. Wilmoth. 1998. "Deceleration in the Age Pattern of Mortality at Older Ages," *Demography*, 35: 391–412; James Carey. 1997. "What Demographers Can Learn from Fruit Fly Actuarial Models and Biology," *Demography*, 34: 17–30; James W. Vaupel, James R. Carey, Kaare Christensen, Thomas E. Johnson, Anatoli I. Yashin, Niels V. Holm, Ivan A. Iachine, Väinö Kannisto, Aziz A. Khazaeli, Pablo Liedo, Valter D. Longo, Yi Zeng, Kenneth G. Manton, and James W. Curtsinger. 1998. "Biodemographic Trajectories of Longevity," *Science*, 280: 855–860; J. R. Wilmoth. 2000. "Demography of Longevity: Past, Present, and Future Trends," *Experimental Gerontology*, 35: 1111–1129; Thomas Perls and Louis M. Kunkel. 2002. "The Genetics of Exceptional Human Longevity," *Journal of the American Geriatrics Society*, 50: 359–368; and Roy L. Walford. 1983. *Maximum Life Span*, New York: Norton, 15.

36. Jennifer Couzin-Frankel. 2011. "A Pitched Battle over Life Span," *Science*, 29: 549–550.

37. GRG Interactive. 2012. *Oldest Living Supercentenarians*, http://www.grg.org/Adams/E.HTM (accessed January 29, 2012).

38. James F. Fries. 1983. "The Compression of Morbidity," *The Milbank Memorial Fund Quarterly. Health and Society*, 61 (Special issue: "Aging: Demographic, Health, and Social Prospects"): 397–419.

39. E. F. Gruenberg. 1977. "The Failures of Success," *Milbank Memorial Fund Quarterly/Health and Society*, 55: 3–24.

40. The data in the figures in this section are based on Ansley J. Coale and Paul Demeny. 1983. *Regional Model Life Tables and Stable Populations*, New York: Academic Press. They refer to the West

model. The values come from a United Nations Population Division extension of these tables to $e_0^0 = 100$, available at http://esa.un.org /unpd/wpp/Model-Life-Tables/download-page .html (accessed June 7, 2011).

41. Gregory C. Wolniak, Tricia A. Seifert, Eric J. Reed, and Ernest T. Pascarella. 2008. "College Majors and Social Mobility," *Research in Social Stratification and Mobility*, 26: 123–139.

42. Stacy J. Rogers and Paul R. Amato. 2000. "Have Changes in Gender Relations Affected Marital Quality?" *Social Forces*, 79: 731–753.

43. James A. Davis. 2004. "Did Growing Up in the 1960s Leave a Permanent Mark on Attitudes and Values? Evidence from the General Social Survey," *The Public Opinion Quarterly*, 68: 161–183.

44. Robert D. Putnam. 2000. *Bowling Alone: The Collapse and Revival of American Community*, New York: Simon & Schuster: 36–38.

45. Duane F. Alwin. 1990. "Cohort Replacement and Changes in Parental Socialization Values," *Journal of Marriage and Family*, 52: 347–360.

46. Wade Hampton Frost. 1940. "The Age Selection of Mortality from Tuberculosis in Successive Decades," *Milbank Memorial Quarterly*, 18: 61–66.

CHAPTER 5

HISTORY AND CONTEXT OF MORTALITY DIFFERENTIALS AND MORTALITY DECLINE

LEARNING OBJECTIVES

- List and briefly explain the four stages of the Epidemiologic Transition.
- Explain how the change from hunting and gathering to pastoral nomadism and settled agriculture, and the rise of periodic markets, affect the level and the causes of mortality.
- Define crisis mortality and explain why it has declined over time.

- List the major proposed causes of mortality decline in Europe in 1750–1900 and assess the evidence for each proposed cause.
- Define the compression of morbidity and explain why it matters for policy whether or not it actually occurs.
- Contrast the main causes of death and of disability in high-income and in low-income countries.

((• Listen to the Chapter Audio

OVERVIEW

In Chapter 4, we looked at mortality levels and risks by age and how these have changed over time. In this chapter, we look at the historical record of mortality decline and set a context for understanding contemporary mortality issues.

We start by discussing the epidemiological transition, which refers to changes in the causes of death over time. Next we look at how social and environmental factors related to mortality have changed over the course of human history from hunting-and-gathering societies to pastoral nomadism and settled agriculture and the kinds of forces affecting mortality through the late nineteenth century. The roles of natural disasters, epidemics, nutrition, war, commerce, government regulations and practices, public health practices, and inoculation and medical care in historical mortality decline are discussed.

After that, we discuss classifications of causes of death and elaborate on the shift over time from communicable to non-communicable diseases. We look at the main causes of death and of disability in countries at different income levels in 2004, as well as at risk factors for death and disability throughout the world.

THE EPIDEMIOLOGIC TRANSITION

In 1971, Omran proposed a three-stage model of the **Epidemiologic Transition**, which describes how causes of death and the age distribution of mortality risks have changed over the course of human history. In 1986, Olshansky and Ault expanded Omran's work by adding a fourth stage. In the late 1960s in more developed countries, e_0^0 was 71 years, and many thought that an upper limit of mortality improvement had been reached. However, in many developed countries, death rates at the older ages continued to decline, reaching levels lower than many had earlier thought possible. By 2000–2005, female e_0^0 in Japan was above 85 years. The fourth stage takes into account the continued progress in mortality decline at advanced ages in more developed countries.[1]

The expanded version of the Epidemiologic Transition can be summarized as follows:

1. **Age of Pestilence and Famine:** Infectious and parasitic diseases are the major causes of deaths, and the population is periodically wracked by epidemics. Famines also periodically lead to large increases in the number of deaths.

146

A large portion of deaths occurs in infancy and childhood.

2. **Age of Receding Pandemics:** Epidemics are less frequent and have a smaller effect on population size. Famines become less common and less severe as the growth of markets reduces the mortality impact of local crop failures. Improved trade networks allow food to be brought in from non-famine areas. Thus, during a famine food is expensive but available. A somewhat smaller portion of deaths occurs in infancy and childhood, while the portion of deaths at older adult ages increases. Those who survive childhood, and thus have not died from infectious or parasitic diseases, tend to die from chronic degenerative diseases.

3. **Age of Degenerative and Manmade Diseases:** Infectious and parasitic diseases become a minor cause of death. Thus, there are relatively few deaths in infancy or childhood. Chronic degenerative diseases, such as stroke, heart disease, and cancer, become the major causes of death. Conditions related to health behaviors, such as smoking, alcohol consumption, a sedentary lifestyle, and obesity, constitute an increasing proportion of causes of death. Deaths are concentrated in the older ages and have become rare in infancy and childhood.

4. **Age of Delayed Degenerative Diseases:** The causes of death remain similar to those in the third stage, but the death rates at older ages decline further, and the average age at death continues to increase. In this stage, it is unclear whether people (1) remain healthy until shortly before death, or (2) become disabled at a relatively young age and remain disabled until death occurs many years later.

The four stages of the Epidemiologic Transition are related both to a shift in death rates by age and to a shift in the distribution of causes of death. The four stages can be roughly linked to the life table patterns shown in Figures 4.38 through 4.41 in Chapter 4, which showed life table measures for female e_0^0 at 25, 50, 75, and 100 years. In the first stage of the epidemiological transition, e_0^0 is about 25 years, and as shown in Figure 4.39, deaths are concentrated under age 10. In the second stage, e_0^0 is about 50 years, and although a large portion of deaths occurs in infancy and childhood, an increased percentage of deaths occurs at older adult ages. In the third stage, with e_0^0 about 75, there are few deaths in infancy and childhood, and almost all deaths occur at the older ages, peaking in the 80–84 age group. In the fourth stage, with e_0^0 of 100 years, 97% of all persons survive to age 80. We see in Figure 4.39 that with very high e_0^0 deaths are concentrated at an advanced age, as was

the case for the third stage. However, in the fourth stage, deaths have shifted to an even older age, and the largest number of deaths occurs in the 105–109 age group.

Causes of death are often divided into three groups: (1) **communicable causes of death**, such as infectious and parasitic diseases, which can be transmitted from one person to another; (2) **non-communicable causes of death**, which are caused by diseases or degenerative conditions and are not transmitted from one person to another, such as cancer or heart disease; and (3) external causes of death, which are caused by human action by the person affected or another person, whether unintentionally as in an accident, or intentionally as in suicide or homicide.

Figure 5.1 presents a schematic representation of how the three categories of causes of death shift in the course of the Epidemiologic Transition. The first panel shows changes in death rates by cause of death. Death rates from communicable diseases decline somewhat between the first and second stages, fall more by the third stage, and are extremely low by the fourth stage. Death rates from non-communicable causes also fall. Death rates from external causes decline after the second stage.

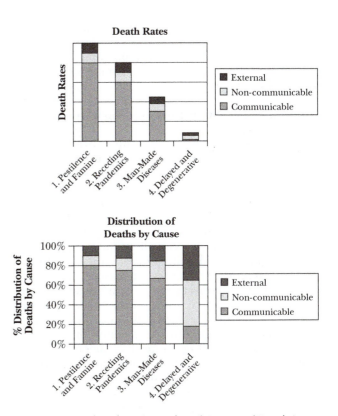

FIGURE 5.1   The Changing Roles of Causes of Death in the Course of the Epidemiologic Transition

While the first panel showed death rates by cause, it is useful to see how the *distribution* of causes of death changes over time. This is shown in the second panel. The percentage of all deaths from communicable causes falls from one stage to the next, and the percentage of deaths from non-communicable causes increases from one stage to the next. In Figure 5.1, external causes comprise a larger percentage of all deaths in later stages.

HISTORICAL MORTALITY DECLINE

Next, we look at what is known about the level of mortality and the causes of mortality decline historically, focusing on the first two stages of the Epidemiologic Transition. First, we look at anthropological work that suggests what mortality conditions might have been in premodern populations. Then, we look at how the development of pastoral nomadism, settled agriculture, commerce, and periodic markets affected mortality. After that, we look at the effect of migration on the spread of disease. Finally, in this section, we discuss the factors thought to influence mortality change historically in what is now the More Developed Region of the world through the early twentieth century.

Premodern Mortality

For most of human history, life expectancy at birth probably was about 20–30 years. About two-thirds of babies survived to their first birthday, and about one-half were still alive at age 5. Around one-tenth of people survived to age 65.[2]

Anthropological Studies of Contemporary Hunters and Gatherers

Researchers have looked at the causes of death and mortality levels of contemporary hunting-and-gathering groups in order to get some idea of mortality conditions in the past when a hunting-and-gathering way of life was common. **Hunters and gatherers** traveled on foot and lived by gathering fruits and vegetables and hunting animals. They moved on to another locale when the local supply of food or game was depleted or when it was thought prudent to move for some other reason.

The study of contemporary hunters and gathers has drawbacks, since contemporary hunting-and-gathering groups are not completely unaffected by the modern world, and because many contemporary hunting-and-gathering groups have been pushed to less desirable locales than where they lived in the past. Nonetheless this approach has value, since we cannot go back and study hunters and gatherers in the past. Three studies of this type were of the !Kung Bushmen in the Kalahari Desert of Southwest Africa, the Yanomama in the rain forests of southern

Venezuela and northern Brazil, and the Ache in the tropical forests of eastern Paraguay.[3]

Howell studied !Kung Bushmen in the Kalahari Desert in the 1960s. Figure 5.2 indicates the area in which the !Kung Bushmen resided. The !Kung were hunter-gatherers and had no regular access to Western medicine, although their lives had not been unchanged over time. Howell's study may be the best demographic study of hunter-gatherers.

Bushmen did not know their ages, but ordering by age was very important in !Kung social structure, and people always knew which group members were older than them and which group members were younger. Using models of age structure, Howell was able to estimate the age distribution and the demographic characteristics of the !Kung.

It seems that causes of death among the !Kung break down as follows:

80%	Infectious and parasitic
10%	Degenerative
10%	Violence
100%	Total

Howell estimated that among !Kung Bushmen, e_0^0 was about 35 years. About 20% of children die before their first birthday, and about 40% die before their fifteenth birthday. The !Kung moved frequently, since after a fairly short time the game and vegetation in an area became depleted. The !Kung walked everywhere, so group members needed to be able to walk under their own power. Older people died or were abandoned when they were no longer able to move with the group. Also, when a group member died for *any reason*, the group moved on. This was a sensible practice since something in that locale, such as contaminated water or another hazard, could have contributed to the person's death.

The Yanomama live in the tropical rain forest between Venezuela and Brazil. They first had contact with the outside world in the 1950s. It was estimated that in the 1970s, e_0^0 was about 20 years. By the 1970s, some aspects of Yanomama life had been substantially affected by the outside world. Bananas and malaria were introduced into the area by outsiders. Bananas have become a staple of the Yanomama diet, and by the mid-1970s bananas contributed 60–70% of the calories in the Yanomama diet. Also, malaria organisms are found in a high proportion of the Yanomama. Malaria debilitates people and makes them susceptible to dying from other causes in addition to causing death directly.[4]

The Ache live in eastern Paraguay. Mortality rates among the Ache were generally similar to those among the !Kung, but the causes of death were different, with substantially more deaths from violence. Among the !Kung, 11% of adult deaths were due to

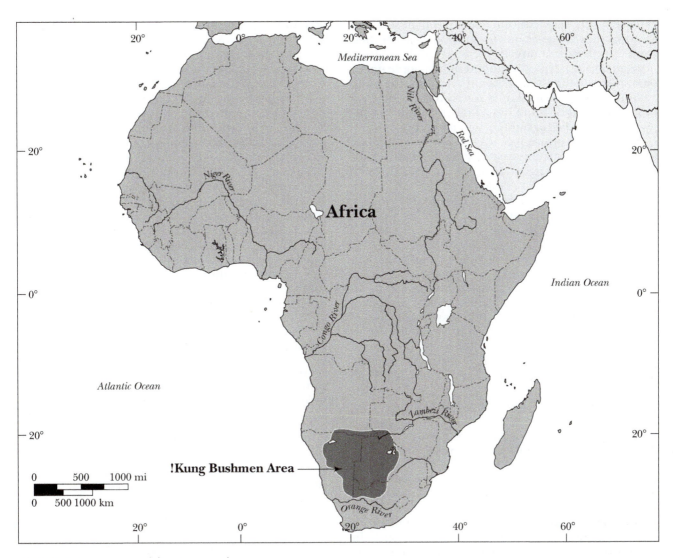

FIGURE 5.2   Location of the !Kung Bushmen Area

warfare or accidents, while among the Ache 73% of adult deaths were due to warfare or accidents.[5]

Estimates of e_0^0 from hunting-and-gathering populations studied in the twentieth century range from 20 years to 37 years. These levels and the distribution of causes of death in these populations provide a background for understanding the history of human mortality change.

Health and Mortality Consequences of the Transition to Pastoral Nomadism and Settled Agriculture

As the wild animals and gatherable fruits and vegetables become depleted in an area, a hunting-and-gathering group needs to move to another area. The circulation of hunting-and-gathering groups means

that a given area can support only a fairly small number of groups. In other words, land used for hunting and gathering has a low carrying capacity. Thus, under hunting and gathering, population density remains low.

Hunting and gathering as a means of support has undergone transitions historically either to pastoral nomadism or to settled agriculture. In **pastoral nomadism**, herds of domestic animals are moved from place to place in order to find grazing land. Pastoral nomadism is possible after animals such as sheep, yaks, or goats have been domesticated. Pastoral nomadism also has persisted in locations where settled agriculture is not possible.[6]

Both pastoral nomadism and settled agriculture give people more control over their environment and their sources of food than is the case for hunters and gatherers. Although pastoral nomads still must search for food, they are searching for grazing areas for their animals rather than directly for food for themselves. Also, an area can typically support more people under pastoral nomadism than it could under hunting and gathering, because land used for pastoral nomadism or for settled agriculture has a higher carrying capacity than land used for hunting and gathering.

Settled agriculture has advantages over hunting and gathering, such as assuring a steady supply of food. When settled agriculture is adopted, cultivated plants provide a more reliable food supply than relying on what is gathered. Settled agriculture also usually involves domesticated animals, which provide a more reliable meat supply than that obtained by hunting wild animals.

Pastoral nomadism also poses new threats to human health and survival. Many serious human diseases have been transmitted from animals to humans, and the change from hunting and gathering to pastoral nomadism makes people susceptible to a new set of diseases.[7]

An early form of agriculture is called **slash-and-burn agriculture**. In this system, after a field has been planted for some years, the yield declines. Then the field is burned and the ash fertilizes the soil. People move on to a new area that they then cultivate. In slash-and-burn agriculture, the land can support a higher population density than under a hunting-and-gathering system, but there are still limitations on population density since land must be left uncultivated for some time to restore the soil's fertility.

Other agricultural techniques allow an area of land to support a higher population density than slash and burn. As agricultural techniques change, fields are left fallow (unplanted) periodically to replenish their soil fertility but not for as long as under slash and burn. In the Middle Ages, the three-field system became common, in which one field was left fallow, a second field was planted with crops such as oats or barley, and a third field was planted with legumes such as peas or beans that improve the soil by capturing nitrogen. When properly applied, agriculture can continue under the three-field system indefinitely without exhausting the soil. In this system, one-third of agricultural land is always uncultivated. Fertilization using animal waste can also replenish soil fertility and increase productivity. The sequence of changes in agricultural technique described here decreases the need for people to relocate, allows higher population density to be supported, and increases agricultural yields. As the population density supported by more intensive forms of agriculture increases, this means that the carrying capacity of the land also increases.

When populations adopted settled agriculture, their calorie consumption rose and their nutritional status improved, but they also encountered new threats from infectious diseases and parasites. There was an increased health risk from poor sanitation. When there is low population density and a small group moves frequently, there is fairly little health risk from contamination of water supplies by human excrement. With settled agriculture, which entails less frequent movement and increased population density, contamination of water supplies becomes an increased hazard. Also, as in pastoral nomadism, close interaction with domestic animals increases the risk of disease transmission from animals to humans.

In sum, with a shift from hunting and gathering to pastoral nomadism or settled agriculture, the combination of causes of death changed. Death rates from some causes increased, while death rates from other causes decreased. It is clear that the population growth rate increased, but whether this was the result of overall mortality decline or whether increased calorie consumption associated with a more reliable food supply resulted in an increase in fertility remains an issue of debate.[8]

Crisis Mortality, Trade, and the Rise of Periodic Markets

A **mortality crisis** occurs when there is a sudden rise in the number of deaths, which is usually followed within a few years by a sharp decline in deaths to about the pre-crisis level. A mortality crisis can be caused by a crop failure, an epidemic, or a war. A time period that includes one or more mortality crises is referred to as a time of **crisis mortality**.

Historically, periodic crop failures led to mortality crises, which resulted in increased death rates. Part of mortality decline in Europe before 1750 was due to the fact that crop failure–caused mortality crises occurred less frequently and became less severe over time.

Figure 5.3 is a schematic representation of the relation between mortality crises and population size. The figure shows the population size, the number of births, and the number of deaths. There is assumed to

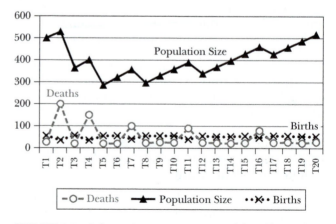

FIGURE 5.3 Schematic Representation of the Effects of Declining Frequency of Mortality Crises on Population Size

be no net migration. Thus, the population at Time 2 is the population at Time 1 plus the births and minus the deaths that occurred between Time 1 and Time 2.

Figure 5.3 illustrates a situation in which, over time, mortality crises become less severe and occur less frequently. In this example, mortality crises occurred at T2, T4, T7, T11, and T16. In non-crisis years, the number of deaths is almost constant. A severe crisis results in a decline in population size. After the crisis, the population size increases until the next crisis occurs. The number of births also declines somewhat during a mortality crisis. The decline in births is because some pregnant women die and more pregnancies end in a miscarriage or a stillbirth in times of crisis than in normal times. When crises become infrequent enough and mild enough, the population grows fairly steadily. When the population gains more in size between crises than it loses during the next crisis, there is population growth.

When a mortality crisis was the result of a crop failure, the crop failure often was a local event. There could be a poor crop in one area and a normal crop yield not many miles away. After there was an increase in trade and the establishment of periodic markets, there was exchange of agricultural products over a larger area. Improved trade meant that food was available after a crop failure, but the cost was higher.

Figure 5.4 shows the relation between grain prices and burials in Mouy, France, during a mortality crisis. The left-hand vertical axis shows the number of burials. The right-hand vertical axis shows the price per unit of wheat in the given year. Wheat prices increased after 1690, probably due to a local crop failure. The increase in deaths lagged the increase in wheat price. As more and more people could not afford to buy food, more deaths occurred. The decline in wheat prices after 1693 was closely tracked by a decline in burials.[9]

Fogel pointed out that an additional cause of mortality crises was government policies related to food distribution. He also presented evidence that poor, but above starvation level, nutrition was the norm even when there was not a crop failure. He argued that this low non-crisis nutritional level was more important than mortality crises in causing the overall high level of mortality. He thought that, before the late 1700s, much of the European population was caught in a situation in which weakness resulting from poor nutritional conditions limited labor productivity and that in turn low agricultural output made it difficult for people's nutritional state to improve.[10]

The development of trade led to less frequent and less severe crop failure–related crises, but populations were still vulnerable to mortality crises that resulted from disease or war. Civil unrest and war can also interact with crop failures to worsen mortality conditions. Violence can interfere with planting and harvesting of crops and can destroy produce. Also, in a time of moderate crop failure, war can interfere with trade and limit the local supply of food. When there are large increases in the price of food, it is thought that usually more people die from eating contaminated or spoiled food than actually starve. Thus, in a time of food shortage, diseases spread by contaminated food can flourish.[11]

Mortality crises caused by epidemics occurred long after commerce was well developed. The crowded and often unsanitary conditions in cities fostered the spread of diseases such as cholera, which is caused by contamination of water by the waste of cholera victims.

Migration and Disease

When there is increased trade and population movement, diseases also can migrate. When people move from one locale to another, they bring diseases with them from the old area to the new area. The population in the new locale can be seriously affected by a disease that is new to them and to which they have little or no resistance. Also, people who come from another area can bring in parasites, such as fleas, that can transmit devastating diseases.[12]

There are two views of how the bubonic plague, also known as the Black Death, entered Europe. One view is that it entered Sicily with sailors in 1347. The other view is that it spread as the result of the first use of biological warfare in 1346, when Mongol warriors who had the Italian city of Caffa under siege catapulted the dead bodies of plague victims into the city. Plague spread in the town either through contact with body fluids or through bites from infected fleas.[13]

After its introduction, the plague proceeded across Europe. Plague killed between 25% and 50% of the population of Europe in 1347–1351. Less serious plague outbreaks through the end of the fifteenth century killed 5–15% of the population.

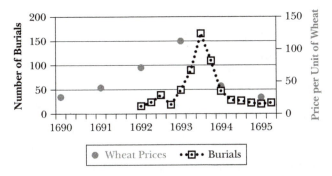

FIGURE 5.4   Crisis Mortality in Mouy, France, in the Late Seventeenth Century

The population decline due to the plague precipitated substantial changes in European social structure. After the epidemic, there was a shortage of agricultural labor. Increased labor demand led to an improvement in the situation of serfs, as they could leave their owner's land and obtain work elsewhere if they were not satisfied. Some have argued that the plague epidemics led to the end of the Middle Ages.[14]

Even in the modern era, movement of persons is a path of disease transmission, and restricting the movement of persons who show any symptoms is a common disease-combating tactic. Severe acute respiratory syndrome (SARS) is a respiratory disease with a high mortality rate: about 15% for people aged 45–64 and 50% for those aged 65 or older. There was a SARS outbreak that began in southern China in November 2002. Between November 2002 and July 2003, over 900 people died of SARS, and SARS spread to 37 countries.

SARS was spread partially through international air travel. Many countries responded to the threat of SARS by screening air travelers. For example, Hong Kong took the temperature of every departing air traveler and did not allow those with a fever to leave. The Philippines encouraged Filipinos abroad not to come home for Christmas. After SARS appeared in Toronto, carried there from travelers from Asia to Canada, most conventions, conferences, and other large meetings in Toronto were canceled.[15]

Columbian Exchange

In the **Columbian Exchange** people, ideas, foods, and diseases were transferred between Europe and the Americas after explorer Christopher Columbus's 1492 voyage. Columbus and other European explorers took many diseases to the Americas, including cholera, smallpox, whooping cough, chicken pox, malaria, measles, and plague. Some diseases moved from the Americas to Europe, including American strains of yellow fever and possibly syphilis.

Although the exact extent of mortality from new diseases in the Americas is not known, it seems clear that the effect on New World populations was devastating. It has been estimated that by 1642, the Native American population was reduced by 80–95%, mainly from disease.[16]

Exchanges of foods were also important. The Americas contributed many crops to Europe, including potatoes, sweet potatoes, corn, cassava, and tobacco, as well as tomatoes, chili peppers, cacao, peanuts, and pineapples. Also, many Old World crops were brought to the Americas, including sugar cane, soybeans, barley, and oranges.

Social Structure, Poverty, and Crop Disease: The Irish Potato Famine

The potato was especially important to the European diet since potatoes along with dairy products comprise a complete diet. Also, a small land area can produce a substantial harvest of potatoes. Thus, potatoes provided an efficient source of calories and contributed to European population growth.

Irish peasants increasingly relied on potatoes from a small plot along with dairy products for almost their entire diet. Most land was owned by large landowners, many of whom lived in England.

Potato blight probably arrived in Europe from Mexico in 1842. It was especially devastating in Ireland in 1846–1847. Even after the blight, yields were low due to a scarcity of seed potatoes for planting. Figure 5.5 shows Bourke's estimates of the yield of Irish potatoes in 1844–1859.[17]

Although some food was supplied by the state, there was massive starvation and death from eating contaminated food. Throughout the famine, corn and livestock for food were exported to England, which further contributed to Irish resentment of the English.

It has been estimated that 1.1–1.5 million people in Ireland died due to the famine between 1846 and 1851.[18] The potato famine also stimulated increased emigration out of Ireland, and the magnitude of increased Irish emigration rivaled the impact of increased mortality in Irish population loss, with an estimated 1.5–2.0 million people emigrating from Ireland in the period 1846–1854.[19] Continued economic problems in Ireland contributed to emigration long after the famine.

Figure 5.6 shows the populations of Ireland and of England in 1801–1911.[20] The values for Ireland are on the left-hand axis and for England are on the right-hand axis. The vertical scale for the two countries is different because the population of England was much larger than that of Ireland. The Irish population decline precipitated by the potato famine is striking.

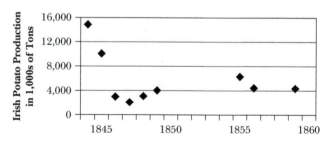

FIGURE 5.5   Irish Potato Production in Thousands of Tons, 1844–1859

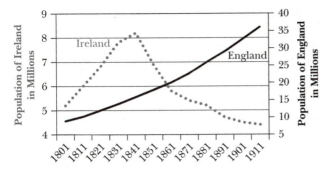

FIGURE 5.6   Population of Ireland and England, 1801–1911

Modern Population Increase in Europe before 1914

In Western Europe, population size began to rise rapidly shortly before 1700. Figure 5.7 shows the estimated population of England and Wales from 850 to 1791.[21] The population grew until the mid-fourteenth century and then was decimated by the Black Death. After 1500, the population grew again. The picture in Figure 5.7 is similar to that shown in the estimates for the world as a whole in Figure 2.1 in Chapter 2.

Civil registration of births and deaths in England began in 1837, long after substantial population growth had begun. There is agreement that population growth was mainly due to declines in mortality rather than increases in fertility. It is also agreed that a decline in deaths from infectious diseases was the main reason for mortality decline.

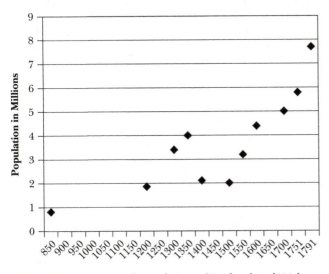

FIGURE 5.7   Estimated Population of England and Wales, 850–1791

Medical Care, Nutritional Improvement, Sanitation Improvements, and Changes in the Nature of Diseases, Such as Plague

Despite the many areas of agreement about the sources of population growth and mortality decline, there has been a debate about the roles of the following factors in mortality decline and population increase in Europe before 1914. We discuss each of these sets of factors:

1. Nutrition
2. Preventive medical care
   a. Improvements in sanitation
   b. Smallpox vaccination
3. Changes in the nature of diseases such as plague and influenza
4. Curative medical care

Nutrition   McKeown has argued that improved nutrition was the main cause of mortality decline and population increase in England and Wales.[22] The argument that nutrition improved in the seventeenth and eighteenth centuries is based on the view that real income increased over time, which led to better diets (more calories). However, there has been controversy about whether real income increased at that time for the bulk of the population or whether the main effect of the increase in per capita income was that those who had been well off became even richer.[23]

Preventive Medical Care   **Preventive medical care** reduces the chance that a person contracts a disease or ailment, or it reduces the chance that the person dies. Preventive medical care includes vaccinations, improvement of water and sanitation systems and removal of a disease-causing agent from the local environment, such as eliminating standing-water pools to reduce the number of mosquitoes and thus reduce the chance of contracting malaria.

Improved Sanitation   As urban populations grew, disease and deaths resulting from poor sanitation became more serious, especially through contamination of drinking water by human waste. This is illustrated in the following example.

John Snow, the Broad Street Pump, and Cholera in London   Cholera was a major problem in England and elsewhere in the nineteenth century. In the early nineteenth century, cholera was thought to be caused by breathing bad air. British physician John Snow thought cholera was transmitted by water contaminated by the waste of cholera sufferers. He published a study of this in 1849.[24]

There was a cholera epidemic in London in 1854. After plotting on a map the location of cholera cases within London, Snow identified the source of the disease as the Broad Street pump. He had the pump handle removed. After that, there were few new cholera cases. The epidemic had slowed before the pump handle was removed, but Snow did a statistical analysis of the geographic spread of the epidemic that supported his theory of disease transmission.[25]

Snow's study was seen as the start of epidemiology and as important in the development of the field of public health. Modern epidemiology continues to map cases of a disease outbreak in order to identify the source of the outbreak. The logic of seeing where diseases occur and the characteristics of people who become ill is a major principle in the use of computerized medical records in detecting outbreaks quickly.[26]

Development of the London Sewers   Although Snow's work increased understanding of how cholera is transmitted, cholera epidemics continued to occur. The summer of 1858 in London was unusually warm, and the stench from untreated sewage was incredibly strong. This was called "The Great Stink." There was an existing sewer system in London, but it was inadequate. In 1859 an engineer, Joseph Bazalgette, developed a plan for improved sewers that was approved, and by 1865 the new system was complete. Even in the new system, however, the sewage was not treated. Sewage was emptied into the Thames, and tides flushed the sewage out to the sea. After the new sewers were in place, the only subsequent cholera outbreak was in 1866, a year after the system was completed.[27]

Change in the Nature of Diseases Such as Plague and Influenza   As discussed in this chapter, plague was a major cause of death in Europe. After the devastating plague epidemic of the fourteenth century, there were subsequent plague epidemics, although they were not as severe. There has been speculation that after the fourteenth century, the plague organism mutated to a less virulent form.[28] Also, influenza had long been known in Europe, but in the 1480s it seemed to become more deadly. It is not clear whether the virus had mutated or whether its greater virulence was due to a climate shift to colder, wetter weather around that time.[29]

Smallpox Vaccination   Smallpox was the first disease for which an effective vaccine was developed. A precursor to vaccination is inoculation or variolation. In an **inoculation**, active disease cells are introduced to produce immunity. In a **vaccination**, cells from a related disease that does not have serious effects in humans or killed or weakened cells from the target disease are introduced to induce immunity.

It has long been known that those who survive smallpox are immune to contracting the disease again. In smallpox inoculation, a small amount of infected matter from a person who has smallpox is placed in a small cut. This practice was widespread in many parts of the world for centuries and was introduced to Europe and North America in 1721, before the development of vaccines.

In smallpox inoculation, there is a risk that the person will contract smallpox. In England in the eighteenth century, about 2% of inoculated people died from smallpox, although between 20% and 60% of those who contracted smallpox naturally died, and about 33% of smallpox survivors became blind. Thus, smallpox inoculation carried a much smaller risk than not being inoculated in a setting in which the chance of contracting smallpox was high. Inoculation also had other risks, including that the inoculated person could contract other diseases that the smallpox donor had, such as syphilis.

Cowpox is a disease related to smallpox that leads to pustules on a cow's udders. In humans, cowpox is a mild skin disease. Dairymaids sometimes contracted cowpox from milking affected cows. It had long been noted that dairymaids rarely contracted smallpox. Benjamin Jesty, an English farmer, applied material from cowpox pustules to small cuts on his family members in 1774. His wife developed a fever but recovered. This was the first instance of vaccination against smallpox.[30]

Edward Jenner played a very important role in the spread of vaccination. He started the promotion of vaccination using cowpox material in 1796. In 1802, the British Parliament gave Jenner a prize for his efforts.[31]

There have been different views of the magnitude of the impact of smallpox vaccination in European mortality decline in the nineteenth century, but there is general agreement that it had a substantial effect. Mercer reports that smallpox caused 8–20% of deaths in Europe in the eighteenth century, and it seems clear that smallpox vaccination and improvements in sanitation were preventive measures that contributed to mortality decline in Europe.[32]

Curative Medical Care   **Curative medical care** is administered after a person has a disease or ailment. There has been a great deal of controversy about whether curative medical care reduced mortality before the discovery of the first modern antibiotic, penicillin, in 1928.[33] Penicillin was not used clinically until 1941. Penicillin is effective against bacteria but is ineffective against viruses.

Infections of wounds and infections as a result of surgery were serious threats to the lives of patients. In 1890, Robert Koch published results of experiments showing that anthrax was caused by bacteria. This was some of the early evidence for the **germ theory of disease**, the theory that microorganisms cause many diseases. The germ theory of disease was a counter to the **miasma theory of disease**, which maintained that most diseases were caused by "bad air." Joseph Lister was also a proponent of the germ theory of disease and in 1867 published protocols for surgery intended to reduce infection resulting from surgery.[34]

Although the importance of cleanliness in caring for wounds and in surgery was understood by the late nineteenth century, the implementation of hygienic practices occurred slowly as many doctors and surgeons did not want to abandon their earlier practices.[35] The dangers of ineffective medical treatment and lack of understanding of the importance of sanitary practices were illustrated after President James Garfield was shot on July 2, 1881. He did not die until September 19. His wounds were not necessarily fatal, but his death was brought on by the failure of doctors to find a bullet lodged in his body and by infections aggravated by unsanitary surgical procedures and wound treatment.[36]

Some researchers have been very skeptical about the contribution of curative medical care to survival before penicillin. McKinlay and McKinlay identified nine infectious diseases that were major causes of death in the past. Death rates from each of these conditions were much higher in 1900 than they were in 1973. For each disease, Table 5.1 shows the decline in the age-adjusted death rate from the disease between 1900 and 1973. It also identifies the vaccine or medicine that was discovered to prevent or treat the disease and the year the vaccine or medicine was first widely or commercially used. Finally, it shows the percentage of the total decline in the age-adjusted death rate from the disease that occurred after the relevant vaccine or medicine was introduced.[37]

McKinlay and McKinlay do not think that the vaccines or medicines listed in Table 5.1 were ineffective. However, they do argue that for each of these diseases, the death rate had fallen substantially before

there was an effective specific medical treatment or vaccine, and they note that only for whooping cough did more than half of the decline occur after the vaccine or medicine was introduced. They speculate that overall improved health and nutrition led to most of the decline in mortality from these diseases before there were specific effective treatments.

Most Important Medical Breakthroughs since 1840
In 2007, the *British Medical Journal* surveyed its readers to ask what readers thought were the most important medical breakthroughs since 1840.[38] The results were as follows:

1. Sanitation (sewers)
2. Antibiotics
3. Anesthesia
4. Vaccines
5. Discovery of structure of DNA

It is interesting that improvement in sanitation was cited as the most important medical breakthrough. Sanitation and vaccines are both public health, preventive measures. Antibiotics and anesthesia are mainly concerned with curative medical care— treatment of a person after he or she has contracted a disease. The discovery of DNA opened a wide range of possibilities for learning about causes of and predispositions to illness and death. Much of the potential from the understanding of DNA is yet to be realized.

MORE CONSIDERATION OF CAUSES OF DEATH AND DISABILITY

As discussed in Chapter 4 and elaborated in the discussion of the Epidemiologic Transition, as mortality conditions improve, the age pattern of risk of death changes. This was shown in Figures 4.39 and 4.40 in Chapter 4

TABLE 5.1 Contribution of Vaccines and Medicines to the Fall in Mortality from Nine Common Infectious Diseases, the United States, 1900–1973

Disease	Fall in age-adjusted death rate from disease, 1900–1973, per 100,000 population	Vaccine or medicine to treat or prevent disease	Year vaccine or medicine was first in widespread or commercial use	% of the decline, 1900–1973, that occurred after vaccine or medicine was introduced
Tuberculosis	200	Isoniazid/Streptomycin	1950	8%
Scarlet fever	10	Penicillin	1946	2%
Influenza	22	Vaccine	1943	25%
Pneumonia	142	Sulphonamide	1935	17%
Diphtheria	43	Toxoid	1930	13%
Whooping cough	12	Vaccine	1930	51%
Measles	12	Vaccine	1963	1%
Typhoid	36	Chloramphenicol	1948	<1%
Polio	3	Vaccine, Salk/Sabin	1955	26%

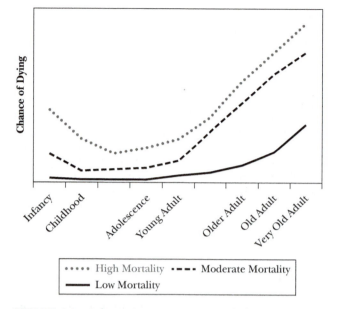

High Mortality ---- Moderate Mortality
Low Mortality

FIGURE 5.8   Schematic Representation of Change in Mortality Risks by Age

and is shown schematically in Figure 5.8. First, the risk of dying in infancy and childhood declines substantially, while the risk of dying declines modestly at older ages. Later, mortality decline is almost entirely due to reductions in the risk of dying at older ages. Eventually, almost all deaths in the population occur at quite advanced ages, as indicated in Figure 4.39.

This change in the pattern of deaths by age is brought about by a shift in the causes of death. In high-mortality conditions, infectious and parasitic diseases, often caused by unsanitary living conditions, take a high toll among infants and children. As death rates at young ages decline, an increasing proportion of deaths occurs at older ages. Increasingly, these deaths at older ages are caused by behaviors whose effects have built up over the course of an entire life, such as smoking, alcohol consumption, and a high-fat diet. Degenerative conditions also become more serious as people grow older and can lead to disability or death.

The rectangularization of mortality is discussed in Chapter 4, in which deaths increasingly become concentrated at advanced ages. **Morbidity** refers to being sick, diseased, generally unhealthy, or disabled. In the third and the fourth stages of the Epidemiologic Transition, researchers and policy makers who had been mainly concerned with mortality turned more of their attention to morbidity, as an increasing proportion of people lived to advanced ages and there became more concern with the capacities and well-being of older people.

There has been a debate about whether in the course of the Epidemiologic Transition there has been a compression of morbidity, analogous to the

rectangularization of mortality. As the age of death increases, does the age at which people become disabled also increase? Has there been a relatively small increase in the average number of years lived in a disabled state as survival to advanced ages has become more common, or has the age of becoming disabled remained relatively unchanged, leading to an increasing proportion of life spent in a disabled state?

As an increasing proportion of people live to advanced ages, often with disabling conditions, the amount of life spent in a disabled or debilitated state has become an issue of increased concern, both due to a desire that every person have as good a quality of life as possible, and due to a concern about strains and costs to relatives and the public in caring for the disabled. For example, there is typically a lag of 7 years between when people are diagnosed with Alzheimer's disease and when they die. In less developed countries, there can be a substantial lag between disability and death, such as with HIV, which has a lag of 6–16 years between infection and death even in the absence of treatment. Also, injuries related to violence and parasitic diseases can disable persons for many years. These concerns have led to efforts to estimate the average number of years lived in a disabled state.

Figure 5.9 depicts the changes in survival and disability that occur when there is a change from moderate-mortality conditions to very-low-mortality conditions. This is shown in the top panel without compression of morbidity and in the bottom panel with compression of morbidity. Each panel shows the number of people out of 100,000 births who survive to various ages. They also show the number of people out of 100,000 births who would be still alive and not disabled at a given age. The example is calculated with moderate mortality represented by $e_0^0 = 50$ and very low mortality represented as $e_0^0 = 100$. The moderate-mortality results are shown in dashed lines, and the very-low-mortality results are shown in solid lines.

The gap between the line for those who are still alive (whether or not they are disabled) and for those who are not disabled indicates the number of people who are alive but disabled. In the moderate-mortality scenario, the lines for those who are alive and the graph for those who are alive and not disabled are close to each other. In the very-low-mortality scenario without compression of morbidity, there is a substantial gap between the lines for those who are alive and for those who are not disabled, especially after age 60. In this example, at moderate mortality on average 5 years are spent alive but disabled. At very low mortality without compression of morbidity, on average 14 years are spent alive but disabled. At very low mortality with compression of morbidity, on average 6 years are spent alive but disabled. Thus, whether or not compression of morbidity occurs and the conditions under which it occurs have substantial implications.

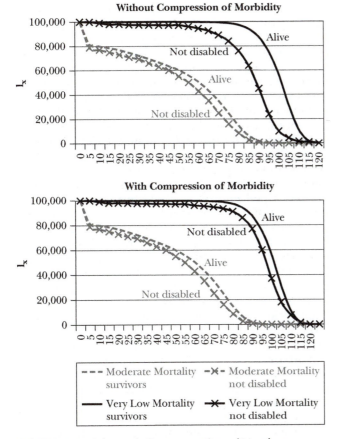

FIGURE 5.9 Schematic Representation of Number Surviving and Number in a Non-Disabled State from 100,000 Births with Moderate Mortality and with Very Low Mortality, without and with Compression of Morbidity

The evidence for the extent to which there has been a compression of morbidity is mixed. Crimmins found, for females in the United States, that e_0^0 increased from 75 to 78 years between 1970 and 1980, but the number of years expected to live in a non-disabled state remained at 60. The entire increment to survival of 3 years was spent in a disabled state.[39] On the other hand, Cambois and colleagues found some evidence in France that as expectation of remaining life at age 65 increased, the proportion of years spent alive and in a non-disabled state also increased. In France between 1980–1981 and 2002–2003, female e_{65}^0 increased by 3 years, from 18.3 years to 21.5 years, but disability-free life expectancy at age 65 increased by 6 years, from 9.8 years to 16.1 years.[40]

Causes of Death

Causes of death are often divided into natural causes of death and external causes of death. **Natural causes of death** are diseases and internal malfunctions of the body, such as heart failure. Death from a natural cause is not directly caused by human action. **External causes of death** are those resulting from human action, either intentional or unintentional. Homicide, suicide, and accidents are the three types of external causes of death. External causes of death are also sometimes called unnatural causes or violent causes of death.

Homicide is a death resulting from the action of another person with the intention of causing the person harm. Death does not need to be the intention. If a person intentionally pushes a person over and the person dies from hitting his head, this is homicide. The perpetrator did not intend for the victim to die, but he or she intended harm. **Suicide** is a death that results from intentional self-harm. An **accidental death** occurs when there is a death from other than natural causes, but no one intended harm.

It can sometimes be difficult to determine whether a death is the result of homicide, suicide, or an accident. When a person dies from a self-inflicted fire-arm shot (if the person shot himself), it could be an accident or suicide. If he or she dies when another person shot the firearm, it also could be an accident or homicide.

The division into natural and external causes is important partly because the policies to decrease natural-cause mortality and the policies to decrease external-cause mortality are different. To attack natural-cause mortality requires things such as immunization programs, the development of new drugs to treat diseases, and health education campaigns to reduce smoking, improve diet, and encourage safe-sex practices. To attack external-cause mortality involves promotion of safe driving practices and safe walking practices for pedestrians, policing programs to reduce homicide, help lines to decrease suicides, and safer housing conditions to reduce fatal accidents in the home.

Diseases or health conditions are often divided into acute conditions and chronic conditions. An **acute condition** is a disease from which a person either recovers fairly rapidly or dies fairly rapidly, such as pneumonia or influenza. **Chronic conditions** last at least a year and require ongoing medical treatment. They often impede the ability of a person to go about his or her daily life.[41] Typically chronic conditions lead to death or contribute to other causes of death only after an extended period of time. Chronic conditions include asthma and arthritis, hypertension (high blood pressure), and high cholesterol. A **degenerative condition** is a chronic condition that tends to worsen with age, such as dementia.

Natural causes of death are also often divided into those caused by communicable diseases and those caused by non-communicable diseases. **Communicable diseases** can be transmitted from one person to another, such as influenza or HIV.

Non-communicable diseases cannot normally be transmitted from one person to another and include heart disease, stroke, and cancer.

When people refer to the cause of death, they usually mean the **underlying cause of death**, which is "the one that started the chain of events leading to the death" or "the circumstances of the accident or violence which produced the fatal injury."[42] Often, many different causes contribute to death. For example, amyotrophic lateral sclerosis (ALS) is a fatal motor neuron disease for which there is no known cure. In the course of ALS, there is progressive paralysis, and most people with ALS die from respiratory failure within 4 years, when the person is no longer able to clear his or her lungs.[43] In this case, ALS is the underlying cause of death, but respiratory failure is a contributory cause of death. A **contributory cause of death** is "a significant condition that unfavorably influences the course of the morbid process and thus contributes to the fatal outcome, but which is not related to the disease or condition directly causing death."[44]

With improved medical care, some diseases that had been acute conditions become chronic conditions. This can happen when medication ameliorates the most serious effects of the disease. For example, highly active antiretroviral therapy (HAART) has changed HIV to a chronic disease for some patients. A person who is HIV-positive is said to have transitioned to AIDS when the symptoms of AIDS, such as weight loss and skin rash, appear. A person can be HIV-positive for many years without showing any symptoms. "Pre-AIDS mortality" occurs when a person dies who is HIV-positive but for whom HIV has not yet developed into AIDS. All HIV-positive persons will die eventually, but not all of those deaths are due to HIV. For example, a person who was HIV-positive could die from being hit by a truck, but it would not be reasonable to attribute that death to HIV. Whether pre-AIDS deaths are related to the person's HIV-positive status is often studied by comparing death rates from a particular cause among HIV-positive persons without AIDS symptoms to death rates for HIV-negative persons. It seems that being HIV-positive does contribute to death rates from some causes, such as pneumonia.[45]

Availability and Limitations of Data on Causes of Death and on Diseases

As discussed in Chapter 3, in less developed countries, there often is very incomplete registration of deaths. In this situation, death rates by age and sex and the related life tables can be estimated by indirect means, using models that were developed using information from countries with more complete and accurate data. In order to study mortality by cause of death, it is necessary not only to have a complete recording of deaths but also to have accurate information about the cause of each death. Many countries that have data that can generate fairly accurate life tables do not have complete and accurate information on causes of death. In such situations, models of causes of death are applied to whatever data are available from the given country to estimate the distribution of causes of death.

The standard categorization of diseases and causes of death is issued by the World Health Organization and is updated periodically.[46] The cause of death is typically obtained from the death certificate. Even in developed countries, there are variations in assignment of causes of death. For example, in some countries a high proportion of deaths that should have been coded with ischemic heart disease as the underlying cause of death were coded with general heart failure as the underlying cause of death.[47] Also, sometimes there is ambiguity as to whether a death is an accident or suicide, such as in a single-vehicle fatal accident with only the driver present.[48] In addition, when a dead body is found, it can be difficult to determine whether the cause is a suicide, an accident, or a homicide.[49] Variation in classification of causes of death is especially likely if there is a negative stigma attached to a particular cause of death, such as suicide in some cultures or HIV.

One approach to determining cause of death in countries with incomplete data has been through verbal autopsies. In a **verbal autopsy**, people are asked if there has been a recent death to a household member. If there has been a recent death, questions are asked about the cause or conditions of the death.[50] Usually there is a coding scheme to assign the cause of death within broad categories. This system is subject to error, but it can yield more information about the cause of death than might be available otherwise. Verbal autopsies have been used to determine causes of infant and child death and to identify maternal deaths. They are more accurate in identifying some causes of death, such as measles and neonatal tetanus, than other causes of death, such as malaria or meningitis. They also have been used to identify deaths from HIV and other causes of adult mortality.[51] Sometimes, they have been used simply to distinguish between natural-cause and external-cause deaths. Concerns have also been expressed that being asked verbal autopsy questions can be very upsetting to family members, causing them to relive the experience of the death.[52]

Data on the prevalence of various diseases or conditions are even more difficult to obtain than data on causes of death. Whether a person has malaria is usually fairly straightforward to determine, but diseases such as HIV typically show no symptoms for many years. In such situations, the incidence of HIV can be reliably determined only through population surveys in which blood or saliva are obtained for testing. As discussed in Chapter 3, surveys that collect biological samples have become common in some developed countries. Also, an increasing number of less developed countries have collected biological samples to test for various conditions, such as HIV, TB, and syphilis, in order to get a better idea of their prevalence in the population, but this is a difficult task. Since people can refuse to participate in such surveys, there are concerns about whether a person's refusal to participate is related to his or her HIV status.[53]

Population surveys are a much better way to determine the prevalence of diseases or conditions than the reports of doctors or other health professionals on the number of cases reported or treated. In a population survey, many people are identified with a condition who would not appear in medical records as having that condition. A population survey that includes a test for a condition can identify people who did not know they had the condition. It also can identify people who knew they had the condition but had not sought health care for the condition.

Many chronic conditions that increase the risk of death, such as hypertension (high blood pressure), usually have no symptoms that are perceivable by the affected person. The presence of such a condition is only discernible through a test such as blood pressure measurement and, like HIV prevalence, can only be reliably known through general population screening. There are large population surveys, such as the National Health and Nutrition Examination Survey (NHANES) that is discussed in Chapter 3, that can produce good estimates of the prevalence of hypertension, but many countries do not have such surveys. Such surveys are rare in less developed countries.

Type II diabetes also is often asymptomatic for many years. Sometimes, diabetes is detected through population screening. For example, a survey of people aged 55–74 in southern Germany in 2000 that included screening for diabetes found that over 16% of the respondents had diabetes, but only one-half of the diabetic respondents had previously been aware of their condition.[54]

As countries implement or extend screening for conditions such as hypertension or diabetes, more hypertensive and more diabetic persons are found. This can lead to the impression that the prevalence of these conditions has increased, when actually this increase results from the identification of people with the condition who earlier would not have been identified.

WHO Global Burden of Disease (GBD) Project

The Global Burden of Disease (GBD) Project is sponsored by the World Health Organization and is headed by Christopher Murray and Alan Lopez.

The first GBD Project results were published in 1990, complete results were published for 2004, and some results have appeared for 2010. The purposes of the project are to develop estimates of the causes of death and disability and to estimate the prevalence and the impact of risk factors contributing to death and disability.[55]

The GBD Project seeks to make estimates on a consistent basis throughout the world, which is a major challenge due to the lack of reliable age-specific mortality data for some countries, the lack of reliable data on causes of death for even more countries, and the lack of reliable data on the prevalence of various disabilities for even more countries. The researchers involved in the GBD Project have been forthright about the data limitations and acknowledge that for low-income countries and for some middle-income countries, there is a great deal of uncertainty in the estimates.

We present the estimates for 2004. This gives a useful picture of the differing causes of death and disability in the world as a whole and by income level of countries, but it does not give a dynamic picture. In Chapter 6, causes of death and disability in the LDR are discussed, and in Chapter 7, the situation in the MDR is discussed.[56]

The Global Burden of Disease Classification of Causes of Death

The GBD Project divided causes of death into three groups. Note also the font coloring, as it will be important to the categorization of data in some of the tables presented in this chapter.

  I. *Communicable and related* diseases, consisting of:
    a. Communicable diseases
    b. Maternal and perinatal conditions
    c. Nutritional deficiencies
 II. **Non-communicable** diseases
III. **External causes**, consisting of:
    a. Accidents
    b. Homicide
    c. Suicide

The **Global Burden of Disease classification** is somewhat different from that distinguishing between communicable and non-communicable causes of death, since maternal and perinatal conditions and nutritional conditions are not communicable diseases. They cannot be transmitted from one person to another, but they are grouped with communicable diseases in the GBD classification scheme. The perinatal period is from the twenty-eighth week of gestation to 28 days of age.

The GBD Project wanted a policy-relevant classification to aid in understanding mortality change. The conditions in Group I, including maternal and perinatal conditions and nutritional deficiencies, usually decline rapidly during the second stage of the epidemiological transition. The conditions in Group II tend to be important in the third and fourth stages of the Epidemiologic Transition.[57]

For 2004, the GBD Project had acceptably complete cause of death data for 76 countries. They had acceptably complete data on deaths, but not on cause of death, for 34 additional countries. For countries without adequate data, the GBD Project estimated cause of death using models based on data from other countries. Some of the data problems encountered in the GBD Project are discussed by Mathers and his colleagues.[58]

Leading Causes of Death

Table 5.2 shows the ten leading causes of death in the world as a whole and in three groupings of countries by per capita income in 2004. The per capita income levels are calculated by the World Bank, and the cutoffs and the countries included in each group can change from year to year. The per capita income cutoffs for 2004 are shown in the table. Per capita income is not adjusted for the cost of living in the given country.

This categorization of countries by per capita income level was made in response to some of the criticisms of the MDR–LDR classification of countries discussed in Chapter 2. The high-income countries are mostly the same countries as in the MDR, except that a few countries, notably South Korea and some Middle Eastern countries such as Saudi Arabia, Kuwait, Qatar, and the United Arab Emirates, are included in the high-income countries even though they are in the UN LDR group. Also, many of the countries in Eastern Europe and the former Soviet Union, such as Russia, Poland, Ukraine, and Latvia, are in the group of middle-income countries, although they are included in the UN MDR group.

In Table 5.2 the causes of death are coded according to the GBD classification and are distinguished by color and font from each other. Table 5.2 also shows the percentage of all deaths in the world and in the given income group due to the given cause.[59]

In the world as a whole, the leading cause of death is ischemic heart disease. Ischemic heart disease occurs when there is a reduced blood supply to the heart, usually because arteries have become clogged by fat deposits. It can be indicated by chest pain, difficulty breathing, or swelling of the extremities, but often it is asymptomatic (has no symptoms) until one or more arteries are almost completely blocked. There is not an easy, low-cost test for ischemic heart disease. The risk of ischemic heart disease is greater for people who are older, who smoke, and who have high cholesterol, diabetes, or hypertension. Prevention of ischemic heart disease has focused on control of cholesterol levels,

TABLE 5.2 Ten Leading Causes of Death in the World and by Income Group of Countries, Classified by Global Burden of Disease Category, 2004

	World	Low-Income Countries (Gross National Income (GNI) per Capita < US$826)	Middle-Income Countries (GNI per Capita US$826–$10,065)	High-Income Countries (GNI per Capita > US$10,065)
1	**Ischemic heart disease 12%**	*Lower respiratory infections 11%*	**Stroke 14%**	**Ischemic heart disease 16%**
2	**Stroke 10%**	**Ischemic heart disease 9%**	**Ischemic heart disease 14%**	**Stroke 9%**
3	*Lower respiratory infections 7%*	*Diarrheal diseases 7%*	**COPD 7%**	**Lung cancer 6%**
4	**Chronic obstructive pulmonary disease (COPD) 5%**	*HIV 6%*	*Lower respiratory infections 4%*	*Lower respiratory infections 4%*
5	*Diarrheal diseases 4%*	**Stroke 6%**	**Lung cancer 3%**	**COPD 4%**
6	*HIV 4%*	**COPD 4%**	**Motor vehicle accidents 3%**	**Alzheimer's and other dementias 3%**
7	*Tuberculosis 3%*	*Tuberculosis 4%*	**Hypertensive heart disease 3%**	**Colon and rectal cancers 3%**
8	Lung cancer 2%	*Neonatal infections 3%*	**Stomach cancer 2%**	**Diabetes 3%**
9	**Motor vehicle accidents 2%**	*Malaria 3%*	*Tuberculosis 2%*	**Breast cancer 2%**
10	*Prematurity and low birth weight 2%*	*Prematurity and low birth weight 3%*	**Diabetes 2%**	**Stomach cancer 2%**

The entries show the percentage of all deaths that were due to a given cause for the world or within each income group.

control of weight, ceasing smoking, and control of hypertension.

Besides ischemic heart disease, other types of heart disease are rheumatic heart disease, hypertensive heart disease, and inflammatory heart disease. In 2004, in the world as a whole, 81% of all heart disease deaths were from ischemic heart disease, and in the high-income countries, 85% of all heart disease deaths were from ischemic heart disease. In middle-income countries, hypertensive heart disease is the seventh leading cause of death. In hypertensive heart disease, hypertension creates a condition that requires a large amount of effort to pump blood, which then results in thickening of the heart muscle. Sometimes deaths are reported in summary statistics for all of the types of heart disease together. Reporting for all types of heart disease together shows basically the same picture as if the data had been reported only for ischemic heart disease.

The second leading cause of death in the world is stroke. Stroke, which is also known as cerebrovascular disease, occurs when there is a loss of blood flow to the brain. Stroke can lead to death, and survivors of a stroke often have limited functions due to problems with moving their limbs, speaking, or understanding speech. Risk factors for stroke include age, hypertension, high cholesterol, diabetes, and smoking. Like ischemic heart disease, prevention of stroke has focused on control of cholesterol levels, ceasing smoking, weight control, and control of hypertension.

Both ischemic heart disease and stroke are noncommunicable causes of death, and a person at risk of dying from these conditions is not likely to be aware of his or her risk unless he or she has been screened for hypertension, high cholesterol, and diabetes. In 2004, it is estimated that 22% of all deaths in the world were due to these two causes.

The third leading cause of death is lower respiratory infections, which are usually complications of pneumonia. Vaccines can prevent childhood pneumonia. Also other conditions, such as HIV or chronic obstructive pulmonary disease (COPD), increase susceptibility to lower respiratory infections. While lower respiratory infections are the leading cause of death in low-income countries, they are the fourth leading cause of death in middle-income and high-income countries.

The fourth leading cause of death in the world is COPD. COPD occurs when the flow of air to the lungs is limited. This restricted air flow is usually a result of smoking, but it can result from air pollution and is exacerbated by infections, such as lower respiratory infections.

The fifth leading cause of death is diarrheal diseases. This is the third leading cause of death in low-income countries and mainly afflicts infants and children, but it is not in the ten leading causes of death in middle-income or high-income countries. Poor sanitation and unsafe drinking water contribute to diarrhea and subsequent death. Lack of adequate treatment to replenish bodily fluids and unavailability of health care also contribute to mortality from diarrheal diseases.

The sixth leading cause of death is HIV, which is mainly a cause of death in low-income countries, although it is also a major cause of death in some middle-income countries, such as South Africa and Botswana. HIV is an infectious disease for which there is not a cure, although there are increasingly effective treatments available. HIV death rates are highest in the middle adult ages, as indicated in Figure 4.23 in Chapter 4, unlike most infectious and parasitic causes of death, which mainly lead to deaths in infancy and childhood and unlike the degenerative causes of death that lead to deaths of the elderly.

The seventh leading cause of death is tuberculosis (TB). There is an effective vaccine available for TB, and most forms of TB can be effectively treated, but in low-income and middle-income countries TB remains a major cause of death. HIV and TB also interact so that a person who has one condition and then acquires the other condition has a substantially higher chance of dying.[60] Also, highly drug-resistant forms of TB have appeared in some parts of the world.

The eighth leading cause of death is lung cancer. While lung cancer is the fifth leading cause of death in middle-income countries and the third leading cause of death in high-income countries, it does not rank in the leading ten causes of death in low-income countries. Lung cancer mortality mainly reflects the impact of smoking. Antismoking campaigns have sometimes had a major effect, such as among men in the United States. However, lung cancer is likely to increase as a cause of death in low-income countries. This is because between 1970 and 1999, tobacco consumption decreased by 2% in the MDR but increased by 75% in the LDR.[61]

Motor vehicle accidents are the ninth leading cause of death. This is the only external cause of death included in the ten leading causes of death. It is especially a problem in middle-income countries, where it is the sixth leading cause of death. In many middle-income and low-income countries, the number of motor vehicles has increased rapidly, but highway safety has not improved enough to keep up with the increase in motor vehicles.[62]

Prematurity and low birth weight comprise the tenth leading cause of death. This reflects a shortage of prenatal care, nutritional inadequacies among pregnant women, deficiencies in medical attendance at birth, and inadequate medical care for newborns in distress. This is a leading cause of death only in low-income countries.

For the world as a whole, five of the leading causes of death are from Group I. Recall that by 2004, about 80% of the world's population lived in the LDR, and thus the results for the world as a whole are heavily weighted by the causes of death in low-income and middle-income countries.

In low-income countries, seven of the leading ten causes of death are communicable and related causes. Diarrhea, neonatal infections, and prematurity and low birth weight stand out as causes of death for infants and children. These causes of death are reflective of poor living conditions and poor preventive and curative health care. Also, the causes of death in low-income countries especially affect infants and children. These causes of death reflect those in the second stage of the Epidemiologic Transition. Malaria and neonatal infections join the list of Group I causes in the leading ten causes of death for low-income countries.

In high-income countries, nine of the ten leading causes of death are non-communicable diseases. These are mainly diseases that afflict the elderly. These causes of death are consistent with the low death rates among those who are not elderly in more developed countries. The causes of death are mainly those in the third and fourth stages of the Epidemiologic Transition.

Alzheimer's and other dementias is the sixth leading cause of death in high-income countries. In Alzheimer's disease there is progressive loss of memory; loss of motor skills, such as swallowing or walking; and progressive incontinence. Being bedridden and incontinent can lead to infections, including pneumonia, which are often fatal. In such cases, Alzheimer's disease would be the underlying cause of death. In Alzheimer's cases, breathing could

eventually be so inhibited that it leads to death, but often death from infection occurs earlier.[63]

In high-income countries, specific cancers form the seventh, ninth, and tenth leading causes of death, while diabetes is the eighth leading cause. While there are genetic predispositions to diabetes, overweight and poor diet contribute to the chance that a person will develop type II diabetes, also called adult-onset diabetes.

In middle-income countries, the causes of death are mixed. Two of the leading causes of death are from Group I of the GBD classification, and seven are from Group II. Motor vehicle accidents, in Group III, constitute the sixth leading cause of death in middle-income countries.

Years of Life Lost

Different causes of death tend to kill people at different ages. Causes of death such as diarrheal diseases or prematurity and low birth weight result in the deaths of infants and young children, while motor vehicle accidents tend to kill young adults, HIV tends to lead to the deaths of persons in the middle adult ages, and stroke and ischemic heart disease mainly lead to the deaths of the elderly.

Years of life lost (YLL) are calculated to take into account the age at which people die. Thus, the younger a person is when he or she dies, the more potential years of life that person has lost. The GBD Project has estimated the YLL in comparison to a standard of attainable life expectancy. The GBD 2004 estimates used a life expectancy at birth of 80 years for men and 82.5 years for women as the standard.[64]

Table 5.3 shows the ten leading causes of YLL for the world as a whole, for the high-income countries and for the middle-income and low-income countries combined.[65] The effect of taking age at death from a given cause into account is seen in the differences

TABLE 5.3 Ten Leading Causes of Years of Life Lost (YLL) by Income Group of Countries, Classified by Global Burden of Disease Category, 2004

	World	Low-Income and Middle-Income Countries	High-Income Countries
1	*Lower respiratory infections 10%*	*Lower respiratory infections 10%*	**Ischemic heart disease 12%**
2	*Diarrheal diseases 7%*	*Diarrheal diseases 8%*	**Lung cancer 7%**
3	**Ischemic heart disease 6%**	*HIV 6%*	**Stroke 6%**
4	*HIV 6%*	**Ischemic heart disease 4%**	**Motor vehicle accidents 5%**
5	**Stroke 4%**	*Prematurity and low birth weight 4%*	**Suicide 5%**
6	*Prematurity and low birth weight 4%*	*Neonatal infections 4%*	**Colon & rectum cancers 3%**
7	*Neonatal infections 4%*	**Stroke 4%**	**Breast cancer 3%**
8	**Motor vehicle accidents 3%**	*Malaria 3%*	**Cirrhosis of the liver 2%**
9	*Malaria 3%*	*Tuberculosis 3%*	**COPD 2%**
10	*Tuberculosis 3%*	**Motor vehicle accidents 3%**	**Diabetes 2%**

between Table 5.2 and Table 5.3. The two leading causes of death in the world in Table 5.2, ischemic heart disease and stroke, mainly lead to deaths at an advanced age. These causes result in a smaller number of YLL for each person who dies than for causes that lead to death at a younger age. Lower respiratory infections can lead to deaths of both the young and the elderly, and deaths from diarrheal diseases almost exclusively lead to deaths of the very young. Thus, we see that ischemic heart disease and stroke move down from the leading two causes of death in Table 5.2 to the third and fifth leading causes of YLL in Table 5.3. We also see that lower respiratory infections move from third place in Table 5.2 to first place in Table 5.3, and diarrheal diseases move from fifth place in Table 5.2 to second place in Table 5.3, reflecting the fairly young ages at which deaths from lower respiratory infections and from diarrheal diseases occur.

In Table 5.2, no external cause of death was among the leading ten causes of death in high-income countries. In Table 5.3, motor vehicle accidents are the fourth leading cause of YLL, and suicide is the fifth leading cause of YLL. This is because the average age of death of those who die in car accidents or who commit suicide is much younger than the age of those who die from degenerative conditions that are the causes of most deaths in high-income countries.

Disabilities and Years Lived Disabled
As deaths have become increasingly concentrated at the older ages, and as death rates at the older ages have become very low in some high-income countries, there has been increased concern with the length of time that people in a population are alive but in a disabled or not fully functional state. In order to determine the extent of disability in a population, it is necessary to know what proportion of people has a given disability and the average duration of that disability for each disabled person.

Some disabilities, such as an amputated arm, are likely to continue from the time the disability first occurs to the end of the person's life. Other disabilities, such as depression or TB, could afflict a person for some time, and then the person could be treated and no longer be disabled. The GBD Project estimated both the prevalence of disabling conditions and the average duration of each disability.

The prevalence and the average duration of each source of disability are used to estimate **years lived disabled (YLD)**. There have been criticisms of some of the estimates of duration and prevalence of conditions such as depression, since the average duration of depression is difficult to know and it is very hard to estimate the prevalence of depression without representative population surveys.[66]

The best source of information on the prevalence of disabilities in a population is population surveys, such as the NHANES, discussed in Chapter 3. General population surveys to assess the presence of disabilities, including physical measurements, such as blood pressure tests, or taking of biological samples, such as saliva or blood to test for high cholesterol or hyperglycemia (high blood sugar), increasingly take place in high-income countries. However, they are less common in middle-income countries and quite uncommon in low-income countries.

Ruzicka and Kane have suggested that mortality data from the population, rather than direct data on morbidity, are the best indicators of health status.[67] This could be a good approach if there were little or no data on morbidity, if the main causes of death were infectious or parasitic diseases, and if effective treatments for these diseases were not available. In that situation, death rates from a disease, such as malaria, could be a good indication of the extent to which the population's health was impacted by malaria. However, this approach is not helpful for understanding the effect of morbidity from the chronic conditions that are very important in the third and fourth stages of the Epidemiologic Transition. Also, this approach is not very useful in situations in which an infectious or parasitic disease is common and influences a person's overall health but treatments limit mortality from the disease.

Different conditions disable people to different extents. The GBD Project assigned weights to different disabilities to indicate the severity of the limitation. These weights range from 0 to 1, with the higher the weight, the more disabling the condition. For example, terminal cancer is given a weight of 0.81, while tuberculosis is given a weight of 0.27, indicating that being in the terminal stages of cancer is more disabling than having tuberculosis.

Table 5.4 shows the GBD estimates of the percentage of people with various moderate or severe disabilities by age group and by income level of countries. Moderate or severe disability was operationalized as having a disability weight of 0.12 of higher. Examples of moderate disabilities include rheumatoid arthritis, deafness, and mild mental retardation. Examples of severe disability include blindness, Down syndrome, acute psychosis, and severe depression. The results are shown separately for those aged 0–59 and for those aged 60 or older, because the kinds of disabilities affecting the elderly and the non-elderly are different.[68]

In Table 5.4, the conditions are ordered from those with the highest percentage of persons affected in the world as a whole to a lower percentage. As in Tables 5.2 and 5.3, the conditions are coded according to the three GBD groups. Conditions that do not fit into any of the three groups, including behaviors

TABLE 5.4 GBD Estimates of the Percentage of Persons with Various Moderate or Severe Disabilities by Age and Income Group, 2004

Disability	High-Income Countries		Low-Income and Middle-Income Countries		World
	Age 0–59	Age 60+	Age 0–59	Age 60+	All Ages
Hearing loss	0.9%	9.7%	1.2%	5.3%	1.9%
Refractive vision errors	1.0%	3.4%	1.5%	4.8%	1.9%
Depression	2.0%	0.3%	1.7%	0.6%	1.5%
Cataracts	0.1%	0.6%	0.5%	3.8%	0.8%
Accidents	0.4%	0.6%	0.8%	0.7%	0.7%
Osteoarthritis	0.2%	4.2%	0.3%	2.3%	0.7%
Alcohol problems	0.9%	0.2%	0.7%	0.2%	0.6%
Infertility from unsafe abortion and maternal infection	0.1%	0.0%	0.7%	0.0%	0.5%
Macular degeneration	0.2%	3.1%	0.2%	1.8%	0.5%
COPD	0.4%	2.4%	0.2%	1.0%	0.4%
Ischemic heart disease	0.1%	1.2%	0.2%	1.4%	0.4%
Bipolar disorder	0.4%	0.2%	0.4%	0.1%	0.3%
Asthma	0.4%	0.3%	0.3%	0.1%	0.3%
Schizophrenia	0.3%	0.2%	0.3%	0.1%	0.3%
Alzheimer's and other dementias	0.1%	3.2%	0.0%	0.8%	0.2%
Panic disorder	0.2%	0.1%	0.2%	0.0%	0.2%
Stroke	0.2%	1.2%	0.1%	0.6%	0.2%
Rheumatoid arthritis	0.2%	0.9%	0.1%	0.4%	0.2%
Drug problems	0.5%	0.1%	0.2%	0.0%	0.2%

The entries show the percentage of all people in the given age group and income group with the given disability.

such as alcohol problems or drug problems, or mental health issues such as depression, schizophrenia or panic disorder, are shown in *italics.*

In the world as a whole, at all ages, hearing loss and refractive vision errors are the most common disabilities. Refractive vision error is blurred vision, caused by the shape of the eye not bending light correctly. It often worsens with age, as the lens of the eye becomes more rigid. Most refractive errors are treatable by eyeglasses or corrective surgery.

Almost all disabilities are more likely to occur for older people than for younger people. Only depression, alcohol problems, bipolar disorder, schizophrenia, and drug problems are more likely to disable those aged 0–59 than those aged 60 or older. Some of the disabling conditions, such as COPD, stroke, and ischemic heart disease, are also among the leading causes of death. Other disabling conditions, such as depression, hearing loss, and cataracts, rarely lead to death.

Most disabilities are more common in low-income and middle-income countries than in high-income countries, but there are some exceptions. Among those aged 0–59, depression, alcohol problems,

COPD, asthma, Alzheimer's and other dementias, stroke, rheumatoid arthritis, and drug problems are more common in high-income than in middle-income or low-income countries. Among those aged 60 or older, hearing loss, osteoarthritis, macular degeneration, COPD, bipolar disorder, asthma, schizophrenia, panic disorder, stroke, rheumatoid arthritis, and drug problems are more common in high-income than in middle-income or low-income countries.

The higher percentage of persons disabled by some conditions in high-income than in low-income or middle-income countries could be real or could be partially the result of lack of data from middle-income and low-income countries. For example, it is not clear whether a higher percentage of people in high-income countries aged 60 or older actually suffer from hearing loss, osteoarthritis, or Alzheimer's or other dementias. However, the higher percentage of older people in high-income countries with osteoarthritis, Alzheimer's, and rheumatoid arthritis could be due to these persons surviving in high-income countries when they would have died in low-income or middle-income countries.

The prevalence of various disabling conditions in a population is combined with an estimate of the average duration of the given disability to calculate the number of YLD in the population.[69] YLD are years in which people are alive but are disabled. YLD is a major focus of policy concern since these are years in which people are not fully functional and require substantial investments of time and money from the state and from family members.

Table 5.5 shows the ten leading contributors to YLD in low-income and middle-income countries combined and in high-income countries. It also shows the ten leading causes of YLD for males and for females. The same coding of conditions is used in Table 5.5 as was used in Table 5.4.

In Table 5.5, depression is the leading cause of YLD for the world as a whole, for both income groups of countries and for both sexes. Depression is a condition that can severely impede normal functioning but that does not usually directly lead to death. Other mental health or neuropsychiatric disorders (schizophrenia and bipolar disorder) also contribute substantially to disability in low-income and middle-income countries and in the world as a whole, as well as for both men and women.

Some non-communicable degenerative conditions that rarely lead to death play a major role in YLD, especially vision loss and hearing loss. Cataracts are an important cause of disability in low-income and middle-income countries but not in high-income countries. This is probably because cataracts are easily corrected with surgery, and this surgery is more readily available in high-income countries than in lower income countries.

The major non-communicable causes of death do not play a substantial role in YLD. For example, although ischemic heart disease and stroke are the major causes of death in the world, and although they are among the top five causes of YLL, they are not in the leading ten causes of YLD.

COPD is the only non-communicable condition that is in the leading ten causes of death, in the leading ten causes of YLL, and in the ten leading causes of YLD, and that is only in high-income countries. The greater role of COPD in YLD in high-income countries could be due to improvements in treatment of COPD so that in high-income countries, more people are alive with COPD because they have not died from it. Thus, although degenerative non-communicable conditions are an increasing source of concern, especially in high-income countries, the specific non-communicable conditions that lead to loss of life and the non-communicable conditions that lead to years spent in a disabled state are not the same.

Alzheimer's and other dementias comprise the sixth leading cause of death in high-income countries, but they comprise the fourth leading cause of YLD in high-income countries. Concerns about the quality of life of people with Alzheimer's and the high psychological and financial cost of caring for people with Alzheimer's make the population with Alzheimer's and related dementias a focus of public attention.

The Group I conditions that are substantial contributors to years of life disabled are birth asphyxia and birth trauma as well as iron deficiency anemia. Birth asphyxia can be eliminated or reduced by

TABLE 5.5   Ten Leading Causes of Years Lived Disabled (YLD) by Income Group and by Sex, 2004

	Low-Income and Middle-Income Countries	High-Income Countries	Males	Females
1	*Depression 10%*	*Depression 15%*	*Depression 8%*	*Depression 13%*
2	**Refractive vision errors 5%**	**Hearing loss 6%**	*Alcohol problems 7%*	**Refractive vision errors 4%**
3	**Hearing loss 5%**	*Alcohol problems 6%*	**Hearing loss 5%**	**Hearing loss 4%**
4	*Alcohol problems 4%*	**Alzheimer's and other dementias 5%**	**Refractive vision errors 5%**	*Cataracts 3%*
5	**Cataracts 3%**	**Osteoarthritis 4%**	*Schizophrenia 3%*	**Osteoarthritis 3%**
6	*Schizophrenia 3%*	**Refractive vision errors 4%**	*Cataracts 3%*	*Schizophrenia 3%*
7	*Birth asphyxia and birth trauma 2%*	**COPD 4%**	*Bipolar disorder 3%*	**Anemia 2%**
8	*Bipolar disorder 2%*	**Diabetes 3%**	**COPD 2%**	*Bipolar disorder 2%*
9	**Osteoarthritis 2%**	**Asthma 3%**	**Asthma 2%**	*Birth asphyxia and birth trauma 2%*
10	*Iron deficiency anemia 2%*	*Drug problems 2%*	**Falls 2%**	**Alzheimer's and other dementias 2%**

The entries show the percentage of total YLDs due to the given cause within the income group or for the given sex.

medical attendance at birth, and in developed countries iron deficiency anemia has been much reduced through iron fortification of bread.

The causes of YLD are also somewhat different for males and for females. Alcohol problems are the second leading cause of YLD for men, while they are not in the top ten causes for women. This is due to the greater tendency of men than women to drink alcohol and to drink alcohol to excess.

Total Loss of Years from Active Life: Disability-Adjusted Life Years

One can also look at the total number of years that a population loses from persons dying prematurely or being disabled. This is the number of **disability-adjusted life years (DALYs)**, which is the sum of the years of life lost (YLL from premature death) and years lived disabled (YLD alive but disabled). It is calculated as:

$$DALY = YLL + YLD$$

Table 5.6 shows the ten leading causes of the GBD DALYs for the world as a whole and by income group of countries. For each cause, the percentage of all DALYs contributed by that cause for the world as a whole or within the given income group of countries is shown.

For the world as a whole, the two leading causes of DALYs are the same as the leading causes of YLL shown in Table 5.3—lower respiratory infections and diarrheal diseases. Depression, which played such a large role in YLD in Table 5.4, is the third leading cause of DALYs. Ischemic heart disease and stroke, which were the leading causes of death overall in Table 5.2 and the third and fifth leading causes of YLL in Table 5.3, are in the fourth and sixth places in terms of DALYs. Vision and hearing problems that were important in YLD play a much smaller role in DALYs.

The Epidemiologic Transition is clear in Table 5.6, with Group I diseases and conditions comprising seven of the leading causes of DALYs in low-income countries, three of the ten leading causes in middle-income countries, and none of the ten leading causes in high-income countries. Depression is an important source of DALYs in all three income groups, but motor vehicle accidents and alcohol problems are important in middle-income and in high-income countries, reflecting some of the negative effects in middle-income countries of economic development, with more motor vehicles and with more availability and consumption of strong alcoholic drinks.

Summary of Causes of Death and Disability

The role of different causes of death and disability is even clearer in Table 5.7, which lists all of the causes of death or disability from Tables 5.2 and 5.3 and Tables 5.5 and 5.6 in alphabetical order. The coding is the same as in Tables 5.5 and 5.6.

TABLE 5.6   Ten Leading Causes of Global Burden of Disease Disability-Adjusted Life Years (DALYs) by Income Group, 2004

	World	Low-Income Countries	Middle-Income Countries	High-Income Countries
1	*Lower respiratory infections 6%*	*Lower respiratory infections 9%*	Depression 5%	*Depression 5%*
2	*Diarrheal diseases 5%*	*Diarrheal diseases 7%*	**Ischemic heart disease 5%**	**Ischemic heart disease 6%**
3	*Depression 4%*	*HIV 6%*	**Stroke 5%**	**Stroke 4%**
4	**Ischemic heart disease 4%**	*Malaria 4%*	**Motor vehicle accidents 4%**	**Alzheimer's and other dementias 4%**
5	*HIV 4%*	*Prematurity and low birth weight 4%*	*Lower respiratory infections 3%*	*Alcohol problems 3%*
6	**Stroke 3%**	*Neonatal infections and perinatal problems 4%*	**COPD 3%**	**Hearing loss 3%**
7	*Prematurity and low birth weight 3%*	**Birth asphyxia and birth trauma 4%**	*HIV 3%*	**COPD 3%**
8	**Birth asphyxia and birth trauma 2%**	*Depression 3%*	*Alcohol problems 3%*	**Diabetes 3%**
9	**Motor vehicle accidents 3%**	**Ischemic heart disease 3%**	**Refractive vision errors 2%**	**Lung cancer 3%**
10	*Neonatal infections and perinatal problems 3%*	*Tuberculosis 3%*	*Diarrheal diseases 2%*	**Motor vehicle accidents 3%**

The entries show the percentage of total DALYs due to the given cause for the world or within the income group.

TABLE 5.7 Comparison of Causes of Death and Disability, Global Burden of Disease, 2004

	(1) Leading Causes of Death				(2) Leading Causes of Years of Life Lost (YLL)			(3) Leading Causes of Years Lived Disabled (YLD)				(4) Causes of Global Burden of Disease Disability-Adjusted Life Years (DALYs)			
	World	Low-Income Countries	Middle-Income Countries	High-Income Countries	World	Low- and Middle-Income	High-Income	Low- and Middle-Income	High-Income	Male	Female	World	Low-Income	Middle-Income	High-Income
Alcohol problems								4	3	2				8	5
Alzheimer's and other dementias				6					4		10				4
Asthma									9	9					
Bipolar disorder								8		7	7				
Birth asphyxia and birth trauma					7	7		7				8	7		
Breast cancer				9			7				4				
Cataracts								5		6	8				
COPD	4	6	3	5			8		7	8				6	7
Cirrhosis of the liver							9								
Colon and rectal cancers				7			6								
Depression								1	1	1	1	3	8	1	1
Diabetes			10	8			10		8						8
Diarrheal diseases	5	3			3	2						2	2		
Drug problems									10						
Falls										10					
Hearing loss								3	2	3	3			10	6
HIV	6	4			4	3						5	3	7	
Hypertensive heart disease			7												
Iron deficiency anemia								10							
Ischemic heart disease	1	2	2	1	1	4	1					4	9	2	2
Lower respiratory infections	3	1	4		2	1						1	1	5	
Lung cancer			5	3			2								9
Malaria		9			10	9							4		
Motor vehicle accidents	9		6		8	10	4					9		4	10
Neonatal infections and perinatal problems		8			9	6						10	6		
Osteoarthritis								9	5		5				
Prematurity and low birth weight	10	10			6	8						7	5		
Refractive vision errors								2	6	4	2			9	
Rheumatoid arthritis											9				
Schizophrenia								6		5	6				
Stomach cancer			8	10											
Stroke	2	5	1	2	5	5	3					6		3	3
Suicide							5								
Tuberculosis	7	7	9										10		

167

Each column shows the leading ten causes of the death or disability indicator for the group being considered, such as low-income countries or males. The rank of each of the top ten causes is shown. The cell for the leading cause of death or disability in a given column has the darkest shading. Looking across a row shows the importance of a given cause across a range of categories of death and disability, by gender and by groups of countries.

Risk Factors for Death and Disability

We just discussed causes of death and disability. A **risk factor** for death or for disability is a variable or condition that increases the chance that death will occur from a particular cause or that the person will have a particular disability. Often risk factors are identified by seeing what is related to death or disability, and sometimes it is not known whether the risk factor actually causes the disease or disability. However, the aim is to identify risk factors that play a causal role in death or disability. Risk factors can operate in a causal chain that leads to death or disability, and it is useful to understand how that chain works.

Figure 5.10 shows a schematic diagram of the causal chain for risk factors for ischemic heart disease, the leading cause of death in the world and in the high-income countries. In Figure 5.10, the causes at each stage influence all of the later stages.[70]

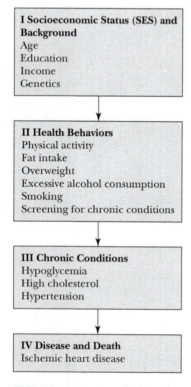

FIGURE 5.10 Causal Chain for Major Causes of Ischemic Heart Disease

Health policy has concentrated on the health behaviors in Part II of Figure 5.10, often involving public information campaigns about the negative health effects of these behaviors, since those behaviors can be influenced by individual action. Much of social science has concentrated on the paths from Part I to the later parts of the diagram.

Leading Risk Factors for Death and Disability

Table 5.8 shows the major risk factors that were important in mortality and disability in the world in 2004 and some of the main outcomes stemming from each risk factor. The risk factors are classified by whether they are mainly the result of *poverty*, are **health behaviors**, are from **other environmental and occupational sources**, or are *caused by other risk factors and by genetic predisposition*. Different colors and fonts are used to distinguish between the different types of risk factors.

Box 5.1 explains the basis of the calculation of the impact of a risk factor on survival and disability. Calculation of the effects of risk factors was based on a large number of studies about the mortality and disability impact of various risk factors as well as estimates of the prevalence of the various risk factors.[71]

Childhood underweight, unsafe water, sanitation and hygiene, vitamin A deficiency, and zinc deficiency are the result of poverty. All of these would be relatively inexpensive to alleviate. Zinc deficiency, although easily treated, also contributes to the body's ability to combat conditions such as diarrhea, pneumonia, and malaria. Indoor smoke from solid fuels relates to use of materials such as wood, dung, and coal. Solid fuels such as wood or charcoal generate a great deal of smoke, which can lead to serious eye and lung disorders, including lung cancer. Replacement of these fuels by gas or electricity can require electrification of areas and requires the financial means to change to more healthy cooking sources.

It is recommended that children be exclusively breastfed until they are 6 months old. Between 6 months and 2 years of age, it is recommended that they be partially breastfed. Breast milk contains antibodies that can help protect against disease, and breast milk is a safe, nutritious source of protein when other sources that small children can easily digest can be scarce. Mortality from suboptimal breastfeeding is that which results from less than the recommended regimen of breastfeeding.

Unsafe water and poor sanitation are aspects of poverty that pose health and survival risks to all persons in the locale. Assuring that drinking water is safe is a great burden on households if there is not a clean drinking water supply. Similarly, poor sanitation poses a risk to survival when there are not sewage systems for safe disposal of human waste. The danger from inadequate sanitation, especially in urban areas

TABLE 5.8   Major Risk Factors for Death and Disability Classified by Type

Risk Factor	Some Death and Disability Outcomes
Poverty	
Unsafe water, sanitation, and hygiene	Diarrheal diseases
Childhood underweight	Diarrhea, malaria, measles, and pneumonia
Indoor smoke from solid fuels	Acute lower respiratory infections, infections in children under age 5, COPD, and lung cancer
Vitamin A deficiency	Blindness, diarrhea, measles, neonatal infections, and prematurity
Zinc deficiency	Diarrhea, pneumonia, and malaria
Health Behaviors	
Smoking	Lung cancer and other cancers, COPD, other respiratory diseases, ischemic heart disease, and stroke
Excessive alcohol use	Ischemic heart disease, hypertensive disease, diabetes, liver cancer and other cancers, cirrhosis of the liver, epilepsy, motor vehicle accidents, and homicide
Suboptimal breastfeeding	Diarrhea, perinatal infections, and acute lower respiratory infections
Overweight and obesity	Ischemic heart disease, stroke, diabetes, osteoarthritis, colon cancer and other cancers, and hypertensive disease
Physical inactivity	Ischemic heart disease, some cancers, and diabetes
Low fruit and vegetable intake	Ischemic heart disease, stroke, and gastrointestinal cancer
Unsafe sex	HIV, other sexually transmitted infections, and cervical cancer
Illicit drugs	HIV, suicide, and trauma
Other Environmental and Occupational Sources	
Urban outdoor air pollution	Respiratory and cardiovascular diseases in adults over age 30, lung cancer, and acute respiratory infection in children under age 5
Occupational risks	Lung cancer, COPD, silicosis, lower back pain, hearing loss, and unintentional injury
Risk Factors Caused by Other Risk Factors and by Genetic Predisposition	
Hypertension	Ischemic heart disease, stroke, hypertensive disease, and other cardiovascular diseases
High cholesterol	Ischemic heart disease and stroke
High blood glucose	Diabetes, ischemic heart disease, and stroke

BOX 5.1
The Logic behind the GBD Calculation of the Impact of a Risk Factor for Death and Disability

For each risk factor considered, the mortality and the disability impact of the given risk factor were calculated in comparison to a theoretical minimum for the presence of the risk factor. These theoretical minima varied. For example, for smoking, alcohol consumption, and illicit drug use, the theoretical minimum was no use of the given substance. For fruit and vegetable consumption, the theoretical minimum was 600 grams per day for an adult. For childhood underweight, the theoretical minimum was the same proportion substantially below the international reference for weight for age as in the international reference group.

where the population is dense, was a reason why the spread of sewers was chosen by *British Medical Journal* readers as the most important medical breakthrough since 1840. The installation of sewers in urban areas in low-income countries could improve survival in those rapidly growing locales.

Health behaviors constitute an important set of risk factors. Smoking is implicated in a wide variety of causes of death and types of disability. Smoking impairs the respiratory system and increases the chance of death and complications from many conditions. Excessive alcohol use also can impair the immune system and contributes to the chance of dying from many causes in addition to those directly related to alcohol consumption, such as cirrhosis of the liver. Excessive alcohol use also leads to impairment of judgment, which leads to higher risk of motor vehicle accidents, whether as a driver or a pedestrian, and makes people more vulnerable to homicide and suicide. Overweight, obesity, and physical inactivity contribute to the risk of diabetes, and they also inhibit the body's ability to deal with ischemic heart disease and some cancers. Low fruit and vegetable intake also contributes to a weakened body, which makes the person more vulnerable to death or disability from a variety of causes.

Smoking, excessive alcohol use, suboptimal breastfeeding, and use of illicit drugs are behaviors that were adopted or increased in less developed countries based on practices common in more developed countries. Also, with development and a shift from rural to urban residence, physical activity often declines. Obesity and overweight are major problems in more developed countries, and changes in types of food consumed in less developed countries have contributed to overweight and obesity. Unsafe sex is a risk factor for death that operates mainly through transmission of the HIV virus. However, unsafe sex also contributes to mortality from cervical cancer, syphilis, gonorrhea, and chlamydia.

Low levels of physical activity are related to occupational changes with development. These effects are increased when calorie consumption is not reduced as activity lessens. Low physical activity contributes to

heart disease, some cancers, and diabetes. Physical activity counters weight gain and lessens symptoms of depression.

Urban outdoor air pollution is a substantial risk factor for survival that is related to industrialization. Fine particles that mainly result from motor vehicles and power plants are especially dangerous. These particles are estimated to lead to 8% of lung cancer deaths in the world and also contribute to a variety of respiratory conditions. Occupational risks include the risk of injury, as well as exposure to substances that can cause cancer and respiratory problems. Back pain related to unhealthy positions at work does not contribute to mortality but is a source of disability and time lost from work.

Hypertension, high cholesterol, and high blood glucose are major contributors to death and disability. It has been estimated that hypertension is the cause of 51% of stroke deaths and 45% of ischemic heart disease deaths in the world. These conditions in turn are related to smoking, overweight and obesity, and diet. There are also genetic predispositions for these conditions.

Table 5.2 showed the ten leading causes of death for the world and by income level. The GBD Project estimated the role of various risk factors in all deaths. For example, smoking contributed to mortality from a variety of causes, including lung cancer and COPD.

Table 5.9 shows the GBD estimates of the ten leading risk factors contributing to mortality for the world

TABLE 5.9 Ten Leading Risk Factors for Death in the World and by Income Group of Countries, 2004

	World	Low-Income Countries	Middle-Income Countries	High-Income Countries
1	*Hypertension 13%*	*Childhood underweight 8%*	**Hypertension 17%**	**Smoking 18%**
2	**Smoking 9%**	**Hypertension 8%**	**Smoking 11%**	*Hypertension 17%*
3	*High blood glucose 6%*	**Unsafe sex 7%**	**Overweight and obesity 7%**	**Overweight and obesity 8%**
4	**Physical inactivity 6%**	*Unsafe water, sanitation, and hygiene 6%*	**Physical inactivity 4%**	**Physical inactivity 8%**
5	**Overweight and obesity 5%**	**High blood glucose 5%**	**Excessive alcohol use 6%**	*High blood glucose 7%*
6	*High cholesterol 5%*	*Indoor smoke from solid fuels 5%*	*High blood glucose 6%*	*High cholesterol 6%*
7	**Unsafe sex 4%**	**Smoking 4%**	*High cholesterol 5%*	**Low fruit and vegetable intake 3%**
8	**Excessive alcohol use 2%**	**Physical inactivity 4%**	**Low fruit and vegetable intake 4%**	**Urban outdoor air pollution 3%**
9	*Childhood underweight 4%*	**Suboptimal breastfeeding 4%**	*Indoor smoke from solid fuels 3%*	**Excessive alcohol use 2%**
10	*Indoor smoke from solid fuels 3%*	**High cholesterol 3%**	**Urban outdoor air pollution 3%**	**Occupational risks 1%**

The entries show the percentage of all deaths due to the given risk factor for the world and within the income group.

TABLE 5.10   Ten Leading Risk Factors for Disability-Adjusted Life Years (Restriction of DALYs) in the World and by Income Group of Countries, 2004

	World	Low-Income Countries	Middle-Income Countries	High-Income Countries
1	*Childhood underweight 6%*	*Childhood underweight 10%*	**Excessive alcohol use 8%**	**Smoking 11%**
2	**Unsafe sex 5%**	*Unsafe water, sanitation, and hygiene 6%*	*Hypertension 5%*	**Excessive alcohol use 7%**
3	**Excessive alcohol use 5%**	**Unsafe sex 6%**	**Smoking 5%**	**Overweight and obesity 7%**
4	*Unsafe water, sanitation, and hygiene 4%*	**Suboptimal breastfeeding 4%**	**Overweight and obesity 4%**	*Hypertension 6%*
5	*Hypertension 4%*	*Indoor smoke from solid fuels 4%*	*High blood glucose 3%*	*High blood glucose 5%*
6	**Smoking 4%**	*Vitamin A deficiency 2%*	**Unsafe sex 3%**	**Physical inactivity 4%**
7	**Suboptimal breastfeeding 3%**	*Hypertension 2%*	**Physical inactivity 3%**	*High cholesterol 3%*
8	*High blood glucose 3%*	**Excessive alcohol use 2%**	*High cholesterol 3%*	**Illicit drugs 2%**
9	*Indoor smoke from solid fuels 3%*	*High blood glucose 2%*	**Occupational risks 2%**	**Occupational risks 2%**
10	**Overweight and obesity 2%**	*Zinc deficiency 2%*	*Unsafe water, sanitation, and hygiene 2%*	**Low fruit and vegetable intake 1%**

and by income level of countries. As in Table 5.2, the percentage which each factor contributes to all deaths is shown for the world as a whole and within each income group. The same coding of types of risk factors (as mainly due to *poverty*, as **health behaviors**, from **other environmental and occupational sources**, or *caused by other risk factors and by genetic predisposition*) is used in Table 5.8 as was used in Table 5.7.

Health behaviors become more important risk factors for death in middle-income and high-income countries, with smoking, overweight and obesity, and lack of physical activity becoming quite important. In middle-income and high-income countries, excessive alcohol use enters the list of the top ten risk factors.

Hypertension is the most important or the second most important risk factor for death in every group of countries considered in Table 5.8. High cholesterol and high blood glucose are also major risk factors for death throughout the world.

Table 5.6 showed the ten leading causes of DALYs, and Table 5.10 shows the ten leading risk factors for years for loss of DALYs for the world as a whole and by income level. The same coding of types of risk factors is used as in Tables 5.8 and 5.9.

Some risk factors that were not among the leading ten risks for survival are among the leading risk factors for loss of DALYs. For example, zinc deficiency and vitamin A deficiency are not among the leading risk factors for survival but are among the leading risk factors for DALYs in low-income countries. This is because these deficiencies are usually not fatal but can lead to a lower quality of life.

In low-income countries, five of the ten leading risk factors for loss of DALYs are poverty related, while only one of the leading risk factors is poverty related in middle-income countries and none is poverty related in high-income countries. Health behaviors are extremely important in middle-income and high-income countries.

In high-income countries, illicit drugs are a major cause of loss of DALYs. Injection drug users have an increased risk of HIV, overdoses, suicide, and accidents. Also, drug addicts often are impaired in their daily functioning.

Hypertension and high blood glucose are important risks for loss of DALYs at all income levels, and high cholesterol is a major risk factor in middle-income and high-income countries.

CONCLUDING COMMENTS

The historical background of mortality decline in Europe provides a context for looking at the similarities and differences with more recent mortality decline in the LDR. Looking at the leading causes of death and disability across the world gives a perspective for assessing the relative importance of various threats to survival across the less developed and the more developed regions of the world that are discussed in Chapters 6 and 7.

☑ Study and Review Online

SUMMARY

1. The Epidemiologic Transition describes the historical change from the dominance of infectious and parasitic causes of death, and of the population being periodically decimated by mortality crises, to less frequent mortality crises. Later deaths from infectious and parasitic diseases decline, and deaths from non-communicable causes, such as heart disease and stroke, increase. Eventually, deaths from communicable causes become rare, and the average age at death increases. Later mortality rates become very low, and non-communicable degenerative diseases become the causes of the vast majority of deaths.

2. In premodern hunting-and-gathering societies, people moved frequently and population density was low. It seems that e_0^0 was about 30 years.

3. With the development of pastoral nomadism and even more so of settled agriculture, more stable sources of food were available, but the risk of transmission of disease from domestic animals increased. Also, with settled agriculture, diseases caused by inadequate sanitation and polluted water became more of a threat.

4. As commerce developed, the impact of local famines on mortality declined.

5. It is difficult to be certain of the relative importance various factors in mortality decline and population increase before 1914. It is likely that increase in calorie consumption and the standard of living played an important role. Improvements in sanitation and smallpox vaccination also contributed to mortality declines. It is unknown whether some diseases, such as plague, mutated to a less deadly form. It is unlikely that changes in curative medical care played a substantial role in mortality decline before the discovery of antibiotics.

6. The compression of morbidity refers to the idea that when there is rectangularization of mortality, the average age of onset of disability could rise, which would result in a small number of years lived in a disabled state. If there were not compression of morbidity, then longer life would mean more years spent in a disabled state without a substantial increase in the number of years lived in a healthy state. There is mixed evidence about whether and to what extent compression of morbidity occurs.

7. Causes of death worldwide have shifted as outlined by the Epidemiologic Transition. However, communicable diseases related to poverty remain important in low-income countries, while non-communicable diseases have become the dominant causes of death in the world as a whole, especially in the middle-income and high-income countries.

8. Poverty and unhealthy environmental conditions remain important for death and disability in low-income and middle-income countries, while in high-income countries health behaviors, especially smoking, are important risk factors for mortality.

9. Improved screening and effective medication for hypertension and high cholesterol have led to lower death rates from these causes than would otherwise occur.

10. Behaviors imported from more developed countries, such as smoking, excessive alcohol use, and limited breastfeeding, have become important risk factors for death in low-income countries.

KEY TERMS

Epidemiologic Transition   146
communicable causes
   of death   147
non-communicable causes
   of death   147
hunters and gatherers   148
pastoral nomadism   149
slash-and-burn agriculture   150
mortality crisis   150
crisis mortality   150
Columbian Exchange   152
preventive medical care   153
inoculation   154

vaccination   154
curative medical care   154
germ theory of disease   154
miasma theory of disease   155
morbidity   156
natural causes of death   157
external causes of death   157
homicide   157
suicide   157
accidental death   157
acute condition   157
chronic conditions   157
degenerative condition   157

communicable disease   157
non-communicable disease   158
underlying cause of death   158
contributory cause of death   158
verbal autopsy   158
Global Burden of Disease
   classification   159
years of life lost (YLL)   162
years lived disabled (YLD)   163
disability-adjusted life years
   (DALYs)   166
risk factor   168

QUESTIONS FOR DISCUSSION AND REVIEW

1. Discuss how changes in the basis of support (from hunting and gathering to agriculture) and the growth of settlements and eventually cities affected the level of mortality and the mix of mortality risks.
2. What is crisis mortality? Why did the frequency and severity of mortality crises decrease over time?

3. What is the "Epidemiologic Transition"?
4. Discuss the role of poverty and of health behaviors in death and disability across countries at various income levels.

NOTES

1. Abdel R. Omran. 1971. "The Epidemiological Transition: A Theory of the Epidemiology of Population Change," *The Milbank Memorial Fund Quarterly*, 49: 509–538; and S. Jay Olshansky and A. Brian Ault. 1986. "The Fourth Stage of the Epidemiologic Transition: The Age of Delayed Degenerative Diseases," *The Milbank Quarterly*, 64: 355–391.
2. J. R. Wilmoth. 2000. "Demography of Longevity: Past, Present, and Future Trends," *Experimental Gerontology*, 35: 1111–1129.
3. Nancy Howell. 2000. *Demography of the Dobe !Kung*, 2nd ed., Chicago: Aldine; J. V. Neel and K. Weiss. 1975. "The Genetic Structure of a Tribal Population, the Yanomama Indians," *American Journal of Physical Anthropology*, 42: 25–52; and Kim Hill and A. Magdelena Hurtado. 1996. *Ache Life History: The Ecology and Demography of a Foraging People*, New York: De Gruyter.
4. Raymond Hames and Jennifer Kuzara. 2004. "The Nexus of Yanomamo Growth, Health, and Demography," in Francisco M. Salzano and A. Magdalena Hurtado, *Lost Paradises and the Ethics of Research and Publication*, New York: Oxford University Press, 110–145.
5. Kim Hill and A. Magdelena Hurtado. 1989. "Hunter-Gatherers of the New World," *American Scientist*, 77: 436–443.
6. David R. Harris, ed. 1996. *The Origins and Spread of Agriculture and Pastoralism in Eurasia*, London: UCL Press; and S. Richard. 1992. *The Origins of Agriculture and Settled Life*, Norman: University of Oklahoma Press.
7. Lee Cronk. 1989. "From Hunters to Herders: Subsistence Change as a Reproductive Strategy among the Mukogodo," *Current Anthropology*, 30: 224–234; Peter Bogucki and Ryszard Grygiel. 1993. "The First Farmers of North-central Europe," *Journal of Field Archaeology*, 20: 399–426; Peter Bogucki. 1996. "The Spread of Early Farming in Europe," *American Scientist*, 84: 242–253; and Jessica M. C. Pearce-Duvet. 2006. "The Origin of Human Pathogens: Evaluating the Role of Agriculture and Domestic Animals in the Evolution of Human Disease," *Biological Reviews*, 81: 369–382.
8. Richard H. Steckel. 2005. "Health and Nutrition in Pre-Columbian America: The Skeletal Evidence," *The Journal of Interdisciplinary History*, 36: 1–32; Jean-Pierre Bocquet-Appel. 2011. "When the World's Population Took Off: The Springboard of the Neolithic Demographic Transition," *Science*, 333: 560–561; and Timothy B. Gage and Sharon DeWitte. 2009. "What Do We Know about the Agricultural Demographic Transition?" *Current Anthropology*, 50: 649–655.
9. E. A. Wrigley. 1969. *Population and History*, New York: World University Library, 67.
10. Robert William Fogel. 1997. "New Findings on Secular Trends in Nutrition and Mortality: Some Implications for Population Theory," in *Handbook of Population and Family Economics*, vol. 1A, ed. Mark R. Rosenzweig and Oded Stark, Amsterdam: Elsevier, 433–481; and Robert William Fogel. 2004. *The Escape from Hunger and Premature Death, 1700–2100: Europe, America and the Third World*, Cambridge: Cambridge University Press.
11. E.A. Wrigley. 1969. *Population and History*, New York: World University Library, 66.
12. R. Mansell Prothero. 1977. "Disease and Mobility: A Neglected Factor in Epidemiology," *International Journal of Epidemiology*, 6: 259–267.
13. Mark Wheelis. 2002. "Biological Warfare at the 1346 Siege of Caffa," *Emerging Infectious Diseases*, 8: 971–975; and C. Claiborne Ray. 2012. "Unearthing the Plague," *The New York Times*, June 19.
14. Barbara Tuchman. 1978. *A Distant Mirror: The Calamitous 14th Century*, New York: Knopf; Suzanne Austin Alchon. 2003. *A Pest in the Land: New World Epidemics in a Global Perspective*, Albuquerque: University of New Mexico Press; and Robert S. Gottfried. 1983. *The Black Death: Natural and Human Disaster in Medieval Europe*, New York: The Free Press.
15. Mark A. Rothstein, M. Gabriela Alcalde, Nanette R. Elster, Mary Anderlik Majumder, Larry I. Palmer, T. Howard Stone, and Richard E.

Hoffman. 2003. *Quarantine and Isolation: Lessons Learned from SARS*, a report to the Centers for Disease Control and Prevention, http://www.iaclea.org/members/pdfs/SARS%20REPORT.Rothstein.pdf (accessed July 1, 2011); and Thomas Crampton. 2003. "Battling the Spread of SARS, Asian Nations Escalate Travel Restrictions," April 12, *New York Times*, http://www.nytimes.com/2003/04/12/news/12iht-a7_20.html?scp=1&sq=SARS%20travel%20restrictions&st=cse (accessed July 1, 2011).

16. N. D. Cook. 1998. *Born to Die: Disease and New World Conquest, 1492–1650*, Cambridge: Cambridge University Press; and Nathan Nunn and Nancy Qian. 2010. "The Columbian Exchange; A History of Disease, Food, and Ideas," *Journal of Economic Perspectives*, 24: 163–188.

17. P. M. Austin Bourke. 1964. "Emergence of the Potato Blight, 1843–46," *Nature*, 203: 805–808; and P. M. Austin Bourke. 1960. "The Extent of the Potato Crop in Ireland at the Time of the Famine," *Journal of the Statistical and Social Inquiry Society of Ireland*, 20: 1–35.

18. Joel Mokyr. 1983. *Why Ireland Starved, A Quantitative and Analytical History of the Irish Economy, 1800–1850*, London: Taylor & Francis.

19. Peter Gray. 1995. *The Irish Famine*, London: Thames & Hudson.

20. Tacitus Historical Atlas, *Population of the British Isles*, http://www.tacitus.nu/historical-atlas/population/british.htm (accessed October 20, 2011); and A Vision of Britain through Time, http://www.visionofbritain.org.uk/data_cube_page.jsp?data_theme=T_POP&data_cube=N_TOT_POP&u_id=10001043&c_id=10001043&add=N (accessed December 1, 2011).

21. Ibid.

22. Thomas McKeown. 1976. *The Modern Rise of Population*, New York: Academic Press.

23. Simon Szreter. 1988. "The Importance of Social Intervention in Britain's Mortality Decline 1859–1940," *Social History of Medicine*, 1: 1–37; and David Cutler, Angus Deaton, and Adriana Lleras-Muney. 2006. "The Determinants of Mortality," *Journal of Economic Perspectives*, 20: 97–120.

24. John Snow. 1849. *On the Mode of Communication of Cholera*, London: John Churchill.

25. John Snow. 1855. *On the Mode of Communication of Cholera*, 2nd ed., London: John Churchill.

26. Milt Freudenheim. 2012. "Fast Access to Records Helps Fight Epidemics," *The New York Times*, June 19.

27. PortCities London, *Bazalgette and London's Sewage*, http://www.portcities.org.uk/london/server/show/ConNarrative.153/chapterId/3178/Bazalgette-and-Londons-sewage.html (accessed December 15, 2011).

28. Robert Steven Gottfried. 1983. *The Black Death: Natural and Human Disaster in Medieval Europe*, London: Collier Macmillan.

29. R. S. Gottfried. 1977. "Population, Plague, and the Sweating Sickness: Demographic Movements in Late Fifteenth-Century England," *Journal of British Studies*, 17: 12–37.

30. Patrick J. Pead. 2003. "Benjamin Jesty: New Light in the Dawn of Vaccination," *The Lancet*, 362: 2104–2109.

31. Stefan Riedel. 2005. "Edward Jenner and the History of Smallpox and Vaccination," *Baylor University Medical Center Proceedings*, 18: 21–25; and Ann Marie Nelson. 1999. "The Cost of Disease Eradication: Smallpox and Bovine Tuberculosis," *Annals of the New York Academy of Sciences*, 894: 83–91, http://onlinelibrary.wiley.com.proxy.lib.umich.edu/doi/10.1111/j.1749-6632.1999.tb08048.x/pdf (accessed July 31, 2011).

32. A. J. Mercer. 1985. "Smallpox and Epidemiological-Demographic Change in Europe: The Role of Vaccination," *Population Studies*, 39: 287–307.

33. Thomas McKeown. 1976. *The Modern Rise of Population*, New York: Academic Press; John P. Bunker, Howard S. Frazier, and Frederick Mosteller. 1994. "Improving Health: Measuring Effects of Medical Care," *The Milbank Quarterly*, 72: 225–258; and John C. Caldwell. 1991. "Major New Evidence on Health Transition and Its Interpretation," *Health Transition Review*, 1: 221–229.

34. Joseph Lister. 1867. "On the Antiseptic Principle of the Practice of Surgery," *British Medical Journal*, 90: 2299; and Agnes Ullmann. 2007. "Pasteur-Koch: Distinctive Ways of Thinking about Infectious Diseases," *Microbe*, 2: 383–387.

35. Michael Worboys. 2000. *Spreading Germs: Diseases, Theories, and Medical Practice in Britain, 1865–1900*, Cambridge: Cambridge University Press.

36. Candice Millard. 2011. *Destiny of the Republic: A Tale of Madness, Medicine and the Murder of a President*, New York: Doubleday.

37. John B. McKinlay and Sonja M. McKinlay. 1977. "The Questionable Contribution of Medical Measures to the Decline of Mortality in the United States in the Twentieth Century," *The Milbank Memorial Fund Quarterly*, 55: 405–428.

38. Annabel Ferriman. 2007. "BMJ Readers Choose the 'Sanitary Revolution' as Greatest Medical Advance since 1840," *British Medical Journal*, 334: 111.

39. Eileen M. Crimmins, Yasuhiko Saito and Dominique Ingegneri. 1989. "Changes in Life Expectancy and Disability-Free Life Expectancy in the United States," *Population and Development Review*, 15: 235–267.

40. Emmanuelle Cambois, Aurore Clavel, Isabelle Romieu and Jean-Marie Robine. 2008. "Trends in Disability-Free Life Expectancy at Age 65 in France: Consistent and Diverging Patterns According to the Underlying Disability Measure," *European Journal of Ageing*, 5: 287–298.

41. Gerard Anderson and Jane Horwath. 2004. "The Growing Burden of Chronic Disease in America," *Public Health Reports*, 119: 263–270.

42. Statistics Canada. 1999. *Vital Statistics Compendium, 1996*, Ottawa: Statistics Canada.

43. National Institute of Neurological Disorders and Stroke (NINDS). 2006. *Amyotrophic Lateral Sclerosis Information Page*, http://www.ninds.nih.gov/disorders/amyotrophiclateralsclerosis/amyotrophiclateralsclerosis.htm (accessed April 12, 2006).

44. OECD, "Compendium of Statistical Terms: Contributory Cause of Death," http://stats.oecd.org/glossary/detail.asp?ID=444 (accessed September 29, 2011).

45. Henri A. Laurichesse, Janet Mortimer, Barry G. Evans, and C. Paddy Farrington. 1998. "Pre-AIDS Mortality in HIV-Infected Individuals in England, Wales and Northern Ireland, 1982–1996," *AIDS*, 12: 651–658; Janice K. Louie, Ling Chin Hsu, Dennis H. Osmond, Mitchell H. Katz, and Sandra K. Schwarcz. 2002. "Trends in Causes of Death among Persons with Acquired Immunodeficiency Syndrome in the Era of Highly Active Antiretroviral Therapy, San Francisco, 1994–1998," *The Journal of Infectious Diseases*, 186: 1023–1027; and Maria Prins, Ildefonso Hernandez Aguado, Raymond P. Brettle, J. Roy Robertson, Barbara Broers, Nicolas Carre, David J. Goldberg, Robert Zangerle, Roel A. Coutinho, and Anneke van den Hoek. 1997. "Pre-AIDS Mortality from Natural Causes Associated with HIV Disease Progression: Evidence from the European Seroconverter Study among Injecting Drug Users," *AIDS*, 11: 1747–1756.

46. World Health Organization. 1994. *International Statistical Classification of Diseases and Related Health Problems*, Geneva: World Health Organization.

47. Rafael Lozano, Christopher J. L. Murray, Alan D. Lopez, and Toshi Satoh. 2001. "Miscoding and Misclassification of Ischaemic Heart Disease Mortality," *Global Programme on Evidence for Health Policy Working Paper No. 12*, Geneva: World Health Organization.

48. Dennis L. Peck and Kenneth Warner. 1995. "Accident or Suicide? Single-Vehicle Accidents and the Intent Hypothesis," *Adolescence*, 30: 463–472.

49. T. A. Holding and B. N. Barraclough. 1978. "Undetermined Deaths—Suicide or Accident?" *British Journal of Psychiatry*, 133: 542–549.

50. World Health Organization. 2007. *Verbal Autopsy Standards: Ascertaining and Attributing Causes of Death*, Geneva: World Health Organization, http://www.who.int/whosis/mort/verbalautopsystandards/en/ (accessed September 11, 2011).

51. R. W. Snow, J. R. Armstrong, D. Foster, M. T. Winstanley, V. M. Marsh, C. R. Newton, C. Waruiru, I. Mwangi, P.A. Winstanley, and K. Marsh. 1992. "Childhood Deaths in Africa: Uses and Limitations of Verbal Autopsies," *The Lancet*, 340: 351–355; and Nadia Soleman, Daniel Chandramohan, and Kenji Shibuya. 2006. "Verbal Autopsy: Current Practices and Challenges," *Bulletin of the World Health Organization*, 84: 239–245, http://www.scielosp.org/pdf/bwho/v84n3/v84n3a20.pdf (accessed September 12, 2011).

52. Daniel Chandramohan, Nadia Soleman, Kenji Shibuya, and John Porter. 2005. "Ethical Issues in the Application of Verbal Autopsies in Mortality Surveillance Systems," *Tropical Medicine & International Health*, 10: 1087–1089.

53. National Academy of Sciences. 2000. *Biological and Clinical Data Collection in Population Surveys in Less Developed Countries*, Washington, DC: Measure Evaluation and USAID, http://www.who.int/hiv/pub/surveillance/en/biomarkers.pdf (accessed October 11, 2011).

54. W. Rathmann, B. Haastert, A. Icks, H. Löwel, C. Meisinger, R. Holle, and G. Giani. 2003. "High Prevalence of Undiagnosed Diabetes Mellitus in Southern Germany: Target Populations for Efficient Screening. The KORA Survey 2000," *Diabetologia*, 46: 182–189.

55. Institute for Health Metrics and Evaluation website. Available at http://www.healthmetricsandevaluation.org/ Accessed March 16, 2013. The findings for 2010 are summarized in the December 13, 2012 issue of *The Lancet*.

56. Unless otherwise indicated, the GBD results in this chapter are from World Health Organization. 2008. *The Global Burden of Disease: 2004 Update*, Geneva: World Health Organization. Available at http://www.who.int/healthinfo/global_burden_disease/2004_report_update/en/index.html Accessed September 12, 2011 or from World Health Organization. 2009. *Global Health Risks: Mortality and Burden of Disease Attributable to Selected Major Risks*, Geneva: World Health Organization Available at http://www.who.int/healthinfo/global_burden_disease/GlobalHealthRisks_report_full.pdf Accessed September 29, 2011.

57. Christopher J. L. Murray and Alan D. Lopez. 1996. "Estimating Causes of Death: New Methods and Global and Regional Applications for 1990," in *The Global Burden of Disease: A Comprehensive*

Assessment of Mortality and Disability from Diseases, Injuries and Risk Factors in 1990 and Projected to 2020, ed. Christopher J. L. Murray and Alan D. Lopez, Cambridge, MA: Harvard University Press, 117–200.

58. Colin D. Mathers, Ties Boerma, and Doris Ma Fat. 2009. "Global and Regional Causes of Death," *British Medical Bulletin*, 92: 7–32.

59. World Health Organization. 2008. *The 10 Leading Causes of Death by Broad Income Group (2004)*, http://www.who.int/mediacentre/factsheets /fs310/en/index.html (accessed July 18, 2010).

60. M. Badri, R. Ehrlich, R. Wood, T. Pulerwitz, and G. Maartens, G. 2001. "Association between Tuberculosis and HIV Disease Progression in a High Tuberculosis Prevalence Area," *International Journal of Tubercular Lung Diseases*, 5: 225–232: and C. Connolly, G. R. Davies, and D. Wilkinson. 1998. "Impact of the Human Immunodeficiency Virus Epidemic on Mortality among Adults with Tuberculosis in Rural South Africa, 1991–1995," *International Journal of Tubercular Lung Diseases*, 2: 919–925.

61. Food and Agriculture Organization (FAO). 2003. *Projections of Tobacco Production, Consumption and Trade to the Year 2010*, Rome: FAO, http://www.fao.org/DOCREP/006/Y4956E/Y4956E00. HTM (accessed November 29, 2011).

62. World Health Organization. 2004. *World Report on Road Traffic Injury Prevention: Summary*, Geneva: World Health Organization, http://www.who .int/violence_injury_prevention/publications /road_traffic/world_report/summary_en_rev. pdf (accessed November 29, 2011).

63. Emily Yoffe. 2001. "How Does Alzheimer's Kill?" *Slate*, April 30, http://www.slate.com/articles /news_and_politics/explainer/2001/04/how _does_alzheimers_kill.html (accessed September 29, 2011).

64. The GBD project made two further modifications in calculating YLL. One is a discounting of YLL in the future, similar to discounting of future income by economists. The other is an application of different weights at different ages, which weights YLL at very young and very old ages less than life lost at other ages. The GBD project presents estimates without discounting and age weights on their website, but the estimates usually presented in the literature include the application of age weights and future discounting. Estimates using age weights and discounting are presented in this chapter. Whether or not these modifications are applied has little effect on the ordering of causes of death in YLL. Also see S. Anand and K. Hanson. 1997. "Disability-Adjusted Life Years: A Critical Review," *Journal of Health Economics*, 16: 685–702; and J. L. Bobadilla. 1996. "Priority Setting and Cost Effectiveness," in *Health Policy and Systems Development: An Agenda for Research*, ed. K. Janovsky, Geneva: World Health Organization, 43–60.

65. World Health Organization, *Regional Burden of Disease Estimates for 2004*, http://www.who.int /healthinfo/global_burden_disease/estimates _regional/en/index.html (accessed October 19, 2011).

66. T. Bedirhan Üstun and Ron C. Kessler. 2002. "Global Burden of Depressive Disorders: The Issue of Duration," *British Journal of Psychiatry*, 181: 181–183.

67. L. T. Ruzicka and P. Kane. 1990. "Health Transition: The Course of Morbidity and Mortality," in *What We Know About the Health Transition: The Cultural, Social and Behavioural Determinants of Health: The Proceedings of an International Workshop, Canberra, May 1989*, ed. J. C. Caldwell, S. Findley, P. Caldwell, G. Santow, W. Cosford, J. Braid, and D. Broers-Freeman, Canberra: Australian National University.

68. Calculated by the author from the number with disability by age and the population by age.

69. As with calculation of YLL, discounting of future years and age weights are used in calculation of YLD.

70. Figure 5.10 is adapted from Figure 1 in World Health Organization. 2009. *Global Health Risks: Mortality and Burden of Disease Attributable to Selected Major Risks*, Geneva: World Health Organization, 11, http://www.who.int/healthinfo /global_burden_disease/GlobalHealthRisks _report_full.pdf (accessed September 29, 2011).

71. WHO Global InfoBase Team. 2005. *The SuRF Report 2. Surveillance of Chronic Disease Risk Factors: Country-Level Data and Comparable Estimates*, Geneva: World Health Organization, https:// apps.who.int/infobase/Publicfiles/SuRF2.pdf (accessed October 14, 2011).

CHAPTER 6

MORTALITY DECLINE IN THE LESS DEVELOPED REGION

LEARNING OBJECTIVES

- Discuss the ways in which the availability of technology has affected the decline of mortality in the LDR since World War II.
- List six pathways through which education of the mother can affect infant and child survival in the Less Developed Region
- Define the double burden of mortality.

- Discuss the role of vaccinations in reducing LDR mortality, why there has been vaccination resistance in both the LDR and the MDR, and the effects of vaccination resistance.
- Describe changes in health behaviors in the LDR and their effects on mortality.
- Explain why some think that many LeastDC populations will be extremely vulnerable to new epidemics in the future.

((• Listen to the Chapter Audio

OVERVIEW

Chapter 5 set a context for mortality in less developed countries by showing what the major causes of death and disability were in low-income and middle-income countries in 2004. In this chapter, we trace the kinds of social changes and programs that have contributed to the large mortality decline in the LDR since World War II, including programs to reduce malaria and vaccination programs. At the same time that public health and vaccination programs have reduced mortality, sanitation and nutrition have been important, as they were in Europe historically. One of the most important factors in reduction of infant and child mortality has been the education of the mother. We discuss some of the mechanisms through which education of the mother might operate to reduce infant and child mortality.

At the same time that per capita income has increased in many less developed countries and mortality from infectious and parasitic causes of death has declined, lifestyles adopted from the more developed countries have caused new health problems. Consumption of tobacco, alcohol, and fatty foods has increased in many less developed countries, which in turn has contributed to unhealthful chronic conditions, such

as high blood pressure, high cholesterol, and type II diabetes. These conditions then contribute to mortality from non-communicable causes. Also, as the number of motor vehicles in less developed countries has increased, a person now is more likely to die in a motor vehicle accident in a less developed country than in a more developed country. Also, violence, crop failure, and natural disasters continue to contribute to death. Some topics, such as vaccinations and vaccination resistance, are important both in the LDR and the MDR. Vaccines and vaccination resistance in both regions are discussed in this chapter to facilitate the flow of the discourse. However, smoking and alcohol consumption in the LDR are also discussed in this chapter. For the MDR, most of the discussion of smoking and alcohol consumption is in Chapter 7.

FACTORS RELATED TO DECLINE FROM HIGH MORTALITY TO MODERATE MORTALITY IN THE LESS DEVELOPED REGION

After World War II, mortality began to decline or its decline accelerated in many parts of the LDR. As was seen in Chapter 4, this was mainly due to the decline in infant and child mortality. The kinds of factors important in mortality decline historically in the MDR, such as poverty, famine, epidemics and war, unclean drinking water, and inadequate sanitation, certainly played a role in the LDR, but a somewhat different set of factors was also important. In the LDR technology, government action, knowledge, preferences, and behavior all were important in mortality decline.

An important difference between mortality decline in the LDR and in the MDR historically has been the availability in the LDR of the results of technology—specifically, vaccines and curative medicines—that were developed in the MDR. Also, LDR governments have implemented public health measures based on MDR experience, such as draining swamps and improving the quality of drinking water and sanitation systems. These measures have been important in LDR mortality decline.

At the same time, practices and substances borrowed from the MDR, such as strong alcohol, manufactured cigarettes, fatty and fast foods, and the spread of motor vehicles, led to new risks to health and survival. The role of imported technology in less developed countries has often been an object of policy and scientific discussion, as both benefits (such as vaccines) and costs (such as moves toward less healthy lifestyles) are simultaneously present.

Many actions taken to reduce mortality, such as draining swamps or spraying for mosquitoes, can be undertaken without the active involvement of the population, and people benefit from these measures whether or not they are aware of them and whether or not they are in favor of them. Other measures, such as vaccination programs, take a small amount of intentional action by people and have sometimes met with resistance when they are seen as a threat to the local culture or as a foreign plot to harm the local population. However, the overall record of acceptance of major vaccines in less developed countries has been good. A change in childbirth practices, such as attendance by a trained health worker and hygienic practices around the birth, requires some knowledge by household members and concrete actions to take mortality-reducing action. The education of the mother has been found to be key to reducing infant and child mortality throughout the developing world. In addition, diseases linked to poor water quality and poor sanitation can be attacked both by the actions of households and families and by the actions of governments and other organizations.

Education of Mother and Infant and Child Survival

Education of the mother is almost always one of the most important factors in infant and child survival.

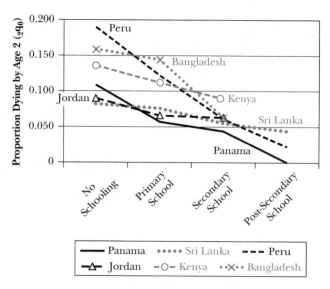

FIGURE 6.1   Proportion of Children Dying by Age 2 by Country and Mother's Education, Late 1970s and Early 1980s

Figure 6.1 shows the proportion of children dying by age 2 ($_2q_0$) in several countries according to the educational attainment of the mother based on data collected in the late 1970s and early 1980s.[1] In every country, a child's chance of dying declines with every incremental increase of the mother's education. This kind of result is typical of studies of the relation of the mother's education to infant and child survival. The result holds up even when other characteristics such as rural versus urban residence and education of the father are taken into account.

How does maternal education affect infant and child survival? There are several possible pathways.[2]

1. More educated mothers could have specific knowledge about health and infant and child care and apply that knowledge more effectively than less educated mothers.
2. More educated mothers could have general skills, such as literacy, that help them to access knowledge and information that contribute to the health of their children.
3. Education could contribute to women having a planning perspective so that more educated mothers recognize signs of illness in children more quickly than less educated mothers, foresee the consequences of these symptoms, and take action.
4. Secular education can have a socializing effect that can work in two ways:
   a. It facilitates the acceptance of Western medical care and adoption of Western health practices. More educated mothers can recognize the importance of actions

such as treating water and are more likely to have their children vaccinated.

    b. It leads women to be less fatalistic about the health and survival of their children and to be more proactive when a child becomes ill.

5. Education is related to women having higher status. This can mean that more educated mothers have more autonomy of action, can take ill children for treatment, and/or can purchase what is needed for treatment without consulting with or getting permission from other family members.

6. Education could be a proxy for household wealth. Wealthier households can afford the costs associated with better health and better survival prospects, such as more plentiful and more nutritious food, the costs of purchasing clean water or treating water, and the costs of medical care.

The extent to which these various explanations are important has implications for policies. To the extent that knowledge of specific child care practices is important (Pathway 1), policy implications for improving infant and child health are fairly clear. If a specific practice is important, that practice could be taught to women perhaps in a fairly short session. However, if literacy or a planning perspective (Pathways 2 and 3) is important, this cannot be imparted quickly or easily to women. The fourth pathway involves changed attitudes or outlooks that can be more difficult to achieve in some settings than in others. The fifth pathway involves autonomy and power of women in the household and the extent to which women's autonomy is related to her education. Although household wealth (Pathway 6) clearly can affect child health, it is unlikely that the relation of the mother's education to infant and child survival operates mainly through household wealth, since usually the mother's education has been found to have a stronger relation to infant and child survival than the father's education or direct measures of household wealth.[3]

Public Health Programs to Reduce Environmental Risk from Diseases

Public health programs to reduce risk from particular diseases have played an important role in less developed countries. In these programs, little individual action is necessary for people to receive the health and survival benefits from the programs. These include malaria reduction programs and efforts to combat cholera and other waterborne diseases through improvements in community water systems.

Malaria and Malaria Reduction Programs

Malaria remains a very important cause of death and disability in low-income countries, being the ninth leading cause of death in low-income countries, as shown in Table 5.2, and the fourth leading cause of disability-adjusted life years (DALYs) in low-income countries, as shown in Table 5.6 in Chapter 5.

After World War II, malaria was a major cause of death in many parts of the world. The pesticide DDT (**di**chloro**di**phenyl**t**richloroethane) was developed during World War II and was found to be very effective against mosquitoes. The campaign to reduce malaria deaths and the changing views of the use of DDT illustrate some of the complications involved in applying technological developments from more developed countries to address health problems in less developed countries.

Mortality Decline in Sri Lanka One of the most studied programs of DDT use in combating malaria was in Sri Lanka, which was called Ceylon until 1972. A large-scale DDT spraying program began in late 1945 and was fully implemented by 1947.

Figure 6.2 shows infant mortality rates (IMRs) and death rates from malaria for Sri Lanka from 1939 to 1956.[4] The IMR is shown on the left-hand axis, and the malaria death rate per 100,000 population is shown on the right-hand axis. It is clear that the decline in infant mortality from all causes closely tracks the trajectory of malaria mortality. Malaria deaths dropped from 12,587 in 1946 to 4,562 in 1947, and there were only 144 annual malaria deaths in 1956.

Some have argued that the decline in malaria was the major factor in overall mortality decline in Sri Lanka, while others see it as only one of several important factors. Among those who think that malaria eradication played a major role in mortality decline, it is estimated that reduction of malaria deaths directly accounted for 20–43% of mortality decline. Newman and Gray argue that the decline in malaria

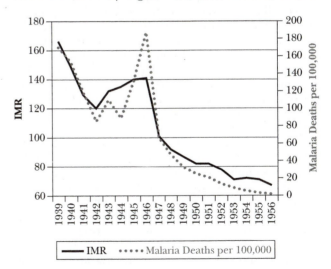

FIGURE 6.2 IMR and Malaria Deaths per 100,000, Sri Lanka, 1939–1956

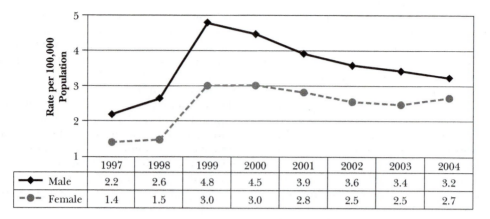

	1997	1998	1999	2000	2001	2002	2003	2004
◆— Male	2.2	2.6	4.8	4.5	3.9	3.6	3.4	3.2
●— Female	1.4	1.5	3.0	3.0	2.8	2.5	2.5	2.7

FIGURE 6.3   Age-Adjusted Death Rates from Malaria, Ages 15–64, South Africa[10]

deaths measures only a part of the effect of malaria reduction on mortality decline. Malaria debilitates people who do not die from it and thus contributes to infant and child mortality from causes of death other than malaria. One of the arguments for the DDT program was that productivity would increase if fewer workers were weakened from malaria.

Meegama argues that mortality had begun to fall before the DDT campaign. He also maintained that at the same time as the malaria campaign, nutritional status and the availability of medical services increased in Sri Lanka, and thus, the decline in malaria deaths was only one aspect of a larger development process that led to mortality decline both from malaria and from other causes that were not influenced by malaria. However, most researchers agree that the DDT spraying campaign was a substantial contributor to mortality decline.[5]

Indoor DDT Spraying and Malaria: The Case of South Africa   Rachel Carson published *The Silent Spring* in 1962, which presented evidence that DDT causes the shells of birds' eggs to thin and often break before the birds hatch. She also claimed that DDT caused cancer.[6] However, there was not scientific work that showed conclusively that DDT caused cancer or other serious problems in humans.[7] Partly in response to Carson's work, DDT was banned in most countries in the 1970s and 1980s. Other pesticides were developed, but the problem was that strains of malaria developed that were resistant to the pesticides, and the pesticides tended not to be as effective as DDT.

During the DDT programs of the 1940s and 1950s, DDT was often sprayed widely over swamps and other areas. Another way to use insecticides to combat mosquitoes is spraying insecticide on the interior walls of residences, which has been an effective way to kill mosquitoes and reduce malaria mortality. Indoor spraying results in much less use of DDT than the earlier approach. In 2006, the World Health

Organization (WHO) recommended DDT as one of the insecticides for indoor spraying.[8]

South Africa began indoor DDT spraying in 1999. Figure 6.3 shows **age-adjusted death rates** from malaria in South Africa for the years 1997–2004.[9] The timing of the drop in malaria death rates in comparison with the date of initiation of indoor DDT spraying is striking.

The Roll-Back Malaria Program and Continuing Efforts to Reduce Malaria   The Roll-Back Malaria Program was launched in 1998 by WHO, the United Nations Children's Fund (UNICEF), United Nations Development Programme (UNDP), and the World Bank to try to decrease the incidence of, and the number of, deaths from malaria.

The Roll-Back Malaria Program pursued a three-pronged approach of spraying insecticide on interior walls of residences, promoting the use of insecticide-treated bednets, and treating those with malaria with medicines based on artemisinin. One drawback of bednets is that to be effective, each person needs a net and they must be used properly. Also, they are not useful when people are moving about in their residences. Another concern about artemisinin-based medications has been the appearance of artemisinin-resistant strains of malaria.[11]

People are only at risk of malaria in parts of the world where the malaria parasite is present in the mosquito population. Figure 6.4 shows the number of malaria deaths per 100,000 people in malarial areas between 2000 and 2010. This decline in malaria mortality is encouraging, but even in 2010 there were more than 650,000 malaria deaths and more than 200 million malaria cases worldwide.[12]

The level and impact of malaria are dependent on the proportion of people in malarial areas who contract malaria and among those who contract malaria the proportion who die. The proportion of people who have a condition or disease, such as malaria, is called the **prevalence** of the condition or disease. The

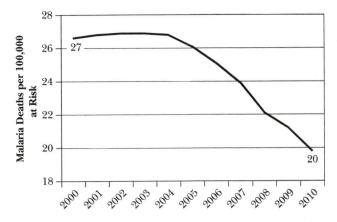

FIGURE 6.4 Malaria Deaths per 100,000 Persons at Risk in the World, 2000–2010

percentage of those with an ailment who die is called the **case fatality rate** for that condition or disease.

Figure 6.5 splits the malaria death rate shown in Figure 6.4 into two parts: (1) among people who live in a malarial area, the number who contracted malaria per 1,000 people at risk of malaria (the prevalence of malaria) and (2) among those who contracted malaria, the percentage who died from malaria in 2000–2010 (the case fatality rate for malaria). Between 2000 and 2010, both the risk that people would have malaria decreased (a decline of 18%) and the chance that a person with malaria died decreased (a decline of 10%).

Parasitism in Less Developed Countries

A **parasite** is an organism that lives on or in a host and gets its food from or at the expense of its host. Parasitic infestation is often a problem in the LDR.

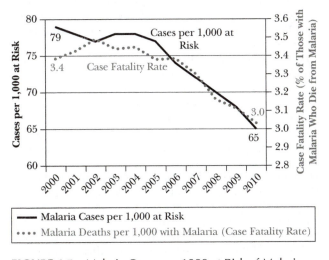

- —— Malaria Cases per 1,000 at Risk
- ···· Malaria Deaths per 1,000 with Malaria (Case Fatality Rate)

FIGURE 6.5 Malaria Cases per 1000 at Risk of Malaria and Malaria Case Fatality Rate in the World, 2000–2010

Parasites other than malaria tend not to kill the host. Rather, they debilitate or weaken the host. Malaria also can debilitate the host when the affected person does not die. Infestation by parasites makes it difficult for people to study or work. Parasites make other conditions, such as infections, more serious. It is difficult to free people of parasites if the parasites are common in the environment, such as in drinking water or local insects. Workers in areas in which parasitism is common are sometimes considered lazy, when the problem could be that their energy is substantially reduced by parasites.

Filariasis is an example of a parasitic disease that rarely leads directly to death but is debilitating and costly in money and suffering. It is transmitted by mosquito bites, is related to elephantiasis, and affects the lymphatic system. A person with filariasis lacks energy, and periodically his or her legs or other parts can swell up, causing discomfort and an inability to function normally. Studies have shown a substantial loss of work time due to filariasis. Filariasis is endemic in much of Middle Africa, Southern Asia, and some parts of Latin America and the Caribbean.[13]

Parasites also lead to other debilitating conditions, such as river blindness, which is caused by a worm transmitted by the bite of a fly. In the body, the worm migrates to the eyes. River blindness is estimated to be the cause of about 10% of the blindness in the world. River blindness is treatable by medication, but that medication is often not available in poor areas.[14]

Drug-Resistant Diseases

When a patient with a disease is treated with a drug, those disease organisms that are less susceptible to the drug will disproportionately survive. This leads to the development of a **drug-resistant strain of a disease**. This is likely to happen when antibiotics are used when they are not necessary or when a patient does not complete a full course of drug treatment. Unnecessary use is especially common when drugs are available without a prescription, which is the situation in many less developed countries.[15]

Tuberculosis (TB) is a major focus of concern about drug-resistant diseases. In early 2012, a strain of TB was reported in India that was resistant to *all* known treatment drugs. To reduce the risk that patients would sell their TB drugs, some countries have adopted a program of directly observed treatment of TB (DOT), in which the patient is not given the drugs to take away but rather has to come to a health facility for each administration of the medication. There is evidence that DOT lowers the level of drug resistance, but there remain concerns about patients who do not return for their full course of treatment. In addition, when patients stop taking drugs before the full course of treatment has been completed, it facilitates the development of drug-resistant disease strains.[16]

There has been concern about the effects that antibiotics fed to farm animals have on the health of humans who eat these animals or their products (such as milk). A 2011 study using data from Denmark showed that antibiotic-resistant bacteria had been transmitted from livestock to people. This is another way in which domestic animals and their care can pose threats to human health, but in different ways than occurred when pastoral nomadism and settled agriculture were first adopted.[17]

Drug-resistant diseases are also an increasingly serious problem in the United States and other developed countries. In 2008, the Infectious Diseases Society of America issued a call to action for support for development of new antibiotics and for physicians to be increasingly careful in not to overprescribe existing antibiotics due to the problem of drug-resistant diseases.[18]

Methicillin-resistant *Staphylococcus aureus* (MRSA) is a bacterium that is resistant to a wide variety of antibiotics and that is common in hospitals and nursing homes. In the United States between 1999 and 2005, MRSA-related hospitalizations increased from 127,036 to 278,036. In England and Wales, deaths involving MRSA increased from 51 in 1993 to 800 in 2002, and the number of laboratory reports of MRSA increased from 210 to 5,309.[19]

Vaccination Programs

Vaccination programs against specific diseases have been very important. As discussed in Chapter 5, smallpox was the first disease for which there was an effective vaccine. Smallpox also is one of the few diseases that has been eradicated. Measles and polio vaccinations in less developed countries also have contributed to a reduction in child mortality. Despite the successful record of vaccines in reducing mortality, there has been suspicion of their safety both in the LDR and in the MDR. Sometimes this suspicion has been unwarranted, but sometimes there have been understandable reasons why people have been concerned.

Problems of Developing Vaccines

Vaccines work in two different ways. Vaccines are produced from either a dead form or a weakened live form of a virus. The dead form is less likely to lead to serious side effects or to mutate to a virulent form, but the weakened live form is likely to be more effective in preventing the disease, and immunity usually lasts longer. Some vaccines are sensitive to heat and thus need to be refrigerated, while others do not need such special measures. Some diseases do not

mutate easily. In these cases, the same vaccine can be used effectively for many years. In other cases, diseases mutate frequently, and a new vaccine must be developed every year.

Flu Vaccine

A vaccine gives the patient a mild case of the disease or a related disease. Every vaccine has side effects, and there is some risk inherent in all vaccines. Vaccines cannot be developed overnight, and good judgment must be used in determining when to launch mass vaccine production and when to call for mass vaccination, especially for a disease that mutates frequently.

Modern strains of flu usually develop in East Asia and travel around the world. In Western countries, such as the United States, the vaccine for the winter flu season needs to be finalized 6 months in advance of flu season in order to have sufficient vaccine grown in time. Also, there is some guesswork involved when the influenza vaccine is formulated. The exact formulation of the vaccine is important, because vaccines are far less effective if they are not developed specific to a given influenza strain.

Smallpox Eradication

By the mid-twentieth century, smallpox had been eliminated from most of the more developed region countries, but it was still an **endemic disease** in most of the less developed region. A disease is endemic in a population if it is present at some level continuously without needing to be reintroduced by an infected person.

In 1966, the World Health Organization launched an intensive smallpox eradication program. In 1967, smallpox was still endemic in 33 countries and led to about 2 million deaths per year. The development of a freeze-dried vaccine was important in the eradication program, since it would not deteriorate in tropical climates. The last countries in which smallpox was found were Ethiopia, where it was eliminated in 1976, and Somalia, where it was eliminated in 1977. The World Health Organization declared that smallpox had been eradicated worldwide in 1980.[20]

Samples of the smallpox virus have been preserved for research purposes. This has been controversial due to concerns about the virus escaping, being stolen, or being used to develop biological weapons.[21]

Measles Vaccination in Less Developed Countries

Measles vaccination has been very important in improving child survival. Measles vaccine became available in 1963. In 2000, there were about 880,000 measles deaths worldwide. By 2006, this had fallen to about 450,000 measles deaths. Almost all measles deaths could be prevented if all children were vaccinated.[22]

Concerns about Vaccination

There have been concerns about the safety of vaccines in both more developed and less developed countries. The bases of the concerns are somewhat different in the two regions.

Opposition to Polio Vaccination in Nigeria   The Salk polio vaccine began being used in 1955, and the Sabin oral polio vaccine began being used in 1962. The number of polio cases fell rapidly as polio vaccines became widely administered throughout the world. In 1980, there were 52,630 polio cases reported worldwide; in 2010, there were 1,348 cases. There were no reported cases in the United States after 1986.

In 2010, polio remained endemic in four countries: Nigeria, Afghanistan, India, and Pakistan. It also was suspected that polio had reestablished itself in Angola, Chad, and the Democratic Republic of the Congo. Polio cases also occurred in 14 other countries where the virus was introduced by an infected person from outside the country. In 2013 polio was reported in Syria. Polio was thought to have been introduced from elsewhere in the Middle East and found a stronghold when the Syrian Civil War disrupted ongoing vaccination campaigns and weakened the entire Syrian medical system.[23]

There have been active campaigns in Nigeria in opposition to polio vaccination, even though the Nigerian central government has supported vaccination. In 2003, leaders in northern Nigeria asked parents to not have their children immunized, claiming that the vaccine could destroy their children's fertility and could be contaminated with materials that lead to HIV or cancer. One reason for the belief that polio vaccine led to infertility was that it was linked in some people's minds with an earlier Nigerian government family-planning program.[24]

Suspicion about the safety of polio vaccine in Nigeria was also fueled by some polio cases that resulted from a mutated vaccine.[25] In addition, suspicion of Western vaccination programs was spurred by findings that some Nigerian children died as a result of a 1996 meningitis drug trial in which there were questions about the application of ethical standards for human subjects. In 2011, the drug company Pfizer made payments to families whose children had died in that drug trial.[26] There were concerns that children had been used as guinea pigs, similar to the situation in Guatemala discussed in Chapter 3.

The World Health Organization and the Nigerian government want to eradicate polio in Nigeria, but it seems to have been increasing. There were only six reported cases of polio in the first half of 2010, but there were 24 cases in the first half of 2011. In August 2011, authorities in northern Nigeria in the area of the boycott announced a policy to jail or fine parents who refused to have their children immunized against polio, but it was unclear how successful this policy would be. While some parents who had initially refused vaccination changed their minds, others complained that Nigerian public health policies had the wrong focus at a time when antimalarial and anti-cholera medicines were often not available.[27]

Vaccination Ruse and the Pursuit of Osama bin Laden   In 2011, when the United States and other countries were pursuing the head of al Qaeda, Osama bin Laden, the CIA launched a hepatitis B vaccination program in an area of Pakistan where it was thought that relatives of Osama bin Laden lived. The purpose of the program was to obtain DNA from bin Laden's relatives to try to verify his whereabouts. No DNA was obtained. Two hundred aid groups protested to the CIA that the program was unethical, undermined the credibility of numerous legitimate vaccination programs, and endangered health workers. It was seen to support the contention that vaccination programs were a Western plot to sterilize Muslims.[28] In June 2012, the Taliban announced that it would not allow a planned polio vaccination program to take place in North Waziristan, a region of Pakistan that was under Taliban control. The announced reasons were that there were concerns that the new vaccination campaign would be used as a cover for espionage, as had happened in 2011.[29] In December 2012, six workers in a polio vaccination campaign in Pakistan were murdered, apparently as a result of Taliban opposition to vaccination programs.[30]

Vaccination Concerns and Herd Immunity in Developed Countries   In American schools, children are required to have had a variety of vaccinations in order to enroll, although individual children can opt out with a parental request. When parents perceive that the chance of contracting a disease is low, they can make a judgment whether their child is at more risk from contracting the disease if the child is not vaccinated or at more risk from a side effect of the vaccine. Many health authorities are concerned about health consequences when a high proportion of parents opt their children out of vaccination programs.[31]

A high level of vaccination in the population is important for the protection of all population members because of the phenomenon of **herd immunity**, also called community immunity or group immunity. When a high proportion of the population is immune to a given disease, the disease cannot become established in that population. The level of vaccination for a population to have herd immunity is generally 83–94%. In Michigan in 2000, more than 3% of children entering school had exemptions from vaccinations, higher than in previous years.[32] In Illinois, the number of schools with less than 90% of children vaccinated for measles went from 31 schools in 2003 to 124 schools in 2010, and the number of schools with less than 90% of children vaccinated for polio increased from 27 to 122 between 2003 and 2010. Even though 98% of all children in Illinois schools were vaccinated against measles and polio, the clustering of unvaccinated children in individual schools led to concerns about the possibility of local outbreaks.[33]

Some parents do not have their children vaccinated because of a concern that a vaccine could have a high risk of serious side effects. Other parents do not have their children vaccinated because they realize that if all other children are vaccinated, then their child has very little chance of contracting the disease, even if their child is not vaccinated. In economics, this is called the free rider problem, which occurs when a person called a **free rider** obtains a benefit without paying the market price or entering into group risk. The problem is that if there are too many "free riders" who remain unvaccinated, herd immunity is lost and all persons are at increased risk.[34]

Vaccines and Fear of Autism　There have been two different sources of concern about vaccines and a possible increased chance that a child will develop autism. One involves the combined measles, mumps, and rubella vaccine (MMR), and the other concerns the preservative used in some vaccines, thimerosal.

In 1998 Wakefield and his colleagues published an article in the British journal *The Lancet* that suggested a possible connection between inflammatory bowel disease, the MMR vaccine, and autism, based on a study of 12 children. A wide variety of studies were published that showed that there was no link between the MMR vaccine and autism. Also, errors, manipulation of the data, and undisclosed conflicts of interest on the part of Wakefield were disclosed. Nonetheless, in many countries MMR immunization rates fell greatly, leading to many deaths that would not have occurred otherwise. Wakefield's 1998 *Lancet* article was partially retracted in 2004 after Wakefield's undisclosed conflicts of interest had been revealed, and it was completely retracted in 2010 after the many problems with Wakefield's study had become known.[35]

Thimerosal contains mercury and has been used as a preservative to prevent the growth of bacteria and fungi in vaccines since the 1930s. In 1997, the U.S. Food and Drug Administration (FDA) required a review to assess the risks of all foods and drugs that contained mercury. The review was completed in 1999 and concluded that there was no evidence of harm from thimerosal in vaccines except for some extremely sensitive individuals. Other research also supported the conclusion that there was no link between thimerosal and autism. Due to the availability of preservatives that do not contain mercury and due to continued public concern about mercury in

vaccines, in 2001 the FDA banned the use of mercury in most childhood vaccines, although some vaccines continued to contain an extremely small amount of mercury.[36]

The UN Environment Programme has recommended the elimination of mercury from all products, which would include thimerosal in vaccines. Some have argued that if thimerosal is too dangerous to be used in vaccines in the United States and other more developed countries, then it is too dangerous to be used in vaccines in less developed countries. In 2012, Chile became the first less developed country to ban the use of mercury in vaccines. However, the WHO's Strategic Advisory Group of Experts on Immunization and the American Academy of Pediatrics argue that the continued use of thimerosal in vaccines in many less developed countries is necessary because it is the only effective preservative for multidose units of vaccine to remain safe without refrigeration. These bodies think that if the use of thimerosal in vaccines is banned, then vaccination rates in many less developed countries will drop greatly. The American Academy of Pediatrics cites the lack of scientific evidence linking thimerosal to negative outcomes and claims that some of those who oppose all use of mercury in vaccines are confusing thimerosal with methylmercury, which is a neurotoxin with well-known serious effects.[37]

Many parents continue to believe that thimerosal has led to autism in their children, and many websites continue to discuss supposed dangers to children from vaccines. A study conducted in 2009 of American parents with at least one child younger than age 18 found that 12% of parents had refused a vaccine for their child that was recommended by a doctor.[38]

It is not completely clear what the source is of the high degree of skepticism about a possible vaccine–autism link, even though almost all medical authorities have concluded that there is no convincing evidence of such a link. Although there is known to be a genetic component to autism, much is not understood about risk factors for autism. Parents are understandably cautious and want to avoid any possible risk for their children. In addition, because more and more information on a variety of subjects is readily available, there can be less confidence in the knowledge of authorities such as the medical community.[39] Using data from the General Social Survey for 1974 through 2010, Gauchet found that there was a decline in confidence in science between 1974 and 2010. This decline in confidence was completely due to lessening confidence in science among political conservatives, who comprised 34% of the combined survey respondents.[40] A feeling that scientific knowledge has been politicized for other ends can lead to skepticism about advice from experts on a variety of topics.

Influenza Epidemics: Past Experience and Future Concerns

Influenza epidemics have played an important role in twentieth-century mortality experience, especially the 1918 epidemic. The devastating effects of that epidemic have led to concerns about when the next serious flu epidemic will occur and to some false alarms. The inherent problems in the development of flu vaccines, as discussed in this chapter, make the problem especially challenging.

The Flu Epidemic of 1918

In 1918, there was a virulent worldwide flu epidemic that is estimated to have killed 50 million people. While most influenza epidemics kill less than 0.1% of infected persons, the 1918 flu killed more than 2.5% of infected persons. In the United States, it killed an estimated 670,000 people.[41] In the United States, e_0^0 in 1918 was 12 years less than it had been in 1917 due to increased flu mortality.[42] The experience of the 1918 flu epidemic led to extensive research on flu and flu vaccines and motivated concern about whether and when the next devastating flu epidemic would occur.

Swine Flu Scare in the United States, in 1976

In February 1976, an army recruit at Fort Dix, New Jersey, became tired and weak and died the next day. Two weeks later, it was announced that the cause of his death was swine flu. There was worry that this was the first death in what would be a new pandemic. Based on research on the time interval between major flu pandemics, it was thought that an especially virulent strain was due to develop by about 1976.

President Ford authorized a major vaccination program against the swine flu. Twenty-four percentage of the U.S. population was vaccinated against swine flu before the program was canceled. No pandemic developed, and about 500 people died from reactions to the vaccine, more than died from swine flu.[43]

Water and Sanitation

In many less developed countries, there are diseases transmitted due to unclean water and inadequate sanitation. These issues are reminiscent of problems that were encountered historically. Unclean water and inadequate sanitation remain a major cause of death and disability, being the fourth most important risk factor for death in low-income countries, as shown in Table 5.9, and the second most important risk factor for death and disability in low-income countries, as shown in Table 5.10 in Chapter 5.

Outbreaks of cholera often signify breakdowns in municipal water systems due to inadequate maintenance, including insufficient treatment of water systems with chemicals. For example, in West Bengal, a cholera outbreak was traced to a faulty water pipe along with irregular treatment of the water with chemicals.[44] Charging for municipal water after it had been free has been cited as a source of a cholera epidemic in South Africa in 2000, when people who could not afford to pay for municipal water turned to contaminated water sources.[45]

Waterborne diseases often break out in situations of social disruption, especially when there is a poor and vulnerable population. The outbreak of cholera in Haiti after the 2010 earthquake resulted from the confluence of various factors that culminated in the deaths of more than 6,000 people. Before 2010, there had not been a cholera outbreak in Haiti for more than 50 years. As a part of the aid effort, UN peacekeepers came from Nepal, a country in which cholera is endemic. There was a spill of raw sewage from the peacekeepers' camp into the Artibonite River, which was a source of drinking water for nearby villages. In countries with clean drinking water and a good sanitation system, the entry of people from cholera-endemic countries would not have resulted in cholera cases and deaths. The combination of long-standing poor sanitation and unclean drinking water, the disruption related to the earthquake, and the temporary migration of Nepalese from a cholera-endemic country combined to result in numerous deaths.[46]

Similarly, one of the major challenges to the health and survival of refugee populations in overcrowded camps is unsanitary conditions and the risk of cholera and other diseases that result from contaminated drinking water. For example, in 2011 many Somali refugees were in crowded camps in Kenya with inadequate sanitation. Some refugees drank from contaminated pools of water. There was a cholera outbreak that affected about 60 people and resulted in at least one death. The provision of soap, encouragement of hand washing, and increased treatment of drinking water alleviated the outbreak.[47]

Sudan was divided into two countries, Sudan and South Sudan, in 2011. In 2012 there were growing numbers of refugees in camps in South Sudan, as a result of conflict between Sudan and South Sudan. The Jamam camp was on a flood plain, which had long been a highly malarial area. Heavy rains led to latrines overflowing, contaminating drinking water, which led to increased deaths from malaria and diarrhea. The child death rates were double what they were otherwise during this conflict. UN officials wanted to move refugees out of Jamam to higher ground with better water supplies, but this effort was complicated by the presence of land mines in the area.[48]

HIV in Less Developed Countries

HIV is an autoimmune disease that often is asymptomatic for many years. If untreated, it transforms into AIDS, which is accompanied by weight loss, skin rash, susceptibility to various infections, and eventually death.

HIV has become a very important cause of death and disability, being the sixth leading cause of death in the world and the fourth leading cause of death in low-income countries, as shown in Table 5.2 in Chapter 5. As shown in Table 5.6, it is the fifth leading cause of death and disability in the world as a whole, the third leading cause in low-income countries, and the seventh leading cause in middle-income countries. HIV has an especially large impact because most of the deaths occur to people in their prime adult ages.

HIV has a number of distinctive features. People can show no symptoms for as long as a decade after they have become HIV-positive and are capable of transmitting the disease to others while they are asymptomatic. In the absence of any treatment, there is an estimated lag of 6–16 years from becoming HIV-positive to death. In sub-Saharan Africa, the region with the highest prevalence, the lag is 8–10 years. HIV could easily be missed in a setting with high incidence of parasitic and infectious diseases, since the early symptoms of HIV include fever, tiredness, headache, and enlarged lymph nodes. These symptoms can result from many causes other than HIV. Also, the early symptoms often disappear after a few weeks and sometimes do not reappear for years.

The HIV epidemic in developed countries often started in the homosexual population and has increasingly become concentrated among injection drug users. However in much of the less developed region, and especially in sub-Saharan Africa, the vast majority of HIV transmission is through heterosexual intercourse. HIV can also be transmitted from an infected woman to her baby either in the labor process or through her breast milk.

Although HIV is a cause of concern in many countries of the world, the percentage of people who are HIV-positive varies enormously by world region and is especially high in Southern Africa. Recall from Figure 2.32 in Chapter 2 that in 2000, 87% of the governments of all the countries in the world regarded HIV as a major concern, and HIV was a major concern among 100% of the governments of countries in the LDR.

As shown in Figure 4.27 in Chapter 4, in countries with a high prevalence of HIV, the age-specific mortality curve is different than that seen in other countries, with a peak in the adult ages. This removes income-producing people in the working ages as well as parents of small children.

Estimates of the percentage of the population who are HIV-positive are often a matter of great uncertainty. Most estimates have been based on tests of pregnant women at prenatal clinics with a

TABLE 6.1   UNAIDS Estimates of the Percentage of Persons Aged 15–49 Who Are HIV-Positive, 2001 and 2009

	2001	2009
World	0.8%	0.8%
North America	0.4%	0.5%
United States	0.6%	0.5%
Western and Central Europe	0.2%	0.2%
Eastern Europe and Central Asia	0.4%	0.8%
Russia	0.5%	1.0%
Caribbean	1.0%	1.1%
Central and South America	0.5%	0.5%
East Asia	<0.1%	0.1%
South and South-East Asia	0.4%	0.3%
Thailand	1.7%	1.3%
Middle East and North Africa	0.1%	0.2%
Sub-Saharan Africa	5.9%	5.0%
South Africa	17.1%	17.8%
Botswana	26.3%	24.8%
Lesotho	24.5%	23.6%
Kenya	8.4%	6.3%
Uganda	7.0%	6.5%
Nigeria	3.8%	3.6%
Ghana	2.3%	1.8%

generalization to the population as a whole. Table 6.1 shows UNAIDS estimates of the percentage of people aged 15–49 who were HIV-positive for some world regions and selected countries for 2001 and 2009.[49]

In the world as a whole, there was no change in the percentage who were HIV-positive between 2001 and 2009. There was enormous variation in the prevalence of HIV among world regions. HIV prevalence was especially high in sub-Saharan Africa, especially in countries of Southern Africa, such as South Africa, Lesotho, and Botswana. Countries in East Africa, such as Kenya and Uganda, had lower HIV prevalence rates than Southern Africa countries, and countries in West Africa, such as Nigeria and Ghana, had even lower HIV prevalence.

South Africa is a high-HIV-prevalence country with better data than similar countries. Figure 6.6 shows among pregnant women in South Africa who visited public prenatal clinics the percentage who were HIV-positive in 1990–2011.[50] HIV prevalence increased rapidly from about 1992 to 2004, and then leveled off.

Figure 6.7 shows age-specific death rates by sex for South Africa in 1997 and 2005 for those aged 15–64.[51] The change in the shape of the age-specific mortality schedule is clear, with a large increase in mortality in the younger adult ages.

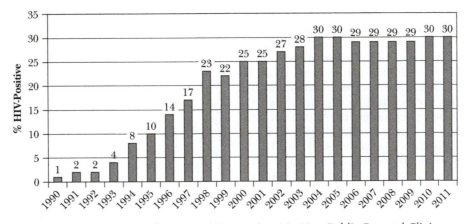

FIGURE 6.6   Percentage of Pregnant Women Age 15–49 at Public Prenatal Clinics in South Africa Who Were HIV-Positive, 1990–2011

The One Health Initiative and the Predict Program

The One Health Initiative is a collaborative effort among physicians, veterinarians, and other health care professionals concerned with the relation between the environment, animals, and human health. As discussed in Chapter 5, there has long been a connection between animal and human health, such as in the transmission of diseases from domestic animals to humans that accompanied the establishment of pastoral nomadism and settled agriculture.

The One Health Initiative was motivated by alarm at emerging infectious diseases and the spread of disease from animals to humans, especially in less developed countries, but also in more developed countries. For example, in 1999, crows in New York City began to die about a month before the West Nile virus outbreak was noticed among humans. The connection was discovered by a veterinarian. The One Health Commission was endorsed by the American Medical Association and the American Veterinary Medical Association in 2007, and there is broad international support for this initiative.[52]

Related to the One Health Initiative, in 2009 the U.S. Agency for International Development (USAID), established the PREDICT program, which was designed to identify and respond to emerging infectious diseases that originated in nonhuman animals.[53]

Maternal Mortality: A Cost of Low Development and High Fertility

Maternal mortality is a cause of concern in much of the world. Not only does it involve the death of a woman in the prime of her life, but also it is very disruptive to the lives of others, including the newborn baby, older children, and other family members. The level of maternal mortality is related both to overall high mortality risks and to high fertility.

The definition of a **maternal death** is as follows:

> The death of a woman while pregnant or within 42 days of termination of pregnancy, irrespective of the duration and site of the pregnancy, from any cause related to or aggravated by the pregnancy or its management but not from accidental or incidental causes.[54]

This definition defines a maternal death as one related to a pregnancy, whether the pregnancy ends in a live birth, a miscarriage, or an induced abortion. As noted in the definition, a maternal death can occur as long as 42 days after the pregnancy ends. However, deaths from causes unrelated to pregnancy and childbirth, such as being hit by a truck a week after a woman has given birth, are not considered maternal deaths.

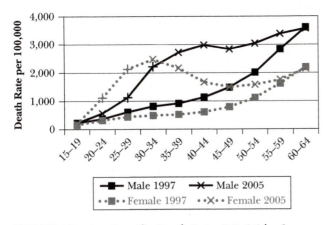

FIGURE 6.7   Age-Specific Death Rates (15–64) by Sex in South Africa, 1997 and 2005

Trends in Maternal Mortality

There are various measures of maternal mortality. Sometimes, the indicator of the level of maternal mortality is the number of maternal deaths per 100,000 women in the childbearing ages, either age 15–44 or age 15–49. More often, measures of maternal mortality are related to the number of births, since without a pregnancy, there cannot be a maternal death. Relating maternal deaths to live births is not ideal, since a pregnancy can end in a miscarriage or an induced abortion and can result in a maternal death. However, reasonable data on the number of miscarriages and on the number of induced abortions are often even less available than data on maternal deaths. One measure of maternal mortality is the **maternal mortality ratio (MMR)**, which is the number of maternal deaths per 100,000 live births.

Figure 6.8 shows estimated maternal mortality ratios in the world, the MDR, the LDR, and the LeastDC in 1990–2008. The MMR declined in every area. In 1990, in the LeastDC, 900 out of every 100,000 live births resulted in a maternal death—almost 1%. The risk of maternal death associated with pregnancy had been almost cut in half by 2008.

The MMR by world region for the years 1990–2008 is shown in Figure 6.9. It decreased between 1990 and 2008, but it was much higher in Africa than in the other regions at every date.

Causes of Maternal Mortality

Data on the cause of maternal deaths are not available for many countries. Khan and his colleagues looked at all the studies that were available in 2006 and estimated the distribution of causes of maternal deaths for developed countries and for regions in the less developed part of the world. Their findings are

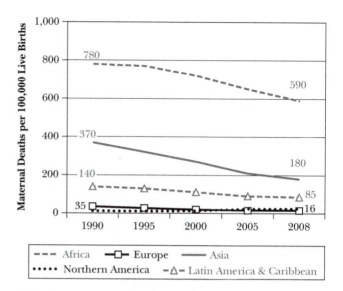

FIGURE 6.9   The Maternal Mortality Ratio in World Regions, 1990–2008

summarized in Table 6.2.[55] The main causes of maternal mortality are hemorrhage, hypertensive disorders, infections, complications of abortion, anemia, obstructed labor, and ectopic pregnancy.

Hemorrhage refers to internal bleeding. Hypertensive disorders result from high blood pressure. Anemia refers to low red blood cell count. Obstructed labor occurs when labor cannot successfully be completed due to the large size of the fetus's head or the small size of the pelvis. Ectopic pregnancy occurs when the embryo implants outside of the uterus. Embolism refers to obstruction of an artery by a foreign substance, such as an air bubble, blood clot, or amniotic fluid.

Some causes of maternal death are related to inadequate health care during labor and delivery, especially hemorrhage, infections, abortion, and obstructed labor.[56] These causes comprise a larger portion of all maternal deaths in less developed countries than in more developed countries. One cause of anemia is hemorrhage, so maternal mortality from anemia is sometimes due to inadequate medical care. Women who are HIV-positive are more prone than other women to infections, so HIV-related maternal mortality also is sometimes due to inadequate medical care.

Hypertensive disorders are generally not related to inadequate labor and delivery care, although they can be related to inadequate prenatal care. Ectopic pregnancies virtually never result in a live birth, and dealing successfully with them can require a high degree of medical expertise. Embolisms associated with labor and delivery can be unpredictable and difficult to deal with even with excellent medical care.

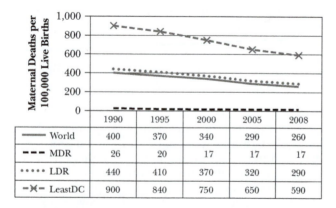

	1990	1995	2000	2005	2008
— World	400	370	340	290	260
- - - MDR	26	20	17	17	17
••••• LDR	440	410	370	320	290
-✕- LeastDC	900	840	750	650	590

FIGURE 6.8   The Maternal Mortality Ratio in the World, MDR, LDR, and LeastDC, 1990–2008

TABLE 6.2   Distribution of Causes of Maternal Deaths by Region, 2006

	Developed Countries	Africa	Asia	Latin America and Caribbean	Related to Inadequate Labor and Delivery Care
Hemorrhage	13	34	31	21	Yes
Hypertensive disorders	16	9	9	26	Sometimes
Infections	2	10	12	8	Yes
Complications of abortion	8	4	6	12	Yes
Obstructed labor	0	4	9	13	Yes
Anemia	0	4	13	0	Sometimes
HIV	0	6	0	0	Sometimes
Ectopic pregnancy	5	1	0	1	Not usually
Embolism	15	2	0	1	Not usually
Other causes	41	27	20	19	
Total	100	100	100	100	

HIV and Maternal Mortality

Especially in less developed countries, women who are HIV-positive have an elevated risk of maternal mortality.[57] Figure 6.10 shows age-specific maternal mortality rates in South Africa in 1997 and in 2004.[58] These rates relate the number of maternal deaths to the number of women by age rather than to the number of live births. In 1997, 17% of pregnant women at public clinics in South Africa were HIV-positive, while in 2004 30% of pregnant women at public clinics were HIV-positive.

When a pregnant woman is HIV-positive, it can increase her risk of maternal death through several mechanisms. People who are HIV-positive are very susceptible to complications or death from infections, including infections that are minor in persons who are not HIV-positive. Pregnancy and delivery can increase that stress. Being HIV-positive also increases susceptibility to and the negative consequences of illnesses such as malaria and TB. HIV also can increase the risk of hemorrhage and anemia. Antiretroviral medications can improve the health of all

HIV-positive persons, including pregnant women, and thus reduce the risk of maternal death.[59]

Changing Pregnancy, Childbirth, and Infant Practices

Childbirth is a dangerous time for the baby as well as for the mother. Nutrition and health in infancy and childhood also can influence the child's later health, ability to learn, and ability to take a role as a productive member of society. Thus, practices around childbirth and decisions about childhood feeding are important for the survival and welfare of children. Especially important have been medical attendance at birth, oral rehydration therapy to combat diarrhea, breastfeeding, and child nutrition.

We saw in Tables 5.2 and 5.6 in Chapter 5 that prematurity and low birth weight, birth trauma and birth asphyxia, neonatal infections, and diarrhea were very important causes of death and disability in low-income countries. We also saw in Tables 5.9 and 5.10 that in low-income countries, suboptimal breastfeeding, and childhood underweight were important risk factors for death and disability.

There is a nexus of considerations around infant feeding practices. Breastfeeding promotes child survival and reduces the chance of diarrhea, but sometimes there is pressure not to breastfeed, and often poor substitutes for breast milk are used. Diarrhea, whether due to lack of breastfeeding or for some other reason, is a major cause of infant and child death and illness. Even when infants and young children survive, poor overall health, inadequate nutrition, and parasitism can contribute to stunting—children being very underweight for age. While infant mortality has declined fairly rapidly throughout the world, we see a much slower decline in the percentage of children who are stunted.

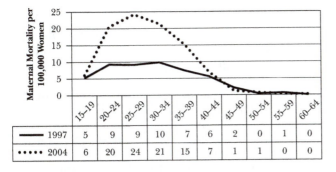

FIGURE 6.10   Maternal Deaths per 100,000 Women in South Africa by Age, 1997 and 2004

Birth Attendance and Neonatal Tetanus

Whether a birth is medically attended and the qualifications of the birth attendant can be very important to the survival of the mother and the baby. One cause of infection and infant death is neonatal tetanus, which is caused when the umbilical cord is cut by an unsanitary knife. In 2001, 30% of the births in the least developed countries were not medically attended. A major way that neonatal tetanus has been attacked is by giving the pregnant woman two doses of medication to immunize her against tetanus during her first pregnancy and one dose in each subsequent pregnancy. This protects both the mother and the newborn.

There has been substantial progress in reducing deaths from neonatal tetanus. In 1988, almost 790,000 newborn babies died from neonatal tetanus. By 2008, there were fewer than 60,000 deaths from neonatal tetanus. In 2000, there were neonatal tetanus deaths in 57 countries; in 2011, there were still neonatal tetanus deaths in 39 countries.[60]

Breastfeeding and Human Milk Substitutes

Breast milk is a high-protein, healthful source of nutrition for infants. Exclusive breastfeeding can protect children from diarrhea in a setting where clean water and easily digestible proteins are not readily available. There is a great deal of evidence that breast milk is the best protein source for infants and that it reduces the chances of death, diarrhea, and infections.[61]

One effect of Western cultural influences has been to make some women in developing countries think that breastfeeding is not "modern." A **human milk substitute** is any substance fed to a baby in place of breast milk. High-quality human milk substitutes (formula) often are not readily available, tend to be expensive, and need to be mixed with clean water in order to be safe. All of these pose substantial problems. Sometimes mothers mix water with corn starch to feed their babies because it looks like milk, even though corn starch has almost no nutritional value.

In the 1970s, the Nestlé Company was accused of promoting the use of formula in developing countries and discouraging breastfeeding. This led to a major campaign against that company. A boycott of Nestlé Company products began in 1977 and lasted into the early 1980s.[62]

UNICEF has recommended exclusive breastfeeding, which is defined as the use of breast milk as the only food for an infant for the first 6 months of life. Besides protecting the child from contaminated food or water, breast milk stimulates the infant's immune system and reduces the chance of diarrhea and acute respiratory infections. The percentage of babies under 6 months of age who were exclusively breastfed in the developing world increased from 34% to 41%

between 1990 and 2004. In sub-Saharan Africa, there was an increase from 15% to 32% in the same time period.[63]

Infant Death, Breastfeeding, and HIV

Decisions about breastfeeding by HIV-positive mothers involve trade-offs. Without the use of drugs to lessen the transmission of HIV from an HIV-positive mother to her infant, about one-third of babies are HIV-positive, which means that about two-thirds of babies born to an HIV-positive mother are HIV-negative.[64] Since the late 1990s, nevirapine, an antiretroviral drug, was found to reduce the chance of HIV transmission during labor and birth by about 50%, and since then more effective combinations of antiretroviral drugs have been developed to help pregnant women and their babies.

It is known that HIV can be transmitted to a baby through breast milk. For a time, the World Health Organization recommended that HIV-positive mothers not breastfeed their infants. But whether that is the best recommendation depends on whether the alternative to breastfeeding would be (1) high-quality formula prepared with clean water or (2) unclean water and a not very nutritious human milk substitute.

WHO has recommended that HIV-positive pregnant women, like all HIV-positive persons, receive antiretroviral therapy (ART) when their CD4 count (which indicates the strength of the immune system) falls below a certain value. In 2009, WHO recommended that HIV-positive pregnant women undergoing ART treatment breastfeed their infants for 12 months. One reason for this recommendation was that WHO became convinced that the ART treatment of the mother provided substantial protection against transmission of HIV to the baby through breast milk. However, in actual circumstances, even without ART treatment, there is a judgment to be made whether the infant of an HIV-positive woman is in more danger from breastfeeding or from using a human milk substitute, depending on the availability of clean water and of nutritious formula.[65]

As of April 2012, South Africa recommended exclusive breastfeeding of all infants for the first 6 months, whether or not the mother is HIV-positive. Earlier the South African government provided free formula to HIV-positive mothers, but this policy was scheduled for termination. The argument of the South African government was that the very low percentage of babies under 6 months of age in South Africa who were exclusively breastfed (8%) contributed to high infant mortality, and that the increased risk of death from diarrhea and pneumonia of formula-fed babies more than outweighs the risk of HIV transmission through breast milk when the mothers are receiving ART. Those opposed to

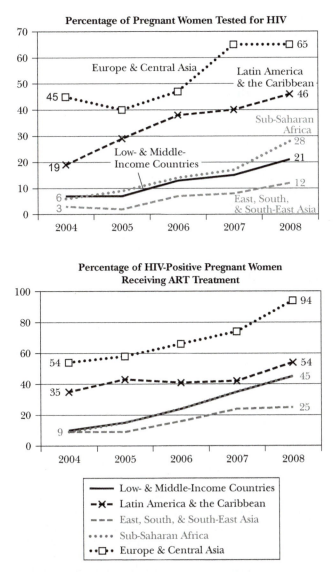

FIGURE 6.11 Testing and Treatment of Pregnant Women in Low- and Middle-Income Countries for HIV, 2004–2008

the change, which include many in the academic and medical community, were concerned that HIV-positive mothers could breastfeed even when they were not receiving ART treatment, thus risking that their babies would become HIV-positive.[66]

The testing of pregnant women for HIV and treatment of HIV-positive pregnant women with ART have increased rapidly, as indicated in Figure 6.11, which refers to low- and middle-income countries. However, even though Table 6.1 showed the highest HIV prevalence in sub-Saharan Africa, the extent of HIV testing and of ART treatment of pregnant women in sub-Saharan African falls below that in the low-income and middle-income parts of Europe and Central Asia and of Latin America and the Caribbean. However, among HIV-positive pregnant women the same percentage

receive ART treatment in sub-Saharan Africa and in low- and middle-income countries as a whole.[67]

Diarrhea, Dehydration, Giving Liquids, and Oral Rehydration Therapy

Diarrheal diseases are the third leading cause of death in low-income countries, as indicated in Table 5.2 in Chapter 5. Diarrhea is defined as three or more loose or liquid stools per day, or more frequent passage than is normal for the person. Diarrhea mainly affects children under age 2, and in 2009 diarrhea was estimated as the second leading cause of death in children under age 5. When an infant has diarrhea, the cause of death usually is dehydration. Diarrhea usually indicates an infection in the intestinal tract, which can be caused by bacteria, viruses, or parasites.[68]

Many mothers in less developed countries believe that when a child has diarrhea, food and liquids, including water, should be withheld or limited. In Haiti in the early 1980s, it was reported that diarrhea was the cause of 50% of all infant deaths and 40% of all deaths to children under age 5.[69] It is important to convince mothers and other caregivers not to withhold liquids from a diarrhetic child. A study in rural Ethiopia in the late 1980s found that 73% of mothers thought that high fluid intake worsened diarrhea, and 69% thought that a diarrhetic child should be given only water.[70] Malnourished children are more susceptible to diarrhea, and withholding of food from a diarrhetic child can contribute to malnutrition, further worsening the child's health and prospects for recovery.

When a child has diarrhea, he or she loses not just water but also essential minerals and salts. If these lost salts are not replenished, the child can die. A major oral rehydration program was begun in 1979 and has spread quickly in less developed countries. This was called **oral rehydration therapy (ORT)** and sometimes was called oral rehydration salts (ORS). It is estimated that in all developing countries in the early 1990s, 40% of children with diarrhea received ORT, while by 2000 69% of diarrhetic children in developing countries received ORT.[71]

In this program, diarrhetic, dehydrated children are brought to a health center where they are given water that has been supplemented with mineral salts to replace the salts lost due to diarrhea. Mothers are often given packets of salts to continue to mix with water and administer to the child after leaving the clinic or to administer to the child in the future if he or she again becomes diarrhetic. Education about the causes of diarrhea and about how to administer the salt-enriched water has been found to improve the behavior of mothers with diarrhetic children, but older mothers tend to administer less ORT liquid, and many mothers remain confused about how ORT should be administered even after some training.[72]

Beliefs about Childhood Nutrition and Stunting

There are sometimes beliefs about proper ways to feed children that are harmful to health. For example, among some groups there was a belief that children should not be fed eggs. Eggs are a good source of protein for children and are easier to digest than other sources of protein that are often available such as groundnuts (peanuts). The source of this belief is that it was important to develop a good character in a child. Eggs were expensive, and it was thought that feeding a child eggs would make the child become a thief or develop bad habits.[73]

A child is considered **stunted** when his or her weight for age is less than would be found for 95% of healthy children of that age according to the World Health Organization Standards. In developed countries, about 6% of children under age 5 are stunted by this definition, slightly higher than the 5% that would be found by chance alone.

Figure 6.12 shows estimates of the percentage of preschool children who were stunted in 1990–2010 in the LDR and in regions of the LDR in 1990–2010.[74] In the LDR as a whole, the percentage of preschool children who were stunted declined by 2010 to two-thirds of the 1990 value. In Asia (excluding Japan) and in Latin American and the Caribbean, there was also a substantial decline in the percentage of children who were stunted. Africa shows a very different pattern. There was essentially no change in the percentage of African children who were stunted between 1990 and 2010.

The lagging of Africa behind other LDR regions in reduction of stunting is similar to the slower decline in the IMR in Africa than in other LDR regions.

Changing Lifestyles in Less Developed Countries

People in the LDR have adopted many MDR behaviors that contribute to death and disability. Increased use of tobacco and alcohol, increased consumption of fatty foods, and increased fatalities from motor vehicle accidents are all behaviors adopted from the MDR that have slowed mortality decline.[75]

These changing behaviors are a major contributor to death and disability in less developed countries. We saw in Table 5.2 in Chapter 5 that diabetes is the tenth leading cause of death in middle-income countries. Also we saw in Table 5.5 that alcohol problems are the fourth leading cause of years of life disabled in low-income and middle-income countries considered together and are the eighth leading cause of DALYs in middle-income countries. Alcohol use is the leading risk factor for loss of life and years disabled in middle-income countries and the eighth leading risk factor for low-income countries (see Table 5.10). The more severe impact of alcohol use in middle-income countries than in low-income countries is consistent with the view that alcohol consumption is an increasingly serious problem in less developed countries. We saw in Table 5.9 that smoking is the second leading risk factor for death in middle-income countries and the seventh leading risk factor in low-income countries. We saw in Table 5.2 that motor vehicle accidents are the sixth leading cause of death in middle-income countries and in Table 5.6 that motor vehicle accidents are the fourth leading cause of DALYs in middle-income countries.

Some less developed countries, including India, have launched antismoking campaigns.[76] This is a difficult effort, since governments collect a substantial amount from cigarette taxes. Also, as the proportion of adults who smoke has declined in many more developed countries, tobacco companies have increasingly turned their attention to less developed countries, where they have fought against restrictive legislation on the sale and advertising of tobacco products.[77]

Diabetes in Nauru and in South Africa

Fatty food and less physical activity have led to increasing problems from overweight in the LDR. The rising levels of type II diabetes in Nauru and in South Africa illustrate this phenomenon.[78]

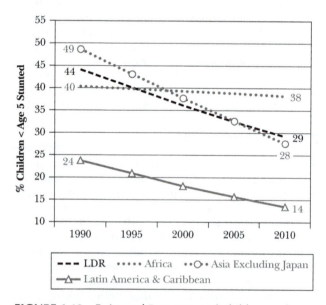

FIGURE 6.12 Estimated Percentage of Children under Age 5 in Less Developed Regions Who Are Stunted, 1990–2010

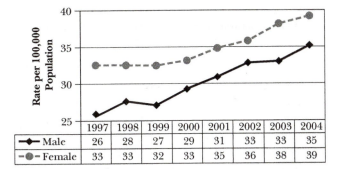

FIGURE 6.13   Age-Adjusted Death Rates from Diabetes and Obesity in South Africa

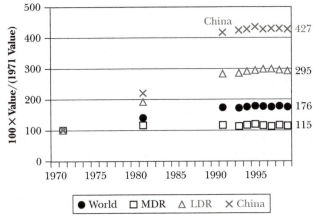

FIGURE 6.14   Cigarette Consumption Relative to Consumption in 1971, 1971–1999

Nauru is an island nation slightly south of the equator and northeast of Australia. It has an area of 8.1 square miles and in 2000 had a population of less than 12,000. In the Pacific Islands, type II diabetes was unknown before World War II. In 2009, 50% of adults on Nauru had type II diabetes.

In South Africa, type II diabetes also has become an increasing problem. Figure 6.13 shows age-adjusted death rates from diabetes and obesity in South Africa for people aged 15–64.[79] The rates have been increasing for each sex. At every date, the female rate is higher than the male rate, although the sex differential narrowed since 2000.

In some African cultures, a woman being obese is a mark of health and of wealth. A man can see a fat wife as an indicator of his prosperity, since he is able to afford for his wife to be well fed.[80] A nickname for HIV is "slim," because HIV leads to weight loss. Thus, in high-HIV-prevalence countries, being fat is sometimes seen as an indicator that you are not HIV-positive.

A survey in South Africa in 1998 found that 49% of White women were overweight or obese, and 59% of African women were overweight or obese. However, while 54% of all White women perceived themselves as overweight or obese, only 15% of all African women perceived themselves as overweight or obese.[81] It is difficult to convince people to undertake activities, such as changing their diet or exercising to lose weight, if they don't think there is any problem with their weight.

Tobacco Use in Less Developed Countries

Cigarette consumption has increased in many less developed countries. One reason is that as more and more developed countries have required warnings against smoking and implemented smoking bans, tobacco companies have shifted their attention to the LDR.

Figure 6.14 shows thousands of tons of cigarette consumption through 1999 relative to cigarette consumption in 1971.[82] In 1999 cigarette consumption

in the MDR was 1.15 times its level in 1971, while in the LDR it had increased to 2.95 times the 1971 level, and in China it had more than quadrupled. The increase in tobacco use in the LDR indicates that the efforts by tobacco companies to increase consumption in the LDR have been successful.[83]

Lopez and his colleagues proposed a model of the stages of the tobacco epidemic, which was elaborated by Esson and Leeder for application to less developed countries.[84] This model is shown in Figure 6.15. The percentage of adults who are smokers is indicated on the left-hand axis, and the percentage of deaths due to smoking is indicated on the right-hand axis.

In Stage 1, smoking is rare, but it increases, especially among men. Only a small percentage of deaths are due to smoking. This stage typifies much

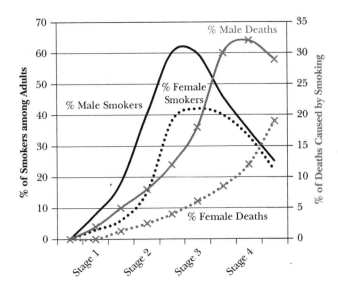

FIGURE 6.15   Stages of the Tobacco Epidemic

of sub-Saharan Africa. In Stage 2, smoking increases, more rapidly among men than women. It often takes 20 years of smoking to lead to death, so although the percentage of deaths due to smoking is higher than in Stage 1, it still is relatively low. This stage typifies China, Japan, much of Latin America, and North Africa. In Stage 3, the percentage of smokers among both men and women reaches a maximum. Smoking starts to decline, more rapidly among men than women. However, the percentage of deaths due to smoking increases rapidly for both sexes due to earlier smoking behavior. This stage typifies the situation in Eastern and Southern Europe and in some parts of Latin America. In Stage 4, the percentage of smokers among both sexes continues to decline, and the gap between the percentage of men who smoke and the percentage of women who smoke becomes small. The percentage of male deaths due to smoking begins to decline, while the percentage of female deaths due to smoking continues to increase. The United States is in Stage 4.

Alcohol Consumption in Less Developed Countries

Alcohol consumption has risen in less developed countries in recent years.[85] Table 6.3 shows estimated per capita alcohol consumption in liters of pure alcohol by income levels of countries in 2005. The higher the income level of countries, the higher the per capita alcohol consumption. However, there are more negative health consequences of alcohol consumption in low- and middle-income countries, partly due to lesser resistance to infection and disease.[86]

Motor Vehicle Accidents in Less Developed Countries

The number of motor vehicles in less developed countries has increased rapidly. Even though motor vehicles are less common in low- or middle-income countries than in high-income countries, the risk of death from a motor vehicle accident is greater in low- or middle-income countries, as shown in Table 6.4, based on regions for which data are available.[87] Also, within each region that included both high-income

TABLE 6.3 Liters of Alcohol Consumed Annually per Adult by Income Level, 2005

Income Group of Country	World	Low Income	Lower-Middle Income	Upper-Middle Income	High Income
Per capita liters of alcohol consumed annually	6.1	3.0	4.4	9.5	10.6

TABLE 6.4 Death Rates from Motor Vehicle Accidents per 100,000 Population, by Income Level and Region, 2002

Region	Low-Income or Middle-Income Countries	High-Income Countries
All countries in category	20	13
Africa	28	—
Americas	16	15
South-East Asia	19	—
Europe	17	11
Eastern Mediterranean	26	19
Western Pacific	19	12

countries and low- or middle-income countries, the death rates were lower in the high-income countries.

There are several sources of high death rates from motor vehicle accidents in low- and middle-income countries, including poorly designed and maintained roads and vehicles, inadequate safety standards for vehicles, poor driver and pedestrian education, and drinking while driving. In addition, inadequate emergency medical services and inadequate trauma care contribute to deaths from motor vehicle accidents.

Vulnerability to New Diseases in Less Developed Countries and the Double Burden of Mortality

There is concern that as infectious and parasitic diseases such as measles and malaria continue to be problems in many less developed countries, the health behaviors just discussed, especially alcohol, tobacco, and fatty foods, that were adopted from the MDR contribute to poor health in the LDR and compound mortality risks. This is sometimes referred to as the **double burden of mortality** in developing countries as death rates from non-communicable diseases increase, while death rates from communicable diseases remain fairly high. Recall that in the Global Burden of Disease estimates shown in Table 5.2, both causes related to poverty, low development and infectious and parasitic causes (such as diarrheal diseases and malaria), and non-communicable diseases (such as ischemic heart disease and stroke) were among the ten leading causes of death in low-income countries. This is an illustration of the double burden of disease at work.[88]

Gwatkin argued in 1980 that if people in the LDR are not very healthy, they are very vulnerable to any new diseases that come along.[89] Poor nutrition makes people vulnerable to new diseases and also increases the chance they will die from existing diseases. Also, alcohol and smoking weaken a poorly nourished and unhealthy person more than a healthier person.

The increased vulnerability to disease and death of those who are unhealthy, whether from poor nutrition, parasitism, or some other cause, is one of the ways in which poverty in many forms contributes to disability and death. There also has been increasing concern about new infectious diseases that have become more prominent in the face of the growing antibiotic resistance of many diseases.[90]

Chagas disease is one infectious disease that could pose an increasing threat to human health. It is mainly found in Central and South America and is transmitted to humans by the bite of a blood-sucking insect that often carries the parasite. Within 4 weeks after the person is bitten, the infection site can become swollen, but sometimes there are no symptoms. Mild early symptoms usually disappear by 8 weeks after infection. Ten years or longer after infection, 10–40% of infected persons show serious digestive or heart problems, such as chronic cardiac disease. There are medications to treat Chagas disease that are effective in over 60% of patients, but these medications are most effective if administered within 2 months of infection. However, many infected persons do not know they are infected until many years later, when serious symptoms develop. Chagas disease has spread to countries outside of Latin America by immigrants, many of whom did not know they were infected.[91]

There continues to be concern about new human diseases that are transmitted from animals. The most common form of HIV, HIV-1, was probably transmitted from chimpanzees or gorillas to humans in the late nineteenth or early twentieth century, probably when the blood of an infected animal got into the wound of the hunter or during meat preparation.[92] It is suspected that diseases often jump from one species to another when meat, especially the brains of wild animals, is consumed without adequate cooking.[93]

Sometimes authorities claim something is a new disease in order to lessen their responsibility. A case of this is described in Box 6.1.[94]

Violence, Crop Failure, Extreme Weather, and Climate Change

In recent times, there also have been mortality crises, and some think that such crises will become more frequent in the future. Next we discuss crises related to the war in Bangladesh, extreme weather, and climate change.

Bangladesh in the Early 1970s

Bangladesh in the early 1970s is an example of when a natural disaster and war combined to cause a mortality crisis. In November 1970, a hurricane, which is also called a tropical cyclone, hit East Pakistan. At that time, East and West Pakistan were parts of the same country. The hurricane killed about half a million people and may have been the worst natural disaster to that point in the twentieth century. There had been political conflicts between East and West Pakistan, and perceptions in East Pakistan of inadequate government response to the natural disaster further exacerbated the situation. A liberation war broke out in March 1971 and ended in December 1971. There was extensive loss of life among both combatants and civilians. In the war, India and West Pakistan fought against East Pakistan. At the end of the war, East Pakistan became an independent country, Bangladesh.[95]

Figure 6.16 shows the expectation of life at birth by sex and the infant mortality rate in Bangladesh in 1950–2010. Expectation of life at birth is indicated on the left-hand axis. In 1970–1975, both male expectation of life at birth fell by 18 years and female expectation of life at birth fell by 9 years. The greater dip in male than female expectation of life at birth was likely because men tended to be combatants in the war. Also note in Figure 5.12 that male expectation of life at birth was higher than female expectation of life at birth in every 5-year period during 1950–1990 except for the crisis period in 1970–1975. Male and female expectation of life at birth were equal in 1990–2005, and female expectation of life

BOX 6.1

Child Deaths in Panama in 2007—New Infectious Disease or Result of Malnutrition?

Sometimes what is reported as the result of a new infectious disease turns out to be something much more mundane.

In 2007, Panama reported that 10 children in a poor area of Panama had died from a "mystery respiratory illness." A UNICEF official in Panama said that the children died from an infectious disease that occurs every year in poor areas of the mountains, but that the children died rather than just becoming ill because of the effects of malnutrition.

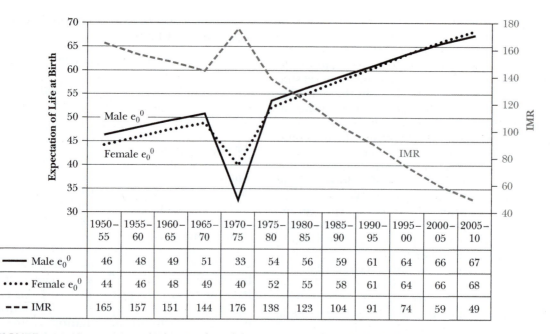

FIGURE 6.16   Expectation of Life at Birth and the IMR in Bangladesh, 1950–2010

	1950–55	1955–60	1960–65	1965–70	1970–75	1975–80	1980–85	1985–90	1990–95	1995–00	2000–05	2005–10
— Male e_0^0	46	48	49	51	33	54	56	59	61	64	66	67
••••• Female e_0^0	44	46	48	49	40	52	55	58	61	64	66	68
– – – IMR	165	157	151	144	176	138	123	104	91	74	59	49

at birth was higher than male expectation of life at birth in 2005–2010. The shift from a male advantage to a female advantage in expectation of life at birth over time is similar to what was shown for India in Figure 4.32.

The infant mortality rate is indicated on the right-hand axis. The IMR spiked in 1970–1975. Infants likely died due to the hurricane, disease, and lack of food related to the aftermath of the hurricane and the war.

Extreme Weather and Climate Change

Extreme weather events can affect mortality whether due to climate change or some other cause. Sometimes extreme heat leads to deaths of otherwise healthy people. However, often mortality rates increase among the frail and the elderly, who might have died in a short time in the absence of a heat wave. Young children and those with other illnesses also are susceptible to dying during heat waves.

An **excess death** is a death that occurred due to some extraordinary event, such as a heat wave or a hurricane, which would not have occurred under normal circumstances. The impact of an extreme weather event is sometimes assessed by estimating the number of excess deaths due to the event. In the Chicago heat wave of July 1995, there were at least 700 excess deaths. Those who were bedridden or lived alone were especially vulnerable.[96] In the French heat wave of August 2003, it was estimated

that there were about 15,000 excess deaths, especially among elderly persons. During a French heat wave in August 2012, authorities warned people to drink fluids and checked on elderly persons living alone, in an attempt to avoid a repeat of what happened in 2003.[97]

The likely implications of global warming include an increase in average temperature, an increase in minimal temperature, changes in average rainfall, sea level rises, and increases in the frequency of extreme weather events. Many of these changes have disease and mortality implications.[98] More frequent extreme weather events, especially extreme heat, can increase excess deaths such as occurred in Chicago and France. Increased average temperature and increased minimal temperature can affect the geographic extent of many parasitic diseases, including malaria, dengue fever, and yellow fever (which are transmitted by mosquitoes); Lyme disease (which is transmitted by ticks); and West African river blindness (which is transmitted by black flies). There is evidence that warmer winter temperatures have led to greater incidence and an expanded geographic range of tick-borne viral encephalitis in Sweden.[99] There is some evidence that increasing temperatures have already led to higher malaria incidence in East Africa, although this is somewhat controversial.[100] Increased rainfall and sea level rises can increase the frequency and severity of floods, which increases the risk from waterborne diseases, such as cholera.

Millennium Development Goals and Mortality Reduction

A set of **Millennium Development Goals (MDGs)** in eight areas was adopted at a conference in New York in 2000. These goals referred to social, population, and health conditions in less developed countries. A pledge was made by 193 countries to seek to attain these goals by 2015.[101] The eight areas and the target foci are as follows:

1. **Goal 1: Eradicate Extreme Poverty and Hunger**

    Target 1A: Halve the proportion of people living on less than $1 a day

    Target 1B: Achieve decent employment for women, men, and young people

    Target 1C: Halve the proportion of people who suffer from hunger

2. **Goal 2: Achieve Universal Primary Education**

    Target 2A: Assure all children—boys and girls—a full course of primary education

3. **Goal 3: Promote Gender Equality and Empower Women**

    Target 3A: Eliminate gender disparity in primary and secondary education and then in tertiary education

4. **Goal 4: Reduce Child Mortality Rates**

    Target 4A: Reduce by two-thirds, between 1990 and 2015, the under-5 mortality rate

5. **Goal 5: Improve Maternal Health**

    Target 5A: Reduce by three-quarters, between 1990 and 2015, the maternal mortality ratio

    Target 5B: Achieve, by 2015, universal access to reproductive health

6. **Goal 6: Combat HIV, Malaria, and Other Diseases**

    Target 6A: Have halted by 2015 and begun to reverse the spread of HIV

    Target 6B: Achieve, by 2010, universal access to treatment for HIV for all those who need it

    Target 6C: Have halted by 2015 and begun to reverse the incidence of malaria and other major diseases

7. **Goal 7: Ensure Environmental Sustainability**

    Target 7A: Integrate the principles of sustainable development into country policies and programs; reverse loss of environmental resources

    Target 7B: Reduce biodiversity loss, achieving, by 2010, a significant reduction in the rate of loss

    Target 7C: Halve, by 2015, the proportion of the population without sustainable access to safe drinking water and basic sanitation (for more information, see the entry on water supply)

    Target 7D: By 2020, to have achieved a significant improvement in the lives of at least 100 million slum dwellers

8. **Goal 8: Develop a Global Partnership for Development**

    Target 8A: Develop further an open, rule-based, predictable, nondiscriminatory trading and financial system

    Target 8B: Address the special needs of least developed countries

    Target 8C: Address the special needs of landlocked developing countries and small island developing states

    Target 8D: Deal comprehensively with the debt problems of developing countries

All of the goals deal directly or indirectly with mortality. Some of the goals address fertility or migration. Goals 4, 5, and 6 concern child mortality, maternal mortality, and deaths from specific diseases. Goal 2 regarding education and Goal 3 regarding gender equality concern some of the main causes of reductions in infant and child mortality—education of the mother. Goal 1 concerns poverty, which affects mortality in a variety of ways, and malnutrition, a cause of childhood mortality and poor health. Target 7C concerns water quality and sanitation, important causes of infant and child mortality.

Goal 5 relates directly to fertility. Goal 7, especially 7D, deals with urbanization, as the main focus of that target is urban slum dwellers. Goals 1, 2, 3, and 7C address directly some of the causes of fertility levels. Goal 8 is clearly in the area of politics, but development is certainly related to mortality, fertility, and migration.

Goals are set for individual countries, and new goals overall and by country are set every 5 years. This gives a way of assessing progress and serves to encourage governments to make explicit efforts in these areas. According to the MDG 2010 report, good progress has been made in most areas.[102]

CONCLUDING COMMENTS

The mortality declines in the LDR since World War II are remarkable. However, poverty still results in high maternal and infant and child mortality in some parts of the world. As smoking, alcohol use, and consumption of fatty foods increase, and as there become more motor vehicles, people in the LDR face a new set of causes of death at the same time that mortality from communicable diseases remains elevated

in some regions. HIV was a shock to the populations of LDR countries, especially in sub-Saharan Africa. It is unknown whether new infectious diseases will develop that will inflict comparable shocks in the future.

✅ Study and Review Online

SUMMARY

1. Technology and medical advances in the more developed countries have been important in mortality declines in the LDR.
2. Many of the programs to reduce mortality have required little action on the part of the individuals and families that benefit.
3. The education of the mother has been one of the most important factors in reduction of infant and child mortality. There is a variety of mechanisms through which mother's education can be important.
4. Development of flu vaccine is complicated and involves some guesses about the nature and the virulence of the flu strain that will be important 6 months or more in the future.
5. Suspicion of vaccination programs has depressed vaccination rates in some countries and has allowed a resurgence of polio.
6. Poverty, including unclean water and inadequate sanitation, remains an important cause of

mortality in the LDR, especially of maternal mortality and infant mortality.
7. Death and disability related to non-communicable causes are increasingly related to health behaviors, such as smoking, excessive alcohol consumption, unhealthy diet, and lack of exercise.
8. The less developed countries have adopted many unhealthy behaviors from more developed countries, which has led to increasing mortality from non-communicable causes at the same time that mortality and disability from infectious and parasitic diseases remain fairly high, leading to a "double burden of mortality."
9. War and extreme weather can lead to mortality crises reminiscent of some of the problems in historical Europe.
10. Global warming could lead to greater variation in weather that could have a substantial mortality impact.

KEY TERMS

age-adjusted death rates 180	endemic disease 182	human milk substitute 190
prevalence 180	herd immunity 183	oral rehydration therapy (ORT) 191
case fatality rate 181	free rider 184	stunted 192
parasite 181	HIV 185	double burden of mortality 194
drug-resistant strain of a disease 181	maternal death 187	excess death 196
	maternal mortality ratio (MMR) 188	Millennium Development Goals (MDGs) 197

QUESTIONS FOR DISCUSSION AND REVIEW

1. Mortality declines since World War II have occurred more rapidly than in Europe historically. Why did this happen?
2. Compare the role of medicine and technology in mortality decline in historical Europe and in the LDR.
3. Mortality from many communicable diseases has declined greatly in the LDR since World

War II. Can we expect communicable disease mortality to fall to a very low level in the LDR, or are there reasons to think that might not happen?
4. Some people are concerned that changing health behaviors in less developed countries will lead to increases in death rates. Why are they concerned about this?

NOTES

1. John Caldwell and Peter McDonald. 1982. "Influence of Maternal Education on Infant and Child Mortality: Levels and Causes," *Health Policy and Education*, 2: 251–267.

2. This discussion of mother's education and child survival is based on Karen O. Mason. 1984. *The Status of Women: A Review of Its Relationships to Fertility and Mortality*, New York: Rockefeller Foundation; and on R. Brent K. Wolff. 1993. *Maternal Education and Community Context in Maternal and Child Health Behavior in Nigeria*, Ph.D. dissertation, Department of Sociology, University of Michigan. The first four pathways are based on Wolff's work; see pp. 6–12.

3. John Hobcraft. 1993. "Women's Education, Child Welfare and Child Survival: A Review of the Evidence," *Health Transition Review*, 3: 159–173.

4. Dallas F. S. Fernando. 1985. "Health Statistics in Sri Lanka," in 1985. *Good Health at Low Cost*, ed. Scott B. Halstead, Julia A. Walsh, and Kenneth S. Warren, proceedings of a conference held at the Bellagio Conference Center, Bellagio, Italy, April 29–May 2, New York: Rockefeller Foundation, 21–32, 79–92.

5. C. M. Langford. 1996. "Reasons for the Decline in Mortality in Sri Lanka Immediately after the Second World War: A Re-examination of the Evidence," *Health Transition Review*, 6: 3–23; S. A. Meegama. 1967. "Malaria Eradication and Its Effect on Mortality Levels." *Population Studies*, 21: 207–237; P. Newman. 1965. *Malaria Eradication and Population Growth*, Ann Arbor: School of Public Health, University of Michigan; R. H. Gray. 1974. "The Decline of Mortality in Ceylon and the Demographic Effects of Malaria Control," *Population Studies*, 28: 205–229; and Peter Newman. 1977. "Malaria and Mortality," *Journal of the American Statistical Association*, 72: 257–263.

6. Rachel Carson. 1962. *The Silent Spring*, Boston: Houghton Mifflin.

7. World Health Organization, Global Malaria Programme. 2007. *The Use of DDT in Malaria Vector Control*, WHO Position Statement, http://www.who.int/ipcs/capacity_building/who_statement.pdf (accessed June 17, 2010).

8. WHO. 2007. *The Use of DDT in Malaria Vector Control*, WHO Position Statement, http://www.scribd.com/doc/53116789/The-Use-of-DDT-in-Malaria-Vector-Control-9789241596305 (accessed July 3, 2011).

9. Many examples from South Africa are shown, such as for malaria death rates and maternal mortality death rates, because South Africa has more plentiful and higher quality data than most less developed countries and better data than any other country in Africa. For South Africa, the standard population for the age-adjusted rates is the South African population in 2001.

10. Figure 6.3 is from Barbara A. Anderson and Heston E. Phillips. 2006. *Adult Mortality (Age 15–64) Based on Death Notification Data in South Africa: 1997–2004*, Pretoria: Statistics South Africa, 81.

11. World Health Organization. n.d. "Roll Back Malaria," http://www.rollbackmalaria.org/index.html (accessed January 17, 2012); and WHO. 2011. *Global Plan for Artemisinin Resistance Containment*, Geneva: World Health Organization, http://www.who.int/malaria/publications/atoz/9789241500838/en/ (accessed February 2, 2012).

12. World Health Organization. 2011. *World Malaria Report 2011*, Geneva: WHO, http://www.who.int/malaria/world_malaria_report_2011/en/ (accessed January 26, 2012).

13. Centers for Disease Control and Infection. 2011. *Parasites—Lymphatic Filariasis*, http://www.cdc.gov/parasites/lymphaticfilariasis/ (accessed July 2, 2011); and Kapa D. Ramaiah, Pradeep K. Das, Edwin Michael, and Helen L. Guyatt. 2000. "The Economic Burden of Lymphatic Filariasis in India," *Parasitology Today*, 16: 251–253, http://www.sciencedirect.com/science/article/pii/S0169475800016434 (accessed July 2, 2011).

14. World Health Organization. 2012. *Onchocerciasis (River Blindness)*, http://www.who.int/blindness/partnerships/onchocerciasis_home/en/ (accessed June 6, 2012).

15. Daniel J. Morgan, Iruka N. Okeke, Ramanan Laxminarayan, Eli N. Perencevich, and Scott Weisenberg. 2011. "Non-prescription Antimicrobial Use Worldwide: A Systematic Review," *The Lancet Infectious Diseases*, 11: 692–701; Iruka N. Okeke, Ramanan Laxminarayan, Zulfiqar A. Bhutta, Adriano G. Duse, Philip Jenkins, Thomas F. O'Brien, Ariel Pablos-Mendez, and Keith P. Klugman. 2005. "Antimicrobial Resistance in Developing Countries. Part I: Recent Trends and Current Status," *The Lancet Infectious Diseases*, 5: 481–493; and Iruka N. Okeke, Keith P. Klugman, Zulfiqar A. Bhutta, Adriano G. Duse, Philip Jenkins, Thomas F. O'Brien, Ariel Pablos-Mendez and Ramanan Laxminarayan. 2005. "Antimicrobial Resistance in Developing Countries. Part II: Strategies for Containment," *The Lancet Infectious Diseases*, 5: 568–580.

16. Matteo Zignol, Mehran S. Hosseini, Abigail Wright, Catharina Lambregts–van Weezenbeek, Paul Nunn, Catherine J. Watt, Brian G. Williams, and Christopher Dye. 2006. "Global Incidence

of Multidrug-Resistant Tuberculosis," *Journal of Infectious Diseases*, 194: 479–485; Richard Knox. 2012. "TB That Resists All Drugs Is Found in India," NPR, January 11, http://www.npr.org /blogs/health/2012/01/12/145027086 /a-dozen-cases-of-tuberculosis-that-resists-all -drugs-found-in-india?ps=sh_sthdl (accessed January 12, 2012); and Stephen E. Weis, Philip C. Slocum, Francis X. Blais, Barbara King, Mary Nunn, G. Burgis Matney, Enriqueta Gomez, and Brian H. Foresman. 1994. "The Effect of Directly Observed Therapy on the Rates of Drug Resistance and Relapse in Tuberculosis," *New England Journal of Medicine*, 330: 1179–1184.

17. Laura García-Álvarez, Matthew T. G. Holden, Heather Lindsay, Cerian R. Webb, Derek F. J. Brown, Martin D. Curran, Enid Walpole, Karen Brooks, Derek J. Pickard, Christopher Teale, Julian Parkhill, Stephen D. Bentley, Giles F. Edwards, E. Kirsty Girvan, Angela M. Kearns, Bruno Pichon, Robert L. R. Hill, Anders Rhod Larsen, Robert L. Skov, Sharon J. Peacock, Duncan J. Maskell, and Mark A. Holmes. 2011. "Methicillin-Resistant *Staphylococcus aureus* with a Novel mecA Homologue in Human and Bovine Populations in the UK and Denmark: A Descriptive Study," *The Lancet Infectious Diseases*, 11: 595–603; and Sabrina Tavernese. 2013. "Study Shows Bacteria Moves from Animals to Humans," *New York Times*, March 27.

18. Brad Spellberg, Robert Guidos, David Gilbert, John Bradley, Helen W. Boucher, W. Michael Scheld, John G. Bartlett, John Edwards, Jr., and the Infectious Diseases Society of America. 2008. "The Epidemic of Antibiotic-Resistant Infections: A Call to Action for the Medical Community from the Infectious Diseases Society of America," *Clinical Infectious Diseases*, 46: 155–164.

19. Eili Klein, David L. Smith, and Ramanan Laxminarayan. 2007. "Hospitalizations and Deaths Caused by Methicillin-Resistant *Staphylococcus aureus*, United States, 1999–2005," *Emerging Infectious Diseases*, 13: 1840–1846; and Clare Griffiths, Theresa L. Lamagni, Natasha S. Crowcroft, Georgina Duckworth, and Cleo Rooney. 2004. "Trends in MRSA in England and Wales: Analysis of Morbidity and Mortality Data for 1993–2002," *Health Statistics Quarterly*, 21: 15–22.

20. World Health Organization. 1980. *The Global Eradication of Smallpox*, Geneva: World Health Organization, http://whqlibdoc.who.int /publications/a41438.pdf (accessed September 13, 2011).

21. Pascal Imperato. 1995. "What to Do with the Smallpox Virus?" *Journal of Community Health*, 20: 1–3.

22. A. Dabbagh, M. Gacic-Dobo, L. Wolfson, D. Featherstone, P. Strebel, J.M. Okwo-Bele, E. Hoekstra, P. Salama, S. Wassilak, and A. Uzicanin, 2007. "Progress in Global Measles Control and Mortality Reduction, 2000–2006," *Morbidity & Mortality Weekly Report. 2007*, 56: 1237–1241.

23. World Health Organization. 2011. *Immunization Surveillance, Assessment and Monitoring: Data, Statistics and Graphics by Subject*, http://www .who.int/immunization_monitoring/data /data_subject/en/ (accessed February 3, 2012); and Aryn Baker. 2013. "Pakistani Polio Hits Syria, Proving That No Country Is Safe Until All Are," Time, November 13, http://world.time .com/2013/11/13/pakistani-polio-hits-syria -proving-no-country-is-safe-until-all-are (accessed November 1, 2013).

24. Ayodele Samuel Jegede. 2007. "What Led to the Nigerian Boycott of the Polio Vaccination Campaign?" *PLoS Medicine*, 4(3): e73, http://www.ncbi.nlm.nih.gov/pmc/articles /PMC1831725/ (accessed June 6, 2010).

25. Donald G. McNeil. 2007. "Polio in Nigeria Traced to Mutating Vaccine," *New York Times*, October 11, http://www.nytimes.com/2007/10/11/world /africa/11polio.html (accessed July 31, 2011).

26. Donald G. McNeil, Jr. 2011. "Nigerians Receive First Payments for Children Who Died in 1996 Meningitis Drug Trial," *New York Times*, August 11, http://www.nytimes .com/2011/08/12/world/africa/12nigeria .html?_r=1&scp=10&sq=Africa%20polio&st=cse (accessed September 13, 2011).

27. Integrated Regional Information Networks, UNHCR. 2011. "Nigeria: Jail Threat for Polio Vaccination Refuseniks," August 16, http://www .irinnews.org/report.aspx?reportid=93480 (accessed September 13, 2011).

28. Mark Mazzetti. 2011. "Vaccination Ruse Used in Pursuit of bin Laden," *New York Times*, July 11, http://www.nytimes.com/2011/07/12 /world/asia/12dna.html?_r=1&hp (accessed November 2, 2011); and Matt Bewig. 2012. "198 U.S. Aid Groups Criticize CIA for Using Fake Polio Vaccine Drive to Kill bin Laden," *AllGov*, March 5, http://www.allgov.com /US_and_the_World/ViewNews/198_US_Aid _Groups_Criticize_CIA_for_Using_Fake_Polio _Vaccination_Drive_to_Kill_Bin_Laden_120305 (accessed June 1, 2012).

29. Declan Walsh. 2012. "Taliban Block Vaccinations in Pakistan," *The New York Times*, June 19.

30. Salman Masood and Declan Walsh. 2012. "Gunmen Kill Anti-Polio Workers in Attacks in Pakistan," *New York Times*, December 18, http:// www.nytimes.com/2012/06/19/world/asia/

taliban-block-vaccinations-in-pakistan.html (accessed December 18, 2012).

31. E. J. Gangarosa, A. M. Galazka, C. R. Wolfe, L. M. Phillips, R. E. Gangarosa, E. Miller, and R. T. Chen. 1998. "Impact of Anti-Vaccine Movements on Pertussis Control: the Untold Story," *The Lancet*, 351: 356–361.

32. Thomas May and Ross D. Silverman. 2003. "'Clustering of Exemptions' as a Collective Action Threat to Herd Immunity," *Vaccine*, 21: 1048–1051; and Daniel R. Feikin, Dennis C. Lezotte, Richard F. Hamman, Daniel A. Salmon, Robert T. Chen, and Richard E. Hoffman. 2000. "Individual and Community Risks of Measles and Pertussis Associated with Personal Exemptions to Immunization," *JAMA*, 284: 3145–3150.

33. Trine Tsouderos, Deborah L. Shelton, and Joseph Germuska. 2011. "Low Vaccination Rates in Some Schools Raise Outbreak Risks," *Chicago Tribune*, June 18, http://articles.chicagotribune.com/2011-06-18/health/ct-met-vaccination-rates-schools-20110618_1_measles-vaccinations-vaccination-rates-herd-immunity (accessed September 18, 2011).

34. M. Zia Sadique. 2006. "Individual Freedom versus Collective Responsibility: An Economic Epidemiology Perspective," *Emerging Themes in Epidemiology*, 3, http://www.biomedcentral.com/content/pdf/1742-7622-3-12.pdf (accessed April 14, 2012).

35. A. J. Wakefield, S. H. Murch, A. Anthony, et al. 1998. "Ileal-lymphoid-nodular Hyperplasia, Non-specific Colitis, and Pervasive Developmental Disorder in Children," *Lancet*, 351: 637–641; Brent Taylor, Elizabeth Miller, C. Paddy Farrington, Maria-Christina Petropoulos, Isabelle Favot-Mayaud, Jun Li, and Pauline A Waight. 1999. "Autism and Measles, Mumps, and Rubella Vaccine: No Epidemiological Evidence for a Causal Association," *The Lancet*, 353: 2026–2029; Brian Deer. 2011. "How the Case against the MMR Vaccine Was Fixed," *British Medical Journal*, 342: 77–84; M. B. Pepys. 2007. "Science and Serendipity," *Clinical Medicine*, 7: 562–578; S. H. Murch, A. Anthony, D. H. Casson, M. Malik, A. P. Dhillon, M. A. Thomson, A. Valentine, S. E. Davies, and J. A. Walker-Smith. 2004. "Retraction of an Interpretation." *Lancet*, 363: 824; and Editors of the Lancet. 2010. "Retraction—Ileal-lymphoid-nodular Hyperplasia, Non-specific Colitis, and Pervasive Developmental Disorder in Children," *Lancet*, 375: 445.

36. L. K. Ball, R. Ball, and R. D. Pratt. 2001. "An Assessment of Thimerosal Use in Childhood Vaccines," *Pediatrics*, 107: 1147–1154; E. Forbonne, R. Zakarian, L. Meng, and D. McLean-Heywood. 2006. "Pervasive Developmental Disorders in Montreal, Canada: Prevalence and Links with Immunizations," *Pediatrics*, 118: e139–e150; and Food and Drug Administration. 2010. *Thimerosal in Vaccines*, http://www.fda.gov/BiologicsBloodVaccines/SafetyAvailability/VaccineSafety/UCM096228 (accessed April 12, 2012).

37. "Chile Stops Use of Mercury in Vaccines," *New York Times*, April 3, http://markets.on.nytimes.com/research/stocks/news/press_release.asp?docTag=201204031149PR_NEWS_USPRX____DC81503&feedID=600&press_symbol=103611 (accessed April 12, 2012); Sabrina Tavernise. 2012. "Vaccine Rule Said to Hurt Health Efforts," *New York Times*, December 17, http://www.nytimes.com/2012/12/17/health/experts-say-thimerosal-ban-would-imperil-global-health-efforts.html?hpw&_r=0 (accessed December 18, 2012); and Alyson Sulaski Wyckoff. 2012. "Ban on All Mercury-Based Products Would Risk Global Immunization Efforts, Say AAP, WHO," *American Association of Pediatrics News*, 33: 4.

38. Gary L. Freed, Sarah J. Clark, Amy T. Butchart, Dianne C. Singer, and Matthew M. Davis. 2010. "Parental Vaccine Safety Concerns in 2009," *Pediatrics*, 125: 654–659.

39. Liza Gross. 2009. "A Broken Trust: Lessons from the Vaccine–Autism Wars," *PloS Biology*, 7:, http://www.plosbiology.org/article/info%3Adoi%2F10.1371%2Fjournal.pbio.1000114 (accessed April 10, 2012; and Sharon R. Kaufman. 2010. "Regarding the Rise in Autism: Vaccine Safety Doubt, Conditions of Inquiry and the Shape of Freedom," *Ethos*, 38: 8–32.

40. Gordon Gauchat. 2012. "Politicization of Science in the Public Sphere: A Study of Public Trust in the United States, 1974–2010," *American Sociological Review*, 77: 167–186.

41. Jeffrey K. Taubenberger and David M. Morens. 2006. "1918 Influenza: The Mother of All Pandemics," *Revista Biomedica*, 17: 69–79, http://www.medigraphic.com/pdfs/revbio/bio-2006/bio061i.pdf (accessed September 18, 2011); and Lynnette Iezzoni. 1999. *Influenza 1918: The Worst Epidemic in American History*, New York: TV Books.

42. Gina Kolata. 1999. *Flu*, New York: Farrar, Straus and Giroux.

43. D. J. Sencer and J. D. Millar. 2006. "Reflections on the 1976 Swine Flu Vaccination Program." *Emerging Infectious Diseases*, http://www.cdc.gov/ncidod/EID/vol12no01/05-1007.htm (accessed March 8, 2010).

44. Rama Bhunia, Ramachandran Ramakrishnan, Yvan Hutin, and Mohan D. Gupte. 2009. "Cholera Outbreak Secondary to Contaminated Pipe Water in an Urban Area, West Bengal,

India, 2006," *Indian Journal of Gastroenterology*, 28: 62–64, http://indianjgastro.com/IJG_pdf /march2009/09_March_SR2.pdf (accessed December 6, 2011).

45. Lean Ka-Min. 29000. "User Fees Blamed for Cholera Outbreak in South Africa," Third World Network, October 26, http://www .twnside.org.sg/title/cholera.htm (accessed December 6, 2011).

46. BBC News. 2010. "Haiti: Cholera Slows but Fears of Spread Remain," October 25, http://www.bbc .co.uk/news/world-latin-america-11622523 (accessed December 6, 2011); and Martin Enserink. 2011. "Whole-Genome Study Nails Haiti-Nepal Link," *ScienceNOW*, August 23, http://news .sciencemag.org/sciencenow/2011/08/whole -genome-study-nails-haiti-n.html (accessed December 6, 2011).

47. Palash R. Ghosh. 2011. "Cholera Outbreak at Dadaab Refugee Camp on Somali-Kenya Border," *International Business Times*, November 15, http://www.ibtimes.com /articles/249829/20111115/kenya-somalia -refugee-cholera-camp-dadaab-famine.htm (accessed December 6, 2011).

48. Jeffrey Gettleman. 2012. "Refugee Children Dying at Alarming Rate in South Sudan, Aid Groups Say," *New York Times*, July 6.

49. UNAIDS. 2010. *Global Report: UNAIDS Report on the Global AIDS Epidemic 2010*, Geneva: UNAIDS, http://www.unaids.org/globalreport /documents/20101123_GlobalReport_full _en.pdf (accessed November 9, 2011).

50. South Africa Department of Health. 2012. *The 2011 National Antenatal Sentinel HIV & Syphilis Prevalence Survey in South Africa*, Pretoria: National Department of Health, http://www .doh.gov.za/docs/presentations/2013 /Antenatal_Sentinel_survey_Report2012_final .pdf (accessed April 25, 2013).

51. Based on Barbara A. Anderson and Heston E. Phillips. 2006. *Adult Mortality (Age 15–64) Based on Death Notification Data in South Africa: 1997– 2004*, Pretoria: Statistics South Africa, with data updated to 2005.

52. One Health Initiative. n.d. http://www .onehealthinitiative.com/index.php (accessed June 28, 2012); an Brendan Howard. 2010. "Biosecurity: Where West Nile Started," *DVM Newsmagazine*, October 1, http://veterinarynews .dvm360.com/dvm/Veterinary+news/Biosecurity -Where-West-Nile-started/ArticleStandard /Article/detail/688918 (accessed June 28, 2012).

53. Jim Robbins. 2012. "Man-Made Epidemics," *New York Times*, July 15; and USAID. 2009. *USAID Launches Emerging Pandemic Threats Program*, October 21, http://www1.usaid.gov/press/releases/2009 /pr091021_1.html (accessed July 15, 2012).

54. World Health Organization. 2010. *Trends in Maternal Mortality: 1990 to 2008*, Geneva: WHO, http://whqlibdoc.who.int/publications /2010/9789241500265_eng.pdf (accessed July 11, 2011). The data in Figures 6.8 and 6.9 are also from this source.

55. Khalid S. Khan, Daniel Wojdyla, Lale Say, A. Metin Gulmezoglu, and Paul F. A. Van Look. 2006. "WHO Analysis of Causes of Maternal Death: A Systematic Review," *The Lancet*, 367: 1066–1074.

56. David A. Grimes, Janie Benson, Susheela Singh, Mariana Romero, Bela Ganatra, Friday E. Okonofua, and Iqbal H. Shah. 2006. "Unsafe Abortion: The Preventable Pandemic," *The Lancet*, 368: 1908–1919; Carine Ronsmans, Wendy J. Graham, and on behalf of The Lancet Maternal Survival Series Steering Group. 2006. "Maternal Mortality: Who, When, Where, and Why," *The Lancet*, 368, 1189–1200; and Lisa B. Haddad and Nawal M. 2009. "Unsafe Abortion: Unnecessary Maternal Mortality," *Reviews in Obstetrics & Gynecology*, 2: 122–126.

57. Georgea Bicego, J. Tiesb Boerma, and Carinec Ronsmans. 2002. "The Effect of AIDS on Maternal Mortality in Malawi and Zimbabwe," *AIDS*, 16: 1078–1081.

58. Barbara A. Anderson and Heston E. Phillips. 2006. *Adult Mortality (Age 15–64) Based on Death Notification Data in South Africa: 1997–2004*, Pretoria: Statistics South Africa.

59. James McIntyre. 2003. "Mothers Infected with HIV," *British Medical Bulletin*, 67: 127–135.

60. J. Vandelaer, M. Birmingham, F. Gasse, M. Kurian, C. Shaw, and S. Garnier. 2003. "Tetanus in Developing Countries: An Update on the Maternal and Neonatal Tetanus Elimination Initiative," *Vaccine*, 21: 3442–3445; and WHO, *Maternal and Neonatal Tetanus (MNT) Elimination*, http://www.who.int/immunization _monitoring/diseases/MNTE_initiative/en /index.html# (accessed November 1, 2011).

61. Alan Berg with Robert J. Muscat. 1973. *The Nutrition Factor: Its Role in National Development*, Washington, DC: The Brookings Institution; and UNICEF. 2008. *Breastfeeding*, http://www.unicef .org/nutrition/index_24824.html (accessed December 16, 2011).

62. John Dobbing (Ed.). 1998. *Infant Feeding: Anatomy of a Controversy 1973–1984*, London and Berlin Heidelberg: Springer Verlag.

63. UNICEF. 2006. *Exclusive Breastfeeding*, http:// www.unicef.org/progressforchildren/2006n4 /index_breastfeeding.html (accessed December 16, 2011).

64. UNAIDS. 2002. *Estimating and Projecting National HIV/AIDS Epidemics, The UNAIDS Reference Group on Estimates, Models and Projections,* UNAIDS/01.83.

65. WHO. 2009. *New HIV Recommendations to Improve Health, Reduce Infections and Save Lives,* http://www.who.int/mediacentre/news/releases/2009/world_aids_20091130/en/ (accessed February 2, 2012).

66. Health Systems Trust. 2012. *Breastfeeding, Not Formula, for South Africa's HIV-Positive Mothers,* April, http://www.hst.org.za/news/breastfeeding-not-formula-south-africas-hiv-positive-mothers (accessed April 13, 2012).

67. World Health Organization. 2010. *PMTCT Strategic Vision 2010–2015: Preventing Mother-to-Child Transmission of HIV to Reach the UNGASS and Millennium Development Goals,* Geneva: World Health Organization, http://whqlibdoc.who.int/publications/2010/9789241599030_eng.pdf (accessed June 6, 2012).

68. World Health Organization. 2009. *Diarrhoeal Disease, Fact Sheet No. 330,* http://www.who.int/mediacentre/factsheets/fs330/en/index.html (accessed December 15, 2011).

69. J. Rohde. 1984. "Accepting ORT, Report from Haiti and Swaziland," *Diarrhoea Dialogue Online,* 19: 4–5, http://rehydrate.org/dd/dd19.htm#page4 (accessed December 4, 2011).

70. Petros Olango and Frances Aboud. 1990. "Determinants of Mothers' Treatment of Diarrhea in Rural Ethiopia," *Social Science & Medicine,* 31: 1245–1249.

71. Cesar G. Victora, Jennifer Bryce, Olivier Fontaine, and Roeland Monasch. 2000. "Reducing Deaths from Diarrhoea through Oral Rehydration Therapy," *Bulletin of the World Health Organization,* 78: 1246–1255, http://www.who.int/bulletin/archives/78(10)1246.pdf (accessed November 1, 2011).

72. Paul Touchette, Edward Douglass, Judith Graeff, Ivy Monoang, Mannuku Mathe, and Lisa Ware Deke. 1994. "An Analysis of Home-Cased Oral Rehydration Therapy in the Kingdom of Lesotho," *Social Science & Medicine,* 39: 425–432.

73. Victor B. Meyer-Rochow. 2009. "Food Taboos: Their Origins and Purposes," *Journal of Ethnobiology and Ethnomedicine,* 5: 18–27.

74. Mercedes de Onis, Monika Blössner, and Elaine Borghi. 2011. "Prevalence and Trends of Stunting among Pre-School Children, 1990–2020," *Public Health Nutrition,* 14: 1–7.

75. S. M. Bah. 1993. "Social Pathologies in Zimbabwe," *Central African Journal of Medicine,* 39: 201–213; Shah Ebrahim and George Davey Smith. 2001. "Exporting Failure? Coronary Heart Disease and Stroke in Developing Countries," *International Journal of Epidemiology,* 30: 201–205; N. Gunawardene. 1999. "Sri Lanka's Double Burden Kills Rich and Poor Alike," *Health for the Millions,* 25: 27; A. R. Walker. 1996. "Urbanisation of Developing Populations: What Are the Health/Ill-Health Prospects Regarding the Diseases of Prosperity?" *Urbanisation and Health Newsletter,* 30: 20–22; Prakash Shetty and Josef Schmidhuber. 2011. *Nutrition, Lifestyle, Obesity and Chronic Disease.* Population Division Expert Paper No. 2011/3, New York: United Nations, http://www.un.org/esa/population/publications/expertpapers/2011-3-shetty.pdf (accessed November 6, 2011); Salim Yusuf, Srinath Reddy, Stephanie Ôunpuu, and Sonia Anand. 2001. "Global Burden of Cardiovascular Diseases: Part I: General Considerations, the Epidemiologic Transition, Risk Factors, and Impact of Urbanization." *Circulation,* 104: 2746–2753; Jacob C. Seidell. 2000. "Obesity, Insulin Resistance and Diabetes—A Worldwide Epidemic." *British Journal of Nutrition,* 83 (Suppl. 1): S5–S8; and Alexander R. P. Walker. 1995. "Nutrition-Related Diseases in Southern Africa: With Special Reference to Urban African Populations in Transition," *Nutrition Research,* 15: 1053–1094.

76. Express India. 2008. "Bill Gates Launches Anti-Smoking Campaign, Focus on India," July 24, http://www.expressindia.com/latest-news/Bill-Gates-launches-antismoking-campaign-focus-on-India/339886/ (accessed November 3, 2011).

77. Duff Wilson. 2010. "Cigarette Giants in Global Fight on Tighter Rules," *New York Times,* November 13, http://www.nytimes.com/2010/11/14/business/global/14smoke.html?pagewanted=all (accessed November 3, 2011).

78. Ruth Colagiuri. 2009. "Diabetes in Nauru: The Price of Economic Wealth and Westernization," March, *Diabetes Voice* 54(1), http://www.diabetesvoice.org/en/articles/diabetes-in-nauru-the-price-of-economic-wealth-and-westernization (accessed June 6, 2010).

79. From Barbara A. Anderson and Heston E. Phillips. 2006. *Adult Mortality (Age 15–64) Based on Death Notification Data in South Africa: 1997–2004,* Pretoria: Statistics South Africa, 102.

80. F. C. Venter, C. M. Walsh, M. Slabber, and C. J. Bester. 2009. "Body Size Perception of African Women (25–44 Years) in Manguang," *Journal of Family Ecology and Consumer Sciences,* 37: 12–23.

81. Thandi Puoane, Krisela Steyn, Debbie Bradshaw, Ria Lauscher, Jean Fourie, Vicki Lambert, and Nolwazi Mbananga. 2002. "Obesity in South

Africa: The South African Demographic and Health Survey," *Obesity*, 10: 1038–1048.

82. Food and Agriculture Organization. 2003. *Projections of Tobacco Production, Consumption and Trade to the Year 2010*, Rome: FAO, http://www.fao.org/DOCREP/006/Y4956E/Y4956E00.HTM (accessed January 14, 2012); what is shown is actually relative to average consumption in 1970–1972.

83. TopForeignStocks.com. 2010. *A Review of the Global Tobacco Industry*, http://topforeignstocks.com/2010/11/14/a-review-of-the-global-tobacco-industry/ (accessed February 4, 2012).

84. Alan D. Lopez, Neil E. Collishaw, and Tapani Pha. 1994. "A Descriptive Model of the Cigarette Epidemic in Developed Countries," *Tobacco Control*, 3: 242–247; and Katherine M. Esson and Stephen R. Leeder. 2004. *The Millennium Development Goals and Tobacco Control*, Geneva: World Health Organization.

85. D. H. Jernigan, M. Monteiro, R. Room, and S. Saxena. 2000. "Towards a Global Alcohol Policy: Alcohol, Public Health and the Role of WHO," *Bulletin of the World Health Organization*, 78: 491–499.

86. World Health Organization. 2011. *Global Status Report on Alcohol and Health 2011*, Geneva: WHO, http://www.who.int/substance_abuse/publications/global_alcohol_report/en/ (accessed January 14, 2011).

87. Charles Mock, Olive Kobusingye, Le Vu Anh, Francis Afukaar, and Carlos Arreola-Risa. 2005. "Human Resources for the Control of Road Traffic Injury," *Bulletin of the World Health Organization*, 83: 294–300.

88. Abdesslam Boutayeb. 2006. "The Double Burden of Communicable and Non-Communicable Diseases in Developing Countries," *Transactions of the Royal Society of Tropical Medicine and Hygiene*, 100: 191–199; and Hoang Van Minh, Peter Bypass, and Stig Wall. 2003. "Mortality from Cardiovascular Diseases in Bavi District, Vietnam," *Scandinavian Journal of Public Health*, 31: 26–31.

89. Davidson R. Gwatkin. 1980. "Indications of Change in Developing Country Mortality Trends: The End of an Era?" *Population and Development Review*, 6: 615–644.

90. Ronald Barrett, Christopher W. Kozawa, Thomas McDade, and George J. Armelagos. 1998. "Emerging and Re-emerging Infectious Diseases: The Third Epidemiologic Transition," *Annual Review of Anthropology*, 27: 247–271.

91. Jan H. F. Remme, Piet Feenstra, P. R. Lever, Andre Nedici, Carlos Morel, Mounkaila Noma, K. D. Ramaiah, Frank Richards, A. Seketeli, Gabriel Schumia, W.H. van Brakel, and Anna Vassali. 2006. "Tropical Diseases Targeted for Elimination: Chagas Disease, Lymphatic Filariasis, Onchocerciasis, and Leprosy," in *Disease Control Priorities in Developing Countries*, 2nd ed., ed. Dean T. Jamison, Joel G. Brennan, Anthony R. Measham, George Alleyne, Mariam Claeson, David B. Evans, Prabhat Jha, Anne Mills, and Philip Musgrovw, Washington, DC: World Bank and Oxfords University Press, http://files.dcp2.org/pdf/DCP/DCPFM.pdf (accessed May 29, 2012); and Danold G. McNeil, Jr. 2012. "Stubborn Infection, Spread by Insects, Is Called 'The New AIDS of the Americas,'" *New York Times*, May 29.

92. AVERT. *The Origins of HIV & the First Cases of AIDS*, http://www.avert.org/origin-aids-hiv.htm (accessed January 20, 2012).

93. William B. Karesh and Eric Noble. 2009. "The Bushmeat Trade: Increased Opportunities for Transmission of Zoonotic Disease," *Mount Sinai Journal of Medicine*, 76: 429–434.

94. *New York Times*. 2007. "World Briefing: The Americas; Panama: U.N. Says Mystery Disease Is Malnutrition." October 6, http://query.nytimes.com/gst/fullpage.html?res=9C0CE5DA1639F935A35753C1A9619C8B63 (accessed July 31, 2011).

95. Reuters. 1970. "Disease Increases in Pakistan Area Swept by Cyclone," *New York Times*, November 18; Tillman Durdin. 1971. "Pakistanis Crisis Virtually Halts Rehabilitation in Cyclone Region," *New York Times*, March 12; and Muniel Islam. 1992. "Natural Calamities and Environmental Refugees in Bangladesh," *Refuge*, 12: 5–10, https://pi.library.yorku.ca/ojs/index.php/refuge/article/view/21639/20312 (accessed October 11, 2011).

96. Jan C. Semenza, Carol H. Rubin, Kenneth H. Falter, Joel D. Selanikio, W. Dana Flanders, Holly L. Howe, and John L. Wilhelm. 1996. "Heat-Related Deaths during the July 1995 Heat Wave in Chicago," *New England Journal of Medicine*, 335: 84–90.

97. Marc Poumadere, Claire Mays, Sophie Le Mer, and Russell Blong. 2005. "The 2003 Heat Wave in France: Dangerous Climate Change Here and Now," *Risk Analysis*, 25: 1483–1494; and AP. 2012. "France: South Struggles with Heat," *New York Times*, August 18.

98. Anthony J. McMichael, Rosalie E. Woodruff, and Simon Hales. 2006. "Climate Change and Human Health: Present and Future Risks," *The Lancet*, 367: 859–869.

99. E. Lindgren, L. Talleklint, and T. Polfeldt. 2000. "Impact of Climatic Change on the Northern

Latitude Limit and Population Density of the Disease-transmitting European Tick *Ixodes ricinus*," *Environmental Health Perspectives*, 108: 119–123.

100. F. Tanser, B. Sharp, and D. le Sueur. 2003. "Potential Effect of Climate Change on Malaria Transmission in Africa," *The Lancet*, 362: 1792–1798; M. Pascual, J. A. Ahumada, L. F. Chaves, X. Rodo, and M. Bouma. 2006. "Malaria Resurgence in the East African Highlands: Temperature Trends Revisited," *Proceedings of the National Academy of Sciences*, 103: 5829–5834; and Jonathan A. Patz, Thaddeus K. Graczyk, Nina Geller, and Amy Y. Vittor. 2000. "Effects of Environmental Change on Emerging Parasitic Diseases," *International Journal for Parasitology*, 30: 1395–1405.

101. United Nations Millennium Development Goals. 2012, http://www.un.org/millenniumgoals / (accessed January 11, 2012).

102. United Nations. 2010. *Millennium Development Goals Report 2010*, New York: United Nations, http://www.un.org/millenniumgoals/pdf /MDG%20Report%202010%20En%20r15%20 -low%20res%2020100615%20-.pdf (accessed January 11, 2012).

CHAPTER 7

MORTALITY ISSUES IN THE MORE DEVELOPED REGION

LEARNING OBJECTIVES

- Discuss the importance of smoking, alcohol consumption, and overweight in mortality risks overall and by sex in more developed countries.
- Discuss the role of screening and of behavioral change in hypertension and high cholesterol.
- Describe the level and pattern of change in external-cause mortality by race and sex in the United States.
- Assess arguments for why the sex differential in mortality in the More Developed Region might narrow in the future.
- Discuss the role of social support, social status, and discrimination in mortality in the United States.

((• Listen to the Chapter Audio

OVERVIEW

The mortality issues in the More Developed Region (MDR) are different than in the Less Developed Region (LDR). We saw in Tables 5.2 through 5.10 in Chapter 5 that in the high-income countries, health behaviors and conditions that mainly affect the elderly have become the most important causes of death and disability.

In this chapter, first we look at the most important public health advances in the United States in the twentieth century. Then we look at how older age mortality in the United States has changed in comparison to some other high-income countries. After that, we look at the shift in mortality from communicable diseases to non-communicable diseases. Then we examine changes in health behaviors that contribute to mortality and at the role of screening for conditions such as high blood pressure, high cholesterol, and high blood sugar. We also consider the role of social causes of mortality, such as the extent of social support and discrimination.

We then examine mortality differentials by age, sex, and race in the United States. We pay special attention to external-cause mortality (homicide, suicide, and accidents) and its large effect on male mortality. Finally, we look at trends and differentials in mortality by race in the United States.

MOST IMPORTANT PUBLIC HEALTH ACHIEVEMENTS IN THE UNITED STATES IN THE TWENTIETH CENTURY

In 1999, the U.S. Centers for Disease Control and Prevention published its list of the ten most important public health achievements in the United States in the twentieth century. In no particular order, they are shown in Table 7.1.[1]

In Chapters 5 and 6, many of these issues were discussed regarding mortality decline in historical Europe and in the LDR. Public health measures that require little voluntary action by the public were important in historical Europe, as seen in the improvement of sewers, and in the LDR in improvement of drinking water quality, draining of swamps, and spraying for insects. The fluoridation of drinking water in the United States fits into this category. Fluoridation drastically reduced dental cavities, but also was an issue of fierce political controversy, as some people did not want anything put into their drinking water without their explicit consent.[2] Vaccination programs in the United States are another public health program that has been very successful in reducing illness and death but that also have been controversial, as discussed in Chapter 6. Control of infectious diseases, healthier mothers and babies,

206

TABLE 7.1   Ten Most Important Public Health Achievements in the United States, 1900–1999

Achievement	Some Specifics
Vaccination	Eradication of smallpox, elimination of polio, control of measles, rubella, tetanus, and diphtheria
Motor vehicle safety	Increased use of seatbelts and child safety seats, motorcycle helmets, and drunk driving awareness and enforcement
Safer workplaces	Control of black lung and silicosis; since 1980, a decline of 40% in occupation-related deaths
Control of infectious diseases	Improvements from clean water and improved sanitation, including for typhoid and cholera. Antimicrobial therapy important for tuberculosis (TB) and sexually transmitted diseases (STDs).
Decline in deaths from coronary heart disease and stroke	More extensive screening and treatment of hypertension; smoking reduction contributed to a decline in deaths from coronary heart disease of 51% since 1972
Safer and healthier foods	Food fortification programs led to elimination of nutritional deficiency diseases such as rickets, goiter, and pellagra
Healthier mothers and babies	Better hygiene and nutrition, as well as antibiotics and advances in medical care, contributed to a 90% decline in infant mortality and a 99% decline in maternal mortality since 1900
Family planning	Contribution to fewer infant, child, and maternal deaths; barrier contraceptives prevent transmission of HIV and other STDs
Fluoridation of drinking water	Began in 1945 and contributed to a more than 40% decline in tooth decay
Recognition of tobacco use as a health hazard	Surgeon General's Report of 1964 initiated antismoking campaigns that contributed to a reduction in cigarette smoking and prevented millions of smoking-related deaths

and decline in mortality from heart disease and stroke involve improvements in medicines and medical care as well as behavioral changes. Healthier food involves behavior as well as government regulation, and mitigating the effects of tobacco involves public campaigns and changed behavior. Motor vehicle safety and safer workplaces involve institutional changes in cars, machinery, and pollution control as well as safer behaviors by drivers, pedestrians, and workers.

OLD AGE MORTALITY TRENDS IN THE UNITED STATES, FRANCE, AND JAPAN

We saw in Chapter 4 that as overall mortality declined in developed countries, deaths became increasingly concentrated at advanced ages. We also saw that e_0^0 has shifted over time from being higher in the United States than the MDR as a whole and higher than in most regions of Europe to being the same or lower in the United States than in the MDR or in most regions of Europe. Figure 7.1 shows changes from 1950 to 2007 in expectation of remaining life at age 50 and expectation of remaining life at age 80 in the United States, France, and Japan. The United States is indicated by a solid line.[3]

The top panel of Figure 7.1 shows expectation of remaining life at age 50. For each sex in every country, e_{50}^0 increased. Also in every country, the female value is always higher than that for males. American

e_{50}^0 in 1950 was as high as that in France and higher than that in Japan for both males and females. By 2007, e_{50}^0 in the United States was the lowest of the three countries for both males and females. American females especially lost ground in comparison to females in the other two countries.

In the bottom panel of Figure 7.1, we see the analogous situation for e_{80}^0. In 1950, Americans of each sex had a higher value of e_{80}^0 than members of the same sex in France or Japan. By 2007, American female e_{80}^0 was the lowest of the three countries, and American male e_{80}^0 in 2007 was lower than for Japan and tied with France. As we look at the sources of mortality in more developed countries, we look at some possible causes of increasingly poor older age mortality in the United States in comparison to other highly developed countries, especially for females.

Illustrative Trends in Communicable, Non-Communicable, and External Causes of Death in the United States

As overall mortality has declined in the MDR, death rates from communicable diseases have become quite low. Non-communicable causes of death have played an increasing role in mortality both because death rates from communicable diseases have declined and sometimes due to an increase in death rates from non-communicable diseases. In some countries, external-cause death rates are quite high, especially

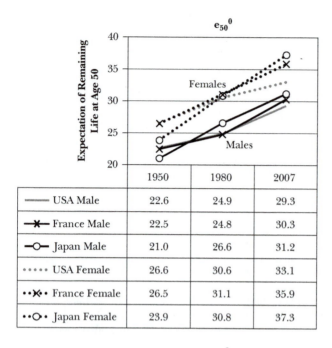

e_{50}^0

	1950	1980	2007
—— USA Male	22.6	24.9	29.3
—✗— France Male	22.5	24.8	30.3
—O— Japan Male	21.0	26.6	31.2
· · · · · USA Female	26.6	30.6	33.1
· ·✗· · France Female	26.5	31.1	35.9
· ·O· · Japan Female	23.9	30.8	37.3

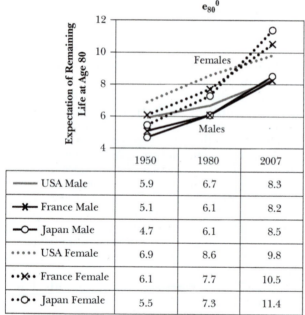

e_{80}^0

	1950	1980	2007
—— USA Male	5.9	6.7	8.3
—✗— France Male	5.1	6.1	8.2
—O— Japan Male	4.7	6.1	8.5
· · · · · USA Female	6.9	8.6	9.8
· ·✗· · France Female	6.1	7.7	10.5
· ·O· · Japan Female	5.5	7.3	11.4

FIGURE 7.1   Expectation of Remaining Life at Age 50 and Age 80 by Sex in the United States, France, and Japan, 1950–2007

for young adult males. In this section, we look at the trend in age-adjusted death rates for one cause within each of the three causes of death categories, influenza and pneumonia combined from the communicable causes of death category; heart disease, stroke, and cancer combined from the non-communicable causes category; and all external-cause deaths.

The top panel of Figure 7.2 shows age-adjusted death rates per 100,000 people for all causes of death and for the selected causes of death from each of the three Global Burden of Disease (GBD) categories for the United States in 1950–2005.[4] The bottom panel of Figure 7.2 shows the change in each cause of death relative to its value in 1950. In the bottom panel, at each date the rate for the given date is divided by the rate in 1950. The changes from 1950 to 2005 reflect the transition from the third to the fourth stage of the epidemiologic transition.

The overall age-adjusted death rate in 2005 was 55% of its value in 1950, a considerable decline. The age-adjusted death rate from the major non-communicable causes of death, heart disease, stroke, and cancer combined, also declined by 2005 to 36% of its value in 1950. Non-communicable causes of death became an increasing proportion of all deaths, but this was mainly because death rates for communicable causes declined even more rapidly than did death rates for non-communicable diseases, rather than because of an increase in mortality from non-communicable causes of death. We see that death rates from influenza and pneumonia declined by 2005 to 26% of the 1950 level, although the death rate from these causes was already low in 1950. In 2005, the death rate from external causes of death (accidents, homicide, and suicide) was 75% of the value in 1950. However, the trajectory of external-cause death rates was variable, increasing to 115% of the 1950 value by 1970 before declining to less than the 1950 value by 2005.

Factors Related to Mortality from Non-Communicable Causes

Non-communicable diseases have become the major causes of death in developed countries.[5] Non-communicable diseases are mainly caused by poor health behaviors, especially smoking, alcohol consumption, poor diet, and lack of exercise. Poor health behaviors and genetic predispositions can lead to chronic conditions, including hypertension (high blood pressure), high cholesterol, and high blood sugar, which in turn increase the risk of death. These chronic conditions typically have no symptoms. Screening of the population for these chronic conditions has increased people's awareness of whether they have a given condition. Also, medication to reduce the effects of these conditions has become increasingly effective and available. Awareness that they have a condition allows people to be treated and also can encourage them to change behaviors that affect the conditions. In turn, health behaviors, such as smoking, alcohol overconsumption, being overweight, and lack of physical activity, are related to the social and economic characteristics of persons.

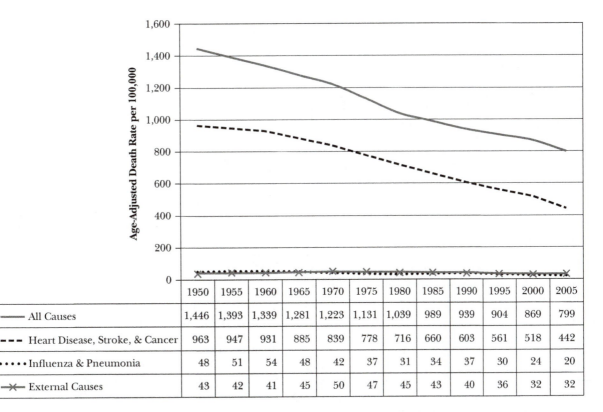

	1950	1955	1960	1965	1970	1975	1980	1985	1990	1995	2000	2005
—— All Causes	1,446	1,393	1,339	1,281	1,223	1,131	1,039	989	939	904	869	799
- - - Heart Disease, Stroke, & Cancer	963	947	931	885	839	778	716	660	603	561	518	442
• • • • Influenza & Pneumonia	48	51	54	48	42	37	31	34	37	30	24	20
—✕— External Causes	43	42	41	45	50	47	45	43	40	36	32	32

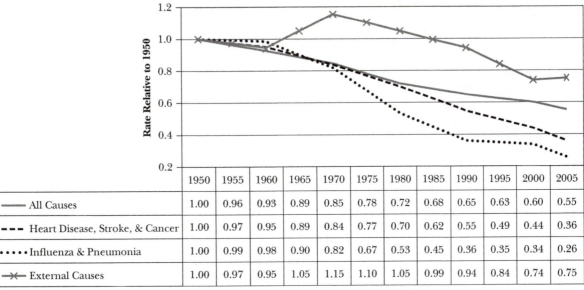

	1950	1955	1960	1965	1970	1975	1980	1985	1990	1995	2000	2005
—— All Causes	1.00	0.96	0.93	0.89	0.85	0.78	0.72	0.68	0.65	0.63	0.60	0.55
- - - Heart Disease, Stroke, & Cancer	1.00	0.97	0.95	0.89	0.84	0.77	0.70	0.62	0.55	0.49	0.44	0.36
• • • • Influenza & Pneumonia	1.00	0.99	0.98	0.90	0.82	0.67	0.53	0.45	0.36	0.35	0.34	0.26
—✕— External Causes	1.00	0.97	0.95	1.05	1.15	1.10	1.05	0.99	0.94	0.84	0.74	0.75

FIGURE 7.2   Age-Adjusted Death Rates from Selected Causes and Change in Rates Relative to 1950, the United States, 1950–2005

We next look at specific behaviors: smoking, excessive alcohol consumption, diet, and overweight and obesity. In each of these areas, there have been active campaigns in the United States to make people aware of the risks of these behaviors and to encourage people to adopt healthier lifestyles. Campaigns intended to change behaviors can focus on (1) encouraging a new behavior to replace the old behavior,

(2) preventing people from starting the undesirable behavior, or (3) ceasing the undesirable behavior. Antismoking campaigns, for example, have focused on replacing smoking by behaviors such as chewing gum, encouraging young people not to commence smoking, and helping smokers quit. Behavior change is especially difficult when it involves an addictive substance, such as tobacco. Ceasing heavy alcohol consumption can lead to withdrawal. Weight loss is also difficult partially because of biological processes that increase hunger and slow down a person's metabolism, which contribute to regaining the lost weight. Thus, behavior change programs often take a substantial time to show effects.[6]

In addition, some negative health behaviors are related. Excessive alcohol consumption and smoking often go together. Also, smoking has been seen as a weight loss strategy, especially among women. Weight gain after quitting smoking confronts former smokers with a new set of challenges.[7]

Smoking, Lung Cancer, and Related Causes of Death
We saw in Table 5.9 in Chapter 5 that smoking is the leading risk factor for death in the high-income countries and in Table 5.10 that it is also the leading risk factor for death and disability in the high-income countries. A great deal of research has found that smoking is related to increased mortality risks, even when other factors are taken into account. Peto and his colleagues estimated that in 44 more developed countries in 1990, about 24% of all male deaths and 17% of all female deaths were due to smoking and that cigarette smokers on average lived 8 years less than nonsmokers.[8]

The Smoking Reduction Campaign in the United States
Through the first half of the twentieth century, cigarette consumption in the United States increased greatly, as shown in Figure 7.3.[9] Cigarettes were promoted as a means to reduce stress. In World War I, the Red Cross dispatched free cigarettes to soldiers, and during World War II, cigarettes were free or very inexpensive for soldiers. Analysis of smoking and the age smoking began in retrospective surveys showed that there was a substantial increase in adolescent and young adult smoking initiation during World War I and again during World War II, especially for men.[10]

A major success story of change in health behavior is the smoking reduction campaign in the United States. There had long been scientific evidence that smoking was dangerous to health, and in 1964 the United States Surgeon General's Report was issued, which warned about the risks that smoking poses to health and survival and marked the beginning of a major antismoking campaign.[11]

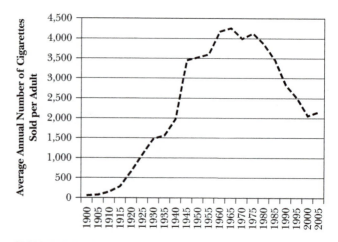

FIGURE 7.3 Average Cigarette Sales per Person Aged 18 or Older, the United States, 1900–2005

Figure 7.4 shows the percentage of Americans interviewed in Gallup polls who agreed that cigarette smoking was one of the causes of heart disease and of lung cancer.[12] Between 1960 and 1969, there was an especially large increase in the percentage of respondents who agreed, perhaps in response to the Surgeon General's report and the subsequent antismoking campaign.

As shown in Figure 7.3, U.S. per capita sales of cigarettes were at a high of 4,345 in 1963. Adult per capita cigarette sales had fallen to 4,141 in 1974 and had fallen further to 3,446 in 1984.[13] Thus, progress in this very successful campaign was not achieved quickly. Warner estimated that in the absence of the Surgeon General's antismoking campaign, cigarette

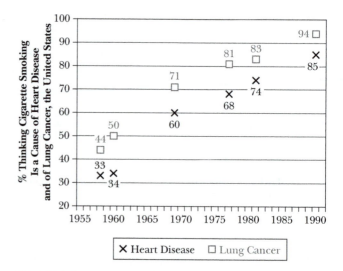

FIGURE 7.4 Percentage Thinking Cigarette Smoking Is a Cause of Heart Disease and of Lung Cancer, the United States, 1958–1990

consumption in 1975 would have been 20–30% higher than its actual level. By 1987, cigarette consumption was 79–89% less than it would have been if earlier trends had continued.[14]

The relation of socioeconomic status to smoking also changed over time. Once information about the health risks of smoking became known, this was understood and acted upon to a greater extent by more educated men than by less educated men. While the proportion smoking among more educated men has declined over time, the decline among less educated men has been much slower.[15]

Figure 7.5 shows the percentage of adults (over age 18) who were current smokers for various years in 1965–2009.[16] The percentage of males who were smokers was always higher than the percentage for women, but the gap narrowed considerably over time. Figure 7.5 looks very much like Stage 4 in Figure 6.15 in Chapter 6.

One reason why the antismoking campaign was less effective for women than for men was that tobacco companies targeted women with special advertising, emphasizing that smoking was a way for women to assert their independence and equality with men. Starting in 1968, Virginia Slims sponsored women's tennis tournaments and other events that promoted smoking as part of an active lifestyle for women.[17]

Although many diseases are related to smoking, a good indicator of the influence of smoking on mortality is lung cancer mortality. Some nonsmokers die of lung cancer due to secondhand smoke or through practices such as cooking in a kitchen with poor ventilation, but smoking is the main cause of lung cancer deaths. It has been estimated that smoking

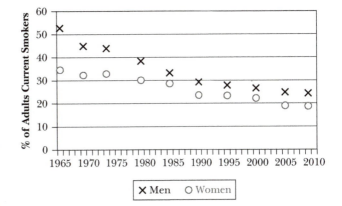

FIGURE 7.5   Percentage of Adults Who Were Current Smokers by Sex, the United States, 1965–2009

leads to more deaths from cardiovascular diseases and chronic obstructive pulmonary disease than from lung cancer. However, lung cancer mortality has often been used as an indicator of the mortality consequences of smoking since only a small percentage of lung cancer deaths have a nonsmoking cause, while many factors other than smoking contribute to deaths from cardiovascular diseases and from chronic obstructive pulmonary disease.[18]

Figure 7.6 shows death rates per 100,000 population by age and sex from lung cancer. Under age 35, death rates from lung cancer are less than 1 per 100,000 for each sex. After age 35, lung cancer death rates increase almost exponentially. The rates are always higher for men than women. By age 65–74, the male rates are more than 50% higher than the

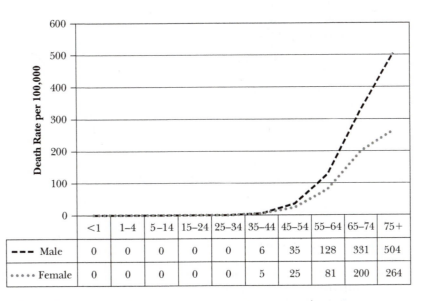

	<1	1–4	5–14	15–24	25–34	35–44	45–54	55–64	65–74	75+
– – – Male	0	0	0	0	0	6	35	128	331	504
••••• Female	0	0	0	0	0	5	25	81	200	264

FIGURE 7.6   Age-Specific Death Rates from Lung Cancer by Sex, the United States, 2005

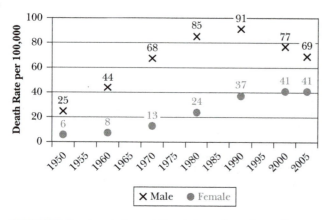

FIGURE 7.7 Age-Adjusted Death Rates from Lung Cancer by Sex, the United States, 1950–2005

female rates, and for those aged 75 or older, the male rates are almost twice as high as the female rates. Although people typically begin smoking in their teens or twenties, it usually takes many years for lung cancer to develop and for people to die from it, resulting in low death rates from lung cancer before about age 45, and a large increase in death rates after about age 55.[19]

Figure 7.7 shows age-adjusted death rates from lung cancer by sex for the United States for 1950–2005. Male rates are higher than female rates at every date. Lung cancer death rates for each sex increased after 1950, consistent with the increase in per capita cigarette sales shown in Figure 7.3. Although Figure 7.5 indicates declines in male smoking from 1965, male lung cancer death rates only began to fall after 1980, again consistent with a long lag time between a change in smoking behavior and its effects on smoking-related mortality. Similarly, although stopping smoking decreases the risk of lung cancer, former smokers have a higher risk of lung cancer than those who have never smoked. Female lung cancer death rates increased until 2000 and then leveled off. This is consistent with the lesser decline in female than male smoking indicated in Figure 7.5.[20]

Figures 7.5 and 7.7 indicate that by 2005, the United States was in the fourth state of the tobacco epidemic shown in Figure 6.15. Male tobacco-related deaths should continue to decline, and hopefully female smoking and female tobacco-related deaths will decline in the near future.

Smoking Trends in the United States, France, and Japan   Figure 7.8 shows cigarette consumption per capita over time in the United States, France, and Japan. The results for the United States are consistent with those in Figure 7.3.[21] Until about 1970, per capita cigarette consumption was higher in the

United States than in France or Japan. Cigarette consumption peaked in Japan in 1977 and then fell, although more slowly than in the United States.

Figure 7.9 compares death rates from lung cancer over time for those aged 65–74 for the United States, France, and Japan. The values for males are shown in the top panel, and those for females in the bottom panel. The vertical scale is different in the two panels, because the female rates are much lower than the male rates.

The lung cancer death rates for France and Japan are always lower than for the United States. However, the gap between male lung cancer death rates in the United States and male rates in France and Japan narrows after 1990, probably due to the patterns of cigarette consumption in the three countries shown in Figure 7.8. Male lung cancer death rates in the United States remained high because of the lag between a change in smoking and a change in lung cancer mortality. It seems likely that in the future, U.S. male lung cancer mortality will fall to the same level as or below that for males in Japan and France. The bottom panel of Figure 7.9 shows that lung cancer mortality for American females is very different from female lung cancer mortality in the other countries, with much higher rates for American women. This is because while female smoking prevalence has approached that of men in the United States, in France and Japan women remain much less likely than men to smoke.

The trend in female smoking in the United States and its associated mortality are a major source of the worsening mortality position for older American females compared to French and Japanese females,

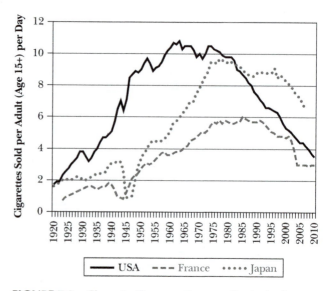

FIGURE 7.8 Cigarette Consumption per Capita in the United States, France, and Japan, 1920–2010

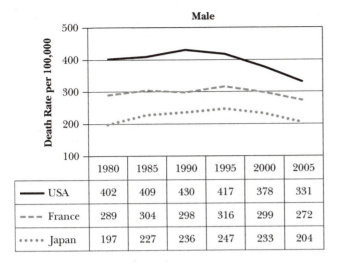

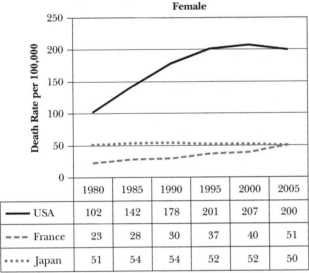

FIGURE 7.9 Death Rates at Ages 65–74 from Lung Cancer in the United States, France, and Japan, 1980–2005

almost the U.S. male level. The percentage of deaths over age 50 due to smoking is also much higher for American females than for females in the other two countries.

Table 7.3 shows the estimated e_{50}^0 by sex in 2003 for the United States, France, and Japan, including smoking and if there were no smoking. Without smoking, female e_{50}^0 in the United States would be almost the same as in France.[23]

Alcohol Consumption, Chronic Liver Disease, Cirrhosis, and Other Consequences of Excessive Drinking

Alcohol consumption is another health behavior related to mortality. Although there is evidence that in small amounts alcohol has a positive effect on health, at higher levels of consumption alcohol contributes to mortality from various diseases and increases the likelihood of motor vehicle fatalities and other external causes of death.[24] As seen in Table 5.9 in Chapter 5, excessive alcohol use is the ninth leading risk factor for death in the high-income countries and, as seen in Table 5.10, is the second leading risk factor for death and disability in the high-income countries.

Heavy drinking and binge drinking are especially dangerous both for disease and for accidental death. Heavy drinking is defined as more than two drinks a day for men or more than one drink a day for women, and binge drinking is defined as more than five drinks at a single occasion for men or four drinks at a single occasion for women.[25] However, there is great individual variability in what amount of alcohol consumption results in a given blood alcohol level.[26]

Figure 7.10 shows per capita alcohol consumption among American adults over time.[27] It is shown as gallons of pure alcohol in order to account for the lower alcohol content of beer and wine than of hard liquor. Consumption is shown for all alcoholic beverages and also separately for hard liquor (spirits), such as vodka or whiskey. Consumption of hard liquor declined after 1975, and overall alcohol consumption declined after 1980. Also, after 1975 there was some shift from consumption of hard liquor to consumption of beer and wine.

shown in Figure 7.1. Table 7.2 shows the percentage of all deaths attributed to smoking by gender in 1955, 1980, and 2003 in the United States, France, and Japan.[22] While there has been a small decline in the percentage of U.S. male deaths due to smoking, the percentage for U.S. females has increased to

TABLE 7.2   Percentage of All Deaths at Age 50+ Due to Smoking in the United States, France, and Japan, 1955–2003

	Male			Female		
	1955	1980	2003	1955	1980	2003
United States	8%	23%	22%	1%	8%	20%
France	5%	17%	19%	0%	0%	2%
Japan	10%	32%	26%	0%	3%	9%

TABLE 7.3   Life Expectancy at Age 50 with and without Smoking in the United States, France, and Japan, 2003

	Male			Female		
	With Smoking	Without Smoking	Difference*	With Smoking	Without Smoking	Difference*
United States	28.5	31.0	2.5	32.3	34.6	2.3
France	28.8	31.0	2.2	34.6	34.9	0.3
Japan	30.5	32.5	2.1	36.7	37.4	0.8

*Difference calculated from more significant figures.

There have been programs intended to encourage people not to overindulge in alcohol, including public awareness campaigns, stiff drunk driving laws, high taxes on alcohol, and restriction of the availability of alcohol. These policies have often been very effective.[28]

There is a tension in alcohol tax policy between intending the policies to (1) lead to less alcohol consumption, and (2) generate more tax revenue. The pressure to increase revenue motivated several American states to increase alcohol taxes and to expand hours when alcohol could legally be sold between 2008 and 2011, since state budgets were under great strain.[29]

Alcohol is a major cause of chronic liver disease and of cirrhosis of the liver. Figure 7.11 shows age-adjusted death rates from chronic liver disease and cirrhosis of the liver by sex in the United States in 1950–2005. For each sex, death rates increase between 1950 and 1970, and they decline after 1970. The timing of the decline of death rates parallels the decline in hard liquor consumption. It is interesting that the mortality response to changes in the risk factor (alcohol consumption) was so rapid.

Figure 7.12 shows age-specific death rates by sex from liver disease and cirrhosis for the United States

in 2005. The rates are very low under age 35 and then increase rapidly. The rates are much higher for males than females, almost certainly due to greater alcohol consumption by men than women.

Alcohol Consumption, Alcohol-Related Mortality, and Gorbachev's Anti-Alcohol Campaign in Russia

Russia has very high alcohol consumption and high death rates related to alcohol. It also is a striking example of the temporary effectiveness of a campaign that restricted the availability of alcoholic beverages.

Figure 7.13 shows annual alcohol consumption in Russia per person aged 15 or older on the left-hand axis.[30] The level of alcohol consumption in Russia was much higher than that shown for the United States in Figure 7.10. When Gorbachev came to power in the Soviet Union in 1985, he was alarmed by the high male mortality, and it was clear to him that alcohol was a major cause. Thus, in June 1985 he declared an anti-alcohol campaign, the major component of which was restriction of the hours of sale of alcoholic beverages and limitation of the amount that could be purchased at one time.

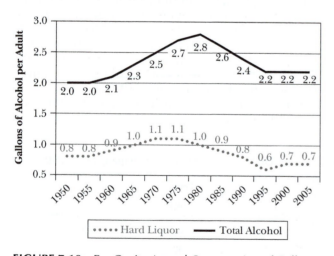

FIGURE 7.10   Per Capita Annual Consumption of Gallons of Alcohol, the United States, 1950–2005

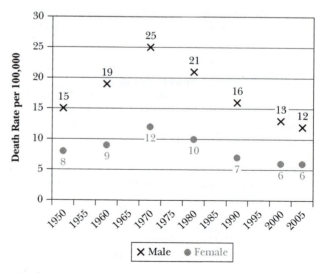

FIGURE 7.11   Age-Adjusted Death Rates from Liver Disease and Cirrhosis by Sex, the United States, 1950–2005

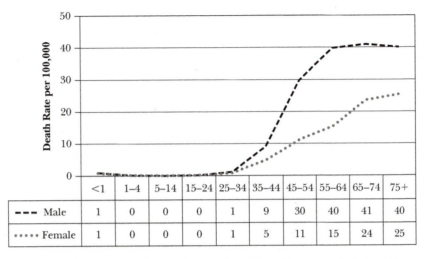

	<1	1–4	5–14	15–24	25–34	35–44	45–54	55–64	65–74	75+
--- Male	1	0	0	0	1	9	30	40	41	40
····· Female	1	0	0	0	1	5	11	15	24	25

FIGURE 7.12   Age-Specific Death Rates from Liver Disease and Cirrhosis by Sex, the United States, 2005

The immediate effects of the anti-alcohol campaign on alcohol consumption and on mortality are clear in Figure 7.13. Alcohol consumption in 1986 had fallen to 74% of the 1984 value. The campaign also had an immediate impact on male and female age-adjusted death rates, which are shown in Figure 7.13, with the values on the right-hand axis. The 1986 male rate was 91% of the 1985 value, while the 1986 female rate was 93% of its 1985 value. The weaker relation between alcohol consumption and the female age-adjusted death rate is almost certainly because female alcohol consumption was much lower than that of males. We saw in Figure 4.12 in Chapter 4

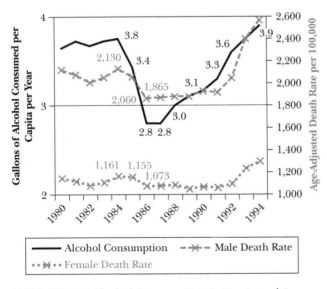

FIGURE 7.13   Alcohol Consumption in Russia and Age-Adjusted Death Rates by Sex in Russia, 1980–1994

that male e_0^0 in Russia increased from 62 years in 1980–1985 to 64 years in 1985–1990, before falling to 61 years in 1990–1995.

The anti-alcohol campaign was very successful but also was extremely unpopular. One reason is that drinking hard liquor, especially vodka, was a major male social activity. In the Soviet Union, a bottle of vodka cost 3 rubles. There was a practice in which a man would stand outside a state liquor store and hold up a finger, indicating he wanted to buy a bottle of vodka along with others. When three men had gathered, they would buy the vodka and share it.

In the Baltic republics of the Soviet Union (Estonia, Latvia, and Lithuania), beer was more popular than vodka. There were complaints that the application of a uniform anti-alcohol policy nationwide was unfair, since beer was not as dangerous as vodka. Soviet Georgia was a major wine-producing region, and wine consumption was quite popular there. Georgians argued, similar to the people in the Baltic republics, that the application of the policy to all alcoholic beverages was unfair.

Another reason for opposition to the campaign from some government authorities was that alcohol taxes were a major source of state revenue, and when alcohol sales declined, revenue from alcohol taxes also declined.[31] Enforcement became somewhat less rigorous over time, and home-brewed alcohol to some extent replaced legally purchased alcohol. The campaign officially ended in 1988.

Even though alcohol consumption fell considerably during the anti-alcohol campaign, it did not become low by international standards. The low point of alcohol consumption in Russia was 2.8 gallons per capita in 1986–1987, which matches the high point of alcohol consumption in the United States in 1980, as shown in Figure 7.10. After the anti-alcohol campaign was relaxed and especially after it ended, alcohol consumption climbed rapidly, reaching its 1984 level by 1994.

Shkolnikov and his colleagues present persuasive evidence that a decline in alcohol consumption was the major cause of the increase in male e_0^0 during the anti-alcohol campaign and that a return to higher levels of alcohol consumption was a major reason for the decline in male e_0^0 after the end of the program.[32] The anti-alcohol policies were curtailed because of their widespread unpopularity in the late 1980s.

With the dramatic declines in male mortality that accompanied the anti-alcohol campaign in the late 1980s, some have wondered what lessons other countries can learn from this campaign. Other countries have found that taxes on alcohol and restriction on hours that alcohol is available for sale can reduce alcohol consumption, but the restriction of alcohol sales during the campaign goes beyond that found elsewhere where alcohol is legal. It is not clear that there are any helpful lessons for other countries. The Soviet Union was dissolved in 1991. Since the program drastically curtailed supply, it was untenable in post-Soviet Russia, when restrictions to the availability of a variety of consumer goods had been eliminated.[33]

In January 2010, Russian president Vladimir Putin announced a plan to raise taxes, restrict alcohol sales and production, and limit advertising in an effort to reduce Russian alcohol consumption by 50% by 2020.[34] However, taxes on alcohol and tobacco remained a major source of government revenue in the post-Soviet period. By September 2010, experiencing the effects of world economic problems, Putin called for Russians to keep consuming alcohol and tobacco as a way to support the Russian state through their taxes.[35]

Other countries have also imposed limitations on alcohol advertising. In South Africa, limitations on alcohol advertising, especially during TV children's programs, have been considered in combination with restrictions on fast-food advertising as part of trying to promote a healthy lifestyle. As in the United States and Russia, there has been pushback related to revenue issues. As the South African health minister said in September 2011:

> The industry, of course, has threatened us with job losses, potential collapse of the sport industry due to lack of revenue if we go ahead with the banning of advertisements of alcohol. I want to make it very clear right now that we shall never be intimidated. It's not going to happen.[36]

Alcohol has contributed to high male mortality in Russia through a number of pathways. We look

briefly at mortality from cirrhosis of the liver in Russia in the next section. Zaridze and colleagues showed that alcohol poisoning has played a substantial role in Russian male mortality trends.[37] Alcohol poisoning does not only occur when someone drinks contaminated alcohol. Alcohol is a poison, and if a person drinks enough alcohol quickly enough, he or she dies of alcohol poisoning. There is particular susceptibility to alcohol poisoning and to binge drinking in Russia and elsewhere in Eastern Europe due to what has been called "the Slavic drinking pattern" in which hard liquor, usually vodka, is consumed rapidly in a down-the-hatch manner without food. It is estimated that in Russia, 63% of alcohol consumption is in the form of hard liquor. It is also estimated that Russia is among the five countries in the world with the riskiest pattern of alcohol consumption.[38]

There is also evidence that alcohol plays a role in motor vehicle fatalities, including deaths to drunk pedestrians wandering into the street. The stresses associated with social disorganization, economic problems, and increased income inequality have also been cited as causes of high external-cause mortality in Russia, since these stresses could have driven some people to suicide or risky behavior.[39]

The pervasiveness of the influence of alcohol on male mortality in Russia can also be seen in data on accidental drowning. Figure 7.14 shows death rates from accidental drowning by age and sex in Russia and the United States. Most countries show a pattern similar to that of the United States, with low rates at most ages but the highest rates for young children. That is also the pattern for Russian females. The picture for Russian males is very different, with the highest rates of accidental drowning for adult men. The most likely explanation of this pattern is that Russian men become drunk, fall into a body of water, and drown.

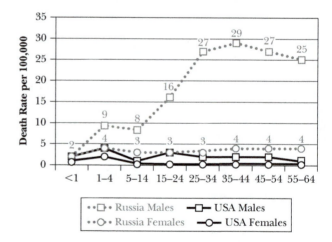

FIGURE 7.14 Death Rates from Accidental Drowning in Russia and the United States, 2002

Diet, Overweight, Obesity, Body Mass Index, and Diabetes Mortality

Diet is another aspect of health behavior related to mortality. In developed counties, starvation or malnutrition is rarely a problem. More consequential is overeating leading to overweight or obesity. Closely related to diet is the issue of lack of exercise or physical activity. Regular exercise lessens the negative effects of a variety of chronic conditions, as well as reduces the chance that people will become overweight or obese.[40] McGee and his associates found that for men, being obese related to a 20% increase in overall mortality and for women to a 28% increase in mortality, and the risks were higher the greater the level of obesity.[41] We saw in Table 5.9 in Chapter 5 that in high-income countries, overweight and obesity were the third leading risk factor for death, and physical inactivity was the fourth leading risk factor. In Table 5.10, we saw that in high-income countries, overweight and obesity were the third leading risk factor for death and disability, and physical inactivity was the sixth leading risk factor.

The main way that overweight or obesity is assessed is through the **body mass index (BMI)**. BMI is calculated as weight in kilograms divided by height in meters squared. BMI is a good measure of obesity and risk for diabetes and other ailments at the population level, but it is much less accurate as an assessment for individuals.[42]

A measure of obesity seeks to indicate the extent of a person's body fat. BMI does not take into account differences in body type or fitness that can affect the relation between an individual's BMI and his or her body fat. However, BMI is easily calculated, and it is minimally intrusive to collect height and weight as compared to skinfold thickness or other indicators of obesity.

Figure 7.15 shows the distribution of the population by overweight and obesity categories of BMI in the United States over time.[43] The data are from the National Health and Nutrition Examination Survey (NHANES), which was discussed in Chapter 3. Those who are not overweight have a BMI of less than 25. Those with a BMI of at least 25 but less than 30 are considered overweight. Those with a BMI of at least 30 but less than 40 are considered obese, and those with a BMI greater than or equal to 40 are considered extremely obese. There has been a decrease between the late 1990s and the late 2000s in the percentage of the American population who are not overweight. There has been an increase in the percentage of the population who are obese and a doubling in the percentage of the population who are extremely obese.

High blood glucose (hyperglycemia) is an indicator of diabetes, and the increase in population screening probably has led to more awareness of the risk of diabetes and more testing for it. Until advanced stages, diabetes often is asymptomatic.

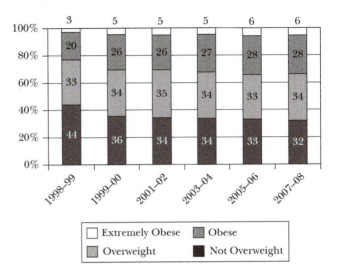

FIGURE 7.15   Obesity in the United States, 1998–1999 through 2007–2008

Although genetic factors are related to susceptibility to diabetes, type II (adult-onset) diabetes has been linked to overweight and obesity and has been linked to patterns of food consumption and lack of exercise that are increasingly common throughout the world. Obesity is also related to a greater risk of death from coronary heart disease, but diabetes mortality is a good indicator of the mortality consequences of overweight and obesity.[44]

Figure 7.16 shows age-adjusted death rates from diabetes by sex for the United States in 1950–2005. In 1950, female death rates from diabetes were much higher than male death rates. The rates for the two sexes were equal in 1980, and after 1980 the male rates were higher than the female rates, even though in 2004, 36% of American women and 30% of American men over age 50 were obese.[45] Diabetes is controllable through diet, exercise, and medication. Women tend to be better at following physicians' instructions

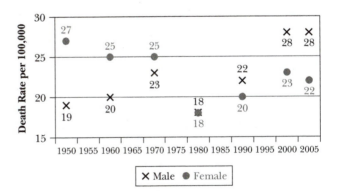

FIGURE 7.16   Age-Adjusted Death Rates from Diabetes by Sex, the United States, 1950–2005

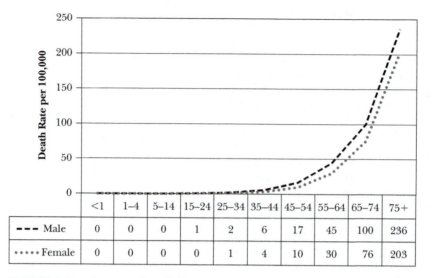

FIGURE 7.17 Age-Specific Death Rates from Diabetes by Sex, the United States, 2005

	<1	1–4	5–14	15–24	25–34	35–44	45–54	55–64	65–74	75+
--- Male	0	0	0	1	2	6	17	45	100	236
····· Female	0	0	0	0	1	4	10	30	76	203

than men, which could be why male diabetes death rates have surpassed female diabetes death rates.

Figure 7.17 shows death rates from diabetes for American men and women by age in 2005. The rates are less than 10 per 100,000 persons below age 45, after which the rates increase exponentially. The male and female rates are similar in each age group, with the male rates always slightly higher than the female rates.[46]

Diabetes Mortality in the United States, France, and Japan Figure 7.18 shows death rates from diabetes for persons aged 65–74 in the United States, France, and Japan. For each sex, the rates in the United States are higher than in the other two countries.

Also, after 1985, the rates in the United States increased for each sex, with a slight decline after 2000 for women. The slowing of the increase in diabetes mortality for men and the decline for women could be related to more effective use of prescription drugs to control diabetes over time.[47]

The differences in diabetes mortality across the three countries are generally consistent with international differences in the percentage of adults who are obese, which in about 2005 was 34% in the United States, 11% in France, and 4% in Japan.[48]

Anti-Obesity Campaigns and Laws There have been programs to promote awareness of the importance

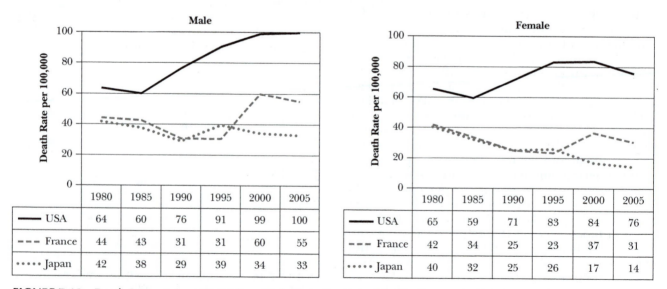

Male

	1980	1985	1990	1995	2000	2005
—— USA	64	60	76	91	99	100
--- France	44	43	31	31	60	55
····· Japan	42	38	29	39	34	33

Female

	1980	1985	1990	1995	2000	2005
—— USA	65	59	71	83	84	76
--- France	42	34	25	23	37	31
····· Japan	40	32	25	26	17	14

FIGURE 7.18 Death Rates at Ages 65–74 from Diabetes in the United States, France, and Japan, 1980–2005

of exercise and the negative effects of obesity, some of which were patterned on the antismoking campaign. Beginning in 2010, First Lady Michelle Obama spearheaded the Let's Move campaign to promote healthier diets. Guidelines for school meals mandate fewer calories and less fat, trans fat, and saturated fat. There was resistance to these changes, as many schoolchildren complained that they did not like the food under the new program. Michelle Obama also promoted a Let's Move initiative to encourage schoolchildren to get more exercise.[49]

There have also been legislative initiatives to ban or limit the sale of foods thought to contribute to obesity. In September 2012, Mayor Michael Bloomberg motivated New York City to pass a ban on the sale of sugared soft drinks larger than 16 ounces in restaurants, delicatessens, and some other venues, to go into effect in March 2013. This ban was opposed by the beverage industry and was also criticized by some consumer groups as interfering excessively in people's lives. In March 2013, shortly before the ban was to go into effect, a New York State judge ruled it void because he questioned whether the New York City Department of Health had the power to impose such a ban and because the ban only covered large sugary drinks sold in some places, but not in other places such as convenience stores. New York City planned to appeal the judge's ruling. In October 2013, Bill DeBlasio, who was newly elected mayor of New York City, stated that he supported a soft drink ban, but it was unclear whether he would pursue the appeal. In reaction to the New York City ban on large sugary drinks, in March 2013 the Mississippi legislature passed a bill that would prevent Mississippi jurisdictions from requiring restaurants to post calorie counts and to put a limit on portion sizes, such as of sugary drinks. In 2013, Mississippi had the highest percentage of adults obese of any state, and some thought that Mississippi needed to limit consumption of fat-inducing foods more than New York City. However, Mississippi politicians saw the issue as one of preserving personal freedom and limiting government interference in people's lives.[50]

In Europe, a taxation approach to modifying diets also has been used. In 2011, Denmark began to tax foods that were high in saturated fats. The tax was revoked in 2012 in the face of political and popular opposition. Many Danes went to nearby Germany to buy the foods they wanted at lower prices. In 2011, Finland placed a tax on confectionary products, and Hungary placed a tax on foods with high sugar, salt, or caffeine content; in 2012, France implemented a tax on sugary soft drinks. A 2012 Organisation for Economic Co-operation and Development (OECD) Report discussed the benefits of taxing unhealthy foods. Although many benefits of a healthier, lower calorie diet in developed countries are clear, some have suggested that the revenue from the

food taxes was a major incentive for adopting these taxes at a time of European financial hardship, similar to the role of alcohol and tobacco taxes in post-Soviet Russia.[51]

Hypertension and High Cholesterol

With the increasing role of chronic conditions such as hypertension and diabetes in morbidity and mortality in more developed countries, screening programs for these asymptomatic conditions have become important. Spread of hypertension screening has increased detection and has aided in making people aware of the risks of hypertension.[52]

Hypertension contributes to mortality from many causes. We saw in Table 5.9 in Chapter 5 that hypertension is second to smoking as a risk factor for death in the high-income countries and in Table 5.10 that it is the fourth leading risk factor for death or disability in the high-income countries.

Figure 7.19 shows the age-adjusted percentage of Americans over age 20 by sex who were not hypertensive, who were hypertensive but their blood pressure was under control, and who were hypertensive and their blood pressure was not under control, based on data from NHANES.[53]

The percentage of men who were hypertensive increased over time, while since the late 1990s there

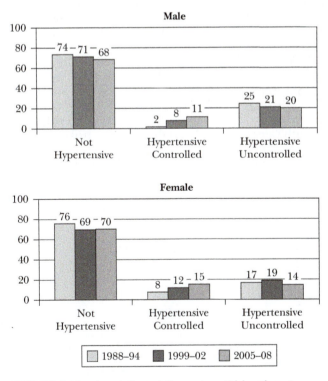

FIGURE 7.19 Age-Adjusted Percentage Older Than Age 20 without Hypertension, with Controlled Hypertension, and with Uncontrolled Hypertension by Sex, the United States, 1988–1994 through 2005–2008

was little change for women. For each sex, the percentage with hypertension under control increased. For men, the percentage with uncontrolled hypertension decreased, while it fluctuated for women. Even in 2005–2008, 20% of all men and 14% of all women had uncontrolled hypertension, putting them at increased risk for stroke and heart disease. The increase over time in the percentage with controlled hypertension and the decrease in the percentage with uncontrolled hypertension are consistent with improved detection and treatment, even as the percentage of hypertensive persons has increased.

Bailey and Goodman-Bacon present evidence that community health centers set up in 1965–1974 as part of the War on Poverty resulted in about a 12% decline in mortality among poor adults aged 50 or over in counties that had a community health center. They estimate that about half of the mortality reduction was due to detection and subsequent treatment of hypertension as the result of a policy that screened all those who came to a center for any reason for hypertension and other conditions.[54]

As shown in Tables 5.9 and 5.10 in Chapter 5, high cholesterol was the sixth leading risk factor for death in the high-income countries and was the seventh leading risk factor for death or disability in the high-income countries. Figure 7.20 shows the age-adjusted percentage of Americans over age 20 by sex who had high cholesterol, based on data from NHANES.[55] The percentage with high cholesterol increased over time for each sex.

Figure 7.21 shows the age-adjusted death rates by sex from heart disease and from stroke, 1950–2005. Male heart disease death rates are substantially higher than female rates, although the death rates from stroke are similar for both sexes. Age-adjusted death rates for both heart disease and stroke for each sex have declined since 1960. This is impressive, since the percentage hypertensive and the percentage with

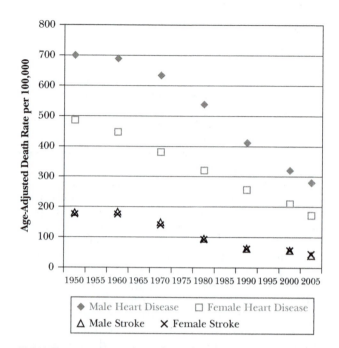

FIGURE 7.21 Age-Adjusted Death Rates from Heart Disease and from Stroke by Sex, the United States, 1950–2005

high cholesterol have increased over time. Treatment of hypertension and high cholesterol along with decreased smoking among American men and improved treatment for heart disease and stroke have probably contributed to the decline in the age-adjusted death rates from heart disease and stroke.

Figure 7.22 shows death rates from heart disease by age and sex in the United States in 2006. The male rates are somewhat higher than the female rates. The age pattern is typical of a cause of death related to poor health behaviors over a life time and to progressive clogging of the arteries with age. The death rates are somewhat elevated among infants, related usually to congenital problems, and then fall to a very low level until rising after age 45 and rising even more rapidly after age 65.

Some Counterintuitive Effects of Short-Term Economic Changes on Mortality in Developed Countries

There is increasing evidence that short-term economic expansion can lead to *increasing* mortality and that short-term economic downturns can lead to *decreasing* mortality in developed countries. Research on the United States since 1900 and on South Korea during the economic crisis of the 1990s confirms these results.

These counterintuitive results stem from the mix of causes of death in developed countries. During times of economic improvement, motor vehicle

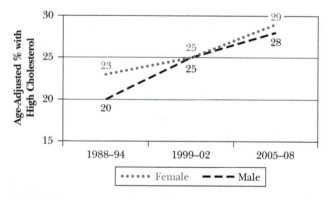

FIGURE 7.20 Age-Adjusted Percentage Age 20 or Older with High Cholesterol, the United States, 1988–1994 through 2005–2008

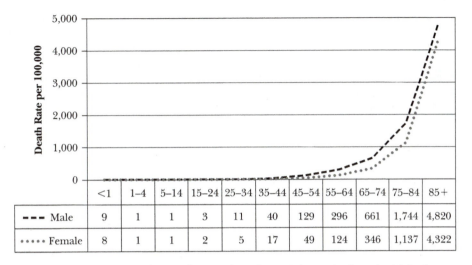

	<1	1–4	5–14	15–24	25–34	35–44	45–54	55–64	65–74	75–84	85+
- - - Male	9	1	1	3	11	40	129	296	661	1,744	4,820
• • • • Female	8	1	1	2	5	17	49	124	346	1,137	4,322

FIGURE 7.22   Age-Specific Death Rates from Heart Disease by Sex, the United States, 2006

fatalities increase, and increased industrial activity results in more work-related deaths. Also, alcohol and cigarette consumption often increases during times of economic expansion. On the other hand, during times of recession, motor vehicle and job-related fatalities decrease, and often consumption of alcohol and cigarettes declines. Suicides increase during economic downturn, which partially offsets declines in other causes of mortality.[56]

These population-level effects of economic change are interesting in light of persistent differentials in mortality among individuals in developed countries, with less educated and lower income persons suffering from worse mortality. These subgroup mortality differentials are discussed in this chapter.

The Roles of Social Support, Socioeconomic Status, Poverty, and Inequality in Mortality in Developed Countries

Two additional factors thought to be important in risks of death are the extent of social support that a person has and various aspects of socioeconomic status (SES). SES can be looked at directly in terms of income or educational attainment but also can be examined in light of poverty, social inequality, and discrimination.

Social Support
Social support has been defined as support that is "provided by other people and arises within the context of interpersonal relationships."[57] It has also been defined as "support accessible to an individual through social ties to other individuals, groups, and the larger community."[58] Researchers have long found that older persons who were currently married and lived with a spouse had lower death rates than others, especially among men. Later, more complex measures of social support were developed than whether a person was currently married and living with his or her spouse.

Uchino and his colleagues discussed how social support influences health and mortality through two pathways. First, greater social support can affect health behaviors and adherence to medical advice. Those with higher levels of social support are more likely to exercise, less likely to smoke, and tend to have healthier eating habits. Second, social support affects a person's psychological processes and general outlook on life. For example, those with more social support are often more able to deal with stress.[59]

One of the first studies that drew attention to the importance of social support in morbidity and mortality is the Alameda County Study. This longitudinal study began in 1965 with about 7,000 adults and traced their behaviors, health, and other characteristics through four follow-up interviews, with the last occurring in 1999. The Alameda County Study found that social ties, including marital status and membership in organizations, such as churches, had a significant influence on mortality. This research helped motivate a large amount of subsequent work on the relation of social support to morbidity and mortality.[60]

Figure 7.23 shows some findings from the Alameda County Study about the relation of age-adjusted death rates to two indicators of social support, marital status and the level of a friends and relatives index. The height of the bars indicates the age-adjusted death rate per 1,000 people. The friends and relatives index is based on answers to questions

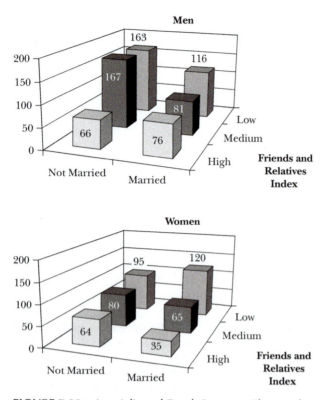

FIGURE 7.23 Age-Adjusted Death Rates per Thousand in Relation to Indicators of Social Support by Sex, Ages 30–64, Alameda County Study, 1965–1974

about how many close friends and relatives a person had and how often the respondent saw these people each month. The same vertical scale is used for both men and women.

For both men and women, being married rather than not married and having a higher rather than a lower level of contact with friends and relatives are related to a lower death rate. However, for each sex, both of these aspects of social support matter. A high level on one aspect of social support is able to at least partially compensate for a low level on the other aspect of social support.

In any study, it can be difficult to be certain whether one variable or condition causes another variable or condition or whether the two factors are related but the direction of causality is unknown. The longitudinal nature of the Alameda County data and the use of other variables in statistical analysis helped disentangle causality and contributed to the conclusion that being married and having strong social support each actually reduced the risk of death.

Socioeconomic Status and Mortality

Many studies have shown strong, persistent educational differentials in mortality. One of the first to do so was that of Kitagawa and Hauser, which found

a strong relationship between male mortality and socioeconomic characteristics such as occupation and education based on data for 1960.[61]

As effective treatments were found for many diseases and as the educational attainment of the population increased, some thought that mortality differentials by education would narrow based on data for 1960.[62] Using data for 1986, Pappas and his colleagues replicated the Kitagawa and Hauser research and found that mortality disparities by SES had widened over time, even as the mix of causes of death had changed. Similar results were found for the United Kingdom, with widening socioeconomic differentials in mortality over time.[63]

Goldman and Smith found that over time, educational differentials became more strongly related to differentials in major diseases, including arthritis, diabetes, and hypertension. They also found that one of the reasons for the widening educational differentials in morbidity was widening educational differentials in health behaviors such as smoking, exercise, and obesity. They restricted their analysis to non-Hispanic Whites in order to avoid the possible influence of different ethnic or racial composition for respondents with different levels of educational attainment.

The relation of education to the percentage who smoke, the percentage who do not get regular intense physical exercise, and the percentage without health insurance appear in Figure 7.24.[64] Figure 7.24 shows results for an addictive negative health behavior (smoking), a non-addictive positive health behavior (regular vigorous exercise), and whether a person has health insurance. Each of these is shown across values of educational attainment for three different time points.

For each behavior or condition, those with more education are likely to have better behaviors or are more likely to have health insurance. Also, the relation with education becomes stronger over time. We see in Figure 7.24 that since the 1970s, after the health risks of smoking were well known, the negative gradient of smoking with education has become steeper. People with less than a high school education were more likely to smoke in 1999–2002 than they were in 1976–1980, while high school graduates were less than half as likely to smoke at the later date. In the second panel of Figure 7.24, we see that in 1976–1980 that there was *no* relation between education and whether a person engaged in vigorous exercise. By 1988–1994, those with more education were more likely to engage in vigorous exercise, and the relation was even stronger by 1999–2002. As the health benefits of exercise became more widely understood, more educated people were much more likely than less educated people to exercise. We also see in the third panel of

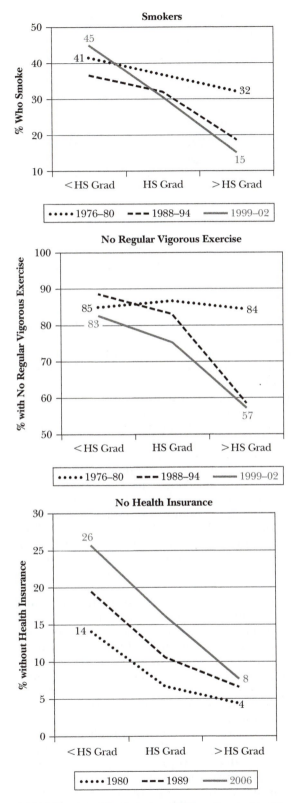

FIGURE 7.24 The Relation of Education to Health Behaviors, 1976–2002, and to Health Insurance, 1980–2006, for Non-Hispanic Whites in the United States

Figure 7.24 that at every date, more educated people were more likely to have health insurance, but as more companies withdrew from offering health insurance to their employees, this mainly affected less educated people.

Fundamental Causes of Disease Approach

In 1995, Link and Phelan proposed the fundamental causes of disease approach.[65] In summary, they write that the fundamental causes approach

> argues that, when a population develops the wherewithal to avoid disease and death, individuals' ability to benefit from that wherewithal is shaped by resources of knowledge, money, power, prestige, and beneficial social connections.[66]

In the **fundamental causes of disease approach**, an individual's or household's resources operate both by affecting whether people engage in healthful behaviors, such as not smoking or not consuming excessive alcohol, and by affecting the kinds of neighborhoods and other environments in which a person functions. Living in less polluted neighborhoods and working in less hazardous occupations lead to lower death rates and less chance of becoming disabled. Much of the fundamental causes of disease approach was motivated by McKeown's work on historical mortality decline and by McKinlay and McKinlay's observations that death rates from many infectious diseases declined considerably before there was any specific treatment or vaccine.

This approach also offers an explanation for the persistent mortality differentials by socioeconomic status even as the causes of death have changed and the level of mortality has declined. The fundamental causes of disease approach argues that people with more resources, whether material or human capital, are always more effective in achieving their ends than people with less resources, including living a long and healthy life. An example of this can be seen in Figure 7.24 in the changing relation over time between education and physical activity.

Miech and colleagues tested the fundamental causes approach in looking at educational differentials in mortality among those aged 40–69 for 1999–2007. They found widening educational differentials in mortality for each sex for Whites, African Americans, and Hispanics. The fundamental causes approach predicts that mortality differentials by SES will emerge whenever there are newly important causes of death, and this study confirmed that prediction in finding that widening educational differentials in mortality were the largest in causes of death that were increasing in their role in overall mortality. For example, death rates from accidental poisoning increased by more than fourfold between 1991 and 2009. Accidental poisoning had the largest widening in educational disparities in mortality among all causes of death.[67]

Poverty, Social Inequality, and Discrimination

Poverty, social inequality, and discrimination are possible sources of high mortality. Some of the ways that poverty can affect mortality are clear. Those with a worse material standard of living, such as unclean drinking water or inadequate, poorly insulated housing, are more susceptible to various diseases that contribute to high mortality. Those without good health insurance are likely to receive less and poorer quality medical care. Also, more educated people typically have more resources to see to their health, but also often pay more attention than less educated people to advice about health behaviors such as smoking and alcohol consumption. Relations between poverty, economic wellbeing, education, and morbidity and mortality are unfortunate but not inexplicable.

The effects of social inequality could be different from the effects of poverty. There would be an effect of poverty when the absolute levels of material wellbeing, quality of housing, and quality of and access to medical care influence mortality risks. There is an effect of inequality to the extent that some resources, such as income, are more or less unequally distributed across households. The least well-off part of a population could improve their absolute level of living, while the extent to which they were more disadvantaged than other parts of the population could remain unchanged or increase.

There are effects of discrimination when one group has worse outcomes than another group even after differences in socioeconomic characteristics and other factors that could reasonably affect the outcome have been taken into account. This can result from systematic differences in health care or treatment decisions as well as being forced to live in less healthy environments.

There is concern with the possible health and mortality effects of inequality even apart from the effects of absolute poverty since the level of economic inequality in the United States is high and is increasing. Figure 7.25 shows the percentage of income in the United States received by the five quintiles of households in 1979 and 2007. If income were evenly distributed, every quintile would receive 20% of the income. In 1979, the bottom three quintiles of households by income received less than their proportionate share of income. In 2007, the bottom four quintiles received less than

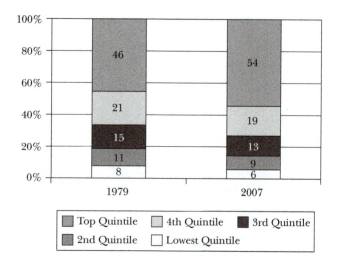

FIGURE 7.25 Distribution of Household Income by Quintile, the United States, 1979 and 2007

their proportionate share—only the highest income quintile received more than its proportionate share. Thus, between 1979 and 2007, income became increasingly concentrated in the highest income households.[68]

Some have suspected that relatively high mortality in the United States could be related to the high level of economic inequality in the United States in comparison to many European countries. This is especially a concern as the degree of inequality in the United States has increased over time.

Crimmins and her colleagues examined the evidence that educational inequality in the United States was one of the reasons for high older age mortality in the United States. They compared e_{65}^0 by sex in the United States and in ten European countries using data from surveys from the late 1990s. Educational attainment was classified in comparable categories.

The results in Figure 7.26 show that for both men and women, there is a large increment to survival from moving from a middle level of education (about high school graduation) to a high level of education. Also, for females, while those with a high educational level fare about the same in the United States and in Europe, those with low education do better in Europe. Thus, there is a greater mortality advantage for American than European women in obtaining a high education, or, to put it another way, there is a higher penalty for American than European women in having a low level of education. American men with high education have a higher e_{65}^0 than European men with high education. There were difficulties in making cross-national comparisons, but Crimmins

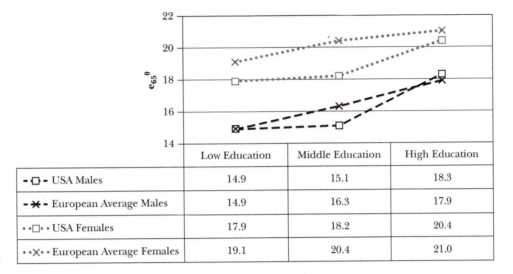

FIGURE 7.26   Expectation of Remaining Life at Age 65 by Sex and Education:
the United States and Average of 10 European Countries, Late 1990s

	Low Education	Middle Education	High Education
- □ - USA Males	14.9	15.1	18.3
- ✱ - European Average Males	14.9	16.3	17.9
• □ • USA Females	17.9	18.2	20.4
• ✕ • European Average Females	19.1	20.4	21.0

and her colleagues concluded that the high level of socioeconomic inequality in the United States contributed to higher mortality in the United States at the older ages.[69]

Researchers think that discrimination probably affects mortality when a substantial difference in mortality remains between groups even after differences in socioeconomic status have been taken into account. Figure 7.27 shows median income by educational attainment for Whites and African Americans in 1996.[70] At every level of education, the median income of Whites is higher than that of African Americans, and the income differential increases with education.

Figure 7.28 shows e_{45}^0 by race, sex, and family income in the United States for 1989–1991. For each sex and each racial group, higher family income is

related to a longer e_{45}^0. However, for a given gender and income level, e_{45}^0 is always higher for Whites than for African Americans.

The results in Figures 7.27 and 7.28 together indicate how racial disadvantage accumulates for African Americans. In Figure 7.27, we see that African Americans do not receive the same income benefits as Whites of education, and we see in Figure 7.28 that within an income category, White survival is higher than African-American survival.

Massey and Denton have argued that racial segregation is a major mechanism though which African-American poverty is perpetuated. They present evidence that an African-American urban underclass emerged in the 1970s that has persisted due to the connection between African-American poverty and urban racial residential segregation.

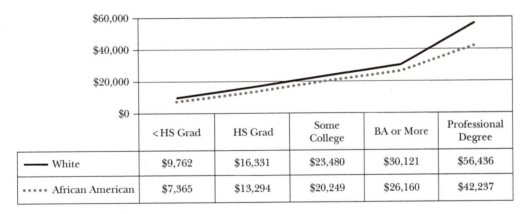

	<HS Grad	HS Grad	Some College	BA or More	Professional Degree
—— White	$9,762	$16,331	$23,480	$30,121	$56,436
••••• African American	$7,365	$13,294	$20,249	$26,160	$42,237

FIGURE 7.27   Median Income by Race and Education, the United States, 1996

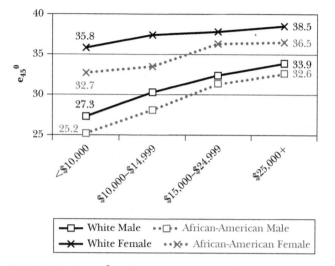

FIGURE 7.28 e_{45}^0 by Race, Sex, and Family Income in 1989–1991, the United States (1980 dollars)

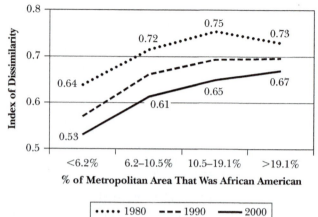

FIGURE 7.29 Index of Dissimilarity for African Americans in 220 U.S. Metropolitan Areas by Percentage of Metropolitan Area That Was African American, 1980–2000

The high level of concentration of African-Amerian neighborhoods in turn led to disappearance of public and commercial services and to increased levels of crime, property abandonment, and school dropouts. They further present evidence that the high level of racial segregation is mainly the result of racial discrimination in the housing market rather than due to African-American SES, housing preferences, or knowledge of the White housing market.[71]

Figure 7.29 shows the index of dissimilarity for African-American residential segregation in 1980–2000. It is computed for 220 metropolitan areas that have a nontrivial African-American population. The **index of dissimilarity** is the proportion of members of one group who would have to move to another location to have the same distribution across locations as some other group. Figure 7.29 shows the proportion of African Americans who would have to move to a different census tract for every census tract to have the same proportion of African Americans as the metropolitan area as a whole. The results are shown according to the percentage of a metropolitan area that was African American.[72]

Across time and across metropolitan areas that differed in the percentage of the population who was African American, between 53% and 75% of African Americans would have needed to move to a different census tract to attain an even African-American population distribution across tracts. The segregation level was generally greater the higher the percentage of the metropolitan area that was African American. There has been some decline in segregation over time, but Williams

and Collins note that this decline has mainly been due to some movement of African Americans into tracts that formerly had included almost no African Americans rather than to a decline in the overwhelmingly African-American composition of many census tracts.

Consistent with Massey and Denton, Williams and his colleagues also argued that one of the major ways that discrimination contributes to high African-American mortality is through residential segregation. They present evidence that heavily segregated African-American neighborhoods lead to poorer quality schools with fewer resources and less qualified teachers and create isolation from good employment opportunities. Although there are more poor Whites than poor African Americans in the United States, poor African Americans are much more geographically concentrated. The proximity of location of poor Whites to non-poor Whites does not result in the same kind of destructive neighborhood characteristics found for poor urban African Americans. Poor segregated neighborhoods tend to have crowded, poorly constructed and maintained housing, with high air pollution levels, all of which contribute to morbidity and mortality. Pharmacies in poor African-American neighborhoods tend to be less well stocked with medications, and urban segregation has been found to contribute to African-American homicide rates.[73]

LaVeist found that the African-American infant mortality rate (IMR) was related to the extent of residential segregation even after SES was taken into account, while residential segregation had a low association with White infant mortality.[74] Some other studies have not found a significant relationship between segregation and African-American infant mortality,[75] but most studies have found a relation between segregation and negative mortality and health outcomes for African Americans. Disentangling individual and neighborhood effects is complex. There is much more research to be done on this topic.[76]

MORTALITY FROM NATURAL CAUSES AND FROM EXTERNAL CAUSES BY SEX: UNITED STATES, 2005

In this section, we look at death rates from all natural causes and from the three kinds of external causes—homicide, suicide, and accidents—by age and sex. We also look at death rates from motor vehicle accidents.[77]

Figure 7.30 shows death rates from natural causes and from external causes per 100,000 people by age and sex for the United States in 2005. As we saw in Figures 4.20 and 4.21 in Chapter 4, the chances of dying are elevated in infancy and after about age 50. It is clear from Figure 7.30 that this age pattern of overall mortality is overwhelmingly caused by the age pattern of death from natural causes. The data table makes clear that although death rates are low between ages 1 and 45, external causes play a major role in mortality between ages 5 and 44, especially for males. In fact, for males aged 5–34 and females aged 15–24, more deaths are from external causes than from natural causes.

The difference in the age pattern of natural and external mortality is even more apparent in Figure 7.31, which shows the base 10 logarithm of the death rates by age. It is clear from the logged values that death rates from both natural and external causes are elevated in infancy. In a study of factors related to infant homicide in the United States in the late 1980s and early 1990s, Overpeck and her colleagues found that infants whose mothers had less education, whose mother was very young when the child was born, who had not had prenatal care, and in which the mother was not married were especially at risk of homicide. African-American and Native American infants also were more likely to be victims of homicide than White or Asian infants.[78] After age 15, death rates from both natural and external causes increase, but the increase in male external-cause death rates between age 15 and 35 is especially striking.

Figure 7.32 shows the percent distribution of all deaths by age and sex according to whether the death was from a natural cause, accident, homicide, or suicide. We saw in Figures 4.18 through 4.21 in Chapter 4 that in the United States, female chances of death are less than male chances of death at every age. We also see in Figure 7.30 that at every age, female death rates from natural causes were lower than male death rates from natural causes, and also female death rates from external causes were lower at every age than male death rates from external causes. Thus, although Figure 7.32 shows the

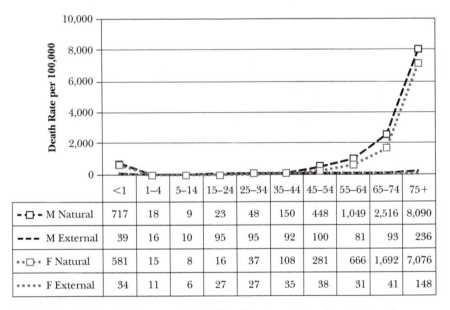

	<1	1–4	5–14	15–24	25–34	35–44	45–54	55–64	65–74	75+
- □ - M Natural	717	18	9	23	48	150	448	1,049	2,516	8,090
- - - M External	39	16	10	95	95	92	100	81	93	236
••□•• F Natural	581	15	8	16	37	108	281	666	1,692	7,076
••••• F External	34	11	6	27	27	35	38	31	41	148

FIGURE 7.30 Death Rates per 100,000 by Sex from Natural and External Causes, the United States, 2005

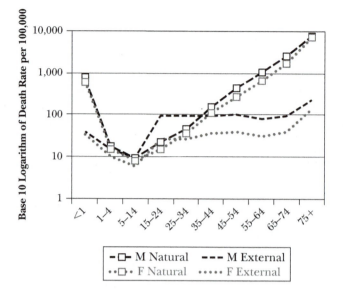

FIGURE 7.31 Base 10 Logarithm of Death Rates per 100,000 by Sex, the United States, 2005

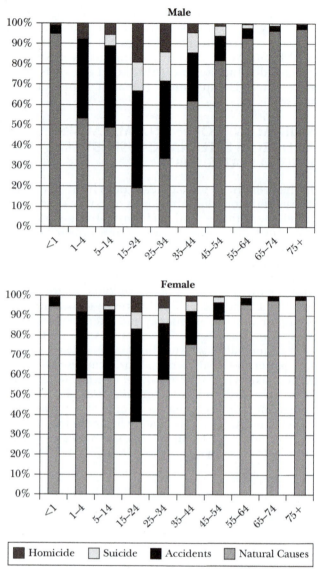

FIGURE 7.32 Percentage Distribution of Deaths from Natural and External Causes by Age and Sex, the United States, 2005

distribution of deaths by cause by age for males and for females, it is important to keep in mind that the level of female mortality is much lower than the level for males.

In Figure 7.32, natural causes comprised more than one-half of the deaths for males except for those aged 5–34 and for females except for those aged 15–24. So it is clear that external-cause mortality is mainly an issue for the young, especially young adults. Homicide comprises less than 10% of deaths for females in every age group, while it comprises more than 10% of all deaths for males aged 15–34.

Figure 7.33 shows the percent distribution of external-cause deaths by age for males and for females for the United States in 2005. For each sex, at every age, accidents comprise more than 50% of all external-cause deaths. Again, keep in mind that Figure 7.30 showed that death rates from external causes for females were lower than for males at every age.

Even though accidents are the major source of external-cause deaths at all ages, the kinds of accidents differ by age and sex. For young adults, accidents related to risky behavior, such as motor vehicle accidents, are common. For the elderly, accidents related to limitations of function and fragility, such as falls, predominate. Figure 7.34 shows the percentage of all external-cause deaths due to motor vehicle accidents and the percentage of all external-cause deaths due to falls by age. The percentage of external-cause deaths occurring in motor vehicle accidents peaks for those aged 15–24 and then tends to fall with age. Less than 4% of all external-cause deaths are due to

falls for those younger than age 35, after which the percentage due to falls rises to 46% for those aged 75 or older.

Figure 7.35 shows age-adjusted death rates from motor vehicle accidents, homicide, and suicide. Throughout 1950–2006, death rates from motor vehicle accidents are higher than from suicide, and death rates from suicide are higher than from homicide.

In Figure 7.36, we see the age-adjusted death rates from motor vehicle accidents, homicide, and suicide relative to their level in 1950. The death rate from homicide more than doubled between 1950 and

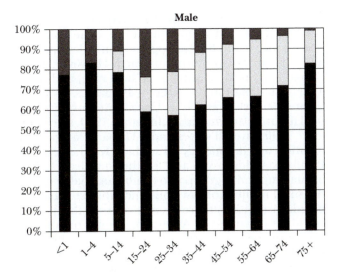

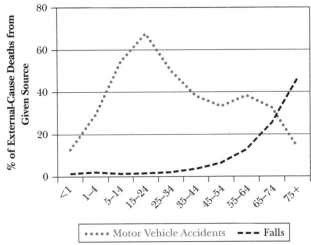

FIGURE 7.34 Percentage of External-Cause Deaths from Motor Vehicle Accidents and from Falls by Age, the United States, 2005

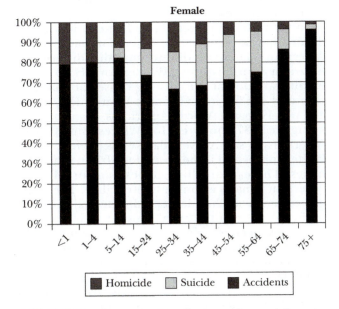

FIGURE 7.33 Percentage Distribution of External-Cause Deaths by Age and Sex, the United States, 2005

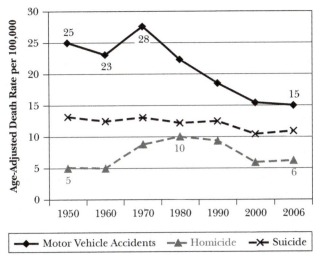

FIGURE 7.35 Age-Adjusted Death Rates per 100,000 from Selected External Causes, the United States, 1950–2006

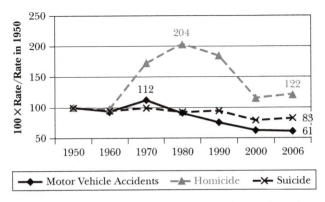

FIGURE 7.36 Age-Adjusted Death Rates from Selected External Causes Relative to 1950 Rates, the United States, 1950–2006

1980, but then fell sharply through the year 2000. In 2006, the homicide rate was 22% higher than its level in 1950. The death rate from suicide declined somewhat to 83% of the 1950 level by 2006. The death rate from motor vehicle accidents rose to 112% of its 1950 value by 1970, but by 2006 the death rate from motor vehicle accidents was only 61% of its 1950 value.

A great deal has been written about the trajectory of increasing and then decreasing homicide rates in the United States since 1960. Both the rise in homicide rates to a peak in 1980 and the subsequent decline seem mainly due to the increased use (and presumably availability) of handguns and then a decline in their use and availability.[79]

The peak in motor vehicle accident deaths in the 1970s was mainly due to an increase in deaths among men aged 15–29. The decline in death rates from motor vehicle accidents seems to have been due to a combination of an increase in the minimum drinking age, enforcement against drunk drivers, graduated license programs for young drivers, better testing of older drivers, mandatory seat belt laws, and car safety improvements such as airbags. Note that the 55 miles per hour national speed limit, which was established in the early 1970s, was abolished between 1987 and 1995. The abolition of this speed limit contributed to higher motor vehicle fatalities, but this was more than offset by other changes. Establishment of improved trauma care also contributed to lower fatalities, although the effect of a new trauma system only became apparent after it had been in use for ten years or more.[80]

Mortality by Race in the United States: Differentials and Trends

There are major differences in mortality in the United States among racial groups. The differences between African Americans and Whites are especially striking, with higher mortality from most causes for African Americans. Some of the sources of racial differences in mortality were discussed in this chapter, such as differences in socioeconomic status and the effects of discrimination, but examination of some of the specific mortality patterns by race is informative.

Table 7.4 shows age-adjusted death rates and infant mortality rates for racial groups and for those of Hispanic origin in the United States for 2006. The African-American age-adjusted death rate is considerably higher than the White rate. The Asian and Pacific Islander rate is lower than the White rate and probably reflects a real mortality difference. The accuracy of the low mortality rates for American Indians or Alaskan Natives has been questioned due to concerns about the fluidity of ethnic identity for members of that group and whether the same population is actually included in the numerator and in the denominator of that rate. This issue is discussed in Chapter 3.

As discussed in Chapter 3, *Hispanic* is considered by the U.S. Census Bureau and the National Center for Health Statistics as an ethnic designation, and Hispanics can be of any race. However, some Hispanics consider Hispanic to be a race, and when a racial designation is chosen by Hispanics, 95% designate themselves as White. Consistent mortality data for Hispanics are only available since 1990, since only after 1990 have all states had a Hispanic origin designation on vital statistics. Estimates for the Asian or Pacific Islander group and for the American Indian or Alaskan Native group also can be unreliable due to the small number of cases on which the estimates are based. In addition, there is some concern that people could be classified as American Indian or Alaskan Native in the census (the denominator of the rate) more easily than in death certificates for vital statistics (the numerator of the rate), which would lead to an underestimation of American Indian or Alaskan Native death rates.

In the rest of this section, we first consider racial differences between White Americans and African Americans. Then, we discuss mortality differences between non-Hispanic Whites and Hispanics. Finally, we look at the leading causes of death by race and sex for non-Hispanic Whites, Hispanics, and non-Hispanic African Americans.

Figure 7.37 shows e_0^0 for Whites and African Americans by sex. At every date, e_0^0 is the highest for White females and is the lowest for African-American males. The e_0^0 for White males and for African-American females is similar at every date. The racial gap for each sex has decreased. The major causes of the decrease in the racial gaps for men in recent years were declines in accidental deaths and in HIV deaths. For women, the main contributors were declines in heart disease and in accidental deaths.[81]

Figure 7.38 shows death rates by age, sex, and race for 2006. The sex differences are clearer in Figure 7.39, which shows ten times the base 10 logarithm of the death rates. The logarithm was multiplied by 10 to make the vertical scale easier to interpret. Thus, the value for White females aged 55–64 in Figure 7.39 appears as 28 rather than as 2.8. It is also clear that, generally, White male and African-American female age-specific death rates are similar.[82]

TABLE 7.4   Age-Adjusted Death Rates and Infant Mortality Rates by Race and Hispanic Origin, the United States, 2006

	White	African American	American Indian or Alaskan Native	Asian or Pacific Islander	Hispanic
Age-Adjusted Death Rate per 100,000	764	982	642	429	564
IMR	5.6	12.9	8.3	4.5	5.4

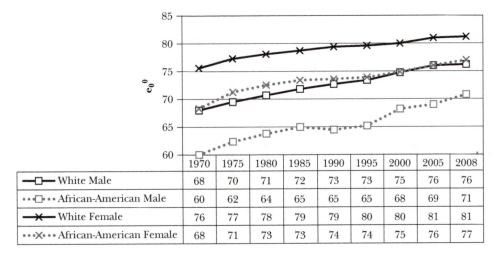

	1970	1975	1980	1985	1990	1995	2000	2005	2008
—□— White Male	68	70	71	72	73	73	75	76	76
••□•• African-American Male	60	62	64	65	65	65	68	69	71
—✕— White Female	76	77	78	79	79	80	80	81	81
••✕•• African-American Female	68	71	73	73	74	74	75	76	77

FIGURE 7.37 Expectation of Life at Birth by Race and Sex, the United States, 1970–2008

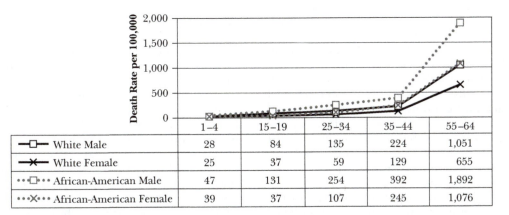

	1–4	15–19	25–34	35–44	55–64
—□— White Male	28	84	135	224	1,051
—✕— White Female	25	37	59	129	655
••□•• African-American Male	47	131	254	392	1,892
••✕•• African-American Female	39	37	107	245	1,076

FIGURE 7.38 Selected Age-Specific Death Rates by Sex and Race, the United States, 2006

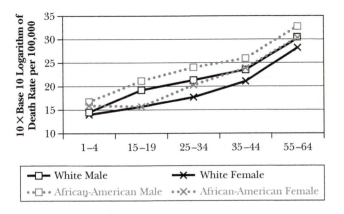

FIGURE 7.39 Ten Times the Base 10 Logarithm of Death Rate per 100,000 People by Race and Sex, the United States, 2006

Figure 7.40 shows age-adjusted death rates from homicide by race and sex over time. Death rates for African-American males are much higher than for the other groups. For each race, male rates are higher than female rates. We see that the decline in overall homicide rates shown in Figures 7.35 and 7.36 was substantially due to the decline for African-American males after 1970. Some decline after 1970 is also shown for African-American females.

The lower socioeconomic status on average of African Americans than of Whites and the poorer neighborhoods in which African Americans live contribute to high African-American homicide rates, but African-American homicide rates are disproportionately high even after such differences have been taken into account. Poverty and economic

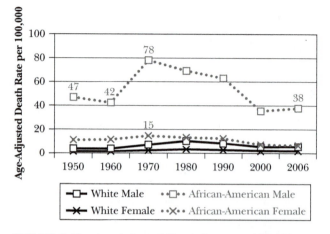

FIGURE 7.40 Age-Adjusted Death Rates per 100,000 People from Homicide by Race and Sex, the United States, 1950–2006

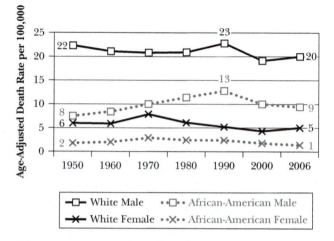

FIGURE 7.41 Age-Adjusted Death Rates per 100,000 People from Suicide by Race and Sex, the United States, 1950–2006

segregation are predictive of both African-American and White homicide rates, but poverty and economic segregation affect a higher proportion of African-American than White households. Also, poorer medical care of African-American compared to White trauma victims contributes to high African-American homicide rates. The magnitude of the impact of homicide on life expectancy also differs by race and gender. In 1975, near the peak of homicide rates, eliminating homicide as a cause of death would have added only 0.1 years of life to White women, 0.4 years of life for non-White women, and 0.2 years of life for White men, but 1.4 years of life for non-White men.[83]

Figure 7.41 shows similar information as in Figure 7.40 but for suicide rather than for homicide. For each sex, African-American suicide death rates

are lower than White suicide rates. This is different than the pattern for e_0^0 seen in Figure 7.37 or the pattern for homicide in Figure 7.40.

There has been much interest in why African-American suicide rates are relatively low. Among the reasons cited are greater social stigma associated with suicide, a higher degree of religiosity, and broader social support networks for African Americans than for Whites.[84]

Figure 7.42 shows infant mortality rates for African Americans and Whites in the United States over time.[85] At every date, the African-American IMR is higher than the White IMR. Some of the reasons for persistently high African-American infant mortality are the high proportion of African-American infants who are born prematurely, the high proportion of infants with low birth weight,

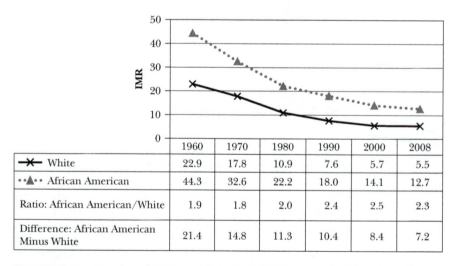

	1960	1970	1980	1990	2000	2008
✕ White	22.9	17.8	10.9	7.6	5.7	5.5
▲ African American	44.3	32.6	22.2	18.0	14.1	12.7
Ratio: African American/White	1.9	1.8	2.0	2.4	2.5	2.3
Difference: African American Minus White	21.4	14.8	11.3	10.4	8.4	7.2

FIGURE 7.42 Trends and Differentials in Racial Differences in Infant Mortality, the United States, 1960–2008

low socioeconomic status, and limitations in access to medical care.[86]

However, rates for both races have declined over time. An important question is, Has the gap or the differential between the African-American and the White IMR widened or narrowed over time?

The answer to that question depends on what measure of the gap is examined. The data table in Figure 7.42 shows two different measures of the gap between the African-American and White IMRs: (1) the ratio of the African-American IMR to the White IMR and (2) the difference between the African-American IMR and the White IMR.

The difference between the African-American and White IMRs has decreased greatly, from 21.4 in 1960 to 7.2 in 2008. This would indicate that the racial gap in IMR has narrowed. However, another way to look at differentials is to look at the ratio of the value for one group to the value for another group. The ratio of the African-American IMR to the White IMR has increased over time, rising from 1.9 in 1960 to 2.5 in 2000, and then was 2.3 in 2008. An argument could be made for the appropriateness of either of these measures, although it seems from looking at the graph that the gap has narrowed, which argues for looking at the difference between the IMR for the two groups. This example illustrates that looking at narrowing or widening of gaps between groups is complicated and that one should look carefully at the measure chosen.

African-American and White Crossover Mortality in the United States

We saw in Figure 7.37 that for each sex, the expectation of life at birth for African Americans is considerably lower than for Whites. We also saw in Figure 7.38 that below age 65, for each sex, age-specific death rates are higher for African Americans than for Whites. However, at advanced ages, the reported age-specific death rates for each sex have often been lower for African Americans than for Whites. When one group has lower death rates than another group at younger ages, but has higher death rates at older ages, this is called **crossover mortality**. The racial crossover has been found for as young as 75 years of age, but the age of crossover seems to have increased over time.

Figure 7.43 shows non-Hispanic African-American $_{10}q_x$ values divided by non-Hispanic White $_{10}q_x$ values by age and sex. Thus, $_{10}q_{30}$ is the proportion of those who are alive on their thirtieth birthday are still alive 10 years later on their fortieth birthday. If the value is greater than 1.0, this means that the non-Hispanic African-American rate is higher than the non-Hispanic White rate; if the value is less than 1.0, it means that the non-Hispanic White rate is higher. With data from 2008, we see that through age 80,

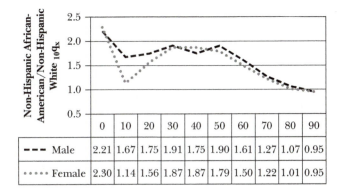

	0	10	20	30	40	50	60	70	80	90
- - - Male	2.21	1.67	1.75	1.91	1.75	1.90	1.61	1.27	1.07	0.95
····· Female	2.30	1.14	1.56	1.87	1.87	1.79	1.50	1.22	1.01	0.95

FIGURE 7.43 Ratio of Non-Hispanic African-American to Non-Hispanic White $_{10}q_x$, the United States, 2008

the chance of surviving 10 more years is less for non-Hispanic African Americans than for non-Hispanic Whites, but that the chance of surviving 10 more years after reaching age 90 is higher for non-Hispanic African Americans than for non-Hispanic Whites of each sex.[87]

There has been a controversy about whether this mortality crossover reflects real differences in the risk of dying by age for African Americans and Whites, or whether this pattern is a result of problems with data quality. One argument is that the crossover represents a true reversal at older ages in the chances of dying by race. This is a selection argument. This view maintains that high death rates at younger ages cause weaker African Americans to die, so that African Americans who survive to old age are very hardy individuals who then experience lower death rates in their old age than Whites of the same age. The counter argument is that the quality of the African-American data is lower than the quality of the White data and that age exaggeration depresses the reported African-American death rates at older ages. That the age of crossover has advanced over time could mean that selection has gotten weaker over time, or it could reflect improving quality of African-American data over time.[88]

The Hispanic Paradox

There also has been controversy about what is called the **Hispanic paradox**. The paradox is that although Hispanics in the United States have relatively low socioeconomic status, they have lower age-specific death rates than non-Hispanic Whites. Similar to the controversy about African-American crossover mortality, there is a controversy about whether the lower reported death rates for Hispanics are real or whether they are an artifact of data problems. The issue of the true mortality risks of Hispanics is also complicated by extensive migration back and forth across the U.S.-Mexico border.[89]

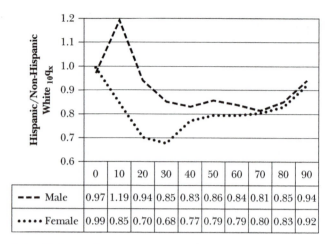

FIGURE 7.44   Ratio of Hispanic to Non-Hispanic White Age-Specific Death Rates, the United States, 2008

Figure 7.44 shows similar information for Hispanics compared to non-Hispanic Whites to that shown for non-Hispanic African Americans and non-Hispanic Whites in Figure 7.43. In every age group, Hispanic females have a lower chance of dying in a ten-year period than non-Hispanic Whites. For males, this is true except for the chance of dying between age 10 and age 20.[90]

As summarized by Palloni and Arias, there have been four proposed explanations for the Hispanic paradox:[91]

1. **Data artifacts:** There are three kinds of data artifacts or data problems that could lead to an underestimation of Hispanic mortality:
   a. **Ethnic identification:** Hispanic identity has often been underreported on death certificates compared to reporting of Hispanic identity in the census, which leads to underestimation of death rates.
   b. **Misreporting of ages:** Hispanic populations have sometimes been found to overstate their ages, which leads to an underestimation of age-specific death rates at older ages.
   c. **Mismatches of records:** In matching of persons alive at one time to later recorded deaths, lack of identification of persons in the death records leads to underestimation of death rates, which could occur for populations trying to avoid authorities or for whom the information used for matching is less complete or accurate.
2. **Healthy-migrant effect:** Healthier persons from origin populations are more likely to migrate, especially when migration is to earn income. Thus, Mexican and other Latin American migrants could be especially healthy individuals and thus have low death rates.
3. **Salmon-bias effect:** Migrants to the United States who become unemployed or who have health problems could be more likely to return to their origin country. The deaths of these somewhat unhealthy persons would then occur in their home country and would lead to the population remaining in the United States being especially healthy, which depresses death rates.
4. **Cultural effect:** Social and cultural characteristics of the Hispanic population, such as a high level of participation in social networks and receipt of substantial social support, are related to lower death rates.

There is more research to be done to disentangle the role of various factors in the Hispanic paradox. Palloni and Arias's work concluded that the Hispanic adult mortality advantage is a result of low death rates among foreign-born Hispanics.

They concluded that the salmon-bias effect played a major role. Some of the evidence that Palloni and Arias looked at is shown in Figure 7.45. The figure shows the distribution of self-reported health status among the responses Poor, Fair, and Good. This is shown for persons interviewed in the United States who were born in Mexico and for Mexican-born individuals interviewed in Mexico who had returned from the United States in the ten years before the interview. This is shown separately for those aged 50–59 and for those aged 60–74. For each age group,

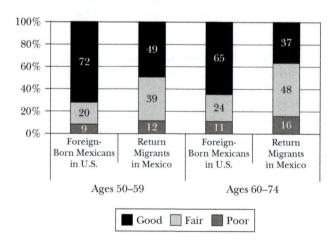

FIGURE 7.45   Distribution of Self-Reported Health among Foreign-Born Mexicans in the United States and among Return Migrants in Mexico, 2000

the return migrants in Mexico have worse reported health than the Mexican migrants in the United States, which is consistent with poor health being a cause of return migration to Mexico.

Leading Causes of Death in the United States by Sex and Age for Non-Hispanic Whites, African Americans, and Hispanics, 2008

In this section we look at the leading causes of death for non-Hispanic Whites, African Americans, and Hispanics in the United States in 2008. This is the most recent year for which these data are available. It takes quite a bit of time for the death registration data for a given year to be collected from all of the states and compiled centrally. Thus, there is a time lag of several years between when data are collected and when they are processed and available.

Table 7.5 shows the leading causes of death for the three groups by sex for all ages and for selected age groups. The causes are coded according to the GBD categories, as shown in Table 5.2 in Chapter 5, as Group 1: *Communicable and Related Causes*; Group 2: **Non-communicable Causes**; and Group 3: **External Causes**.[92]

In the first panel with results for all ages, non-Hispanic White females have a higher overall death rate than non-Hispanic White males, even though at every age non-Hispanic White females have lower age-specific death rates than non-Hispanic White males. The higher overall rate for non-Hispanic White females than non-Hispanic White males is due to the older age distribution of non-Hispanic White females than non-Hispanic White males. This is a similar phenomenon to the sometimes higher crude death rate in more developed countries than in less developed countries, even though death rates at every age are lower in the more developed country.

Heart disease and cancer are the two leading causes of death for all six groups. For males, accidents are among the leading four causes of death, and for non-Hispanic African-American males, homicide is also important. The cause of death results point to the fact that males engage in more risky behavior than females. For children aged 1–4, accidents are the leading cause of death for every group. What is perhaps more disturbing is that homicide is the second leading cause of death for non-Hispanic African-American males and females and is the fourth leading cause of death for non-Hispanic Whites and Hispanics. Congenital malformations are an important cause of death for all six groups. Children who die from congenital malformations had noticeable problems from the time of their birth.

External causes of death are the leading causes for all six groups of teenagers (ages 15–19). This is partially because overall death rates for teenagers are relatively low, since teenagers rarely die from natural causes. For non-Hispanic African-American males, homicide is the leading cause of death, while for the other five groups accidents are the leading causes of death. Homicide rates are several times higher for males than females and are also much higher for non-Hispanic African-American than for non-Hispanic White or Hispanic males.

Much has been written about suicides of teenage girls, so it is perhaps surprising that for all three groups, male suicide rates are higher than female suicide rates. Depression is a major cause of suicide, and women seem more willing than men to seek help for depression, which contributes to lower suicide rates for women. Also, although men have higher suicide rates, women have higher rates of attempted suicide. For women, a suicide attempt could often be a call for help. It also could contribute to less deadly means being used for women attempting suicide than for men.[93]

External causes are still the leading cause of death for young adults aged 25–34, except for non-Hispanic African-American females, for whom heart disease is the leading cause of death. Again, homicide is the leading cause of death for non-Hispanic African-American males. The role of degenerative and chronic conditions—heart disease and cancer—as causes of death becomes somewhat more important in the 25–34 age group than at younger ages. For both male and female non-Hispanic African Americans, by ages 25–34 HIV enters the five leading causes of death, and the HIV death rates are higher for non-Hispanic African-American males than for non-Hispanic African-American females. One reason for higher male than female non-Hispanic African-American HIV death rates is that injection drug use is a major source of HIV in the United States, and males are more likely than females to use injection drugs.

For those aged 35–44, degenerative and chronic conditions hold the leading place for all groups except non-Hispanic White and Hispanic males, for whom accidents remain the leading cause of death. Heart disease and cancer are important causes of death for all groups. HIV is an important cause of death for non-Hispanic African-American males and females.

For all six groups of those aged 55–64, cancer and heart disease are the leading causes of death, which are chronic and degenerative conditions of the elderly. No infectious diseases are among the leading causes of death for this age group, and although accidents are still among the leading five causes for males, their ranking is much lower. The nature of accidents has also changed. As shown in Figure 7.34, for younger adults, motor vehicle accidents are a

TABLE 7.5 Five Leading Causes of Death by Age and Sex and Rate per 100,000 People for Non-Hispanic Whites, Non-Hispanic African Americans, and Hispanics, All Ages and by Age Group, the United States, 2008

All Ages

	Non-Hispanic White		Non-Hispanic African American		Hispanic	
	Male 978	Female 986	Male 794	Female 701	Male 317	Female 275
1	Heart disease 255	Heart disease 244	Heart disease 191	Heart disease 174	Heart disease 64	Cancer 60
2	Cancer 241	Cancer 213	Cancer 179	Cancer 153	Cancer 63	Heart disease 59
3	Chronic lower respiratory disease 60	Chronic lower respiratory disease 65	Accidents 45	Stroke 47	Accidents 35	Stroke 17
4	Accidents 60	Stroke 63	Stroke 39	Diabetes 33	Stroke 14	Diabetes 14
5	Stroke 42	Alzheimer's disease 50	Homicide 39	Nephritis 33	Diabetes 14	Accidents 12

Ages 1–4

	Non-Hispanic White		Non-Hispanic African American		Hispanic	
	Male 29	Female 23	Male 50	Female 38	Male 28	Female 22
1	Accidents 10	Accidents 7	Accidents 14	Accidents 9	Accidents 10	Accidents 6
2	*Congenital malformations 3*	*Congenital malformations 3*	Homicide 7	Homicide 5	*Congenital malformations 3*	*Congenital malformations 3*
3	Cancer 3	Cancer 2	*Congenital malformations 5*	*Congenital malformations 4*	Cancer 2	Cancer 3
4	Homicide 2	Homicide 2	Cancer 3	Heart disease 2	Homicide 2	Homicide 2
5	Heart disease 1	Heart disease 1	Heart disease 3	Cancer <1	Heart disease <1	*Influenza and pneumonia <1*

Ages 15–19

	Non-Hispanic White		Non-Hispanic African American		Hispanic	
	Male 73	Female 33	Male 124	Female 39	Male 77	Female 28
1	Accidents 40	Accidents 19	Homicide 63	Accidents 10	Accidents 31	Accidents 10
2	Suicide 13	Suicide 3	Accidents 27	Homicide 8	Homicide 22	Cancer 4
3	Homicide 4	Cancer 3	Suicide 9	Cancer 3	Suicide 8	Homicide 3
4	Cancer 3	Homicide 1	Heart disease 5	Heart disease 3	Cancer 1	Suicide 3
5	Heart disease 2	Heart disease 1	Cancer 4	Suicide 2	Stroke <1	*Congenital malformations <1*

Ages 25–34

	Non-Hispanic White		Non-Hispanic African American		Hispanic	
	Male 140	Female 62	Male 234	Female 102	Male 107	Female 42
1	Accidents 63	Accidents 20	Homicide 82	Heart disease 15	Accidents 42	Accidents 10
2	Suicide 26	Cancer 8	Accidents 44	Accidents 13	Homicide 18	Cancer 8
3	Heart disease 10	Suicide 6	Heart disease 24	Cancer 11	Suicide 10	Homicide 4
4	Cancer 9	Heart disease 4	Suicide 16	*HIV 10*	Cancer 8	Heart disease 3
5	Homicide 6	Homicide 3	*HIV 13*	Homicide 9	Heart disease 6	Suicide 2

(Continued)

236

TABLE 7.5 (Continued)

Ages 35–44

	Non-Hispanic White		Non-Hispanic African American		Hispanic	
	Male 225	Female 134	Male 361	Female 230	Male 159	Female 82
1	Accidents 60	Cancer 34	Heart disease 71	Cancer 50	Accidents 40	Cancer 26
2	Heart disease 37	Accidents 27	Accidents 52	Heart disease 39	Heart disease 18	Accidents 10
3	Suicide 31	Heart disease 15	Homicide 40	HIV 22	Cancer 17	Heart disease 7
4	Cancer 27	Suicide 10	HIV 37	Accidents 19	Homicide 12	Chronic liver disease and cirrhosis 4
5	Chronic liver disease and cirrhosis 8	Chronic liver disease and cirrhosis 4	Cancer 36	Stroke 11	Suicide 11	Stroke 3

Ages 55–64

	Non-Hispanic White		Non-Hispanic African American		Hispanic	
	Male 1067	Female 652	Male 1869	Female 1053	Male 831	Female 477
1	Cancer 353	Cancer 272	Cancer 545	Cancer 348	Cancer 227	Cancer 179
2	Heart disease 274	Heart disease 106	Heart disease 504	Heart disease 246	Heart disease 195	Heart disease 80
3	Accidents 54	Chronic lower respiratory disease 44	Stroke 92	Stroke 61	Chronic liver disease and cirrhosis 57	Diabetes 35
4	Chronic lower respiratory disease 47	Accidents 24	Diabetes 79	Diabetes 57	Diabetes 50	Chronic liver disease and cirrhosis 17
5	Chronic liver disease and cirrhosis 36	Diabetes 22	Accidents 77	Nephritis 36	Accidents 49	Nephritis 15

Ages 75–84

	Non-Hispanic White		Non-Hispanic African American		Hispanic	
	Male 6167	Female 4420	Male 7234	Female 4897	Male 4264	Female 3119
1	Heart disease 1641	Heart disease 1053	Heart disease 1997	Heart disease 1354	Heart disease 1140	Heart disease 769
2	Cancer 1625	Cancer 1029	Cancer 1916	Cancer 1032	Cancer 1063	Cancer 658
3	Chronic lower respiratory disease 511	Chronic lower respiratory disease 390	Stroke 453	Stroke 405	Stroke 273	Stroke 239
4	Stroke 322	Stroke 305	Chronic lower respiratory disease 359	Diabetes 270	Diabetes 242	Diabetes 197
5	Alzheimer's disease 184	Alzheimer's disease 224	Diabetes 318	Nephritis 187	Chronic lower respiratory disease 212	Chronic lower respiratory disease 136

large part of accident deaths, while for older persons, falls and other conditions related to age play a larger role in accident mortality.

Non-communicable causes of death are the leading five causes of death for every group aged 75–84. Heart disease and cancer predominate, and Alzheimer's disease is the fifth leading cause of death for both male and female non-Hispanic Whites.

Diabetes is among the leading causes of death for non-Hispanic African Americans and for Hispanics of both sexes, which could reflect poorer medical care for the elderly or lesser adherence to physicians' instructions in these groups than for non-Hispanic Whites.

CONCLUDING COMMENTS

For most people in the MDR, advances in medicine have made communicable diseases unimportant. As non-communicable diseases increasingly become the predominant causes of death, motivating and enabling healthy behaviors becomes key to further mortality reductions. In addition, the development of policies to counter the mortality effects of poverty, inequality, and racial discrimination remains important.

✓ Study and Review Online

SUMMARY

1. The United States moved from being a leader among developed countries in low mortality to a middle or poor position. This has become a cause of substantial concern.

2. In the United States, the antismoking campaign is related to large declines in cigarette consumption, especially among men. This has led to male declines in lung cancer mortality.

3. Alcohol consumption has declined in the United States, with accompanying declines in cirrhosis of the liver. In Russia, male alcohol consumption remains high and is a major cause of high adult male mortality.

4. The American population has become increasingly overweight or obese. Male death rates from diabetes have increased, while there has been some decline in female diabetes death rates. This is perhaps related to better adherence to physicians' instructions among women than men.

5. While the prevalence of hypertension has increased, improvements in detection and treatment of hypertension have contributed to declines in death rates from heart disease and stroke.

6. As mortality has declined, differentials in mortality by socioeconomic status have not decreased. As new medical treatments are developed and there is new knowledge about healthful behaviors, these treatments and behaviors are more likely to be adopted the higher a person's socioeconomic status.

7. In the United States, racial residential segregation exacerbates the negative effects of poverty and contributes to higher African-American mortality.

8. Racial differences in mortality in the United States remain large, with a substantial difference in death rates between White Americans and African Americans. Homicide death rates for African-American males are especially high. On the other hand, African Americans have lower death rates from suicide than White Americans of the same sex.

KEY TERMS

body mass index (BMI)   217
social support   221

fundamental causes of disease approach   223
index of dissimilarity   226

crossover mortality   233
Hispanic paradox   233

QUESTIONS FOR DISCUSSION AND REVIEW

1. Discuss the kinds of causes of death that are prevalent in less developed countries and the kinds of causes of death that are prevalent in more developed countries. How does the difference in the distribution of causes of death relate to different patterns of age-specific mortality rates in more developed and in less developed countries?

2. What do differences in mortality by sex typically look like? What do we know about the sources of sex differentials in mortality? What is the role

of external causes of death in sex differentials in mortality? What is the role of health behaviors in sex differentials in mortality?

3. What is the role of health behaviors in mortality change in more developed countries?

4. What is the fundamental causes of disease approach? How does this relate to thinking about the social causes of death?

SUGGESTED PAPER TOPICS

1. For the United States, discuss the effects of the differences in mortality between non-Hispanic whites and African Americans and how these differences affect the life situation and opportunities of members of these groups. What policies would you recommend to reduce mortality differentials for members of these groups?

2. In the area of smoking, alcohol consumption, or diet and exercise, trace death rates from related causes and policies designed to influence that health behavior in a country of your choice. Assess how successful the policies have been.

3. Discuss the antismoking campaign in the United States, the prevalence of smoking, and related causes of death. Why might a similar campaign work or not work in a country such as China, India, or Russia?

NOTES

1. CDC. 2001. *Ten Great Public Health Achievements—United States, 1900–1999*, http://www.cdc.gov/about/history/tengpha.htm (accessed February 2, 2012).

2. Herschel S. Horowitz. 1996. "The Effectiveness of Community Water Fluoridation in the United States," *Journal of Public Health Dentistry*, 56: 253–258.

3. Eileen M. Crimmins, Samuel H. Preston, and Barney Cohen, eds. 2011. *Explaining Divergent Levels of Longevity in High-Income Countries*, Washington, DC: National Academies Press, Table 1.1.

4. The tables in this chapter with age-adjusted death rates starting in 1950 for the United States are from National Center for Health Statistics. 2011. *Health, United States, 2010: With Special Feature on Death and Dying*, Hyattsville, MD: Government Printing Office, http://www.cdc.gov/nchs/hus.htm (accessed November 9, 2011).

5. The cross-national comparisons and the death rates from specific conditions since 1980 in this section are from WHO, Mortality database, http://apps.who.int/whosis/database/mort/table1.cfm (accessed July 8, 2011).

6. Leslie B. Snyder, Mark A. Hamilton, Elizabeth W. Mitchell, James Kiwanuka-Tondo, Fran Fleming-Milici, and Dwayne Proctor. 2004. "A Meta-Analysis of the Effect of Mediated Health Communication Campaigns on Behavior Change in the United States," *Journal of Health Communication*, 9: 71–96; and Rudolph L. Leibel, Michael Rosenbaum, and Jules Hirsch. 1995. "Changes in Energy Expenditure Resulting from Altered Body Weight," *New England Journal of Medicine*, 332: 621–628.

7. Robert J. Battjes. 1988. "Smoking as an Issue in Alcohol and Drug Abuse Treatment," *Addictive Behaviors*, 13: 225–230; Simone A. French, Cheryl L. Perry, Gloria R. Leon, and Jayne A. Fulkerson. 1994. "Weight Concerns, Dieting Behavior, and Smoking Initiation among Adolescents: A Prospective Study," *American Journal of Public Health*, 84: 1818–1820; and Paul Froom, Samuel Melamed, and Jochanan Benbasset. 1998. "Smoking Cessation and Weight Gain," *Journal of Family Practice*, 46: 460–464.

8. Richard Peto, Alan D. Lopez, Jillian Boreham, Michael Thun, Clarke Heath, Jr., and Richard Doll. 1996. "Mortality from Smoking Worldwide," *British Medical Bulletin*, 52: 12–21.

9. American Lung Association. 2011. *Trends in Tobacco Use*, http://www.lungusa.org/finding-cures/our-research/trend-reports/Tobacco-Trend-Report.pdf (accessed September 29, 2011).

10. John P. Pierce and Elizabeth A. Gilpin. 1995. "A Historical Analysis of Tobacco Marketing and the Uptake of Smoking by Youth in the United States: 1890–1977," *Health Psychology*, 14: 500–508.

11. U.S. Public Health Service. 1964. *Smoking and Health: Report of the Advisory Committee to the Surgeon General of the Public Health Service*, Public Health Service Publication No. 1103, Washington, DC: Government Printing Office, http://profiles.nlm.nih.gov/ps/access/NNBBMQ.pdf (accessed March 28, 2013).

12. David M. Cutler and Srikanth Kadiyala. 2003. "The Return to Biomedical Research: Treatment and Behavioral Effects." In *Measuring the Gains from Medical Research*, ed. R. Topel and K. Murphy, Chicago: University of Chicago Press.

13. U.S. Surgeon General. 1989. *Reducing the Health Consequences of Smoking: 25 Years of Progress*, Washington, DC: Government Printing Office, 268.

14. K. E. Warner. 1977. "The Effects of the Anti-Smoking Campaign on Cigarette Consumption," *American Journal of Public Health*, 67: 645–650; and K. E. Warner. 1989. "Effects of the Antismoking Campaign: An Update," *American Journal of Public Health*, 79: 144–151.

15. L. G. Escobedo and J. P. Peddicord. 1996. "Smoking Prevalence in US Birth Cohorts: The Influence of Gender and Education," *American Journal of Public Health*, 86: 231–236; and Alexander Schulze and Ute Mons. 2006. "The Evolution of Educational Inequalities in Smoking: A Changing Relationship and a Cross-over Effect among German Birth Cohorts of 1921–70," *Addiction*, 101: 1051–1056.

16. American Lung Association. 2011. *Trends in Tobacco Use*, http://www.lungusa.org/finding-cures/our-research/trend-reports/Tobacco-Trend-Report.pdf (accessed September 29, 2011).

17. B. A. Toll and P. M. Ling. 2005. "The Virginia Slims Identity Crisis: An Inside Look at Tobacco Industry Marketing to Women," *Tobacco Control*, 14: 172–180, http://www.ncbi.nlm.nih.gov/pmc/articles/PMC1748044/pdf/v014p00172.pdf (accessed September 30, 2011).

18. Y. C. Ko, C. H. Lee, M. J. Chen, C. C. Huang, W. Y. Chang, H. J. Lin, H. Z. Wang, and P. Y. Chang. 1997. "Risk Factors for Primary Lung Cancer among Non-smoking Women in Taiwan," *International Journal of Epidemiology*, 26: 24–31; Takeshi Hirayama. 2000. "Non-smoking Wives of Heavy Smokers Have a Higher Risk of Lung Cancer: A Study from Japan," *British Medical Journal*, 282: 940–942; and Majid Ezzati and Alan D. Lopez. 2003. "Estimates of Global Mortality Attributable to Smoking in 2000," *The Lancet*, 362: 847–852.

19. The death rates in this section are discussed as being from lung cancer. Actually, they are from cancer of the trachea, bronchus, and lung.

20. Thomas E. Novotny, Michael C. Fiore, Evridiki J. Hatziandreu, Gary A. Giovino, Sherry L. Mills, and John P. Pierce. 1990. "Trends in Smoking by Age and Sex, United States, 1974–1987: The Implications for Disease Impact," *Preventive Medicine*, 19: 552–561; Samuel Preston and Haidong Wang. 2006. "Sex Mortality Differences in the United States: The Role of Cohort Smoking Patterns," *Demography*, 434: 631–646; and Fred C. Pampel. 2002. "Cigarette Use and the Narrow-ing Sex Differential in Mortality," *Population and Development Review*, 28: 77–104.

21. International Smoking Statistics. 2012. http://www.pnlee.co.uk/iss.htm (accessed April 16, 2012).

22. Eileen M. Crimmins, Samuel H. Preston, and Barney Cohen, eds. 2011. *Explaining Divergent Levels of Longevity in High-Income Countries*, Washington, DC: National Academies Press, Table 5.1.

23. Eileen M. Crimmins, Samuel H. Preston, and Barney Cohen, eds. 2011. *Explaining Divergent Levels of Longevity in High-Income Countries*, Washington, DC: National Academies Press, Table 5.2.

24. Michael G. Marmot, G. Rose, M. J. Shipley, and B. J. Thomas, 1981. "Alcohol and Mortality: A U-Shaped Curve," *The Lancet*, 317: 580–583.

25. Arthur L. Klatsky, Mary Anne Armstrong, and Gary D. Friedman. 1992. "Alcohol and Mortality," *Annals of Internal Medicine*, 117: 646–654; and Robert D. Brewer and Monica H. Swahn. 2005. "Binge Drinking and Violence," *Journal of the American Medical Association*, 294: 616–618.

26. Brian O'Neill, Allan F. Williams, and Kurt M. Dubowski. 1983. "Variability in Blood Alcohol Concentrations: Implications for Estimating Individual Results," *Journal of Studies on Alcohol*, 44: 222–230; and J. R. Wilson and R. Plomin. 1985. "Individual Differences in Sensitivity and Tolerance to Alcohol," *Biodemography and Social Biology*, 21: 162–184.

27. National Institute on Alcohol Abuse and Alcoholism. 2009. *Apparent per Capita Ethanol Consumption for the United States, 1850–2007. (Gallons of Ethanol, Based on Population Age 15 and Older prior to 1970 and on Population Age 14 and Other Thereafter)*, http://www.niaaa.nih.gov/Resources/DatabaseResources/QuickFacts/AlcoholSales/Pages/consum01.aspx (accessed October 27, 2011).

28. D. H. Jernigan, M. Monteiro, R. Room, and S. Saxena. 2000. "Towards a Global Alcohol Policy: Alcohol, Public Health and the Role of WHO," *Bulletin of the World Health Organization*, 78: 491–499.

29. Kim Severson. 2011. "States Putting Hopes in 'Bottoms Up' to Help the Bottom Line," *New York Times*, September 28, http://www.nytimes.com/2011/09/29/us/alcohol-laws-eased-to-raise-tax-money.html?_r=1&scp=1&sq=alcohol%20taxes&st=cse (accessed September 29, 2011).

30. A. V. Nemtsov. 1999. "Alcohol-Related Human Losses in Russia in the 1980s and 1990s," *Addiction*, 97: 1413–1425.

31. V. G. Treml. 1997. "Soviet and Russian Statistics on Alcohol Consumption and Abuse," in *Premature Death in the New Independent States*, ed. J. L. Bobadilla, C. A. Costello, and F. Mitchell, Washington, DC: National Academy Press, 220–238.

32. Vladimir Shkolnikov, Martin McKee, and David A Leon. 2001. "Changes in Life Expectancy in Russia in the Mid-1990s." *The Lancet*, 357: 917–921.

33. Vladimir Shkolnikov, France Mesle, and Jacques Vallin.1996. "Health Crisis in Russia II. Changes in Causes of Death: A Comparison with France and England and Wales (1970 to 1993)," *Population: An English Selection*, 8: 155–189; and Daniel Tarschys. 1993. "The Success of a Failure: Gorbachev's Alcohol Policy, 1985–88," *Europe-Asia Studies*, 45: 7–25.

34. Reuters. 2010. "Putin Calls Time on Russians' Alcohol Habit," Reuters, January 14, http://www.reuters.com/article/idUSTRE60D4N620100114 (accessed September 6, 2010).

35. Scott Baker. 2010. "Russian Finance Minister Encourages More Smoking & Drinking," *The Blaze*, September 4, http://www.theblaze.com/stories/russian-finance-minister-encourages-more-smoking-drinking/ (accessed June 3, 2011).

36. Health Systems Trust. 2011. "Moves towards a Healthy Lifestyle," http://www.hst.org.za/news/moves-towards-healthy-lifestyle (accessed September 30, 2011).

37. David Zaridze, Dimitri Maximovitch, Alexander lazarev, Vladimir Igitov, Alex Boroda, Jillian Boreham, Peter Boyle, Richard Peto, and Paolo Boffeta. 2009. "Alcohol Poisoning Is a Main Determinant of Recent Mortality Trends in Russia: Evidence from a Detailed Analysis of Mortality Statistics and Autopsies," *International Journal of Epidemiology*, 38: 143–153.

38. World Health Organization. 2011. *Global Status Report on Alcohol and Health*, Geneva: World Health Organization, http://www.who.int/substance_abuse/publications/global_alcohol_report/msbgsruprofiles.pdf (accessed October 31, 2011).

39. Elizabeth Brainerd and David M. Cutler. 2005. "Autopsy on an Empire: Understanding Mortality in Russia and the Former Soviet Union." *The Journal of Economic Perspectives*, 19: 107–131; Lincoln C. Chen, Frederike Wittgenstein, and Elizabeth McKeon. 1996. "The Upsurge of Mortality in Russia: Causes and Policy Implications," *Population and Development Review*, 22: 517–530; William Alex Pridemore. 2004. "Weekend Effects in Binge Drinking and Homicide: The Social Connection between Alcohol and Violence in Russia," *Addiction*, 99: 1034–1041; Vladimir Shkolnikov, France Mesle, and Jacques Vallin.1996. "Health Crisis in Russia II. Changes in Causes of Death: A Comparison with France and England and Wales (1970 to 1993)," *Population: An English Selection*, 8: 155–189; and P. Walberg, M. McKee, V. Shkolnikov, and L. Chenet. 1998. "Economic Change, Crime, and Mortality Crisis in Russia: Regional Analysis," *British Medical Journal*, 317: 312–318.

40. Richard G. Rogers, Robert A. Hummer, and Charles B. Nam. 2000. *Living and Dying in the USA: Behavioral, Health and Social Differentials of Adult Mortality*, San Diego, CA: Academic Press.

41. Daniel L. McGee and Diverse Populations Collaboration. 2005. "Body Mass Index and Mortality: A Meta-Analysis Based on Person-Level Data from Twenty-Six Observational Studies," *Annals of Epidemiology*, 15: 87–97.

42. National Obesity Laboratory. 2009. *Body Mass Index as a Measure of Obesity*, UK National Health Service, http://www.noo.org.uk/uploads/doc789_40_noo_BMI.pdf (accessed January 17, 2012).

43. Cynthia L. Ogden and Margaret D. Carroll. 2011. *Prevalence of Overweight, Obesity, and Extreme Obesity among Adults: United States, Trends 1960–1962 through 2007–2008*, Washington, DC: Centers for Disease Control and Prevention, http://www.cdc.gov/NCHS/data/hestat/obesity_adult_07_08/obesity_adult_07_08.pdf (accessed November 4, 2011).

44. Tavia Gordon, William P. Castelli, Marthana C. Hjortland, William B. Kannel, and Thomas R. Dawber. 1977. "Diabetes, Blood Lipids, and the Role of Obesity in Coronary Heart Disease Risk for Women: The Framingham Study," *Annals of Internal Medicine*, 87: 393–397.

45. Dawn E. Alley, Jennifer Lloyd, and Michelle Shardell. 2010. "Can Obesity Account for Cross-National Differences in Life Expectancy Trends?" in *Explaining Divergent Levels of Longevity in High-Income Countries*, ed. Eileen M. Crimmins, Samuel H. Preston, and Barney Cohen, Washington, DC: National Academies Press, 164–192.

46. Lorraine L. Lipscombe and Janet E. Hux. 2007. "Trends in Diabetes Prevalence, Incidence, and Mortality in Ontario, Canada 1995–2005: A Population-Based Study," *The Lancet*, 369: 750–756; and S. F. Wetterhall, D. R. Olson, F. DeStefano, J. M. Stevenson, E. S. Ford, R. R. German, J. C. Will, J. M. Newman, S. J. Sepe, and F. Vinicor. 1992. "Trends in Diabetes and Diabetic Complications, 1980–1987," *Diabetes Care, 15:* 960–967.

47. Judith Charlton, Radoslav Latinovic, and Martin C. Gulliford. 2008. "Explaining the Decline in Early Mortality in Men and Women with Type 2 Diabetes," *Diabetes Care*, 31: 1761–1766.

48. National Obesity Observatory. 2009. *International Comparisons of Obesity Prevalence*, http://www.noo.org.uk/uploads/doc799_2_International_Comparisons_Obesity_Prevalence2.pdf (accessed November 10, 2011).

49. Mark Landler. 2012. "In Iowa, Michelle Obama Says, 'Let's Move!'" *New York Times*, February 9; Ron Nixon. 2012. "New Rules for School Meals Aim at Reducing Obesity," *New York Times*, January 25; and Christine Kearney. 2012. "Michelle Obama's School Lunch Plan Is Unpopular," *Medical News Today*, September 26, http://www.medicalnewstoday.com/articles/250732.php, (accessed March 4, 2013).

50. Michael M. Grynbaum. 2012. "Health Panel Approves Restrictions on Sale of Large Sugary Drinks," *New York Times*, September 13; Michael M. Grynbaym. 2013. "Judge Blocks New York City's Limits on Bug Sugary Drinks," *New York Times*, March 11; Tara Culp-Ressler. 2013. "State with Highest Obesity Rate Passes 'Anti-Bloomberg Bill' to Ban Food Regulation," *Think-Progress*, March 12, http://thinkprogress.org/health/2013/03/12/1703081/mississippi-anti-bloomberg-bill-obesity/?mobile=nc (accessed March 12, 2013); and Michael M. Grynbaum. 2013. "New York Soda Ban to Go before State's Top Court," *New York Times*, October 17.

51. William Harless. 2012. "Taxes on Unhealthy Foods Gain Traction in Europe," PBS NewsHour, June 7, http://www.bbc.co.uk/news/world-europe-20280863 (accessed March 4, 2013); OECD. 2012. *Obesity Update 2012*, http://www.oecd.org/health/health-systems/49716427.pdf (accessed March 4, 2013); BBC News, 2012. "Denmark to Abolish Tax on High-Fat Foods," November 10, http://www.bbc.co.uk/news/world-europe-20280863 (accessed March 4, 2013); and Suzanne Daley. 2013. "Hungary Tries a Dash of Taxes to Promote Healthier Eating Habits," *New York Times*, March 2.

52. Eileen M. Crimmins. 1981. "The Changing Pattern of American Mortality Decline, 1940–77, and Its Implications for the Future," *Population and Development Review*, 7: 229–254; and Sundar Natarajan and Paul J Nietert. 2003. "National Trends in Screening, Prevalence, and Treatment of Cardiovascular Risk Factors," *Preventive Medicine*, 36: 389–397.

53. National Center for Health Statistics. 2011. *Health, United States, 2010: With Special Feature on Death and Dying*, Hyattsville, MD: Government Printing Office, http://www.cdc.gov/nchs/hus.htm (accessed November 9, 2011).

54. Martha J. Bailey and Andrew Goodman-Bacon. 2011. "The War on Poverty's Experiment in Public Medicine: Community Health Centers and the Mortality of Older Americans," unpublished paper, Department of Economics, University of Michigan.

55. National Center for Health Statistics. 2011. *Health, United States, 2010: With Special Feature on Death and Dying*, Hyattsville, MD: Government Printing Office, http://www.cdc.gov/nchs/hus.htm (accessed November 9, 2011).

56. Jose A. Tapia Granados. 2005. "Increasing Mortality during the Expansions of the US Economy, 1900–1996," *International Journal of Epidemiology*, 34: 1194–1202; Young-Ho Khang, John W. Lynch, and George A. Kaplan. 2005. "Impact of Economic Crisis on Cause-Specific Mortality in South Korea," *International Journal of Epidemiology*, 34: 1291–1301; and Jose A. Tapia Granados and Ana V. Diez Roux. 2009. "Life and Death during the Great Depression," *Proceedings of the National Academy of Sciences*, 106: 17290–17295.

57. B. J. Hirsh. 1981. "Social Networks and the Coping Process: Creating Personal Communities," in *Social Networks and Social Support*, ed. B. Gottlieb, Beverly Hills, CA: Sage, 151.

58. N. Lin, R. S. Simeone, W. M. Ensel, and W. Kuo. 1979. "Social Support, Stressful Life Events and Illness: A Model and an Empirical Test," *Journal of Health and Social Behavior*, 20: 108–119.

59. Bert Uchino. 2006. "Social Support and Health: A Review of Physiological Processes Potentially Underlying Links to Disease Outcomes," *Journal of Behavioral Medicine*, 29: 377–387.

60. Lisa F. Berkman and Lester Breslow. 1983. *Health and Ways of Living: The Alameda County Study*, New York: Oxford University Press; and Julianne Holt-Lunstad, Timothy B. Smith, and J. Bradley Layton. 2010. "Social Relationships and Mortality Risk: A Meta-Analytic Review," *PLoS Medicine*, 7, http://www.plosmedicine.org/article/info%3Adoi%2F10.1371%2Fjournal.pmed.1000316 (accessed April 20, 2012).

61. Evelyn M. Kitagawa and Philip M. Hauser. 1972. *Differential Mortality in the United States: A Study in Socioeconomic Epidemiology*, Cambridge, MA: Harvard University Press,

62. Charles Kadushin. 1964. "Social Class and the Experience of Ill Health," *Sociological Inquiry*, 34: 67–80.

63. Gregory Pappas, Susan Queen, Wilbur Hadden, and Gail Fisher. 1993. "The Increasing Disparity in Mortality between Socioeconomic Groups in the United States," *The New England Journal*

of Medicine, 329: 103–109; and G. D. Smith, M. Bartley, and D. Blane. 1990. "The Black Report on Socioeconomic Inequalities in Health 10 Years On," *British Medical Journal*, 301: 373–377.

64. Dana Goldman and James P. Smith. 2011. "The Increasing Value of Education to Health," *Social Science & Medicine*, 72: 1728–1737.

65. Bruce G. Link and Jo Phelan. 1995. "Social Conditions as Fundamental Causes of Disease," *Journal of Health and Social Behavior*, 35 (Extra Issue): 80–94.

66. Bruce G. Link and Jo C. Phelan. 2002. "McKeown and the Idea That Social Conditions Are Fundamental Causes of Disease," *American Journal of Public Health*, 92: 730.

67. Richard Miech, Fred Pampel, Jinyoung Kim, and Richard G. Rogers. 2011. "The Enduring Association between Education and Mortality: The Role of Widening and Narrowing Disparities," *American Sociological Review*, 76: 913–934.

68. Congressional Budget Office. 2011. *Trends in the Distribution of Household Income between 1979 and 2007*, Washington: Congressional Budget Office, http://www.cbo.gov/ftpdocs/124xx /doc12485/10-25-HouseholdIncome.pdf (accessed October 26, 2011); and Rebecca M. Blank. 2011. *Changing Inequality*, Berkeley: University of California Press.

69. Eileen M. Crimmins, Samuel H. Preston, and Barney Cohen, eds. 2011. *Explaining Divergent Levels of Longevity in High-Income Countries*, Washington, DC: National Academies Press, 117–141.

70. David R. Williams. 1999. "Race, Socioeconomic Status, and Health: The Added Effects of Racism and Discrimination," *Annals of the New York Academy of Sciences*, 896: 173–188, Table 7.

71. Douglas S. Massey and Nancy A. Denton. 1993. *American Apartheid: Segregation and the Making of the Underclass*, Cambridge, MA: Harvard University Press.

72. John Iceland, Daniel H. Weinberg, and Erika Steinmetz. 2002. *Racial and Residential Segregation in the United States: 1980–2000*, Washington, DC: Government Printing Office, 64.

73. David R. Williams and Chiquita Collins. 2001. "Racial Residential Segregation: A Fundamental Cause of Racial Disparities in Health," *Public Health Reports*, 116: 404–416; and David R. Williams, Selina A. Mohammed, Jacinta Leavell, and Chiquita Collins. 2010. "Race, Socioeconomic Status, and Health: Complexities, Ongoing Challenges, and Research Opportunities," *Annals of the New York Academy of Sciences*, 1186: 69–101.

74. Thomas A. LaVeist. 1989. "Linking Residential Segregation to the Infant Mortality Race Disparity," *Sociology and Social Research*, 73: 90–94.

75. Mary O. Hearst, J. Michael Oakes, and Pamela Jo Johnson. 2008. "The Effect of Racial Segregation on Black Infant Mortality," *American Journal of Epidemiology*, 168: 1247–1254.

76. Michael R. Kramer and Carol R. Hogue. 2009, "Is Segregation Bad for Your Health?" *Epidemiological Reviews*, 31: 178–194.

77. Figures 7.30 through 7.36 are based on data from World Health Organization, WHO Statistical Information System, http://apps.who.int /whosis/database/mort/table1_process.cfm (accessed September 17, 2011).

78. Mary D. Overpeck, Ruth A. Brenner, Ann C. Trumble, Lara B. Trifiletti, and Heinz W. Berendes. 1998. "Risk Factors for Infant Homicide in the United States," *New England Journal of Medicine*, 339: 1211–1216.

79. Reynolds Farley. 1980, "Homicide Trends in the United States," *Demography*, 17: 177–188; and Alfred Blumstein, Frederick P. Rivara, and Richard Rosenfeld. 2000. "The Rise and Decline of Homicide and Why," *Annual Review of Public Health*, 21: 505–541.

80. Avery B. Nathens, Gregory J. Jurkovich, Peter Cummings, Frederick P. Rivara, and Ronald V. Maier. 2000. "The Effect of Organized Systems of Trauma Care on Motor Vehicle Crash Mortality," *Journal of the American Medical Association*, 15: 1990–1994; David C. Grabowski and Michael A. Morrisey. 2001. "The Effect of State Regulations on Motor Vehicle Fatalities for Younger and Older Drivers: A Review and Analysis," *The Milbank Quarterly*, 79: 517–545; and Guohua Li, Cyrus Shahpar, Jurek George Grabowski, and Susan P. Baker. 2001. "Secular Trends of Motor Vehicle Mortality in the United States, 1910–1994," *Accident Analysis & Prevention*, 33: 423–432.

81. Data in Figure 7.37 are from Arialdi M. Minino, Sherry L. Murphy, Jiaquan Xu, and Kenneth D. Kochanek. 2011. "Deaths: Final Data for 2008," *National Vital Statistics Reports*, Hyattsville, MD: National Center for Health Statistics, http://www.cdc.gov/nchs/data/nvsr/nvsr59 /nvsr59_10.pdf (accessed June 8, 2012); also see Sam Harper, Dinela Rushani, and Jay S. Kaufman. 2012. "Trends in Black-White Life Expectancy Gap, 2003–2008," *Journal of the American Medical Association*, 307: 2257–2259.

82. The results in Figures 7.38 and 7.39 are from M. Heron. 2010. "Leading Causes of Death for 2006," *National Vital Statistics Reports*, March 31, National Center for Health Statistics, http://www.cdc.gov/nchs/data/nvsr/nvsr58 /nvsr58_14.pdf (accessed June 8, 2012).

83. David Eitle, Stewarrt J. D'Alessio, and Lisa Stolzenberg. 2006. "Economic Segregation, Race, and Homicide," *Social Science Quarterly*, 87: 638–657; David R. Williams and Pamela Braboy Jackson. 2005. "Social Sources of Racial Disparities in Health," *Health Affairs*, 24: 325–334; and Reynolds Farley. 1980, "Homicide Trends in the United States," *Demography*, 17: 177–188.

84. Leigh A. Willis, David W. Coombs, Patricia Drentea, and William Cockerham. 2003. "Uncovering the Mystery: Factors of African American Suicide," *Suicide and Life-Threatening Behavior*, 33: 412–429; and Shawn O. Utsey, Joshua N. Hook, and Pia Stanard. 2007. "A Re-Examination of Cultural Factors That Mitigate Risk and Promote Resilience in Relation to African American Suicide: A Review of the Literature and Recommendations for Future Research," *Death Studies*, 31: 399–416.

85. Data from Arialdi M. Minino, Sherry L. Murphy, Jiaquan Xu, and Kenneth D. Kochanek. 2011. "Deaths: Final Data for 2008," *National Vital Statistics Reports*, Hyattsville, MD: National Center for Health Statistics, http://www.cdc.gov/nchs/data/nvsr/nvsr59/nvsr59_10.pdf (accessed June 8, 2012).

86. Centers for Disease Control and Prevention. 2011. "CDC Health Disparities and Inequalities Report—United States, 2011," *Morbidity and Mortality Weekly Report*, 60(Suppl.), January 14, http://www.cdc.gov/mmwr/pdf/other/su6001.pdf (accessed February 6, 2012); and Marian F. MacDorman and T. J. Matthews. 2008. "Recent Trends in Infant Mortality in the United States," *NCHS Data Brief* (9), October, http://198.246.98.21/nchs/data/databriefs/db09.pdf (accessed February 6, 2012).

87. Elizabeth Arias. 2010. *United States Life Tables by Hispanic Origin*, National Center for Health Statistics, Vital and Health Statistics, series 2, no. 152, October, http://www.cdc.gov/nchs/data/series/sr_02/sr02_152.pdf (accessed September 27, 2012). Many of the earlier graphs on mortality by race compared all African Americans to all Whites. These figures compare non-Hispanic African Americans to non-Hispanic Whites. When data are shown for trends over time, it is often not possible to show data separately by Hispanic ethnicity due to the recency of uniform collection of demographic data by Hispanic ethnicity.

88. Nan Johnson. 2000. "The Racial Crossover in Comorbidity, Disability, and Mortality, *Demography*, 37: 267–283; Samuel Preston, Irma Elo, Ira Rosenwaike, and Mark Hill. 1996. "African-American Mortality at Older Ages: Results of a Matching Study," *Demography*, 33: 193–209; and Scott M. Lynch, J. Scott Brown, and Katherine G. Harmsen. 2003. "Black-White Differences in Mortality Compression and Deceleration and the Mortality Crossover Reconsidered," *Research on Aging*, 25: 456–483.

89. Alberto Palloni and Jeffrey D. Morenoff. 2001. "Interpreting the Paradoxical in the Hispanic Paradox," *Annals of the New York Academy of Sciences*, 954: 140–174.

90. United States Census Bureau. 2012. *The 2012 Statistical Abstract*, http://www.census.gov/compendia/statab/cats/births_deaths_marriages_divorces.html (accessed September 16, 2012).

91. Alberto Palloni and Elizabeth Arias. 2004. "Paradox Lost: Explaining the Hispanic Adult Mortality Advantage," *Demography*, 41: 385–415.

92. The results in Table 7.5 are from M. Heron. 2012. "Leading Causes of Death for 2008," *National Vital Statistics Reports*, Hyattsville, MD: National Center for Health Statistics, http://www.cdc.gov/nchs/data/nvsr/nvsr60/nvsr60_06.pdf (accessed June 8, 2012).

93. George E. Murphy. 1998. "Why Women Are Less Likely Than Men to Commit Suicide," *Comprehensive Psychiatry*, 39: 165–175; and Anna Maria Moller-Leimkuhler. 2003. "The Gender Gap in Suicide and Premature Death or: Why Are Men So Vulnerable." *European Archives of Psychiatry and Clinical Neuroscience*, 253: 1–8.

CHAPTER 8

FERTILITY PATTERNS IN THE MODERN ERA

LEARNING OBJECTIVES

- Describe changes in the level of fertility in the LDR and in the MDR since 1950.

- Define natural fertility and controlled fertility. Explain the behavioral changes that lead to the shift from natural fertility to controlled fertility.

- List the proximate determinants of fertility and the main indicators of each.

- Describe how different patterns of marriage and different patterns of fertility control lead to different age-specific fertility patterns.

- Explain the difference between the gross reproduction rate and the net reproduction rate and how mortality influences the differences between the two.

((• Listen to the Chapter Audio

OVERVIEW

While death is inevitable, it is a source of sadness to those close to the deceased. On the other hand, the birth of a child is usually a joyous event. Although it is always good for mortality to be lower, how many children women and couples want and what fertility level is seen as desirable are the result of a balancing of the level of fertility with the level of mortality. Often what is desired by parents is a certain number of surviving children, and what is desired by governments is a moderate positive growth rate. Thus when women, couples, and governments form a view of what level of fertility is desirable, this is often dependent on their perception of the level of infant and child mortality and what they expect the level of infant and child mortality will be in the future.

This is the first of three chapters that discusses fertility. Although they address distinct topics, they are clearly interrelated. In addition, the meaning of these chapters cannot be fully understood without the earlier material in the chapters about mortality.

In this chapter, we look at the definition and interpretation of measures of fertility and of population growth. We also look at variations in fertility across world regions and at changes in fertility since 1950. We then look at how fertility and mortality work

together to result in different levels of population growth. This is a more complicated version of looking at how the crude birth rate and the crude death rate work together to produce the rate of natural increase, which was discussed in Chapter 2. After that, we examine how age patterns of female marriage, union formation, and childbearing have varied across countries and over time.

Chapter 9 discusses fertility change in historical Europe and in the least developed region (LDR) since 1950. A major concern has been what motivates couples to limit their fertility. Chapter 10 discusses fertility issues in the most developed region (MDR). Increasingly, the main fertility concern in the MDR is fertility that is so low that it will lead to population decline, a situation that most countries want to avoid. Thus, many MDR governments have been trying to induce women to have more children. These efforts have yielded mixed results.

THE GENERAL FERTILITY RATE, THE CHILD–WOMAN RATIO, AND THE TOTAL FERTILITY RATE

Chapter 2 traced the course of the crude birth rate. The crude birth rate looks at the total number of births per 1,000 people of all ages. A demographic, behavioral approach would concentrate more directly on the experiences and decisions of the people most directly involved in childbearing.

Women between their 15th and their 50th birthdays are usually able to bear children. Ages 15–49 are often called the **childbearing ages**. A slightly more refined measure of fertility than the crude birth rate is the **general fertility rate**, which is the number of births per 1,000 women aged 15–49. To calculate the general fertility rate, all you need is information about the number of births and about the population by age and sex. You do not need information on the number of births by age of the mother.

Sometimes researchers calculate the **child–woman ratio**, which is the number of children aged 0–4 per 1,000 women aged 15–49. An advantage of the child–woman ratio is that you do not need *any* direct information about births in order to calculate it. The information on children and women by age can be obtained from household listings in censuses or surveys without any direct questions on fertility. With information on child mortality, the child–woman ratio can be converted into a general fertility rate for the previous 5 years.

Within the childbearing ages, the chance that a woman has a baby is not the same at all ages. The **age-specific fertility rate (ASFR)** is the rate of childbearing by age of women, usually considered in 5-year age groups, and usually expressed per 1,000 women in the age group. In all populations, the chance of bearing a child increases after age 15 and declines after some age in the twenties or thirties. An example of this is shown in Figure 8.1. Different age patterns of marriage, entry into sexual intercourse, and postponement of the birth of the first child, as well as different patterns of voluntary fertility control lead to differences in the age pattern of fertility. These differences are discussed later in this chapter.

One could look at the fertility situation in a population by looking at the age-specific fertility rates for each of the seven 5-year age groups in the childbearing ages (from 15–19 through 45–49). However, the fertility situation is often summarized through the **total fertility rate (TFR)**, which is the number of children that a woman would have if she passed through the childbearing ages having children at each age at the rate prevalent in that population at every age. One can think of the TFR as the average number of children born over the life of a woman in a particular population if she survives through the childbearing ages. Thus, the total fertility rate does not adjust for female mortality.

If the age-specific fertility rates are presented for 5-year age groups of women, the TFR is the sum of the age-specific fertility rates multiplied by 5. While age-specific fertility rates are usually presented per 1,000 women, the TFR is usually presented per individual woman. For the age-specific fertility rates shown in Figure 8.1, the TFR would be 3.00. The TFR for this example is calculated as shown in Box 8.1.

It takes both a male and a female to produce a child. In principle, one could look at ASFRs of men and then calculate a male TFR. Although there has been research on fertility by age of men, a male TFR is rarely calculated.[1] One reason why a male TFR is rarely calculated is that the beginning and ending of the childbearing ages are clearer for women than for men. Another reason is that while it is almost always clear who the mother of a child is, it is sometimes not known who the father is.

Figure 8.2 shows the TFR in the world as a whole, in the United States, and in major groupings of countries. The world TFR was almost 5 from 1950–1955 through 1965–1970. World TFR fell after 1965–1970. By 2005–2010, the world TFR had fallen to 50% of the 1950–1955 value. The TFR in the LDR had begun to fall in the 1970s. By 2005–2010, the TFR in the LDR had declined to 44% of the 1950–1955 value. The TFR in the LeastDC was essentially unchanged between 1950–1955 and 1980–1985. In fact, the TFR in the LeastDC rose somewhat between the early 1950s and the 1970s. The TFR in the LeastDC began to fall in the 1990s, about 20 years later than in the LDR as a whole. The 2005–2010 value of the TFR in the LeastDC was 68% of the 1950–1955 value.

The TFR in the more developed region (MDR) declined from 2.8 in 1950–1955 to 1.7 in 2005–2010. The MDR TFR in 1950–1955 was slightly higher than the LDR TFR was in 2005–2010. The TFR in the United States was noticeably higher than in the MDR before 1970 and after 1990. The higher TFR in the United States than in the MDR 1950–1965 reflects the Baby Boom that occurred in the United States between the late 1940s and the mid-1960s. In a low mortality population, a TFR of less than 2.07 will result in long-term population decline, no matter how low death rates become. A low mortality population with a TFR less than 2.07 is said to be in

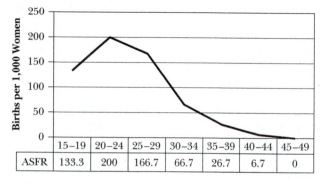

	15–19	20–24	25–29	30–34	35–39	40–44	45–49
ASFR	133.3	200	166.7	66.7	26.7	6.7	0

FIGURE 8.1 Age-Specific Fertility Rates Resulting in a Total Fertility Rate of 3.00

BOX 8.1
Calculation of the Total Fertility Rate

Calculation of the total fertility rate from the age-specific fertility rates in Figure 8.1 is done by summing the age-specific fertility rates. Then this sum is multiplied by 5, because there are 5 years of age in each age group. If age-specific fertility rates were given for every individual year of age 15–49, the total fertility rate would be calculated by summing up the values for each single year of age 15–49.

Although the crude birth rate is typically presented per 1,000 persons, the total fertility rate is shown per woman. Thus, the sum of the age-specific fertility rates times five is divided by 1,000 to present the TFR per individual woman. The TFR is interpreted as the number of children a woman would have if she went through life having children at the rate prevalent in the population.

Age Group	Age-Specific Fertility Rate per 1,000 Women
15–19	133.3
20–24	200.0
25–29	166.7
30–34	66.7
35–39	26.7
40–44	6.7
45–49	0.0
Sum	600.1

5 × Sum   = TFR per 1,000 women = 3,000.5

5 × Sum/1,000 = TFR per individual woman = 3.00

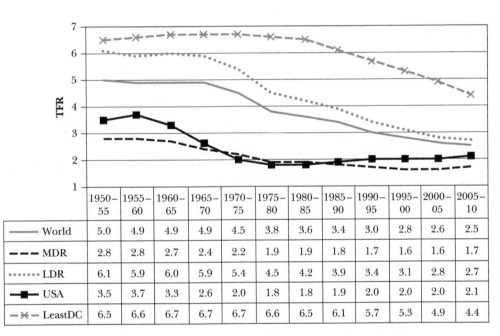

	1950–55	1955–60	1960–65	1965–70	1970–75	1975–80	1980–85	1985–90	1990–95	1995–00	2000–05	2005–10
World	5.0	4.9	4.9	4.9	4.5	3.8	3.6	3.4	3.0	2.8	2.6	2.5
MDR	2.8	2.8	2.7	2.4	2.2	1.9	1.9	1.8	1.7	1.6	1.6	1.7
LDR	6.1	5.9	6.0	5.9	5.4	4.5	4.2	3.9	3.4	3.1	2.8	2.7
USA	3.5	3.7	3.3	2.6	2.0	1.8	1.8	1.9	2.0	2.0	2.0	2.1
LeastDC	6.5	6.6	6.7	6.7	6.7	6.6	6.5	6.1	5.7	5.3	4.9	4.4

FIGURE 8.2   Total Fertility Rate (TFR) for the World, MDR, LDR, the United States, and LeastDC, 1950–2010

a situation of below-replacement fertility. The MDR had a TFR of less than 2.07 in the entire period of 1975–2010.

Figure 8.3 shows the TFR in world regions. At every date, the TFR is the highest in Africa. The gap in the TFR between Africa, on the one hand,

and Asia and Latin America and the Caribbean, on the other hand, increased over time. In 1950–1955, the TFR in Asia and in Latin America and the Caribbean was 0.7 children less than in Africa; in 2005–2010, the difference was 2.3 children. The TFR in Africa did not begin to decline noticeably

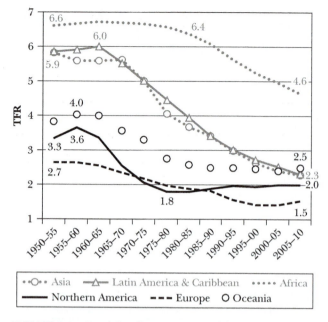

FIGURE 8.3   Total Fertility Rate in World Regions, 1950–2010

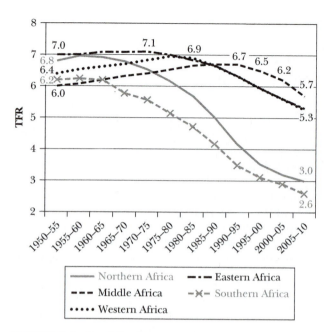

FIGURE 8.4   Total Fertility Rate in Regions of Africa, 1950–2010

until after 1985, while in Latin America and the Caribbean, a decline was noticeable after 1965 and in Asia after 1970.

TFR in Europe was lower at almost every date than in the MDR as a whole. The value of the TFR for Northern America mainly reflects the value for the United States. Again, the impact of the American Baby Boom is clear in the relatively high TFR in Northern America. Europe did not have an elevated TFR in 1950–1965 because unlike the United States, many European countries did not have a post–World War II Baby Boom. After 1990, Europe had substantially below-replacement fertility. Australia, New Zealand, and Canada had similar Baby Booms after World War II as occurred in the United States. The effects of the Baby Boom in Australia and New Zealand are reflected in the results for Oceania.

Trends in the Total Fertility Rate by Region of Africa

We see in Figure 8.3 that fertility in Africa is much higher than in other world regions. Figure 8.4 shows that there is great variability in fertility among African regions.

Sub-Saharan Africa includes all African regions except Northern Africa. When people talk about the demographic situation in Africa, they often mean sub-Saharan Africa.

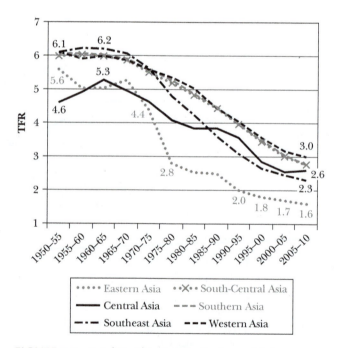

FIGURE 8.5   Total Fertility Rate in Regions of Asia, 1950–2010

After 1975, the TFR in Northern Africa was lower than in every other African region except Southern Africa. The fertility trajectory in Northern Africa is similar to that shown in Western Asia in Figure 8.5.

Both Northern Africa and Western Asia are mainly composed of traditionally Muslim countries. The pattern and causes of fertility change in Algeria, which is in Northern Africa, are discussed in Chapter 9.

In Middle Africa and Western Africa, there was a marked increase in the TFR from the early 1950s through the early 1980s or early 1990s. This increase is likely due to improving health, which reduced the extent of subfecundity. **Subfecundity** occurs when women have difficulty in becoming pregnant and carrying a pregnancy through to result in a live birth. Subfecundity has long been a concern in much of sub-Saharan Africa.[2]

Many of the TFR patterns in Figure 8.4 mirror trends in mortality in African regions seen in Figure 4.8, except that the sharp drop in survival in Southern Africa due to HIV is not seen in fertility trends in Southern Africa. There has been controversy about the extent to which HIV has depressed fertility in Southern Africa. This is difficult to know with certainty, since estimates of the extent to which fertility is depressed among untreated HIV-positive women range from a small amount to about 20% and because the TFR had been declining in Southern Africa since the late 1960s, well before HIV had any population impact.[3]

In 2005–2010, Middle Africa had the highest TFR, with slightly lower TFR in Eastern Africa and Western Africa. However, in all three regions, the TFR was at least one child less than it had been at its peak value. Thus, although fertility remains high in these three regions, it had begun a downward trajectory by the 1990s. In 2005–2010, the TFR in Middle Africa was only slightly lower than it had been in 1950–1955 (5.7 vs. 6.0). If one only looked at the values of the TFR in 1950–1955 and 2005–2010, one might conclude that there had been no fertility decline in Middle Africa. However, by looking at the entire trajectory of the TFR, one can see there has been substantial change. By 2005–2010, a question for sub-Saharan Africa, including Middle Africa, was no longer "What can be done to begin a fertility decline?" but rather "What can be done to continue and accelerate a fertility decline?" We saw in Table 2.4 in Chapter 2 that in 2005–2010, the growth rate in Africa was 23 per 1,000 population and the natural rate of increase was 24 per 1,000. With a crude birth rate of 36 per 1,000 and a TFR of 4.6, if fertility does not decline further in Africa, then many African countries, especially in Eastern and Middle Africa, face very high growth rates and accompanying challenges to social and economic development. The different fertility trajectories in Kenya (in Eastern Africa) and in Nigeria (in Western Africa) are discussed in Chapter 9.

Trends in the Total Fertility Rate by Region of Asia

As seen in Figure 8.3, Asia and Latin America and the Caribbean have had similar values of the TFR for 1950–2010. In this section, we look at trends in TFR by region of Asia, and in the next section we look at trends in the TFR by regions of Latin America and the Caribbean.

As shown in Figure 8.5, there has been great variability in TFR by region of Asia. Western Asia, South-Central Asia, and Southern Asia had similar values of TFR throughout the period. Southeast Asia had similar values to the other three regions until 1975 but then experienced more rapid fertility decline.

Central Asia had the lowest TFR among Asian regions in 1950–1955, but the TFR increased until 1960–1965, when it reached a value higher than for Eastern Asia in 1960–1965. The picture for Central Asia is somewhat similar to that for Western Africa in Figure 8.4, in which TFR increased for some time after 1950–1955. In both cases, improved nutritional status and health could have contributed to higher fertility. Many of the countries in Central Asia were formerly in the Soviet Union. The drop in the TFR in the 1990s in Central Asia was likely related to the social and economic disruption that followed the dissolution of the Soviet Union.[4]

Eastern Asia had moderately high fertility in the early 1950s, but it had the lowest fertility among Asian regions after 1970. In Eastern Asia, the TFR fell from 4.4 in 1970–1975 to 2.8 in 1975–1980. Eastern Asia had below replacement fertility after 1990, with no sign of an increase in the TFR to replacement level. The trajectory for Eastern Asia is mainly determined by China with a TFR of 1.6 in 2005–2010, but Japan and the Republic of Korea (South Korea) are also in Eastern Asia, both of which had an even lower TFR than China at 1.3 in 2005–2010. Chapter 10 discusses the pattern and causes of fertility change in Japan.

Trends in the Total Fertility Rate by Region of Latin America and the Caribbean

Figure 8.6 shows the TFR by region of Latin America and the Caribbean. Like Middle Africa and Central Asia, the TFR increased after 1950–1955 in the Caribbean. Caribbean fertility declined after 1960–1965.

Fertility began to decline in Central America after 1970–1975, later than in the other regions of Latin America and the Caribbean. Mexico comprises a major part of Central America. The lag in decline in fertility in Mexico compared to other less developed countries is discussed more in Chapter 9.

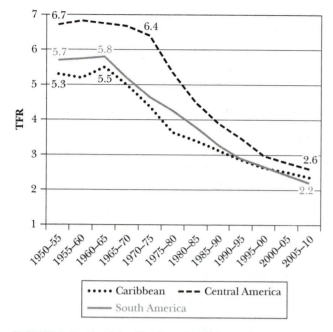

FIGURE 8.6 Total Fertility Rate in Regions of Latin America and the Caribbean, 1950–2010

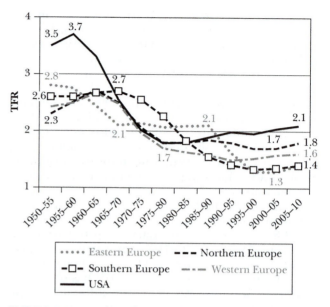

FIGURE 8.7 Total Fertility Rate in Regions of Europe and the United States, 1950–2010

In South America, fertility increased slightly from 1950–1955 through 1960–1965, after which it declined. The TFR in South America in 2005–2010 was 2.2, slightly above replacement level. South America includes Chile, Argentina, and Brazil, which have experienced fairly rapid economic development.

Trends in the Total Fertility Rate by Region of Europe

Europe and Northern America include most of the more developed countries. We see in Figure 8.2 that the United States has had a higher TFR than the MDR as a whole since the late 1980s, and we see in Figure 8.3 that Northern America (comprised overwhelmingly of the United States) also has had a higher TFR than Europe since the late 1980s. The diversity of the trends in the TFR in Europe and how the TFR in regions of Europe compare to the TFR in the United States are shown in Figure 8.7.

In Figure 8.7, we see that the TFR in the United States is above that of every European region from 1950–1955 through 1960–1965. This reflects the elevated fertility after World War II during the Baby Boom in the United States. After dipping below the TFR in several European regions, by 1990–1995, the U.S. TFR was again higher than in any European region.

In Eastern Europe, the TFR declined in 1950–1970, which was almost unchanged until 1990, and then declined rapidly after 1990. The decline of fertility in Eastern Europe after 1990 was related to the dissolution of the Soviet Union in 1991. The period after 1991 was not a good time to have children, due to dire economic conditions, which only gradually improved. In Chapter 10, there is more discussion of fertility in Ukraine, which is in Eastern Europe.

Northern Europe had the lowest fertility among European regions in 1950–1955, but it had the highest fertility among European regions in 2005–2010. Chapter 10 discusses the pattern and causes of fertility in Sweden, which is in Northern Europe.

Fertility in Western Europe was similar to that in Northern Europe until 1980, after which it was considerably lower than in Northern Europe. The TFR in Western Europe was below replacement after 1975. In Chapter 10, there is more discussion of changes in fertility in France, which is in Western Europe.

In Southern Europe, the TFR increased slightly between 1950–1955 and 1965–1970, and then steadily declined. The TFR in Southern Europe was tied with Eastern Europe for the lowest among European regions in 2005–2010 at 1.4. In Chapter 10, there is more discussion of the pattern and causes of low fertility in Italy, which is in Southern Europe.

In 2005–2010, every region of Europe had a TFR too low to prevent population decline in the long run, although there was a slight increase in the TFR in every European region between 2000–2005 and 2005–2010. The low TFR in Europe has been a source of great policy anxiety, since almost every country wants to avoid actual population decline. Low fertility and a low or negative growth rate also result in substantial population aging, which presents challenges for how to support the elderly population. Consequences of population aging are discussed in Chapter 11.

THE SEX RATIO AT BIRTH

The TFR looks at the total number of children (both boys and girls) born to a woman as she passes through the childbearing ages. In populations in which nothing is done to interfere with the sex of children who are born, slightly more baby boys than baby girls are born. In Chapter 9, we discuss sex-selective abortion, which has had a major effect on the ratio of baby boys to baby girls in some Asian countries.

In all populations in which nothing is done to influence the sex of babies, there are 104–107 baby boys born for every 100 baby girls born. The **sex ratio at birth** is the number of baby boys born per 100 baby girls who are born. This value of 104–107 is as close to a constant as almost anything found in human behavior.

There are some naturally occurring variations in the sex ratio at birth. First births are slightly more likely to be male than later births, and African-background populations tend to have a slightly lower sex ratio at birth than other racial groups. It is thought that the sex ratio at conception could be as high as 130, and evidence of gender of fetuses that die in miscarriages shows a higher proportion of males than females.[5]

THE GROSS REPRODUCTION RATE

The **gross reproduction rate (GRR)** is the number of daughters that a woman will have if she goes through her life having daughters by age at the rate occurring in that population at that time. It is basically a TFR that refers to bearing daughters.

The GRR could be calculated by tabulating births by sex and then calculating an ASFR for having baby girls. However, usually the GRR is calculated as follows:

$$GRR = TFR \times (100/(100 + \text{sex ratio at birth}))$$

That calculation of the GRR multiplies the TFR times the proportion of births that are female.

Figure 8.8 shows the GRR for the same regional divisions as Figure 8.2 showed for the TFR. The GRR was calculated as $0.4878 \times TFR$, which is consistent with a sex ratio at birth of 105.

Since the GRR is essentially the TFR multiplied by a constant, the picture shown in Figure 8.8 is identical to that in Figure 8.2. A major reason the GRR is calculated is as a step in the calculation of the net reproduction rate, which is discussed next.

THE NET REPRODUCTION RATE

The **net reproduction rate (NRR)** is the gross reproduction rate adjusted for female mortality. It is the number of daughters that a woman would have in the course of her life, given fertility and mortality rates at a given time. It takes into account the chance that a woman will survive through the childbearing ages and thus have the possibility of having children as long as she is biologically capable of bearing a child. The NRR contrasts with the TFR and the GRR, which assume that all women live to age 50—the end of the childbearing ages. Thus, the NRR is a measure that combines fertility and mortality. Infant mortality

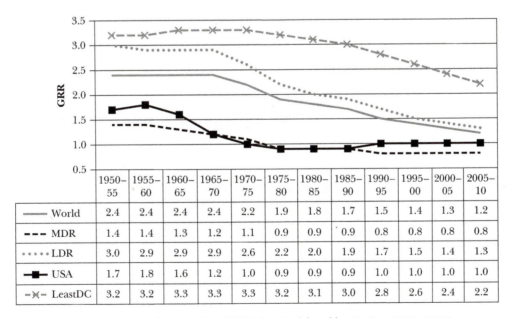

	1950–55	1955–60	1960–65	1965–70	1970–75	1975–80	1980–85	1985–90	1990–95	1995–00	2000–05	2005–10
World	2.4	2.4	2.4	2.4	2.2	1.9	1.8	1.7	1.5	1.4	1.3	1.2
MDR	1.4	1.4	1.3	1.2	1.1	0.9	0.9	0.9	0.8	0.8	0.8	0.8
LDR	3.0	2.9	2.9	2.9	2.6	2.2	2.0	1.9	1.7	1.5	1.4	1.3
USA	1.7	1.8	1.6	1.2	1.0	0.9	0.9	0.9	1.0	1.0	1.0	1.0
LeastDC	3.2	3.2	3.3	3.3	3.3	3.2	3.1	3.0	2.8	2.6	2.4	2.2

FIGURE 8.8   Gross Reproduction Rate (GRR), by World and by Region, 1950–2010

and child mortality are the main causes of the difference between the GRR and the NRR; in high- and moderate-mortality populations, many baby girls do not survive to age 15 to even begin the childbearing years.

A net reproduction rate of 1.00 implies **zero population growth (ZPG)**, which means an unchanging population size in the long run. When NRR = 1.00, the population is said to have **replacement fertility**. When the NRR < 1 the population has < 1.00, it is said that the population has **below-replacement fertility**.

When NRR = 1.00, this means that after mortality has been taken into account, on average each woman replaces herself with one daughter. This situation will lead to an unchanging population size if fertility and mortality rates by age remain unchanged. It is reasonable to calculate the NRR based only on females because women bear children and because of the near constancy of the sex ratio at birth. In principle, a male-based NRR could be calculated based on male mortality and male ASFRs. In that case, a male NRR = 1.00 would also imply zero population growth in the long run.

Figure 8.9 shows the NRR for the world and for major world divisions. For the world as a whole, the NRR increased between 1950–1955 and 1965–1970, after which it has steadily declined. The world GRR was unchanged between 1950–1955 and 1965–1970, as shown in Figure 8.8. The NRR increased in that period because mortality was declining. As shown in Figure 4.3, between 1950–1955 and 1965–1970, female e_0^0 increased from 49 to 53 years. Thus, more daughters were surviving in 1965–1970 than in 1950–1955, even though the GRR, indicating the number of daughters born, was identical in 1950–1955 and 1965–1970 at 2.4.

The NRR in the LDR increased from 1950–1955 through 1965–1970, even though the GRR in 1965–1970 was slightly lower than in 1950–1955. Again, this was due to mortality decline, mainly a decline in infant and child mortality, so that more females survived through the childbearing ages. Female e_0^0 in the LDR was 43 in 1950–1955 and was 53 in 1965–1970. After 1965–1970, the NRR in the LDR declined, consistent with the decline in the GRR in the LDR. The decline in the NRR occurred because fertility declined more rapidly than infant and child mortality declined. In the LeastDC, the NRR peaked in 1980–1985.

The increase in the NRR in the LeastDC is even more striking than the increase in the LDR, increasing by 22% from 1950–1955 to 1980–1985, even though the GRR in the LeastDC was 3.2 in 1950–1955 and was 3.1 in 1980–1985. However, female e_0^0 in the LeastDC also increased from 38 in 1950–1955 to 50 in 1980–1985. Even in 2005–2010, after adjusting for mortality, every woman in the LeastDC was replacing herself by 1.74 daughters, implying high positive population growth rates in these countries for some time in the future unless fertility declines or mortality increases.

In the MDR, female e_0^0 was 68 in 1950–1955, and further mortality decline had little effect on the NRR. Female mortality before age 50 affects the difference between the GRR and the NRR, and with female e_0^0 of 70, typically 88% of women survive to their fiftieth birthday. The NRR increased slightly between 1950–1955 and 1955–1960 from 1.27 to 1.28, while female e_0^0 increased from 68 to 71 between 1950–1955 and 1955–1960. At its high point, each woman in the

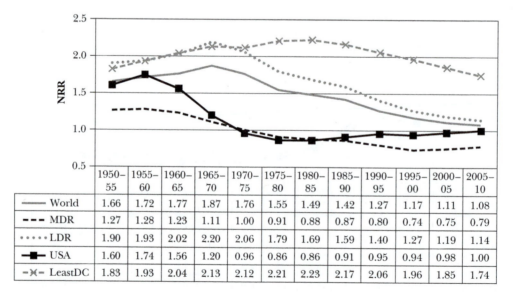

	1950–55	1955–60	1960–65	1965–70	1970–75	1975–80	1980–85	1985–90	1990–95	1995–00	2000–05	2005–10
—— World	1.66	1.72	1.77	1.87	1.76	1.55	1.49	1.42	1.27	1.17	1.11	1.08
- - - MDR	1.27	1.28	1.23	1.11	1.00	0.91	0.88	0.87	0.80	0.74	0.75	0.79
·····LDR	1.90	1.93	2.02	2.20	2.06	1.79	1.69	1.59	1.40	1.27	1.19	1.14
—■— USA	1.60	1.74	1.56	1.20	0.96	0.86	0.86	0.91	0.95	0.94	0.98	1.00
-✕- LeastDC	1.83	1.93	2.04	2.13	2.12	2.21	2.23	2.17	2.06	1.96	1.85	1.74

FIGURE 8.9 Net Reproduction Rate (NRR) for the World, MDR, LDR, the United States, and LeastDC, 1950–2010

MDR was replacing herself by 1.28 daughters, after adjusting for mortality. An NRR of 1.28 means that each generation would have 28% more women than the previous generation. By 2005–2010, in the MDR, each woman was replacing herself by 0.79 daughters, implying long-term population decline.

We see that the path of the NRR for the United States has been substantially different than for the MDR as a whole. The NRR in the United States increased from 1950–1955 to 1955–1960, but the GRR in the United States also increased from 1.7 to 1.8 between those two periods. Through the end of the Baby Boom in the 1960s, the United States NRR was higher than for the MDR. Then, in 1970–1990, the values of the NRR in the United States and the MDR were almost identical. After 1995, the NRR in the United States increased at the same time it was declining in the MDR. The value of the NRR for the United States 1990–2010 has been close to 1.00, which would lead in the long run to an unchanging population size. Thus, the United States, unlike the MDR as a whole, does not currently face long-term population loss.

The population growth rate does not immediately fall to zero as soon as the NRR reaches 1. It takes some time for the growth rate to decline due to the existing age structure of the population. This effect on population growth of the existing age structure is called population momentum and is discussed in Chapter 11.

Figure 8.10 shows the NRR in regions of the world. Through the early 1960s the NRR was the highest in Latin America and the Caribbean, reaching a maximum value of 2.4 in 1960–1965, after which it declined fairly quickly to a value of 1.1—only slightly above replacement—in 2005–2010. The NRR peaked 5 years later in Asia, in 1965–1970, at a maximal value of 2.1. By 2005–2010, the NRR in Asia was also near replacement at 1.1. Thus, by 2005–2010, much of the LDR—Latin America and the Caribbean and Asia—was near replacement fertility, implying long-term unchanging population size. The situation in Africa is very different. The NRR reached a maximum in Africa in 1980–1985, and in 2005–2010 was still quite high at 1.8. The NRR peaked so late in Africa because, as shown in Figure 4.4, mortality decline occurred later in Africa than elsewhere in the LDR.

If you compare the trajectory of the NRR for Africa in Figure 8.10 with the TFR for Africa in Figure 8.3, you can see why some policy makers act as if nothing has happened with fertility decline in Africa, because long-term population growth (the NRR) in Africa was virtually identical in 1950–1955 and in 2005–2010. The TFR reflects behavior by women and couples. Since the TFR declined, this behavior changed. This addresses the causal or microbehavioral approach discussed in Chapter 1, in which the behaviors that

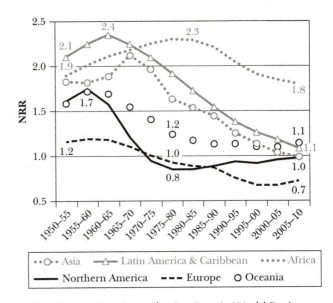

FIGURE 8.10 Net Reproduction Rate in World Regions, 1950–2010

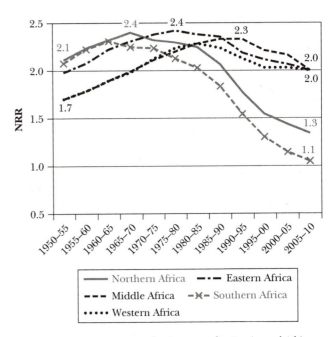

FIGURE 8.11 Net Reproduction Rate by Region of Africa, 1950–2010

people engage in and the choices they make change. The NRR addresses a concern from the aggregate approach discussed in Chapter 1, in which countries face the problems of population growth, regardless of the source.

Figure 8.11 shows the NRR by region of Africa. The large variations in the NRR by region are somewhat similar to variations in the TFR across regions of Africa shown in Figure 8.4. The vertical scale is the same as

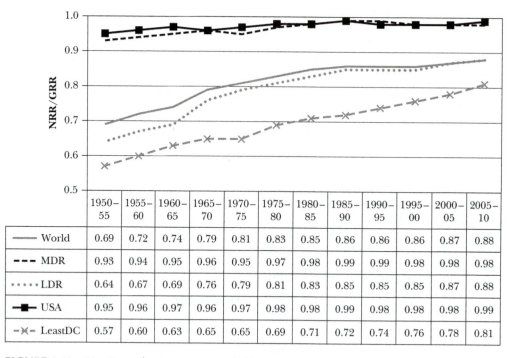

	1950– 55	1955– 60	1960– 65	1965– 70	1970– 75	1975– 80	1980– 85	1985– 90	1990– 95	1995– 00	2000– 05	2005– 10
—— World	0.69	0.72	0.74	0.79	0.81	0.83	0.85	0.86	0.86	0.86	0.87	0.88
--- MDR	0.93	0.94	0.95	0.96	0.95	0.97	0.98	0.99	0.99	0.98	0.98	0.98
····· LDR	0.64	0.67	0.69	0.76	0.79	0.81	0.83	0.85	0.85	0.85	0.87	0.88
■— USA	0.95	0.96	0.97	0.96	0.97	0.98	0.98	0.99	0.98	0.98	0.98	0.99
✗ LeastDC	0.57	0.60	0.63	0.65	0.65	0.69	0.71	0.72	0.74	0.76	0.78	0.81

FIGURE 8.12   Net Reproduction Rate Divided by Gross Reproduction Rate (NRR/GRR) for the World, MDR, LDR, the United States, and LeastDC, 1950–2010

in Figure 8.10. The differences between the TFR in African regions in Figure 8.4 and the NRR in African regions in Figure 8.11 are due to differences in the level and decline in mortality, especially infant mortality, across regions of Africa. We see in Figure 8.4 that Southern Africa had close to the lowest TFR among African regions in 1950–1955, but Southern Africa and Northern Africa had the highest NRR in 1950–1955. That is because, as shown in Figure 4.8 in Chapter 4, Southern Africa had the lowest IMR and the highest e_0^0 in Africa in 1950–1955. Thus, more female babies in Southern Africa were surviving into the childbearing ages than in the rest of sub-Saharan Africa.

As noted in this chapter, the NRR is the GRR adjusted for mortality, while the GRR assumes that all women survive to age 50. In low-mortality populations, there are few female deaths before age 50. In typical mortality patterns, with female expectation of life at birth of 80 years, 98% of all women survive to their fiftieth birthday. One can calculate how much the NRR is depressed by female mortality before age 50 by dividing the NRR by the GRR. One way to interpret this ratio is: How much could the NRR increase with further female mortality decline? This ratio is shown in Figure 8.12.

In the MDR, female mortality was fairly low even in the early 1950s. In 1950–1955, in the MDR the NRR was 93% of what its value would have been if there were no female deaths before age 50. By 2005–2010, in the MDR the NRR was 98% of the value of the GRR.

All of the lines in Figure 8.12 trend upward over time, reflecting female mortality decline. However, in the LeastDC, NRR/GRR in 2005–2010 was 0.81, reflecting a substantial potential for further increases in the NRR as a result of future mortality decline. If fertility were unchanged in the LeastDC and mortality continued to decline, the NRR would increase to 1.23 times its 2005–2010 value. This would result in an NRR of 2.15, which is about what the NRR was in the LeastDC in the 1970s. Thus, the future course of the NRR for the LeastDC is uncertain, and it depends on changes both in fertility and in mortality. UN population projections, including projected mortality and fertility levels, are discussed in Chapter 11. Although these projections are based on best guesses about the future, it is not possible to know whether these projections will prove to be accurate.

CALCULATION OF THE NET REPRODUCTION RATE

The net reproduction rate is the gross reproduction rate adjusted for female mortality. The net reproduction rate is approximated by the gross reproduction rate multiplied by the proportion of females who survive to the mean age of childbearing, which is about 30 years of age.

Thus:

$$NRR = (l_{30}/l_0) \times GRR$$

TABLE 8.1   Basis of Calculation of the Net Reproduction Rate

(1)	(2)	(3)
Age	ASFR	ASFR (100/205)
15–19	133.3	65.0
20–24	200.0	97.6
25–29	166.7	81.3
30–34	66.7	32.5
35–39	26.7	13.0
40–44	6.7	3.3
45–49	0.0	0.0
Sum	600.1	292.7
5 × Sum	3,000.5	1,463.7

Total Fertility Rate = 5 × Sum(ASFR)/1,000 = 3.00
Gross Reproduction Rate = (5 × Sum(ASFR)/1,000) × (100/205) = 1.46
With Female $e_0^0 = 50, l_{30}/l_0 = 0.722$
Net Reproduction Rate = (l_{30}/l_0) × GRR = 0.722 × 1.46 = 1.06

Table 8.1 shows the basis for calculation of the NRR. Column (1) shows the childbearing ages in 5-year age groups. Column (2) shows the number of births per year per 1,000 women in each age group, which is called the age-specific fertility rate (ASFR). Column (3) shows the number of female births per 1,000 women in each age group. Column (3) is obtained by multiplying the total number of births by the proportion of births that are female, assuming a sex ratio at birth of 105.

Summing up the age-specific fertility rates and multiplying by 5 yields 3000.5 births per 1,000 women and 1463.7 female births per 1,000 women. Looking at this on the basis of one woman rather than one 1,000 women yields a total fertility rate of 3.00 and a GRR of 1.46. Multiplying the GRR by the proportion of women who survive to their thirtieth birthday yields a NRR of 1.06. In this example, each woman is slightly more than replacing herself with daughters under the given mortality and fertility regime. In the absence of migration, this would result in a low positive growth rate.

FERTILITY AND FERTILITY CHANGE IN THE TEN MOST POPULOUS COUNTRIES: FROM 1950–1955 TO 2005–2010

Table 8.2 looks at fertility change between 1950–1955 and 2005–2010 in each of the ten most populous countries in 2010. All of these countries had an NRR considerably above 1.0 in 1950–1955, while by 2005–2010 the NRR was below 1.0 in four countries and was at 1.0 in two additional countries. The declines in the TFR and the NRR are especially striking in China, Indonesia, and Brazil.

The NRR declined between 1950–1955 and 2005–2010 in each of the countries except Nigeria, where the NRR increased from 1.7 to 2.0. In Nigeria, the NRR increased, even though over the same time span the TFR declined by almost one child, from 6.4 to 5.6. The NRR increased while the TFR decreased because the magnitude of improvement in female survival below age 50 in Nigeria more than compensated for the decline in fertility. Between 1950–1955 and 2005–2010, female e_0^0 increased from 37 to 51 years and the IMR decreased from 189 to 96.

The NRR/GRR also increased in each of the ten largest countries. The NRR/GRR will increase whenever female mortality below age 50 declines. In 2005–2010, it was at least 0.88 in every country except Nigeria. Nigeria has a substantial potential for further mortality declines to lead to further increases in the NRR.

TABLE 8.2   Fertility and Fertility Change, from 1950–1955 to 2005–2010, in the Ten Most Populous Countries

(1)	(2)	TFR 1950–1955	TFR 2005–2010	NRR 1950–1955	NRR 2005–2010	NRR/GRR 1950–1955	NRR/GRR 2005–2010
		(3)	(4)	(5)	(6)	(7)	(8)
1	China (PRC)	6.1	1.8	2.0	0.7	0.67	0.89
2	India	5.9	2.8	1.7	1.2	0.57	0.88
3	USA	3.5	2.1	1.6	1.0	0.95	0.99
4	Indonesia	5.5	2.2	1.6	1.0	0.59	0.95
5	Brazil	6.2	1.9	2.3	0.9	0.75	0.96
6	Pakistan	6.6	3.7	1.9	1.6	0.59	0.88
7	Nigeria	6.4	5.6	1.7	2.0	0.55	0.73
8	Bangladesh	6.4	2.4	2.0	1.1	0.65	0.92
9	Russia	2.9	1.4	1.3	0.7	0.90	0.97
10	Japan	3.0	1.3	1.3	0.6	0.87	0.99

THE GROWTH RATE RESULTING FROM COMBINATIONS OF EXPECTATION OF LIFE AT BIRTH AND THE TOTAL FERTILITY RATE

Table 8.3 shows the population growth rate that would result from various combinations of female expectation of life at birth and the total fertility rate (TFR) if both were maintained over a long time. For a given TFR, the lower the mortality rates (i.e., the higher the expectation of life at birth), the higher the resulting population growth rate.[6]

With a female expectation of life at birth of 20 years, women on average would need to have between six and seven children in order to result in a growth rate of zero—an unchanging population size. With female expectation of life at birth of 20 years, if women on average had 5 or fewer children, the population would eventually decline in size. If mortality risks were lower and female expectation of life at birth were 40 years, the same TFR of 6–7 would result in an annual growth rate of over 2%. If mortality risks were even lower and female expectation of life at birth were 60 years, a TFR of 6–7 would result in a growth rate of over 3%.

The numbers bolded and underlined in Table 8.3 bracket in each column what the TFR would need to be to result in a zero rate of population growth for a given female expectation of life at birth. For example, with female $e_0^0 = 50$, a TFR of 3.0 would result in a growth rate of 0.03%, and a TFR of 2.5 would result in a growth rate of −0.03%. Thus, a TFR between 2.5 and 3.0 (about 2.75) would result in a growth rate of 0.

With low mortality, a TFR of 2.07 is necessary for a zero rate of population growth. With female e_0^0 of 60 or higher, very few people die before age 50, and almost all subsequent mortality improvement occurs above the childbearing ages, which has no effect on population growth.

Table 8.3 illustrates the Demographic Transition. At one point in time, a combination of expectation of life at birth and the TFR would result in a low or zero growth rate, for example, $e_0^0 = 30$ and TFR = 5.5. If mortality risks subsequently fell and fertility behavior did not change, the population growth rate would increase. For example, $e_0^0 = 50$ and TFR = 5.5 result in a growth rate of about 2.4%. In order to avoid a high population growth rate, if expectation of life at birth increases, the TFR needs to fall.

THE NET REPRODUCTION RATE RESULTING FROM COMBINATIONS OF EXPECTATION OF LIFE AT BIRTH AND THE TOTAL FERTILITY RATE

Table 8.4 shows the same information as in Table 8.3, but with the entries in Table 8.4 the NRR results from a given combination of an expectation of life at birth and a TFR, rather than the growth rate. In Table 8.4, looking down columns of the table, the values are underlined and bolded that bracket an NRR = 1.

Looking across a row, a higher value of e_0^0 with a given TFR results in a higher NRR. This illustrates how the increases in the NRR occurred in Figures 8.9, 8.10, and 8.11, even when the TFR was unchanging or declining.

HIGHEST TOTAL FERTILITY RATE AND HIGHEST NET REPRODUCTION RATE COUNTRIES: 2005–2010

When thinking about high-fertility countries, sometimes people are thinking about the TFR, and sometimes they are thinking about the NRR. It is useful to look at what countries had the highest TFR and what countries had the highest NRR in 2005–2010 and to look at the difference between the two lists.

TABLE 8.3   Growth Rate (%) for Combinations of e_0^0 and TFR

		Female e_0^0						
		20	**30**	**40**	**50**	**60**	**70**	**80**
TFR	8.0	0.09%	2.24%	3.16%	3.83%	4.35%	4.75%	4.95%
	7.0	**0.04%**	1.76%	2.67%	3.34%	3.86%	4.25%	4.45%
	6.0	**−0.02%**	**1.20%**	2.11%	2.77%	3.29%	3.68%	3.88%
	5.0	−0.08%	**0.06%**	1.45%	2.11%	2.63%	3.02%	3.22%
	4.0	−1.62%	−0.03%	**1.20%**	1.31%	1.83%	2.21%	2.41%
	3.0	−2.61%	−1.25%	**−0.04%**	**0.03%**	0.08%	1.19%	1.39%
	2.5	−3.23%	−1.88%	−0.10%	**−0.03%**	**0.02%**	**0.06%**	**0.07%**
	2.0	−3.99%	−2.64%	−1.76%	−1.11%	**−0.60%**	**−0.22%**	**−0.03%**
	1.6	−4.73%	−3.39%	−2.51%	−1.87%	−1.37%	−0.99%	−0.79%

NOTE: Bolded and underlined numbers indicate what the TFR would need to be to result in a zero rate of population growth for a given female expectation of life at birth; see the text for more information.

TABLE 8.4   Net Reproduction Rate for Combinations of e_0^0 and TFR

		Female e_0^0						
		20	**30**	**40**	**50**	**60**	**70**	**80**
TFR	8.0	1.27	1.87	2.41	2.90	3.36	3.75	3.97
	7.0	**_1.11_**	1.63	2.11	2.54	2.94	3.28	3.48
	6.0	**_0.95_**	1.40	1.81	2.18	2.52	2.81	2.68
	5.0	0.79	**_1.17_**	1.50	1.81	2.10	2.35	2.48
	4.0	0.63	**_0.93_**	**_1.20_**	1.45	1.68	1.88	1.99
	3.0	0.48	0.70	**_0.90_**	**_1.09_**	1.26	1.41	1.49
	2.5	0.40	0.58	0.75	**_0.91_**	**_1.05_**	**_1.17_**	**_1.24_**
	2.0	0.32	0.47	0.60	0.73	**_0.84_**	**_0.94_**	**_0.99_**
	1.6	0.25	0.37	0.48	0.58	0.67	0.75	0.79

Values that are underlined and bolded bracket an NRR = 1.

Table 8.5 shows the ten countries with the highest TFR in 2005–2010. The country's TFR rank 2005–2010 is shown (Column 1), as well as the TFR 2005–2010 (Column 3), the TFR 1950–1955 (Column 4), and the highest TFR for any 5-year period 1950–2010 (Column 5). The region in which each country is located (Column 7) and whether it is a LeastDC are also indicated (Column 8). Female e_0^0 2005–2010 (Column 9) and NRR 2005–2010 (Column 10) are also shown as well as the country's world rank in NRR 2005–2010 (Column 11).

The first ten rows of Table 8.5 are the countries with the highest TFR 2005–2010 in descending order. There are seven countries that are both in the ten highest TFR countries and in the ten highest NRR countries. In the last three rows of the table are the three countries that are in the ten countries with the highest NRR but are not included in the ten countries with the highest TFR.

In 2005–2010 each of the ten countries with the highest TFR had a TFR of at least 6.00. In Niger, Timor-Leste, Chad, and the Democratic Republic of the Congo, the TFR in 2005–2010 was higher than in 1950–1955. In Afghanistan, Mali, Uganda, Zambia, and Malawi, the TFR in 2005–2010 was lower than in 1950–1955, but the TFR was higher in some 5-year periods than it was in 1950–1955. This increase in the TFR before it declined is consistent with the increases

TABLE 8.5   Some Characteristics of the Ten Countries with the Highest TFR and Ten Countries with the Highest NRR, 2005–2010

(1)	(2)	(3)	(4)	(5)	(6)	(7)	(8)	(9)	(10)	(11)
TFR Rank 2005–2010	**Country**	**TFR 2005–2010**	**TFR 1950–1955**	**Highest TFR**	**% Decline from Highest TFR**	**Region**	**LeastDC**	**Female e_0^0 2005–2010**	**NRR 2005–2010**	**NRR Rank 2005–2010**
1	Niger	7.2	6.9	7.8	8%	Western Africa	X	54	2.70	2
2	Afghanistan	6.6	7.7	8.0	17%	Southern Asia	X	48	2.23	10
3	Timor-Leste	6.5	6.4	7.0	6%	Southeast Asia		62	2.71	1
4	Mali	6.5	6.5	7.1	9%	Western Africa	X	51	2.33	5
5	Somalia	6.4	7.3	7.3	12%	Eastern Africa	X	52	2.29	7
6	Uganda	6.4	6.9	7.1	10%	Eastern Africa	X	53	2.44	3
7	Zambia	6.2	6.8	7.4	17%	Eastern Africa	X	47	2.17	14
8	Chad	6.2	6.1	6.8	8%	Middle Africa	X	50	2.19	12
9	Democratic Republic of the Congo	6.1	6.0	7.1	15%	Middle Africa	X	49	2.12	17
10	Malawi	6.0	6.8	7.5	20%	Eastern Africa	X	52	2.29	6
11	Burkina Faso	5.9	6.1	7.1	16%	Western Africa	X	55	2.25	8
14	Tanzania	5.6	6.7	6.8	18%	Eastern Africa	X	56	2.23	9
15	Yemen	5.5	7.3	9.2	41%	Western Asia	X	65	2.38	4

in the TFR for Middle Africa and Western Africa in Figure 8.4 and for Central Asia in Figure 8.5 before the TFR eventually declined.

The percentage decline in the TFR from its highest value to its 2005–2010 value is shown in Column 6. That was calculated as $100 \times$ (Highest TFR–TFR 2005–2010)/(Highest TFR). Sometimes a decline of at least 10% in the TFR from its highest value is seen as an indicator that a long-term fertility decline has begun. By that standard, although the TFR in 2005–2010 is high in these countries, all except Niger, Timor-Leste, Mali, and Chad had begun a long-term fertility decline.

The ten countries with the highest NRR are somewhat different from the ten countries with the highest TFR. As seen in Table 8.4, for a given TFR, the lower mortality, the higher the NRR. The TFR rank for Yemen is 15, while its rank for NRR is 4. This is because Yemen has relatively low mortality, with female $e_0^0 = 65$. Most of the high-TFR countries have relatively high mortality. This means that as mortality falls further in these countries, the NRR will rise considerably even if the TFR is unchanged. This makes the need for a decline in the TFR even more urgent if extremely high population growth is to be avoided.

All of the countries listed in Table 8.5 are in sub-Saharan Africa except Afghanistan, Yemen, and Timor-Leste. Timor-Leste, also known as East Timor, is in Southeast Asia and was formerly part of Indonesia. It achieved full independence in 2002. All of the countries in Table 8.5 except Timor-Leste are LeastDCs.

COHORT FERTILITY

As discussed in Chapter 4 on mortality, a **cohort** is a group of people who start something at the same time. A birth cohort is people who were born in the same year (or in the same range of years). When people use the term "cohort" without any additional modifier (such as high school graduation cohort or first marriage cohort), they usually mean **birth cohort**. You can take a cohort approach to the study of either mortality or fertility, but the implications of a cohort approach to fertility are easier to understand.

Cohort fertility traces ASFRs of women as they go through their lives. You can calculate a cohort total fertility rate, just as you can calculate a period total fertility rate. A cohort total fertility rate takes postponement of childbearing into account. Women in a cohort might think that it is not a good time to have a child and could postpone having a child until later, when they are also somewhat older. They could postpone having a child due to a bad economy, a turbulent political situation or for some other reason. If they eventually have that child, the cohort TFR is unaffected. A cohort total fertility rate also is unaffected by the speeding up of childbearing resulting from

TABLE 8.6 Age-Specific Fertility Rates to Calculate Period TFR for 1990 (O) and to Calculate Cohort TFR of Those Aged 30–34 in 1990 (X)

	1975	1980	1985	1990	1995	2000	2005
15–19	X			O			
20–24		X		O			
25–29			X	O			
30–34				X O			
35–39				O	X		
40–44				O		X	
45–49				O			X

new pro-natalist policies or especially good economic conditions, as long as women do not increase the total number of children they bear over the course of their lives.

Table 8.6 shows how age-specific fertility rates are strung together to calculate a period total fertility rate and how ASFRs are strung together to calculate a cohort total fertility rate. For a period total fertility rate, the age-specific fertility rates for a given year are added together and multiplied by 5, as was explained in Box 8.1. These values are indicated by circles (**O**) in Table 8.6. In Table 8.6, a period total fertility rate is calculated by summing ASFRs down a column and multiplying the value by 5, to reflect that 5-year age groups are being used. There would be no need to multiply by 5 if 1-year age groups were used.

For a cohort total fertility rate, the age-specific fertility rates of the same group of women as they pass through their lives are added together and multiplied by 5. These values are indicated in Table 8.6 by bold Xs (**X**). A cohort total fertility rate is calculated by summing the age-specific fertility rates down a diagonal. In the example in Table 8.6, the values are for those women who were age 30–34 in 1990. These women would all have been born in 1955–1959. Age 30 is close to the mean age of childbearing in almost all populations. Thus the cohort total fertility rate for women born in 1955–1959 is indexed by the year in which that birth cohort was aged 30–34.

PERIOD AND COHORT TOTAL FERTILITY RATES IN THE UNITED STATES: THE GREAT DEPRESSION AND THE BABY BOOM

In the United States, the total fertility rate was low in the 1930s during the Great Depression and was high in the Baby Boom. The Baby Boom lasted from the late 1940s through the mid-1960s. The fluctuations in fertility related to the Great Depression

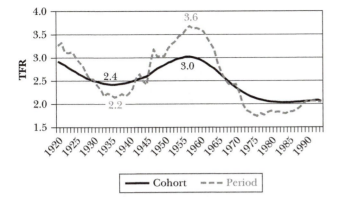

FIGURE 8.13 U.S. Period and Cohort Total Fertility Rates, 1920–1994

and to the Baby Boom are clear from Figure 8.13, which shows the total fertility rate in the United States for 1920–1994. The typical total fertility rate (for periods of time) is shown with a dashed line. The cohort total fertility rate is shown with a solid black line. The cohort total fertility rates are associated with the time period for which the cohort was age 30–34.[7]

The same general picture appears from both the period TFRs and the cohort TFRs. However, the period TFRs dip lower in the 1930s and rise higher in the 1950s and 1960s than the cohort TFRs. This difference in the period TFR and cohort TFR is due to shifts in the timing of childbearing.

The Great Depression in the 1930s was not a good time to have a child. This could have convinced women and couples to have fewer children over their entire lives than they would have otherwise. Alternatively, the woman or couple might have decided that the current time was not good for having a child, and they would postpone some or all or their childbearing until after the economic situation improved. The somewhat minor dip in the cohort TFR in the 1930s indicates declines in lifetime childbearing. The larger dip in period TFR in the 1930s reflects postponement in childbearing, which was made up for later in the women's lives.

Similarly, in the good economic situation in the 1950s and 1960s after World War II, couples could have decided to have more children in total in their lives than they would have had otherwise. Alternatively, they could have decided that then was a good time to have children, but they might not have changed the total number of children they wanted to have.

After World War II, many marriages occurred when men came home from the war, and the good economic situation encouraged shorter spacing between children than had occurred earlier. The fairly substantial increase in cohort TFR in the 1950s and

1960s indicates that women and couples decided to have a larger number of children over the course of their lives than women had earlier. However, the larger increase in period TFR than in cohort TFR in the 1950s and 1960s also indicates that the 1950s and early 1960s were seen as an especially favorable time to have children and couples decided to have children then rather than somewhat earlier or somewhat later.[8]

POPULATION DYNAMICS AND CRISIS IN RWANDA

We next look at how fertility, mortality, and migration changed in the course of a catastrophe, the Rwandan Civil War of 1993–1994. Rwanda is a country in Middle Africa that had a population of 7 million in 1990. It has been estimated that 800,000 people died in the civil war. Besides the deaths, many Rwandans fled the country.[9] This was not a good time to have a child.

Figure 8.14 shows the crude birth rate, crude death rate, and net migration rate in Rwanda in 1950–2010. The effects of the 1993–1994 Rwandan Civil War are clear in the increase in the crude death rate and in the decline in the net migration rate (to a high level of out-migration) in 1990–1995. We also see a decline in the crude birth rate. However, after 1990–1995, the crude death rate declined rapidly, and by 2000–2005 the crude death rate was lower than the 1985–1990 level. The crude birth rate declined after 1985–1990, but once the crude birth rate declined (from 49 to 41 per 1,000), it remained essentially unchanged through 2005–2010. Thus, the Rwandan Civil War almost certainly contributed to the decline in the crude birth rate from 1985–1990 to 1990–1995, but after the war, the CBR did not increase.

The net migration rate rebounded in 1995–2000 to more than compensate for its decline in 1990–1995. The behavior of the net migration rate is consistent with the observation that most international refugees return to their home country within 5 years after the disaster that caused their initial emigration.[10] By 2000–2005, the net migration rate was 0 per 1,000.

Figure 8.15 shows the roles of the natural rate of increase and the net migration rate in the overall population growth rate in Rwanda. In 1950–1985, the net migration rate was close to zero, so in that period the growth rate was almost totally determined by the natural rate of increase. In 1990–1995, at the time of the Rwandan Civil War, the population growth rate was almost totally determined by the net migration rate because the natural rate of in crease was close to zero. The growth rate spiked to 78 per 1,000 population in 1995–2000 because, during that period, (1) net immigration was high (due to the return of refugees), and (2) the natural rate of increase had almost recovered to its 1985–1990 level.

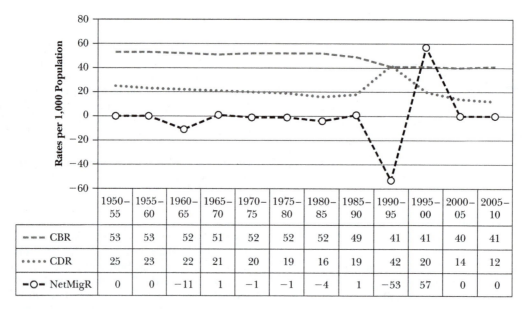

FIGURE 8.14 Population Dynamics in Rwanda and the 1993–1994 Rwandan Civil War

	1950–55	1955–60	1960–65	1965–70	1970–75	1975–80	1980–85	1985–90	1990–95	1995–00	2000–05	2005–10
--- CBR	53	53	52	51	52	52	52	49	41	41	40	41
••••• CDR	25	23	22	21	20	19	16	19	42	20	14	12
–O– NetMigR	0	0	−11	1	−1	−1	−4	1	−53	57	0	0

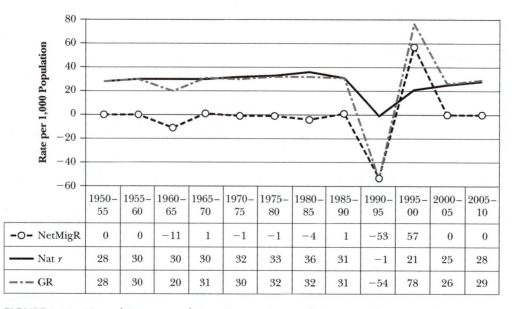

FIGURE 8.15 Natural Increase and Net Migration in Population Growth in Rwanda and the 1993–1994 Rwandan Civil War

	1950–55	1955–60	1960–65	1965–70	1970–75	1975–80	1980–85	1985–90	1990–95	1995–00	2000–05	2005–10
–O– NetMigR	0	0	−11	1	−1	−1	−4	1	−53	57	0	0
—— Nat *r*	28	30	30	30	32	33	36	31	−1	21	25	28
–·– GR	28	30	20	31	30	32	32	31	−54	78	26	29

Figure 8.16 shows the decline and the recovery in expectation of life at birth that caused the increase and then the decline in the crude death rate shown in Figure 8.14. The Rwandan Civil War led to a sharp decline in expectation of life at birth in 1990–1995, but the effects on expectation of life at birth were short-lived and were gone by 2000–2005.

Figure 8.17 shows the total fertility rate in Rwanda. As was shown for the crude birth rate in Figure 8.14, Figure 8.17 shows that the total fertility rate declined somewhat between 1980–1985 and 1985–1990, before the Rwandan Civil War. The decline in the TFR accelerated during the civil war, but after the civil war the TFR continued to decline and, unlike the expectation of life at birth, did not rebound to its pre–civil war level. The results for Rwanda are consistent with the view that once fertility starts to decline in a less developed country, it is likely to remain at its lower level or continue to decline, even if its decline had been accelerated by events such as a war

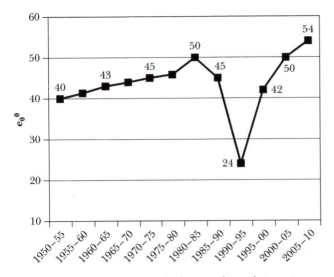

FIGURE 8.16 Expectation of Life at Birth (Both Sexes) in Rwanda and the 1993–1994 Rwandan Civil War

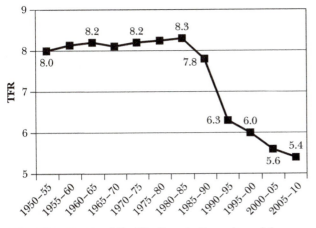

FIGURE 8.17 Total Fertility Rate in Rwanda and the 1993–1994 Rwandan Civil War

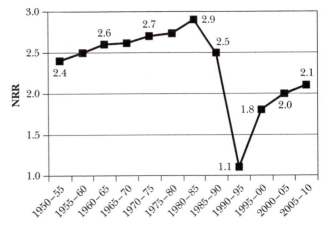

FIGURE 8.18 Net Reproduction Rate in Rwanda and the 1993–1994 Rwandan Civil War

THE FEMALE REPRODUCTIVE PERIOD

Females are able to become pregnant after they reach **menarche** (when a woman begins to ovulate and thus begins to have menstrual periods), although there is often a period of time after menarche when the chance of conception is low. Menarche can start at age 10 or younger, but more typically occurs at about 12 years of age. Age at menarche has declined over time in more developed countries, and in developed countries it usually occurs between 12 and 13 years of age.[11] It tends to be older in populations who are not well nourished. In a rural area of Bangladesh in the 1970s, age at menarche was found to be on average 16 years.[12]

Females stop being able to become pregnant at **menopause**, when they no longer ovulate. The average age at menopause is about 51 in developed countries, and seems to have become older over time in developed countries. There is evidence that menopause tends to occur earlier in the LDR. Thus, women in the MDR have lower fertility than women in the LDR, even though women in the MDR are at risk of having a child for more years than are women in the LDR.[13]

FERTILITY AND FECUNDITY

It is important to distinguish between (1) the biological ability for a woman to become pregnant and have a live birth, and (2) factors related to whether a woman who is biologically capable of bearing a child actually has a child. Although most women between menarche and menopause are capable of becoming pregnant and bearing a child, usually children are not born at the maximum level that would be possible for women in that population.

Fecundity is the biological ability to have children, which rises after menarche and then declines until

or other disaster. This could be because of changes in views about how many children are needed, even when the initial fertility decline was not totally a matter of choice. This is related to the role of changing attitudes and values in fertility decline, which is discussed in Chapter 9.

Figure 8.18 shows how the changes in expectation of life at birth and in the total fertility rate worked together to result in the net reproduction rate. The NRR declined between 1985–1990 and 1990–1995 mainly due to the large decline in the expectation of life at birth. When the expectation of life at birth recovered, the NRR increased, but it did not attain its pre–civil war level, due to the continued decline in the total fertility rate.

menopause. **Fertility** is the actual having of children, which is influenced not only by the level of fecundity but also by whether the woman has sexual intercourse, whether she uses contraception to prevent becoming pregnant, and whether a pregnancy ends before the child's birth, either naturally through a miscarriage or stillbirth or through an induced abortion.[14] The increase in the TFR in many high-fertility countries shown in Table 8.5 could be due to an increase in fecundity, related to improving health over time.

BIRTH INTERVALS

A **birth interval** is the amount of time between one live birth that a woman has and the next live birth. It is often expressed in months. One way to view fertility is to think about the components of the interval between births. Among women who are not permanently sterile and who are exposed to sexual intercourse, the components of birth intervals appear as in Figure 8.19.

There is a waiting time to conception. Then the woman becomes pregnant. The pregnancy ends in a birth, a miscarriage, or an abortion. Then, the cycle starts again with a wait to conception and the beginning of the next pregnancy.

Adding up the length of time in these components of a birth interval gives the total length of the birth interval. If a pregnancy lasts 9 months, in those 9 months, the woman cannot become pregnant again. Typically, women do not ovulate for some period of time after the birth of a child. When a woman is not able to get pregnant after the birth of a child or when a pregnancy ends for some other reason, ovulation does not resume for some time. When the woman is not pregnant and not ovulating, it is said that she is in a state of **postpartum amenorrhea**. The period of postpartum amenorrhea is often extended by breast-feeding.[15] It is thought that breastfeeding extends the period of postpartum amenorrhea less if a woman is very well nourished. In more developed countries, the period of postpartum amenorrhea can be very short.[16]

A pregnancy that results in a full-term live birth removes 9 months and a little more time from the possibility of becoming pregnant again. An induced abortion or miscarriage removes somewhat less time, because the period of pregnancy is less than 9 months and because the woman is not breastfeeding. Thus, each induced abortion or miscarriage prevents less than one birth, in a birth interval sense, because the woman is removed from the risk of

pregnancy for a shorter amount of time than if there were a live birth.

PROXIMATE DETERMINANTS OF FERTILITY

In order to for a woman to have a child, she must be exposed to the risk of pregnancy through sexual intercourse, and she needs to be biologically able to become pregnant and carry the pregnancy to result in a live birth—that is, she must be fecund.[17] The risk that a woman who is fecund and engages in regular sexual intercourse becomes pregnant is also influenced by other factors, such as use of contraception, tendency to have a miscarriage, and willingness to have an induced abortion.

With these kinds of considerations in mind, Bongaarts divided factors related to fertility into three types, which he termed the **proximate determinants of fertility**:[18]

1. Exposure to sexual intercourse (intercourse variables)
2. Exposure to conception (conception variables)
3. Gestation and carrying the pregnancy to birth (gestation variables)

In Bongaarts's work, "exposure to sexual intercourse" is usually operationalized as whether a woman is currently married or not. Thus, this aspect of the proximate determinants looks at:

a. Formation and duration of marriage
b. Whether a woman marries and the age at marriage
c. Marital dissolution (divorce and widowhood)

More generally, the exposure to sexual intercourse variables refer to formation and dissolution of sexual unions, whether in a marriage or other stable cohabiting relationship or in a less regular sexual relationship. Exposure to sexual intercourse also involves coital frequency, voluntary abstinence, and involuntary abstinence. Involuntary abstinence can be caused by impotence, illness, or temporary separation of partners, such as due to labor migration.

Exposure to conception variables include use (or not) of contraception and the effectiveness of any contraceptive method used. Conception variables

---

Wait to conception → Pregnancy → Birth, miscarriage, or abortion → Wait to conception → Pregnancy

→ Time →

FIGURE 8.19 Schematic Picture of Components of Birth Intervals

also include periods of infecundity, such as those affected by breastfeeding or by sterilization or medical treatment. The main aspects of the gestation and carrying the pregnancy to birth variables are the tendency to have a miscarriage (also called spontaneous abortion) and induced abortion.

MARRIAGE AND MARITAL FERTILITY

In many historical societies and in some current societies, sexual intercourse outside of marriage is rare. In those situations, it is reasonable to think of fertility as a two-stage process: (1) entry into exposure to the risk of pregnancy through marriage; and (2) childbearing among married women, which is called **marital fertility**. As will be discussed in Chapter 10, non-marital fertility has comprised an increasing portion of all childbearing in the more developed countries. As an increasing proportion of unmarried women are in relationships, some of which are indistinguishable from marriage and some of which involve more irregular sexual intercourse, thinking about exposure to the risk of pregnancy becomes much more complicated.

The factors related to early or late marriage and factors related to early or late beginning of sexual activity are thought to be different from the factors related to the control of fertility within marriage, and demographers have usually thought about them separately. In this chapter, we next discuss the exposure to sexual intercourse variables, usually seen as entry into marriage. After that, we look at factors related to variations in fertility among women exposed to the risk of conception, which is usually addressed by looking at marital fertility. Factors related to the risk of conception are Bongaarts's "conception variables." After that, we discuss factors related to whether marriage age is early or late, whether or not almost all women eventually marry, and factors related to the initiation of sexual activity. Finally, we look at changes in the age pattern and level of fertility that have been observed in some very-low-fertility developed countries and possible pathways and shifts in the age pattern of fertility that can accompany an increase from very low fertility to simply low fertility.

CHANGES IN THE AGE PATTERN OF FIRST MARRIAGE

Malthus considered abstention from sexual intercourse until marriage and delay of marriage as the only acceptable means of controlling population growth after mortality has declined from a high level.

In high-mortality populations, high fertility is usually achieved partially by women entering into regular sexual intercourse (usually through marriage) at a young age. A high proportion of women in the childbearing ages being exposed to the risk of pregnancy can be

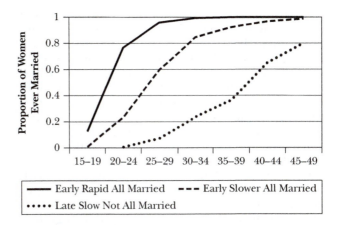

FIGURE 8.20 Proportion of Women Ever Married under Different Conditions

accomplished through a combination of (1) a young age at which marriage begins, (2) rapid entry into marriage once a woman has reached the age at which marriage begins, and (3) a very high proportion of women eventually marrying. Coale and McNeil developed a model of the female age pattern of first marriage in which these three factors are manipulated.[19]

Figure 8.20 shows the proportion of women ever married by age under different combinations of the three factors. In the early, rapid marriage scenario (Early Rapid All Married) all women eventually marry, and the proportion ever married increases rapidly. In the early beginning age of marriage but slower progression scenario (Early Slower All Married), although all women eventually marry, the proportion of women ever married at each age is much lower. In the first scenario, 96% of women age 25–29 have married, but in the second scenario, only 60% of women age 25–29 have married. In the third scenario, marriage begins at a later age, it proceeds slowly, and only 80% of all women ever marry (Late Slow Not All Married). In the third scenario, only 7% of those aged 25–29 have married.

An early beginning of marriage and rapid progression of marriage until almost all women have married has been found in some less developed countries. This pattern is often found in arranged-marriage systems. It has been argued that the only way that marriage can proceed as rapidly as in the Early Rapid All Married scenario in Figure 8.20 is if marriages are planned while the future spouses are children and where the partners have little say in the process. As people have more say about whom they will marry, marriage typically begins somewhat later and proceeds more slowly, as it takes time for young people to find a spouse.[20]

Age of Sexual Debut

In some groups in Africa, marriage is a process rather than a discreet event. In a study in the Ivory Coast, van de Walle and Meeker found that among the Baule ethnic group, if one considered a birth illegitimate if it occurred before the marriage ceremony, then 50% of births were illegitimate. However, if one only considered a birth illegitimate if it occurred before the woman first had sex with the man she eventually married, only 17% of births would be considered illegitimate. Having a child with a man whom a woman eventually married was not met with disapproval. In fact, if a woman has had a child with a man, this can increase the chance that they marry, since she has demonstrated that she is fecund.[21]

In settings in which subfecundity is a major concern, having demonstrated fertility is especially important. Larsen estimated that in Cameroon in 1978, 28% of women aged 25–29 were sterile, and in Nigeria in 1981–1983 18% of women aged 25–29 were sterile.[22] This has led to research on the **age of sexual debut**, which is the age of first sexual intercourse.[23] Looking at infertility across 27 African countries, early sexual debut was positively related to infertility, especially when there was more than one partner. A major cause of infertility is sexually transmitted diseases, and sexual relations with several persons increases the risk of such infections.[24]

Early sexual debut among girls in sub-Saharan Africa is a concern also because of the risk of contracting HIV. Those with early sexual debut are more likely to have multiple sexual partners, which is also a substantial risk factor for HIV. This finding is consistent with earlier research about other sexually transmitted diseases. In addition, those with early sexual debut were more likely to have problems with drinking alcohol, smoking, and strained relationships with their parents.[25]

NATURAL FERTILITY AND CONTROLLED FERTILITY

In all populations, the chance that a woman who is exposed to the risk of pregnancy has a child increases after menarche and then declines after some age until it reaches zero at menopause. Researchers have been interested in the shape of the age pattern of fertility of women who are married or who regularly engage in sexual intercourse and what influences that shape. It has long been observed that in very-high-fertility populations with little indication of a desire to limit fertility, the shape of the age-specific marital fertility schedule is different than in lower fertility settings where there is substantial effort to limit fertility.

The French demographer Louis Henry was interested in the age pattern of marital fertility in populations in which little or nothing was done to limit fertility. He looked at the fertility of married women in 13 populations in which he thought there was little or no action to limit childbearing.

Henry was especially interested in the Hutterites, who are a religious group that came from Eastern

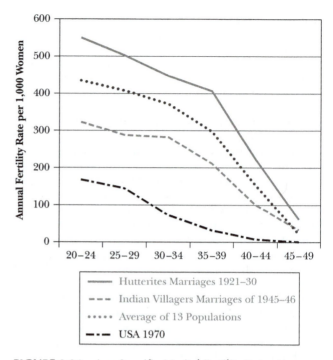

FIGURE 8.21 Age-Specific Marital Fertility Rates (Ages 20–49) among Populations with Little Limitation of Fertility and for the United States, 1970

Europe and settled in the northwest United States and southwest Canada. They believe that it is morally wrong for a married couple to do anything to prevent a pregnancy. Hutterite women breastfeed for a very short time, which leads to a short period of postpartum amenorrhea. Most Hutterites have a high school education, and they have as good survival chances as the general U.S. and Canadian populations. As a result of these beliefs and practices, Hutterites have short intervals between births and have a large number of children.[26]

Populations with high fertility and little effort to control their fertility often have low educational attainment and very poor-quality data. Due to the relatively high education and good health of Hutterites, the quality of the fertility data from Hutterites is thought to be more accurate than in other populations with little limitation of fertility.

Figure 8.21 shows age-specific fertility rates for Hutterites who were married in 1921–1930 and for women in Hindu villages in Bengal in India who married in 1945–1946. The Hutterites and the Indian villagers were two of the 13 populations that Henry examined. The average of the age-specific fertility rates across the 13 populations is also shown. Age-specific fertility rates for American women in 1970 are also shown for comparison.

The age-specific fertility rates are shown by 5-year age groups for women age 20–49. Hutterites had almost no non-marital childbearing, and marriage

age was about 20. Henry noted that marital fertility rates for women aged 15–19 are often very strongly influenced by premarital pregnancies that caused the marriage to occur. He was trying to develop a general model of fertility of women exposed to regular sexual intercourse because they were married, and he was not trying to explain differences among populations in rates of premarital pregnancy that led to marriage. Thus, he did not include the 15–19 age group in his analysis. Rather, he looked at marital fertility by age, starting at age 20.

The Hutterites had the highest ASFRs among the 13 populations that Henry examined. Women in Indian villages who married in 1945–1946 had the lowest ASFRs among the 13 populations. The three lines shown for populations that Henry examined vary in level, but they all decline gradually with age until after age 40, and all three graphs show a convex shape. The graph for American women in 1970 has lower ASFRs than in the populations that Henry examined, but also the shape of the line differs, showing a concave shape after age 30.

Figure 8.22 shows the information on ASFRs for the same four populations as in Figure 8.21, but in a different way. In Figure 8.22, the rates for women aged 25–49 are shown relative to the value for women aged 20–24. When looked at this way, it is clear that the shapes of the age-specific fertility schedules for the populations studied by Henry are virtually identical, and the convex shape for these

populations is even more apparent than it was in Figure 8.21. The concave shape of the age-specific fertility schedule for American women is also clearer than it was in Figure 8.21.

Henry argued that in populations with little or no fertility limitation, the shape of their age-specific fertility schedules is the same, in the sense illustrated by Figure 8.22. But these populations showed a large variation in the value of the TFR. If one calculated a total fertility rate based on fertility experience of women aged 20–45, Hutterite women have a TFR of 10.9 and the Indian village women a TFR of 6.2.

Henry argued that the change from the shape seen in the Hutterites and other 12 populations to the shape seen in the American data resulted from a change in women's behavior. He argued that substantial voluntary control of fertility among women who are not celibate results from women adopting behaviors that reduce the chance of pregnancy and birth (and thus increase the interval to the next birth) and that the extent to which women engage in these behaviors increases as the women have more children. After women have had the number of children they want, they act to decrease the chance of a subsequent birth.

Henry coined the term **natural fertility** for populations in which women and couples do not vary behaviors that affect the chance of a subsequent birth or the interval to the next live birth dependent on how many children have already been born.[27] A woman's **parity** is the number of live births she has had. Natural fertility does *not* mean having children at the biological maximum. A couple or population is exhibiting natural fertility behavior even if their actions reduce the chance of a subsequent pregnancy if that behavior is not parity dependent.

Parity is the numbering of a birth—after having one child, a woman is at parity 1, and after the second birth, she is at parity 2. If she acts in ways that influence the time to the next birth, but she behaves the same way after each subsequent birth as after the first birth, then her behavior is not parity dependent.

One behavior that might or might not be parity dependent is prolonged breastfeeding. Another is postpartum abstinence from sexual intercourse. Prolonged breastfeeding tends to delay the return of ovulation after a birth and thus increases the interval to the next birth. A population in which all women breastfeed a child for a year will tend to have longer interbirth intervals—and thus a lower total fertility rate—than a population in which all women breastfeed children for one month. However, if the long-breastfeeding population breastfeeds *every* newborn for a year, then that population is still exhibiting natural fertility behavior. The Gainj of New Guinea are a natural fertility population but have a total fertility rate of only 4.3, mainly because of long periods of amenorrhea after births as a result of prolonged breastfeeding.[28]

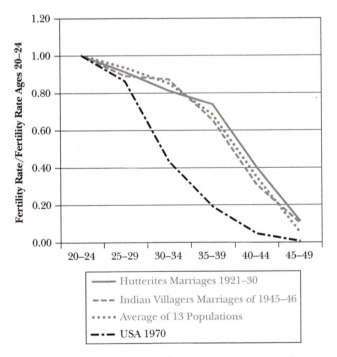

FIGURE 8.22   Age-Specific Marital Fertility Rates Relative to the Value at Ages 20–24, among Populations with Little Limitation of Fertility and for the United States, 1970

However, if women in a population breastfeed the firstborn child for 1 month, the second-born child for 3 months, and the third-born and later-born children for a year, then the population is not exhibiting natural fertility behavior. It is exhibiting **controlled fertility** behavior because the behavior that influences the interval to the next live birth is parity dependent. In controlled fertility behavior, women are more likely to be engaged or more intensively engaged in fertility-delaying behavior after higher order births.

For a population to exhibit natural fertility behavior, women and couples do not need to be ignorant of the effects of their behavior. It is only necessary that behaviors that influence the interval to the next live birth are not parity dependent.

Henry's choice of the term "natural fertility" to characterize childbearing where behavior that influences the interval to the next birth is not parity dependent is perhaps unfortunate. Some have criticized the concept by saying, "There is nothing natural about natural fertility," since even a population that consciously behaves in a way that influences the interval to the next live birth is still a natural fertility population if that behavior is not parity dependent. However, women in a population in which there is prolonged breastfeeding after every birth are still practicing natural fertility, even if they understand that this behavior prolongs interbirth intervals. Modern contraception can even be a part of natural fertility behavior if its use is not parity dependent, as is illustrated by the following discussion of postpartum abstinence in sub-Saharan Africa.

Postpartum Abstinence in Africa and a Shift to Contraception: Behavior to Reduce Infant and Child Mortality

In many parts of sub-Saharan Africa, there is a belief that it is risky to a baby's survival if the mother becomes pregnant and has another child too soon after the earlier child's birth. This belief is sensible. Although breastfeeding reduces the risk of pregnancy, it is not totally effective. When a woman becomes pregnant, her breast milk dries up.[29]

In many LDR settings, breast milk is the safest food for young babies. It is a clean, high-calorie, easily digestible source of protein. Breast milk is a better food for infants than any substitute, and high-quality formula is often unavailable or extremely expensive. Easily digestible protein sources for infants can be difficult to find. In some countries, nuts are a major source of protein, but nuts are very difficult for babies and young children to digest. Thus, if a woman has a baby and becomes pregnant while she is still breastfeeding, it is reasonable to think that the new pregnancy will increase the chance that the already-born child will die.[30]

Due to concerns about the survival of a child who was recently born, in some populations in sub-Saharan Africa there is a postpartum taboo against the new mother having sexual intercourse for a prolonged period of time after the birth, sometimes as long as 2 years or more. This is called a period of **postpartum abstinence**. In some cultures, the taboo is until the recently born child has reached some developmental stage such as "until the child can walk" or "until the child is weaned." These practices lengthen interbirth interval and thus depress fertility, but they also improve the survival chances of the child who has already been born. The postpartum intercourse taboo applied to the mother but did not necessarily apply to the father, who often had sexual intercourse with other women while his wife was practicing postpartum abstinence.[31]

In these settings, modern contraceptives can be a convenient substitute for abstinence. For example, a 1973 survey in Ibadan City, Nigeria, found that among women who were using contraception, over 75% of the women stated that the purpose was spacing—lengthening the interval to the birth of the next child—rather than part of an attempt to limit the total number of children they would bear.[32] In Gambia, it is a source of shame for there to be less than years between the births of a woman's children. A study in one region of Gambia found substantial use of modern contraceptives, mainly the injectable contraceptive Depo-Provera. The overwhelming reason for use of modern contraception was to prolong the interbirth interval.[33] Often, the mother or mother-in-law would move in with the couple to help enforce postpartum abstinence. Fertility decline in sub-Saharan Africa in the 1980s and 1990s was substantially due to increases in birth spacing.[34]

AGE PATTERNS OF NATURAL AND CONTROLLED FERTILITY

Coale and Trussell built on Henry's work to model age-specific fertility rates for natural fertility populations. They also modeled a pattern of deviation by age from natural fertility, which included increasingly intense behavior to limit fertility after age 25.

The indicator of the intensity of fertility control is called "m." The higher the value of m, the more intensively parity-dependent fertility control is being exercised. The value of m indicates the extent to which fertility after the 20–24 age group adopts a concave shape, rather than a convex, shape. In Figure 8.22, the natural fertility populations have a convex shape, while the United States in 1970 has a concave shape. In a natural fertility population, m = 0.[35]

Figure 8.23 shows age-specific fertility rates relative to the age-specific fertility rate for those aged 20–24. It is shown for a natural fertility population and for populations with intentional fertility control. Populations with intentional fertility control have positive

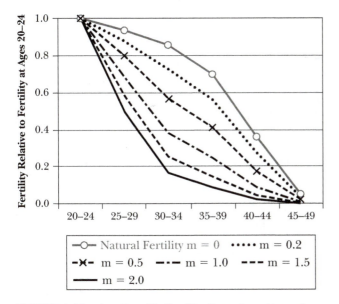

FIGURE 8.23   Age-Specific Fertility Rates for a Natural Fertility Population and for Varying Levels of Fertility Control Relative to Fertility at Ages 20–24

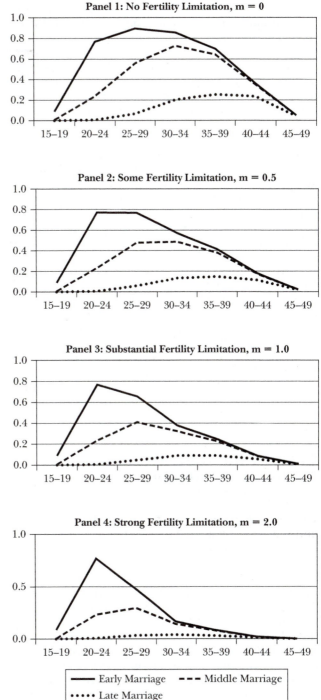

FIGURE 8.24   Age-Specific Fertility Rates with Different Marriage Patterns and Different Levels of Fertility Limitation

values of m. The higher the value of m, the more concave the shape of the age-specific fertility schedule.

The change in the shape of the age-specific marital fertility schedule shown in Figure 8.23 is thought to result from women shifting to a pattern of controlled fertility, in which behaviors are increasingly adopted to stop childbearing or postpone the birth of the next child, as women have more children. This would be even clearer if parity were on the x-axis rather than age, but parity data are much rarer than data on age, so Henry formulated his model in terms of a woman's age rather than in terms of her parity.

Control of fertility is one of the few social changes that is typically adopted by older persons before younger persons. The idea is that women adopt controlled fertility behavior because they have reached or are approaching the total number of children that they want to bear. Thus, generally women who have reached their desired number of children are older than women who have not reached their desired number of children.

THE CONTRIBUTION OF CHANGES IN MARRIAGE AGE AND FERTILITY CONTROL TO THE SHAPE OF THE FERTILITY SCHEDULE

Coale and Trussell combined variations in the age pattern of marital fertility (just discussed here) with variations in the age pattern of first marriage portrayed in Figure 8.20 to develop a model of variation in age-specific fertility rates.[36] In their model, the shape of the schedule is determined by (1) how early marriage begins, (2) how rapidly marriage proceeds, and (3) the extent of fertility control.

Figure 8.24 shows age-specific fertility rates under various conditions of the earliness and rapidity of marriage and at different levels of fertility limitation. These graphs are shown assuming no non-marital fertility. The marriage patterns are shown for an Early Marriage pattern, which has an early start to marriage and rapid progress of marriage; a Middle Marriage pattern with marriage beginning somewhat later and progressing more slowly; and a Late Marriage pattern with marriage beginning even later and progressing even more slowly.

In Panel 1, there is no parity-dependent fertility limitation. Thus, in Panel 1, age-specific fertility rates are determined by fecundity by age and the age pattern of marriage. In Panel 2, we see shifts in age-specific fertility rates when there is some parity-dependent fertility limitation. When early marriage persists, we see that age-specific fertility rates decline substantially after age 30, when some fertility limitation is adopted. In Panel 3, we see that age-specific fertility rates become quite peaked due to the influence of the age pattern of fertility control. The peak occurs at a younger age if marriage is early than if there is a pattern of later age at marriage. The peaking of fertility is even more apparent in Panel 4 with strong fertility limitation. Overall, the shape of the left-hand side of the age-specific fertility curve is mainly influenced by how early or late marriage is. The right-hand side of the age-specific fertility curve is mainly influenced by the extent of fertility limitation in the population.

SHIFTS IN THE AGE PATTERN OF FERTILITY IN HIGHLY DEVELOPED, LOW-FERTILITY SETTINGS

We saw in Figures 8.2, 8.3, and 8.7 that fertility in many more developed countries fell to very low levels after 1990. In 2005–2010, the TFR in Europe as a whole was 1.5, far below replacement level, and the TFR also was below replacement level in every European region. Many countries reached a TFR of 1.3 or less, a level that has been referred to as **lowest-low fertility**. In the countries in which the TFR became very low, modern contraceptives were readily available, and women were very effective at preventing pregnancy and birth. These populations show age patterns of fertility that had not been envisioned by Coale and Trussell. Fertility at younger ages declined considerably due to an increase in the age at first birth. The level of fertility also declined due to an increase in permanent childlessness.

These new patterns of age-specific fertility are shown in Figure 8.25. At Time 1, the age pattern of fertility looks similar to the Middle Marriage scenario in Panel 4 of Figure 8.25. The schedule at

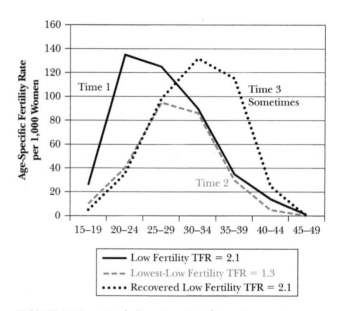

FIGURE 8.25 A Path from Low Fertility to Lowest-Low Fertility and Back to Low Fertility

Time 2 results in a very low TFR of 1.3. The lowest-low fertility scenario at Time 2 reflects what has been seen in several highly developed countries, with a decline in fertility rates at younger ages and no increase in fertility rates at older ages. The age-specific fertility schedule at Time 2 in Figure 8.25 is consistent with a late marriage pattern that is even later than shown in the late marriage scenario in Panel 4 of Figure 8.24.

Between 2000–2005 and 2005–2010, some more developed countries showed a substantial increase in fertility from very low fertility to simply low fertility. As shown in Figure 8.7, the TFR in every European region increased from 2000–2005 to 2005–2010. On the other hand, we saw in Figure 8.5 that in Eastern Asia, the TFR continued to decline. Thus, the TFR did not increase after 2005 in all more developed or high-income countries.

Questions that have been raised include the following: (1) When is very low fertility followed by an increase to merely low fertility? and (2) when in such an increase the result of a shift in the age pattern of fertility with little change in cohort TFR? Recall from Figure 8.13 that in the United States through the Great Depression and the Baby Boom, cohort TFR varied much less than did period TFR.

In Figure 8.25, the age pattern that has often occurred in populations that have recovered from lowest-low fertility to simply low fertility is shown. In those situations, the age pattern of fertility shifts to a much older age, reaching a peak for women in their thirties, rather than for women in their twenties. This is labeled as "Time 3 Sometimes" because sometimes this fertility recovery has happened and sometimes it has not happened. The TFR at Time 1 and at Time 3 are the same, with only a shift in the timing of childbearing. Cohort fertility could have been constant from Time 1 through Time 3.

Theories and mechanisms concerning changes in the level and the age pattern of fertility are discussed in Chapter 10, including examination of the social changes and mechanisms that have led to very low fertility in some settings and to a recovery from very low fertility to low fertility in other settings.

CONCLUDING COMMENTS

Fertility decline in much of the LDR is impressive, although fertility remains high in much of Africa. Given the low value of NRR/GRR for the LeastDC shown in Figure 8.12, as mortality continues to decline, the NRR will continue to rise in the LeastDC unless there is further decline in the TFR. The very low fertility in some MDR countries has had a major influence on the policy concerns of many governments. The complex changes in patterns of marriage and fertility by age discussed in this chapter provide a background for understanding the discussion of fertility change in the following chapters.

✔ Study and Review Online

SUMMARY

1. The total fertility rate (TFR) is the number of children that a woman would have if she went through her life having children at the rates that women in that population experience.

2. TFR in the world declined starting in the 1970s. The TFR in Latin America and the Caribbean began to decline in the late 1960s, in Asia in the 1970s, and in Africa in the 1980s.

3. In populations where nothing is done to affect the sex of babies (no sex-selective abortion), the sex ratio at birth is virtually always 104–107 baby boys born for every 100 baby girls. The gross reproduction rate (GRR) is the number of daughters that a woman would have if she went through her life having daughters at the rates that women in that population experience. It is a TFR for daughters.

4. The net reproduction rate (NRR) is the GRR adjusted for female mortality. It is a measure of the extent to which women replace themselves with daughters, taking both fertility and mortality into account.

5. When NRR = 1, it is said that the population has attained replacement fertility or zero population growth. When NRR = 1, in the long run the population size will not change.

6. World NRR declined from 1.66 in 1950–1955 to 1.08 in 2005–2010, slightly above replacement fertility. The MDR was below replacement fertility since 1975–1980, and in 2005–2010 in the United States, NRR = 1.00. NRR in the LDR peaked in 1965–1970 and then declined, while NRR in the LeastDC peaked in 1980–1985 and then declined, although even in 2005–2010 NRR was quite high in the LeastDC at 1.74. NRR in Latin America and the Caribbean peaked in 1960–1965, in 1965–1970 in Asia, and in 1980–1985 in Africa. NRR was highest in Africa among world regions since 1970–1975.

7. In order to maintain a given growth rate, as mortality declines fertility must also decline. At $e_0^0 = 20$, a TFR of about 6.5 is necessary for a growth rate of zero. At $e_0^0 = 40$, the same TFR would result in a growth rate of about 2%, and at $e_0^0 = 60$, a TFR = 6.5 would result in a growth rate of about 3%. At $e_0^0 = 60$ or higher, a TFR of about 2.07 would result in a growth rate of zero.

8. One can study cohort fertility as one can study cohort mortality. Cohort TFR is the TFR that would result if a woman went through her life having children at the rate by age that was experienced by women born in a given time period.

9. When conditions are not favorable for having children, women and couples can postpone having a child and then have the child when they perceive that conditions are better. When one looks at fertility during and after the Great Depression of the 1930s in the United States, there is evidence that there was postponement of childbearing. Period TFR is much more variable over time than cohort TFR. The lesser variability of cohort TFR suggests that much of the decline in period TFR during the Great Depression was due to postponement of childbearing to a somewhat more favorable time.

10. When looking at the 1993–1994 Rwandan Civil War catastrophe, it is clear that during crises demographic processes change, but they do not all change in the same way. Mortality increased during the civil war and then returned to pre–civil war levels. Fertility declined during the civil war and then remained at the new lower level. There was substantial emigration from Rwanda during the civil war, but this was almost completely offset by immigration in the 5-year period after the civil war.

11. Females become able to reproduce at menarche, which usually occurs at about age 12, and women cease to be able to reproduce at menopause, which usually occurs at about age 50.

12. Intervals between births can be divided into different parts. There is a waiting time to conception, which is then followed by pregnancy. The pregnancy can end in a live birth, a miscarriage, or an induced abortion. Then there is another waiting time to the next conception.

13. The division of the interbirth interval into parts is useful when thinking about the proximate determinants of fertility, which are (1) exposure to sexual intercourse, (2) exposure to conception, and (3) gestation and carrying the pregnancy to birth. Exposure to sexual intercourse has usually been indicated by whether a woman is married, exposure to conception is usually indicated by the use of contraception, and gestation and carrying the pregnancy to birth are usually indicated by the tendency to miscarry and the use of induced abortion.

14. One can model the pattern of female marriage by age as the result of three components: (1) the age at which females begin to marry, (2) how rapidly marriage proceeds once a marriageable age is reached, and (3) the proportion of females who ever marry. These three factors can be varied to see how patterns of first marriage can change.

In some societies, the age when marriage begins has increased, the pace of marriage has slowed, and the proportion of women eventually marrying has declined.

15. Among women having regular sexual intercourse, one can model age patterns of fertility, often viewed as age patterns of marital fertility. A distinction is between natural fertility and controlled fertility. A couple or a population is practicing natural fertility if behaviors that increase the interval to the next live birth are not related to the number of children the woman has already borne—her parity. A couple or population is practicing controlled fertility if behaviors that prolong the interval to the next birth are positively related to how many children have already been born—that is, the behavior is parity dependent. In populations that have shifted from natural fertility to controlled fertility, age-specific fertility rates decline increasingly rapidly with the age of the woman, as more women have borne the number of children they desired.

16. Different patterns of marriage and different patterns of marital fertility work together to produce a variety of patterns of age-specific fertility. The left-hand side of the age-specific fertility curve is mainly influenced by the age pattern of entry into marriage or other union. The right-hand side of the age-specific fertility curve is mainly influenced by the extent of the control of fertility among married women or women in other unions.

17. When societies are highly developed and women have a high level of control over their fertility, childbearing often shifts to an older age, resulting in an older age pattern of childbearing than occurred earlier. Sometimes age-specific fertility rates increase at older ages and compensate for the decline in age-specific fertility rates at younger ages.

KEY TERMS

childbearing ages   246
general fertility rate   246
child–woman ratio   246
age-specific fertility rate
    (ASFR)   246
total fertility rate (TFR)   246
subfecundity   249
gross reproduction rate
    (GRR)   251
net reproduction rate
    (NRR)   251
sex ratio at birth   251

zero population growth
    (ZPG)   252
replacement fertility   252
below-replacement
    fertility   252
birth cohort   258
cohort   258
cohort fertility   258
menarche   261
menopause   261
fecundity   261
fertility   262

birth interval   262
postpartum amenorrhea   262
proximate determinants of
    fertility   262
marital fertility   263
age of sexual debut   264
natural fertility   265
parity   265
controlled fertility   266
postpartum abstinence   266
lowest-low fertility   268

QUESTIONS FOR DISCUSSION AND REVIEW

1. How can it be that fertility behavior in a country is unchanged but the rate of population growth increases over time?
2. What is a "cohort"? What difference does it make to look at cohort fertility as compared to period fertility? Is the interpretation of behavior of American women and families during the Great Depression and during the Baby Boom different if one uses a cohort perspective rather than a period perspective?

NOTES

1. Barbara A. Anderson. 1975. "Male Age and Fertility Results from Ireland prior to 1911," *Population Index*, 41: 561–567; and Isabelle Bray, David Gunnell, and George Davey Smith. 2006. "SHORT REPORT: Advanced Paternal Age: How Old Is Too Old?" *Journal of Epidemiology and Community Health*, 60: 851–853.

2. John Bongaarts, Odile Frank, and Ron Lesthaeghe. 1984. "The Proximate Determinants of Fertility in Sub-Saharan Africa," *Population and Development Review*, 10: 511–537.

3. S. Gregson. 1994. "Will HIV Become a Major Determinant of Fertility in Sub-Saharan Africa?" *Journal of Development Studies*, 30: 650–679; and UNAIDS. 2002. *Estimating and Projecting National HIV/AIDS Epidemics*, UNAIDS Reference Group on Estimates, Models and Projections UNAIDS/01.83, January, Geneva: UNAIDS.

4. Appendix A lists the countries in each United Nations region.

5. Anouch Chanazarian. 1988. "Determinants of the Sex Ratio at Birth: Review of Recent Literature," *Social Biology*, 35: 214–235; M. M. McMillen. 1979. "Differential Mortality by Sex in Fetal and Neonatal Deaths," *Science*, 204: 89–91; and T. Hassold, S. D. Quillen, and J. A. Yamane. 1983. "Sex Ratio in Spontaneous Abortions," *Annals of Human Genetics*, 47: 39–47.

6. From Ansley J. Coale and Paul Demeny. 1983. *Regional Model Life Tables and Stable Populations*, New York: Academic Press. West model life tables are used.

7. Norman B. Ryder. 1986. "Observations on the History of Cohort Fertility in the United States," *Population and Development Review*, 12: 617–643; and OPR data archive, http://opr.princeton.edu/archive/cpft/ (accessed July 10, 2012).

8. Frank D. Bean. 1983. "The Baby Boom and Its Explanations," *The Sociological Quarterly*, 24: 353–365.

9. Linda Melvern. 2004. *Conspiracy to Murder: The Rwandan Genocide*, London: Verso.

10. Manuel Angel Castillo and James C. Hathaway. 1997. "Temporary Protection," in *Reconceiving International Refugee Law*, ed. James C. Hathaway, The Hague: Martinus Nijhoff, 1–21.

11. Margaret A. McDowell, Debra J. Brody, and Jeffery P. Hughes. 2007. "Has Age at Menarche Changed? Results from the National Health and Nutrition Examination Survey (NHANES) 1999–2004," *Journal of Adolescent Health*, 40: 227–231; R. V. Short. 1976. "The Evolution of Human Reproduction," *Proceedings of the Royal. Society—Biological Sciences*, 195: 3–24; P. H. Whincup, J. A. Gilg, K. Odoki, S. J. C. Taylor, and D. G. Cook. 2001. "Age of Menarche in Contemporary British Teenagers: Survey of Girls Born between 1982 and 1986." *British Medical Journal*, 322: 1095–1096; J. L. Boldsen and B. Jeune. 1990. "Distribution of Age at Menopause in Two Danish Samples," *Human Biology*, 62: 291–300; and Kenneth Hill. 1996. "The Demography of Menopause," *Maturitas*, 23: 113–127.

12. A. Foster, J. Menken, A. Chowdhury, and J. Trussell. 1986. "Female Reproductive Development: A Hazards Model Analysis," *Social Biology*, 33: 183–198.

13. Ellen B. Gold, Joyce Bromberger, Sybil Crawford, Steve Samuels, Gail A. Greendale, Sioban D. Harlow, and Joan Skurnick. 2001. "Factors Associated with Age at Natural Menopause in a Multiethnic Sample of Midlife Women," *American Journal of Epidemiology*, 153: 865–874; and Julia Dratva, Francisco Gómez Real, Christian Schindler, Ursula Ackermann-Liebrich, Margaret Gerbase, Nicole Probst-Hensch, Cecilie Svanes, Ernst Raidar Omenaas, Françoise Neukirch, Matthias Wjst, Alfredo Morabia, Deborah Jarvis, Bénédicte Leynaert, and Elisabeth Zemp. 2009. "Is Age at Menopause Increasing across Europe? Results on Age at Menopause and Determinants from Two Population-Based Studies," *Menopause*, 16: 385–394.

14. The terms *fertilite* and *fecondite* in French have the opposite meaning of those terms in English. *Fertilite* means fecundity, and *fecondite* means fertility.

15. Sandra L. Huffman, Kathleen Ford, Hubert A. Allen Jr., and Peter Streble. 1987. "Nutrition and

Fertility in Bangladesh: Breastfeeding and Post Partum Amenorrhoea," *Population Studies.* 41: 447–462; and J. Bongaarts and R. G. Potter. 1983. *Fertility, Biology and Behavior*, New York: Academic Press.

16. P. G. Lunn, M. Watkinson, A. M. Prentice, P. Morrell, P. Austin, and R. G. Whitehead. 1981. "Maternal Nutrition and Lactational Amenorrhoea," *The Lancet*, 1928–1929; and K. Prema, A. Nadamuni, E. Neelakumari, and B. A. R. Ramalakshmi. 1981. "Nutrition–Fertility Interaction in Lactating Women of Low Income Groups," *British Journal of Nutrition*, 45: 461–467.

17. Other ways for a woman to be exposed to the risk of pregnancy are artificial insemination and in vitro fertilization.

18. John Bongaarts. 1978. "A Framework for Analyzing the Proximate Determinants of Fertility," *Population and Development Review*, 4: 105–132.

19. A. J. Coale and D. R. McNeil. 1972. "The Distribution by Age of the Frequency of First Marriage in a Female Cohort," *Journal of the American Statistical Association*, 67: 743–749.

20. R. Lesthaeghe. 1971. "Nuptiality and Population Growth," *Population Studies*, 25: 415–432.

21. Etienne van de Walle and Dominique Meekers. 1988. "Marriage Drinks and Kolanuts," paper presented at the International Union for the Scientific Study of Population Seminar on Nuptiality in Sub-Saharan Africa: Current Changes and Impact on Fertility, Paris, November 14–17; and Caroline E. Bledsoe and Barney Cohen, eds. 1993. *Social Dynamics of Adolescent Fertility in Sub-Saharan Africa*, Washington, DC: National Academy Press.

22. Ulla Larsen. 1994. "Sterility in Sub-Saharan Africa," *Population Studies*, 48: 459–474.

23. Linda Richter and Saadhna Panday. 2006. "Youth Conceptions of the Transition to Adulthood in South Africa: Barriers and Opportunities," *Sexuality in Africa*, 3: 3–5; and B. Zaba, E. Pisani, E. Slaymaker, and J. Ties Boerma. 2004. "Age at First Sex: Understanding Recent Trends in African Demographic Surveys," *Sexually Transmitted Infections*, 80(Supplement II): ii28–ii35.

24. Karen Ericksen and Tracy Brunette. 1996. "Patterns and Predictors of Infertility among African Women: A Cross-national Survey of Twenty-seven Nations," *Social Science & Medicine*, 42: 209–220.

25. K. Zuma, G. Setswe, T. Kelye, T. Mzolo, T. Rehle, and N. Mbelle. 2010. *African Journal of Reproductive Health*, 14: 47–54; and Karl Peltzer. 2010. "Early Sexual Debut and Associated Factors among In-School Adolescents in Eight African Countries," *Acta Paediatrica*, 99: 1242–1247.

26. Before 1950, it is thought that Hutterites did not engage in practices that prevented pregnancy. The data that Henry used for Hutterites referred to marriages that occurred during 1921–1930, so the women would have completed their childbearing before 1950. J. W. Eaton and A. J. Mayer. 1953. "The Social Biology of Very High Fertility among the Hutterites: The Demography of a Unique Population," *Human Biology*, 25: 206–264; and Katherine J. Curtis White. 2002. "Declining Fertility among North American Hutterites: The Use of Birth Control within a Dariusleut Colony," *Social Biology*, 49: 58–73.

27. Louis Henry. 1961. "Some Data on Natural Fertility," *Eugenics Quarterly*, 8: 81–89.

28. James W. Wood, Patricia L. Johnson, and Kenneth L. Campbell. 1985. "Demographic and Endocrinological Aspects of Low Natural Fertility in Highland New Guinea," *Journal of Biosocial Science*, 17: 57–79.

29. Ron H. Gray. 1981. "Birth Intervals, Postpartum Sexual Abstinence and Child Health," in *Child-Spacing in Tropical Africa: Traditions and Change*, ed. Hilary J. Page and Ron Lesthaeghe, New York: Academic Press, 93–109.

30. Mark VanLandingham, James Trussell, and Laurence Grummer-Strawn. 1991. "Contraceptive and Health Benefits of Breastfeeding: A Review of the Recent Evidence," *International Family Planning Perspectives*, 17: 131–136.

31. R. Schoenmaeckers, I. H. Shah, R. Lesthaeghe, and O. Tambashe. 1981. "The Child-Spacing Tradition and the Postpartum Taboo in Tropical Africa: Anthropological Evidence," in *Child-Spacing in Tropical Africa: Traditions and Change*, ed. Hilary J. Page and Ron Lesthaeghe, New York: Academic Press, 26–27; Hilary J. Page and Ron Lesthaeghe, eds.1981. *Child-Spacing in Tropical Africa: Traditions and Change*, New York: Academic Press; and John C. Caldwell and Pat Caldwell. 1987. "The Cultural Context of High Fertility in Sub-Saharan Africa," *Population and Development Review*, 13: 409–437.

32. J. C. Caldwell and P. Caldwell. 1981. "Cause and Sequence in the Reduction of Postnatal Abstinence in Ibadan City, Nigeria," in *Child-Spacing in Tropical Africa: Traditions and Change*, ed. Hilary J. Page and Ron Lesthaeghe, New York: Academic Press, 190–191.

33. Caroline H. Bledsoe, Allan G. Hill, Umberto D'Alessandro, and Patricia Langerock. 1994. "Constructing Natural Fertility: The Use of Western Contraceptive Technologies in Rural Gambia," *Population and Development Review*, 20: 81–113.

34. Dudley Kirk and Bernard Pillet. 1998. "Fertility Levels, Trends, and Differentials in Sub-Saharan Africa in the 1980s and 1990s," *Studies in Family Planning*, 29: 1–22.

35. Ansley J. Coale and T. James Trussell. 1974. "Model Fertility Schedules: Variations in the Age Structure of Childbearing in Human Populations," *Population Index*, 40: 185–258.

36. Ansley J. Coale and T. James Trussell. 1974. "Model Fertility Schedules: Variations in the Age Structure of Childbearing in Human Populations," *Population Index*, 40: 185–258.

CHAPTER 9

THEORY AND PRACTICE OF FERTILITY DECLINE IN HISTORICAL EUROPE AND IN THE LESS DEVELOPED REGION

LEARNING OBJECTIVES

- Describe the historical difference between the pattern of marriage in Western Europe and in Eastern Europe and the effects of this difference on overall fertility, on the age at marriage, and on marital fertility.

- List Coale's three preconditions for fertility limitation.

- List the main theories of why fertility declines from a high to a moderate or low level.

- Describe the main reasons why women in the LDR are thought to adopt or not adopt contraception.

- Discuss the main differences between mortality policy and fertility policy.

((· Listen to the Chapter Audio

OVERVIEW

In Chapter 8, we looked at indicators of the level of fertility and at typical patterns of change in the age pattern of childbearing. In this chapter, we look at the causes of fertility levels and trends in historical Europe and in current less developed countries. We also examine theories about why fertility declines. We discuss preconditions for fertility limitation. Theories of decline from high fertility and some reasons for the persistence of high fertility are discussed. We also look at contraceptive use and the development of family-planning programs.

At the end of this chapter, we look at sex-selective abortion in some East Asian countries. In Chapter 10, which mainly focuses on more developed countries, we discuss the level of abortion use throughout the world, including in the least developed region (LDR). That LDR discussion is in the context of abortion use and attitudes toward abortion in the United States and other developed countries.

Fertility is determined by whether a woman is at risk of pregnancy and the chance of having a child among women who are at risk of pregnancy. In many

settings, this reduces to (1) factors related to marriage, and (2) factors related to the level of fertility of married women. This is a convenient division of factors in populations in which almost all children are born to married women, as was the case in much of historical Europe and the LDR.

FERTILITY CHANGE IN HISTORICAL EUROPE

In this section, we look at the age pattern of female marriage and of marital fertility, and how these two influences on fertility changed in Europe historically. There are differences and similarities with the situation in current less developed countries.

Variations in the Age at Marriage and the Proportion Ever Marrying in Historical Europe

In eighteenth-century Europe, before there was substantial voluntary control of fertility, there were large variations in the total fertility rate. This variation mainly resulted from differences in marriage

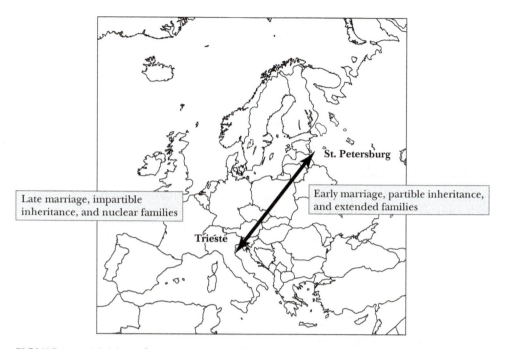

FIGURE 9.1   Division of Europe into Hajnal's Areas of Early and Late Marriage

patterns. In some parts of Europe, such as Ireland, female marriage commenced late, proceeded slowly, and a high proportion of women never married. This resulted in a moderate Total Fertility Rate (TFR) in Ireland, even though married women had very high fertility. On the other hand, in Hungary women began to marry at a young age, marriage proceeded rapidly, and almost all women eventually married. Young and universal marriage combined with moderate fertility among married women resulted in a moderate TFR in Hungary.

Hajnal was a European demographer who was interested in historical marriage patterns. He drew a line between Trieste in northeast Italy and St. Petersburg in Russia. He noted that to the east of the line, early and almost universal marriage was common, while to the west of the line late marriage was common, and a substantial proportion of women never married. This division is shown in Figure 9.1.[1] The areas to the west of Hajnal's line and to the east of Hajnal's line also tended to differ in inheritance patterns and in household structure.[2] Differences in inheritance patterns and household structure are thought to be the sources of the different marriage patterns.

In the West impartible inheritance was common, and in the East partible inheritance was common. With **impartible inheritance**, one child (almost always a son) inherits all of the land. Usually this was the oldest son (in a system called **primogeniture**), but it could be the youngest son (in a system called

ultimogeniture). In an impartible inheritance system, non-inheriting sons needed to accumulate resources in order to marry, and often they were never able to marry. This resulted in a high proportion of women never marrying and, depending on conventions about age differences of spouses, could result in an advanced age at marriage for women. In a **partible inheritance** system, the holdings are equally divided among all children, or more often among all sons. In this system, there was no incentive for sons to postpone marriage, since the earlier children were born, the earlier the households had additional labor to work the land.

Differences in household structure between the West and the East also contributed to differences in marriage patterns. In the West, a newly married couple tended to set up a separate household. Thus, most households were **nuclear households**, including only parents and minor children. In the East, a newly married couple tended to reside in an **extended household**, with parents or other relatives, such as married siblings. Due to these differences in household arrangements, more resources were required in order to marry in the West than in the East.

As discussed in Chapter 8, marriage is important as a proxy for exposure to the risk of pregnancy in populations in which almost all births occur to married women. However, there always have been non-marital births. For England, it is estimated that between 1540 and 1834, between 1% and 5% of births occurred to unmarried women. Also, many European brides were already pregnant. In France and Belgium in the eighteenth century, it has been estimated that as high as 34% of brides were pregnant at the time of marriage, depending on the region. In England in 1550–1799, it is estimated that 16–33% of brides were premaritally pregnant. However, in historical Europe, the vast majority of births occurred to married women, so dividing fertility into looking at marriage and then looking at marital fertility makes some sense.[3]

Historical Voluntary Fertility Limitation

Evidence of voluntary fertility limitation was first found in studies of elite families in France and in Geneva in the seventeenth century. The evidence for fertility limitation is that there were changes in the age pattern of fertility from a natural fertility pattern to a controlled fertility pattern, as discussed in Chapter 8. These well-off families had much lower infant and child mortality than poorer families and could have observed that they were having more surviving children than were needed to assure the survival of a male heir.[4]

The **Theory of the Demographic Transition** which was discussed in Chapter 2, describes a pattern of fertility decline in Europe after there had been substantial mortality decline, which eventually resulted in a decline in the natural rate of increase. Generally fertility declined as populations became more urban, as infant mortality declined, as industrialization proceeded, and as educational levels increased. Thus, many assumed that aspects of economic development such as urbanization, industrialization, and education directly led to fertility decline.

The Princeton European Fertility Project, under the direction of Ansley Coale, sought to further specify and test whether fertility behavior actually changed as described by the Theory of the Demographic Transition by looking at data from the eighteenth through the early twentieth centuries. That project examined how marriage and marital fertility patterns changed on the level of provinces in a large number of individual European countries. It looked at these aspects of fertility in relation to the changes in the factors thought to drive the demographic transition—infant mortality, education, industrialization, and urbanization. It also examined the timing of changes in aspects of development, such as an increase in education and a decrease in infant mortality and urbanization, to see whether they plausibly could have caused fertility decline.[5]

Teitelbaum summarized the findings of the Princeton European Fertility Project as follows:[6]

> From a broad macrohistorical view it is correct to say that in the two centuries from the mid-1700s onward there were widespread and substantial declines in marital fertility which were associated with major social and economic transformations in European societies. However, the more specific and explanatory propositions derived from [demographic] transition theory cannot explain all of the salient features of the European experience. In particular, the theory fails to explain fundamental phenomena such as variations in pre-transition levels of fertility and in the timing of onset and the pace of fertility decline which eventually became universal.

As Teitelbaum observed, fertility behavior did not conform well to the predictions of the Theory of the Demographic Transition. Substantial marital fertility limitation occurred in France about 70 years before it occurred in England. At that time France was less urban, less industrialized, and less educated than England. In Denmark, the timing of fertility decline was unrelated to the decline in infant mortality but showed a strong relation to increases in the proportion surviving from birth to age 15. Apparently, people in Denmark wanted to be sure that survival beyond infancy had actually improved before they were willing to risk having fewer children.[7] Similarly, Knodel found for Germany that infant mortality decline sometimes preceded fertility decline, sometimes occurred at the same time, and sometimes occurred after fertility decline. However in Germany marital fertility decline was related to the timing of decline in mortality of children aged 1–4.[8]

William Leasure was a graduate student at Princeton who was interested in demographic change in historical Spain. He looked at a map of Spanish provinces on which the date of substantial fertility decline was coded. There were distinct regional patterns, but the pattern did not correspond to regional differences in development level. When he showed the map to an expert on languages and culture in Spain, he received the comment, "Oh, that is a map of Spanish dialects." In an analysis of marital fertility levels and of the timing of marital fertility decline in Spain, Leasure found that region was more important in the timing of Spanish fertility decline than a variety of socioeconomic factors, such as education and industrialization. This observation helped convince Coale to launch the European Fertility Project. It also foreshadowed the importance of project findings that regional and cultural factors often were more important than indicators of development in precipitating fertility decline. This led to a more nuanced understanding of the interplay of social, economic, cultural, and psychological factors in fertility decline. It also stimulated continuing cooperation between sociologists, economists, anthropologists, and psychologists in the effort to more fully understand the factors that lead to fertility decline both in historical Europe and in less developed countries.[9]

TABLE 9.1   Year of a 10% Decline in Marital Fertility from Highest Level for Countries of Europe

France	1827	Denmark	1898	Greece	1913
Belgium	1881	Sweden	1902	Italy	1913
Switzerland	1887	Norway	1903	Portugal	1916
Germany	1888	Europe median	1903	Spain	1920
England & Wales	1892	Austria	1907	Ireland	1922
Scotland	1884	Hungary	1910	European Russia	1922
Netherlands	1887	Finland	1912		

Table 9.1 shows the approximate date by which marital fertility had declined at least 10% from its highest level. A 10% decline was seen as substantial and almost certainly indicated that long-term fertility decline in a population had begun. As mentioned, substantial marital fertility decline in England and Wales began about 70 years after it began in France.

The earliness of the fertility decline in France is striking. The evidence that French marital fertility declined in response to intentional actions by couples is strong. For example, one indication of a change from a natural fertility pattern to a controlled fertility pattern is a decline in the age of women at the birth of their last child. In France, based on studies of village parish records, the average age of women at the birth of their last child declined from 40 years of age before 1750, to 39 years of age in the period 1740–1790, to 37 years of age in 1780–1820. Also for French women married at ages 25–29, the marital total fertility rate declined from 6.9 children before 1750, to 6.5 in 1740–1790, and to 5.3 children in 1780–1820.[10]

There have been many ideas about why French fertility declined so early, but this is still a subject of scholarly controversy. Most scholars agree that substantial marital fertility limitation among the population as a whole, and not just the elite, began shortly after the French Revolution, but the ideas of the French Revolution were also well known elsewhere. The main methods of marital fertility decline seem to have been abstinence after the desired number of children had been born and coitus interruptus (withdrawal). Coitus interruptus was also known in many other parts of Europe. Those areas did not show substantial fertility limitation until much later.[11]

Before the Princeton European Fertility project, many demographers subscribed to the **characteristics hypothesis**. This hypothesis maintains that any behavioral difference among groups related to cultural or regional variables will disappear once socioeconomic characteristics have been taken into account. Cultural variables include language, ethnicity, and religion. Socioeconomic variables include education,

urban residence, and industrial development. In this view, the *real* cause of the relation between the cultural variable and behavior is socioeconomic differences among groups that have not yet been taken into account.

A major contribution of the Princeton European Fertility Project was that it convinced many demographers that the characteristics hypothesis was not always true and that cultural and regional factors could be very important even after socioeconomic characteristics had been taken into account. These findings did not immediately reveal what it was about cultural or regional factors that led to the differences in behavior, but it pointed to new lines of research that were more closely coordinated with cultural history, anthropology, and social psychology. Next, we describe some of the European Fertility Project findings.

In many European countries, cultural factors were more strongly related to the decline of marital fertility than were socioeconomic factors, such as education, infant mortality, or industrialization. Table 9.2 indicates regional and cultural factors that were important in explaining differences among provinces in the level and the timing of decline in marital fertility even after socioeconomic characteristics had been taken into account. "Region" refers to variation in marital fertility by groups of provinces. The characteristic that distinguishes regions is shown under "Region" in the table.[12]

For example, Belgium had a French-speaking population and a Flemish-speaking population. These populations were located in different regions of the country, and the connections between socioeconomic characteristics and fertility differed among the regions. For example, in provinces in the Flemish-speaking area, the percentage of the population that was literate was positively related to fertility, while in provinces in the French-speaking region, the percentage of the population that was literate was negatively related to fertility. It seems that in the French-speaking area, education was an agent of modernization and attitude change, while in the Flemish-speaking region, education tended to reinforce Catholic pronatalist values.

TABLE 9.2   Regional and Cultural Factors in the Decline of Marital Fertility in Some European Countries

Country	Region	Religion and Religiosity	Ethnicity	Language
Belgium	Language	% Non-Catholic vote 1910		
Switzerland	Language and religion	% Protestant		% German speaking
Germany	Language	% Catholic	% Poles and % Danes	
Austria			% Germans, Austrians, or Czechs, and % Poles or Ukrainians	
England & Wales	% Catholic		% born in France	
Scotland			% born in Ireland	
Italy		Divorce vote 1974		
Portugal	% Catholic marriage	% Catholic		

In Austria, the ethnic composition of provinces was important in the level of marital fertility and the timing of marital fertility decline. Provinces in which over 90% of the population was composed of Poles or Ukrainians had higher marital fertility and a later fertility decline; provinces in which over 90% of the population was composed of Austrians, Czechs, or Germans had lower marital fertility and an earlier fertility decline. These differences remained even after socioeconomic characteristics of provinces had been taken into account.

In Italy in 1974, there was a national referendum on whether a somewhat liberal divorce law that had been passed 3 years earlier should be repealed. The proportion by province that voted against the repeal of the law in 1974 was more strongly related to the historical provincial pattern of decline in marital fertility than were differences among Italian provinces in socioeconomic characteristics such as the percentage that lived in a rural area, the level of industrialization, or the percentage of illiterate males. The interpretation was that the vote in 1974 reflected the extent of attachment to the traditional view of marriage and the family.[13]

In Portugal, the north was more industrialized than the south, but marital fertility declined first in the south. The north was seen as having a higher level of Catholic religiosity than the south, which was indicated by a higher percentage of marriages performed in a Catholic service in the north than in the south. In fact, the provincial level of industrial development was *positively* related to marital fertility. Even in 1960, the fertility level by province was positively related to the percentage of the population of a province that declared that they were Catholic.

COALE'S PRECONDITIONS FOR FERTILITY LIMITATION

Coale proposed three **preconditions for fertility limitation** that he thought were necessary for fertility to decline from a high to a moderate level.[14] His preconditions referred to intentional fertility control among women or couples who believe they are fecund and engage in regular sexual intercourse. Sometimes the three conditions are referred to in a shorthand way as "Ready, Willing, and Able" (to control fertility). The conditions are as follows:

1. Acceptance of the possibility and moral acceptability of control of fertility (Willing)
2. Perception of advantages from reduced fertility (Ready)
3. Knowledge and mastery of an effective and acceptable technique of fertility control (Able)

Acceptance of the Possibility and Moral Acceptability of Control of Fertility (Willing)

In order to limit fertility, women and couples need to (1) believe it is possible for humans to take actions to control fertility, and (2) find it personally and morally acceptable to do so. Referring to the first situation, in some populations there has been little understanding of human reproduction, and it has seemed that control over whether and when childbearing occurs was impossible. In this situation, there is little possibility of effective voluntary fertility control. The Hutterites, discussed in Chapter 8 in the context of natural fertility, are a group that understands human reproduction but finds it morally unacceptable to do anything to reduce the chance that a married woman becomes pregnant and bears a child.

Perception of Advantages from Reduced Fertility (Ready)

Women and couples can find it acceptable to control their fertility, but if they do not see that it is in their interest to control their fertility, they will not take actions to do so. During the Baby Boom in the United States, the total fertility rate increased. This was not because American women forgot how to control their fertility, but because they wanted more children than they had wanted somewhat earlier. Westoff and Potvin found that in the late 1950s, college-educated Catholic women in the United States had more children than college-educated non-Catholic American women not mainly due to an unwillingness of Catholic women to use contraception but because they wanted more children than did non-Catholic Americans. Also, those Catholic women who attended Catholic colleges wanted more children than Catholic women who attended non-sectarian colleges. It seemed that this was because Catholic women who attended Catholic colleges had a more positive view toward having several children than other college-educated Catholic women and had more children mainly because they wanted more children.[15]

Knowledge and Mastery of Effective Techniques of Fertility Control (Able)

Even if women or couples are willing to control their fertility, and they think that doing so would be in their interest, they need to have access to an acceptable and effective method of fertility limitation. The main methods used in the historical decline of marital fertility in Europe almost certainly were coitus interruptus (withdrawal) and abstinence.[16] Neither of these methods requires modern technology, but people need to learn how to practice coitus interruptus, and both withdrawal and abstinence exact a high psychological cost because of the level of commitment it requires to stop sexual intercourse midway through when practicing withdrawal or to abstain from sexual intercourse with a partner to whom one is very attracted.

Much of the rationale behind family-planning programs that were instituted in the 1960s and 1970s was based on the belief that there were many women and couples who were ready and willing to limit their fertility but lacked an effective, convenient contraceptive method. The experience of the family-planning program in Taiwan, discussed later in this chapter, supports this view. However, the experience of family-planning programs in other settings suggests that this has not always been the case.

Sometimes women want to limit their fertility and have no moral objections to doing so, but the available contraceptive methods have unacceptable side effects. This can limit fertility control when otherwise women would be happy to use contraception.

Need to Have All Three Preconditions Satisfied for Voluntary Fertility Limitation to Occur

In Coale's view, women and couples will not adopt voluntary fertility limitation unless all three preconditions are met. One can think of situations in which

two of the three conditions are met, but because the third is not met, there will not be voluntary fertility limitation.

A couple can want to limit their fertility, and there can be a method available to them that they think would be effective and not difficult to use, but they will not limit their fertility if they think that it is morally unacceptable ever to limit fertility or that none of the available effective methods are morally acceptable. A Catholic couple who find artificial birth control unacceptable and for whom natural family planning does not work would not intentionally limit their fertility because the first condition (Willing) was not satisfied. Jennings and others have conducted research on improving effectiveness of natural family-planning methods. Their aim was to improve the control of fertility by couples with objections to contraceptives. These methods are based on abstinence on some days of a woman's monthly cycle.[17]

A couple can find contraceptive use acceptable and can have an acceptable and effective method available, but if they want more children they will not intentionally limit their fertility. This was the situation during the Baby Boom in the United States after World War II, during which the total fertility rate increased because women wanted more children than earlier cohorts of American women had wanted. In this situation, the first and the third preconditions are satisfied (Willing and Able), but the second is not (Ready).

A couple can find contraceptive use acceptable and can want to limit their childbearing, but will not do so if there is no acceptable method available. There could be a lack of availability of any supplies, or there could be unacceptable side effects from the available methods. In the Soviet Union, the supply of modern contraceptives was sporadic. It does not work well to begin to use contraceptive pills when the woman does not know if they will still be available in three months. Similarly, it is risky to rely on condoms if there is concern that they could be of poor quality and prone to breakage.[18] In these situations, the first two preconditions are met (Willing and Ready), but the third is not (Able). Situations in which the first two conditions are met but contraceptives are not used is the main concern of the area called the "unmet need for family planning," which is discussed later in this chapter.

AGE AT MARRIAGE IN LESS DEVELOPED COUNTRIES

Many less developed countries had earlier and more universal marriage even than found in Eastern Europe historically. For example, in Bangladesh before 1930 the average age of female marriage was

12 years, in Pakistan it was 17 years, and in India it was 14 years. Often the husbands were much older than their wives. Coale argued that this very early and universal pattern of marriage could only occur in an arranged-marriage system where the marriages had been planned when the bride and groom were children. Then, when the children reached what was considered marriageable age, the wedding could take place without a delay caused by a search for a spouse.[19]

In some less developed countries, non-marital childbearing has long been common, and sometimes marriage or a marriage-like arrangement has not been seen as important for childbearing. This is especially true in the Caribbean and in sub-Saharan Africa.

In some parts of the Caribbean, when a woman first enters a sexual relationship, she does not co-reside with her partner. This is called a "visiting union." Later, there can be a common-law union in which the partners live together, and later there can be a legal marriage.[20] In any type of union a child can be born, and a woman's exposure to the risk of pregnancy does not relate well to whether or not she considers herself in a union or the type of union.

In some parts of sub-Saharan Africa, although almost all women marry and their age at marriage is young, marriage has also often not been seen as a prerequisite to childbearing. One reason for this is that there has long been a fear of subfecundity in parts of sub-Saharan Africa. Subfecundity is the inability to become pregnant or a very low chance of becoming pregnant even with no contraceptive use and with regular sexual intercourse. There has been widespread fear of **childlessness**, and childlessness is a common reason for divorce. In this situation, if a woman has had a live birth, even if she is not married, this can make her a more desirable marriage partner since she has demonstrated that she is fecund.[21]

Changes in women's status have often contributed to an increase in female age at marriage. More educated women tend to marry later, and as educational attainment in the LDR has increased, this has led to later age at marriage. If women gain enough education, educational attainment directly affects age at marriage, since women who are still in school do not tend to marry.

There are also other mechanisms related to female education and age at marriage. Often before a woman marries, the benefits of her economic activity go to her **family of orientation**, which is the family into which she was born. Once the woman is married, the benefits of her economic activity go to her **family of procreation**, which is the family to which the woman, her husband or partner, and any children belong. Often the greater a woman's educational attainment, the greater her economic productivity.

In cities in less developed countries, a major economic activity for women has been selling goods on the street, such as fruit. Even a small amount of education can increase a woman's knowledge of the national language or the former colonial language and thus can increase her income. In these situations, her father can be reluctant for her to marry, because marriage would lead her family of orientation to lose her income to her family of procreation.[22]

THEORIES OF DECLINE FROM HIGH TO MODERATE OR LOW FERTILITY

Although age at marriage can be important, marital fertility or the fertility of women in a regular sexual union is the focus of most theories about the causes of fertility decline from a high to a moderate or low level.[23] Some theories have been based on economic considerations, while other theories have focused on balancing competing demands on women or on changes in the goals, desires, and worldview of women and couples.

Becker's New Home Economics Model

Gary Becker, a Nobel Prize–winning economist, developed the **New Home Economics Model** in the 1960s. It focused on the value of women's time. His idea was that care of children takes a great deal of time and that this time is virtually always contributed by the mother. Caring for children, especially young children, is seen as being incompatible with the mother working for pay. As women's education increases and opportunities for paid work outside the home for women increase, it is more expensive for families with more educated wives to have several children, because they must forego the income-producing activities that women could engage in if they had fewer children. The higher the wage rate a woman would receive if she worked, the more expensive it is to the family for her not to work, since she is giving up a larger amount of income. This loss of income due to women with children not working for pay is called the **opportunity cost** of childbearing, where more educated women have higher opportunity costs. The main determinant of a woman's wage rate is her educational attainment.

Some had proposed that with increasing societal standard of living, families have a wider variety of things on which to expend resources besides children. Some raised the question of whether children were shifting from being "superior goods" to being "inferior goods." In economic terms, an **inferior good** is something that is seen as desirable only when people have a low income and cannot afford more desirable goods. A **superior good** is something for which the demand persists with increased income.

Becker saw children as superior goods. He saw children as inherently desirable and thought that there was no available substitute for children. Becker further thought that over time and with higher income, people shifted their preferences from having more children to having higher quality children. This is often termed as a shift from **child quantity** to **child quality**. Consistent with the rest of Becker's model, the more highly educated the mother, the more expensive each child is. Assuming that more educated mothers produce higher quality children, this also means that more educated mothers have children who are higher in quality although fewer in number. In addition, as costs associated with children rise, including costs of education, music lessons, and summer camp, each child is more expensive, even apart from the cost of the foregone income of the mother. These changes over time in female education and the costs of raising children then lead to couples having fewer children. Becker's model was originally formulated with developed countries in mind but has also been applied to less developed countries.[24]

A Challenge to Whether Women's Labor Force Participation and Fertility Are Always Incompatible in Less Developed Countries

One of the main ideas behind Becker's model was that work for pay by mothers was incompatible with childrearing. **Role incompatibility** refers to whether and the extent to which the demands of different roles, especially the role of being a mother and the role of being a worker for pay, conflict with or are incompatible with each other.

Mason looked at labor force activity of mothers. She observed that in some less developed countries, higher female labor force participation rates of women did not result in lower fertility. In some less developed countries, women's income-producing activities are commonly either home production of goods, such as beer, or selling goods on the street, such as buying fruits wholesale and selling them retail. In these kinds of pursuits, children are often present, and the economic activity does not occupy the women's complete attention, especially if other women with children engaging in similar pursuits are also present. The argument is that these activities produce income, but there is little incompatibility between these activities and child care. Thus, there is little reason to expect engagement in these activities to depress fertility.[25]

When women's labor force participation is incompatible with child care, such as for most formal sector jobs; when child care is not easily available; when interruption of work for pay jeopardizes further employment or advancement opportunities; and when

the satisfaction that women receive from work for pay is high compared to the likely satisfaction from having additional children, female labor force participation is likely to lead to lower fertility.[26]

Easterlin's Relative Income Model

Easterlin's model of fertility, called the **Relative Income Model**, is based on changing preferences for a given number of children across generations. He thought that when people are young, they observe the resources that their parents expend on each child and think that this defines the resources needed to raise a child. Later, when these same people are older and making fertility decisions, they observe the amount of resources available. If the resources available are less than they remember from their childhood, they feel they cannot afford as many children as their parents had and thus have lower fertility than did the parental generation. If their income is greater than their parents, then they feel relatively rich and think they can afford more children than their parents had. Easterlin observed that members of a small birth cohort are likely to see themselves as relatively rich in resources when adults, since a small number of workers would be available for a large number of jobs, which should lead to people on average having better jobs. On the other hand, members of a large birth cohort would feel relatively resource poor, as when they are starting their adult lives a relatively large number of people are competing for a relatively small number of jobs, which should lead to people on average having worse jobs. Easterlin's theory combines classic economic thinking about resources with sociological thinking about changing preferences. Easterlin further posited that later generations have higher consumption expectations for themselves, and this tends to decrease fertility apart from relative income fluctuations.[27]

The Value of Children Study and Reasons Why People Have or Do Not Have Children

The Value of Children Study (VOC) conducted research in several countries. It looked at the reasons why people had children and how these reasons differed across countries and changed over time. Part of the motivation for the VOC Study was the sentiment expressed by Edwards in 1975:

> A fundamental weakness of [Becker's] approach, and indeed of others, is its assumption that basic tastes and preferences do not change with income. . . . It is a major lacuna [i.e., gap] in the social sciences that we lack a theory of preferences and must therefore

base our theories of choice on the assumption of given tastes. The cost in terms of our understanding of what determines family size and how it can be reduced seems very great indeed. If we knew more about preferences, perhaps policy variables could be manipulated in ways which would have direct effects on them.[28]

The VOC Study began with a decision by the American Psychological Association in 1969 to propose a specific psychological alternative to the then existing economically based theories of fertility. The first survey was in 1972, with several later surveys. The VOC Study investigated the perceived economic, social, and psychological costs and benefits of having children from the viewpoint of parents. It was extended in the VOC-IR studies, which looked more broadly at the relation between value orientations and parent–child relations.

The benefits from children include (1) instrumental assistance, such as help with housework or helping the parents in their old age; (2) rewarding interactions, such as love, fun, or strengthening the marital bond; and (3) psychological appreciation, such as living through your children, fulfillment, or an incentive to succeed. The costs of children include (1) financial costs, such as education or other costs; (2) childrearing demands, such as the work involved, emotional strains, or dealing with a child's sickness; (3) restrictions on parents, such as tying down parents and restricting the mother's opportunity to work; and (4) costs to social relations, such as marital strains. Across several studies, it was found that voluntary fertility control was related to (1) lesser importance of instrumental assistance, (2) increased importance of rewarding interactions, and (3) increased concern with the restrictions that children place on parents.[29]

Thornton's Developmental Idealism Model

Thornton proposed the **Developmental Idealism Model** as a way to integrate thinking and interpret findings about cultural and socioeconomic factors in voluntary fertility limitation. This model has been applied to changes both in less developed countries and in more developed countries.[30] There are four parts of the developmental idealism model:

1. Modern society is good, and its characteristics include that it is
   a. Industrialized
   b. Urbanized
   c. Highly educated
   d. Highly knowledgeable
2. The modern family is good and includes
   a. Individualism
   b. Nuclear households
   c. Relatively old age at marriage
   d. Youthful autonomy
   e. Courtship leading to marriage
   f. Gender egalitarianism
   g. Use of family planning
   h. Low fertility
3. The modern family is a cause and an effect of a modern society.
4. Individuals have the right to be free and equal.

The principles of developmental idealism have been disseminated through several mechanisms, including scholarly writings, mass education, mass media, Christianity, colonization, democratic movements, UN activities, nongovernmental organizations, U.S. foreign policy, international aid programs, the spread of civil rights, the spread of women's rights, and the spread of family planning.

Thornton is the head of a research program that has found evidence of developmental idealism in a wide variety of countries. He and his colleagues published the results of surveys in six very different countries. These surveys asked identical or similar questions about norms and expectations related to developmental idealism and fertility. All the surveys were conducted between 2006 and 2009. The six countries and some of the countries' and the surveys' characteristics are shown in Table 9.3. They are ordered from the lowest to the highest gross domestic product per capita.[31]

TABLE 9.3   Some Characteristics of Six Developmental Idealism Surveys

	GDP per Capita, 2007	% Adults Literate, 2007	Sample
Nepal	$1,049	56%	Chitwan Valley adults
Egypt	$5,349	66%	Two district adults
China	$5,383	93%	Gansu Province adults
Iran	$10,955	82%	Yazd City women
Argentina	$13,328	98%	Adults in large urban agglomerates
United States	$45,592	99%	National adults

TABLE 9.4   Views of the Relation between Fertility Decline and Development in Six Countries, 2006–2009

	Nepal	Egypt	China	Iran	Argentina	United States
% agreeing that development would decrease couples having many children	83%	80%	95%	90%	73%	75%
% agreeing that fertility reduction would increase the standard of living	94%	92%	99%	95%	84%	84%
% agreeing that fertility reduction would decrease infant mortality	86%	87%	98%	89%	89%	86%
% agreeing that fertility reduction would increase the fraction of people being educated	98%	93%	96%	95%	83%	91%
% agreeing that fertility reduction would increase love and understanding between parents and children	NA	86%	86%	83%	57%	79%
% agreeing that fertility reduction would increase respect for elders	76%	86%	79%	64%	51%	60%

NA: Not available.

Table 9.4 shows the percentage of survey respondents in each country who agreed with various statements about fertility decline. Agreement indicates support of the developmental idealism view. In each of the six countries, a majority of respondents agreed with each statement. This is interpreted as meaning that the majority of people in these six countries agreed with the main tenets of developmental idealism.

There have often been clashes between developmental idealism and some elements of local cultures. Huntington argued that after the Cold War, the major source of world conflict at the institutional and individual levels would be cultural differences, especially resistance to what was seen as attempts at imposition of Western cultural values.[32] The opposition of the Taliban in Afghanistan to education for girls and the destruction of Muslim shrines by the Ansar Dine in Mali can be seen in part as opposition of the type that Huntington wrote about.[33] However, it is clear that the values of developmental idealism have spread and that this has produced a variety of changes in families, including lower fertility, higher age at marriage, partner choice rather than arranged marriage, gender egalitarianism, nuclear families, sexual freedom, and increased divorce.

A Shift from a Concern with Child Quantity to Child Quality and a Change in Intergenerational Resource Flows

Most of the theories discussed here explicitly or implicitly see a shift from a concern with child quantity (having many children) to child quality (having fewer children but with better characteristics). Often increasing child quality requires money and other resources, especially as a result of the costs of education. However, assuring that children have sufficient nutritious food and receive preventive and curative health care also requires money and other resources. The economic models of fertility decline see that when there is a shift to a desire for child quality, each child is more expensive, so the family limits its fertility because it cannot afford as many children as they could have earlier with the same resources. This shift to child quality is especially possible after infant and child mortality rates have fallen, so parents can have some certainty that a high proportion of their children will survive and that they do not need to have many "extra" children to ensure that at least one will survive to adulthood.

An idea related to the change from child quantity to child quality is the shift in the direction of intergenerational obligations and resource flow from the younger generation to the older generation (from adults to their elderly parents) to resource flow from the older generation to the younger generation (from adults to their children). As Caldwell wrote,[34]

> Two types of society can be distinguished: one of stable high fertility, where there would be no net economic gain accruing to the family (or to those dominant within it) from lower fertility levels, and the other in which economic rationality alone would dictate zero reproduction. The former is characterized by "net wealth flows" from younger to older generations, and the latter by flows in the opposite direction. These flows are defined to embrace all economic benefits both present and anticipated over a lifetime.

This shift in the direction of resource flows is consistent with an increased focus on the education of children. In a society in which it is not clear that education leads to higher income and in which the basis of production is subsistence agriculture, more children means more productivity. However, when the basis of the economy changes and increased skills are related to a higher income, education becomes important. In that situation, investing in the education of a relatively small number of children becomes rational. It also accompanies a change from a concern with having many children in order to assure there will be at least one adult child when the parent reaches old age to a concern that there will be sufficient resources for education and other investments seen as necessary for all children.

SOME REASONS FOR THE PERSISTENCE OF HIGH FERTILITY

Another side to the question of what leads to fertility decline from a high level is: What social and economic arrangements, attitudes, and beliefs contribute to the persistence of fertility at a high level? Whether continuation of high fertility is desirable depends on the social and economic organization. Based on looking at fertility in European countries historically, Lesthaeghe and Wilson argue that for fertility to remain high, couples must see continued high fertility as in their interests, Coale's second precondition. In Western Europe before voluntary fertility decline, often there was what they call the family labor-intensive mode of production (FLIMP), in which more labor is always helpful, and high fertility is seen as a desirable choice. In FLIMP situations, the household, which is often engaged in agriculture, is the unit of production. They further argue that for this view of the desirability of high fertility to change, there needs to be a shift in the calculation of whether high fertility continues to be in the household's interest. In the course of the nineteenth century, with changes accompanying industrialization, education became increasingly important for income-producing activity, and the proportion of households with FLIMP social organization decreased. As these

changes occurred, having fewer children came to be perceived as in the household's interests.[35]

Sub-Saharan Africa has the highest fertility among world regions. Figure 9.2 shows the TFR and the Net Reproduction Rate (NRR) in sub-Saharan Africa in 1950–2010. The TFR only began to decline after 1980, before which many had despaired whether it would ever begin to decline. The NRR began to decline after 1990. The growth rate of 2.45% in 2005–2010 would result in a doubling of the population in 28 years if the growth rate does not decline further. The NRR declined less than the TFR after 1980–1985 because after 1985 fertility declined more rapidly than mortality.

There have been specific cultural explanations offered for the persistence of high fertility in sub-Saharan Africa after it had begun to decline elsewhere. These explanations could also be relevant to the pace of fertility decline in sub-Saharan Africa in the future. Preston-Whyte argued that among many African groups, the idea of having "too many children" is an alien concept. Based on work both in sub-Saharan Africa and in South India, Caldwell argued that sometimes persistent high fertility is rational. He refers to the fear among many African groups that even four or five children might all die and then the parents would be left childless, a prospect that is met with horror. He also argued that although child labor has often been viewed as of little economic value, in many poor settings this view is not accurate. In South India, the poorest people are widows with no surviving sons. In this situation, it is rational for women to attempt to have as many children as possible, especially as many sons as possible.[36]

Even after infant and child mortality has declined, a disaster can lead to the death of all of a woman's children. In 2004 a strong tsunami (hurricane) struck Southern Asia, including parts of India, Indonesia, and Thailand. All the children of many families died in the tsunami. Thus, mothers who had been sterilized after they had borne two, three, or even five

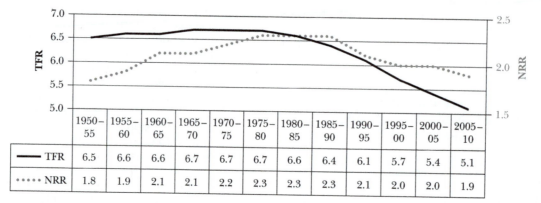

	1950–55	1955–60	1960–65	1965–70	1970–75	1975–80	1980–85	1985–90	1990–95	1995–00	2000–05	2005–10
—— TFR	6.5	6.6	6.6	6.7	6.7	6.7	6.6	6.4	6.1	5.7	5.4	5.1
····· NRR	1.8	1.9	2.1	2.1	2.2	2.3	2.3	2.3	2.1	2.0	2.0	1.9

FIGURE 9.2   Total Fertility Rate (TFR) and Net Reproduction Rate (NRR) in Sub-Saharan Africa, 1950–2010

children suddenly found themselves childless. Some women had operations to reverse their sterilizations, a procedure that was often successful.[37]

KAP SURVEYS, FERTILITY INTENTIONS, AND WANTEDNESS OF CHILDREN

Knowledge, Attitude, and Practice (KAP) surveys of family planning originated in the 1950s. They have been used to investigate issues related to Coale's three preconditions for voluntary fertility limitation. The Knowledge questions address knowledge of family-planning methods but also tap understanding of reproductive physiology, which relates to Coale's first condition. The Attitude questions relate to views of the desirability of having various numbers of children, which is related to Coale's second condition. The Practice aspect relates to use of family-planning methods, which is related to Coale's third condition.

Among the attitude questions asked was a question about desired family size. To try to estimate a desired or ideal number of children, women are asked a question such as the following:

> If you were talking to a young woman similar to yourself who was just beginning her adult life, how many children would you tell her was the best number of children to have?

The question is asked this way so that the respondent can state a number smaller than her actual number of children without seeming to say that she did not want or does not love the later-born children.

Questions were also developed about fertility intentions. Women can act to reduce their fertility either because they want to stop having children or because they want to lengthen the interval between the birth of one child and the birth of the next child. In the case of postpartum abstinence in Africa, which was discussed in Chapter 8, the intention is to lengthen interbirth intervals, rather than to limit the total number of children. A woman is engaging in **fertility-stopping behavior** if she is acting to limit her further fertility and wants no more children. A woman is engaging in **fertility-postponing behavior** if she does not want to bear a child right away, but she wants to bear another child at some time in the future. This is the situation in some sub-Saharan African populations in which postpartum abstinence is common. In surveys, women were asked whether they wanted to become pregnant and have a child as soon as possible, whether they wanted to become pregnant and have a child at some time in the future but not right away, or if they wanted to have no more children. Fertility-postponing behavior is also called **fertility-spacing behavior**.

Sometimes in surveys, women are also asked about the wantedness status of each child. Referring to each live birth, a woman is asked whether just before she got pregnant with that child, she had wanted to get pregnant as soon as possible, wanted another child but wanted to get pregnant later, or did not want any more children. If she wanted another child but not right away, that birth is classified as a timing error, and if she never wanted another child, the child is classified as an unwanted birth. A pregnancy might not have been wanted at the time the woman became pregnant, but that does not mean she does not love the child once she became pregnant or once the child was born.

There have been mixed opinions about the value of the results of KAP surveys regarding desired family size. The results in Asia and in sub-Saharan Africa have been different. Some of the concern has been motivated by a high percentage of respondents replying "up to God" or "don't know" to the desired family size questions in surveys in sub-Saharan Africa. Among the interpretations of why women answered "up to God" was that some women thought it was not within the purview of human activity to influence fertility. That was the interpretation given for the 50% of the respondents who replied "up to God" to the desired family size question in a KAP survey in Nigeria in 1983–1984. Qualitative interviews in Mali in 1983 of women who replied "up to God" indicated that the women felt it was inappropriate to try to tell God how many children they should have. The women answering "up to God" do not meet Coale's first precondition for voluntary fertility limitation, that is, thinking it is acceptable for humans to try to control the number of children they have.

Another interpretation of "don't know" responses is that people do not tend to think about the number of children they might want in numerical terms until they are on the verge of being willing to take some action to influence the number of children they have. In the 1963 Ghana KAP survey, 45% of rural respondents and 36% of urban respondents replied "don't know" to the question about desired family size. In the 1988 Ghana DHS, only 13% replied "don't know" to the desired family size question. The 1988 survey did not interview the same people as the 1963 survey, but this is a substantial decline in 25 years.[38] In 1960–1965, the TFR in Ghana was 6.8 and there seemed to be almost no voluntary fertility control. By 1985–1990, Ghanaian TFR had fallen to 5.9 and had begun a slow decline facilitated by some voluntary fertility limitation. Sometimes, the response "as many as possible" is common. In the Kenya 1966 KAP, 13% of women gave that answer. An interpretation of those responses was that in settings where infant and child mortality were high and where sterility and subfecundity were concerns, women could not imagine being able to have more children than they wanted.[39]

In Asia, the answers to the desired family size question seem very plausible, and there is little indication of any lack of understanding. Longitudinal KAP survey results about desired family size for Taiwan from 1967 were quite predictive of individual fertility behavior between 1967 and 1970.[40] An analysis of KAP surveys in Thailand that were conducted in 1969 and 1970 indicated that only a small proportion of rural or urban respondents did not give a numerical response to the question about desired family size, and the numerical responses agreed well with answers about whether more children were wanted.[41]

We next discuss an early family-planning program in Asia that has been seen as a model of how these programs have often operated. Many have questioned why family-planning programs in Africa did not have the same results as these programs did in much of Asia. Later in this chapter we discuss some reasons why adoption of family planning in some parts of the world has not followed the pattern observed in Asia.

THE FAMILY-PLANNING PROGRAM IN TAIWAN: AN EARLY SUCCESS STORY

One of the first family-planning programs took place in Taiwan. This program was in the Taichung area of Taiwan in 1963–1964. It was extensively studied by Freedman and Takeshita.[42]

When one studies the effects of a family-planning program, it is important to know the situation before the program was implemented. This study conducted a survey to determine the relation between parity and whether women wanted more children before the program was implemented.

Figure 9.3 shows that before the program, the higher a woman's education and the more live births she had experienced, the more likely she was to want no more children. This suggests that more educated

TABLE 9.5   Percentage of Women Wanting No More Children before the Family-Planning Program, by Number of Sons and Total Number of Children, Taichung, Taiwan

No children	0
One child—no sons	0
One son	1
Two children—no sons	2
One son	15
Two sons	7
Three children—no sons	2
One son	25
Two or more sons	56
Four children—no sons	24
One son	51
Two or more sons	83
Five or more children	91

women and higher parity women were more likely to be receptive to participation in a family-planning program than less educated or lower parity women.

Table 9.5 shows that the gender of the children already born influenced whether a woman stated that she wanted no more children before the family-planning program began. It is clear that almost all women wanted two or more children, and they very much wanted to have at least one son, preferably at least two sons. Almost no women without sons wanted no more children. Among women with four children, less than one-quarter of those with no sons wanted no more children, and one-half of those with four children with one son wanted no more children, illustrating the strong desire to have at least one son.

Often, some women would have used contraception or taken other actions to limit their fertility before any organized family-planning program had started. Studies of the adoption of family planning and of other social innovations show that early adopters of an innovation are important in influencing others to adopt the new behavior. The presence of these early adopters also indicates that the innovation is not a completely new or unacceptable idea in the particular social setting.[43]

Figure 9.4 shows the percentage of women by educational attainment and parity who had ever used contraception, had an abortion, or were sterilized before the family-planning program began. As for women who wanted no more children (shown in Figure 9.3), Figure 9.4 shows that the higher a woman's education and the higher her parity, the more likely she was to have taken action to limit her fertility, even before the family-planning program began.

Figure 9.5 looks at the same information as shown in Figure 9.4 divided according to whether the woman had the number of children she wanted, more children than she wanted, or fewer children than she wanted. This is shown by the educational attainment of the woman. If a woman wanted more

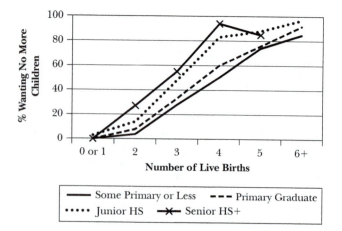

FIGURE 9.3   Percentage of Women Wanting No More Children before the Family-Planning Program, by Number of Live Births and Education, Taichung, Taiwan

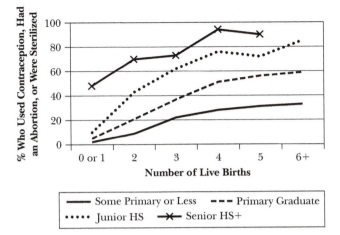

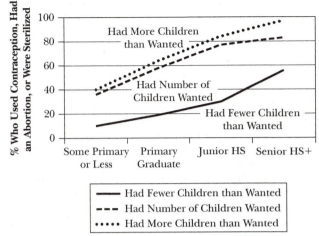

FIGURE 9.4 Percentage of Women Who Reported They Had Ever Used Contraception, Had an Abortion, or Were Sterilized before the Family-Planning Program, by Number of Live Births and Education, Taichung, Taiwan

FIGURE 9.5 Percentage of Women Who Limited Their Fertility before the Family-Planning Program by Education and Whether the Women Had More Children, Fewer Children, or the Number of Children Wanted, Taichung, Taiwan

children, then it was unlikely she would have used contraception, had an abortion, or been sterilized. On the other hand, women who had as many or more children than they wanted would be expected to be more likely to have done something to limit their fertility. Perhaps what is surprising in Figure 9.5 is the *small* difference in behavior between women with the number of children they wanted and those women with more children than they wanted. Both groups were quite likely to have acted to limit their fertility.

Figure 9.6 looks at the extent to which women accepted contraception in the organized family-planning program according to their education and number of living children. The more living children the woman had and the higher her educational attainment, the more likely she was to have accepted contraception in the family-planning program.

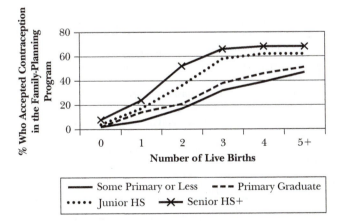

FIGURE 9.6 Percentage of Women Who Accepted Contraception in the Family-Planning Program, by Education and Number of Live Births, Taichung, Taiwan

Policy makers typically want some measure of the success of a program. In the case of a family-planning program, it can look at how many births were averted by each woman who accepted family planning in the program. This is not a straightforward question to answer. How many births the acceptance of contraception averts depends on the age of the woman. The older the woman, the fewer children she would have been likely to have subsequently borne.

Also, women can discontinue contraceptive use. In Taichung, the main contraceptive method promoted was insertion of an intrauterine device (IUD). IUDs are sometimes spontaneously expelled, and some women have them removed because of unacceptable side effects. Even if a woman does not have an IUD removed or does not intentionally discontinue use of another contraceptive method, no contraceptive method is 100% effective in preventing pregnancy. Sometimes this is due to a failure of the method, and sometimes it is because people do not always use a method perfectly. Thus, people discuss the "use effectiveness" of a method. For example, sometimes women using foam do not apply it properly or a condom might break while a couple was using it. Thus, a method as used is not as effective as it would be if everything went perfectly.

In addition, if fertility has been falling and some women have adopted contraception before the program, it is important to compare the results of the program to what one estimates would have been the situation in the absence of the program. If women were already adopting contraception before the program, contraceptive use probably would have increased even in the absence of the program. The question becomes: How much more contraceptive use occurred and how many more births were prevented due to the program? Assessment of program effectiveness is discussed more in Chapter 11. Taking these various considerations into account, Potter estimated that every IUD that a woman had inserted in the Taiwan family-planning program averted 0.88 of a birth. Another way to put this is that in order to avert one birth, 1.14 IUDs needed to be inserted.[44]

The Taiwan program is viewed as having been very successful. Freedman and Takeshita's study covered the situation in Taichung through the mid-1960s. By 1973, 55% of married women in the childbearing ages in Taiwan used contraception, and 38% of these women had obtained contraception through the family-planning program. The educational differentials in contraceptive use in the early years of the program are clear in Figure 9.6. However, by 1973, 71% of Taiwanese women with no education used contraception, a level that would have been unlikely to have been attained without the program.[45]

After the analysis of this early family-planning program, some thought that promoting fertility control throughout the less developed region would just be a matter of educating women about family planning and making effective contraceptive methods available. In some less developed countries, especially in Asia, fertility decline proceeded as in Taiwan. However, in many other less developed countries, fertility decline was more complicated. This is discussed regarding Kenya, Nigeria, India, Algeria, and Mexico later in this chapter. In each of these countries, convincing women and couples to substantially reduce their fertility proved to be more complicated than in Taiwan.

EDUCATION OF WOMEN AND THE FERTILITY TRANSITION

Almost everywhere in the LDR, more educated women have lower fertility than less educated women. Education can influence fertility through the mechanisms listed in Table 9.6.[46]

TABLE 9.6   Possible Mechanisms for Female Education to Affect a Shift from High Fertility to Moderate or Low Fertility

Mechanism	Direction of Effect	Rationale
Exposure to Intercourse Variables		
Age at menarche	+	Education is related to better health, and healthier girls have earlier menarche.
Arranged marriage	−	More educated girls can be less likely to have an arranged marriage.
Pre-marriage work	−	Marriage can be delayed due to more educated women being more likely to work outside the home, and an unmarried woman's income is directed to the family of orientation.
Delay due directly to education	−	Being in school can postpone marriage.
More autonomy	−	More education can lead to less arranged marriage or more say in choice of spouse, which can delay marriage.
Exposure to Conception Variables		
Postpartum amenorrhea	+	Education is related to better health, and healthier women have a shorter period of amenorrhea.
Post-marriage work	−	More educated women are sometimes more likely to work outside the home after marriage, which can lead to lower fertility.
Infant and child mortality	−	Children of more educated mothers have lower mortality, which can lead the mother to have fewer children to assure a certain number of surviving children.
Desired family size	−	More educated women often have a lower desired family size.
Concern with child quality	−	More educated women can perceive that the costs of children can be higher, leading to fewer children.
Receptivity to use of contraception	−	More educated women are often more receptive to contraceptive use.
Effectiveness of use of contraception	−	More educated women are likely to use contraception more effectively.
Ability to afford costs of children	+	Likely higher household income means that expenses of children can be afforded more easily.
Communication with husband	−	More educated women are likely to have more power in the family and more effective communication with the husband.
Gestation Variables		
Miscarriage	+	Healthier women have lower miscarriage rates.

Table 9.6 is organized according to Bongaarts's three areas of proximate determinants of fertility. As discussed in Chapter 8, the proximate determinants operate through biological and social pathways. In the biological pathways, having more education contributes to higher fertility, since more educated women are likely to be healthier, which can result in menarche at a younger age, a shorter period of postpartum amenorrhea, and a lower chance of miscarriage.

In almost all of the social pathways, higher female education leads to lower fertility. The exception is that more educated women are likely to have higher household income, which makes the family more able to afford the costs associated with children and thus could contribute to higher fertility.

We saw in the Taiwan program that more educated women were more likely to have used contraception than less educated women even before the implementation of the family-planning program, and also that more educated women were more likely to adopt contraception during the program. This is consistent with what has been found regarding education of women and contraceptive use throughout the world. In almost all settings, the net effect of education is that more education contributes to lower fertility.

Figure 9.7 shows the relation between education and various aspects of fertility in four sub-Saharan African countries. The African examples are interesting because of the high fertility in sub-Saharan Africa and the later fertility decline in sub-Saharan Africa than in Asia and other parts of the LDR. The results are based on surveys conducted in the late 1980s and early 1990s.[47]

The first panel shows the relation between women's years of schooling and the TFR. There is a generally negative relation in all four countries. The second panel shows the relation between years of schooling and one of Bongaarts's major exposure variables, age at marriage. The higher the number of years of schooling, the higher the median age of marriage. The bottom panel shows the relation between education and one of Bongaarts's "major exposure to conception" variables, contraceptive use. The higher the education of married women, the more likely they were to use contraception.

Figure 9.8 shows the relation between the percentage of women of an appropriate age enrolled in secondary school and the percentage of women of childbearing age using any contraceptive method for less developed countries that had the required data for about the year 2000.[48]

The relation between female secondary school enrollment and contraceptive use is strong. A fitted

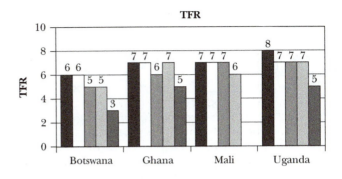

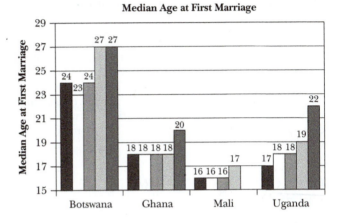

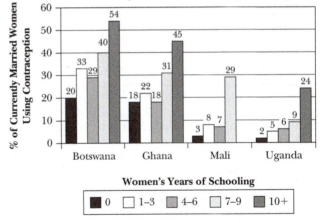

FIGURE 9.7 The Relation of Women's Years of Schooling to Aspects of Fertility in Four Sub-Saharan African Countries, Late 1980s–Early 1990s

linear trend line is shown, as well as the equation defining that line. An increase of 0.57% in female secondary school enrollment on average is related to a 1% increase in the percentage of women in the childbearing ages using any contraceptive. Fifty-four percentage of the variation in contraceptive

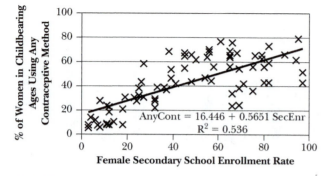

FIGURE 9.8   Female Education and Contraceptive Use for 74 Less Developed Countries, circa 2000

Contraceptive methods are divided into **modern contraceptive methods** and **traditional contraceptive methods**. Modern methods are those that have been developed through the use of modern technology or medical research or that include procedures that have been developed through medical research, such as sterilization. They include sterilization, contraceptive pills, IUDs, condoms, injectable methods, vaginal barrier methods (such as foam), and implants (such as Depo-Provera). Traditional methods have long been known in many populations as ways to limit fertility. Traditional methods include rhythm, withdrawal, douching, and abstinence.

use is accounted for by variation in female secondary school enrollment. It is possible that there are characteristics of countries that contribute both to female education and to contraceptive use, but Figure 9.7 indicates that the relation between education and contraceptive use also holds at the individual level.

DEVELOPMENT OF CONTRACEPTIVE METHODS

Some methods of preventing pregnancy have long been known. Other methods have been developed or improved by the application of modern technology.

Contraception is the prevention of conception. Conception can be prevented through the use of drugs, devices, or sexual practices. When there is understanding of the basics of reproduction, abstinence from sexual intercourse can effectively prevent pregnancy. Related to this is coitus interruptus, also called withdrawal. It is thought that coitus interruptus was the major method used in the historical decline in marital fertility in Europe.[49] Condoms have long been known. Technology has improved condoms, so they are easier to use and less likely to break. One of the earliest truly modern contraceptive methods was the diaphragm, which, like a condom, is a barrier method that prevents sperm from reaching the egg.

Another way to think about contraceptive methods is those in which something must be done at or near the time of sexual intercourse and methods whose use is far removed from the act of intercourse. Condoms, coitus interruptus, foam, and diaphragms are all applied near the time of intercourse, while injectable contraceptives, a birth control patch, a contraceptive ring, IUDs, and birth control pills do not require action close to the time of actual intercourse.

CONTRACEPTIVE USE

We saw that in Taiwan, there was substantial contraceptive use before there was any organized family-planning program. Although contraceptive use has increased throughout the world, the level and rate of increase in contraceptive use have differed.

Figure 9.9 shows the percentage of women aged 15–49 who were married or in a marriage-type relationship who used any type of contraception. The percentage using contraception increased over time, with a persistent large gap between the LDR as a whole and the least developed countries (LeastDC).[50]

Figure 9.10 shows similar information about contraceptive use for world regions. The low percentage of married women using contraception in Africa is

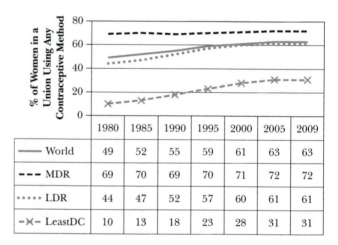

	1980	1985	1990	1995	2000	2005	2009
—— World	49	52	55	59	61	63	63
--- MDR	69	70	69	70	71	72	72
..... LDR	44	47	52	57	60	61	61
-✕- LeastDC	10	13	18	23	28	31	31

FIGURE 9.9   Percentage of Women Who Used Any Contraceptive Method among Those Aged 15–49 Who Were Married or in a Union, in the World, MDR, LDR, and LeastDC, 1980–2009

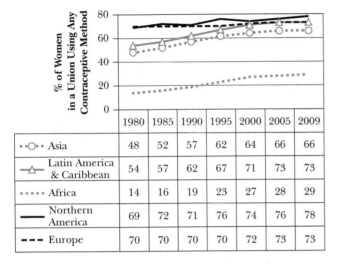

FIGURE 9.10   Percentage of Women Who Used Any Contraceptive Method among Those Aged 15–49 Who Were Married or in a Union in World Regions, 1980–2009

striking. The low level of contraceptive use in the LeastDC shown in Figure 9.8 is mainly due to a low level of use in Africa.

UNMET NEED FOR FAMILY PLANNING

A woman is considered to have an **unmet need for family planning** if she does not want any more children (wants to stop having children) or if she wants to become pregnant and have another child at some time but not right away (wants to postpone having more children) but she is not using any method of contraception.[51] There can be several reasons for this unmet need. She can think that she is not at risk of becoming pregnant because of infrequent sexual intercourse, subfecundity, or being in postpartum amenorrhea. Contraceptives can be unavailable or too expensive, family-planning workers or other health personnel can be insensitive, there can be unacceptable side effects from methods that are available, the woman could not know about contraceptive methods, or she or her relatives could be opposed to the use of contraception.[52]

Figure 9.11 shows the percentage of women in the childbearing ages using a modern contraceptive method, women using a traditional contraceptive method, and the percentage of women with an unmet need for family planning at five dates. The difference between the total height of a column in the figure and 100% is those women who wanted to become pregnant and have a birth immediately. Results are shown for the entire LDR

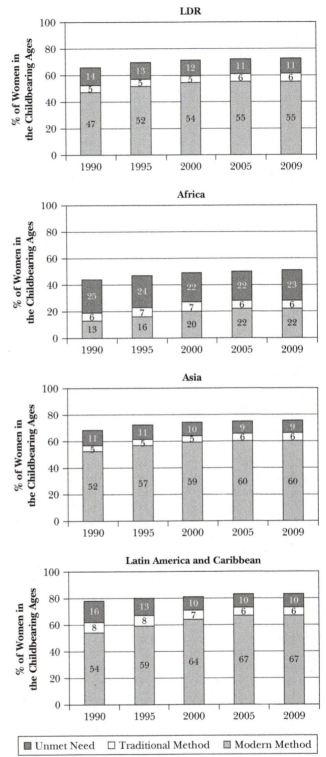

FIGURE 9.11   Percentage of Women in the Childbearing Ages Who Used a Modern or Traditional Contraceptive Methods and Percentage with an Unmet Need for Family Planning by World Region, 1990–2009

as well as for Africa, Asia, and Latin America and the Caribbean.

The total height of each bar can be interpreted as the percentage of women who see limitation of their fertility as in their interest, since these are women who either are using some form of contraception or are not using any contraceptive method but do not want to become pregnant and have a child immediately. In every region, the percentage of women seeing fertility limitation as in their interest increased over time. Also, in every region, the percentage of women in the childbearing ages using some contraceptive method increased over time, and the total percentage of women using or in need of contraception increased. The most striking increase was in the percentage of women using modern contraceptives. There is little change over time in the percentage of women using traditional methods, being 5–8% of women in the LDR and in each region at every date. The percentage of women using modern contraceptive methods is highest in Latin America and the Caribbean and somewhat lower in Asia.

The levels of contraceptive use and of unmet need for contraception are much lower in Africa. In Asia and in Latin America and the Caribbean, the percentage of women with an unmet need for family planning is much lower than the percentage using contraception, but in Africa in 1990 and 1995, the percentage of women with unmet need was larger than the percentage using contraception, and the percentage of women using contraception was only slightly larger than the percentage with unmet need in 2005 and 2009. That the percentage with unmet need is so large in Africa could indicate the potential for large increases in contraceptive use as new methods are developed that might be more convenient for or acceptable to African women.

Some have wondered whether African countries in principle could be expected to follow the trajectory of contraceptive use and fertility decline seen first in Asia and later in Latin America and the Caribbean. Caldwell and others have argued that the widespread use of contraception in Africa to space children is very different than what happened in Asia and Latin America. Also, the high value placed on children and the fear of infertility in Africa can make it difficult to convince women to adopt contraception in order to limit the total number of children.[53]

Table 9.7 shows information about the level of intentions to postpone and to stop childbearing by family status for several less developed countries across world regions. The results are based on Demographic and Health Surveys. The year of the given survey is indicated in Column (2).[54]

Column (3) shows the percentage of all women in the survey who want to postpone childbearing but are not using any form of contraception, and Column (4) shows similar information for women who want to stop childbearing but are not using any form of contraception. The values in Column (3) are bolded if the value in Column (3) is greater than the value in Column (4). In most of the countries, the percentage of women with an unmet need for stopping childbearing is greater than the percentage with an unmet need for postponing the birth of the next child. The main exception is sub-Saharan Africa, in which for each country considered the unmet need for postponement is greater than for stopping. For India, the value in Column (3) is slightly higher than the value in Column (4).

Columns (5) and (6) show similar information to that in Columns (3) and (4), but for women who are currently using some contraceptive method. In most countries, a much higher percentage of women are using contraception to stop childbearing than are using contraception to postpone the birth of the next child. Again, the situation in sub-Saharan African countries is different than in other world regions. The value in Column (5) is bolded if it is greater than the value in Column (6). In three of the four sub-Saharan countries, more women are using contraception to postpone childbearing than are using contraception to stop childbearing. The strong interest in postponing the birth of the next child in sub-Saharan African countries is related to the concern with elevated infant and child mortality if the next child is born too soon, as was discussed in Chapter 8.[55]

The interest in postponing childbearing compared to stopping childbearing is also clear in Columns (7) and (8). In most countries, a much higher percentage of women want to stop childbearing than want to postpone childbearing. Again, in Table 9.7 the sub-Saharan African countries show a different pattern, with much more interest in postponement than in stopping.

The high percentage of women with an unmet need for family planning shown in Figure 9.11 and Table 9.7 means that understanding the distribution of reasons for not using a contraceptive method when a woman does not want to have a child immediately can be important in determining how to address unmet need.

Sedgh and her colleagues analyzed reasons for lack of contraceptive use among women with an unmet need for contraception based on surveys in 39 countries conducted in 2000–2005. They grouped the reasons into three categories:

1. **Exposure:** This set of reasons includes women who thought they were at low risk of

TABLE 9.7   Postponing (PP) and Stopping (ST) Fertility Intentions by Family-Planning Status for Some Less Developed Countries

(1)	Year (2)	Unmet Need		Current Use		Total %PP (7)	Total %ST (8)
		%PP (3)	%ST (4)	%PP (5)	%ST (6)	(3) + (5)	(4) + (6)
South and Southeast Asia							
Bangladesh	2004	5.1	6.3	16.2	41.8	21.3	48.1
India	1998–1999	**8.3**	7.5	3.5	44.7	11.8	52.2
Indonesia	2002–2003	4.0	4.6	24.2	36.2	28.2	40.8
Uzbekistan	1996	6.6	7.0	20.2	35.4	26.8	42.4
Vietnam	2002	2.0	2.8	13.9	64.6	15.9	67.4
Latin America and Caribbean							
Brazil	1996	2.6	4.7	14.0	62.8	16.6	67.5
Colombia	2005	2.5	3.3	16.9	61.3	19.4	64.6
Haiti	2000	16.0	23.8	9.8	18.3	25.8	42.1
Middle East and Northern Africa							
Egypt	2005	3.6	6.7	12.4	46.8	16.0	53.5
Morocco	2003–2004	3.5	6.6	22.3	40.6	25.8	47.2
Turkey	2003	2.3	3.7	15.8	55.2	18.1	58.9
Sub-Saharan Africa							
Ghana	2003	**21.7**	12.3	**13.7**	11.4	**35.4**	23.7
Kenya	2003	**14.4**	10.1	14.3	25.0	28.7	35.1
Mali	2001	**20.9**	7.6	**5.1**	3.0	**26.0**	10.6
Nigeria	2003	**11.8**	5.1	**7.8**	4.8	**19.6**	9.9

Numbers are shown in **bold** when the percentage for those undertaking the behavior for postponing is higher than the percentage for those undertaking the behavior for stopping.

pregnancy. This could be because they rarely had sexual intercourse, they were in a state of postpartum amenorrhea, or they thought they were infertile or subfecund.

2. **Supply:** This set of reasons includes lack of knowledge of contraceptive methods, lack of access to contraceptive methods, or the high cost of contraceptives. It also includes lack of use due to unacceptable side effects of contraceptives.

3. **Opposition:** This set of reasons includes women whose non-use of contraception was the result of their opposition to the use of contraception or opposition to the use of contraception on the part of another influential person, such as their husband or another relative.

Figure 9.12 shows the distribution of reasons for non-use of contraception that Sedgh and her colleagues found within four world regions. The top panel shows the distribution across all reasons. Across

regions, between 38% and 59% of women with an unmet need across regions were not using contraception because they thought they were at low risk of becoming pregnant.

The lower panel of Figure 9.12 excludes women who thought they were at low risk of becoming pregnant. Thus, it shows the distribution of reasons for non-use of contraception between supply and opposition. The supply problems are the reasons that family-planning programs are designed to address. A family-planning program can make women aware of the characteristics of contraceptive methods and how to use them, and can facilitate easy, low-cost access. Also, a family-planning program can help a woman find an acceptable method if she has had bad side effects from a method she has tried.[56]

Among women who thought they were at risk of becoming pregnant, over 60% of women in each region were not using a contraceptive due to supply problems. However, while only about 25% of women outside of sub-Saharan Africa who thought they were

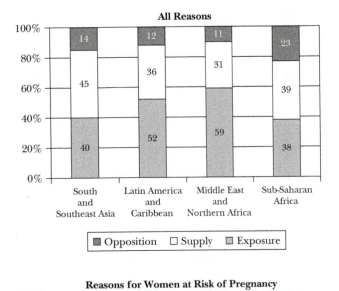

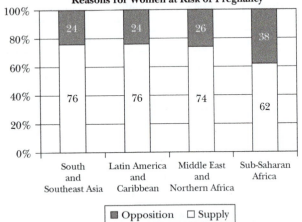

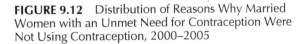

FIGURE 9.12 Distribution of Reasons Why Married Women with an Unmet Need for Contraception Were Not Using Contraception, 2000–2005

at risk of pregnancy were not using a contraceptive due to opposition, opposition was the reason for almost 40% of the non-use in sub-Saharan Africa. Family-planning programs have been less successful in addressing opposition reasons than supply reasons, partially because opposition is often religiously or culturally based.

LINKING ADOPTION OF CONTRACEPTION TO OTHER CONTACTS WITH THE HEALTH CARE SYSTEM

Two strategies to encourage the adoption of contraception by women in less developed countries take advantage of other contacts women have with the health care system. They are (1) when children

are taken for health care, such as vaccinations; and (2) in the postpartum period immediately after a birth, which increasingly often is medically attended, even in less developed countries.

Linking Child Health and Survival to Contraceptive Use in Less Developed Countries

One successful family-planning promotion strategy has linked child health and survival with contraceptive use. An idea motivating this approach is that women do not want to *bear* a certain number of children, but rather they want a certain number of *surviving* children. Maternal and child health (MCH) programs discuss with women the link between improved child health and survival. Since infant and child survival is better than it was in the past, women do not need to have as many children in order to have a certain number of surviving children.[57]

Convincing Immediately Postpartum Women to Adopt Contraception

In many less developed countries, women are encouraged to adopt a contraceptive method shortly after they have delivered a child. If women have had prenatal care, discussion of contraception options during prenatal care can also increase the chance of postpartum contraceptive use. Women are often in a health facility at the time of the delivery, and health advice and contraception are more easily available at that time than at most other times.[58]

Immediately postpartum, women often are very aware of the complications of pregnancy and childbirth and the commitments involved in an additional child. Often, women are sterilized immediately after giving birth. The procedure is medically easier at this time than at a time far removed from a birth, but if the woman had not decided on sterilization before the birth, there are issues raised about informed consent. Also, IUDs are often inserted immediately after a woman had given birth. A World Health Organization (WHO) review concluded that this practice was safe. However, a problem with the IUD is that it is sometimes spontaneously expelled, and the chance of expulsion is higher when it is inserted immediately postpartum than at other times.[59]

Some contraceptive methods are not recommended immediately postpartum. For example, the manufacturer's recommendations for Depo-Provera, an injectable contraceptive that is given every 3 months, recommends that for women who are exclusively breastfeeding, Depo-Provera should not be started until at least 6 weeks after birth.[60]

THE DIFFERENCE BETWEEN MORTALITY POLICY AND FERTILITY POLICY

According to Demeny, **population policies** are "deliberately constructed or modified institutional arrangements and/or specific programs through which governments influence, directly or indirectly, demographic change."[61] Both mortality and fertility policies can have important effects on demographic outcomes, but the issues and controversies about policies in these two areas differ. Moral and philosophical issues play a much smaller role in mortality policies than in fertility policies.

Policies to reduce mortality are usually relatively noncontroversial. The benefit to the individual or the household is fairly clear. Controversies usually revolve around the safety or possible side effects of vaccines and other treatments, not about whether mortality reduction is a good idea.

Often policies to reduce mortality can be implemented without active participation by the individual or household. For example, if a swamp is drained and the incidence of mosquito-borne diseases lessens, this increases the survival chances of all residents of the area, whether or not they would have been willing to take some action to reduce the chance they contracted particular mosquito-borne diseases.

When the aim of a fertility policy is to reduce the population growth rate, the benefit to the individual or household can be unclear. Implementation of fertility policies requires the cooperation or active engagement of the individual or household. Also, to actively cooperate in implementing a fertility policy, people need to think that reducing (or increasing) their fertility is in their interest.

For mortality policies, the goals of societal mortality reduction and household mortality reduction are consistent. However, the kinds of arguments that motivate changes in fertility behavior by individual women or couples are different than the arguments for societal fertility change. For example, policy makers in a society can see a high population growth rate as a threat to the society's future prosperity, but it can be difficult to convince women or couples that they should limit their fertility if they are concerned that an unanticipated mortality crisis due to a war or an epidemic might kill all their children. Also, in a society with a low or negative rate of population growth, higher fertility can seem to be in the society's interest, but it might not be in a woman's or a couple's interest as they face increasing costs of child raising related to child care, postsecondary education and other kinds of enrichment activities.

Often fertility policies are motivated by concern with a too high (or too low) rate of population growth. Thus, whether a fertility policy aims to lower or raise fertility is decided in light of the mortality situation rather than mainly motivated by concerns with fertility itself. Also, fertility raising policies often conflict or seem to conflict with labor force participation policies. As is discussed in Chapter 10, many high-income, very-low-fertility countries are struggling with how to both encourage female labor force participation and raise fertility from a below-replacement level, as their aging populations have reduced the number of working-age people compared to retirement-age people, and as they face the prospect of long-term population decline.

There are often ethical or religious objections to fertility limitation. Sometimes the main objections are to the goal of fertility reduction, but more often objections are to the methods used in the program. Since at least the eighteenth century, there have been objections to actions to reduce the chance of a conception that leads to a live birth. Malthus thought that fertility limitation was important in order to prevent a high rate of population growth, but he also thought that postponement of marriage and celibacy before marriage were the only acceptable ways to limit fertility.

The Roman Catholic Church and some other religious groups have objected to the use of "artificial contraception." Since there are times in a woman's monthly cycle when there is a low chance of conception, natural family planning, also called the rhythm method, directs couples to only have sexual intercourse during times with a low chance of conception. The rhythm method has the approval of the Catholic Church. Although effective use of natural family planning can be difficult, there have been some successful programs in development of and instruction in the effective use of natural family planning.[62]

Family-planning programs often had difficulty in traditionally Catholic countries not only because some women and couples found contraception objectionable, but also because of institutional opposition of the Catholic Church. Under Ferdinand Marcos, in the late 1960s, a family-planning program was instituted in the Philippines. In 1986, Corazon Aquino became president with the substantial backing of Catholic bishops. The family-planning program was downgraded in 1987. The program that had dealt with family planning refocused on health generally.[63]

Often the Catholic Church has not been able to prevent the implementation of government-sponsored family-planning programs, but the Church still has been able to impact their effectiveness. Often in traditionally Catholic countries, the schools are run by the Catholic Church. There was a program in Guatemala sponsored by a Japanese nongovernmental organization (NGO) that combined education about family planning and about parasite control in Guatemala.

The Catholic-run Guatemalan schools would not even let information about the antiparasite program be disseminated in the schools.[64]

Sometimes there is a reluctance to use contraception because members of a couple think that the partner would object. A study in Puerto Rico in the 1950s found that 36% of respondents had never discussed family size preferences with their spouse. Sometimes there are large misperceptions of the views that the spouse holds. In separate interviews with the two spouses, 15% of husbands thought that their wives wanted as many children as God would send, but only 5% of the wives actually reported this preference.[65]

Sometimes, family-planning programs have been opposed because they have been seen as an attempt at genocide. **Genocide** is the deliberate and systematic destruction, in whole or in part, of an ethnic, racial, religious, or national group. In South Africa under apartheid, family planning was promoted for all groups and the total fertility rate for all groups declined. However, since much of the White power structure in South Africa was worried about high rates of population growth among Africans, the motives behind the family-planning program were suspect.[66]

Sometimes there are objections to particular contraceptive methods because of how they work. There have been moral objections to the use of IUDs due to evidence that they operate by preventing the fertilized egg from becoming implanted in the vaginal wall. People who view the fertilized egg as a human being see an IUD as a method of abortion. The "morning-after pill" is taken within 72 hours after sexual intercourse to prevent pregnancy. It has widely been thought by the public that it operates by preventing the fertilized egg from implanting in the uterine wall. However, medical research shows that it operates by postponing ovulation or slowing the progress of sperm. Thus, "morning-after" means the morning after sexual intercourse rather than the morning after fertilization.[67]

SHIFTS IN FERTILITY POLICY

There have been two main rationales for fertility policies. One rationale is the welfare of the population as a whole. In this rationale, when there is a high population growth rate, a decline in fertility would result in a lower population rate, which would foster economic growth, increase school enrollment, and allow higher per capita calorie consumption. When there is a very low growth rate, a more rapidly growing population as the result of higher fertility would counter the aging of the population, increase the proportion of the population in the working ages, and increase the demand for goods, thus fostering economic growth. The other rationale is the welfare or interests of women and families. A lower fertility rate allows families to afford school fees and other costs to educate their children. A higher fertility rate allows families to be more certain of having a living heir, of providing enough labor for household production, and of support in their old age.

Malthus advocated fertility limitation after growth rates in Europe had increased due to mortality decline. He thought that massive starvation would be a likely result if fertility did not decline. He thought the only acceptable method was celibacy among the unmarried and postponement of marriage until the couple could afford to support children. This had a distinctly eugenic cast, as Malthus thought that selectivity for fertility on the basis of economic success would be good for the population.

Support for birth control in the United States began in the 1800s among feminist groups that wanted to liberate women from the drudgery of work in the home. Some of this was a part of a movement for "voluntary motherhood" in which women wanted to have control over their bodies and their lives. The motivation for this was serving women's own interests, which is quite different from that of some of the neo-Malthusians who advocated fertility control in the interest of society generally.[68]

Some of the rationale for birth control shifted in the Progressive Era, which lasted from the 1880s through the 1920s. The Progressive Era was a time of social, political, and municipal reform; the rooting out of corruption; and increasing respect for science and technology. In this era, there were calls for improvement of the American population. Means to achieve this improvement were seen as reducing crime, prostitution, and illegitimacy; restricting immigration; and promoting birth control and sterilization, especially among undesirable elements of the population. Margaret Sanger, a leader of the birth control movement, criticized the provision of free maternity care, because "Instead of decreasing and aiming to eliminate the stocks that are most detrimental to the future of the race and the world, it tends to render them to a menacing degree dominant."[69]

Thus, the birth control movement developed strong eugenic connections. In the 1930s, the Rockefeller Foundation began planning birth control field studies to be carried out in less developed countries. After World War II, eugenicists remained closely associated with fertility limitation and population control efforts. Many people involved in birth control and population limitation programs were not at heart eugenicists, and John D. Rockefeller III founded the Population Council in 1952 partially as a counterweight to some of the more extremist arguments for population control. The Population Council was to support medical research and train population experts to help develop fertility limitation programs in developing countries. Rockefeller also advocated the improvement of agricultural productivity in developing countries.[70]

In the 1960s, concern about the possible serious consequences of high population growth rates in the LDR increased interest in birth control programs in order to reduce population growth. This view at first was mainly put forward by policy analysts and academics in the more developed countries. However, over time most LDR governments came to agree that high fertility and a high rate of population growth jeopardized their country's future. This is indicated by the increasing percentage of LDR governments that viewed their country's population growth rate and fertility as too high, as shown in Figures 2.30 and 2.33. Direct governmental support of family planning also increased. In 1976, 6% of LDR governments limited access to contraception; by 2009, no LDR governments limited access to contraception. Also in 1976, 62% of LDR governments directly supported contraceptive use through dissemination of information and supplies through governmental facilities, while in 2009 87% of LDR countries provided such governmental support of contraceptive use.[71]

The only African country that in 2009 thought its fertility level was too low was Gabon, which is in Middle Africa and has its western border on the Atlantic Ocean. It had a growth rate in 2005–2010 of 1.9% and a TFR of 3.4. However, Gabon had very low population density, and in 1950–1965 the growth rate was less than 0.7%. A rapid decline in mortality after 1970 led to a higher growth rate. Expectation of life at birth increased from 37 years in 1950–1955 to 49 years in 1970–1975 to 61 years in 2005–2010. Mortality reduction was financed by funds from oil, which was extracted in the Atlantic Ocean off the Gabon coast beginning in the early 1970s. Due to its use of oil income, Gabon had the highest score on the Human Development Index of any sub-Saharan African country, and the GNI per capita in 2010 was $13,190 using the PPP method, which adjusts for differences among countries in the cost of living and was discussed in Chapter 2. Gabon was second in GNI per capita only to Botswana in sub-Saharan Africa at $13,910 and higher than Brazil at $10,880. With a recently achieved high level of economic prosperity, the Gabon government saw no reason to try to limit population growth.[72]

The concerns of MDR governments and organizations about high fertility and a high rate of population growth in the LDR were motivated by macrolevel concerns, and it sometimes seemed that the desires and aspirations of women and families were unimportant. These policies were sometimes seen as condescending or semicolonial.[73]

A wide variety of fertility-limitation policies were considered that evoked ethical objections. These ethical objections were often discussed in the context of a balance between ethics and what was seen as a pressing need for growth rates and thus fertility to decline in much of the LDR.[74] The range of policies that governments had implemented or seriously considered as of 1979 was summarized as part of a discussion of the ethical issues in fertility limitation as follows:[75]

1. *Manipulate public and private access* to modern methods of fertility control, including not only oral contraceptives, IUDs, and condoms but also sterilization and abortion.
2. *Change the perceived socioeconomic determinants* of fertility behavior: popular education and literacy, infant and child mortality and life expectancy, industrialization and urbanization, income and income equity, status of women, and housing, among others.
3. *Make propaganda* and/or limit opposing views.
4. *Manipulate incentives and disincentives* in the desired directions, through child assistance stipends, maternity leaves and costs, tax benefits, direct monetary subsidies to individual families for "correct" fertility behavior (e.g., fees for vasectomies), and community incentives or disincentives for "correct" fertility behavior (e.g., roads or schools).
5. *Exert sociopolitical pressure or impose direct sanctions,* from minimum age at marriage to limits on family size.

Many of these policies were seen as ethically questionable. The issue that was raised in 1979 was whether fertility would decline quickly "enough" in response to educational campaigns and other voluntary aspects of family-planning programs. As shown in Figures 8.9 and 8.10 in Chapter 8, in 1975–1980, the NRR in the LDR had declined somewhat to 1.8 from a high of 2.2 in 1965–1970, but in Africa the NRR was still increasing, with a value of 2.3. Some viewed the situation as justifying extreme and often coercive measures that otherwise would be unacceptable, similar to the reasoning about necessities for extreme actions in a war or in fighting terrorism.

Several heavy-handed and ethically questionable policies are discussed for Singapore, China, and India later in this chapter. The reaction to these tactics was mixed from the MDR, with criticism of China being most common. Western criticism of Singapore and India was more sporadic.[76]

As fertility and rates of population growth declined in much of the LDR, there was less impetus for heavy-handed fertility reduction programs. Note in Figures 8.9 and 8.2 in Chapter 8 that in 1990–1995, the NRR in the LDR was 1.4 and the TFR in the LDR was 3.4, much lower than earlier fertility levels.

There was also increased criticism of family programs for ignoring the wishes of women and dismissing complaints about unacceptable side effects of some contraceptive methods.[77]

At the International Conference on Population and Development (ICPD) in 1994, often called the Cairo Conference, there was a clear shift from a concern with controlling population growth to a concern with reproductive health and reproductive rights.[78] **Reproductive health** concerns the reproductive processes, functions, and system at all stages of life. It is concerned with assuring that people are able to have a responsible, satisfying, and safe sex life and that they have the capability to reproduce and the freedom to decide if, when, and how often to do so.

The ICPD agreed on the following points:

1. **Universal Education:** A goal of universal primary education by 2015 and a goal for women to have increased access to secondary and higher education.
2. **Reduction of Infant and Child Mortality:** A goal of reducing infant and child mortality by one-third by 2000.
3. **Reduction of Maternal Mortality:** A goal of cutting in half the 1990 level of maternal mortality by 2000.
4. **Access to Reproductive and Sexual Health Services, Including Family Planning:** There should be access to family-planning counseling, prenatal care, safe delivery, prevention and treatment of infertility, prevention of abortion and management of consequences of abortion, and treatment of reproductive tract infections and other reproductive health conditions. Abortion was not supported as a method of family planning, and the legality of abortion was seen as an issue for each individual country. There should be education and counseling on human sexuality, reproductive health, and responsible parenthood. There should be services available for HIV, breast cancer, infertility, and delivery. There should be active discouragement of female genital mutilation.

The first point is a goal that is facilitated by lower population growth rates, although increasing education of women can also require a shift in values. The second and third points continue longstanding goals regarding mortality reduction. The content of the fourth goal was new at the Cairo Conference, since it advocated not only family planning but also infertility treatment and attention to women's problems related to reproductive health. Although many hailed the changes at the Cairo Conference as a step forward, there were also concerns raised about whether there would be sufficient funds available to address all of the areas in the fourth point and whether there would continue to be sufficient family-planning effort in areas of sub-Saharan Africa in which population growth and fertility remained high. Note in Figures 8.10 and 8.3 that in 1990–1995, the NRR in Africa was 2.0 and the TFR was 5.6, meaning that much of Africa had a long way to go to reach replacement fertility.[79]

CONTROVERSIES ABOUT THE ROLES OF DEVELOPMENT AND FAMILY-PLANNING PROGRAMS IN FERTILITY DECLINE IN LESS DEVELOPED COUNTRIES

As early as 1974, some expressed skepticism about the role and effectiveness of family-planning programs in reducing fertility. At the 1974 World Population Conference in Bucharest, Romania, Dr. Karan Singh, who headed the Indian delegation, coined the phrase, "Development is the best contraceptive." This became the slogan of those who thought that organized family-planning programs were unnecessary or even harmful.[80]

In 1994, Pritchett argued that the desired number of children controls fertility decisions and that family-planning programs have little effect on the desired number of children. He was essentially arguing that family-planning programs are effective when the problem is lack of availability of an effective and acceptable means for fertility limitation (Coale's third precondition), but they are ineffective when the problem is that people see no advantage to limiting their fertility (Coale's second precondition). He contended that when women and couples want to reduce their fertility, they will do so. He dismissed data on the unmet need for family planning, partially due to the large proportion of women with unmet need who think they are not susceptible to pregnancy, many of whom are in postpartum amenorrhea.[81]

Bongaarts and Sinding in 2009 argued that it was easy by the end of the twentieth century to claim that family-planning programs were unnecessary, after fertility had declined in much of the less developed world. In response to the argument that fertility had been impervious to family-planning programs in sub-Saharan Africa, Bongaarts pointed to cases such as Kenya, in which the desired number of children had declined.[82]

Some of the controversy about the importance of development compared to the importance of family-planning programs seems to result from an inappropriate framing of the question. In Coale's three preconditions for voluntary fertility limitation, in some countries such as in Taiwan, family-planning programs are very effective when an impediment to fertility decline is the lack of available, inexpensive, convenient contraceptive methods. This is also the situation when the reason for an unmet need for family planning is supply issues, as shown in Figure 9.12. However, when opposition to family planning in principle is the impediment, traditional family-planning programs are not likely to be effective. When the impediment is that women and couples do not perceive limiting the number of children as in their interest, family-planning programs can play a role, but development as manifested in reduced infant and child mortality and especially in increased female education is likely to be very important. This is similar to the argument that Meadows has made.[83]

FERTILITY CANNOT BE LOWERED AND RAISED INSTANTLY LIKE TURNING A WATER TAP OFF OR ON: THE CASE OF SINGAPORE

Singapore is an example of a country that drastically changed its fertility policy and has not been totally happy with the results. Figure 9.13 shows the total fertility rate in Singapore for 1950–2010. In 1950–1955, with a TFR of 6.6 and a NRR of 2.82, there was reason for Singapore to be concerned about population growth. At that time, the population growth rate was consistent with a population doubling time of 14 years. Singapore achieved full independence from Malaysia in 1965. Although fertility had declined, it was still considered high. In 1960–1965, the TFR was 3.7, and the NRR was 2.4. By 1975–1980, the TFR at 1.8 was below-replacement fertility, and the NRR was 0.9. It was reasonable for Singapore at that time to be concerned about low fertility and population growth. These low-fertility concerns were similar to those in many more developed countries, but the approach that Singapore took was different than that in many other countries.

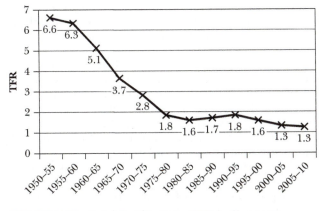

FIGURE 9.13   Total Fertility Rate (TFR) in Singapore, 1950–2010

Efforts to Decrease Fertility in Singapore

After independence from Malaysia, Singapore authorities saw problems of the newly independent country such as high unemployment and increasing demand for social services as the result of a high population growth rate. In 1966, a National Family Planning Program was launched. Policies were implemented to discourage women from having more than two or, in some cases, three children. These policies included the following:

1. **Maternity Policies:** Fees for prenatal care and delivery fees increased with parity, while maternity leave was not given for third and later births. There was no delivery fee if the woman was sterilized after delivery.
2. **Education Policies:** Priority in choice of school was given to first and second children if a parent was sterilized before age 40 and if no more than three children were born.
3. **Income Tax Policies:** Income tax deductions were lower or not given for the third and later children.
4. **Housing Policies:** Large families no longer had priority in obtaining larger units in public housing, and those families with no more than three children were allowed to sublet rooms.
5. **Other Policies:** Government employees got paid leave after sterilization, and abortion and sterilization were heavily subsidized.[84]

A Shift to Trying to Increase Fertility in Singapore

Although fertility in Singapore began to decline in 1957, governmental policies seem to have accelerated the decline. By the mid-1980s, Singapore authorities were disturbed at the low fertility rate and the low growth rate. However, in addition to wanting a higher total fertility rate, they especially wanted higher fertility among well-educated women and men, who were thought to have "better" and more economically productive children. To that end, a number of incentives to promote marriage and childbearing among the well-educated were implemented in 1984:[85]

1. A program was instituted to give priority in access to high-quality public schools to the children of women who had attended a university and who had at least three children.
2. A governmental Social Development Unit was established to encourage men and women who were university graduates to marry.
3. The very selective nature of the program in encouraging well-educated women to have children is emphasized by the implementation of a program of cash payments to poor women with low educational attainment who became sterilized.

In 1987, some policies were implemented to overturn earlier fertility reduction policies that had discouraged couples from having more than two children. For example, the income tax deduction for third-born children was increased, and discrimination in school enrollment against third-born children was removed. A child care subsidy was implemented, and maternity leave was increased. In 2000, 2004, and 2008, pronatalist policies were strengthened with further increases in tax benefits, maternity leave, child care subsidies, baby bonus payments, and housing preference for married couples.[86]

Singapore implemented severe policies to reduce fertility, and these policies were more successful than the Singapore government had expected, leading in a shift from concerns about a rapidly growing population to concerns about the prospect of population decline. Since 1984, the series of pronatalist measures that the Singapore government has implemented have not been successful, since in 2005–2010 the TFR was 1.3 and the NRR was 0.6.

CHANGES IN FERTILITY IN PAIRS OF LESS DEVELOPED COUNTRIES

In this section, we look at fertility changes in pairs of less developed countries to illustrate some of the paths that countries have taken. First, we look at China and India, the two largest countries in the world. Both countries have experienced substantial fertility decline, but their trajectories have differed. Also, the family-planning programs in both countries have been severely criticized on ethical grounds. Then, we compare Nigeria and Kenya, two sub-Saharan African countries that have pursued somewhat different paths and that still have a substantial way to go before reaching replacement fertility. After that, we compare Mexico and Algeria. In these countries, fertility has declined but in 2005–2010 was still above replacement level.[87]

China and India

Both China and India implemented vigorous fertility limitation programs that were motivated by real policy concerns. However, the two countries implemented different policies and also differed in the timing and speed of fertility decline.

Figure 9.14 shows the total fertility rates in China and India in 1950–2010. In 1950–1955, the TFR was about 6.0 in each country.

The very high TFR in China in the late 1960s alarmed Chinese government officials. In an effort to reduce fertility and thus reduce the population growth rate, in 1971 China launched the Later-Longer-Fewer program. This program was designed to motivate women to begin childbearing later, have

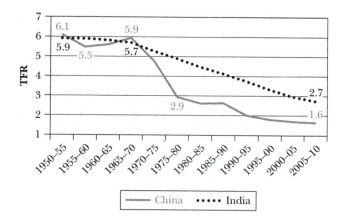

FIGURE 9.14 Total Fertility Rate (TFR) in China and India, 1950–2010

longer interbirth intervals, and have a smaller total number of children.

In 1979, the one-child policy was announced, which was designed to encourage couples, especially Han Chinese couples (who comprise more than 90% of the population of China), to have only one child. This policy was implemented differentially according to location, and although the TFR in China dropped rapidly, it never was close to 1.0. With a TFR of 1.6 in 2004–2010, most women were having more than one child.

The number of children that women could have without being penalized differed by rural or urban location and by the ethnicity of the mother. Also, the nature and severity of penalties for violating fertility limitations also differed. In some areas, the fine was modest. For example, among rural ethnic Kazakhs in Xinjiang, the fine for having a child beyond the plan was about the value of one sheep. In other places, the fine was as much as half the income of the husband and wife for as long as 14 years.

There were also benefits for urban residents who pledged to have only one child. Sometimes a group of about 20 couples would form a one-child club, with each couple committing to have no more than one child. If any member of the club had a second child, all club members lost their benefits. This amounted to forced abortion.

A Marriage Law implemented in 1980 required every Chinese couple to use birth control. Although continuing high growth rates would have posed serious obstacles to increasing economic growth and to improving the standard of living of the Chinese people, many critics have viewed these Chinese fertility limitation policies as draconian.[88]

Since 1990–1995, China has had below-replacement fertility. This gradually led to concerns about possible negative effects of a declining and aging population. In 2007, in all but one province, all couples in which both persons were only children were allowed to have a second child. and this was the situation in all provinces by 2011. After a Chinese Communist Party Conference in 2013, it was announced that the policy would be further relaxed to allow all couples in which either parent was an only child to have a second child.[89]

High fertility and high population growth rates also alarmed Indian officials. India had the first governmental fertility limitation program. In 1950, the Indian government appointed a Population Policy Committee, and in 1952 it implemented the First Five-Year Plan for family limitation and population control. This plan provided for study of the population problem in India but also included giving advice on family planning to government hospitals and public agencies.[90]

Family-planning efforts in India were intensified in the Second and the Third Five-Year Plans (1956–1966), and in 1965 the IUD was introduced to India. However, the IUD program was not very successful due to problems with inadequate medical follow-up and a large number of unacceptable and mainly unanticipated side effects. Ten percent of women with IUDs reported excessive bleeding, and for 6% of women IUDs were involuntarily expelled. Another major part of the program beginning in 1963 was both male and female sterilizations. In the late 1960s, condoms were added to the program, although there were persistent problems with condom distribution. In the late 1960s, contraceptive pills became available in India, but they were never very popular due to the expense, concern about side effects, and the necessity to take a pill every day.

Indira Gandhi was actively involved in family planning in India. As prime minister, in 1967 Gandhi supported an intensified family-planning program, which was mainly based on sterilizations. By the mid-1970s, Indira Gandhi and her son, Sanjay Gandhi, had become even more concerned about population growth fueled by high fertility. Due to mortality decline, the growth rate in India had increased from 1.8% in 1960–1955 to 2.4% in 1975–1980, reflecting a decrease in population doubling time from 39 years to 29 years.

Thus, Indira Gandhi launched a program in 1976 that included incentives for sterilization (especially vasectomies for men) and disincentives for resisting sterilization that many saw as coercive. The implementation of the family-planning programs depended heavily on local initiative, and there were regional variations, but there are reports of very questionable ethnical practices. Each state was given a quota of persons who were to be sterilized. In the Indian state of Rajasthan, sterilization was required after a couple had two or three children, and in the states of Haryana and Punjab, government employees with two or more children were denied benefits,

including loans and maternity leave, if they were not sterilized. The great pressure to find people to sterilize also led to some ineffective actions. It was reported that in Uttar Pradesh, over 60% of the sterilizations were performed on elderly men, men whose wives were past the childbearing ages, or men who were not married.

In the 1977 elections, Indira Gandhi was defeated, and her Congress Party lost power. One reason for the political defeat was probably criticism of the implementation of family planning. After 1977, India's family-planning program was recast as part of a broad-based health and welfare program.

We see in Figure 9.14 that India's TFR declined after the early 1960s. Perhaps the extreme family-planning efforts helped start fertility decline, but fertility decline continued at a steady pace after the late 1970s.

Figure 9.15 shows the proportion of women ever married by age in China and India in the early 1980s and around 2000. In China, the legal minimum age for female marriage was set at 18 in 1950, whereas formerly marriages could occur much earlier. The motivation for the minimum age was not population limitation but rather to counter what were seen as negative consequences of arranged marriages with very young brides. In 1962, a campaign began to convince young people to postpone marriage, but the legal minimum age was not raised, although permission from the work unit (basically the place of employment) was necessary in order for people to marry. Women were encouraged not to marry until they were at least 23 years old in rural areas and at least 25 years old in urban areas. In 1981, a law allowed women to marry at age 20 without work unit permission. It is clear in Figure 9.15 that both in 1982 and in 2000, almost no women aged 15–19 in China were married, although in 2000, 43% of women aged 20–24 were married.

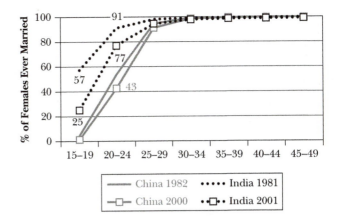

FIGURE 9.15   Percentage of Females Ever Married by Age in China and India, in about 1980 and about 2000

In 1978, the minimum legal age for marriage of females was established at 18 in India. However, since 57% of women aged 15–19 in India were married in 1981, and 25% of women aged 15–19 in India were married in 2001, it is clear that this law was not vigorously enforced. Marriage began later in China than in India at both dates, but in India there was more of a change in age at marriage between the two dates. However, since 1981, the proportion of women under age 25 who are married has declined substantially in India.

The **singulate mean age at marriage (SMAM)** is the average age at marriage of those women who eventually marry. It is a life table–based measure, similar to expectation of life at birth. It is based on the proportion of women ever married by age. It can be thought of as the average number of years lived single among those who eventually marry.[91]

Table 9.8 shows the SMAM in China and in India at the two dates. The SMAM increased by about 1 year in both countries. It was about 3 years later in China than in India.

Figure 9.16 shows age-specific fertility rates in China and India in the early 1970s and in 2006. In both countries, the rates became lower and increased more gradually with age across younger ages. This was a result of an increase in the age of marriage, resulting in an increase in the age of first birth. China's policy promoting extensive birth

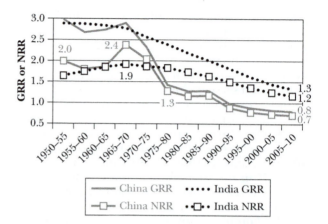

FIGURE 9.17   Gross Reproduction Rate (GRR) and Net Reproduction Rate (NRR) in China and India, 1950–2010

spacing also contributed to the more gradual rise in age-specific fertility rates with age at the later date. In both countries, the shape of the right-hand side of the age-specific fertility curve (across older ages) changed from being convex to concave, reflecting the impact of substantial fertility limitation. It is striking that around 1970 age-specific fertility rates were higher in China than in India at most ages, while in 2006 age-specific fertility rates were lower at every age in China than in India.

Figure 9.17 compares the Gross Reproduction Rate (GRR) and the NRR in China and India. Declining mortality in both countries has resulted in the NRR changing from slightly more than half of the GRR to the NRR and the GRR being almost the same. The closeness of the values of the NRR and the GRR in 2005–2010 in each country shows that further decline in mortality in China and India will have little effect on the NRR; in each country, the value of the NRR in 2005–2010 was about 88% of the value of the GRR. China has had an NRR below 1.00 since 1995–2000, and India's NRR is expected to fall below 1.00 in 2025–2030. Thus, although these two largest countries in the world will remain large, their declining fertility limits their future population growth.

Nigeria and Kenya

Nigeria and Kenya are sub-Saharan African countries in which the idea of fertility limitation was more difficult for people to accept than it was in China or India. Also, people in Nigeria and Kenya were more skeptical that limiting their total number of children was in their interests than had been the people in China or India. The two countries differ in the timing and reasons for fertility decline. Kenya seems to be in an early stage of substantial voluntary fertility limitation, while there is little indication that this process has begun in Nigeria.[92]

TABLE 9.8   Singulate Mean Age at Marriage (SMAM) in China and India, in about 1980 and about 2000

	About 1980	About 2000
China	22.4	23.3
India	18.7	20.2

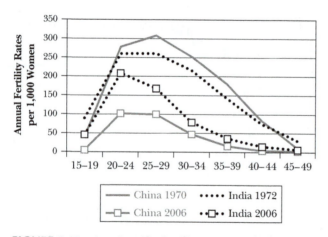

FIGURE 9.16   Age-Specific Fertility Rates in China and India, in about 1970 and in 2006

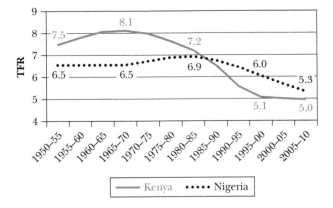

FIGURE 9.18 Total Fertility Rate (TFR) in Nigeria and Kenya, 1950–2010

The population growth of 3.8% in 1980–1985 in Kenya was the highest rate reliably recorded for a country. This growth rate implies a population doubling time of 18 years. The highest growth rate for Nigeria was 3.0% in 1975–1980, with an implied population doubling time of 23 years.

Figure 9.18 shows the TFR in Nigeria and Kenya. The TFR in Kenya increased between the early 1950s and the late 1960s, after which it fell by more than three children through 2005–2010. The TFR also increased slightly in Nigeria from the early 1950s to the early 1980s. The TFR in Nigeria was lower than in Kenya until about 1990, when the Kenyan TFR fell below that of Nigeria. In 2005–2010, the TFR in Nigeria was 1.6 children lower than it had been at its maximum. By 2005–2010, the TFRs in the two countries were close to each other.[93]

The family-planning association of Kenya was established in 1962, and the Kenyan government started a 5-year family-planning program in 1975. After 1980, it seems that Kenyan women became more interested in limiting their fertility. Table 9.9 shows the estimated percentage of married Kenyan women using some form of contraception, the average ideal number of children, and the percentage desiring no more children for various years based on KAP surveys.[94]

After the late 1970s in Kenya, contraceptive use increased, the ideal number of children declined, and

the percentage desiring no more children increased. Clearly, the views of many Kenyan women about fertility had changed by the 1980s. This was after TFR had begun to decline, but was at about the same time that population growth rates in Kenya peaked.

After the mid-1990s, the decline in the TFR in Kenya stagnated. Using data from the 2003 Kenya Demographic and Health Survey, Magadi and Agwanda investigated whether HIV could have played a role in the stagnation of Kenyan fertility decline. In Kenya in 2003, 7% of all adults and 9% of adult women were HIV-positive. Table 6.1 in Chapter 6 showed that the level of HIV prevalence in Kenya was somewhat above the average for sub-Saharan Africa but was lower than in countries in Southern Africa. Analysis showed that although HIV-positive women had lower fertility than women who were not HIV-positive, the stagnation in fertility decline was especially pronounced in those regions of Kenya with a relatively high HIV prevalence rate. It could be that HIV-negative women in regions with high HIV prevalence felt that they needed to have more children than they would have otherwise because of the uncertainty of the future mortality risks for those children.[95]

Figure 9.19 shows the percentage of women of childbearing age who used a modern contraceptive method, who used a traditional contraceptive method, who had an unmet need for contraception and wanted to stop their childbearing, and who had an unmet need for contraception and wanted to delay their next pregnancy and live birth. The gap between the top of each column and 100% indicates the percentage of women who wanted to become pregnant and have a child as soon as possible. Results are shown for each country for four different dates.[96]

The percentage of childbearing age women in Kenya using a modern contraceptive method more than doubled between 1988–1989 and 2008–2009. The total percentage who were either using a contraceptive method or stated an unmet need (the total height of the column) only increased from 65% in 1988–1989 to 72% in 2008–2009. Thus, it seems that in Kenya, women with some desire to stop or postpone their childbearing were increasingly turning to the use of contraception.

For Nigeria, the level of modern contraceptive use and the total percentage of women in the

TABLE 9.9 Percentage of Married Women in Kenya with Various Behaviors and Views: 1977–1978 through 2003

Year	% of Married Women Using Contraception	Average Ideal Number of Children	% Desiring No More Children
1977–1978	7%	6.2	17%
1984	17%	5.8	32%
1989	27%	4.4	50%
1998	39%	NA	NA
2003	39%	NA	NA

NA: Not available.

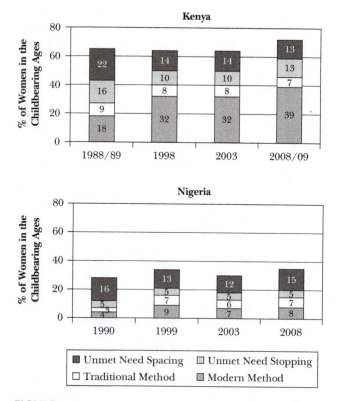

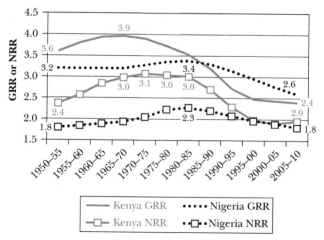

FIGURE 9.20 Gross Reproduction Rate (GRR) and Net Reproduction Rate (NRR) in Nigeria and Kenya, 1950–2010

FIGURE 9.19 Percentage of Women in the Childbearing Ages Who Used Contraception and with an Unmet Need for Family Planning in Kenya and Nigeria, in about 1990 to about 2008

We see in Figure 9.21 that between 1969 and 2003, the proportion of females under age 30 in Kenya who had ever married declined considerably, while there was little change in marriage patterns in Nigeria between 1986 and 2003.

Figure 9.22 shows that age-specific fertility rates declined considerably in both Kenya and Nigeria between about 1970 and about 2000. Kenya shifted from a natural fertility pattern to a more controlled fertility pattern, as discussed in Chapter 8. Although age-specific fertility rates in Nigeria declined, the changing shape of fertility by age does not suggest increased limitation of the total number of children born.

We saw in Table 9.7 that current contraceptive use was more for stopping than for postponing in Kenya and more for postponing than stopping in Nigeria. We also saw that the percentage of women wanting to stop childbearing was higher than the percentage

childbearing ages who were either using a contraceptive method or stated an unmet need were **much** lower than in Kenya. Although the percentage using a modern contraceptive method doubled between 1990 and 2008, even in 2008 it was only 8%. Thus, even in 2008 in Nigeria, 65% of women in the childbearing ages neither were using contraception nor expressed a desire to stop or postpone further childbearing, while this was only true for 28% of Kenyan women.

Figure 9.20 shows the GRR and the NRR in Kenya and Nigeria. Mortality declined enormously in both countries. The IMR in Kenya declined from 147 per 1,000 births in 1950–1955 to 65 per 1,000 births in 2005–2010; in Nigeria, the IMR declined from 189 to 96. These declines in the IMR brought the graphs of the GRR and the NRR for the two countries closer together over time, although as the IMR declines further, the NRR will increase if the TFR remains unchanged. The NRR in Nigeria is the same in 2005–2010 as it was in 1950–1955 because although the TFR was lower in 2005–2010, mortality was also lower in 2005–2010. Since the NRR and the population growth rate are the result of both fertility and mortality, the growth rate and the NRR continued to increase even after the TFR had begun to decline, due to the decline in mortality.

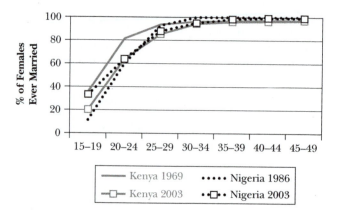

FIGURE 9.21 Percentage of Females Ever Married by Age in Nigeria and Kenya, 1969 or 1986 and 2003

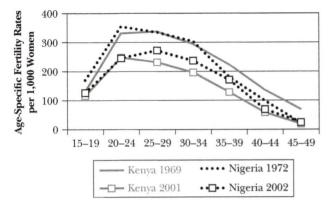

FIGURE 9.22 Age-Specific Fertility Rates in Kenya and Nigeria, in about 1970 and about 2001

wanting to postpone the next birth in Kenya, while the opposite was true in Nigeria. It seems that Kenya has begun a trajectory of lowered desired number of children and increased contraceptive use, which, if continued, will result in a much lower population growth rate. In Nigeria, contraceptive use is helping women and families achieve their goals of spacing children, substantially as a substitute for postpartum abstinence. Also, surveys in Nigeria that asked about unmet need for family planning in 2000–2005 found that among women who stated opposition or supply reasons for non-use of contraception, 48% stated opposition to family planning as the reason. This was true for only 32% of Kenyan women.[97] Whether the increased use of contraception in Nigeria will lead to substantial voluntary fertility limitation is yet to be seen, while a large portion of women in Nigeria continue to be opposed to contraception in principle.

Mexico and Algeria

Both Mexico and Algeria have moved from high to moderate fertility. The reasons for and the mechanisms of the fertility decline differ in the two countries.

Figure 9.23 shows the TFR in Mexico and Algeria. In both countries, fertility was very high in the 1950s. There was no sign of a fertility decline in Mexico until after 1975 and in Algeria until after 1980. However, in 2005–2010, both countries had a TFR of 2.4.

People have wondered why fertility in Mexico remained high long after substantial economic development had occurred. Between 1940 and 1970, the percentage of the economically active Mexican population that was in agriculture declined from 58% to 41%, while the percentage in trade, finance, and other services increased from 24% to 33%. The percentage rural declined from 72% to 48%, and the percentage literate among those at least aged 15 increased from 43% to 76%.

Many thought that substantial fertility decline would have started before a country reached the development level shown by Mexico in 1970. However, Mexico had a number of policies in place that cushioned families from feeling incentives to limit childbearing, such as public investment in industry, state provision of social services, and subsidization of urban food costs.

In 1973, the Mexican government decided that the high rate of population growth, caused by high fertility, constituted a threat to social development and economic growth. A substantial family-planning program was launched, and contraceptive use increased rapidly, from 29% of women in unions in 1976, to 38% in 1979, to 48% in 1982. There is substantial reason to believe that the family-planning program provided the trigger to the decline in Mexican fertility.[98]

Kouaouci sees the high fertility in Algeria through 1970 as a result of very early marriage and high marital fertility. The age structure of Algeria also had a high proportion of women in the reproductive ages. By 1986, there had been a substantial increase in the age of female marriage, a decline in marital fertility rates, and an increase in contraceptive prevalence.[99] Sutton argues that the information and experiences of the many Algerians who became labor migrants in Europe contributed to changing views that led to the kind of change in thinking that Thornton writes about in the context of developmental idealism. This kind of change can motivate fertility limitation.[100]

Figure 9.24 shows the percentage of women ever married by age in Mexico and Algeria in about 1980 and about 2000. There was little change in the trajectory of female marriage in Mexico, and the SMAM in Mexico increased only from 22 in 1980 to 23 in 2000. In Mexico, 93% of women aged 45–49 had married in 1980, and this had declined trivially to 92% in 2000. However, in Algeria, female marriage became MUCH later in the last 20 years of the twentieth century.

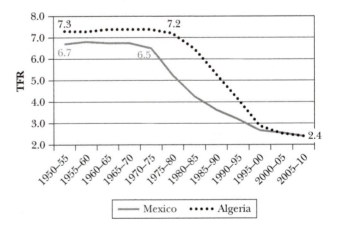

FIGURE 9.23 Total Fertility Rate (TFR) in Mexico and Algeria, 1950–2010

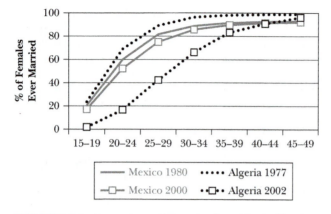

FIGURE 9.24 Percentage of Females Ever Married by Age in Mexico and Algeria, in about 1980 and about 2000

The SMAM was 21 in 1977 but was 30 in 2002. However, in Algeria both in 1977 and in 2002, almost all women had married by their late forties.

Figure 9.25 shows age-specific fertility rates in Mexico and Algeria in 1970 and 2005. The major change in the age-specific fertility schedule in Mexico was the large decline in rates at almost all ages between 1970 and 2006. Also, the shape of the age-specific fertility schedule changed from a typical natural fertility shape to a typical controlled fertility shape, with childbearing shifted to a younger age. In Algeria, the rates also were lower at every age in 2006 than in 1970, and the age pattern of fertility had shifted to an older age, with ages 30–34 having the highest rate in 2006.

Figure 9.26 shows the GRR and NRR in Mexico and Algeria. Of course, the trajectory of the GRR reflects that of the TFR. The NRR increased until the early 1970s in Mexico and until the late 1970s in Algeria, reflecting substantial mortality decline in both countries. In 2005–2010, the NRR in Algeria was 1.1 and in Mexico was 1.2. By

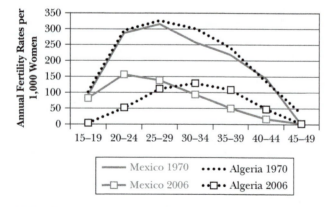

FIGURE 9.25 Age-Specific Fertility Rates in Mexico and Algeria, 1970 and 2006

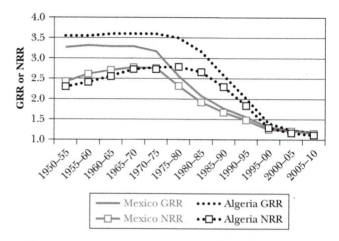

FIGURE 9.26 Gross Reproduction Rate (GRR) and Net Reproduction Rate (NRR) in Mexico and Algeria, 1950–2010

2015–2020, the NRR in both countries is expected to be below 1.00.

UNWANTED PREGNANCIES, UNWANTED CHILDREN, AND ABORTION

In every population, there are unwanted pregnancies and unwanted children. These are issues of concern in both less developed and more developed countries. Induced abortion is a way to prevent an unwanted pregnancy from resulting in a live birth. In this section, we discuss abortion and other ways that women and couples have responded when there was an unwanted pregnancy or unwanted birth and the woman or couple were not willing to have the birth or raise the child themselves.

Ways of Dealing with Unwanted Children and Unwanted Births

Once an unwanted pregnancy is detected, some of the main ways that the pregnancy or the subsequent unwanted birth has been dealt with are (1) abortion, (2) infanticide, (3) fosterage, (4) adoption, and (5) abandonment.

Induced abortion has long been known. An **abortion** is the termination of a pregnancy resulting in the death of the fetus. An **induced abortion** is an abortion that is brought about intentionally. An abortion that is not brought about intentionally is called a **miscarriage**. When used without a modifier, "abortion" usually refers to induced abortion.

Historically, an abortion was often induced by the pregnant women ingesting or otherwise introducing poison into her body. Abortions were dangerous to the pregnant woman because the aim was to introduce enough poison to kill the fetus but not enough to kill the woman. The English folk song "Scarborough Fair," with the lyrics

> Are you going to Scarborough Fair?
> Parsley, sage, rosemary, and thyme;
> Remember me to one who lives there,
> For once she was a true lover of mine.[101]

may be about induced abortion. Parsley, sage, rosemary, and thyme are all herbs that were used in various ways to induce an abortion. Abortion was often illegal, but most scholars believe that it has long been widely practiced. Often a distinction about illegality and moral judgment has been made related to how early in the pregnancy the abortion occurs. There is usually much less moral objection to an abortion that occurs very early in the pregnancy than to an abortion that occurs late in the pregnancy.[102]

Infanticide is the killing of a child under one year of age. Infanticide usually occurs very soon after birth. In some societies, it has been an accepted practice to kill newborn twins. Sometimes the practice has been to kill one of the twins, based on the argument that it would be impossible to care for two babies at the same time, partially due to the difficulty of procuring enough food. Sometimes the practice has been to kill both twins, under the view that twins were unlucky. Closely related to infanticide is general neglect, inattention, or exposure that leads to early death.[103] Sometimes, unwanted children would be abandoned in the forest with the idea that there was a chance the child would survive, even though survival was quite unlikely. This is what the "Hansel and Gretel" story is about. It has been argued that in some cultures, infanticide of newborns is viewed as a continuation of abortion.[104] There is evidence that infanticide was common in the past and that even when there were penalties, they were fairly light.[105] In some cultures, a child is not seen as fully human until a short time after birth. Sometimes naming and other birth ceremonies are delayed, possibly to prevent investing too much emotional energy in an infant who might die, especially in a setting of high infant mortality.[106]

Fosterage is the placing of a child with another household that needs the child or can afford to raise the child. There are several different forms and reasons for fosterage. This placement can be permanent and can involve adoption of the child, or it can be temporary. Fosterage is also used to promote the moral and practical education of wanted children. In historical Europe, sometimes children from poorer households were placed as servants in richer households for economic reasons. It was thought that often parents were too lenient with their children and that being raised to adulthood in the parental home was not good for the child's moral development. Children, sometimes as young as age 7, were placed in the households of relatives and often worked there essentially as apprentices. This was viewed as in the best interests of the child. In some less developed countries, especially in sub-Saharan Africa, it has been common for children in rural areas to live with urban relatives. Some reasons for this are the greater availability of education in urban areas and the higher quality of urban than rural schools. These practices also were seen as in the best interests of the child. In Senegal, children have been given over to Muslim teachers, called marabouts, for the purpose of education, although marabouts have often been criticized for exploiting the children. In addition, with the HIV epidemic, relatives, especially grandparents, have assumed care of children not only when the child's mother has died, but also when the mother is alive but is too ill to care for the child.[107]

A child can be given up for **adoption**. An adoption occurs when a person other than a biological parent assumes parental and legal responsibilities for a person. An adoption can involve a formal procedure, such as when a pregnant woman decides that she cannot care for a child and arranges with an adoption agency before the child is born. Smith showed that in Japan in the eighteenth and early nineteenth centuries, families who had no sons often adopted a boy from a family with two or more sons.[108]

Abandonment involves anonymously leaving a child at an institution such as a hospital or a convent. As of May 2010, 49 American states and Puerto Rico had provisions called Safe Haven Laws that specify that a small baby can be left at a hospital or other location without fear of legal recriminations.[109]

Trexler presented evidence that in medieval Florence, abandonment of babies at convents was common. Usually, the abandoned babies were overwhelmingly girls. However, in times of economic hardship, a higher proportion of the babies were boys than in normal times.[110]

There has been concern that unwanted children suffer in later life even if they stay with their biological mother. An example of this is discussed in Box 9.1.[111]

Sex-Selective Abortion in East Asia

A **sex-selective abortion** occurs when the decision to abort the fetus is based on the gender of the fetus. This most often occurs with abortion of female fetuses. Since the spread of ultrasound machines across much of the world, sex-selective abortion has been widely used in Asia to prevent unwanted female births.

Throughout the world, it is common for couples to have sex preferences about their children. Westoff and his colleagues studied American women who had their second child in 1957. They followed these women for 3 years to see whether they had an additional child. This was at a time when the American TFR was 3.7. The factor most strongly related to whether a woman had a third child was if the first two

BOX 9.1

An Extreme Example of Unwantedness: Children Born to Women Denied Abortion in Czechoslovakia

There were studies of children born in Czechoslovakia in 1961–1963 to women who had twice been denied permission to abort the pregnancy. Seeking to abort a given pregnancy twice is a strong indication that the birth is not wanted. Although most abortions were legal in Czechoslovakia, about 2% of requests for abortion were denied, for reasons such as health concerns, the fetus was at more than 12 weeks gestation, or the woman had had an abortion in the previous 6 months. The 220 children in the study were matched with 220 children whose mother had not requested to abort the pregnancy. The matches were made on

many characteristics, including age, sex, birth order, and number of siblings. The children were given social and psychological tests at ages 9, 14–16, and 22–23. The children whose mothers had been denied the requested abortion did not differ from the control children on IQ, but they showed significantly worse psychological adjustment, more behavioral problems in school, and worse school performance than the control group of children. When the children were 22–23, the study group young adults showed more conflict at work, in their marriages, and with friends than the control group children.

children were the same sex. At that time, Americans seemed to want at least one son and one daughter. If the couple's first two children were the same sex (whether boys or girls), the couple were much more likely to have a third child in an effort to balance the sex composition of their children.[112]

In many Asian societies, there are strong cultural and economic motivations for a couple to have at least one son. Caldwell and his colleagues found that in South India, a major determinant of whether a widow fell into poverty was if she did not have a surviving son. Thus, it was economically rational for women in that setting to be very motivated to have at least one son and to do everything possible to try to increase the chance that at least one son would survive.[113]

Traditionally, in Confucian-influenced societies, the concept of filial piety obligates sons to care for the welfare of their parents, especially when the parents are elderly. Confucian norms direct that the oldest son's family should reside with his parents. Thus couples in those settings could be motivated to have at least one son.[114] In Korean culture, there are rituals that can only be performed by sons. Thus, also for religious reasons, Koreans could be quite motivated to have at least one son.[115]

Taeuber found in an analysis of births in Japan 1947–1949 that the proportion of births that were male increased with the age of the mother and with parity.[116] She related the disproportionate number of male births to the higher value placed on sons than daughters and attributed this to female infanticide. Even in a setting in which infanticide related to sex preference is not completely unacceptable, sex-selective abortion is a more attractive alternative than female infanticide.

Guilmoto has suggested that three conditions are necessary for there to be an excessively high (masculine) sex ratio at birth:[117]

1. There must be a strong traditional preference for sons within the context of a patriarchal society (Readiness).
2. There must be access to a modern sex-selective method (Ability).
3. There must be pressure to have a small number of children (Squeeze).

China, South Korea, and other Asian societies have strong male preference and a strong patriarchal tradition, satisfying Guilmoto's first condition. Ultrasound machines became widely available in East and South Asia in the mid-1980s. With some degree of error, the sex of the fetus is discernible from an ultrasound by late in the first trimester of pregnancy.[118] The wide availability of ultrasound satisfies Guilmoto's second condition. In many Asian societies, with increasing aspirations for children's education, there is a strong desire for increased child quality, and increasingly couples to want to have fewer high-quality children rather than many lower quality children, satisfying Guilmoto's third condition.

In China and other countries, the sex ratio at birth is the major indicator of sex-selective abortion. Recall that the normal range for the sex ratio at birth, which is the number of male births per 100 female births, is 104–107. One does not see a sex ratio at birth of above 107 in the absence of sex-selective abortion or unreported female infanticide.

Figure 9.27 shows sex ratios at birth in China and in South Korea for various years between 1980 and

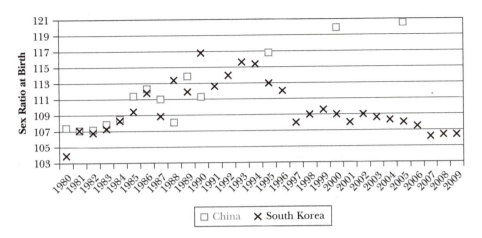

FIGURE 9.27   Sex Ratios at Birth for China and South Korea, 1980–2009

2009. In both China and South Korea, sex-selective abortion was illegal, but this was extremely difficult to enforce. Abortion was freely available in both countries, and a side payment could be made to the ultrasound operator for some sort of signal indicating the sex of the fetus.

In both countries, the sex ratios at birth rose in the late 1980s. The ratios remained high through the mid-1990s, after which the sex ratio at birth for South Korea declined, reaching 107 by 2006.

Figure 9.28 shows sex ratios at birth by parity for China, that is, the sex ratio is shown for the firstborn, second-born, third-born, fourth-born, and fifth- or later-born child.[119] In every year, the sex ratio at birth for the first birth is within or slightly above the normal range. However, by 1987, the sex ratios at birth for second and later births are far above the normal range, indicating substantial sex-selective abortion for the second and later births.

In the presence of strong fertility limitation policies in China, one might wonder why there is little evidence of sex-selective abortion for the first birth. One explanation is that although there is much discussion of China's one-child policy, this policy was strongly enforced mainly in large urban areas. Recall from Table 8.2 that in 2005–2010, the total fertility rate in China was 1.6. If all fecund women had one child, the TFR would be slightly less than 1.0 rather than more than 1.5. Another factor in the infrequent use of sex-selective abortion for the first pregnancy could be fear that an induced abortion would lead to subsequent sterility.

There is evidence that experiencing an induced abortion increases the risk that a woman will become sterile. Chinese women and couples probably generally preferred to have a son to a daughter for their first child, but they preferred to have a daughter to having no children at all. After having a girl as the first child, a woman could continue to become pregnant but abort the pregnancy if the fetus were female, until she was pregnant with a boy. In China, one of the main factors related to whether a subsequent birth was male was the sex composition of earlier-born children, especially if there were no sons among earlier births. This implies that earlier pregnancies in which the fetus was female often ended in an abortion.[120]

Figure 9.29 shows sex ratios by parity for South Korea. The top panel shows the results for the first-, second-, third-, and fourth- and later-born children. The bottom panel shows the same results but only for the first- and second-born children. The vertical scale is expanded in the second panel to make it easier to see the difference in the values. We see in Figure 9.29 results through 1994 similar to those for China in Figure 9.28, with a sex ratio within or slightly above the normal range for the first birth, but with sex ratios at birth considerably above the normal range for second and later births. After the mid-1990s, we see the sex ratios at birth decline for second and

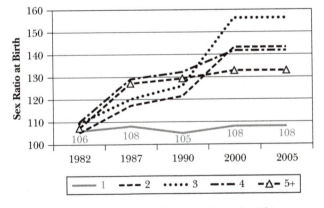

FIGURE 9.28   Sex Ratios at Birth by Parity for China, 1982–2005

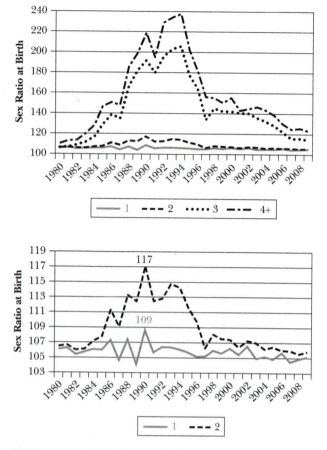

FIGURE 9.29 Sex Ratios at Birth by Parity for South Korea, 1980–2008

later births. After 1997, the sex ratios for the second birth are within the normal range, although even in 2009, the sex ratio for the third birth was 144, and the sex ratio for fourth and later births was 123, both of which were far above the normal range. Thus, it seems that the extent of male preference in South Korea, as manifested in sex-selective abortion, diminished after the mid-1990s, although it had not disappeared by 2009.

Looking at Figures 9.27, 9.28, and 9.29, China and South Korea exhibited similar behavior linking sex-selective abortion and parity from the mid-1980s through the mid-1990s. The two countries have also had similar trajectories in the TFR, with below-replacement fertility in China since 1995–2000 and in South Korea since 1985–1990. South Korea had an active family-planning program since the mid-1960s. There were some monetary incentives for couples who were sterilized before they had three children, but it was mainly a program of information, education, and contraceptive method availability, without the coercive aspects of the Chinese program.[121] Since the courses of fertility and of sex-selective abortion were so similar in China

and in South Korea from about 1985 through about 1995, even though fertility limitation policies were very different in the two countries, it seems unlikely that Chinese state policy was the main reason for sex-selective abortion in China.

Das Gupta and her colleagues argue that state policies and the low status of women supported high sex ratios at birth in both China and South Korea. They think that changes in policies and in women's roles in South Korea led to the decline in sex-selective abortion in South Korea since the mid-1990s. They note that education and urban residence were rising rapidly in South Korea, and that survey results on whether women felt it was necessary to have a son indicated a decline since 1985. However, the availability of an easy technology to implement son preference (ultrasound) led to the increase in the sex ratio at birth after the mid-1980s. Social policies in South Korea, such as the implementation of more gender-egalitarian inheritance laws along with ever-progressing higher educational attainment, seem to have finally led to a decline in the intensity of son preference.[122]

Li looked at the sex ratio at birth in China and described governmental programs to try to reduce it, but little evidence has been seen of the effectiveness of these programs. However, Das Gupta and colleagues saw some evidence of an incipient decline in sex ratios at birth based on a leveling off or decline in sex ratios at birth in some provinces of China. They also argue that the kinds of changes in South Korea that led to less sex-selective abortion could soon have an effect in China.[123]

Jha and his colleagues found substantial evidence of sex-selective abortion in India in 1990–2005 and that it had increased in recent years. As in China and South Korea, the sex ratio for the first birth was generally within the normal range, but for the second birth the sex ratio at birth was higher, especially if the first child was a girl. The likely explanation is that if the first child was a girl, the next fetus was aborted if it was also female. The couple would continue to try to have a son until the fetus was male.[124]

CONCLUDING COMMENTS

In many parts of Asia, fertility declined rapidly once family-planning programs were introduced, and contraceptive use increased rapidly, especially to stop childbearing. In some of sub-Saharan Africa, contraception has been more popular for spacing of children than for stopping childbearing. After much wringing of hands, fertility has begun to be voluntarily limited in much of sub-Saharan Africa. However, in many African regions, growth rates remain high, and it is unclear what the future will bring.

Economic arguments about why people would want more or less children have long been persuasive, but it is not always clear how people in a given situation will assess their interests regarding fertility. There is increasing evidence that attitudes and views of a desirable future and what constitutes a good life for themselves and their children are important for parents and prospective parents in deciding whether they want a large or a small number of children. It seems that both a desire to limit the number of children and access to an acceptable, convenient means to limit fertility are necessary for a decline from high to moderate or low fertility. As in the case of infant mortality decline, the status of women seems to be a very important factor in fertility decline, both for changing desires about the number of children and also in the use of contraceptive methods.

 Study and Review Online

SUMMARY

1. In historical Europe there were different patterns of marriage in different regions, with marriage early and close to universal in Eastern Europe, and later marriages with many women never marrying in Western Europe. These different marriage patterns were related to patterns of inheritance and co-residence, with equal division of property among all sons and intergenerational co-residence common in the East, while in the West inheritance of all property by one son was common, and intergenerational co-residence was less common.

2. Voluntary limitation of fertility by married couples was probably first achieved through a combination of coitus interruptus (withdrawal) and abstinence. An increase in the age of female marriage also contributed to fertility decline in some areas.

3. Cultural differences among areas of Europe were often found to be more important in the initiation of limitation of marital fertility than differences among areas in indicators of development, such as literacy or industrialization.

4. Coale proposed three preconditions that need to be simultaneously satisfied in order for there to be substantial voluntary fertility limitation. They are (1) acceptance of the possibility and moral acceptability of control of fertility (Willing), (2) perception of advantages from reduced fertility (Ready), and (3) knowledge and mastery of an effective and acceptable method of fertility control (Able).

5. Age at marriage in some less developed countries has been even earlier than it was in Eastern Europe historically. In the LDR, female age at marriage often increased as arranged marriage became less common and as there was some increase in female education.

6. Becker's New Home Economics Model saw a major cost of having children as the time the mother spent caring for the children, which was seen as incompatible with the mother working for pay. As women's education increases, a family is forgoing more income due to the wife not working for pay. Thus, the higher the wife's education, the fewer children a couple has. In addition, as people came to desire higher quality, more educated children, the cost of raising children increased, and people had fewer children.

7. Easterlin's Relative Income Model saw people forming an idea of the resources needed to raise a child when they are young. When they are adults, they compare their resources to those available when they are young and feel relatively rich or poor and able to afford more or fewer children than their parents had. Increased consumption aspirations over time generally led to lower fertility over time.

8. Mason pointed out that women's labor force participation and fertility are not necessarily incompatible in less developed countries, depending on the nature of the labor force participation.

9. The Value of Children study (VOC) looked at what parents and potential parents see as the costs and benefits of having children. It was developed by psychologists and found that the perceived costs and benefits of having children changed with fertility limitation, with (1) less importance of the economic benefits that children could provide becoming less important, (2) increased importance of rewarding interactions with children, and (3) increased concern with the restrictions children place on parents.

10. Thornton's Developmental Idealism Model describes a set of values that have been found to spread across the word and lead to lower fertility. They are as follows: (1) Modern society is good. Modern society is urban, industrialized, and highly educated. (2) The modern family is good. The modern family includes use of family planning and low fertility. (3) The modern family is a cause and an effect of modern society. And (4) individuals have the right to be free and equal.

11. Caldwell proposed that a shift from a concern with child quantity to child quality often occurs when there is a change in the direction of inter-generational obligations from the younger generation mainly having obligations to the older generation to the older generation mainly having obligations to the younger generation. This shift often occurs as education becomes more important.

12. Sub-Saharan Africa had the highest fertility of any region. The TFR began to decline in about 1980, and the NRR began to decline in about 1990. In 2005–2010, the growth rate if continued would lead to the population doubling in 28 years.

13. Some were concerned whether fertility would ever decline in sub-Saharan Africa, but the cultural arguments about continuation of high fertility in sub-Saharan Africa could be relevant to the pace of future fertility decline. In some settings, having "too many children" is an alien concept. Also, in settings where the elderly depend on adult children, there are incentives to have many children.

14. Knowledge, Attitude, and Practice (KAP) surveys of family planning have been used across the LDR to help understand how many children women see as desirable to have and to understand what might motivate women to adopt family planning.

15. The family-planning program in Taiwan in the early 1960s is a model of how policy planners hoped family-planning programs would operate. Many women had taken actions to limit their fertility before the program began. Many people were not limiting their fertility because of the absence of Coale's third precondition. With the family-planning methods available through the program, fertility limitation increased.

16. Female education is strongly related to fertility and to contraceptive use throughout the LDR.

17. Contraceptive use and the use of modern contraceptive methods have increased over time in every region. Contraceptive use and use of modern contraceptive methods are much lower in Africa than in other regions.

18. A woman has an unmet need for family planning if she thinks she can become pregnant and does not want to become pregnant immediately, but she is not using any method to prevent pregnancy. A major challenge to family-planning programs is to understand why women with an unmet need are not using any contraceptive method.

19. Contraceptive use has been promoted through contacts with the health care system that occur for reasons other than family planning, such as when a child is brought for vaccinations or immediately after a woman has given birth.

20. Mortality policy and fertility policy are fundamentally different, since mortality decline is always a good idea. Policies can advocate lower fertility or higher fertility, depending on the population growth rate. Also, while many policies to reduce mortality can be implemented with little or no involvement of individuals or households, fertility policies cannot be implemented without the active participation of individuals and households.

21. Fertility policies have either a population-level, macrosocial rationale or the rationale of serving the interests of women and families. The 1994 Cairo Conference marked a major shift from the first rationale to the second rationale.

22. There have been many ethically questionable fertility policies. Whether they were justified depends partially on how the likelihood of and danger from continued high fertility was assessed.

23. Sex-selective abortion has been common in much of East Asia, including China and South Korea since the early 1980s, although it has decreased in South Korea since the mid-1990s. It might have begun to decrease in some parts of China.

KEY TERMS

impartible inheritance   275
primogeniture   275
partible inheritance   275
ultimogeniture   275
nuclear household   275
extended household   275
Theory of the Demographic
   Transition   276
characteristics hypothesis   277
preconditions for fertility
   limitation   278
childlessness   280
opportunity cost   280

family of procreation   280
family of orientation   280
New Home Economics
   Model   280
inferior good   280
superior good   280
child quantity   281
child quality   281
role incompatibility   281
Relative Income Model   281
Developmental Idealism
   Model   282
fertility-stopping behavior   285

fertility-postponing
   behavior   285
fertility-spacing
   behavior   285
contraception   290
modern contraceptive
   methods   290
traditional contraceptive
   methods   290
unmet need for family
   planning   291
Population policies   295
genocide   296

QUESTIONS FOR DISCUSSION AND REVIEW

1. What are Coale's three preconditions for fertility limitation? Give an example (hypothetical or actual) for each precondition in which the other two are met but lack of meeting of the remaining precondition leads to no intentional fertility limitation.
2. Discuss the different motivations behind actions to space births and actions to limit the total number of births in some parts of sub-Saharan Africa.
3. Compare and contrast the considerations that less developed country policy makers need to take into account in devising and implementing mortality policy and devising and implementing fertility policy.
4. Discuss the controversy about individual human rights in the area of mortality policy and in the area of fertility policy.
5. What is meant by an "unmet need for family planning"? How does the presence of this unmet need relate to Coale's three preconditions for fertility control?

SUGGESTED PAPER TOPICS

1. Pick a country that experienced a tumultuous event, such as a civil war or a natural disaster. Look at the demographic indicators for that country, and discuss how the tumultuous event influenced mortality, fertility, and international migration and what possible explanations might be for the observed patterns.
2. Pick a country in the LDR. Discuss its history of mortality and fertility policies in light of social, cultural, and political conditions in the country. Relate this policy history to mortality and fertility rates.

NOTES

1. Map from About.com Geography, http://geography.about.com/library/blank/blxeurope.htm (accessed December 17, 2011).
2. John Hajnal. 1953. "Age at Marriage and Proportions Marrying," *Population Studies*, 7: 111–136; and John Hajnal. 1982. "Two Kinds of Preindustrial Household Formation System," *Population and Development Review*, 8: 449–494.
3. Edward Shorter. 1973. "Female Emancipation, Birth Control, and Fertility in European History," *The American Historical Review*, 78: 605–640; Edward Shorter, John Knodel, and Etienne Van De Walle. 1971. "The Decline of Non-Marital Fertility in Europe, 1880–1940," *Population Studies*, 25: 375–393; and Peter Laslett. 1980. "Introduction: Comparing Illegitimacy over Time and between Cultures," in *Bastardy and Its Comparative History*, ed. Peter Laslett, Karla Oosterveen, and Richard M. Smith, Cambridge: MA: Harvard University Press, 1–68.
4. Louis Henry. 1956. *Anciennes familles genevoises. Etude demographique XVIe–XXe siècle*, Paris: Presses universitaires francaises; J. Dupaquier, J. Dupâquier, and M. Lachiver. 1969. "Sur les débuts de la contraception en France ou les deux malthusianismes," *Annales. Histoire, Sciences Sociales*, 24: 1391–1406; and Natalie Zemon Davis. 1976. "'Women's History' in Transition: The European Case," *Feminist Studies*, 3: 63–103.
5. Ansley J. Coale and Susan Cotts Watkins, eds. 1986. *The Decline of Fertility in Europe: the Revised Proceedings of a Conference on the Princeton European Fertility Project*, Princeton, NJ: Princeton University Press.
6. Michael Teitelbaum. 1975. "Relevance of Demographic Transition Theory for Developing Countries," *Science*, 188: 420–425, 424.
7. Poul C. Matthiessen. 1985. *The Limitation of Family Size in Denmark*, Copenhagen: Royal Danish Academy of Sciences and Letters.
8. John Knodel. 1974. *The Decline of Fertility in Germany, 1871–1939*, Princeton, NJ: Princeton University Press.
9. J. William Leasure. 1963. "Factors Involved in the Decline of Fertility in Spain 1900–1950," *Population Studies*, 16: 271–285.
10. Michael W. Flinn. 1981. *The European Demographic System, 1500–1820*, Baltimore: Johns Hopkins University Press, 84–86.
11. Rudolph Binton. 2001. "Marianne in the Home, Political Revolution and Fertility Transition in France and the United States," *Population: An*

English Selection, 13: 165–188; and Etienne van de Walle. 1980. "Motivations and Technology in the Decline of French Fertility," in *Family and Sexuality in French History*, ed. Robert Wheaton and Tamara K. Hareven, Philadelphia: University of Pennsylvania Press, 135–178.

12. Barbara A. Anderson. 1986. "Regional and Cultural Factors in the Decline of Marital Fertility in Western Europe," in *The Decline of Fertility in Europe*, ed. Ansley J. Coale and Susan Cott Watkins, Princeton, NJ: Princeton University Press.

13. Massimo Livi-Bacci. 1977. *A History of Italian Fertility*, Princeton, NJ: Princeton University Press.

14. Ansley J. Coale. 1973. "The Demographic Transition Reconsidered," in *International Population Conference, Liege, 1973*, Vol. 1, Liege: International Union for the Scientific Study of Population, 53–72.

15. Charles F. Westoff and Raymond H. Potvin. 1967. *College Women and Fertility Values*, Princeton, NJ: Princeton University Press.

16. John Knodel and Etienne van de Walle. 1979. "Lessons from the Past: Policy Implications of Historical Fertility Studies," *Population and Development Review*, 5: 217–245.

17. Irit Sinai, Rebecka Lundgren, Marcos Arévalo, and Victoria Jennings. 2006. "Fertility Awareness-Based Methods of Family Planning: Predictors of Correct Use," *International Family Planning Perspectives*, 32: 94–100.

18. Andrej A. Popov, Adriaan P. Visser, and Evert Ketting. 1993. "Contraceptive Knowledge, Attitudes, and Practice in Russia during the 1980s," *Studies in Family Planning*, 24: 227–235.

19. Ansley J. Coale. 1992. "Age of Entry into Marriage and the Date of the Initiation of Voluntary Birth Control," *Demography*, 29: 333–341.

20. Digest. 1983. "WFS Surveys Show Three Caribbean Nations Differ Widely in Levels of Fertility and Contraceptive Use," *International Family Planning Perspectives*, 9: 58–61; and James Allman. 1985. "Conjugal Unions in Rural and Urban Haiti," *Social and Economic Studies*, 34: 27–57.

21. Ester Boserup. 1985. "Economic and Demographic Interrelationships in Sub-Saharan Africa," *Population and Development Review*, 11: 383–397; Uche C. Isiugo-Abanihe. 1998. "Stability of Marital Unions and Fertility in Nigeria," *Journal of Biosocial Science*, 30: 33–41; and John C. Caldwell and Pat Caldwell. 1987. "The Cultural Context of High Fertility in Sub-Saharan Africa," *Population and Development Review*, 13: 409–437.

22. Barbara A. Anderson and James L. McCabe, 1977. "Nutrition and the Fertility of Younger Women in Kinshasa, Zaire," *Journal of Development Economics*, 4: 343–363.

23. Warren C. Robinson. 1997. "The Economic Theory of Fertility over Three Decades," *Population Studies*, 51: 63–74; and John C. Caldwell and Pat Caldwell. 1988. "Is the Asian Family Planning Program Model Suited to Africa?" *Studies in Family Planning*, 19: 19–28.

24. Gary S. Becker. 1960. "An Economic Analysis of Fertility," in *Demographic Change and Economic Change in Developed Countries*, National Bureau of Economic Research, Princeton, NJ: Princeton University Press; Gary S. Becker. 1965. "A Theory of the Allocation of Time," *Economic Journal*, 75: 493–517; and Gary S. Becker. 1991. *A Treatise on the Family*, rev. and enlarged ed., Cambridge, MA: Harvard University Press.

25. Karen Oppenheim Mason et al. 1971. *Social and Economic Correlates of Family Fertility: A Survey of the Evidence*, Research Triangle Park, NC: Research Triangle Institute.

26. Lin Lean Lim. 2009. "Female Labour Force Participation," in United Nations, *Completing the Fertility Transition*, New York: United Nations, 195–212, http://www.un.org/esa/population/publications/completingfertility/RevisedLIM paper.PDF (accessed March 13, 2012).

27. Richard A. Easterlin. 1966. "On the Relation of Economic Factors to Recent and Projected Fertility Change," *Demography*, 3: 131–153; Richard Easterlin. 1974. "Does Economic Growth Improve the Human Lot? Some Empirical Evidence," in *Nations and Households in Economic Growth*, ed. Paul A. David and Melvin W. Reder, New York: Academic Press; and Richard A. Easterlin. 1987. *Birth and Fortune*, Chicago: University of Chicago Press.

28. Edgar O. Edwards. 1975. "Population-Related Choices and Development Strategy," in *Social Science Research on Population and Development*, New York: Ford Foundation, 18.

29. James T. Fawcett, ed. 1972. *The Satisfactions and Cost of Children: Theories, Concepts and Methods*, Honolulu, HI: East-West Population Institute; Rudolf A. Bulatao. 1979. *On the Nature of the Transition in the Value of Children*, East-West Population Institute Paper No. 60-A, Honolulu, HI: East-West Population Institute; and Gisela Trommsdorff and Bernhard Nauck. 2010. "Introduction to Special Section for Journal of Cross-Cultural Psychology: Value of Children: A Concept for Better Understanding Cross-Cultural Variations in Fertility Behavior and Intergenerational Relationships." *Journal of Cross-Cultural Psychology*, 41: 637–651.

30. Arland Thornton. 2005. *Reading History Sideways: The Fallacy and Enduring Impact of the Developmental Paradigm on Family Life*, Chicago: University of Chicago Press. Much of this discussion is based on a presentation by Arland Thornton at the

50th Reunion of the Population Studies Center, Ann Arbor, Michigan, on October 22, 2011.

31. Arland Thornton, Georgina Binstock, Kathryn M. Yount, Mohammad Jamal Abasi-Shavazi, Dirgha Ghimire, and Yu Xie. 2012. "International Fertility Change: New Data and Insights from the Developmental Idealism Framework," *Demography*, 49: 677–698.

32. Samuel P. Huntington. 1993. "The Clash of Civilizations?" *Foreign Affairs*, 72: 22–49.

33. *New York Times*. 2006. "Suspected Taliban Rebels Behead an Afghan Teacher," January 4; and Reuters. 2012. "Islamist Militants in Mali Continue to Destroy Shrines," *New York Times*, July 1.

34. John C. Caldwell. 1978. "A Theory of Fertility: From High Plateau to Destabilization," *Population and Development Review*, 4: 553.

35. Ron Lesthaeghe and Chris Wilson. 1986. "Modes of Production, Secularization, and the Pace of the Fertility Decline in Western Europe, 1870–1930," in *The Decline of Fertility in Europe*, ed. Ansley J. Coale and Susan Cotts Watkins, Princeton, NJ: Princeton University Press, 261–292.

36. John C. Caldwell, P. H. Reddy, and Pat Caldwell. 1984. "The Determinants of Family Structure in Rural South India," *Journal of Marriage and Family*, 46: 215–229; John C. Caldwell and Pat Caldwell. 1987. "The Cultural Context of High Fertility in Sub-Saharan Africa," *Population and Development Review*, 13: 409–437; and Eleanor Preston-Whyte. 1988. "Culture, Context and Behaviour: Anthropological Perspectives on Fertility in Southern Africa," *Southern African Journal of Demography*, 2: 13–23.

37. Saritha Ray. 2005. "New Start for Young Indian Families," *New York Times*, December 26.

38. Etienne van de Walle. 1992. "Fertility Transition, Conscious Choice, and Numeracy," *Demography*, 29: 487–502.

39. Donald F. Heisel. 1968. "Attitudes and Practice of Contraception in Kenya," *Demography*, 5: 632–641; and Donald Heisel, personal conversation, July 1971.

40. Ronald Freedman, Albert I. Hermalin, and Ming-Cheng Cheng. 1975. "Do Statements about Desired Family Size Predict Fertility? The Case of Taiwan, 1967–1970," *Demography*, 12: 407–416.

41. John Knodel and Visid Prachuabmoh. 1973. "Desired Family Size in Thailand: Are the Responses Meaningful?" *Demography*, 10: 619–637.

42. Ronald Freedman and John Takeshita. 1969. *Family Planning in Taiwan*, Princeton, NJ: Princeton University Press.

43. Nan Lin and Ralph Hingson. 1974. "Diffusion of Family Planning Innovations: Theoretical and Practical Issues," *Studies in Family Planning*, 5: 189–194; Thomas W. Valente. 1996. "Social Network Thresholds in the Diffusion of Innovations," *Social Networks*, 18: 69–89; and Marlene E. Burkhardt and Daniel J. Brass. 1990. "Changing Patterns or Patterns of Change: The Effects of a Change in Technology on Social Network Structure and Power," *Administrative Science Quarterly*, 35: 104–127.

44. Robert G. Potter, Jr. 1969. "Estimating Births Averted in a Family Planning Program," in *Fertility and Family Planning: A World View*, ed. S. J. Behrman, Leslie Corsa, Jr., and Ronald Freedman, Ann Arbor: University of Michigan Press, 413–434.

45. Ronald Freedman and Bernard Berelson. 1976. "The Record of Family Planning Programs," *Studies in Family Planning*, 7: 1–40.

46. Karen O. Mason. 1984. *The Status of Women: A Review of Its Relationships to Fertility and Mortality*, New York: Rockefeller Foundation; Mary Beth Weinberger. 1987. "The Relationship between Women's Education and Fertility: Selected Findings from the World Fertility Surveys," *International Family Planning Perspectives*, 13: 35–46; Kristi McClamroch. 1996. "Total Fertility Rate, Women's Education, and Women's Work: What Are the Relationships?" *Population and Environment*, 18: 175–186; and Susan Hill Cochrane. 1979. *Fertility and Education: What Do We Really Know?* World Bank Staff Occasional Paper No. 26, Washington, DC: International Bank for Reconstruction and Development.

47. Teresa Castro Martin. 1995. "Women's Education and Fertility: Results from 26 Demographic and Health Surveys," *Studies in Family Planning*, 26: 187–202. Data are not shown for women in Mali with 10 or more years of schooling because of the small number of cases in that category in the survey.

48. Female education data from UNESCO, Institute of Statistics. n.d. http://stats.uis .unesco.org/unesco/TableViewer/tableView .aspx?ReportId=182 (accessed April 3, 2012). Contraceptive use data from United Nations. 2011. *World Contraceptive Use 2010*. New York: United Nations, http://www.un.org/esa /population/publications/wcu2010/Main.html (accessed April 3, 2012).

49. Gigi Santow. 1995. "Coitus Interruptus and the Control of Natural Fertility," *Population Studies*, 49: 19–43.

50. Data in Figures 9.9 through 9.11 are from United Nations. 2011. *World Contraceptive Use 2010*, New York: United Nations, http://www.un.org/esa /population/publications/wcu2010/Main.html (accessed December 23, 2011).

51. John B. Casterline and Steven W. Sinding. 2000. "Unmet Need for Family Planning in Developing Countries and Implications for Population Policy," *Population and Development Review*, 26: 691–723.

52. Digest. 1986. "Clinic Staff's Insensitive Attitudes Deter Low-Caste Nepalese Women from Practicing Family Planning," *International Family Planning Perspectives*, 12: 31.

53. Dudley Kirk and Bernard Pillet. 1998. "Fertility Levels, Trends, and Differentials in Sub-Saharan Africa in the 1980s and 1990s," *Studies in Family Planning*, 29: 1–22; and John C. Caldwell and Pat Caldwell. 1988. "Is the Asian Family Planning Program Model Suited to Africa?" *Studies in Family Planning*, 19: 19–28.

54. Charles F. Westoff. 2006. *New Estimates of Unmet Need and the Demand for Family Planning*, DHS Comparative Reports No. 14, December, Calverton, MD: Macro International, http://www.measuredhs.com/pubs/pdf/CR14/CR14.pdf (accessed July 2, 2012).

55. Gbolahan A. Oni and James McCarthy. 1986. "Use of Contraceptives for Birth Spacing in a Nigerian City," *Studies in Family Planning*, 17: 165–171.

56. Gilda Sedgh, Rubina Hussein, Akinrinola Bankole, and Susheela Singh. 2007. *Women with an Unmet Need for Contraception in Developing Countries and Their Reasons for Not Using a Method*, Occasional Report No, 37, June, New York: Guttmacher Institute, http://www.guttmacher.org/pubs/2007/07/09/or37.pdf (accessed July 2, 2012). The distribution of reasons has been adjusted to sum to 100.

57. Howard C. Taylor and Robert J. Lapham. 1974. "A Program for Family Planning Based on Maternal/Child Health Services," *Studies in Family Planning*, 5: 71–82.

58. Howard C. Taylor and Bernard Berelson. 1970. "Maternity Care and Family Planning as a World Program," in *Post-partum Family Planning: Report on the International Program*, ed. Gerald I. Zatuchni, New York: McGraw Hill, 385–399; and Sarah L. Barber. 2007. "Family Planning Advice and Postpartum Contraceptive Use among Low-Income Women in Mexico," *International Family Planning Perspectives*, 33: 6–12.

59. World Health Organization (WHO) Reproductive Health Library (RHL). 2012. *Immediate Postpartum Insertion for Intrauterine Devices*, http://apps.who.int/rhl/fertility/contraception/cd003036_muthalrathorea_com/en/index.html (accessed July 4, 2012).

60. Pharmacia & Upjohn. 1999. *Physician Information: Depo-Provera Contraceptive Injection*, http://www.whale.to/vaccine/depo-doctors.pdf (accessed July 4, 2012).

61. Paul Demeny. 2003. *Population Policy: A Concise Summary*, Policy Division Working Paper No. 173, New York: Population Council, http://www.popcouncil.org/pdfs/wp/173.pdf (accessed April 5, 2012).

62. Irit Sinai, Rebecka Lundgren, Marcos Arévalo, and Victoria Jennings. 2006. "Fertility Awareness-Based Methods of Family Planning: Predictors of Correct Use," *International Family Planning Perspectives*, 32: 94–100.

63. Terence H. Hull and Ann Larson. 1987. "Dynamic Disequilibrium: Demographic Policies and Trends in Asia," *Asian-Pacific Economic Literature*, 1: 25–59; Ledivina V. Carino. 1995. "Population Policy in the Philippines," *Philippine Journal of Public Administration*, 39: 88–112; Alejandro N. Herrin. 2007. "Development of the Philippines' Family Planning Program: The Early Years, 1967–80," in *The Global Family Planning Revolution: Three Decades of Population Policies and Programs*, ed. Warren C. Robinson and John A. Ross, Washington, DC: World Bank, http://siteresources.worldbank.org/INTPRH/Resources/GlobalFamilyPlanningRevolution.pdf (accessed July 6, 2012).

64. P. Poppe and L. M. Aller Atucha. 1992. *Integrated Project and IEC Materials in Guatemala and Mexico and Their Dissemination throughout the Region*, Evaluation Report RLA/88/P14, Tokyo: JOICFP.

65. Reuben Hill, J. Mayone Stycos, and Kurt W. Back. 1959. *The Family and Population Control: A Puerto Rican Experiment in Social Change*, Chapel Hill: University of North Carolina Press.

66. Carol E. Kaufman. 2000. "Reproductive Control in Apartheid South Africa," *Population Studies*, 54: 105–114.

67. *New York Times*. 2012. "How Morning-After Pills Really Work," June 28.

68. Linda Gordon. 1973. "Voluntary Motherhood: The Beginnings of Feminist Birth Control Ideas in the United States," *Feminist Studies*, 1: 5–22.

69. Margaret Sanger. 1922. *The Pivot of Civilization*, New York: Brentano's, 177.

70. Linda Gordon. 1976. *Woman's Body, Woman's Right: Birth Control in America*, New York: Grossman; Thomas C. Leonard. 2005. "Eugenics and Economics in the Progressive Era," *Journal of Economic Perspectives*, 19: 207–224; and Donald T. Critchlow. 1995. "Birth Control, Population Control, and Family Planning: An Overview," *Journal of Policy History*, 7: 1–20.

71. United Nations Population Division. 2010. *World Population Policies 2009*, New York: United Nations, http://www.un.org/esa/population/publications/wpp2009/wpp2009.htm (accessed June 12, 2011).

72. World Bank. 2011. *Gross National Income per Capita 2010, Atlas Method and PPP*, http://siteresources.worldbank.org/DATASTATISTICS/Resources/GNIPC.pdf (accessed June 9, 2012).

73. Susan Greenhalgh. 1996. "The Social Construction of Population Science: An Intellectual,

Institutional, and Policy History of Twentieth-Century Demography," *Comparative Studies in Society and History*, 38: 26–66.

74. Bernard Berelson. 1969. "Beyond Family Planning," *Studies in Family Planning*, 1: 1–16; and Daniel Callahan. 1972. "Ethics and Population Limitation," *Science*, 175: 487–494.

75. Bernard Berelson and Jonathan Lieberson. 1979. "Government Efforts to Influence Fertility: The Ethical Issues," *Population and Development Review*, 5: 581–613, quote from 582.

76. Rosanna Ledbetter. 1984. "Thirty Years of Family Planning in India," *Asian Survey*, 24: 736–758; J. John Palen. 1986. "Fertility and Eugenics: Singapore's Population Policies," *Population Research and Policy Review*, 5: 3–14; and Penny Kane and Ching Y. Choi. 1999. "China's One Child Family Policy," *British Medical Journal*, 319: 992–994.

77. Sandra D. Lane. 1994. "From Population Control to Reproductive Health: An Emerging Policy Agenda," *Social Science & Medicine*, 39: 1303–1314; and Seamus Grimes. 1998. "From Population Control to 'Reproductive Rights': Ideological Influences in Population Policy," *Third World Quarterly*, 19: 375–393.

78. The Linkages website, *United Nations International Conference on Population and Development (ICPD) 5–13 September 1994, Cairo, Egypt*, contains extensive background material about the 1994 ICPD; see http://www.iisd.ca/cairo.html (accessed June 9, 2012). The full report from the conference appears as United Nations. 1995. *Report of the International Conference on Population and Development, Cairo, 5–13 September 1994*, New York: United Nations, http://www.unfpa.org/public/publications/pid/1973 (accessed June 9, 2012).

79. C. Alison McIntosh and Jason L. Finkle. 1995. "The Cairo Conference on Population and Development: A New Paradigm?" *Population and Development Review*, 21: 223–260; and Jason L. Finkle and Alison McIntosh. 1996. "Cairo Revisited: Some Thoughts on the Implications of the ICPD," *Health Transition Review*, 6: 110–113.

80. Steven W. Sinding. 2007. "Overview and Perspective," in *The Global Family Planning Revolution: Three Decades of Population Policies and Programs*, ed. Warren C. Robinson and John A. Ross, Washington, DC: World Bank, http://siteresources.worldbank.org/INTPRH/Resources/GlobalFamilyPlanningRevolution.pdf (accessed July 6, 2012).

81. Lant H. Pritchett. 1994. "Desired Fertility and the Impact of Population Policies," *Population and Development Review*, 20: 1–55.

82. John Bongaarts and Steven W. Sinding. 2009. "A Response to Critics of Family Planning Programs," *International Perspectives on Sexual and Reproductive Health*, 35: 39–44; and John Bongaarts. 2011. "Can Family Planning Programs Reduce High Desired Family Size in Sub-Saharan Africa?" *International Perspectives on Sexual and Reproductive Health*, 37: 209–216.

83. Donella Meadows. 1994. *Is Development the Best Contraceptive—or Are Contraceptives?* Donella Meadows Archive, http://www.sustainer.org/dhm_archive/index.php?display_article=vn543famplanninged (accessed July 4, 2012).

84. James T. Fawcett. 1979. "Singapore's Population Policies in Perspective," in *Public Policy and Population Change in Singapore*, ed. P. Chen and J Fawcett, New York: Population Council, 3–17; and James T. Fawcett and Siew-Ean Khoo. 1980. "Singapore: Rapid Fertility Transition in a Compact Society," *Population and Development Review*, 6: 549–579.

85. Sharon M. Lee, Gabriel Alvarez, and J. John Palen. 1991. "Fertility Decline and Pronatalist Policy in Singapore," *International Family Planning Perspectives*, 17: 65–69, 73; S-H. Saw. 1985. "New Population Policies for More Balanced Procreation," *Contemporary Southeast Asia*, 17: 2; Paul Cheung. 1988, "Singapore," in *Comparative Study of Population Policies in Asia—Focus on Eight Asian Countries*, Tokyo: Asian Population and Development Association, 155–160; L. T. Lyons-Lee. 1998. *The 'Graduate Woman' Phenomenon: Changing Constructions of the Family in Singapore*, University of Wollongong, http://ro.uow.edu.au/artspapers/96 (accessed June 25, 2011); and Theresa Wong and Brenda S. A. Yeoh. 2003. *Fertility and the Family: An Overview of Pro-natalist Population Policies in Singapore*, Asian MetaCentre Research Paper No. 12, Singapore: Asia Research Institute, National University of Singapore, http://www.populationasia.org/Publications/ResearchPaper/AMCRP12.pdf (accessed June 25, 2011).

86. Saw Swee-Hock. 2012. *The Population of Singapore*, 3rd ed., Singapore: Institute of Southeast Asian Studies, 209–251.

87. The data on marriage in this section are from United Nations. 2009. *World Marriage Data 2008*, http://www.un.org/esa/population/publications/WMD2008/Main.html (accessed June 14, 2012).

88. The discussion of China's fertility limitation program is based on John Bongaarts and Susan Greenhalgh. 1985. "An Alternative to the One-Child Policy in China," *Population and Development Review*, 11: 585–617; Judith Banister. 1984. "Population Policy and Trends in China, 1978–83," *The China Quarterly*, 100: 717–741; K. Basu. 2009. "China and India: Idiosyncratic Paths to High

Growth," *Economic and Political Weekly*, 44: 43–56; Amitrejeet A. Barabyal. 2004. "Desirable Properties of an Unconventional Population Control Policy," *Canadian Journal of Regional Science*, 27: 273–22; Susan Greenhalgh. 1994. "Controlling Births and Bodies in Village China," *American Ethnologist*, 21: 3–30; Jiali Li. 1995. "China's One-Child Policy: How and How Well Has it Worked? A Case Study of Hebei Province, 1979–88," *Population and Development Review*, 21: 563–585; and H. Yuan Tien. 1983. "Age at Marriage in the People's Republic of China," *The China Quarterly*, 93: 90–107.

89. Sina. 2007. "Family Planning Commission Spokesman: More than 11% of the Population May Have Two Children (in Chinese)", *Sina*, July 10, http://news.sina.com.cn/c/2007-07-10/154513416121.shtml (accessed November 23, 2013); Chinese People's Daily. 2011. "China's Most Populous Province Amends Family-Planning Policy," *People's Daily Online*, November 25, http://english.peopledaily.com.cn/90882/7657026.html (accessed November 23, 2013); and Jonathan Kaiman. 2013. "China's One-Child Policy to be Relaxed as Part of Reforms Package," *The Guardian*, November 15, http://www.theguardian.com/world/2013/nov/15/china-one-child-policy-relaxed-reforms (accessed November 23, 2013).

90. The discussion of family planning programs in India is based on the following sources: Rosanna Ledbetter. 1984. "Thirty Years of Family Planning in India," *Asian Survey*, 24: 736–758; K. Srinivasan. 1995. *Regulating Reproduction in India's Population*, New Delhi: Sage; Davidson R. Gwatkin. 1979. "Political Will and Family Planning: The Implications of India's Emergency Experience," *Population and Development Review*, 5: 29–59; and Harry W. Blair. 1980. "Mrs Gandhi's Emergency, The Indian Elections of 1977, Pluralism and Marxism: Problems with Paradigms," *Modern Asian Studies*, 14: 237–271.

91. John Hajnal. 1953. "Age at Marriage and Proportions Marrying," *Population Studies*, 7: 111–136.

92. Stephen Ndegwa, Pamela Onduso, and Linda Casey. 2008. *Reproductive Health and Family Planning in Kenya: The Pathfinder International Experience*, Pathfinder International, http://www.pathfind.org/site/DocServer/RH_and_FP_in_Kenya__the_Pathfinder_Experience_2008.pdf?docID=13081 (accessed April 6, 2012); African Institute for Development Policy Website. 2011. *Kenya Moves to Revitalize Its Family Planning and Population Program*, http://www.afidep.org/2011/02/kenya-moves-to-revitalize-its-family-planning-and-population-program/ (accessed April 6, 2012); Robert A. Miller, Lewis Ndhlovu, Margaret M. Gachara, and

Andrew A. Fisher. 1991. "The Situation Analysis Study of the Family Planning Program in Kenya," *Studies in Family Planning*, 22: 131–143; John C. Caldwell and Pat Caldwell. 2002. "Africa: The New Family Planning Frontier," *Studies in Family Planning*, 33: 76–86; John Cleland, Stan Bernstein, Alex Ezeh, Anibal Faundes, Anna Glasier, and Jolene Innis. 2006. "Family Planning: The Unfinished Agenda," *The Lancet*, 368: 1810–1827; Ann Duerr, Stacey Hurst, Atena P. Kouris, Naomi Rutenberg, and Denise J. Jamieson. 2005. "Integrating Family Planning and Prevention of Mother-to-Child HIV Transmission in Resource-Limited Settings," *The Lancet*, 366: 261–263; Odile Frank and Geoffrey McNicoll. 1987. "An Interpretation of Fertility and Population Policy in Kenya," *Population and Development Review*, 13: 209–243; Warren C. Robinson. 1992. "Kenya Enters the Fertility Transition," *Population Studies*, 46: 445–457; Thomas E. Dow, Jr., Linda Archer, Shansiya Khasiani, and John Kekovole. 1994. "Wealth Flow and Fertility Decline in Rural Kenya, 1981–92," *Population and Development Review*, 20: 343–364; John Blacker, Collins Opiyo, Momodou Jasseh, Andy Sloggett, and John Ssekamatte-Ssebuliba. 2005. "Fertility in Kenya and Uganda: A Comparative Study of Trends and Determinants," *Population Studies*, 59: 355–373; and Joanna Crichton. 2008. "Changing Fortunes: Analysis of Fluctuating Policy Space for Family Planning in Kenya," *Health Policy and Planning*, 23: 339–350.

93. National Population Commission Nigeria and ICF Macro. 2009. *Nigeria Demographic and Health Survey, 2008*, Abuja, Nigeria: National Population Commission and ICF Macro, http://www.measuredhs.com/publications/publication-FR222-DHS-Final-Reports.cfm (accessed May 6, 2012); Muyiwa Oladosu. 2002. "Prospects for Fertility Decline in Nigeria: Comparative Analysis of the 1990 and 1999 Nigeria Demographic and Health Survey Data," *Prospects for Fertility Decline in High Fertility Countries, Population Bulletin of the United Nations*, (Special Issue 46/47): 223–237; and Kenya National Bureau of Statistics (KNBS) and ICF Macro. 2010. *Kenya Demographic and Health Survey 2008–09*, Calverton, MD: KNBS and ICF Macro, http://www.measuredhs.com/pubs/pdf/fr229/fr229.pdf (accessed May 6, 2012).

94. Warren C. Robinson. 1992. "Kenya Enters the Fertility Transition," *Population Studies*, 46: 445–457; and UN 2009 contraceptive prevalence.

95. Monica Akinyi Magadi and Alfred O. Agwanda. 2010. "Investigating the Association between HIV/AIDS and Recent Fertility Patterns in Kenya," *Social Science & Medicine*, 71: 335–344.

96. United Nations. 2011. *World Contraceptive Use 2010*, http://www.un.org/esa/population/publications/wcu2010/Main.html (accessed June 10, 2012).

97. Gilda Sedgh, Rubina Hussein, Akinrinola Bankole, and Susheela Singh. 2007. *Women with an Unmet Need for Contraception in Developing Countries and Their Reasons for Not Using a Method*, June, Occasional Report No. 37, New York: Guttmacher Institute, http://www.guttmacher.org/pubs/2007/07/09/or37.pdf (accessed July 2, 2012).

98. Francisco Alba and Joseph E. Potter. 1986. "Population and Development in Mexico since 1940: An Interpretation," *Population and Development Review*, 12: 47–75; and Ansley J. Coale. 1978. "Population Growth and Economic Development: The Case of Mexico," *Foreign Affairs*, 56: 415–429.

99. Ali Kouaouci. 1993. "Fertility in Algeria between 1970 and 1986: Trends and Factors," *Population: An English Selection*, 5: 21–42; and Ali Kouaouci. 1994. "Study of Contraceptive Practice in Algeria, 1967–87," *Population: An English Selection*, 6: 1–22.

100. Keith Sutton. 1999. "Demographic Transition in the Maghreb," *Geography*, 84: 111–118; Dominique Tabutin, Bruno Schoumaker, Godfrey Rogers, Jonathan Mandelbaum, and Catriona Dutreuilh. 2005. "The Demography of the Arab World and the Middle East from the 1950s to the 2000s. A Survey of Changes and a Statistical Assessment," *Population (English Edition, 2002–)*, 60: 505–591, 593–615.

101. Wikipedia. 2014. "Scarborough Fair (ballad)," http://en.wikipedia.org/wiki/Scarborough_Fair_(ballad) (accessed February 15, 2014).

102. J. M. Riddle. 1992. *Contraception and Abortion from the Ancient World to the Renaissance*, Cambridge, MA: Harvard University Press; J. M. Riddle. 1997. *Eve's Herbs: A History of Contraception and Abortion in the West*. Cambridge, MA: Harvard University Press; THLady Maimuna al-Bukhariyya. 2009. "Parsley, Sage, Rosemary and Thyme: An Historical Examination of Birth Control Methods from the Medieval and Renaissance Periods," www.florilegium.org/files/PERSONAL/Birth-Control-art.rf (accessed July 18, 2011).

103. Gary Granzberg. 1973. "Twin Infanticide: A Cross-Cultural Test of a Materialistic Explanation," *Ethos*, 1: 405–412; and Helen L. Ball and Catherine M. Hill. 1996. "Reevaluating 'Twin Infanticide'," *Current Anthropology*, 37: 856–863.

104. Leigh Minturn and Jerry Stashak. 1982. "Infanticide as a Terminal Abortion Procedure," *Cross-Cultural Research*, 17: 70–90.

105. William L. Langer. 1974. "Infanticide: A Historical Survey," *History of Childhood Quarterly*, 1: 353–365.

106. Nancy Scheper-Hughes. 1989. "Death without Weeping," *Natural History*, October: 8–16.

107. Grant McCracken. 1983. "The Exchange of Children in Tudor England: An Anthropological Phenomenon in Historical Context," *Journal of Family History*, 8: 303–313; Edmund S. Morgan. 1966. *The Puritan Family*, New York: Harper & Row; Uche C. Isiugo-Abanihe. 1985. "Child Fosterage in West Africa," *Population and Development Review*, 11: 53–73; Caroline Bledsoe. 1990. "'No Success without Struggle': Social Mobility and Hardship for Foster Children in Sierra Leone," *Man*, 25: 70–88; Dorte Thorsen. 2012. *Children Begging for Quranic School Masters*, UNICEF Briefing Paper No. 5, April, http://www.unicef.org/wcaro/english/Briefing_paper_No_5_-_children_begging_for_Quranic_school_masters.pdf (accessed October 6, 2012); and Barbara A. Anderson and Heston E. Phillips. 2006. *Trends in the Percent of Children Who Are Orphans in South Africa: 1995–2005*, Pretoria: Statistics South Africa.

108. Thomas C. Smith. 1977. *Nakahara: Family Farming and Population in a Japanese Village, 1717–1830*, Stanford, CA: Stanford University Press.

109. U.S. Department of Health and Human Services. 2010. "Infant Safe Haven Laws: Summary of State Laws," http://www.childwelfare.gov/systemwide/laws_policies/statutes/safehaven.cfm (accessed June 23, 2011).

110. Richard Trexler. 1973. "The Foundlings of Florence," *History of Childhood Quarterly*, 1: 78–85.

111. Henry P. David. 1992. "Born Unwanted: Long-Term Developmental Effects of Denied Abortion," *Journal of Social Issues*, 48: 163–181.

112. Charles F. Westoff, Robert G. Potter, Jr., and Philip C. Sagi. 1963. *The Third Child: A Study in the Prediction of Fertility*. Princeton, NJ: Princeton University Press.

113. John C. Caldwell, P. H. Reddy, and Pat Caldwell. 1988. *The Causes of Demographic Change: Experimental Research in South India*, Madison: University of Wisconsin Press, esp. 190–195.

114. Kyu-taik Sung. 1995. "Measures and Dimensions of Filial Piety in Korea," *The Gerontologist*, 35: 240–247.

115. Roger L. Janelli and Dawnhee Yim Janelli. 1982. *Ancestor Worship and Korean Society*, Stanford, CA: Stanford University Press.

116. Irene B. Taeuber. 1958. *The Population of Japan*, Princeton, NJ: Princeton University Press, 278–280.

117. Christophe Z. Guilmoto. 2009. "The Sex Ratio Transition in Asia," *Population and Development Review*, 35: 519–549.

118. Gunther Mielke, Ludwig Kiesel, Claudia Backsch, Winfried Erz, and Markus Gonser. 1998. "Fetal Sex Determination by High Resolution Ultrasound in Early Pregnancy," *European Journal of Ultrasound*, 7: 109–114.

119. Data for China in Figures 9.27 and 8.28 are from Shuzuo Li. 2007. "Imbalanced Sex Ratio at Birth and Comprehensive Intervention in China," paper presented at the 4th Asia Pacific Conference on Reproductive and Sexual Health and Rights, Hyderabad, India, October 29–31, http://www .unfpa.org/gender/docs/studies/china.pdf (accessed July 6, 2011); and Gu Bao Chang and Li Yong Ping. 1996. "Sex Ratio at Birth and Son Preference in China," in Korean Institute for Health and Social Affairs (KIHASA), *Sex Preference for Children and Gender Discrimination in Asia*, Seoul: KIHASA, 43–70. Data for Korea in Figures 9.27 and 9.29 for 1980 from Nam-Hoon Cho and Moon-Sik Hong. 1996. "Effects of Induced Abortion and Son Preference on Korea's Imbalanced Sex Ratio at Birth in China," in KIHASA, *Sex Preference for Children and Gender Discrimination in Asia*, Seoul: KIHASA, 90–112. Data for 1981–2009 from Korean Statistical Information Service, http://kosis.kr/abroad /abroad_01List.jsp (accessed July 6, 2011).

120. D. Trichopoulos, N. Handanos, J. Danezis, Anna Kalandidi, and Victoria Kalapothaki. 1976. "Induced Abortion and Secondary Sterility," *BJOG: An International Journal of Obstetrics & Gynaecology*, 83: 645– 650; Barbara A. Anderson and Jinyun Liu. 1997. "Son Preference and Excess Female Infant Mortality among Koreans and non-Koreans in Yanbian Prefecture, Jilin Province, China, with Implications for the Republic of Korea," in *Population Process and Dynamics for Koreans in Korea and China*, ed. Doo-Sub Kim and Barbara A. Anderson, Seoul: Hanyang University Press, 189–243.

121. Taek Il Kim and John A. Ross. 2007. "The Korean Breakthrough," in *The Global Family Planning Revolution: Three Decades of Population Policies and Programs*, ed. Warren C. Robinson and John A. Ross, Washington, DC: World Bank, http://siteresources.worldbank.org/INTPRH /Resources/GlobalFamilyPlanningRevolution .pdf (accessed July 6, 2012).

122. Woojin Chung and Monica Das Gupta. 2007. "The Decline of Son Preference in South Korea: The Roles of Development and Public Policy," *Population and Development Review*, 33: 757–783; Monica Das Gupta, Jiang Zhenghua, Li Bohua, Xie Zhenming, Woojin Chung, and Bae Hwa-Ok. 2003. "Why Is Son Preference So Persistent in East and South Asia? A Cross-Country Study of China, India and the Republic of Korea," *Journal of Development Studies*, 40: 153–187; and Monica Das Gupta, Sunhwa Lee, Patricia Uberoi, Danning Wang, and Xiaodan Zhang. 2004. "State Policies and Women's Agency in China, the Republic of Korea and India 1950–2000: Lessons from Contrasting Experiences," in *Culture and Public Action: A Cross-Disciplinary Dialogue on Development Policy*, ed. V. Rao and M. Walton, Stanford, CA: Stanford University Press, 234–259.

123. Shuzhuo Li. 2007. "Imbalanced Sex Ratio at Birth and Comprehensive Intervention in China," paper presented at the 4th Asia Pacific Conference on Reproductive and Sexual Health and Rights, October 29–31, Hyderabad, India, http://www.unfpa.org/gender/docs/studies /china.pdf (accessed July 3, 2011); Therese Hesketh and Zhu Wei Xing. 2006. "Abnormal Sex Ratios in Human Populations: Causes and Consequences," *Proceedings of the National Academy of Sciences (PNAS)*, 103: 13271–13275, http://www.pnas.org/content/103/36/13271. full.pdf+html (accessed July 3, 2011); and Monica Das Gupta, Woojin Chung, and Li Shuzhuo. 2009. "Evidence for an Incipient Decline in Numbers of Missing Girls in China and India," *Population and Development Review*, 35: 401–416.

124. Prabhat Jha, Maya A. Kesler, Rajesh Kumar, Faujdar Ram, Usha Ram, Lukasz Aleksandrowicz, Diego G Bassani, Shailaja Chandra, and Jayant K. Banthia. 2011. "Trends in Selective Abortions of Girls in India: Analysis of Nationally Representative Birth Histories from 1990 to 2005 and Census Data from 1991 to 2011," *The Lancet*, 377: 1921–1928.

CHAPTER 10

FERTILITY IN THE MORE DEVELOPED REGION

LEARNING OBJECTIVES

- Describe the similarities and differences in abortion policies in the LDR and in the MDR.

- Discuss change and stability in the views of Americans about abortion since the 1960s.

- List the main proposed reasons for below-replacement fertility in many more developed countries since 1990.

- Explain why some researchers think that the status of women is strongly related to fertility in high-income countries.

- Describe the relation of changes in fertility, female labor force participation, and availability of child care in the United States since the 1960s.

((Listen to the Chapter Audio

OVERVIEW

In more developed countries, almost all women have access to very effective means to limit their fertility. In this situation, intentions to have children and judgments about whether the woman or the couple consider the present to be a good time to have a child or whether they should wait become very important. Fertility has been related to a nexus of changes in female labor force participation, access to nonfamily child care, changing sex roles, and changes in views of cohabitation and marriage. This has sometimes resulted in substantially below-replacement fertility.

CONTRACEPTIVE USE AND ABORTION IN MORE DEVELOPED COUNTRIES

In most developed countries, the vast majority of women think that contraception is morally acceptable. Even though the Catholic Church officially opposes the use of artificial birth control, increasingly, this official view is not reflected in the behavior of Catholic women. Analysis of National Survey of Family Growth data for 1965–1988 for currently married White Protestant and Catholic women in the United States found that in 1965 and 1973, the Protestant women were significantly more likely than the Catholic women to be using contraception

(72% vs. 67% in 1973). However, in 1982 and 1988, there was no significant difference between Protestant and Catholic women (77% vs. 75% in 1988).[1] Data from the 2006–2008 National Survey of Family Growth showed that among all American women who had ever had sexual intercourse, 99% have used a contraceptive method, and 98% of Catholic women who had ever had sexual intercourse had used contraception. Among sexually active women who were not pregnant, had not just had a baby, and did not want to get pregnant right away, 89% both of all women and of Catholic women were using contraception. Thirty-one percent both of all American women and of Catholic women used birth control pills or another hormonal contraceptive. Only 1% of all women and 2% of Catholic women were using natural family planning.[2] We also saw in Figure 9.9 that 72% of women aged 15–49 in the MDR in 2009 who were in a marriage or other union used a contraceptive method. Thus, among women in the MDR as a whole and in the United States specifically, the vast majority of women at risk of pregnancy used contraception. Gallup Poll results from 2012 also showed that 82% of Catholics and 90% of non-Catholics thought that use of contraception was morally acceptable.[3] Thus, in the United States, the contraceptive attitudes and behavior of Catholics have come to differ little from those of all Americans.

Abortion is a different issue. As we will see, people in all countries, including the United States, differentiate strongly among the situations in which they think abortion should be legal. However, even though the Catholic Church opposes abortion more strongly than birth control, there is little difference in the United States between Catholic and non-Catholic views of whether abortion is morally acceptable. A 2009 Gallup poll found that 40% of Catholics and 41% of non-Catholics thought that abortion was morally acceptable. However, only 24% of Catholics who attended church weekly or almost weekly thought that abortion was morally acceptable.[4]

Next, we look at abortion policies across the world. Then we look in some detail at trends in abortion attitudes in the United States. After that, we look at patterns and trends in the use of induced abortion in the United States and some other countries.

Abortion Policies throughout the World

Since 1980, UN surveys have asked about the grounds on which abortion was legal in each country. The results for the MDR countries and for the LDR countries are shown in Figure 10.1.[5] Reasons directly

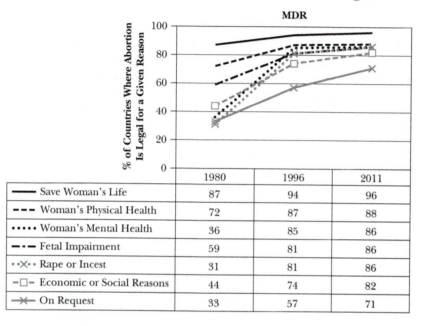

MDR	1980	1996	2011
——— Save Woman's Life	87	94	96
– – – Woman's Physical Health	72	87	88
••••• Woman's Mental Health	36	85	86
—•—• Fetal Impairment	59	81	86
••×•• Rape or Incest	31	81	86
–□– Economic or Social Reasons	44	74	82
—×— On Request	33	57	71

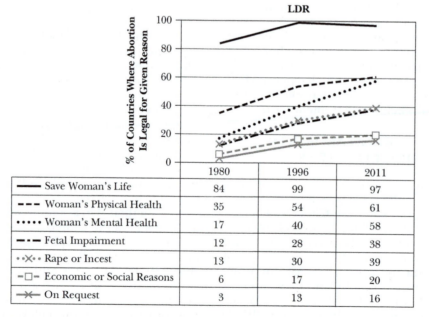

LDR	1980	1996	2011
——— Save Woman's Life	84	99	97
– – – Woman's Physical Health	35	54	61
••••• Woman's Mental Health	17	40	58
—•—• Fetal Impairment	12	28	38
••×•• Rape or Incest	13	30	39
–□– Economic or Social Reasons	6	17	20
—×— On Request	3	13	16

FIGURE 10.1 Percentage of Countries in the MDR and the LDR That Permit Abortion on Various Grounds: 1980, 1996, and 2011

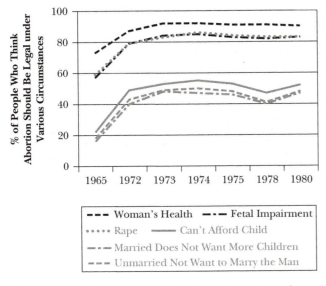

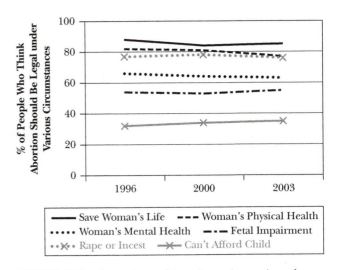

FIGURE 10.3   Percentage of Americans Approving of Abortion Being Legal under Various Circumstances, 1996–2003

FIGURE 10.2   Percentage of Americans Approving of Abortion Being Legal under Various Circumstances, 1965–1980

related to the health or the life of the mother or the fetus are shown in lines without markers, while reasons less closely related to the health or life of the mother or fetus are shown in lines with markers.

In almost all countries in both the LDR and the MDR, abortion has been legal to save a woman's life at least since 1980. All other reasons for an abortion have been legal in a smaller proportion of countries. As shown in Figure 10.1, while a woman's health approaches a woman's life as legal grounds for abortion in MDR countries, there is a large gap between the number of countries in which abortion is legal to protect the woman's life and *all* other reasons in LDR countries. In 1980, in both the MDR and the LDR, abortion was considerably less likely to be legal to protect a woman's mental health than her physical health, but by 2011, this distinction was relatively unimportant in both the MDR and the LDR. However, even in 2011, abortion to protect a woman's health (if her life was not in danger) was much more likely to be legal in the MDR than in the LDR.

MDR and LDR countries have very different laws about abortion due to fetal impairment. In the MDR, by 2011 fetal impairment was as likely to be legal grounds for abortion as the woman's mental health (86%). However, in the LDR in 2011, in only 38% of countries was fetal impairment legal grounds for abortion, while the woman's mental health was legal grounds in 58% of LDR countries.

The MDR and LDR countries also differ in whether the pregnancy being the result of rape or incest is grounds for abortion. In MDR countries by 2011, rape or incest is legal grounds for an abortion in as many countries as a woman's mental health (86%), while in LDR countries rape or incest is much

less likely to be grounds for abortion than a woman's mental health (39% versus 58%).

In MDR countries, there has been a large increase over time in the percentage of countries allowing abortion for economic or social reasons or on request (for any reason), reaching 82% for economic or social reasons and 71% on request by 2011. However, in LDR countries, in 2011 only 20% of countries allow abortion for economic or social reasons and 16% on request.

Reasons for Approval or Disapproval of Abortion in the United States

As elsewhere in the world, Americans have highly differentiated views about the conditions under which abortion should be legal. Figures 10.2, 10.3, and 10.4 show Americans' views of the conditions under which abortion should be legal at various dates. Note that completely consistent questions were not asked in

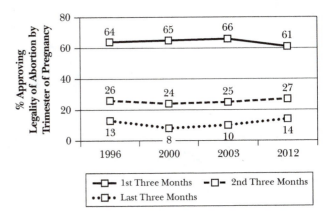

FIGURE 10.4   Percentage of Americans Approving of Abortion Being Legal by Trimester of Pregnancy, 1996–2012

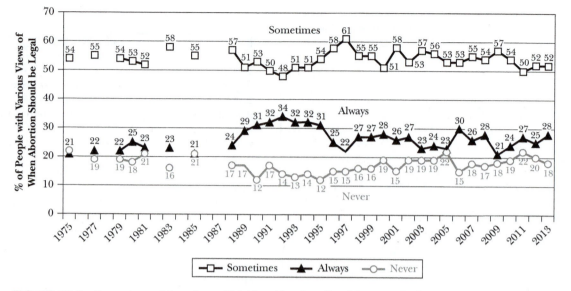

FIGURE 10.5 Percentage of Americans Thinking Abortion Should Be Legal Always, Sometimes, or Never, 1975–2013

large surveys in all years. Then, Figures 10.5 and 10.6 look at whether Americans more generally approved of abortion being legal.

Summarizing findings from surveys from 1975 to 2001, a Gallup poll analysis concluded that Americans were supportive of the legality of abortion:[6]

1. In the first trimester of pregnancy
2. When the health of the mother or of the baby is seriously at risk

Most Americans think that abortion should not be legal:

1. After the first trimester of pregnancy
2. When the reason for the abortion is a matter of choice, such as that the family cannot afford the child

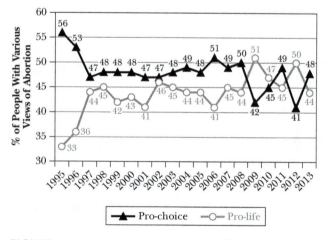

FIGURE 10.6 Percentage of Americans Characterizing Themselves as Pro-Choice or Pro-Life, 1995–2013

Figure 10.2 shows survey results from Americans who were asked questions about the conditions under which abortion should be legal in various years between 1965 and 1980. Recall that the *Roe v. Wade* decision that legalized abortion in the United States occurred in 1973.[7]

By 1972, shortly before the *Roe v. Wade* decision, Americans were more favorable to abortion being legal under every circumstance than they had been in 1965. Approval of abortion for various reasons increased between 1965 and the early 1970s and then remained fairly stable. However, at every survey date, Americans tended to favor the legality of abortion to protect the health of the mother, if the pregnancy was the result of rape, or if there was a strong chance the baby would have a serious defect. There was far less support of the legality of abortion if the reason for the abortion was that the family was poor, the mother wanted an abortion because she was unmarried, or the woman did not want any more children. Although Figure 10.1 refers to legality in countries and Figure 10.2 refers to the views of individuals, the results of the two analyses are generally consistent, with the U.S. survey respondents holding somewhat less accepting views about the legality of abortion than the laws in MDR countries but more accepting of the legality of abortion than the laws in LDR countries.

Figure 10.3 shows Americans' views on the legality of abortion in response to slightly different survey questions that were asked at various dates between 1996 and 2003.[8] The responses are amazingly stable over time. There is strong approval of abortion to save the woman's life, to protect the woman's physical health, or if the pregnancy is the result of rape or incest. Support for the legality of abortion falls if the reason is the woman's mental health and falls even more if there is a serious chance of fetal impairment. Less than 40% of respondents thought abortion should be legal if the reason for the abortion was that the woman or couple could not afford the child.

Figure 10.4 shows approval of the legality of abortion among Americans dependent on the trimester of pregnancy.[9] About two-thirds of Americans think abortion should be legal in the first trimester of the pregnancy, but this falls to one-fourth for the second trimester and about one-tenth in the third trimester.

Figure 10.5 shows Gallup Poll results on the percentage of Americans thinking abortion should be legal always, sometimes, or never. Since at least 1975, about 20% of Americans have thought abortion should always be legal, about 20% thought abortion should never be legal, but over 50% thought that abortion should be legal under some circumstances but not under other circumstances. These percentages have fluctuated over time, with an increase in the 1990s in the percentage who thought abortion should always be legal, after which the curves again approached each other and were almost equal (22–23%) in 2005. At every date, the percentage that thought abortion should sometimes be legal and sometimes not be legal vastly exceeded the percentage who either thought abortion should always be legal or who thought abortion should never be legal. The high percentage thinking abortion should sometimes be legal and sometimes not be legal is not surprising given the results in Figures 10.2, 10.3, and 10.4.[10]

After 1995, the Gallup Poll began to ask people to classify themselves as pro-choice or pro-life. People could refuse to choose one or the other, but the question was designed to try to force a choice. In 1995, 11% did not choose one of the two options, and in 2012, 9% did not choose one of the options.

Figure 10.6 shows the results of this poll for 1995–2013.[11] At most dates, the percentage characterizing themselves as pro-choice exceeded the percentage characterizing themselves as pro-life. In 2009, 2010, and 2012, this was reversed, with the percentage pro-life exceeding the percentage pro-choice, but in 2011 and 2013, the percentage pro-choice exceeded the percentage pro-life. In May 2009, after the Gallup Poll results appeared when the percentage declaring themselves pro-life exceeded the percentage declaring themselves pro-choice for the first time, there was speculation about whether this signaled a major shift in Americans' attitudes about abortion.[12] However, noting the substantial stability of the results in Figure 10.5 and noting the preponderance of respondents who thought abortion should "sometimes" be legal, it seems that the shifts in Figure 10.6 between those who are pro-choice and those who are pro-life

might be less important than they first appear to be, since the percentage in each group depends on how those who think abortion should sometimes be legal choose to interpret the question or classify themselves.

Saad looked further at the similarities and differences in the positions of Americans who characterized themselves as pro-choice or pro-life in 2011. Not surprisingly, in light of the results in Figures 10.3 and 10.4, members of both groups tend to agree that abortion should be legal when the woman's life or health is in danger or if the pregnancy is the result of rape or incest. They also tend to agree that abortion should be illegal after the first trimester. They disagree about whether abortion should be legal in the first trimester, when the family cannot afford to have the child, when the woman's mental health is endangered, or when the baby might be physically or mentally impaired.[13]

Despite the stability of abortion attitudes in the United States, there have been some clear trends by age. Based on Gallup Poll research, Figure 10.7 shows trends in the percentage of Americans by age who think that abortion should be legal under all circumstances. At every date, those aged 65+ were the least likely to agree that abortion should always be legal, and those aged 50–54 were usually the next most unlikely to agree that abortion should always be legal. However, there was no discernible difference in the attitudes of those aged 30–49 and of those aged 18–29. Also, in every age group, the percentage thinking abortion should always be legal increased until the early 1990s and then declined.[14]

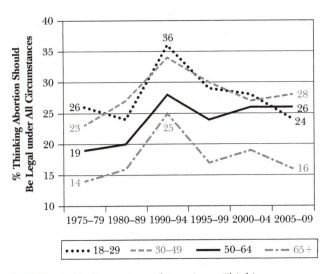

FIGURE 10.7 Percentage of Americans Thinking Abortion Should Be Legal under All Circumstances by Age, 1975–2009

Abortion Patterns and Reasons for Abortion throughout the World

The reasons why women have abortions tend to fall into three categories:

1. Abortion can be used as a way for unmarried women to avoid having a child before they are ready or when their situation for having a child is not good. This pattern has been common in the West, including the United States, where abortion is often used by young unmarried women who did not expect to become pregnant.
2. Abortion can be used as a backup to contraceptive failure. This can occur for women of all ages, whether married or unmarried, but is especially common among women who have already had all the children they want. Abortion as a backup for contraceptive failure has become more common in developed countries.
3. Abortion can be the major method of fertility regulation. This was common in Eastern Europe and the Soviet Union, where contraceptives were unavailable or irregularly available. This historical pattern of abortion as a first choice for fertility limitation seems to have contributed to continuing high levels of abortion in Eastern Europe.

Abortion Levels in 2003

There are two major indicators of the level of abortion in a society. One is the **abortion rate**, which is usually calculated as the number of abortions per 1,000 females aged 15–44. The other is the **abortion ratio**, which is the number of abortions per 100 live births. Sometimes, the percentage of all pregnancies that end in an abortion is also calculated. This measure is intended to take into account pregnancies that end in a miscarriage or a stillbirth. However, often the calculation actually does not include miscarriages or stillbirths because it is very difficult to obtain reliable information on this in most countries.

Table 10.1 shows the abortion rates and abortion ratios for regions of the world in 2003. There were about half as many abortions as live births in the MDR and almost one-third as many abortions as live births in the LDR. In the MDR, abortions were especially common in Eastern Europe, where there were more abortions than live births. This is likely because during the state socialist period in Eastern Europe, abortion was the major method of fertility limitation, and use of abortion remained common after the end of state socialism. When one looks at the MDR without Eastern Europe, the abortion rate declines from 26 to 19.[15]

Figure 10.8 shows age-specific abortion rates in 1996 and 2003 for Russia, the United States, and

TABLE 10.1   Abortion Rates and Ratios by World Regions, 2003

Region	Abortion Rate (abortions/ 1,000 × women aged 16–44)	Abortion Ratio (abortions/ 100 × live births)
World	29	31
MDR	26	50
LDR	29	29
Africa	29	17
Asia	29	34
Europe	28	59
Eastern Europe	44	105
Northern Europe	17	31
Southern Europe	18	38
Western Europe	12	23
Latin America and Caribbean	31	35
Northern America	21	33
Oceania	15	22

Sweden. The abortion rates in Russia fell substantially between 1996 and 2003, but even in 2003 they were much higher than in the United States or Sweden. There was little change between 1996 and 2003 in the United States or Sweden.

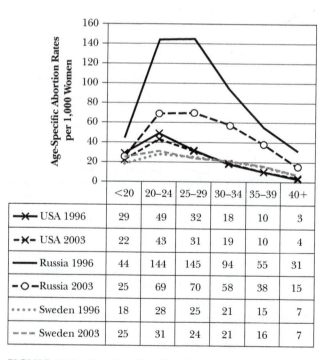

	<20	20–24	25–29	30–34	35–39	40+
—✳— USA 1996	29	49	32	18	10	3
-✖- USA 2003	22	43	31	19	10	4
—— Russia 1996	44	144	145	94	55	31
—○— Russia 2003	25	69	70	58	38	15
····· Sweden 1996	18	28	25	21	15	7
--- Sweden 2003	25	31	24	21	16	7

FIGURE 10.8   Age-Specific Abortion Rates in Russia, the United States, and Sweden, 1996 and 2003

The high abortion rates in Russia are consistent with the use of abortion as the major means of fertility limitation during the Soviet period. In Eastern Europe and the Soviet Union under state socialism, contraceptive methods were either unavailable or sporadically available. Sometimes, birth control pills were available, but since it was uncertain whether they would be available in future months, it was risky for a woman to begin taking birth control pills. Also, although condoms were sometimes available, they had a reputation of being low quality and prone to breaking.[16]

The decline in the rates between 1996 and 2003 in Russia was probably because of increased availability and acceptability of contraceptives. In Russia, even in 2003 abortion was used readily by women at all ages.

Sweden in 2003 shows much lower rates of abortion at every age than Russia, but also shows an age pattern consistent with abortion being used throughout the reproductive ages as a way to limit fertility. In the United States, there was little change in the level or the age pattern of abortion between 1996 and 2003. The age pattern of abortion is younger in the United States than in either Russia or Sweden and is consistent with abortion being used more often as a way to delay the beginning of childbearing than in Russia or Sweden.[17]

Abortion in the United States

Figure 10.9 shows the abortion ratio for all women in the United States. This is also shown for currently married women and for unmarried women.[18]

Results are shown from shortly after abortion became legal in the United States in 1973 through 2005. After rising between 1975 and 1980, the abortion ratio declined from 36 to 23. The most notable feature is the large decline in the abortion ratio for

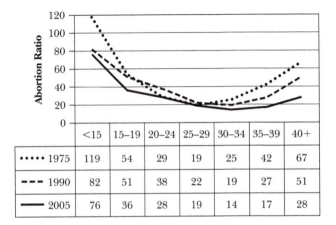

	<15	15–19	20–24	25–29	30–34	35–39	40+
····· 1975	119	54	29	19	25	42	67
--- 1990	82	51	38	22	19	27	51
— 2005	76	36	28	19	14	17	28

FIGURE 10.10 Abortion Ratio by Age of Woman in the United States: 1975, 1990, and 2005

unmarried women. This reflects both greater acceptability of non-marital childbearing and more effective use of contraception by unmarried women to avoid unwanted births over time.

Figure 10.10 shows the abortion ratio by the age of the woman in 1975, 1990, and 2005. In every year, the curve of the ratio is U-shaped. Young pregnant women are quite likely to end a pregnancy in an abortion. In 1975, more women under age 15 had abortions than had live births. Also, older pregnant women, especially those over age 40, are fairly likely to end a pregnancy in an abortion. Many of these women already would have had all the children they wanted.

Figure 10.11 shows the abortion ratio by the number of previous live births. The level of abortions is elevated for those with no previous live births, declines for those who have had one child, and then increases for those who have had two or more previous live births. Women who have not had any

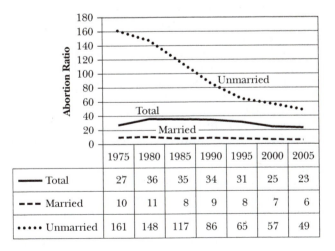

	1975	1980	1985	1990	1995	2000	2005
— Total	27	36	35	34	31	25	23
--- Married	10	11	8	9	8	7	6
····· Unmarried	161	148	117	86	65	57	49

FIGURE 10.9 Abortion Ratio by Marital Status in the United States, 1975–2005

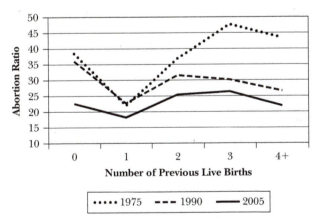

FIGURE 10.11 Abortion Ratio by Number of Previous Live Births in the United States: 1975, 1990, and 2005

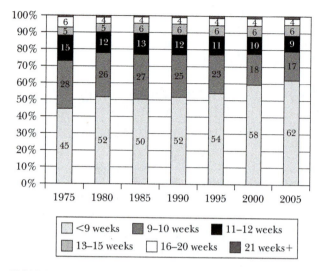

FIGURE 10.12 Distribution of Legal Abortions by Gestational Age in the United States, 1975–2005

children and find themselves pregnant, especially those who are young and unmarried, are likely to have abortions. Women who have already had children and do not want to have any more children are also likely to have an abortion. Those with no previous children often are using abortion to postpone childbearing, while those with two or more children often are using abortion to stop their childbearing. We also see that over time, the tendency for pregnant women to have an abortion has generally declined for women at all parities.

Figure 10.12 shows the distribution of abortions by gestational age of the fetus in the United States from 1975 to 2005. Abortions tend to happen very early in a pregnancy. Since 1980, at least half of all abortions occurred at less than 9 weeks of gestational age. We saw in Figure 10.4 that Americans are much more approving of abortions that occur in the first 12 weeks of a pregnancy (in the first trimester) than those that occur later in a pregnancy. Over 85% of all abortions occurred in the first 12 weeks of pregnancy at every date for 1975–2005. Also at every date, 1% of all abortions occurred at 21 weeks or more gestational age. Thus, although there is a very high level of disapproval of abortions after the first trimester, less than 15% of abortions occur after the first trimester, and a very small portion of abortions occur in the third trimester.

THEORIES OF FERTILITY DECLINE FROM LOW TO VERY LOW FERTILITY

The emergence of very low fertility in many countries led to thinking about what could have motivated this behavior. Some scholars saw this new phenomenon as a logical extension of earlier fertility decline, while others saw it as the result of a change

in the underlying processes that lead to childbearing decisions. Developmental idealism, which is discussed in Chapter 9 as a possible cause of decline from moderate fertility to low fertility, can explain a decline from low to very low fertility. However, several other explanations have been proposed.

Second Demographic Transition

One explanation for below-replacement fertility is called the **Second Demographic Transition**. This explanation was motivated by looking at the experience of Western European countries, such as the Netherlands and France. The main components of the Second Demographic Transition are as follows:[19]

1. Increase in non-marital births
2. Increase in age at first birth
3. Increase in permanent childlessness
4. Increase in cohabitation
5. Decrease in and postponement of marriage

The behavioral explanation embodied in the Second Demographic Transition is that in the modern world, women have many more options for finding fulfillment and meaning in life than raising a family. The availability of these options motivates many women to be permanently childless and results in a late age at first birth for many women who have children. Some have argued that while it used to be that women tended to not feel completely adult until they had borne a child, this is no longer true. Also, it is thought that with increased opportunities for paid work, many women want to establish themselves in their careers before they have a child. This delays the age at first birth, even among women who do not remain childless. Also, the increase in non-marital births, the increase in cohabitation, and the postponement and decrease in marriage are seen as manifestations of the decreasing importance of the family and the increasingly secular nature of more developed countries.

The Second Demographic Transition explanation of below-replacement fertility is related to an economic explanation of changes in how children are viewed. Traditionally, economists such as Becker have viewed children as "superior goods." This means that, with other things being equal, people see it as desirable to have children. In economic terms, an "inferior good" is something that is seen as desirable only when people have a very low income and cannot afford more desirable goods. Some think that with the kinds of changes in views described in the Second Demographic Transition, children have shifted from being superior goods to being inferior goods and that the material and psychological benefits that people receive from their children can be obtained by other means.[20]

Too Much Family

Another explanation of very low fertility was proposed by the Italian demographer Massimo Livi-Bacci and is called **Too Much Family**.[21] His explanation was motivated by conditions in Italy. As indicated in Table 10.2, Italy had below-replacement fertility from 1975 to 2010 and had lowest-low fertility from 1990 to 2005. Recall that, as explained in Chapter 8, if the TFR is less than 1.3, the country is considered to have lowest-low fertility. Livi-Bacci observes that in Italy, as the rate of economic growth declined, it became more difficult and took longer for young people to complete their education, obtain a good job, and buy a house, with each of these milestones achieved at an older age than previously. At the same time, Italian young people felt that completion of education, securing of a good job, and home ownership were necessary preconditions for having children. These economic conditions and views of necessary prerequisites for marriage and childbearing combined with strong ties within Italian families and feelings of obligations to their adult children on the part of parents. Parents were willing for their adult children to live with them for many years with little or no pressure to marry and set up an independent household. All of these factors together contributed in Italy to a late age at marriage, a high proportion of women permanently childless, and low fertility among those women who have children. Policies related to fertility in Italy are discussed later in this chapter.

Low Fertility but Little Childlessness in Eastern Europe

Yet another explanation of very low fertility was motivated by looking at the experience of Russia and Ukraine. These countries have very low fertility, but this has been mainly the result of very few women having more than one child, while almost all women have one child and have that child at a fairly young age. This pattern shows that there is another way to achieve low fertility and even lowest-low fertility without the adoption of all Second Demographic transition behaviors.

These Eastern European examples show that there is more than one path to lowest-low fertility. Perelli-Harris finds that in Ukraine, the ideal age for the birth of a first child is between 20 and 25, and that in any case it was thought that a woman should have her first child before age 30. Almost all Ukrainian women reported that their first child was wanted at the time of their pregnancy, suggesting that early childbearing was not the result of accidental pregnancies. Ukrainian women were also reluctant to end their first pregnancy with an abortion due to fear of secondary sterility. However, especially in a time of economic uncertainty after the dissolution of the Soviet Union in 1991, there was little motivation to have a second or third child.[22]

CHANGES IN ASPECTS OF FERTILITY IN LOW-FERTILITY COUNTRIES

In Chapters 2 and 8, we looked at some of the fertility changes in low-fertility countries, and we just discussed some of the explanations that have been proposed for these changes. Next, we look in more detail at the empirical patterns that have motivated concern about very low fertility and led to theories about the causes.

Changes in the Total Fertility Rate in Low-Fertility Countries

Replacement fertility is the level of TFR in a population that results in NRR = 1. With low mortality, that means TFR = 2.07. In 2005–2010, all countries in the MDR had below-replacement fertility, that is, a TFR < 2.07, except the United States, Ireland, Iceland, and New Zealand. Several countries had lowest-low fertility, which is a TFR of 1.3 or less.[23]

Table 10.2 shows the TFR for 1950–2010 for every country that had a TFR of 1.3 or less in at least one 5-year period and for several other more developed countries. This list includes South Korea and Singapore which are classified as less developed countries. A country is indicated as having lowest-low fertility only if the TFR was 1.3 or less for a 5-year period. Thus, countries that had a lowest-low TFR only for 1–2 years but did not have lowest-low TFR for a 5-year period are not considered to have been lowest-low fertility countries. Lowest-low fertility periods are indicated by *italics*. Other periods in which fertility was below replacement (TFR < 2.07) but was above 1.3 are indicated by **bold**. The values for the MDR as a whole are shown for comparison. The TFR is also shown for several other more developed countries that never had lowest-low fertility in any 5-year period.

We see in Table 10.2 that many countries had lowest-low fertility for some five-year period between 1990 and 2005. However, the only countries that still had lowest-low fertility in 2005–2010 were South Korea, Singapore, Bosnia and Herzegovina, and Slovakia. Thus, this period of extremely low fertility could be over. However, even in 2005–2010 among the countries listed, only New Zealand and the United States had above-replacement fertility. In addition, in 2005–2010, three countries (Australia, France, and Sweden) had fertility that was below replacement but was 1.9 or higher, which is close to replacement level.

TABLE 10.2   TFR in Some MDR and Low-Fertility Countries, 1950–2010

	1950–1955	1955–1960	1960–1965	1965–1970	1970–1975	1975–1980	1980–1985	1985–1990	1990–1995	1995–2000	2000–2005	2005–2010
MDR	2.81	2.78	2.66	2.36	2.16	1.93	1.85	1.81	1.66	1.56	1.58	1.66
All Countries That Had Lowest-Low Fertility (TFR Less Than or Equal to 1.3) in at Least One 5-Year Period												
Asia												
Japan	3.00	2.16	**1.99**	**2.02**	2.13	1.83	1.75	1.66	1.48	1.37	*1.30*	1.32
South Korea	5.05	6.33	5.63	4.71	4.28	2.92	2.23	1.60	1.70	1.51	*1.22*	*1.29*
Singapore	6.61	6.34	5.12	3.65	2.82	1.84	1.59	1.70	1.84	1.58	1.33	*1.25*
Former Soviet Union												
Belarus	2.61	2.73	2.69	2.38	2.25	2.09	2.09	2.05	1.68	1.31	*1.24*	1.39
Russia	2.85	2.82	2.55	**2.02**	2.03	**1.94**	2.04	2.12	1.55	*1.25*	*1.30*	1.44
Ukraine	2.81	2.70	2.20	2.04	2.16	2.00	2.02	2.03	1.64	*1.23*	*1.15*	1.39
Latvia	2.00	1.95	1.85	1.81	2.00	2.00	2.00	2.09	1.63	*1.17*	*1.25*	1.41
Lithuania	2.71	2.66	2.40	2.27	2.32	2.12	2.03	2.09	1.81	1.47	*1.28*	1.41
Eastern European Countries												
Bosnia and Herzegovina	4.82	4.28	3.81	3.17	2.63	2.24	1.99	1.90	1.53	1.54	*1.28*	*1.18*
Bulgaria	2.48	2.27	2.18	2.15	2.17	2.17	2.01	1.92	1.51	*1.22*	*1.25*	1.46
Czech Republic	2.68	2.37	2.24	**1.96**	2.19	2.32	2.00	1.93	1.66	*1.18*	*1.19*	1.41
Hungary	2.73	2.21	**1.82**	**1.98**	2.09	2.12	1.81	1.82	1.73	1.38	*1.30*	1.34
Poland	3.62	3.29	2.65	2.27	2.25	2.26	2.33	2.15	1.89	1.48	*1.27*	1.32
Romania	2.87	2.62	**2.04**	2.96	2.62	2.52	2.25	2.27	1.50	1.35	*1.28*	1.33
Slovakia	3.50	3.24	2.91	2.54	2.51	2.46	2.27	2.15	1.87	1.41	*1.22*	*1.27*
Slovenia	2.80	2.39	2.32	2.32	2.19	2.20	1.88	1.66	1.36	*1.25*	*1.23*	1.39
Other European Countries												
Greece	2.29	2.27	2.20	2.38	2.32	2.32	1.96	1.53	1.37	*1.30*	*1.28*	1.46
Italy	2.36	2.29	2.47	2.52	2.35	**1.94**	1.54	1.34	*1.28*	*1.22*	*1.25*	1.38
Spain	2.53	2.70	2.81	2.84	2.85	2.55	1.88	1.46	*1.28*	*1.19*	*1.29*	1.41
Germany	2.16	2.30	2.49	2.32	1.64	1.52	1.46	1.43	*1.30*	1.34	1.35	1.36
Some Developed Countries That Never Had Lowest-Low Fertility in Any Five-Year Period												
Austria	2.08	2.50	2.78	2.57	**2.04**	1.65	1.59	1.44	1.47	1.37	1.39	1.38
Australia	3.18	3.41	3.27	2.87	2.54	**1.99**	1.91	1.86	1.86	1.78	1.75	1.93
Canada	3.65	3.88	3.68	2.61	**1.98**	1.73	1.63	1.62	1.69	1.56	1.52	1.65
Denmark	2.55	2.55	2.58	2.27	**1.96**	1.68	1.43	1.54	1.75	1.76	1.76	1.85
France	2.76	2.70	2.85	2.65	**2.31**	1.86	1.87	1.80	1.71	1.76	1.88	1.97
Netherlands	3.05	3.10	3.17	2.80	**2.06**	1.60	1.51	1.55	1.58	1.60	1.73	1.74
New Zealand	3.69	4.07	4.02	3.35	2.84	2.18	1.97	2.03	2.07	1.95	1.95	2.14
Portugal	3.10	3.12	3.19	3.12	2.83	2.55	2.01	1.62	1.51	1.48	1.45	1.36
Sweden	2.21	2.23	2.32	2.16	**1.89**	1.66	1.65	1.91	2.01	1.56	1.67	1.90
United Kingdom	2.18	2.49	2.81	2.57	**2.01**	1.73	1.78	1.84	1.78	1.74	1.66	1.83
United States	3.45	3.71	3.31	2.55	**2.02**	1.79	1.80	1.89	1.99	1.96	2.04	2.07

TFR 2.07 or greater is given in plain black ink; TFR > 1.3 but < 2.07 in **bold**; and TFR 1.3 or less in *italics*.

Increases in the Age of Childbearing and a Decline to Lowest-Low Fertility

In many more developed countries, the age at first birth has increased, and thus childbearing has shifted to older ages. This is a reversal in the changes in age patterns of fertility usually seen when there is a shift from natural to controlled fertility. With the shift to controlled fertility, childbearing shifts to younger ages, as women who have had all the children they want are able to stop having children.

We saw in the discussion of period and cohort fertility in the U.S. Baby Boom that period total fertility varies more than cohort total fertility. If period fertility shifts to an older age but cohort fertility is unchanged, there will be a temporary decline in the period TFR. After a while, the period TFR will rebound to match the cohort TFR. This is called a change in the **tempo of fertility**. Bongaarts and Feeney divided changes in period TFR into changes in the tempo (changes in how early or late childbearing occurs) and changes in the **quantum of fertility** (changes in cohort TFR).[24]

Some of the fall from below-replacement fertility to lowest-low fertility seen in Table 10.2 is the result of changes in the tempo of fertility, with women postponing childbearing to an older age. This phenomenon has been called the "postponement transition," as postponement of childbearing leads to a temporary decline in the period TFR. Fertility postponement in a low-fertility situation is illustrated in Figure 8.25 in Chapter 8.[25]

Changes from Low Fertility to Persistent Lowest-Low Fertility or to a Fertility Rebound

In Table 10.2, almost all countries in the MDR had below-replacement fertility in 2005–2010 and some had lowest-low fertility. However, the TFR in 2005–2010 varied between 1.18 in Bosnia and Herzegovina and 2.14 in New Zealand, which is a large range. Also, in all the countries shown in Table 10.2, the TFR increased at least slightly between 2000–2005 and 2005–2010 except for Singapore, Bosnia and Herzegovina, Austria, and Portugal.

Observations of the patterns in Table 10.2 led several researchers to propose conditions under which low or very low fertility would increase to merely low fertility in highly developed countries. Feyrer and his colleagues thought that changes in women's status led to changes in fertility rather than changes in fertility leading to changes in women's status. They related fertility changes to changes in the amount of work in the home done by men. They proposed a three-stage model of the relation between female labor force participation and fertility related both to development level and to the extent of gender equity in the society. The stages in **Feyrer's model of women's status and fertility** are as follows: [26]

1. **Early phase:** In this phase, women's wage rates are much lower than men's, and women are expected to do virtually all the work involved at home, including child care. Women have low labor force participation rates. This was the situation in the United States in the 1950s and 1960s.
2. **Intermediate phase:** In this phase, women's labor force opportunities have improved, but their opportunities are still not as good as men's. Women still have most of the burden of child care and other home activities. Female labor force participation is higher than in the first phase, and there is a strong negative relation between female labor force participation and fertility. This is the situation in Italy and Japan.
3. **Final phase:** In this phase, women's labor force opportunities become equal or nearly equal to those of men. Men also take on more child care and other home responsibilities than in earlier phases. Female labor force participation is higher than in the intermediate phase, but this interferes less with having and raising children due to greater participation in home activities by men and increased availability of child care than in the intermediate phase, so fertility rises. This is the situation in Sweden and the Netherlands and could be the situation developing in the United States.

Consistent with Feyrer's views, Myrskylä and his colleagues used the global gender gap measure to assess gender inequality. They concluded that in high-development countries, when there is substantial gender equity, fertility rises from the very low levels that it has attained. Goldstein and his colleagues made a similar argument.[27]

As discussed in many of the theories covered here, in many developed countries fertility rates at younger ages have declined, often more drastically than at older ages, which led to a decrease in the period TFR. Figure 8.25 showed how this could indicate a long-term change in cohort TFR, or it could simply be a case of a shift in the tempo or timing of childbearing from younger ages to older ages. If it is only a shift in timing, there should be little change in the cohort TFR.

The work on gender equity and role incompatibility suggests that in populations in which there is a high level of gender equity and in which there are behavioral patterns and social policies that make it possible for women to both have children and pursue other aspects of their lives, such as paid work, the TFR should rebound, at least to some extent. It also suggests that in situations in which there is a low level of gender equity and in which combining childbearing and childrearing with activities such as work for women is difficult, the TFR should remain low or perhaps fall even further.

Short-Term Fluctuations in Fertility in Populations with a High Degree of Fertility Control

Once a high proportion of women have effective control of whether they become pregnant, the level of fertility can become much more volatile. Women and couples can decide to postpone childbearing if the national or family economic situation is not good, and they can decide to have more children than they would have otherwise if they feel prosperous or if something changes their view of the desired number of children.

Easterlin's relative income theory, discussed in Chapter 9, provides an interpretation of why fertility can fluctuate across generations, including rising at least temporarily after a substantial decline. When there are effective methods available to prevent conception and birth and when short-term economic fluctuations occur, the result can be large variations in fertility. We saw this in the rapid decline in fertility in Russia and other countries after the economic hardships that followed the dissolution of the Soviet Union in 1991.

We see evidence of the short-term responsiveness of fertility to economic conditions in declines in fertility in the United States during the severe recession that began in late 2007. A Pew Research Center analysis related the general fertility rate to U.S. per capita income for every year from 2000 through 2008. A further analysis of fertility and per capita income in 25 individual states supported the overall conclusion that per capita income and fertility were closely related. Figure 10.13 shows the general fertility rate for 2000–2009 and per capita income in the United States in 2000–2008. They track each other very closely. It will be interesting to see whether the GFR increases when per capita income increases.[28]

Postponement of Marriage and a Decline in the Proportion Ever Marrying

Women in more developed countries usually have a higher female age at marriage and a lower percentage ever marrying than in less developed countries,

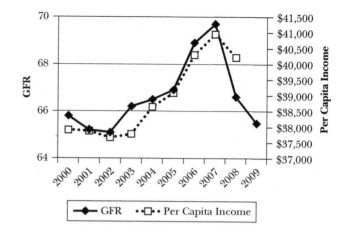

FIGURE 10.13 General Fertility Rate and Per Capita Income in the United States, 2000–2009

but in many more developed countries the female age at marriage has increased greatly, and the percentage ever marrying has declined.

Table 10.3 shows data about changes in female age at marriage in several more developed countries as well as in South Korea and Singapore. In every country in Table 10.3, the singulate mean age of marriage (SMAM) increased over time. Thus, all of the countries examined exhibited the Second Demographic Transition characteristics of postponement of marriage to some extent.[29]

Ranges of female SMAM are indicated in Table 10.3. Values through 25 are shown in a normal black font, values greater than 25 but less than 30 are indicated in **bold**, and values of 30 or greater are shown in *italics*. In about 1970, female SMAM was 25 or less in every country shown. Only in Japan was the SMAM 25. By about 1995, it was still 25 or less in Eastern European countries, but it was above 25 in most Northern, Southern, and Western European countries, as well as in Canada and in the East Asian countries shown. The United States and New Zealand were similar to Eastern European countries with a SMAM of 25. In about 1995, the SMAM was age 30 or greater in some Northern and Western European countries. By about 2008, the SMAM was above 25 in almost all countries shown, and was 30 or higher in most Northern and Western European countries. Some Eastern European countries, Canada, the United States , New Zealand, and the Eastern Asian countries retained a SMAM less than 30. Thus, Western and Northern Europe remain distinctive in how late marriage occurs, even among women who eventually marry.

Table 10.4 shows the percentage of women aged 40–44 who have never married for the same set of

TABLE 10.3 Female Singulate Mean Age of Marriage (SMAM): about 1970, 1995, and 2008

	About 1970	About 1995	About 2008		About 1970	About 1995	About 2008
Eastern Europe				**Southern Europe**			
Belarus	—	23	25	Greece	23	25	—
Bosnia and Herzegovina	—	—	25	Italy	23	**26**	*30*
				Portugal	23	**26**	—
Bulgaria	21	24	**26**	Spain	24	**26**	—
Czech Republic	21	22	**29**	**Western Europe**			
Hungary	21	22	*30*	Austria	22	**26**	*31*
Poland	22	24	25	Belgium	21	25	*30*
Romania	21	22	**26**	France	22	*31*	*32*
Russia	21	22	24	Germany	—	**28**	*31*
Slovakia	—	23	**28**	Netherlands	22	**28**	*31*
Slovenia	—	25	*31*	Switzerland	23	**28**	**29**
Ukraine	21	22	23	**Northern America**			
Northern Europe				Canada	22	**26**	**27**
Denmark	22	25	*31*	United States	22	25	**27**
Estonia	22	—	25	**Oceania**			
Finland	23	**28**	*31*	Australia	22	—	*30*
Iceland	24	*31*	**28**	New Zealand	22	25	**26**
Ireland	24	**29**	*31*	**Eastern Asia**			
Latvia	22	—	**29**	Japan	25	**28**	**29**
Lithuania	—	—	**27**	South Korea	23	**26**	**29**
Norway	22	*30*	*32*	Singapore	24	**27**	**27**
Sweden	24	*31*	*32*				
United Kingdom	21	**26**	*32*				

SMAM 25 or less is given in plain black ink; SMAM > 25 but < 30 in **bold**; and SMAM 30 or greater in *italics*. — indicates data not available.

countries considered in Table 10.2. Not marrying by age 40–44 is taken as an indicator that women will never marry. Also, 40–44 is close to the end of the childbearing ages, so any children these women ever have likely would all have been born to an unmarried woman. These data were not readily available for some countries in some years.

Ranges of the percentage of women never married at age 40–44 are indicated in Table 10.4. Values through 8% are shown in a normal black font, values greater than 8% but less than 15% are indicated in **bold**, and values of 15% or greater are shown in *italics*.

In most countries, the percentage of women never married at age 40–44 increased, indicating that most developed countries exhibited this aspect of Second Demographic Transition behavior to some extent. In about 1970, only Ireland had 15% or more of women never married at age 40–44, probably reflecting long-standing Irish patterns of delayed marriage and non-marriage, as discussed in Chapter 9. By about 2008, most

countries in Northern and Western Europe had 15% or more of women aged 40–44 who had never married. In Eastern Europe, except for Slovenia, the percentage never marrying was much lower.

Shift in Childbearing to Older Ages

Table 10.5 shows the average age at first birth in about 1970, about 1995, and about 2008. The average age at first birth increased over time in almost every country shown, which again is consistent with Second Demographic Transition behavior.[30]

As in other aspects of marriage and childbearing, there was great variation in the extent of this increase. To highlight differences, values greater than 25 are **bold**, and values of 30 or greater are in *italics*.

The increase in the average age at first birth was large in many countries in Northern, Western, and Southern Europe, as well as in Japan,

TABLE 10.4 Percentage of Women Aged 40–44 Never Married: about 1970, 1995, and 2008

	About 1970	About 1995	About 2008		About 1970	About 1995	About 2008
Eastern Europe				**Western Europe**			
Belarus	—	4	6	Austria	**10**	**9**	**14**
Bosnia and Herzegovina			4	Belgium	7	6	**14**
Bulgaria	2	4	**9**	France	8	*17*	*24*
Czech Republic	4	4	6	Germany	—	8	*19*
Hungary	5	4	**10**	Netherlands	8	**9**	*20*
Poland	6	7	7	Switzerland	**11**	**12**	*16*
Romania	3	4	**9**	**Northern America**			
Russia	3	7	5	Canada	7	**10**	**13**
Slovakia	—	7	**10**	United States	5	**13**	**18**
Slovenia	—	**9**	*21*	**Oceania**			
Ukraine	4	2	2	Australia	5	—	*20*
Northern Europe				New Zealand	4	7	**13**
Denmark	7	**9**	*21*	**Eastern Asia**			
Estonia	7	**9**	—	Japan	5	7	**12**
Finland	**12**	**12**	*26*	South Korea	0	2	4
Iceland	**9**	*15*	*16*	Singapore	3	**12**	**14**
Ireland	*18*	**12**	*18*				
Latvia	6	—	**13**				
Lithuania	7	—	**11**				
Norway	7	**11**	*25*				
Sweden	8	*21*	*33*				
United Kingdom	8	6	*22*				
Southern Europe							
Greece	—	6	—				
Italy	**13**	8	*15*				
Portugal	**13**	7	—				
Spain	**12**	**9**	—				

Never married 8 or less is given in plain black ink; never married > 8 but < 15 in **bold**; and never married 15 or greater in *italics*. — indicates data not available.

South Korea, and Australia. The increase was less in much of Eastern Europe and the United States. Specifically, only in Sweden, Canada, and Japan was the average age at first birth in about 1970 greater than 25. By about 1995, it was greater than 25 in most Northern European countries and in all Southern and Western European countries. By about 2008, it was age 30 or greater in the United Kingdom, Germany, Switzerland, Australia, and South Korea. The relatively low age at first birth in the United States and in Eastern Europe is striking. The only Northern European countries in which the age at first birth was younger than 26 in about 2008 were Estonia, Latvia, and Lithuania, all of which were formerly part of the Soviet Union.

Increase in Non-Marital Childbearing

Table 10.6 shows the percentage of all births that occurred to unmarried women in about 1970, 1995, and 2008 in the more developed countries than were shown in earlier tables as well as in some less developed countries. In every country for which there were data, non-marital childbearing increased over time, consistent with Second Demographic Transition behavior. However, we see several different patterns. In Japan and South Korea, non-marital childbearing was rare even in 2008, at 2% or less of all births. In Martinique, El Salvador, and Panama, over half of all births occurred to unmarried women in 1970. In these countries, non-marital childbearing had long been common.[31]

TABLE 10.5   Average Age at First Birth: about 1970, 1995, and 2008

	About 1970	About 1995	About 2008		About 1970	About 1995	About 2008
Eastern Europe				**Western Europe**			
Belarus	—	23	24	Austria	—	**26**	**28**
Bosnia and Herzegovina	23	24	25	Belgium	24	**28**	**28**
Bulgaria	22	22	25	France	24	**28**	**29**
Czech Republic	23	23	**27**	Germany	24	**28**	*30*
Hungary	23	23	**28**	Netherlands	25	**28**	**29**
Poland	23	24	**26**	Switzerland	25	**28**	*30*
Romania	23	23	25	**Northern America**			
Russia	23	23	—	Canada	**27**	**29**	—
Slovakia	23	22	**26**	United States	23	25	25
Slovenia	24	25	**28**	**Oceania**			
Ukraine	22	23	23	Australia	24	**29**	*31*
Northern Europe				New Zealand	24	**29**	**28**
Denmark	24	**27**	**28**	**Eastern Asia**			
Estonia	24	23	25	Japan	**26**	**28**	**29**
Finland	24	**27**	**28**	South Korea	24	**27**	*30*
Iceland	21	25	**26**	Singapore	—	**29**	**29**
Ireland	25	**27**	**29**				
Latvia	23	24	25				
Lithuania	24	23	25				
Norway	—	**27**	**28**				
Sweden	**26**	**27**	**29**				
United Kingdom	—	—	*30*				
Southern Europe							
Greece	25	**27**	**29**				
Italy	25	**28**	—				
Portugal	24	**26**	**27**				
Spain	25	**28**	**29**				

Average age at first birth less than 26 in plain black; average age at first birth at least 26 but less than 30 in **bold**; and average age at first birth 30 or greater in *italics*. — indicates data not available.

In many more developed countries, non-marital childbearing was relatively uncommon in 1970 but increased rapidly over time. In about 1970, in none of the more developed countries shown did 20% or more of births occur to unmarried women. Even in 1970, in many of the Latin American countries shown, the percentage of births that occurred to unmarried women was very high. By about 1995, more than 20% of births occurred to unmarried women in most Northern European countries, Northern America, and Oceania. By about 2008, the percentage of all births that occurred to unmarried women increased, and in France and several Northern European countries, more than 50% of births occurred to unmarried women.

Changes in the Relation between Women's Education and Fertility in Norway

As the changes documented here were occurring in highly developed countries, there is evidence that the relation between women's education and fertility was changing. Kravdal and Rindfuss looked at cohort fertility for Norway for women born between 1940 and 1964. They looked at fertility experience up to 2003, using Norwegian population register data. The existence of a high-quality population register in Norway allowed an analysis that would be very difficult in most countries.[32]

Figure 10.14 shows the number of births women had by birth cohort and education. This is shown for five levels of educational attainment, from compulsory (the lowest level with 10 years of education) to

TABLE 10.6 Percentage of Births That Occurred to Unmarried Women: about 1970, 1995, and 2008

	About 1970	About 1995	About 2008		About 1970	About 1995	About 2008
Eastern Europe				**Northern America**			
Czech Republic	5	16	**36**	Canada	10	**30**	**31**
Hungary	5	**21**	40	United States	11	**32**	39
Poland	5	10	20	**Oceania**			
Romania	4	20	**27**	Australia	8	**27**	**34**
Russia	11	**21**	**27**	New Zealand	13	**41**	**47**
Ukraine	9	14	**21**	**Eastern Asia**			
Northern Europe				Japan	1	1	2
Denmark	11	**46**	**46**	South Korea	—	—	2
Estonia	14	**44**	*59*	**Caribbean**			
Finland	6	**33**	**41**	Bahamas	**29**	*56*	*63*
Iceland	**30**	*61*	*64*	Martinique	*51*	*66*	*73*
Ireland	3	**22**	**33**	**Central America**			
Latvia	11	**30**	**43**	Costa Rica	**29**	**47**	*65*
Lithuania	4	13	**29**	El Salvador	*68*	*70*	*74*
Norway	7	**48**	*55*	Mexico	**27**	**37**	*55*
Sweden	19	*52*	*55*	Panama	*71*	*76*	*84*
United Kingdom	8	**34**	**42**	**South America**			
Southern Europe				Argentina	**26**	**46**	—
Greece	1	3	6	Chile	19	**41**	*61*
Italy	2	8	18	Venezuela	**39**	—	*83*
Portugal	7	19	**36**				
Spain	1	11	**32**				
Western Europe							
Austria	13	**27**	**39**				
Belgium	3	14	**39**				
France	7	**38**	*52*				
Germany	7	16	**32**				
Netherlands	2	16	**41**				
Switzerland	4	7	17				

% Births non-marital 20 or less in plain black; % births non-marital at least 20 but less than 50 in **bold**; and % births non-marital greater than 50 in *italics*. — indicates data not available.

holding a college degree. Although for every cohort, women with more education had fewer children than women with less education, the educational differential narrowed considerably over time. Thus, there was a convergence in lifetime fertility over time, with educational attainment mattering less than it had earlier.

Kravdal and Rindfuss suggest several reasons for this educational convergence in fertility. One set of reasons has to do with lessening of the assumption in Becker's fertility model that it is incompatible for a woman to have a young child and work for pay, with a greater economic penalty for more educated women who could command a higher wage rate. The wage penalty for working mothers in Norway declined over time, and high-quality subsidized child care with flexible hours and paid maternity leave became increasingly available. These changes substantially reduced the role incompatibility. Also, Norwegian men have increased their contribution to work in the home. Finally, it became easier for women to increase their educational attainment after they had borne children. In the most recent birth cohort, 21% of women acquired additional education between when they had their first child and when they reached age 39.

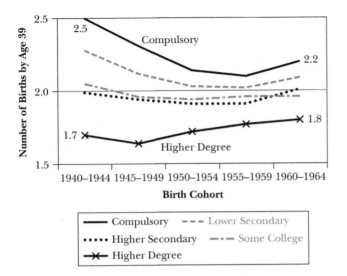

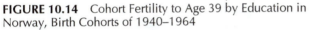

FIGURE 10.14 Cohort Fertility to Age 39 by Education in Norway, Birth Cohorts of 1940–1964

MARRIAGE, COHABITATION, AND FERTILITY CHANGES IN THE UNITED STATES

In this section, we look at recent important trends related to marriage, cohabitation, and fertility in the United States. This elaborates on some of the earlier trends presented for many more developed countries. It also looks at topics of special interest in this area, such as whether non-marital births occur to women who are cohabiting and the dynamics of teen-age fertility.

Cohabitation, Non-Marital Childbearing, and Consequences for Children

As the age of marriage has increased, more women remain unmarried, and an increasing proportion of children are born to unmarried women. This does not necessarily mean a shift in the lives of women from living with a partner to living alone or only with minor children. In many countries, there has been a large increase in **cohabitation**, which is when people of the opposite sex live together in a committed sexual relationship without being married.

Although cohabitation is an important emerging phenomenon, it has been difficult to study trends, since data on cohabitation have only been collected systematically in most countries recently. In Great Britain, government surveys began collecting data on cohabitation in 1979. In the United States, the National Survey of Families and Households, which is discussed in Chapter 3, began collecting data on cohabitation in 1987–1988, although retrospective questions in that survey provide some information on earlier cohabitation levels.

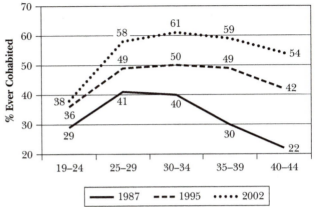

FIGURE 10.15 Percentage of Women Who Ever Cohabited by Age in the United States, 1987–2002

Using data for women aged 15–44 from the National Survey of Families and Households, Bumpass and his colleagues looked at trends in cohabitation between 1987 and 2002. Figure 10.15 shows by age group for three time points the percentage of women who had ever cohabited. The increases across time are striking. In 2002, more than 50% of all women aged 25–44 had cohabited at some time in their lives.[33]

Figure 10.16 shows how the percentage of women who have ever cohabited over time differs by educational attainment. In every year, those with less education were more likely to have cohabited than those with more education. But within every educational category the percentage who ever cohabited has increased over time. In 2002, women with 4 years or more of college were more likely to have cohabited than were women with less than 12 years of education in 1987.

Figure 10.17 shows how the percentage of women who have ever cohabited differs by race and ethnicity.

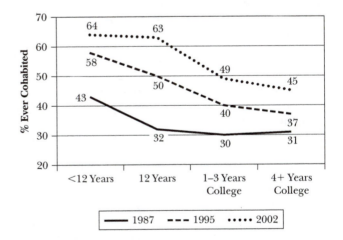

FIGURE 10.16 Percentage of Women Aged 15–44 Who Ever Cohabited by Education in the United States, 1987–2002

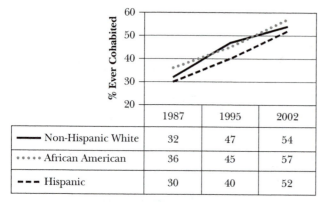

FIGURE 10.17 Percentage of Women Aged 15–44 Who Ever Cohabited by Race and Ethnicity in the United States, 1987–2002

The percentage increases over time for every group. However, at any point in time, there are small and inconsistent differences among race and ethnic groups.

Young people could cohabit before they have children and then marry once they decide to start a family. Figure 10.18 shows, for all women and by race and ethnicity, the distribution of the marital and cohabitation statuses of mothers of children at three points in time. As shown in the first panel, the percentage of children born to married women has decreased, consistent with the results shown in Table 10.6. However, the percentage of children born to single (not cohabiting) women remained almost unchanged between the early 1980s and the late 1990s. The decrease in the percentage born to married women is completely accounted for by the increase in the percentage of children born to cohabiting women.

The last three panels of Figure 10.18 show large differences in the marital and cohabitation statuses of mothers at the time their children are born between non-Hispanic White women, African-American women, and Hispanic women. Children of non-Hispanic White women are more likely to be born to married mothers than are children of Hispanic women, whose children are more likely to be born to married mothers than are African-American children. The trends in births to single women differ among the three groups. Among all groups, the percentage of births that occur to married women has declined. Among non-Hispanic White and African-American women, there has been fairly little change in the percentage of births to single (non-cohabiting) women, but an increase in the percentage of births to cohabiting women, as in seen for all women. For Hispanic women, there has been an increase in the percentage of births both to single (not cohabiting women) and to cohabiting women.

As cohabitation and non-marital childbearing have increased, factors related to when and

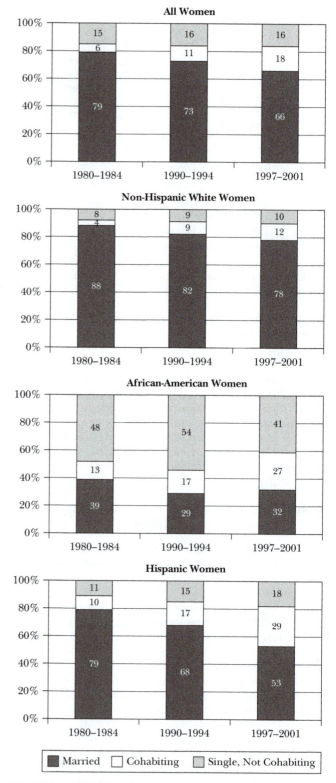

FIGURE 10.18 Distribution of Marital and Cohabitation Status of Women Aged 25–44 at the Births of Their Children by Race and Ethnicity in the United States, 1980–1984 to 1997–2001

whether cohabiting couples marry have changed. Figure 10.19 shows what happens after a couple begins to cohabit. At the time cohabitation begins (time 0), all couples are cohabiting. After each year of elapsed time, the percentages who are still cohabiting, who have married, and for whom the union has dissolved are shown. The situation is shown for 1990–1994 and also for 1997–2001. Over time, cohabiting relationships have become more stable, with somewhat lower chances of dissolution and lower chances of transitioning to marriage. In 1990–1994, 2 years after a cohabitation began, 40% of the cohabitations had changed to marriage, while in 1997–2001 only 32% had changed to marriage. The percentage of unions that dissolved after 2 years declined from 29% in the first period to 24% in the second period.[34]

Cohabitations have a higher chance of dissolution than marriages do of divorce or separation. Table 10.7 compares the chance that a cohabitation either persists as a cohabitation or is

TABLE 10.7   Percentage of Cohabitations and of Marriages Surviving after 1, 3, and 5 Years in the United States, 1997–2002

	1 Year	3 Years	5 Years
Cohabitations, 1997–2001	87	70	63
Marriages, 2002	94	85	78

transformed into a marriage after 1, 3, and 5 years for 1997–2001 (from Figure 10.19) and the chance that a marriage is intact after 1, 3, and 5 years based on data for 2002. After 5 years, 78% of marriages are still intact, but only 63% of cohabitations are either still intact as cohabitations or changed into marriages.[35]

Manning and her colleagues found that for children born to a married mother, 4% of the marriages had ended by the time the child was 1 year old and 15% by the time the child was 5 years old. Among children born to a cohabiting mother, 15% of the cohabitations had dissolved by the child's first birthday and 50% by the child's fifth birthday. If the cohabiting parents marry, this decreases the chance of the dissolution of the union, but the chance of dissolution is still greater than for children whose parents were married when they were born.[36]

Whether a child lives with a married or a cohabiting couple matters because there are often negative results for children whenever a partnership dissolves, whether through divorce or through the dissolution of the cohabitation. The higher rates of dissolution of cohabitations than marriages account for most of the worse outcomes for children in a cohabiting-couple than in a married-couple household. The more partnership transitions of the parent, the more aggressive the behavior of the child and the more likely the child is anxious or depressed.[37]

The proportion of same-sex households and of children living in same-sex households over time also has increased. In 2010, in households with a couple, about 1% were a same-sex couple. Nineteen percent of same-sex households included one or more children. Being raised by two adults rather than one adult seems to be good for children. Also, being raised by a same-sex couple seems to have the same effect on child well-being as being raised by a heterosexual married or cohabiting couple.[38]

Teenage Fertility, Age of Sexual Debut, Contraceptive Use, and Abortion

Teenage sexual activity and fertility comprise an area of special interest. In the United States and other developed countries, as the age at first birth

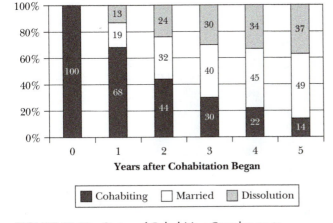

FIGURE 10.19   Status of Cohabiting Couples up to 5 Years after the Cohabitation Began in the United States, 1990–1994 and 1997–2001

FIGURE 10.20   Births per 1,000 Teenage Girls in the United States, 1940–2010

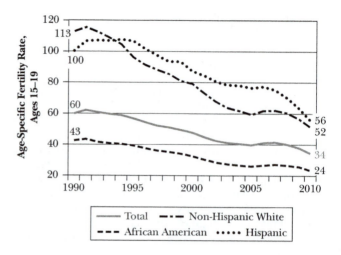

Total	Non-Hispanic White
African American	Hispanic

FIGURE 10.21   Teenage Birth Rates by Race and Ethnicity in the United States, 1990–2010

increases, teenage childbearing has become a somewhat unusual event. Even in the United States, the average age at first birth in 2008 was 25 years. Often teenage pregnancy and childbearing are unplanned, sometimes resulting from teenagers thinking that they are invulnerable to becoming pregnant. Teenage childbearing often ends the mother's schooling. Increasingly, those with low educational attainment, especially with less than high school graduation, fare very poorly in the labor market, causing problems for the women and often placing burdens on their relatives and the state.

Teenage sexual activity and childbearing are areas of moral conflict, with some arguing that detailed sex education and availability of contraceptives can prevent unintended teenage fertility, while others think that advocacy of abstinence is the only acceptable sex education for teenagers. Some think that discussion of sexual activity and the availability of contraceptives encourage sexual activity and pregnancy among teenagers who would remain celibate otherwise.

In light of these concerns, it is useful to look at the history of teenage fertility. Figure 10.20 shows

teenage birth rates in the United States. They have declined considerably, reaching their lowest level in more than 70 years in 2010. Figure 10.21 shows that teenage birth rates have declined since 1990 for African Americans, Hispanic Whites, and non-Hispanic Whites.[39]

Thinking about Bongaarts's proximate determinants of fertility that are discussed in Chapter 8, teenage fertility rates are a combination of exposure to the risk of pregnancy, use of contraception, and use of abortion. We next look at trends in teenage sexual activity, contraceptive use among the sexually active, and abortion.

Figure 10.22 shows the percentage of unmarried teenage girls who had ever had sexual intercourse at four time points. The **age of sexual debut** is the age at which a person first has sexual intercourse. We see that for every group except Hispanic teenagers, the

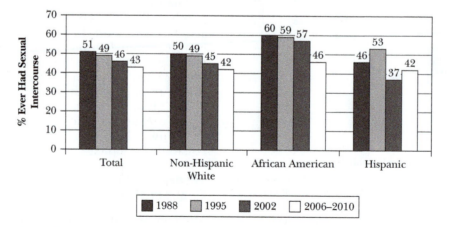

1988	1995	2002	2006–2010

FIGURE 10.22   Percentage of Unmarried Teenage Girls Who Ever Had Sexual Intercourse by Race and Ethnicity in the United States, 1988 through 2006–2010

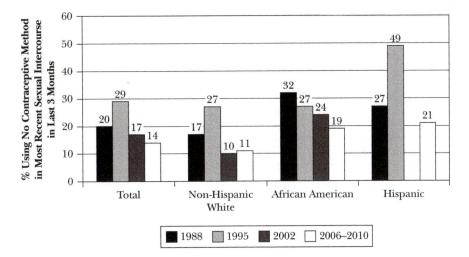

FIGURE 10.23   Percentage of Sexually Active Teenage Girls Who Used No Contraceptive Method in Most Recent Sexual Intercourse in Previous 3 Months in the United States, 1988 through 2006–2010

NOTE: The data for Hispanic women were not available for 2002.

age of sexual debut has gotten older over time. This increase in the age of sexual debut contributes to lower teenage fertility rates.

We see in Figure 10.23 that since the mid-1990s, for all groups, there was a decline in the percentage of sexually active teenage girls who used no contraceptive method when they last had sexual intercourse. No data were available for Hispanics in 2002. The greater use of contraception among sexually active teenagers also contributes to lower teenage birth rates.

Figure 10.24 shows the abortion ratio for teenagers. The number of abortions per 100 live births has declined since 1980, and it is much lower in 2005 than it was in 1975, shortly after the *Roe v. Wade* decision. Thus, the decline in teenage fertility has not been due to an increase in the use of abortion.

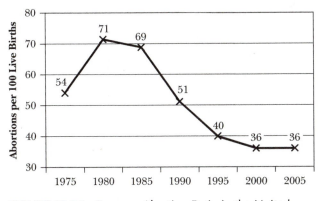

FIGURE 10.24   Teenage Abortion Ratio in the United States, 1975–2005

Changes in Female Labor Force Participation and Fertility

In order to understand changes in fertility, it is useful to briefly discuss changes in the United States in the relation between female labor force participation and fertility, including some of the relevant legal restrictions.

At one time, it was legal to bar married women or women with children from certain jobs. For example, in 1930, 77% of public schools in the United States would not hire married women as teachers, and 61% of schools required women who married to resign, 33% at once and 28% at the end of the school year. Even in 1950, 8% of American public schools would not hire married women as teachers.[40]

The Equal Pay Law of 1963 required equal pay for men and women performing the same jobs, although there has been much litigation about this. The Civil Rights Act of 1964 made discrimination on the basis of sex in hiring illegal except when sex was a relevant occupational consideration. There has been a great deal of controversy and litigation about when sex is a relevant consideration. The Lilly Ledbetter Equal Pay Act of 2009 changed the 180-day period for filing a discrimination complaint from starting when the first discriminatory paycheck is issued to when the most recent discriminatory paycheck is issued.[41]

Figure 10.25 shows female labor force participation rates by age for 1950–2008. The **labor force** is composed of those people above some age (such as age 16) who are working for pay or are actively seeking work for pay. Those who are not working for pay but are seeking work for pay are considered **unemployed**. Those who are not in the labor force

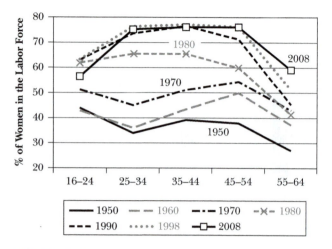

FIGURE 10.25   Female Labor Force Participation Rates by Age in the United States, 1950–2008

include persons who are full-time students, are retired, are in prisons or other institutions, and are working in the home not for pay. The **labor force participation rate** is the percentage of those aged 16 or older who are in the labor force. The labor force does not include **discouraged workers**, who are people who would like to work for pay but who have stopped actively looking for employment because they do not think they would be able to find a job.[42]

Over time, female labor force participation rates by age have increased. Also the shape of labor force participation by age has changed. Female labor force participation rates were relatively high for women aged 16–24 in 1950–1970 because many of these young women had not yet married or started a family, and many did not attend college. By ages 25–34, most of the women were married with children. Labor force participation fell for women aged 25–34 as many women dropped out of the labor force to marry and to care for their children. The rates increased for women aged 35–44 as their children became older and some children had left home. By ages 55–64, the rates dropped as women who had worked for pay retired. By 1980, the dip for those aged 25–34 had disappeared, as children had become less of a barrier to female labor force participation.

Figure 10.26 shows the percentage of women in the labor force by the age of their youngest child. At every date, the labor force participation rates are lowest for women with a child under age 3 and are highest for mothers whose youngest child is aged 6–17. But for mothers in each age group of children, the labor force participation rates have tended to increase over time, with some leveling off in about 2000. However, a woman with a child younger than age 3 in 2007 was

more likely to be in the labor force than was a woman in 1975 whose youngest child was aged 6–17.[43]

Some of the increased female labor force participation even for women with young children has been related to increased availability of commercial child care. Figure 10.27 shows the distribution of child care arrangements for mothers who were employed in various years between 1965 and 2010. This is shown for children younger than 3 years old and for children aged 3–4. The data for 1965 refer to children aged 3–5.[44]

Child care arrangements are shown in three categories: relatives, non-relatives, and group care. Relatives include fathers, grandparents, and other relatives, whether the care takes place in the child's home or the relative's home. Non-relative care includes both non-relatives coming to the child's home and care elsewhere, including in family day care. Group care includes nursery schools and day care centers. The results are shown for children whose mothers are employed, whether full time or part time.

Child care by relatives is acceptable to almost all people, and no special institutions are required. The percentage of children of employed mothers cared for by relatives declined over time, with the proportion always higher for younger than for older children. Group care increased over time, hitting a plateau of about 20% of all child care for those under age 3 and about 35% of all child care for those aged 3 or 4. The increase in group care for very young children is the result of a combination of willingness to place very young children in group care and the availability of commercial group care for very young children. Before the 1980s, it was difficult to locate group care for very young children.

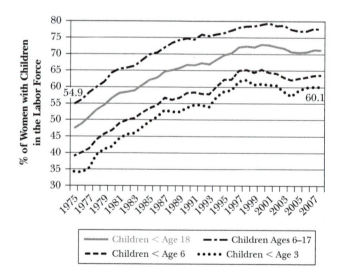

FIGURE 10.26   Children and Female Labor Force Participation (Women Age 16+) in the United States, 1975–2008

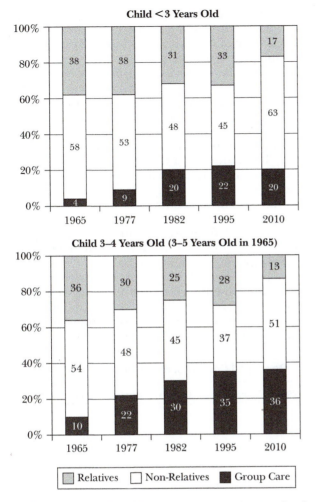

FIGURE 10.27 Child Care Arrangements for Preschool Children of Women Who Were Employed in the United States, 1965–2010

Fertility, Female Labor Force Participation, and Pro-natalist Policies in Highly Developed Countries

Usually, it has been assumed that female labor force participation and fertility will be negatively related. The more children on average a woman has, the more time she must spend out of the labor force if, as assumed by Becker and other economists, mothers must take time out of the labor force.

However, several researchers have documented a change over time in the relation between the female labor force participation rate and fertility in high-income countries.[45] The shift in the relation between fertility and female labor force participation in developed countries is illustrated in Figure 10.28.

The figure shows the relation between TFR and the percentage of females age 15 or older in the

labor force for 19 European countries that never had a state socialist system, as well as the United States, Canada, Australia, New Zealand, and Japan. In state socialist countries, women had very high labor force participation rates, and the dynamics of the relation between fertility and female labor force participation were different than in market economies. By 2008, the former state socialist countries in Europe had market economies, but they did not in 1982.

This relationship is shown in about 1982 and in about 2008.[46] The linear trend line and the one variable regression equation relating the female labor force participation rate and the TFR are also shown in each figure.

In 1982, the relation between fertility and female labor force participation was weak but negative. The higher a country's female labor force participation rate, the lower the country's total fertility rate. This is the relation that Becker and other economists would have expected. Doing a similar analysis for 1970, Brewster and Rindfuss find an even stronger negative relation between the TFR and the female labor force participation rate in 1970.[47]

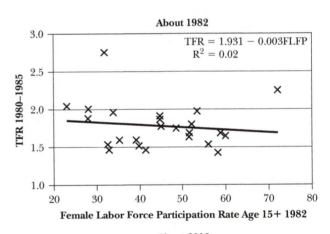

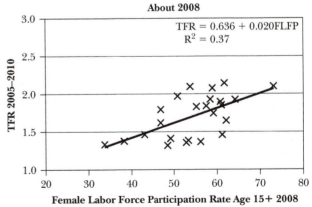

FIGURE 10.28 Relation of Female Labor Force Participation Rate and TFR in 24 More Developed Countries, about 1982 and about 2008

By 2008, the relationship had reversed so that the higher a country's female labor force participation rate, the higher its total fertility rate. Brewster and Rindfuss found a similar reversal in data for 1996. Within individual countries, women with young children were less likely to be in the labor force than women without young children, as is shown in Figure 10.26 for the United States. However, it seems that by 2008, and even by 1996, countries that made it relatively easy for women both to have children and to work for pay ended up with both relatively high female labor force participation and relatively high fertility. At the same time, countries in which women found it very difficult to combine the roles of paid worker and mother ended up with many women choosing one role or the other. Consequently, countries in which women found it difficult to combine the roles of mother and worker for pay ended up with both less female labor force participation and lower fertility than in countries where the roles of mother and paid worker were more compatible.

Table 10.8 shows the data on female labor force participation and the TFR at two points in time for the 24 more developed countries shown in Figure 10.28. The countries are shown in order of the percentage of females aged 15 or older who were in the labor force in 1982.

Table 10.8 also shows each country's gender gap measure in 2009. The gender gap measure is an index based on differences between the two sexes in each country in four areas: (1) economic participation and opportunity, (2) educational attainment, (3) political empowerment, and (4) health and survival. The index has a range of 0.0 to 1.0, with a higher value indicating a more equitable situation: the higher the value of the gender gap measure, the greater the extent of gender equity. As discussed in this chapter, Feyrer and Myrskylä thought that the higher the level of gender equity in a developed country, the higher both fertility and female labor force participation were likely to be.

In each column in Table 10.8, values above the mean for the column are shown in *italics*. We see in that in the early 1980s, those countries with low rates of female labor force participation tended to have high fertility, while by the late 2000s, many countries

TABLE 10.8 Female Labor Force Participation and TFR in Some More Developed Countries, about 1982 and about 2008

	FLFP15+ 1982	TFR 1980–1985	FLFP15+ 2008	TFR 2005–2010	Gender Gap Measure 2009
Malta	23	*2.04*	34	1.33	0.664
Portugal	28	*2.01*	*56*	1.36	0.701
Spain	28	*1.88*	49	1.41	0.735
Ireland	32	*2.76*	54	*2.10*	*0.760*
Italy	33	1.54	38	1.38	0.680
Luxembourg	33	1.47	47	1.62	0.689
Greece	34	*1.96*	43	1.46	0.666
Belgium	35	1.60	47	*1.79*	0.717
Austria	39	1.59	53	1.38	0.703
Netherlands	40	1.52	*59*	*1.75*	*0.749*
Germany	41	1.46	53	1.36	*0.745*
France	*45*	*1.87*	51	*1.97*	0.733
United Kingdom	*45*	*1.78*	*55*	*1.83*	*0.740*
Australia	*45*	*1.91*	*58*	*1.93*	0.728
Japan	*49*	1.75	49	1.32	0.645
Canada	*52*	1.63	*62*	1.65	0.720
United States	*52*	*1.80*	*59*	*2.07*	0.717
Norway	*52*	1.69	*64*	*1.92*	*0.823*
New Zealand	*54*	*1.97*	*62*	*2.14*	*0.788*
Switzerland	*56*	1.54	*61*	1.46	*0.743*
Denmark	*58*	1.43	*61*	*1.85*	*0.763*
Finland	*59*	1.69	*58*	*1.84*	*0.825*
Sweden	*60*	1.65	*61*	*1.90*	*0.814*
Iceland	*72*	*2.25*	*73*	*2.10*	*0.828*
Mean	44	1.78	54	1.70	0.737

Values above the mean for each column are shown in *italics*.

with high rates of female labor force participation also had relatively high fertility. We also see that those countries with high female labor force participation tended to have a small gender gap, which means a high value of the gender gap measure.

Figure 10.29 shows the gender equity gap measure for 2009 plotted against the TFR 2005–2010 and against the female labor force participation rate in 2008, using the data from Table 10.8. We can see in Table 10.8 that Ireland had relatively high fertility in both periods, but female labor force participation increased enormously, from 32% to 54%. We also note in Table 10.8 that in 2009, Ireland had a high level of gender equity, which could have contributed to its maintenance of relatively high fertility even as female labor force participation increased. Both relations are positive and very strong, consistent with Feyrer's and Myrskylä's arguments.

In light of the low TFRs in many highly developed countries seen in Table 10.2, many countries have implemented pro-natalist policies. We saw in Figure 2.33 in Chapter 2 that in 2011, 65% of countries in the MDR thought their fertility level was too low. Also, 67% of MDR countries had explicit policies intended to raise fertility.[48]

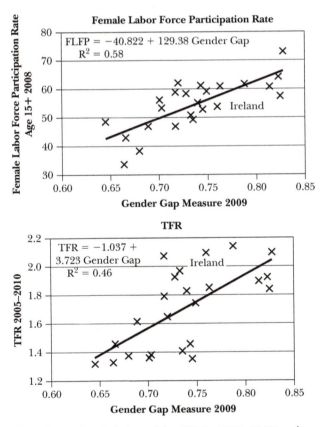

FIGURE 10.29 Relation of the TFR in 2005–2010 and Female Labor Force Participation in 2008 to the Gender Gap in 2009 in 24 More Developed Countries

Kalwij examined the effectiveness of three kinds of pro-natalist policies in 16 Western European countries. They were: (1) family child allowances, (2) maternity and paternity leave benefits for employed parents, and (3) child care subsidies for young children of employed women. He looked at the relation of each of these kinds of policies to the probability that a woman has a first birth and the probability that a woman has a second or later birth. He found that family child allowances had little effect on either how early women had children or the total number of children a woman had, but that the other two policies had significant positive effects on childbearing. Maternity and paternity leave programs were significantly related to a woman having a child at an earlier age than otherwise, while child care subsidization programs were significantly related to a woman having a larger total number of children.[49]

Sometimes whether public child care leads to higher fertility and higher female labor force participation depends on how the child care program is structured. There have been two rationales for preschool child care: (1) It can be intended to facilitate labor force participation by the mothers of young children, or (2) it can be intended to provide educational enrichment for young children. The first approach encourages wide availability of child care slots and full-day care availability, while the second approach is more concerned with the quality of the educational program at the child care facility and has little concern with provision of full-day care. Looking at data for Western Germany in the 1980s and 1990s, Hank and Kreyenfeld found that access to informal child care, such as from relatives, increased the chance of having a child, but that access to public child care had no relation to fertility. They speculated that their result could have been due to problems in the public child care system. For example, at that time the main purpose of German preschool child care was to contribute to the child's education rather than to facilitate female labor force participation. Public child care was available only in the morning, and the hours were not the same every day. Thus, the availability of public child care did not make it much easier for the mother of a young child to hold a full-time paid job.[50]

EXAMPLES OF POLICY EFFORTS TO RAISE FERTILITY

We next look at some examples of government efforts to lower or raise fertility. First, we look at Romania, where in the state socialist period restrictions on abortion were implemented in an effort to raise fertility. These policies had a short-term impact. Then we look at Italy, where a stated government aim was to increase fertility, but some government policies had exactly the opposite effect. Finally, we look at an unusual pro-natalist program in Denmark.

Efforts to Raise Fertility in Romania in the 1960s: Abolition of Abortion and Limitation of Availability of Contraception

The experience since 1966 in Romania suggests that government policy changes that make fertility limitation more difficult can affect fertility. However, the effects last for only a short time if the views and desires of the population do not change. Figure 10.30 shows the crude birth rate (CBR) in Romania for every year in the period 1955–2010.[51]

Abortion on request was legalized in Romania in 1957. Abortion became the main means of fertility limitation in Romania, as was the case at that time in much of Eastern Europe. In 1965, about 80% of all pregnancies ended in an induced abortion. As can be seen in Figure 10.30, the CBR declined rapidly through 1966. In 1957 the TFR was 2.7, and by 1966 the TFR was 1.9, below-replacement level.

The Romanian government was very concerned about low fertility and incipient population decline. In order to try to raise fertility, in October 1966 a government decree was issued that drastically limited access to abortion. The fertility response was immediate, with the crude birth rate rising in 1967 to a value greater than it had been in 1955. The TFR in 1967 was 3.7. However, by 1969, the CBR had declined considerably, and by 1969 the TFR was 3.2.

The CBR declined after 1967 and by 1984 it was 14.3—the same value as in 1966. The Romanian government responded to this fertility decline by further tightening restrictions on abortion, including issuing directives in 1984 and1985 that included periodic gynecological exams of women at work. A woman who was pregnant at one exam and was not pregnant at the next exam was interrogated about what

had happened to her pregnancy. All contraceptive methods were illegal. There was a tax on unmarried women over age 25 and on childless couples who did not have a medical reason for their childlessness. The CBR did increase from 14.3 in 1984 to 16.7 in 1987, but it is clear that the fertility response to tightening of abortion regulations was far less than what occurred after 1966.

It seems that illegal abortion was the main response to the tightening of abortion regulations. Between 1965 and 1985, the maternal mortality ratio (the number of maternal deaths per 100,000 live births) increased from 85 to 170. An illegal abortion is more likely to result in sterility than a legal abortion. It has been estimated that as a result of illegal abortions, almost 20% of reproductive age women in Romania could have become infertile.

In 1989, the state socialist government in Romania ended. In December 1989, restrictive abortion legislation was repealed, and abortion again became available on demand. Contraceptive methods also became legal. In 1990, the maternal mortality ratio had declined to 83 per 100,000 live births. The decline in fertility after the end of state socialism in 1989 was immediate. In 1990, the crude birth rate was 13.6, lower than its 1984 value. After 1990, the CBR continued to decline, similar to what occurred in many other European countries. By 2000–2005, the CBR was 10, and the TFR was 1.3, placing Romania among the lowest-low fertility countries.

Policy Conflicts with Fertility, Child Care Policy, and Female Labor Force Participation: The Case of Italy

Italy, like many other more developed countries, would like to both increase female labor force participation and increase fertility. Within Europe, Italy has both very low TFR and very low female labor force participation. The old age dependency ratio is the number of people aged 65 or older per 100 people aged 15–64. In Italy in 2010 it was 31, which was the second highest old age dependency ratio in the world, second only to Japan's. Thus, Italy has a great need for women to work for pay to support its elderly population. However, policies in Italy make achievement of these goals difficult or impossible. Italy's aging population is discussed further in Chapter 11.

Policies related to child care are a particular area of difficulty. Private child care in Italy is rare. There are limited public child care spaces available for children under age 3, meaning that Italian families cannot rely on being able to obtain a space in public child care for a young child. Also, public child care for children under age 3 costs about twice as much as child care for children age 3 or older. Public child care facilities are usually open 8 hours per day, which

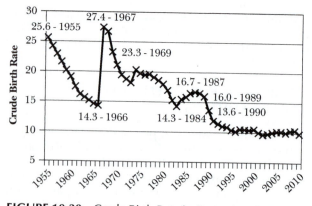

FIGURE 10.30   Crude Birth Rate in Romania, 1955–2010

is not enough time for a mother to deliver and pick up her child and work a full 8-hour day. Thus, somewhat similar to the situation in Germany, public child care only facilitates work by mothers to a limited extent.

Female unemployment rates are about twice as high as male unemployment rates, and it is difficult for women to return to paid work after leaving the labor force for some years to care for a young child. Also, in most of Italy there is little part-time work available for women.

In the past, most child care was provided by relatives, such as the child's grandmother. Increasingly, young couples do not live close to their parents, which makes this kind of child care less available. It seems that one reason for the rules related to public child care is the belief by Italian authorities that it is not good for a young child to be cared for by anyone other than the child's mother or another close relative, such as the grandmother.[52]

Although the Italian authorities want both higher female labor force participation and higher fertility, the situation with child care seems to have led to women choosing between having children *or* working for pay. The unintended result is that even in comparison to other European countries, Italy has both a low female labor force participation rate and low fertility.

A Free Child Care Evening and Encouragement of Higher Fertility in Denmark

There also have been less systematic efforts to encourage higher fertility. In Denmark in September 2012, some nursery workers offered free child care for two hours on one evening "so that the parents can go to bed and make more babies."[53]

CHANGES IN FERTILITY IN PAIRS OF MORE DEVELOPED COUNTRIES

In this section, we compare the fertility and marriage situation over time in pairs of more developed countries.[54] These detailed comparisons are intended to make some of the discussion of the divergence of fertility trajectories in more developed countries clearer. First we look at Sweden and Japan, two highly developed countries that have both similarities and differences in fertility and marriage behavior. Sweden is a country with a high level of gender equity, while Japan has a low level of gender equity. We then look at Ukraine and Italy, two low-fertility countries that have pursued very different trajectories. Italy motivated Livi-Bacci's thinking about alternatives to the Second Demographic Transition, and Russia and Ukraine were motivations for Perelli-Harris's thinking about

this topic. Finally, we look at France and the United States. The French fertility experience contributed to thinking about the Second Demographic Transition, while the United States has been seen as having persistently high fertility among developed countries.

Sweden and Japan

In this section, we compare the fertility trajectories of Japan and Sweden, the countries with the lowest mortality in the world. They have had very different fertility experiences since 1950.

Figure 10.31 shows the TFR in the two countries since 1950. Although Japan had a much higher TFR in the early 1950s, from 1955 to 1985 the TFR in the two countries was similar, with both countries usually under replacement level after 1970. After 1985, fertility in the two countries diverged with steady decline in Japan, reaching a lowest-low level during 2005–2010. In Sweden, fertility increased during 1985–1995, dropped and then rebounded after the mid-1990s to reach almost replacement fertility level during 2005–2010. Japan is a prime example of a lowest-low fertility country with little sign of an increase to replacement fertility. Sweden is an example of a country where fertility has increased close to replacement fertility, which is a development to which many more developed countries aspire.

Figure 10.32 compares the percentage of women ever married and the percentage of women currently married in 1970 and in 2005 or 2006 in Japan and Sweden. In 1970, the curve of the percentage of women ever married was nearly identical in the two countries, with 96% of all women marrying before age 50. The difference between the percentage ever married and the percentage currently married reflects marital dissolution, whether through divorce or widowhood. With the low mortality levels in these countries, marital dissolution was almost

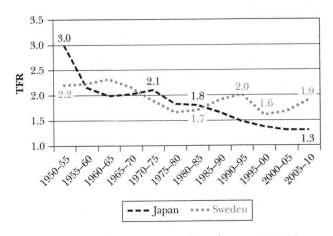

FIGURE 10.31   TFR in Japan and Sweden, 1950–2010

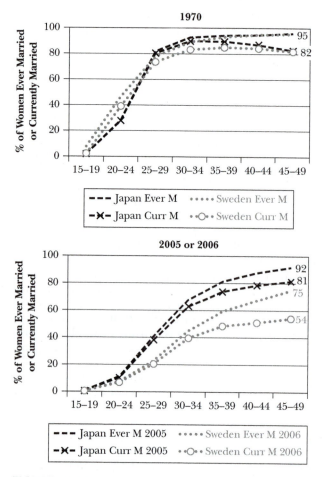

FIGURE 10.32 Percentage of Women Ever Married and Currently Married by Age in Japan and Sweden, 1970 and about 2006

totally due to divorce. In 1970, in both countries 82% of women aged 45–49 were currently married. By 2005 or 2006, the pattern of marriage in the two countries had diverged. The percentage of women ever married aged 45–49 had only declined slightly in Japan, to 92%. However, in Sweden, only 75% of women aged 45–49 had ever married. Also, there was much greater marital dissolution in Sweden, with only 54% of women aged 45–49 currently married. In both countries, the pace of first marriage proceeded more slowly in the mid-2000s than in 1970, and this reduction in the pace of marriage was much greater in Sweden than in Japan. Thus, in terms of Second Demographic Transition considerations, Sweden was a prime example of the lesser importance of marriage over time, while this was much less true for Japan.

Figure 10.33 shows age-specific fertility rates in Japan and Sweden in 1970 and 2006. In both countries, there was a substantial shift in childbearing to older ages, with the highest rates in 2006 at ages 30–34. The shift in childbearing to an older age in

both countries is consistent with Second Demographic Transition ideas about postponement of childbearing.

However, in Japan, the decrease in age-specific fertility rates at ages 20–29 was accompanied by a trivial increase in the age-specific fertility rate at ages 35–39, while in Sweden the decline in age-specific fertility rates at ages 20–24 was met by a substantial increase at ages 30–39. In Japan, the shift in the age pattern of fertility shown in Figure 10.33 resulted in a decline in the TFR from 2.1 to 1.3, while in Sweden it reflected a TFR of 1.9 in both 1970 and 2006. Thus, in Sweden, these changes in the age pattern of fertility reflected a change in timing but not in the average number of children born, and thus little change in cohort total fertility rates. In Japan, the shift to childbearing at older ages was accompanied by a substantial reduction both in period and cohort TFR. Hoem showed that cohort TFR in Sweden was almost unchanged for cohorts born in 1940 through 1965.[55] Thus, Japan reflects the first situation in Figure 8.25 in Chapter 8 of a country falling into very low fertility with unclear prospects for recovery, while Sweden is an example of the second situation in Figure 8.25, where a shift in timing of childbearing results in a decline in period TFR but little or no change in cohort TFR.

The higher age-specific fertility rates in Sweden and the lower proportions currently married by age are partially explained by the results shown in Table 10.6. Around 1970 1% of all births in Japan occurred to unmarried women, and this had increased only to 2% of all births by about 2008. On the other hand, in Sweden about 1970 19% of all births occurred to unmarried women, and this had increased to 55% of all births by about 2008. Thus, in Japan, childbearing has remained closely tied to marriage, while in Sweden it has become increasingly dissociated from marriage.

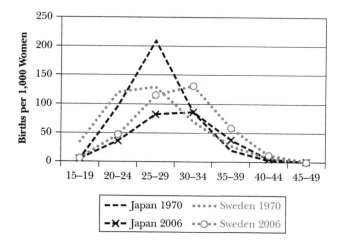

FIGURE 10.33 Age-Specific Fertility Rates in Japan and Sweden, 1970 and 2006

The marked increase in the period TFR in Sweden after the mid-1990s and the fact that in Sweden the TFR never reached a lowest-low low level are consistent with ideas about gender equity and fertility policy. Both Japan and Sweden have wanted to increase their fertility and at least to avoid very low fertility. However, these efforts were much more successful in Sweden than in Japan.

Table 10.9 compares indicators of gender equity for Japan and Sweden. These indicators are based on ratios. Thus, the female labor force participation rate is divided by the male labor force participation rate. An estimate of the female wage rate is divided by an estimate of the male wage rate for similar work, and female estimated earned income is divided by male estimated earned income. Besides the values of these ratios, the gender equity rank is shown among the 134 countries for which these indicators were calculated. A lower rank indicates a more equitable situation.[56]

On every indicator, Sweden had a more gender-equitable situation than Japan. Thus, the difference in the trajectories of fertility in the two countries is consistent with Japan being in the second stage of Feyrer's model, where female labor force participation and childbearing are in substantial conflict, and Sweden being in stage 3 of Feyrer's model, where fertility increases over its earlier value as it becomes more manageable for women to be both mothers and workers for pay.

Ukraine and Italy

Ukraine and Italy present interesting contrasts that are different in important ways from the Japan–Sweden comparison. Ukraine was formerly in the Soviet Union and experienced social and economic shocks when the Soviet Union dissolved in 1991. Italy has a substantial elderly population, along with

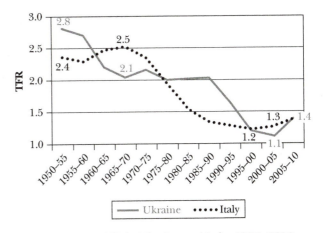

FIGURE 10.34 TFR in Ukraine and Italy, 1950–2010

extremely low mortality. Figure 10.34 shows the TFR in Ukraine and Italy in 1950–2010. The total fertility rate has declined in both countries and has been almost identical since 1995.[57]

TFR in Ukraine was much higher than in Italy in the early 1950s. But fertility in Ukraine declined rapidly until the late 1960s, when it was near replacement level. The TFR declined slightly to the late 1970s and then increased to about replacement level in the 1980s. After the early 1990s, the TFR dropped rapidly to 1.1 during 2000–2005, only recovering slightly in 2005–2010. The rapid decline from 1985–1990 to 1990–1995 was almost certainly mainly due to the serious economic and social disruptions after the dissolution of the Soviet Union in 1991. The course of fertility change in Italy was somewhat smoother than in Ukraine. After the late 1960s, TFR in Italy declined gradually through 2000 with only a slight increase after 2000.

Figure 10.35 shows the percentage of women ever married and the percentage currently married by age in Ukraine and Italy in about 1980 and in about 2006. In about 1980, the patterns are similar in the two countries, with somewhat later marriage in Italy and somewhat greater marital dissolution (mainly divorce) in Ukraine. By about 2006, patterns of marriage and marital dissolution in the two countries had become more dissimilar. By that time, marriage occurred **much** later in Italy than in Ukraine, and 10% fewer women had ever married by ages 45–49 in Italy than in Ukraine (88% vs. 98%). In addition, marital dissolution (mainly divorce) was much more common in Ukraine than in Italy.

Figure 10.36 shows age-specific fertility rates in the two countries in 1970 and about 2007. Italy shows a substantial decline in age-specific fertility rates at younger ages, with no increase at older ages. In Italy, the age pattern of fertility also shifted to older ages, with the highest age-specific fertility rate at

TABLE 10.9 Gender Equity Indicators for Japan and Sweden, about 2008

	Japan		Sweden	
	Value	**Rank out of 134 Countries**	**Value**	**Rank out of 134 Countries**
Ratio female/ male labor force participation	0.72	83	0.95	7
Ratio female/ male wage rate for similar work	0.59	99	0.72	41
Ratio female/ male estimated earned income	0.46	100	0.84	1

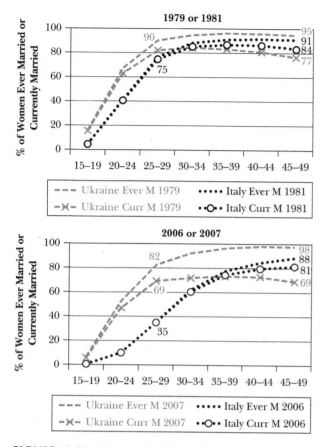

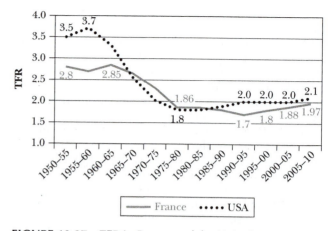

FIGURE 10.37 TFR in France and the United States, 1950–2010

FIGURE 10.35 Percentage of Females Ever Married and Currently Married by Age in Ukraine and Italy, about 1980 and about 2006

ages 30–34. In Ukraine, age-specific fertility rates declined at almost all ages, but the age group 20–24 remained the age interval with the highest rate.

Italy displays many Second Demographic Transition characteristics, with a shift to an older age at first birth and of all births and a high proportion

permanently childless. Ukraine deviates from the Second Demographic Transition model with a persistent low age at first birth and a low proportion permanently childless, illustrating Perelli-Harris's argument about how low fertility with little childlessness was achieved in Ukraine and Russia.

France and the United States

France and the United States present another interesting pair of contrasts in fertility behavior. France is often characterized as a Second Demographic Transition country with low TFR, low marriage rates, and postponed childbearing, while high American TFR has been seen as desirable but very unusual among more developed countries.

Figure 10.37 shows the TFR in France and the United States in 1950–2010. In 1950–1965, both countries were well above replacement fertility, with higher fertility in the United States than in France. Through the mid-1960s, the United States was still in the Baby Boom. TFR was slightly higher in France than in the United States 1965–1990, but was higher in the United States after 1990. By 2005, TFR was similar in both countries, with the United States slightly above replacement and France slightly below replacement. The increase in TFR in France after 1990 looks similar to what occurred in Sweden and is consistent with a shift across cohorts to later childbearing, since in 2005–2010, the TFR is slightly higher than it was in 1975–1980. TFR in the United States was almost constant throughout 1990–2010.

Figure 10.38 shows the percentage of females ever married and the percentage currently married in the two countries in 1970 and in 2006. In 1970, the age pattern of marriage in the two countries was similar, with marriage occurring slightly earlier in the

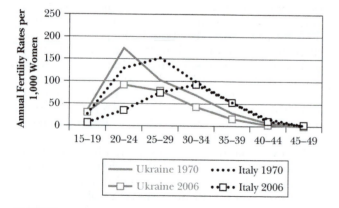

FIGURE 10.36 Age-Specific Fertility Rates in Ukraine and Italy, 1970 and 2006

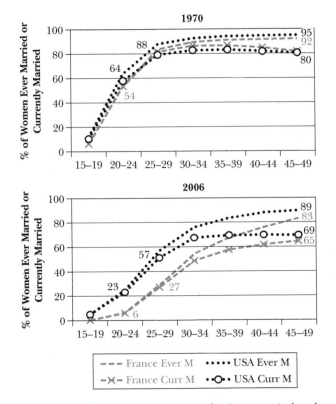

FIGURE 10.38   Percentage of Females Ever Married and Currently Married by Age in France and the United States, 1970 and 2006

United States. The SMAM in both countries was 22. In 1970, at ages 45–49, a slightly higher percentage of American than French women had ever married (95% vs. 92%), but in both countries 80% of women aged 45–49 were currently married.[58]

By 2006, the marriage patterns in the two countries had diverged. In both countries marriage occurred later and was less universal in 2006 than in 1970. While in the United States in 1970, 64% of women aged 20–24 and 88% of women aged 25–29 had married, by 2006, only 23% of women aged 20–24 and 57% of women aged 25–29 had married. In the United States, the percentage ever married at age 45–49 dropped slightly between 1970 and 2006 from 95% to 89%, but the percentage currently married at age 45–49 dropped more, from 80% to 69%. The changes in marriage pattern in France between 1970 and 2006 were similar to those in the United States but larger. The percentage ever married among those aged 20–24 dropped from 54% to 6%, and the percentage ever married among those aged 25–29 dropped from 79% to 27%. In both countries, in 2006 less than 70% of women aged 45–49 were currently married.

Figure 10.39 shows age-specific fertility rates in France and the United States in 1970 and 2006.

Rates were similar in the two countries in 1970, but the age pattern had diverged considerably in the two countries by 2006. In both countries, rates declined at younger ages and increased at ages 30–39. In 1970, the TFR in each country was 2.5, and in 2006 it was 2.0 in France and 2.1 in the United States. In 2006, the mean age of childbearing was 27 in the United States and 30 in France. Thus we see some increase in the age of childbearing in the United States, but a greater shift in childbearing to older ages in France.

There has been discussion about whether the United States has been experiencing or is about to experience the Second Demographic Transition. The relatively high fertility and relatively young age pattern of fertility in the United States would argue against the United States becoming a Second Demographic Transition country.

It has often been noted that the United States is distinguished by a high degree of religious belief and religious observance in comparison to other developed countries. In a 2002 poll, 59% of Americans agreed that religion was important to them in their lives, while only 11% of the French respondents held this view. The highest value among European countries was for the Polish respondents at 36%. Studies in the United States and Europe have found higher fertility among more religious than among less religious women.[59] These observations suggest that the greater importance of religion in the United States than in Europe might account for higher American fertility. Carlson thought that American demographic exceptionalism accounted for high American fertility in comparison to other developed countries.[60]

Lesthaeghe and Neidert argue that the Second Demographic Transition has arrived in some parts of the United States. Their analysis divides states

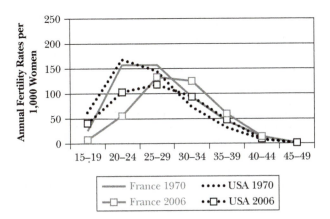

FIGURE 10.39   Age-Specific Fertility Rates in France and the United States, 1970 and 2006

into two groups. One group, which is mainly in the Midwest, Great Plains, and the South, has high fertility and can be characterized as exhibiting "American exceptionalism." In comparison to the rest of the United States, these states are more rural, less highly educated, and have a high proportion of Evangelical Christians. The other group of states exhibit low fertility similar to Europe and seem to have entered into the Second Demographic Transition.[61] However, the rebound in some developed countries, such as France and Sweden, to close to replacement levels suggests that the Second Demographic Transition ideas about the decreasing importance of children can mean a change in the timing of childbearing through postponement rather than permanently low fertility levels.

CONCLUDING COMMENTS

We saw in earlier chapters that the role of women in reducing infant and child mortality is crucial, as is the decline from high fertility to moderate or low fertility. Economic opportunities for women and the status of women are clearly important both in the decline from low to very low fertility and whether fertility increases from very low to low fertility or replacement fertility. In the possible recovery to low or replacement fertility, it seems important that policies be implemented that not only relieve the financial burdens of childbearing but also take seriously the multiple roles that women fill and make functioning in all these roles simultaneously easier.

✔️ Study and Review Online

SUMMARY

1. Almost all women in the MDR who are at risk of pregnancy and who do not want to get pregnant and have a child right away use contraception.

2. In both the MDR and the LDR, the most common legal grounds for abortion are saving the woman's life, followed by the woman's physical health.

3. There has been great stability in American views of when abortion should be legal, with support for legality of abortion (1) in the first trimester of pregnancy or (2) when the health or life of the mother or the health of the baby is at risk; and opposition to legality of abortion (1) after the first trimester or (2) when the reason is a matter of choice, such as the family cannot afford the child.

4. Throughout the world, abortion has mainly been used (1) by young unmarried woman to avoid having a child; (2) as a backup to contraceptive failure, such as when a woman has had all the children she wants; or (3) as a major method of fertility regulation, especially in Eastern Europe.

5. Although the level of abortion has fallen in Eastern Europe, it still remains higher there than in other world regions, probably as a legacy of its common use under state socialism.

6. In the United States, the use of abortion has declined since 1980, especially among young, unmarried women and among older women who have had several children.

7. In the United States, abortion tends to occur early in the pregnancy. In 2005, 88% of abortions occurred at 12 week or less of gestational age, and 98% occurred at 20 weeks or less of gestational age.

8. The Second Demographic Transition describes a set of changes that occurred in some Western European countries that resulted in below-replacement fertility. Many countries entered a situation of lowest-low fertility, which is when the TFR is 1.3 or lower. These changes are (1) increase in non-marital births, (2) increase in age at first birth, (3) increase in permanent childlessness, (4) increase in cohabitation and (5) decrease in and postponement of marriage.

9. Some scholars think that the Second Demographic Transition changes are inevitable in all MDR countries.

10. Observation of Italy led to an alternative path to below-replacement fertility, called Too Much Family. In Italy, below-replacement fertility resulted from acceptance of prolonged co-residence of unmarried adult children with their parents and very high standards for setting up an independent home and starting a family, which delays marriage and childbearing.

11. Observation of Russia and Ukraine led to another alternative path to below-replacement fertility. In those countries, childbearing continued to occur early, and there was little childlessness. However, few women proceeded to a second or a third birth.

12. In 2005–2010, the TFR increased in many MDR countries. Most countries that had been in a situation of lowest-low fertility changed to merely low fertility.

13. Some MDR countries that experienced very low fertility had an almost unchanging cohort TFR, revealing the dip in TFR to be a result of timing, in which lifetime fertility was unchanged, but was shifted to an older age. Other countries remained at very low fertility, with little or no increase in fertility at older ages.

14. Highly developed countries in which there was a high level of gender equity experienced a recovery in TFR, while in those with a low level of gender equity tended to remain at a very low fertility level. With a high level of gender equity, women could combine childbearing, labor force participation, and other aspects of self-expression, and fertility and female labor force participation were both fairly high.

15. The percentage of women who have ever cohabited in the United States has increased over time and is similar for non-Hispanic White women, African-American women, and Hispanic women. The percentage of children born to cohabiting women has increased over time, mainly taking away from the percentage of children born to married women.

16. Cohabitation is related to worse outcomes for children than marriage, mainly because cohabiting relationships are more likely to dissolve than marriages are to divorce, and family disruptions have negative consequences for children.

17. In the United States teenage fertility was lower in 2010 than it has been since 1940. Teenage fertility rates declined since 1990 among non-Hispanic Whites, African Americans, and Hispanics. The teenage abortion ratio has declined to its lowest level since 1975, the percentage of teenage girls who have ever had sex has declined among most groups, and sexually active teenagers have become more likely to use contraception.

18. Female labor force participation in the United States has increased since 1950. Until 1970, female labor force participation rates dipped for women in the early childbearing ages and then increased for women in their late forties as children left home. After 1970, this dip related to childrearing disappeared.

19. Women with young children are less likely to be in the labor force than women without young children or women with only older children. However, female labor force participation rates have increased over time, even for women with a child less than age 3.

20. Across more developed countries there has been a shift from a negative relation between the TFR and the female labor force participation rate to a positive relation. In every country, women with young children are less likely to be in the labor force than women without young children. However, countries in which it is relatively easy for women to combine the roles of mother and a worker for pay tend to have both higher fertility and higher female labor force participation than in countries where combining those roles is more difficult.

KEY TERMS

abortion rate 326	quantum of fertility 331	labor force 341
abortion ratio 326	Feyrer's model of women's	unemployed 341
Second Demographic Transition 328	status and fertility 331	labor force participation rate 342
Too Much Family 329	cohabitation 337	discouraged worker 342
tempo of fertility 331	age of sexual debut 340	

QUESTIONS FOR DISCUSSION AND REVIEW

1. What is the "Second Demographic Transition"? Where is it applicable? Is there evidence that the Second Demographic Transition model is not relevant for some low-fertility countries? What are some alternative explanations of very low fertility?

2. Briefly describe the major changes in fertility and fertility-related behavior in the less developed region and in the more developed region of the world in the last 50 years. How have the concerns with fertility-related issues changed over time and how have the policies pursued to address fertility-related issues changed over time?

3. Imagine the following countries:

	Country A	Country B	Country C	Country D
Total fertility rate	6.0	6.0	1.6	2.2
Proportion of women aged 15–19 married	0.65	0.65	0.07	0.15
Proportion of women aged 40–44 ever married	0.95	0.95	0.75	0.85
Proportion of women living to age 30	0.50	0.75	0.98	0.95
Proportion of women exposed to the risk of pregnancy who are using some contraceptive method	0.07	0.30	0.97	0.85
Percentage of births to unmarried women	5%	7%	45%	25%
Expectation of life at birth	35	55	75	70

a. Rank the countries from highest to lowest in growth rate. Explain your reasoning. Speculate on the characteristics of each country.
b. Which countries are likely to have reduction of mortality as a priority? Which countries are likely to have reduction of fertility as a priority? Which countries are likely to have increase of fertility as a priority? What actions or policies would each country be likely to implement in order to try to achieve that country's priorities?
c. Draw a graph of the age-specific fertility rate for each country. Discuss each graph.
4. Discuss the role of attitudes and perceptions in fertility decision making in the LDR and in the MDR.
5. How are the role of thinking about opportunities and the likely future in fertility decision making the same or different in a less developed country with a moderate fertility level and in a highly developed country with a low or very low fertility level?
6. Comment on the following statement:

"Higher female education always leads to lower fertility."

7. Comment on the following statement:

"Higher female labor force participation education always leads to higher fertility."

8. Discuss the similarities and differences in the relation of female education to fertility in the LDR and in the MDR.
9. Discuss how changing gender roles have influenced fertility decisions in highly developed countries.

SUGGESTED PAPER TOPICS

1. Discuss the changes in age-specific fertility rates, childlessness, non-marital childbearing, and cohabitation in a developed country since 1950. How have the media and social groups, such as religious groups or political parties, viewed these changes? Has the country implemented any policies to influence these changes? Have these policies been successful and why or why not?
2. Pick a highly developed country. Discuss its history of fertility policies and how these policies have related to the political and cultural situation in the country.

NOTES

1. Calvin Goldscheider and William D. Mosher. 1991. "Patterns of Contraceptive Use in the United States: The Importance of Religious Factors," *Studies in Family Planning*, 22: 102–115.
2. Rachel K. Jones and Joerg Dreweke. 2011. *Countering Conventional Wisdom: New Evidence on Religion and Contraceptive Use*, New York: Guttmacher Institute, http://www.guttmacher.org/pubs /Religion-and-Contraceptive-Use.pdf (accessed May 30, 2012).
3. Frank Newport. 2012. "Americans, Including Catholics, Say Birth Control Is Morally OK," Gallup Poll, May 22, http://www.gallup.com /poll/154799/Americans-Including-Catholics -Say-Birth-Control-Morally.aspx (accessedApril15, 2013).

4. Frank Newport. 2009. "Catholics Similar to Mainstream on Abortion, Stem Cells," Gallup Poll, March 30, http://www.gallup.com/poll/117154/Catholics-Similar-Mainstream-Abortion-Stem-Cells.aspx (accessed April 15, 2013).

5. United Nations Population Division. 2010. *World Population Policies 2009*, New York: United Nations, http://www.un.org/esa/population/publications/wpp2009/wpp2009.htm (accessed June 12, 2011); and United Nations Population Division. 2012. *World Population Policies 2011*, New York: United Nations, http://www.un.org/en/development/desa/population/publications/policy/world-population-policies-2011.shtml (accessed April 15, 2013).

6. Lydia Saad. 2002. *Public Opinion about Abortion: An In-Depth Review*, http://www.gallup.com/poll/9904/Public-Opinion-About-Abortion-InDepth-Review.aspx#1 (accessed June 16, 2010).

7. Donald Granberg and Beth Wellman Granberg. 1980. "Abortion Attitudes, 1965–1980: Trends and Determinants," *Family Planning Perspectives*, 12: 250–261.

8. Gallup Poll, http://www.gallup.com/poll/1576/abortion.aspx#2 (accessed July 7, 2011).

9. Gallup Poll, http://www.gallup.com/poll/1576/abortion.aspx#2 (accessed July 7, 2011); and Lydia Saad. 2013. "Majority of Americans Still Support Roe v. Wade Decision," Gallup Poll, January 22, http://www.gallup.com/poll/160058/majority-americans-support-roe-wade-decision.aspx (accessed April 15, 2013).

10. The question asked whether abortion should be legal under all circumstances, no circumstances, or some circumstances. From Gallup Poll, http://www.gallup.com/poll/1576/Abortion.aspx (accessed April 15, 2013).

11. From Gallup Poll, http://www.gallup.com/poll/1576/Abortion.aspx (accessed April 15, 2013). The value for 2013 was from a survey conducted December 27–30, 2012.

12. Lydia Saad. 2009. "More Americans 'Pro-Life' Than 'Pro-Choice' for First Time," Gallup Poll, May 15, http://www.gallup.com/poll/118399/More-Americans-Pro-Life-Than-Pro-Choice-First-Time.aspx (accessed June 28, 2011); and Steve Benon. 2009. "A National Shift on Abortion?" *Washington Monthly*, May 15, http://www.washingtonmonthly.com/archives/individual/2009_05/018194.php (accessed June 28, 2011).

13. Lydia Saad. 2011. "Plenty of Common Ground Found in Abortion Debate," Gallup Poll, August 8, http://www.gallup.com/poll/148880/Plenty-Common-Ground-Found-Abortion-Debate.aspx (accessed May 5, 2012).

14. Lydia Saad. 2010. "Generational Differences on Abortion Narrow," Gallup Poll, March 12, http://www.gallup.com/poll/126581/generational-differences-abortion-narrow.aspx (accessed April 15, 2013).

15. Gilda Sedgh, Stanley K. Henshaw, Susheela Singh, Elisabeth Ahman, and Iqbal H. Shah. 2007. "Induced Abortion: Estimated Rates and Trends Worldwide," *The Lancet*, 370: 1338–1345.

16. Tomas Frejka. 1983. "Induced Abortion and Fertility: A Quarter Century of Experience in Eastern Europe," *Population and Development Review*, 9: 494–520.

17. Gilda Sedgh, Stanley K. Henshaw, Susheela Singh, Akinrinkkola Bankole, and Joanna Drescher. 2007. "Legal Abortion Worldwide: Incidence and Recent Trends," *International Family Planning Perspectives*, 33: 106–116; and Associated Press. 2011. "Russia: Abortion Restrictions Adopted," *New York Times*, October 21.

18. Data in the graphs in this section are from information in National Center for Health Statistics. 2011. *Health, United States, 2010: With Special Feature on Death and Dying*, Hyattsville, MD: Government Printing Office, http://www.cdc.gov/nchs/hus.htm (accessed November 9, 2011).

19. Dirk J. van de Kaa. 2001. "Postmodern Fertility Preferences: From Changing Value Orientation to New Behavior," *Population and Development Review*, 27 (Supplement: Global Fertility Transition): 290–331.

20. Jason M. Lindo. 2010. "Are Children Really Inferior Goods? Evidence from Displacement-Driven Income Shocks" *Journal of Human Resources*, 45: 301–327.

21. Massimo Livi-Bacci. 2001. "Too Few Children and Too Much Family," *Daedalus*, 130: 139–155.

22. Brienna Perelli-Harris. 2005. "The Path to Lowest-Low Fertility in Ukraine," *Population Studies*, 59: 55–70.

23. Hans-Peter Kohler, Francesco C. Billari, and José Antonio Ortega. 2002. "The Emergence of Lowest-Low Fertility in Europe during the 1990s," *Population and Development Review*, 28: 641–680.

24. John Bongaarts and Griffith Feeney. 1998. "On the Quantum and Tempo of Fertility," *Population and Development Review*, 24: 271–291.

25. Joshua R. Goldstein, Tomas Dobotka, and Aiva Jasilioniene. 2009. "The End of 'Lowest-Low' Fertility?" *Population and Development Review*, 35: 663–699.

26. James Feyrer, Bruce Sacerdote, and Ariel Dora Stern. 2008. "Will the Stork Return to Europe and Japan? Understanding Fertility within

Developed Nations," *The Journal of Economic Perspectives*, 22: 3–22.

27. Mikko Myrskylä, Hans-Peter Kohler, and Francesco C. Billari. 2009. "Advances in Development Reverse Fertility Declines," *Nature*, 460: 741–743; Mikko Myrskylä, Hans-Peter Kohler, and Francesco Billari. 2011. "High Development and Fertility: Fertility at Older Reproductive Ages and Gender Equality Explain the Positive Link." Population Studies Center, University of Pennsylvania, PSC Working Paper Series PSC 11-06, http://repository.upenn.edu/psc_working_papers/30 (accessed December 29, 2011); Ricardo Hausmann, Laura D. Tyson, and Saadia Zahidi. 2009. *The Global Gender Gap Report 2009*, Geneva: World Economic Forum, https://members.weforum.org/pdf/gendergap/report2009.pdf (accessed January 3, 2012); and Joshua R. Goldstein, Tomas Sobotka, and Aiva Jasilioniene. 2009. "The End of 'Lowest-Low' Fertility?" *Population and Development Review*, 35: 663–699.

28. Gretchen Livingston and D'Vera Cohn. 2010. *U.S. Birth Rate Decline Linked to Recession*, Washington, DC: Pew Research Center, http://www.pewsocialtrends.org/files/2010/10/753-birth-rates-recession.pdf (accessed December 26, 2011); and B. Tejada-Vera and P. D. Sutton. 2010. *Births, Marriages, Divorces, and Deaths: Provisional Data for 2009*, National Vital Statistics Reports, vol. 58, no. 25, Hyattsville, MD: National Center for Health Statistics, http://www.cdc.gov/nchs/data/nvsr/nvsr58/nvsr58_25.pdf (accessed December 26, 2011).

29. Data in Tables 10.3 and 10.4 are from United Nations. 2013. *World Marriage Data 2012*, http://www.un.org/esa/population/publications/WMD2012/MainFrame.html (accessed March 15, 2013).

30. Data in Table 10.5 are from United Nations. 2011. *World Fertility Report 2009 Country Profiles*, http://www.un.org/esa/population/publications/WFR2009_Web/Data/CountryProfiles_WFR2009.pdf (accessed December 25, 2011).

31. Data in Table 10.6 are from United Nations, Department of Economic and Social Affairs, Population Division (2011). *World Fertility Report 2009*, http://www.un.org/esa/population/publications/WFR2009_Web/Data/DataAndSources.html (accessed December 25, 2011).

32. Øystein Kravdal and Ronald R. Rindfuss. 2008. "Changing Relationships between Education and Fertility: A Study of Women and Men Born 1940 to 1964," *American Sociological Review*, 73: 854–873.

33. Figures 10.15 through 10.19 are based on data in Larry Bumpass and Hsien-Hen Lu. 2000. "Trends in Cohabitation and Implications for

Children's Family Contexts in the United States," *Population Studies*, 54: 29–41; and S. Kennedy and L. Bumpass. 2008. "Cohabitation and Children's Living Arrangements: New Estimates from the United States," *Demographic Research*, 19: 1663–1692.

34. Pamela J. Smock and Fiona Rose Greenland. 2010. "Diversity in Pathways to Parenthood: Patterns, Implications, and Emerging Research Directions," *Journal of Marriage and Family*, 72: 576–593.

35. Data for marital dissolution from P. Y. Goodwin, W. D. Mosher, and A. Chandra. 2010. "Marriage and Cohabitation in the United States: A Statistical Portrait Based on Cycle 6 (2002) of the National Survey of Family Growth," National Center for Health Statistics, *Vital and Health Statistics*, Ser. 23, No. 28, Table 16.

36. Wendy D. Manning, Pamela J. Smock, and Debarun Majumdar. 2004. "The Relative Stability of Cohabiting and Marital Unions for Children," *Population Research and Policy Review*, 23: 135–159.

37. Cynthia Osborne and Sara McLanahan. 2007. "Partnership Instability and Child Well-Being," *Journal of Marriage and the Family*, 69: 1065–1083.

38. U.S. Census Bureau. 2011. *Same-Sex Couples Households*, American Community Survey Brief, September, Washington, DC: U.S. Census Bureau, http://www.census.gov/prod/2011pubs/acsbr10-03.pdf (accessed July 9, 2012); David K. Flaks, Ilda Ficher, Frank Masterpasqua, and Gregory Joseph. 1995. "Lesbians Choosing Motherhood: A Comparative Study of Lesbian and Heterosexual Parents and Their Children," *Developmental Psychology*, 31: 105–114; Ellen C. Perrin and the Committee on Psychosocial Aspects of Child and Family Health. 2002. "Technical Report: Coparent or Second-Parent Adoption by Same-Sex Parents," *Pediatrics*, 109: 341–344; and American Psychological Association. 2012. *APA on Children Raised by Gay and Lesbian Parents*, June 11, http://www.apa.org/news/press/response/gay-parents.aspx (accessed March 21, 2013).

39. Figures 10.20 through 10.24 are from the following sources: Brady E. Hamilton and Stephanie Ventura. 2012. *Birth Rates for U.S. Teenagers Reach Historic Lows for All Age and Ethnic Groups*, NCHS Data Brief, No. 89, Hyattsville, MD: National Center for Health Statistics, http://www.cdc.gov/nchs/data/databriefs/db89.pdf (accessed April 10, 2012); Stephanie J. Ventura, T. J. Mathews, and Brady E. Hamilton. 2001. *Births to Teenagers in the United States, 1940–2000*, National Vital Statistics Reports, Vol. 49, No. 10, Hyattsville, MD: National Center for Health Statistics, http://www.cdc.gov/nchs/data/nvsr/nvsr49/nvsr49_10.pdf (accessed April 10, 2012); Brady E. Hamilton, Joyce A. Martin, and Stephanie

Ventura. 2011. *Births: Preliminary Data for 2010*, National Vital Statistics Report, Vol. 60, No. 2. Hyattsville, MD: National Center for Health Statistics, http://www.cdc.gov/nchs/data/nvsr/nvsr60/nvsr60_02.pdf (accessed April 10, 2012); and G. Martinez, C. E. Copen, and J. C. Abema. 2011. *Teenagers in the United States: Sexual Activity, Contraceptive Use, and Childbearing, 2006–2010*, National Survey of Family Growth, Vital and Health Statistics, Ser. 23, No. 11, http://www.cdc.gov/nchs/data/series/sr_23/sr23_031.pdf (accessed April 10, 2012).

40. Valerie Kincade Oppenheimer. 1976. *The Female Labor Force in the United States*, Westport, CT: Greenwood Press; Chinhui Juhn and Simon Potter. 2006. "Changes in Labor Force Participation in the United States," *Journal of Economic Perspectives*, 20: 27–46; and Claudia Goldin. 1994. "Understanding the Gender Gap: An Economic History of American Women," in *Equal Employment Opportunity; Labor Market Discrimination and Public Policy*, ed. Paul Burstein, Hawthorne, NY: Aldine de Gruyter, 17–26.

41. Robert Stevens Miller, Jr. 1966–1967. "Sex Discrimination and Title VII of the Civil Rights Act of 1964," *Minnesota Law Review*, 51: 877–89; and Sheryl Gay Stolberg. 2012. "Obama Signs Equal Pay Legislation," January 28, *New York Times*.

42. Data through 1998 from Howard N. Fullerton, Jr. 1999. "Labor Force Participation: 75 Years of Change, 1950–98 and 1998–2025," *Monthly Labor Review*, December: 3–12, http://www.bls.gov/mlr/1999/12/art1full.pdf (accessed March 14, 2012); and data for 2008 from Mitra Toossi. 2009. "Employment Outlook 2008–18, Labor Force Projections to 2018: Older Workers Staying More Active," *Monthly Labor Review*, November: 30–51, http://www.bls.gov/opub/mlr/2009/11/art3full.pdf (accessed March 14, 2012).

43. Bureau of Labor Statistics. 2009. *Labor Force Participation of Women by Presence and Age of Youngest Child*, March 1975–2008, http://www.bls.gov/opub/ted/2009/ted_20091009_data.htm#a (accessed April 17, 2013).

44. Marjorie Lueck, Ann C. Orr, and Martin O'Connell. 1982. *Trends in Child Care Arrangements of Working Mothers*, Current Population Report P-23, No. 117, June, http://www.census.gov/hhes/childcare/data/cps/trends-in-childcare.pdf (accessed July 3, 2012); Martin O'Connell and Carolyn C. Rogers. 1983. *Child Care Arrangements of Working Mothers: June 1982*, Current Population Report P-23, No. 129, November, http://www.census.gov/hhes/childcare/data/cps/childcare-arrangements.pdf (accessed July 3, 2012); Census Bureau. 2011.

Who's Minding the Kids? Child Care Arrangements: Spring 1995—Detailed Tables, http://www.census.gov/hhes/childcare/data/sipp/1995/tables.html (accessed July 5, 2012); and U.S. Census Bureau. 2011. *Who's Minding the Kids? Child Care Arrangements: Spring 2010—Detailed Tables*, http://www.census.gov/hhes/childcare/data/sipp/2010/tables.html (accessed July 5, 2012). Data for 1995 and 2010 are for employed mothers, whether full- or part-time.

45. Karin L. Brewster and Ronald R. Rindfuss. 2000. "Fertility and Women's Employment in Industrialized Nations," *Annual Review of Sociology*, 26: 271–296; Ronald R. Rindfuss, Karen Benjamin Guzzo, and S. Philip Morgan. 2003. "The Changing Institutional Context of Low Fertility," *Population Research and Policy Review*, 22: 411–438; and Henriette Engelhardt and Alexia Prskawetz. 2004. "On the Changing Correlation between Fertility and Female Employment over Space and Time," *European Journal of Population*, 20: 35–62.

46. TFR from United Nations. 2011. *World Population Prospects the 2010 Revision*. Female labor force participation data from World Bank. 2012. http://data.worldbank.org/indicator/SL.TLF.CACT.FE.ZS (accessed April 3, 2012).

47. Karin L. Brewster and Ronald R. Rindfuss. 2000. "Fertility and Women's Employment in Industrialized Nations," *Annual Review of Sociology*, 26: 271–296.

48. United Nations Population Division. 2012. *World Population Policies 2011*, New York: United Nations, http://www.un.org/en/development/desa/population/publications/policy/world-population-policies-2011.shtml (accessed April 15, 2013).

49. Adriaan Kalwij. 2010. "The Impact of Family Policy Expenditure on Fertility in Western Europe," *Demography*, 47: 503–519.

50. Karsten Hank and Michaela Kreyenfeld. 2003. "A Multilevel Analysis of Child Care and Women's Fertility Decisions in Western Germany," *Journal of Marriage and Family*, 65: 584–596.

51. Information in this section is from Michael S. Teitelbaum. 1972. "Fertility Effects of the Abolition of Legal Abortion in Romania," *Population Studies*, 26: 405–417; B. Berelson. 1979. "Romania's 1966 Anti-Abortion Decree: The Demographic Experience of the First Decade," *Population Studies*, 33: 209–222; and Charlotte Hord, Henry P. David, France Donnay, and Merrill Wolf. 1991. "Reproductive Health in Romania: Reversing the Ceausescu Legacy," *Studies in Family Planning*, 22: 231–240; National Institute of Statistics of Romania, http://www.insse.ro/cms/rw/pages/index.en.do (accessed January 2, 2012).

52. Daniela Del Boca. 2002. "The Effect of Child Care and Part Time Opportunities on Participation and Fertility Decisions in Italy," *Journal of Population Economics*, 15: 549–573; Daniela Del Boca and Daniela Vuri. 2007. "The Mismatch between Employment and Child Care in Italy: The Impact of Rationing," *Journal of Population Economics*, 20: 805–832; and Ylenia Brilli, Daniela Del Boca, and Chiara Pronzato. 2011. *Exploring the Impacts of Public Childcare on Mothers and Children in Italy: Does Rationing Play a Role?* Working Paper No. 2011-038. Human Capital and Economic Opportunity Working Group, Economic Research Center, University of Chicago.

53. BBC News. 2012. "Danish Nursery Offers Parents Time for Making Babies," BBC News, September 13, http://www.bbc.co.uk/news/world-europe-19585136 (accessed September 13, 2012).

54. Marriage data from United Nations, Department of Economic and Social Affairs, Population Division (2009). *World Marriage Data 2008 (POP/DB/Marr/Rev2008)*, http://www.un.org/esa/population/publications/WMD2008/Main.html (accessed June 15, 2010). Age-specific fertility rates from United Nations. 2010. *World Fertility Patterns 2009*, http://www.un.org/esa/population/publications/worldfertility2009/worldfertility2009.htm (accessed June 15, 2010); and TFR, NRR, and GRR data from United Nations. 2011. *World Population Prospects 2010*, http://esa.un.org/unpd/wpp/unpp/p2k0data.asp (accessed June 10, 2011).

55. Jan Hoem. 2005. "Why Does Sweden Have Such High Fertility?" *Demographic Research*, 13: 559–572, http://www.demographic-research .org/volumes/vol13/22/13-22.pdf (accessed March 20, 2012).

56. Ricardo Hausmann, Laura D. Tyson, and Saadia Zahidi. 2009. *The Global Gender Gap Report 2009*, Geneva: World Economic Forum, https://members.weforum.org/pdf/gendergap/report2009.pdf (accessed January 3, 2012).

57. Fertility and marriage patterns in Ukraine and Russia are similar. Results are shown here for Ukraine because more recent data on some aspects of marriage were available for Ukraine than for Russia.

58. Marital status for the United States estimated from Statistical Data Base, United Nations Economic Commission for Europe, http://w3.unece.org/pxweb/dialog/varval.asp?ma=005_GEPOPop5YearMaSta_r&path=../database/STAT/30-GE/01-Pop/&lang=1&ti=Population%2C+5-year+age+groups%2C+by+marital+status+and+sex (accessed March 13, 2012).

59. Tomas Frejka and Charles Westoff. 2008. "Religion, Religiousness and Fertility in the US and in Europe," *European Journal of Population*, 24: 5–31.

60. A. C. Carlson. 2005. "The Fertility Gap: Recrafting American Population," *Family Policy Lectures*, Family Research Council.

61. R. Kelly Raley. 2001. "Increasing Fertility in Cohabiting Unions: Evidence for the Second Demographic Transition in the United States?" *Demography*, 38: 59–66; and Ron J. Lesthaeghe and Lisa Neidert. 2006. "The Second Demographic Transition in the United States: Exception or Textbook Example?" *Population and Development Review*, 32: 669–698.

CHAPTER 11

AGE AND SEX STRUCTURE
AND POPULATION PROJECTIONS

LEARNING OBJECTIVES

■ Explain the effects of declining mortality and declining fertility on the age distribution of a population.

■ List three reasons why many governments are concerned about having an aging population.

■ Give two examples of how historical events, such as a war or a famine, have affected the age distribution of an actual population.

■ Discuss four uses of population projections.

■ Define population momentum. Explain how it results from changes in mortality and fertility and its effect on population growth.

((• Listen to the Chapter Audio

OVERVIEW

Earlier chapters examined how mortality and fertility separately affect population. This chapter discusses how they work together to influence the population by age and sex. Specifically, this chapter looks at the population's median age and the division of a population by age roughly into those in the working ages, those younger than the working ages (and thus in need of support by others), and those older than the working ages (and thus in need of support from others).

Then it looks at the long-term implications of a combination of an age-specific fertility schedule and an age-specific mortality schedule for the population's age structure. This is done through a discussion of stable populations. A stable population has the age distribution that would result if a given age-specific fertility schedule and a specific age-specific mortality schedule were in effect for a very long time. We also look at the growth of the elderly population in the MDR, especially of the oldest old, which are those aged 85 or older.

After that, population pyramids for several countries over time are examined to see how the age structure of particular populations has changed. In

this, the long-term impact of historical events such as the Great Depression, World War II, and rapid fertility reduction on the age structure of a population is seen.

Next, population projections are discussed, including how they are done and for what purposes. The factors related to, as well as some consequences of, population aging are examined. The differing effects of declining mortality and declining fertility on the age structure are explained. When mortality first declines, the age structure of the population becomes somewhat younger, since decline from high to moderate mortality is mainly the result of a decline in infant and child mortality. As fertility declines, the age structure becomes older. Declines in mortality at the older ages also contribute to population aging.

Populations in more developed countries have grown considerably older in recent years, and population aging is increasingly viewed as a social problem. However, populations in the least developed countries (LeastDC) have remained quite young, and there has been fairly little aging of the populations of the less developed countries. Growing young adult populations provide opportunities for less developed countries but also can contribute to social unrest.

Population projections are important to plan for the future, but they are not necessarily predictions. A projection says that if population processes A, B, and C are in effect for X years in the future, then the population will look like this after X years. A population projection does not predict singular events such as famine or wars that can have a large effect on a population's age structure. Also, the results of a population projection can stimulate implementation of policies that change a population's future. Population momentum is also discussed, in which, due to the age structure, a population can continue to grow for many years after the age-specific mortality and fertility schedules that would eventually lead to an unchanging or a declining population have come into effect.

MEDIAN AGE

One useful way to think about the age of a population is to look at the median age. The **median age** is the age at which there is an equal number of people above that age and below that age.

Figure 11.1 shows the median age of the population for the world, the more developed region (MDR), the less developed region (LDR), and the least developed countries (LeastDC). The median age for the world population declined from 1950 through 1965–1975 and then increased through 2010. Even in 2010, over one-half the world's population was below age 30. The median age of the MDR has steadily increased since 1950, rising from 29 years to 40 years. In the LDR, as in the world, the median age declined during 1950–1965 and then increased during 1975–2010. In 2010 the median age was lower in the LDR than it was in the MDR in 1950. In the LeastDC, after a decline in the median age between 1960 and 1965,

the median age increased slightly from 2000 through 2010. In 2010, the median age in the LeastDC was 20, one year older than it was in 1950–1955. The differences in median age indicate why the MDR countries are concerned about population aging, while in the LeastDC producing the resources for education of children continues to be a pressing problem.

Figure 11.2 shows the median age of the population by world region. Europe and Northern America had the same median age in 1950, but by 1960, the median age in Europe was higher than in Northern America. This is mainly because of the substantially lower fertility in Europe than in Northern America since 1990, as shown in Figure 8.3 in Chapter 8. Median age in Oceania is somewhat lower than in Northern America. The median age in Asia, Africa, and Latin America and the Caribbean was lower than in Europe, Northern America, or Oceania at every date. After 1970, the values of the median age in Asia and in Latin America and the Caribbean were similar, but were slightly higher at every date in Asia. After 1970, the median age increased in both regions. The values of the median age in Africa are very similar to those for the LeastDC shown in Figure 11.1. The gap between the median age in Africa and in other regions increases over time, especially after 1970, because fertility was considerably lower in other regions than in Africa, as shown in Figure 8.3.

Figure 11.3 shows the median age for five individual countries. Japan is shown because in 2010 it had the highest median age in the world. Italy had the third highest median age in 2010, just behind Germany which had a median age of 44. In 1950, the median age in Japan was 7 years younger than in Italy, but by 1990, the median age in Japan was the same as in Italy, and by 2010 the median age in Japan was

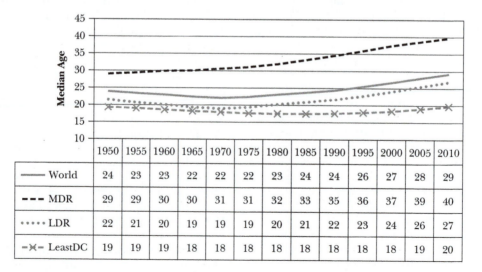

	1950	1955	1960	1965	1970	1975	1980	1985	1990	1995	2000	2005	2010
——— World	24	23	23	22	22	22	23	24	24	26	27	28	29
- - - MDR	29	29	30	30	31	31	32	33	35	36	37	39	40
••••• LDR	22	21	20	19	19	19	20	21	22	23	24	26	27
-✕- LeastDC	19	19	19	18	18	18	18	18	18	18	18	19	20

FIGURE 11.1 Median Age of the Population in the World, MDR, LDR, and LeastDC, 1950–2010

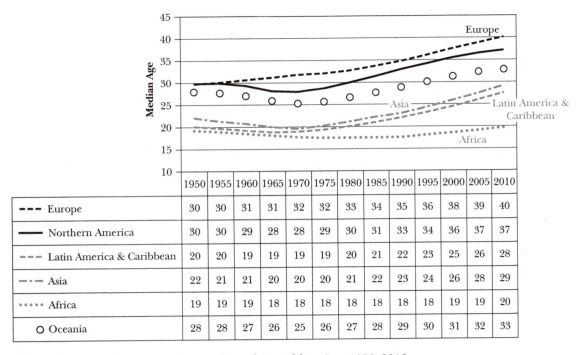

	1950	1955	1960	1965	1970	1975	1980	1985	1990	1995	2000	2005	2010
- - - Europe	30	30	31	31	32	32	33	34	35	36	38	39	40
—— Northern America	30	30	29	28	28	29	30	31	33	34	36	37	37
- - - Latin America & Caribbean	20	20	19	19	19	19	20	21	22	23	25	26	28
—·— Asia	22	21	21	20	20	20	21	22	23	24	26	28	29
····· Africa	19	19	19	18	18	18	18	18	18	18	19	19	20
O Oceania	28	28	27	26	25	26	27	28	29	30	31	32	33

FIGURE 11.2   Median Age of the Population by World Region, 1950–2010

2 years older than in Italy. The United States is shown for comparison. In 1950, the median age in the United States was higher than in Italy or Japan, but by 1970, it was lower than in Japan or Italy. The United States had a lower median age due to the higher fertility in the United States than in Italy or Japan.

In 2010, Mali, Uganda, and Niger were the countries with the lowest median ages in the world, at

16 years. In Mali, the median age has declined over time. Mali is a very poor Western African country and is a member of the LeastDC. The median age declined in Mali because infant and child mortality declined, while fertility was almost unchanged. Kenya is in East Africa, and although it is in the LDR, it is not a member of the LeastDC. In Kenya, the median age declined between 1950 and 1975 (to a low value

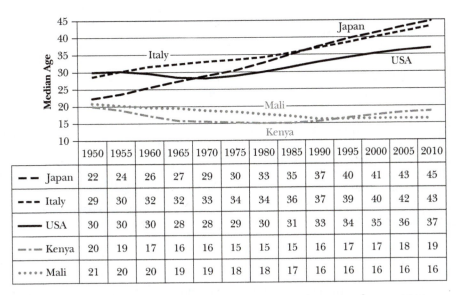

	1950	1955	1960	1965	1970	1975	1980	1985	1990	1995	2000	2005	2010
- - Japan	22	24	26	27	29	30	33	35	37	40	41	43	45
- - - Italy	29	30	32	32	33	34	34	36	37	39	40	42	43
—— USA	30	30	30	28	28	29	30	31	33	34	35	36	37
—·— Kenya	20	19	17	16	16	15	15	15	16	17	17	18	19
····· Mali	21	20	20	19	19	18	18	17	16	16	16	16	16

FIGURE 11.3   Median Age of the Population in Selected Countries, 1950–2010

of 15), and then increased after 1985 to a value of 19 in 2010. The increase was due to fertility decline in Kenya, as shown in Figure 9.18 in Chapter 9.

YOUNG, WORKING AGE, AND OLDER POPULATIONS

To assess the role of the age distribution in economic activity it is useful to divide the population into three broad age groups: the young, those in the working ages, and the older population. The larger the young and the older population relative to those in the working ages, the greater the burden on the working age population. Although people can contribute productive work at all but the youngest and oldest ages, to assess the economic impact of the age distribution it is convenient to divide the population roughly into the young, who are mainly supported by others; the working age population, who provide most of the productive work; and the older population, who are mainly supported by others. These divisions are related to likely potential for productive economic activity rather than to whether people are actually working for pay or engaged in home production.

The **young population** is usually defined as those aged 0–14. The **working age population** is defined either as those aged 15–59 or as those aged 15–64, and the **older or elderly population** as those aged 60+ or 65+. We are showing the age break between the working ages and the older ages as 65. Although much of the world has had a retirement age of 60, in the United States the age of full retirement has been at least 65. Since 1986 there has been no mandatory retirement age in the United States for most jobs. Also, as mortality at older ages declines, many countries that previously had retirement at age 60 have raised that age and similarly have raised the age for payment of pensions.

Growth of Broad Age Groups by Region

Figure 11.4 shows the growth of population in the three age groups for the world as a whole and by region. The working ages are shown as those age 15–64, and the older population as those age 65+. The data through 2010 are population estimates, and the results for 2015–2050 are UN Population Division projections as of 2011.[1] The projections are based on assumptions about mortality, fertility, and migration patterns after 2010. How projections are produced is discussed later in this chapter.

In the figures, the estimates for 2015–2050 are indicated by solid graph markers, since these projections will differ from what will occur if the actual fertility, mortality, and migration patterns differ from those in the assumptions for time periods after 2010.

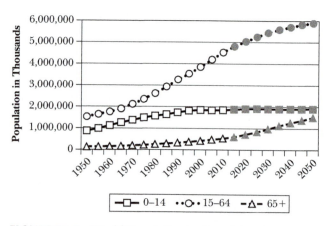

FIGURE 11.4   World Population by Broad Age Groups, 1950–2050

We see in Figure 11.4 that between 1950 and 2010, the world population in the working ages grew rapidly, especially after 1970. The older population also grew. However, the growth rate of the young population declined after about 1970, and the size of the young population was almost unchanged after 2000. After 2010, the working age population is projected to continue to increase through 2050, although the rate of growth will slow after 2010. The older population is expected to grow ever more rapidly after 2010, while the young population is expected to decline slightly after 2030. It is expected that the size of the older population will be 79% of the size of the young population in 2050.

The changes in the age composition of the world seen in Figure 11.4 are the result of very different patterns in different world regions. Figure 11.5 shows similar information to that in Figure 11.4 but referring to the LDR. The patterns in the LDR are similar to those in the world as a whole. However, according to the UN projections, in 2050 in the LDR, the older population is expected to be 69% the size of the young population.

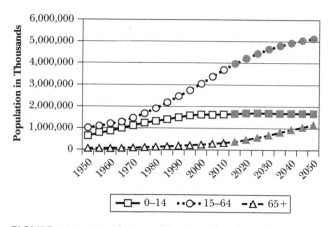

FIGURE 11.5   Population of the Less Developed Region by Broad Age Groups, 1950–2050

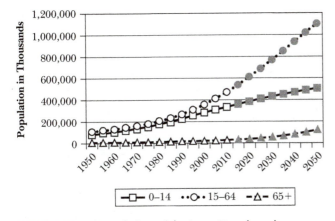

FIGURE 11.6 Population of the Least Developed Countries by Broad Age Groups, 1950–2050

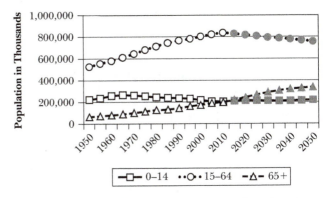

FIGURE 11.7 Population of the More Developed Region by Broad Age Groups, 1950–2050

The situation in the LeastDC is shown in Figure 11.6. In the LeastDC, the size of the working age population is expected to increase at an accelerating rate through 2050, while the growth rate of the older population is seen to increase after about 2030. The growth rate of the young population declines after about 2000 and is expected to decline further after about 2030. However, the population of the LeastDC remains very young. In 2050, the older population is projected to be 24% of the size of the young population.

Figure 11.7 shows a very different situation for the MDR. In the MDR, the size of the young population peaked in 1965. The size of the working age population peaked in 2010 and is expected to decline steadily through 2050. By 2015, in the MDR, the size of the older population is expected to exceed the size of the young population, and in 2050 the older population is expected to be more than 50% larger than the young population.

Figure 11.8 shows comparable information for Japan, the country with the oldest population in the world in 2010. The situation in Japan is a more extreme version of what we see for the MDR as a whole in Figure 11.7. In Japan, the size of the young population generally declined from 1955, with a brief increase between 1970 and 1980. By 2000, the size of the older population exceeded the size of the young population. In 2050, the older population is expected to be 267% the size of the young population, and by 2050, the size of the older population in Japan is expected to be 70% the size of the working age population.

Population Composition by Broad Age Groups

Another way to look at the composition of the population by three broad age groups is to look at the total size of population, divided into the three age groups. This is shown in Figure 11.9 for the MDR, the LDR, and the LeastDC. For each date, the height of the

column represents the total population at the given date. Each column is divided into the size of the three population age groups: 0–14, 15–64, and 65+. The results are shown 1950–2010 and are not shown for projected values after 2010. In the MDR, the population age 65+ has clearly been growing, while the population younger than age 15 has been shrinking. In the LDR and the LeastDC, all age groups are growing.

Percentage Distribution of Population by Broad Age Groups

Figure 11.10 shows the percentage distribution of the population across the three age groups. Again, this is shown for the MDR, the LDR, and the LeastDC. The same shading of age groups is shown in Figures 11.9 and 11.10.

In the top panel of Figure 11.10, the increase in the percentage of the population in the older age group and the decrease in the young age group in the MDR are striking. The percentage of the population in the older age group doubled between 1950 and 2010, and the percentage in the younger age group in 2010 was 63% of the 1950 value. There is fairly little change in

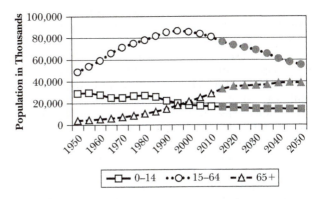

FIGURE 11.8 Japan's Population by Broad Age Groups, 1950–2050

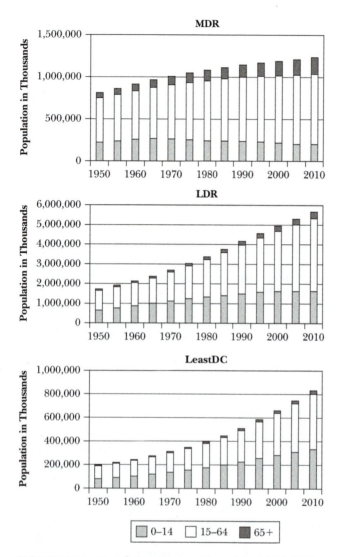

FIGURE 11.9 Population Composition of the MDR, LDR, and LeastDC in Broad Age Groups, 1950–2010

the percentage of the population in the working ages, only varying from 63% to 68% across time.

In the LDR, the percentage of the population in the older age group increased by 50% between 1950 and 2010, but only from 4% to 6%. Thus, although the older population is an increasing percentage of the population in the LDR, by 2010 it still constituted a small portion of the total population. In the LDR, the percentage of the population at young ages increased from 1950 through 1970 and then decreased between 1970 and 2010, declining from 42% to 29%. This decline in the percentage at the younger ages resulted in an increase in the percentage in the working ages from 55% in 1975 to 65% in 2010.

In the LeastDC, there was essentially no change in the percentage of the population above age 65

between 1950 and 2010, with older persons constituting 3% of the population at every date. After 1985, the percentage at young ages declined from 45% to 40%, which resulted in an increase in the percentage in the working ages from 52% to 56%, an increase similar to, but more modest than, the increase in the LDR as a whole.

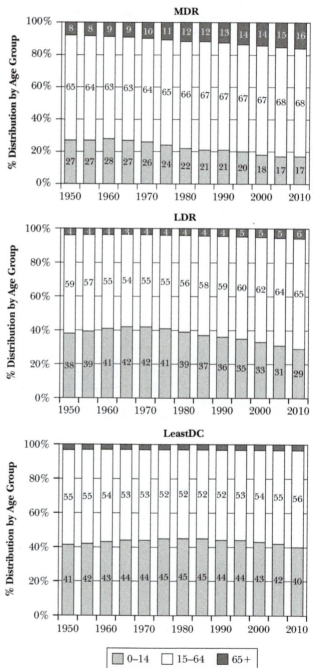

FIGURE 11.10 Percentage Distribution of the World Population in Broad Age Groups, 1950–2010

Dependency Ratios

Another way to look at the age structure of the population across three broad age groups is through dependency ratios. The overall **dependency ratio** is the number of people aged 0–14 plus the number of people 65+ divided by the number of people aged 15–64. This is multiplied by 100, so that the dependency ratio is interpreted as the number of people in the dependent ages per 100 people in the working ages. The **youth dependency ratio** is the number of people aged 0–14 per 100 people aged 15–64. The **old age dependency ratio** is the number of people aged 65+ per 100 people aged 15–64.

Figure 11.11 shows the overall dependency ratio 100 × ((aged 0–14) + (aged 65+))/ (aged 15–64), the young dependency ratio 100 × ((aged 0–14)/ (aged 15–64)) and the old age dependency ratio 100 × ((aged 65+)/(aged 15–64)) for the world as a whole, the MDR, the LDR, and the LeastDC. The overall dependency ratio is the sum of the young dependency ratio and the old age dependency ratio. The values that appear for 1950–2010 are estimates of the actual values of the ratios for those dates. The values for 2015–2050 are based on UN Population Division projections of likely future populations by age. The values based on projections are further designated by solid markers on the graph lines. All of the graphs in Figure 11.11 have the same vertical scale in order to facilitate comparisons.

In the world as a whole between 1950 and 2010, the overall dependency ratio increased from 65 people in the dependent ages per 100 people in the working ages in 1950 to 75 people in the dependent ages per 100 people in the working ages in 1965 and then declined to 52 by 2010. It is expected to increase to 58 by 2050. After 1970, the old age dependency ratio contributed an increasing proportion of the overall dependency ratio. In 2050, the contribution of the young dependency ratio and the old age dependency ratio to the overall dependency ratio is expected to be almost equal, with the old age dependency ratio contributing 45% of the overall dependency ratio.

In the MDR, in 1950, the young dependency ratio contributed 78% of the overall dependency ratio, but by 2010 the young dependency ratio and the old age dependency were equal at 24 per 100 persons in the working ages. The overall dependency ratio in the MDR is expected to increase by 52% between 2010 and 2050, and 84% of that increase is expected to be due to an increase in the old age dependency ratio. By 2050, the old age dependency ratio is expected to be 55% larger than the young dependency ratio.

In the LDR, the old age dependency ratio increased slowly over time between 1950 and 2010 and is expected to increase more rapidly after 2015. The young dependency ratio declined steadily after

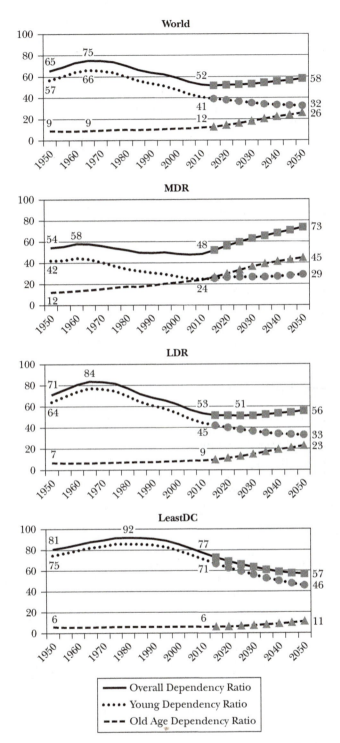

FIGURE 11.11   Dependency Ratios in the World, MDR, LDR, and LeastDC, 1950–2050

1965. The overall dependency ratio peaked in 1965, due to the peak in the young dependency ratio. The overall dependency ratio declined after 1965 and is expected to be 51 in 2025. The overall dependency ratio is expected to increase between 2025 and 2050 due to the influence of the increasing old age dependency ratio.

In the LeastDC, the trajectories of the dependency ratios are similar to in the LDR as a whole, but with certain exceptions. The young dependency ratio and the overall dependency ratio peaked in 1980 in the LeastDC, 15 years later than in the LDR. In the LeastDC, the old age dependency ratio is expected to increase from 6 to 11 between 2010 and 2050. Although this would represent an 83% increase in the old age dependency ratio, the absolute increase of 5 per 100 persons in the working ages is more than offset by the expected decline in the young dependency ratio between 2010 and 2050 from 71 to 46.

Potential Support Ratios and the Demographic Dividend

When looking at the working age population relative to the dependent age population, potential support ratios are sometimes discussed. The **old age potential support ratio** is the inverse of the old age dependency ratio. It is the number of people aged 15–64 per every person aged 65 or older. This is often interpreted as the number of working age people there are to support each retirement age person. The overall **potential support ratio** is the number of people aged 15–64 divided by the sum of the number of people aged 0–14 and aged 65+. This is the number of working age people there are to support every dependent age person.[2]

Figure 11.12 shows the old age potential support ratio for the world, MDR, LDR, and LeastDC. It communicates a similar picture (but the inverse) to that in Figure 11.11 for the old age dependency ratio. In the LeastDC, the old age potential support ratio is expected to decline to almost 50% of its 2010 value by 2050, but even in 2050, there are expected to be more than eight people in the working ages for every person aged 65+. In the MDR, by 2050 there are expected to be two working age persons for every person aged 65+, which makes it clear why there are strong concerns about support of the elderly in the MDR. Recall from Figure 2.34 in Chapter 2 that in 2011, 88% of MDR countries considered population aging a major concern. In a pay-as-you-go social security system, where those retired at a given point in time are supported by contributions from those in the working ages, the potential support ratio often plays a major role in policy discussions of whether to raise the retirement age and how to generate financial support for retired persons, as many pension funds run out of money and others are projected to run out of money in the future.

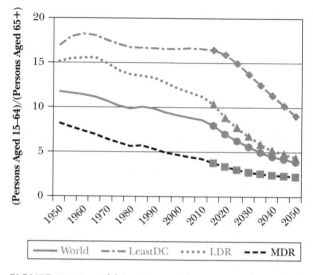

FIGURE 11.12 Old Age Potential Support Ratio in the World, MDR, LDR, and LeastDC, 1950–2050

Figure 11.13 shows the overall potential support ratio for the world, MDR, LDR, and LeastDC. In the MDR, the potential support ratio declined between 1950 and 1960 and then increased, reaching a maximum of 2.1 working age persons for every dependent age person in 2010. The potential support ratio is expected to decline to 1.4 by 2050 in the MDR. If the old age group began at age 70 rather than at age 65, the overall support ratio in the MDR would have been 2.6 in 2010 and 1.8 in 2050, and if the old age group began at age 75 rather than at age 65, the overall support ratio in the MDR would have been 3.2 in 2010 and 2.2 in 2050.

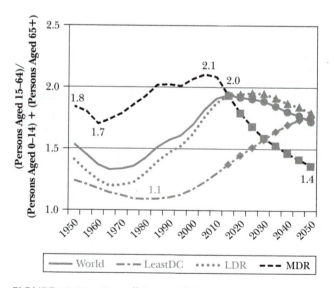

FIGURE 11.13 Overall Potential Support Ratio in the World, MDR, LDR, and LeastDC, 1950–2050

The temporary high value of the overall potential support ratio that is seen in the MDR in 1980–2010 has been termed a **demographic dividend**.[3] When the size of the working age population is high relative to the size of the dependent age population, there is the potential for a high level of economic productivity. The period when the potential support ratio has a high value is also sometimes termed a **demographic window**. The demographic window has been defined as the period when the percentage of the population aged 0–14 is less than 30% and the percentage of the population aged 65+ is less than 15%.[4] This period of time is seen as a window of opportunity because this favorable potential support ratio only translates into economic growth if there are jobs to productively employ the working age population and if the relatively small number of child dependents is capitalized on by increasing educational attainment. It is also sometimes termed a window because, after a time, the potential support ratio declines. The window "closed" for the MDR after 2010.

The LDR is expected to experience a demographic window between about 2010 and 2040. The overall potential support ratio in the LeastDC is expected to increase through 2050, although it only reaches a value of 1.8 in 2050. Sometime after 2050, the demographic window in the LeastDC is expected to begin to close.

The mere presence of a demographic window does not assure economic growth. Bloom and his colleagues point out that to take advantage of a demographic window, there must be sufficient investment and sufficient human capital to translate this opportunity into economic growth.[5] Ingle and Suryawanshi estimate that India is experiencing a demographic window from 2010 through about 2050.[6] They argue that the Indian state needs to develop policies to take advantage of this opportunity.

Less Developed Countries and the Youth Bulge

Related to the idea of a "demographic dividend" is what is called a **youth bulge**. In the course of development, often the size of the young adult population and the proportion of the population who are young adults increase and then decline. When the young adult population is large or increasing, the population is said to have a youth bulge.

There have been various indicators for the presence of a youth bulge. Sometimes researchers have looked at the proportion of the population aged 15–24 or the change in the size of the population aged 12–24. At other times, they have looked at the percentage of those at least aged 15, who are aged 15–24, or who are aged 15–29. Urdal has argued that the most appropriate indicator of the extent of the youth bulge is the percentage of those aged 15 or older who are aged 15–24. The rationale for this rather than looking at those aged 15–24 as a percentage of the total population is that most of the arguments about why a youth bulge can lead to social unrest or violence have to do with competition between younger and older adults.[7] We follow Urdal's suggestion and indicate the extent of the youth bulge as the percentage of those aged 15+ who are aged 15–24.

It has been argued that a youth bulge can contribute to unrest such as campus demonstrations and that an excessive concern with the problems of young adults can influence government spending and social welfare programs in a way that might not be best for society as a whole. As educational attainment has increased in many countries, young adults are increasingly well educated. This can have economic benefits if these educated young adults can be productively employed. However, if the economy is not doing well, a lack of a job or of an acceptable job can be extremely frustrating to the educated youth and can contribute to social unrest or violence. Also, in a poor economic situation, young adults are typically more likely to be unemployed than more experienced workers. In the Middle East and North Africa, there is a concern that educated youth without acceptable jobs and without the economic means to marry and start a family could be especially susceptible to radical appeals and could feel that it would be virtuous to devote themselves to a larger cause, especially if they do not see a possibility for success through a more socially acceptable path.[8] Some countries have raised the minimal age of marriage to offset the fertility-increasing effects of a large number of people in the prime childbearing ages as a result of the youth bulge, but such actions could increase the frustrations of unmarried youth.[9]

Figure 11.14 shows the indicator of the youth bulge for 1950–2010 and as projected to 2050 for the world, the MDR, the LDR, the LeastDC and the USA. Those who were 15–24 in 1950 were born in 1925–1940, while in 1975, those aged 15–24 were born in 1950–1965.

The time of the youth bulge was over by about 1980 in the MDR. In the LDR, the youth bulge began to lessen after 1990 and was considerably less by 2000. In the LeastDC, the youth bulge was unabated through 2005 and is expected to lessen gradually after 2010.

It has been argued that the larger the size of this youth bulge, the higher the potential for social unrest, including violence. The peak of the youth bulge in the United States generally coincides with the period of high campus unrest in the 1960s and 1970s. The youth bulge in the LDR lasted longer than in the MDR, and the level of the youth bulge was higher in the LDR than the MDR at every date. The youth

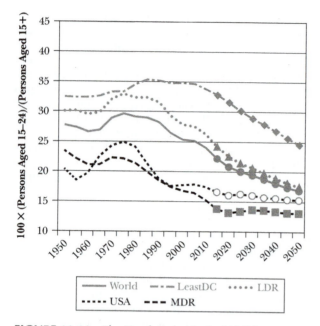

FIGURE 11.14 The Youth Bulge in the World, MDR, LDR, LeastDC, and in the United States, 1950–2050

bulge in the LeastDC occurred later than in the LDR and also lasted longer.

Figure 11.15 shows the extent of the youth bulge in six individual countries. Each of the countries has experienced substantial social unrest, and it is useful to see whether the size of the youth bulge could be related to unrest in those countries. In South Korea the youth bulge peaked in the 1980s, which was also

a period of unprecedented campus unrest in that country.[10] In South Africa, the youth bulge was at a high plateau in 1975–1990, which was a period of vigorous political and violent activity in opposition to apartheid.

Figure 11.15 shows results for two North African countries, Egypt and Tunisia, that experienced Arab Spring activities in 2010–2011. In 2000–2010, there was a substantial youth bulge in Egypt and a somewhat smaller youth bulge in Tunisia. There were larger youth bulges in these countries in 1975–1985. The two Middle Eastern countries shown, Yemen and Jordan, show strong evidence of a youth bulge, especially Yemen, which in 2012 had become the center of the al Qaeda organization.[11]

Stable and Stationary Populations

If a population has an unchanging age-specific mortality schedule and an unchanging age-specific fertility schedule for a long time, then that population will have an unchanging age distribution. Such a population is called a **stable population**. As discussed in Chapter 2, in the course of the demographic transition, typically mortality falls (first in infancy and childhood). This leads to an increase in the population growth rate. Later fertility falls. As the gap between fertility and mortality narrows, the population growth rate declines. That growth rate can become zero or even negative. Stable populations are calculated assuming no migration.

If a stable population has mortality and fertility rates that result in a positive growth rate, even though the age distribution is unchanged, the population size will increase over time. If the population has a growth rate of 2%, then every year there will be 2% more births than there were the previous year, and in fact the total population size will be 2% greater than it was the previous year. Also, at every age, there will be 2% more people than there were the previous year.

Figure 11.16 shows population pyramids for stable populations generated by typical age-specific death rates that lead to a female $e_0^0 = 40$ and male $e_0^0 = 37.3$. Recall that in almost all populations, female death rates are lower than male death rates at every age, and female e_0^0 is higher than male e_0^0. This example represents a typical relationship between male and female mortality in a high-mortality population. In a **population pyramid**, the number of persons or the percentage of the population by age is shown.

In Figures 11.16, 11.17, and 11.18, the percentage distribution by age for each sex is shown, with the results for males on the left and for females on the right. The distribution by age is shown from age 0 at the bottom to age 90+ at the top. The percentages

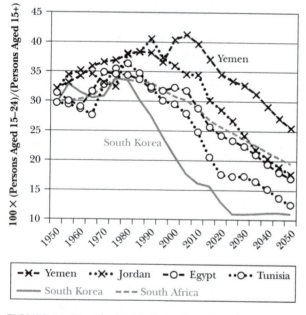

FIGURE 11.15 The Youth Bulge in Selected Countries, 1950–2050

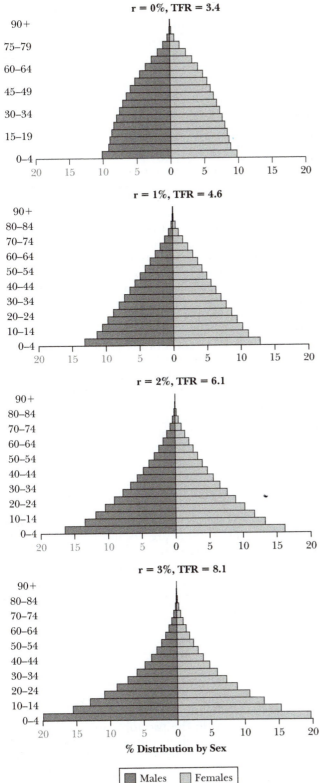

FIGURE 11.16   Population Pyramids for Stable Populations with High Mortality: Female $e_0^0 = 40.0$, Male $e_0^0 = 37.3$

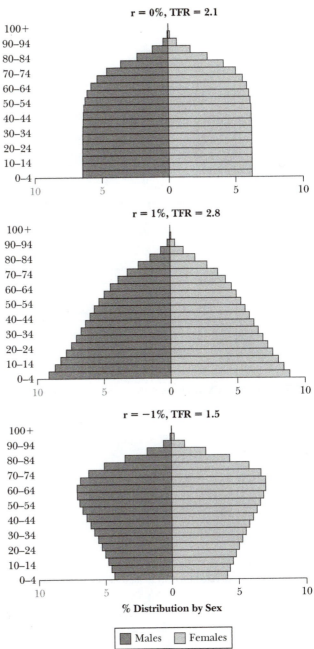

FIGURE 11.17   Population Pyramids for Stable Populations with Low Mortality: Female $e_0^0 = 80.0$ and Male $e_0^0 = 76.6$

for males sum to 100%, and the percentages for females sum to 100%.

The pyramids show the stable population age distributions implied by a combination of a given expectation of life at birth (with the associated typical schedule of age-specific death rates) and a given growth rate. The total fertility rate (TFR) needed to

Panel 1: High Mortality and High Fertility, r = 0

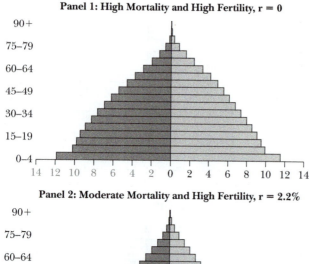

Panel 2: Moderate Mortality and High Fertility, r = 2.2%

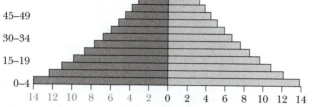

Panel 3: Moderate Mortality and Moderately High Fertility, r = 1%

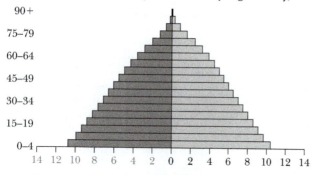

Panel 4: Moderate Mortality and Moderate Fertility, r = 0%

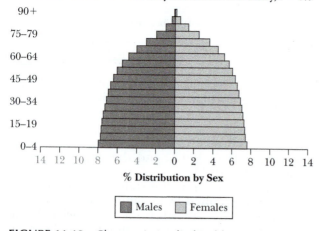

% Distribution by Sex

☐ Males ☐ Females

FIGURE 11.18 Changes in Implied Stable Populations through the Demographic Transition

attain that growth rate with the given expectations of life at birth is also shown.[12]

The first panel of Figure 11.16 shows the population pyramids for the stable populations by sex that result from the given age-specific mortality schedules and a growth rate of 0. This would happen with a total fertility rate of 3.4. That this population has a growth rate of zero means that the size of the total population is constant. Since a stable population has an unchanging age distribution, when a stable population has a growth rate of zero, then there are the same number of people in every age group at all times. Thus, if a stable population with a growth rate of zero had 12,000 people aged 3 in one year, it would also have 12,000 people aged 3 in the next year and in the year after that.

A stable population with a growth rate of zero is also called a **stationary population**. In a stationary population, the age distribution is the same as the $_nL_x$ column of the population's life table, which was discussed in Chapter 4. In the first panel with a growth rate of zero, there are many more people aged 0–4 than aged 5–9 due to high mortality below aged 5 when expectation of life at birth is about 40 years. In the life tables used, only 72% of females and 70% of males survive to their fifth birthday.

The second panel of Figure 11.16 shows the stable populations resulting from the same life tables used in the first panel and a growth rate of 1%. With those life tables, a total fertility rate of 4.6 results in a growth rate of 1%. While in a stationary population there is the same number of births every year, in a stable population with a growth rate of 1% every year there are 1% more births than there were the previous year (i.e., every birth cohort is 1% larger than the birth cohort of the previous year). Also in every age group (5–9, 60–64, etc.), there are 1% more persons than there were in that age group in the previous year. Notice that with a growth rate of 1%, the age distribution curves in more rapidly with increasing age than when the growth rate is zero. This is because when the growth rate is 0 in a stable population, the number of people declines with age only due to mortality, while in a stable population with a positive growth rate, the number of people declines by age both due to mortality and because every successive birth cohort is larger than the birth cohort of the previous year.

The third panel of Figure 11.16 shows the population pyramids for the stable populations with the same life tables as in the two top panels and with a growth rate of 2%, while the fourth panel shows the stable populations for the same life tables and a growth rate of 3%. The higher the growth rate, the more steeply the population pyramid declines with age.

It is clear with a given life table that the higher the growth rate, the younger the age distribution. Recall that the population pyramids in Figure 11.16 add to 100% for each sex. With expectation of life at birth of about 40 years and with a growth rate of zero, the associated stable population has about 10% of the population of each sex in the 0–4 age group. With the same life table and a growth rate of 3%, about 20% of the population of each sex is in the 0–4 age group.[13]

Figure 11.17 is similar to Figure 11.16 but shows the stable populations consistent with a low-mortality life table at different population growth rates. The female life table with $e_0^0 = 80$ years and the male life able with $e_0^0 = 76.6$ years are used, again reflecting a typical mortality difference between the sexes.

The first panel of Figure 11.17 shows the population pyramids for the stable populations produced by these low-mortality life tables and a growth rate of zero. This is a stationary population in which the population size remains unchanged over time. A total fertility rate of only 2.1 would be necessary for a growth rate of zero in these low-mortality life tables, in contrast to the situation shown in Figure 11.16 in which for high-mortality life tables, a total fertility rate of 3.4 was necessary for a growth rate of zero. With a growth rate of zero, the age distribution in the first panel is affected only by the life table. The number of people in each 5-year age group is almost unchanged until age 50. This is because in the life tables used, 98% of females and 97% of males survive to their fiftieth birthday.

The second panel of Figure 11.17 shows the stable populations resulting from the same life tables but with a growth rate of 1%. A total fertility rate of 2.8 would be necessary to attain a growth rate of 1%. With a growth rate of 1%, the population is much younger than with a growth rate of zero, because every year there are 1% more births than in the previous year,

and at every age there are 1% more people than in the previous year.

The third panel of Figure 11.17 shows the population pyramids for stable populations with the given life tables but with a population growth rate of -1%. Every year, this stable population is 1% *smaller* than it was the previous year. This third population pyramid increases with age until about age 50. The age groups increase in size because every year, there are 1% *fewer* births than there were the previous year. This means that the people aged 30 are survivors of a birth cohort that is 35% larger than the current year's birth cohort. Thus, below age 50 the population pyramid mainly reflects the relative size of the different birth cohorts. After age 70, the size of age groups begins to decrease, as age-specific death rates become large enough to diminish the size of age groups.

Population Pyramids for Stable Populations Simulating the Demographic Transition

In Chapter 2, there is a discussion of the demographic transition, in which at first both fertility and mortality are high and the growth rate is near zero. Then mortality falls, while fertility remains high, and the growth rate increases. Later fertility falls, eventually falling low enough to result in a growth rate again of about zero.

Table 11.1 shows the expectation of life at birth and the total fertility rate across four stages of the demographic transition. Mortality is unchanged in the last three stages. Thus, changes across the last three stages are completely determined by changes in fertility. Between the first and second stages, the young dependency ratio shoots up, but across the last three stages the young dependency ratio falls, while the old age dependency ratio increases. Figure 11.18

TABLE 11.1   Characteristics of Stable Populations Consistent with Conditions at Various Stages of the Demographic Transition

	High Mortality and High Fertility, r = 0.0%	Moderate Mortality and High Fertility, r = 2.2%	Moderate Mortality and Moderately High Fertility, r = 1.0%	Moderate Mortality and Moderate Fertility, r = 0.0%
Female e_0^0	30	60	60	60
Male e_0^0	27.7	56.5	56.5	56.5
IMR	276	79	79	79
TFR	4.4	4.4	3.3	2.4
% Age 0–4	12	14	11	8
% Age 0–14	31	37	30	23
% Age 15–64	64	58	63	66
% Age 65+	5	5	8	12
Young Dependency Ratio	49	64	47	35
Old Age Dependency Ratio	7	8	12	18
Overall Dependency Ratio	57	72	60	53

shows the population pyramids for the stable populations implied by the given values of e_0^0 and of TFR at each stage.

Variation in the Percentage of a Stable Population Aged 65 + by Fertility and Mortality Level

Table 11.2 shows how the percentage of the population aged 65+ varies across stable populations characterized by the age-specific mortality schedule associated with the given expectation of life at birth and the age-specific fertility schedule typically associated with the given total fertility rate. Cells are marked with an "a" if the given fertility and mortality schedule has never been found in any known actual population. You never find very high-mortality populations with relatively low fertility over a sustained time period. If such populations existed for a long time, they would disappear due to a negative growth rate.

For a given expectation of life at birth, the higher the total fertility rate, the smaller the percentage of the population aged 65 or older. All babies are born at age 0. The effect of a higher fertility level for a given life table is to increase the growth rate, and thus to increase the number of babies who are born each year, relative to the number of babies born the previous year. This is because for a given expectation of life at birth, the higher the TFR, the higher the population growth rate. The higher the population growth rate, the larger each successive birth cohort, and thus the smaller the percentage of the population above any given age. Note that with $e_0^0 = 50$ and with TFR = 3, 8.8% of the population is aged 65 or older, while with $e_0^0 = 50$ and with TFR = 6, only 2.6% of the population is aged 65 or older.

For a given TFR, a change from e_0^0 of 30 years to 60 years is actually associated with a *decrease* in the percentage of the population above age 65. When mortality improves, the effect on the age distribution depends on the mortality level. This is because when mortality declines, death rates decline both at the youngest ages and at the oldest ages. When mortality declines from a high to a moderate level, most of the decline in age-specific death rates is among infants and children; when mortality declines from a moderate to a low level, most of the decline in the age-specific death rates is at old ages, resulting in an older population. Note that with a TFR of 5 and with $e_0^0 = 30$, 3.9% of the population is over age 65, while at the same TFR but with $e_0^0 = 60$, only 3.7% of the population is above age 65. This is because at fairly low values of e_0^0 (such as younger than 60 years), the change in the age-specific death rates is almost all in infancy and childhood. The effect on the age distribution of a decline in mortality in this situation is virtually identical to an increase in fertility—rather than dying by 3 months of age, the child survives, so it is as if an additional child had been born. With e_0^0 of 60 or higher, a large part of mortality decline is a decrease in death rates at older ages. The effect of such a mortality change is to increase the percentage of the population at older ages.

With low mortality, a TFR of 2 is about at replacement fertility, while a TFR of 1.64 will result in a declining population. With e_0^0 of 60 or higher, the higher the value of e_0^0, the higher the percentage of the population above age 65. The situation in the lower left-hand corner of Table 11.2, with $e_0^0 = 80$ and TFR = 1.64, is similar to the situation in some highly developed low-fertility countries in Europe and Asia since the 1990s.

A Very-High-Mortality Population

Next we look at the age distribution and other characteristics of a stable population with expectation of life at birth of 40 years, but we vary the growth rate from 0 to 0.025 (or positive 2.5%). These calculations are related to the situation in less developed countries. For simplicity, we look at both sexes together. One can look at the population pyramids in Figure 11.16 to see how the age distribution changes with a varying growth rate in a high-mortality population. The results are shown in Table 11.3.

With an unchanging mortality schedule, a higher growth rate is the result of higher fertility—a higher

TABLE 11.2 Percentage of a Stable Population Age 65 + by TFR and e_0^0

Expectation of Life at Birth (e_0^0)	Total Fertility Rate (TFR)					
	1.64	2	3	4	5	6
30	a	a	a	a	3.9%	2.8%
40	a	a	a	5.6%	3.8%	2.7%
50	a	a	8.8%	5.5%	3.7%	2.6%
60	20.1%	15.0%	8.8%	5.4%	3.6%	2.5%
70	21.2%	16.5%	9.2%	5.7%	3.7%	2.6%
80	25.9%	20.9%	12.3%	7.9%	5.4%	3.9%

NOTE: "a" indicates a combination that is never found in an actual population.

TABLE 11.3   Population Characteristics and Dependency Ratios with $e_0^0 = 40$

r	0	0.005	0.010	0.015	0.020	0.025
TFR	3.4	3.9	4.5	5.2	6.0	6.9
Average Age	32	29	27	25	24	22
% Age 65+	8	6	5	4	3	2
% Age 70+	5	4	3	2	2	1
% Under Age 15	27	31	34	38	41	45
% Age 5–9	9	10	11	12	13	14
% Age 5–14	18	19	21	23	25	27
$100 \times (0\text{–}14/15\text{–}64)$ Young Dependency Ratio	42	49	56	64	74	84
$100 \times (65+/15\text{–}64)$ Old Age Dependency Ratio	12	10	8	7	6	5
$100 \times ((0\text{–}14 + 65+)/15\text{–}64)$ Overall Dependency Ratio	54	59	65	71	80	89

TFR. The higher the growth rate, the younger the average age of the population. Also, the higher the growth rate, the lower the percentage of the population above any age (such as age 65 or 70) and the higher the percentage below any age. If we think of ages 5–14 as the main ages for school enrollment, it is worth noting that with a growth rate of 0.0%, 18% of the population is aged 5–14, but with a growth rate of 2.5%, 27% of the population is aged 5–14. Thus, the higher the growth rate, the greater the challenge of maintaining or increasing school enrollment rates. Similarly, the higher the growth rate, the higher the young dependency ratio and the lower the old age dependency ratio. Although with an increasing growth rate the increase in the young dependency ratio is somewhat compensated by the decline in the old age dependency ratio, overall, with a higher growth rate the overall dependency ratio increases.

A Very-Low-Mortality Population

Now we look at the age distribution and other characteristics of a stable population with $e_0^0 = 80$ years, but we vary the growth rate from −0.01 (which is negative 1%) to 0.01 (which is positive 1%). These calculations are related to the situation in many developed countries. Again, for simplicity, we look at both sexes together. One can look at the population pyramids in Figure 11.17 to see how the age distribution changes with a varying growth rate in a low-mortality population.

The results are shown in Table 11.4. In a low-mortality population, varying the growth rate has little effect on the overall dependency ratio, but it has a tremendous effect on the composition of the dependent population. With a growth rate of 1%, two-thirds of the dependency ratio is due to the young population; with a growth rate of −1%, two-thirds of the dependency ratio is due to the older population.

Problems of Elderly Populations

Many countries have a pay-as-you-go pension or social security plan. In such a system, current workers pay into a fund for pensions or social security for current retirees. In the discussion of the rising old age dependency ratio and the financial problems of pay-as-you-go pension or social security plans, there has been much discussion of raising the retirement age or the age at which full benefits begin.

In the United States, for most jobs mandatory retirement below age 70 was made illegal in 1978, and for most jobs, any mandatory retirement age became illegal in 1986. At the same time, the age at which full Social Security payments begin in the United States has gradually increased. For many years, the minimal age for full Social Security benefits was 65. Starting for

TABLE 11.4   Population Characteristics and Dependency Ratios with $e_0^0 = 80$

r	−0.010	−0.005	0	0.005	0.010
TFR	1.5	1.8	2.1	2.4	2.8
Average Age	47	44	41	38	35
% Age 65+	28	24	20	17	14
% Age 70+	21	17	15	12	10
$100 \times (0\text{–}14/15\text{–}64)$ Young Dependency Ratio	22	26	30	36	42
$100 \times (65+/15\text{–}64)$ Old Age Dependency Ratio	46	39	33	27	23
$100 \times ((0\text{–}14\ \&\ 65+)/15\text{–}64)$ Overall Dependency Ratio	68	65	63	63	64

TABLE 11.5   Effect on Old Age Dependency Ratios with $e_0^0 = 80$ of Increasing Working Ages to 70 or 75 (Retirement Age Increased to 70 or 75) at Various Values of r

r	−0.010	−0.005	0	0.005	0.010
Old Age Dependency Ratios					
$100 \times (65+/15\text{–}64)$ *(retirement age 65)*	46	39	33	27	23
$100 \times (70+/15\text{–}69)$ *(retirement age 70)*	31	26	22	18	15
$100 \times (75+/15\text{–}74)$ *(retirement age 75)*	19	16	13	11	9

those born in 1938, that age has gradually increased and will be 67 for those born in 1959 or later. Raising the pension age has been a subject of great controversy in Europe. After substantial discussion, in 2010 France decided to raise its pension age from 60 to 62, and in 2011, Spain raised its retirement age from 65 to 67.[14]

Effects of Increasing the Retirement Age in a Low-Mortality Population

As an illustration of the impact of raising the retirement age in low-mortality populations, Table 11.5 shows the stable population old age dependency ratios under different population growth rates. The dependency ratios are also varied by whether age 65, 70, or 75 is the retirement age. Regardless of the growth rate, a 5-year increase in the retirement age from 65 to 70 decreases the old age dependency ratio to about 66% of its earlier value, and a 10-year increase in the retirement age from 65 to 75 decreases the old age dependency ratio to about 40% of its earlier value.

Although raising the retirement age lowers the old age dependency ratio, this action is not without costs. Older workers tend to occupy more senior positions. If the retirement age increases, younger workers can anticipate a longer wait to promotion to

a senior position than when the retirement age was lower, which can result in demoralization of younger workers.

Table 11.6 shows the effect on promotion opportunities of increasing the oldest working age from 65 to 70 to 75. In this hypothetical example, people begin working at age 25. They are divided into two groups, younger workers (those aged 25–49) and older workers (those aged 50 through retirement age). The top part of Table 11.6 shows the ratio of the number of older workers to the number of younger workers under different population growth rates and different retirement ages. The calculations were done for stable populations determined by $e_0^0 = 80$ and the indicated growth rates.

The higher the population growth rate, the lower the ratio of older workers to younger workers, whether the retirement age is 65, 70, or 75. This is because, as we saw in Figures 11.16 and 11.17, in a stable population with a given life table, the higher the growth rate, the lower the percentage above any given age. Increasing the retirement age from 65 to 70 increases the ratio of older workers to younger workers for every rate of population growth. Increasing the retirement age to 75 increases the ratio of older to younger workers further. With a retirement age of 75 and a growth rate of −0.5% or less, there are more workers aged 50–74 than there are aged 25–49.

The lower part of Table 11.6 looks at a work situation in which there are two ranks, an upper rank and a lower rank. Real-life examples similar to this include tenured and untenured faculty members, officers and non-officers in the military, and workers and supervisors. In some such situations, there is a set ratio of the number of workers in the upper rank to the number in the lower rank. For example, there might be one supervisor for every three workers. Imagine that there is a set ratio of the number of people in the upper rank to the number of people in the lower rank. Also imagine that all members of the upper rank are older than all members of the lower rank. Although most

TABLE 11.6   Effect on Promotion Opportunities with $e_0^0 = 80$ of Increasing Oldest Working Age from 65 to 70 or to 75

r	−0.010	−0.005	0	0.005	0.010
Number of Older Workers per 100 Younger Workers					
$100 \times (50\text{–}64/25\text{–}49)$ *(retirement age 65)*	71	64	58	52	47
$100 \times (50\text{–}69/25\text{–}49)$ *(retirement age 70)*	95	85	76	68	61
$100 \times (50\text{–}74/25\text{–}49)$ *(retirement age 75)*	118	104	92	81	72
Age of Promotion for ¼ of Workers to Be in the Upper Rank					
Age at which ¼ of those are above that age among those 25–65	56	55	55	54	53
Age at which ¼ of those are above that age among those 25–69	60	59	58	57	56
Age at which ¼ of those are above that age among those 25–74	63	62	61	60	59

job situations are not this clear-cut, this hypothetical situation has some resemblance to reality.

In the hypothetical situation in Table 11.6, 75% of the workers are in the lower rank and 25% are in the upper rank. The age of promotion is the age for which 25% of workers are above that age. Thus, the older the retirement age, the older the age of promotion. In addition, the older the age distribution of the overall working population (that is the lower the growth rate), the older the age of promotion. This example is shown comparing stable populations with $e_0^0 = 80$ with various retirement ages and various growth rates. Raising the retirement age from 65 to 70 increases the age at promotion about 3 years, and raising the retirement age to 75 increases the age at promotion by a further 3 years. Also, varying the growth rate from -1% to $+1\%$ affects the age at promotion by about 3 years.

As technological requirements of many jobs increase, facility with computers is increasingly valuable, and it can be difficult for some older workers to adapt to these new technological requirements. Without a mandatory retirement age, there is no limit to how long an individual can remain in a job, and the organization has no certain future date at which he or she will retire. In this situation, the only way to end a person's employment who has become less capable of performing their work is termination for cause, a situation that is often unpleasant and destructive to workplace morale.[15]

The uncertainty about when older workers will retire has also influenced norms about raises in some workplaces. For example, in the past, in some universities, for faculty an equivalent raise for two different faculty members (with different salaries) was seen as an equal-percentage raise. Older faculty members tend to have higher salaries than younger faculty members. Of course, an equal-percentage raise means a larger absolute raise for higher salaried individuals. Some universities have changed the criterion from an equal raise being seen as the same percentage raise to an equal raise being the same dollar amount of raise. Especially in a situation in which an academic department or school has a certain total number of dollars to devote to raises, the norm in dollars (rather than a percentage) keeps the higher salaried faculty from depleting the raise pool and makes the pace of salary increases better for lower salaried (and usually younger) faculty, which helps avoid demoralization of the lower-salaried faculty members.

The Growth of the Oldest-Old Population in More Developed Countries

In the MDR, not only has the population above age 65 increased in size and percentage of the population, but also the population age 85+, often called

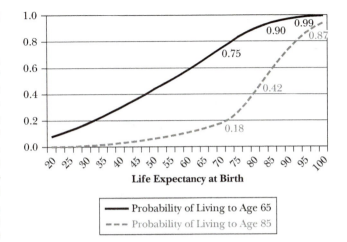

FIGURE 11.19 Female Proportion Surviving to Age 65 (l_{65}) and Proportion Surviving to Age 85 (l_{85}) across Values of e_0^0 20 to 100

the oldest-old population, has increased very rapidly. In fact, in the United States between 1980 and 2010, the population aged 90 and older nearly tripled, and among those aged 65 and older, those aged 90 and older increased from 2.8% to 4.7%.[16]

The increasing proportion of the population at very old ages is related to fertility declines in the past, to increasing proportions surviving to an advanced age, and to the average number of years a person lives given the person survives to an advanced age. Figure 11.19 shows how the probability of surviving to age 65 and the probability of surviving to age 85 changes across typical life tables for female populations. The probability of surviving to age 85 increases rapidly when e_0^0 increases above 70 years. Figure 11.20 shows how the average number of years a

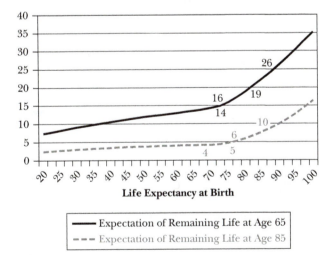

FIGURE 11.20 Female Expectation of Remaining Life at Age 65 (e_{65}^0) and at Age 85 (e_{85}^0) across Values of e_0^0 20 to 100

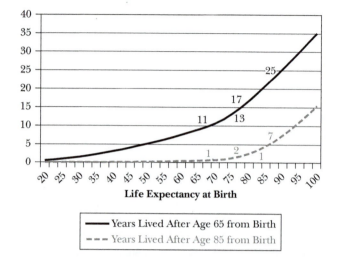

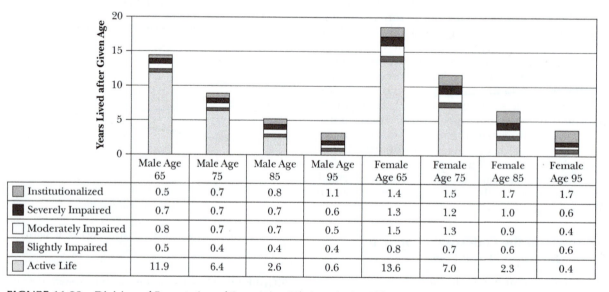

FIGURE 11.21 From Birth, the Number of Years a Female Can Expect to Live Past Her Sixty-Fifth Birthday (T_{65}/l_0) and Past Her Eighty-Fifth Birthday (T_{85}/l_0) across Values of e_0^0 20 to 100

woman is expected to live given she is alive on her sixty-fifth birthday and given she is alive on her eighty-fifth birthday changes with increasing e_0^0. Recall that the expectation of remaining life at age x is the average number of years a person will live after age x, if they survive to their xth birthday. The number of years a person is expected to live after reaching age 85 doubles between $e_0^0 = 75$ and $e_0^0 = 90$.

Putting the results of Figures 11.19 and 11.20 together, Figure 11.21 shows across values of e_0^0, the average number of years lived above age 65 and the average number of years lived above age 85 from

birth. The values in Figure 11.21 are a result both of the chance of surviving to age 65 or 85 and of the average number of ears lived after age 65 or 85 among survivors to age 65 or 85. The number of years that a baby girl can expect to live after age 65 increases gradually until e_0^0 is about 70, after which there is a more rapid increase. A baby girl can expect to live less than 1 year past her eighty-fifth birthday until $e_0^0 = 75$. After that, the number of years she can expect to live past age 85 increases fairly rapidly, the higher the expectation of life at birth. Survival to the oldest-old ages and continued survival beyond age 85 only becomes substantial in low- or very-low-mortality populations. Since in 2005–2010 female e_0^0 was 86 years in Japan, 83 years in Sweden, 81 years in the United States, and 80 years in the MDR as a whole, it is easy to see why growth of the oldest-old population is an area of concern in developed countries.

Active Life Expectancy and the Elderly

One reason for concern about the growth of the older population and especially of the oldest-old population involves the concept of active life expectancy.[17] **Active life expectancy**, sometimes called **healthy life expectancy** or **disability-free life expectancy,** refers to the number of years that a person can expect to live from birth or from some particular age free of any of various disabilities or limitations on activity.[18] This is closely related to the years lived disabled concept discussed in Chapter 5 and the discussion of compression of morbidity in Chapter 4.

Figure 11.22 shows estimates that Manton and colleagues produced by sex for the U.S. population in 1983.[19] Expectation of remaining life is shown by sex at

	Male Age 65	Male Age 75	Male Age 85	Male Age 95	Female Age 65	Female Age 75	Female Age 85	Female Age 95
Institutionalized	0.5	0.7	0.8	1.1	1.4	1.5	1.7	1.7
Severely Impaired	0.7	0.7	0.7	0.6	1.3	1.2	1.0	0.6
Moderately Impaired	0.8	0.7	0.7	0.5	1.5	1.3	0.9	0.4
Slightly Impaired	0.5	0.4	0.4	0.4	0.8	0.7	0.6	0.6
Active Life	11.9	6.4	2.6	0.6	13.6	7.0	2.3	0.4

FIGURE 11.22 Division of Expectation of Remaining Life into Active Life Expectancy and Various Types of Impaired Life Expectancy by Sex in the United States, 1982

ages 65, 75, and 85, divided into active life expectancy and impaired life expectancy. Impaired life expectancy is divided into slightly impaired life expectancy (such as needing help with heavy work or rheumatism), moderately impaired life expectancy (such as needing help taking medicine or getting about outside), heavily impaired but non-institutionalized life expectancy (such as needing help getting about inside or using the toilet), and years lived in an institution.

In the example in Figure 11.22, at age 65, over 70% of remaining years of life will be spent in active life, while at age 85, 50% of the remaining years for men and 30% of the remaining years for women are in active life. For women at age 85, 26% of remaining years of life are expected to be spent in an institution, and 42% of remaining years are expected to be spent in an institution or not in an institution but in a severely impaired state. Traphagan has written about how fear of senility among elderly Japanese can lead to suicide.[20]

POPULATION PYRAMIDS FOR ACTUAL POPULATIONS

Next we look at population pyramids for real populations. First we look at population pyramids for these populations through 2010. Later in this chapter, we look at population pyramids for real populations according to projections into the future. We separate these to help keep in mind that a projection into the future is not a certain prediction of what will happen. The horizontal axis for each graph shows the number of persons in millions.

The Population of the World

Figure 11.23 shows population pyramids for the world as a whole in 1950, 1970, 1990, and 2010. The scale is the same in all four panels.

As we know from the discussion in earlier chapters, there was a large decline in mortality between 1950 and 1970. As shown in Figures 4.3 and 4.5, e_0^0 increased for each sex by about 10 years between 1950–1955 and 1970–1975, and as shown in Figure 4.1, the IMR declined from 133 per 1,000 to 86 per 1,000. At the same time, as shown in Figure 8.2, the TFR only declined from 5.0 to 4.5. Thus with the decline in infant mortality, there was considerable improvement in infant and child survival, which is reflected in the population pyramid for 1970 being younger, with a higher proportion of people at young ages than in 1950. This is similar to the effects of the decline from high mortality to moderate mortality, while fertility remains high as illustrated in the first two panels of Figure 11.18.

Between 1970–1975 and 1990–1995, fertility declined, with the TFR decreasing from 4.5 to 3.0 with

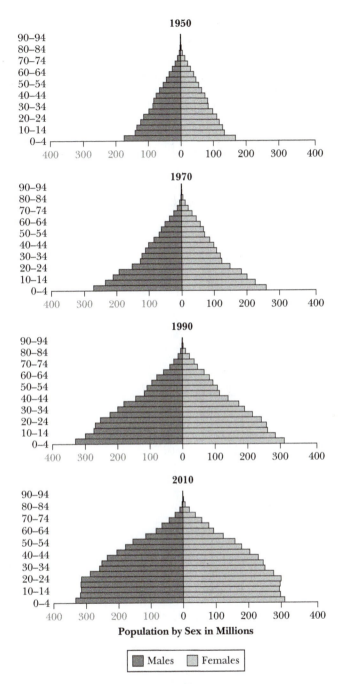

FIGURE 11.23 Population Pyramids for the World: 1950, 1970, 1990, and 2010

a further decline in the TFR to 2.5 by 2005–2010. The change in the population pyramids for the world between 1970 and 1990 shown in Figure 11.23 is similar to the change between Panel 2 and Panel 3 in Figure 11.18. By 2010, with the further decline in fertility, the population pyramid looked somewhat like that in Panel 4 of Figure 11.18.

The Population of Mali: A Young and Rapidly Growing Country

Figure 11.24 shows the population pyramids for Mali for 1950, 1970, 1990, and 2010. The horizontal bars are the number of people in the given 5-year age group by sex in millions, as in Figure 11.23 for the world.

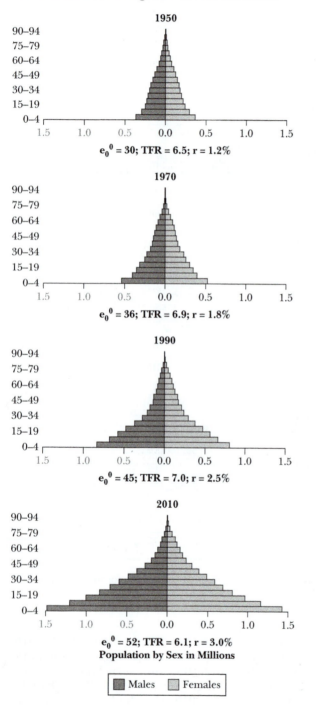

FIGURE 11.24   Population Pyramids for Mali: 1950, 1970, 1990, and 2010

Recall that Mali is a member of the LeastDC and in 2010 was one of three countries with the youngest median age in the world at 16 years. Expectation of life at birth in Mali increased over time between 1950–1955 and 2010–2015, while the TFR increased from 1950–1955 (at 6.5) to 1990–1995 (at 7.0) and only declined slightly to 6.1 in 2010–2015. The more rapid decline of mortality than fertility is reflected in the increase over time in the population growth rate. In 2010, the population doubling time was 23 years.

The age pyramids for Mali for each date resemble those for high-growth-rate stable populations. Since the same horizontal scale is used for the pyramids for Mali for all four dates, it is easy to see that the Mali population was growing rapidly, and there was a large increase in every age group. There were 4.0 times as many children aged 0–4 in Mali in 2010 as there were in 1950, but the total population of Mali in 2010 was 3.3 times its size in 1950. In 2010, the rapid decrease in the width of the 5-year age groups with increasing age makes clear why Mali had such a low median age. This steep decline in the population with increasing age shown for Mali in 2010 is typical of countries with a high population growth rate. This situation occurs when mortality, especially infant and child mortality, has declined, but fertility has declined very little. The population pyramid for Mali in 2010 resembles that in Panel 2 of Figure 11.18, which shows the population pyramid for a moderate-mortality, high-fertility population.

The United States: The Great Depression, the Baby Boom, and Other Events

Figure 11.25 shows the U.S. population pyramids for 1950, 1970, 1990, and 2010. Unlike the population pyramids for Mali, the population pyramids for the United States do not look much like stable populations. Rather, the population pyramids for the United States are distinguished by the bulges and gouges that were mainly caused by fluctuations in fertility.

The pyramid for 1950 shows a gouge for those aged 10–24, reflecting the small number of births during the Great Depression. Recall that Figure 8.13 shows the dip in American fertility during the Depression. The large number of people aged 0–4 in 1950 in the population pyramid reflects the beginning of the postwar Baby Boom. Figure 8.13, which tracked the TFR in the United States, also showed the increase in fertility after World War II, which was the beginning of the Baby Boom.

In the pyramid for 1970, those born during the Great Depression were aged 30–44, and the gouge caused by those small birth cohorts is still apparent. The Baby Boom ended with the birth cohort of

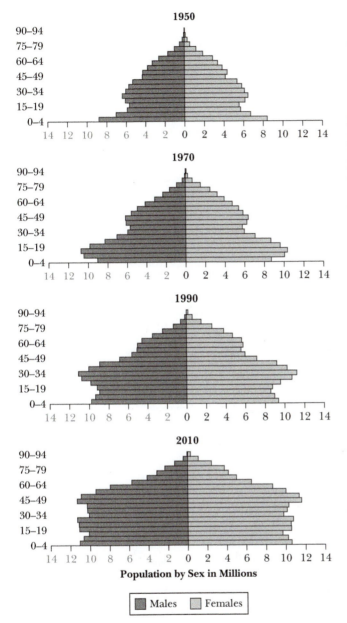

FIGURE 11.25   U.S. Population Pyramids: 1950, 1970, 1990, and 2010

1964, so in 1970 the Baby Boomers were aged 5–24. The Baby Boom birth cohorts are shown as a distinct bulge in 1970. The decline in the number of births between 1960–1965 and 1965–1970 is clear in the pyramid for 1970 for those aged 0–4.

By 1990, the Baby Boomers were in the prime childbearing ages. Thus, in the pyramid for 1990, we see the bulge of the Baby Boom birth cohorts and also what is called the echo of the Baby Boom in the larger number of people aged 0–4 and aged 5–9 than aged 10–14. The echo of the Baby Boom is the

increase in births in the 1980s due to the fertility of the large number of women of childbearing age who were born during the Baby Boom.

In 2010, we can still see the Baby Boom, although its prominence in the population pyramid has declined, since those born early in the Baby Boom had entered ages with relatively high age-specific death rates. The jag in the age distribution created by the echo of the Baby Boom is still apparent for those aged 20–29. In 2010, the oldest Baby Boomers were in the 60–64 age group. It is clear that when more of the Baby Boomers enter retirement ages, the proportion of the population at older ages will increase substantially. By 2010, we can see some rectangularization of the age distribution.

The Russian Empire, the Soviet Union, and the Former Soviet Union: Very Jagged Population Pyramids

Next we look at population pyramids for the Russian Empire, the Soviet Union, and the former Soviet Union. These population pyramids are more affected by bulges and gouges than perhaps any other population in the world. The population pyramids for 1959 and 1970 have sometimes been referred to as resembling Christmas trees. Also, although the bulges and gouges for the United States were mainly the result of fluctuations in fertility, the bulges and gouges for the Russian Empire and successor states are the result both of fluctuations in fertility and in mortality. We look at population pyramids for 1897, 1927, 1959, 1970, 1990, 2000, and 2010.

Figure 11.26 shows population pyramids for the Russian Empire and for the Soviet Union in 1897, 1927, and 1959. These countries suffered a variety of disasters that had a strong impact on the population by age and sex.

The first population pyramid is for the Russian Empire in 1897. This pyramid and those for 1927, 1959, and 1970 are shown for single years of age, as estimated by the French demographer, Biraben.[21] The only census in the Russian Empire was conducted in 1897. The 1897 pyramid looks somewhat like a life table l_x column for a high-mortality population. It looks similar to the situation with an expectation of life at birth of about 40 years and a growth rate of 2% in Figure 11.16. One exception to the stable population shape is that the pyramid jags in for those age 4. This jag for both males and females is the result of deaths in the 1892 famine. Babies who were very young at the time of the famine died at high rates, and pregnant women at the time of the famine were probably more likely to miscarry than in more normal times. Thus, there were relatively few members of the birth cohort of 1892 in 1897 both due to fewer live births and due to high infant mortality rates compared to slightly earlier or later birth cohorts.

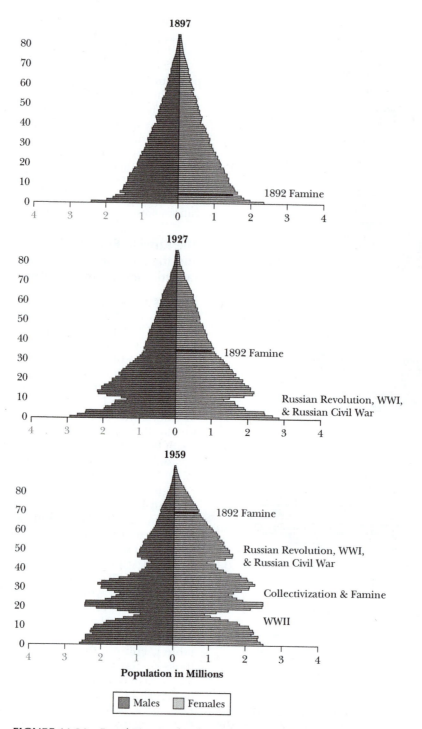

FIGURE 11.26 Population Pyramids for the Russian Empire and the Soviet Union, Single-Year Age Groups: 1897, 1927, and 1959

The next population pyramid is for 1927. The birth cohort of 1892 was age 35 in 1927. In 1927, there were fewer people aged 35 than aged 34 or 36. The effects of a small birth cohort or of a cohort that experienced unusually high death rates remain with the population and are seen long after the period of exceptionally high mortality or exceptionally low fertility. The population pyramid for 1927 was also seriously affected by the Russian Revolution, World War I, and the Russian Civil War. These events lasted from

1917 through 1923. Although people of all ages died as a result of these events, they had an especially high mortality toll on infants and young children. These effects can be seen in the gouge for both males and females for those who were aged 4–10 in 1927.

Next we look at the population pyramid for the Soviet Union for 1959. By 1959, the 1892 birth cohort was age 66. By that age, mortality over so many years had made the jag in the population pyramid for that birth cohort much less noticeable. We still see the gouge for those who were born during the Russian Revolution, World War I, and the Russian Civil War, and those birth cohorts have moved up the population pyramid. By 1959, the Soviet population pyramid had two additional gouges. Collectivization of agriculture occurred in the Soviet Union in 1928–1940. Associated with the collectivization of agriculture was a severe famine. In the pyramid for 1959, a substantial gouge can be seen, especially for

those aged 25, who would have been born in 1934, at the height of the famine. The effects of World War II on births and on survival of the young can also be seen in the gouge for those aged 13–18 in 1959 (born in 1941–1946).

Another effect of World War II can also be seen in the population pyramid for 1959. At the older adult ages, the left-hand side (the male side) of the pyramid has many fewer people than the right-hand side (the female side), indicating a substantial male deficit at older ages. This is because of the much greater mortality among adult men than women in the Soviet Union due to World War II. After World War II, there was great concern about a deficit of men to marry young women, leading to a decrease in marriage among women for a period of time.[22]

Figure 11.27 shows the population pyramid for the Soviet Union in 1970 in two ways. First it

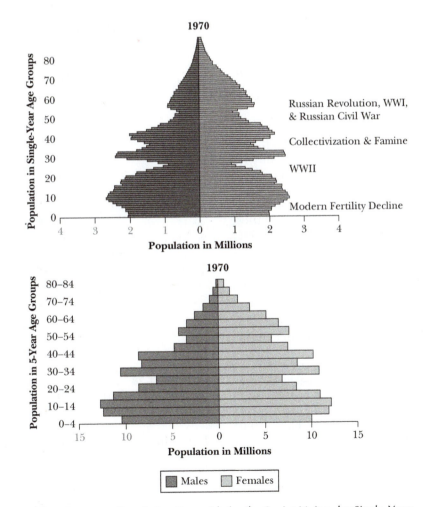

FIGURE 11.27   Population Pyramids for the Soviet Union, by Single-Year and 5-Year Age Groups, 1970

is shown for single-year age groups, and then it is shown for 5-year age groups.[23] The two versions for 1970 look quite similar, although of course more detail is apparent in the pyramid by single year of age. The horizontal scale for the second panel of Figure 11.27 is about five times greater than in the first panel, due to the 5-year age groups in the second panel. By 1970, the birth cohort of 1892, which was age 76, no longer appears distinctive. We still see the gouges associated with the Russian Revolution, World War I, and the Russian Civil War, with collectivization and famine, and with World War II. We also see the number of people declining with more recent birth cohorts for those under age 10 in 1970. This decline below age 10 is the result of modern fertility decline.[24]

Figure 11.28 shows population pyramids for the Soviet Union and the former Soviet Union for 1990, 2000, and 2010. In the pyramid for 1990, we see the impact of the events that caused gouges in the earlier population pyramids. In 1990, there was a relatively large number of people under age 10. This was partially due to a pro-natalist campaign in the 1980s, which was accompanied by an increase in fertility.[25]

The Soviet Union dissolved in 1991, and the pyramid for 2000 shows the effects of the aftermath of that political change on the population of the former Soviet Union. As was shown in Table 10.2, fertility in Russia plummeted after 1991, and a similar fertility decline occurred elsewhere in the former Soviet Union. The effects of this sharp fertility decline are seen in the pyramid for 2000 in the small number of people aged 5–9 and aged 0–4 compared to those age 10–14. The larger number of people aged 0–4 in the pyramid for 2010 compared to those aged 5–9 reflects that by 2005–2010, there had been a slight recovery in fertility in the former Soviet Union.

China: Famine, Population Growth, and Fertility Reduction

The population pyramids for China are interesting due to the effects of famine and of sharp declines in fertility. Figure 11.29 shows population pyramids for China in 1950, 1970, 1990, and 2010. In 1950, the 0–4 age group is much larger than the 5–9 age group. This is because there was some recovery of births in 1945–1949 compared to during World War II when fertility was depressed. Except for the 0–4 age group, the pyramid for 1950 looks similar to that for a stable population.

The pyramid for 1970 shows more deviations from a stable population shape than did the pyramid for 1950. The birth cohort of 1945–1949, who were aged 0–4 in 1950, were aged 20–24 in 1970. This cohort is

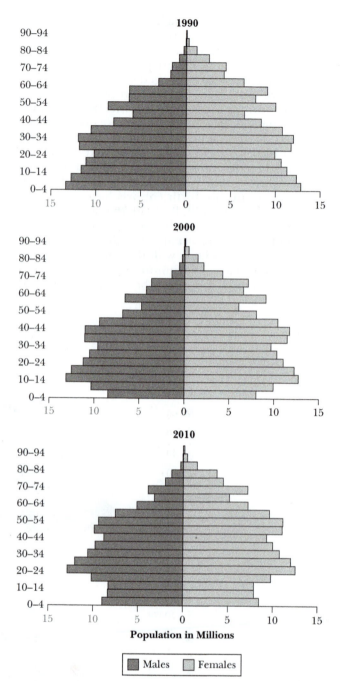

FIGURE 11.28 Population Pyramids for the Soviet Union and the Former Soviet Union: 1990, 2000, and 2010

larger in 1970 than those slightly older or younger. What is more striking in the pyramid for 1970 is the large number of people aged 0–4. This corresponds with the high growth rate seen in China in 1965–1970 (2.7%), which led to alarm among Chinese authorities about population growth.

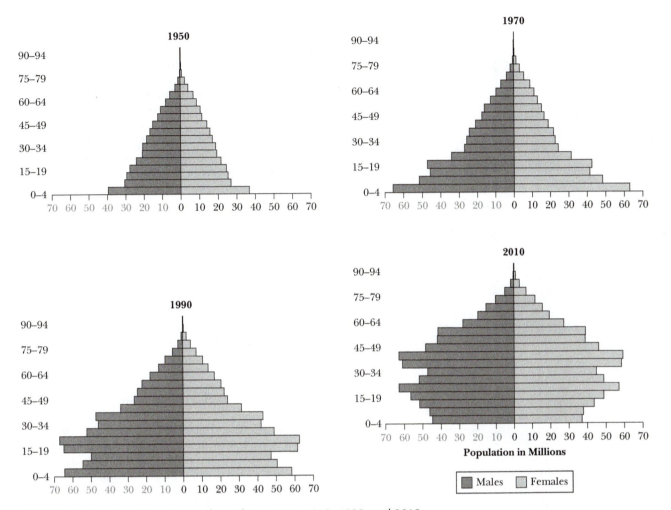

FIGURE 11.29   Population Pyramids in China: 1950, 1970, 1990, and 2010

The impact of the fertility limitation policies implemented after 1970 is striking and can be seen in the pyramid for 1990. Each 5-year age group born between 1970 and 1980 is smaller than the next older 5-year age group. There was some recovery in fertility in 1980–1990. The 1990 population pyramid does not look at all like that of a stable population.

The pyramid for 2010 shows a gouge at ages 25–34. This is the result of the small number of people who were born during the first fertility limitation campaign after 1970. These are the people who were aged 5–14 in 1990. It also shows a new gouge at ages 0–9 for those born after 1990. Unlike the major gouges for the Soviet Union, which mainly resulted from wars and famines related to policies, the gouges in Chinese population pyramids are mainly the result of government fertility policies.

Italy: A Decline from Fairly High Fertility to Concern about Demographic Collapse

The population pyramids for Italy are interesting because Italy went from TFR = 2.4 in 1950 to TFR = 1.5 in 2010, far below replacement fertility. Figure 11.30 shows population pyramids for Italy for 1950, 1990, and 2010. There is a gouge in 1950 for those aged 30–34, who were born during World War I, when there were fewer births and higher infant mortality than in non-war years. Similarly, there is a gouge for those aged 5–9, who were born during World War II.

The pyramid for 1990 shows the effects of the substantial fertility decline in Italy that occurred starting in about 1970. The pyramid for 2010 shows the effects of continued fertility decline, with only a slight fertility increase after 2000. The population

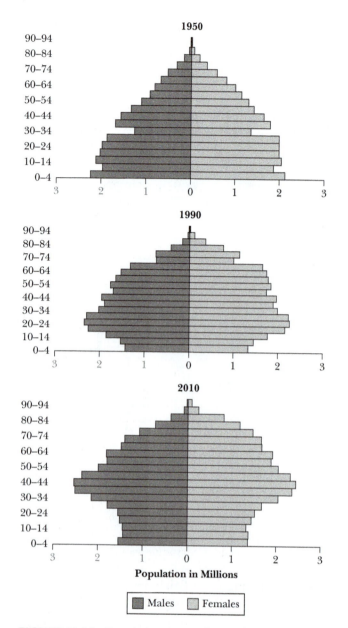

FIGURE 11.30   Population Pyramids in Italy: 1950, 1990, and 2010

pyramids for Italy in 1990 and 2010 do not look much like population pyramids for any stable populations.

POPULATION PROJECTIONS

In a **population projection**, you start with a population by age and sex. You take a specified life table (mortality schedule) by age and sex, a specified age-specific fertility schedule, and (sometimes) a specified schedule of migration by age and sex. Using these mortality, fertility, and migration schedules, you estimate what the population you started with

would look like by age and sex after a certain number of years if these mortality, fertility, and migration schedules were in effect. You can change any of the schedules you wish as you continue to project the population. Usually populations are projected for 5 years at a time. You can project an actual population or a hypothetical (made-up) population.

The Difference between a Population Projection and a Comparison of Stable Populations: Dynamic Analysis versus Comparative Statics

A comparison of stable populations with different fertility and mortality schedules is an exercise in comparative statics. Comparative statics is sometimes called comparison of steady-state conditions. Comparative statics compares the equilibrium or long-term implications of a set of underlying conditions. This approach has often been used in economics, such as in determining what the equilibrium price would be under two different combinations of supply and demand.[26] Similarly, Frenkel and Razin looked at the short-term and the steady-state implications of government spending and budget deficits on interest and consumption.[27] The steady-state results are what would occur if the spending and deficit conditions were in effect for a long time, because the effect on any real economy would depend on the time span over which they were implemented. In all of these steady-state or equilibrium analyses, the equilibrium value is not attained instantly.

When we want to know what happens to a population with a TFR of 4 that goes from an expectation of life at birth of 30 to 45, we can look at the stable population implied by $e_0^0 = 30$ and TFR = 4 and the stable population implied by $e_0^0 = 45$ and TFR = 4. Then, we would know what the two stable populations that had those fertility and mortality conditions for a long time would look like. This stable population comparison does not show what an actual population would look like if we started with an actual population at one point in time and if the age-specific mortality and fertility schedules changed in a particular way. However, as was shown in the population pyramids for actual countries just discussed here, the detailed impact of changing fertility and mortality conditions on a population depends on the timing and duration of those conditions and cannot be answered in a straightforward and simple way. This is one reason why people sometimes use a stable-population, comparative statics approach.

The only way to answer the question of the effects of a particular mortality and fertility trajectory on an actual population is to take the actual population by age and sex (such as shown in the population pyramids in this chapter) and to perform a population projection. The resulting population by age and sex and the characteristics of the population at time 2, such as its growth rate, will depend on the composition of the population by age and sex at time 1 and on the sequence of mortality, fertility, and migration schedules that are used to project the population. Slightly later in this chapter, we look at projected populations for several countries, using the UN Population Division projections.

Purposes of Population Projections

There are a number of reasons to do population projections, including to predict or forecast the future, to see the results of alternative futures, to see the implications of population growth for some other phenomenon, and as counterfactual history. Each of these is discussed in this section.

A Prediction or Forecast

The most obvious purpose of a population projection is to produce a prediction or forecast. A **prediction** or a **forecast** is a population projection that yields the best guess of what the population will actually be at a time in the future. Examples of questions that can be answered by a prediction or forecast include the following:

1. What will the population of Michigan by age and sex be in 2025? This can help in many types of governmental and business planning.
2. What will the number of students by grade be in a district's public schools in 2025? This can help in planning for school construction and staffing. To answer this question, the number of births in the future must be estimated, as well as migration in and out of the district. Enrollment in parochial and other private schools also can be important. Morrison estimated future public school enrollment in Santa Ana, California, where the task was complicated by frequent migration of school children between Mexico and the United States.[28]

To See the Results of Alternative Likely Futures

Another purpose is to see the results or implications of possible or likely alternative futures or to see whether a hypothetical future is possible. Examples of questions that fall in this area include the following:

1. What will the regional distribution of population be under various internal migration scenarios? Van der Gaag and colleagues estimated the effects on the projected population of the European Union by region to 2050 using alternative internal migration assumptions.[29] Wetrogan projected the population of states of the United States using four alternative migration assumptions.[30]

2. What will the distribution of seats among states be in the U.S. House of Representatives in 2050 under various scenarios of economic growth for various U.S. regions, resulting in various fertility and migration patterns?

To Determine the Implications of a Proposed Policy

Another purpose of a population projection is to see the implications of a possible or proposed policy. Examples of questions in this area include the following:

1. What would the effects on Europe's future population be of various possible immigration policies? Is it possible for the magnitude of immigration to Europe to be large enough to avert population decline or to achieve a desirable old age potential support ratio? These are the questions addressed in the UN *Replacement Migration* study, which is discussed later in this chapter for the case of Italy.[31]
2. What would the effect on the world population have been if there had been no family-planning programs? What would the effect on the world population have been if women had no unwanted births? In 1990, Bongaarts and colleagues estimated what the population of the world would be in 2100 if there had been no family-planning programs and then estimated what the world population in 2100 would be if women had no unwanted births.[32] When they wrote their article, the world population in 2100 was projected to be 10 billion. In the absence of family-planning programs, they estimated that the world population in 2100 would be 14.6 billion. In the absence of unwanted births, the world population was projected to be 7.8 billion in 2100.
3. What would alternative immigration policies mean for the future U.S. population? Martin and Fogel[33] projected the U.S. population to the year 2050 under four different immigration scenarios that ranged from no immigration to an amnesty program. The range of estimates for 2050 differed by 135 million people.

To Determine the Implications of a Pattern of Population Growth for a Given Phenomenon

Yet another purpose is to see the implications of a particular pattern of population growth. Examples of questions in this area include the following:

1. The lower the population growth rate of a country or a region, the lower the future demand for food. What effect would the attainment of various lower growth rates (including zero growth rate) have on the adequacy of future food supplies in sub-Saharan Africa? Heilig and Krebs projected the population of sub-Saharan Africa under

various scenarios, including attainment of zero population growth, in order to see the effects of alternative patterns of population growth on the adequacy of African food supply.[34]

2. What will the effect of the future population of Michigan by age and sex be on state government revenue? In 2002 Menchik looked at the projected population of Michigan to the year 2025 to estimate how changes by age and sex, including the aging of the population, affected estimates of future state revenues.[35]

3. What will the projected future population of a state mean for demand for services? In 2003, Murdock used projections of the population of Texas to the year 2040 to estimate the demand for services such as education and prisons.[36]

4. What is the effect of modifying fertility assumptions on likely future demand for services? Udjo estimated the effect of high versus low future fertility assumptions on the demands for housing, education, and health care in Botswana in 2011, as projected from 1991.[37]

As Counterfactual History

A major use of population projections is as an exercise in counterfactual history. **Counterfactual history** examines what would have occurred if the past had been different than it actually was, for example if a war had not occurred. When a policy is implemented, after the policy has been in place for some time, it is possible to know what actually happened. But it is more difficult to know what would have happened if the policy had not been implemented. In order to evaluate the impact of the policy, it is necessary to estimate what would have occurred if the policy had not been implemented. This kind of projection says,

If the past had been different, this is what the population would have looked like today or at some other date.

Examples of questions in this area include the following:

1. What would the population of Europe be today if World War II had not occurred?

2. Often when some event has a large impact on mortality, people use a projection to assess its effects. Andreev and colleagues estimated how many excess deaths there were in World War II—people who died who would not have died otherwise.[38] Anderson and Silver estimated how many excess deaths were there due to Stalin's regime in the 1930s,[39] Heuveline estimated how many people died due to the Khmer Rouge in Cambodia,[40] and Rooney and colleagues estimated how many excess deaths there were during a severe heat wave in Great Britain.[41]

3. What would the population of the United States be in 2030 if cancer were eliminated?

4. What would the population of Taiwan have been in 2000 if there had not been a government family-planning program?

5. What portion of fertility decline in a country was due to participation in the national family-planning program? In Tunisia, crude birth rates declined considerably from the early to the late 1960s. A national family-planning program was implemented in Tunisia in the mid-1960s. Lapham estimated that based on the births averted due to participation in the national family-planning program, the program accounted for about one-third of the fertility decline. The rest of the decline was due to a decrease in the proportion of women in the prime childbearing ages (related to changes in birth rates in the past) and due to a decline in the proportion of women aged 15–19 who were married.[42]

UN Population Division Estimates and Projections

Since 1951, the UN Population Division has produced estimates and projections. Estimates are necessary because some countries do not have good-quality data collection systems, so that calculation of accurate demographic measures using vital statistics and census data is not possible.

Sometimes new information leads to a modification of a population estimate for an earlier time. For example, Keilman discussed why the estimates of the population of China were revised after 1950. This was mainly because the 1953 Census of China counted many more people than experts had thought there were in China.[43] In addition, as surveys collect data about recent fertility and mortality in a country, this can lead to revisions of estimates of total population size as well as of fertility and mortality indicators for that country.

When projections are done, there need to be specified schedules of age-specific mortality, fertility, and migration for the future. These schedules can be changed over the projection period. A projection is a "what if" exercise. It says that if fertility, mortality, and migration develop in a given way, then this will be the population by age and sex at a given date in the future.

A projection can be wrong for a variety of reasons. The development of a new vaccine can lead to unexpected decline in infant and child mortality. Before World War II, few would have anticipated the mortality decline that accompanied use of DDT in reducing malaria mortality. In the 1960s, projections of the population of less developed countries would have been too high if they did not anticipate the success of family-planning programs in some parts of the world.

Assumptions behind UN Population Division Projections

The most important part of a population projection is the assumption about future fertility. As discussed in Chapter 10, when women and couples have a high degree of control over childbearing, fertility can be quite volatile in response to short-term changes in the economic outlook or other kinds of uncertainty.

Also disasters, such as famines and war, can lead to substantial gouges in the age distribution. A projection cannot anticipate such short-term changes in conditions. Thus, projected age distributions are likely to look smoother than the actual future age distributions that will have been influenced by unanticipated events.

When the UN Population Division does projections, they have usually done them under three sets of assumptions, a low, medium, and high variant. The mortality assumption used in the three variants is the same. The variants differ by the fertility assumption used. The medium-variant assumption is the one that the population division thinks is most likely to occur. When people talk about the UN Population Division projections for a country, they almost always mean the medium-variant assumption. All of the projections shown in this chapter use the medium variant.

The only situation in which the UN Population Division does projections under different mortality assumptions is for countries with high HIV prevalence. For those countries, projections have been made with and without HIV mortality.

If the projection is made for many years into the future, a major question is: What is the level of fertility that will be approached? For many years, the UN Population Division assumed that fertility was approaching replacement level, that is, a TFR of 2.1 children per woman, when mortality is low. This leads to a net reproduction rate of 1.0, which is replacement fertility.

However, as a larger and larger number of more developed countries maintained below-replacement fertility and the ideas about the Second Demographic Transition developed, many demographers wondered whether less developed countries, especially those with intermediate fertility rather than high fertility, could be moving toward below-replacement fertility. In 2002, the UN Population Division held a major conference that resulted in a change in the fertility assumptions behind UN projections. They adopted the assumption that the TFR was moving asymptotically to a level of 1.86 children per woman.[44] This change was implemented in the *2004 World Population Prospects* and remained in effect through the *2008 World Population Prospects*. The change in the fertility projection assumption resulted from a change in thinking among demographers and an assessment and interpretation of fertility trends, but there was not an identifiable single event that led to this change.

The fertility projection assumptions were again changed in the *2010 World Population Prospects*. All countries were again assumed to move toward a TFR of 2.1, as was the assumption before 2004. For low-fertility countries, the projections assumed that even if the total fertility rate had fallen far below 2.1, the total fertility rate would approach 2.1 and then fluctuate around that level.[45] This new procedure was motivated by fertility increases between 2000 and 2010 in some low-fertility countries. For example, as discussed in Chapter 10 and as seen in Table 10.2, in France, Spain, Sweden, and several other highly developed, low-fertility countries, the TFR increased between 2000–2005 and 2005–2010. Between 2000–2005 and 2005–2010, the NRR increased from 0.60 to 0.66 in Italy, from 0.91 to 0.95 in France, and from 0.80 to 0.91 in Sweden.

The fertility assumptions in population projections have also differed due to differences in the administrative arrangements and worldviews of the persons making the projections. An example of this is discussed in Box 11.1.[46]

BOX 11.1

Fertility Assumptions for Population Projections in Great Britain and France, 1945–2005

Marshall showed that although the level and the trajectory of the total fertility rate were almost identical in Great Britain and France since World War II, the future fertility assumptions used by French demographers were consistently lower than those used by British demographers. She attributed this to different institutional arrangements in the two countries. French demographers making official projections typically were in non-governmental research institutes, while British demographers making official projections were typically in government departments. Also, a tradition of concern with the possibility of very low fertility in French thought and a concern with the problems stemming from high fertility in British thought contributed to different prognoses about future fertility.

POPULATION PROJECTIONS FOR THE WORLD, ITALY, THE UNITED STATES, CHINA, AND MALI

Next, we look at population projections for the world and for several countries for which we have already examined actual population pyramids: Italy, the United States, China, and Mali. Recall that although the projections are based on reasonable assumptions about the future course of fertility, mortality, and migration, no one has a crystal ball. It is possible that the factors affecting fertility could change, or a new disease with similar effects to that of HIV could emerge. The future course of the world economy is unknown, which can influence fertility decisions. In addition, drought, famine, war, and natural disasters can affect the populations of countries by age and sex and could render these projections inaccurate.

For example, there was civil unrest and violence in Mali in 2011 and 2012 related to regime change and the activity of dissident groups. Political and social development in Mali could affect the course of fertility, mortality, and migration and thus affect the size and the age distribution of the future Mali population.[47]

Projected World Population in 2030 and 2050

Figure 11.31 shows the projected population pyramids for the world in 2030 and 2050.[48] If we compare Figure 11.23 to Figure 11.31, the projected aging of the world population is clear. By 2050, the population pyramid for 5-year age groups is expected to be essentially a vertical line from birth to age 35. By 2030 and even more by 2050, the world population pyramid resembles Panel 4 in Figure 11.18.

Table 11.7 shows some population characteristics of the world from 1950 through 2050. Rates are shown in the top part of Table 11.7 for time periods, such as 1990–1995, while in the bottom part of Table 11.7 the population size and characteristics of the age distribution for single years, such as 1990, are shown. Measures such as the TFR are more reliably estimated for a range of years, while the population size and the age distribution can be effectively estimated for a single year, using a source such as a census.

Table 11.7 documents the large mortality decline through 2010 and the projected further mortality decline for the world as a whole. By 2050–2055, it is expected that the IMR in the world will be the same as it was in the United States in the 1960s, and world e_0^0 by 2050–2055 is expected to be the same as it was in the United States in 1990–1995. The world growth rate fell from 1.82% in 1950–1955 to a projected rate of 0.36% by 2050–2055, which implies an

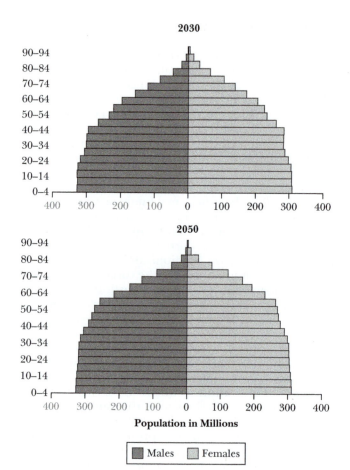

FIGURE 11.31   The Projected Population of the World, 2030 and 2050

increase in population doubling time from 38 years to 173 years.

The world TFR declined from 5.0 in 1950–1955 to 2.5 in 2010–2015, and it is expected to fall further to 2.2 in 2050–2055 to yield replacement fertility (NRR = 0.99). We also see the aging of the world population, with 16% of the population expected to be age 65+ and 2% of the population expected to be age 85+ in 2050. We will have to see whether mortality continues to fall as expected and, more controversially, whether fertility falls to replacement level by 2050–2055.

Replacement Migration: Can Immigration Solve the MDR's Aging Population Challenge? The Case of Italy

Recall from Figure 2.23 in Chapter 2 that net migration has comprised an increasing portion of population growth in Europe since the mid-1980s. When migration occurs across international boundaries, it is called immigration into the receiving country. Since the early 1990s, without

TABLE 11.7   Some Population Characteristics of the World, 1950–1955 through 2050–2055

	1950–1955	1970–1975	1990–1995	2010–2015	2030–2035	2050–2055
e_0^0	48	59	64	69	73	76
IMR	133	86	60	42	30	22
TFR	5.0	4.5	3.0	2.5	2.3	2.2
NRR	1.68	1.76	1.27	1.06	1.01	0.99
% Growth Rate	1.8%	2.0%	1.5%	1.1%	0.7%	0.4%
% Net Migration Rate	0	0	0	0	0	0
	1950	**1970**	**1990**	**2010**	**2030**	**2050**
Population in Millions	2,532	3,696	5,306	6,896	8,321	9,306
% Age 65+	5.1%	5.3%	6.2%	7.6%	11.7%	16.2%
% Age 85+	0.2%	0.2%	0.4%	0.6%	1.0%	2.0%
% Age 0–14	34.3%	37.5%	32.7%	26.8%	22.9%	20.5%
% Age 15–29	25.9%	24.8%	27.1%	24.7%	22.1%	20.1%
Young Dependency Ratio	56.7	65.5	53.6	40.8	35.1	32.4
Old Age Dependency Ratio	8.5	9.3	10.2	11.6	17.9	25.7
Overall Dependency Ratio	65.2	74.8	63.8	52.4	53.0	58.1

immigration Europe would not have had a positive rate of population growth. Because of the population aging implications of a negative growth rate and concerns with an increasing old age dependency ratio, some have wondered whether immigration could plausibly alleviate the problems that arrive from an old age structure and negative rate of natural increase.

To answer this question, the UN Population Division carried out a project, the results of which were published in 2000. They wanted to know how large immigration to more developed countries would need to be in order to attain various goals.[49] Thus, they looked at the projected age–sex pyramids associated with six scenarios:

1. **Scenario I:** These projections are from the medium variant of the *UN World Population Prospects 1998 Revision.* This was the comparative referent for *no change in immigration.*
2. **Scenario II:** These projections are from the medium variant of the *UN World Population Prospects 1998 Revision,* except there was assumed to be *no net immigration* after 1995.
3. **Scenario III:** These projections result from assuming sufficient immigration to keep the population at the *highest total size* that it would have achieved in the absence of net immigration after 1995 (the situation in Scenario II).
4. **Scenario IV:** These projections result from assuming sufficient immigration to maintain the *size of the working age population* (15–64) *at the highest level* that it would have achieved in the absence of net immigration after 1995 (the situation in Scenario II).
5. **Scenario V:** These projections result from assuming sufficient immigration to keep the *old age potential support ratio* (those aged 15–64)/(those aged 65+) *from falling below 3.0.*
6. **Scenario VI:** These projections result from assuming sufficient immigration to keep the *old age potential support ratio at the highest level* that it would have achieved in the absence of net immigration after 1995 (the situation in Scenario II).

Scenarios II–VI reflect various policy objectives related to the size of the population or the size of the working age population compared to the size of the retirement age population that governments have seen as desirable.

In order to make the projections for Scenarios III–VI, one needs an assumption about the age–sex distribution of net immigrants. Net immigrants are the number of people migrating into the country by age and sex minus the number of people migrating out of the country by age and sex.

To obtain a distribution by age and sex of net immigrants, the average of the age distributions for each sex for immigrants to the three countries with high levels of immigration (Australia, Canada, and the United States) was used. The age pattern for each of the three countries was given equal weight.

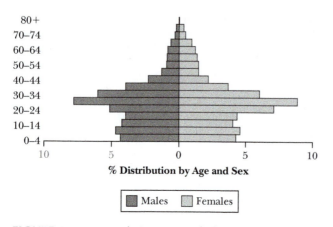

% Distribution by Age and Sex

■ Males ☐ Females

FIGURE 11.32 Population Pyramid of Age–Sex Distribution of Net Immigrants Assumed in UN Replacement Migration Project

Figure 11.32 shows the population pyramid assumed for net immigrants. The values across all ages and both sexes sum to 100%. The immigrants at arrival are concentrated in the younger adult ages (20–39). These people are in the prime childbearing ages. The relatively large number of net immigrants under age 15 reflects the children of the adult immigrants. The projections assume that upon arrival in the destination country, immigrants immediately are subject to the age-specific death rates and age-specific fertility rates in the destination country.

Projections under the six scenarios were made for France, Germany, Italy, the Republic of Korea, the Russian Federation, the United Kingdom, the United States, Europe, and the European Union. In this section, we discuss the results for Italy.

Table 11.8 shows some results of the *Replacement Migration* projections for Italy. Scenarios V and VI are based on a ratio of the working age population to the older population. It is clear that requiring this ratio results in a much larger 2050 population and much higher population growth than Scenarios III and IV, which require a constant (non-declining) either total population or working age population. The number of net immigrants required to achieve any of Scenarios III–VI would require a substantial increase in net immigration. Even Scenario III would require the number of net immigrants under Scenario I to increase almost 20-fold (from 12,000 to 235,000).

In light of substantial anti-immigrant sentiment in Italy, as in many other developed countries, it is unclear what level of immigration would be socially and politically acceptable. In Scenarios V and VI, over one-half of the 2050 population of Italy would be post-1995 immigrants or their descendants. Although immigration can alleviate some of the problems of an aging, low-fertility population, it does not seem possible that it can solve all of the problems of the size and age distribution of the population.

Figure 11.33 shows Italy's projected population for 2030 and 2050, according to the United Nations' *2010 World Population Prospects*. The pyramids in Figure 11.33 should be viewed in the context of the earlier population pyramids for Italy in Figure 11.30.

TABLE 11.8   Population and Age Consequences of Various Replacement Migration Scenarios for Italy

		Scenario			
I	**II**	**III**	**IV**	**V**	**VI**
1998 World Population Prospects medium variant	Medium variant with zero net immigration	Constant total population	Constant age group 15–64	Ratio 15–64/65+ not less than 3.0	Constant ratio 15–64/65+
Total Population in Thousands, 2050					
41,197	40,722	57,338	66,395	87,345	193,518
Average Annual Net Number of Immigrants in Thousands, 2000–2050					
12	0	235	357	638	2,176
% of Population in 2050 Post-1995 Migrants and Their Descendants					
1%	0%	29%	39%	53%	79%
Average Annual Growth Rate in %, 1995–2050					
−0.60%	−0.62%	0.00%	0.27%	0.77%	2.21%
Old Age Potential Support Ratio 15–64/65+ in 2050					
1.52	1.52	2.03	2.25	3.00	4.08

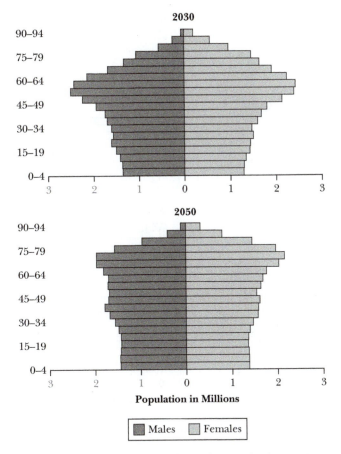

2030

2050

Population in Millions

■ Males   ☐ Females

FIGURE 11.33   The Projected Population of Italy, 2030 and 2050

The bulge in the population pyramid for Italy for 2010 for those in their thirties shown in Figure 11.30 has moved up to become a bulge for those in their fifties in 2030, as shown in Figure 11.33. Above age 50, age-specific death rates increase more rapidly than at younger ages, so by 2050, when the same cohort is in their seventies, the bulge is much less apparent. By 2050, the age distribution is expected to be almost rectangular. The economic advantages of an increased retirement age become clear as the Italian age distribution changes from that in 2010 to that in 2030 to that in 2050.

Table 11.9 shows some characteristics of the population of Italy over time and as projected to 2050. The increasing e_0^0 over time in Italy is one reason for the rectangularization of the Italian population pyramid, and the declining growth rate resulting from declining fertility is another reason. Compare the changing Italian population pyramids in Figures 11.30 and 11.33 with the stable population age distributions with $e_0^0 = 80$ shown in Figure 11.17 to see how with a high e_0^0, the lower the growth rate the higher the proportion of the population at older ages.

The aging of the Italian population is clear from the increase in the percentage of the population over age 65 and in the increase in the percentage of the population over age 85. At the same time, the percentage of the population below age 15 is expected to be almost reduced by half between 1950 and 2050. The young dependency ratio declines from 1950 to 2010, and then is expected to rise between 2010 and 2050.

TABLE 11.9   Some Population Characteristics of Italy, 1950–1955 through 2050–2055

	1950–1955	1990–1995	2010–2015	2030–2035	2050–2055
e_0^0	66	77	82	84	86
IMR	60	8	3	3	3
TFR	2.4	1.3	1.5	1.8	1.9
NRR	1.0	0.6	0.7	0.8	0.9
% Growth Rate	0.75%	0.05%	0.23%	−0.10%	−0.28%
% Net Migration Rate	−0.09%	0.05%	0.34%	0.22%	0.20%
	1950	**1990**	**2010**	**2030**	**2050**
Population in Thousands	46,367	56,832	60,551	60,851	59,158
% Age 65+	8%	15%	20%	26%	33%
% Age 85+	0%	1%	3%	4%	7%
% Age 0–14	27%	16%	14%	13%	14%
% Age 15–29	26%	24%	16%	15%	14%
Young Dependency Ratio	41.0	24.0	21.5	22.0	27.0
Old Age Dependency Ratio	12.4	21.7	30.9	43.7	61.5
Overall Dependency Ratio	53.4	45.7	52.4	65.7	88.5

The young dependency ratio will rise between 2010 and 2050 if the TFR in Italy increases from 1.5 in 2010–2015 to 1.9 in 2050–2055, as the UN Population Division expects. Recall from Chapter 8 that a net reproduction rate (NRR) of 1.00 is necessary for the population to have an unchanging size over the long run. This is called replacement fertility. In 1950–1955 Italy was at replacement fertility, but the NRR was considerably lower in 1990–1995. If things occur in Italy as expected, the NRR will increase from 0.6 in 1990–1995 to 0.9 in 2050–2055, almost at replacement fertility level. However, note that the population growth rate continues to decline through 2050–2055, even as the NRR is increasing. The NRR reflects the long-term implications of the age-specific fertility and mortality schedules in a given time period, and is unaffected by the population's history. The Italian age distribution is influenced by its history of low fertility, even after the NRR has increased. This is discussed later under the topic population momentum.

Note also that the Italian population increases through 2030 but then is expected to decline between 2030 and 2050. Net migration to Italy is expected to remain positive. Without net immigration, the Italian population would have begun to decline by 1990–1995. The Italian growth rate is expected to become negative by 2020–2025, by which time expected continued immigration is expected to not be sufficient to counter the excess of deaths over births.

The old age dependency ratio increases with each later date. In 2050, it is expected that there will be 62 persons over age 65 for every 100 persons in the working ages. The overall dependency ratio declined between 1950 and 1960, but then increased by 2010. By 2010, the demographic window for Italy had closed.

The Projected U.S. Population

Figure 11.34 shows the population of the United States, as projected to 2030 and 2050. This figure should be viewed as a continuation of Figure 11.25, which shows population pyramids for the United States in 1950–2010.

The expected rectangularization of the United States population pyramids by 2030 and even more so by 2050 is clear. By 2030, the youngest Baby Boomers will be in their late sixties. There is still a slight bulge visible for those aged 65–69 in the pyramid for 2030. We still see some bulge for the echo of the Baby Boom for those aged 40–49 in 2030. The population projections do not anticipate any unevenness in fertility or mortality in the future, and by 2050, the U.S. age distribution is quite rectangular and below age 50 is fairly smooth. However, unforeseen circumstances, such as prolonged economic problems, could lead to a fertility reduction that would cause a gouge in the age distribution. Recall the year-to-year fertility

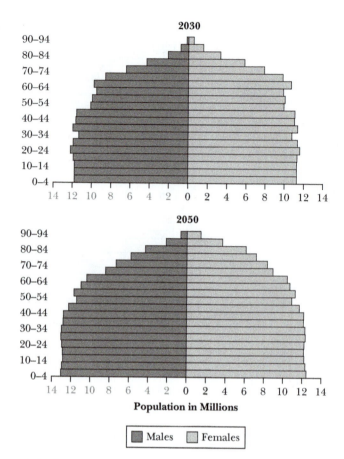

FIGURE 11.34   The Projected Population of the United States, 2030 and 2050

fluctuations in the United States in step with economic changes in 2000–2008, shown in Figure 10.13 in Chapter 10.

Table 11.10 shows some demographic characteristics of the United States in the period 1950 through 2050. We see that the percentage of the population age 65+ and the old age dependency ratio increased rapidly between 1950 and 2010 and are expected to continue to increase through 2050. However, comparing Table 11.10 for the United States with Table 11.9 for Italy, we see that by 2050 the percentage of the population age 65+ is expected to be 57% higher in Italy than in the United States, and the old age dependency ratio in Italy is expected to be 74% higher than the United States. The overall dependency ratio is expected to be about one-third higher in Italy than in the United States in 2050.

Thus, although there has been much concern about the aging of the American population, this is a much less serious problem than that which faces Italy. Italy has an older population than the United States due to the lower fertility and the lower mortality in Italy than in the United States. The net migration

TABLE 11.10   Some Population Characteristics of the United States, 1950–1955 through 2050–2055

	1950–1955	1970–1975	1990–1995	2010–2015	2030–2035	2050–2055
e_0^0	69	72	76	79	81	84
IMR	31	18	9	7	5	5
TFR	3.5	2.0	2.0	2.1	2.1	2.1
NRR	1.6	1.0	1.0	1.0	1.0	1.0
% Growth Rate	1.62%	0.90%	1.00%	0.85%	0.61%	0.45%
% Net Migration Rate	0.14%	0.25%	0.34%	0.31%	0.25%	0.19%
	1950	**1970**	**1990**	**2010**	**2030**	**2050**
Population in Thousands	157,813	209,464	253,339	310,384	361,680	403,101
% Age 65+	8%	10%	13%	13%	20%	21%
% Age 85+	1%	1%	1%	2%	2%	5%
% Age 0–14	27%	28%	22%	20%	19%	19%
% Age 15–29	23%	24%	23%	21%	19%	19%
Young Dependency Ratio	41.7	45.9	33.0	30.0	31.4	31.4
Old Age Dependency Ratio	12.7	15.9	19.0	19.5	32.6	35.4
Overall Dependency Ratio	54.5	61.8	51.9	49.6	63.9	66.8

rate in both countries is high and about the same. However, due to Italy's much lower fertility, net migration has been and is expected to remain more important in Italy in averting population decline.

China's Likely Population Future: A Path to Declining Population

Figure 11.35 shows China's population projected to 2030 and to 2050. These population pyramids should be viewed as a continuation of the population pyramids for China for 1950–2010, as shown in Figure 11.29.

The jag for those aged 25–34 in 2010, shown in Figure 11.29, is apparent in the pyramid for 2030 for those aged 45–54. As shown in Table 11.11, the NRR is expected to remain below 1 through 2050–2055, and by 2030–2035, the growth rate in China is expected to become negative. This is reflected in the population pyramids for 2030 and 2050 in the narrowing of the pyramids at the younger ages. The pyramids look much like the third panel of Figure 11.17 for a low-mortality population with a negative growth rate. The values in Table 11.11 for China in the future are consistent with those used in the projections shown in Figure 11.35. The rapid decline in mortality and likely further future decline is striking. Additionally impressive is the fertility decline since the 1970s. Like many more developed countries, the TFR in China is anticipated to increase slightly by 2050–2055. If the TFR does not increase, the population of China will be even smaller, and the population pyramid will be more pinched in at younger ages than is shown for 2050 in Figure 11.35.

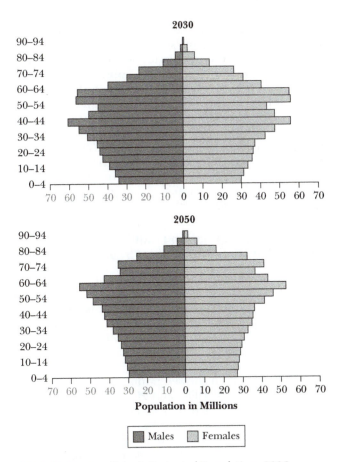

FIGURE 11.35   China's Projected Population, 2030 and 2050

TABLE 11.11 Some Population Characteristics of China, 1950–1955 through 2050–2055

	1950–1955	1970–1975	1990–1995	2010–2015	2030–2035	2050–2055
e_0^0	45	65	70	74	77	80
IMR	122	47	30	20	13	10
TFR	6.1	4.8	2.0	1.6	1.6	1.8
NRR	2.0	2.0	0.9	0.7	0.8	0.9
% Growth Rate	1.99%	2.33%	1.17%	0.42%	−0.17%	−0.54%
% Net Migration Rate	0.00%	0.00%	−0.01%	−0.03%	−0.03%	−0.03%
	1950	**1970**	**1990**	**2010**	**2030**	**2050**
Population in Thousands	550,771	814,623	1,145,195	1,341,335	1,393,076	1,254,854
% Age 65+	5%	4%	6%	8%	17%	26%
% Age 85+	0%	0%	0%	1%	1%	3%
% Age 0–14	34%	39%	28%	20%	15%	14%
% Age 15–29	25%	26%	30%	24%	17%	15%
Young Dependency Ratio	55.8	69.7	42.4	26.9	21.2	22.1
Old Age Dependency Ratio	7.3	7.1	9.0	11.3	23.8	41.8
Overall Dependency Ratio	63.2	76.8	51.4	38.2	45.1	63.8

Whether there is any increase in the TFR in China by 2050 likely will depend on both Chinese governmental policies and what happens to the status of women in China. After such low fertility, it is not clear if the Chinese population would increase their fertility, even though new state policies announced in 2013 and discussed in Chapter 9 allow somewhat higher fertility. The old age dependency ratio in China increased between 1950 and 2010, to 11.3 older people per 100 people in the working ages. This is expected to double to 23.6 by 2030 and to almost double again to 41.8 by 2050. That would yield a higher old age dependency ratio in China in 2050 than in the United States, although lower than is expected for Italy in 2050.

Mali's Likely Population Future: Continuing High Population Growth

Figure 11.36 shows the population of Mali as estimated for 2010 and as projected to 2030 and 2050. The 2010 pyramid is shown on the same horizontal scale as the pyramids for the projected populations in 2030 and 2050 in order to make population growth by age and sex clear.

Figure 11.36 should be seen as a continuation of Figure 11.24, which showed population pyramids for Mali in 1950, 1970, 1990, and 2010. In Figure 11.24, a different scale was used to facilitate comparisons of the Mali population in 2010 with that since 1950. The projections anticipate a modest decline in the growth rate, from 3% in 2010–2015 to 1.9% in 2050–2055. Even though the TFR is expected to decline from 6.1 to 3.2 in that same period, the effect

on population growth of fertility decline is muted by the effect of the expected large decline in IMR from 92 to 37.

Table 11.12 shows demographic indicators for Mali for 1950–2050. Mortality declined considerably between 1950–1955 and 2010–2015, as indicated by the increase in the expectation of life at birth and the decline in the infant mortality rate. Fertility had not declined much by 2010–2015, and the NRR and the population growth rate increased between 1950–1955 and 2010–2015. Thus, in 2010, Mali remained a high-fertility, high-growth-rate country.

In 2010, almost one-half of the population was under age 15, and a trivial percentage of the population was at advanced ages. About one-fourth of the population was young adults (aged 15–29). These young people would be eager for employment opportunities and increasingly concentrated in cities. The high proportion of children presents substantial challenges to the educational system, and the high proportion of young adults, especially in urban areas, could be a source of concerns about potential social unrest on the part of authorities. The UN projections anticipate continued mortality decline after 2010 to an expectation of life at birth of 67 by 2050–2055 and a decline in the infant mortality rate to 37 per 1,000. Only time will reveal whether mortality in Mali declines as rapidly as expected.

The projections anticipate considerable decline in the TFR after 2010. Even with the TFR expected to be almost cut in half by 2050–2055, Mali would still have a population growth rate of almost 2% in 2050–2055, with an implied population doubling time of 37 years.

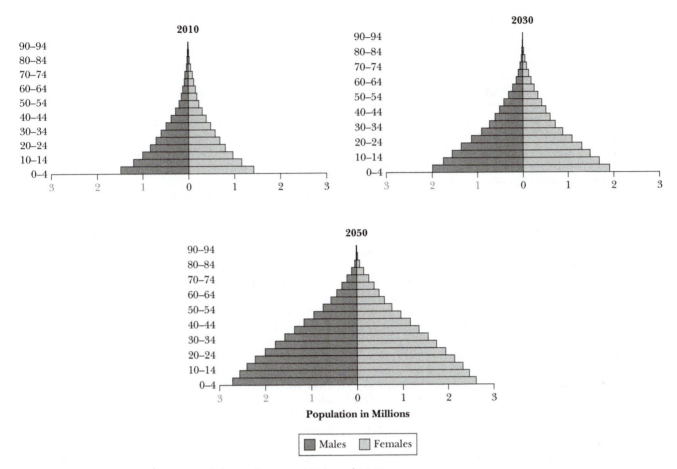

FIGURE 11.36   Population Pyramids for Mali: 2010, 2030, and 2050

TABLE 11.12   Some Population Characteristics of Mali, 1950–1955 through 2050–2055

	1950–1955	1970–1975	1990–1995	2010–2015	2030–2035	2050–2055
e_0^0	30	36	45	52	60	67
IMR	175	156	127	92	61	37
TFR	6.5	6.9	7.0	6.1	4.5	3.2
NRR	1.5	1.9	2.3	2.3	1.9	1.5
% Growth Rate	1.2%	1.8%	2.5%	3.0%	2.5%	1.9%
% Net Migration Rate	−0.2%	−0.3%	−0.4%	−0.2%	−0.1%	−0.1%
	1950	**1970**	**1990**	**2010**	**2030**	**2050**
Population in Thousands	4,638	6,034	8,673	15,370	26,784	42,130
% Age 65+	3%	2%	2%	2%	2%	4%
% Age 85+	0%	0%	0%	0%	0%	0%
% Age 0–14	39%	42%	48%	47%	39%	36%
% Age 15–29	27%	26%	26%	27%	25%	28%
Young Dependency Ratio	66.7	76.6	93.5	93.2	82.2	59.2
Old Age Dependency Ratio	4.8	4.3	3.3	4.3	3.9	6.2
Overall Dependency Ratio	71.5	81.0	96.8	97.5	86.1	65.4

Between 1986 and 1996, the official position of the government of Mali changed from the view that the population growth rate was satisfactory to the view that the growth rate was too high and from the view that the fertility level was satisfactory to thinking it was too high. In 2003, the Mali government declared a new population policy identifying "controlling population growth" as a goal, and the 2006 Poverty Reduction Strategy Paper saw reducing the population growth rate and reducing the unmet need for family planning as part of a poverty reduction strategy. The TFR did decline from a high of 7.1 in 1985–1990 to 7.0 in 1990–1995 to 6.5 in 2005–2010, and contraceptive prevalence increased from 5% in 1987 to 8% in 2006. These changes in positions, policies, and behaviors could result in programs that would lead to a decline in the TFR equal to or greater than what is projected.[50]

Although Mali has experienced considerable mortality decline, Mali in 2010 remains a relatively high-mortality, high-fertility, high-growth-rate country with a very young population. In 2050, Mali is still expected to be a high-growth-rate country with a young population. Mali is an example of a less developed country in which the demographic transition had progressed only partway by 2010 and in which the demographic transition is not expected to be over by 2050.

THE ACTUAL GROWTH RATE, THE INTRINSIC GROWTH RATE, AND POPULATION MOMENTUM

Every population has age-specific mortality rates and age-specific fertility rates that together determine a unique, stable population. That stable population has a growth rate, which can be different from the population's actual growth rate. The growth rate of the stable population implied by the age-specific fertility rates and age-specific mortality rates in an actual population is called that population's **intrinsic growth rate**. As shown in Table 11.11, in 1990–1995 China had an $e_0^0 = 70$ and TFR = 2.0. The net reproduction rate was 0.9. The actual growth rate in China was 1.17%. However, when NRR = 0.9, the implied stable population has an intrinsic growth rate of −0.19%. The difference between the actual population growth rate and the intrinsic growth rate was not due to migration, since for China the net migration rate is close to zero at every date.

Discussing populations in which fertility has been above replacement, Keyfitz noted that when fertility declines to NRR = 1 and then remains unchanged for a long time, the population will eventually have a growth rate of zero. It would be a stable population and, in fact, it would be a stationary population.[51]

Even if fertility instantly fell to the level necessary for a net reproduction rate of 1.0, the growth rate would not instantly fall to zero. This is because a population's age structure at any point in time is the result of the population's fertility and mortality history. A population that has had a positive growth rate for some time has a large proportion of women in the childbearing ages, which leads to a crude birth rate that is higher than the crude birth rate in the stationary population implied by the age-specific fertility and age-specific mortality rates.

Writing in 1971, Keyfitz estimated that if Chile in 1965 had instantly reduced its fertility to a level giving NRR = 1, the eventual stationary population produced by the age-specific rates would have been 50% larger than the 1965 Chilean population size. If the United States in 1966 had instantly reduced its fertility to yield NRR = 1, the eventual American stationary population would have been 35% larger than the 1966 U.S. population size. The population pyramid for the United States in 1990, shown in Figure 11.25, reveals the high number of births to women born in the Baby Boom, called the "echo of the Baby Boom." This is an example of how age distributions that are a result of the past affect birth rates at a given point in time.

Building on Keyfitz's work, **population momentum** has sometimes been defined as the amount above its current size that a population would grow if fertility instantly fell to result in NRR = 1. Others have defined population momentum more generally as the effect on population growth (or decline) of a population's age structure that results in the difference between the actual growth rate of a population and the population's intrinsic growth rate. If a population has had below-replacement fertility for some time and then the NRR increases to 1.00, the growth rate will continue to be negative for some time. Writing in 2003, Lutz and his colleagues[52] looked at the negative rate of natural increase in Europe since the late 1990s. This was also shown in Figure 2.23. They looked at the effect of the age structure, which was produced by low fertility, on the ultimate size of Europe's population if fertility rose to a point where NRR = 1. They estimated that for every decade that fertility in the 15 countries of the European Union as of 2003 remained at its low level before rising to replacement level, there would be 25–40 million fewer people in Europe when it eventually became a stationary population with a growth rate of 0.0.

CONCLUDING COMMENTS

Actual age distributions are the result of a complicated interplay of past fertility and mortality. In addition, no matter how successful family-planning programs might be, the population's history means that the effects of these programs are not immediately fully apparent. In addition, a population's history has effects long after the events that caused a change in the age distribution have

occurred. A jagged age distribution, whether the result of famine, war, temporarily increased fertility, or rapid fertility decline, can present challenges for many years.

✔ Study and Review Online

SUMMARY

1. With declines in mortality throughout the world since the early 1950s, but little decline in fertility in the LDR until the 1970s, the age structure of the world's population has changed considerably.

2. In the world as a whole, the median age declined until the 1970s and then gradually increased. In the MDR, the median age increased between 1950 and 2010, going from 29 in 1950 to 40 in 2010. In the LDR, there was some increase in the median age, but in the LeastDC there was little change. The LeastDC continued to have a very young population, with a median age of 20 in 2010. Individual countries reached more extreme values; in Japan, the median age reached 45 in 2010, while in Mali it was 16 in 2010.

3. Changes in the age distribution are reflected in the percentage of the population in broad age groups: the young (ages 0–14), the working ages (ages 15–64), and the older population (ages 65+). The effects of changes in these broad age groups are captured by dependency ratios: the young dependency ratio (the number aged 0–14 per 100 aged 15–64), the old age dependency ratio (the number aged 65+ per 100 aged 15–64), and the overall dependency ratio (the sum of the young dependency ratio and the old age dependency ratio). The different dependency ratios are important because they reflect different social challenges. The overall dependency ratio reflects the number of people in all dependent ages per hundred people in the working ages. The young dependency ratio reflects the demands of children, while the old age dependency ratio reflects the needs of the retired population.

4. In the world as a whole, the young dependency ratio increased between 1950 and 1965 and then declined. At the same time, the old age dependency ratio in the world increased after 2005, leading to less variation in the overall dependency ratio than in the young or the old age dependency ratio. In the MDR, the young dependency ratio declined after 1960, and the old age dependency ratio increased since 1950. In the LDR, the young dependency ratio increased sharply through 1965 and then decreased, while the old age dependency ratio increased after

1990. In the LeastDC, the young dependency decreased after 1995 and the old age dependency ratio is expected to increase slowly after 2020.

5. There is a demographic dividend when the proportion of the population in the working ages increases. This occurs when the proportion at young ages has declined due to fertility declines, but the proportion at old ages has not yet increased. The MDR experienced a demographic dividend from 1980 through 2010, and the LDR will experience a demographic dividend from about 2010 through 2040. During the period of a demographic dividend, there is the potential for a high rate of economic growth, if there are productive economic activities available for the working age population.

6. A youth bulge occurs when the proportion of the adult population that is comprised of young adults is high. This can occur nationally after fertility has declined for about a decade. Also, rural-urban migration contributes to a youth bulge in urban places. A youth bulge is thought to increase the potential for social unrest and has been seen as contributing to unrest in some Middle Eastern and North African countries.

7. A stable population has an unchanging age distribution and an unchanging growth rate. A stationary population is a stable population with a growth rate of zero and thus an unchanging population size. A set of age-specific mortality rates and age-specific fertility rates implies a given stable population. Looking at the stable population implied by various mortality and fertility rates can provide insight into the implications of changing mortality and fertility.

8. As a population ages and the old age dependency ratio increases, substantial burdens are placed on society. Increasing retirement age can ease these burdens, but also can create new problems. An older work force and an older retirement age can stifle promotion opportunities for younger workers, and some think that it can impede innovation and the application of technology.

9. Those age 85 or older are called the oldest-old. As fertility and mortality decline in developed countries, the proportion of the population in the oldest-old ages increases rapidly. As people

grow older, there is an increased chance that they will be physically or mentally disabled. Thus, whether the oldest-old are able to live an active life and care for themselves or whether they need substantial help in carrying out the requirements of daily living has large social and financial implications for their relatives and for society.

10. As mortality declines, the population first becomes somewhat younger and then becomes older. As fertility declines, the population becomes older. These general trends in age distributions affect all populations, but particular historical events, such as wars and famines, affect the detailed age distributions of populations, sometimes resulting in a very jagged age distribution.

11. Population projections show what the age distribution and demographic characteristics of a population would be in the future if mortality, fertility, and migration rates changed in particular ways. Unforeseen events, such as wars, can cause the actual population to differ from the projected population. Also, the implications of the projected population can lead to policy changes that alter the course of demographic change, especially future fertility. Concern about population projections from the 1960s and 1970s resulted in family-planning programs that led to lower fertility and less population growth than what was projected.

12. Population projections are also used as an exercise in counterfactual history. They can answer questions such as "How many births were averted by a family-planning program?" Or "What was the effect of World War II on the population of Europe?"

13. The age-specific fertility and mortality rates in an actual population imply a unique stable population. The growth rate of that implied stable population is called the actual population's intrinsic growth rate. The actual population's growth rate and the intrinsic growth rate can differ because of the effects of the actual population's history on the age distribution.

14. In a growing population, if age-specific fertility rates instantly decline to result in NRR = 1, then eventually the population size will be unchanged. However, the population actually will continue to grow for some time due to the age distribution. The age distribution does not instantly change to that in the stable population implied by the age-specific mortality and fertility rates. This is called population momentum. The population continues to grow because the actual population has a higher proportion of women in the childbearing ages than does the implied stable population.

KEY TERMS

median age   360
young population   362
working age population   362
older or elderly population   362
dependency ratio   365
youth dependency ratio   365
old age dependency ratio   365
old age potential support
   ratio   366

potential support ratio   366
demographic dividend   367
demographic window   367
youth bulge   367
stable population   368
population pyramid   368
stationary population   370
active life expectancy   376

healthy life expectancy   376
disability-free life expectancy   376
population projection   384
prediction   385
forecast   385
counterfactual history   386
intrinsic growth rate   396
population momentum   396

QUESTIONS FOR DISCUSSION AND REVIEW

1. Discuss how the age distribution of a population changes as mortality and fertility go from a high level to a moderate level to a very low level. What are some of the consequences for society of these changes in the age distribution? What kinds of policies have been proposed to address problems raised by these changes in the age distribution?

2. Discuss the following statement: "Policy discussions about fertility and about immigration in developed countries are actually discussions about desirable and undesirable age distributions."

3. Discuss changes in age distributions in the last 50 years in the less developed region and in the more developed region of the world and how mortality, fertility, and migration changes have influenced changes in these age distributions. How have policies that governments have proposed or

pursued changed in response to observed or anticipated changes in the age distribution?

4. Why do countries consider it problematic to have a large proportion of the population above age 65?

5. Some have suggested raising the retirement age in more developed countries to achieve a lower old age dependency ratio. What are the main arguments for and against raising the retirement age?

SUGGESTED PAPER TOPICS

1. Pick a country. Look at the projected population size, total fertility rate, infant mortality rate, and the expectation of life at birth for 2010 as projected in 1980, 1990, 2000, and 2004. Compare the earlier projections with the estimates made in 2008. Discuss the extent and the possible reasons for changing projected values over time and for discrepancies with the estimated values for 2010.

2. Pick a country. Estimate the youth dependency ratio and the old age dependency ratio since 1950. Discuss what problems or opportunities these changing dependency ratios presented to the country and any policies that the country considered or implemented to address perceived dependency ratio problems.

NOTES

1. All the graphs of population by age group in this section are based on data from United Nations. 2011. *World Population Prospects: The 2010 Revision*, New York: United Nations.

2. Often, the term "potential support ratio" is used when what is meant is the old age potential support ratio.

3. Andrew Mason. 2007. *Demographic Transition and Demographic Dividends in Developed and Developing Countries*, New York: United Nations; David E. Bloom and Jeffrey G. Williamson. 1998. "Demographic Transitions and Economic Miracles in Emerging Asia," *World Bank Economic Review*, 12: 419–455; and David E. Bloom, David Canning, and Jaypee Sevilla. 2003. *The Demographic Dividend: A New Perspective on the Economic Consequences of Population Change*, Population Matters Monograph MR-1274, Santa Monica, CA: RAND.

4. United Nations. 2004. *World Population to 2300*. New York: United Nations.

5. David E. Bloom, David Canning, and Jaypee Sevilla. 2003. *The Demographic Dividend: A New Perspective on the Economic Consequences of Population Change*, Population Matters Monograph MR-1274, Santa Monica, CA: RAND.

6. Arun Ingle and P. B. Suryawanshi. 2011. *India's Demographic Dividend—Issues and Challenges*, paper presented at the International Conference on Technology and Business Management, March 28–30, Dubai, United Arab Emirates, http://www.trikal.org/ictbm11/pdf/Marketing/D1151-done.pdf (accessed July 29, 2011).

7. Henrik Urdal. 2012. *A Clash of Generations? Youth Bulges and Political Violence*, Population Division Expert Paper No. 2012/1, New York: United Nations, http://www.un.org/esa/population/publications/expertpapers/Urdal_Expert%20Paper.pdf (accessed March 28, 2012).

8. Colleen McCue and Kathryn Haahr. 2008. "The Impact of Global Youth Bulges on Islamist Radicalization and Violence," *CTC Sentinel*, 1(11): 12–14, http://www.innovative-analytics.com/docs/GlobalYouthCTCSentinel.pdf (accessed April 5, 2012).

9. Peter Xenos, Midea Kabamalan, and Sidney B. Westley. 1999. "A Look at Asia's Changing Youth Population," *Asia-Pacific Population and Policy*, January(48): 1–4.

10. Gary Fuller and Forrest R. Pitts. 1990. "Youth Cohorts and Political Unrest in South Korea," *Political Geography Quarterly*, 9: 9–22.

11. Anna Mulrine. 2012. "US Sends Troops to Yemen as Al Qaeda Gains Ground," *Christian Science Monitor*, May 11, http://www.csmonitor.com/USA/Military/2012/0511/US-sends-troops-to-Yemen-as-Al-Qaeda-gains-ground (accessed May 14, 2012).

12. The stable populations shown are from Ansley J. Coale and Paul Demeny. 1983. *Regional Model Life Tables and Stable Populations*, 2nd ed., New York: Academic Press. The stable populations shown in Figure 11.16 are based on West model life tables level 9, and those in Figure 11.17 are based on West model life tables level 25.

13. For more discussion of the age distribution of a stable population, see Samuel H. Preston, Patrick Heuveline, and Michel Guillot. 2001. *Demography: Measuring and Modeling Population Processes*, Malden, MA: Blackwell.

14. Till von Wachter. 2002. *The End of Mandatory Retirement in the US: Effects on Retirement and Implicit Contracts*, Working Paper No. 49, Berkeley: Center for Labor Economics, http://www.eea-esem.com/papers/eea-esem/2003/1037/tvw_mr.pdf (accessed December 4, 2013); France24. 2010. "Pension Reform across Europe," http://www.france24.com/en/20100616-pension-reform-across-europe-france-england-germany-spain# (accessed June 20, 2011); and Raphael Minder. 2011. "Spain to Raise Retirement Age to 67," *New York Times*, January 17, http://www.nytimes.com/2011/01/28/world/europe/28iht-spain28.html?_r=1&scp=7&sq=pension%20reform%20Europe&st=cse (accessed June 20, 2011).

15. Nelson D. Schwartz. 2011. "Easing Out the Gray-Haired. Or Not," *New York Times*, B1, B4, May 28, http://www.nytimes.com/2011/05/28/business/economy/28worker.html?_r=1&scp=1&sq=Schwartz%20Gray-Haired&st=cse (accessed October 3, 2011).

16. Wan He and Mark N. Muenchrath. 2011. *90+ in the United States: 2006–2008*. U. S. Census Bureau, American Community survey Reports, ACS-17, Washington, DC: Government Printing Office, http://www.census.gov/prod/2011pubs/acs-17.pdf (accessed November 17, 2011).

17. S. Katz, L. G. Branch, M. H. Branson, J. A. Papsidero, J. C. Beck, and D. S. Greer. 1983. "Active Life Expectancy," *New England Journal of Medicine*, 309: 1218–1224.

18. The calculation of the number of years of active life expectancy can be sensitive to what particular disabilities or conditions are included.

19. Kenneth G. Manton and Eric Stallard. 1991. "Cross-sectional Estimates of Active Life Expectancy for the U.S. Elderly and Oldest-Old Populations," *Journal of Gerontology*, 46: S170–S182. Figure based on table on page S179.

20. J. W. Traphagan. 2000. *Taming Oblivion: Aging Bodies and the Fear of Senility in Japan*, New York: State University of New York Press.

21. Jean-Noël Biraben. 1976. "Naissances et répartition par age dans l'Empire russe et en Union Sovietique," *Population* (French ed.), 31: 441–478.

22. Barbara A. Anderson and Brian D. Silver, 1985. "Demographic Effects of World War II on the Non-Russian Nationalities of the Soviet Union," in *The Impact of World War II on the Soviet Union*, ed. Susan J. Linz, Totowa, NJ: Rowman and Allanheld, 207–242; and E. Brainerd. 2007. *Uncounted Costs of World War II: The Effect of Changing Sex Ratios on Marriage and Fertility of Russian Women*, Department of Economics, Williams College, http://web.williams.edu/Economics/faculty/brainerd-rfwomen.pdf (accessed June 20, 2011).

23. The data for the population pyramids by 5-year age groups for the Soviet Union and the former Soviet Union are from the U.S. Census Bureau, International Database, http://www.census.gov/ipc/www/idb/ (accessed June 14, 2011).

24. Ansley J. Coale, Barbara A. Anderson, and Erna Harm. 1979. *Human Fertility in Russia since the Nineteenth Century*, Princeton, NJ: Princeton University Press.

25. Barbara A. Anderson. 2002. "Russia Faces Depopulation? Dynamics of Population Decline," *Population and Environment*, 23: 437–464; and S. V. Zakharov and E. I. Ivanova. 1996. "Fertility Decline and Recent Changes in Russia: On the Threshold of the Second Demographic Transition," in *Russia's Demographic "Crisis,"* ed. J. DaVanzo, Conference Report CF-124-CRES, Santa Monica, CA: RAND, 36–82.

26. cf. Andreu Mas-Colell. 1977. "On the Equilibrium Price Set of an Exchange Economy," *Journal of Mathematical Economics*, 4: 117–126; and John H. Nachbar. 2002. "General Equilibrium Comparative Statics," *Econometrica*, 70: 2065–2074.

27. Jacob A. Frenkel and Assaf Razin. 1986. "Fiscal Policies in the World Economy," *Journal of Political Economy*, 94: 564–594.

28. Peter A. Morrison. 2000. "Forecasting Enrollments for Immigrant Entry-Port School Districts," *Demography*, 37: 499–510.

29. Nicole van der Gaag, Evert van Imhoff, and Leo van Wissen. 2000. "Internal Migration Scenarios and Regional Population Projections for the European Union," *International Journal of Population Geography*, 6: 1–19.

30. Signe I. Wetrogan. 1990. *Projections of the Population of States, by Age, Sex, and Race: 1989 to 2010*, Current Population Reports, Series P-25: Population Estimates and Projections, No. 1053, January, Washington, DC: U.S. Bureau of the Census.

31. United Nations. 2000. *Replacement Migration*, New York: United Nations.

32. John Bongaarts, W. Parker Mauldin, and James F. Phillips. 1990. "The Demographic Impact of Family Planning Programs," *Studies in Family Planning*, 21: 299–310.

33. Jack Martin and Stanley Fogel. 2006. *Projecting the U.S. Population to 2050: Four Immigration Scenarios*, Federation for American Immigration Reform, http://76.227.221.63/articles/2006,0717-martin.pdf (accessed July 28, 2011).

34. G. Heilig and T. Krebs. 1987. "Bevolkerungswachstum und Nahrungsversorgung in Schwarzafrika: Modellrechnungen zur kunftigen Entwicklung" [Population Growth and Food Supply in Africa South of the Sahara: Models of Future Development], *Zeitschrift fur Bevolkerungswissenschaft*, 13: 81–119.

35. Paul L. Menchik. 2002. *Demographic Change and Fiscal Stress on States: The Case of Michigan*, Michigan State University, Michigan Applied Public Policy Research Program, http://www.ippsr.msu.edu/Publications/ARDemographic.pdf (accessed July 28, 2011).

36. Steven H. Murdock. 2003. *The New Texas Challenge: Population Change for the Future of Texas*, College Station: Texas A & M University Press.

37. Eric O. Udjo. 1998. "Fertility and Mortality Trends and Implications for Social Demands in Botswana," *Southern African Journal of Demography*, 5: 1–10.

38. E. Andreev, L. Darskii, and T. Khar'kova. 1990. "Otsenka lyudskikh poter' v period Velikoi Otechestvennoi voiny" [An Assessment of Population Losses during World War II], *Vestnik Statistiki*, (10): 25–27.

39. Barbara A. Anderson and Brian D. Silver. 1985. "Demographic Analysis and Population Catastrophes in the USSR," *Slavic Review*, 44: 517–536.

40. Patrick Heuveline. 1998. "L'insoutenable incertitude du nombre: estimations de décès de la période Khmer rouge" [The Unbearable Uncertainty of Numbers: Estimating the Deaths in the Khmer Rouge Period], *Population*, 53: 1103–1117.

41. C. Rooney, A. J. McMichael, R. S Kovats and M. P. Coleman. 1998. "Excess Mortality in England and Wales, and in Greater London, During the 1995 Heatwave," *Journal of Epidemiology and Community Health*, 52: 482–486.

42. Robert Lapham. 1970. "Family Planning and Fertility in Tunisia," *Demography*, 7: 241–253.

43. Nico Keilman. 1998. "How Accurate Are the United Nations World Population Projections?" *Population and Development Review*, 24 (Supplement: Frontiers of Population Forecasting): 15–41.

44. United Nations Population Division. *Completing the Fertility Transition*, http://www.un.org/esa/population/publications/completingfertility/completingfertility.htm (accessed July 10, 2011).

45. United Nations Population Division. *Assumptions Underlying the 2010 Revision*, http://esa.un.org/unpd/wpp/Documentation/WPP2010_ASSUMPTIONS_AND_VARIANTS.pdf (accessed July 29, 2011).

46. Emily A. Marshall. 2012. *Population Problems? Demographic Knowledge and Fertility in Great Britain and France, 1945–2005*, doctoral dissertation, Department of Sociology, Princeton University.

47. Daniel Politi. 2012. "Chaos in Mali," *New York Times*, April 6.

48. The projections in the remainder of this chapter are based on United Nations. 2011. *World Population Prospects 2010*, http://esa.un.org/unpd/wpp/unpp/p2k0data.asp (accessed June 10, 2011).

49. United Nations. 2000. *Replacement Migration*, New York: United Nations.

50. United Nations. 2009. *What Would It Take to Accelerate Fertility Decline in the Least Developed Countries?* United Nations Policy Brief No. 2009/1 March, http://www.un.org/esa/population/publications/UNPD_policybriefs/UNPD_policy_brief1.pdf (accessed July 6, 2012); and United Nations. 2010. *World Population Policies 2009*, New York: United Nations, http://www.un.org/esa/population/publications/wpp2009/Publication_complete.pdf (accessed July 10, 2012).

51. Nathan Keyfitz. 1971. "On the Momentum of Population Growth," *Demography*, 8: 71–80.

52. Wolfgang Lutz, Brian C. O'Neill, and Sergei Scherbov. 2003. "Europe's Population at a Turning Point," *Science*, 299: 1991–1992.

CHAPTER 12

MIGRATION AND URBANIZATION

LEARNING OBJECTIVES

- Define migration and residential mobility, and explain the difference between the two.
- Explain why laws have a greater effect on international than on internal migration.
- List the two main kinds of international migrants, and explain the differences in the response of receiving countries to the two kinds of migrants.

- Discuss the main economic and social theories of migration.
- List the factors that are taken into account in defining whether a place is urban.
- Describe the history of the growth or decline of central cities, suburbs, and nonmetropolitan areas in the United States since 1910.

(((Listen to the Chapter Audio

OVERVIEW

This chapter examines internal and international migration and urbanization. Urbanization is not a component of population growth, but it is extremely important in demographic processes. Life is very different in urban areas from that in rural areas. One of the major variables related to standard of living, educational opportunities, and quality of life in the least developed region (LDR) is whether a person lives in an urban or a rural area. Also, although developments in infrastructure and communication have narrowed the differences between urban and rural areas in the most developed region (MDR), many opportunities are only available in urban areas, or are more widely available in urban than in rural areas.

Migration and urbanization are interrelated since throughout the world, rural-to-urban migration (also called **rural-urban migration**) is a major source of urban growth, and the desire for an urban job and for urban educational and cultural opportunities are major reasons for migration. The nature of rural areas is often strongly affected by the composition of the out-migrants, since migration is selective of the young and the relatively well off, leaving rural areas older and poorer than they would have been otherwise.

In addition, in the LDR urban poverty is fueled by the influx of poor migrants from rural areas. Urban programs to alleviate poverty can seem futile as ever more poor migrants replace earlier rural-urban migrants in the ranks of the urban poor. As the standard of living is higher in urban than rural places, the living standards of poor urban-rural migrants are higher than if they had remained at their rural origin, which attracts subsequent rural-urban migrants. Also, remittances sent to rural households by household members in urban places often are a major source of income in rural areas.

Throughout the world, economic development and industrialization have been accompanied by net movement from rural to urban places. In some developing countries, this has mainly resulted in growth of one or a small number of very large cities. In many countries, this has also been accompanied by growth of middle-sized cities and often by substantial growth of suburbs. Some countries have tried to restrict urban growth, but this effort has usually not been very successful.

International migration has mainly been from the LDR to the MDR. International migration into a country is called **immigration**, and international migration out of a country is called **emigration**. While the vast majority of the populations of the United States, Canada, and Australia are immigrants or the descendants of immigrants, and these countries still receive many international migrants, many other MDR countries have been less receptive to immigrants.

Immigration policy has been an issue of great conflict in developed countries. Whereas internal migration is mainly governed by the desires and actions of individuals and families, international migration is very much influenced by laws related to immigration. Recent world economic problems make it clear that labor demand does not always increase, and the economic situation has an influence on immigration policies.

Migration is often considered the stepchild of demography, and many demographers do not want to think about migration. Although there are some ambiguities about what is a death and what is a live birth, the definition of what is an instance of migration is much more subjective.

Also, the models and factors influencing migration are different from those affecting mortality and fertility. Mortality and fertility occur to members of a population, and the results of mortality and fertility are manifested in the rate of natural increase. The effects of mortality and fertility can be modeled as occurring in a population that is closed to migration, where only internal processes (fertility and mortality) affect the result. Migration out of a population is caused by decisions and behavior of members of the population, but migration into a population is the result of decisions and behaviors of people who are **not** members of the population. This makes modeling of migration and its effects on population growth much more uncertain and complicated than for the effects of mortality and fertility in a population completely or mainly closed to migration.

In addition, immigration to a country is substantially affected by the laws of the receiving country. Who enters a country can be much more affected by these laws than by the desires of potential immigrants from other countries. Analysis of immigration laws falls into the areas of political science and the study of legislation, which are topics that demographers typically do not deal with. However, due to the increased importance of migration in population growth, as was discussed for Europe in Chapter 2, and related interest in migration policy, especially in the MDR, all researchers and policy makers interested in population, including demographers, have needed to take the subject of migration seriously.[1]

DEFINING MIGRATION

Migration always involves some geographic move. It also involves some aspect or intention of a long-term stay or permanent move. Migration is distinguished from residential mobility (such as moving to an apartment down the hall or a home three blocks away). Migration and residential mobility are also distinguished from vacationing, tourism, or a temporary work assignment.

Goldscheider's Definition of Migration

Calvin Goldscheider has a conceptually based definition of migration. He defined migration as "detachment from the organization of activities at one place and the movement of the total round of activities to another."[2]

Application of Goldscheider's definition presents some challenges. Imagine a family of four in which the father works for pay, and the mother does not work for pay. There are two children in grade school. Imagine that the family moves 20 miles to a new, slightly larger home. The father does not change jobs. He spends his non-work time at home with his family. His total round of activity has not changed, and according to Goldscheider's definition he would not be considered to have migrated. The children have changed their schools and have new friends. Their total round of activity has changed, and they might be considered to have migrated. The mother has new neighbors, but she retains social contacts with some of her old friends. She might or might not be considered to have migrated. A direct application of Goldscheider's definition could lead to the conclusion that in this family of four, one person did not migrate, two migrated, and another member might have migrated. This would not be a sensible conclusion. Thus, although Goldscheider's definition of migration is highly regarded, it is almost never directly applied to individuals to decide whether people have migrated or whether they have experienced residential mobility. **Residential mobility** occurs when a person or a household changes their place of residence without a major change in most aspects of their lives.

Duration of Residence and Intention to Stay in a Place

Definitions of migration almost always include an aspect of duration of residence or intention to remain at the destination for an extended time. As mentioned earlier in this chapter, visitors to a place, such as tourists or those visiting relatives, are not considered to have migrated from their usual place of residence.

There can be complications in deciding whether migration has occurred. Imagine that Helen from Ann Arbor, Michigan, has gone to stay with her ill aunt, who lives in Toledo, Ohio. She only plans to stay in Toledo until her aunt's health improves, perhaps a month or two. When Helen first arrives in Toledo, if she were asked if she planned to remain in Toledo for 6 months or more, her answer would have been, "No, I am only going to be in Toledo for a short time until my aunt gets better." Imagine that her aunt's condition does not improve, and Helen is interviewed after she has been in Toledo for 6 months. She again replies that she has not migrated to Toledo, she still considers her permanent residence to be in Ann Arbor, and she plans to return to Ann Arbor soon. Imagine she is still in Toledo after one year and gives a similar response. Imagine further that she is still in Toledo after 5 years and replies the same way. At what point in time did Helen "migrate" to Toledo?

MEASURING MIGRATION

We just discussed conceptual definitions of migration, but researchers and policy planners need some way to estimate the number of migrants using the data that they have or can collect fairly easily. An **operational definition** of something is an indicator of an underlying concept that uses data that are readily available and that can be calculated to give an unambiguous result. In this section, we discuss operational definitions of who is a migrant and measures of different kinds of migration rates.

Operational Definitions of Who Is a Migrant

Estimation of the number of migrants by governments and other bodies does not rely on surveys about people's views of the permanency of their moves. For a move to be defined as a migration in official statistics typically requires a move across some administrative boundary. There is often a requirement of a particular duration of residence or planned residence, often 6 months or more.

The U.S. Census Bureau defines a migrant as a person who has moved to a different county within the United States. From the standpoint of a local school district, a migration would involve moving into or out of the school district's boundaries. A person has experienced residential mobility (but is not considered to have migrated) if he or she changes his or her usual place of residence to a new location in the same county. The idea of the Census Bureau definition is that it is fairly easy for people to report whether they have moved across the boundary of a county. Also, if a person has moved within one county, it is thought that it is usually possible for a person to retain the same job and the same total round of activity.

Analysis of the reasons for moving within a county and moving to another county gives some support for the distinction between residential mobility and migration.[3] Table 12.1 shows that over half of the moves within the same county are mainly for reasons of housing, which accords with them being cases of residential mobility. Also, while employment was the main reason for 10% of within-county moves, it was the main reason for 36% of between-county moves.

Estimates of the number of migrants in the last year or in the last 5 years typically come from

TABLE 12.1 Reasons for Moving within a County and to a Different County, the United States, 2010–2011

	Within the Same County	To a Different County
Housing	55%	24%
Employment	10%	36%
Family or other reason	35%	40%
Total	100%	100%

questions about the current place of residence and about the place of residence 1 year or 5 years earlier. The assumption is that people had substantial subjective ties at the earlier place of residence while they lived there. If a person's place of residence 1 year earlier was Chicago, but the person was actually on vacation at the Grand Canyon 1 year earlier, it is not thought that he or she would claim to have resided in Arizona, where the Grand Canyon is located, and that person also should not claim that his or her place of residence 1 year earlier was at the Grand Canyon.

There are some conceptual problems with the definition of migration as changing the usual place of residence from one county to another county. Let us think about the New York metropolitan area, which includes parts of the states of New York, New Jersey, Connecticut, and Pennsylvania. Also, New York City includes five counties: the boroughs of Manhattan, Bronx, Brooklyn, Queens, and Staten Island. A person could live in Brooklyn and work in Manhattan. Also, a person could live anywhere in the New York metropolitan area and work in New York City. Thus, a move within the metropolitan area could reasonably be residential mobility rather than migration, even if it involved changing the place of residence to a different county or even to a different state. Metropolitan areas are discussed further later in this chapter.

Despite these ambiguities, to have consistent, easily applied definitions of migration for all parts of the United States, it is reasonable to define migration as involving a change of place of residence across county lines and to define residential mobility as change of place of residence within a county.

Gross and Net Migration

Gross migration between place A and place B involves two migration streams:

1. Gross migration from A to B is the number of people who migrate from A to B.
2. Gross migration from B to A is the number of people who migrate from B to A.

Net migration between place A and place B is the difference between the two gross migration streams. Net migration to place A is the number of migrants into place A from anywhere minus the number of migrants out of place A to anywhere. Net migration from place A is the number of migrants out of place A to anywhere minus the number of migrants into place A from anywhere. When people talk about net migration, they usually mean the number of net migrants into the place. If more migrants came into the place than left, then the number of net migrants is a positive number. If more people migrated out of the place than migrated into the place, then the number of net migrants is a negative number.

Estimating Net Migration

As discussed in Chapter 2, if you have the population of a place at Time 1(P1) and Time 2 (P2) and you have the number of births (B) and the number of deaths (D) in the time interval between Time 1 and Time 2, you can estimate the number of net migrants to the place and the net migration rate, using the population balancing equation:

$$P2 = P1 + B - D + \text{Net Migrants}$$

Using this equation, you can estimate the number of net migrants for a country as a whole and for any subdivisions of the country for which you have the required data or estimates without any direct information about the number of people who migrated. You can calculate the net migration rate into place A as follows:

(Number of Net Migrants into Place A)/ (Mid-period Population of Place A)

Estimating Gross Migration

Estimating gross migration (migration flows) is much more difficult than estimating net migration. There are several ways that the number of gross migrants and thus the gross migration rate from place A to place B are estimated:

1. If you have a population registration system, you can use that, since most population registers are supposed to record out-migrants and in-migrants. However, as discussed in Chapter 3, population registers are often deficient in recording migration, especially if the person is expected to return to his or her place of origin.
2. You can do a survey and ask a migration history, although you need to get the respondent to understand what you mean. You need to be clear about whether the respondent is supposed to include time away at college, time in the military, or time at a temporary job assignment in the migration history, Usually, such moves are not considered acts of migration.
3. You can ask about residence at two time points, such as at the time of the census or survey and 1 year earlier or 5 years earlier. In the United States, the Current Population Survey and the American Community Survey, which were discussed in Chapter 3, are used to estimate gross migration between counties, states, and regions. The responses to a question about place of residence 1 year earlier are used to calculate gross migration between places.
4. You can ask about place of birth and place of residence. People who do not live in their place of birth have migrated at least once in their lives. A problem with this indicator is that you know that migration occurred at least once since birth, but you do not know when the migration occurred. Sometimes people look at the place of birth and place of residence of children younger than 5 years old. If a child lives in a different place than his or her place of birth, you know that the migration happened sometime in the previous 5 years.

Once you know the number of gross migrants from place A to place B, you can calculate the **gross out-migration rate** from A to B as follows:

(Number of Migrants from Place A to Place B)/ (Mid-period Population of Place A)

People sometimes estimate the **gross in-migration rate** from place A to place B as follows:

(Number of Migrants from Place A to Place B)/ (Mid-period Population of Place B)

Stocks versus Flows

The movement of people from one place to another represents the **migration flow**. This is a measure of migration that occurs in a particular period of time. In-migrants to a country are called **immigrants**, and out-migrants from a country are called **emigrants**. The flow of immigrants to a country in a year is equal to the number of immigrants to the country in that year.

For a country, the **migrant stock** changes as people move into and out of the country. This is a measure of the cumulative number of migrants over the lives of people in an area. The indicator of the migrant stock of a country is usually the percentage of the population of the area that was born in a different country, which is often referred to as the percentage foreign-born. The migrant stock is affected both by the number of people who immigrated to the country and are still alive and by emigration of earlier immigrants.

MIGRATION THEORIES

Many migration theories apply both to internal migration and to international migration. A major difference is that for legal international migration, the receiving country must agree that the person or household can immigrate. For undocumented international migration, theories are complicated since the movement is not legal. Another difference is that for international migration, the destination is often more distant, fewer people at the destination are known to the potential migrant before the migration, and, if the migrant is undocumented, there can be a great deal of risk attached to the migration.[4]

Ravenstein's Laws of Migration

The first hypotheses or generalizations about migration were set forth by E. G. Ravenstein. Writing in the 1880s, he proposed a set of "Laws of Migration."[5]

1. Most migrations are over a short distance.
2. Migration often occurs in steps.
3. Long-range migrations are usually to urban areas.
4. Each migration flow produces a countermigration flow in the opposite direction.
5. Rural residents are more likely to migrate than urban residents.
6. Women are more often internal migrants than men. Men are more likely to be long-distance or international migrants.
7. Most migrants are adults.
8. Urban places grow more by migration than by natural increase.
9. Migration increases with economic development.
10. Migration is usually motivated by economic reasons.

Some of Ravenstein's laws, such as the first law, are empirical generalizations. Ravenstein's fourth law refers to **return migration**. Typically, a substantial proportion of people who migrate from place A to place B return to place A at some point in time. The primacy of economic considerations is clear in the tenth law. Ravenstein also thought that although unpleasant or undesirable conditions at an origin could encourage migration, the attraction of destinations was more important in motivating migration.[6]

Gravity Models of Migration

Gravity models of migration are based on Sir Isaac Newton's law of gravity, which states,

Any two bodies attract each other with a force that is proportional to the product of their masses and inversely proportional to the square of the distance between them.

In such formulations, the populations of two places are viewed as their masses. Thus the greater the population of two places, and the closer they are to each other, the greater the expected amount of migration between the two places. E. C. Young, George Zipf, and Samuel Stouffer built gravity models of migration, and Lee then expanded on their work.

In 1924, using a somewhat broad definition of attraction, Young proposed that

$$m = a \times X/D$$

where:

m is the number of migrants between two places.

X is the "force of attraction" between the two places.

D is the distance between the two places.

a is a constant.[7]

In 1946, Zipf modified Young by restricting attraction to population size. He proposed that migration between Place 1 and Place 2 is

$$m = k \times P1 \times P2/D$$

where:

m is the number of migrants between two places.

P1 is the population of place 1.

P2 is the population of place 2.

D is the distance between the two places.

k is a constant.[8]

Stouffer and Intervening Opportunities

Stouffer took a different approach than Young and Zipf. He wrote,

The number of persons going a given distance is directly proportional to the number of opportunities at that distance and inversely proportional to the number of intervening opportunities.[9]

He thought that the amount of migration between two places was more dependent on the spatial distribution of opportunities, some of which might not be physically between the two places under consideration. For example, the existence of New York City can influence the amount of migration between Philadelphia and Washington, DC, even though New York City is not between Philadelphia and Washington, DC. These "intervening opportunities" can be more important in the amount of migration between two places than the size of the two places and the distance between the places.

Lee and the Factors Affecting Migration

Everett Lee integrated earlier work on migration and in 1966 proposed a typology of the factors affecting migration:[10]

1. **Origin Factors:** This includes positive aspects of the origin, such as the inertia that inhibits migration. It also includes characteristics of the origin that can either inhibit or encourage migration, such as climate, threat of violence, and educational and employment opportunities. Aspects of the origin that encourage migration, such as poor educational and income-producing opportunities, are often called **push factors** for migration.
2. **Destination Factors:** This includes positive aspects of the destination, such as a good climate or educational and income-producing opportunities. These positive aspects of a destination are often called **pull factors** for migration.
3. **Intervening Obstacles:** This includes the distance between places, barriers such as the Berlin Wall, and immigration laws.
4. **Personal Factors:** This includes intelligence, education, stage of the life cycle, and knowledge about the destination. The role of personal factors such as education, health, and age is discussed later in this chapter under the topic of migrant selectivity.

Zelinsky's Model of the Mobility Transition

Wilbur Zelinsky observed the history of migration and in 1971 proposed a model of what he called the mobility transition. The mobility transition has the following five phases:[11]

Phase one ("Premodern traditional society"): There is very little migration. Natural increase rates are about zero (i.e., births approximately equal deaths).

Phase two ("Early transitional society"): There is a high level of rural-urban migration and migration to agricultural frontiers. There is a high level of emigration from European countries to colonies. This occurs during the period of the demographic transition after mortality has declined but before fertility has declined, when there is a high rate of natural increase. There is some circulation migration, in which a migrant returns to his or her place of residence once a week or more infrequently. Circulation migration is discussed further later in this chapter.

Phase three ("Late transitional society"): Rural-urban migration is lower than in the previous phase, and there is less emigration to colonies. Circulation migration increases. The natural rate of increase is lower than in the previous phase but is still fairly high.

Phase four ("Advanced society"): Rural-urban migration is lower than in the previous phase. Urban-urban and migration within large urban areas increases. The natural rate of increase is low. There is immigration from less developed places. There is very little settlement migration.

Phase five ("Future superadvanced society"): Almost all migration and residential mobility are between and within urban places. There is less immigration from less developed places. Legal controls on internal and international migration can emerge.

Economic Perspectives on, and Theories of, Migration

Most people acknowledge the relevance of gravity models of migration. For example, most would agree that some measure of the distance between two places needs to be taken into account in modeling migration between places. However, beyond gravity model considerations, economic models have been dominant in thinking about migration, especially in decisions about whether to migrate and choice of destination.

Neoclassical Economics

Neoclassical economic ideas emerged in the nineteenth century and were further developed in the twentieth century.[12] The basic idea of neoclassical economics is that people make decisions in order to maximize their income. As applied to migration, this means that people decide whether to migrate and choose a destination based on a comparison of (1) their expected income or wage rate if they remained at their current location, and (2) their expected income or wage rate if they migrated to a particular destination. If the expected increase in their income or wage rate is sufficiently large, it is likely that the person will migrate.

Dual Labor Market Theory

The development economist W. Arthur Lewis argued in 1954 that in urban areas of less developed countries, there is a **dual labor market**. There is a modern or capitalist sector in which people are hired and paid wages. In the modern sector, people are hired and continue to be employed based on the characteristics of the potential employee, such as his or her education or seeming aptitude. The other sector, which is sometimes called the traditional sector or the murky sector, includes income-producing activities that do not entail actual employment, such as buying fruit wholesale in order to sell it retail on the streets.[13]

Peter Doeringer and Michael Piore modified Lewis's concept of a dual labor market to distinguish between a primary sector with relatively high pay and good working conditions and a secondary sector in which jobs have low pay, little job security, and poor working conditions. Many undocumented migrants in more developed countries and many rural-urban migrants in less developed countries work in this secondary sector.[14]

Piore applied the dual labor market concept to the situation in advanced industrial countries, in which jobs can be divided into stable, highly skilled jobs and low-skilled, low-wage jobs. Highly skilled jobs are sought by citizens of advanced countries, but they are sometimes occupied by highly skilled immigrants. Low-skilled, low-wage jobs often attract international migrants. Citizens of the advanced countries often are unwilling to hold such jobs.[15]

Economic Theories of Expected Increase in the Wage Rate Due to Migration

Building on Lewis's dual labor market concept, and applying ideas of neoclassical economics, John Harris and Michael Todaro developed a model of rural-urban migration in less developed countries that sees the potential migrant in the rural area assessing his (or her) likely wage rate if he remained in the rural area and the likely wage rate if he or she migrated to an urban destination. If the likely increment to the wage rate is sufficient, the person will migrate. This model assumes there is a virtually unlimited supply of rural residents available and eager to become rural-urban migrants and to work in the murky sector. The Harris-Todaro model remains the dominant model of rural-urban migration in less developed countries.[16]

Lewis defined a turning point in economic development when there is no longer an unlimited supply of rural migrants seeking urban jobs because the rural wage rate has risen sufficiently that it exceeds the wage rate from murky sector urban jobs. Minami argued that Japan reached this turning point in the late 1950s, and Cai argued that China reached this turning point in about 2004.[17] After the turning point, urban wage rates increase because there is no longer an unlimited supply of labor available in rural areas to become rural-urban migrants and work in the murky sector.

The New Economics of Labor Migration

Oded Stark and David Bloom are economists who in 1985 expanded the range of factors affecting the decision whether a person migrates. While the Harris-Todaro model acted as if the potential migrant were the sole decision maker, Stark and Bloom thought the migration decision was made by the entire household, with the decision of whether anyone would migrate and who would migrate made with the interests of *all* household members in mind.[18]

Relative Deprivation

In 1989, Oded Stark and J. Edward Taylor further developed the role of all household members in migration decisions and further expanded the set of factors considered in economic models of migration decision making. In the relative deprivation perspective, migration decisions are made by households with the standard of living and opportunities of the household's reference group in mind. If other households in the community have obtained particular goods such as a television, a bicycle, or an automobile, this can motivate a household to aspire to have those goods when otherwise they would not have thought obtaining the goods was feasible or desirable. One way that the relative deprivation approach applies is when some households have members who have become internal or international labor migrants. These household members send money (remittances) to their household of origin, which raises the standard of living of those households and makes other households aspire to a similar standard of living, which in turn increases migration. The relative deprivation approach was developed with international migration in mind, but it also applies to internal migration, especially labor migration from rural areas.[19]

Sociological Perspectives on, and Theories of, Migration

Sociologists, social psychologists, and other non-economists agree that economic motivations are usually the main reasons for migration. The difference between the views of many non-economists and the views of economists arises in whether factors other than an increase in expected income influence migration decisions. For example, sociological and social psychological perspectives focus on factors that decrease the perceived risk associated with migration, such as the education of the potential migrant and whether relatives have migrated earlier and have conveyed relevant information to potential migrants.

Selectivity of Migration by Education, Health, Age, and Gender

Migration is said to exhibit **migrant selectivity** on some characteristic if people with that characteristic are more (or less) likely to migrate than people without that characteristic.

Selection by Education   Migration has often been found to be selective of those at the origin with relatively high education. Figure 12.1 shows the migration propensity by age and educational attainment for males in Java, Indonesia, in 1969–1973. The migration propensity is the proportion of male migrants to urban areas who are a given age and educational attainment divided by the proportion of rural male non-migrants of that same age and educational attainment.[20]

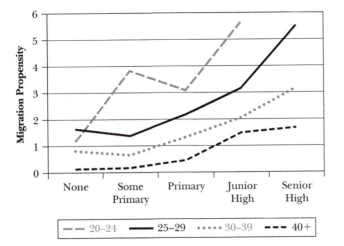

FIGURE 12.1 Migration Propensity to Cities by Age and Education, Java, Indonesia, 1969–1973

Figure 12.1 indicates the selectivity of migration by education. Men aged 25–29 with junior high school education were 3.2 times more likely to be found among rural-urban migrants than among rural residents. Men aged 30–39 with some primary education were only 0.65 times as likely to be found among rural-urban migrants as among rural residents. There is no value shown for men aged 20–24 with a senior high education because there were very few cases in the study.

Migrant selectivity also relates to perceptions and reactions of rural-urban migrants and urban natives. Even though rural-urban migrants are often selected from among rural residents for relatively high education, the educational attainment of urban natives is still often higher than that of rural-urban migrants, due to the overall higher educational attainment of urban than rural residents. Thus, despite the educational selectivity of rural-urban migrants, they still can seem to urban natives to be "country bumpkins."

Selection by Health Both internal and international migrants have often been found to be positively selected for those who are healthy and thus less likely to die early in comparison to the non-migrant population at the origin. This is especially true of younger migrants who are seeking increased economic or personal opportunities. Sometimes older migrants are less healthy, since sometimes they are migrating to receive health care. Sometimes younger migrants are so healthy that they have lower death rates than natives at the destination. As was discussed in Chapter 7, this has been one proposed explanation for the Hispanic paradox, in which Hispanics in the United States have lower reported aged-specific death rates than natives of the United States.[21]

Selection by Age Figure 11.32 in Chapter 11 showed the age and sex distribution of immigrants to the

United States, Canada, and Australia. Immigrants to these developed countries were common in the younger adult ages, 20–34. Migrants were also common among children aged 5–9, who were the offspring of the migrants.

Andrei Rogers and Luis Castro summarized age patterns of migration in a model shown in Figure 12.2. The migration rate declines after young ages, peaks in adulthood, and then falls. A retirement migration peak often is present in populations where migration related to retirement is common. The age pattern of migration is shown with and without a retirement peak.

The highest migration rate is for those in the younger working ages. The relatively high rates for children appear because although people often migrate when they are single or they move without their families, young families are also more likely than others to move. Also, as is discussed under the topic of chain migration a little later in this chapter, often one family member moves first and then other family members join this first migrant later. The retirement peak appears in populations in which migration often occurs in association with retirement. This can be in order for the older person to live with younger relatives, or it can be a move to some other part of the country due to a better climate, a lower cost of living or some other reason.[22]

New communities, such as new housing developments, often have an age distribution similar to that in Figure 12.2 without a retirement peak. As the development ages, the bulge of people in the working ages becomes older, and the entire population of the development can become older, unless there is a high level of turnover of residents and the new residents have a similar age distribution to those when the development was first opened. This is one reason why there are often groups of children in a given age group in suburban developments.[23]

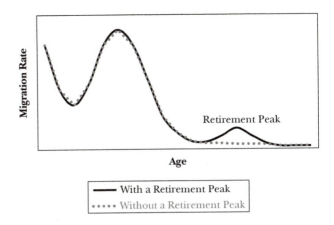

FIGURE 12.2 Rogers and Castro's Model of Migration by Age

Selection by Gender In most cases of labor migration, males are more likely to migrate than females. However, when there are many jobs available in urban places for maids and other household workers, females can be more likely to migrate than males. Females have long predominated in rural-urban migration in Latin America.[24]

Also, some industries that require fine motor skills for assembly of products prefer female to male workers. For example, in the Foxconn plant in China that assembles iPhones, a worker told the *Daily Mail* reporter,[25]

> Our supervisor said that these works were actually being assigned to female workers with nimbler fingers, but due to too many workers reassigned lately they have no choice but to assign these jobs to male workers.

When entire families migrate, there is little selectivity by sex. This is the case in settlement migration, discussed later in this chapter.

Changes Caused by Earlier Migration

The fact of earlier migration changes the context for later migration in several ways, both through connections among individuals and families and through institutional changes. Three theories that involve the effects of earlier migration are cumulative causation, network theory, and institutional theory.

Cumulative Causation In 1957, Gunnar Myrdal proposed the idea of cumulative causation, which states that once a migration stream exists between two places, this in itself alters the context in which subsequent migration decisions are made and typically increases the volume of migration.[26] Building on Myrdal's work, in 1993 Douglas Massey and his colleagues point out that there are six ways in which prior migration changes the social context of migration decision making:[27]

1. **Income Distribution:** As some families have members who have migrated and have sent back remittances, the income distribution in rural areas often becomes more unequal, which provides additional incentives for migration, related to the relative deprivation theory discussed earlier in this chapter.
2. **Land Distribution:** Internal and international migrants often purchase land for use in their later retirement or for prestige. This removes land from agriculture and reduces the demand for agricultural labor, which provides additional incentives for rural residents to migrate.
3. **Agricultural Organization:** Rural households with migrant members who contribute to household income are more likely to invest in agricultural machinery and to use commercial fertilizer. These investments change the nature of rural agricultural production and reduce the demand for agricultural labor. These changes increase rural income inequality and provide additional incentives for rural out-migration.
4. **Cultural Changes:** As there is increased migration out of an area, information received from the migrants makes the prospect of migration less risky. Also, the very idea of migration becomes more acceptable. Migrants from the area could have initially migrated while planning to return after a fairly short time, but exposure to urban life or life in a more prosperous country decreases the chance that the migrant will permanently return. All of these changes increase out-migration. This is similar to the relative deprivation argument, discussed earlier in this chapter.
5. **Distribution of Human Capital:** Migration is selective of those who are more educated, very ambitious, or highly skilled. Thus, as migration proceeds, places of origin becomes less educated and less skilled in comparison to potential migration destinations, which makes migration more attractive to those who are relatively highly educated, ambitious, or skilled at the origin.
6. **Social Labeling of Jobs:** For international migration and sometimes for internal migration, some jobs become defined as "migrant jobs." As natives of the destination become unwilling to hold these jobs, they become reserved for migrants, which can increase migration, depending on the number of people needed to fill these jobs.

Network Theory of Migration Graeme Hugo saw rural-urban migration as a response to the stress resulting from the large socioeconomic differences between rural and urban places. He argued that whether a potential migrant decides to migrate is related to the context in which the decision is made. He thought that there are three intervening variables between stress and the migration decision that influence whether people migrate:[28]

1. **Information:** People vary in the amount of information they have about potential migration destinations. Much of the information that potential migrants have is through personal links with people at the urban destination. Information also operates to promote **chain migration**, in which one person migrates and later relatives and friends migrate. Sometimes

the relatives are waiting until the first migrant finds housing and some money is accumulated to facilitate the move of the later migrants, and sometimes information from the first migrant directly influences the later migration decision of relatives and friends. In the case of international migration, immigration laws sometimes make it much easier for people to immigrate if they have relatives who are already in the destination country.

2. **Characteristics of the Individual:** The potential migrant's education, socioeconomic characteristics, and outlook on life will influence how he or she evaluates information in making the decision whether or not to migrate.

3. **Characteristics of the Community of Origin:** The potential migrant will evaluate information about potential migration destinations in light of comparison of the social and economic characteristics of the community of origin with the characteristics of potential destinations.

Institutional Theory   Hugo showed in Indonesia and Caldwell showed in Ghana that networks in urban destinations, sometimes based on ethnic group membership, can ease the adjustment process for new migrants from rural areas. This is an aspect of cumulative causation, but it is manifested though institutional change and is related to institutional theory.[29]

Massey and his colleagues point out that the development of networks and institutions have facilitated international migration. Pathways to smuggle undocumented migrants and to arrange marriage for the purpose of obtaining visas have emerged. Also, organizations develop information to help potential migrants obtain visas through legal means.[30]

World Systems Theory

Immanuel Wallerstein developed world systems theory based on the development of modern world markets. One of his major ideas is that there is a set of core countries and a set of peripheral countries. Michael Hechter applied similar ideas to an urban core and a rural periphery within countries, especially in less developed countries or in currently developed countries prior to substantial development. He called his formulation "internal colonialism." The core exploits the labor and resources of the periphery to the benefit of development and profit for the capitalists in core countries or in core areas within countries. In this neo-Marxist theory, capitalist economies create a system that motivates international migration from peripheral, dependent societies or from peripheral, dependent areas within a society.[31]

Massey and his colleagues have summarized the various ways in which world systems theory applies to theories of international migration. Many of these mechanisms also can be applied to rural-urban migration in less developed countries:[32]

1. **Land:** Capitalist farmers in peripheral areas mechanize production and increase the use of commercial fertilizer. This decreases the demand for agricultural labor. Land consolidation and a change to cash crops by capitalist farmers motivate migration. This is similar to the argument of how changes in agricultural organization motivate migration under the earlier discussion of cumulative causation.

2. **Raw Materials:** Development of extractive industries for raw materials draws migrants from rural areas to domestic and international destinations.

3. **Labor:** Capitalist companies establish manufacturing sites in peripheral countries due to the low cost of labor. The relatively high wages paid in these factories attract workers from traditional agriculture, weaken social ties in rural areas, and increase migration domestically and internationally. This is similar to the argument about how cultural changes motivate migration under the earlier discussion of cumulative causation.

4. **Material Links:** In order to move agricultural goods, raw materials, or manufactured goods from peripheral countries to core countries, capitalists from core nations improve transportation systems between core and periphery countries. These systems facilitate the movement of persons for labor as well as goods.

5. **Ideological Links:** There are ideological and cultural links between core and peripheral countries, often because of a former colonial relationship. These links encourage migration from particular peripheral countries to particular core countries.

6. **Global Cities:** A small number of cities in core countries manage the world economy. These cities have a highly skilled workforce, but a large number of low-skilled jobs are also created. These low-skilled jobs attract migrants, whether legal or undocumented, from peripheral countries, since natives of the core countries are not willing to take these low-skilled jobs.

Consistent with world systems theory, Alejandro Portes and Craig Gurian argue that the international system creates a situation in which there is a high demand for workers to fill low-wage, unskilled jobs, and that many people migrate from the LDR to the MDR whether legally or not. They argue that there is little enforcement of any relevant immigration laws due to the high demand for low-skilled workers in areas such as agricultural labor and domestic service.[33]

MOVERS AND STAYERS

People can be roughly divided into **movers and stayers**. The movers migrate frequently, and the stayers rarely move. Sidney Goldstein first pointed out that in 1954 a high proportion of incidents of migration and of residential mobility is the result of frequent moves by "movers," while the vast majority of the population remains at the same place of residence.[34] This is partially the result of selectivity of migration, in which people who have characteristics related to migration at one point in time are also likely to migrate at a later point in time.

Using a longitudinal data set, Peter Morrison looked at moves in the United States in the early 1960s. Figure 12.3 shows the proportion of males who moved in 1966–1967 according to their duration of residence at their previous place of residence. The results are shown for men for whom 7 or more years of data were available.

Among those who had been at their residence for less than 1 year, 43% moved, while for those at their residence for 6 years, only 5% moved. People are not born with a stamp on their foreheads that says "mover" or "stayer," but which category they are likely to fall into is revealed by their migration behavior, as indicated in Figure 12.3. Those who had been at their residence for a short time were much more likely to subsequently move than those who had been there for several years, which is consistent with the idea that the short-term residents tended to be movers and always would have a higher propensity to move than those who at any point in time had resided in one place for several years.[35]

MIGRATION AND MORTALITY

Several links between migration and mortality have been discussed in earlier chapters. In Chapter 5, we saw that the !Kung Bushmen moved after there was a death to a group member. In Chapter 5, there also was discussion of the spread of disease by migrants, including the plague in the fourteenth century and SARS in the twenty-first century. Chapter 5 also discussed how the nineteenth-century potato famine in Ireland caused some people to die, while it led other people to migrate out of Ireland. Migration in the face of high mortality and attendant problems is an example of Davis's theory of multiphasic response, discussed in Chapter 1. Also, as discussed in this chapter, migration for economic or personal betterment is often selective of healthier individuals, who have lower mortality risks than non-migrants.

Sometimes mortality is associated with complex humanitarian emergencies. Charles Keely and his colleagues have classified mortality and migration in the context of these emergencies into the following categories:[36]

1. **Rural Famine or Refugee Paradigm:** This occurs among poor populations, often in high-density refugee camps. People moved to the camps because they were refugees due to a famine or other cause. People, especially children, die from communicable diseases exacerbated by malnutrition.
2. **Ethnic Cleansing or Genocide:** In this situation, civilians are attacked to kill them or induce them to move. People die mostly from physical injury. The 1993–1994 Rwandan Civil War, discussed in Chapter 8, is an example.
3. **Urban Services Collapse or Urban Depopulation:** This occurs when generally healthy urban residents become refugees because of violence. Deaths are often due to chronic diseases and disruption of medicine or treatment, such as dialysis.
4. **Conflict among Combatants:** This is mortality among combatants in a conflict. It can be directly due to injuries or due to communicable diseases exacerbated by war. Angola in the 1980s and 1990s is an example.
5. **Short-onset, Short-duration Natural Disaster:** Natural disasters, such as hurricanes or earthquakes, can lead to many deaths when they occur, and can later result in famine or disease if adequate steps are not taken. Haiti after the 2010 hurricane, discussed in Chapter 6, is an example.

MIGRATION AND CLIMATE CHANGE

People have speculated on the possible future effects of climate on migration based on information about responses to temporary climate changes, such as droughts in the Sahel area of Northern Africa and the dustbowl in eastern Oklahoma in the 1930s.[37]

The Intergovernmental Panel on Climate Change (IPCC) did an assessment in 2007 of the likelihood of various climate change events occurring. All of the aspects of climate change listed that contribute to

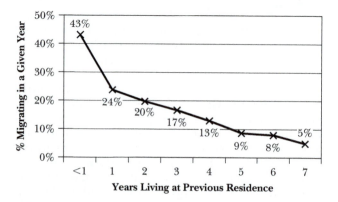

FIGURE 12.3   Percentage of Males Moving by Years Living at Previous Residence, the United States, 1966–1967

migration also contribute to mortality. The six most likely climate change events are listed below, along with their relation to migration:[38]

1. **Warmer and More Frequent Hot Days and Nights over Most Land Areas (>99% Chance of Happening):** This can lead to worse urban air quality, increased evaporation leading to drought, and increased wildfires. All of these can induce migration.

2. **Increases in Warm Spell and Heat Wave Frequencies over Most Land Areas (90–99% Chance of Happening):** This can lead to increased wildfires and deteriorating water quality, which can contribute to migration.

3. **Increases in Heavy Precipitation over Most Areas (90–99% Chance of Happening):** This can lead to soil erosion, which decreases agricultural productivity, contamination of water, and flooding, all of which can contribute to migration.

4. **Increases in Areas Affected by Drought (66–89% Chance of Happening):** This can lead to crop damage, livestock deaths, and water shortages, which can lead to migration. It also can affect power generation, which can contribute to migration.

5. **Increasingly Intense Tropical Cyclone Activity (66–89% Chance of Happening):** This can lead to flooding, wind damage, power outages, and crop damage, all of which can contribute to migration.

6. **Rising Sea Level (66–89% Chance of Happening):** This can require relocation of people from areas, including cities newly underwater. It can also contribute to salinization of water sources, affecting agriculture and drinking water.

Most theories of rural-urban migration discussed earlier in this chapter would expect that the level of rural-urban migration and improvement in development indicators would be strongly related. Salvador Barrios and his colleagues present evidence that the relation between climate change and migration is different in sub-Saharan Africa than in other regions of the world. Specifically, they note that high levels of rural-urban migration and growth of the urban population in sub-Saharan Africa have not been accompanied by improvement in development indicators, unlike the situation elsewhere in the world. In much of sub-Saharan Africa, agricultural production has long been dependent on low and often unpredictable levels of rainfall. The unpredictability of rainfall and periods of drought have created additional incentives for people to leave their rural origins to seek income-producing activities in urban areas. They also relate high levels of

rural-urban migration to the removal of colonial-era restrictions on movement of Africans and the removal of apartheid-era restrictions in South Africa. The apartheid-era restrictions on migration in South Africa are discussed later in this chapter.[39]

MIGRATION AND FERTILITY

It has often been noted that recent migrants have lower fertility than urban natives. Sometimes with longer duration of residence, the fertility of the rural-urban migrants rises (and sometimes surpasses) to that of the urban natives. When people compare the fertility of migrants and natives, sometimes they compare the number of children ever born (which reflects lifetime childbearing), and sometimes they compare the age-specific fertility rate (which reflects recent childbearing).

Three kinds of explanations of the lower fertility of recent rural-urban migrants than urban natives have been proposed. They are as follows:[40]

1. **Migration selection:** Migrant selectivity was discussed in this chapter. Since migrants are selected for higher education than the general population at the origin, they could also be selected for lower fertility.

2. **Migration disruption:** The experience of migration could disrupt a woman's life, leading to lower fertility. Migration could be associated with temporary separation of spouses, or a woman could temporarily restrict her fertility in anticipation of migration or after migration to cope with the new setting. The fertility of recent migrants could be higher if migrant women were unable to find at the new location the contraceptives they had used before migration.

3. **Migration adaptation:** A migrant could adjust her behavior to be more similar to that of natives at the destination, including lower fertility due to adoption of contraception or by some other mechanism.

Studies have found support for all three mechanisms. Figure 12.4 shows the number of children ever born to urban natives and to rural-urban migrant women in Puerto Rico in 1960.[41] Younger migrant women had a substantially lower number of children ever born than urban natives. This relationship changed at older ages, with a higher number of children ever born among migrant women. The phenomenon when one group of people has higher fertility than another group at a younger age but lower fertility at an older age is called **crossover fertility**.

Among all women, there was almost no difference between urban native and migrant women in the number of children ever born (3.47 vs. 3.36).

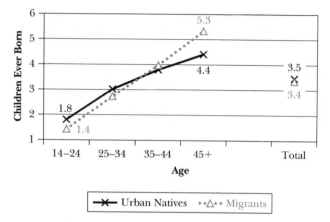

FIGURE 12.4 Children Ever Born among Migrants and Urban Natives in Puerto Rico by Age of Woman, 1960

Recent selection of migrants could account for the low fertility of young migrant women, but disruption seems a more likely explanation. Shortly after having migrated might not have been a good time to have children, or the spouses could have been temporarily separated. The migrant women later made up for their low fertility when they were younger.

Eric Jensen and Dennis Ahlburg found for the Philippines for 1993 that migrant women had lower fertility than urban natives. However, in that case the first two factors, selection and disruption, seemed to play a minor role. Rather, the lower fertility of migrant women seemed to be explained by the third factor, adaptation. This was especially relevant to the lower fertility of migrant women who were working for pay. Women who migrated to cities wanted to better their families' situation. They tended to work for pay and in doing so ended up reducing their fertility.

INTERNAL MIGRANTS

Internal migrants move within the same country. People migrate within a country for a variety of reasons, including for marriage, relocating the household to a place where land is more available, and finding work. Some of the major kinds of internal migrants are marriage migrants, settlement migrants, and labor migrants.

Marriage Migrants

Marriage migration occurs when people migrate in order to marry and live with the new spouse. Movement of the bride to the place of residence of the groom is most common, but in some cultures, such as Thailand, the norm is for the groom to move to the place of residence of the bride.

Many cultures have a tradition or norms that require people to marry outside of the local group. This is one of the largest sources of migration in many less developed countries. It often has been ignored by researchers, except anthropologists. One reason is that it has been thought to have little overall population impact, because the characteristics of persons migrating from Place A to Place B for marriage are thought to be about the same as the people migrating from Place B to Place A for marriage, and the numbers moving in each direction are thought to be approximately equal. If these assumptions are true, then marriage migration has little effect on the characteristics of the populations in Place A and in Place B.[42]

Settlement Migrants

Settlement migration occurs when people migrate for the purpose of pursuit of agriculture in a place where land is more readily available than in the earlier place of residence. Migration is usually undertaken by entire families, villages, or a large part of villages. For example, the wagon trains in the settlement of the American West consisted of a large number of families travelling together, rather than individuals or individual families.

This westward movement is indicated by changes over time in the center of the U.S. population, as shown in Figure 12.5. In 1790, it was east of Baltimore, Maryland; by 1860, it was in eastern Ohio; in 1910, it was in Bloomington, Indiana; in 1960, it was near Centralia, Illinois; and in 2010, it was in central Missouri.[43]

Settlement migration is often a response to population pressure at the origin. Settlement migration has been encouraged by governments to relieve what is seen as high population density in some areas and is intended to populate locations that have low population density. Examples of settlement migration are the large-scale migrations to the American West in the nineteenth century; Siberia and Kazakhstan in the Russian Empire, also in the nineteenth century; and Indonesia in the twentieth century. In the United States, the Homestead Act of 1862 provided 160 acres of land to qualifying settlers. In the Russian Empire, laws regulating migration to Siberia and Russian Central Asia were eased in 1881, and the annual number of migrants to Siberia and Russian Central Asia for settlement increased from 28,000 in the 1880s to 108,000 in the 1890s. Starting in 1893, Frederick Jackson Turner argued that the American frontier and its settlement were the source of distinctive American characteristics, including egalitarianism, democracy, aggression, and innovation.[44]

Internal Labor Migrants

Internal labor migrants migrate within a country for the purpose of work. This often is rural-urban migration, but it can be migration between urban places.

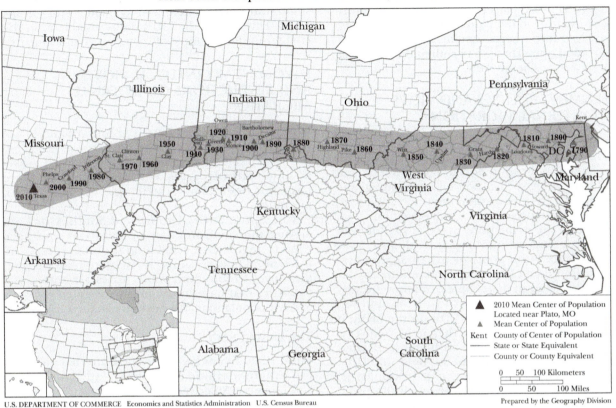

Mean Center of Population for the United States, 1790 to 2010

FIGURE 12.5 Mean Geographic Center of the United States Population, 1790–2010

There also can be rural-rural labor migration when people migrate to work in mines or to be agricultural laborers.

Rural-Urban Labor Migration
Development economists have been very concerned with the causes and effects of rural-urban migration in the LDR. The desire for income is clearly a major factor in rural-urban labor migration. As discussed by Skeldon, and in line with selectivity of migration, rural-urban migrants tend to have better skills and be younger than those who remain in rural areas, but they have fewer skills than urban natives.[45]

In response to the higher expected wage rate in urban places than at rural origins, migrants have moved into LDR cities in massive numbers. These migrants often live in unsightly conditions in shacks and sometimes in cardboard boxes. LDR national and city governments often feel overwhelmed as improvement of living conditions and provision of services and housing only seem to attract more migrants. Often, the migrants are competing for income from murky sector jobs, such as reselling fruit or coat hangers. These workers are not employed by anyone, and

there is no limit on their number. However, the more workers who are competing to sell a particular good, the lower the income of all similar workers. This can lead to intense competition and even violence, sometimes against members of particular ethnic groups or against those from other countries who are also seeking income in the murky sector.[46]

Labor migrants often move with the intention of returning permanently to their place of origin after a short time. Technically, such movement should not qualify as "migration," but these moves are usually considered acts of migration. One reason for this is that although the rural-urban migrants say they intend to return to their rural place of origin, they often remain at the urban destination for many years, and many never return permanently to their rural origin.

Circulation Migrants
Circulation migration occurs when people move from their place of origin to a place of destination but frequently return to the place of origin. With poor transport systems, a person's rural home could be 20 or 30 miles from the urban workplace, but

daily commuting is not feasible. Often circulation migrants go to urban places for work, but they return weekly or monthly to their rural place of origin for a few days. As transportation systems improve, circulation migration often changes to **commuting**, in which the worker returns home daily.[47]

GOVERNMENT POLICIES AND VIEWS ABOUT INTERNAL MIGRATION

With some exceptions, governments do not make laws to regulate internal migration, although they often implement policies to encourage or discourage internal movement, such as policies to encourage the settlement of a frontier or movement to rural areas, or to discourage movement to very large cities.

Figure 12.6 shows the percentage of LDR and of MDR governments with policies intended to lower migration from rural areas to urban agglomerations at various dates. Urban agglomerations are discussed further later in this chapter, but they are very large urban areas. The concern with rural-urban migration has increased in the LDR. In the MDR, it decreased until about 2000 and then increased. This could be because in the LDR, problems associated with a high level of migration of the poor into large cities have become more apparent. In the MDR, there has been increasing concern with the problems of very large cities. Middle-sized cities often have had higher growth rates in the MDR than very large cities.

There has been more interest in motivating migration from urban to rural areas. In 2009, 38% of LDR governments and 23% of MDR governments had policies intended to increase migration from urban to rural areas.[48] These policies have not been

very effective in the LDR, although there has been some shift to rural areas and to smaller cities in the MDR. This shift in the MDR is discussed later in this chapter under the topic of "counterurbanization."

INVOLUNTARY INTERNAL MOVES AND RESTRICTIONS ON INTERNAL MIGRATION

Internal migration is usually voluntary and is not regulated by the government, although as indicated in Figure 12.6, governments have favored movement to particular areas. With few exceptions, there have not been legal restrictions on rural-urban migration.

China, the Soviet Union, and South Africa are among the small number of countries that have tried to regulate internal migration to cities. Also, the United States, China, Russia (and, before that, the Soviet Union), and South Africa are among the countries that have involuntarily relocated portions of their populations. We next discuss these cases.

The United States

The United States has compelled internal moves of two different ethnic minorities, Native Americans and Japanese Americans. The relocation and restriction of residence of Native Americans can be seen as the result of a desire by European Americans to improve their access to land and other resources. The relocation of Japanese Americans during World War II can be seen as a war-inspired fear of subversive behavior, influenced by racism.

Relocation of Native Americans and Establishment of the Indian Reservation System

Between 1800 and 1850, about 100,000 Native Americans who lived east of the Mississippi River, including the Cherokee, Chickasaw, Choctaw, Creek, and Seminole, were relocated to west of the Mississippi, especially to Oklahoma. Groups that refused to move were required to live in very small areas that became reservations. These dislocations were precipitated by the Indian Removal Act of 1830. The relocation of Native Americans from the southeastern United States to Oklahoma was called the "Trail of Tears." Even after Native American groups had moved West, European settlers wanted large parts of Native American land, and Native American groups were forced to live on smaller and smaller tracts of what was regarded as the worst land in the area. The discovery of large natural resource deposits, especially related to energy, on Indian reservations in the twentieth century has changed and complicated the relation between Native American groups, the U.S. government, and third parties who want to obtain Indian land.[49]

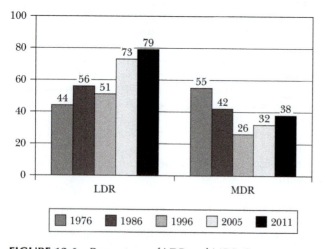

FIGURE 12.6 Percentage of LDR and MDR Governments with Policies to Lower Migration from Rural Areas to Urban Agglomerations, 1976–2011

The U.S. reservation system has been emulated by other countries. Chile won independence from Spain in 1880. In 1881, the new Chilean government implemented a system to restrict members of indigenous groups to a small amount of land and to free other land for the use of European immigrants, based on the American reservation system.[50]

Internment of Japanese Americans during World War II

In 1942, following the Japanese attack on Pearl Harbor in December 1941, over 100,000 Japanese and Japanese Americans who lived on the west coast of the United States were moved to "War Relocation Camps." Sixty-two percent of those who were interred were American citizens. There have been accusations of racism, since there was no similar internment of German Americans or Italian Americans. In 2000, the U.S. Census Bureau admitted that it had cooperated in locating Japanese and Japanese Americans for internment. This admission was made after researchers found incontrovertible evidence of the cooperation. In 1988, the U.S. Congress apologized to those who had been interred, and over $1.6 billion was paid in reparations to those who had been interred and their descendants.[51]

Russia and the Soviet Union

The Russian Empire restricted movement in various ways, and the Soviet Union continued to restrict and compel internal movement. In the Russian Empire, Jews were limited in where they could live. The relocation of ethnic groups in the Caucasus during World War II can be seen as the result of concern with subversive or collaborationist activity with the Nazis combined with racism. The restriction of internal movement of collective farmers, also referred to as peasants, can be seen as a lack of concern with collective farmers, encouraged by the Marxist emphasis on the importance of workers and suspicion of the peasantry. The restrictions on urban residence stemmed from a perhaps excessive concern with the negative consequences of too-rapid urban growth and of too-large cities.

Restriction of Residence of Jews in the Nineteenth Century

In 1835, most Jews were restricted to living in the "Pale of Settlement," which was a set of provinces in the western Russian Empire, most of which had been part of Poland. In addition, merchants and townspeople, which were legal categories, were required to live in the town in which they were registered. Almost all Jews were in these two categories, so this rule essentially barred Jews from residing in rural areas and restricted the areas of the Russian Empire in which they could live.[52]

Forced Relocation of Ethnic Groups from the Baltic and the Caucasus in the 1930s and 1940s

In World War II, the Soviet Union involuntarily relocated members of many ethnic groups from the Baltic and Caucasus regions to Siberia and Soviet Central Asia. Finns, Estonians, Lithuanians, Poles, and members of other non-Slavic ethnic groups were relocated from the western border of the Soviet Union beginning in 1935. This involved about 1.5 million people.

The first of the deportations from the Caucasus region was of the Volga Germans in 1941. Other groups (Karachai, Kalmyks, Chechen, Ingush, Crimean Tatars, and Meshkhetians) were deported in 1943–1944. The rationale for the Baltic deportations was that the Soviet state saw these groups as inherently unreliable and worried that their many relatives outside of the Soviet Union would be conduits for anti-Soviet propaganda. The rationale for the deportations from the Caucasus was that members of these groups were thought to be potential collaborators with the invading Nazi army.

After Stalin's death in 1953, most members of the Baltic groups and of five of the groups from the Caucasus were allowed to return to their earlier regions of residence. However, the Germans, Crimean Tatars, and Meshketians were not allowed to move back to their earlier areas at that time. The Crimean Tatars were allowed to return to the Crimea only in 1989. This resulted in a variety of problems, including that the land and homes that the families had previously held were occupied by other people.[53]

Internal Passports and Restriction of Internal Movement by Collective Farmers

In the Soviet Union, people officially belonged to one of three "social groups": employees, workers, and peasants. Employees were mainly white-collar workers, and workers were blue-collar workers and those on what were called state farms. Peasants were collective farmers. In order to travel and stay overnight in a hotel or to migrate, a person needed a Soviet internal passport. Peasants did not have internal passports until 1974 and thus were severely restricted in their travel and internal migration.[54]

Restricted-Residence Cities and Closed Cities

The Soviet Union had a set of "closed cities" and "restricted-residence cities." For residence in both kinds of cities, a special permit was required. The closed cities were often locations of defense installations or defense plants. One such city was Gorky, which was later renamed Nizhny Novgorod.

Many large cities were designated as restricted-residence cities to try to restrict their growth, because Soviet planners thought that a high rate of growth had negative consequences for a city. A person could legally reside in a restricted-residence city

BOX 12.1

An Extreme Example of Efforts to Obtain a Permit to Live in a Restricted-Residence Soviet City

In the 1980s, a Latvian woman who lived in Riga, the capital of Latvia and a restricted-residence city, was studying at Moscow State University. She met and married a Russian man while at school. They moved to Riga, where he received a residence permit due to his marriage. Within 6 months of moving to Riga, the husband filed for divorce. It was clear that he had engineered the marriage in order to obtain a residence permit for Riga. The wife was devastated. The man was able to keep his residence permit for Riga.

if he or she had been born there, but if a person were born elsewhere, obtaining a residence permit could be difficult or impossible. Restricted-residence cities included Moscow, Leningrad, Minsk, Kiev, Rostov-on-Don, and Vladivostok. Although these restrictions prevented some people from migrating where they wished, there is general agreement that these cities grew more rapidly than Soviet planners had desired. Box 12.1 presents an extreme example of the efforts that some people made to obtain a residence permit for a restricted-residence city.[55]

China

China has employed several policies to influence internal movements. The relocation of many Han Chinese to China's northern border provinces was seen as an issue of military security in light of a perceived Soviet threat. The sending of urban youth to rural areas during the Cultural Revolution was part of an effort by Mao to "purify" society and to reduce the influence of all alternative power bases. The household registration system and educational requirements for becoming an urban resident were seen as ways to exercise control over local populations, limit urban growth and the possible negative effects of rapid urban growth, and help assure that China's urban population was composed of educated persons.

Relocation of Han Chinese to Northern Border Provinces

In the period 1953 through 1982, the Chinese government encouraged and sometimes required migration by Han Chinese to three provinces on China's northern border, especially Xinjiang. It was seen as an issue of national security to increase the proportion of residents of that region who were Han Chinese rather than members of Muslim ethnic minorities. Part of the motivation for the migration of Han Chinese to the Xinjiang border was a concern with possible threats from the Soviet Union that bordered these provinces. Han Chinese were viewed by the Chinese government as more reliable than members of the local indigenous groups, many of whom were Muslim. Mainly as a result of this policy, the percentage of the population of Xinjiang increased from 6% Han Chinese in 1953 to 40% Han Chinese in 1982.[56]

The nature of the incentives to migrate to the northern frontier varied. Discussion with a young Han Chinese woman in Xinjiang in the late 1980s revealed that both of her parents had been required to move to Xinjiang from southern China. Her mother had been told that she had a choice. She could move to Xinjiang and have normal educational and occupational opportunities, or she could remain in southern China and have no desirable educational or occupational opportunities. Her father had been told to move to Xinjiang and that he had no choice in the matter.[57]

Relocation of Youth to the Countryside during the Cultural Revolution

During China's Cultural Revolution in 1967–1978, 17 million urban young people were sent to rural areas. Usually, these people had graduated from junior or senior high school. Those sent to rural areas comprised about one-third of urban youth entering the labor force in that period. It was thought that these youth needed to be reeducated by rural residents and needed to align their thinking more with that of Mao Zedong. Many of these people eventually returned to urban areas, but this experience had major negative effects on their later education and careers.[58]

The Household Registration System and Restriction of Migration to Cities

China also has tried to restrict the growth of urban areas through limiting migration into cities.[59] In 1955, China established the household registration (*hukou*) system. This system was intended to limit rural-urban migration. Every person had either rural or urban registration. A child inherited his or her mother's registration at birth. If a person did not have urban registration at birth, education was a pathway to urban registration. A person with rural registration could obtain urban registration if he or she gained admission to a specialized secondary school or to a postsecondary educational institution. Rural members of the Chinese Communist Party and those who had served in the People's Liberation Army also sometimes could obtain urban registration.[60]

In the late 1970s, China implemented economic reforms that generated a need for more urban labor. Rural residents were brought into urban places as "temporary contract workers," but they did not obtain urban registration. Without official urban registration, they had no access to urban social services and were disadvantaged in comparison to those with urban registration. The number of these "temporary contract workers" in Chinese urban areas increased greatly over time. Temporary labor migrants to cities worked in construction, waitressing, and child care. They also worked in factories. Some of these temporary workers engaged in entrepreneurial activity, such as opening small restaurants. Since these workers were away from their household's place of permanent residence, their children could not enroll in school, or the parents had to pay substantial fees to enroll. Since the mid-1990s, local governments have obtained more discretion in awarding urban registration to temporary contract workers.[61]

Xiushi Yang and Sidney Goldstein have argued that the influx of temporary migrants to Chinese urban areas has substantially countered the restrictions on permanent movement imposed by the household registration system. However, Chun-Chung Au and Vernon Henderson argue that restriction of migration to China's cities impeded economic productivity, and that China would have been more productive if there had been no restrictions on movement.[62]

In 2013, Chinese leaders appeared to be changing to a policy that would be more permissive of rural-urban migration with the migrants obtaining permanent residence, especially in small and medium-sized cities. Such migration was seen to contribute to economic growth. Also in 2013, Shanghai, China's largest city, announced that it would ease procedures for migrants into the city to obtain legal permanent residence.[63]

South Africa

The National Party won the 1948 South African elections, which led to the progressive implementation of apartheid laws. Although there had been laws that limited the free movement of non-Whites in South Africa for 300 years, the apartheid laws brought the regulation of the movement of non-Whites to a new level. The creation of homelands served to help move Africans out of areas that Whites wanted for their own uses, to fragment groups to minimize possibilities of political organizing and coordination, and to create additional incentives for Africans to become workers in mines and other White-owned enterprises. The restrictions on African residence in cities and restrictions against Africans being in cities at night catered to White fears of violence and of sullying of their neighborhoods.

Creation of Homelands

The Bantu Homelands Citizenship Act of 1970 declared that every African was a citizen of one of ten "homelands" and was not a citizen of South Africa. Africans in South Africa were members of Bantu-language groups that had long resided in Africa. The homelands comprised 14% of the land area of South Africa; at that time, Africans comprised about 70% of the population of South Africa. Many Africans in South Africa were forced to relocate to the homelands, which were in rural areas. It was impossible for all Africans in homelands to procure a living within the homelands. The homeland policy was an incentive for African males to work in the mines.[64]

Restrictions on Residence of Africans in South African Cities

South Africa tried to limit growth of its cities under apartheid and especially severely limited the residence of Africans in cities. Under apartheid, laws and policies were determined by the White minority. Africans were no longer allowed to live in cities, with exceptions for live-in domestic servants. Africans without permits to live in cities were not allowed to be in cities at night; if they were found in a city at night, they were subject to arrest. Even during the apartheid period, Africans were allowed to live in townships, which had many urban characteristics and often were close to cities.

In apartheid South Africa, there were four official population groups: Whites, Africans, Coloured persons, and Asians. Coloured persons were a mixed-race group that dates back 300 years to the descendants of Dutch, Malay, African, and other groups. Most Asians were descendants of persons from India, although some Asians were descendants of those from other Asian countries. Although Coloured persons and Asians were never banned from cities, they were often relocated from one part of a city to another, as White groups wanted exclusive control over neighborhoods where non-Whites lived.

In 1985, the law against Africans living in cities was repealed. In 1991, most other apartheid policies were reversed, and the new South African government was founded in 1994, in which all citizens had the right to vote and participate in the South African Parliament.[65]

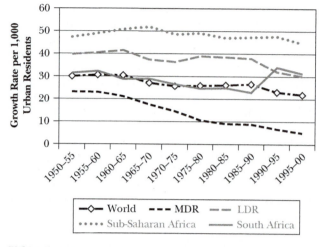

FIGURE 12.7 Rate of Growth of Urban Population in South Africa and Some World Regions, 1950–2000

Figure 12.7 shows the growth rate of the urban population in the world as a whole, the MDR, the LDR, all of sub-Saharan Africa, and South Africa. Throughout 1950–2000, the growth rate of the urban population in sub-Saharan Africa was higher than in the LDR as a whole, and the growth rate of the urban population in the LDR was higher than in the MDR.

South Africa had an extremely low urban growth rate during 1950–1990 in comparison to the LDR or sub-Saharan Africa. The urban growth rate increased substantially from 1985–1990 to 1990–1995, due to the abolition of apartheid-era restrictions on African movement to cities.

The increased growth rate of the urban population after 1990 was viewed by some South Africans, especially White South Africans, as an unprecedented rush of Africans into South African cities. However, from Figure 12.7 it is clear that after 1985, the urban growth rate changed to a typical level for the LDR and to a level that was still low in comparison to the rest of sub-Saharan Africa.

FAMILY MIGRATION DECISIONS IN THE UNITED STATES

There has been considerable work to determine the influence of different family members on family migration decisions. It has often been assumed that when an entire family in a more developed country moves, it is done mainly because of the interests of the husband. The husband has often been called the "primary migrant," and the wife and children have been called "secondary migrants." Clearly, children migrate because of their parents. However, the argument about the wife as a secondary migrant is less clear. The rationale for this assumption is that the husband more often works for pay than the wife, and

even if the wife works for pay, the husband usually has a higher income. It is analytically easier to think of the migration of a household as dependent only on the characteristics of one person (the husband) rather than to figure out a way to also take the wife's characteristics into account.

This way of thinking about things has become less common as female labor force participation rates have increased, as we saw in Figure 10.25 in Chapter 10. In 1978, the economist Jacob Mincer thought that maximization of income was a family's main goal in migration decisions, and thus, since husbands tended to have higher incomes than wives, the husband's job interests would be the primary factor in family migration decisions. He also thought that as wives' labor force participation and incomes increased, characteristics of wives would increasingly matter in family migration decisions.[66]

In 1982, Daniel Lichter analyzed the effect of the wife's labor force participation on migration. He found that in families in which the wife worked for pay, the family was less likely to migrate. Among families in which the wife worked for pay, the only characteristic of the wife that mattered was her job seniority, with holding a more senior position related to less chance of moving. Her income, her income relative to her husband's income, whether she was in a professional or managerial job, whether she worked full-time, and her job satisfaction did not significantly affect whether the family migrated.[67]

In 2010, Steven Tenn analyzed the influence of husband's characteristics and wife's characteristics on family migration in 1960–2000. He had expected that the wife's characteristics would have become more important in migration decisions over time, as women's labor force participation and wages increased and as women generally had more voice in society. Between 1960 and 2000, the percentage of married women in the labor force increased from 34% to 71%, and the percentage of household wages contributed by the wife increased from 13% to 30%. Nonetheless, Tenn found that there was little change in the 40-year period in the influence of the wife's characteristics on migration and that the husband's characteristics remained much more important than the wife's.[68]

In light of Mincer's view of migration decision making and income maximization, one would have expected a greater change. In 1990, in households in which both the husband and wife had earnings, 19% of wives with earnings earned more than their husbands; in 2000, 23% of wives earned more than their husbands; and in 2010, it had increased to 29%. It is yet to be seen whether after 2000, wives' characteristics became more important in migration decisions. In the results for data through 2000, it seems that a wife working could inhibit family migration, but that migration was rarely due to job opportunities for the wife.[69]

PATTERNS OF U.S. INTERREGIONAL MIGRATION

There have been many shifts in the regional distribution of the American population. Much of this has been fueled by interregional migration. The eighteenth, nineteenth, and twentieth centuries were characterized by a shift in population to the West, mainly due to migration.

Figure 12.8 shows the division of the United States into four major regions and into more detailed divisions. The regions are NE (Northeast), MW (Midwest), S (South), and W (West).[70]

Figure 12.9 shows the distribution of the American population across the four regions: 1910–2010. The top panel shows the number of people in each region. The total population more than tripled between 1910 and 2010, and the number of people in each region also increased over time.

The bottom panel shows the distribution of population across the four regions. The shift to the West and the South is very clear in the bottom panel. This shift was mainly caused by interregional migration, but international migration, both legal and undocumented, contributed to changes in the population distribution over time.[71]

Figure 12.10 shows migration among American regions from 1960–1961 through 2010–2011. The results are based on surveys that asked about a person's place of residence at the time of the survey and also asked about his or her place of residence 1 year earlier. The number of migrants in thousands among those at least 1 year old at the survey date is shown. The top panel shows the number of migrants out of each region to any other region. The second panel shows the number of migrants into each region from any other region, and the bottom panel shows the number of net migrants in thousands into each region. The results are shown for people who changed their place of permanent residence between a year ending in 0 (1960, 1970, etc.) and their location 1 year later (in 1961, 1971, etc.).[72]

In the top panel of Figure 12.10, we can see that the number of migrants out of every region increased between the early 1960s and the early 1970s, and then usually declined after that. There is a similar pattern in the second panel for migrants into each region. The third panel, which shows the number of net migrants by region, indicates that the Northeast and the Midwest generally lost population on balance, while the South and the West tended to gain population. The number of net migrants to the South and the

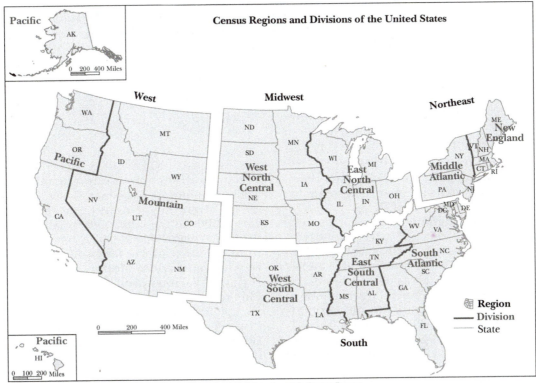

U.S. Department of Commerce Economics and Statistics Administration U.S. Census Bureau

FIGURE 12.8   Major U.S. Census Regions

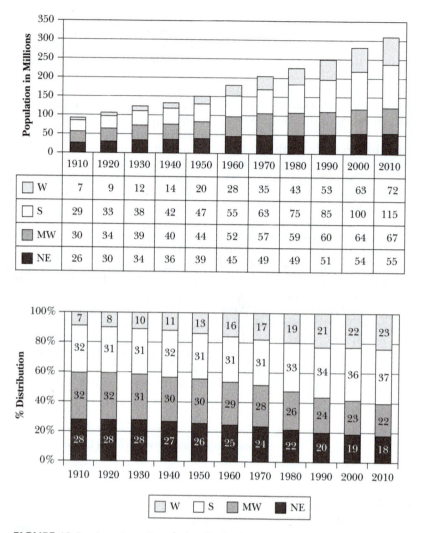

	1910	1920	1930	1940	1950	1960	1970	1980	1990	2000	2010
☐ W	7	9	12	14	20	28	35	43	53	63	72
☐ S	29	33	38	42	47	55	63	75	85	100	115
■ MW	30	34	39	40	44	52	57	59	60	64	67
■ NE	26	30	34	36	39	45	49	49	51	54	55

FIGURE 12.9 American Population by Region, 1910–2010

West tended to decline after the 1970s or the 1980s, reflecting a general decline in American geographic mobility.

Differences in net migration among areas show something about the relative attractiveness of different areas. However, it is clear from the bottom panel of Figure 12.10 that the number of net migrants is usually a relatively small number that is the difference between two much larger numbers. For example, the largest number of net migrants into a region was for the South in 1980–1981. There were 486,000 net migrants, which is the difference between 1,377,000 in-migrants and 891,000 out-migrants.

Figure 12.11 shows the total number of interregional migrants, based on the data source used in Figure 12.10, but here it is shown for 5-year intervals rather than 10-year intervals. The number of interregional migrants has generally declined since the 1970s. Migration also declined rapidly from the early 2000s to the late 2000s, related to economic problems beginning in 2007, but this can be seen in the context of the long-term decline in interregional migration. Molloy, Smith, and Wozniak reviewed various proposed explanations of the long-term decline in American geographic mobility, including the aging of the population, changes in the housing market, and a return to equilibrium after the massive shift to the South shown in Figure 12.10. They concluded that although all of these factors could have played some role in declining geographic movement, none seemed adequate to fully explain the long-term decline since the 1980s.[73]

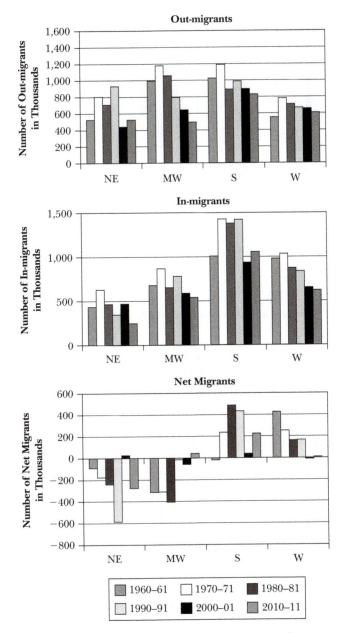

FIGURE 12.10 Interregional Migrants by Region, the United States, 1960–1961 through 2010–2011

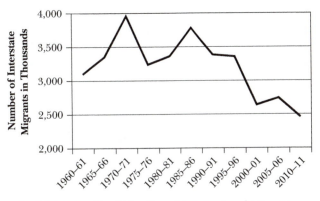

FIGURE 12.11 Total Number of Interregional Migrants, the United States, 1960–1961 through 2010–2011

The Great Migration and the Second Great Migration: African-American Migration from the South to the North, and Its Subsequent Reversal

Between 1900 and 1930, there was a large exodus of African Americans from the South to Northern cities. This movement has often been called "The Great Migration." A period of further high levels of African-American migration out of the South in the period 1940 through 1970 is sometimes called "The Second

Great Migration." However, by the late twentieth century, African Americans on balance had begun to return to the South.

Figure 12.12 shows the regional distribution of the African-American population over time. The regional definitions are the same as those in Figure 12.8. Sometimes, the regions of the Midwest, Northeast, and West are referred to collectively as the "North." Although differences among regions in African-American fertility, mortality, and international migration contribute to the regional share of the African-American population, the main source of changes in the regional distribution is migration among regions.[74]

Through 1970, the South continued to lose its African-American population, but this net loss stabilized from 1970 through 1990, and the results of an African-American migration reversal are shown in the increased percentage of African Americans residing in the South after 1990.

There have been three main reasons proposed for the mass African-American Great Migration of 1900–1930:[75]

1. **Economic Forces, Including Higher Wage Rates and Expanding Employment Opportunities in the North:** Most African Americans in the South worked in a plantation economy, with low wages and little opportunity for upward mobility. There were increasing economic opportunities in the North, especially with the growth in the economy accompanying World War I.

2. **Social Forces, Such as Better Educational Opportunities in the North and Response to Racial Violence and Voter Disenfranchisement in the South:** There were limited educational opportunities for African Americans in the South. Also, social and legislative changes in the South, such as the passage of Jim Crow laws, voting restrictions, poor funding of schools

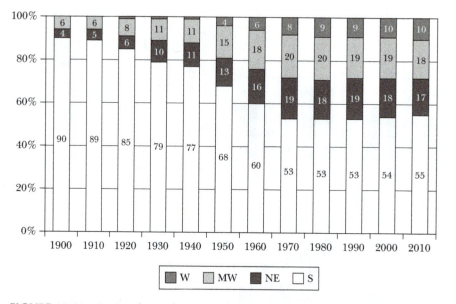

FIGURE 12.12   Regional Distribution of the U.S. African-American Population, 1900–2010

attended by African Americans, and an increase in lynchings, made life in the South increasingly difficult for many African Americans.

3. **Precipitous Events in the South:** Floods, including the Great Mississippi Flood of 1927, destroyed land and housing in many areas, and boll weevil infestation reduced cotton production, which made remaining in the South unattractive.

We see in Figure 12.12 that African Americans increasingly were located in the Midwest and the Northeast in the period 1900 through 1930. Few African Americans went to the West, with 1% of all African Americans living in the West in 1930.

Between 1930 and 1940, there was little change in the regional distribution of the African-American population. However, net migration from the South increased in the 1940–1950 period, beginning the Second Great Migration. The perception of less racial prejudice and the absence of Jim Crow laws made the North an attractive migration destination. Movement out of the South in the period 1940 through 1970 was related to increased employment opportunities as a result of World War II, along with federal government fair-employment practices. In this period, more African Americans settled in the West, where there were many employment opportunities, especially in defense industries.

Throughout the 1900–1970 period, African-American migration was selective of those who were better educated. This was probably partially due to the costs of migration and partially due to general migration selectivity for education related to willingness to take risks, as was discussed earlier in this

chapter. Better educated Southern African Americans also could have been less willing to accept discrimination and other racially related restrictions and indignities.[76]

In the summer of 1967, there were race riots in Detroit, Newark, and more than 20 other northern cities. A government-appointed commission investigated the causes of the riots and concluded that the rioters tended not to be recent migrants from the South who were overwhelmed by urban life but were natives of the North. In Detroit and Newark, about three-quarters of the rioters had grown up in the North. Although the North did not have the outward trappings of discrimination that were apparent in the South, the presence and the effects of discrimination and segregation in the North were clear. These riots and the disillusionment of many Northern African Americans could have contributed to the decreasing attractiveness of Northern cities to Southern African Americans.[77]

By 1975–1980, there was positive net migration to the South from the Northeast and the Midwest, and there was positive net migration from the West by 1995–2000. In 1965–1970, California led all states with 91,425 African-American net in-migrants; California had 63,180 African-American net out-migrants in the 1995–2000 period.[78]

There have been various reasons proposed for the shift to African-American net migration to the South. Just as the Great Migration and the Second Great Migration were selective for educated African Americans, so was migration to the South in the late twentieth and early twenty-first century. At least one-half of the African-American migrants to the South in the late twentieth century were return migrants who had earlier moved from the South to the North. Many persons returned to their Southern state of birth. However, whereas many earlier African-American migrants from the South came from rural areas, African-American return migrants tended to move to metropolitan areas, especially suburbs. Some have seen African-American return migration to the South as a return to cultural roots, but at a time when economic opportunities in the urban South were perceived as equaling or exceeding opportunities in the North.[79]

INTERNATIONAL MIGRANTS

Since the late twentieth century, international migration from less developed countries has been averting population decline in many developed countries. This was discussed in Chapter 2. Demographers and policy makers might ask, "What is motivating this movement?" and "What are the motivations for migration for skilled versus unskilled migrants?" While internal migration has usually been unaffected by laws, legal international migration from the LDR to the MDR often becomes a question of how many people (with what characteristics) a more developed country will allow to enter. Many developed countries have had programs that allow workers from less developed countries to come and work for some period of time, but without the chance of permanent residence or citizenship. Another relevant question is "How well have these programs worked?"

Often, immigration to more developed countries becomes an issue of policy formation and legislation in the more developed country rather than an issue of the desires and motivations of potential international migrants. Other relevant demographic and sociological questions are as follows:

- Are fears about the consequences of increased cultural heterogeneity in the developed region leading to policies that will heavily influence international migration in the future?
- Developed countries also experience substantial illegal or undocumented migration. What are the effects of this migration? How have countries tried to deal with it?
- What are the effects of migration from the LDR to the MDR? How have countries tried to deal with it?

Natural disasters and political disturbances have led to large movements of refugees. Most refugees from less developed countries move temporarily to other less developed countries. This can cause a major strain on the resources of the receiving countries. In addition, while international laws promote consideration of refugees for permanent residence, many MDR countries struggle with the question "Who is a true refugee?" as they perceive a much larger number of people who would like to immigrate than they are willing to admit.

Emigration and Immigration throughout the World

Table 12.2 shows the leading ten countries of emigration, the leading ten countries of immigration, and the leading ten migration corridors in 2010. The emigration countries tend to be in the LDR, and the immigration countries in the MDR. Mexico and India, in the LDR, are the two leading countries of emigration, and the United States and Russia, in the MDR, are the two leading countries of immigration.

Russia, the United Kingdom, and India are leading countries of both immigration and emigration. For Russia, much of the immigration and emigration were with other countries of the former Soviet Union. All ten of the countries that were the largest sources of immigration to Russia were countries of the former Soviet Union, and seven of the leading ten countries of emigration from Russia were countries of the former Soviet Union. Ukraine, Kazakhstan, and Belarus were the top three countries of both immigration and emigration. Israel, the United States, and Germany were also among the top ten countries of emigration from Russia. Six of the leading countries of immigration to the United Kingdom were former British colonies or Commonwealth members, with the leading source of immigration being India. The leading destination for emigrants from the United Kingdom was Australia, followed by the United States. The only LDR countries that were from the United Kingdom among the leading ten emigration destinations were Saudi Arabia at number 4 and India at number 10. Saudi Arabia was the destination of many labor migrants. The five leading sources of immigrants to Saudi Arabia were India, Egypt, Pakistan, Yemen, and the Philippines. Most of the leading sources of immigrants to India were countries in the region, with Bangladesh, Pakistan, Nepal, Sri Lanka, and Myanmar as the five leading sources of immigrants. The leading emigration destination from India was the United Arab Emirates, followed by the United States.

The leading migration corridor is from Mexico to the United States. Four of the leading corridors are between countries of the former Soviet Union (Russia, Ukraine, and Kazakhstan), reflecting the long-standing family and economic ties between these countries.[80]

The Migrant Stock of Countries

Table 12.2 showed the countries with the highest inflow of immigrants in 2010. Another important aspect of international migration is the level of migrant stock, which is the percentage of the population

TABLE 12.2   Leading Countries of Emigration and Immigration, and Leading Migration Corridors, 2010

	Top Emigration Countries	Emigrants in Millions	Top Immigration Countries	Immigrants in Millions	Top Migration Corridors	Migrants in Millions
1	Mexico	12	United States	43	Mexico–United States	12
2	India	11	Russia	12	Russia–Ukraine	4
3	Russia	11	Germany	11	Ukraine–Russia	4
4	China	8	Saudi Arabia	7	Bangladesh–India	3
5	Ukraine	7	Canada	7	Turkey–Germany	3
6	Bangladesh	5	United Kingdom	7	Kazakhstan–Russia	3
7	Pakistan	5	Spain	7	Russia–Kazakhstan	2
8	United Kingdom	5	France	7	India–United Arab Emirates	2
9	Philippines	4	Australia	6	China–United States	2
10	Turkey	4	India	5	Philippines–United States	2

that was born in another country. The magnitude of migrant stock can influence attitudes of natives toward immigrants, and if immigrants have a reasonable chance of obtaining citizenship, migrants who become citizens can affect government policies.

Table 12.3 shows the percentage migrant stock, also called the percentage foreign-born (i.e., the percentage born in another country) in three broad age groups in the world, in regions, and for selected countries. In the world as a whole, the migrant stock under age 20 is low. Migrant stock is higher among older people. It is approximately the same in the main working ages (20–64) and among retirement age people (those aged 65+). We also see that at all ages, the migrant stock is much greater in the MDR than in the LDR, which is consistent with international migration mainly flowing from the LDR to the MDR.[81]

The regional pattern is also consistent, with a low percentage migrant stock in Africa, Asia, and Latin America and the Caribbean, and a high percentage migrant stock in Europe, Northern America, and Oceania. Within regions, individual countries show interesting results. South Africa, with the best economy in sub-Saharan Africa and a long history of White immigration, has a relatively high percentage migrant stock. China, with its growing economy, contains only a small percentage of immigrants. Japan, unlike most other high-income countries, also has less than 3% foreign-born in each of the three age groups. This probably reflects long-standing anti-immigrant attitudes in Japan. Singapore has a high percentage of its population who are foreign-born, mainly reflecting immigration from China. Israel has a very high percentage foreign-born, reflecting the high level of immigration since its founding in 1948. Kuwait, Qatar, and Saudi Arabia are wealthy states in

TABLE 12.3   Percentage Migrant Stock by Age, by Region, and for Selected Countries, 2010

	Age		
	0–19	20–64	65+
World	1.3	4.0	4.7
MDR	4.8	12.8	8.5
LDR	0.9	1.8	2.4
LeastDC	0.8	2.0	1.6
Africa	1.0	2.8	2.3
South Africa	1.2	5.1	7.9
Asia	0.9	1.7	2.3
China	0.0	0.1	0.1
Japan	1.3	2.3	0.5
Singapore	29.0	47.3	24.0
Israel	11.5	49.7	91.1
Kuwait	51.6	77.8	26.7
Qatar	73.3	90.6	68.4
Saudi Arabia	15.9	37.9	5.7
Europe	4.9	11.5	8.1
United Kingdom	4.6	13.6	7.4
France	3.0	13.4	12.4
Germany	5.9	17.0	8.1
Switzerland	13.1	29.9	11.8
Latin America and Caribbean	0.8	1.5	2.3
Northern America	5.2	18.6	12.8
Canada	9.5	23.8	29.1
United States	4.8	18.0	10.9
Oceania	5.9	20.8	27.5
Australia	8.3	25.8	30.2
New Zealand	13.2	25.9	25.5

which a large amount of labor is performed by sometimes long-resident foreigners who have little or no chance of obtaining citizenship.

The four European countries listed have experienced substantial immigration; in the cases of the United Kingdom and France, this is often from former colonies. Germany and Switzerland have extensively employed international temporary labor migrants. In the case of Germany, many of these earlier temporary migrants, especially from Turkey, have become citizens. As is discussed later in this chapter, efforts by Muslim immigrants to Switzerland to practice their religion and culture and to gain citizenship have often been strongly resisted.

The United States, Canada, and Australia have often been characterized as traditional countries of immigration, and as discussed in Chapter 11 and shown in Figure 11.32, the age pattern of immigrants to these three countries was used by the United Nations to model the age pattern of immigrants. New Zealand probably should have been included in that group.

International Labor Migrants

There are two main kinds of international labor migrants. One group fills low-skilled jobs, such as working as agricultural laborers or as domestic servants, that citizens of the destination country are unwilling to take. The other group consists of highly skilled persons, such as doctors and nurses, who can obtain much higher wage rates in more developed countries than they could if they had remained in their home country. The policies of potential destination countries regarding these two categories of migrants are quite different.

Low-Skilled International Labor Migrants

A large number of low-skilled international migrants move for purposes of work. Often their intentions are to remain in the destination country temporarily, and often a large portion of their earnings is sent back to relatives in their home country. Their motivations are often similar to those of rural-urban internal labor migrants. As discussed by Portes and Gurian, they often seek jobs in high-income countries that citizens of those countries are unwilling to hold, especially not at the relatively low wage rates that are often paid. These include agricultural labor in the United States and many other countries, as well as work as domestic servants in the Middle East and other regions.

There have been a variety of legal provisions for low-skilled temporary labor migration, but there is often a high degree of undocumented migration for these purposes. Since such undocumented migrants fill a need for business and often also fill the personal needs of well-off citizens, there is often lax and vacillating enforcement of immigration laws.[82]

Some international labor migrants are in the destination country legally, and some are not. **Undocumented migrants**, also called **illegal immigrants**, come to a country without the required authorization to move to the country. Sometimes there is vigorous pursuit and deportation of undocumented migrants, and sometimes the receiving country mainly ignores their presence.

There are many undocumented workers, especially in more developed countries. In the United States, it is estimated that in 2011 there were 11.5 million undocumented migrants.[83] In the European Union in 2008, it is estimated there were between 1.9 and 3.8 million undocumented migrants.[84]

Different prevailing wage rates in different countries have resulted in a chain of international labor migrants. In Romania in 2007, the average monthly wages after taxes for Romanian workers were $375. Factory owners in Romania brought laborers from China to Romania, for whom average monthly wages after taxes were $347. At the same time, many Romanian workers became labor migrants in Italy and Spain, where the wages paid to Romanian workers were less than what Italian or Spanish workers would have accepted, but higher than wages in Romania.[85]

A large number of Filipino citizens have been engaged in labor migration, often in the Middle East. There have been concerns about abuse of Filipinos, especially women employed as domestic servants. In 2007, the Philippines signed a pact with the United Arab Emirates that provided for some vetting of potential labor migrants while still in the Philippines and also provided some labor protections for Filipino labor migrants. The Philippines pursued similar agreements with other countries, including one signed with Lebanon in 2010.[86]

After the world economic downturn began in 2007, many thought that legal and undocumented international labor migration would plummet. That seems to have happened to a much lesser degree than was expected. In 2010, there seemed to have been little, if any, decline in the international demand for Filipino labor migrants. Some recipient countries facing economic problems, such as Spain, Japan, and the Czech Republic, tried to convince legal labor migrants to go home, including offering foreign workers money to go home. But few migrants accepted the offers. One reason for reluctance to go home is that many saw the economic prospects in their home countries as worse than in the countries in which they were working.[87]

Low-skill undocumented migrants have some legal rights in the United States, although often they do not know what rights they have, and they often fear they will be deported if they assert any of these rights.

BOX 12.2

Undocumented Workers Successfully Assert Their Rights in New York City

In 2007, Asian restaurant deliverymen successfully filed suit against many New York City Asian restaurants for below minimum wage pay. The deliverymen were mainly Chinese immigrants, many of whom were undocumented. The New York State minimum wage laws cover both documented and undocumented workers, but threats from restaurant owners and fear of deportation put the restaurant owners in a position in which many workers thought they had no recourse to accepting pay as low as $1.40 per hour. In 2008, a New York State judge found for the deliverymen in the case of the Saigon Grill and ordered that restaurant to reinstate workers who had been illegally fired for filing wage complaints and that the restaurants needed to pay the deliverymen at least the minimum wage. The Saigon Grill owners were ordered to pay $4.6 million for wage violations.

In 2008, a factory in Queens in New York City that employed mainly Chinese immigrants was found guilty of forcing workers to falsify timesheets and to lie to government inspectors to cover up the far below minimum wage pay. The workers were threatened with firing if they did not cooperate. The factory was found to owe workers $5.3 million. The factory manufactured apparel for many firms, including Macy's, Banana Republic, and Victoria's Secret.

Box 12.2 gives two examples of some success that undocumented workers have had in asserting their rights in New York City.[88]

Brain Drain

Although the more developed countries are good locations for people from throughout the world to gain advanced training, less developed countries can least afford to lose highly qualified individuals. The United Kingdom has a highly skilled category of potential labor immigrants who do not even need to show they have a job offer in order to come to the United Kingdom.[89]

The migration of highly educated and highly skilled persons from less developed countries to more developed countries is called **brain drain**. Those who have come to the United States on J-1 visas, which many graduate students and visiting scholars hold, must return to their home country for 2 years before coming back to the United States. Although there can be some exceptions to this rule, it discourages brain drain to some extent. This rule is in place due to the interests of the home countries of the students and scholars, especially less developed countries, rather than due to the interests of the United States.

An area of great concern has been the migration of physicians and other health care professionals from countries that are already underserved by physicians to more developed countries where they can earn higher incomes. Vujicic and his colleagues analyzed whether the size of the wage differential for physicians between origin and destination countries affected the amount of physician brain drain. They found that the wage differential was not strongly related to the magnitude of physician migration because the wage differential between *all* destination countries and *all* origin countries was so large that relatively small differences between origin countries had little effect on the amount of physician emigration. They speculated that differences between the origin and destination countries in living and working conditions were also important in the international migration decisions of physicians.[90]

Ghana is a prime example of physician brain drain, with many Ghanaian doctors working in the United States, Jamaica, and Canada. This is good for the mobility of the individual doctors, but it does not help the health care situation in Ghana. Between 1999 and 2004, 54% of newly trained Ghanaian doctors left Ghana to work in other countries. One compensating factor was an increase in remittances sent to Ghana from Ghanaians working in other countries.[91]

Table 12.4 shows the top countries in terms of the percentage of those with tertiary education who emigrated, the top ten countries in terms of the number of physicians who emigrated in 2000, the top ten countries for the percentage of physicians, who emigrated, and the top ten countries for the percentage of physicians trained in the country who emigrated.[92] All of the top ten countries in the percentage of the tertiary-educated population who migrated are in the less developed regions, and Haiti is a Least Developed Country. These countries can ill afford to lose these individuals. On the other hand, opportunities for highly educated persons in these countries can be sparse.

TABLE 12.4   Top Countries for Emigration of Those with Tertiary Education and of Physicians, 2000

	Top Countries % of Tertiary-Educated Emigrating	% of Tertiary-Educated Emigrating	Top Countries for Number of Physicians Emigrating	Number of Physicians Emigrating (in Thousands)	Top Countries for % of Physicians Emigrating	% of Physicians Trained in Country Emigrating
1	Guyana	89%	India	20	Grenada	98%
2	Grenada	85%	United Kingdom	12	Dominica	97%
3	Jamaica	85%	Philippines	10	St. Lucia	66%
4	St. Vincent and the Grenadines	85%	Germany	9	Cape Verde	54%
5	Haiti	84%	Italy	6	Fiji	48%
6	Trinidad and Tobago	79%	Mexico	6	Sao Tome and Principe	43%
7	St. Kitts and Nevis	79%	Spain	5	Liberia	34%
8	Samoa	76%	South Africa	4	Papua New Guinea	32%
9	Tonga	75%	Pakistan	4	Iceland	26%
10	St. Lucia	71%	Iran	4	Ethiopia	26%

Grenada, Dominica, and St. Lucia are all in the Caribbean, and a substantial portion of the medical students there are from the United States or Canada. They typically return to those countries after graduation. However, for most of the other countries on the list, most medical students were natives of the country.

Several of the top suppliers of physicians to other countries are in the LDR, such as India and the Philippines, but the United Kingdom, Germany, and Italy are also major suppliers of physicians to other countries, many of whom go to the United States or Australia. A Canadian Medical Association study published in 2007 found that one out of every nine Canadian-trained physicians was practicing medicine in the United States. Higher physician income in the United States was probably one of the reasons for relocation of Canadian doctors to the United States.[93]

Non-physician professionals also migrate between more developed countries. In 2012, when the economic situation in Europe outside of Germany was not good, there was concern about many professionals migrating from Southern Europe to Germany. This movement was facilitated by the membership in the European Union of all the countries involved.[94]

Remittances

Remittances are very important in international migration and are also important in internal migration in some countries. International remittances are funds sent back to the home country by both legal and undocumented migrants. Remittances are also sent from labor migrants to relatives in their place of origin within a country.

These remittances contribute to income in the origin country, but there are various implications of these remittances, including an increase in inequality in the origin country between households with access to international remittances and households without such access. The observation of the higher standard of living of families with remittances is one reason for both internal and international migration in the relative deprivation model of migration.[95]

Table 12.5 shows the top remittance-sending and remittance-receiving countries. It also shows the top countries in terms of remittances as a percentage of the gross domestic product in 2009.[96]

Worldwide, international remittances tend to go to countries with a large population outside of the country, either from people who had permanently emigrated or from international labor migrants. Based on surveys in 135 countries conducted in 2009–2010, 3% of adults worldwide had received an international remittance in the previous month. However, in 35 countries, 10% or more of adults had received an international remittance, and in three countries, more than 30% of adults received remittances: Somaliland (40%), Comoros (35%), and Zimbabwe (32%). These three countries have all experienced extensive political and social turmoil, and have a large portion of their population living abroad.[97]

Immigration of Family Members

Often one person migrates internationally and then is joined by family members. Sometimes the first person assesses the situation in the destination country and then advises relatives whether to come.

TABLE 12.5 Top Remittance-Sending and Remittance-Receiving Countries, 2009

	Top Remittance-Sending Countries	Remittances in Billions $	Top Remittance-Receiving Countries	Remittances in Billions $	Top Countries for Remittances as a % of GDP	% of GDP
1	United States	48	India	55	Tajikistan	35
2	Saudi Arabia	26	China	51	Tonga	28
3	Switzerland	20	Mexico	23	Lesotho	25
4	Russia	19	Philippines	21	Moldova	23
5	Germany	16	France	16	Nepal	23
6	Italy	13	Germany	12	Lebanon	22
7	Spain	13	Bangladesh	11	Samoa	22
8	Luxembourg	11	Belgium	10	Honduras	19
9	Kuwait	10	Spain	10	Guyana	17
10	Netherlands	8	Nigeria	10	El Salvador	16

In developed countries, immigration laws have often been more lenient for those joining relatives who immigrated earlier than they are for people who apply to immigrate on their own, although these laws have been a source of controversy in many destination countries. Sometimes one member of a family has a strong desire to migrate to another country, and other family members go along to keep the family together, even if they had no strong desire to become an international migrant. This spurs chain migration.

Migration between Mexico and the United States

As indicated in Table 12.2, Mexico–United States is the highest volume migration corridor in the world, three times the magnitude of the second largest migration corridor. Some of this migration is legal, but a substantial part of the migration flow is undocumented.

According to Jeffrey Passel and his colleagues, the annual number of immigrants from Mexico to the United States rose from 370,000 in 1991 to 770,000 in 1999, after which it declined, especially after 2005, to 140,000 in 2010. This decline between 2005 and 2010 was the result of both less migration from Mexico to the United States (a decline from 3 million in 1995–2000 to 1.4 million in 2005–2010) and an increase in the number of people who moved from the United States to Mexico (from less than 670,000 million in 1995–2000 to 1.4 million in 2005–2010), most of whom had probably earlier immigrated from Mexico to the United States. In 2011–2012, there could have been net migration from the United States to Mexico. The turnaround and possible reversal in the migration flow were due both to voluntary movements from the United States to Mexico related to problems in the U.S. economy, and to increased enforcement of the U.S.–Mexico border and increased deportations.[98]

Typically undocumented labor migrants from Mexico to the United States have made the move with the intention of sending remittances home to their relatives in Mexico. During the economic downturn in the United States that began in 2007–2008, unemployment increased, including unemployment for undocumented migrants. At the same time, monitoring of the U.S.–Mexico border increased, making free movement across the border more difficult. Thus, while some undocumented migrants returned to Mexico, others were reluctant to return to Mexico, because they thought it would be more difficult to come back to the United States later. Many stayed in the United States in the hope that the economy would improve and that it would be worthwhile for them to remain in the United States until that happened. In the meantime, many relatives in Mexico began sending money to their relatives who were in the United States, in the hope that the economic downturn would be temporary. It often had been difficult for the family in Mexico to raise the money necessary to fund migration, and there often was a reluctance to lose that investment.[99]

With the hope that there will be substantial immigration reform, some undocumented workers have tried to put themselves in a good position in case of any reform. Since at least 2005, there was an increase in the paying of federal income tax among undocumented migrants in the United States. A major rationale was the desire by many undocumented migrants to fulfill rules for qualification for legal residency in any possible future immigration bill, since many of the immigration bills that had been discussed included payment of taxes as one of the criteria. Although undocumented migrants cannot legally obtain Social Security numbers, they can obtain individual taxpayer numbers. There has been an effective separation between the Internal Revenue Service and other parts of the U.S. government, such as the Department of Homeland Security, so undocumented migrants face very little risk that paying income taxes will increase their chance of deportation.[100] The purpose of this separation is to motivate payment of taxes.

Refugees, Forced Migrants, and Internally Displaced Persons

There are various kinds of migrants who have moved due to disaster, violence, or the threat of persecution. A **forced migrant** is someone who has been forced to leave his or her home because of a real or perceived threat to life and wellbeing. A **refugee** is defined by the United Nations (and by most countries of the world) as "any person who is outside his or her country of nationality and is unable or unwilling to return to that country because of persecution or a well-founded fear of persecution."

Refugees usually move to countries in the same region and typically return to their home country within 5 years. If refugees do not return to their country of origin within 5 years, it is considered a "protracted refugee situation." Closely related to refugees are **internally displaced persons**, who flee their homes to avoid violence but do not cross an international border.

Many countries feel an obligation to accept refugees, but the extent of that obligation has varied among countries and across time. The focus on refugees in international discourse appeared after World War II. Article 33 of the 1951 UN Refugee Convention stated that

> no Convention State shall expel or return a refugee in any manner whatsoever to the frontiers of a territory where his life or freedom would be threatened on account of his race, religion, nationality, membership in a particular group or political opinion.[101]

Although the convention had been written with European refugees in mind, a 1967 UN Protocol expanded the coverage to all refugees. One hundred and forty-seven countries signed the convention, the protocol, or both documents. However, many countries have pulled back on their obligations to accept refugees. As discussed in this chapter, the motivations are somewhat different in LDR than in MDR countries. Also, the UN High Commission for Refugees (UNHCR) acknowledges that it cannot compel any country to receive refugees. However, the UNHCR can try to apply moral force. For example, in 2012, the UNHCR commissioner chastised Israel for refusing to admit 21 refugees from Eritrea who were on the Israeli–Egyptian border. The commissioner said that Israel could not simply "shut the door" and accused Israel of effectively violating the UN Convention Relating to the Status of Refugees. The group included two women and a teenage boy. Israel eventually admitted those three while refusing the other 18, who were men.[102]

Table 12.6 shows the ten largest countries as a source of refugees, the ten largest countries that received refugees, and the ten countries with the largest number of displaced persons in 2010.[103] The LDR produces the vast majority of refugees and internally displaced persons but also hosts the majority of refugees. All of the top refugee-producing countries, and seven of the top ten refugee-hosting countries are in the LDR. All of the top ten countries with internally displaced persons, except Georgia are in the LDR. Iraq, Somalia, the Democratic Republic of the Congo, Colombia, and Sudan are both in the top

TABLE 12.6 Ten Leading Refugee-Producing Countries, Refugee-Hosting Countries, and Countries with Internally Displaced Persons, 2010

	Refugee-Producing Countries		Refugee-Hosting Countries		Internally Displaced Persons	
1	Afghanistan	3,054,700	Pakistan	1,900,600	Colombia	3,672,054
2	Iraq	1,683,600	Iran	1,073,400	Democratic Republic of the Congo	1,721,382
3	Somalia	770,100	Syria	1,005,500	Sudan	1,624,100
4	Democratic Republic of the Congo	476,700	Germany	594,300	Somalia	1,463,780
5	Myanmar	415,700	Jordan	450,900	Iraq	1,343,568
6	Colombia	395,600	Kenya	402,900	Pakistan	952,035
7	Sudan	387,200	Chad	347,900	Azerbaijan	592,860
8	Vietnam	338,700	China	301,000	Ivory Coast	514,515
9	Eritrea	222,500	United States	264,600	Georgia	359,716
10	China	184,600	United Kingdom	238,100	Afghanistan	351,907

ten countries producing refugees and in the top ten countries producing internally displaced persons, supporting the view that the process of producing these two groups of migrants is similar.

LDR countries face a challenge when a large number of refugees, often from neighboring countries, come in with few possessions and resources. The receiving country, which often has limited resources, can feel overwhelmed. In 2012, refugees from war-torn Syria strained the resources of many nearby countries, especially Turkey. In August 2012, there were almost 80,000 registered refugees from Syria in Turkey. Turkey stated that it would not admit more than a total of 100,000 Syrian refugees, because that was the maximum number they could accommodate. Also, many members of an ethnic minority, the Kachin, fled from a civil war in Myanmar into China. There were mixed reports about whether they were involuntarily expelled back to Myanmar or whether they had voluntarily returned.[104]

Australia is a more developed country that is fairly close to many less developed countries of Asia. Often, desperate people seeking asylum are rescued from unsafe boats trying to reach Australia. In 2012, the Australian government planned to place asylum seekers in detention centers in Nauru and Papua New Guinea that had been closed in 2007. This plan was widely criticized as being inhumane. Subsequently in 2012, Australia increased the quota of refugees it would receive, but continued to try to formulate policies that would reduce the flow of asylum seekers while treating those who arrived humanely.[105]

Many refugees could not have entered more developed countries under normal immigration rules but are admitted because they are defined as refugees. There has been much discussion about whether some migrants from the LDR to the MDR are refugees or whether they are actually economic migrants, who have migrated mainly to enhance the educational or economic opportunities of themselves or their children. Many MDR countries have implemented very strict criteria for who is a refugee and have subjected those applying for refugee status to what some consider unreasonable conditions. Matthew pointed out that in the United Kingdom, some asylum seekers were destitute by the time they were granted refugee status.[106]

An example of migrants with mixed refugee and economic motives is migrants from Zimbabwe to South Africa. South Africa has the best economy in sub-Saharan Africa and has long been a magnet for labor migrants. However, the violent and repressive conditions in Zimbabwe have produced refugees, and many migrants to South Africa clearly have mixed motives. Many in South Africa have little sympathy with the Zimbabwean migrants and see them as a drain on South African resources and as economic competitors. Since Zimbabwe borders on South Africa, it also is an example of refugees going to neighboring countries.[107]

Proposed Solutions to the Problem of Refugee Populations

There have been three proposed solutions to the problem of refugee populations:[108]

1. **Repatriation to the Country of Origin:** This is seen as the most desirable option, when it is feasible. However, for this to occur successfully, the country of origin needs to be sufficiently safe for the former refugees, and often these refugees will need financial assistance, help in finding employment, and counseling or emotional help.

2. **Integration in the Country to Which They Initially Fled:** For this option to work, the former refugees need to become economically integrated into the new country and also need to be accepted socially and culturally by the natives of the destination country. Sometimes this involves convincing the destination country that the migrants were actually refugees. To be successful, the refugees need to be integrated into society, rather than remaining in refugee camps.

3. **Resettlement in a Third Country:** This can be quite challenging and involves all the issues in point 2. An argument for resettlement in a third country is when the original destination country is seen as excessively burdened with refugees.

Violence-Inspired Migration in Nepal

Many have assumed that people facing extreme violence have no choice but to migrate. This is also reflected in the term "forced migration." However, in virtually every situation of forced migration, less than half of the people actually leave. Thus, although there are pressing reasons to migrate, there is some choice in whether or not to actually leave.

Nathalie Williams wanted to apply social science theory to gain a better understanding of what was related to who leaves and who stays in a violent situation. She looked at migration in the Chitwan Valley of Nepal during the Maoist insurrection, which began in 1996. Looking at migration before and during the insurrection, she had many interesting findings.

The level of violence varied greatly over time. When there was a moderate increase in violence, the level of out-migration decreased. In that situation, people apparently hunkered down and waited. However, when the level of violence became high, the rate of out-migration increased. At some point, the threat of violence became so great that many people left.

Assets also had a complicated role in the decision to migrate in violent situations. Williams distinguished immovable assets, such as land, from moveable assets, such as livestock. Moveable assets could be readily sold for cash. She found that the higher the level of immovable assets, the less likely people were to migrate, while the higher the level of moveable assets, the more likely they were to migrate. Apparently, cash and the capacity to obtain cash facilitated migration, while people remained reluctant to abandon assets such as land, since they would lose all of the benefit of such assets if they left. This work indicated that even in violent situations that are often characterized as situations of forced migration, people behave in understandable, non-random ways.[109]

International Human Trafficking

Human trafficking involves an act of recruiting, transporting, transferring, harboring, or receiving a person through the use of force, coercion, or other means, for the purpose of exploiting them. It includes forced prostitution, sexual exploitation, forced labor, slavery or similar practices, and the removal of organs. It often involves undocumented migration and the crossing of international borders. In 2010, the United Nations established a fund to combat human trafficking, with the aims of preventing trafficking, protecting victims, and prosecuting trafficking offenders.[110] The UN Office of Drugs and Crime reported that in 2005, about 2.4 million people worldwide had been drawn into forced labor, the total market value of which was about $32 billion. Victims come from at least 127 countries and have been found in at least 37 countries.[111]

There has been a great deal of concern about sex trafficking, in which young women are lured into prostitution, often under the expectation that they would work as *au pairs* or in other reputable occupations. Many of the women are from Eastern Europe and end up elsewhere in Europe or in the United States. In 2002, there was a European effort with American cooperation to identify victims of sex trafficking and arrest sex traffickers, many of whom were thought to pass through Bosnia. The operation identified 237 victims and arrested 293 traffickers. However, the operation was seen as having, at best, mixed success. One problem was election-related political turmoil at that time in some countries, including Serbia, Bosnia, and Macedonia.[112]

In West Africa, many children travel long distances to take risky jobs. The question has been raised as to whether this qualifies as human trafficking. It has been argued that the work these children are doing often is not as grueling as the work they would have done if they had stayed at home. In

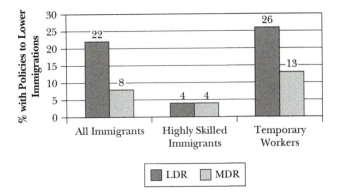

FIGURE 12.13 Percentage of LDR and MDR Governments with Policies to Lower Various Types of Immigration, 2009

addition, if they returned home, they rarely would have enrolled in school, and the family would be poorer than if they had remained in their work situation. Some argue that the problem is poverty, especially rural poverty, rather than trafficking. Others argue that this clearly is human trafficking and should be stopped regardless of the underlying causes.[113]

GOVERNMENT POLICIES ABOUT INTERNATIONAL MIGRATION

Governments often have policies and usually have laws about immigration. Figure 12.13 shows the percentage of LDR and MDR governments that had policies to lower various kinds of immigration. A higher percentage of LDR than MDR governments wanted to lower the overall level of immigration. However, governments differentiated between kinds of immigrants. Almost no governments (4%) wanted to lower the number of highly skilled immigrants. However, 26% of LDR governments and 13% of MDR governments wanted to lower the number of temporary immigrant workers.[114]

IMMIGRATION TO THE UNITED STATES

Immigration to the United States has varied over time. Figure 12.14 shows the number of legal immigrants to the United States by decade, 1820–2009. Immigration generally increased from the early nineteenth century through the first decade of the twentieth century, dropped through the 1940s, and then increased again.[115]

Figure 12.15 shows the number of immigrants to the United States by region of origin by decade for 1820–2009, and Figure 12.16 shows the percentage distribution of immigrants by region over time.

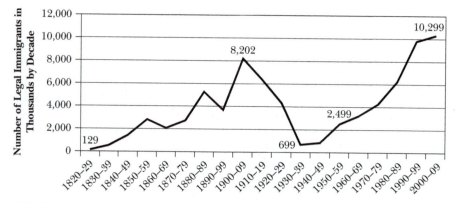

FIGURE 12.14 Number of Legal Immigrants to the United States in Thousands, 1820–2009

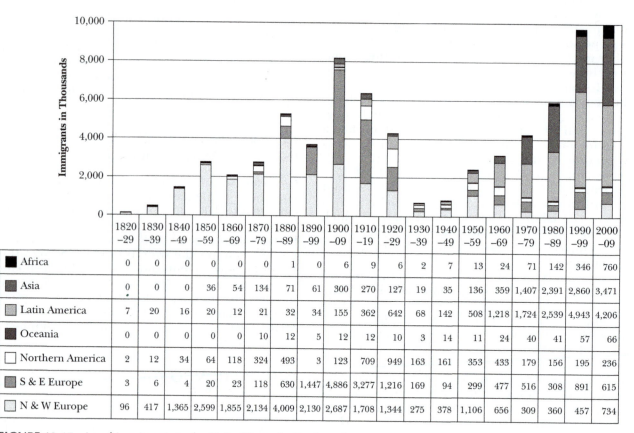

FIGURE 12.15 Legal Immigrants to the United States by Region of Origin, 1820–2009

Immigration from Northern America is almost totally from Canada, and the vast majority of migration from Oceania is from Australia.

The trajectory of immigrants was affected both by world events and U.S. immigration laws. Immigration peaked in the 1860s after the failed Revolutions of 1848 across Europe. This wave of immigration led to the founding of numerous towns in the Midwest. Immigration fell after 1910 due to World War I, restrictive immigration laws, the Great Depression, and World War II. Immigration then increased after World War II.

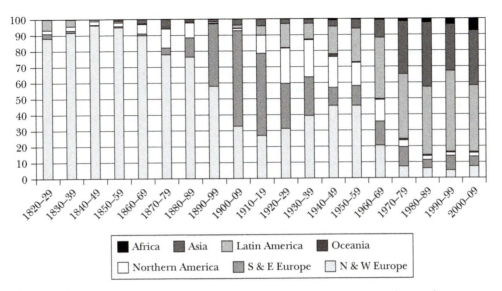

FIGURE 12.16 Percentage Distribution of Legal Immigrants to the United States by Region of Origin, 1820–2009

History of U.S. Immigration Laws

Inspection of the history of American immigration laws shows that this has been an arena of political decision making from the start of the United States. Cheryl Shanks pointed out that U.S. immigration laws have been erratic partially because the people most directly concerned—potential international migrants—have no voice in legislation and are not part of the voting public that legislators need to consider. Even though residents of some countries have advocates in the United States, support from these groups has often been variable, even among people who themselves or whose ancestors came from the given country.[116] Both domestic and foreign policy considerations have played a role in legislation about who can legally migrate to the United States or who can become a citizen.

This section discusses major U.S. immigration legislation and decrees that influenced the volume of immigration and the origins of immigrants. These laws are summarized in Table 12.7.[117]

Naturalization Act of 1790
This act established rules for naturalized citizenship. It was passed March 26, 1790, and limited naturalization to "free white persons" and thus left out indentured servants, slaves, free African Americans, Native Americans, and later Asian Americans. The 1790 act also limited naturalization to persons of "good moral character" and required a set period of residence in the United States prior to naturalization, specifically 2 years in the country and 1 year in the state of residence when applying for citizenship. The act also

established U.S. citizenship for children born abroad of U.S. citizen parents.

Act to Prohibit Importation of Slaves of 1807
This act prohibited the importation of slaves as of January 1, 1808. It was the first law that regulated immigration. Importation of slaves was deemed to be "piracy" in an act passed in 1819.

Chinese Exclusion Act of 1882
This act excluded Chinese laborers from immigrating to the United States for 10 years. Chinese laborers in the United States and laborers with work visas received a certificate of **residency** and were allowed to travel in and out of the United States. Amendments made in 1884 clarified that the law applied to ethnic Chinese regardless of their country of origin. The act was renewed and only repealed by the 1943 Magnuson Act, which allowed a national quota of 105 Chinese immigrants per year, although large-scale Chinese immigration did not occur until the passage of the Immigration Act of 1965.

The act was passed in reaction to the large number of Chinese who had immigrated to the western United States as a result of unsettled conditions in China, the availability of jobs working on railroad construction, and the gold rush that was going on at that time in California. Most came on 5-year labor contracts. It was the first immigration law passed in the United States targeted at a specific ethnic group. The impact of this law can be seen in the drop in the number of immigrants from Asia shown in Figure 12.15 from 134,000 in 1870–1879 to 71,000 in 1880–1889.

TABLE 12.7   Some Major U.S. Immigration Laws and Decrees

Law or Decree	Description
Naturalization Act of 1790	This act established rules for naturalized citizenship.
Act to Prohibit Importation of Slaves of 1807	This was the first act to regulate immigration. It stopped the importation of slaves.
Chinese Exclusion Act of 1882	This was the first race-based immigration act and severely limited Chinese immigration.
Gentleman's Agreement of 1907	This was an agreement between Japan and the United States to limit Japanese immigration and was seen as a way to avoid a "Japanese Exclusion Act."
Emergency Quota Act of 1921	This act was intended to limit the number of immigrants from Southern and Eastern Europe. Immigration was based on the number of people of each origin in the 1910 U.S. Census.
Immigration Act of 1924 (Asian Exclusion Act)	This act was intended to limit the number of immigrants from Southern and Eastern Europe and from Asia. Immigration was based on the number of people from each origin in the 1890 U.S. Census.
National Origins Formula of 1929	A maximum of 150,000 annual immigrants was established, based on national origins in the 1920 U.S. Census. Asians were excluded from immigration, but there were no restrictions on immigrants from the Americas.
Bracero Program with Mexico, 1942–1964	This was a temporary contract labor program in which Mexican workers came to the United States.
Chinese Exclusion Act Repeal of 1943 (Magnuson Act)	The Chinese Exclusion Act was repealed, but immigration from China was restricted to 105 people a year.
Immigration Act of 1952	This was a Cold War-inspired law that somewhat liberalized immigration of Asians but strengthened government power to restrict entry and eased deportation of suspected Communists. It is also called the McCarren-Walter Act.
Immigration and Naturalization Act of 1965	This act discontinued quotas based on national origin. Immigration became based on skills and on having relatives in the United States. It contributed to a major change in the racial composition of the United States.
Refugee Act of 1980	This act liberalized rules for refugees to the United States.
Immigration Reform and Control Act of 1986	This act implemented a variety of conditions aimed to reduce illegal immigration. It established an amnesty program for undocumented migrants, which led to legalization of the status of almost 3 million people.
Illegal Immigration Reform and Responsibility Act of 1996	This act made deportation of undocumented and legal immigrants easier.
Real ID Act of 2005	This act was implemented in response to the 9/11 attacks. It made border enforcement and deportation of undocumented and legal immigrants easier.
Obama's Deportation Policy of 2012	This decree protected young undocumented migrants who had entered the United States before age 16 and who met certain criteria from deportation for two years.

Gentlemen's Agreement of 1907

This was an informal agreement between the United States and Japan regarding immigration and racial segregation. After the Japanese victory over Russia in the Russo-Japanese War, anti-Japanese feeling in California increased. In 1906, the San Francisco (California) Board of Education required that children of Japanese descent attend racially segregated separate schools. Japanese immigrants made up approximately 1% of the population of California.

Japan agreed not to issue new passports for Japanese citizens to come to the United States to work. The United States agreed to accept Japanese immigrants already in the United States; to permit the immigration of wives, children, and parents; and to avoid segregation of Japanese children in California schools. Japan did not want the United States to pass a "Japanese Exclusion Act" similar to the Chinese Exclusion Act. President Theodore Roosevelt, who had a positive opinion of Japan, accepted the agreement as proposed by Japan as an alternative to more formal, restrictive immigration legislation. The agreement was nullified by the U.S. Immigration Act of 1924.

Emergency Quota Act of 1921

This act established national quotas on immigration based on the number of foreign-born residents of each nationality who were living in the United States as of the 1910 Census. The act limited the annual number of immigrants who could be admitted from any country to 3% of the number of persons from that country living in the United States in 1910. This totaled about 357,802 immigrants. Of that number, just over half was allocated for Northern and Western Europeans, and the remainder for Eastern and Southern Europeans, a 75% reduction from prior years. Professionals were allowed in regardless of their origins.

The act was passed in a time of increasing isolationism following World War I, and the belief that the large number of immigrants from Southern and

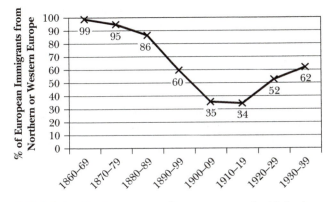

FIGURE 12.17 Percentage of Immigrants to the United States from Europe Who Were from Northern or Western Europe, 1860–1939

Eastern Europe in recent years had negative wage effects on native-born Americans. The Emergency Quota Act had been proposed several times before, but never passed until 1921.

Figures 12.15 and 12.16 show that the act and the Immigration Act of 1924, which is discussed next, were successful in changing the distribution of origins of European immigrants, and it is even clearer in Figure 12.17, which shows the percentage of all immigrants from Europe who were from Northern or Western Europe. In 1880–1889, 86% of immigrants from Europe to the United States were from Northern or Western Europe. This fell to 34% by 1910–1919. As a result of the 1921 and 1924 acts, the percentage from Northern and Western Europe rose to 52% in 1920–1929 and further to 62% in 1930–1939.

Immigration Act of 1924 (Asian Exclusion Act)
The aim of this act was to freeze the ethnic distribution as of 1924. This was in response to negative reactions to rising immigration from Southern and Eastern Europe, as well as from Asia. This act was also known as the Asian Exclusion Act. It limited the number of immigrants from any country to 3% of the number of people from that country who were in the United States in 1890, which was much more restrictive than the 1921 act. It also prevented Japanese Americans from legally owning land and barred immigration from all of Asia, including Japan, China, the Philippines, Laos, Siam, Cambodia, Singapore, Korea, Vietnam, Indonesia, Burma, India, Ceylon, and Malaysia. These immigrants were deemed to have an "undesirable" race. This act was related to the overall decline in the number of immigrants in the 1920s.

In 1900–1910, about 200,000 Italians immigrated every year. After 1924, only 4,000 per year were allowed. The annual quota for Germany was over 57,000. Eighty-six percent of the 165,000 permitted entries were from the British Isles, France, Germany,

and other Northern European countries. The act set no limits on immigration from Latin America. The quotas remained in place with minor alterations until the Immigration and Nationality Act of 1965.

National Origins Formula of 1929
This act capped total annual immigration at 150,000 and set quotas based on the national origin of U.S. residents in 1920. Asians were excluded from immigration, but immigration by residents of nations in the Americas was not restricted. Figure 12.15 shows that the number of immigrants from Asia dropped from 127,000 in the 1920s to 19,000 in the 1930s.

Bracero Program with Mexico, 1942–1964
This was a program of contract labor in which Mexican workers came to work in American agriculture. There were some worker protections written into the program, although it is not clear they were always observed.[118]

Chinese Exclusion Act Repeal of 1943 (Magnuson Act)
This act repealed the 1882 Chinese Exclusion Act, but allowed for only 105 Chinese immigrants per year. The act also allowed some Chinese residents of the United States to become citizens, which was not previously allowed.

Immigration and Nationality Act of 1952
This act liberalized immigration from Asia, but increased government power to deport illegal immigrants suspected of Communist sympathies. As shown in Figure 12.15, the number of migrants from Asia increased from 35,000 in the 1940s to 136,000 in the 1950s.

Immigration and Nationality Act of 1965
This act discontinued quotas based on national origin. It gave preference to those with skills and those with U.S. relatives. Also, for the first time Mexican immigration was restricted. An annual limitation of 170,000 visas was established, with no more than 20,000 per country. By 1968, the annual quota from the Western Hemisphere was set at 120,000 immigrants. However, the number of family reunification visas was unlimited, which led to a large amount of chain immigration.[119]

The act was influenced by the Civil Rights Movement. The act's supporters claimed that the law would not change the United States' ethnic makeup and that such a change would be undesirable. But the ethnic composition of American society changed enormously as a result of this act. In 1965, 89% of the United States was composed of Whites of European descent, with the only minority group of significant size being African Americans (10%). The proportion of the population of White European background has declined, and Whites are projected to lose their majority status in the twenty-first century. Hispanics are the largest minority in the United States. As shown in Figures 12.15 and 12.16, there has been enormous growth in the number of immigrants and the percentage of all immigrants from non-European countries.

The change from an emphasis on national origins to an emphasis on skills especially helped immigrants from Asia. Figures 12.15 and 12.16 show that the number of immigrants from Asia and the percentage of all immigrants who came from Asia grew rapidly after the 1960s, increasing by almost tenfold from the 1960s to the 2000s (from 359,000 to 3,471,000), and increasing from 11% to 34% of all immigrants.

Refugee Act of 1980

This act modified the procedure for admission of refugees who came from extreme humanitarian situations. It regularized the status of refugees as permanent resident aliens, rather than relegating them to a temporary status. It also provided funds for resettlement of these refugees. It was quickly applied to a large influx of Cuban refugees to Florida, although many Cuban immigrants were admitted under other legal provisions. The law also was applied in the immigration of over 200,000 Jews from the Soviet Union.[120]

Immigration Reform and Control Act of 1986

This act aimed to reduce illegal immigration. It established a 1-year amnesty program for undocumented immigrants who had worked and lived in the United States since January 1982. Those eligible could apply for regularization of status and eventually full citizenship. Over 2.7 million undocumented migrants and others not qualifying for visas were legalized under this amnesty. The law also criminalized knowingly hiring an undocumented migrant and established financial and other penalties for those employing undocumented migrants. These sanctions only applied to employers who had more than three employees and who did not make a sufficient effort to determine the legal status of the worker. Reflections on the consequences of this act have motivated some with concerns about the possible negative effects of large-scale immigration to argue against any subsequent major immigration reform that would make regularization of status easier.[121]

Illegal Immigration Reform and Immigrant Responsibility Act of 1996

This act changed asylum law, immigration detention, criminal-based immigration, and many forms of immigration relief, including the following:

1. A 1-year filing deadline for political asylum applications
2. Renamed deportation proceedings and exclusion proceedings "removal proceedings"

3. Made major changes to the immigration consequences of being involved in a criminal case
4. Required mandatory detention for immigrants convicted of certain crimes
5. Made a permanent bar to permanent residence for those who falsely claimed to be U.S. citizens
6. Authorized the U.S. Attorney General to hire at least 1,000 new U.S. Border Patrol agents and 300 new support personnel each year from 1997 to 2001

Real ID Act of 2005

This act was the main legislative response to the September 11, 2001, attacks related to immigration. The act restricted political asylum, curtailed habeas corpus for immigrants, increased immigration enforcement, altered judicial review, and imposed federal restrictions on the issuance of state driver's licenses to immigrants.[122]

This legislation was intended to deter terrorism by the following:

1. Establishing national standards for state-issued driver's licenses and non–driver's identification cards
2. Waiving laws that interfere with construction of physical barriers at the borders
3. Updating and tightening the laws on application for asylum and deportation of aliens for terrorist activity
4. Introducing rules covering "delivery bonds" (rather like bail bonds, but for aliens who have been released pending hearings)

Obama's Deportation Policy of 2012

President George W. Bush and President Barack Obama tried unsuccessfully to pass a liberalized immigration law, especially with undocumented migrants from Mexico in mind. In 2012, President Obama issued a decree that directed that children of undocumented migrants would not be deported as long as they came to the United States before age 16, were under age 30, and had resided continuously in the United States for at least 5 years. In addition, they needed a high school diploma, a GED, or an honorable discharge from the military; have had no felony or other serious conviction; and not be considered a security risk. Qualifying young people could register and would not be deported for 2 years. They could subsequently apply for an additional 2 years, and they could obtain a work permit. There was no assurance that registering would help them to eventually become American citizens, but many people viewed this decree as a stopgap solution in the hope that wide-ranging immigration reform legislation would be passed.[123]

CITIZENSHIP LAWS IN VARIOUS COUNTRIES

Countries differ greatly in citizenship laws. In this section, we discuss the various bases of granting of citizenship.

Citizenship by Territory, by Blood, and by Ethnic Ties

Citizenship can be from being born on a territory, by blood (descent from a citizen), or by a combination (requiring that at least one parent be a citizen for those born in the territory, or it can be by ethnic descent). Citizenship by descent is called *jus sanguinis* (right of blood). This system is common in most of the world outside of the Americas.[124]

By Birth on Territory

Citizenship acquired by being born on the territory of a country is called *jus soli* (right of soil). It is common in the Americas. Countries practicing this principle include the following:

Northern America: United States and Canada

Latin America: Argentina, Barbados, Belize, Bolivia, Brazil, Chile, Colombia, Ecuador, El Salvador, Grenada, Guatemala, Honduras, Jamaica, Mexico, Nicaragua, Panama, Paraguay, Peru, Uruguay, and Venezuela

Asia: Cambodia and Pakistan

Africa: Lesotho

Oceania: Fiji

Some Countries Have Modified Citizenship by Birth to Require Citizenship or a Period of Permanent Residence by at Least One Parent

Some countries earlier had citizenship conferred by birth in the country but have modified the law to require that at least one parent has been a permanent resident for at least a certain amount of time or is a citizen of the country. Some groups have called for a similar modification of U.S. law, although that would require a constitutional amendment. There has been concern about pregnant women who are not U.S. citizens coming to the United States for their deliveries and having what are called "anchor babies" in order to gain U.S. citizenship for the child and then to enhance the chance of other family members becoming U.S. citizens. Some think this is a major problem, while others think this occurs rarely.[125] In 2010 and 2011, Florida passed laws that denied children who were U.S. citizens by virtue of birth but whose parents were undocumented migrants the right to in-state tuition at public colleges and universities.

The out-of-state tuition was sometimes three times the in-state rate. In 2012, a Florida court ruled these laws were unconstitutional because they "create a second-tier status of U.S. citizenship."[126]

Countries that have changed their laws and the date of the change include the following:

United Kingdom, 1983: The law requires that at least one parent be a British citizen or legal resident.

Australia, 1986: The law requires that at least one parent be an Australian citizen or permanent resident. On his or her tenth birthday, an Australian-born child can become an Australian citizen, regardless of the parents' status.

Dominican Republic, 2010: Dominicans of Haitian origin are excluded from citizenship, even if they were previously recognized as citizens.

France, 1993: Children of non-citizens can request French citizenship at age 16.

India, 1986: The law requires that at least one parent be a citizen of India.

Malta, 1989: The law requires that at least one parent be a citizen of Malta.

Ireland, 2005: The law requires that at least one parent be an Irish or a British citizen or a permanent resident of Ireland or be the child of a legal resident and have resided in Ireland at least 3 of the last 4 years.

New Zealand, 2006: The law requires that at least one parent be a New Zealand citizen or legal resident.

Portugal, 1981: The law made it difficult for immigrants as well as the children and grandchildren of immigrants to acquire Portuguese citizenship. The law was somewhat liberalized in 2006. A child whose parents have lived legally in Portugal for at least 10 years can acquire Portuguese citizenship, after 6 years if the parents' country of citizenship has Portuguese as an official language.

Some Countries with Citizenship by Blood Have Eased Immigration for Those with Ethnic Ties

Some countries have had citizenship conferred by blood but have eased immigration for those with ethnic ties to the country. Countries that have made these kinds of changes include the following:

Eastern Europe and the Former Soviet Union: Armenia, Bulgaria, Croatia, Hungary, Poland, Romania, Russia, Serbia, Slovakia, and Ukraine

Asia: China, India, Japan, South Korea, and Turkey

Elsewhere in Europe: Finland, Germany, Greece, Ireland, Italy, and Spain

By Religion: Israel Right of Return for those with a Jewish parent or grandparent or Jewish by conversion

Swiss Naturalization

Citizenship in Switzerland can be obtained by a permanent resident who lives in Switzerland for 12 years (any years spent in Switzerland between the tenth and the twentieth years are counted double), and has lived in the country for the last 3 out of 5 years before applying for citizenship. One should be able to speak fluently in German (preferably Swiss German), French, Italian, or Romansch (depending on the community) and show the following:

1. Integration into the Swiss way of life
2. Familiarity with Swiss habits, customs, and traditions
3. Compliance with the Swiss rule of law
4. Pose no danger to Switzerland's internal or external security

The decision on citizenship is made at the level of the 26 cantons that comprise Switzerland. Cantons and municipalities, some as small as a village of 400 people, can impose their own residence and other requirements, in addition to those imposed by the Swiss Confederation. Switzerland is probably the only country in which decisions on citizenship applications are made by municipalities.

Between 1980 and 2008, there were three national referenda that proposed to make citizenship easier for the children and grandchildren of non-citizen immigrants. All of these referenda were defeated. The process of examination of applicants for Swiss citizenship can include questions about Swiss history and politics, as well as an exam in the language of the Swiss region.

Muslim applicants and applicants from Muslim countries are especially likely to be rejected. In 2000, the Swiss town of Emmen rejected 48 out of 56 persons who applied for Swiss citizenship. All of those who were approved were of Italian background. Most of those who were rejected were Muslims from the former Yugoslavia.[127]

German Citizenship

Germany is one of a small number of countries that have made citizenship easier to acquire for persons whose parents are not citizens. Some of these changes were motivated by German experiences with Turkish immigrants.

Germany has had a long and variable history of migration from Turkey. Starting in the 1950s, West Germany had temporary labor migration programs called guest worker, or *Gastarbeiter*, with many countries. In 1961, an agreement was signed with Turkey. Originally the agreement stated that Turkish workers could remain in Germany at most 2 years, but this provision was removed in 1964 at the urging of German industry. Most of these guest workers were males from rural Turkey, and the assumption was that they would work in Germany for a few years and then return home. The German-Turkish guest worker agreement ended in 1973, but many Turkish workers remained in Germany and brought their families to Germany. Many German schools with a large number of Turkish students instituted Turkish language classes to facilitate the entry or re-entry of the students into Turkish society, and the German state repeatedly stated that it was not pursuing a policy of integration.[128]

Before 2000, citizenship in Germany was completely based on descent by blood. Partially due to the increasing number of persons of Turkish background in Germany, many of whom were born and lived their entire lives in Germany, leftist parties pushed for liberalization of naturalization laws. There were unsuccessful laws proposed several times in the 1980s. The naturalization law was slightly liberalized in 1990. In 1998, the Social Democratic Party and the Greens came to power, and in 2000 a new naturalization law was passed. Children born on or after January 1, 2000, to non-German parents acquire German citizenship at birth if at least one parent has lived in Germany for at least 8 years. Some had pressed for an even more liberal law, but public opinion polls showed a high degree of opposition to liberalized laws, and the Christian Democratic Party had strongly opposed even the law that finally passed.[129]

RESENTMENT TOWARD IMMIGRANTS

Immigration has prevented population decline in Europe and elsewhere, but there has also been substantial anti-immigrant sentiment. Sometimes the concern has been competition for jobs, and sometimes it has been related to fear or antagonism toward an ethnic or religious group that differs from that of the majority of the country's population. After the 9/11 attacks and the rise of al Qaeda, prejudice against Muslim immigrants has also been conflated with fear of terrorism. We next discuss three examples of anti-immigrant sentiment, in Switzerland, Greece, and Singapore.

Anti-Muslim Sentiment in Switzerland

Anti-Muslim sentiment in Switzerland is consistent with the high rejection rates of Muslim applicants for Swiss citizenship discussed earlier in this section. In Switzerland in November 2009, there was a referendum on whether new mosques constructed

FIGURE 12.18 Poster in Swiss Anti-Minaret Campaign ("Stop! Yes to Ban Minarets")

in Switzerland could include minarets. Minarets are tall spires that are often on top of mosques. They are architecturally distinctive, and the Muslim call to prayer is typically broadcast from the minaret. At that time, four mosques in Switzerland had minarets. Figure 12.18 shows an ad from the anti-minaret campaign, which portrayed minarets resembling missiles on a Swiss flag along with a veiled woman. The text on the ad says, "Stop, Yes to the minaret ban."[130] The referendum passed with 58% of the vote.[131]

Perceived Job Competition with Immigrants in Greece

Especially in difficult economic times, anti-immigrant sentiment can become intense. In July 2012, when Greece was facing severe economic problems, a right-wing party targeted immigrants as the cause of Greece's problems. A legal immigrant from Pakistan said,

> They said: "You're the cause of Greece's problems. You have seven days to close or we'll burn your shop—and we'll burn you."

When the man called the police, he was told that the police didn't have time to help immigrants like the caller.[132]

In a similar incident, in January 2013, Greek police handcuffed and beat up a South Korean tourist whom they had wrongly assumed was an illegal immigrant. This was part of an even harsher law enforcement strategy than earlier, which had been implemented to detain and export illegal migrants.[133]

Cultural and Language Differences between Immigrants and Natives in Singapore

In view of Singapore's very low fertility, discussed in Chapter 9, the Singapore government decided to ease immigration and temporary labor migration requirements. This was intended to help prevent population decline, increase the labor force, and counter population aging.

In many ways, the policies were successful. Figure 12.19 shows the natural rate of increase and the net migration rate per thousand population in Singapore in 1950 through 2010. The natural rate of increase and the net migration rate together comprise the population growth rate. It also shows the percentage contribution of each to Singapore's population growth rate. We see in the top panel that the growth rate declined until the late 1970s and then increased, with some fluctuations. The increase was almost entirely due to increases in the net migration rate. We see in the bottom panel that the net migration rate jumped from contributing less than 10% of the population growth rate in the late 1970s to over 50% of the population growth rate in the early 1980s, and by 2005–2010 the net migration rate contributed 88% of the population growth rate.

The newcomers were composed both of highly educated persons and of persons with low educational attainment who entered on temporary work permits and who took low-skilled jobs that native Singaporeans were reluctant to fill. The future will reveal whether the low-skilled workers return to their home countries, as the Singapore government intends.

There were complaints about the new arrivals, including about the highly educated immigrants who were on a path to permanent residency and citizenship. Although the majority of the immigrants were from China, and in 2010 76% of Singapore's citizens were ethnic Chinese, there were still cultural differences. English is the main language of Singapore, and many of the Chinese immigrants spoke only Mandarin Chinese. Also, social norms about politeness and public interactions differed among the two groups of Chinese, which led the Singaporean Chinese to view the Chinese immigrants as rude and ill mannered, even if the immigrants were wealthy and contributed substantially to Singapore's economy.

World economic problems that affected Singapore in 2011 also led to criticisms of the new arrivals and accusations that they were taking desirable jobs from Singapore natives. Thus, in 2011, new restrictions were placed on highly skilled newcomers.

This is an example of Singapore trying to fine-tune its population policies, as it did in the case of fertility.[134] A Singaporean government policy white paper issued in January 2013 described the demographic challenges facing Singapore and argued that substantial immigration was the only viable solution. In February 2013, there was a public demonstration protesting the new immigration plans. Such public protests are very rare in Singapore. Protestors complained that immigration had already led to lower salaries and higher property prices.[135]

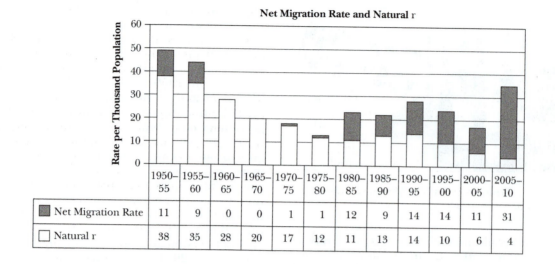

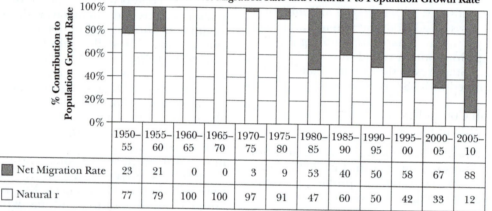

FIGURE 12.19 The Net Migration Rate and Natural Rate of Increase in Singapore, 1950–2010

STATELESS PERSONS

Although legal and undocumented immigrants often face discrimination and legal difficulties, stateless persons often face even greater obstacles. A **stateless person** is not recognized as a citizen of any country. Stateless persons cannot vote in any country and cannot obtain a passport or other documents for legal international travel. In many countries, they are denied any social services and cannot legally work. It is estimated that in 2013, there were 12 million stateless persons in the world.[136]

Statelessness results from the following:[137]

1. **Discriminatory Legislation and Decrees against Minority Ethnic Groups:** In 1980, the Faili Kurds of Iraq lost their citizenship as the result of a Saddam Hussein decree. Many

Roma in Europe, who have long been subjects of discrimination, are stateless.

2. **Legislative Problems When a New State Is Formed:** When the Soviet Union and Yugoslavia were dissolved in the early 1990s, many people found themselves stateless in their new countries of residence. Often, new citizenship laws relating to place of birth, ethnicity, or language left people without citizenship. Also, thousands of people in former colonies in Africa and Asia remain stateless.

3. **Discrimination against Women:** In some countries, citizenship is passed on from the father. Children of women who marry foreigners can be stateless.

4. **Complex Laws and Legal Requirements:** In some countries, extended residence outside the country can lead to loss of citizenship.

Also, the lack of a birth certificate can lead to statelessness, which is a possibility as long as there is not complete birth registration.

There were UN Conventions in 1954 and 1961 that specified some protections for stateless persons, but as of 2013 only 66 states had signed the 1954 Convention and 38 states had signed the 1961 Convention.

POLITICAL SHIFTS AND INTERNATIONAL MIGRATION

When there are major political changes, the net immigration rate can change substantially. In interpreting the meaning of such changes, it is important to keep in mind that a net migration rate is the difference between the gross immigration rate and the gross emigration rate.

Figure 12.20 shows the immigration rate, the emigration rate, and the estimated net immigration rate to South Africa in 1950 through 2000. In 1960, the South African government began to actively recruit White immigrants from Europe, partly motivated by concern about the decreasing proportion of the South African population that was White. This is reflected in the large increase in the immigration rate from 1955–1960 to 1960–1965. The immigration rate declined fairly steadily from its peak in 1965–1970. The emigration rate also generally declined, with some increase in the late 1970s. Recall that the net immigration rate is the immigration rate minus the emigration rate.[138]

The net immigration rate is negative if there are more emigrants than immigrants. In 1995–2000, the number of emigrants exceeded the number of immigrants, which resulted in a negative net immigration rate. This net emigration from South Africa

was viewed by many as indicating that dissatisfied South Africans fleeing the country in droves. However, it is clear from Figure 12.20 that the net emigration was more due to a decrease in immigration than due to an increase in emigration.

Figure 12.20 makes it clear that interpreting the meaning of a net migration rate can be complicated, since it is the difference between two rates. Often, the magnitude of both gross migration rates is larger than that of the net migration rate. This means that relatively small changes in the gross rates can result in a substantial change in the net rate. In South Africa in 1950–1960 and 1985–2000, both gross rates were larger than the net rate. This is a similar point to that made about net and gross migration in and out of American regions for Figure 12.10.

The remainder of this chapter discusses urban places, the differences between rural and urban areas, and increasing urbanization in the world. These topics are strongly related to migration and need to be read with consideration of migration in mind.

WHAT IS URBAN?

Simply put, urban means nonagricultural. **Rural** means any place that is not urban. Whether a place is **urban** is a function of the following:

1. **Population Size:** Often, there is a minimum required settlement size.
2. **The Ratio of Population to Space (Population Density):** Sometimes, there is a minimum required population density.
3. **Economic, Political, and Social Organization:** Sometimes, there are requirements that there are commercial, political, or administrative institutions or services in the place or that a minimum percentage of the working population be engaged in non-agricultural activities.

It makes sense that places that are considered urban have larger and denser populations than places that are considered rural. Also, urban places fill certain functions, such as in commerce, administration, and manufacturing, which are usually not filled in rural places.

However, whether a place is officially designated as urban is something that is determined by individual countries, and the definitions are not consistent across countries. Also, many countries have further divisions of urbanness besides just a rural-urban divide. One question is: Should a fairly large settlement in which almost everyone works on their agricultural land near the settlement be considered rural or urban? As seen in this section, countries have made different decisions about whether to include a criterion about the percentage of the population who obtain economic support from agriculture.

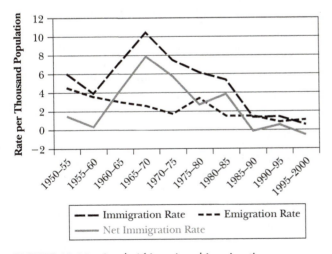

FIGURE 12.20 South African Legal Immigration, Emigration, and Net Migration Rates, 1950–2000

Many countries have a minimum population requirement. However, every region, such as a state or province, needs an administrative and judicial center. Sometimes a region has no large settlements, so the place where most administrative and judicial functions are located is designated as urban, even if it has a small population.

It is clear from the examples of country-specific definitions of urban that data on the percentage of the population in urban places can have a vastly different meaning in different countries. For example, in Benin an urban place has to have at least 10,000 persons, while in Norway a place needs only 200 persons to be classified as urban, and in Ecuador the definition of urban is completely based on administrative functions. In Burundi, only the capital city is considered urban. Many countries, such as Canada, Germany, and India, have a density criterion, and several countries have a requirement related to the economic activity of inhabitants, including Botswana, Democratic Republic of the Congo, India, and Japan. Some countries have a requirement related to the availability of urban services, including Costa Rica and Cuba. Lesotho has a rapid population growth criterion. In some places, including Bermuda and the Cayman Islands, the entire population is considered urban.

Definition of Urban in Various Countries

Although countries differ widely in their exact definitions of urban, they virtually all include aspects of the three areas listed above: population size, population density, and economic, political, and social organization. Some examples of the definitions of urban in individual countries follow. We see that the minimal population among countries listed varies from 200 to 50,000, and that some countries require a minimum population density or a maximal proportion of people deriving their livelihood from agriculture. Some countries just designate national or provincial capitals as urban:[139]

Argentina: Population centers with 2,000 inhabitants or more.

Benin: Localities with 10,000 inhabitants or more.

Bermuda: Entire population is considered urban.

Botswana: Agglomerations of 5,000 inhabitants or more where 75% or more of the economic activity is non-agricultural.

Burundi: Population of Bujumbura (the capital).

Canada: Settlements that have more than 400 people per square kilometer and more than 1,000 people in the settlement.

Cayman Islands: The entire population.

Costa Rica: Administrative centers of cantons, including adjacent areas with clear urban characteristics such as streets, urban services, and electricity.

Cuba: Places with 2,000 inhabitants or more, and places with fewer inhabitants but with paved streets, street lighting, piped water, sewage, a medical center, and educational facilities.

Democratic Republic of the Congo: Places with 2,000 inhabitants or more where the predominant activity is non-agricultural, and places with fewer inhabitants that are considered urban because of their predominantly non-agricultural economic activity.

Denmark: Localities with 200 or more inhabitants.

Ecuador: Capitals of provinces and cantons.

Germany: Communes with population density of 150 people per square kilometer or more.

Ghana: Localities with 5,000 inhabitants or more.

Iceland: Localities with 200 or more inhabitants.

India: Places that are urban by statute due to being the center for a municipality or other designated area and places with 5,000 or more inhabitants, a density of not less than 400 persons per square kilometer, and at least three-quarters of the adult male employed population working in pursuits other than agriculture.

Israel: All settlements of more than 2,000 inhabitants, except those where at least one-third of households participating in the civilian labor force earn their living from agriculture.

Japan: Settlements with 50,000 or more inhabitants in which 60% or more of the houses are located in the main built-up areas and 50% or more of the employed population are engaged in manufacturing, trade, or another urban type of business.

Lesotho: District headquarters and other settlements with rapid population growth and with facilities that tend to encourage people to engage in non-agricultural economic activities.

Nigeria: Towns of 20,000 or more whose occupations are not mainly agrarian.

Norway: Localities of 200 or more inhabitants.

Poland: Towns and settlements of an urban nature (e.g., workers' settlements, fishermen's settlements, and health resorts).

Senegal: Agglomerations of 10,000 inhabitants or more.

Sweden: Built-up areas with at least 250 inhabitants and where houses are at most 200 meters separated from each other.

U.S. Urban Definitions

The 2010 U.S. definition of urban places encompasses many of the considerations discussed here. There are density and population size requirements, although low-density areas between dense areas are also considered urban. "Rural" is a residual category, defined as "not urban." As the Census Bureau writes,

> The Census Bureau's urban-rural classification is fundamentally a delineation of geographical areas, identifying both individual urban areas and the rural areas of the nation. The Census Bureau's urban areas represent densely developed territory, and encompass residential, commercial, and other non-residential urban land uses.
>
> For the 2010 Census, an urban area will comprise a densely settled core of census tracts and/or census blocks that meet minimum population density requirements, along with adjacent territory containing non-residential urban land uses as well as territory with low population density included to link outlying densely settled territory with the densely settled core. To qualify as an urban area, the territory identified according to criteria must encompass at least 2,500 people, at least 1,500 of which reside outside institutional group quarters. The Census Bureau identifies two types of urban areas:
>
> - Urbanized Areas (UAs) of 50,000 or more people
> - Urban Clusters (UCs) of at least 2,500 and less than 50,000 people
>
> "Rural areas" encompass all population, housing, and territory not included within an urban area.[140]

IDEAS ABOUT THE DEVELOPMENT OF URBAN PLACES AND THE NATURE OF URBAN AND RURAL LIFE

Based on archaeological data available through the early twentieth century, V. Gordon Childe discussed the transition from subsistence agricultural life to the rise of urban places, related to larger and denser population and specialization and division of labor based on an agricultural surplus. This transition was discussed in Chapter 5 in terms of its effects on the level and mixture of causes of mortality.[141]

Social scientists have often discussed the essential differences between rural and urban life:

1. A rural area has low population density and long-term residents, and the primary means of support are agriculture, fishing, or mining (which are called "primary industry"). Often, a high proportion of rural residents are supported by subsistence agricultural production with a small part of the produce sold to others.
2. An urban area has high population density, a shifting group of residents, and very differentiated occupations, based on the production and provision of goods and services to others, with almost no engagement in agriculture or other primary industries.

Scholars have differed considerably on whether urban life or rural life is better for people and especially whether urban life is destructive of human sensitivity and human interaction. These different views are important in understanding why people migrate to urban places and in understanding the different challenges that urban and rural places face.

Ferdinand Tönnies was a German scholar who saw urban life, especially in large cities, as destructive of human interaction. He developed a dichotomy of ways to organize social life:[142]

1. *Gemeinschaft* (community), in which people cooperated for the common good and had a sense of integration of all parts of their lives. This was seen as characterizing village or rural life.
2. *Gesellschaft* (association), in which people pursued their individual goals with little sense of community and interacted with different sets of people in different aspects of their lives. This was seen as characterizing urban life.

Other scholars had a mixed view of the effects of urban life on people. Marx and Engels saw the development of cities as an inevitable part of the course of history. They also saw the capitalist city as a major venue in which workers were degraded and kept in a state of poverty, although urban work removed people from "the idiocy of rural life." The city was seen as destroying the positive social ties that existed in rural communities.[143] Max Weber saw the city as dehumanizing but also as key to the development of capitalism, which he saw as crucial to social and economic development. He saw the city as characterized by anonymity in personal relations and the center for markets as well as political, administrative, and judicial functions.[144]

Georg Simmel also had a mixed view of the effects of urban life. He saw urban life as extremely stimulating, which increased people's powers of observation, increased rationality in the division of labor, and resulted in money—rather than labor or bartered goods—as the primary medium of exchange. These stimuli and adaptations to urban life were seen as making people calculating and insensitive to the needs of others.[145]

Some scholars had a more positive view of urban life. Émile Durkheim produced a dichotomy about how social life is organized that has some similarities to that of Tönnies but was much less critical of urban life. He distinguished between the following:[146]

1. **Mechanical Solidarity,** in which social bonds are based on similarities between individuals and common beliefs and practices. This typifies rural life.
2. **Organic Solidarity,** in which social bonds are based on differences between individuals and in which the division of labor in society allows more complex tasks to be accomplished. This typifies urban life.

Geographers have been concerned with what determines the location and relative size of urban places. Walter Christaller, a German geographer, proposed central place theory in 1933. In this formulation, a town is the center of a region, which serves as a distribution center for various goods and services. Over time, larger urban places emerge for the dispersal and coordination of higher level services and the marketing of goods that are less needed at smaller urban places. The theory involved the idea of the range of a good, which predicted the distance between places at which the good would be found. The ideas of central place theory were the basis of the development of theories of urban networks from geography that predict the location and size of urban places.[147]

URBANIZATION AND URBAN GROWTH

Definition of Urbanization

The level of **urbanization** is the percentage of the population that lives in urban places. Urbanization is a relative measure ranging from 0%, if a population is entirely rural or agricultural, to 100%, if a population is entirely urban.

Definition of Urban Growth

The rate of **urban growth** is the growth rate of the urban population. This is calculated the same way the rate of growth of the total population is calculated:

$$U_2 = U_1 e^{rt}$$

where:

U_2 is the size of the urban population at Time 1.

U_1 is the size of the urban population at Time 1.

t is the number of years between Time 1 and Time 2.

r is the rate of growth of the urban population.

Sources of Urban Growth

There are three sources of growth of urban places:

1. **Rate of Natural Increase of Urban Places:** The excess of urban births over urban deaths will contribute to urban growth.
2. **Rural-Urban Internal Migration and International Migration to Urban Places:** Typically, there are more internal and international migrants into urban places than out of urban places.
3. **Reclassification (Usually of Areas From Rural To Urban):** When an area that has formerly been classified as rural becomes reclassified as urban, the population of that area becomes part of the urban population. Reclassification can motivate migration either into or out of the reclassified area.

Sources of Urbanization

Similarly to the sources of urban growth, there are three sources of urbanization:

1. **The Difference Between the Rate of Natural Increase in Urban Places and Rural Places Is One Source of Urbanization:** If the urban area has a lower rate of natural increase than the rural area, then differences in the rate of natural increase will slow urbanization, while if the rate of natural increase is higher in the urban area, this will contribute to urbanization. Urban places often have a lower crude birth rate than rural places, but sometimes urban places also have a lower crude death rate than rural areas. However, the rate of natural increase is usually higher in rural places due to a higher rural crude birth rate, so this source usually depresses the rate of urbanization.
2. **Rural-Urban Internal Migration and International Migration Almost Always Contribute to Urbanization:** Since there is almost always net rural-urban migration and urban places are disproportionately the destinations of international migrants, migration contributes to urbanization.
3. **Reclassification of Areas Between a Rural Designation and an Urban Designation:** This contributes to urbanization, since the reclassification is almost always from rural to urban rather than from urban to rural.

Growth of Cities and Rural-Urban Reclassification

The **reclassification** of areas from rural to urban and the growth of the boundaries of cities are common processes, as the population concentrated around

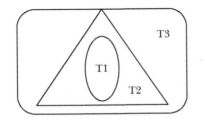

FIGURE 12.21   Schematic Representation of Reclassification and Urban Growth over Time in Center City

cities increases. Figure 12.21 shows this schematically in a hypothetical city, Center City. At Time 1 (T1), the boundaries of the city are an oval. By Time 2 (T2), the population has grown and spread out, and the urban boundaries now form a larger area in the shape of a triangle. By Time 3 (T3), the urban place has grown further and forms a rounded rectangle. People who live at T1 in the area of the triangle for T2 but outside of the oval at T1 become urban residents between T1 and T2, even if they still live in the same place at T2. They have not migrated from a rural to an urban place, but the place where they live has been reclassified from being a rural place to being an urban place.

The situation depicted in Figure 12.21 raises the issue of what definition of an urban place should be used in comparisons over time. Does a researcher or policy maker want to compare the population of Center City across time in terms of the city as defined at each time, as defined at the first date (T1), or as defined at the last date (T3)? Comparing anything other than the city as defined at each time (comparing T1 to T2 to T3) can present difficult and sometimes insurmountable technical problems. However, the answer to what geographical area should be compared depends on the question asked. If one wanted to look at the changing urban setting as experienced by urban dwellers over time in relation to the physical environment, one might want to compare the residents of T1 at all three time points. Perhaps there were physical features, such as streams or ponds, in the area included in Center City at T3 but not included in Center City at T2 and one wanted to look at how the presence of these features affected urban policies. In that case, one might want to look at the area included in Center City at T3 at all three time points.

URBAN AND RURAL POPULATIONS IN THE WORLD: 1950–2010

Figure 12.22 shows the population living in urban areas and the population in rural areas from 1950 through 2010. It is clear that the urban population of the world has grown more rapidly than the rural population. While in 1950 more than twice as many people

lived in rural than in urban places, by 2005, as many people lived in urban as in rural places, and by 2010 more people lived in urban than in rural places.[148]

Figure 12.23 shows the urban and rural populations of the MDR, while Figure 12.24 shows similar information for the LDR. The urban and rural

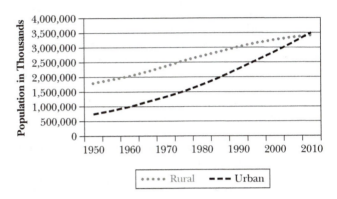

FIGURE 12.22   Urban and Rural Populations in the World, 1950–2010

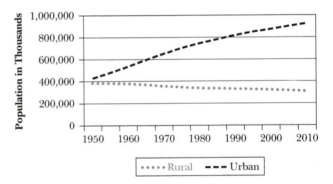

FIGURE 12.23   Urban and Rural Populations in the MDR, 1950–2010

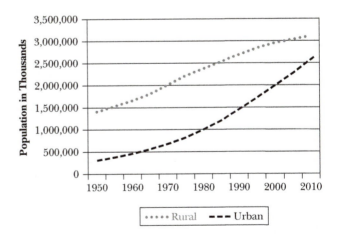

FIGURE 12.24   Urban and Rural Populations in the LDR, 1950–2010

definitions applied are those of each individual country. In the MDR, even in 1950, there were slightly more people in urban than in rural places. Also, since 1950, in the MDR the rural population has progressively declined in size, while the urban population has continued to grow, although at a decreasing rate after about 1980. While in 1950 in the MDR, the urban and rural populations were approximately the same size, in 2010, there were three times as many people in urban than in rural places.

In the LDR since 1950, there have always been more people in rural than in urban places. However, as shown in Figure 12.24, by 2010 the LDR population in urban places has approached that in rural places. In the LDR, the rate of growth of the rural population has slowed since the 1970s, while the rate of growth of the urban population increased.

We see in Figure 12.25 that in both the more developed region and in the less developed region, the percentage of the population living in urban areas has increased. Even in 1950, over half of the population in the MDR lived in urban places, while by 2010 45% of the population of the LDR lived in urban places, and 75% of the MDR lived in urban places.

Figure 12.26 shows the percentage urban by world region in 1950–2010. At every date, Northern America had the highest percentage of its population living in urban areas, despite the extensive sparsely populated parts of the United States and Canada. Asia and Africa had a similar percentage living in urban areas at every date, and the percentage urban in these two regions was substantially lower than in other regions. In 1950, a higher percentage of the population of Europe than of Latin America and the Caribbean lived in urban areas, but Europe, Latin America, and the Caribbean each had 70% of their populations in urban areas in 1990, after which a higher percentage of the population of Latin America and the Caribbean than

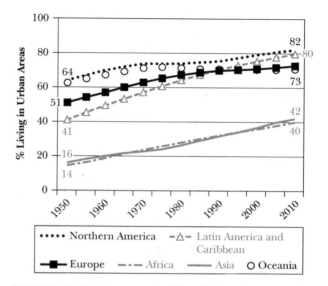

FIGURE 12.26 Percentage of Population Living in Urban Areas by World Region, 1950–2010

of Europe lived in urban places. Oceania had 62% of its population in urban places in 1950, similar to Northern America, but by 2010 Oceania had 71% of its population in urban areas, similar to Europe.

Urbanization in Large Countries

Figure 12.27 shows the percentage of the population living in urban places in the ten largest countries in the world in 2010. The percentage urban has increased in all countries. Even in Nigeria, with a very low development level, half of the population lived in an urban area (using Nigeria's definition) in 2010. In 2010, Brazil was the most urbanized large country, followed closely by the United States.

URBAN AGGLOMERATIONS

The United States and other countries sometimes define masses of urban population, such as metropolitan areas. A metropolitan area can be a city and the nearby suburban areas, or it can include two or more cities and the nearby area. The United States defines two kinds of clusters of urban areas: metropolitan areas and micropolitan areas.

Both metropolitan areas and micropolitan areas are groups of counties. The counties included in a metropolitan or micropolitan area can change after each decennial census. Also, there can be areas within a metropolitan area that have a distinctly rural character.

Metropolitan statistical areas (MSAs) are based on a central urbanized area (contiguous area of relatively high population density). Adjacent counties are included in the MSA if they have strong social and

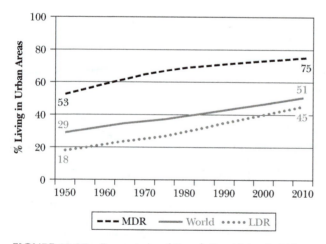

FIGURE 12.25 Percentage of Population Living in Urban Areas in the World, MDR, and LDR, 1950–2010

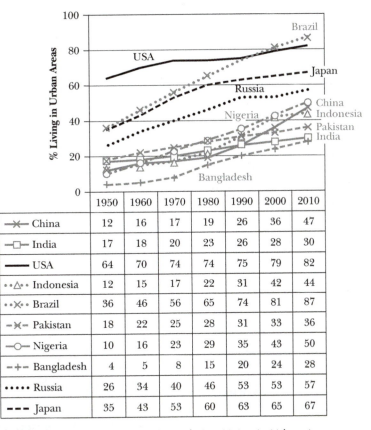

	1950	1960	1970	1980	1990	2000	2010
—✕— China	12	16	17	19	26	36	47
—☐— India	17	18	20	23	26	28	30
—— USA	64	70	74	74	75	79	82
··△·· Indonesia	12	15	17	22	31	42	44
··✕·· Brazil	36	46	56	65	74	81	87
–✕– Pakistan	18	22	25	28	31	33	36
—◯— Nigeria	10	16	23	29	35	43	50
–+– Bangladesh	4	5	8	15	20	24	28
····· Russia	26	34	40	46	53	53	57
– – – Japan	35	43	53	60	63	65	67

FIGURE 12.27   Percentage of Population Living in Urban Areas for Ten Largest Countries in 2010, 1950–2010

economic ties to the central counties as measured by commuting and employment. Entire adjacent counties can be rural in character when considered on their own.

Micropolitan statistical areas were designated starting in 2003. They are urban areas around a core city with a population of 10,000–49,999.[149] An example of a micropolitan statistical area is Galesburg, Illinois. The U.S. Census Bureau also has a designation called a combined statistical area, which is similar to a metropolitan or micropolitan statistical area, but the economic and social ties do not need to be as strong as within a metropolitan or micropolitan statistical area.

An example of the changing composition of counties in an MSA can make this clearer. Table 12.8 shows the counties comprising the Chicago MSA in 1950 and in 2010 and the population of each county at both dates. There were five counties in the Chicago MSA in 1950 and 13 counties in the Chicago MSA in 2010, even though the county boundaries did not change between 1950 and 2010.

Table 12.9 shows the population of Cook County, which includes Chicago, in 1950 and 2010. It also shows the population of the Chicago MSA at both dates as well as the population of the counties that were included in the Chicago MSA in 1950 at both dates and the population of the counties included in the Chicago MSA in 2010 at both dates. The population of Cook County increased by 15% between 1950 and 2010. Cook County was fairly densely settled by 1950 and had limited potential for further population growth. The Chicago MSA grew by 74% between 1950 and 2010. However, if the Chicago MSA boundaries had remained unchanged between 1950 and 2010, it would have only grown by 50% in the same time period. If the boundaries of 2010 had been in force in 1950, it would have grown by 64% in the period. This is an example of urban growth due to reclassification, as was discussed earlier in this chapter regarding city boundaries.

The United Nations compares urban agglomerations that are similar to U.S. metropolitan areas. A very large city or urban area that is a significant economic, political, and cultural center for a country or region, and an important hub for regional or international connections and communications, is also called a **metropolis**.

TABLE 12.8 Comparison of Counties Comprising the Chicago Metropolitan Statistical Area in 1950 and 2010

Counties in Chicago MSA, 1950	Counties in Chicago MSA, 2010	Population in 1950	Population in 2010
Cook County, IL	Cook County, IL	4,508,792	5,194,675
Du Page County, IL	Du Page County, IL	143,599	916,924
Will County, IL	Will County, IL	134,336	677,560
Lake County, IL	Lake County, IL	179,097	703,462
Lake County, IN	Lake County, IN	368,152	496,005
	DeKalb County, IL	40,781	105,160
	Grundy County, IL	19,217	50,063
	Kane County, IL	150,388	515,269
	Kendall County, IL	12,115	114,736
	McHenry County, IL	50,656	308,760
	Jasper County, IN	17,031	33,478
	Newton County, IN	11,006	14,244
	Porter County, IN	40,076	164,343

TABLE 12.9 Population of Cook County and of Chicago MSA with Boundary Definitions of 1950 and 2010

	1950	2010	Percent Increase 1950–2010
Cook County, including Chicago	4,508,792	5,194,675	15%
Chicago MSA with boundaries of given year	5,333,976	9,294,679	74%
Chicago MSA with boundaries of 1950	5,333,976	7,988,626	50%
Chicago MSA with boundaries of 2010	5,675,246	9,294,679	64%

The United Nations uses the following definition of an **urban agglomeration**:[150]

The term "urban agglomeration" refers to the population contained within the contours of a contiguous territory inhabited at urban density levels without regard to administrative boundaries. It usually incorporates the population in a city or town plus that in the suburban areas lying outside of, but being adjacent to, the city boundaries. Whenever possible, data classified according to the concept of urban agglomeration are used. However, some countries do not produce data according to the concept of urban agglomeration but use instead that of metropolitan area or city proper. If possible, such data are adjusted to conform to the concept urban agglomeration. When sufficient information is not available to permit such an adjustment, data based on the concept of city proper or metropolitan area are used.

World Urban Agglomerations: 1950–2010

Table 12.10 shows the ten largest urban agglomerations in the world at 10-year intervals for 1950–2010. The population of each agglomeration in millions is also shown. Urban agglomerations in the LDR are shown in *italic*.

It is clear that, increasingly, these large agglomerations are in the LDR. In 1950, seven of the ten were in the MDR; by 2010, only two were in the MDR. If one looks at the 30 largest agglomerations, none are located in Africa until 1960, when Cairo, Egypt, with 4 million people ranked eighteenth. In 2000, Lagos, Nigeria was the first agglomeration in sub-Saharan Africa among the largest 30 urban agglomerations. With 7 million people, Lagos ranked twenty-seventh. By 2010, Kinshasa, the capital of the Democratic Republic of the Congo, was the second sub-Saharan African urban agglomeration among the largest 30 with 9 million people. Kinshasa ranked twenty-ninth. Even in 2010, there was no African urban agglomerations among the 10 largest.

The size of urban agglomerations also increased over time. In 1950 the largest urban agglomeration, New York City–Newark, had 12 million people. In 2010, an urban agglomeration with 12 million people would not have made the list of the ten largest urban agglomerations.

TABLE 12.10 Largest World Urban Agglomerations and Population in Millions, 1950–2010[151]

	1950	Population	1960	Population	1970	Population	1980	Population	1990	Population	2000	Population	2010	Population
1	NYC–Newark, USA	12	Tokyo, Japan	17	Tokyo, Japan	23	Tokyo, Japan	29	Tokyo, Japan	33	Tokyo, Japan	34	Tokyo, Japan	37
2	Tokyo, Japan	11	NYC–Newark, USA	14	NYC–Newark, USA	16	NYC–Newark, USA	16	NYC–Newark, USA	16	*Mexico City, Mexico*	18	*Delhi, India*	22
3	London, UK	8	London, UK	8	Osaka–Kobe, Japan	9	*Mexico City, Mexico*	13	*Mexico City, Mexico*	15	NYC–Newark, USA	18	*Sao Paulo, Brazil*	20
4	Paris, France	7	Paris, France	7	*Mexico City, Mexico*	9	*Sao Paulo, Brazil*	12	*Sao Paulo, Brazil*	15	*Sao Paulo, Brazil*	17	*Mumbai (Bombay), India*	20
5	Moscow, USSR	5	*Shanghai, China*	7	Los Angeles–Long Beach–Santa Ana, USA	8	Osaka–Kobe, Japan	10	*Mumbai (Bombay), India*	12	*Mumbai (Bombay), India*	16	*Mexico City, Mexico*	19
6	*Buenos Aires, Argentina*	5	*Buenos Aires, Argentina*	7	Paris, France	8	Los Angeles–Long Beach–Santa Ana, USA	10	Osaka–Kobe, Japan	11	*Delhi, India*	16	NYC–Newark, USA	19
7	Chicago, USA	5	Los Angeles–Long Beach–Santa Ana, USA	7	*Buenos Aires, Argentina*	8	*Buenos Aires, Argentina*	11	*Kolkata (Calcutta), India*	13	*Shanghai, China*	13	*Shanghai, China*	17
8	*Kolkata (Calcutta), India*	5	Osaka–Kobe, Japan	6	*Sao Paulo, Brazil*	8	*Kolkata (Calcutta), India*	11	Los Angeles–Long Beach–Santa Ana, USA	13	*Kolkata (Calcutta), India*	13	*Kolkata (Calcutta), India*	16
9	*Shanghai, China*	4	Chicago, USA	6	London, UK	8	Paris, France	9	*Seoul, Republic of Korea*	11	*Buenos Aires, Argentina*	12	*Dhaka, Bangladesh*	15
10	Osaka–Kobe, Japan	4	Moscow, USSR	6	Moscow, USSR	7	*Mumbai (Bombay), India*	9	*Buenos Aires, Argentina*	11	Los Angeles–Long Beach–Santa Ana, USA	12	*Karachi, Pakistan*	13

Urban agglomerations in the LDR are shown in *italic*.

MEGALOPOLISES

Oswald Spengler coined the term megalopolis in 1918, and Jean Gottmann in the 1950s used the term in reference to the large urbanized area between Boston and Washington, DC, which is sometimes referred to as Boswash. Other American megalopolises that Gottmann identified are from Chicago to Pittsburgh and the Ohio River (which he called Chipitts), and from San Francisco to San Diego (which he called Sansan).[152]

A **megalopolis** is sometimes called a **mega-region**. Megalopolises or mega-regions are "integrated sets of cities and their surrounding suburban hinterlands across which labor and capital can be reallocated at very low cost."[153]

In 1976, Gottman suggested that a megalopolis be defined as having a minimum of 25 million people. He stated that at that time, there were six megalopolises in the world:[154]

1. American Northeastern Megalopolis
2. Great Lakes Megalopolis
3. Tokaido Megalopolis in Japan
4. English Megalopolis
5. Northwestern Europe Megalopolis from Amsterdam to the Ruhr and northern France
6. Urban constellation centering on Shanghai in China

In 2008, Richard Florida and his colleagues identified 40 mega-regions in the world. Their work was based on inspection of light emitted as recorded by satellite photographs. Based on this, they defined the geographic limits of each mega-region and calculated the population and the economic activity within each mega-region.

Florida and his colleagues considered the magnitude of economic activity more important than population in ranking of mega-regions. Table 12.11

shows the largest ten world mega-regions as defined by Florida and his colleagues ranked by economic activity, and Table 12.12 shows the largest ten mega-regions ranked by population.

Whether mega-regions are ranked by economic activity or by population size clearly makes a difference. The leading two mega-regions by population size shown in Table 12.12 are not among the top ten in terms of economic activity shown in Table 12.11. Mega-regions in the less developed region are shown in *italic*. None of the top ten mega-regions ranked by economic activity are in the LDR, while four of the top ten mega-regions ranked by population are in the LDR. The top ten mega-regions by economic activity contributed 43% of world economic activity and 7% of the world population, while the top ten mega-regions by population size contributed about 25% of world economic activity and 11% of the world population.

A regional planning association, America 2050, identified 11 megalopolises or emerging megalopolises in the United States. Some of them extend into Canada or Mexico. They are shown in Table 12.13. While Gottman considered there to be one megalopolis that extended from San Francisco to San Diego, America 2050 divides this into two megalopolises, Northern California and Southern California. A total of 234 million people lived in American megalopolises in 2010, which constituted 75% of the U.S. population.[155]

OVERBOUNDED CITIES, UNDERBOUNDED CITIES, AND ALTERNATIVE CITY BOUNDARY DEFINITIONS

A city is overbounded if the city includes within its boundaries substantial area that does not have urban characteristics. China is well known for having

TABLE 12.11   Ten Largest World Mega-Regions Ranked by Economic Activity, about 2005

Rank	Name	Economic Activity (in Billions of Dollars)	Population (in Millions)
1	Greater Tokyo (Japan)	2,500	55
2	Boston–Washington (USA)	2,200	54
3	Chicago–Pittsburgh (USA)	1,600	46
4	Amsterdam–Rotterdam–Brussels–Antwerp–Ruhr–Cologne (Netherlands, Belgium, and Germany)	1,500	59
5	Osaka–Nagoya (Japan)	1,400	36
6	London–Leeds–Manchester (UK)	1,200	50
7	Rome–Milan–Turin (Italy)	1,000	48
8	Charlotte–Atlanta (USA)	730	22
9	Southern California (USA)	710	21
10	Frankfurt–Stuttgart (Germany)	630	23

TABLE 12.12 Ten Largest World Mega-Regions Ranked by Population Size, about 2005

Rank	Name	Economic Activity (in Billions of Dollars)	Population (in Millions)
1	*Delhi–Lahore (India and Pakistan)*	110	122
2	*Shanghai (China)*	130	66
3	Amsterdam–Rotterdam–Brussels–Antwerp–Ruhr–Cologne (Netherlands, Belgium, and Germany)	1,500	59
4	Greater Tokyo (Japan)	2,500	55
5	Boston–Washington (USA)	2,200	54
6	London–Leeds–Manchester (UK)	1,200	50
7	Rome–Milan–Turin (Italy)	1,000	48
8	*Seoul–Busan (South Korea)*	500	46
9	Chicago–Pittsburgh (USA)	1,600	46
10	*Mexico City (Mexico)*	290	46

Mega-regions in the LDR are shown in *italic*.

TABLE 12.13 American Megalopolises, 2010

Rank	Name	Population in Millions	Major Cities
1	Arizona Sun Corridor	5.7	Phoenix and Tucson
2	Cascadia	8.4	Portland, Seattle, and Vancouver
3	Florida	17.3	Miami, Orlando, Tampa, and Jacksonville
4	Front Range	5.5	Albuquerque, Santa Fe, Colorado Springs, and Denver
5	Great Lakes (Chipitts)	55.5	Chicago, Detroit, Toronto, Montreal, Pittsburgh, Cleveland, Minneapolis, St. Louis, and Indianapolis
6	Gulf Coast	13.4	Houston, New Orleans, Baton Rouge, Biloxi, and Pensacola
7	Northeast (Boswash)	52.3	Boston, New York, Philadelphia, Baltimore, Washington, DC, Norfolk, and Richmond
8	Northern California	14.0	Oakland, Reno, Sacramento, Fresno, San Jose, and San Francisco
9	Piedmont Atlantic	17.6	Atlanta, Birmingham, Chattanooga, Huntsville, Memphis, Knoxville, Nashville, Raleigh-Durham, and Charlotte
10	Southern California	24.4	Los Angeles, San Diego, Anaheim, Riverside, Long Beach, Las Vegas, and Tijuana
11	Texas Triangle	19.7	Austin, Dallas–Fort Worth, Houston, and San Antonio

overbounded cities. Sometimes there is a large area with completely rural characteristics within city boundaries. One reason is that Chinese urban places are defined based on administrative functions, and city boundaries conform to political boundaries. When city boundaries have been expanded, the new areas included often are substantially rural. In fact, there sometimes are designations of an "urban part" of a city and a "rural part" of a city. Sometimes the rural part of a city is included in the definition of the urban population, and sometimes it is not. Differences in the incidence of overbounded cities among countries introduce an additional aspect of incomparability in comparing the urban populations of different countries.[156]

There are also overbounded cities in other countries, including the United States. The largest city in geographic area in the United States is the City and Borough of Yakutat, Alaska, which in 2010 had a population of 662 but an area of 7,650 square miles, giving a population density of 0.1 persons per square mile. Yakutat is larger in area than the state of New Hampshire.[157]

As cities have expanded, suburbs have developed that are urban areas but are outside the city boundaries. When people refer to the size of a city, sometimes they mean the population within the city limits, and sometimes they mean some other definition of the urbanized area. What is meant depends on which definition of a city is used.

TABLE 12.14 Population of Some Large Cities According to Alternative Definitions, about 1990

City	Population	City Definition
Beijing, China	2,336,544	Four inner-city districts, including the historic old city
	~5,400,000	Core city
	6,325,722	Inner-city and inner-suburban districts
	10,819,407	Inner-city, inner- and outer-suburban districts, and eight counties
Mexico City, Mexico	1,935,708	Central city
	8,261,951	Federal District
	14,991,281	Mexico City Metropolitan Area
	~18,000,000	Mexico City Megalopolis
London, United Kingdom	4,230	Original "city" of London
	2,343,133	Inner London
	6,393,568	Greater London (32 boroughs and the City of London)
	12,530,000	London Metropolitan Region
Los Angeles, United States	3,000,000	Los Angeles City
	8,700,000	Los Angeles County
	8,863,000	Los Angeles–Long Beach Primary Metropolitan Statistical Area
	14,532,000	Los Angeles Consolidated Metropolitan Statistical Area

David Satterthwaite pointed out the alternative populations of several cities in about 1990, depending on which definition is used. The results for a few cities are shown in Table 12.14.[158] The variation between what population is referred to can be enormous. The central city of Mexico City included less than 2 million people, but the Mexico City Metropolitan Area included almost 15 million people, while there were about 18 million people in the Mexico City megalopolis.

SIZE DISTRIBUTIONS OF CITIES

There have been ideas about what describes the size distribution of cities in a country and also what the size distribution of cities should be. Two that have been important are the rank-size rule of city sizes and the concept of the primate city.

Rank-Size Rule

The **rank-size rule**, proposed by Zipf in 1949, states that in a country or in a region, the second largest city is one-half the size of the largest city, and the third largest city is one-third the size of the largest city. In general, if the population of the largest city is P, then the population of the ith largest city, P_i, is $P_i = P/i$.[159] There has been controversy about whether city size distributions typically follow the rank-size rule and about whether it is desirable for the distribution of city sizes in a country to follow the rank-size rule. However, many governments think a distribution in keeping with the rank-size rule is desirable and think that problems result from the dominance of one city.

Primate Cities

Mark Jefferson defined a **primate city** as follows:[160]

A country's leading city is always disproportionately large and exceptionally expressive of national capacity and feeling. The primate city is commonly at least twice as large as the next largest city and more than twice as significant.

Thus, a primate city usually exceeds the rank-size rule, sometimes by a large amount. A primate city also plays a dominant role in the country's business and culture.

It is often thought, especially in less developed countries, that the presence of a primate city impedes development across the country as a whole. Primate cities have been thought to contribute to serious problems in the areas of housing, transportation, service provision, pollution, and employment. Also, a system of smaller cities has been thought to contribute to more equitable national development.[161]

Some MDR countries have also seen problems arising from large, and especially primate, cities. For example, London instituted a congestion charge in 2003, in which people who drive into central London during business hours on a weekday must pay a fee. In 2014 the fee was 10 British pounds (about $16.50).[162]

Table 12.15 shows information about the largest and the second largest city in some countries with primate cities and some countries without primate cities. In all of the countries listed with a primate city, that city plays a dominant role in the culture and business of the country. Except for Egypt, the largest

TABLE 12.15 Some Countries with and without Primate Cities, 2012

(1) Country	(2) Largest City	(3) Population of Largest City (in Millions)	(4) Second Largest City	(5) Population of Second Largest City (in Millions)	(6) (3)/(5) Ratio of Largest to Second Largest City	(7) Other Major Cities
			Some Countries with a Primate City			
United Kingdom	London	7.2	Birmingham	1.0	7.2	
United Kingdom	London Agglomeration	13.7	Manchester–Liverpool Agglomeration	5.6	2.4	
France	Paris	2.2	Marseilles	0.8	2.8	
France	Paris Agglomeration	12.1	Lyon Agglomeration	1.8	6.7	
Mexico	Mexico City	8.4	Ecatepec de Morelos	1.7	4.9	
Chile	Santiago	5.3	Puente Alto	0.9	5.9	
Chile	Santiago Agglomeration	5.3	Conception Agglomeration	1.1	4.8	
Thailand	Bangkok	5.9	Samut Prakan	0.5	11.8	
Indonesia	Jakarta	9.8	Surabaya	2.8	3.5	
Indonesia	Jakarta Agglomeration	19.9	Bandung Agglomeration	6.7	3.0	
Egypt	Cairo	8.3	Alexandria	4.5	1.8	
Kenya	Nairobi	3.5	Mombasa	1.0	3.5	
			Some Countries without a Primate City			
United States	New York City	8.2	Los Angeles	3.8	2.2	Chicago and Washington, DC
United States	New York Agglomeration	23.6	Los Angeles Agglomeration	18.2	1.3	
Canada	Toronto	5.2	Montreal	3.4	1.5	Vancouver and Ottawa
Germany	Berlin	3.5	Hamburg	1.8	1.9	Munich and Frankfurt
Italy	Rome	2.4	Milan	1.3	1.7	Naples
Italy	Milan Agglomeration	4.4	Rome Agglomeration	4.2	1.0	
India	Mumbai	14.3	Delhi	11.3	1.3	Hyderabad and Bangalore
Saudi Arabia	Riyadh	5.2	Jeddah	3.4	1.5	Damman/Dhahran/Al-Khobar
Australia	Sydney	3.8	Melbourne	3.6	1.1	Brisbane and Perth

city is more than twice as large as the second largest city. Cairo is considered to be a primate city despite the size of Alexandria due to the dominant importance of Cairo in Egypt.[163]

For some countries, the largest and second largest cities are shown both as comparisons of individual cities and sometimes as metropolitan areas or other urban agglomerations. This is related to the issues discussed earlier in this chapter about city boundaries and urban agglomerations.

The United States is not considered to have a primate city. Although New York City has more than twice the population of Los Angeles, the urban agglomeration including New York City is only 1.3 times the size of the urban agglomeration including Los Angeles. Also, New York City is not considered to play the overall dominant role that a primate city plays, especially since Washington, DC, rather than New York, is the national capital. For countries without a primate city, one or two cities in addition to the two largest cities are listed that play an important role in the country's business and culture, and they are part of the reason why the country is not considered to have a primate city. For Italy, whether one considers the city alone or considers urban agglomerations reverses whether Rome or Milan is the larger city. In any case, Italy does not have a primate city.

CENTRAL CITIES, SUBURBANIZATION, TRANSPORTATION IMPROVEMENT, AND NONMETROPOLITAN GROWTH IN THE UNITED STATES AND OTHER MDR COUNTRIES

In discussing urban places, it is useful to distinguish between central cities and suburbs. A **central city** is a densely populated place that provides a variety of urban functions. It is often the principle city in a metropolitan area. A **suburb** is a less densely populated

urban place near a central city, which is primarily residential.

Figure 12.28 shows the population of the United States in central cities, in suburbs, and in nonmetropolitan (rural) areas at ten-year intervals from 1910 through 2010. The top panel shows the number of people in each type of area, and the bottom panel shows the distribution of the population among the three areas. The size of the nonmetropolitan population grew during the period 1910 through 1940 and then declined after 1940, while the size of the central city and the suburban populations grew in every decade since 1910. The percentage of the total population that lived in central cities increased after 1910 and then declined slowly between 1950 and 2000, with some increase by 2010. The percentage in nonmetropolitan areas has steadily declined,

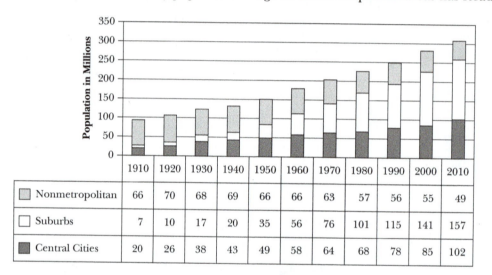

	1910	1920	1930	1940	1950	1960	1970	1980	1990	2000	2010
Nonmetropolitan	66	70	68	69	66	66	63	57	56	55	49
Suburbs	7	10	17	20	35	56	76	101	115	141	157
Central Cities	20	26	38	43	49	58	64	68	78	85	102

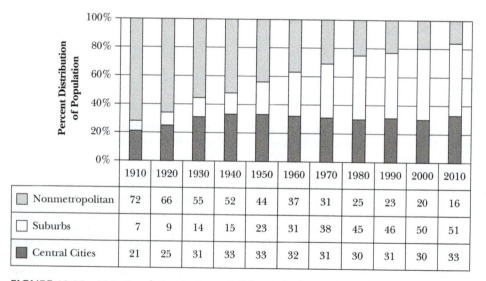

	1910	1920	1930	1940	1950	1960	1970	1980	1990	2000	2010
Nonmetropolitan	72	66	55	52	44	37	31	25	23	20	16
Suburbs	7	9	14	15	23	31	38	45	46	50	51
Central Cities	21	25	31	33	33	32	31	30	31	30	33

FIGURE 12.28   U.S. Population in Central Cities, Suburbs, and Nonmetropolitan Areas, 1910–2010

and the percentage in suburbs has steadily increased. Thus, we see a progressive move out of rural areas, an increase in suburbs that are less densely populated than central cities, and fluctuations in the percentage living in central cities.[164]

In the United States, as cities grew and transportation improved, mainly through commuter railroad lines, wider ownership of cars, and improved highways, it was not necessary for those working in central cities to live as close to their place of work. This led to the growth of suburbs.

In 1956, the U.S. Congress authorized construction of an interstate highway system to interconnect the nation with high-speed, limited-access highways. Construction began in 1956, and the system was essentially complete in 1992. These highways pass through many large cities and provide high-speed commuting corridors. This in turn contributed to the spread of suburbs to counties that had earlier been considered too far from the central city for commuting. The growth of suburbs led to the reclassification of many counties from nonmetropolitan to metropolitan.

With suburbs, people see a trade-off between housing amenities and travel time to work. Across many more developed countries, the average amount of time spent daily on travel is slightly over 1 hour.[165] The development of the interstate highway system in the United States facilitated improved long-distance motor vehicle travel across the country but also further increased the viable commuting distance. At the same time, some previously urban enterprises moved their facilities to suburbs within the metropolitan area. With improved communication and transport, it was increasingly less necessary for many urban services and manufacturing enterprises to be located in central cities.[166] This shift of enterprises from central cities contributed to what Brian Berry called **counterurbanization**, in which the rate of growth of large cities declines, smaller urban places grow, and some nonmetropolitan areas grow rapidly.[167]

In the 1970s in the United States, there was what was called a nonmetropolitan turnaround, as many nonmetropolitan areas that had earlier lost population gained population. Some have argued that access to the interstate highway system contributed to this turnaround. A great deal of this growth was in counties that were classified as nonmetropolitan but were adjacent to metropolitan counties. Many of these nonmetropolitan counties were reclassified as metropolitan after the subsequent census.[168]

In other MDR countries, rural-urban migration has led to rural depopulation and aging. In some countries, such as Spain, a negative natural rate of increase also contributed both to aging and to depopulation. However, sometimes immigrants have settled in rural areas and small towns, countering both depopulation and aging.[169]

Urban places virtually always have a wider variety of available services and have a more developed infrastructure than rural places. Schools, especially postprimary and postsecondary schools, are much more available in urban areas. The quality of life is typically higher in urban areas, drinking water is likely to be cleaner, and often sanitation is better. Rural residents can obtain a comparable material standard of living to those in urban places through having an individual well and water purification system and by having a septic field, but the cost can be considerable, and the individual household is responsible for maintenance.

THE CHANGING NATURE OF RURAL PLACES

With progressive urbanization, rural areas in both the LDR and the MDR have experienced challenges. In both regions, there has been a problem of attracting physicians to rural areas. In the LDR, rural areas increasingly have become areas of concentrated poverty, while in the MDR, the aging of the population is often much more extreme in rural than in urban areas.

Rural Areas in the LDR

People from the LDR who visit the MDR often comment that urban places throughout the world, especially large cities, look similar, but they are amazed at the prosperity and the development level of the rural parts of the MDR.

Rural areas and towns often experience brain drain akin to that which occurs from less developed to more developed countries. Many teachers and physicians came from rural areas, were educated in urban areas, and are reluctant to return to the more limited facilities and infrastructure that they would encounter in rural areas. Salaries for professional positions, such as teachers and health care providers, are typically lower in rural than in urban places. In many less developed countries, a major impediment to staffing rural schools and health care facilities is the lack of infrastructure and the lack of (and lower quality of) rural schools. Unmarried teachers, doctors, and nurses can be attracted to rural areas, but once they marry and have children, they often are reluctant to remain in a rural location.[170]

Along with the good facilities in parts of urban places in less developed countries, urban places often include extremely poor areas that are considered eyesores by the government and that often have very bad living conditions. After a disaster, such as the Haiti earthquake, urban places can become centers of destitution.[171]

Extreme poverty has declined in much of the world, but the poor and the extremely poor are concentrated in rural areas in the LDR. It is estimated that in 2005, 1.4 billion people lived in extreme poverty (less than $1.25 per day), and 70% of the extremely poor lived in rural areas. For example, in South Asia, the percentage of households living in extreme poverty declined from 52% to 39% between 1988 and 2008, but at both dates, about 80% of all extremely poor people in South Asia lived in rural areas.[172] Urban poverty and the presence of unsightly slums in cities in the LDR are objects of legitimate concern. But often rural areas, which can appear green and beautiful, mask much deeper poverty than urban slums. Despite the problems of urban places in the LDR, rural-urban migration, with its selectivity for young adults and the educated, leaves the rural area with an older and less educated population. In 2011, Haiti announced a plan to try to attract people from Haitian cities to rural areas.[173]

Remittances play a similar role in the rural areas of some countries that they do for the origins of international migrants. A set of surveys in 11 sub-Saharan African countries in 2011 found that 32% of adults received remittances in the previous month from friends or relatives elsewhere in the same country, while only 4% of adults received remittances from friends or relatives outside the country. Thirteen percent of adults sent remittances domestically. Domestic remittances were mainly composed of funds sent from urban residents to relatives in the rural area.[174] These remittances can increase inequality within the rural origin, but they probably contribute to an overall increase in the standard of living at the rural origin.

Even though the populations of the LDR are generally much younger than in the MDR, the removal of young adults from rural areas of the LDR due to migration makes the rural populations older than they would have been in the absence of migration. The relative scarcity of health care professionals in rural areas exacerbates problems of the rural elderly in accessing health care.[175]

Rural Areas in the MDR

More developed countries also have had large problems attracting professionals, especially physicians, to rural areas and small urban places. In 2010, there were one-fourth as many doctors per capita in rural as in urban areas in the United States.[176] Similar to concerns in the United States, rural Australians face a severe shortage of doctors. In 2006, in Australia, it was proposed that medical students be required to work in rural areas for a certain length of time after becoming doctors. This was intended to relieve rural doctor shortages. The Australian Medical Association opposed the plan because they maintained that such programs were not a good way to staff rural areas and that doctors who were in rural areas unwillingly would not do a good job.[177]

Wilson and his colleagues reviewed studies that focused on the United States, Canada, and Australia and discussed interventions intended to increase the number of health care professionals, especially physicians, in rural and remote areas. The five strategies that they identified, and the findings of their effectiveness in increasing the supply of physicians working in rural areas, are as follows:[178]

1. **Selection:** This included recruiting medical students from rural areas, or members of underserved ethnic groups. Also, it included a preference for applicants who reported volunteer activities in their applications that indicated a desire to serve others.

   Finding: Rural origin was found to be strongly related to pursuing a rural medical practice.

2. **Education:** This included attention to the content of the medical school curriculum, clinical rotation in a rural setting, fellowships for rural or family physician training, and location of medical schools in rural areas.

   Finding: There was some evidence that encouraging students to become family physicians and providing fellowships in rural health increases the supply of rural physicians.

3. **Coercion:** This included requiring "community service" in order to be certified as a physician, requiring rural experience before pursuing medical specialization, and requiring that foreign physicians practice in a rural area.

   Finding: Besides being objectionable to many people, there was little evidence that coercive measures were effective in more than the very short term. Physicians forced to practice in rural areas often suffer from lack of experience while working in an isolated setting and leave that setting as soon as possible after the term of required service.

4. **Incentives:** This included providing scholarships linked to later practice in a rural area and supplementing the income or providing other financial incentives for practicing in a rural area.

   Finding: There was modest evidence that scholarships with required rural service and directly increasing financial compensation increased the supply of rural physicians.

5. **Support:** This included creating opportunities for the continued professional development of rural physicians, providing sabbaticals and other periods of rest and relief for rural physicians, and facilitating flexible work schedules,

subsidized accommodations, and schooling of children.

Finding: There was weak evidence that supporting the lifestyle of rural physicians has an effect on the supply of physicians working in rural areas.

A similar concern to the shortage of physicians in rural areas has arisen about the shortage of lawyers in rural areas of the United States. Although in 2013, it had been widely reported that nationally there was a surplus of lawyers, at the same time there was a severe shortage of lawyers in many rural areas. For example, 70% of the lawyers in Georgia were in the Atlanta area, and with the retirement of an 86-year-old attorney in Bennett County, South Dakota, there would be no practicing lawyers within 120 miles. In response to the rural lawyer shortage, in 2013 South Dakota passed a law that offered a subsidy to lawyers who agreed to live and practice in rural South Dakota. The program was modeled on incentives for physicians to live and practice in rural areas. However, the size of the subsidy ($12,000 a year) does not approach the incentives offered to physicians. Other states, including Iowa and Nebraska, have instituted summer programs to induce law students to spend time in rural areas. The degree of success of these programs is yet to be seen.[179]

Rural-urban migration has contributed to the aging of rural populations in many MDR countries. Population decline and aging in rural areas of Japan are exacerbated by migration of the young to urban places. Some provincial cities are suffering the same fate as the young move to large cities. Increasingly, rural areas of Russia are populated by older women.[180]

Men who are committed to remaining in rural areas, such as farmers, sometimes have a difficult time finding women willing to marry them and commit to a rural life. In 2012, the town of Candeleda, Spain, held a weekend fiesta intended to attract urban women to marry rural men and thus hopefully to stem rural out-migration. Candeleda has a population of 6,000 and is mainly supported by agriculture. The fiesta was sponsored by the group Asocamu, which was founded in 1995 to encourage rural repopulation.[181]

CONCLUDING COMMENTS

Migration has become increasingly important in the world. Both rural-urban migration and LDR-to-MDR migration present opportunities for the upward mobility of individuals and can result in the flow of remittances to relatives at the place of origin. However, migration can be seen as a source of blight at the destination, as some rural-urban migrants live in unappealing informal settlements. Similarly, low-skilled immigrants are often discriminated against and viewed negatively whether they are in the destination country legally or not. Also, international brain drain helps the MDR destination, while taking needed professionals from the LDR.

The world is becoming increasingly urban, and soon even the LDR population will mainly live in urban areas. Large cities in the LDR continue to grow, while in many MDR countries, middle-sized cities are growing more rapidly than the largest cities. At the same time, rural areas throughout the world suffer from a shortage of professionals, especially health personnel. A variety of schemes to achieve a more equitable geographic distribution of health care professionals has yielded at best mixed results.

✓ Study and Review Online

SUMMARY

1. Migration always involves a geographic move. It also involves a permanent or long-term change of place of residence with a substantial change in daily life. It is sometimes defined as a change of residence across county lines.

2. Residential mobility occurs when a person or a household changes their place of residence without a major change in most aspects of their lives. It is sometimes defined as a residential move within the same county.

3. Gross migration from place A and place B is the number of people who migrated from A to B in the relevant time period. Gross migration from place B to place A is the number of people who migrated from B to A in the relevant time period. Net migration between place A and place B is the difference between the migration stream from A to B and the migration stream from B to A. If more people migrate from place A to place B than from place B to place A, there is positive net migration to place B and negative net migration from place A.

4. Gravity models of migration are based on models of the attraction between particles in physics, in which the distance between and the mass of particles are interpreted as the distance between places and the populations of the two places in order to estimate the migration stream between two places.

5. In economic models of migration, the decision whether to migrate is thought to mainly depend on the extent to which the potential migrant is likely to increase his or her income or wage rate by migrating, as opposed to remaining at the place of origin.

6. Sociological models of migration introduce personal and contextual factors that influence the perception of the desirability of migration. This includes factors that reduce or increase the perceived risk involved in migration.

7. Political science and political considerations are very important in international migration, due to the key role of immigration laws.

8. Migration is selective by education, with more educated people more likely to migrate than less educated people.

9. Migrants have a distinct age pattern, with elevated migration rates for young children and high migration rates in the younger working ages. If there is substantial migration associated with retirement, there can be a minor peak in migration rates around the normal retirement age.

10. A population's overall migration rate and residential mobility rate are composed of frequent moves by a portion of the population, called "movers," and infrequent moves by the rest of the population, called "stayers."

11. Internal migration occurs within one country. Much internal migration occurs for marriage, for settlement of sparsely populated areas, or for work, including temporary migration to urban places.

12. Most countries would like to slow down rural-urban migration and increase urban-rural migration, but only a few countries have had laws restricting or requiring internal movement.

13. The geographic center of the U.S. population has moved west since the eighteenth century, mostly due to internal migration. The South and West have mainly gained population from internal migration, while the Northeast and Midwest have mainly lost population.

14. Since the 1970s, the magnitude of internal migration in the United States has declined.

15. There was substantial migration of African Americans from the South to other regions in 1900–1970. This flow was reversed after 1990, with more African Americans migrating to the South than leaving the South.

16. International migration has generally flowed from the LDR to the MDR.

17. Most international migrants from the LDR can be divided into (1) those with low skills who often hold jobs that MDR citizens are unwilling to perform, and (2) highly skilled persons whom MDR countries are eager to receive. The "brain drain" of highly skilled persons is costly to their origin countries.

18. Most refugees have come from the LDR and have been taken in by other LDR countries. Most refugees return to their home countries within 5 years.

19. U.S. immigration policies have changed over time. Often, they have discriminated against people from particular parts of the world, such as Southern or Eastern Europe or Asia. The Immigration and Nationality Act of 1965 shifted from preferences based on national origins to preferences based on skills and family ties. This law contributed to a large increase in the racial diversity of the United States.

20. Some theorists have seen urban life as dehumanizing and destructive, while others have seen urban places as centers of opportunity, economic betterment, and open-mindedness.

21. By 2010, a majority of the world's population lived in urban places, and 45% of the population of the LDR lived in urban places.

22. Population in much of the world has become increasingly concentrated in urban agglomerations, and these agglomerations have become larger over time.

23. In some more developed countries, there has been a falling off of the growth of large cities and an increase in the size of smaller urban places, in a phenomenon called counterurbanization.

24. In the LDR, poverty is increasingly concentrated in rural areas, although remittances, whether domestic or international, raise the standard of living of some rural households.

25. Rural areas in both the LDR and MDR face challenges in attracting and retaining needed professionals, especially physicians.

26. In both the LDR and the MDR, rural-urban migration contributes to the aging of the rural population.

KEY TERMS

QUESTIONS FOR DISCUSSION AND REVIEW

1. Discuss the factors that are considered in designating a move as an instance of migration.
2. What are the advantages and disadvantages to a less developed country of having a high rate of emigration?
3. What are the reasons why many people in developed countries oppose immigration?
4. What are the advantages and disadvantages to a developed country of having a high rate of immigration?
5. Discuss the following statement: "In the next few decades, population policy will shift its focus from fertility to migration."
6. Discuss the following statement: "Seasonal migration of agricultural workers from Mexico to the United States should not be defined as migration."
7. Discuss how a change from low net in-migration to high net in-migration would affect population growth and the proportion of the population over age 60 in a population.
8. Discuss the role of individual motivations to migrate and of laws restricting migration in internal migration and in international migration.
9. Discuss the factors that are considered in designating a place as urban.

NOTES

1. S. Goldstein. 1976. "Facets of Redistribution: Research Challenges and Opportunities," *Demography*, 13: 423–443; Leon F. Bouvier, Dudley L. Poston, Jr., and Nanbin Benjamin Zhai. 1997. "Population Growth Impacts of Zero Net International Migration," *International Migration Review*, 31: 294–311; and R. Skeldon. 2005. "Migration and Mobility," *Asia-Pacific Population Journal*, 20: 5–9.
2. Calvin Goldscheider. 1971. *Population, Modernization and Social Structure*, Boston: Little, Brown, 64.
3. U.S. Census Bureau. 2011. *Migration Data from the U.S. Census Bureau*, Webinar, November 15, http://www.census.gov/newsroom/releases/pdf/2011-11-15_migration_slides.pdf (accessed August 26, 2012).
4. Ian Molho. 1986. "Theories of Migration: A Review," *Scottish Journal of Political Economy*, 33: 396–419; Calvin Goldscheider. 1987. "Migration and Social Structure: Analytic Issues and Comparative Perspectives in Developing Nations," *Sociological Forum*, 2: 674–696; and Subrata Ghatak, Paul Levine, and Stephen Wheatley Price. 1996. "Migration Theories and Evidence: An Assessment," *Journal of Economic Surveys*, 10: 159–198.
5. E. G. Ravenstein. 1885. "The Laws of Migration," *Journal of the Statistical Society of London*, 48:

167–235; and E. G. Ravenstein. 1889. "The Laws of Migration, Part II," *Journal of the Statistical Society of London*, 52: 241–301.
6. D. B. Grigg. 1977. "E. G. Ravenstein and the 'Laws of Migration,'" *Journal of Historical Geography*, 3: 41–54.
7. E. C. Young. 1924. *The Movement of Farm Population*, Bulletin 426, Ithaca, NY: Cornell Agricultural Experiment Station.
8. George Kingsley Zipf. 1946. "The Hypothesis: On the Intercity Movement of Persons," *American Sociological Review*, 11: 677–686.
9. Samuel A. Stouffer. 1940. "Intervening Opportunities: A Theory Relating Mobility and Distance," *American Sociological Review*, 5: 845–867; and Samuel A. Stouffer. 1960. "Intervening Opportunities and Competing Migrants," *Journal of Regional Science*, 2: 1–26.
10. Everett S. Lee. 1966. "A Theory of Migration," *Demography*, 3: 47–57.
11. Wilbur Zelinsky. 1971. "The Hypothesis of the Mobility Transition," *Geographical Review*, 61: 219–249.
12. Robert B. Ekelund, Jr., and Robert F. Hébert. 2002. "Retrospectives: The Origins of Neoclassical Microeconomics," *The Journal of Economic Perspectives*, 16: 197–215.

13. W. Arthur Lewis. 1954. "Economic Development with Unlimited Supplies of Labor," *The Manchester School*, 22: 139–191; W. Arthur Lewis. 1955. *The Theory of Economic Growth*, Homewood, IL: Richard D. Irwin; and Gary S. Fields. 2004. "Dualism in the Labor Market: A Perspective on the Lewis Model after Half a Century," *The Manchester School*, 72: 724–735.

14. M. B. Doeringer and M. J. Piore. 1971. *Internal Labor Markets and Manpower Analysis*, Lexington, MA: D. C. Heath.

15. Michael J. Piore. 1979. *Birds of Passage: Migrant Labor in Industrial Societies*, Cambridge: Cambridge University Press.

16. John R. Harris and Michael P. Todaro. 1970. "Migration, Unemployment and Development: A Two-Sector Analysis," *The American Economic Review*, 60: 126–142; S. V. Lall, H. Selod, and Z. Shalizi. 2006. *Rural-Urban Migration in Developing Countries: A Survey of Theoretical Predictions and Empirical Findings*, Policy Research Working Paper No. 3915, Washington, DC: World Bank, http://www-wds.worldbank.org/external/default/WDSContentServer/IW3P/IB/2006/05/05/000016406_20060505110833/Rendered/PDF/wps (accessed November 14, 2013); and Gary S. Fields. 1975. "Rural-Urban Migration, Urban Unemployment and Underemployment, and Job-Search Activity in LDCs," *Journal of Development Economics*, 2: 165–187.

17. Ryoshin Minami. 1973. *The Turning Point in Economic Development: Japan's Experience*, Tokyo: Kinokuniya Bookstore; Ryoshin Minami. 1968. "The Turning Point in the Japanese Economy," *The Quarterly Journal of Economics*, 82; 380–402; and Fang Cai. 2011. "*Hukou* System Reform and Unification of Rural-Urban Social Welfare," *China & World Economy*, 19: 33–48.

18. Oded Stark and David E. Bloom. 1985. "The New Economics of Labor Migration," *The American Economic Review*, 75: 173–178.

19. Oded Stark and J. Edward Taylor. 1989. "Relative Deprivation and International Migration," *Demography*, 26: 1–14.

20. Alden Speare, Jr., and John Harris. 1986. "Education, Earnings and Migration in Indonesia," *Economic Development and Cultural Change*, 34: 223–244.

21. Yao Lu. 2008. "Test of the 'Healthy Migrant Hypothesis': A Longitudinal Analysis of Health Selectivity of Internal Migration in Indonesia," *Social Science & Medicine*, 67: 1331–1339; Guillermina Jasso, Douglas S. Massey, Mark R. Rosenzweig, and James P. Smith. 2004. "Immigrant Health: Selectivity and Acculturation," in *Critical Perspectives on Racial and Ethnic Differences in Health in Late Life*, ed. N. B. Anderson, R. A. Bulatao, and B. Cohen, Washington, DC: National Academies Press, 227–266; and Alberto Palloni and Elizabeth Arias. 2004. "Paradox Lost: Explaining the Hispanic Adult Mortality Advantage," *Demography*, 41: 385–415.

22. Andrei Rogers and Luis J. Castro. 1981. *Model Migration Schedules*, Research Report 81-30, November, Laxenburg, Austria: International Institute for Applied Systems Analysis.

23. Herve Le Bras and Jean-Claude Chesnais. 1976. "Cycle de l'habitat et age de habitants," [The housing cycle and age of inhabitants] *Population*, 31: 269–200.

24. M. Tienda and K. Booth. 1991. "Gender, Migration and Social Change," *International Sociology*, 6, 51–72; and Pierette Hondagneu-Sotelo and Cynthia Cranford. 2006. "Gender and Migration," in *Handbook of the Sociology of Gender*, Part II, ed. Jane Saltman Chavetz, New York: Springer, 105–125.

25. Eddie Wrenn. 2012. "'Humiliating Punishments for Working Too Slow, Bars on the Windows and Squalid Dorms': Inside the Factory That Makes iPhone 5," *Mail Online*, September 12, http://www.dailymail.co.uk/sciencetech/article-2202170/iPhone-5-release-Inside-shocking-conditions-Foxconn-factory.html (accessed September 29, 2012).

26. Gunnar Myrdal. 1957. *Rich Lands and Poor*, New York: Harper and Row.

27. Douglas S. Massey, Joaquin Arango, Graeme Hugo, Ali Kouaouci, Adela Pellegrino, and J. Edward Taylor. 1993. "Theories of International Migration: A Review and Appraisal," *Population and Development Review*, 19: 431–466.

28. Graeme J. Hugo. 1981. "Village-Community Ties, Village Norms, and Ethnic and Social Networks: A Review of Evidence from the Third World," in *Migration Decision Making: Multidisciplinary Approaches to Microlevel Studies in Developed and Developing Countries*, ed. Gordon F. De Jong and Robert W. Gardner, New York: Pergamon, 186–225.

29. Graeme J. Hugo. 1981. "Village-Community Ties, Village Norms, and Ethnic and Social Networks: A Review of Evidence from the Third World," in *Migration Decision Making: Multidisciplinary Approaches to Microlevel Studies in Developed and Developing Countries*, ed. Gordon F. De Jong and Robert W. Gardner, New York: Pergamon, 186–225; and John Charles Caldwell. 1969. *African Rural-Urban Migration*, New York: Columbia University Press.

30. Douglas S. Massey, Joaquin Arango, Graeme Hugo, Ali Kouaouci, Adela Pellegrino, and J. Edward Taylor. 1993. "Theories of International Migration: A Review and Appraisal," *Population and Development Review*, 19: 431–466.

31. Immanuel Wallerstein. 1974. *The Modern World System: Capitalist Agriculture and the Origins of the European World Economy in the Sixteenth Century*, New York: Academic Press; and Michael Hechter. 1975. *Internal Colonialism: The Celtic Fringe in British National Development*, Berkeley: University of California Press.

32. Douglas S. Massey, Joaquin Arango, Graeme Hugo, Ali Kouaouci, Adela Pellegrino, and J. Edward Taylor. 1993. "Theories of International Migration: A Review and Appraisal," *Population and Development Review*, 19: 431–466.

33. Alejandro Portes. 1997. "Immigration Theory for a New Century: Some Problems and Opportunities," *International Migration Review*, 31: 799–825; Alejandro Portes and John Walton. 1981. *Labor, Class, and the International System*, New York: Academic Press; and Craig Gurian. 2012. *On Population: U.S. Remains in Full Denial Mode*, Remapping Debate, May 2, http://www.remappingdebate .org/article/population-us-remains-full-denial -mode (accessed May 4, 2012).

34. Sidney Goldstein. 1954. "Repeated Migration as a Factor in High Mobility Rates," *American Sociological Review*, 19: 536–541.

35. Peter A. Morrison. 1971. "Chronic Movers and the Future Redistribution of Population: A Longitudinal Analysis," *Demography*, 8: 171–184.

36. Charles B. Keely, Holly E. Reed, and Ronald J. Waldman. 2001. "Understanding Mortality Patterns in Complex Human Emergencies," in *Forced Migration and Mortality*, ed. Holly E. Reed and Charles B. Keely, Washington DC: National Academies Press.

37. Jon Pedersen. 1995. "Drought Migration and Population Growth in the Sahel: The Case of the Malian Gourma: 1900–1991," *Population Studies*, 49: 111–126; and R. McLeman and B. Smit. 2006. "Migration as an Adaptation to Climate Change," *Climatic Change*, 76: 31–53.

38. Susana B. Adamo and Alexander de Sherbinin. 2011. "The Impact of Climate Change on the Spatial Distribution of the Population and on Migration," in United Nations, *Population Distribution, Urbanization, Internal Migration and Development: An International Perspective*, New York: United Nations, 161–195, http://www.un.org /esa/population/publications/PopDistrib Urbanization/PopulationDistribution Urbanization.pdf (accessed July 21, 2012).

39. Salvador Barrios, Luisito Bertinelli, and Eric Strobl. 2006. "Climatic Change and Rural–Urban Migration: The Case of Sub-Saharan Africa," *Journal of Urban Economics*, 60: 357–371.

40. Eric R. Jensen and Dennis A. Ahlburg. 2004. "Why Does Migration Decrease Fertility? Evidence from the Philippines," *Population Studies*, 58: 219–231.

41. John J. Macisco, Jr., Leon F. Bouvier, and Martha Jane Renzi. 1969. "Migration Status, Education and Fertility in Puerto Rico, 1960," *The Milbank Memorial Fund Quarterly*, 47: 167–186.

42. Susan J. Watts. 1983–1984. "Marriage Migration: A Neglected Form of Long-Term Mobility: A Case Study from Ilorin, Nigeria," *International Migration Review*, 17: 682–698; and Rajni Palriwala and Uberoi. 2005. "Marriage and Migration in India: Gender Issues," *Indian Journal of Gender Studies*, 12: v–xxix.

43. U.S. Census Bureau. 2011. *Mean Center of Population for the United States: 1790 to 2010*, http://www.census.gov/geo/www/2010census /centerpop2010/centerpop_mean2010.pdf (accessed September 4, 2012).

44. Donald W. Treadgold. 1957. *The Great Siberian Migration*, Princeton, NJ: Princeton University Press; George J. Demko. 1969. *The Russian Colonization of Kazakhstan*, Bloomington: Indiana University Press; Colin MacAndrews. 1978. "Transmigration in Indonesia: Prospects and Problems," *Asian Survey*, 18: 458–472; Frederick J. Turner. 1921. *The Frontier in American History*, New York: Henry Holt, http://xroads.virginia .edu/~HYPER/TURNER/ (accessed September 3, 2012); and Richard Hofstadter and Seymour Martin Lipset, eds. 1968. *Turner and the Sociology of the Frontier*, New York: Basic Books.

45. Ronald Skeldon. 1997. "Rural-to-Urban Migration and Its Implications for Poverty Alleviation," *Asia-Pacific Population Journal*, 12: 3–16.

46. Brij Maharaj. 2009. "Migrants and Urban Rights: Politics of Xenophobia in South African Cities," *L'Espace Politique*, 8, http://espacepolitique .revues.org/index1402.html (accessed September 14, 2012).

47. Murray Chapman and R. Mansell Prothero. 1983–1984. "Themes on Circulation in the Third World," *International Migration Review*, 17: 597–632.

48. Data in this section are from United Nations Population Division. 2010. *World Population Policies 2009*, New York: United Nations, http:// www.un.org/esa/population/publications /wpp2009/wpp2009.htm (accessed September 2, 2012); and United Nations Population Division. 2012. *World Population Policies 2011*, New York: United Nations, http://www .un.org/en/development/desa/population /publications/policy/world-population -policies-2011.shtml (accessed April 15, 2013).

49. Jeannette Wolfley. 1991. "Jim Crow, Indian Style: The Disenfranchisement of Native Americans," *American Indian Law Review*, 16: 167–202; Russell Thornton. 1984. "Cherokee Population Losses during the Trail of Tears: A New Perspective and a New Estimate," *Ethnohistory*, 31: 289–300;

Gary D. Sandefur. 1989. "American Indian Reservations: The First Underclass Areas?" *Focus*, 12: 37–41, http://www.irp.wisc.edu/publications/focus/pdfs/foc121f.pdf (accessed August 9, 2012); and C. Matthew Snipp. 1986. "American Indians and Natural Resource Development: Indigenous Peoples' Land, Now Sought After, Has Produced New Indian-White Problems," *American Journal of Economics and Sociology*, 45: 457–474.

50. Larry Rohter. 2004. "Mapuche Indians in Chile Struggle to Take Back Forests," *New York Times*, August 11; and Jane Newbold. 2004. "Balancing Economic Considerations and the Rights of Indigenous People: The Mapuche People of Chile," *Sustainable Development*, 12: 175–182.

51. J. R. Minkel. 2007. "Confirmed: The U.S. Census Bureau Gave Up Names of Japanese-Americans in WW II," *Scientific American*, March 30, http://www.scientificamerican.com/article.cfm?id=confirmed-the-us-census-b&sc=I100322 (accessed July 19, 2012); and Alan Taylor. 2011. "World War II: Internment of Japanese Americans," *The Atlantic*, August 21, http://www.theatlantic.com/infocus/2011/08/world-war-ii-internment-of-japanese-americans/100132/ (accessed July 19, 2012).

52. Yoav Peled. 1989. *Class and Ethnicity in the Pale: The Political Economy of Jewish Workers' Nationalism in Late Imperial Russia*, New York: St. Martin's Press.

53. Isabelle Kreindler. 1986. "The Soviet Deported Nationalities; A Summary and an Update," *Soviet Studies*, 38: 387–405; Brian Glyn Williams. 2010. "Hidden Ethnocide in the Soviet Muslim Borderlands: The Ethnic Cleansing of the Crimean Tatars," *Journal of Genocide Research*, 4: 357–373; and Michael Gelb. 1996. "The Western Finnic Minorities and the Origins of the Stalinist Nationalities Deportations," *Nationalities Papers*, 24: 238–265.

54. Ira N. Gang and Robert C. Stuart. 1999. "Mobility Where Mobility Is Illegal: Internal Migration and City Growth in the Soviet Union," *Journal of Population Economics*, 12: 117–134: and Marc Garcelon. 2001. "Colonizing the Subject: The Genealogy and Legacy of the Soviet Internal Passport," in *Documenting Individual Identity: The Development of State Practices in the Modern World*, ed. Jane Caplan and John C. Torpey, Princeton, NJ: Princeton University Press.

55. Cynthia Buckley. 1995. "The Myth of Managed Migration: Migration Control and Market in the Soviet Period," *Slavic Review*, 54: 896–916; Ira N. Gang and Robert C. Stuart. 1999. "Mobility Where Mobility Is Illegal: Internal Migration and City Growth in the Soviet Union," *Journal of Population Economics*, 12: 117–134; and Michael Gentile. 2004. "Former Closed Cities and Urbanisation in the FSU: An Exploration in Kazakhstan," *Europe-Asia Studies*, 56: 263–278. The example in Box 12.1 is based on a personal conversation that took place in 1989.

56. Rose Maria Li. 1989. "Migration to China's Northern Frontier 1953–82," *Population and Development Review*, 15: 503–538.

57. Personal conversation in 1989.

58. Xueguang Zhou and Liren Hou. 1999. "Children of the Cultural Revolution: The State and the Life Course in the People's Republic of China," *American Sociological Review*, 64: 12–36.

59. Kam Wing Chan and Ying Hu. 2003. "Urbanization in China in the 1990s: New Definition, Different Series, and Revised Trends," *The China Review*, 3: 49–71.

60. Xiaogang Wu and Donald J. Treiman. 2004. "The Household Registration System and Social Stratification in China: 1955–1996," *Demography*, 41: 363–384.

61. Kam Wing Chan. 2010. "The Household Registration System and Migrant Labor in China: Notes on a Debate," *Population and Development Review*, 36: 357–364; and Xiaogang Wu. 2005. *Registration Status, Labor Migration, and Socioeconomic Attainment in China's Segmented Labor Markets*, Population Studies Center Research Report 05-579, July, Ann Arbor: Population Studies Center, University of Michigan.

62. Xiushi Yang and Sidney Goldstein. 1990. "Population Movement in Zhejiang Province, China: The Impact of Government Policies," *International Migration Review*, 24: 509–533; and Chun-Chung Au and J. Vernon Henderson. 2006. "How Migration Restrictions Limit Agglomeration and Productivity in China," *Journal of Development Economics*, 80: 350–388.

63. Bob Davis. 2013. "Beijing Puzzles Over Urban Growth," Wall Street Journal, May 9, http://online.wsj.com/news/articles/SB10001424127887323361804578389943868485434 (accessed December 8, 2013); Xinhua News Agency. 2013. "China's Largest City Relaxes Residency Policies for Migrants," June 20, *People's Daily Online*, http://english.people.com.cn/90882/8291585.html (accessed December 8, 2013).

64. Leonard Thompson. 2001. *A History of South Africa*. New Haven: Yale University Press. Townships, which had many urban characteristics, were not considered cities in South Africa during apartheid.

65. Figure 12.7 is based on Barbara A. Anderson. 2005. "Migration in South Africa in Comparative Perspective," in *Migration in South and Southern Africa: Dynamics and Determinants*, ed. Pieter Kok, Derik Gelderblom, John O. Oucho, and Johan van Zyl, Pretoria: Human Sciences Research Council, 97–117.

66. Jacob Mincer. 1978. "Family Migration Decisions," *Journal of Political Economy*, 86: 749–773.

67. Daniel T. Lichter. 1982. "The Migration of Dual-Worker Families: Does the Wife's Job Matter?" *Social Science Quarterly*, 63: 48–57.

68. Steven Tenn. 2010. "The Relative Importance of the Husband's and Wife's Characteristics in Family Migration, 1960–2000," *Journal of Population Economics*, 23: 1319–1337.

69. Bureau of Labor Statistics. 2012. *Wives Who Earn More Than Their Husbands, 1987–2010*, http://www.bls.gov/cps/wives_earn_more.htm (accessed July 22, 2012).

70. http://www.census.gov/geo/www/us_regdiv.pdf (accessed April 23, 2013).

71. U.S. Census Bureau. 2012. *Current Population Survey Data on Geographical Mobility/Migration*, http://www.census.gov/hhes/migration/data/cps.html (accessed August 30, 2012).

72. U.S. Census Bureau. 2012. *Current Population Survey Data on Geographical Mobility/Migration*, http://www.census.gov/hhes/migration/data/cps.html (accessed August 30, 2012).

73. William H. Frey. 2009. *The Great American Migration Slowdown: Regional and Metropolitan Dimensions*, Washington, DC: Brookings Institution; and Raven Molloy, Christopher L. Smith, and Abigail Wozniak. 2011. *Internal Migration in the United States*, Finance and Economics Discussion Series 2011-30, May, Washington, DC: Federal Reserve Board, http://www.federalreserve.gov/pubs/feds/2011/201130/201130pap.pdf (accessed April 18, 2013).

74. Campbell Gibson and Kay Jung. 2002. *Historical Census Statistics on Population Totals by Race, 1790 to 1990, and by Hispanic Origin, 1970 to 1990, for The United States, Regions, Divisions, and States*, Working Paper Series No. 56, September, Washington, DC: U.S. Census Bureau, http://www.census.gov/population/www/documentation/twps0056/twps0056.html (accessed October 29, 2012); U.S. Census Bureau. 2001. *The Black Population: 2000*, Census 2000 Brief, August, Washington, DC: U.S. Census Bureau, http://health-equity.pitt.edu/766/1/The_Black_Population_2000.pdf (accessed October 29, 2012); and Census Bureau. 2001. *The Black Population: 2010*, Census 2010 Briefs, September, Washington, DC: U.S. Census Bureau, http://www.census.gov/prod/cen2010/briefs/c2010br-06.pdf (accessed October 29, 2012).

75. Stewart E. Tolnay and E. M. Beck. 1990. "Black Flight: Lethal Violence and the Great Migration, 1900–1930," *Social Science History*, 14: 347–370; and Richard Hornbeck and Suresh Naidu. 2012. *When the Levee Breaks: Black Migration and Economic Development in the American South*, NBER Working Paper 18296, August, Cambridge, MA: National Bureau of Economic Research, http://www.nber.org/papers/w18296 (accessed October 29, 2012).

76. Jacob L. Vigdor. 2002. "The Pursuit of Opportunity: Explaining Selective Black Migration," *Journal of Urban Economics*, 51: 391–417.

77. U.S. Kerner Commission. 1968. *Report of the National Advisory Commission on Civil Disorders*, Washington, DC: Government Printing Office.

78. Kevin E. McHugh. 1987. "Black Migration Reversal in the United States," *Geographical Review*, 77: 171–182; and William H. Frey. 2004. *The New Great Migration: Black Americans' Return to the South 1965–2000*, Washington, DC: Brookings Institution, http://www.brookings.edu/~/media/research/files/reports/2004/5/demographics%20frey/20040524_frey (accessed October 29, 2012).

79. William W. Falk, Larry L. Hunt, and Matthew O. Hunt. 2004. "Return Migrations of African-Americans to the South: Reclaiming a Land of Promise, Going Home, or Both?" *Rural Sociology*, 69: 490–509; Larry L. Hunt, Matthew O. Hunt, and William W. Falk. 2008. "Who Is Headed South? U.S. Migration Trends in Black and White, 1970–2000," *Social Forces*, 87: 95–119; and Stewart E. Tolnay. 2003. "The African American 'Great Migration' and Beyond," *Annual Review of Sociology*, 29: 209–232.

80. World Bank. 2011. *Migration and Remittances Factbook 2011*, Washington, DC: World Bank, http://siteresources.worldbank.org/INTLAC/Resources/Factbook2011-Ebook.pdf (accessed August 6, 2012).

81. Table 12.3 is from United Nations. 2011. *The Age and Sex of Migrants 2011*, http://www.un.org/esa/population/publications/2011Migration_Chart/2011IttMig_chart.htm (accessed January 2, 2012).

82. Wayne A. Cornelius. 1981. "Mexican Migration to the United States," *Proceedings of the Academy of Political Science*, 34: 67–77; and Martin Ruhs. 2006. "The Potential of Temporary Migration Programmes in Future International Migration Policy," *International Labour Review*, 145: 7–36.

83. Michael Hofer, Nancy Rytina, and Bryan Baker. 2012. *Estimates of the Unauthorized Immigrant Population Residing in the United States: January 2011*, March, Washington, DC: Office of Immigration Statistics, Department of Homeland Security, http://www.dhs.gov/xlibrary/assets/statistics/publications/ois_ill_pe_2011.pdf (accessed September 2, 2012).

84. Clandestino Research Project. 2009. *Size and Development of Irregular Migration to the EU*, European

Union, October, http://irregular-migration.net//fileadmin/irregular-migration/dateien/4.Background_Information/4.2.Policy_Briefs_EN/ComparativePolicyBrief_SizeOfIrregular-Migration_Clandestino_Nov09_2.pdf (accessed August 7, 2012).

85. Matthew Brunwasser. 2007. "Romania, a Poor Land, Imports Poorer Workers," *New York Times*, April 11.

86. Veronica Uy. 2007. "RP-UAE Sign Pact to Boost Filipino Workers' Welfare," Inquirer.net, http://services.inquirer.net/print/print?article_id=20070410-59502 (accessed October 26, 2010); and OFWNgayon. 2010. "RP, Caritas Lebanon Sign Pact to Assist OFW's" October 4, http://www.ofwngayon.com/2010/10/rp-caritas-lebanon-sign-pact-assist-ofws/ (accessed November 25, 2011).

87. Jason DeParle. 2010. "Downturn Does Little to Slow Migration," *New York Times*, May 27.

88. Steven Greenhouse. 2008. "Queens Factory Is Found to Owe Workers $5.3 Million," *New York Times*, July 23; Steven Greenhouse. 2007. "Where Delivery Is a Mainstay, a Rebellion over Pay," *New York Times*, April 15; and Steven Greenhouse. 2008. "Restaurant Owners Charged on More Than 400 Counts," *New York Times*, December 3.

89. Migration Information Source. 2009. *United Kingdom: A Reluctant Country of Immigration*, Migration Information Source Website, July, http://www.migrationinformation.org/Profiles/display.cfm?ID=736 (accessed August 7, 2012).

90. Marko Vujicic, Pascal Zum, Khassoum Diallo, Orvill Adams, and Mario R. Dal Poz. 2004. "The Role of Wages in the Migration of Health Care Professionals from Developing Countries," *Human Resources for Health, Biomed Central*, 2: 3, http://www.human-resources-health.com/content/pdf/1478-4491-2-3.pdf (accessed September 12, 2012).

91. Ghana Home Page. 2007. "Brain Drain Killing Healthcare Sector," http://www.ghanaweb.com/GhanaHomePage/News Archive/artikel.php?ID=211302 (accessed November 25, 2011).

92. World Bank. 2011. *Migration and Remittances Factbook 2011*, Washington, DC: World Bank, http://siteresources.worldbank.org/INTLAC/Resources/Factbook2011-Ebook.pdf (accessed August 6, 2012).

93. Robert L. Phillips, Jr., Stephen Petterson, George E. Fryer, Jr., and Walter Rosser. 2007. "The Canadian Contribution to the US Physician Workforce," *Canadian Medical Association Journal*, 176: 1083–1087.

94. Suzanne Daley and Nicholas Kulish. 2012. "Brain Drain Feared as German Jobs Lure Southern Europeans," *New York Times*, April 28.

95. Richard H. Adams, Jr., and John Page. 2005. "Do International Migration and Remittances Reduce Poverty in Developing Countries?" *World Development*, 33: 1645–1669.

96. World Bank. 2011. *Migration and Remittances Factbook 2011*, Washington, DC: World Bank, http://siteresources.worldbank.org/INTLAC/Resources/Factbook2011-Ebook.pdf (accessed August 6, 2012).

97. Anita Pugliese and Julie Ray. 2011. *Three Percent Worldwide Get International Remittances*, Gallup Poll, May 6, http://www.gallup.com/poll/147446/Three-Percent-Worldwide-International-Remittances.aspx (accessed June 19, 2012).

98. Jeffrey Passel, D'Vera Cohn, and Ana Gonzalez-Barrera. 2012. *Net Migration from Mexico Falls to Zero—and Perhaps Less*, Washington, D.C.: Pew Research Center, http://www.pewhispanic.org/files/2012/04/Mexican-migrants-report_final.pdf (accessed February 11, 2014).

99. Marc Lacey. 2009. "Money Trickles North as Mexicans Help Relatives," *New York Times*, November 16.

100. Nina Bernstein. 2007. "Tax Returns Rise for Immigrants in U.S. Illegally," *New York Times*, April 16.

101. Paul H. Nitze School of Advanced International Studies. 2011. *International Refugee Law*, Johns Hopkins, http://www.sais-jhu.edu/cmtoolkit/issues-in-practice/safe-havens/intl-refugee-law.htm (accessed September 3, 2012).

102. UN High Commission for Refugees. *States Parties to the 1951 Convention Relating to the Status of Refugees and the 1967 Protocol*, http://www.unhcr.org/protect/PROTECTION/3b73b0d63.pdf (accessed September 3, 2012); UN High Commission for Refugees. *Information on Refugee Resettlement*, http://www.unhcr.org.ua/img/uploads/.../14%20ENG%20RST%20Brochure.doc (accessed September 3, 2012); BBC News. 2012. "Israel Urged to Admit African Migrants on Egypt Border," *BBC News*, September 6, http://www.bbc.co.uk/news/world-middle-east-19503736 (accessed September 6, 2012); and Isabel Kershner. 2012. "Israel to Admit 3 of 21 Africans Waiting in Desert," *New York Times*, September 7.

103. United Nations. 2011. *UNHCR Statistical Yearbook 2010: Trends in Displacement, Protection and Solutions*, Geneva: UN High Commission for Refugees, http://www.unhcr.org/4ef9cc9c9.html (accessed December 27, 2011).

104. Damien Cave. 2012. "Strategy for Syrian Refugees in Turkey Is on Clinton Agenda," *New York Times*,

August 10; Rick Gladstone and Damien Cave. 2012. "Torrent of Syrian Refugees Strains Aid Effort and Region," *New York Times*, August 24; Edward Wong. 2012. "China Forces Ethnic Kachin Refugees back to a Conflict Zone in Myanmar's North," *New York Times*, August 23; and Edward Wong. 2012. "Chinese Deny Forcing Kachin Refugees Back to Myanmar," *New York Times*, August 25.

105. Matt Siegel. 2012. "130 Rescued after Shipwreck South of Indonesia," *New York Times*, June 27; Reuters. 2012. "Australia's Plan for Migrants Draws Warning," *New York Times*, August 17; and Matt Siegel. 2012. "Australia Increases Refugee Quota," *New York Times*, August 23.

106. Penelope Matthew. 2012. "They're Not 'Economic Migrants'—Why Refugees and Asylum-Seekers Have the Right to Work," Asylum Access, http:// rtwasylumaccess.wordpress.com/2012/01/25 /theyre-not-economic-migrants-why-refugees-and -asylum-seekers-have-the-right-to-work/ (accessed August 26, 2012).

107. Monika Kiwanuka and Tamlyn Monson. 2009. *Zimbabwean Migration into Southern Africa: New Trends and Responses*, Forced Migration Studies Program, Wits University, November, http://www.polity.org.za/article/zimbabwean -migration-into-southern-africa-new-trends-and -responses-november-2009-2009-12-03 (accessed September 15, 2012).

108. UN High Commission for Refugees. 2003. *Framework for Durable Solutions for Refugees and Persons of Concern*, Geneva: UNHCR, http://www.unhcr .org/partners/PARTNERS/3f1408764.pdf (accessed August 6, 2012).

109. Nathalie E. Williams. 2009. *Living with Conflict: The Effect of Community Organizations, Economic Assets and Mass Media Consumption on Migration during Armed Conflict*, PhD dissertation, Department of Sociology, University of Michigan; and Nathalie E. Williams. 2008. *Betting on Life and Livelihood: The Role of Employment and Assets in the Decision to Migrate during Armed Conflict*, paper presented at the Fourth Annual Workshop of the Households in Conflict Network, Yale University, October, http://www.yale.edu /macmillan/ocvprogram/hicn_papers /FourthAnnualWorkshop_Williams.pdf (accessed August 5, 2012).

110. Raymond Bechard. 2010. "Human Trafficking Victims Assisted by United Nations Fund," examiner.com, http://www.examiner. com/human-trafficking-in-national/human- trafficking-victims-assisted-by-united-nations-fund (accessed November 25, 2011).

111. United Nations Office on Drugs and Crime (UNDOC). 2010. *Factsheet on Human Trafficking*, http://www.unodc.org/documents/human -trafficking/UNVTF_fs_HT_EN.pdf (accessed September 8, 2012).

112. David Binder. 2002. "In Europe, Sex Slavery Is Thriving Despite Raids," *New York Times*, October 20.

113. IRIN Africa. 2009. "West Africa: But Is It Really Trafficking?" January 6, http://www.irinnews .org/report.aspx?reportid=82225 (accessed November 25, 2011).

114. United Nations Population Division. 2010. *World Population Policies 2009*, New York: United Nations, http://www.un.org/esa/population /publications/wpp2009/wpp2009.htm (accessed September 2, 2012).

115. Figures 12.14 and 12.15 are from U.S. Department of Homeland Security. 2011. *Yearbook of Immigration Statistics: 2010*, Washington, DC: U.S. Department of Homeland Security, Office of Immigration Statistics, http://www.dhs.gov /xlibrary/assets/statistics/yearbook/2010/ois _yb_2010.pdf (accessed July 27, 2012).

116. Cheryl Shanks. 2001. *Immigration and the Politics of American Sovereignty*, 1890–1990, Ann Arbor: University of Michigan Press.

117. Much of the discussion of U.S. immigration laws through the Immigration and Nationality Act of 1965 is based on Michael C. LeMay. 1987. *From Open Door to Dutch Door*, New York: Praeger; and Jane Guskin and David L. Wilson. 2007. *The Politics of Immigration*, New York: Monthly Review Press, http://thepoliticsofimmigration.org /pages/chronology.htm (accessed September 29, 2012).

118. Texas State Historical Association. 2013. "Bracero Program," http://www.tshaonline.org /handbook/online/articles/omb01 (accessed February 16, 2013).

119. Jorge Durand, Douglas S. Massey, and Emilio A. Parrado. 1999. "The New Era of Mexican Migration to the United States," *The Journal of American History*, 86: 518–536.

120. Edward M. Kennedy. 1981. "Refugee Act of 1980," *International Migration Review*, 15: 141–156.

121. David North. 2010. *A Bailout for Illegal Immigrants? Lessons from the Implementation of the 1986 IRCA Amnesty*, Center for Immigration Studies, http://www.cis.org/irca-amnesty (accessed August 7, 2012).

122. National Conference of State Legislatures. 2012. *Real ID Act of 2005*, http://www.ncsl.org/issues -research/transport/real-id-act-of-2005.aspx (accessed August 6, 2012).

123. Margaret Talbot. 2012. "Future Voters," *The New Yorker*, June 21, http://www.newyorker .com/online/blogs/comment/2012/06 /new-obama-deportation-policy.html (accessed September 29, 2012).

124. NumbersUSA. 2012. *Nations Granting Birthright Citizenship*, https://www.numbersusa.com/content/learn/issues/birthright-citizenship/nations-granting-birthright-citizenship.html (accessed August 6, 2012); Wikipedia. 2012. *Jus soli*, http://en.wikipedia.org/wiki/Jus_soli (accessed August 6, 2012); and Wikipedia. 2012. *Jus sanguinis*, http://en.wikipedia.org/wiki/Jus_sanguinis (accessed August 6, 2012).

125. The Debate Room. 2009. "'Anchor' Babies: No More U.S. Citizenship," *Businessweek*, July 24, http://www.businessweek.com/debateroom/archives/2009/07/anchor_babies_no_more_us_citizenship.html (accessed August 26, 2012); and Reynolds Holding. 2011. "'Anchor Babies': No Getting around the Constitution." *Time*, February 1, http://www.time.com/time/nation/article/0,8599,2045617,00.html (accessed August 26, 2012).

126. Julia Preston. 2012. "Court Rulings Help Illegal Immigrants' College-Bound Children," *New York Times*, September 5.

127. Susanne Wessendorf. 2008. "Culturalist Discourses on Inclusion and Exclusion: the Swiss Citizenship Debate," *Social Anthropology*, 16: 187–202; Marc Helbling. 2008. *Practising Citizenship and Heterogeneous Nationhood*. Amsterdam: Amsterdam University Press; and Elizabeth Olson. 2000. "A Swiss Town Votes to Reject Dozens of Would-Be Citizens," *New York Times*, March 13.

128. Stephen Castles. 1985. "The Guests Who Stayed—The Debate on 'Foreigners Policy' in the German Federal Republic," *International Migration Review*, 19: 517–534; Marc Morje Howard. 2008. "The Causes and Consequences of Germany's New Citizenship Law," *German Politics*, 17: 41–62; and Matthias Bartsch, Andrea Brandt, and Daniel Steinvorth. 2010. "Turkish Immigration to Germany: A Sorry History of Self-Deception and Wasted Opportunities," *Der Spiegel*, September 7, http://www.spiegel.de/international/germany/0,1518,716067-2,00.html (accessed July 20, 2011).

129. European Citizenship: German Citizenship. http://www.immigrationcitizenship.eu/2005/12/german-citizenship.html (accessed June 30, 2011).

130. From Boing-Boing, http://boingboing.net/2009/11/30/the-poster-that-conv.html (accessed August 6, 2011).

131. swissinfo. 2009. *Minaret Result Seen as "Turning Point,"* November 29, http://www.swissinfo.ch/eng/Specials/Islam_and_Switzerland/Minaret_vote/Minaret_result_seen_as_turning_point.html?cid=7793740 (accessed April 28, 2012).

132. Liz Alderman. 2012. "Greek Far Right Hangs a Target on Immigrants," *New York Times*, July 11; and Fraser Nelson. 2004. "Poll Shows Britons Fear Immigration Has Damaged UK," *The Scotsman*, May 27.

133. Max Fisher. 2013. "Greek Police Beat Up Another 'Illegal immigrant' Who's Actually a Tourist," *Washington Post*, January 10.

134. Andrew Jacobs. 2012. "In Singapore, Vitriol against Chinese Newcomers," *New York Times*, July 27; and Brenda S. A. Yeoh and Weiqiang Lin. 2012. *Rapid Growth in Singapore's Immigrant Population Brings Policy Challenges*, April, Migration Information Source, http://www.migrationinformation.org/Profiles/display.cfm?ID=887 (accessed July 27, 2012).

135. BBC News. 2013. "Rare Mass Rally over Singapore Immigration Plans," February 16, http://www.bbc.co.uk/news/world-asia-21485729 (accessed April 22, 2013).

136. UN High Commissioner for Refugees. 2013. *Stateless People*, http://www.unhcr.org/pages/49c3646c155.html (accessed April 23, 2013).

137. UNHCR. 2013. *Media Backgrounder: Millions Are Stateless, Living in Legal Limbo*, http://www.unhcr.org/4e54ec469.html (accessed April 23, 2013).

138. Figure 12.20 is based on Barbara A. Anderson. 2005. "Migration in South Africa in Comparative Perspective," in *Migration in South and Southern Africa: Dynamics and Determinants*, ed. Pieter Kok, Derik Gelderblom, John O. Oucho, and Johan van Zyl, Pretoria: Human Sciences Research Council, 97–117.

139. The following source has each UN member country's definition of urban: United Nations. 2012. *World Urbanization Prospects, the 2011 Revision: Data Sources/ Statistical Concepts (Definitions)*, http://esa.un.org/unpd/wup/CD-ROM/Data-Sources.htm (accessed August 22, 2012).

140. U.S. Census Bureau. 2012. *2010 Census Urban and Rural Classification and Urban Area Criteria*, http://www.census.gov/geo/www/ua/2010urbanruralclass.html (accessed July 30, 2012).

141. V. Gordon Childe. 1950. "The Urban Revolution," *The Town Planning Review*, 21: 3–17.

142. Jose Harris, ed. 2001. *Tönnies: Community and Civil Society*, Cambridge: Cambridge University Press.

143. Karl Marx and Friedrich Engels. 1848/1967. *The Communist Manifesto*, trans. A. J. P. Taylor, London: Penguin; and Friedrich Engels. 1845/1968. *The Condition of the Working Class in England*, Stanford, CA: Stanford University Press.

144. Fritz Ringer. 2007. "Max Weber on the Origins and Character of the Western City," *Critical Quarterly*, 36: 12–18; and A. I. Mahbub Uddin Ahmed. 2004. "Weber's Perspective on the City and Culture, Contemporary Urbanization and Bangladesh," *Bangladesh e-Journal of Sociology*,

1: 1–13, http://www.bangladeshsociology .org/Max%20Weber%20-%20Mahbub%20 Ahmed,%20PDF.pdf (accessed August 29, 2012).

145. Georg Simmel. 1902/1964. "The Metropolis and Mental Life," in *The Sociology of Georg Simmel*, ed. Kurt H. Wolff, New York: Free Press, 409–424.

146. Emile Durkheim. 1893. *De la division du travail social; étude sur l'organisation des sociétés supérieures* [The Division of Labor in Society: A Study of the Higher Organization of Societies], Paris: F. Alcan.

147. Arthur Getis and Judith Getis. 1966. "Christaller's Central Place Theory," *Journal of Geography*, 65: 220–226; and Geraldine Pflieger and Celine Rozenblat. 2010. "Urban Networks and Network Theory: The City as the Connector of Multiple Networks," *Urban Studies*, 47: 2723–2735.

148. Data in Figures 12.22–12.27 are from United Nations. 2012. *World Urbanization Prospects, the 2011 Revision*, http://esa.un.org/unpd/wup/unup /index_panel1.html (accessed April 21, 2013).

149. United States Census Bureau. 2012 *Metropolitan and Micropolitan Statistical Areas Main*, http:// www.census.gov/population/metro/ (accessed July 30, 2012).

150. United Nations. 2012. "Frequently Asked Questions," in *World Urbanization Prospects: The 2011 Revision*, http://esa.un.org/unpd/wup /Documentation/faq.htm (accessed July 30, 2012).

151. United Nations Population Division. *World Urbanization Prospects 2009*, http://esa.un.org /unpd/wup/index.htm (accessed June 29, 2011).

152. Oswald Spengler. 1918/1991. *The Decline of the West*, trans. Charles F. Atkinson. New York: Oxford University Press; and Jean Gottmann. 1961. *Megalopolis: The Urbanized Northeastern Seaboard of the United States*, New York: The Twentieth Century Fund.

153. Richard Florida, Tim Gulden, and Charlotta Mellander. 2008. "The Rise of the Mega-Region," *Cambridge Journal of Regions, Economy and Society*, 1: 459–476.

154. Jean Gottman. 1976. "Megalopolitan Systems around the World," *Ekistics*, 41: 109–113.

155. America2050. 2012. *Megaregions*, http://www .america2050.org/megaregions.html (accessed August 11, 2012).

156. Mei-Ling Hsu. 1985. "Growth and Control of Population in China: The Urban-Rural Contrast," *Annals of the Association of American Geographers*, 75: 241–257; and Judith Banister. 1993. "China's Population Changes and the Economy," in *China's Economic Dilemmas in the 1990s: The Problems of Reforms, Modernization and Interdependence*, ed. Joint Economic Committee of the United States Congress. Armonk, NY: M. E. Sharpe, 234–251.

157. About.com Geography. 2012. *Largest City in the United States*, http://geography.about.com/od /specificplacesofinterest/a/sitkaarea.htm (accessed August 2, 2012); and U.S. Census Bureau. 2012. *Yakutat City and Borough, Alaska*, http:// quickfacts.census.gov/qfd/states/02/02282 .html (accessed August 2, 2012).

158. David Satterthwaite. 2005. *The Scale of Urban Change Worldwide 1950–2000 and Its Underpinnings*, International Institute for Environment and Development, Human Settlements Discussion Paper Series, http://pubs.iied.org /pdfs/9531IIED.pdf (accessed June 30, 2011).

159. George K. Zipf. 1949. *Human Behavior and the Principle of Least Effort*, Reading, MA: Addison-Wesley; and Cesar A. Vapnarsky. 1969. "On Rank-Size Distributions of Cities: An Ecological Approach," *Economic Development and Cultural Change*, 17: 584–595.

160. Mark Jefferson. 1939. "The Law of the Primate City," *Geographical Review*, 29: 226–232.

161. Dennis A. Rondinelli. 1983. "Towns and Small Cities in Developing Countries," *Geographical Review*, 73: 379–395; Low Kwai Sim and G. Balamurugan. 1991. "Urbanization and Urban Water Problems in Southeast Asia: A Case of Unsustainable Development," *Journal of Environmental Management*, 32: 195–209; and Vernon Henderson. 2002. "Urbanization in Developing Countries," *The World Bank Research Observe*, 17: 89–112.

162. Transport for London. Charging zone, http:// www.tfl.gov.uk/roadusers/congestioncharging /6709.aspx (accessed February 11, 2014).

163. World Gazetteer. 2012. http://world-gazetteer .com/wg.php?x=&lng=en&des=wg&geo=-85&sr t=p1nn&col=abcdefghinoq&msz=1500&sbj=pg (accessed September 4, 2012).

164. Frank Hobbs and Nicole Stoops. 2002. *Demographic Trends in the 20th Century*, Census 2000 Special Reports CENSR-4, November, Washington, DC: U.S. Government Printing Office; and Mark Mather, Kelvin Pollard, and Linda A. Jacobsen. 2011. *First Results from the 2010 Census*, July, Washington, DC: Population Reference Bureau.

165. David Metz. 2004. "Travel Time: Variable or Constant?" *Journal of Transport Economics and Policy*, 38: 333–344.

166. David Keeble. 1984. "The Urban-Rural Manufacturing Shift," *Geography*, 69: 163–166.

167. Brian J. L. Berry. 1980. "Urbanization and Counterurbanization in the United States," *Annals of the American Academy of Political and Social Science*, 451: 13–20; Keith H. Halfacree. 1994. "The Importance of 'the Rural' in the Constitution of Counterurbanization: Evidence from England

in the 1980s," *Sociologia Ruralis*, 34: 164–189; and Paul Cloke. 1985. "Counterurbanisation: A Rural Perspective," *Geography*, 70: 13–23.

168. John Wardwell and C. Gilchrist. 1980. "Employment Deconcentration in the Nonmetropolitan Migration Turnaround," *Demography*, 17: 145–158; Glenn V. Fuguitt and Calvin L. Beale. 1996. "Recent Trends in Nonmetropolitan Migration: Toward a New Turnaround?" *Growth and Change*, 27: 156–174; William H. Frey. 1987. "Migration and Depopulation of the Metropolis: Regional Restructuring or Rural Renaissance?" *American Sociological Review*, 52: 240–257; Daniel T. Lichter and Glenn V. Fuguitt. 1980. "Demographic Response to Transportation Innovation: The Case of the Interstate Highway," *Social Forces*, 59: 492–512; and Kenneth M. Johnson and Calvin L. Beale. 1994. "The Recent Revival of Widespread Population Growth in Nonmetropolitan Areas of the United States," *Rural Sociology*, 59: 655–667.

169. Vicente Pinilla, María-Isabel Ayuda, and Luis-Antonio Sáez. 2008. "Rural Depopulation and the Migration Turnaround in Mediterranean Western Europe: A Case Study of Aragon," *Journal of Rural and Community Development*, 3: 1–22.

170. Patrick J. McEwan. 1999. "Recruitment of Rural Teachers in Developing Countries: An Economic Analysis," *Teaching and Teacher Education*, 15: 849–859; and Uta Lehmann, Marjolein Dieleman, and Tim Martineau. 2008. "Staffing Remote Rural Areas in Middle and Low-Income Countries: A Literature Review of Attraction and Retention," *Biomed Central*, 8: 19–28, http://www.biomedcentral.com/1472-6963/8/19 (accessed September 6, 2012).

171. UN General Assembly. 2010. *Global Action Needed to Tackle Urban Squalor as Number of Slum-Dwellers Continues Rising Worldwide, Second Committee Told*, November 2, http://www.un.org/News/Press /docs/2010/gaef3294.doc.htm (accessed September 16, 2012).

172. International Fund for Agricultural Development. 2011. *Agriculture—Pathways to Prosperity in Asia and the Pacific*, March, http://www.ifad.org /pub/apr/pathways.pdf (accessed September 15, 2012); and International Fund for Agricultural Development. 2011. *Rural Poverty Report 2011*, Rome: IFAD, http://www.ifad.org/rpr2011 /report/e/print_rpr2011.pdf (accessed September 12, 2011).

173. Randal C. Archibald. 2011. "A Quake-Scarred Nation Tries a Rural Road to Recovery,"

New York Times, December 25, http://www .nytimes.com/2011/12/25/world/americas /in-countryside-stricken-haiti-seeks-both-food -and-rebirth.html?_r=1&scp=2&sq=Haiti&st=cse (accessed December 25, 2011).

174. Jake Kendall and Jan Sonnenschein. 2012. *Many Sub-Saharan Africans Receive Domestic Remittances*, Gallup Poll, June 18, http://www.gallup.com /poll/155213/Sub-Saharan-Africans-Receive -Domestic-Remittances.aspx?version=print (accessed June 19, 2012).

175. L. B. Shrestha. 2000. "Population Aging in Developing Countries," *Health Affairs*, 19: 204–212.

176. David Wahlberg. 2010. "Rural Health Risk Factor: A Shortage of Doctors," *Wisconsin State Journal*, March 6.

177. Ninemsn. 2006. "AMA Rejects Doctor Shortage Plan," April 20, http://news.ninemsn.com.au /health/96550/ama-rejects-rural-doctor -shortage-plan (accessed April 11, 2007).

178. N. W. Wilson, I. D. Couper, E. De Vries, S. Reid, T. Fish, and B. J. Marais. 2009. "A Critical Review of Interventions to Redress the Inequitable Distribution of Healthcare Professionals to Rural and Remote Areas," *Rural and Remote Health*, 9: 1–21.

179. David Segal. 2011. "Is Law School a Losing Game?" *New York Times*, January 8; Ethan Bronner. 2013. "To Place Graduates, Law Schools Are Opening Firms," *New York Times*, March 7; and Ethan Bronner. 2013. "No Lawyer for 100 Country Miles, So One Rural State Offers to Pay," *New York Times*, April 8.

180. Glenn V. Fuguitt and Timothy B. Heaton. 1995. "The Impact of Migration on the Nonmetropolitan Population Age Structure, 1960–1990," *Population Research and Policy Review*, 14: 215–232; Kevin Kinsella. 2001. "Urban and Rural Dimensions of Global Population Aging: An Overview," *The Journal of Rural Health*, 17: 314–322; William Hollingworth. 2007. "Capitalism Decimated Japan's Rural Youth," *Japan Today*, April 17, http://www.japantoday.com/news/jp/e/tools /print.asp?content=comment&id=1084 (accessed April 16, 2007); and United Nations. 2009 *World Population Aging*, http://www.un.org/esa /population/publications/WPA2009 /WPA2009_WorkingPaper.pdf (accessed September 16, 2012).

181. Alberto Di Lolli and Harold Heckle. 2012. "Women Visit Spanish Town to Ease a Bride Shortage," *Businessweek*, April 22, http://www .businessweek.com/ap/2012-04/D9UA0KRG0.htm (accessed April 24, 2012).

APPENDIX A

UNITED NATIONS CLASSIFICATION OF COUNTRIES[1]

Africa

Eastern Africa	Middle Africa	Northern Africa	Western Africa	Southern Africa
Burundi	Angola	Algeria	Benin	Botswana
Comoros	Cameroon	Egypt	Burkina Faso	Lesotho
Djibouti	Central African Republic	Libya	Cape Verde	Namibia
Eritrea	Chad	Morocco	Cote d'Ivoire	South Africa
Ethiopia	Congo	Sudan	Gambia	Swaziland
Kenya	Democratic Republic of the Congo	Tunisia	Ghana	
Madagascar	Equatorial Guinea	Western Sahara	Guinea Bissau	
Malawi	Gabon		Liberia	
Mauritius	Sao Tome and Principe		Mali	
Mayotte			Mauritania	
Mozambique			Niger	
Reunion			Nigeria	
Rwanda			Saint Helena	
Seychelles			Senegal	
Somalia			Sierra Leone	
South Sudan			Togo	
Uganda				
United Republic of Tanzania				
Zambia				
Zimbabwe				

[1]From United Nations Population Division, http://esa.un.org/unpd/wup/CD-ROM/definition-of-regions.htm (accessed July 25, 2012).

Asia

Eastern Asia	Central Asia	Southern Asia	Southeast Asia	Western Asia
China	Kazakhstan	Afghanistan	Brunei Darussalam	Armenia
China, Hong Kong	Kyrgyzstan	Bangladesh	Cambodia	Azerbaijan
China, Macao	Tajikistan	Bhutan	Laos	Cyprus
Democratic People's Republic of Korea	Turkmenistan	India	Malaysia	Georgia
Japan	Uzbekistan	Iran	Myanmar	Iraq
Mongolia		Maldives	Philippines	Israel
Republic of Korea		Nepal	Singapore	Jordan
		Pakistan	Thailand	Kuwait
		Sri Lanka	Timor-Leste	Lebanon
			Vietnam	Occupied Palestinian Territory
				Oman
				Qatar
				Saudi Arabia
				Syrian Arab Republic
				Turkey
				United Arab Emirates
				Yemen

Europe

Eastern Europe	Northern Europe	Southern Europe	Western Europe
Belarus	Channel Islands	Albania	Austria
Bulgaria	Denmark	Andorra	Belgium
Czech Republic	Estonia	Bosnia and Herzegovina	France
Hungary	Faeroe Islands	Croatia	Germany
Poland	Finland	Gibraltar	Liechtenstein
Republic of Moldova	Iceland	Greece	Luxembourg
Romania	Isle of Man	Holy See	Monaco
Russian Federation	Latvia	Italy	Netherlands
Slovakia	Lithuania	Malta	Switzerland
Ukraine	Norway	Montenegro	
	Sweden	Portugal	
	United Kingdom	San Marino	
		Serbia	
		Slovenia	
		Spain	
		The former Yugoslav Republic of Macedonia	

Latin America and the Caribbean

Caribbean	Central America	South America
Anguilla	Belize	Argentina
Antigua and Barbuda	Costa Rica	Bolivia
Aruba	El Salvador	Brazil
Bahamas	Guatemala	Chile
Barbados	Honduras	Colombia
British Virgin Islands	Mexico	Ecuador
Cayman Islands	Nicaragua	Falkland Islands
Cuba	Panama	French Guinea
Dominica		Guyana
Guadeloupe		Paraguay
Haiti		Peru
Jamaica		Suriname
Martinique		Uruguay
Montserrat		Venezuela
Netherlands Antilles		
Puerto Rico		
Saint Kitts and Nevis		
Saint Lucia		
Saint Vincent and the Grenadines		
Trinidad and Tobago		
Turks and Caicos Islands		
United States Virgin Islands		

Northern America

Bermuda
Canada
Greenland
Saint Pierre and Miquelon
United States of America

Oceania

Australia/New Zealand	Melanesia	Micronesia	Polynesia
Australia	Fiji	Guam	American Samoa
New Zealand	New Caledonia	Kiribati	Cook Islands
	Papua New Guinea	Marshall Islands	French Polynesia
	Solomon Islands	Micronesia (Federated States of)	Niue
	Vanuatu	Nauru	Samoa
		Northern Mariana Islands	Tokelau
		Palau	Tuvalu
			Wallis and Futuna Islands

Sub-Saharan Africa

Angola	Congo	Guinea-Bissau	Namibia	South Africa
Benin	Côte d'Ivoire	Kenya	Niger	South Sudan
Botswana	Democratic Republic of the Congo	Lesotho	Nigeria	Swaziland
Burkina Faso	Djibouti	Liberia	Reunion	Togo
Burundi	Equatorial Guinea	Madagascar	Saint Helena	Uganda
Cameroon	Eritrea	Malawi	Sao Tome and Principe	United Republic of Tanzania
Cape Verde	Ethiopia	Mali	Senegal	Zambia
Central African Republic	Gabon	Mauritania	Seychelles	Zimbabwe
Chad	Guinea	Mayotte	Sierra Leone	
Comoros	Ghana	Mozambique	Somalia	

Least Developed Countries[2]

Afghanistan	Gambia	Rwanda
Angola	Guinea	Samoa
Bangladesh	Guinea-Bissau	Sao Tome and Principe
Benin	Haiti	Senegal
Bhutan	Kiribati	Sierra Leone
Burkina Faso	Laos	Solomon Islands
Burundi	Lesotho	Somalia
Cambodia	Liberia	South Sudan
Central African Republic	Madagascar	Sudan
Chad	Malawi	Timor-Leste
Comoros	Mali	Togo
Democratic Republic of the Congo	Mauritania	Tuvalu
Djibouti	Mozambique	Uganda
Equatorial Guinea	Myanmar	United Republic of Tanzania
Eritrea	Nepal	Vanuatu
Ethiopia	Niger	Yemen
		Zambia

[2]These are the Least Developed Countries as of April 26, 2012.

APPENDIX B

WEBSITES WITH USEFUL POPULATION INFORMATION

National Center for Health Statistics http://www.cdc.gov/nchs/

Population Reference Bureau http://www.prb.org

UNAIDS http://www.unaids.org/en/

United Nations Population Division http://www.un.org/esa/population/unpop.htm

United States Census Bureau http://www.census.gov

World Bank http://www.worldbank.org

World Health Organization http://www.who.int/en/

APPENDIX C

MAJOR POPULATION JOURNALS

Following are some of the major population journals. They are those journals that 5% or more of demographers worldwide reported they read "often" based on a survey in 2009. They are listed in descending order of the percentage of demographers who read the journal often.[1] Population articles also often appear in major sociology journals such as the **American Sociological Review**, the **American Journal of Sociology**, and **Social Forces**; in economics journals such as the **Journal of Development Economics** and **Journal of Population Economics**; and in public health journals such as the **American Journal of Public Health**.

Population and Development Review: This has been published by the Population Council since 1975.

Demography: This has been published by the Population Association of America since 1964.

Population Studies: This has been published by the London School of Economics since 1948.

Population: This has been published by Institut national d'études démographiques (INED) in Paris in French since 1946. An English edition also has been published since 1996.

Demographic Research: This is an online-only journal that is available at http://www.demographic-research.org. It has been published by the Max Planck Institute for Demographic Research in Rostock, Germany, since 1999. This is an open-access journal.

Studies in Family Planning: This has been published by the Population Council since 1963.

Genus: This has been published by the University of Rome since 1934. It is available only online by subscription.

International Perspectives on Sexual and Reproductive Health: This was formerly **International Family Planning Perspectives**. The name of the journal changed in 2009. This has been published by the Alan Guttmacher Institute since 1975.

Population Bulletin of the United Nations: This has been published by the United Nations Department of Economic and Social Affairs since 1951.

European Journal of Population: This was formerly **European Demographic Information Bulletin**. The name of the journal changed in 1984. This has been published by the European Association of Population Studies since 1970.

Journal of Population Research: This has been published by Springer since 1984.

International Migration Review: This has been published by the Center for Migration Studies since 1965.

Population Policy and Research Review: This has been published by the Southern Demographic Association since 1980.

International Perspectives on Sexual and Reproductive Health: This was formerly **International Family Planning Perspectives**. The name of the journal changed in 2002. This has been published by the Alan Guttmacher Institute since 1969.

Journal of Marriage and the Family: This has been published by the National Council on Family Relations since 1938.

Population and Environment: This has been published by Springer since 1978.

International Migration: This has been published by the International Organization for Migration since 1961.

---

[1]Henrik P. van Dalen and Kene Henkens. 2012. "What Is on a Demographer's Mind? A Worldwide Survey," *Demographic Research*, 26: 363–408.

Asia-Pacific Population Journal: This has been published by the United Nations Economic and Social Commission for Asia and the Pacific since 1969.

Journal of Population Economics: This has been published by Springer since 1988.

Journal of Biosocial Science: This has been published by Cambridge University Press since 1969.

Population, Space and Place: This has been published by Wiley since 1995.

African Population Studies: This has been published by the Union for African Population Studies since 1987. Articles appear in English and in French.

GLOSSARY

abandonment This involves anonymously leaving a child at an institution such as a hospital or a convent.

abortion This is the termination of a pregnancy resulting in the death of the fetus. An abortion can be a spontaneous abortion or an induced abortion. When the term is used without a modifier, it is typically interpreted as an induced abortion. See **induced abortion.** See **spontaneous abortion.**

abortion rate The abortion rate is calculated as the number of abortions per 1,000 women in the childbearing ages. Usually the denominator is women aged 15–44.

abortion ratio This is the number of abortions per 100 pregnancies. It is usually estimated as 100 × abortions/ (abortions + live births).

accidental death An accidental death occurs when there is a death from other than natural causes, but it was not the result of anyone intending harm to the person who died.

active life expectancy This refers to the number of years that a person can expect to live from birth or from some particular age free of any of various disabilities or limitations on activity.

acute condition This is a disease from which a person recovers or dies fairly rapidly, such as pneumonia or influenza.

adoption An adoption occurs when a person other than a biological parent assumes parental and legal responsibilities for a person.

age When used without further specification, age means **age last birthday.**

age-adjusted death rate This is also called an age-standardized death rate. It is a death rate that adjusts for changes in the age structure over time in one population or for differences in the age structure between populations.

age last birthday This is how many years of age a person was on his or her last birthday. This is in contrast to **exact age.**

age of sexual debut This is the age of first sexual intercourse.

age-specific death rate This is the number of deaths per 1,000 people in an age group.

age-specific fertility rate This is the number of births per 1,000 women in an age group. This is typically calculated for 5-year age groups aged either 15–49 or 15–44.

age-specific mortality rate See **age-specific death rate.**

AIDS See **HIV.**

area of destination This is the place to which a migrant moves.

area of origin This is the place from which a migrant moves.

Baby Boom This period in the United States extended from 1946 through 1964. Birth rates were higher than they were earlier or later. Some other countries also experienced baby booms after World War II that included a slightly different set of years.

base 10 logarithm If $x = 10^p$, then p is the base 10 logarithm of x. The base 10 logarithm is the power to which the number 10 must be raised to yield the given number. The base 10 logarithm is also called the common logarithm.

below-replacement fertility This is when the population's **net reproduction rate** (NRR) is less than 1.00.

birth cohort These are people all of whom were born in the same time period.

birth interval A birth interval is the amount of time between when a woman has one live birth and when she has her next live birth. This is also called an **interbirth interval.**

Body Mass Index (BMI) This is calculated as weight in kilograms divided by height in meters squared. BMI is a good measure of obesity and risk for diabetes and other ailments at the population level, but it is much less accurate as an assessment for individuals.

carrying capacity This is the maximum population size that the environment can sustain, given the food, habitat, water, and other necessities available in the environment.

case fatality rate This is the percentage of those with an ailment who die from that condition or disease.

cause of death This is the disease or injury that led to death. Usually, what is meant is the **underlying cause of death.**

census A census is an official enumeration of an entire population. It is usually taken every 10 years, but sometimes is taken every 5 years. Besides counting the population, it usually includes other information about each person, such as age, sex, education, marital status, and occupation.

central city This is a densely populated city at the core of a large metropolitan area.

characteristics hypothesis   This hypothesis maintains that any behavioral difference among groups related to cultural or regional variables will disappear once socioeconomic characteristics have been taken into account. In this view, the *real* cause of the relation between the cultural variable and behavior is socioeconomic differences among groups that have not yet been taken into account.

childbearing ages   This typically means the childbearing ages for females. It is usually considered as ages 15–49 or 15–44, although it is possible for women younger than 15 or older than 49 to bear a child.

childlessness   A woman or a couple who have never had a child are childless.

child mortality rate   The child mortality rate is, out of 1,000 births, the number of children who die before their fifth birthday.

child quality   This refers to a concern with the characteristics of children, such as whether children have at least a certain amount of education.

child quantity   This refers to the number of children, or a desire to have many children.

child–woman ratio   This is the number of children aged 0–4 divided by the number of women in the childbearing ages, either ages 15–49 or 15–44. It gives an indication of the fertility level of a population and can be calculated from information on the population by age and sex without special questions about fertility.

chronic condition   It is a condition that lasts at least a year and requires ongoing medical treatment. It often impedes the ability of a person to go about his or her daily life.

circulation migration   This is when people move from their place of origin to a place of destination and frequently return to the place of origin. Usually, the people are working at the place of destination. Often, the labor migrants return weekly or monthly to the place of origin. As transportation systems improve, circulation migration often changes to commuting. See **commuting**.

closed population   In a closed population, there is no migration in or out of the population. The population's size and age structure are influenced only by fertility and mortality. No population, except the world as a whole, is completely closed. A closed population is often used in producing models.

cohabitation   This is when people live together in a sexual relationship without being legally married.

cohort   Those who begin something at the same time or in the same time period constitute a cohort. When the term cohort is used without any modifier, it means a **birth cohort**, which means those who were born in the same year or the same time period. There are also cohorts defined by other events, such as marriage cohorts and college graduation cohorts.

cohort component projection   This is a projection method in which cohorts are projected using a schedule of age-specific fertility rates, age-specific death rates, and age-specific migration rates. This is typically done by 5-year periods. This method is in contrast to other projection methods, such as assuming exponential growth.

cohort fertility   This traces the fertility of a cohort of women as they go through the reproductive ages. A cohort total fertility rate can be calculated from cohort age-specific fertility rates. Also see **period fertility**.

cohort mortality   This traces the mortality of a cohort of persons from birth through the death of the longest-living members of the cohort. A cohort life table can be constructed from the death rates of the cohort as it goes through its life. Also see **period mortality**.

coitus interruptus   This is a method of prevention of pregnancy in which the male withdraws before sperm is ejaculated. It is also called withdrawal.

Columbian Exchange   The Columbian Exchange refers to the populations, ideas, foods, and diseases that were transferred between Europe and the Americas after Christopher Columbus's 1492 voyage.

communicable and related causes of death   This is the Global Burden of Disease category of causes of death that includes communicable diseases as well as some non-communicable causes of death, specifically some causes of maternal mortality and conditions that originate in the perinatal period as well as deaths that result from nutritional deficiencies.

communicable causes of death   These are deaths caused by communicable diseases.

communicable disease   This is a disease that can be transmitted under normal circumstances from one person to another.

community immunity   See **herd immunity**.

commuting   This occurs when the place of work is at some distance or travel time from the place of residence. People who commute typically sleep each night at their place of residence. People who commute typically do so 5 days a week and typically travel by car, bus, or train.

components of population growth   Births, deaths, and migrants are the components of population growth. A population changes between two times due to the births that add to the population, the deaths that subtract from the population, and the net number of migrants into the area.

compression of morbidity   This concept was proposed by Fries. It is the idea that as mortality falls to very low levels and as deaths become concentrated at an advanced age, the average age of onset of various disabling conditions also increases, leading to a smaller number of years lived in a disabled state than if the age of onset of the disability had not increased.

conception   The beginning of a pregnancy, when an ovum is fertilized by a sperm.

contagion theory of disease   This is the view that many diseases are caused by transmission from one ill person to another.

contraception   This is the prevention of pregnancy when sexual intercourse occurs. This is also called **family planning**.

contraceptive method   These are any of various methods to prevent pregnancy when sexual intercourse occurs, including withdrawal, IUDs, birth control pills, and sterilization.

contributory cause of death   This is a disease or injury that played a role in the death but was not the **underlying cause of death**.

controlled fertility   A population is practicing controlled fertility when actions related to the time to the next pregnancy are positively related to the number of births that a woman has already had. See **natural fertility**.

counterfactual history   This examines what would have occurred if the past had been different than it actually was, for example if a war had not occurred.

crisis mortality   A time period that includes one or more **mortality crises** is referred to as a time of crisis mortality.

counterurbanization   This is a process in which rural areas or small urban places gain population, while large cities lose population.

crossover fertility   This occurs when members of one group have higher fertility below a certain age but members of that group have lower fertility above that age. Sometimes rural-urban migrants have lower fertility than urban natives at younger ages but higher fertility than natives at older ages.

crossover mortality   This occurs when members of one group have higher mortality below a certain age but members of that group have lower mortality above that age. It has sometimes been found that African Americans in the United States have higher mortality than Whites below a certain age but lower mortality than Whites at advanced ages.

cross-sectional survey   This is a survey in which the same people or households are interviewed one time. Often, cross-sectional surveys are repeated over time with new respondents but with similar questions asked.

crude birth rate   The crude birth rate is the number of births to a population in a given year divided by the midyear population. The crude birth rate is typically expressed per 1,000 population. For example, a crude birth rate of $((4,000 \text{ births})/(\text{population of } 100,000)) = .040$ would be expressed as 40 per 1,000 population or just expressed as 40. More exactly, the crude birth rate is the number of births over a given period divided by the person-years lived by the population over that period.

crude death rate   The crude death rate is the number of births to a population in a given year divided by the midyear population. The crude death rate is typically expressed per 1,000 population. For example, a crude death rate of $((2,000 \text{ deaths})/(\text{population of } 100,000)) = .020$ would be expressed as 20 per thousand population or just expressed as 20. More exactly, the crude death rate is the number of births over a given period divided by the person-years lived by the population over that period.

curative medical care   This is medical care that is administered after a person has a disease or ailment. See **preventive medical care**.

death   Death is the cessation of life. Brain death is "irreversible unconsciousness with complete loss of brain function."[1] Brain death is the official definition of death in the United States.

de facto population   The de facto population of a place is the number of people who are physically in that place at a given time. This is in contrast to the **de jure population**. The de facto–de jure distinction is important for census counts. See **de jure population**.

degenerative condition   This is a chronic condition that tends to worsen with age, such as dementia.

de jure population   The de jure population of a place is the number of people whose usual place of residence is in a given place, whether or not they are physically present in the place at a given time. This is in contrast to the **de facto population**. The de facto–de jure distinction is important for census counts. See **de facto population**.

demographic dividend   This occurs when the proportion of the population in the working ages increases. This occurs after fertility has declined substantially, leading to a decrease in the proportion of the population younger than the working ages and before the proportion of the population at older ages has increased substantially. The increase in the population in the working ages provides an opportunity for a high rate of economic growth if there are jobs available to take advantage of the large proportion of the population in the working ages. See **demographic window**.

demographic transition   This is a description of the change in population growth rates in Europe historically in which death rates declined, which resulted in an increase in the growth rate. After some time, birth rates declined finally to the point where the birth rate and the death rate are approximately equal, and thus the growth rate is near zero.

demographic window   This is the period of time when the potential support ratio is temporarily high due to the demographic dividend. If there are not sufficient jobs for working-age persons during this period of opportunity, there will not be the economic growth that the demographic dividend could facilitate. See **demographic dividend**.

demography   This is the study of the growth, structure, and composition of human populations and the study of the determinants and consequences of these aspects of population.

dependency ratio   The total dependency ratio is the ratio of the sum of the population aged 0–14 and that aged 65+ to the population aged 15–64. The child dependency ratio is the ratio of the population aged 0–14 to the population aged 15–64. The old age dependency ratio is the ratio of the population aged 65 years or over to the population aged 15–64. All ratios are presented as number of dependents per 100 persons of working age (15–64).

Developmental Idealism Model   This is a model developed by Thornton that includes four elements: (1) Modern society is good, (2) the modern family is good, (3) the modern family is a cause and effect of a modern society, and (4) individuals have the right to be free and equal.

disability-adjusted life years (DALYs)   This is the sum of **years of life lost** (YLL from premature death) and **years lived disabled** (YLD alive but disabled). See **years of life lost** and **years lived disabled**.

disability-free life expectancy   See **active life expectancy**.

---

[1]U.S. Legal. *Brain Death Law & Legal Definition*, http://definitions.uslegal.com/b/brain-death (accessed September 7, 2011)

discouraged worker   This is a person who would like to work for pay but who has stopped actively looking for employment because the person does not think he or she would be able to find a job.

double burden of mortality   This occurs when mortality from infectious and parasitic diseases is still high but mortality from non-communicable diseases related to health behaviors has risen.

drug-resistant strain of a disease   This is a version of a disease that does not respond to the drugs that have been effective in treating the disease. These strains can develop when a particular drug has been used for an extended time. Their development is promoted when the disease is treated with the drug for too short a time to kill the bacteria or viruses and the resistant organisms are thus selected and form a resistant version of the disease. This has been a problem with many diseases, including tuberculosis.

dual labor market   This is the view that the labor market is divided into two sectors. In Lewis's conceptualization, there is a modern sector with well-paying jobs for which people are hired and in which qualifications such as education matter, and a traditional sector with low-income jobs, often for which there are no employers, such as hawkers. In Doeringer and Piore's view, there is a primary sector with well-paying jobs with promotion possibilities and a secondary sector in which the jobs are low paying, with poor working conditions and poor pay. Some of the secondary-sector jobs have employers, and some do not. Piore applied the dual labor market to the situation in advanced industrial countries, in which jobs can be divided into stable, highly skilled jobs and low-skilled, low-wage jobs; the latter attract international migrants and are jobs that citizens of the advanced countries are unwilling to hold.

emigrant   This is a person who migrates out of a country.

emigration   This is migration out of a country.

employed population   This refers to persons who engaged in income-producing activity as an employee, were self-employed, or did substantial work (usually 15 hours a week or more) as an unpaid worker in a family business, or who had jobs but were temporarily not at them due to circumstances such as vacation, illness, parental leave, job training, or a labor dispute.

endemic disease   A disease is endemic in an area when it afflicts people in that area frequently, without the need for its introduction by infected people entering the area.

epidemic disease   A disease is epidemic in an area when the number of cases increases rapidly above the level that it was a short time earlier.

Epidemiologic Transition   This refers to the long-term shifts in health and disease patterns that occur as mortality moves from high to low levels. It involves a shift in the causes of death from infectious and parasitic diseases (and, more generally, communicable diseases) to chronic diseases (and, more generally, non-communicable diseases). The epidemiologic transition has been divided into four stages: (1) age of pestilence and famine, (2) age of receding pandemics, (3) age of degenerative and man-made diseases, and (4) age of delayed degenerative diseases.

eugenics   Eugenics is a science that deals with the improvement, through breeding, of hereditary qualities of humans or other animals.

exact age   This is the exact number of years since a person was born. On a person's fifth birthday, the person is exact age 5. Three months after his or her fifth birthday, that person is exact age 5.25.

excess death   An excess death is one that occurs under certain conditions, when it would not have occurred under normal conditions. For example, in a heat wave there are deaths that would not have occurred during normal weather. The number of excess deaths is calculated by comparing the actual number of deaths to the number of deaths that would have been expected to have occurred. It is usually not possible to identify any individual death as an excess death.

expectation of life at birth   This is the average number of years that a hypothetical cohort of individuals would live if they were subject through their lives to the age-specific mortality rates of a given period.

expectation of remaining life at age x   Given that a person survives to his or her xth birthday, this is the average number of years that person would live, given age-specific death rates above age x.

exponential growth   Growth is exponential when

$$P2 = e^{rt} \, \text{Pop1}$$

where:

$P1$ = Population at time 1

$P2$ = Population at time 2

   r = Growth rate between T1 and T1

   t = number of years between T1 and T2

   e = base of natural logarithm, approximately 2.73

Populations typically grow exponentially. Exponential growth occurs when there is continuous compounding at the growth rate of the population.

extended household   An extended household includes members other than those who would be in one nuclear family. It can be vertically extended through the inclusion of members of a parental, child, and/or grandparent generation, or it can be extended horizontally through the inclusion of siblings of the parental generation and sometimes members of their families.

external causes of death   External causes of death are deaths that occur from the intentional or unintentional actions of humans. They are accidents, homicides, and suicides. They are also called **unnatural causes of deaths** or **violent causes of death**.

family of orientation   This is the family into which a person is born.

family of procreation   This is the family to which a woman, her husband or partner, and any children belong.

family planning   See **contraception**.

fecundity   This is the biological ability of a woman to become pregnant and have a live birth.

fertility   This is the extent to which people or couples have live births. It usually refers to women having live births.

fertility-postponing behavior   This occurs when a woman does not want to have a child immediately but wants to bear another child at some time in the future and she acts to avoid becoming pregnant immediately.

fertility-spacing behavior   See **fertility-postponing behavior**.

fertility-stopping behavior   This occurs when a woman is acting to limit her fertility and wants no more children.

Feyrer's model of women's status and fertility   This is a three-stage model, in which the stages are as follows. (1) Early phase: In this phase, women's wage rates are much lower than men's, and women are expected to do virtually all the work involved at home, including child care. Women have low labor force participation rates. (2) Intermediate phase: In this phase, women's labor force opportunities have improved, but their opportunities are still not as good as men's. Women still have most of the burden of child care and other home activities. Female labor force participation is higher than in the first phase, and there is a strong negative relation between female labor force participation and fertility. (3) Final phase: In this phase, women's labor force opportunities become equal or nearly equal to those of men. Men also take on more child care and other home responsibilities than in earlier phases. Female labor force participation is higher than in the intermediate phase, but this interferes less with having and raising children due to greater participation in the home by men and an increased availability of child care compared to the intermediate phase, so fertility rises.

forced migrant   This is someone who has been forced to leave his or her home because of a real or perceived threat to life and well-being.

forecast   See **prediction**.

fosterage   This occurs when a child resides with and is cared for by someone other than the child's biological parents. This can be because the child is an orphan, because the parents are ill, or to provide opportunities for schooling or training of the child. Usually the child is not legally adopted.

free rider   This is a person who obtains a benefit without paying the market price or entering into group risk. This concept is often invoked in discussions of vaccinations. If there are too many "free riders" who are not vaccinated, **herd immunity** is lost and all persons are at increased risk.

fundamental causes of disease approach   This is an approach developed by Link and Phelan. In this framework, an individual's or household's resources operate both by affecting whether people engage in healthful behaviors, such as not smoking or not consuming excessive alcohol, and by affecting the kinds of neighborhoods and other environments in which a person functions. Residence in less polluted neighborhoods and working in less hazardous occupations lead to lower death rates and a lower chance of becoming disabled.

general fertility rate   The general fertility rate (GFR) is the number of births per thousand women in the **childbearing ages**. See **childbearing ages**.

genocide   This is the deliberate and systematic destruction, in whole or in part, of an ethnic, racial, religious, or national group.

germ theory of disease   This states that many diseases are caused by microscopic organisms.

gestation   This is the period between when a pregnancy occurs and when the pregnancy ends, whether the result is a live birth, miscarriage, induced abortion, or stillbirth.

gestational age   This is the time elapsed since conception, while the pregnancy is still viable.

Global Burden of Disease classification   This classification was developed by a World Health Organization project. Causes of death are divided into (1) communicable and related diseases (including maternal and perinatal conditions and nutritional deficiencies), (2) noncommunicable diseases, and (3) external causes.

gross in-migration rate   This is the number of migrants into an area in a time period divided by the mid-period population in thousands if the period of time is 1 year, or divided by the person-years lived in the area in the time period in thousands.

gross migration   Gross migration between place A and place B in a time period consists of two migration flows. One is the total number of migrants from A to B in the time period, and the other is the total number of migrants from B to A in the time period. Also see **net migration**.

gross national income   Gross national income (GNI) is the total value of goods and services produced by the domestic economy of a country, within a given period of time, usually a year.

gross out-migration rate   This is the number of migrants out of an area in a time period divided by the mid-period population in thousands if the period of time is 1 year, or divided by the person-years lived in the area in the time period in thousands.

gross reproduction rate   The gross reproduction rate (GRR) is the number of daughters that would be born to a woman if the current age-specific fertility rates remained constant and the woman survived through the childbearing ages. It is usually calculated as the total fertility rate multiplied by the proportion of births that are female. See **total fertility rate**.

group quarters   A group quarters is a place where people live or stay in a group living arrangement; it is owned or managed by an entity or organization providing housing and/or services for the residents. Group quarters include institutions, such as correctional facilities and nursing homes, and non-institutional settings, such as college residence halls, adult group homes, and workers' dormitories.

growth rate   See **population growth rate**, and see **exponential growth**.

healthy life expectancy   See **active life expectancy**.

herd immunity   A population has herd immunity to a contagious disease when a large enough proportion of the population has been vaccinated against the disease, so that susceptible members of the population are unlikely to contract the disease. The proportion vaccinated that is necessary for herd immunity depends on the virulence of the disease, the efficacy of the vaccine, and the nature of contact in the population. The herd immunity threshold for many diseases, including diphtheria and polio, is about 85%. This is also called **community immunity**.

high-income countries   This is a World Bank classification based on per capita income. The per capita income cutoff that is used changes over time. In 2004, countries with more than US$10,065 per capita income were high-income countries.

Hispanic paradox   The paradox is that although Hispanics in the United States have relatively low socioeconomic status, they have lower age-specific death rates than non-Hispanic Whites. Possible explanations include data quality, healthy migrant selection, salmon-bias return migration, and cultural practices.

HIV   The human immunodeficiency virus (HIV) is an autoimmune disease that often is asymptomatic for many years. If untreated, it transforms into **AIDS**, which is accompanied by weight loss, susceptibility to various infections, and eventually death.

homicide   This is a death that results from the action of another person who intended to cause harm to the person who died. The person who caused harm did not necessarily intend that the person would die.

household   This is a living arrangement made by persons, individually or in groups, for providing themselves with food or other essentials for living. The persons in the group may pool their incomes and have a common budget to a greater or lesser extent; they may be related or unrelated persons, or a combination of both.

human milk substitute   This is any substance fed to a baby in place of breast milk. It includes formula, cow's milk, and cornstarch mixed with water.

human subjects   Research using human subjects includes surveys as well as interviews and focus-group participation, as well as analysis of biological samples or other medical studies. There has been increasing concern with the protection of human subjects in research.

hunters and gatherers   In a hunter-gatherer society, almost all food is obtained from wild plants and animals.

hypothetical cohort   See **synthetic cohort**.

ideational factors   Ideational factors in behavior or decision making refer to a person's perceptions of his or her interests or changes in perceptions of interests.

illegal immigrant   See **undocumented migrant**.

immigrant   This is a person who migrates into a country.

immigration   This is migration into a country.

impartible inheritance   This is a practice in which one child, almost always a son, is the sole heir. See **primogeniture**.

index of dissimilarity   This is the proportion of members of one group who would have to move to another location to have the same distribution across locations as some other group.

induced abortion   This is an abortion that is brought about intentionally. See **abortion**.

infanticide   This is the intentional killing of a child younger than 1 year of age. It usually occurs shortly after birth.

infant mortality   Infant mortality occurs when a child younger than 1 year of age dies.

infant mortality rate   This is the number of infants who die before their first birthday out of every 1,000 births.

infectious disease   This is a disease than can be transmitted from one person to another under normal conditions.

inferior goods   This is something that is seen as desirable only when people have a low income and cannot afford more desirable goods.

in-migration rate   See **gross in-migration rate**.

inoculation   In an inoculation, active disease cells are introduced to a cut or by injection to produce immunity. It is also called **variolation**.

institution   In an institution, there is formally supervised care of inmates or patients. Examples include prisons and nursing homes.

interbirth interval   See **birth interval**.

internal migrant   This is a person who migrates within the boundaries of a country.

internal migration   This is migration that occurs within the boundaries of a country.

internally displaced person   This is someone who is forced to flee his or her home but who remains within his or her country's borders.

international migration   This is migration that occurs between one country and another country.

international migrant   This is a person who migrates from one country to another country.

intrauterine device (IUD)   This is a contraceptive method in which a device is inserted into a woman's vagina. It is thought to prevent pregnancy by preventing a fertilized egg from implanting in the uterine wall.

intrinsic growth rate   This is the growth rate that would occur in the stable population implied by a population's age-specific birth rates and age-specific death rates.

labor force   This is composed of those people above some age (such as age 16) who are working for pay or are actively seeking work for pay. Those who are not working for pay but are seeking work for pay are considered unemployed but are part of the labor force. Those who are not in the labor force include persons who are full-time students, are retired, are in prisons or other institutions, and are working in the home not for pay, as well as those who would like to have a job but are not making active efforts to find a job, possibly because they do not think they would be successful in finding a job. See **discouraged worker**.

labor force participation rate   This is the percentage of those aged 16 or older who are in the labor force.

labor migrant   This is a migrant who has moved primarily because of a job or the prospect of engaging in income-producing activity at the place of destination.

least developed countries (LeastDC)   This is a UN designation of countries defined by a combination of low income, human resource weakness, and economic vulnerability. Countries can move on and off this list.

legal immigrant   This is a person who migrates into a country legally, with the knowledge and permission of the receiving country.

less developed region (LDR)   This is a UN classification. It includes all of the countries except those in the **more developed region (MDR)**.

life expectancy at birth   This is the average number of years that a person would live if he or she were subject to the chances of dying by age in a given population. It is usually calculated separately by sex.

life span   This is the maximal age to which humans can survive. It was once thought to be 110 years, but now is thought to perhaps be as old as 130 years.

life table   This is a way of presenting the mortality risks by age in a population. It usually depicts the conditions at a particular point in time, but it can be constructed for a birth cohort.

live birth This is the birth of an infant, whatever the duration of gestation, that shows any sign of life, such as respiration, heartbeat, umbilical pulsation, or movement of voluntary muscles.

longitudinal survey This is a survey in which the same people or the same households are interviewed two or more times.

lowest-low fertility This is when the total fertility rate is 1.3 or less.

low-income countries This is a World Bank classification based on per capita income. The per capita income cutoff that is used changes over time. In 2004, countries with less than US$826 per capita income were low-income countries.

marital fertility This is childbearing among married women.

marital status A full listing of marital status is never married, married, widowed, and divorced. Sometimes those who are separated are listed separately, and sometimes those who are separated are grouped with the divorced. A shorter marital status division is into those currently married and those not currently married. Those not currently married include those who have never married, who are widowed, and who are divorced.

marriage cohort Members of a marriage cohort are those who were married in the same time period.

marriage migration This is migration for the purpose of relocation due to marriage. Usually the wife migrates to the husband's place of residence, but in some cultures the husband migrates to the wife's place of residence. Many groups have had norms that people had to marry members of a different group or from a different geographic area.

maternal death A maternal death is the death of a woman while pregnant or within 42 days of termination of pregnancy, irrespective of the duration and site of the pregnancy, from any cause related to or aggravated by the pregnancy or its management but not from accidental or incidental causes.

maternal mortality ratio (MMR) This is the number of maternal deaths per 100,000 live births.

median age This is the age for which one-half the population is younger than that age and one-half the population is older than that age.

megalopolis A megalopolis is an integrated set of cities and their surrounding suburban hinterlands across which labor and capital can be reallocated at very low cost.

mega-region See **megalopolis**.

menarche Menarche occurs when a girl begins to ovulate. It is usually accompanied by her first menstrual cycle. It marks the beginning of time when a girl is physiologically capable of becoming pregnant and bearing a child.

menopause Menopause occurs when a woman no longer ovulates and thus no longer has menstrual cycles. It usually occurs between age 45 and age 55.

mercantilism This economic doctrine contends that government control of foreign trade and a positive balance of trade is of paramount importance for a state's prosperity and safety. This view was dominant in Western Europe from the sixteenth to late eighteenth centuries. Mercantilism was a major rationale for colonialism and related occurrences, such as the **triangle trade**.

metropolis This is a very large city or urban area that is a significant economic, political, and cultural center for a country or region, and an important hub for regional or international connections and communications.

metropolitan statistical area This is the set of counties that comprise a core urban area and any surrounding counties that are tightly socially or economically integrated with it. In the United States, the counties included in a Standard Metropolitan Statistical Area can be changed after each census.

miasma theory of disease This is the view that many diseases are caused by a miasma or mist, often from decomposing materials.

micropolitan statistical area This is an urban area in the United States based around an urban cluster (urban area) with a population of 10,000–49,999.

middle-income countries This is a World Bank classification based on per capita income. The per capita income cutoff that is used changes over time. In 2004, countries with US$826–US$10,065 per capita income were middle-income countries.

midyear population This is the population of an area in the middle of the year. The midyear population, or an estimate of the midyear population, is often used as the denominator for rates, such as the crude birth rate or the crude death rate.

migrant This is a person who migrates. See **migration**.

migrant adaptation This occurs when migrants, especially rural-urban migrants or international migrants, change their behavior to become more similar to natives or long-time residents of the place they have migrated to.

migrant selectivity This occurs when people with certain characteristics, such as a particular age, gender, or level of educational attainment, are more likely to migrate than others.

migrant stock This is persons in a country who were born in a different country.

migration There is a variety of definitions of migration. Migration always involves a geographic move. It also involves a permanent or long-term change of place of residence that involves a substantial change in daily life. It is sometimes defined as a change of residence across county lines.

migration disruption This occurs when the behavior of migrants shortly after migration changes because of disruption in some aspects of life. For example, fertility might increase because of lack of knowledge of where to obtain contraceptives at the new location.

migration flow The migration flow from place A to place B is the migrants who move from place A to place B in a specific time period.

migration selection This occurs when there is **migrant selectivity**.

Millennium Development Goals (MDGs) These are eight goals that were adopted at a conference in New York in 2000. These goals referred to social, population, and health conditions in less developed countries. A pledge was made by 193 countries to seek to attain goals in the eight areas by 2015.

miscarriage   This is when a pregnancy ends spontaneously before the fetus can survive, typically before the fetus is 20 or 22 weeks of gestational age. It is also called a spontaneous abortion. It is estimated that 15–20% of all pregnancies end in miscarriages.

modern contraceptive methods   Modern contraceptive methods are those that have been developed through the use of modern technology or medical research or that include procedures that have been developed through medical research, such as sterilization. They include sterilization, contraceptive pills, intrauterine devices (IUDs), condoms, injectable methods, vaginal barrier methods (such as foam), and implants (such as Depo-Provera).

moral restraint   See **preventive check**.

morbidity   This refers to being sick, diseased, generally unhealthy, or disabled.

more developed region (MDR)   This is a UN classification. It comprises the countries of Europe, the United States, Canada, Japan, Australia, and New Zealand. The other countries are in the **less developed region (LDR)**.

mortality   Mortality refers to death as well as measures of the level of dying in a particular population.

mortality crisis   A mortality crisis occurs when there is a sudden rise in the number of deaths, which is usually followed within a few years by a sharp decline in deaths to about the pre-crisis level. A mortality crisis can be caused by a crop failure, an epidemic, or a war. See **crisis mortality**.

movers and stayers   This refers to the observation that some people move frequently (movers), while others rarely move (stayers). A large part of migration and residential mobility is due to the frequent moves of movers.

natural causes of death   These are deaths caused by disease or other natural processes, such as degeneration.

natural fertility   This concept was developed by the French demographer, Louis Henry. A population is practicing natural fertility when actions related to the time to the next live birth are not related to the number of births that a woman has already had. See **controlled fertility**.

natural logarithm   If $x = e^p$, then p is the natural logarithm of x. The natural logarithm is the power to which e must be raised to yield the given number; e is approximately 2.72.

neonatal period   This is the first 28 days of life.

net migration   Net migration between place A and place B in a time period is the difference between two migration flows: the number of migrants from A to B, and the number of migrants from B to A. If there are 20 migrants from A to B and 30 migrants from B to A, there are 10 net in-migrants from B to A and −10 net in-migrants from A to B.

net migration rate   This is actually the net in-migration rate. It is the number of migrants into an area in a time period minus the number of migrants out of the area in a time period, divided by the mid-period population of the area in thousands if the period of time is 1 year or divided by the person-years lived in the area in the time period in thousands.

net percent undercount   This is the percentage of the actual population that is estimated to have been missed by a census.

net reproduction rate   The net reproduction rate (NRR) is a measure of generational replacement. It is the average number of daughters that would be born to a woman, given the age-specific fertility rates and age-specific mortality rates in a given year. The net reproduction rate takes into account mortality of the generation of mothers. It is approximated by the **gross reproduction rate (GRR)** multiplied by the probability that a woman survives to the mean age of childbearing. A population with an NRR of 1.00 is said to have replacement fertility or to be at zero population growth. A population can continue to grow for several years, even in the absence of international migration, after attaining an NRR of 1.00. See **population momentum**.

New Home Economics Model   This was proposed by Becker as a model of whether and to what extent couples limit their fertility. It focused on the value of women's time. His idea was that care of children takes a great deal of time and that time is virtually always contributed by the mother. As women's education increases and opportunities for paid work outside the home for women increase, it is more expensive for families with more educated wives to have several children, because they are seen as forgoing the income-producing activities that women could engage in if they had fewer children.

non-communicable causes of death   These are deaths from non-communicable diseases.

non-communicable disease   This is a disease that is not normally transmitted from one person to another. Non-communicable diseases include cancer, stroke, and heart disease.

non-institutional household   This is an ordinary residential household and contains one or more persons.

nonmetropolitan area   This is a location in a county that is not part of a metropolitan area. See **metropolitan statistical area**.

nuclear household   This is a household that consists of a pair of adults in a continuing sexual relationship with or without their minor children.

old age dependency ratio   This is the number of people above the working ages per 100 persons in the working ages. It is usually calculated as

100 × (Persons aged 65+)/(Persons aged 15–64)

old age potential support ratio   See **potential support ratio**.

older or elderly population   This is defined as those aged 60+ or 65+.

oldest-old ages   This refers to those aged 85 or older.

operational definition   This is an easily obtainable indicator of an underlying concept that can be calculated to give an unambiguous result.

opportunity cost   This is the cost, often in terms of forgone income, of pursuing one activity instead of another activity. This is often applied to calculation of a major part of the cost of childbearing as income that a woman with children does not earn, under the assumption that she cannot both care for children and work for pay.

oral rehydration therapy (ORT)   In this treatment, salts are dissolved in water and given to persons, usually infants and children, who have become dehydrated, usually due to diarrhea. The salts replenish essential minerals that were lost due to diarrhea.

out-migration rate   This is the number of migrants out of an area in a time period per 1,000 persons in the area at the midpoint of the time period.

overcount   This is the percentage by which the population of a country as a whole or of some population subgroups is overestimated in a census enumeration. There is rarely an overcount of an entire population, but population subgroups, such as persons with two homes, can be overcounted. See **undercount**.

parasite   This is an organism that lives on or in a host and gets its food from or at the expense of its host. Parasites include malaria and hookworm.

parity   This is the number of live births that a woman has already had. If she has never had a live birth, she is zero parity.

partible inheritance   This is an inheritance system in which all children, or more often all sons, are heirs.

pastoral nomadism   In this form of economic organization, herds of domestic animals are moved from place to place in order to find grazing land.

perinatal period   This is the period of time from the 28th week of gestation to 28 days of age.

period fertility   This refers to fertility conditions at a given point in time across all ages. The total fertility rate as typically calculated is a period fertility measure. Also see **cohort fertility**.

period mortality   This refers to the mortality conditions at a given point in time across all ages. The expectation of life at birth as typically calculated is a period mortality measure. Also see **cohort mortality**.

person-years of life   This is a concept used in calculation of a life table. A person-year of life is 1 year of life per one person. It can be composed of 1 year lived by one person, 6 months each lived by two people, 1 month lived by each of 12 persons, or any other combination that ends up with a year of exposure to risk. Person-years of life are used as the denominator for many rates. The person-years lived in a population in a year are often estimated by the midyear population.

place of destination   This is the location to which a migrant moves.

place of origin   This is the place from which a person moves.

population   The population of a geographic area, such as a city or a country, is the number of people in that geographic area at a particular time. The population can be counted on a **de facto** or a **de jure** basis. See **de jure population** and **de facto population**.

population at risk   This is the set of people to whom something logically could happen. Although all persons are at risk of death, only those who are currently married are at risk of divorce. The population at risk of an event is the proper denominator for the rate at which the event, such as divorce, occurs.

population-balancing equation $P_{T2} = P_{T1} + B - D + I - O$ is the population-balancing equation, where all numbers refer to the country or region of interest, and where:

P_{T2} = Population at Time 2

P_{T1} = Population at Time 1

B = Number of births between Time 1 and Time 2

D = Number of deaths between Time 1 and Time 2

I = Number of migrants into the country or region between Time 1 and Time 2

O = Number of migrants out of the country or region between Time 1 and Time 2

This equation shows all of the sources of population increase and population decline for a given geographic area between two dates.

population composition   This refers to the distribution of a population according to some characteristic, such as age, educational attainment, or ethnic group membership.

population density   This is the number of people per unit of land area. It is typically expressed as the population per square mile or as the population per square kilometer.

population doubling time   This is the number of years it would take for the size of the population to double if the population growth rate at a given point in time is positive and persisted indefinitely. The population doubling time can be calculated by dividing the population growth rate (expressed as a decimal, not per 1,000 population) into the natural logarithm of 2, which is 0.693. The population doubling time is a synthetic measure; it does not imply that the population will continue to grow at a given rate for any specific number of years. It provides a way to interpret the magnitude or the implications of different population growth rates. See **population halving time**.

population growth rate   The growth rate of a population is the number per 1,000 population by which a population grows in a year. If P1 is the population at the beginning of the year and P2 is the population at the end of the year, it can be calculated as $1,000 \times (P2 - P1)/$ (midyear population). Since a population grows exponentially, it can be calculated as $1,000 \times (\ln(P2/P1)$. It also can be calculated as

(crude birth rate) − (crude death rate) +
    (in-migration rate) − (out-migration rate)

which is the same as the rate of natural increase plus the net migration rate. If there are no migrants in or out of the population or if the number of in-migrants equals the number of out-migrants, the growth rate is equal to the rate of natural increase.

population halving time   This is the number of years that it would take for the size of the population to be reduced to one-half its size if the population growth rate at a given point in time is negative and persisted indefinitely. The population halving time can be calculated by dividing the population growth rate (expressed as a decimal, not per 1,000 population) into the natural logarithm of 2, which is 0.693. The population halving time is a synthetic measure; it does not imply that the population will continue to shrink at a given rate for any specific number of years. It provides a way to interpret the magnitude or the implications of different population growth rates. See **population doubling time**.

population health   This is the health outcomes of a group of people, including the distribution of these outcomes within the group.

population momentum   This refers to population growth at the national level that would occur even if levels of childbearing immediately declined to replacement level (NRR = 1.00). In countries with NRR < 1.00, population momentum is the population decline at the national level that would occur if the NRR immediately changed to 1.00. Population momentum occurs because of the age distribution of the population, which is a result of fertility, mortality, and migration in the past.

population policy   This is a policy or set of actions by a government intended to influence fertility, mortality, migration, or population growth.

population pressure   This is the force exerted by a growing population upon its environment, resulting in dispersal or reduction of the population.

population projection   This is the calculation of a population's size at one point in time, given its size at an earlier point in time. A projection can be done assuming an exponential population growth rate. More typically, a population projection is done using the cohort component method.

population pyramid   This is a graphical display of the age and sex composition of a population at a given point in time. The ages are displayed vertically, with the youngest ages at the bottom and the oldest ages at the top. Data for males are shown on the left, and for females on the right.

population register   This is a continuously maintained record of the members of the population and of events that occur to them, including births and deaths and sometimes including other events, such as marriages, divorces, and migrations.

population sex ratio   This is the number of males per 100 females in the population as a whole.

positive check   This concept was formulated by Thomas Malthus. Increased mortality, whether from famine, disease, or war, is a positive check to population growth. Malthus thought that if preventive checks were not employed in a population, then positive checks would emerge to counter a high rate of population growth. See **preventive check**.

post-enumeration survey   This is a large survey, conducted shortly after a census, which is intended to assess the percentage of people who were undercounted or overcounted in the census overall and by geographic and personal characteristics.

postpartum   This is the period shortly after childbirth.

postpartum abstinence   Postpartum abstinence occurs when, after the birth of a child, a woman abstains from sexual intercourse for a period of time, sometimes for a year or longer. Sometimes, there is one act of sexual intercourse shortly after the child is born before the period of abstinence begins.

postpartum amenorrhea   This is the period of time after the birth of a child or after the conclusion of a pregnancy when the woman does not ovulate and thus cannot become pregnant.

potential support ratio   This is the number of people in the working ages divided by the number of people not in the working ages. Sometimes it is calculated as the number of people in the working ages divided by the number of people older than the working ages, although when that is done, it should be called the **old age potential support ratio**.

preconditions for fertility limitation   Coale proposed three preconditions for a substantial decline in fertility due to voluntary fertility limitation by women or couples. They are (1) acceptance of the possibility and moral acceptability of control of fertility (willing), (2) perception of advantages from reduced fertility (ready), and (3) knowledge and mastery of an effective and acceptable technique of fertility control (able).

prediction   This is a population projection that yields the best guess of what the population will actually be at a time in the future.

prevalence   This is the proportion of the members of a population who have a condition or disease.

preventive check   This concept was formulated by Thomas Malthus. Postponement of marriage and celibacy among the unmarried are preventive checks to population growth. Preventive checks are also called **moral restraint**. See **positive check**.

preventive medical care   This is medical care that reduces the chance that a person contracts a disease or ailment or reduces the chance that the person dies. Preventive medical care is administered before a person has a disease or ailment. See **curative medical care**.

primary sterility   This occurs when a woman who has never borne a child is unable to become pregnant and bear a child.

primate city   This is the largest city in a country, which is usually more than twice the size of the second-largest city and which plays a dominant role in the country's culture and economy. Some countries have a primate city, and some countries do not have a primate city.

primogeniture   This is an inheritance practice in which the oldest son is the sole heir. **See impartible inheritance.**

pronatalist   This refers to policies or positions favoring high or higher fertility.

proximate determinants of fertility   Bongaarts divided factors related to fertility into three types: (1) exposure to sexual intercourse (intercourse variables), (2) exposure to conception (conception variables), and(3) gestation and carrying the pregnancy to birth (gestation variables). These factors are referred to as the proximate determinants of fertility.

purchasing power parity (PPP)   PPP is an adjustment to a country's gross national income to account for differences among countries in the cost of living.

quantum of fertility   This is the cohort TFR. When the age pattern of fertility shifted to older ages in the 1990s and 2000s in some more developed countries, although period TFR declined, cohort TFR changed little. In these situations, the quantum of fertility was unchanged. See **tempo of fertility**.

radix   The radix of a life table is the number of people assumed to be exact age 0. The radix is often chosen as

100,000 or 1,000. So if the radix is 100,000, then $l_0 = 100,000$.

rank-size rule   This is the proposition that the second largest city in a country is half the size of the largest city, the third largest city is one-third the size of the largest city, and generally the nth largest city is $1/n$ times the size of the largest city. The distribution of city sizes in some countries closely follows the rank-size rule, while in other countries it does not.

rate   A rate is the chance that an event will occur to members of a population at risk of the event occurring. If the number of deaths in a year is D, and the mid-period population is P, the rate of deaths to the population is D/P.

rate of natural increase   This is the number (typically, per 1,000 people) by which the population grows due to the excess of births over deaths. It is the crude birth rate minus the crude death rate.

ratio   If there are two quantities, A and B, the ratio of A to B is A/B.

reclassification   Reclassification occurs when a person or an area changes from one category to another. Individuals can be reclassified by changing their ethnic or racial identification. Areas can be reclassified from being rural areas to being urban areas, or vice versa. See **urban-rural reclassification**.

rectangularization of mortality   This is the phenomenon that as mortality approaches a very low level, the l_x graph increasingly resembles half of a rectangle. In this situation, few deaths occur until an advanced age, after which the population is rapidly depleted by mortality.

refugee   This is a person who is outside of his or her country of citizenship and is unable or unwilling to return to that country because of persecution or a well-founded fear of persecution.

Relative Income Model   This model, which was proposed by Easterlin, is an explanation of why fertility fluctuates in developed countries. It is based on changing preferences for a given number of children across generations. When people are young, they observe the resources that their parents expend on each child and think that this defines the resources needed to raise a child. Later, when these same people are older and making fertility decisions, they observe the amount of resources available. If the resources available are less than they remember from their childhood, they feel they cannot afford as many children as their parents had and thus have lower fertility than did the parental generation. If their income is greater than their parents' income, then they feel relatively rich and think they can afford more children than their parents had. Easterlin also proposed that consumption expectations increase across time, which leads to a general decrease in the number of that people desire.

remittances   These are monies sent by a migrant to relatives or friends at the migrant's place or country of origin.

replacement fertility   When a population has a net reproduction rate of 1.00, it has replacement fertility. In the long run, the population will remain at the same size. Even at replacement fertility, however, a population typically continues to grow for some time. See **net reproduction rate** and **population momentum**.

reproductive health   This addresses the reproductive processes, functions, and system at all stages of life. It is concerned with assuring that people are able to have a responsible, satisfying, and safe sex life and that they have the capability to reproduce and the freedom to decide if, when, and how often to do so.

residence   This is where a person normally resides. It is sometimes defined as where a person typically eats their meals or where the person typically sleeps. In some countries, a person's place of residence is legally defined. In the United States, a person's place of residence can differ for some purposes. For example, a person can have a place of residence that qualifies that person to vote or to obtain a public library card but may not satisfy the residency requirements for in-state college tuition.

residential mobility   This occurs when a person or a household changes their place of residence without a major change in most aspects of their lives. It is sometimes defined as a residential move within the same county.

retrospective questions   These are questions that are asked in a survey about experiences in the past, such as when births occurred or when a person migrated.

return migrant   A return migrant is a person who migrates to a place of destination and then migrates back to the place of origin.

return migration   This occurs when a person migrates from place A to place B and later migrates back to place A. Usually it occurs after the person has been in place B for some considerable time, and the return to A was not anticipated when the migrant first migrated from A to B.

risk factor   A risk factor for death or for disability is a variable or condition that increases the chance that death will occur from a particular cause or that a person will have a particular disability. Smoking is a risk factor for death from lung cancer and for emphysema.

role incompatibility   This is whether and the extent to which the demands of different roles, especially the role of being a mother and the role of being a worker for pay, conflict with or are incompatible with each other.

rural   An area is rural if it is not urban. See **urban**.

rural-urban migrant   This is a person who migrates from a rural place of origin to an urban place of destination.

rural-urban migration   This is migration from a rural place of origin to an urban place of destination.

secondary sterility   This occurs when a woman has borne one or more children but is unable to become pregnant and bear a subsequent child.

Second Demographic Transition   This is a description and proposed explanation for below-replacement fertility. It is characterized by (1) an increase in the proportion of births that occur to unmarried women, (2) an increase in the age at first birth, (3) an increase in permanent childlessness, (4) an increase in cohabitation, and (5) a decrease in and postponement of marriage. It is based on experience in Western and Southern Europe beginning in the late twentieth century.

settlement migration   This is migration to a sparsely populated area, often for the pursuit of agriculture in a frontier area.

sex ratio   This is the number of males per 100 females. It can be calculated for the population as a whole, for births, or for an age group.

sex ratio at birth   The sex ratio at birth is the number of male births per 100 female births. The normal sex ratio at birth is in the range of 104–107.

sex-selective abortion   This occurs when the decision to abort the fetus is based on the gender of the fetus. Sex-selective abortion most often occurs with abortion of female fetuses.

singulate mean age at marriage (SMAM)   This is the average age of marriage among those who ultimately marry given the proportion single by age in a population. It is usually calculated for females.

slash-and-burn agriculture   In this system, after a field has been planted for some years, the yield declines. Then the field is burned, and the ash fertilizes the soil. People move on to a new area that they then cultivate.

social Darwinism   This is the position that underlying, and largely irresistible, forces act in societies like the natural forces that operate in animal and plant communities. These social forces produce evolutionary progress through natural conflicts between social groups. The best-adapted and most successful social groups survive these conflicts, raising the evolutionary level of society generally (the "survival of the fittest").

social epidemiology   This is the branch of epidemiology that studies the social determinants of health.

social support   This is support that is provided by other people and arises within the context of interpersonal relationships.

spacing behavior   A woman or a couple are practicing spacing behavior when they take actions to prevent having a live birth in the near future.

spontaneous abortion   This is a **miscarriage**.

stable population   This is the population that would result if a given set of age-specific death rates and a given set of age-specific fertility rates were in effect for a very long time. This assumes there is no migration. In a stable population with a given growth rate, for example 2%, each year the population is 2% larger than in the previous year, each year there are 2% more births than in the previous year, and each year there are 2% more persons in each age group than in the previous year.

stateless person   This is a person who is not considered a citizen of any country.

stationary population   This is a stable population with a population growth rate of zero. A stationary population has a constant population size. It has the same number of births as deaths each year and the same population in a given age group in every year. It has the age distribution of the $_nL_x$ column of the life table.

sterility   This is when a woman is unable to become pregnant and bear a child. It can be either **primary sterility** or **secondary sterility**.

sterilization   This is an operation in which a person is rendered unable to become pregnant or to father a child.

stillbirth   This is when a fetus dies in the uterus, typically after 20 or 22 weeks of gestational age. Most stillbirths occur to full-term pregnancies.

stopping behavior   A woman or a couple are practicing stopping behavior when they take actions to prevent having any further live births.

stunting   A child is considered stunted when his or her weight for age is more than two standard deviations below the World Health Organization standards. This means that the child weighs less than what would be found for 95% of healthy children of that age. The level of stunting in a population is the proportion of children who are stunted.

subfecundity   This is when women have difficulty in becoming pregnant and carrying a pregnancy through to result in a live birth.

suburb   This has a less dense population than does a central city. It is mainly residential and is located near a central city.

suicide   This is a death that results from intentional self-harm.

superior goods   This is something that is inherently desirable to possess. It is scarce and has a high price.

survey   In a survey, a sample of the population is asked a set of questions. See **cross-sectional survey** and **longitudinal survey**.

synthetic cohort   The experience of a synthetic cohort is calculated when the effect of the age-specific rates at a given time (in a particular period) is calculated as if it were applied to a cohort. This is what happens in a period life table in the calculation of expectation of life at birth for a particular year. A synthetic cohort is also called a hypothetical cohort.

tempo of fertility   This is how early or late in women's lives childbearing occurs. In the 1990s and 2000s, childbearing shifted from the early twenties to the late twenties and early thirties in some countries. In these countries, the tempo of fertility changed. See **quantum of fertility**.

Theory of Demographic Change and Response   This is the view that when there is population increase due to mortality decline, people have a variety of options as to how to respond in addition to voluntary fertility limitation. Some of the other options include migration, abortion, and infanticide.

Theory of the Demographic Transition   This is a descriptive model of the process by which the decline in death rates results in an increase in the rate of population growth, after which the growth rate declines once birth rates have declined. It was based on historical experience in Europe.

Too Much Family   This is an explanation proposed by Massimo Livi-Bacci for very low fertility in Italy and possibly in some other countries. Family ties are seen as unintentionally promoting low fertility through behaviors such as allowing unmarried children to live with their parents into their thirties or older and the presence of extremely high economic thresholds for getting married and beginning a family.

total fertility rate   The total fertility rate (TFR) is the number of children who would be born to a woman if the current age-specific fertility rates remained constant and the woman survived through the childbearing ages.

traditional contraceptive methods   These methods have long been known in many populations as a way to limit fertility. They include rhythm, withdrawal, douching, and abstinence.

triangle trade   This was a system in which slaves were bought in West Africa in exchange for New World sugar, cotton, and tobacco, which were exchanged in Europe for textiles, rum, and other manufactured goods, which were traded in Africa for slaves.

ultimogeniture   This is an inheritance practice in which the youngest son is the sole heir. **See impartible inheritance.**

undercount   This is the percentage of the population or of a population subgroup that is omitted in a census enumeration.

underlying cause of death   This is the disease or injury that initiated the chain of events that resulted in death.

undocumented migrant   This is a person who migrates into a country without the proper documents for immigration or in violation of immigration rules.

unemployed population   These are people who are actively seeking paid work but have not yet found such work. They are part of the **labor force.** See **labor force.**

unmet need for family planning   Women with an unmet need for family planning are those who not using any method of contraception, and report not wanting any more children or wanting to delay the birth of their next child. The unmet need for family planning is expressed as a percentage of women of reproductive age who are married or in a union.

unnatural causes of death   This is another term for **external causes of death.**

urban   This is an official definition that varies among countries. The definition of urban usually relies on a combination of (1) population size, (2) space (land area), (3) ratio of population to space (population density), and (4) economic, political, and social organization.

urban agglomeration   This is a UN designation, which is similar to the American designation of a metropolitan area.

urban growth   This is growth of the urban population.

urban growth rate   If the urban population is U1 at time 1 and U2 at time 2, and there are t years between time 1 and time 2, the urban growth rate per 1,000 urban residents is $1,000 \times (\ln(U2/U1)/t)$. See **population growth rate.**

urban-rural reclassification   This occurs when a geographic area is classified as rural to one point in time and as urban at another point in time. Usually this is a reclassification from rural to urban as cities expand, as population density increases, and as the basis of the economy changes.

urbanization   This is the percentage of the population living in urban places.

vaccination   This is the administration of killed or weakened living organisms that are prepared to produce or artificially increase immunity to a particular disease.

validity   An indicator, such as a demographic measure, is intended to accurately represent some underlying concept. The validity of a measure is the extent to which it accurately represents the underlying concept.

variolation   See **inoculation.**

verbal autopsy   This is a research method that helps determine the probable cause of death based on answers to questions asked of household members or other persons familiar with the situation when a person died. Sometimes questions are asked to determine whether a person died of natural or external causes. Sometimes questions are asked to determine whether a person died of HIV or of malaria.

violent causes of death   See **external causes of death.**

vital statistics   Vital statistics are records of births, deaths, and often marriages and divorces that are recorded in a timely manner, usually shortly after the given event has occurred. This is a governmental function, sometimes located in a department concerned with health or population and sometimes in a department of justice, concerned with the establishment of legal rights. In many countries, vital statistics are under federal authority, while in the United States, their collection, and exactly what information is collected about each event, such as the age or education of the mother, is under the control of each state.

withdrawal   See **coitus interruptus.**

working age population   Typically the working age population is defined as those aged 15–64. Sometimes it is defined as those aged 15–59.

years lived disabled (YLD)   This is an estimate of the number of years alive but disabled from a particular condition based on the prevalence and the average duration of the disabling condition.

years of life lost (YLL)   This is an estimate of the number of years lost due to premature death from a given cause of death in comparison to a standard of attainable life expectancy.

young dependency ratio   See **youth dependency ratio.**

young population   This is usually defined as those aged 0–14.

youth bulge   The youth bulge is usually indicated by the proportion of those at least aged 15 who are aged 15–24. It can occur when there has been substantial labor migration to an area, in which a large proportion of the migrants are young adults. It also can occur when a Baby Boom cohort reaches the 15–24 age group.

youth dependency ratio   This is the number of people in the population younger than the working ages per 100 people in the working ages. It is usually calculated as $100 \times$ (Population aged 0–14)/(Population aged 15–64). This is also called **the young dependency ratio.**

zero population growth (ZPG)   See **replacement fertility.**

INDEX

A

Abandonment, 307
Abortion, 97
  approval/disapproval reasons, in the
    U.S., 323–325
  attitudes according to age group
    towards, 325
  deemed as illegal, 307
  defined, 306
  by gestational age in the U.S., 328
  induced, 262, 263, 306
  legality of, 324–325
  levels in 2003, 326–327
  miscarriage, 306
  in more developed countries,
    321–328
  patterns, 326–328
  permission of abortion in LDR, 322
  permission of abortion in MDR,
    322
  policies throughout the world,
    322–323
  rates and ratios by world regions
    (2003), 326
  ratio, teenage, 341
  reasons for, 326–328
  risk of, 306–307
  sex-selective, 251
  sex-selective, in East Asia, 307–310
  spontaneous, 263
  in the U.S., 327–328
Abortion rate, 326
Abortion ratio, 326
Abstinence, 277, 279, 290
  involuntary, 262
  postpartum, 266, 285, 305
  voluntary, 262
Accidental death, 157
Accidents, motor vehicle. *See* Motor
  vehicle accidents

Ache, 148, 149
ACS. *See* American Community
  Survey (ACS)
Active life expectancy, 376–377
Act to Prohibit Importation of
  Slaves of 1807, 435
Actual nonvoters, 5
Acute condition, diseases, 157
Administration, Census, 70–73
Administrative data, 85–86
Adoption, 307
Advanced society, 407
Advances in computing, 24
Africa
  median age, 360, 361
  mortality trends by region of,
    114–116
  NRR in, 253–254
  postpartum abstinence in, 266
  TFR in, 247, 248–249
  youth bulge, 367, 368
African-Americans
  age-adjusted death rate for, 230
  child living with single parent, 5
  crossover mortality of, 233
  economic forces, 423
  Great Migration, 423–425
  homicide rates of, 227, 231–232
  imprisonment, rate of, 6
  infant mortality rate (IMR) among,
    227, 232, 233
  population census, 72
  population distribution of, 424
  poverty and, 226
  precipitous events in South,
    424
  residential segregation of, 226
  social forces, 423–424
  suicide death rates of, 232
  in Tuskegee Study, 94
  voting behavior of, 5

Age
  definition, 124
  of degenerative and manmade
    diseases, 147
  of delayed degenerative diseases, 147
  effects of HIV by, 128–129
  exact, 124
  last birthday, 124
  of pestilence and famine, 146–147
  of receding pandemics, 147
  sex differences in mortality by, 131–132
  sex ratios and, 132–134
Age-adjusted death rates, 123–124, 180
Age at marriage. *See also* Marriage
  female educational attainment and,
    280
  in less developed countries, 279–280
  singulate mean, 302
  variations in the, in historical
    Europe, 274–276
Age composition, 3
Age last birthday, 124
Age of sexual debut, 263–264, 340
Age patterns
  controlled fertility, 266–267
  of fertility in highly developed, low-
    fertility settings, shifts in, 268–269
  of first marriage, changes in,
    263–264
  of marital fertility, 264, 267–268
  natural fertility, 266–267
Age-specific death rates, 125
Age-specific fertility rate (ASFR), 246,
  255
Age structure, CDR influence on,
  55–56
Aggregate approach, 3
Aging, 55–56. *See also* Older/elderly
  population
  of the American population, 392
  government views on, 59